KV-622-085

THE LAW OF RESTITUTION

AUSTRALIA
The Law Book Company
Brisbane • Sydney • Melbourne • Perth

CANADA
Carswell
Ottawa • Toronto • Calgary • Montreal • Vancouver

Agents
Steimatzky's Agency Ltd., Tel Aviv;
N.M. Tripathi (Private) Ltd., Bombay;
Eastern Law House (Private) Ltd., Calcutta;
M.P.P. House, Bangalore;
Universal Book Traders, Delhi;
Aditya Books, Delhi;
MacMillan Shuppan KK, Tokyo;
Pakistan Law House, Karachi, Lahore

012536478

LIVERPOOL UNIVERSITY LIBRARY

WITHDRAWN
FROM
STOCK

LIVERPOOL UNIVERSITY LIBRARY

LAW LIBRARY

Please return or renew, on or before the last
date below. A fine is payable on late returned
items. Books may be recalled after one week for
the use of another reader. Unless overdue, or
during Annual Recall, books may be renewed by
telephone:- 794-2832.

LAW

CANCELLED

2 2 AUG 1996

DUE FOR RETURN

1 3 JAN 1995

3 0 JUN 1997

1 4 AUG 1997

2 2 JAN 1997

3 0 JUN 1995

5 FEB 1997

2 9 JUN 1996

2 1 APR 1997

CANCELLED

THE LAW
OF
RESTITUTION

by

Lord Goff of Chieveley, P.C., D.C.L., F.B.A.

A Lord of Appeal in Ordinary; Honorary Fellow
of Lincoln College and of New College, Oxford,
and sometime Tutorial Fellow of Lincoln College;
High Steward of Oxford University;
A Master of the Bench of the Inner Temple;
Chairman of the British Institute
of International and Comparative Law

and

Gareth Jones, Q.C., LL.D., F.B.A.

Downing Professor of the Laws of England
in the University of Cambridge;
Fellow of Trinity College, Cambridge;
Honorary Bencher of Lincoln's Inn

Fourth Edition
edited by
Gareth Jones

LONDON
SWEET & MAXWELL
1993

First Edition 1966   Third Edition 1986
Second Edition 1978   Fourth Edition 1993

Published in 1993 by
Sweet & Maxwell Limited of
South Quay Plaza, 183 Marsh Wall, London E14 9FT
Phototypeset by MFK Typesetting Ltd., Hitchin, Herts
Printed and bound in Great Britain by Hartnolls Ltd., Bodmin

No natural forests were destroyed to make this product;
only farmed timber was used and replanted

A CIP catalogue record for
this book is available
from the British Library

ISBN 0-421-42560-1

All rights reserved. UK statutory material in this publication is acknowledged
as Crown copyright.

No part of this publication may be reproduced or transmitted in any form or
by any means, or stored in any retrieval system of any nature without prior
written permission, except for permitted fair dealing under the Copyright,
Designs and Patents Act 1988, or in accordance with the terms of a licence
issued by the Copyright Licensing Agency in respect of photocopying and/or
reprographic reproduction. Application for permission for other use of
copyright material including permission to reproduce extracts in other
published works shall be made to the publishers. Full acknowledgment of
author, publisher and source must be given.

©
Sweet & Maxwell
1993

PREFACE

The Third Edition of this work was published in 1986. Since that date there have been very significant developments in this branch of the law. Most importantly, the House of Lords has recognised, quite unequivocally, the principle of unjust enrichment: see *Lipkin Gorman (A Firm)* v. *Karpnale Ltd.* and *Woolwich Equitable Building Society* v. *The Inland Revenue Commissioners.* Many other notable recent decisions are fully discussed in the text of this edition.

During these years there have been many scholarly books and articles on the law of restitution. Two volumes of essays, edited respectively by Professor Finn and Mr. Burrows, have been published. Mr. Beatson's articles have been revised and collected together in *The Use and Abuse of Unjust Enrichment.* The pages of the learned journals continue to demonstrate the interest which the subject has excited; Professor Birks' challenging contributions to the debate on the structure of the subject deserve particular mention. It was a matter of regret that Mr. Andrew Burrows' *The Law of Restitution* was published when this edition was in galley proof; this work deserved, if space and time had allowed, fuller recognition in these pages.

Much of the text has been rewritten in light of the developing case law and academic criticism. Very few chapters remain as they were. The text is only 44 pages longer because of the omission of the chapter on Fraudulent and Voluntary Dispositions; it had become a mere catalogue of statutory provisions.

The most important changes are to be found in the following chapters. Chapter 1 on General Principles reflects the increasing academic and professional awareness of the role of the principle of unjust enrichment in English law. Proprietary Claims (Chapter 2) concludes with further thoughts on the nature of restitutionary proprietary claims; the proofs only allowed a short analysis of *Barlow Clowes International Ltd.* v. *Vaughan*, C.A., *Lord Napier and Ettrick* v. *R. F. Kershaw Ltd.*, H.L., and Millett J.'s judgment in *El Ajou* v. *Dollar Land Holdings plc.*

Mistake of Fact (Chapter 3) questions whether *ignorance* can be a ground of a restitutionary claim and there is an expanded section on the defence of change of position. Chapter 4 on Mistake of Law speculates on the future of the "no recovery" rule, in the light of dicta in *Woolwich* and its rejection, most recently, in South Africa and Australia; there is also an expanded section on change of position. The case law on proprietary estoppel and the emergence of the concept of *unconscionability*, in this country and Australia, influences the text of Chapter 5 on Services Rendered Under Mistake as well as those on Breach (Chapter 18) and on Anticipated Contracts (Chapter 25).

Chapter 9 on Duress concludes that it may be premature to jettison the *colore officii* line of cases; and the House of Lords' decision, *The Evia Luck*, finds a prominent place both here and in Chapter 38 on Tort and Restitutionary Claims. In Chapter 10 on Undue Influence, in the section on Third Party Rights, there is much new and controversial law; space compelled only a brief discussion of *Barclays Bank plc* v. *O'Brien*, C.A. *The Esso Bernicia*, H.L. is discussed in Chapter 12 on Contribution or Recoupment and in Chapter 14 on Compulsory Discharge; in Chapter 13 on Contribution the Privy Council decision, in *Eagle Star Insurance plc* v. *Provincial Insurance plc*, could only be briefly considered.

The section on Necessity suggests limits to any possible restitutionary claim, and discusses the implications of *Re T*, C.A. and *Re F*, H.L.

Chapter 18, Contracts Discharged through Breach or Frustration, examines the inter-relationship of money claims and claims for services rendered and goods delivered and returns to the problem of the scope of the innocent party's *quantum meruit* and *quantum valebat* claims. The significant cases include *Stern* v. *McArthur* (High Court of Australia). The enactment of the Law of Property (Miscellaneous Provisions) Act 1989 necessitated a chapter (19) on Contracts for the Sale or Disposition of Land which are Void for Lack of Writing. *Tinsley* v. *Milligan*, H.L. and the two "swap" cases were reported after the galleys arrived, so are only briefly considered: see, respectively, Chapters 22 (Illegality) and 23 (Incapacity). *Woolwich Equitable Building Society* v. *The Inland Revenue Commissioners* merits its own chapter (24).

Chapter 31 on Subrogation contains a full discussion of *Lord Napier and Ettrick* v. *R. F. Kershaw Ltd.* and *Re T.H. Knitwear (Wholesale) Ltd.*, C.A.

Chapter 33 on Benefits Acquired in Breach of Fiduciary Relationships discusses *Guinness plc* v. *Saunders*, H.L. (see also Chapter 20 on Contracts Void for Want of Authority) and concludes with a section on the personal liability of a stranger who receives trust property transferred in breach of trust. There is now a short chapter (34), entitled Benefits Acquired in Breach of an Undertaking to hold Property for the Benefit of Another. Chapter 36 on Benefits Acquired in Breach of Another's Confidence analyses the House of Lords' decisions in the *Spycatcher* litigation. Chapter 37, on Benefits Accruing to a Criminal from his Crime, has a new section on the disgorgement of profits; and Chapter 38 on Tort and Restitutionary Claims, formerly entitled Waiver of Tort, has been recast; it includes *Stoke-on-Trent City Council* v. *W. J. Wass Ltd.*, C.A.

The Section on Defences gives prominence to the defence of change of position (Chapter 40), as interpreted in *Lipkin Gorman*. It is predictable that estoppel will in the future play a minor role in the law of restitution and, for that reason, much of the common law is only summarised.

This book is, and always has been, an empirical but critical text on English law; there are, however, not infrequent references to the experience of other common law and some civilian jurisdictions. In recent years the complex of rules which forms the law of restitution has become more systematic and more coherent, although perfect symmetry and coherence have yet to be achieved.

I much regret that Lord Goff could not play a fuller part in the preparation of the text of this edition; but his work in the House of Lords and the Privy Council, as well as his extra-judicial activities, have absorbed all his considerable energies. His contribution has nonetheless been a real one. For his innovative and closely reasoned speeches have done much to mould the modern law and consequently the text of the Fourth Edition of *Goff and Jones on The Law of Restitution*.

Both Lord Goff and I would like to thank the publishers and their representatives for their courteous and patient assistance.

Gareth Jones   September 1, 1993
Trinity College, Cambridge

NOTE BY LORD GOFF

I have come to the conclusion that the Fourth Edition of *Goff and Jones* should appear with a statement on the title page that it is the work of Gareth Jones alone; and my co-author has, with becoming reluctance, agreed that this should be so.

Three circumstances have combined to force me to take this step. First, there is the explosive growth of published material on the subject by judge and jurist, and indeed of the subject itself, which continues despite the professed anxiety of some, wedded to the old order of things, to play the part of King Canute. Second, there is my work as a Law Lord, which dominates my life. Few perhaps realise how absorbing and time-consuming this is: indeed, newly appointed members of the Appellate Committee of the House of Lords habitually discover, to their surprise, how demanding is the work of a final appellate tribunal. Third, there are the public engagements of a senior judge— engagements which I am reluctant to refuse, and to the preparation for which I devote what I suspect to be an inordinate amount of time. In the result, I have discovered that I can no longer claim to have properly fulfilled the role of editor of a work such as this.

This is a moment of sadness for me. It is however softened by the knowledge that future editions of this book, the writing of which occupied so great a part of my early career as a lawyer, will remain in the hands of my admired co-author, who is bound to me by the closest ties of friendship.

Robert Goff   September 28, 1993
House of Lords

CONTENTS

ix

TABLE OF CASES

xv

TABLE OF STATUTES

NON-U.K. STATUTES

TABLE OF ABBREVIATIONS

A.L.J. . . . . *Australian Law Journal*
American L.R. . . . . *American Law Review*
Calif.L.R. . . . . . . *California Law Review*
Can.B.R. . . . . . . *Canadian Bar Review*
C.L.J. . . . . *Cambridge Law Journal*
C.L.P. . . . . *Current Legal Problems*
Col.L.R. . . . . . *Columbia Law Review*
Conveyancer (N.S.) . . . *Conveyancer*, New Series
Cornell L.Q. . . . . *Cornell Law Quarterly*
Crim.L.R. . . . . . *Criminal Law Review*
Fordham L.R.. . . . *Fordham Law Review*
Harv.L.R. . . . . . *Harvard Law Review*
Ill.L.R. . . . . . . *Illinois Law Review*
J.S.P.T.L.. . . . . . *Journal of the Society of Public Teachers of Law*
Jo. of Bus.L. . . . . *Journal of Business Law*
L.Q.R. . . . . . . *Law Quarterly Review*
L.T.Jour . . . . . . *Law Times Journal*
Mel.Univ.L.R. . . . *Melbourne University Law Review*
Mich.L.R. . . . . . *Michigan Law Review*
Minn.L.R.. . . . . *Minnesota Law Review*
M.L.R. . . . . . . *Modern Law Review*
New York Univ.L.R. . *New York University Law Review*
S.A.L.J. . . . . . . *South African Law Journal*
S.J. . . . . *Solicitors' Journal*
Stan.L.R. . . . . . *Stanford Law Review*
Tasmania L.R. . . . *Tasmania Law Review*
Texas L.R.. . . . . *University of Texas Law Review*
Tulane L.R. . . . . *Tulane Law Review*
Univ. of Pa.L.R. . . . *University of Pennsylvania Law Review*

PART I

INTRODUCTION

CHAPTER 1

GENERAL PRINCIPLES

1. RESTITUTION AND QUASI-CONTRACT

THE law of restitution is the law relating to all claims, quasi-contractual or
otherwise, which are founded upon the principle of unjust enrichment. Restitutionary claims are to be found in equity[1] as well as at law. But the common
law of quasi-contract is the most ancient and significant part of restitution and,
for that reason, restitution is more easily understood if approached through
that topic.

We understand quasi-contract to be that part of restitution which stems
from the common *indebitatus* counts for money had and received and for
money paid, and from *quantum meruit* and *quantum valebat* claims. The *action
for money had and received* lay to recover money which the plaintiff had paid to
the defendant, on the ground that it had been paid under a mistake or
compulsion, or for a consideration which had wholly failed. By this action the
plaintiff could also recover money which the defendant had received from a
third party, as when he was accountable or had attorned to the plaintiff in
respect of the money, or the money formed part of the fruits of an office of the
plaintiff which the defendant had usurped. The action also lay to recover
money which the defendant had acquired from the plaintiff by a tortious act;
and, in the very rare cases, where the defendant had received money which the
plaintiff could identify as his own[2] at the time of receipt and for which the
defendant had not given consideration, the plaintiff could assert his claim by
means of this action.

The *action for money paid* was the appropriate action when the plaintiff's
claim was in respect of money paid, not to the defendant, but to a third party,
from which the defendant had derived a benefit. Historically, the plaintiff had
to show that the payment was made at the defendant's request; but we shall
see[3] that the law was prepared to "imply" such a request on certain occasions,
in particular where the payment was made under compulsion of law or, in
limited circumstances, in the course of intervention in an emergency on the
defendant's behalf, which in this book we shall call necessitous intervention.

---

[1] See below, pp. 4–5.
[2] The plaintiff has a limited right at law "to follow" his property into its product: see below,
    pp. 75–83.
[3] See below, pp. 29–30 *et seq.*

Quantum meruit and *quantum valebat* claims lay respectively to recover reasonable remuneration for services and a reasonable price for goods supplied by the plaintiff. Since, like a payment to a third party, services can be rendered and goods supplied without the co-operation of the defendant, something more than the mere supply of the services or goods must be shown to make the defendant liable to pay for them. So here, too, the plaintiff had to prove, and indeed must still plead, a request by the defendant. But again the notion of request has been extended.[4] It is now enough[5] that the defendant has either freely accepted[6] or that he has incontrovertibly benefited from the services rendered or the goods delivered.[7]

To draw the boundaries of quasi-contract, it is necessary to refer to the limits of these old forms of action. But these limits, though relevant, are not definitive. Not every right enforced by these remedies can be classified as quasi-contractual. Each one of the remedies might be used to enforce purely contractual claims. Thus the action for money had and received was used to compel a contracting party, such as an agent, to account; and the action for money paid lay to enforce the contractual right of indemnity, for example, by a surety against his principal debtor. *Quantum meruit* and *quantum valebat* claims were employed to recover reasonable remuneration for services or a reasonable price for goods which had been rendered or supplied under a contract in which the remuneration or price had not been agreed. Moreover, as we have seen, the action for money had and received also lay in respect of money as property; and the action could be used to recover miscellanea such as statutory penalties and judgment debts, these claims being part of the inheritance which *indebitatus assumpsit* received from *debt* in the seventeenth century. Historical accident is an unsatisfactory basis for classification and, to arrive at a satisfactory description of quasi-contract, jurists have been forced to search for a predominant principle which will enable them to reject a minority and unify the majority of the claims enforced by these forms of action. This principle is widely accepted to be *unjust enrichment*.

Quasi-contractual claims are, therefore, those which fall within the scope of the actions for money had and received or for money paid, or of *quantum meruit* or *quantum valebat* claims, and which are founded upon the principle of unjust enrichment. There are, however, other claims of different origin which are also based on that principle. So, for example, there are claims in equity analogous

---

[4] See below, pp. 18–19. *Craven-Ellis* v. *Canons Ltd.* [1936] 2 K.B. 403; *William Lacey (Hounslow) Ltd.* v. *Davis* [1957] 1 W.L.R. 932; *Société Franco-Tunisienne D'Armement* v. *Sidermar S.P.A.* [1961] 2 Q.B. 278 (later overruled on a different point: see *Ocean Tramp Tankers Corp.* v. *V/O Sovfracht ("The Eugenia")* [1964] 2 Q.B. 226); *Greenwood* v. *Bennett* [1973] 1 Q.B. 195.
[5] See below, pp. 18 *et seq.*
[6] See below, pp. 18–19.
[7] See below, pp. 22–26. It has long been accepted that, at least in some circumstances, a restitutionary claim may lie if services have been rendered or goods delivered in an emergency even though the defendant neither freely accepted them nor benefited from them: see below, Chap. 15.

to quasi-contractual claims to recover money paid under a mistake; there are claims for profits made from a breach of trust; equitable relief from undue influence is a rational extension of the limited relief which the common law once provided in cases of duress; catching bargains may be set aside in equity as unconscionable; and proprietary claims are granted in equity to revest title in the plaintiff, to protect his equitable title or to allow him the additional advantages which spring from the recognition of a right of property. Some restitutionary claims outside the scope of quasi-contract are known to both law and equity; these include two of the more important topics in restitution, namely, contribution[8] and subrogation. Other restitutionary claims, notably general average and salvage, were adopted by the Court of Admiralty. But the substantive link between these and quasi-contractual claims are hidden by the artificial barriers of the forms of action. It is now over a century since the forms of action were abolished.[9] They should no longer be allowed to obstruct a unified treatment of all claims, quasi-contractual or otherwise, which are founded on the principle of unjust enrichment and which compose the law of restitution.[10]

2. THE LEGACY OF HISTORY. THE "IMPLIED CONTRACT THEORY"

In the past restitution was considered to be no more than a heterogeneous collection of unrelated topics.[11] It was even suggested that quasi-contractual claims should, on principle, receive separate treatment from the other matters considered in this book on the ground that it is the special characteristic of

---

[8] There is now a statutory right: see The Civil Liability (Contribution) Act 1978, below, Chap. 15.
[9] Common Law Procedure Act 1852, s.3, provided that it should no longer be necessary to mention any form or cause of action in the writ. For the effect of this Act on the common *indebitatus* counts, see Bullen & Leake's *Precedents of Pleadings* (3rd ed., 1868), p. 36. "But even after this Act the form of action remains of vital importance to the pleader for each action retains its own precedents, and although the choice of the proper form of action need no longer be made in the choice of writ it is merely deferred until the declaration": see F. W. Maitland, *The Forms of Action at Common Law*, p. 81. The final demise of the forms of action was effected by the Judicature Acts 1873–1875, which introduced a new code of civil procedure (see Sched. I to the Judicature Act 1875). Cf. *United Australia Ltd.* v. *Barclays Bank Ltd.* [1941] A.C. 1, 53, *per* Lord Porter; [1964] C.L.J. 234, 252–253 [M. J. Prichard]. See also (1941) 57 L.Q.R. 184, 196–198 [Lord Wright].
[10] The concept of unjust enrichment may be influential in other areas of the law; for example, in trust and property law: see, *e.g.* Chap. 26. It has also been suggested that the principle of unjust enrichment may be the explanation for the tortious liability of enterprises which create abnormally high risks: see 72 Harv.L.Rev. 401 (1959) [R. Keeton]. See also (1988) 13 Queen's L.J. 126 [Wingfield]. But we have restricted our inquiry to those situations where the prevention of unjust enrichment is "the central objective" of the claim: see generally "Restitution of Damages?" 20 Ohio St. L.J. 175, 177 [Dawson], and contrast Atiyah, *The Rise and Fall of Freedom of Contract*, p. 768.
[11] At one time a similar charge was levelled against the law of tort. "We are inclined to think that tort is not a proper subject for a law book": see 5 Am.L.Rev. 340–341 (1871) [O. W. Holmes Jr.], reviewing an abridged edition of Addison's *Torts*. Three years later Holmes came "to recognise there were satisfactory reasons, both historical and analytical, for including the subject in the *corpus juris*": Mark De Wolfe Howe, *Mr. Justice Holmes, The Proving Years*, 1870–1882, pp. 65, 184.

these claims that they are founded upon an implied contract by the defendant
to pay to the plaintiff the money claimed by him.

The "implied contract theory,"[12] as it is usually called, has little or no
immediate attraction. There are, it is true, some contexts in which an implied
contract for repayment can, with not too much artificiality, be imputed to the
parties. So if the plaintiff had paid money to the defendant under a contract,
subsequently discharged by reason of the defendant's breach, it can be argued
that the defendant should be taken to have impliedly contracted that, in such
an event, he would repay the money to the plaintiff. But in most situations
recourse to the theory becomes so absurd that serious doubts about its validity
are aroused. It is difficult to understand, for example, how the recipient of
money paid under a mistake, still less a thief who has stolen money, could be
held to have impliedly contracted to repay it. Yet at one time it was argued[13]
that all quasi-contractual claims are founded upon an implied contract, and
this argument used to be reflected in the language of some members of the
judiciary.[14] It is impossible, therefore, to ignore the implied contract theory;
and to assess its validity we must first briefly examine the historical background of quasi-contract.[15]

English lawyers did not originally distinguish between contractual and
quasi-contractual claims. Their classification was founded on remedies; and
the medieval registers contained precedents of writs whose functions included
both the enforcement of what are now called contracts and, occasionally, the
prevention of unjust enrichment. So *debt*, which lay for a certain sum,[16] could
be employed to recover not only rent, or the price of goods sold or a loan of
money,[17] but also money paid to the defendant's use or for a consideration
which had failed[18]; and debt was also used to recover the miscellaneous items

---

[12] The theory has provoked a disproportionately large literature: see, *e.g.* (1924) 40 L.Q.R. 31,
34–36 [H. G. Hanbury]; (1937) 53 L.Q.R. 302 [P. A. Landon], 447 [Winfield], 449 [W. A.
Friedman]; (1938) 54 L.Q.R. 24 [G. R. Y. Radcliffe], 201, 202–209 [C. K. Allen]; (1938) 6
C.L.J. 305, 312–326 [Lord Wright]; (1939) 55 L.Q.R. 37, 45–53 [W. S. Holdsworth]; R. M.
Jackson, *History of Quasi-Contract*, 117–124; Winfield, *Province of the Law of Torts*, 124–141,
The Law of Quasi-Contracts, 14–21; S. J. Stoljar, *The Law of Quasi-Contracts*, pp. 1 *et seq.* (2nd
ed., 1989).

[13] See, *e.g.* (1939) 55 L.Q.R. 37 [Holdsworth].

[14] See, *e.g. Re Simms* [1934] Ch. 1, 20, *per* Lord Hanworth M.R., 31–32, *per* Romer L.J.; *Morgan
v. Ashcroft* [1938] 1 K.B. 49, 62, *per* Sir W. Greene M.R.; *Transvaal & Delagoa Bay Investment
Co. Ltd. v. Atkinson* [1944] 1 All E.R. 579, 583–584, *per* Atkinson J.; *Re Diplock* [1947] Ch. 716,
724, *per* Wynn Parry J., [1948] Ch. 465, 480, *per curiam*, C.A. *Cf. Morris v. Tarrant* [1971] 2
Q.B. 143. The adoption by the Court of Appeal in *Re Diplock* of the "implied contract theory"
led them to interpret the common law right of following property into its product in a manner
inconsistent with earlier authority. *Cf.* below, p. 81, n. 50.

[15] For the history of quasi-contract generally, see Jackson, *History*; Holdsworth, *History of English
Law*, III, pp. 424–454, VI, pp. 637–640, VIII, pp. 88–98; C. H. S. Fifoot, *History and Sources
of the Common Law*, pp. 222–223, 272–273, 363–367; 2 Harv.L.Rev. 1, 53 (1888) [J. B. Ames];
J. B. Ames, *Lectures*, p. 149; A. W. B. Simpson, *A History of the Common Law of Contract*,
Chap. 8.

[16] Glanvil, Bk. 10, Chap. 7.

[17] See, generally, Fifoot, *History and Sources*, Chap. 10; Ames, *Lectures*, Chap. 8.

[18] Y.B. 21 & 22 Edw. I (R.S.) 598, *per* Metingham C.J. See, generally, Jackson, *History*,
pp. 18–24, and cases cited.

already mentioned, such as penalties due under statute or by-law, customary obligations and judgment debts.[19] *Account*, though founded on a special relationship between the parties,[20] was extended, before it was superseded by debt and then by *indebitatus assumpsit*, to render the defendant accountable to the plaintiff in the absence of a special relationship between them[21] and, exceptionally, to enable a person to recover money paid under a mistake.[22] But these developments were piecemeal and pragmatic. They neither presupposed nor disclosed the growth of any general principle. Bracton's reference in his *Tractatus* to *obligationes quasi ex contractu*[23] was no more than a "brief and meagre"[24] summary of a passage in Justinian's *Institutes*,[25] which the contemporary lawyer would certainly have found foreign and probably have dismissed as irrelevant.[26]

It was the growth of *indebitatus assumpsit* which provided the opportunity for the development of quasi-contract as we know it. This action superseded debt and account in the sixteenth century. Why and how this happened is somewhat obscure, although the clue is certainly to be found in the traditional rivalry between the Courts of King's Bench and Common Pleas.[27] Debt and account were returnable only in the Common Pleas, *assumpsit* in the King's Bench. The King's Bench judges were more progressive, and were eager to manipulate *assumpsit* to enable it to do the work of debt. They did this by finding that the defendant was indebted to the plaintiff in a certain sum and had promised, at the time of the contract or afterwards, to pay that sum to him. If this promise were broken, loss would occur and so case would lie.[28] Most importantly, they did not require the jury to find an express promise; the promise could be implied from the defendant's conduct. Actions so pleaded were known as *indebitatus assumpsit*. Litigants were also anxious to bring their action in the King's Bench; the bill procedure was cheaper, wager of law could be avoided and they did not have to set out so precisely the facts giving rise to the debt.

In the last quarter of the sixteenth century the Common Pleas began to attack the King's Bench use of *assumpsit*. They did so on a number of grounds, the most significant of which was that the *assumpsit* was a mere fiction and a

---

[19] Winfield, *Province*, pp. 150, 178–181, and cases cited.
[20] Its origin is to be found in the Statute of Marlborough 1267, c. 23: see, generally, Langdell, *Equity Jurisdiction*, p. 75; Jackson, *History*, pp. 8–17, 32–34; Ames, *Lectures*, pp. 117–119.
[21] See, generally, Jackson, *History*, pp. 9–17, 30–31, and cases cited.
[22] *Framson* v. *Delamare* (1595) Cro.Eliz. 458; *Hewer* v. *Bartholomew* (1598) Cro.Eliz. 614.
[23] Fol. 100b.
[24] Maitland, *Bracton and Azo* (1894) 8 Selden Society 158.
[25] Inst. 3.27.
[26] H. G. Richardson, *Bracton*, pp. 6–7, 53.
[27] For the scholarship on which this paragraph is based, see [1954] C.L.J. 105 [S. F. C. Milsom]; (1958) 74 L.Q.R. 381 [A. W. B. Simpson]; (1968) 81 L.Q.R. 422, 539, (1969) 82 L.Q.R. 81 [H. K. Lücke]; [1971] C.L.J. 51, 213 [J. H. Baker]; [1975] 91 L.Q.R. 406 [Helmholz]; [1982] C.L.J. 142 [Ibbetson]; S. F. C. Milsom, *Historical Foundations of the Common Law*, pp. 339–356; A. W. B. Simpson, *A History of the Common Law of Contract*, Chaps. 3 and 8; J. H. Baker, *Spelman's Reports*, Vol. II (Selden Society, Vol. 94), Chaps. II and IX; G. E. Palmer, *History of Restitution in Anglo-American Law*, Vol. X *International Encyclopedia of Comparative Law*.
[28] [1954] C.L.J. 105 [Milsom].

flagrant attempt to avoid wager of law. It was not, however, until the creation
of a new Exchequer Chamber in 1585, to review the judgments of the King's
Bench, that it became possible to resolve the conflict between the courts. After
the decision of that Chamber in 1602, in *Slade's* case,[29] there was no further
attempt to frustrate the use of *assumpsit* as an alternative to debt, and so the
view of the King's Bench prevailed.

In *Slade's* case the promise was implied from facts sufficient to support a
writ of debt; the case was one which a modern lawyer would characterise as
contractual. Whether it influenced the extension of *assumpsit* to enforce quasi-
contractual actions is conjectural, for the "notion that an executory contract, in
the old technical sense, imported an *assumpsit* in itself, does not lead logically to
the implication of fictional subsequent promises in cases where there is no
contract at all."[30] What is certain is that by the Restoration[31] *indebitatus
assumpsit* had become fully concurrent with debt and account and, since these
old *praecipe* writs cut across the boundaries of the modern contract and
quasi-contract, *indebitatus assumpsit* was employed to enforce those quasi-
contractual claims which had previously been enforced by debt and account.[32]
In these cases, the "contract" or "promise" alleged in the pleading was a
complete fiction. It was not even a tacit though genuine promise implied from
the facts, but an entirely fictitious promise; a so-called "contract implied in
law." This did not, however, deter the lawyers of the time and, indeed,
indebitatus assumpsit proved so popular that it gradually spread beyond the
boundaries of the *praecipe* writs. It was soon to become available in cases of
improper application of legal process,[33] of waiver of tort,[34] and of duress of
goods.[35] By the end of the eighteenth century, the foundations of the modern
law of quasi-contract had been laid.

The victory of *indebitatus assumpsit* over the *praecipe* writs was highly beneficial to the growth of quasi-contract. But the fictitious promise which lay at its
root has left a legacy of confusion which has seriously hindered the development of a law of restitution. Lord Mansfield, at least, had no doubts about the
status of this so-called promise. In the celebrated case of *Moses* v. *Macferlan*[36]
counsel argued that no action would lie because *assumpsit* lay only on an express
or implied contract, and on the facts of the case it was impossible to presume
any contract to refund the money claimed by the plaintiff. Lord Mansfield

---

[29] (1602) 4 Co. Rep. 92a.
[30] [1971] C.L.J. 213, 235 [Baker]. And see Simpson, *History*, Chap. 8.
[31] See Jackson, *History*, pp. 40–41; Fifoot, *History and Sources*, pp. 363–367. The history between
Slade's case and the Restoration is obscure; but indications that *indebitatus assumpsit* might lie in
quasi-contractual cases are to be found in, *e.g. Lady Cavendish* v. *Middleton* (1628) Cro.Car. 141.
[32] Recovery of money paid for a consideration which wholly failed: see *Martin* v. *Sitwell* (1690) 1
Show. K.B. 156; *Holmes* v. *Hall* (1704) 6 Mod. 161. Recovery of money paid under a mistake:
see *Bonnel* v. *Foulke* (1657) 2 Sid. 4. See, generally, Simpson, *History*, pp. 494 *et seq.*; Stoljar,
The Law of Quasi-Contracts, (2nd ed.) pp. 11, 12.
[33] *Newdigate* v. *Davy* (1693) 1 Ld.Raym. 742.
[34] *Lamine* v. *Dorrell* (1705) 2 Ld.Raym. 1216.
[35] *Astley* v. *Reynolds* (1731) 2 Str. 915.
[36] (1760) 2 Burr. 1005; see below, Chap. 42.

gave this answer[37]: " . . . if the defendant be under an obligation, from the ties of natural justice, to refund; the law implies a debt, and gives this action, founded in the equity[38] of the plaintiff's case, as it were upon a contract (*quasi ex contractu*, as the Roman law expresses it)."[39]

While the forms of action continued in existence, it is not surprising that lip-service should have continued to be paid to the notion of "implied contract," for it was only through that fiction that quasi-contractual claims were enforceable at all in *indebitatus assumpsit*.[40] But its demise might have been expected after the abolition of the forms of action in the nineteenth century,[41] and the provision in the Common Law Procedure Act 1852, that fictitious and needless averments, including "the statement of promises which need not be proved, as promises in *indebitatus* counts," were not to be pleaded.[42] Yet the fiction grew rather than diminished in importance. The abolition of the forms of action, which had for so long provided the skeleton of the law, forced lawyers to find some new method of classifying claims. This they found in the dichotomy of contract and tort[43]; and the apparently intractable quasi-contractual claims were relegated to the status of an appendix to the law of contract. If the historical connection of these claims with the contractual action of *assumpsit* provided the justification for this step, the means lay in giving substance to the fictitious contract by which they were enforced; and positivist fear of uncertainty encouraged lawyers to take refuge behind a concept whose name at least was familiar. The "implied contract" ceased to be simply an undesirable means to a desirable end. It became the "basis of the law of quasi-contract."[44]

Yet there is no reason why the common law should be rigidly stratified into contract and tort[45]; and the assertion that the requirement of implied contract leads to certainty is unintelligible. When is a contract to be implied? No logical answer can be given to the question when recourse should be had to a fiction. Moreover, study of the cases reveals that emphasis on implied contract, and the spurious connection with contract which it implies, did, in the past, inhibit

---

[37] (1760) 2 Burr. 1005, 1008; *cf. City of York* v. *Toun* (1699) 5 Mod. 444, where Holt C.J. was puzzled that there could be "any privity or assent implied when a fine is imposed on a man against his will."

[38] Lord Mansfield's habit of referring to the action for money had and received as an equitable action led to adverse criticism in the 19th and early 20th centuries: see Winfield, *Province*, pp. 129–131 and cases cited.

[39] On English and Roman learning in *Moses* v. *Macferlan*, see [1984] C.L.P. 1 [Birks]; see also below n. 40.

[40] See (1986) 6 Oxford Jo. of Legal Studies 46 [Birks and McLeod].

[41] See above, p. 5, n. 9.

[42] s.49; see *Fibrosa Spolka Akcyjna* v. *Fairbairn Lawson Combe Barbour Ltd.* [1943] A.C. 32, 63–64, *per* Lord Wright.

[43] See, *e.g. Sinclair* v. *Brougham* [1914] A.C. 398, 415, *per* Viscount Haldane.

[44] The new emphasis on implied contract was accompanied by a revival of interest in the concept of "privity"; see, *e.g.* pp. 55–57.

[45] (1938) 6 C.L.J. 305, 312–326 [Lord Wright]; p. 12 n. 64. Contrast Gilmore, *The Death of Contract*; Atiyah, *The Rise and Fall of the Freedom of Contract*.

discussion of substantive issues. In *Sinclair* v. *Brougham*,[46] the House of Lords held that money deposited under contracts of deposit which were *ultra vires* the "banking" company were not recoverable in an action for money had and received because, *inter alia*, "the law cannot *de jure* impute promises to repay, whether for money had and received or otherwise, which, if made *de facto*, it would inexorably avoid."[47] This resort to implied contract prevented any discussion of the real point at issue, namely, whether the rule of policy which precludes unjust enrichment should override the rule of policy which underlies the *ultra vires* doctrine.[48] In other cases, reliance on implied contract led to serious injustice. Thus, in *Cowern* v. *Nield*,[49] the plaintiff failed to recover money paid by him to the infant defendant under a contract of sale void under the Infants' Relief Act 1874, although the consideration for his payment had wholly failed because the defendant had not delivered part of the goods and the plaintiff had rightly rejected the remainder as not in accordance with the contract. The court held that the action failed because the action for money had and received was in form *ex contractu* and was, therefore, in this case, caught by the Act.[50] Yet consideration of the substance, rather than the form, of the claim would have revealed that there was no question here of a quasi-contractual claim being used indirectly to enforce a contract avoided by statute.

In our view, the concept of implied contract is, in this context, a meaningless, irrelevant and misleading anachronism. Even at the end of the last century, some support for this view can be found in the cases. In *Re Rhodes*,[51] a case concerned with necessitous intervention to support a lunatic, Cotton L.J. said[52]:

> " . . . Now the term 'implied contract' is a most unfortunate expression, because there cannot be a contract by a lunatic. But whenever necessaries are supplied to a person who by reason of disability cannot himself contract, the law implies an obligation on the part of such person to pay for such necessaries out of his property. It is asked, can there be an implied contract by a person who cannot himself contract in express terms? The answer is, that what the law implies on the part of such a

---

[46] [1914] A.C. 398. See below, pp. 83–86, and (1938) 6 C.L.J. 305 [Lord Wright], reprinted in Lord Wright's *Legal Essays*, Chap. 1.

[47] [1914] A.C. 398, 452, *per* Lord Sumner.

[48] See below, pp. 83–86, 540–542.

[49] [1912] 2 K.B. 419; see below, p. 531. See also *Chandler* v. *Webster* [1904] 1 K.B. 493, where the Court of Appeal held that money paid under a contract thereafter frustrated was irrecoverable in the absence of any express or implied provision in the contract for its recovery. This erroneous approach was corrected by the House of Lords nearly 40 years later in *Fibrosa Spolka Akcyjna* v. *Fairbairn Lawson Combe Barbour Ltd.* [1943] A.C. 32, when Viscount Simon pointed out (at p. 47) that, in such a case, the claim arises "not because the right to be repaid is one of the stipulated conditions of the contract, but because, in the circumstances that have happened, the law gives the remedy."

[50] [1912] 2 K.B. 419, 423–424, *per* Phillimore J.

[51] (1890) 44 Ch.D. 94.

[52] *Ibid.* at 105; see below, p. 380.

person is an obligation, which has been improperly termed a contract, to repay money spent in supplying necessaries. I think that the expression 'implied contract' is erroneous and very unfortunate."

Expressions of this kind have become more frequent in recent years. Lord Atkin, in a much-quoted dictum,[53] castigated "these fantastic resemblances of contracts invented in order to meet requirements of the law as to forms of action which have now disappeared," and suggested that when the "ghosts of the past stand in the path of justice clanking their medieval chains the proper course of the judge is to pass through them undeterred." Lord Wright,[54] Lord Denning,[55] Lord Pearce[56] and Winn L.J.[57] have joined judges in other common law jurisdictions[58] in asserting that the fiction should now be disregarded. Such a course was, indeed, followed by the Court of Appeal in *Craven-Ellis* v. *Canons Ltd.*,[59] where the plaintiff was held entitled to recover upon a *quantum meruit* in respect of services rendered by him to the defendant company under a supposed contract which was void because the directors who had caused the company's seal to be affixed to it were not qualified so to act. The fact that no contract could be implied did not deter the court. Greer L.J. said[60]: "In my judgment, the obligation to pay reasonable remuneration for the work done when there is no binding contract between the parties is imposed by a rule of law, and not by an inference of fact arising from the acceptance of services or goods." It is reasonable, therefore, to expect that references to "implied contract" in cases of quasi-contract will cease, and that the fiction will no longer be allowed to affect substantive rights.[61]

It follows that attention can now be diverted from this barren topic[62] to the substantive principle of unjust enrichment which underlies not only quasi-contractual claims but also the other related claims which, with quasi-contract, make up the law of restitution.

---

[53] *United Australia Ltd.* v. *Barclays Bank Ltd.* [1941] A.C. 1, 28–29.
[54] *Brook's Wharf and Bull Wharf Ltd.* v. *Goodman Bros.* [1937] 1 K.B. 534, 545; *Fibrosa Spolka Akcyjna* v. *Fairbairn Lawson Combe Barbour Ltd.* [1943] A.C. 32, 63; (1941) 57 L.Q.R. 184, 199–200.
[55] *Kiriri Cotton Co.* v. *Dewani* [1960] A.C. 192, 204; (1949) 65 L.Q.R. 37, 38–39.
[56] *Nissan* v. *Att.-Gen.* [1970] A.C. 179, 228.
[57] *Nissan* v. *Att.-Gen.* [1968] 1 Q.B. 286, 352.
[58] American courts have long treated it as fiction; and it was rejected by the Supreme Court of Canada in *Deglman* v. *Guaranty Trust Co. of Canada* [1954] S.C.R. 725 and by Windeyer J. in *Mason* v. *The State of New South Wales*, 102 C.L.R. 105, 146 (1959). For the history of the development of Canadian law, see Maddaugh and McCamus, *The Law of Restitution*.
[59] [1936] 2 K.B. 403; see below, pp. 478 *et seq.*
[60] *Ibid.* at 412; *cf.* (1939) 55 L.Q.R. 54, 62–63 [A. T. Denning].
[61] But see *Guinness plc.* v. *Saunders* [1990] 2 A.C. 663 at 689, *per* Lord Templeman.
[62] Lord Simonds called it a "rather arid dispute": *Ministry of Health* v. *Simpson* [1951] A.C. 251, 275.

3. THE PRINCIPLE OF UNJUST ENRICHMENT[63]

Most mature systems of law have found it necessary to provide, outside the fields of contract and civil wrongs, for the restoration of benefits on grounds of unjust enrichment.[64] There are many circumstances in which a defendant may find himself in possession of a benefit which, in justice, he should restore to the plaintiff. Obvious examples are where the plaintiff has himself conferred the benefit on the defendant through mistake or compulsion. To allow the defendant to retain such a benefit would result in his being unjustly enriched at the plaintiff's expense, and this, subject to certain defined limits, the law will not allow. "Unjust enrichment" is, simply, the name which is commonly given to the principle of justice which the law recognises and gives effect to in a wide variety of claims of this kind.[65]

It has been said[66] that the principle of unjust enrichment is too vague to be of any practical value. Nevertheless, most rubrics of the law disclose, on exam-

---

[63] See, generally, (1934) 5 C.L.J. 204 [Gutteridge and David]; (1938) 16 Can. Bar Rev. 247, 365 [Friedmann]; (1939) 55 L.Q.R. 37 [Holdsworth]; 36 Tulane L.R. 605 (1962), 37 Tulane L.R. 49 (1962) [Nicholas]; J. P. Dawson, *Unjust Enrichment: A Comparative Analysis*; (1968) 3 *Israel Law Review* 526 [Elman]; (1969) 47 Can.B.R. 1 [Samek]; 8 Ottowa L. Rev. 156 (1976) [Fridman]; (1982) 5 Otago L.R. 187 [Sutton]; 67 Texas L.R. 1277 (1989) [Laycock]. On the Louisiana Law of Unjustified Enrichment, see [1991–1992] *Tulane Civil Law Forum* 3 [Barry Nicholas]. "The Province of the Law of Restitution" [1992] Can. B.R. 673 [Lionel Smith]. Contrast (1985) 5 *Legal Studies* 56 [Hedley].
In recent years Professor Birks has provided a highly influential, analytical framework for the law of restitution, without accepting the desirability of a general right of unjust enrichment: see his *Introduction to the Law of Restitution* (1985), (1982) 35 C.L.P. 53, (1983) 36 C.L.P. 141, and (1985) 5 *Legal Studies* 67.
There have also been attempts to explain and rationalise restitution through such economic concepts as "least-cost avoiders," "market-encouragement," and "wealth-dependency": see 71 Virginia L.R. 65 (1985) [Levmore]; 94 Yale L.J. 415 (1984) [Long]; 49 La.L.R. 71 (1988) [Huper]; (1990) 19 Jo. of Legal Studies 691 [Levmore].
The law of restitution developed more quickly in the U.S.A. than in England, and was undoubtedly helped to do so by the publication of the *Restatement of Restitution* in 1937. The Reporters were Professors Seavey and Scott. The writings of Professors J. P. Dawson and G. E. Palmer have been most influential. In 1978 Professor Palmer published his scholarly four-volume treatise on *Restitution*. It comprehensively analyses the American case law; but an English reader will learn much from its text.
[64] *Fibrosa Spolka Akcyjna* v. *Fairbairn Lawson Combe Barbour Ltd.* [1943] A.C. 32, 61, *per* Lord Wright. It has been argued that it is now unsatisfactory, if not misleading, to perpetuate the divisions of the law into contract, tort and restitution: see Atiyah, *Rise and Fall of the Freedom of Contract*, 764–770, following G. Gilmore, *The Death of Contract*. It is said that the case law demonstrates that the courts have been principally concerned to compensate a person for his reliance loss, and that an independent study of restitution fails to recognise the close relationship between contractual and restitutionary liabilities. These arguments do less than justice to the body of case law which protects a person's contractual expectation interest (see (1983) 99 L.Q.R. 217, 263–267 [Burrows]); and to recognise the independent existence of the law of restitution is not to deny the "very substantial and close relationship" between contract and restitution: see below, p. 9 and Chap. 17, for a discussion, and generally, Birks, *Introduction*, pp. 28–74.
[65] See, generally, (1983) 99 L.Q.R. 217, 232–239 [Burrows].
[66] "To ask what course would be *ex aequo et bono* to both sides never was a very precise guide": *Baylis* v. *Bishop of London* [1913] 1 Ch. 127, 140, *per* Hamilton L.J. See, generally, Winfield, *Province*, pp. 131 *et seq.*; (1939) 55 L.Q.R. 37, 51–53 [Holdsworth]; and *cf.* Birks, *Introduction*, pp. 22–25.

ination, an underlying principle which is almost invariably so general as to be incapable of any precise definition. Moreover, in a search for unifying principle at this level we should not expect to find any precise "common formula," but rather an abstract proposition of justice which is "both an aspiration and a standard for judgment."[67] Unjust enrichment is no more vague than the tortious principle that a man must pay for harm which he negligently causes[68] another, or the contractual principle that *pacta sunt servanda*.[69] The search for principle should not be confused with the definition of concepts.[70]

The principle of unjust enrichment is placed to the forefront of the American *Restatement of Restitution*. Paragraph 1 states that "a person who has been unjustly enriched at the expense of another is required to make restitution to the other."[71] Similar statements of principle had been made by Lord Mansfield in a number of cases[72] concerning the action for money had and received. His conclusion was that "the gist of this kind of action is, that the defendant, upon the circumstances of the case, is obliged by the ties of natural justice and equity to refund the money."[73] We have only to substitute "make restitution" for the last three words of his statement to make it appropriate for the whole law of restitution.

For many years Lord Mansfield's views gained acceptance.[74] But the change of climate which encouraged or accompanied the advance of the implied

---

[67] Dawson, *Unjust Enrichment*, p. 5, is speaking of Pomponius' statement in D. 50. 17. 206.

[68] *Problems of Restitution*, 7 Okla.L.Rev. 257 (1954) [W. Seavey].

[69] *Cf. Carl Zeiss Stiftung* v. *Herbert Smith (No. 2)* [1969] 2 Ch. 276, 301, *per* Edmund Davies L.J.

[70] For some definitions of quasi-contract, see Winfield, *Province*, pp. 119–120. Winfield concluded that "genuine quasi-contract signifies liability not exclusively referable to any other head of the law, imposed upon a particular person to pay money to another particular person on the ground of unjust benefit" (see *Province*, p. 119). This definition is, like many other definitions, open to criticism. The words, "not exclusively referable to any other head of law" are curious. Obviously, if the liability is exclusively referable to a head of law other than quasi-contract, it cannot be quasi-contractual; a definition which defines by excluding everything else is not very helpful. But, in any event, what is meant by another "head of law"? It is impossible to tell whether such matters as salvage, general average, subrogation, contribution, or equitable claims analogous to claims for money had and received, do or do not fall within the definition. Moreover, if claims are to be included which were not enforced by the common *indebitatus* counts, it is difficult to see why the field should be restricted to money claims. Winfield's attempt appears, therefore, to provide another warning against the hazards of definition, on which see (1954) 70 L.Q.R. 37 [H. L. A. Hart].

[71] § 1 of the Tentative Draft of the *Restatement of Restitution 2d* states "A person who receives a benefit by reason of an infringement of another person's interest, or of loss suffered by the other, owes restitution to him in the manner and amount necessary to prevent unjust enrichment". *Cf.* the Canadian cases of *Deglman* v. *Guaranty Trust of Canada* (1954) S.C.R. 725; *Pettkus* v. *Becker* (1980) 117 D.L.R. (3rd) 257, and *Sorochan* v. *Sorochan* (1986) 29 D.L.R. (4th) 1; the BGB, § 812(1), discussed in Zweigert and Kötz, *An Introduction to Comparative Law* (trans. Weir), pp. 578 *et seq.*; Israeli Unjust Enrichment Law, 5739–1979, s.1.

[72] See, *e.g. Moses* v. *Macferlan* (1760) 2 Burr. 1005, 1012; *Sadler* v. *Evans* (1766) 4 Burr. 1984, 1986; *Jestons* v. *Brooke* (1778) 2 Cowp. 793, 795.

[73] *Moses* v. *Macferlan* (1760) 2 Burr. 1005, 1012.

[74] See, *e.g. Munt* v. *Stokes* (1792) 4 T.R. 561, *per* Lord Kenyon; *Edwards* v. *Bates* (1844) 7 Man. & G. 590, 597–598, *per* Tindal C.J.; Bullen & Leake's *Precedents of Pleadings* (3rd ed., 1868), p. 44. Professor Dawson dates the reaction against Mansfield to the 1850s: see *Unjust Enrichment*, pp. 15–16.

contract theory also led to a reaction against his enunciation of principle. Scrutton L.J., no doubt with Lord Mansfield's influence in mind, went so far as to describe the history of the action for money had and received as a "history of well-meaning sloppiness of thought."[75] Earlier, in 1913, Hamilton L.J. had said that "whatever may have been the case 146 years ago, we are not now free in the twentieth century to administer that vague jurisprudence which is sometimes attractively styled 'justice as between man and man.' "[76] Such remarks are merely pejorative. Others are more revealing of the error under which these critics were labouring. In *Sinclair* v. *Brougham*, Lord Sumner, as Hamilton L.J. had now become, confessed[77] that "it is hard to reduce to one common formula the conditions upon which the law will imply a promise to repay money received to the plaintiff's use," a view with which Scrutton L.J. was later to express agreement.[78] It is indeed impossible to produce any such common formula in this branch, as in other branches, of the law. The principle of unjust enrichment "may defy definition and yet the presence in or absence from a situation of that which [it denotes] may be beyond doubt."[79]

Lord Sumner's opinion[80] that the scope of the action for money had and received was fixed by the decided cases was expressed at a time when the legacy of the forms of action inhibited the development of the law of restitution. Few, if any, English judges would now endorse it. The insistence on any notional promise no longer closes "the door to any theory of unjust enrichment in English law."[81] The old common law counts should be seen as "a practical and useful, if not complete or ideally perfect instrument to prevent unjust enrichment, aided by the various methods of technical equity which are also available."[82]

The case law[83] now demonstrates that the courts recognise that the principle of unjust enrichment unites restitutionary claims, and that the law is not con-

---

[75] *Holt* v. *Markham* [1923] 1 K.B. 504, 513.
[76] *Baylis* v. *Bishop of London* [1913] 1 Ch. 127, 140, referring to *Sadler* v. *Evans* (1766) 4 Burr. 1984, 1986, *per* Lord Mansfield.
[77] [1914] A.C. 398, 454.
[78] *Holt* v. *Markham* [1923] 1 K.B. 504, 514.
[79] *Carl Zeiss Stiftung* v. *Herbert Smith (No. 2)* [1969] 2 Ch. 276, 301, *per* Edmund Davies L.J.
[80] *Sinclair* v. *Brougham* [1914] A.C. 398, 453.
[81] *Nissan* v. *Att.-Gen.* [1968] 1 Q.B. 286, 352, *per* Winn L.J., endorsing Lord Wright's observations in *Legal Essays and Addresses* (1939, C.U. Press).
[82] *Ibid.*
[83] See, *e.g. Craven-Ellis* v. *Canons Ltd.* [1936] 2 K.B. 403 (see below, pp. 478 *et seq.*; *Morgan* v. *Ashcroft* [1938] 1 K.B. 49 (see below, pp. 119–121); *Fibrosa Spolka Akcyjna* v. *Fairbairn Lawson Combe Barbour* [1943] A.C. (see below, pp. 408–409, 449); *Larner* v. *London County Council* [1949] 2 K.B. 683 (see below, p. 118); *William Lacy (Hounslow) Ltd.* v. *Davis* [1957] 1 W.L.R. 932 (see below, p. 555); *Shamia* v. *Joory* [1958] 1 Q.B. 448 (see below, p. 573); *Kiriri Cotton Co. Ltd.* v. *Dewani* [1960] A.C. 192 (see below, p. 151); *Greenwood* v. *Bennett* [1973] 1 Q.B. 195 (see below, p. 172); *British Petroleum Exploration Co. (Libya) Ltd.* v. *Hunt (No. 2)* [1982] 1 W.L.R. 783, (aff'd). [1981] 1 W.L.R. 232, C.A.; [1983] A.C. 352 (see below, pp. 449 *et seq.*); *Barclays Bank Ltd.* v. *W. J. Simms & Son* [1980] Q.B. 677 (see below, pp. 447 *et seq.*); *Lipkin Gorman (A Firm)* v. *Karpnale Ltd.* [1991] 2 A.C. 548 (see below, Chap. 24); *Woolwich Equitable Building Society* v. *Commissioners of Inland Revenue* [1993] A.C. 70 (H.L.).

demned to "no further growth in this field."[84] This growth will continue. Some years ago, however, Lord Diplock denied the existence of any "general doctrine" of unjust enrichment,[85] and this has hitherto been the received view. But we are of the opinion that English law is now sufficiently mature to follow the example of other common law jurisdictions and to recognise that the principle of unjust enrichment unites all restitutionary claims.[86] The recognition of the principle of unjust enrichment should not absolve the courts from determining what is the basis of a particular restitutionary claim. But not all cases where a restitutionary claim has been granted can be readily categorised under such accepted grounds of recovery as mistake, compulsion, necessity, total failure of consideration, free acceptance, or wrongdoing. There are some decisions, including those of the House of Lords,[87] which are best explained on the basis that it is manifest that the defendant has been enriched and that it would be unjust to allow him to retain that enrichment, even though the plaintiff's claim did not fall within these accepted grounds.[88] The law of restitution is not petrified, as recent decisions of the House of Lords dramatically demonstrate.[88a] The courts may well recognise new grounds to found a restitutionary claim; unconscionability may be one such ground.[88b] The judicial recognition of the unifying principle of unjust enrichment should encourage them to do so.

It cannot be too strongly emphasised that this recognition does not, and should not, give judges carte blanche to adjudicate disputes in accordance with their own conception of justice. In Professor Dawson's words, "The aims of . . . this common enterprise are obviously to scale down the apparently unlimited mandate of the general clause, to restructure it into distinct sub-

---

[84] *Re Cleadon Trust* [1939] Ch. 286, 314, *per* Scott L.J.; see also *Morgan* v. *Ashcroft* [1938] 1 K.B. 49, 74, *per* Scott L.J.

[85] *Orakpo* v. *Manson Investments Ltd.* [1978] A.C. 95, 104, *per* Lord Diplock. See also *Re Byfield* [1982] Ch. 267, 276, *per* Goulding J. But *cf.* Lord Browne-Wilkinson's observations in *Woolwich Equitable Building Society* v. *Commissioners of Inland Revenue* [1993] A.C. 70, 196–197: "Although as yet there is in English law no general rule giving the plaintiff a right of recovery from a defendant who has been unjustly enriched at the plaintiff's expense, the concept of unjust enrichment lies at the heart of all the individual instances in which the law does give a right of recovery."

[86] See, *e.g. Government of India* v. *Taylor* [1955] A.C. 491, 513, *per* Lord Keith of Avonholm (see below, pp. 159–160); *Nissan* v. *Att.-Gen.* [1968] 1 Q.B. 286, 352, *per* Winn L.J. (see above, n. 81); *Greenwood* v. *Bennett* [1973] 1 Q.B. 195, 202, *per* Lord Denning M.R. (see below, pp. 172–174); see also the cases cited in n. 88a.

[87] *Cf. Thurstan* v. *Nottingham Permanent Benefit Building Society* [1903] A.C. 6 (see below p. 632); *Sinclair* v. *Brougham* [1914] A.C. 398 (see below, p. 83).

[88] *Cf.* Deane J. in *Pavey and Matthews Pty.* v. *Paul* (1987) 162 C.L.R. 221, 256–257, who described unjust enrichment as a "unifying legal concept, which explains why the law recognises, in a variety of distinct categories of case, an obligation on the part of the defendant to make fair and just restitution for a benefit derived at the expense of a plaintiff and which assists in the determination, by the ordinary processes of legal reasoning, of the question whether the law should, in justice, recognise such an obligation in a new or developing category of case."

[88a] *Lipkin Gorman* v. *Karpnale Ltd.* and *Woolwich Equitable B.S.* v. *I.R.C.* at n. 83.

[88b] See below, pp. 43–44.

ordinate norms that become intelligible and manageable through their narrowed scope and function."[89]

In restitution, as in other subjects, recourse must be had to the decided cases in order to transfer general principle into concrete rules of law. As Lord Wright once said of Lord Mansfield's famous dictum in *Moses* v.*Macferlan*: "Like all large generalisations, it has needed and received qualifications in practice ... The standard of what is against conscience in this context has become more or less canalised or defined, but in substance the juristic concept remains as Lord Mansfield left it."[90]

As might be expected a close study of the English decisions, and those of other common law jurisdictions, reveals a reasonably developed and systematic complex of rules. It shows that the principle of unjust enrichment is capable of elaboration and refinement. It presupposes three things. First, the defendant must have been enriched by the receipt of a *benefit*. Secondly, that benefit must have been gained *at the plaintiff's expense*. Thirdly, it would be *unjust* to allow the defendant to retain that benefit. These three subordinate principles are closely interrelated, and cannot be analysed in complete isolation from each other. Examination of each of them throws much light on the nature of restitutionary claims and the principle of unjust enrichment. We will consider these subordinate principles in turn.

(a) *The Benefit Conferred*

(A) What is a benefit?

A restitutionary claim is for the *benefit*, the *enrichment*, gained by the defendant at the plaintiff's expense; it is not one for loss suffered.[91] As will be seen,[92] the concept of *benefit* is in English law not synonymous with that of objective enrichment (in the sense that the wealth of the defendant has increased), but also embraces expense saved and "requested for performance."

Whether a plaintiff's claim is successful may depend on the nature of the benefit conferred. Different principles govern claims arising from the payment of money from claims based on the receipt of services or the delivery of goods.[93]

---

[89] Professor Dawson was commenting on the concept of *unconscionability* in Article 2–302 of the Uniform Commercial Code: *"Unconscionable Coercion: The German Version,"* 89 Harvard L.R. 1041, 1042–1044. But his comment is equally apt to describe the role of *unjust enrichment* in English law. *Cf.* Ernst von Caemmerer and Detlef König: "According to the modern German view the task of transforming the general principle into concrete rules of law can only be achieved by elaborating typical fact situations of unjust enrichment and refining the conditions and extent of recovery for each type individually."

[90] *Fibrosa Spolka Akcyjna* v. *Fairbairn Lawson Combe Barbour Ltd.* [1943] A.C. 32, 62–63.

[91] *English* v. *Dedham Vale Properties Ltd.* [1978] 1 W.L.R. 93, 112, *per* Slade J. *Cf. Sorrell* v. *Finch* [1977] A.C. 728 (estate agents absconding with deposit), noted in [1976] C.L.J. 237, 239 [Markesinis]; and contrast *Anglia T.V.* v. *Reed* [1972] 1 Q.B. 60; *Lloyd* v. *Stansbury* [1971] 1 W.L.R. 538.

[92] See below, pp. 17 *et seq.*

[93] Jurists have suggested that this asymmetry is indefensible, given the abolition of the forms of action and the development of the modern law of restitution, see below, p. 400, nn. 3–4.

Moreover, at one time it was thought that a plaintiff had to demonstrate that the defendant had gained a positive, as distinct from a negative, benefit.[94] Today few would deny that the saving of expense is a legal as well as an economic benefit. So, if you use my chattel without my consent you must compensate me for its use[95]; and it has been long recognised that the essence of a claim for contribution or recoupment is that the plaintiff has discharged the defendant's duty to make a payment to a third party.[96]

Money

The most common example of a positive benefit is *money*, which has the peculiar character of a universal medium of exchange. The mere receipt of money is therefore a benefit to the recipient. It is for this reason that restitutionary claims for money had and received are so frequent. Such claims are generally personal rather than proprietary[97] for the legal title to money, being currency,[98] will generally have passed to the recipient with delivery. The defendant may also benefit if money is paid not to him but to a third party, to his use.[99] But at common law he will only benefit if the plaintiff's payment discharges a debt which he owes to a third party.[1] It is not, however, easy to discharge another's debt in English law. This will occur only if the debtor authorised, or subsequently ratified, the payment.[2] There are few exceptions

---

[94] *Phillips* v. *Homfray* (1883) 24 Ch.D. 439, 454–455, *per* Bowen L.J.: see below, p. 717; and *Government of India* v. *Taylor* [1955] A.C. 491, 513, *per* Lord Keith: see below, pp. 159–160. But *cf. Re Wyvern Developments Ltd.* [1974] 1 W.L.R. 1097, 1105–1106, *per* Templeman J.

[95] *Strand Electric and Engineering Co.* v. *Brisford Entertainments Ltd.* [1952] 2 Q.B. 246: see below, p. 727.

[96] See below, Chaps. 12–14.

[97] Exceptionally a restitutionary proprietary claim may be granted in equity: see below, Chap. 2.

[98] *Miller* v. *Race* (1758) 1 Burr. 452, 457–458, *per* Lord Mansfield.

[99] See above, p. 3.

[1] See below, n. 2, and Chaps. 12–14.

[2] In spite of dicta to the contrary (see *Cook* v. *Lister* (1863) 13 C.B.(N.S.) 543, 594–597, *per* Willes J.; *Hirachand Punamchand* v. *Temple* [1911] 2 K.B. 330, 339, *per* Fletcher Moulton L.J.), it is probably now settled that if A, a stranger, pays B's debt to C, such payment will not of itself discharge B's liability to C, unless it has been made on B's behalf and has been subsequently ratified by him (see *James* v. *Isaacs* (1852) 12 C.B. 791; *Simpson* v. *Eggington* (1855) 10 Ex. 845; *Lucas* v. *Wilkinson* (1856) 1 H. & N. 420; *Re Rowe* [1904] 2 K.B. 483; *Smith* v. *Cox* [1940] 2 K.B. 558; see also *M'Intyre* v. *Miller* (1845) 13 M. & W. 725; *Jones* v. *Broadhurst* (1850) 9 C.B. 173; *Belshaw* v. *Bush* (1851) 11 C.B. 191; *Kemp* v. *Balls* (1854) 10 Ex. 607; *Purcell* v. *Henderson* (1885) 16 L.R.Ir. 213). The cases in which a plaintiff is entitled to restitution in respect of payment of the defendant's debt are, therefore, fairly limited; see below, Chaps. 12–14 and, in particular, *Esso Petroleum Co. Ltd.* v. *Hall Russell & Co.*, *"The Esso Bernicia"* [1989] 1 A.C. 643: see below, p. 344. There are several cases in which a claim by A to reimbursement by B has failed (see, *e.g. Stokes* v. *Lewis* (1785) 1 T.R. 20; *Tappin* v. *Broster* (1823) 1 C. & P. 112; *Ram Tahul Singh* v. *Biseswar Lall Sahoo* (1875) L.R. 2 Ind.App. 131; *Re National Motor Mail-Coach Co. Ltd.* [1908] 2 Ch. 515; *Re Cleadon Trust Ltd.* [1939] Ch. 286). In cases where A's payment is ineffective to discharge B's liability to C, it is prima facie still open to C to sue B for his debt, despite A's payment (*Lucas* v. *Wilkinson* (1856) 1 H. & N. 420), unless such an action would be a fraud on A and would constitute an abuse of the process of the court, or for some other similar reason (see *Welby* v. *Drake* (1825) 1 C. & P. 557; *Cook* v. *Lister* (1863) 13 C.B.(N.S.) 543, 594, *per* Willes J.; *Hirachand Punamchand* v. *Temple* [1911] 2 K.B. 330; *Re L. G. Clarke Ltd.* [1967] Ch. 1121; *Snelling* v. *John Snelling & Co.* [1973] Q.B. 87, 98–99; *cf. Arnett and Wensley Ltd.* v. *Good,*

to this principle,[3] which appears to be of little merit now that debts are freely assignable. The most important common law exception is where the plaintiff is compelled to make the payment by compulsion of law.[4-5]

Services

(1) *The principle of free acceptance*

The receipt of money always benefits the defendant. But *services* may not do so. From their very nature services cannot be restored; and the defendant may never have wished to receive them or, at least, to receive them if he had to pay for them. As Pollock C.B. laconically once remarked: "One cleans another's shoes. What can the other do but put them on?"[6] For that reason the common law originally concluded that a defendant could be said to have benefited from the receipt of services only if he had requested them. A true request will normally lead to the conclusion that the defendant who requested the services has contractually bound himself to pay for them.[7] But a defendant, who is not contractually bound, may have benefited from services

---

64 D.L.R. (2d) 181 (1967). If it is open to C to sue B and he does so, B will in all probability ratify A's payment, but if he does not do so and pays C, A should be entitled to recover his money from C on grounds of total failure of consideration, or alternatively to recover B's payment from C on the grounds that C received it as a trustee for him, A (see *Hirachand Punamchand* v. *Temple* [1911] 2 K.B. 330, 337, *per* Vaughan Williams L.J., 342, *per* Farwell L.J.). Even if C simply keeps A's payment and does not sue B, A can claim reimbursement from B, and if B refuses to ratify A's payment, A may be entitled to recover his money from C on grounds of total failure of consideration (*Walter* v. *James* (1871) L.R. 6 Ex. 124, 127, *per* Kelly C.B.).

It has been said that C is entitled to retain A's payment, and to disregard B's repudiation unless B also offers to pay him the same debt: see (1983) 99 L.Q.R. 534 [Friedmann], who also argues that A's payment discharges B's debt to C but that C may revive it by repaying A. In other cases, A may protect himself by taking an assignment from C of B's debt. (*Williston on Contracts*, §§ 1857–1860, concludes, on the weight of American authority, that C, after accepting A's tender, cannot sue B; but the basis of his conclusion is accord and satisfaction, not legal discharge). Contrast Birks and Beatson, *Unrequested Payment of Another's Debt* (1976) 92 L.Q.R. 188, discussing *Owen* v. *Tate* [1976] 1 Q.B. 402; and for a rejoinder to Friedmann, see Beatson, *The Use and Abuse of Unjust Enrichment*, pp. 200–205. See below, pp. 597–598 on whether A can be subrogated to C's rights against B.

[3] It would appear that, in these exceptional cases, B is deemed to have been benefited because he adopted the benefit conferred by A: see below, pp. 622 *et seq.* And *cf.* the situation where A without authority pays B's debt to C, where the debt is due under an executory contract for the sale of goods, and subsequently C delivers goods to B who accepts them: see (1983) 99 L.Q.R. 534, 542–543 [Friedmann], arguing that A may then recover from B. *Cf. Restitution for Benefits conferred without Request*, 19 Vand.L.Rev. 1183, 1206–1208 (1966) [Wade].

[4-5] See below, Chaps. 12–14.

[6] *Taylor* v. *Laird* (1856) 25 L.J. Ex. 329, 332.

[7] *Ellis* v. *Hamlen* (1810) 3 Taunt. 52, 53, *per* Sir James Mansfield C.J. In cases of money paid, such a request will often arise by virtue of some relationship between the parties. It is the foundation of the right of indemnity which, for example, an agent has against his principal, a surety against his principal debtor, an assignor of a lease against his immediate assignee, and a transferor of shares against his immediate transferee; and since the right is founded on contract, it may entitle the plaintiff to be indemnified against expenditure which has not in fact benefited the defendant: see *Brittain* v. *Lloyd* (1845) 14 M. & W. 762 (see below, p. 360, n. 17). Similarly, in case of services rendered or goods supplied, a true request, express or tacit, by the defendant to the plaintiff to render the services or supply the goods will, in the absence of special

rendered in circumstances in which the court holds him liable to pay for them. Such will be the case if he *freely accepts* the services.[8] In our view, he will be held to have benefited from the services rendered if he, as a reasonable man, should have known that the plaintiff who rendered the services expected to be paid for them, and yet he did not take a reasonable opportunity open to him to reject the proffered services.[9] Moreover, in such a case, he cannot deny that he has been *unjustly* enriched.[10]

It is said that the recognition of free acceptance, so defined, is in principle objectionable for it erodes the right of a person to determine his own choices; only if he has *requested* services has he chosen and so benefited.[11] If a principle of free acceptance is recognised, a defendant may be compelled to pay for services which he asserts, honestly if perversely, are of no benefit to him; or he may be indifferent, not caring one way or the other, whether the services are rendered or not.[12] Again, the defendant may concede that the services are beneficial but plead that he had "more important things on which to spend his money."[13] But, in these exceptional circumstances, the burden should be on the defendant, who is not the reasonable man, immediately to tell the plaintiff that he is perverse, indifferent or that he has more important things to do with his money. If he does not do so, he cannot deny that he has gained a benefit.

It is true that few judges have explicitly adopted a principle of *free acceptance*.[13a] But the principle enshrined in that concept is the most satisfactory explanation of those decisions which recognised the plaintiff's claim that his services, which had not been requested,[14] had benefited the defendant. Many of the successful claims have arisen in the context of ineffective contracts.[15] A plaintiff who rendered services under a contract which was void because the parties had not agreed on essential terms was awarded a sum which was "what

---

circumstances which show that they were not intended to be paid for, impose on the defendant a contractual obligation to pay for services rendered or goods supplied pursuant to such request.

[8] See below, pp. 19–20.

[9] *Cf. Restatement of Contracts 2d*, § 69(1).

[10] See below, p. 41.

[11] *Cf.* "Freedom, Unrequested Improvements, and Lord Denning" [1981] C.L.J. 340 [Matthews].

[12] "Free Acceptance and the Law of Restitution" (1988) 104 L.Q.R. 576, 577–580 [Burrows]. (". . . [A] defendant is just as likely to accept what the plaintiff is conferring on him where he considers it neither beneficial nor detrimental as where he considers it beneficial"; and Burrows, *the Law of Restitution*, pp. 11–15. See also "Free Acceptance: Some Further Conclusions" (1989) 105 L.Q.R. 460 [Mead]; and Birks in *Essays on the Law of Restitution* (ed. Burrows), Chap. 5, pp. 127 *et seq.*; Burrows, *The Law of Restitution*, pp. 11–15.

[13] "The Role of Subjective Benefit in the Law of Unjust Enrichment" (1990) 10 Oxford Jo. of Legal Studies 42 [Garner] who argues that it must be shown that the defendant wanted, and was willing to pay for, the services.

[13a] See Burrows, above p. 19, n. 12. In Professor Birks' view, free acceptance is the explanation of a cluster of earlier cases, including *Lamb* v. *Bunce* (1815) 4 M. & S. 275; *Weatherby* v. *Banham* (1832) 5 C. & P. 228; *Paynter* v. *Williams* (1833) 1 Cr. & M. 810; *Alexander* v. *Vane* (1836) 1 M. & W. 511: see Birks, *Essays on the Law of Restitution*, (ed. Burrows) *Chap.* 5.

[14] In some situations the defendant may have gained an incontrovertible benefit from the rendering of the services: see below, pp. 22–26.

[15] It must also be demonstrated that the defendant's enrichment is unjust: see below, pp. 39 *et seq.*

the services were worth"[16]; a builder who did extra work, thinking that a contract was about to be made, recovered a "reasonable price"[17]; and the High Court of Australia has granted a restitutionary claim for services rendered under a contract which was executed but was unenforceable by action.[18]

The principle of free acceptance may also explain the line of authority which holds that a *quantum meruit* claim will lie for the value of services rendered under an entire contract which had not been substantially performed and which the defendant had wrongfully repudiated.[19] It should not be open to the party in breach to deny that he had been benefited when it was his breach which prevented full performance.[20] Conversely, as the law now stands, if the plaintiff was in breach his restitutionary claim will normally fail.[21] The Law Commission has, however, proposed that he should be granted a restitutionary claim to the extent that his services have benefited the defendant.[22] It is a distinct and difficult question how the benefit gained by the defendant is to be valued and what is the ground of his claim.[23]

As will be seen,[24] in equity the principle of free acceptance finds its expression in the equitable doctrine of acquiescence which protects the mistaken improver of land in circumstances where the landowner encouraged him to improve the property, or stood by and allowed him to do so.[25] In such a situation it is unconscionable for the landowner to deny that he has received a benefit.[26]

It is more controversial to conclude that the defendant has received a benefit simply because he requested services, in circumstances where he gained no objective benefit from what the plaintiff has done or, possibly, is yet to do. The germ of this principle is to be found in the well-known case of *Planché* v. *Colburn*,[27] at least as subsequently interpreted by the courts.[28] The defendant publisher had wrongfully repudiated the contract before the author, the plaintiff, had delivered a single page of the manuscript. Nevertheless, the author recovered on a *quantum meruit*. A more recent illustration, in a different context, is *William Lacey (Hounslow) Ltd.* v. *Davis*.[29] In that case the

---

[16] *Way* v. *Latilla* [1937] 3 All E.R. 759 at 765, *per* Lord Wright, H.L.: see below, pp. 484–485.
[17] *Cf. William Lacey (Hounslow) Ltd.* v. *Davis* [1957] 1 W.L.R. 932 at 934: see below, p. 555.
[18] *Pavey & Matthews Pty. Ltd.* v. *Paul* (1987) 162 C.L.R. 221. Contrast Birks, *Essays* (ed. Burrows), pp. 109–112: see below, p. 65.
For the argument that these cases are best explained through the principle of failure of consideration: see (1988) 104 L.Q.R. 576 [Burrows].
[19] See below, pp. 425–428. *Cf.* Birks, *op. cit.* pp. 126–127, who describes this acceptance as "limited acceptance"; see also *Essays on Restitution* (ed. Burrows), pp. 127–141.
[20] *Cf.* (1988) L.Q.R. 576, 582–583 [Burrows].
[21] See below, p. 446.
[22] See below, pp. 438–440.
[23] See below, pp. 28–35.
[24] See below, Chap. 5.
[25] The improver may recover even if the landowner shared his mistake: see below, pp. 169–170.
[26] See below, Chap. 5. *Cf.* Birks, *Essays* (ed. Burrows), *op. cit.* pp. 128–132.
[27] (1831) 8 Bing. 14: see below, p. 425.
[28] See below, p. 426, n. 35.
[29] [1957] 1 W.L.R. 932.

plaintiff had done work in the expectation that a contract was about to be made; in fact the parties failed to reach any agreement. He recovered on a *quantum meruit*, for "the party from whom the payment was sought requested the work and obtained the benefit of it."[30] It has been argued that this is in essence a claim for reliance loss and not one for an enrichment gained at the plaintiff's expense.[31] But, as an Italian scholar, Professor Gallo, has pointed out,[32] common lawyers characterise *benefit* not only in terms of a benefit which has in fact been received but in terms of "requested for performance." It may be tempting for a plaintiff to claim that the defendant has received a benefit, for a restitutionary claim may succeed when a claim based on the contract for damages must fail. So, in *Planché* v. *Colburn*, the plaintiff's claim to recoup his reliance loss would have failed if he would have made a greater loss from the entire performance of the contract[33]; and in *William Lacey* v. *Davis* since there was no contract there could be no claim for damages based on its breach.[34] As the latter case demonstrates, the concept of "requested for performance" may be sufficiently generous to embrace the situation where a plaintiff incurred expenses, anticipating that he and the defendant would soon enter into a contract, in circumstances where the defendant, knowing that he expected to be recompensed for the services rendered, withdrew from the contractual negotiations.[35]

The concept of benefit is consequently extended to embrace services which have been requested but which have not been rendered.[36] In our view, a defendant should be deemed to have received a benefit only if he has received an objective benefit, in the sense that he cannot deny that he has made a realisable gain or has been saved an expense.[37] This conclusion will, moreover, avoid the awkward question of construction, which has troubled courts in the United States,[38] namely, whether the plaintiff has performed part of the performance, for which he bargained, or has only performed acts preparatory to performance. Common lawyers have, as has been seen, accepted that the defendant may gain a benefit "even though there was never any product created by the service that

---

[30] At p. 939, *per* Barry J. See below, p. 555.
[31] See "Benefit, Reliance and the Structure of Unjust Enrichment" [1987] C.L.P. 71 [Beatson] and Beatson, *The Use and Abuse of Unjust Enrichment*, Chap. 2: see below, pp. 424–425.
[32] *L'Arricchimento Senza Causa* (Padova 1990), pp. 87 *et seq.* We are indebted to Professor Gallo for the text and to Luigi Chessa Ll.M. (Cantab.) for the translation.
[33] *Cf. CCC Films (London) Ltd.* v. *Impact Quadrant Films Ltd.* [1984] 3 All E.R. 298.
[34] In the United States a plaintiff has successfully argued that his claim, which was essentially for reliance loss, was a restitutionary claim and was therefore outside the Statute of Frauds: see Farnsworth, *Contracts*, §§6.11–6.12.
[35] See below, Chap. 25. *Cf. Essays* (ed. Burrows), pp. 141–143 [Birks], discussing, *inter alia*, *Sabemo Pty. Ltd.* v. *North Sydney Municipal Council* [1977] 2 N.S.W.L.R. 880.
[36] Contra *Restitution without Enrichment* (1981), 61 Boston Univ.L.R. 563 [Dawson]: followed by Birks, *Essays* (ed. Burrows), pp. 137–141.
[37] If he has freely accepted services, he cannot deny these facts. Contrast the concept of "incontrovertible benefit": see below, p. 22.
[38] Palmer, *op. cit.* Vol. I, para. 4.2.

added to the wealth of the defendant."[39] A court may more readily question this principle if it is perceived that a claim based on benefits conferred may conceal a claim for loss suffered, in reliance on the defendant's performance of a contract which is or has become ineffective.[40]

There is the related question: can D be said to have received a benefit if P performs services which benefit a third person, T, but not D? If these services are requested by D under an agreement which is or becomes ineffective, a court may well find that D has benefited from the services rendered; and the Law Commission has recommended that a person who, having partly performed a contract, then wrongfully repudiates it, should be entitled to claim the value of the benefit conferred if he has benefited a third person at the defendant's request.[41]

Finally, a defendant may receive a benefit even though the plaintiff's services do not leave a "marketable residuum" or increase his "human capital".[42] "Pure" services will generally have a market value. It surely cannot be denied that P who regularly cuts D's hair or feeds him has rendered services which can be valued and which, if freely accepted, have benefited D.

We discuss later in this Chapter how services which have been freely requested are valued.[43-44] It is sufficient here to say that the value is normally the reasonable value of the services at the date when the services were rendered, although the price, or a proportion of it,[45] agreed by the parties may, in many cases, be the ceiling to any award even if that price is embodied in a contract which is or becomes ineffective.[46]

(2) *The principle of incontrovertible benefit*

At one time English courts did not generally inquire whether a defendant had been incontrovertibly benefited; he was not deemed to have received a benefit unless he requested or freely accepted the services. But other jurisdictions did consider it critical that he had been incontrovertibly benefited, even though he had not requested the services. The Indian Contract Act[47] provides that: "Where a person lawfully does anything for another person, or delivers any-

---

[39] The (First) *Restatement of Contracts*, para. 348, comment (a), which the American courts still accept: see Palmer, *op. cit.* Vol. I, para. 4.2.

[40] See below, p. 426 for a fuller discussion; and contrast Birks, *Essays* (ed. Burrows) *op. cit.* pp. 140–141.

[41] Law Commission *Report, No. 121, Law of Contract: Pecuniary Restitution on Breach of Contract* (1983), para. 2.47: see below, pp. 444–447.

[42] Contrast Beatson, p. 21, n. 31 of this text.

[43-44] See below, pp. 28 *et seq.*

[45] *Cf.* (1989) 12 Sydney L.R. 76 [Hunter].

[46] See below, pp. 29–30.

[47] § 70, which has also been adopted in Malaya. But no compensation will be granted unless "(1) the thing must be done lawfully; (2) it must be done by a person not intending to act gratuitously; and (3) the person for whom the act is done must enjoy the benefit of it": Pollock and Mulla, *The Indian Contract Act*, p. 245. (This principle is then wider than that of incontrovertible benefit). *Cf. Siow Wong Fatt* v. *Susur Rotan Mining Co. Ltd.* [1967] 2 A.C. 269, 276, *per* Lord Upjohn, P.C. The principles of Scots law are somewhat comparable: see *The Lawrence Building Co. Ltd.* v. *Lanarkshire C.C.*, 1977 S.L.T. 110, 111, 113, *per* Lord Maxwell.

thing to him, not intending to do so gratuitously, and such other person enjoys the benefit thereof, the latter is bound to make compensation to the former in respect of, or to restore, the thing so done or delivered." The Supreme Court of Canada had held that a defendant was benefited when the plaintiff mistakenly discharged, without the defendant's knowledge, the defendant's statutory duty to support an indigent[48]; and, in the United States, some states, following the civilians, have granted restitution to the mistaken improver of land.[49] There is much to be said for the view that a person has been incontrovertibly benefited[50] if a reasonable person would conclude that he has been saved an expense which he otherwise would necessarily have incurred or where he has made, in consequence of the plaintiff's acts, a realisable financial gain.[50a]

Any principle of incontrovertible benefit will, of course, be refined by judicial decisions. In determining what is a *necessary* expense the Supreme Court of New South Wales has accepted[51] Professor Birks' qualification that unrealistic or fanciful possibilities should be discounted.[52] Again, it is sufficient, in our view, that the benefit is *realisable*; it should not be necessary to demonstrate that it has been *realised*. It may not be unreasonable, in some circumstances, to compel a person to sell an asset which another has mistakenly improved.[53] But not every financial gain may be said to be *realisable*.[53a] It is long established that, subject to the application of the equitable doctrine of acquiescence,[54] a landowner is not obliged to make restitution to the mistaken improver even though the land can, of course, be sold or mortgaged.

To accept the principle of incontrovertible benefit will not be to recognise a novel principle. There are a number of decisions which are best explained on this ground, even though the courts may not always have explicitly adopted that principle.

There is, for example, nineteenth-century and modern authority which holds that a trustee, who improved property which he improperly bought from the trust, can obtain restitution for the benefit conferred if the beneficiaries set aside the purchase[55]; and a purchaser who improved land, in circumstances in which both vendor and purchaser mistakenly thought the contract of sale was

---

[48] *County of Carleton* v. *City of Ottawa* (1963) 39 D.L.R. (2d) 11: see below, p. 177. And *cf. Weldon* v. *Canadian Surety Co.*, 64 D.L.R. (2d) 735 (1966).

[49] See below, p. 167, n. 6.

[50] Contrast the position if there is a "free acceptance" of services: see above, pp. 18–19.

[50a] *Cf.* Burrows, *The Law of Restitution*, pp. 10–11 and see below, n. 53a.

[51] *Monks* v. *Poynice Pty. Ltd.* (1987) 11 A.C.L.R. 637, 640.

[52] Birks, *Introduction*, p. 120.

[53] This was accepted by Judge Bowsher Q.C. in *Marston Construction Co. Ltd.* v. *Kigass Ltd.* [1989] *Construction Industry Law Letter*, 476. For a different view, see Birks, *Introduction*, pp. 121–124.

[53a] Contrast Burrows, *The Law of Restitution*, p. 10, who takes an intermediate view: a defendant will be incontrovertibly benefited if the court regards it as "reasonably certain that he will realise the positive benefit."

[54] See below, Chap. 5.

[55] The authorities, which are somewhat conflicting, are collected in *Holder* v. *Holder* [1968] Ch. 373–374, *per* Cross J. (reversed on a different point in [1968] Ch. 353); see below, p. 652 for a fuller discussion.

valid, was held entitled to recover the value of the improvements.[56] In *Société Franco Tunisienne D'Armement* v. *Sidermar SPA*[57] Pearson J. held that shipowners were entitled to reasonable freight on a *quantum meruit*, though the contract of carriage had been frustrated by the closure of the Suez Canal; the cargo had been carried to its destination and the cargo owners had therefore undoubtedly been benefited. Lord Denning M.R.[58] allowed a person who mistakenly improved another's chattel a restitutionary claim against the owner; and now, by statute,[59] in "proceedings for wrongful interference with goods" the court must make the improver an allowance to "the extent to which . . . the value of the goods is attributable to the improvement." Again, the Law Commission[60] has proposed that an innocent party should make restitution for benefits conferred by a party in breach of contract even though those benefits have been conferred under an entire contract which was not wholly performed.[61] Restitution is granted in all these cases because it is apparent that the defendant has been incontrovertibly benefited.[62] Indeed this may be the only satisfactory explanation of the leading decision of *Craven-Ellis* v. *Canons Ltd.*[63] In that case the plaintiff, whose contract of employment with the defendant company was void, was allowed a *quantum meruit* claim even though there was "nobody for want of authority, at any material time, who could act for the company . . . who could make requests for the company, or who could enter into any contract express or implied."[64] The company had benefited because it had received services which it "would have had to get some other agent to carry out."[65]

More recently, in *The Manila*,[66] Hirst J. expressly accepted the principle of incontrovertible benefit, although he held on the facts that there was no such benefit. The question had arisen some years before in *The Winson*.[67] Salvors salvaged cargo, depositing it on a wharf. They asked the cargo owners for instructions and received no reply. Consequently they stored the cargo in order to preserve it, and subsequently sued the cargo owners for the expenses which

---

[56] *Lee-Parker* v. *Izett (No. 2)* [1972] 1 W.L.R. 775. But the vendor was entitled to a set-off for the rental value of the purchaser's occupation: see below, p. 486.

[57] [1961] 2 Q.B. 278, overruled on other grounds in *Ocean Tramp Tankers Organisation* v. *V/O Soyfracht ("The Eugenia")* [1964] 2 Q.B. 226. *Cf.* the deviation cases: see below, pp. 442–443.

[58] *Greenwood* v. *Bennett* [1973] 1 Q.B. 195, 202: see below, pp. 172–174. *Cf. The Swan* [1968] 1 Lloyd's Rep. 5.

[59] Torts (Interference with Goods) Act 1977, ss.1 and 6: see below, p. 174.

[60] Report, No. 121. *Law of Contract: Pecuniary Restitution on Breach of Contract*: see below, pp. 446–447.

[61] The innocent party will have, of course, his action for damages.

[62] *Cf.* Birks, *Introduction*, pp. 116 *et seq.* for a somewhat similar principle.

[63] [1936] 2 K.B. 403: see below, pp. 478–480 and see Birks, *Introduction*, pp. 119–120. But *cf. Kepong Prospecting Ltd.* v. *Schmidt* [1968] A.C. 810, P.C.

[64] [1936] 2 All E.R. 1066, 1069, *per* Croom-Johnson K.C., *arguendo*; this passage does not appear in the law reports.

[65] [1936] 2 K.B. 403, 412, *per* Greer L.J. See generally on this point Birks, *Negotiorum Gestio and the Common Law* [1971] C.L.P. 110.

[66] [1988] 3 All E.R. 843, 855, noted in [1989] L.M.C. L.Q. 397, 401.

[67] *China Pacific S.A.* v. *Food Corporation of India (The Winson)* [1982] A.C. 939. *Cf.* the cases on compulsory discharge of another's liability: see below, Chap. 14.

they had incurred. At first instance Lloyd J. held that the salvors had the right as bailees to be reimbursed these expenses even though there was no emergency and it was not essential to store the cargo.[68] But he also went on to say, following *Craven Ellis* v. *Canons Ltd.*,[69] *Société Franco Tunisienne D'Armement* v. *Sidermar SPA*[70] and Lord Denning M.R.'s judgment in *Greenwood* v. *Bennett*,[71] that, even if the salvage agreement had come to an end, the salvors would have succeeded on the ground that the cargo owners had nonetheless gained a benefit at the salvors' expense and it would be unjust to allow them to retain it.[72] The House of Lords held[73] that there was a direct pre-existing relationship of bailor and bailee between the cargo owners and the salvors and that that relationship continued to subsist after the cargo had been deposited. The salvors would have been liable in damages for any diminution in the value of the goods; and, having fulfilled their duty to preserve the cargo, they had a correlative right to charge expenses reasonably incurred in preserving the cargo where the owner had failed to give any instructions what should be done with it. But Lord Diplock also cited with approval the decision of the Court of Session in *Garriock* v. *Walker*,[74] where the cargo owner did not acquiesce in the steps taken by his bailee to preserve the cargo. "Nevertheless he took the benefit of them by taking delivery of the cargo thus preserved at the conclusion of the voyage."[75]

Given the history of the law of restitution, it is not surprising that until recently the courts did not rationalise these decisions in terms of incontrovertible benefit. Today, as we have seen, they are more ready to do so.

To allow recovery because a defendant has been incontrovertibly benefited is to accept that he may have to make restitution[76] even though he did not request or freely accept the benefit. In the past, the principle embodied in Bowen L.J.'s well-known dictum in *Falcke's* case,[77] that "liabilities are not to be forced on people behind their backs any more than you can confer a benefit upon a man against his will," has been regarded as paramount. Free choice must be preserved inviolate.[78] To accept the principle of incontrovertible benefit is to admit a limited and, in our view, desirable exception. The burden

---

[68] [1979] 2 All E.R. 35; and see the arguments for the salvors before the House of Lords: [1982] A.C. 939, 947–948.
[69] [1936] 2 K.B. 403: see below, p. 478.
[70] [1961] 2 Q.B. 278: see above, p. 24.
[71] [1973] Q.B. 195, 202: see below, pp. 172–174.
[72] [1979] 2 All E.R. 35, 43–44.
[73] [1982] A.C. 939, reversing the Court of Appeal.
[74] (1973) 1 R. (Ct. of Session) 100.
[75] [1982] A.C. 939, 961.
[76] But the enrichment must be an *unjust* enrichment on which see below, pp. 39 *et seq.*
[77] *Falcke* v. *Scottish Imperial Insurance Co.* (1886) 34 Ch.D. 234, 248: see below, p. 369.
[78] See [1981] C.L.J. 340 [Matthews]. In his *Unjust Enrichment*, pp. 58–60 and 95–98, Klippert draws a distinction between irrebuttable benefit (the unofficious discharge of obligations) and incontrovertible benefit. Such a distinction is drawn in an attempt to reconcile such cases as *County of Carleton* v. *City of Ottawa* (1963) 39 D.L.R. (2d) 11 (see below, p. 177) with the principle of free choice. But it cannot accommodate the facts of *Greenwood* v. *Bennett* [1973] Q.B. 195 (see below, p. 172), and for that reason we would reject it.

will always be on the plaintiff to show that he did not act officiously,[79] that the particular defendant has gained a realisable financial benefit or has been saved an inevitable expense and that it will not be a hardship to the defendant, in the circumstances of the case, to make restitution.

(3) *Necessitous intervention*

There is one situation where a defendant may be deemed to have benefited from services even if he did not freely accept them and received no actual benefit from them. Decisions in other common law jurisdictions suggest that a plaintiff who intervenes in an emergency to save another's life and (possibly) his property may obtain restitution even though the services did not benefit the defendant because the plaintiff's intervention was unavailing.[80] But the recognition of this claim, which has received only a limited recognition in this country,[80a] may simply reflect society's concern to encourage intervention in an emergency rather than its desire to deprive a defendant of an unjust benefit.

Goods

The receipt of *goods* may also benefit the defendant. Unlike services, goods can be returned. Consequently, a restitutionary claim is never appropriate if the property still remains in the plaintiff and the defendant is in a position to return the goods; the plaintiff then has his remedies for wrongful interference.

(1) *The principle of free acceptance*

Conversely, when property in goods has passed to the defendant, a restitutionary claim may fail because the defendant consumed the goods not knowing that he had to pay for them.[81] It is for this reason that the plaintiff must normally show that the defendant has requested or freely accepted the goods. As in the case of services, a restitutionary claim for the price of the goods delivered will lie if the defendant had a reasonable opportunity to reject the goods but consumed them in circumstances in which, as a reasonable man, he should have known that the plaintiff expected to be paid for them. This may occur if the defendant consumes goods which have been delivered under a contract void for want of authority[82] or under a contract which is ineffective because the parties have failed to agree the price. In such cases it is evident that he has received a benefit which has enriched him. It is another question, which we discuss later, how the enrichment is valued.[83]

(2) *The principle of incontrovertible benefit*

The analogy of the cases on services also suggests that an English court may

---

[79] On which see below, p. 58.
[80] See below, p. 377.
[80a] See below, Chap. 15.
[81] *Cf. Boulton* v. *Jones* (1857) 2 H. & N. 564: see below, p. 488.
[82] See below, Chap. 20.
[83] See below, pp. 28 *et seq.*

impose a *quantum valebat* claim for goods delivered, in the absence of a request or free acceptance, if their delivery has incontrovertibly benefited the defendant.[84]

(3) Necessitous intervention

Finally, if goods are delivered in an emergency, the defendant may possibly be bound to make restitution even though the goods did not in fact benefit him.[85]

Land

Land is a very special case. If property has passed to another, the requisite formalities ensure that a conveyance, or at least a contract, must have been executed. Restitution, if necessary, can only, therefore, be effected by rescission or rectification of the contract, by rectification of the conveyance or by rectification of the land register. A plaintiff may have improved another's property in circumstances where title to that property has not passed to him. Whether he will then obtain restitution will depend on whether the defendant has requested or freely accepted the services or acquiesced in what he did. As the law now stands, it is generally not enough that he has incontrovertibly benefited the defendant by improving the defendant's land.[86] Moreover, it is, on the present authorities,[87] doubtful whether he can be held liable in a restitutionary action[88] to restore any benefit accruing to him from the use and occupation of the land.

Other benefits

Money, services, goods and land are the principal, though not the exclusive, types of benefit which may give rise to a claim in restitution. The cases provide many other examples of benefits which have been recognised as restitutionary benefits. A defendant's contractual or statutory liability to a third party may be discharged[89]; his chattel my be improved[90]; he may use profitably another's asset[91]; he may utilise confidential information[92]; he may profit from a position of trust[93]; he may save himself expense[94]; or he may receive the benefit of a chose in action.[95]

---

[84] See above, pp. 23–26 for a discussion of the concept of incontrovertible benefit.
[85] See above, pp. 26 *et seq.*
[86] See below, Chap. 5.
[87] See below, pp. 166–167.
[88] But there may be an action for mesne profits.
[89] See below, Chap. 14.
[90] See below, pp. 172–174.
[91] See below, p. 726.
[92] See below, Chap. 33.
[93] See below, Chap. 36.
[94] See, *e.g.* below, pp. 717–720.
[95] *e.g.* under a contract subsequently rescinded for misrepresentation, duress or undue influence: see below, Chaps. 9–11.

(B) The valuation of the benefit

Money

Money claims rarely present any problem of valuation if the plaintiff simply seeks to make the defendant personally liable to make restitution. If the plaintiff is successful, the defendant will be required to repay a sum equivalent to that received or applied for his benefit. His assets have been increased to that extent, and that is the value of his benefit.

Difficulties can arise, however, if a plaintiff seeks to recover profits which, he alleges, the defendant has gained at his expense. First, a plaintiff has no right to an account. It is an equitable remedy granted at the court's discretion[96]; for example, it may be denied if a defendant acted innocently in using another's trade secret.[97] Secondly, it is a personal remedy which renders a defendant liable to pay over a sum of money, consisting of the profits which he made. Thirdly, it is said that to order an account is to set in train a "complex and protracted" inquiry.[98] But that should not be in itself a sufficient reason for denying an account in an appropriate case.[99] So, in the *Spycatcher* case, the House of Lords ordered what was in fact a "complex and protracted" inquiry when it required the *Sunday Times* to account for the profits made from the issue of the newspaper containing extracts from Mr. Peter Wright's memoirs.[1] We discuss later in this Chapter the extent to which a wrongdoer can claim an allowance for his skills and expenditure in earning the profits for which he must account.[2]

A claim that a defendant is a trustee of money for the plaintiff or that the plaintiff is entitled to a lien over a fund in his hands presents more complex questions which we discuss in the following Chapter of this book, entitled "Proprietary Claims".

Services rendered and goods supplied

(1) *Services and goods freely accepted*

If a defendant has freely accepted services or goods, then the general rule is that he must pay their reasonable value at the date they were rendered or delivered respectively. Reasonable value is normally market value, that is the sum which a willing supplier and buyer would have agreed upon; any sum awarded will generally include a figure which represents a profit element,[3] although excep-

---

[96] By the middle of the 18th century the common law action of account had fallen into desuetude. Thereafter, account was always sought in equity: Story, *Equity Jurisprudence* (Boston 1836), Vol. I, pp. 427 *et seq.*

[97] *Seager* v. *Copydex Ltd.* [1967] 1 W.L.R. 923: see below, p. 692.

[98] *Siddell* v. *Vickers* (1892) 9 R.P.C. 152, 162–163, *per* Lindley L.J.

[99] *My Kinda Town* v. *Soll* [1982] F.S.R. 147, 156, *per* Slade J.

[1] *Att.-Gen.* v. *Guardian Newspapers Ltd. (No. 2)* [1990] 1 A.C. 109: see below, p. 691.

[2] See below, pp. 32–34.

[3] *Cf. Rover International Ltd.* v. *Cannon Film Sales Ltd.* [1989] 1 W.L.R. 912, 922, *per* Kerr L.J.

tionally a court has granted only the actual cost of services and goods.[4] The "special position" of the parties may also be taken into account in determining what is the reasonable value of the services and goods.[5]

It has been argued[6] that the award should be limited to the value of the benefit to the particular defendant, which may be less than its market value. But the application of the principle of subjective devaluation (to adopt Professor Birks' terminology)[7] may result in hardship to the plaintiff. For example, a rogue persuades D that P will render services for £100 and P that D will pay him £200. On such facts the courts have awarded P the reasonable value of his services.[8] Both are the innocent victims of the rogue; and D should not be allowed successfully to say that he would not have entered into the agreement if he knew that he would have to pay more than £100.

If the defendant has freely accepted services or goods, which have been rendered or supplied under a contract which is or has become ineffective, it may be proper to look to the price which the parties have agreed should be paid in respect of the benefit so conferred. The contract price provides evidence of the reasonable value of services rendered in part performance of a contract which the defendant has wrongfully repudiated.[9] But it is only evidence, and the sum awarded may exceed the contract price.[10] In contrast, Deane J., in the High Court of Australia,[11] was of the view that the contract price should provide a ceiling of any award to the plaintiff for services rendered under a contract which was unenforceable by him and which the defendant had wrongfully repudiated. Again, in litigation arising out of a contract which had been frustrated,[12] it has been held that the consideration agreed upon is relevant as providing some evidence of the "just" sum to be awarded and may "provide a limit to the sum to be awarded."[13] The price agreed may also be held to provide the ceiling of an award if a contract is held to be void, for example, if the parties failed to agree on an essential term of the bargain or if there was some unresolved ambiguity in a fundamental contractual term.[14] It is not surprising that a court should look to the agreed price if the contract failed because some other essential term had not been agreed upon or was fatally equivocal. But in *Way* v. *Latilla*[15] the parties had not agreed on what the

---

[4] As in the Massachusetts case of *Vickery* v. *Ritchie* (1909) 88 N.E. 835: see below, p. 491.

[5] As it was in *Seager* v. *Copydex Ltd.* (*No. 2*) [1969] 2 All E.R. 718, C.A.

[6] (1989) 9 Legal Studies 121, 131–132 [Arrowsmith]; *Essays* (ed. Burrows), pp. 129, 136–137 [Birks].

[7] *Introduction.*

[8] See below, p. 491.

[9] See below, pp. 424 *et seq.*

[10] *Ibid.* for a further analysis and criticism.

[11] *Pavey & Matthews Pty. Ltd.* v. *Paul* (1987) 162 C.L.R. 221, 257; *cf. Scarisbrick* v. *Parkinson* (1869) 20 L.T. 175.

[12] *British Exploration Co. (Libya) Ltd.* v. *Hunt (No. 2)* [1979] 1 W.L.R. 783, [1981] 1 W.L.R. 232, C.A., [1983] 2 A.C. 352, H.L. Henceforth referred to in the notes as *B.P.* v. *Hunt.*

[13] [1979] 1 W.L.R. 783, 805–806, *per* Robert Goff J.: see below, pp. 458–459.

[14] See below, Chap. 21.

[15] [1937] 3 All E.R. 759.

plaintiff's remuneration should be. Nonetheless, Lord Atkin was of the opinion that the

> "court may take into account the bargainings between the parties, not with a view to completing the bargain for them, but as evidence of the value which each of them puts upon the services. If the discussion had ranged between three per cent. on the one side and five per cent. on the other, all else being agreed, the court would not be likely to depart from somewhere about those figures, and would be wrong in ignoring them altogether and fixing remuneration on an entirely different basis, upon which, possibly, the services would never have been rendered at all."[16]

Only in exceptional circumstances should a court ignore the terms of the ineffective agreement.[17]

(2) *Services rendered and goods delivered which have incontrovertibly benefited the defendant*

A defendant may be incontrovertibly benefited[18] even though he has not freely accepted the services or goods. How that benefit is valued will depend on the facts of the particular case. To take a few examples:

(1) Necessary services may be rendered under a contract which is void for want of authority; it is then proper to grant the plaintiff a reasonable sum which may be measured by the sum which the parties had agreed upon.[19]

(2) P thinks that he is the owner of a car and improves it without the true owner's, D's, knowledge. P should recover from D the reasonable value of his services or the increased value of the car, whichever is the lower figure.[20]

(3) P mistakenly delivers oil to D who consumes it, not knowing of P's mistake. P should have delivered it to T who has a standing contract with him. The value of D's incontrovertible benefit is the market value of the oil (including a profit element), the sum which D regularly pays his supplier, or possibly the sum which T had agreed to pay P,[21] whichever is the lowest figure.

(4) P wrongfully repudiates an entire contract before he has substantially performed his side of the bargain. He has, however, rendered valuable

---

[16] At p. 764.

[17] For such a case, see *Rover International Ltd.* v. *Cannon Film Sales Ltd.* [1989] 1 W.L.R. 912, 927–928, *per* Kerr L.J. ("All remedies must necessarily lie in the area of restitution".) See below, pp. 543–544 for a discussion of the decision.

[18] For a definition of incontrovertible benefit, see above, pp. 26 *et seq.*

[19] *Cf. Craven-Ellis* v. *Canons Ltd.* [1936] 2 K.B. 403: see below, pp. 478–480.

[20] Or possibly the sum, adjusted for inflation, which D had agreed, in the past, to pay a third party for a similar improvement.
In *Greenwood* v. *Bennett* [1973] 1 Q.B. 195, the Court of Appeal awarded the reasonable value of the services rendered, without any consideration of alternative awards: see below, pp. 172 *et seq.*

[21] This award may ensure that P does not profit from his mistake. D is not a wrongdoer, but an innocent defendant.

services which D had bargained for. As English law now stands, he is without a remedy.[22] But the Law Commission has proposed[23] that, as in some other common law jurisdictions,[24] P should be allowed to recover the value of the benefit conferred, subject to the innocent party's, D's, counterclaim for loss suffered. In these circumstances D's incontrovertible benefit should be a sum which represents the reasonable value of P's services, the increased value of D's assets or a rateable proportion of the contract price, whichever is the lowest figure.

(3) *Services rendered in an emergency*

There is very little, if any, English authority to support a restitutionary claim. The case law of other common law jurisdictions suggest that the intervener may recover reasonable expenses and, if a professional, (for example, a doctor), reasonable remuneration.[24a]

Is the determination of the value of the benefit gained by the defendant dependent upon whether the defendant has acted wrongfully?

An accounting of profits

There is some English authority,[25] as there is in the United States,[26] that a defendant who has consciously exploited another's trade mark or trade secret must account for the profits which he thereby made,[27] as must a conscious infringer of another's patent or copyright.[28] But it is not every conscious wrongdoer who must account for profits. As will be seen, some torts cannot form the basis of a restitutionary claim,[29] and a defendant who wrongfully repudiates a contract is under no obligation to account for profits made from the breach.[30]

In contrast, the honest defendant may be required to make restitution, but not necessarily to account for profits. The defendant who honestly but unwittingly betrayed another's confidence had only to pay "damages" which were measured by the reasonable value of the confidential information which he had

---

[22] See below, pp. 444–447 for a full discussion.

[23] Report, No. 121, Law of Contract, *Pecuniary Restitution on Breach of Contract*: see below, pp. 428 *et seq.* for a full discussion.

[24] *e.g.* in the U.S.A.

[24a] See below, pp. 377–378.

[25] *Seager* v. *Copydex Ltd. (No. 2)* [1969] 1 W.L.R. 809, C.A. (innocent exploitation, no account), with which contrast *Peter Pan Manufacturing Corp.* v. *Corsets Silhouette Ltd.* [1963] R.P.C. 45 45 (conscious exploitation, account ordered): see below, Chap. 36.

[26] *Olwell & Nye* v. *Nye & Nissen Co.* 173 P. 2d 652, especially at 654, following *Restatement of Restitution*, pp. 595–596.

[27] *Edelsten* v. *Edelsten* (1863) 1 De G. J. & Sm. 185, 189, *per* Lord Westbury.

[28] Patents Act 1977, ss.61–62; Copyright Designs and Patents Act 1988, ss.96 and 97.

[29] See below, Chap. 38.

[30] Only the Israeli Supreme Court has reached a different conclusion: see below, pp. 415–417.

used.[31] Similarly, the Copyright, Designs and Patents Act 1988[32] treats more harshly the conscious infringer than the infringer who did not know and had no reason to believe that he was infringing copyright; it is a defence to an action for damages, but not to any other remedy, that he did not know and had no reason to believe that he was infringing copyright. If these common law and statutory analogies are followed, then the extent of the wrongdoers liability, and in particular that of tortfeasors, may depend on the court's characterisation of the conduct of the wrongdoer.

If it is the general rule that the innocent wrongdoer will not be obliged to account for profits, then there are important exceptions to it. First, if the defendant is a fiduciary and is said to have breached his fiduciary duty of loyalty, then not only is he personally liable to account for any profit but he is a constructive trustee of any identifiable benefit. It matters not that he acted honestly and in his principal's best interests, that his principal also benefited from what he did, and that his principal would not have been in a position to acquire the benefit which he gained.[33] This equitable principle is well established and admits few exceptions. As will be seen, the class of fiduciary relationships is never closed, and exceptionally even a person who wrongfully repudiates his contractual obligations may be said to owe a fiduciary duty to the person he wronged.[34]

Secondly, the plaintiff may have interests which the courts wish to protect. These include such economic interests as title to property and, in other common law jurisdictions, the right to exploit one's own personality.[35] A court may then, for this reason, deprive even an innocent wrongdoer of his profits.

In determining the *quantum* of profits for which the wrongdoer must account, a court may have to consider whether a wrongdoer should be granted an allowance for his skills in earning that profit and whether he should be reimbursed his necessary expenses. It has been recently said that only in "exceptional circumstances"[36] should a court remunerate, or grant an allowance to, a fiduciary. The claim must be "overwhelming" and "not provide any encouragement to trustees to put themselves in a position were their duties as trustees conflicted with their interests."[37] In *Boardman* v. *Phipps*,[38] if Mr. Boardman, the fiduciary, had not done what he did, "the beneficiaries would have had to employ (and would, had they been well advised, have employed) an expert to do it for them ... It seems ... inequitable now for the beneficiaries to step in and take

---

[31] See above, n. 28.
[32] ss. 96 and 97.
[33] See below, Chap. 33.
[34] *Cf. LAC Minerals Ltd.* v. *International Corona Resources* (1989) 61 D.L.R. (4th) 14: see Chap. 3.
[35] See below, pp. 643–644.
[36] *Guinness plc.* v. *Saunders* [1990] 2 A.C. 663, 694, *per* Lord Templeman; said in context of Mr. Ward's claim for an equitable allowance.
[37] *Op. cit.* at 701, *per* Lord Goff.
[38] [1967] 2 A.C. 46: see below, pp. 663–664.

the profit without paying for the skill and labour which has produced it."[39] In that case Mr. Boardman was as honest as the day is long. In *Guinness plc*. v. *Saunders*, Mr. Ward was assumed to be just as honest,[40] but he was granted neither remuneration nor an allowance. The House of Lords proceeded on the basis that, in the context of Guinness's successful application for summary judgment, £5.2 million was a proper reward for Mr. Ward's services, and that he "acted in good faith, believing that his services were rendered under contract binding on the company" and, in that mistaken belief, he "may have rendered services to Guinness of great value and contributed substantially to the enrichment of the shareholders of Guinness."[41] Nevertheless, that mistake, in particular his failure to realise that he could not use his position as a director to obtain a contingent fee of £5.2 million, authorised by a sub-committee of Guinness directors (which included Mr. Ward) but not disclosed to the full Guinness board, did not "excuse him or enable him to defeat the rules of equity which prohibit a trustee from putting himself in a position in which his interests and duty conflict and which insist that a trustee or any other fiduciary shall not make a profit out of his trust."[42] The House of Lords held that Guinness was entitled to recover the fee. Mr. Ward was not entitled to reasonable remuneration, and the House declined to exercise its equitable jurisdiction to grant him an allowance. It would not in the circumstances be "inequitable . . . for the beneficiaries to step in and take the profit without paying for the skill and labour which has produced it."[43] Given the assumptions made in Mr. Ward's favour, this case provides another illustration of the strict application of equity's draconian rules.[44]

This decision is to be contrasted with that of the Court of Appeal in *O'Sullivan* v. *Management Agency and Music Ltd*.[45] which was not discussed in the judgments of the House of Lords in *Guinness plc*. v. *Saunders*, although it was cited in argument. In that case the Court of Appeal set aside a publishing contract on the ground of undue influence. The publisher was in a fiduciary relationship to the composer so that there arose a presumption of undue influence which the publisher failed to rebut. Both Dunn and Fox L.JJ. concluded, however, that the Court should exercise its discretion to grant the publisher an allowance for his skill and labour, an allowance which:

> "could include a profit element in the way that solicitors' costs do . . . [T]his would achieve substantial justice between the parties because it would take account of the contribution made by the defendants to [the

---

[39] *Phipps* v. *Boardman* [1964] 1 W.L.R. 993, 1018, *per* Wilberforce J., cited in *Guinness plc*. v. *Saunders* [1990] 2 A.C. 663, 700–701, *per* Lord Goff.

[40] [1990] 2 A.C. 663 see below, pp. 664–665.

[41] At p. 695, *per* Lord Templeman; *cf*. Lord Goff at p. 696.

[42] At p. 695, *per* Lord Templeman.

[43] At p. 701, *per* Lord Goff.

[44] See below, pp. 664–665 for a further discussion.

[45] [1985] Q.B. 428.

plaintiff's] success. It would not take full account of it in that the allowance would not be at all as much as the defendants might have obtained if
the contracts had been properly negotiated between fully advised
parties."[46]

No doubt, the exercise of the discretion to grant an allowance depends upon
the circumstances of the particular case. Although it is plain that the *Guinness*
case does not preclude the possibility of the grant of an allowance in an
appropriate case, it demonstrates a continuing anxiety that the exercise of the
jurisdiction should not be allowed to undermine the principle that a fiduciary
must not place himself in a position in which his duty and interests conflict,
and indicates that the discretion should only be exercised in exceptional
circumstances.

It follows that only rarely can an honest fiduciary be remunerated or granted
an allowance. But it is another question whether he should be reimbursed for
what he spent in earning any profits. If a trustee acquires an asset using his own
as well as the trust's money, then both he and the trust will enjoy a proportionate interest in the asset so acquired, although the burden is on him to demonstrate that he used his money in its acquisition.[47] Again, in patent and
copyright law, the court frequently directs an apportionment of profits, in
order to reflect the contribution, ideas and financial input of the infringer. As
Lord Watson once said: "it would be unreasonable to give the patentee profits
which were not earned by the use of his invention"[48] and he accepted that, in
many cases, "[t]his is obviously a matter which cannot be determined by
mathematical calculation or with absolute accuracy. At best, the result can
only be an approximation."[49] But the line between the fiduciary's "ideas", for
which he is granted an allowance, and his "skill and labour," for which he is
not,[50] may be a thin one.

The wrongdoer should normally be reimbursed any expenditure incurred in
making the profits.[51] Exceptionally, however, it appears that a court may be
prepared to reject his claim for reimbursement. Both Lord Keith and Lord

---

[46] At p. 469, *per* Fox L.J. See also dicta in such cases as *Redwood Music Ltd.* v. *Chappell Co. Ltd.*
[1982] R.P.C. 109, 132, *per* Robert Goff J. and *My Kinda Town* v. *Soll* [1982] F.S.R. 147,
156–158, *per* Slade J.; but *cf.* Templeman L.J.'s dicta, in *Queen Productions* v. *Music Sales*
(1981), unrep., that a court should not allow "any deduction from those profits as reward to
defendants for their own efforts which they should never have employed," cited by Lionel
Bently in [1991] E.I.P.R. 5.

[47] *Cf. Re Tilley's Will Trusts* [1967] Ch. 1179, 1188–1189, *per* Ungoed-Thomas J.: see below,
p. 87.

[48] *The United Horse Shoe and Nail Co. Ltd.* v. *Stewart & Co.* (1888) 5 R.P.C. 260, 266–267, *per*
Lord Watson.

[49] *Watson, Laidlaw & Co. Ltd.* v. *Pott, Cassels and Williamson* (1914) 31 R.P.C. 104, 114, *per* Lord
Atkinson: see below, p. 691. Lionel Bently discusses, in [1991] E.I.P.R. 5, 11–12 *et seq.*, in the
context of claims for breach of copyright, some of the difficulties which arise in determining
what is the appropriate contribution of the wrongdoer.

[50] See above, p. 33.

[51] For the American authorities, see Laycock, *Modern American Remedies* (Boston 1985),
pp. 502–505.

Jauncey refused to allow the *Sunday Times* to deduct the payments made to Peter Wright for the right to reproduce extracts from *Spycatcher*, on the ground that the newspaper could have resisted Wright's claim to those payments.[52] But the payments had been made. Consequently, they were items which should arguably have been deductible in assessing the newspaper's profits.[53]

(b) *The Benefit must be Gained at the Plaintiff's Expense*

The second subordinate principle of the general principle of unjust enrichment is that the benefit, the enrichment, must be gained *at the plaintiff's expense*.

In many cases it will not be difficult to discharge the burden of demonstrating that it has been so gained; it will be evident that the plaintiff has paid money, rendered services or delivered goods to the defendant. But on occasions it may. For example, the plaintiff makes a payment, under mistake or under protest, in pursuance of the defendant's demand, which is subsequently held to be *ultra vires*. He sues to recover his payments,[54] to be met by the defence that he has "passed on" the tax to his customers; consequently, it has been argued, he suffered no loss and the defendant's enrichment was not gained at his expense. These precise facts have not yet arisen in England. But they have in other common law jurisdictions and in the European Court of Justice; and these courts have come to different conclusions.[55] In principle, the burden should be on the defendant to prove that the plaintiff suffered no loss because he passed on the tax. The economic variables are so many and complex that it cannot be presumed that he suffered no loss because he did so. However, if the plaintiff's payment is the product of the defendant's illegitimate pressure or other wrongful act, it may well be that it is never a defence that the tax has been passed on, and the defendant must make restitution of the payment.[56]

Similarly, a defendant may submit that the benefit is the product, wholly or in part, of his own ideas and financial input. As has been seen, the burden is then on him to substantiate that submission.[57]

D may benefit at P's expense even though P does not directly benefit D. It is settled law that if P discharges a debt owed by D to T under compulsion of law, then P has a right to look to D for reimbursement[58]; and if P discharges more than a proportionate share of a common obligation which he and D owed to T, he can seek contribution from D.[59] Indeed, P may obtain restitution if he

---

[52] *Att.-Gen.* v. *Guardian Newspapers Ltd.* (*No. 2*) [1990] 1 A.C. 109, p. 262, *per* Lord Keith, 293–294, *per* Lord Jauncey. No other member of the House of Lords discussed this point.

[53] For this reason Lord Donaldson M.R. would have allowed the deduction: [1990] 1 A.C. at p. 198; see also Dillon L.J. at p. 211.

[54] *Cf. Woolwich Equitable Building Society* v. *Commissioners of Inland Revenue* [1993] A.C. 70, discussed below, Chap. 00.

[55] For a discussion of the case law in these jurisdictions, where the legal and economic arguments are explored, see Jones, *Restitution in Public and Private Law* (1991), pp. 28–40.

[56] *Mason* v. *The State of New South Wales* (1958) 102 C.L.R. 108, 146, *per* Windeyer J.: see below, Chap. 24.

[57] See below, p. 691.

[58] See below, Chap. 14.

[59] See below, Chap. 13.

36

mistakenly renders services to T and, in doing so, discharges D's statutory or contractual duty so to do.[60]

However, in two situations, the inquiry whether the benefit has been gained at the plaintiff's expense is more complex. These are (i) where the benefit was gained from a third party; and (ii) where the benefit was gained from the defendant's wrongful act.

Where the benefit was gained from a third party

T pays money to D, a stranger, intending thereby to discharge a debt which he owes P. D makes no payment to P. T's debt remains undischarged and T can normally recover his payment from D, the consideration for the payment having wholly failed.[61] It must follow that P never had any claim against D. D has not gained his benefit at P's expense; it has been gained at T's. It is T, not P, who has suffered the loss. The conclusion that P has no claim against D is, as a general rule, a wise one. At one time it was held that P's claim failed because there was no "privity" between P and D. As Professor Dawson said, the invocation of the fiction of privity reflected a "dimly felt situation that it was a mistake to become involved in these multi-party confusions when quasi-contract would short circuit a series of interconnected transactions, without joinder of the parties at intermediate stages."[62] Take, for example, the case where T mistakenly gives £300 to D, intending to give P that sum. If T demands the money from D before he has paid it to P, D cannot resist that demand. T is allowed to change his mind. The gift to P is still imperfect and, for that reason, P has no claim against either T or D. Again, T mistakenly pays D, thinking that he is his creditor or his creditor's agent; his creditor is in fact P. D becomes insolvent before T and P discover the true facts. If it were held that T's payment had the effect of discharging the debt owed to P, P would have to look to an insolvent D, not to a solvent T, for reimbursement. P would have good reason to feel aggrieved if that were the case.[63]

However, there are situations where P has successfully recovered from D the sum which T paid to D and where D's gain was commensurate with P's loss.

First, there are a number of old cases where D had usurped P's office and where he was obliged to make restitution of the sums which he had received from T "in the way of profits." There are other examples in the reports where D has been held to be accountable because he had assumed to act with P's authority, for example, purporting to be his agent or his executor.[64] It is not clear what is the basis of these decisions. The fact that D was liable to make restitution to P suggests T's obligation to P was thereby discharged. Any other

---

[60] See below, pp. 177–178.
[61] See above, p. 17, n. 2.
[62] *Unjust Enrichment*, p. 126.
[63] Admittedly, P would argue differently if D was solvent and T insolvent. *Cf.* (1991) 11 Oxford Jo. of L.S. 481 [Lionel Smith]. It appears that some American jurisdictions are now prepared, in some circumstances, to "short-circuit" the interconnected transactions: see Palmer, *op. cit.* Vol. IV, pp. 300–301.
[64] See above, Chap. 28.

result would be bizarre. If T's debt to P was not discharged, T would be able to recover his payment from D, on the ground of mistake or total failure of consideration. On this hypothesis D may find himself in the position of having to make restitution both to P and T.[65]

Secondly, there are the cases on attornment. If T transferred a "fund" to D to hold to the use of P and D has assented so to hold it, then it is well established that D must hold the fund to P's use if he has by some act attorned to P. In the nineteenth century unconvincing attempts were made to rationalise the case law by finding a contract between P and D. Today these cases are of very limited importance. It may well be that they find their way into the modern law of restitution simply because, in the seventeenth century, *indebitatus assumpsit* superseded account which had formerly been P's appropriate writ. The happiest explanation of this body of law is that the act of attornment is effective to vest the equitable title in the fund in the plaintiff.[66]

Thirdly, there is an isolated English dictum which suggests that, if T dies, intending to bequeath P £300 but, by mistake, bequeathed £300 to D, then P is entitled to restitution from D.[67] This is fragile authority. The bequest is imperfect; and, unless the will can be rectified,[68] to perfect it would frustrate the policy embodied in the Wills Act 1837.

Fourthly, there is the law of secret trusts. Its origin lies in the principle that no statute, and in particular the Wills Act 1837,[69] can be invoked as a cloak for fraud.[70] The possibility of fraud in equity, D's breach of his undertaking to hold property for the benefit of another, P, "converts the party who has committed it into a trustee for the party who is injured by that fraud."[71] The law of secret trusts is not wholly reconcilable with the policy underlying the Wills Act. It is one thing to prevent D benefiting from his own fraud. It is another to enforce the trust in favour of P. If historically English lawyers enforced the trust on the ground that there was a possibility that D might repudiate his undertaking to the testator and therefore benefit from his own (equitable) fraud, today fraud may no longer be "an essential ingredient" of the law of secret trusts.[71a] D holds on trust for P from the moment of the testator's death or possibly even earlier, from the date when he gave his undertaking.[72]

---

[65] *King* v. *Alston* (1848) 17 L.J.Q.B. 59. For a further discussion, see pp. 578–579. It has recently been suggested that these *special* cases are characterised by the fact that D, in receiving the payments, was authorised to act, or purported to act, on behalf of P; D could not then deny that he had received money to the plaintiff's use. The corollary of that conclusion is that T's payment discharged the debt which he owed to P: see (1991) Oxford 11 Jo. of L.S. 481 [Lionel Smith].

[66] See below, Chap. 27.

[67] *Lister* v. *Hodgson* (1867) L.R. 4 Eq. 30, 34–35, *per* Romilly M.R. See also *M'Mechan* v. *Warburton* [1896] 1 I.R. 435, 439, *per* Chatterton V.-C.

[68] Administration of Justice Act 1982, s.20: see above, p. 222, n. 30.

[69] See also Law of Property Act 1925, s.53: below p. 473.

[70] *Cf. Bannister* v. *Bannister* [1948] 2 All E.R. 133, C.A., following *Rochefoucauld* v. *Boustead* [1897] 1 Ch. 196, C.A.: see below, p. 473.

[71] *McCormick* v. *Grogan* (1869) L.R. 4 H.L. 82, 97, *per* Lord Westbury.

[71a] *Re Snowden (deceased)* [1979] Ch. 528, 536, *per* Sir Robert Megarry V.-C.

[72] *Re Gardner (No. 2)* [1923] 2 Ch. 230, which is a much criticised decision.

Finally, if a fiduciary diverts an opportunity from a third party to himself which equity decrees should have been acquired for his principal, then he holds any asset gained thereby as a constructive trustee. It is irrelevant that his principal did not have the power, the means or the desire to acquire it on his own behalf. But these are very special cases. Equity deems the opportunity to belong to the principal from the moment of its acquisition. It does so, not only to prevent the fiduciary's unjust enrichment, but to deter all fiduciaries from the temptation of using their fiduciary office for their own profit.[73]

Benefits gained from wrongdoing

In the situations hitherto discussed, the benefit gained by the defendant is the loss suffered by the plaintiff, for he has paid money, rendered services or delivered goods which the defendant has indubitably received from the plaintiff. In contrast, if the plaintiff's claim is based upon the defendant's wrongful act, there is no necessary equation between what the plaintiff has lost and what the defendant wrongdoer has gained. Yet that benefit *may*[74] be deemed to have been gained *at the plaintiff's expense*.

Some tortfeasors must make restitution of profits made from their torts, even though the injured party has suffered no loss.[75] Criminals must not be allowed to benefit from their crimes[76]; benefits gained through duress or undue influence must be disgorged[77]; and a fiduciary who abuses his duty of loyalty is a constructive trustee of the profits which he has made, as may be the cynical confidant and trade mark and copyright infringer.[78] In all these cases, to adopt Windeyer J.'s rhetorical question, in *Mason* v. *The State of New South Wales*[79]: "if the defendant be improperly enriched, on what legal principle can it claim to retain its ill-gotten gains merely because the plaintiffs have not . . . been correspondingly impoverished?"

As has been seen, the defendant may be said to be a wrongdoer even though he acted honestly and the plaintiff suffered no loss.[80] For example, it is no defence to my claim, based on your conversion of my chattel, that you thought that you had title to it; and a fiduciary who has broken his duty of loyalty cannot resist the principal's claim by saying that he acted honestly and in his principal's best interests.[81]

However, not all conscious wrongdoers must disgorge benefits obtained by their wrongful acts, even though they made the gain through the cynical

---

[73] See below, Chap. 33. Query if the *Diplock* personal claim (below Chap. 29) is an illustration of a benefit conferred by a third party: *cf.* Smith, *op. cit.* p. 37 n. 63 of this text. Burrows' *The Law of Restitution*, pp. 51–53.

[74] See below, p. 641.

[75] See below, Chap. 38. As will be seen, not all tortfeasors will be compelled to disgorge.

[76] See below, Chap. 37.

[77] See below, Chaps. 9 and 10.

[78] See below, Chaps. 33 and pp. 690–694.

[79] (1959) 102 C.L.R. 108, 146.

[80] See below, p. 641.

[81] See below, pp. 643–647.

exploitation of the plaintiff's rights.[82] For example, Wass Ltd., which persistently and consciously infringed Stoke-on-Trent City Council's exclusive right to hold a market, was not liable to pay substantial damages measured by the licence fee which Stoke-on-Trent would have demanded[83]; seemingly no restitutionary claim would have succeeded. Similarly, no common law court has ever held that a person who wrongfully repudiates his contractual obligations should make restitution to the innocent party of the profits made thereby.[84] The possibility of a restitutionary claim would, in these cases, revolutionise respectively the law of tort and the law of contract.[85] To grant a restitutionary claim would be without authority or principle.[86] The claim for loss suffered is said to be an adequate remedy, given the nature of the interest which had been infringed. However, it is open to the House of Lords to conclude that tortfeasors and those who wrongfully repudiate their contractual obligations should in principle disgorge benefits which are the product of their wrongful acts and that such benefits have been gained at the expense of those whom they have wronged.[87]

(c) *Unjust Retention of the Benefit*

It is not in every case where a defendant has gained a benefit at the plaintiff's expense that restitution will be granted. It is only when a court concludes it would be unjust for him to retain the benefit that he must make restitution to the plaintiff. It is necessary, therefore, to give content to the concept of *unjust* enrichment. The grounds and boundaries of restitutionary claims were originally formed by the old forms of action. For that reason money claims have hitherto been treated differently from claims based on services rendered and goods supplied.[88-89] Nowadays it is possible to identify substantive categories which form the basis of the restitutionary claim that the defendant has received a benefit which it is *unjust* for him to retain.

(d) *The Grounds which Found the Basis of the Restitutionary Claim*

Benefits which are not voluntarily conferred

A benefit may be conferred on another under mistake, compulsion or necessity. As Professor Birks has said, the transfer[90-91] of the benefit is then non-

---

[82] See below, p. 641.
[83] *Stoke-on-Trent City Council* v. *W. J. Wass Ltd.* [1988] 3 All E.R. 394: see above, pp. 772–773.
[84] See below, pp. 414–417.
[85] *Stoke-on-Trent City Council* v. *W. J. Wass Ltd.* [1988] 3 All E.R. 394.
[86] *The Siboen and The Sibotre* [1976] 1 Lloyd's Rep. 293, 337, ("no basis" for the claim), *per* Kerr J., who rejected the submission that a contract-breaker should disgorge his profits.
[87] See below, pp. 414–417.
[88-89] See (1989) 99 L.Q.R. 217 [Burrows].
[90-91] *Introduction*, Chap. 6.

voluntary, in the sense that the benefit would not have been conferred but for the mistake, the compulsion or the necessity for the intervention.[92] In these cases, the other's enrichment is prima facie an unjust enrichment. We say *prima facie* because, as will be seen,[93] there are limits and defences to the restitutionary claim, *e.g.* a claim will fail if the plaintiff has submitted to the defendant's honest claim, or if public policy precludes restitution, or if the defendant cannot be restored to his original position.[94]

Benefits which have been voluntarily conferred

A benefit may be voluntarily conferred, but the defendant may nonetheless be held to have received an enrichment which is an *unjust* enrichment. Commonly, but not exclusively, such claims arise out of contracts which are or become ineffective. At common law the plaintiff's ground of recovery is determined by the nature of the benefit conferred.

Money paid is recoverable only if there has been a total failure of consideration. The defendant's performance of his promise is the consideration which the payer expects in return.[95] In the past, the courts have applied the principle stringently so as to deny recovery by the plaintiff if he has received from the defendant a benefit, no matter how small, which he can no longer restore and which forms part of the defendant's promised performance under the contract. Conversely, if the benefit received does not form part of the promised performance, there is a total failure of consideration.[96] Statutory provisions apart, therefore, a payer cannot recover in restitution money paid if the consideration for the payment has only partially failed. This regrettable limitation is the product of the common law's reluctance to make any allowance, and to give credit to the defendant, for benefits which the plaintiff can no longer restore to him.[97]

Historically, these principles were formulated in the context of claims for money had and received between contracting parties. But there is no reason why claims should be so limited, and they are not. There is a total failure of consideration when money has been paid on the basis of any assumption which is or becomes falsified. Money may be paid in anticipation of the parties entering into a contract which in fact never materialises[98]; under an arrangement which was never intended to create legal relations and where the payer did not get his expected returns[99]; or on the footing that there is a legal demand

---

[92] *Cf. Woolwich Equitable Building Society* v. *Commissioners of Inland Revenue* [1993] A.C. 70, 179 *et seq., per* Lord Jauncey.

[93] See below, pp. 44 *et seq.* and see Chaps. 39–43.

[94] *Ibid.*

[95] *Fibrosa Spolka Akcyjna* v. *Fairbairn Lawson Combe Barbour* [1943] A.C. 32, 48, *per* Viscount Simon: see below, p. 408.

[96] For such a case, see *Rover International Ltd.* v. *Cannon Film Sales Ltd.* [1989] 1 W.L.R. 912: see below, pp. 543–544.

[97] See below, pp. 402–404.

[98] See below, Chap. 25.

[99] *Rose & Frank Co.* v. *J. R. Crompton & Bros. Ltd.* [1925] A.C. 445, *semble.*

but where it transpires that the legal demand is a nullity.[99a] The payment may then be recoverable, the consideration for that payment having failed.

There is an analogous principle in equity, which finds its expression in the law of resulting trusts. For example, a testator bequeaths property on trusts which do not exhaust the beneficial interests, or on trusts which fail for one reason or another.[1] In both these cases the resulting trust for the benefit of the testator's estate arises, not because it is presumed that the testator intended it to arise, but because it is imposed by law. The resulting trust is the automatic consequence of the testator's failure to dispose of what is vested in him; and it arises because the testator did not anticipate the event which caused the declared trusts to fail.[2]

In contrast, different principles determine whether it would be unjust to deny a plaintiff's restitutionary claim based on services rendered or goods delivered. Under the old *quantum meruit* and *quantum valebat* counts,[3] a plaintiff had to plead and prove a request by the defendant. The notion of request has now been extended. It is now enough to demonstrate that the defendant has freely accepted the benefit conferred.[4] Not only is he then enriched,[5] but his enrichment is in law an *unjust* enrichment.[6] For if he ought to have known that the plaintiff expected to be paid and if he had a reasonable opportunity of rejecting the goods or services and did not do so, the plaintiff may legitimately say that his failure to do so is the ground of the plaintiff's restitutionary claim. Of course, the claim may fail for other reasons; for example, the plaintiff may have acted officiously,[7] he may have taken the risk that the defendant would not pay him,[8] or his claim, if admitted, would frustrate the policy of the statutory or common law rule which rendered the contract ineffective.[9]

Benefits which are conferred in consequence of a wrongful act

A wrongdoer may be required to make restitution of benefits gained from a wrongful act. A wrongdoer may be: a fiduciary or one who abuses another's confidence; a criminal; some tortfeasors and perhaps even the defendant who wrongfully repudiates his contractual obligations. These questions are discussed in *Part II*, Section Three of this book.

Claims based on title to property

The plaintiff may seek to base his claim on his legal or equitable title to

---

[99a] *Woolwich Equitable Building Society* v. *Commissioners of Inland Revenue* [1993] A.C. 70, 197, *per* Lord Browne-Wilkinson (a payment "without consideration"); see below, p. 548.
[1] See below, Chap. 26.
[2] *Re Vandervell's Trusts (No. 2)* [1974] Ch. 269, 289–290, *per* Megarry J.
[3] See above, pp. 3–4.
[4] See above, pp. 18 *et seq.*
[5] See above, p. 19.
[6] See Birks, *Introduction*, Chap. 8.
[7] See below, p. 58.
[8] *Ibid.*
[9] See below, p. 62.

property. Legal title to land and chattels is generously protected.[10] But claims
at law based on the defendant's receipt of money are especially difficult to
sustain since money has no ear-mark and passes into currency. Any text on
restitution should arguably eschew that body of law which deals with questions
relating to legal title to property. But a knowledge of the common law is
necessary for two distinct reasons. First, the plaintiff's legal title may ground
an action for money had and received against a defendant who has received his
money and who cannot plead the defence of bona fide purchase.[10a] Secondly,
an understanding of the common law is necessary to an understanding of
equitable proprietary claims.[11]

In some cases a plaintiff may be able to identify property in the defendant's
hands, and claim that property as his. Whether he must do so may depend on
whether his claim is at law or in equity. These questions form the subject
matter of Chapter 2 of this book, where we discuss proprietary claims which
are restitutionary proprietary claims.

But the plaintiff may not be able to identify his property, even though he can
demonstrate that at one time the defendant did receive it. Again, the success of
any claim may depend on whether it is at law or in equity. A simple hypothetical example illustrates the problem. A pays money to B under mistake; the
mistake is induced by B's fraudulent misrepresentation. B decides that he does
not need the money, opens a bank account in the name of his adult son C and
pays the money directly into that account. B is now insolvent and not worth
suing. Does A have any claim against C at law or in equity?

The legal title to the money passes from A to B because A intended that it
should pass. But there is well-established authority[12-13] that, on discovering the
fraud, A can rescind the transaction. The legal title then revests in A, and A has
a claim at law against B (who is not worth suing) and C. To use the language of
the old pleaders, A can successfully bring an action for money had and received
for he can, on these facts, demonstrate that C did receive *his* money.[14] A's claim
is personal, although it is based on his legal title to the money.[15] C must,
therefore, make restitution of a like sum. C cannot successfully plead that he is
a bona fide purchaser and, in the example just given, he has not changed his
position. But if B had mixed A's money with his own money in his bank
account, which is in credit, and pays C from that account, A's claim will fail.[15a]

---

[10] See below, p. 75.

[10a] See below, pp. 82–83.

[11] See below, p. 75, where this argument is developed.

[12-13] See below, Chap. 2 for the rules and presumptions which determine whether property can be
recovered at law, and identified in equity.

[14] As will be seen (below, pp. 79–82), if A's money is mixed in B's bank account with B's money,
then A's claim at law against C will normally fail.

[15] See below, p. 78.

[15a] See below, p. 79.

There is authority which holds that, in consequence of the mistake, the equitable title to the money paid to B is deemed to remain in A.[16] A may be able to identify his money in C's hands, in which case he will be entitled to claim at least a lien over the fund in which the money is deposited. If he cannot, then his equitable proprietary claim will fail. But there are slender dicta which suggest that he may have a direct personal claim in equity against C.[17]

However, if A makes the payment under mistake and the mistake has *not* been induced by B's wrongful act, then A's common law claim against C will normally fail. The legal title to the money has passed to B, and from B to C. On these facts it cannot revest in A since he cannot rescind the transaction. In contrast, the equitable claim may succeed if he can identify his money. Because A made the payment under mistake, he is deemed to retain the equitable title to the money.[18] Moreover, he may have a personal claim in equity.[18a]

Courts have at times assumed, without spelling out the precise ground of the restitutionary claim, that the benefit, gained at the plaintiff's expense, is an *unjust* enrichment. Most cases can now be rationalised on the grounds of involuntary payment, total failure of consideration, free acceptance or title to property. A few cannot, and yet it is evident that it is just to require the defendant to make restitution.

Public policy

Public policy may ground a restitutionary claim; for example, it is a good thing to encourage, even by offering the carrot of a reward, maritime salvors to intervene in an emergency.[19]

Unconscionability

A ship deviates but nevertheless delivers the cargo on time at the agreed port of discharge. The shipowner is not entitled to claim the agreed freight; but influential dicta suggest that the shipowner is entitled to reasonable freight.[20] Money paid under an *ultra vires* agreement may be traced in equity; to do so will not frustrate the policy underlying the *ultra vires* rule. A loan to an infant, to enable him to purchase land, was void under the Infants Relief Act 1874; the lender was nonetheless subrogated to the vendor's lien for unpaid purchase money.[21]

---

[16] *Chase Manhattan Bank NA Ltd.* v. *Israel-British Bank (London) Ltd.* [1981] Ch. 105: see below, pp. 130–131.
[17] See below, Chap. 29. As will be seen, the personal action may be subject to certain irrational limitations, on which see below, pp. 584–585.
[18] See below, p. 585.
[18a] See below, Chap. 29.
[19] See below, Chap. 16; Birks, *op. cit.* Chap. 9. Conversely, it may defeat a restitutionary claim: see below, pp. 62–68.
[20] *Hain Steamship Co. Ltd.* v. *Tate & Lyle Ltd.* (1936) 41 Com.Cas. 350, 358, 368, 373: see below, p. 440.
[21] *Nottingham Permanent Benefit Building Society* v. *Thurstan* [1903] A.C. 6: see below, p. 595.

A defendant who received, in these circumstances, the benefit of the delivery of the goods or the payment of money and then refused to make restitution may be said to behave unconscionably. Similarly, *unconscionability* may be the happiest rationalisation of the equitable doctrine of proprietary estoppel.[22]

(e) *The Limits to a Restitutionary Claim based on Another's Unjust Enrichment*

We have now identified the principal grounds of restitutionary claims. A plaintiff who can establish one such ground is prima facie entitled to restitution, for the defendant's encrichment is an unjust enrichment. However, the restitutionary claim may nonetheless fail. The court may conclude that the benefit gained has not been unjustly gained. What then are the circumstances which form the limits of the restitutionary claim? We shall identify the following limits, which are of necessity generously drawn:

(1) the plaintiff conferred the benefit as a valid gift or in pursuance of a valid common law, equitable or statutory obligation which he owed to the defendant;
(2) the plaintiff submitted to the defendant's honest claim or entered into a compromise;
(3) the plaintiff conferred the benefit while performing an obligation which he owed to a third party or otherwise while acting voluntarily in his own self-interest;
(4) the plaintiff acted officiously in conferring the benefit;
(5) the defendant cannot be restored to his original position or is a bona fide purchaser;
(6) public policy precludes restitution.

These broad limits form the boundaries of restitution, derived from the subordinate principle that a restitutionary claim will succeed only if it can be said that the defendant's enrichment is an *unjust* enrichment. As will be seen, some are more firmly drawn than others.[23-24]

The plaintiff conferred the benefit as a valid gift or in pursuance of a valid common law, equitable or statutory obligation which he owed to the defendant

In principle the fact that a benefit has been conferred as a valid gift should always preclude restitution. For that reason a person who renders services gratuitously to another, hoping that he might then obtain a benefit under that

---

[22] See below, Chap. 5 and *Lord Napier and Ettrick* v. *R. F. Kershaw Ltd.* [1993] 1 All E.R. 385, 397–398, *per* Lord Templeman; *cf. Liggett* v. *Kensington* [1993] 1 N.Z.L.R. 257 (see below, p. 94, n. 36a).
[23-24] *Cf. The Lawrence Building Co. Ltd.* v. *Lanarkshire C.C.*, 1977 S.L.T. 110. 111–113, *per* Lord Maxwell.

other's will, should be denied a *quantum meruit* claim if that expectation is not fulfilled. But the line between the situation where the plaintiff conferred a benefit hoping to be recompensed and where he acted because he thought that he was promised recompense can be a thin one. A plaintiff may succeed even if any agreement is ineffective, if he can show that his reasonable expectation was that a testator would leave him property in his will, but the testator never did so. In recent years the Canadian courts have been faced with such problems in the context of claims for services rendered by relatives and neighbours to the aged or the infirm.[25]

Benefits are never rendered gratuitously if they are rendered under mistake, in such circumstances that they would not have been rendered but for the mistake. However, whether the plaintiff can obtain restitution may depend on the nature of the benefit conferred, *e.g.* if A pays money to B under mistake, believing him to be C, he will recover his payment.[26] But if he renders services or delivers goods, he may succeed only if B knew or ought to have known of the mistake. For B will never be in a position to restore services and he may have consumed the goods before he learns of A's mistake.[27] In such cases B will be deemed to have freely accepted the services or goods respectively. But if he did not know and could not have known of the mistake, then A's claim should succeed only if B has gained an incontrovertible benefit.[28]

Circumstances other than mistake may prevent the gift being a valid gift. The gift may have been made under undue influence or under duress[29]; or the donor may have given property to trustees on trusts which fail or which do not exhaust the beneficial interest, in which case equity will normally imply a resulting trust for the donor.[30]

The plaintiff's restitutionary claim will also fail if it is shown that he was under a common law, equitable or statutory *obligation* to confer the benefit. The most important illustration is where he had contracted either to confer the benefit on another or, conversely, to forgo his right of restitution from another.

If A confers a benefit on B under a valid contract, he must seek his remedy under that contract and not in restitution. The parties' rights and duties are governed by the contract. That is the general principle, which has been affirmed by the courts on a number of occasions.[31] However, there are dicta to

---

[25] See Maddaugh and McCamus, *op. cit.* pp. 474–481.

[26] *Cf. Morgan* v. *Ashcroft* [1938] 1 K.B. 49, 66–67, *per* Greene M.R.; see below, pp. 119–120.

[27] *Cf. Boulton* v. *Jones* (1857) 2 H. & N. 564; see below, pp. 488 *et seq.*

[28] See above, pp. 22–27.

[29] See below, Chaps. 9 and 10.

[30] See below, Chap. 26.

[31] See below, pp. 59–60. *Weston* v. *Downes* (1778) 1 Doug. 23; *Toussaint* v. *Martinnant* (1787) 2 T.R. 100, 105, *per* Buller J.; *Gompertz* v. *Denton* (1832) Cromp. & M. 207; *Restatement of Restitution*, § 107; 2 *Smith's Leading Cases*, p. 9. The principle is sometimes stated in terms of implied contract. Reference is often made to Brett L.J.'s dictum in *Britain* v. *Rossiter* (1879) 11 Q.B.D. 123, 127, that "no new contract can be implied from acts done under an express contract, which is still subsisting." That case was concerned, however, with an attempt to recover damages for wrongful dismissal under a contract caught by the Statute of Frauds. Brett L.J.'s language is nowadays inappropriate to determine whether a restitutionary claim should

the effect that a *quantum meruit* claim may lie if the plaintiff, who has entered
into an entire contract, only offers partial performance which the defendant
accepts, not voluntarily, but because he has no option but to do so.[32] For
example, there is an industrial dispute and an employee determines to "go
slow"; the employer may have no real option but to agree to accept the services
on the employee's terms. In such a case, the contract of employment remains in
force; it has not been superseded by a new agreement to pay a reasonable
sum.[33] If the original contract has not been terminated, then any claim must be
brought on the contract.[34] No restitutionary claim should succeed in such a
case.[35]

The general principle has been most influential in determining the success of
claims arising under building contracts. If an architect or a builder agrees to
supervise work for a lump sum but supervises extra work which was not
included in the original contract, he must show that there is a "new contract"
before he can obtain recompense for the extra work; and "in order to have a
new contract you must get rid of the old contract."[36] Where he agrees to do
work for a lump sum there is, therefore, no necessary implication that, if there
is extra work, any further payments are due to him.[37] The Canadian case of
Webb and Knapp (Canada) Ltd. v. *City of Edmonton*[38] is an unusual illustration
of the application of the general principle to a development contract. The
plaintiff, a land development corporation, offered to spend $100,000 on pre-
paring a plan for a new civic centre. The plan was to belong to the defendants
when completed; only if the defendants accepted the plan would they become
obliged to provide land at a fair market value for development by the plaintiff.
After a lengthy study the defendants rejected the plan but publicly expressed
the view that the plan would be the basis of a new plan and that the plaintiff
would suffer no loss. This new plan was, however, never implemented. The
Alberta Supreme Court held that the plaintiff's restitutionary claim must fail.

---

lie; once again implied contract disguises the substantive principles in dispute between the
parties.

[32] *Miles* v. *Wakefield Metropolitan D.C.* [1987] A.C. 539, 553, *per* Lord Brightman, 561, *per* Lord
Templeman; *contra*: Lord Bridge at p. 552. Lord Brandon and Lord Oliver reserved their
opinions. (In the case, the plaintiff was a superintendent registrar of births, marriages and
deaths. The terms of the tenure of his office were said to be closely analogous to a contract of
employment. He refused to carry out marriage ceremonies on Saturday mornings as part of
industrial action, although he performed other duties. He was not paid for work done on
Saturday mornings. The House of Lords held that he could not recover the amount withheld,
for his employer had, without terminating his appointment, declined to accept the partial
performance offered by him.)

[33] At p. 552, *per* Lord Bridge.

[34] See above, p. 45.

[35] *Cf.* Treitel, *The Law of Contract*, (8th ed., 1991), p. 719, who points out that, if the employer
voluntarily accepts the services, he can deduct from the wages any loss suffered in consequence
of the employee's breach. But the loss may be difficult to quantify.

[36] *Gilbert and Partners* v. *Knight* [1968] 2 All E.R. 248, 250, *per* Harman L.J., citing *The Olanda*
[1919] 2 K.B. 728n., 730, *per* Lord Dunedin.

[37] *Ibid.*

[38] [1969] 3 D.L.R. (3d) 123.

"The city acted strictly within its rights under the contract and the obligations of the city ceased when it rejected the plan, and these obligations were not revived by the subsequent conduct of the parties . . . There can be no claim for *quantum meruit* where the city acted according to its rights under the contract."[39] Similar principles apply even if the contract is held to be unenforceable.[40]

A party can also contract out of a right to restitution. At common law a surety may agree not to seek contribution from a co-surety[41]; a principal may allow an agent to retain a secret profit[42]; and a purchaser of land may agree that a deposit be forfeited if he fails to complete the contract.[43] Moreover, a party may, by contract, modify his statutory right to restitution of benefits conferred under a frustrated contract.[44]

In the past, hardship has been caused by overstrict interpretation of such contractual provisions.[45] For example, at common law a person who has failed to complete the performance of his obligations under an entire contract has been held unable to obtain restitution for benefits conferred on the other party by his partial performance.[46] In principle the contractual rules relating to entire contracts should not necessarily prevent the party in breach recovering in restitution. These rules no longer prevent restitution if the contract is frustrated[47]; and the Law Commission has proposed[48] that they should no longer do so if there is a breach of an entire contract.

It is not always easy to determine whether the parties did intend to exclude a restitutionary claim. For example an event may occur which the parties could have anticipated, but probably did not anticipate, when they entered into the contract and which produces what is, arguably, a windfall for one of them. The Court of Appeal's decision in *Henshall* v. *Fogg*[49] forms an interesting contrast with the Canadian case of *James More & Sons Ltd.* v. *The University of Ottawa*[50] In *Henshall* v. *Fogg* the plaintiffs conveyed land to T and covenanted to indemnify T, and subsequent purchasers claiming through him, against any liability which they might incur as frontage owners to the local authority. After the conveyance, the plaintiffs deposited with the local authority a sum of money in respect of that potential liability. T then sold the land to the defendant. Subsequently the local authority repaid the defendant part of the

---

[39] At p. 138, *per curiam*. But *cf. William Lacey (Hounslow) Ltd.* v. *Davis* [1957] 1 W.L.R. 93; see below, p. 555.
[40] *Cf. Smith* v. *Hartshorn* [1960] S.R. (N.S.W.) 391.
[41] See below, pp. 307 *et seq.*
[42] See below, pp. 666 *et seq.*
[43] See below, pp. 426 *et seq.*
[44] See below, pp. 462–464.
[45] *Cf. Re Richmond Gate* [1965] 1 W.L.R. 335.
[46] See below, pp. 428 *et seq.*
[47] See below, pp. 449 *et seq.*
[48] Report No. 121, *Law of Contract, Pecuniary Restitution on Breach of Contract* (1983): see below, pp. 445–446.
[49] [1964] 1 W.L.R. 1127.
[50] (1974) 49 D.L.R. (3d) 666.

deposit which had been paid by the plaintiffs; it was under a statutory obligation to make any repayment to the frontage owner for the time being. The
Court of Appeal held that the plaintiffs' claim for the return of that payment
must fail. The plaintiffs should have reserved any such right in the contract of
sale with T and they had not done so. The Court rejected the argument that the
deposit had been paid in pursuance of the plaintiffs' obligation to indemnify
the defendant and that "by analogy with cases of insurance any receipt by the
person indemnified over and above what was required to indemnify is a receipt
for which the recipient must account to the indemnifier."[51] The defendant may
have taken into account his statutory right to the repayment in making his bid
for the land, although there was no evidence that he had done so; it was not
correct therefore to describe the repayment as "a windfall at the expense of the
plaintiffs."[52]

In reaching its decision the Court of Appeal was undoubtedly influenced by
the complications which would arise in the statutory scheme if it ordered a
repayment, even though it is probable that the defendant had never anticipated
any repayment by the local authority. Moreover, the defendant had acted in
good faith and had bought the land from T and not from the plaintiffs. In
contrast, in *James More & Sons Ltd.* v. *The University of Ottawa*,[53] The
defendants' agent had innocently misled the plaintiffs. In that case the defendants accepted the plaintiffs' tender for certain building works. After the
contract had been made the defendants' architect promised the plaintiffs that
any increase in taxes on building materials, for which the plaintiffs would
become liable, would be borne by the defendants; he acted outside the scope of
his authority in making that promise. The taxes were increased and were paid
by the plaintiffs. As an educational institute the defendants were entitled by
statute to recover the taxes, and they did so. They then refused to reimburse
the plaintiffs. The Ontario High Court held that the plaintiffs' claim on the
contract failed since the architect had acted without authority. But their
restitutionary claim succeeded. The defendants had gained a benefit, the
refund of the taxes, at the plaintiffs' expense. Their duty to disgorge sprang
from "the principle of unjust enrichment. . . . There is definitely nothing in the
legislation preventing the operation of the law of restitution in this case."[54]
Unlike the Court of Appeal in *Henshall* v. *Fogg*, the Ontario High Court was
not persuaded by the argument that the parties must have contracted with the
provisions of the statute in mind; the defendants had received more than they
had bargained for.[55] The facts would have been more delicately poised if there
had been no misrepresentation by the architect but the taxes had unexpectedly

---

[51] [1964] 1 W.L.R. 1227, 1135, *per* Russell L.J.
[52] *Ibid.* (The court assumed, but did not decide, that the covenant ran with the land: see p. 1136.)
[53] (1974) 49 D.L.R. (3d) 666.
[54] At pp. 676–677, *per* Morden J.
[55] *Cf.* an earlier decision of the same court, which was not cited, *McCarthy Milling Co.* v. *Elder Packing Co.* (1973) 33 D.L.R. (3d) 52 (selling price adjusted on erroneous assumption that vendor would get government subsidy; recovery from purchaser allowed). And contrast *Simplot Chemical Co. Ltd.* v. *Govt. of Manitoba* [1975] 1 W.W.R. 289, 3 W.W.R. 480.

been increased. The Supreme Court of Minnesota allowed recovery in comparable circumstances.[56] But as a general rule it is not desirable to rewrite the terms of the contract. The risk that taxes might be increased is a risk which in law the builder should bear even though neither party foresaw that he would have to do so.[57]

In the Canadian case just discussed the plaintiffs succeeded because their restitutionary claim was said to fall outside the limits of the contract between them and the defendants. But if the benefit has been conferred under the contract, the contract governs. Then the plaintiff can bring a restitutionary claim only if the contract can be brought to an end, rectified, rescinded or otherwise set aside. A contract may be brought to an end by reason of breach or frustration.[58] It may be rectified if it does not reflect the agreement of the parties[59]; and it may be rescinded for misrepresentation,[60] bad faith,[61] duress,[62] undue influence[63] or breach of fiduciary relationship.[64] Moreover equity has, as yet, an ill-defined jurisdiction to set aside contracts for mistake, even though the mistake was not induced by misrepresentation,[65] and to set aside contracts for unconscionability. Equity's jurisdiction to declare a bargain unconscionable has hitherto been severely limited. The Court of Chancery mends no man's bargain.[66] However, there have always been exceptional cases where equity has intervened; for example, improvident bargains with expectant heirs and with the poor and ignorant can be reopened and set aside on terms[67] Equity may, in very limited circumstances, order the repayment of a deposit if it would be unconscionable to allow the recipient to retain it.[68]

There is some slight evidence that the courts may be more ready than they were to inquire whether bargains are unconscionable. In *Schroeder Music Publishing Co. Ltd.* v. *Macauley*[69] the House of Lords set aside an employment contract because its terms were oppressive and in restraint of trade. In that context, Lord Diplock expressed the view that the courts should be prepared

---

[56] *Klass* v. *Twin City Federal Savings and Loan Associations*, 190 N.W. 2d 493 (1971), and the authorities there cited.

[57] Contrast *The Isle of Mull*, 278 F. 131 (4th Cir. 1921) (ship requisitioned while on charter; contract discharged, owner entitled to higher freight paid on requisition).

[58] See below, Chap. 18.

[59] See below, Chap. 8.

[60] *Ibid.*

[61] See below, p. 151.

[62] See below, p. 230.

[63] See below, Chap. 9.

[64] See below, Chap. 33.

[65] See below, Chap. 11.

[66] *Maynard* v. *Moseley* (1676) 3 Swanst. 651, 655, *per* Lord Nottingham L.C. But *cf. Parker* v. *South Eastern Ry.* (1877) 2 C.P.D. 416, 427–428, *per* Bramwell L.J.; *John Lee & Son (Grantham) Ltd.* v. *Railway Executive* [1949] 2 All E.R. 581, 584, *per* Denning L.J.

[67] See below, Chap. 11. *Cf.* the Court of Admiralty's power to set aside salvage agreements where the agreed terms were inequitable: see below, pp. 297–298.

[68] *Stockloser* v. *Johnson* [1954] 1 Q.B. 476, 490–492. *Cf. The Scraptrade* [1983] 2 A.C. 694, 702, *per* Lord Diplock; *Sport International Bussum BV* v. *Inter-Footwear Ltd.* [1984] 1 W.L.R. 776; *BICC plc* v. *Burndy Corp.* [1985] Ch. 232, below, p. 437; *Stern* v. *McArthur* below, pp. 434–435.

[69] [1974] 1 W.L.R. 1308; see above, pp. 43–44 and below, p. 259.

to scrutinise such standard form contracts which have not been subject to arm's-length negotiation,[70] and the existence of statutory provisions, such as section 3 of the Unfair Contract Terms Act 1977,[71] may possibly encourage them to do so more frequently.[72] In *Lloyds Bank Ltd.* v. *Bundy*[73] Lord Denning M.R. went further and suggested that equity had a general jurisdiction to grant relief if the terms of a contract appeared to be unfair, where the consideration was grossly inadequate, and where one of the parties' bargaining power was grievously impaired. But in *National Westminster Bank* v. *Morgan*[74] Lord Scarman doubted whether the courts should "erect a general principle of relief against inequality of bargaining power. Parliament has undertaken the task— and it is essentially a legislative task—of enacting such restrictions on freedom of contract as are in its judgment necessary to relieve against the mischief." Litigation *inter partes* is an imperfect means of determining whether contractual terms which may be widely accepted in the particular business or profession are "unconscionable." A standard form contract may be advantageous for most persons in the plaintiff's position. Products may be marketed more cheaply, and it may well be that more favourable terms could not have been obtained from competitors in the market.[75]

The plaintiff submitted to an honest claim or entered into a compromise

A defendant confers a benefit in pursuance of an honest claim made by the defendant, or he enters into a compromise with the defendant.[76] The general principle is that the benefit is irrecoverable and the compromise cannot be set aside.[77] A person upon whom a claim is made is not allowed to choose his own

---

[70] *Ibid.* 1315–1316.

[71] See below, pp. 294 *et seq. Cf. Walker* v. *Boyle* [1982] 1 W.L.R. 495: see below, p. 187, n. 40.

[72] *Cf.* the "passing-off" case of *Erven Warnink Besloten Vennootschap* v. *J. Townend & Sons (Hull) Ltd.* [1979] A.C. 731, 743, *per* Lord Diplock: "where over a period of years there can be discerned a steady trend in legislation which reflects the view of successive Parliaments as to what the public interest demands in a particular field of law, development of the common law in that part of the same field which has been left to it ought to proceed upon a parallel rather than a diverging course."

[73] *Lloyds Bank Ltd.* v. *Bundy* [1975] 1 Q.B. 326, 339; see below, p. 290. *Cf. Levison* v. *Patent Steam Carpet Cleaning Co.* [1977] 3 W.L.R. 90, 95, 96–97, *per* Lord Denning M.R.; *Shiloh Spinners Ltd.* v. *Harding* [1973] A.C. 691, 726–727, *per* Lord Simon of Glaisdale.

[74] [1985] A.C. 686, 708. The other members of the House simply agreed with Lord Scarman. These remarks were made in the context of a claim that a transaction should be set aside because of undue influence: see below, p. 290.

[75] *Cf. Pao On* v. *Lau Yiu Long* [1980] A.C. 614, 634, *per* Lord Scarman. And see the critique of the *Schroeder Music Publishing Co.* case (see above, n. 69) by Michael Trebilcock in (1976) 26 Univ. of Toronto L.J. 359.

[76] See generally, "Mistaken settlements of disputable claims" (1989) 4 L.M.C.L.Q. 431 [Andrews]; S. Arrowsmith, *Mistake and the Role of the "Submission to an Honest Claim"* in *Essays* (ed. Burrows), Chap. 2.

[77] A court may find that the parties have impliedly reached a contractually binding agreement to settle a claim or dispute (see Andrews, *op. cit.* above, n. 76). But A may resolve to pay B in circumstances where B has made no demand on A. He may do so for a number of reasons; *e.g.* to settle a potential claim which he thinks B is likely to make or, perhaps, to avoid litigation. He then waives his right to recover: *cf. Woolwich Equitable Building Society* v. *Inland Revenue*

time for litigation[78]; moreover, the courts lean in favour of settlements,[79] and to allow a party to reopen a transaction of this kind serves to promote rather than to allay disputes.

Although there is no reason why a benefit so conferred should not take other forms,[80] in fact it generally consists of a payment of money. Such a payment is usually called a voluntary payment.[81] In the words of Gibbs J.[82]: "Where a man demands money of another as a matter of right, and that other, with a full knowledge of the facts upon which the demand is founded, has paid a sum, he can never recover back that sum he has so voluntarily paid." The test is whether "the money is intentionally paid without reference to the truth or falsehood of the fact, ... meaning to waive all inquiry into it, and that the person receiving shall have the money at all events, whether the fact be true or false."[83] If so, the payment is voluntary and can be retained by the defendant,[84] even though the fact in question is different from what the plaintiff believed it to be. On this basis, insurance companies who settle honest claims, waiving further investigation and taking the risk that they may be mistaken, should be unable to recover their payments.[85] But it may be difficult to establish that an insurance company took the risk that it might be mistaken and, consequently, that the payment was in the nature of a compromise of a doubtful liability.[86] Consequently, if it can be shown that, even if the insurance company had doubts about the validity of the claim, it would not have made the payment but for its mistaken belief, it should be granted restitution.[87]

Payments made under mistake of law

Money paid under a mistake of law is irrecoverable.[87a] Even if the legislature or

---

Commissioners [1991] S.T.C. 364, 401–402, *per* Ralph Gibson L.J., dissenting. *Cf.* Arrowsmith, *op. cit.*: see above, n. 76, pp. 29–33.

[78] See, *e.g. Cam & Sons Pty. Ltd.* v. *Ramsay* (1960) 104 C.L.R. 247.

[79] On the unwillingness of courts to reopen compromises, see *Callisher* v. *Bischoffsheim* (1870) L.R. 5 Q.B. 449.

[80] Such as services; see, *e.g. Peter Kiewit Sons' Co. of Canada Ltd.* v. *Eakins Construction Co.* [1960] S.C.R. 361.

[81] *Cf.* below, pp. 143–144.

[82] *Brisbane* v. *Dacres* (1813) 5 Taunt. 143. 152.

[83] *Kelly* v. *Solari* (1841) 9 M. & W. 54, 59, *per* Parke B.

[84] *Beevor* v. *Marler* (1898) 14 T.L.R. 289; see also *Simpson* v. *Swann* (1812) 3 Camp. 291. Moreover, if the defendant has brought legal proceedings to recover money from the plaintiff, who thereupon pays the money to the defendant, the plaintiff cannot reopen the transaction and recover his money on the grounds that he paid it under a mistake of fact (*Moore* v. *Vestry of Fulham* [1895] 1 Q.B. 399; see also *Marriot* v. *Hampton* (1797) 7 T.R. 269; *Hamlet* v. *Richardson* (1833) 9 Bing. 644); and the same may apply where the payment is made under threat of legal proceedings (*Moore* v. *Vestry of Fulham* [1895] 1 Q.B. 399, 404, *per* A. L. Smith L.J.).

[85] *New York Life Insurance Co.* v. *Chittenden*, 134 Iowa L.Rep. 613, 112 N.W. 96 (1907); *Meeme Mutual Protection Fire Insurance Co.* v. *Lorfeld*, 194 Wis. 322, 216 N.W. 507 (1927): see below, pp. 127–130.

[86] *Pilot Insurance* v. *Cudd*, 208 S.C. 6, 36 S.E. 2d 860 (1945) is representative: see below, p. 129. Contrast Andrews, *op. cit.* above, n. 76 at pp. 443–444.

[87] Palmer, *op. cit.* Vol. III, pp. 166 *et seq.*

[87a] See below, Chap. 4.

the House of Lords were to repudiate this long standing rule, a payment made under a mistake of law, with full knowledge of the material facts, may be characterised as voluntary and therefore irrecoverable.[88] Payments made in satisfaction of honest claims or under bona fide compromises should not be set aside merely because the payer mistook the law. He has had his opportunity to investigate his legal rights and to take legal advice; and to allow recovery "would open a fearful amount of litigation,"[89] and would impose an "intolerable hardship"[90] on the recipient who had made the honest demand. This is a sound principle which ought to be sustained, though it has in the past been too stringently applied.[91]

But there are many instances where recovery has been allowed despite a mistake of law. Most of these can be explained on the ground that money was paid involuntarily. For that reason, we suggest, it is better to stress the underlying principle that only if the payments are made in satisfaction of an honest claim are they irrecoverable, rather than to emphasise that *ignorantia juris non excusat*.[92] For example, this underlying principle has no application where there is something in the recipient's conduct "which shows that he is the one primarily responsible for the mistake," for example, where he made a misrepresentation or where the duty of observing the law is placed on the recipient rather than the payer, or where the recipient has misled the payer when he ought to have known better.[93] Moreover, the recipient must not have lacked bona fides[94]; a claim settled in such circumstances may be reopened and money paid thereunder recovered.

Payments made in consequence of an ultra vires demand

In *Woolwich Equitable Building Society* v. *Commissioners of Inland Revenue*[95] the House of Lords held, Lord Keith and Lord Jauncey dissenting, that a taxpayer was entitled to recover payments, with interest, which it had paid under protest in pursuance of a demand by the Revenue which was subsequently held to be *ultra vires*.

Ralph Gibson L.J., in his dissent in the Court of Appeal,[96] could not see, if the restitutionary claim is grounded simply on the illegality of the demand, "on what basis the payer could be taken to have paid to close the transaction." Nor could he see that "repetition over time of such payments would by itself

---

[88] *Bilbie* v. *Lumley* (1802) 2 East 469. See, generally, below, Chap. 4. But see *Woolwich Equitable Building Society* v. *Commissioners of Inland Revenue* [1993] A.C. 70: see below, Chap. 24.
[89] *Rogers* v. *Ingham* (1876) 3 Ch.D. 351, 356, *per* James L.J.
[90] *Derrick* v. *Williams* [1939] 2 All E.R. 559, 565, *per* Greene M.R.
[91] See below, pp. 143–144. Contrast Arrowsmith, *op. cit.* above, n. 76 at pp. 34–37.
[92] *Kiriri Cotton Co.* v. *Dewani* [1960] A.C. 192: see below, pp. 151–153.
[93] *Ibid.* at 204, *per* Lord Denning.
[94] *Ward & Co.* v. *Wallis* [1900] 1 Q.B. 675, 678, *per* Kennedy J.
[95] [1993] A.C. 70, discussed below, Chap. 24.
[96] [1993] A.C. 70, 121–122.

amount to waiver. For such a waiver, it would be essential . . . to prove that the payer knew of the point as to the illegality of the demand and nevertheless made the payment with the apparent intention of not seeking to recover it." He added that it was not clear to him how an intention not to seek recovery would be demonstrated.[97] These dicta echo those of Wilson J., dissenting, in the Supreme Court of Canada, in *Air Canada* v. *British Columbia*.[98] But neither Lord Goff nor Lord Slynn suggested that a payment in submission to an honest, but *ultra vires*, claim would necessarily be irrecoverable.[98a]

Payments induced by misrepresentation or made under duress or undue influence

A settlement can, of course, be set aside if it was induced by misrepresentation, duress or undue influence. In recent years the courts have been confronted with claims that payments were made, or agreements entered into, under economic duress. In response, defendants have argued that they acted in good faith in making their threats, and the plaintiffs gave in and settled their claim. For example, a vendor and a purchaser may dispute whether the purchaser is liable to pay a water rate under the terms of a contract for the sale of land. The vendor, acting in good faith, threatens not to complete the contract, and the purchaser capitulates because the sum in dispute is relatively small and he wants a speedy end to the litigation. On such facts Australian courts have held that, since the purchaser's interpretation of the contract was correct, he could recover his payment.[99] However, the Supreme Court of Canada has held that a party cannot go on "with the performance of the contract according to the other party's interpretation and then impose a liability on a different con-tract."[1] But that is, in our view, too unsophisticated a conclusion which ignores the reality of the economic pressure which is the consequence of the threat not to perform. Other common law jurisdictions have reached a different conclu-sion.[2] There are two questions involved. First, was the threat a wrongful act? Secondly, if it was, did the defendant only succumb because of the threat or because he did not want to "dispute the matter further"?[3] The first question is one of law; as we shall see a bona fide threat not to perform a contract may be held to be a wrongful act if a court later determines that the defendant was not entitled to make it.[4] But the second question is essentially one of fact. In resolving the factual question a court may take into account such factors as

---

[97] Contrast Glidewell L.J. at p. 98.
[98] [1989] 4 W.W.R. 97, 107: see below, p. 550.
[98a] See below, Chap. 24.
[99] See, *e.g. Re Hooper and Grass's Contract* [1949] V.L.R. 269.
[1] *Peter Kiewit Sons' Co.* v. *Eakins Construction Co.* [1960] S.C.R. 361, 367, *per* Judson J.: see below, pp. 258–259.
[2] These are discussed below, p. 259. See *inter alia, Molloy* v. *Liebe* (1910) 102 L.T. 616 and *Re Hooper & Grass's Contract* [1949] V.L.R. 269.
[3] *Mason* v. *The State of New South Wales* (1959) 102 C.L.R. 108, 143, *per* Windeyer J.
[4] See below, pp. 258 *et seq.*

whether the defendant plaintiff protested[5]; was given independent advice[6]; promptly repudiated the transaction as soon as the improper pressure was removed[7]; and the adequacy of alternative remedies.[8] The threatener's knowledge of the plaintiff's financial or personal circumstances may also be relevant.[9]

Payments under protest

A person may make a payment knowing that another is not entitled to it. If he makes the payment because he cannot be bothered to challenge the other's demand, he will be deemed to have made a voluntary payment. Similarly, he will be denied restitution if he made the payment simply because he could not prove that he has already paid the sum demanded.[10]

But what if a payment is made under protest and with a vigorous statement that the payee is not entitled to it? It has been said that there is "no magic in a protest; for a protest may accompany a voluntary payment or be absent from one compelled . . . Moreover the word 'protest' is itself equivocal. It may mean the serious assertion of a right or it may mean no more than a statement that payment is grudgingly made."[11] If the court finds on the facts that the protest is unequivocal evidence that the payment was involuntary, it is recoverable.[12] The protest may also be some evidence that the payee had impliedly promised to repay the money if it was later held that he was not entitled to have made his demand.[13] In contrast, a court may be more ready to hold that payments were voluntary if there were a series of payments, even though each payment was accompanied by a protest and it was subsequently held that the recipient was not entitled to the money demanded.[14]

---

[5] *Maskell* v. *Horner* [1915] 3 K.B. 106, 120 ("some evidence"), *per* Lord Reading C.J.: see below, pp. 268–270.

[6] *Universe Tankships Inc. of Monrovia* v. *International Transport Workers' Federation* [1983] 1 A.C. 366, 400: see below, pp. 252–253.

[7] *Universe Tankships Inc. of Monrovia* v. *International Transport Workers' Federation* [1981] I.C.R. 129, 143.

[8] *Alec Lobb (Garages) Ltd.* v. *Total Oil G.B. Ltd.* [1985] 1 W.L.R. 303, C.A., reversing in part [1983] 1 W.L.R. 87: see below, p. 288.

[9] *Cf.* Palmer, *op. cit.* Vol. II, § 9.12(d).

[10] See below, p. 267.

[11] *Mason* v. *The State of New South Wales* (1959) 102 C.L.R. 108, 143, *per* Windeyer J.: see below, p. 271.

[12] *Cf. Woolwich Equitable Building Society* v. *Commissioners of Inland Revenue* [1993] A.C. 70.

[13] *Cf. Sebel Products Ltd.* v. *Commissioners of Customs and Excise* [1949] Ch. 409; *Woolwich Building Society* v. *Inland Revenue Commissioners* [1989] S.T.C. 111, 119, *per* Nolan J.; [1993] A.C. 70, 113–117, *per* Ralph Gibson L.J.; [1993] A.C. 70, 165–166, *per* Lord Goff.

[14] *Cf. Maskell* v. *Horner* [1915] 3 K.B. 106, 120, *per* Lord Reading C.J., cited in *Woolwich Equitable Building Society* v. *Commissioners of Inland Revenue* [1993] A.C. 70, 114, *per* Lord Goff: see below, Chap. 24.

The plaintiff conferred the benefit while performing an obligation which he owed to another or while acting voluntarily in his own self-interest

A garage, believing that a thief is the owner of a car, undertakes certain repairs at his request. The true owner then retakes possession of the car.[15]

A builder contracts with a third party, whom he mistakenly but reasonably believes owns Blackacre, to build a swimming pool on Blackacre. He does so. The third party who has not paid the builder is evicted by the true owner.[16]

A sub-contractor contracts with the main contractor to instal light fittings in the owner's house. He does so. The contractor is unable to pay him.[17]

English as well as American courts will deny the garage, the builder and the sub-contractor any claim against the owner.[18] At first it was said that the claim must fail because there was no privity between the parties[19]; but that requirement, which is a relic of the heresy of implied contract, has been justly condemned as "unintelligible."[20] In more recent years less formalistic reasons have been suggested for rejecting any restitutionary claim; in particular, that a plaintiff can never recover in restitution if the benefits were conferred on the defendant while discharging an obligation which the plaintiff owed to a third party.[21] Underlying that principle is the assumption that it is unwise to cut across contractual boundaries and to redistribute to a stranger, such as the owner, the risks which the plaintiff implicitly agreed to bear when he contracted with a third party (the thief, the apparent owner, the contractor).[22] In some cases a defendant may be liable to pay a third party for services rendered even though they were rendered by the plaintiff, for such may be the case where the sub-contractor seeks restitution from the landowner who is contractually bound to make payments for the sub-contractor's services to the head contractor. Moreover, in the third of our examples, to allow the sub-contractor a direct claim against the landowner may result in the sub-contractor gaining priority over the contractor's general creditors in the event of the contractor's insolvency.[23]

---

[15] *Cf. Tappenden* v. *Artus* [1964] 2 Q.B. 185; *Brown and Davies Ltd.* v. *Galbraith* [1972] 1 W.L.R. 997 (garage repairing car for insurer cannot recover from owner). But *cf.* now Torts (Interference with Goods) Act 1977, s.6(4): see below, p. 174.

[16] *Cf.* the cases on mistaken improvement: see below, Chap. 5. This hypothetical problem is based on the facts of the South African case of *Gouws* v. *Jester Pools Ltd.*, 1968 (3) S.A. 563 (T.).

[17] *Cf. Hamptom* v. *Glamorgan C.C.* [1917] A.C. 13. And for principals and sub-agents, see *Cobb* v. *Becke* (1845) 6 Q.B. 930; *Robbins* v. *Fennell* (1847) 11 Q.B. 248.

[18] See above, n. 15, for the English cases; and *cf.* Chap. 12 for a discussion of comparable problems in the context of claims for contribution. For the American cases, see 87 Harv.L.Rev. 1409 (1974).

[19] *Cf.* above, pp. 5 *et seq.*

[20] Jackson, *History*, p. 103.

[21] *Cf. Ruabon Steamship Co.* v. *The London Assurance Co.* [1900] A.C. 6: see below, p. 56.

[22] *Cf.* Dawson, *Unjust Enrichment*, pp. 126–127.

[23] The sub-contractor's claim is, however, more persuasive if there is no insolvency and the owner has not paid the general contractor: *cf.* the succeeding paragraph of the text and *Costanzo* v. *Stewart*, 453 P. 2d. 526 (1969).

It is irrelevant that, in some of these situations, the defendant knew that the plaintiff would enter into a contract with the third party to render services for his benefit. It also appears to be irrelevant that the plaintiff's intervention has incontrovertibly benefited the defendant. Consequently at common law[24] the garage has no redress against the real owner, even though the garage was mistaken and the repairs made at the thief's request were essential if the real owner were to obtain an M.O.T. certificate, which he fully intended to obtain. This is a hard case,[25] and a court may one day be persuaded to grant the garage relief in such a case. But a restitutionary claim should be contemplated only if the plaintiff can show that, but for the repairs, the defendant must have entered into a contract similar to that entered into by the thief with the garage. This may even outweigh any argument that contractual risks are in consequence redistributed. The court should, of course, then subrogate the owner to the garage's rights against the thief, although, in practice, this will be a paper remedy.[26]

In all these examples the plaintiff rendered services. But the plaintiff, A, has similarly been denied subrogation to B's claim against C in the following circumstances. A entered into a contract with T to indemnify B in the event of loss caused by the tortious act of a third party, C. B suffers that loss, and accepts payment from A. A is said to have voluntarily conferred the benefit and consequently his payment did not discharge C's liability to B.[27] A cannot therefore recover directly from C. This is a regrettable conclusion, which is the product of English law's over-inclusive notion of what is a voluntary payment.[28]

A person who confers a benefit on another while acting in his own self-interest cannot obtain restitution from that other. In *Ruabon Steamship Company* v. *The London Assurance Co.*,[29] insurers of a vessel, which was in dock to enable the owner to make repairs for which the insurers were liable, failed to recover contribution from the owner towards the expenses of docking, the owner having taken the opportunity, while the ship was docked, of making a survey to renew the ship's classification. The Earl of Halsbury L.C. could not "understand how it can be asserted that it is part of the common law that where

---

[24] *Quaere* if the garage may now be able to recover under Torts (Interference with Goods) Act 1977, s.6(4), which is equivocally worded: see below, p. 174.

[25] For a hard and even more difficult case, see *Re Nott and Cardiff Corp.* [1918] 2 K.B. 146: see below, p. 359. And *cf. Bowstead on Agency* pp. 134–135, for a suggestion that a sub-agent should now account to his principal (*cf.* above, n. 49). *Cf. Charles B. Kane* v. *Motor Vessel Leda*, 355 F.Supp. 796, 804–805 (1972); the well-known fertiliser case before the *Cour de Cassation*, D.92.1.596, S.93.1.281, discussed in Dawson, *Unjust Enrichment*, pp. 100 *et seq.* and Zweigert and Kötz, *An Introduction to Comparative Law*, Vol. II, pp. 213 *et seq.* (trans. T. Weir, 1977). *Cf.* the South African decisions of *New Club Garage* v. *Milborrow & Son* (1931) G.W.L. 85 and *Klug and Klug* v. *Perkin* (1932) C.P.D. 401 (a restitutionary claim allowed.)

[26] For a case where D represented to P, a sub-contractor, that D would put T, the main contractor, in funds and where P's restitutionary claim succeeded, see *Atlas Cabinets & Furniture Ltd.* v. *National Trust Co.* (1990) 68 D.L.R. (4th.) 161 (B.C.C.A.).

[27] See *"The Esso Bernicia"* [1986] A.C. 643: see below, pp. 344–345.

[28] See above, pp. 50–51; see below, Chap. 4.

[29] [1900] A.C. 6; and *cf. The Acanthus* [1902] P. 17.

one person gets some advantage from the act of another a right of contribution towards the expense from that act arises." He thought that otherwise there would be ludicrous results. "So that if a man were to cut down a wood which obscured his neighbour's prospect and gave him a better view, he ought upon this principle to be compelled to contribute to cutting down the wood."[30] Consistently, in the United States, a Maine quarry owner, who pumped dry his own quarry and thereby freed his neighbour's quarry of an accumulation of water, was refused any recompense from the neighbour.[31] There are sound reasons for denying restitution in such cases. The defendant may not have received an incontrovertible benefit, in the sense that he had been saved an expense which he would inevitably have incurred. But, more fundamentally, to grant restitution in every case where a plaintiff had acted in his own self-interest would be to open a Pandora's box of claims. Self interest is manifestly not a sufficient ground of a restitutionary claim.

The predominant reason why the Maine quarry owner acted as he did was to advance his own interests.[32] But there may be other situations where a person acts, not only from self-interest, but for other reasons. A restitutionary claim may then succeed. Claims for contribution and recoupment may arise from payments made out of self-interest.[33] In *Exall* v. *Partridge*[34] the plaintiff, who met the landlord's demand for rent, did so because he wanted to recover his goods seized under distress, but he recovered his payment from the lessees; a person who has rendered services in an emergency may obtain restitution where he intended to charge for them[35]; and in Canada a person who rendered services to another, in the expectation that she would be paid for them in some form or another, recovered on a *quantum meruit*, despite her evidence that she stayed with the defendant because she wanted a roof over her head.[36] In all these cases there is present an element of self-interest. But it is subservient to other more compelling factors, such as compulsion, necessity and request.

In German law, a distinction is made between direct enrichment, for which restitution must be made, and indirect enrichment, for which no restitution need be made.[37] Indeed a similar principle is sometimes expressed by common lawyers in the statement that a person cannot obtain restitution for benefits which are "incidentally" conferred on another. In our view this latter proposition, so formulated, may be too imprecise. For there are situations where English courts have granted a restitutionary claim even though the defendant's

---

[30] At p. 10; see also p. 12.
[31] *Ulmer* v. *Farnsworth*, 15 A. 65 (1888). Cf. *Sinclair Canada Oil* v. *Pacific Petroleum Ltd.* (1969) 2 D.L.R. (3d) 338.
[32] Dawson, "The Self Serving Intermeddler," 87 Harv.L.Rev. 1409 (1974).
[33] See below, Chaps. 13 and 14.
[34] (1799) 8 T.R. 308: see below, p. 346.
[35] Cf. *Re Rhodes* (1890) 44 Ch.D. 94, below, p. 380; *Matheson* v. *Smiley* [1932] 2 D.L.R. 787: see below, p. 377.
[36] Cf. *Hinck* v. *Lhenen* (1974) 52 D.L.R. (3d) 301.
[37] A discussion of the German law is to be found in Dawson, *Indirect Enrichment, Jus Privatum Gentium* (Festschrift für Max Rheinstein) (Tübingen, 1969), Vol. II, p. 789.

enrichment may be characterised as indirect. The defendant may have acquired property from a third person in breach of his fiduciary duty or his undertaking to hold property for the benefit of another.[37a] He may have received a payment, such as a rent, which should have been paid to the plaintiff.[38] The *Diplock*[39] personal action, to recover money paid by executors under a mistake, may lie not only against the immediate recipient but against any third party claiming through him other than a bona fide purchaser[40]; and a claimant may be able to trace in equity his property into its product and into the hands of any third party other than a bona fide purchaser.[41] In principle a defendant who has gained an undoubted benefit should make restitution if it has been gained at the plaintiff's expense, whether the benefit was directly or indirectly conferred. Consequently, we prefer to describe the limiting principle as denying restitution in cases where the plaintiff conferred the benefit on the defendant while acting voluntarily in his own self-interest.

The plaintiff acted officiously in conferring the benefit

Judges and jurists have sought to express this limiting principle in a number of other ways.[42] Other statements of the same principle are that recovery will be denied because the plaintiff was a *mere volunteer*, or a person who had *thrust himself* on the defendant, or who had intervened without "*adequate justification.*"[43]

Such expressions as "officiousness," "mere volunteer" or "thrust himself on another" are simply a "form of legal shorthand"[44] which conceals the conclusion that a defendant should not be required to pay for benefits which the plaintiff knows that the defendant neither solicits nor desires. He takes the risk that the defendant will pay him for the benefit which he conferred on him. Because the risk is on his head, he has no cause to complain if his hope is disappointed.[45] Consequently, it is irrelevant whether or not the defendant has gained an incontrovertible benefit.[46]

Many examples will be found in this book of restitutionary claims which have been denied because a claimant has so acted. For that reason a stranger who improves another's land,[47] knowing that the land belongs to that other, is

---

[37a] See Chap. 33.

[38] See Chap. 29, for other examples. Contrast the Israeli Unjust Enrichment Law, 5739–1979, s.1(b): "It shall be immaterial whether the benefit was obtained through an act of the beneficiary or an act of the benefactor or in any other way."

[39] *Ministry of Health* v. *Simpson* [1951] A.C. 251: see below, p. 583.

[40] See below, p. 585.

[41] See below, Chaps. 2 and 40.

[42] See also Hope, "Officiousness," 15 Cornell L.Q. 25 and 205 (1930).

[43] Contrast Birks, *Introduction*, pp. 102–103.

[44] Dawson, *Unjust Enrichment*, pp. 127 *et seq.*; *Cf.* Palmer, *op. cit.* Vol. I, § 1.7.

[45] *Cf.* Birks, *Essays* (ed. Burrows), pp. 120–124.

[46] See above, p. 22. Contrast Birks, *Introduction*, p. 103.

[47] See below, Chap. 5.

without remedy; "if without an antecedent request a person assumes an obligation or makes a payment for the benefit of another, the law will, as a general rule, refuse him a right of indemnity."[48] And a plaintiff who consciously discharges, without compulsion of law, another's statutory or contractual duty to a third party cannot obtain restitution.[49] In all these cases the restitutionary claim failed because the plaintiff knew that the defendant did not want him to intervene.[50]

In contrast, the case law suggests that a plaintiff who acts mistakenly[51] or under compulsion will not generally be stigmatised as a mere volunteer or officious even though the defendant did not ask him to act. This will also be the case if he confers a benefit on the defendant, at the defendant's request, in the course of a transaction which proves to be ineffective. In particular, a restitutionary claim will not be defeated solely on the grounds of officiousness in the following cases, which are not exhaustive:

(1) if money has been paid under a mistake of fact;
(2) if land has been mistakenly improved with the defendant's acquiescence;
(3) if chattels have been mistakenly improved;
(4) if services have been mistakenly rendered;
(5) if benefits have been conferred under duress, or undue influence, or compulsion of law;
(6) if benefits have been conferred under contracts void for want of authority, mistake or uncertainty;
(7) if benefits have been conferred in anticipation of a transaction which does not materialise.

Moreover, a restitutionary claim should only be defeated on this ground if the plaintiff's conduct is officious vis-à-vis the defendant. For that reason it may be proper to refuse to require a debtor to indemnify a plaintiff who, without authority, became his surety and paid the creditor.[52] But if the creditor willingly accepted the surety's payment, it can hardly be said that the surety has acted officiously vis-à-vis the creditor; there should, arguably, be no objection to subrogating the surety to the creditor's rights against the debtor.[53] Only if the creditor would never have assigned the debt to the plaintiff, but accepted the payment in the reasonable but mistaken belief that the plaintiff

---

[48] *Owen* v. *Tate* [1976] Q.B. 402, 411–412, *per* Scarman L.J.
[49] *Macclesfield Corp.* v. *Great Central Ry.* [1911] 2 K.B. 528: see below, p. 371, n. 65. For other cases where officiousness has defeated a restitutionary claim, see *Stokes* v. *Lewis* (1785) 1 T.R. 20 (below, p. 368, n. 52); *Re Cleadon Trust* [1939] Ch. 286 (see below, p. 622); *Boulton* v. *Jones* (1857) 2 H. & N. 564 (see below, p. 488).
[50] *Cf.* Birks, "Negotiorum Gestio and the Common Law" [1971] C.L.P. 110.
[51] Probably even if the mistake is one which no reasonable man would make.
[52] *Owen* v. *Tate* [1976] 1 Q.B. 402: see below, p. 35. The debtor's debt is not discharged by the plaintiff's payment. See above, p. 17.
[53] But see *Owen* v. *Tate* [1976] 1 Q.B. 402, 411–412, *per* Scarman L.J.: see below, p. 598.

intended to confer a gratuitous benefit on the debtor by discharging the debt,[54] should subrogation be denied.

There is at least one possible exception to this limiting principle.[55] Restitution should be awarded if services have been rendered to another in an emergency, for the public interest, at least in the preservation of life, is so great that it overrides the defendant's vigorous and positive dissent.[56] But even then it is conceivable that the plaintiff may act officiously; he may have intervened knowing that there was near another person who was better qualified to help and was ready to do so.[57]

The defendant cannot be restored to his original position or is a bona fide purchaser

An important application of this principle has been the limit imposed upon the right to rescind transactions. Consequently, a party claiming rescission must be able to make, and must in fact make, *restitutio in integrum*. There is a comparable principle which governs money claims: money cannot be recovered unless the plaintiff can show that there has been a total failure of consideration.

"As a condition to a rescission there must be a *restitutio in integrum*. The parties must be put *in statu quo*."[58] This principle was applied both at law and in equity, though the power of courts of equity to order accounts of profits and to make allowances for deterioration rendered the application of the principle less rigorous in these courts than in courts of law. Today, however, all divisions of the High Court can give effect to the more flexible equitable doctrine.[59]

In cases at law concerned with recovery of money, however, the principle of *restitutio in integrum* has not been given full scope. Thus, where a claimant seeks to recover money which he has paid under an ineffective transaction, the general rule is that he can only recover his money if the consideration for his payment has totally failed. Conversely, he will be denied recovery if the failure of consideration is only partial.[60] In cases of breach of contract a conflict developed between the principle of *restitutio in integrum* and the principle of total failure of consideration. So it was held, in the past, that if the innocent

---

[54] These were the facts of *Norton* v. *Haggett*, 85 A.2d 571 (1952), where a restitutionary claim was denied: see below, p. 599, n. 80.

[55] *Cf.* Birks, *Introduction*, Chap. IX.

[56] *Matheson* v. *Smiley* [1932] 2 D.L.R. 787, a suicide. (But what if the intervener knew that the injured person was a Christian Scientist who would not want the aid which was administered?) For property intervention, see *Great Northern Ry.* v. *Swaffield* (1874) L.R. 9 Ex. 132. See below, Chap. 15 for a discussion of these questions.

[57] See below, pp. 374 *et seq.*

[58] *Erlanger* v. *New Sombrero Phosphate Co.* (1878) 3 App.Cas. 1218, 1278, *per* Lord Blackburn. *Cf.* Birks, *Introduction*, pp. 415 *et seq.*

[59] Supreme Court Act 1981, s.49. For a recent illustration of the application of this flexible doctrine, in the context of a claim of undue influence, where the contract was wholly performed, see *O'Sullivan* v. *Management Agency and Music Ltd.* [1985] Q.B. 428 C.A.: see below, p. 284.

[60] For a criticism of the common law, see below, pp. 400–404.

party elected to determine the contract, he rescinded it *ab initio*, but that he could only rescind it *ab initio* if he could put the party in breach *in statu quo*.[61] These cases,[62] which are in part the product of the semantic confusion surrounding the concept of *rescission*,[63] have now been overruled. In *Johnson v. Agnew*,[64] the House of Lords confirmed that an innocent party may, in appropriate circumstances, bring the contract to an end, without rescinding it *ab initio*, and that the contract, when terminated, is terminated only prospectively.[65] At one time it was thought that, where a contract had been brought to an end in this way, any benefits previously conferred under it would be irrecoverable since they had already accrued due and since the contract had not been rescinded *ab initio*; on this basis, it was held that the benefits conferred under contracts thereafter frustrated could not be recovered.[66] But it is now established that money paid by an innocent party under a contract which one party has wrongly repudiated is recoverable at common law provided that the consideration for the payment has wholly failed.[67]

No doubt it is right that a party who has received the very thing which he has contracted to receive should be unable to reopen the transaction to recover his money.[68] But where he has received only part of the consideration for his payment, application of the principle of total failure of consideration may be productive of injustice.[69] In such a situation, the less rigid principle of *restitutio in integrum* would be better adapted to adjust the rights of the parties and, in cases of frustrated contracts, the legislature has intervened to give the courts a statutory power of adjustment[70]; and there are some indications[71] that the courts will, on occasion, interpret that principle in a manner more akin to the principle of *restitutio in integrum*. Furthermore, whether there has been a total failure of consideration is for the court to determine as a matter of construction. It may interpret the contract narrowly, to enable the plaintiff to recover on the ground that he has not received any part of the bargained-for performance.[72] But this is rough justice. The plaintiff may have received some benefit from the defendant's performance of his contractual obligation, and it may

---

[61] *Hunt* v. *Silk* (1804) 5 East 449; *Chandler* v. *Webster* [1904] 2 K.B. 419; *Rowland* v. *Divall* [1923] 2 K.B. 500, 503, *per* Bankes L.J.

[62] *Berchem* v. *Wren* (1904) 21 R.P.C. 683; *Thorpe* v. *Fasey* [1949] Ch. 649; *Horsler* v. *Zorro* [1975] Ch. 302.

[63] (1975) 91 L.Q.R. 33 [Albery].

[64] [1980] A.C. 367.

[65] See also *Fibrosa Spolka Akcyjna* v. *Fairbairn Lawson Combe Barbour Ltd.* [1943] A.C. 32, 65.

[66] *Chandler* v. *Webster* [1904] 1 K.B. 793; *Blakeley* v. *Muller & Co.* [1903] 2 K.B. 760n., 761–762, *per* Wills J.; (1939) 55 L.Q.R. 54, 60 [A. T. Denning].

[67] *Fibrosa Spolka Akcyjna* v. *Fairbairn Lawson Combe Barbour Ltd.* [1943] A.C. 32: see below, pp. 408–409.

[68] See, *e.g.* *Steinberg* v. *Scala (Leeds) Ltd.* [1923] 2 Ch. 452.

[69] *Cf.* Law Commission, Working Paper, No. 65, §§ 48–56.

[70] Law Reform (Frustrated Contracts) Act 1943, s.1(2): see below, pp. 447 *et seq.*

[71] See, *e.g.* *Valentini* v. *Canali* (1889) 24 Q.B.D. 166, 167, *per* Lord Coleridge C.J. (see below, p. 527); *Rowland* v. *Divall* [1923] 2 K.B. 500 (see below, p. 421).

[72] *Cf.* *Rover International Ltd.* v. *Cannon Film Sales Ltd.* (*No. 3*) [1989] 1 W.L.R. 912, C.A.: see below, pp. 401, 543–544.

well be that he will not be required to recompense the defendant for the benefit which he has received.

The essence of the limiting principle that *restitutio in integrum* must be possible is that it is unjust to grant restitution if the defendant cannot be restored to his original position. But its application is not confined to the rescission of transactions or to actions for the recovery of money paid. It is now recognised to be a general defence to all restitutionary claims that the defendant is able to show that, after the receipt of the benefit, his position has so changed that it would be inequitable to require him to make restitution.[73] For example, a person may incur a loss because he believes that a benefit which has been conferred on him is his to deal with as he likes[74]; or an agent may pay money over to his principal in ignorance of the fact that the payment was exacted under duress.[75] In both cases, his change of position should be a defence to a claim for restitution.[76] Statute may recognise a defence of change of position. On one view this is the principle which underlies section 1(3) of the Law Reform (Frustrated Contracts) Act 1943, which requires the court to have regard to any expenditure incurred by the benefited party in, or for the purpose of, the performance of the contract, in determining the value of the benefit gained by him.[77]

Bona fide purchase provides another example of this limiting principle. It is a defence particularly appropriate to pure proprietary claims.[78] But it has its part in the law of restitution; it is a defence to restitutionary money claims both at law and in equity and is distinct from that of change of position.[79]

For convenience we have discussed change of position, estoppel and bona fide purchase in that part of this book entitled Defences.

Public policy may preclude a restitutionary claim[80]

A restitutionary claim will fail if it is against public policy to enforce it. There are many illustrations of this limiting principle. There are the specific defences to restitutionary claims, which are discussed later in this book, such as *res judicata*[81] and the statutes of limitation and laches.[82] Illegality may also be pleaded as a bar to restitution. The court will not assist a party who has to rely upon an illegal act as a necessary part of his claim. The principal examples of

---

[73] *Lipkin Gorman (A Firm)* v. *Karpnale Ltd.* [1991] 2 A.C. 548: see below, Chap. 40.

[74] See below, pp. 740–741; and *cf.* (1981) 61 Boston U.L.R. 563, 568–576 [Dawson].

[75] *D. Owen & Co.* v. *Cronk* [1895] 1 Q.B. 265: see below, p. 739, which suggests that the defence may be an independent defence.

[76] Depending on the facts, it may be a complete or partial defence: see below, pp. 740–741.

[77] *BP Exploration Co. (Libya) Ltd.* v. *Hunt (No. 2)* [1982] 1 W.L.R. 783, 800, 804, *per* Robert Goff J.

[78] See below, Chap. 41.

[79] See below, p. 762.

[80] Conversely, it may be the ground of a restitutionary claim: see above, p. 43.

[81] See below, Chap. 42.

[82] See below, Chap. 43.

the application of that defence are to be found in the cases where a party seeks to recover benefits rendered under a contract ineffective because of illegality.[83] But other instances occur throughout the law of restitution; for example, a contribution claim may be defeated on that ground.[84] Because a successful plea of illegality allows a defendant to retain an enrichment which may be manifestly unjust, it should succeed only in the clearest cases. Illegality is no bar if the parties are not *in pari delicto* or if the illegal agreement is still executory.[85] Moreover, exceptionally, equity may give relief even if the parties are *in pari delicto* and the contract is executed.[86]

Such defences apart, public policy reflects itself most significantly in the principle that restitution will not be awarded if the award would lead to the enforcement of a transaction which statute or common law refuses to enforce. There have been a number of cases where a plaintiff's claim has failed for this reason. Occasionally a statute will prohibit any claim whatsoever.[87] More frequently, the courts will have to decide whether the recognition of the claim will indirectly frustrate the policy of a particular statute or common law rule.

At times the courts have tended too readily to deny a restitutionary claim on this ground. Such a case was *Sinclair* v. *Brougham*[88] The House of Lords held that bank depositors, who sought to recover money deposited by them under *ultra vires* contracts of deposit, could not recover their money in a personal action either at law or in equity; for to have allowed their claim would have circumvented the "doctrine of *ultra vires* as established in the jurisprudence of this country."[89] The depositors were, however, allowed to follow their money in equity, although they were compelled to recognise the equities of the shareholders in the society which carried on the *ultra vires* banking business. It is strange that the principle should have been held to preclude a personal but not a proprietary claim. In the majority of cases, where the limiting principle applies, both claims should be barred.

---

[83] See below, Chap. 22.
[84] See below, p. 332.
[85] See below, pp. 505 *et seq. Cf. Re Ferguson* (1969) 14 F.L.R. 311, 317, *per* Gibbs J.
[86] See below, pp. 517 *et seq.*
[87] See, *e.g. Butler* v. *Broadhead* [1975] Ch. 97 (see below, p. 586), interpreting s.264 of the Companies Act 1948 and the Companies (Winding Up) Rules 1949, r. 106, made under the Companies Act 1948, s.273(*e*).
Conversely, a statutory provision may specifically provide that restitution may be granted even though a contract is ineffective. For example, the Financial Services Act 1986, s.3 renders an agreement made by or through unauthorised persons "unenforceable against the other party;" but also states that the other party shall be "entitled to recover any money or other property paid or transferred by him under the agreement, together with any compensation for any loss sustained by him as a result of having parted with it." See also s.61 which empowers the court to make an order requiring the person concerned to pay into court such sums as appear to be just having regard to the profits accruing from the statutory contravention or to the extent of the loss or other adverse effect.
For a general discussion, see J. Beatson, *Should there be Legislative Development?* in *Essays* (ed. Burrows), pp. 292 *et seq.*
[88] [1914] A.C. 398: see below, pp. 83–85.
[89] *Ibid.* 414, *per* Viscount Haldane L.C. See below, pp. 540–542 (recovery not prevented).

In contrast, in *R. Leslie Ltd.* v. *Sheill*,[90] the Court of Appeal properly[91] dismissed a quasi-contractual claim to recover money lent by an adult to an infant; for if the claim had been allowed, the infant would have been indirectly compelled to perform his primary obligation under a contract of loan which the Infants Relief Act 1874 had declared to be void. Another example is *Boissevain* v. *Weil*.[92] There, the House of Lords held that money lent to a British subject, contrary to the Defence (Finance) Regulations 1939, was irrecoverable. Lord Radcliffe[93] said that if the claim, based on the respondent's unjust enrichment, were

> "a valid one, the court would be enforcing on the respondent just the exchange and just the liability, without her promise, which the Defence Regulation has said that she is not to undertake by her promise. A court that extended a remedy in such circumstances would merit rather to be blamed for stultifying the law than to be applauded for extending it. I would borrow the words which Lord Sumner used in *Sinclair* v. *Brougham*: 'the law cannot *de jure* impute promises to repay, whether for money had and received or otherwise, which, if made *de facto*, it would inexorably avoid.' His principle is surely right whether the action for money had and received does or does not depend on an imputed promise to pay."

The principle, if applicable, enables the recipient to retain a benefit which in other circumstances he would be bound to restore. It should, therefore, only be applied where absolutely necessary. Yet in the authorities which have just been cited no real attempt was made by the courts to weigh the policy underlying the rule which rendered the transaction ineffective against the policy which requires restitution of unjust benefits; and there is much to be said for the view that, in cases of *ultra vires* contracts at least, the latter policy should have prevailed.

In other cases express consideration has been given to the question whether a restitutionary claim would indirectly enforce a transaction which the law declares to be ineffective. Benefits conferred under contracts which were unenforceable because of the want of a corporate seal[94] or evidence in writing[95]

---

[90] [1914] 3 K.B. 607.

[91] Query, however, if the legislature, in avoiding the contract of loan, intended to permit the infant's unjust enrichment: see below, pp. 531–532.

[92] [1950] A.C. 327; *cf. Re H.P.C. Productions Ltd.* [1962] Ch. 466.

[93] [1950] A.C. 327, 341. See also *Kasumu* v. *Baba-Egbe* [1956] A.C. 539, 549, *per* Lord Radcliffe; and *cf. Restatement of Restitution*, § 62.

[94] *Lawford* v. *Billericay R.D.C.* [1903] 1 K.B. 772.

[95] *Scott* v. *Pattison* [1923] 2 K.B. 723, where services had been rendered under a contract unenforceable because of the Statute of Frauds and the plaintiff recovered remuneration in quasi-contract. To allow the plaintiff's claim did not conflict with the policy of the statute, which was to prevent the setting up, by means of fraud and perjury, of contracts or promises by parol, upon which parties might otherwise have been charged for their whole lives: see *Souch* v. *Strawbridge* (1846) 2 C.B. 808, 814, *per* Tindal C.J. Unlike the claim in *Britain* v. *Rossiter* (1879) 11 Q.B.D. 123, the claim was not for damages for breach of a contract sought to be implied in the teeth of an unenforceable contract. It was a quasi-contractual claim for benefits conferred: *cf. Phillips* v. *Ellinson Bros. Pty. Ltd.* (1941) 65 C.L.R. 221, 246, *per* Williams J.

have been recovered because the courts were satisfied that the restitutionary claim did not frustrate the legal policy which rendered the particular transaction ineffective.[96]

More recently, the High Court of Australia was required to consider whether a New South Wales statute, under which a building contract is not enforceable by the builder against the other party to the contract unless the contract is "in writing signed by each of the parties or his agent in that behalf, and sufficiently describes the building work the subject of the contract," barred a restitutionary claim in circumstances where the builder had completed the building in accordance with the terms of the oral contract.[97] The High Court, Brennan J. dissenting, held that it did not; and granted the builder reasonable remuneration, which was fortuitously the sum which the defendant had orally promised to pay, for the work requested by him. In the view of the High Court, the intent of the legislature had to be gleaned from the bare language of the statute. The statute was enacted so as to ensure that the other party could not be forced to comply with the terms of the contract; it did not embrace the situation where the other party requested and accepted the building work. The builder was not deprived of his common law right to recover fair and reasonable remuneration for work done and accepted, for the statute was not intended to penalise the builder beyond making the agreement unenforceable by him. The Court did not analyse why the defendant was unjustly enriched; seemingly it was because she had requested and freely accepted the services.[97a]

The High Court gave a further reason for its decision, namely, that dismissal of the builder's claims would be so draconian a result that it is difficult to suppose that the legislature intended it.[98] In England the courts, when asked to determine whether the grant of a restitutionary claim would frustrate the policy of a particular statute, have also been moved, on some but not all occasions, by the consideration that the defendant would be unjustly enriched if the plaintiff's claim were rejected. For example, in *Congresbury Motors Ltd.* v. *Anglo-Belge Finance Co. Ltd.*,[99] the defendant had lent the plaintiff money to

---

[96] *Ciz* v. *Hauka* (1953) 11 W.W.R. (N.S.) 433 (money paid recoverable though, by statute, a contract made on Sunday was void); *Tuck Construction Ltd.* v. *Wappa County* [1967] N.Z.L.R. 781 (illegality). In the United States the question has arisen whether a municipality can be held liable in restitution for benefits conferred on it under a contract which was ineffective because it had not complied with provisions requiring the contract to be awarded only after competitive bidding. Many States have denied recovery. But some have allowed a *quantum meruit* claim for the reasonable value of the goods or services; the "contract" price is, however, a ceiling on recovery. The cases are collected in 33 A.L.R. 3d 1164 (1970).

[97] *Pavey & Matthews Pty. Ltd.* v. *Paul* (1987) 162 C.L.R. 221.

[97a] At p. 228, *per* Mason C.J. and Wilson J. Her conduct may be characterised as unconscionable: *cf.* Birks, *Essays* (ed. Burrows), Chap. 5.

[98] For a fuller discussion of the reasons given by the High Court and that of the New South Wales Court of Appeal, whose decision was reversed, see (1988) 1 Jo. of Contract Law 8 [Jones] and (1988) 8 Oxford J.L.S. 312 [Ibbetson].

[99] [1971] Ch. 81. *Cf. Bradford Advance Co.* v. *Ayers* [1924] W.N. 152 (money advanced under a bill of sale void under Bills of Sale Act 1882, recoverable).

buy certain property. On the plaintiff's instructions the defendant handed the
money over to the vendor who conveyed the title to the plaintiff. Contemporaneously a legal mortgage was executed in the defendant's favour. Both the loan
and the mortgage were declared to be unenforceable under section 6 of the
Moneylenders Act 1927 since no proper memorandum had been executed.
Nevertheless the Court of Appeal allowed the defendant's counterclaim, and
held that they should be subrogated to the vendor's lien for unpaid purchase
money; for the defendant was not attempting to enforce a contract of repayment for money lent and the statute only required formalities for such a
contract. The Court did not consider it decisive that the defendant must be
assumed to have known that the contract of repayment was unenforceable; and
it held that the acceptance of the invalid legal mortgage did not mean that the
valid lien had been waived, abandoned or superseded.[1]

In the Court's view, the facts were similar to those in *Thurstan* v. *Nottingham
Permanent Benefit Building Society*.[2] There the defendant had lent money to the
plaintiff, who was then an infant. On the infant's instructions part of the loan
was applied to the purchase of land; the vendor conveyed the land to the infant
and a legal mortgage was contemporaneously executed in the defendant's
favour. Both the loan and the security were void under the Infants Relief Act
1874. The plaintiff brought an action against the defendant, seeking a declaration that the mortgage was void and claiming delivery of title deeds and
possession of the property. The House of Lords held that the defendant should
be subrogated to the vendor's lien for unpaid purchase money. This did not
conflict "with the legislation or its policy."[3] The plaintiff's claim was without
"ethical merits."[4]

However, in *Orakpo* v. *Manson Investments Ltd.*[5] the House of Lords was not
moved by the prospect of the defendant's unjust enrichment. The House
overruled *Congresbury Motors* and held that it was improper to allow subrogation if the result was to enable the moneylender "to escape from the
consequences of his breach of the statute."[6] The Court of Appeal, in the latter
case, had paid "too little attention . . . to a consideration of the construction of
section 6 of the Act of 1927."[7] Its terms were manifestly different from those of
the Infants Relief Act 1874. The Moneylenders Act rendered the loan unenforceable; the Infants Relief Act made the loan void. In one case, the lender had a
valid security; in the other, he had none. *Thurstan's* case was, therefore,
"decided correctly."[8] But there can be no doubt that the policy of the Infants

---

[1] At p. 94, *per curiam*.
[2] [1902] 1 Ch. 1 C.A., [1903] A.C. 6: see below, pp. 595–596.
[3] [1971] Ch. 81, 93, *per curiam*, commenting on *Thurstan's* case.
[4] [1971] Ch. 81, 90, *per curiam*.
[5] [1978] A.C. 95. *Cf. Menaka* v. *Lum Kum Chum* [1977] 1 W.L.R. 267, P.C.
[6] *Ibid.* at p. 111, *per* Lord Salmon.
[7] *Ibid.* at p. 118, *per* Lord Keith of Kinkel.
[8] *Ibid.* at pp. 114–115, *per* Lord Edmund-Davies. For another distinction between the two cases,
see *ibid.* at pp. 120–121, *per* Lord Keith of Kinkel; and *cf.* Birks, *Introduction*, pp. 390–393,
who suggests that *Thurstan's* case can only be explained on the basis that the Building Society

Relief Act is stronger than that of section 6 of the Moneylenders Act 1927; and it is for that reason that the lender "obtains nothing"[9] for his loan to an infant. Yet, as the law now stands, he can be subrogated to an unpaid vendor's lien while a moneylender who falls foul of section 6 cannot. This is a strange result.[10]

Similarly, in *Re Byfield*, Goulding J. stopped his ears to "the siren song of unjust enrichment," and dismissed the creditor's claim.[11] A bank had paid out, on its customer's instructions, money in the customer's account to her mother. It did so in good faith, not knowing that a receiving order had been made and gazetted against its customer. The mother used some of the money to pay off some of the customer's creditors. Subsequently the bank paid the customer's trustee in bankruptcy a sum equivalent to that paid out to the mother. Goulding J. rejected the bank's claim to be subrogated to the rights of creditors paid off by the mother, and to lodge the proof of debt which the creditors could have put in if they had not been paid off. Section 4 of the Bankruptcy (Amendment) Act 1926, provided that where money of a bankrupt has, after the date of the receiving order and "before it has been gazetted in the pre-scribed manner, been paid or transferred by a person having possession of it to some other person," then if the payer can prove that he had no notice of the receiving order, "any right of recovery which the trustee may have against him shall not be enforced by any legal proceedings. . . ." The judge could not see that "good conscience and equity" demanded any further relief. Section 4 was the limit of the bank's protection, and the bank was not protected by it. Consequently its payment was void against the trustee in bankruptcy.

But it is a distinct question whether it would offend the policy underlying the Bankruptcy Act to have allowed subrogation to the claims of creditors whose debts were discharged by the bank's payment. In our view it did not. The creditors, if they had not been paid, could have lodged proof; and to allow subrogation is to allow the bank to succeed to their claims when it is just to do so. To deny subrogation is, in these circumstances, to allow the bankrupt's estate to retain a windfall.[12]

The policy underlying the common law rule will be found in the decisions which formulated and refined that rule. But, as has been seen, the courts must normally[12a] seek the intention of the legislature from the language of the statute. In these circumstances there is much to be said for the view that, in

---

had dealt with the vendors over the purchaser's head. But query if the facts support this interpretation.

[9] *Ibid.* at p. 110, *per* Lord Salmon.

[10] *Ibid.* at p. 114, *per* Lord Edmund-Davies. See below, p. 596. The House of Lords (Lord Diplock dissenting on this point) also held that the moneylender's claim must fail because the relief sought through subrogation was essentially a proceeding "for the recovery . . . of any money lent" within s.13 of the Moneylenders Act 1927.

[11] [1982] Ch. 267 at 276: see below, p. 158. Nowadays the bank is protected: see Insolvency Act 1986, ss.284(5) and 307(4).

[12] *Cf.* Burrows, *The Law of Restitution*, pp. 90–92.

[12a] But see now *Pepper* v. *Hart* [1992] 3 W.L.R. 1032 (H.L.).

cases of doubt, the courts should be guided by the principle that a defendant should make restitution of a payment, gained at the plaintiff's expense, which it would be manifestly unjust for him to retain.

4. PERSONAL AND PROPRIETARY CLAIMS

Restitutionary claims are either personal or proprietary.[13] Most are personal and seek to impose upon the defendant a personal obligation to pay the plaintiff a sum of money. The obligation is normally a legal obligation, but it may also arise in equity.[14]

There are, however, occasions when a plaintiff may seek a proprietary claim. A restitutionary proprietary claim may be granted in order to revest title in the plaintiff[15]; a plaintiff may, in an action for money had and received, rely on his legal title, having rescinded a contract. In equity he may submit that the defendant is a constructive trustee of, or that a lien be imposed over, certain assets; or he may seek to be subrogated to another's secured claim. Whether, and under what conditions, a court will grant such a remedy is a question of considerable complexity and uncertainty. Moreover, in equity it must be possible to identify an asset in the defendant's hands.[16] Consequently, as a matter of convenience we have treated this subject at length in the succeeding Chapter. Such a restitutionary claim must be carefully distinguished from a pure proprietary claim where the plaintiff asserts that the property which he has identified in the defendant's hands belongs, and has always belonged, to him.[17] The law of property forms no part of the law of restitution. But the historical development of the forms of action has at times blurred the boundaries of the two subjects; for that body of law which determines "title" to property may incidentally prevent the defendant's enrichment at the plaintiff's expense.[18]

Subrogation should also be regarded as a restitutionary remedy. But English judges have, on occasions, regarded subrogation as a right, not as a remedy, which a plaintiff may enjoy, in certain specific situations, where the defendant has acquired a benefit from a third party for which he must account to the

---

[13] See Stoljar, *Law of Quasi-Contract*, for a theory that the non-contractual source of quasi-contract is to be found in the rules which protect "basic proprietary interests." For convincing criticisms, see (1969) 47 Can. B.R. 1 (Samek); (1965) 16 Univ. of Toronto L.J. 473 (Wade).

[14] See above, pp. 4–5.

[15] See [1983] C.L.P. 141, 145 [Birks]; *e.g.* a contract may be rescinded for fraud.

[16] See below, Chaps. 2 and 27.

[17] *Cf.* Birks, in [1983] C.L.P. 141, 144, 146. "Both rights in personam and in rem are restitutionary if they are created when a defendant receives an enrichment at the expense of the plaintiff and have the effect of causing him to yield up that enrichment to the plaintiff ... The key [to the distinction between restitution and property] is the isolation of the phenomena of reversal of as opposed to deterrence and anticipation of, unjust enrichment." Birks develops this argument in his *Introduction*, pp. 49–73.

[18] A good illustration is provided by the law of attornment, which is discussed below, Chap. 27. The history of that subject is part of the history of the action for money paid; for that reason we have set out the law in this book. But, in principle, there is much to be said for the view that attornment should belong to the law of property. For that reason we have concluded that the topic of conditional gifts does not belong to the law of restitution; and history no longer compels us to treat is as such.

plaintiff. Consequently we have felt compelled to treat the topic of subrogation in a later Chapter of this book.[19] In our view, however, the development of the law of restitution will ultimately lead to the acceptance of the principle that subrogation is a restitutionary remedy.[19a] Whether a plaintiff should be subrogated to a personal claim or to a lien or charge over another's property must depend on the facts of the particular case. The court should not regard it as a fatal objection that the personal claim or lien has been discharged by the plaintiff's payment. The cases demonstrate that the plaintiff may be subrogated in equity to a claim analogous to that discharged at law,[20] and that a lien may be resurrected if it is necessary to do justice to the plaintiff.[21]

5. THE CLASSIFICATION OF RESTITUTIONARY CLAIMS

Restitutionary claims can be classified in various ways.[22] Those who have attempted to classify quasi-contracts have generally done so, though seldom consistently, in terms of remedy.[23] But such a classification is unrevealing and harmful. It is unrevealing because it tells us nothing about why or when the plaintiff is entitled to recover.[24] It is harmful because it preserves and even emphasises archaic pleading requirements which have outgrown their original function; to this extent the accent on remedy is misleading and inhibits rational development of principle. The classical example of this development is the "request" which is usually said to be an essential requirement not only of the action for money paid, but also of *quantum meruit* and *quantum valebat* claims. But, as has been seen, the requirement has been so interpreted and extended over the years that in some cases it no longer bears any relation to the ordinary meaning of the word "request."[25]

Moreover, the wider range of restitutionary claims makes it impracticable to adopt a classification of restitution founded upon remedy. Other restitutionary remedies are not easily accommodated within the common *indebitatus* counts; and equitable claims are scarcely susceptible to classification in terms of remedy. We are compelled, therefore, to follow natural instinct and divert attention from remedy to right.

---

[19] Chap. 31.
[19a] See *Lord Napier and Ettrick* v. *R. F. Kershaw Ltd.* [1993] 1 All E.R. 385, H.L.: see below, pp. 74, 100, 590, 606–607.
[20] See below, pp. 621 *et seq.*
[21] See below, pp. 631 *et seq.*
[22] See, *e.g.* Palmer, *op. cit.* Vol. I, § 1.7.
[23] See, *e.g.* Munkman, *Quasi-Contracts*.
[24] The same might be said of a classification founded on the character of the benefit received by the defendant. Moreover, the difficulty of drawing up a complete list of the different types of benefit makes such a classification impracticable.
[25] See above, pp. 18–22. Extensions of this kind are not irrational; they reflect a legitimate desire on the part of the courts to develop the law to meet the needs of justice. The sensible course is to accept the fact that the old criterion no longer suffices, and to attempt to isolate and identify the new principle which has emerged. But it is precisely this course which is inhibited by clinging to the old forms of pleading.

English courts have traditionally provided "specific remedies in particular cases of what might be classified as unjust enrichment in a legal system that is based upon the civil law."[26] As a matter of history this statement cannot be faulted. But these "particular cases" are now sufficiently numerous to enable a court to recognise that they are united by, and are representative of, a general principle of unjust enrichment. However, for reasons already explained, attention must still be concentrated on the substantive grounds for recovery.

It will be found that different considerations apply in cases where the plaintiff himself conferred the benefit on the defendant as opposed to cases where the benefit came into the defendant's hands from a third party. This is the main division in restitution. In both situations the defendant's benefit gained at the plaintiff's expense is normally commensurate with the loss suffered by the plaintiff.[27] But together with these two principal categories we must recognise a third, more limited in scope, which is concerned with cases where the benefit has come into the hands of the defendant in consequence of some wrongdoing on his part. In this category a restitutionary claim may be alternative to some other type of claim. Moreover, there is here no necessary equation between benefit gained and loss suffered. Indeed one of the principal objects of the restitutionary claim is to strip the defendant of a gain, even though the circumstances may be such that the plaintiff has suffered little or no loss.[28]

(a) *Where the Plaintiff has Himself Conferred the Benefit on the Defendant*

Within this category the cases fall naturally into groups which reflect the fact that benefits have been unofficiously conferred by the plaintiff on the defendant. There are four of these groups:

(1) Where the plaintiff was *mistaken.*
(2) Where the plaintiff acted under *compulsion.*
(3) Where the plaintiff intervened as a matter of *necessity.*
(4) Where the plaintiff conferred a benefit under an *ineffective transaction.*

The law in these four groups of cases is in varying stages of development. Perhaps it is most highly developed in the last group, concerned principally with contracts but also with trusts. Certainly it is most unbalanced in the third group of cases, concerned with necessity, where there is a sharp contrast between the highly developed law of maritime salvage and an embryonic set of rules relating to common law claims. Our arrangement of the various topics within these four groups has been based simply on convenience, being largely dictated by the manner in which, and the extent to which, the law has developed.

---

[26] *Orakpo* v. *Manson Investments Ltd.* [1978] A.C. 95, 104, *per* Lord Diplock.
[27] See above, pp. 35–38.
[28] See above, p. 38.

(b) *Where the Defendant has Received the Benefit from a Third Party*

In cases of this kind, the plaintiff will generally be entitled to recover from the defendant only if some special relationship existed between the parties, or if the plaintiff can assert a right of property in money, or in an object whose receipt has benefited the defendant. Such cases do not ordinarily fall within the law of restitution. Exceptionally, however, restitution will be ordered. For example, the plaintiff may be subrogated to the rights of another; subrogation is not always dependent upon a contractual or other relationship between the plaintiff and the defendant.[29] Subrogation apart,[30] the topics include claims arising out of the administration of an estate or under an *inter vivos* trust, attornment (where, it can be argued, there is a particular relationship between the plaintiff and the defendant created by the attornment), and certain special cases in which benefits have come into the defendant's hands which were intended for the plaintiff.[31] These claims are of limited importance.

(c) *Where the Defendant has Acquired the Benefit through his own Wrongful Act*

Special rules have been developed in the cases of benefits acquired from crime, from a tortious act, or from a breach of fiduciary relationship, or from a breach of confidence. These topics call for separate treatment. Where, however, benefits are conferred under contracts discharged through breach, the applicable principles are in general similar to those which apply in other cases of benefits conferred under ineffective contracts; all such cases, are accordingly treated together in the first category.

If benefits have been acquired through a tortious act or rendered under contracts discharged through the defendant's breach, the restitutionary right may be of limited practical importance because of the availability of alternative tortious or contractual remedies. To a lesser extent this is also true of cases of benefits acquired through crime, where there may be an alternative remedy in tort. But there may be other cases, such as those where a person has betrayed another's confidence,[32] when the only possible claim is in restitution; and, as we have seen, there are occasions when a defendant acquires a benefit from his wrongful act, in circumstances where the plaintiff suffers no loss.[33]

That there may, on occasion, be an overlap between restitutionary and other claims simply reflects the fact that the rubrics of the law are not watertight

---

[29] See below, Chap. 31.

[30] When subrogation becomes recognised as a general remedy to prevent unjust enrichment, this category may wither away. Attornment belongs rather to the law of property and finds itself in restitution only for historical reasons (see below, Chap. 27).

[31] *e.g.* where the defendant has usurped the plaintiff's office and has received profits to which the plaintiff was entitled (see below, Chap. 28), or where the assets of a trust, or the estate of a deceased person, have been wrongly paid over to the defendant instead of to the plaintiff (see below, Chap. 29). For a different analysis, see Birks, *Introduction*, pp. 138–139.

[32] The Law Commission has recommended that the confider should have a tortious claim: see Report No. 110, *Breach of Confidence* (1981) (see below, p. 702); *cf. Dowson & Mason Ltd.* v. *Potter* [1986] 2 All E.R. 418, C.A.

[33] See above, pp. 38–39.

compartments, so that the same set of facts may well give rise to alternative claims. A similar overlap often occurs between claims in contract and tort, as, for example, when a bailee negligently damages goods, or a carrier negligently injures passengers in his care.

CHAPTER 2

PROPRIETARY CLAIMS

1. INTRODUCTION

RESTITUTIONARY claims are generally personal; in order to prevent the defendant's unjust enrichment the law imposes upon him a personal obligation to make restitution to the plaintiff. In most cases a plaintiff will be satisfied with a personal claim. But exceptionally he may not. He may seek to rescind a transaction, or he may claim that the defendant should be made a constructive trustee of property for him or that he should have a lien, or that he should be subrogated to another's lien, over the defendant's property. He will be particularly anxious to establish an equitable proprietary claim if the defendant is insolvent, for he may then obtain priority over general creditors.[1] He may also wish to recover the profits made by the defendant.[2] Moreover, a limitation period governing proprietary claims may be longer[3]; a limit to a personal claim may occasionally not constitute a bar to a proprietary claim[4]; an order may be obtained for the preservation of the property pending the hearing of the action,[5] he may be awarded compound interest on any sum awarded[6]; and, if the defendant is resident out of the jurisdiction, service of the writ may be permissible.[7]

In this book it would not be appropriate to discuss every situation in which a proprietary claim can be asserted by a claimant.[8] For that reason we do not discuss in detail a claim that the plaintiff has never been divested of his property in chattels (pure proprietary claims[9]). In contrast, there are

---

[1] For an example of such a claim, see below, pp. 130–132.

[2] For examples of such a claim, see cases cited on pp. 83 *et seq.*

[3] This is a possibility since equitable claims are barred only by laches. However, the analogy of the statutes of limitation is generally followed: see below, pp. 756–766.

[4] *Sinclair* v. *Brougham* [1914] A.C. 398: see below, p. 83.

[5] R.S.C., Ord. 29, r. 2. *Cf. Lister* v. *Stubbs* (1890) 45 Ch.D. 1: see below, pp. 765–766. For a significant extension of the court's powers, see the *Mareva* line of cases, now legitimatised in the Supreme Court Act 1981, s.37(3).

[6] See *Wallersteiner* v. *Moir* (No. 2) [1975] Q.B. 373.

[7] Ord. 11, r. 1(1)(*t*).

[8] For another view, see Elias, *Explaining Constructive Trusts*, p. 17.

[9] *Whittaker* v. *Campbell* [1983] 3 All E.R. 582, 586, *per* Robert Goff L.J.; Birks, *Introduction*, pp. 49–73, 377–396.

proprietary claims which are restitutionary. Claims for rescission on the ground of misrepresentation, duress, fraud or undue influence may be so characterised since they seek to revest title in the plaintiff.[10] The plaintiff may also seek to vindicate his title to property, generally money. His title may be his legal title or, more commonly, his equitable title. At law he must show that the defendant has received his money. In equity he must identify (trace) *his* property. If he succeeds in doing so, then at law the defendant must make restitution; in equity the court may declare that the defendant holds a fund as a constructive trustee for his benefit or may grant a lien over that fund to secure his title.

In other situations where a plaintiff has been granted an equitable remedy it is not easy to support the court's decision on the ground that it was protecting the plaintiff's existing equitable title. For example, it has been held that ultra vires depositors could trace their deposits into the hands of the liquidator of an insolvent building society[11]; and that a bank could trace its money, which it had paid under a mistake of fact, into the hands of another bank, now insolvent[12]; in both cases it was said that the plaintiffs, the ultra vires depositors and the bank respectively, had retained an equitable interest in the moneys which they had paid the recipients.[13] In these contexts, the constructive trust and the equitable lien were in reality remedies imposed by the court because it was thought just to do so. They are "nothing more than a formula for equitable relief".[13a] Similarly, it has been held that an insurer has a lien over a fund, namely, moneys paid by a third party in settlement of the assured's claim

---

[10] We have considered, as a matter of convenience, the remedy of rescission elsewhere in this book: see below, Chap. 8.

[11] *Sinclair* v. *Brougham* [1914] A.C. 398: see below, p. 83.

[12] *Chase Manhattan Bank N.A. Ltd.* v. *Israel-British Bank (London) Ltd.* [1981] Ch. 105: see below, p. 130.

[13] See below, p. 94. But contrast R. Goode, *Property and Unjust Enrichment in Essays* (ed. Burrows), pp. 215 *et seq.*

[13a] *Cf. Selangor United Rubber Estates Ltd.* v. *Cradock* [1968] 1 W.L.R. 1555, 1582, *per* Ungoed-Thomas J. ("The court of equity says that the defendant shall be liable in equity, as though he were a trustee. He is made liable in equity as trustee by the imposition or construction of the court of equity"). *Cf.* Lord Denning M.R.'s observations in *Hussey* v. *Palmer* [1972] 1 W.L.R. 1286, 1289–1290 (he has made similar remarks in many cases); *Chase Manhattan Bank N.A.* v. *Israel-British Bank (London) Ltd.* [1981] Ch. 105, 117–118, *per* Goulding J. (followed in *Neste Oy* v. *Lloyds Bank plc* [1983] 2 Lloyd's Rep. 658, 665–666, *per* Bingham J., citing Story's *Commentaries on Equity Jurisprudence* (2nd ed., 1839), Vol. 2, § 1225); *Metall und Rohstoff* v. *Donaldson Inc.* [1990] 1 Q.B. 391, 479, *per* Slade L.J.: see below, p. 94.

English lawyers have traditionally thought of the constructive trust as akin to an express trust, carrying with it at least some of the ordinary duties of trusteeship. So an express trustee who makes an unauthorised profit from his trusteeship is a constructive trustee of that profit. See, generally, Lord Wright, *Legal Essays* p. 7; (1959) 75 L.Q.R. 234 [Maudsley]; A. J. Oakley, *Constructive Trusts*, Chap. 1. This is not to deny that a constructive trust may be imposed for other reasons: *cf.* Elias, *op. cit.* n. 8, Chap. 1.

against him, in the hands of the assured's agents. It would be unconscionable not to impose the lien since the assured had been fully indemnified.[13b]

In equity, no proprietary claim can succeed unless a plaintiff can identify his property in the defendant's hands, and in the following sections of this Chapter we describe the complex body of law which has developed to identify property, particularly money, in the hands of another. Equity's rules and presumptions were created in the context of litigation between beneficiaries of a trust and a bankrupt trustee who, having mixed his own money and trust money in a bank account, had dissipated part of the fund. The sums involved were small and the activity of the bank account modest. The rules and presumptions which identified the trust money were created to ensure that the beneficiaries gained priority over the trustee's general creditors. It has been hitherto assumed that equity's rules and presumptions are of general application, governing restitutionary claims which arise otherwise than from a breach of trust. But they should not be regarded as immutable, and from time to time the courts have, in the context of new fact situations, modified them to do justice to the claims, not only of beneficiaries,[14] but also of innocent volunteers.[15]

2. RESTITUTIONARY PROPRIETARY CLAIMS

(a) *Protecting Title: at Law and in Equity*

The very great majority of restitutionary proprietary claims are concerned to protect equitable title to property. But it is first necessary to describe the principles of common law, particularly those which seek to protect title to money. A plaintiff's action for money had and received may be grounded on his legal title. More importantly, the equitable rules and presumptions were fashioned to remedy what was perceived to be the inadequacy of the common law rules.[16]

(A) "Tracing" at common law

Property in land and chattels, other than money and negotiable instruments, is widely protected.[17] In ejectment a plaintiff must establish that he has a better

---

[13b] *Lord Napier and Ettrick* v. *R. F. Kershaw Ltd.* [1993] 1 All E.R. 385, 397–398, *per* Lord Templeman, H.L.: see below, p. 100.

[14] *Neste Oy* v. *Lloyds Bank plc* [1983] 2 Lloyds Rep. 658, 665–666, *per* Bingham J.

[15] See below, p. 83.

[16] See below, p. 90.

[17] For a general discussion of the nature and scope of the common law right "to follow" property, see "Tracing at Common Law" (1965–1966) 7 W.A.L.R. 463 [Scott]; "A Tracing Paper" (1976) 40 Conv. 277 [Pearce]; "The Right to Trace and its Impact in Commercial Transactions" (1976) 92 L.Q.R. 360, 528 [Goode]; *Tracing Confusion* (1979) 95 L.Q.R. 78 [Kurshid and Mathews].

right to possess the land than the defendant; if he can do so he will not be defeated by any defence of bona fide purchase although his action may become statute-barred under the Limitation Act 1980. Claims to chattels, other than money or negotiable instruments, are nowadays enforced through the tortious action for "wrongful interference with goods"[18] or in quasi-contract through the action for money had and received. Bona fide purchase will rarely be a defence to such claims.[19] A successful plaintiff is not entitled to specific restitution; but the court has a discretion to order the chattel to be restored.

The plaintiff must, however, be able to demonstrate that the defendant received his property. Where the plaintiff is claiming non-fungible chattels, this important practical limitation will create little difficulty. But the identity of fungibles may become easily lost by their becoming mixed with other fungibles. Consequently if grain has become mixed in a ship or in a warehouse, the common law applies the special rules, akin to those developed in Roman law, of *commixtio* and *confusio*.[20] Where A's property has become inseparably[21] mixed with B's, the resultant mass will belong, in proportion to their contributions, to A and B as tenants in common.[22] But if the mixing was due to the wrongful act of either A or B, there is some authority which suggests that English law makes a significant and punitive departure from the Roman doctrine and will give the whole mass to the innocent party.[23] However, in

---

[18] Torts (Interference with Goods) Act 1977, s.1. The tort is also described as "wrongful interference."

[19] But see Sale of Goods Act 1979, ss.22(1) and 23; Consumer Credit Act 1974. It is very rarely, too, that a defendant can defeat a claim to such a chattel by invoking the doctrine of estoppel.

[20] Inst. 2.1 27–28; D.6.1.3.2, 5 pr. These should be distinguished from *accessio* (where two things are so united that the identity of one is merged and lost in the identity of the other) and *specificatio* (where one person makes a *nova species* on his own account out of another's materials). Here, too, a person may be divested of his property without his consent. In the case of *accessio* of a movable to land, the maxim *quicquid plantaur solo, solo cedit* still applies, subject to modifications (*Gough* v. *Wood & Co.* [1894] 1 Q.B. 713, 718–719, *per* Lindley L.J.); and in the case of inseparable *accessio* of movable to movable it appears that, in the absence of contrary intention, the property in the acceding movable will pass to the owner of the movable to which it has acceded (*Appleby* v. *Myers* (1867) L.R. 2 C.P. 651, 659–660, *per* Blackburn J.). (For an argument that *accessio* has no application to personalty, see [1981] C.L.P. 159 [Matthews]). There is little English authority on *specificatio*; but it is likely that, at least where there is a true *nova species* which is irreducible to its original materials, the manufacturer will become owner (2 Bl.Comm. 404–405). In all these cases, the deprived owner may be able to recoup his loss by an action of trover. See, generally, (1964) 27 M.L.R. 505 [A. G. Guest].

[21] On separable mixing, see *Colwill* v. *Reeves* (1811) 2 Camp. 575.

[22] *Buckley* v. *Gross* (1863) 3 B. & S. 566, 575, *per* Blackburn J.; *Spence* v. *Union Marine Insurance Co.* (1868) L.R. 3 C.P. 427; *Sandeman & Sons* v. *Tyzack & Branfoot S.S. Co.* [1913] A.C. 680, 695, *per* Lord Moulton; *Gill & Duffus (Liverpool) Ltd.* v. *Scruttons Ltd.* [1953] 1 W.L.R. 1407; 2 Bl.Comm. 404. See also *Jones* v. *Moore* (1841) 4 Y. & C. Ex. 351.

[23] *Spence* v. *Union Marine Insurance Co.* (1868) L.R. 3 C.P. 427, 437–438, *per* Bovill C.J.; but see *Sandeman & Sons* v. *Tyzack & Branfoot S.S. Co.* [1913] A.C. 680, 695, *per* Lord Moulton; 2 Bl.Comm. 405. Similar principles apply in equity: see *Lupton* v. *White* (1808) 15 Ves. 432; *Cooke* v. *Addison* (1869) L.R. 7 Eq. 466: see below, p. 86. For a discussion, see (1981) 34 C.L.P. 159 [Matthews].

Indian Oil Corp. Ltd. v. *Greenstone Shipping SA*,[24] Staughton J., after comprehensively reviewing the case law, concluded that[25]:

" . . . where it is totally unknown how much of the innocent party's goods went into the mixture, the whole should belong to him. But I do not see that they require or justify the same result where it is known how much was contributed by the innocent party, or even what the maximum quantity is that he can have contributed, being something less than the whole."

In the latter circumstances A and B should then hold any admixture as tenants in common, in proportion to their contributions. To this conclusion there must be a further qualification, which the judge accepted: if the wrongdoer prevents the innocent party proving how much of his property has been taken, then the wrongdoer is liable to the greatest extent that is possible in the circumstances.[26]

Money Claims at Common Law

Claims for money[27] (or for instruments which are of value to their owners not simply as concrete objects but for the choses in action which they represent,[28] such as a debt,[29] negotiable instruments and cheques[30]) present special problems, given that money is not easily identifiable and normally passes into currency so that its holder is able to invoke a defence of bona fide purchase.[31]

---

[24] [1987] 3 All E.R. 893; [1987] C.L.J. 369 [Stein].

[25] At p. 906.

[26] *Ibid.* citing *Armory* v. *Delamire* (1722) 1 Stra. 505. See, generally, (1990) 10 Jo.L.S. 293 [McCormack].

[27] Coins are not the only chattels that are money. It has been suggested (Mann, *The Legal Aspect of Money*, 5th ed., 1992, p. 8) that, in law, "the quality of being money is to be attributed to all chattels which, issued by the authority of the law and denominated with reference to a unit of account, are meant to serve as universal means of exchange in the state of issue." In particular, a banknote is treated as money: see *Miller* v. *Race* (1758) 1 Burr. 452; *Wookey* v. *Pole* (1820) 4 B. & Ald. 1, 6, *per* Best C.J.; *Suffell* v. *The Bank of England* (1882) 9 Q.B.D. 555, 559, *per* Jessel M.R.: see below, n. 28.

[28] Including banknotes (*Miller* v. *Race* (1758) 1 Burr. 452: see above, n. 27); bills of exchange (*Atkins* v. *Owen* (1836) 5 A. & E. 819; *Fenton Textile Association Ltd.* v. *Thomas* (1929) 45 T.L.R. 264; *cf. Palmer* v. *Jarmain* (1837) 2 M. & W. 282; guarantees (*M'Leod* v. *M'Ghie* (1841) 2 Man. & G. 326); life policies (*Watson* v. *McLean* (1858) E.B. & E. 75; and a similar principle has been applied to documents published in infringement of copyright. (Copyright, Designs and Patents Act 1988, s.96(1)). The owner will be entitled to recover by way of damages for the conversion of such an instrument the value of the right represented thereby: see, generally, *Bavins, Jnr. & Sims* v. *London & South Western Bank Ltd.* [1900] 1 K.B. 270; and *cf. Ernest Scragg & Sons Ltd.* v. *Perseverance Banking and Trust Co. Ltd.* [1973] 2 Lloyd's Rep. 101, 103, *per* Lord Denning M.R.

[29] *Lipkin Gorman (A Firm)* v. *Karpnale Ltd.* [1991] 2 A.C. 548, 573–574, *per* Lord Goff.

[30] See *Morison* v. *London County & Westminster Bank Ltd.* [1914] 3 K.B. 256, 379, *per* Phillimore L.J.

[31] *Higgs* v. *Holiday* (1600) Cro.Eliz. 746; *Miller* v. *Race* (1758) 1 Burr. 452, 457–458, *per* Lord Mansfield; *Clarke* v. *Shee and Johnson* (1774) 1 Cowp. 197, 200, *per* Lord Mansfield; *Calland* v. *Loyd* (1840) 6 M. & W. 26. The defence applies to claims to negotiable instruments. See, generally, *below*, Chap. 41.

A money claim was at common law enforceable by an action for money had and received[32] or, occasionally, in trover.[33] Either action results in a personal judgment,[34] based on the plaintiff's proprietary right, against the defendant. Since the claim is based on the claimant's legal title, it is not necessary to inquire whether there is in existence a fiduciary relationship.

The claim can only succeed if the plaintiff can demonstrate that the defendant received *his* money and that he did not, as a result of that receipt, obtain good title to it.[35] Given the defence of bona fide purchase, successful claims are rare.

It is commonly said that the plaintiff's money ceases to be identifiable if it has become mixed with the money of another person.[36] But the common law claim is based on the plaintiff being able to show that the defendant received his money. It is not necessary for him to take the further step of proving that the defendant still has his money.[37] So, where A's money has been paid without his authority into B's bank account, A can still maintain an action for money had and received against B.[38] The fact that the relationship between B and his bank is, in consequence of the payment, creditor and debtor, the property in the money deposited having passed to the bank, will not defeat A's claim.

---

[32] See above, pp. 3–4.

[33] It is sometimes said that trover will not lie for money, because money has no ear-mark. But this is not correct. Trover will lie for money provided that it can be shown that the defendant has converted to his own use coins or notes which can be identified as belonging to the plaintiff: see *Miller* v. *Race* (1758) 1 Burr. 452, 457–458, *per* Lord Mansfield. The fact that money has no ear-mark will not prevent trover lying for money until it has passed into currency. Conversely, once a man's money has passed into currency, trover will not lie for it even though it may for some particular reason have an ear-mark. "The true reason of this rule is that by the use of money the interchange of all other property is most readily accomplished. To fit it for its purpose the stamp denotes its value, and possession alone must decide to whom it belongs": *Wookey* v. *Pole* (1820) 4 B. & Ald. 1, 7, *per* Best C.J. Trover will lie for money, even though it is not in a container such as a chest or bag: *Hall* v. *Dean* (1601) Cro.Eliz. 841. It will lie, for example, against a man who has stolen money (*Thomas* v. *Whip* (1714) Buller N.P. 130a, *semble*); and against a person to whom money has been entrusted for use in a certain way but which he converts to his own use (*Taylor* v. *Plumer* (1815) 3 M. & S. 562; *Orton* v. *Butler* (1822) 5 B. & Ald. 652, *semble*; *Sinclair* v. *Brougham* [1914] A.C. 398, 411, *per* Lord Parker).

[34] *Lipkin Gorman (A Firm)* v. *Karpnale Ltd.* [1991] 2 A.C. 548, 572, *per* Lord Goff. See (1976) 40 Conv. 277, 284 [Pearce]; (1979) 95 L.Q.R. 78, 93 [Kurshid and Mathews] and above, p. 74. Even on an insolvency the tortious or quasi-contractual action may not be less effective than equity's lien, since judgment will be against the trustee in bankruptcy personally. Indeed it may be more effective since it will not be necessary to show that the trustee still has that property: see (1965–1966) 7 W.A.L.R. 480–483 [Scott]; see below, pp. 82–83.

[35] *Cf. Agip (Africa) Ltd.* v. *Jackson* [1991] Ch. 547; *Lipkin Gorman (A Firm)* v. *Karpnale Ltd.* [1991] 2 A.C. 548, H.L.

[36] *Cf.*, for example, *Re J. Leslie Engineers & Co. Ltd.* [1976] 1 W.L.R. 292; *Agip (Africa) Ltd.* v. *Jackson* [1991] Ch. 547, 564–565, *per* Fox L.J.; *Lipkin Gorman (A Firm)* v. *Karpnale Ltd.* [1991] 2 A.C. 548, 573, *per* Lord Goff.

[37] *Agip (Africa) Ltd.* v. *Jackson* [1991] Ch. 547, 563, *per* Fox L.J.

[38] *Marsh* v. *Keating* (1834) 1 Bing. (N.C.) 198; *Reid* v. *Rigby & Co.* [1894] 2 Q.B. 40; *Banque Belge pour l'Etranger* v. *Hambrouck* [1921] 1 K.B. 321; *Lipkin Gorman (A Firm)* v. *Karpnale Ltd.* [1991] 2 A.C. 548. *Cf. Agip (Africa) Ltd.* v. *Jackson* [1991] Ch. 547, 563–564, *per* Fox L.J. And see below, p. 79, particularly n. 39.

The claim is normally against B who received A's money. But there are a number of nineteenth century cases which hold that an action for money had and received also may lie against C, where A's money is paid to B who then pays it over to C. In all these cases A succeeded because he could show that the legal title to the money remained or was revested in him and that C received his and not B's money and gained no title to it, neither B nor C being bona fide purchasers.[39] In contrast, if A's money is paid by B into his bank account and then money is paid from that account into C's account, A's claim against C will fail if his money was mixed with B's money in B's bank account. A cannot then prove that C received his money. Conversely, if the only money in B's account was A's, A can successfully claim that C must have received his money. These were the facts of *Banque Belge pour l'Etranger v. Hambrouck.*[40]

In that case Hambrouck fraudulently obtained over £6,000 from the plaintiff bank by means of cheques payable to himself which purported to be drawn on the bank *per pro* his employers but which were drawn without the authority of that firm. Hambrouck paid the cheques into his account at Farrow's bank which credited his account and duly cleared the cheques through another bank, through which the amount of the cheques was collected from the plaintiff bank. In substance, no other money was paid into Hambrouck's account at Farrow's bank. From that account Hambrouck drew sums which he paid over to his mistress, a Mademoiselle Spanoghe, in consideration of the continuance of their illicit co-habitation. These sums were paid into her

---

[39] Subject to the requirements of identifiability and the defence of bona fide purchaser, the action for money had and received should be available to enable A to recover from C in the following circumstances: (1) Where A's money is lost or stolen and is paid over to C (*Thomas* v. *Whip* (1714) Buller N.P. 130a); (2) Where A pays his money to B under a fundamental mistake of fact, and B then pays it over to C; (3) Where A, under a contract void for want of the other party's agent's authority, pays money to such agent, who then pays it over to C (*Reid* v. *Rigby & Co.* [1894] 2 Q.B. 40; *Sinclair* v. *Brougham* [1914] A.C. 398, 441, *per* Lord Parker); (4) Where A's money is obtained by B under a voidable transaction, *e.g.* through B's fraud, and B pays it over to C, provided A is still entitled to, and does, rescind the transaction (*Marsh* v. *Keating* (1834) 1 Bing. (N.C.) 198; *Reid* v. *Rigby & Co.* [1894] 2 Q.B. 40; *Banque Belge pour l'Etranger* v. *Hambrouck* [1921] 1 K.B. 321); (5) Where A has entrusted his money to B to take care of, and B pays it over to C (*Calland* v. *Loyd* (1840) 6 M. & W. 26); (6) Where A has entrusted his money to B to be used by B for a specific purpose on A's behalf, and B instead pays it over to C for another purpose (*Litt* v. *Martindale* (1856) 18 C.B. 314; *Taylor* v. *Plumer* (1815) 3 M. & S. 562, *semble* (see below, p. 81, n. 50); *Holt* v. *Ely* (1853) 1 E. & B. 795, *semble*; see also *Reid* v. *Rigby & Co.* [1894] 2 Q.B. 40; *Sinclair* v. *Brougham* [1914] A.C. 398, 441, *per* Lord Parker); (7) Where A's servant (*Clarke* v. *Shee and Johnson* (1774) 1 Cowp. 197) or even, possibly, his agent (*Littlewood* v. *Williams* (1815) 6 Taunt. 277) receives money on behalf of A and pays it over to C; (8) Where a person who was adjudicated bankrupt had, by an act of bankruptcy or under a settlement avoided by s.42 of the Bankruptcy Act 1914, paid money to a third party, his trustee in bankruptcy, in whom the property in the money had vested by virtue of the doctrine of "relation back," could recover the money from the third party (*Trustee of Rousou (a bankrupt)* v. *Rousou* [1955] 1 W.L.R. 545). In these cases the action for money had and received "goes almost into the region of trover" (*Holt* v. *Ely* (1853) 1 E. & B. 795, 799, *per* Erle J.). The cases are not, however, treated as cases of waiver of tort; indeed, the action for money had and received may be available in these cases although trover would not lie (*Reid* v. *Rigby & Co.* [1894] 2 Q.B. 40; *Holt* v. *Ely* (1853) 1 E. & B. 795, 800, *per* Erie J.; *Banque Belge pour l'Etranger* v. *Hambrouck* [1921] 1 K.B. 321, 333, *per* Atkin L.J.).

[40] [1921] 1 K.B. 321.

deposit account in yet another bank. At the time of the action some £315 remained in this deposit account. This sum was paid into court by the bank concerned; the plaintiff bank asked for the sum to be paid out to them, and they also claimed a declaration that the £315 was their property. Salter J., who treated the claim as one for money had and received, gave judgment against Mademoiselle Spanoghe and ordered that the sum in court should be paid out to the plaintiff bank. The Court of Appeal affirmed his decision.

It was assumed that the money had been obtained by means of a voidable transaction under which title passed to Hambrouck until the plaintiff bank avoided that title by commencing proceedings.[41] Moreover Mademoiselle Spanoghe had given no consideration in law and could not be regarded as a bona fide purchaser of the money. The only difficulty was whether the money could be traced through Hambrouck's account at Farrow's bank into the deposit account at Mademoiselle Spanoghe's bank.

All three Lords Justices agreed that Banque Belge could trace its money into Mademoiselle Spanoghe's account. Bankes L.J. held that it could be traced at common law because Mademoiselle Spanoghe never paid any money into her account except part of the proceeds of Hambrouck's fraud; in any event there would be "no difficulty" in following the money in equity.[42] Scrutton L.J. relied upon the equitable doctrine of tracing.[43] There was no common law right to trace; it "was not the money of the *Banque Belge*; for payment into Hambrouck's bank, and his drawing out other money in satisfaction, had changed its identity."[44] Atkin L.J. considered that the common law right to trace was available even if the plaintiff bank's money had been mixed with other money in Hambrouck's bank. If it could be ascertained that the money in the defendant's bank is "the product of, or substitute for, the original thing then it still follows the nature of the thing itself"[45]; on the facts tracing was admittedly not difficult because no other money had been mixed with the proceeds of the fraud. Atkin L.J. was therefore prepared to hold[46] that even if the fund had been increased by the admixture of the plaintiff's money, the plaintiff bank could still trace into any sum which was demonstrably the product of that mixed fund; it could then claim that the product was its money.[47]

---

[41] *Cf. Agip (Africa) Ltd.* v. *Jackson* [1991] Ch. 547, C.A., where it was the defrauded plaintiff who sued at law. But in that case the plaintiff's bank had debited the plaintiff's account. Consequently, the plaintiff had title to sue at law. In contrast in *Banque Belge* the bank was disputing its liability.

[42] [1921] 1 K.B. 321, p. 328.

[43] On which see below, pp. 83 *et seq.*

[44] *Ibid.* pp. 329–330.

[45] [1921] 1 K.B. 321, 335, quoting *Taylor* v. *Plumer* (1815) 3 M. & S. 562, 575, *per* Lord Ellenborough C.J.: see below, p. 82.

[46] But see *Agip (Africa) Ltd.* v. *Jackson* [1991] Ch. 547, 564–566, *per* Fox L.J., preferring the judgment of Bankes L.J.

[47] A majority of the Court of Appeal (Bankes and Atkin L.JJ.) held, therefore, that the mere fact that money has passed through a bank account did not defeat the common law right to trace.

By their statement of claim the plaintiffs asked for an order that the sum of £315 should be paid out to them. Salter J. treated the claim as one for money had and received; and in the Court of Appeal both Bankes and Atkin L.JJ. agreed, as has been seen, that the bank succeeded at law. It would appear, therefore, that *Banque Belge pour l'Etranger* v. *Hambrouck* is authority for the proposition that the common law claim may lie against C, who received A's money from B, who had first received the money. Moreover, in principle A should recover what C received from B and not simply what sum remained in her hands.[48-49]

Finally, there is the question whether A can claim from B, who is not a bona fide purchaser, an asset which he can show was bought with his money. In *Taylor* v. *Plumer*,[50] Lord Ellenborough said that:

[48-49] But contrast *Agip (Africa) Ltd.* v. *Jackson* [1990] Ch. 265, 287–288, *per* Millett J.; and see, on the effect of Mlle. Spanoghe's insolvency (1976) 92 L.Q.R. 360, 528 [Goode]; (1979) 95 L.Q.R. 78 [Kurshid and Matthews].

[50] (1815) 3 M. & S. 562, 575 *et seq*. See also *Golightly* v. *Reynolds* (1772) Lofft. 88. In *Taylor* v. *Plumer*, the defendant gave W, the stockbroker, a draft to buy Exchequer bills. With part of the draft W bought American securities and doubloons. Being apprehended, he surrendered the securities and the doubloons to the defendant. His assignees in bankruptcy failed to recover them or their value from the defendant.

It was argued by counsel for the plaintiff assignees that property cannot be followed into its product when it is tortiously converted into another form for the use of the factor himself because the principal cannot, "for his own private advantage, and to the prejudice of all the other creditors, aver what has been done in fraud of his trust to have been done in execution of it": see (1815) 3 M. & S. 562, 567, 574. Lord Ellenborough, however, rejected this argument as being "mischievous in principle, and supported by no authorities of law."

It is true that, if the original property is still ascertainable and has passed into the hands of another who cannot take advantage of the defence of bona fide purchaser, the owner may abandon his right to the original property and assert his right to the product: see *Marsh* v. *Keating* (1834) 1 Bing. (N.C.) 198. Nevertheless, *Taylor* v. *Plumer* clearly decided that the common law right does not rest on any theory of ratification. Had it done so, the defendant could not have succeeded as, in Lord Ellenborough's view, his subsequent conduct was inconsistent with ratification of W's act of converting the proceeds of the draft and banknotes into the securities and doubloons; and, in any event, the act of conversion was not done on behalf of the defendant.

Yet in *Re Diplock* [1948] Ch. 465, 518, the Court of Appeal, following Lord Parker in *Sinclair* v. *Brougham* [1914] A.C. 398, 441, resurrected the theory of ratification to explain the common law right "to follow" property into its product. This was motivated by a concern to reconcile the right with so-called "implied contract theory"; but money can be followed at law in an action of trover, in which an "implied contract" has never been said to be relevant, and even in an action for money had and received privity is, in this context, irrelevant (see *Litt* v. *Marindale* (1856) 18 C.B. 314). It is not surprising, therefore, that Lord Denning has, extra-judicially, dismissed the theory as "fanciful": see (1949) 65 L.Q.R. 37, 41. *Cf.* (1979) 95 L.Q.R. 78, 89–91 [Kurshid and Matthews]; *Lipkin Gorman (A Firm)* v. *Karpnale Ltd.* [1991] 2 A.C. 548, 572, *per* Lord Goff. Many of the cases relied upon by Lord Ellenborough in his judgment were authorities only for the proposition that property in the hands of the bankrupt was the property of the defendant in equity; and indeed it was irrelevant to the decision in this case whether the defendant had a legal or equitable interest in the product of his property while it was in the hands of W, for in either case he was entitled to it as against the assignees and, having repossessed himself of it, could resist an action of trover brought by them in respect of it. It may well be, however, that the defendant was in fact the legal owner of the securities and doubloons even while they were in W's hands; for the banknotes, of which they were the product, had been entrusted by the defendant to W for a specific purpose which he did not perform: see above, p. 79, n. 39, example (6); and "the product of or substitute for the original thing still follows the nature of the thing itself, as long as it can be ascertained to be such, and the right only ceases when the means of ascertainment fail, which is the case when the subject is turned into money and confounded in a general mass of the same description."

This case and these words have been traditionally interpreted to mean that at common law the legal title to the product passes to A, if he so elects.[51] A dramatic and important illustration of this principle is the decision of the House of Lords in *Lipkin Gorman (A Firm)* v. *Karpnale Ltd.*[51a] Cass was a partner in the plaintiff firm of solicitors. He had authority to draw cheques on the firm's clients' account. He did so, without the firm's authority, in order to satisfy his craving for gambling. The cheques were normally drawn for cash, which he then gambled away at the defendant club. It was conceded that he did not mix any of that money with his own money in his bank account, although it was at the same branch of the same bank. It was also clear that he had used some of his own money to gamble. The plaintiff firm brought an action for money had and received against the defendant club; the ground of the claim was that the defendant club had received the plaintiff's money and that its legal title was not defeated because the defendant club was not a bona fide purchaser. The House of Lords accepted this submission.[51b]

Lord Goff held that the plaintiff firm could trace or follow its "property into its product"; for this "involves a decision by the owner of the original property to assert title to the product in place of his original property".[51c] What was that original property? It was the firm's chose in action, the bank's debt owed to the firm. And the firm could "trace their property at common law in that chose in action, or in any part of it, into its product, i.e. cash drawn by Cass from the clients' account at the bank. Such a claim is consistent with their assertion that the money so obtained by Cass was their property at common law."[51d] It is, of course, true that the plaintiff firm did not discover the inquity of Cass' conduct until after the money had been gambled away. But this did not defeat the claim

---

Winch v. *Keeley* (1787) 1 T.R. 619. See generally (1976) 40 Conv. 277 [Pearce]; (1976) 92 L.Q.R. 360, 528 [Goode] and (1979) 95 L.Q.R. 78 [Kurshid and Matthews].

[51] *Lipkin Gorman (A Firm)* v. *Karpnale Ltd.* [1991] 2 A.C. 548, 573, *per* Lord Goff; *Re J. Leslie Engineers Co. Ltd.* [1976] W.L.R. 292. See also *Clarke* v. *Shee and Johnson* (1774) 1 Cowp. 197, 200, *per* Lord Manfield; *Taylor* v. *Plumer* (1815) 3 M. & S. 562; *cf. Ryall* v. *Rolle* (1749) 1 Atk. 165.

This traditional interpretation of *Taylor* v. *Plumer* has been challenged in (1979) 95 L.Q.R. 78 [Kurshid and Matthews], who argue that the plaintiff can claim the "product" only if property has passed to him or has been specifically appropriated to him, following (1976) 92 L.Q.R. 360, 528 [Goode]. Moreover, they submit that the plaintiff's claim was in equity and not at law. These arguments, which are not unattractive, do not find support in the later case law.

[51a] [1991] 2 A.C. 548.

[51b] The defendant club was allowed to defend itself by pleading that it had changed its position: see below pp. 741–742.

[51c] At p. 573.

[51d] At p. 574.

of the plaintiff firm which could, when the facts came to light, assert its title to the product of its chose in action.[51e]

(B) Tracing in equity

The equitable rules and presumptions to identify the plaintiff's property in the hands of another were developed in the nineteenth century, generally in the context of litigation between the beneficiaries of a trust and the trustee in bankruptcy of a bankrupt trustee. It is always said that equity's significant contribution was its readiness to allow the beneficiaries to trace into a mixed fund; the banker's door did not bar their claim, as it would, so it was thought, a comparable claim at common law.[52]

In these cases the plaintiffs, being beneficiaries under a trust, asked the court to protect their equitable title, and to declare that the defendant, the trustee in bankruptcy of a trustee, held identifiable property on trust for them or to impose a lien over a fund to secure their claim. The Court of Chancery never sought to question the defendant's legal title. As a matter of history, therefore, the plaintiff has to show that the equitable title was vested in him before he could trace in equity. Today that condition is formulated in this way: it is said that the plaintiff must show that the defendant, or a third party through whose hands the trust money had passed on the way to the defendant, is in a fiduciary relationship to him. Whether the courts should still insist on this condition is, however, another and debatable question.[53]

The Requirement of Fiduciary Relationship

The decision of the House of Lords in *Sinclair* v. *Brougham*[54] is said to be[55] authority for the proposition that a fiduciary relationship is necessary before property can be followed in equity. *Sinclair* v. *Brougham* involved a contest between shareholders, depositors and outside creditors arising out of the liquidation of the Birkbeck Permanent Building Society. The Society carried on an *ultra vires* banking business with which the depositors had deposited money. An order was made for the winding-up of the Society and the courts were asked how the assets were to be distributed. It was agreed that the outside creditors should be paid off first. The litigation, therefore, concerned only the shareholders[56] and the depositors. Neville J.,[57] having decided that the banking business was *ultra vires*, held that the depositors could not recover in a

---

[51e] *Cf. Banque Belge pour l'Etranger* v. *Hambrouck* [1921] 1 K.B. 321: above p. 79; and Burrows, *The Law of Restitution*, pp. 65–69.

[52] But see above, pp. 77 *et seq.* for the common law.

[53] See below, pp. 93–94.

[54] [1914] A.C. 398.

[55] As interpreted by the Court of Appeal in *Re Diplock* [1948] Ch. 465, 532.

[56] There were in fact two classes of shareholders, A and B. But an arrangement had been made under which general creditors were paid off first and the A shareholders ranked *pari passu* with the depositors. In the House of Lords, the contest was between the B shareholders and the depositors: see [1912] 2 Ch. 183, 199.

[57] [1912] 2 Ch. 183.

personal claim either at law or in equity for no debt could be created by an *ultra vires* borrowing.[58] His decision was affirmed by the Court of Appeal.[59] The House of Lords rejected the personal claim for similar reasons. But the analogy of *Hallet's* case,[60] as suggested by Viscount Haldane in the course of argument,[61] persuaded the House to allow the depositors to follow their money in equity into the Society's hands; at the same time the depositors were forced to recognise the equities of the shareholders and to accept that the shareholders must rank *pari passu* with them.[62] Consequently the depositors were in law[63] in a better position than the general creditors. If their loan had been *intra vires* no one would have doubted that their only claim would have been as general creditors; like the general creditors, they had merely given credit to the Society. In our view a proprietary claim should never lie where a person has merely given credit to another, whether the loan transaction is valid or ineffective.[64]

It is questionable whether *Sinclair* v. *Brougham* is authority for the proposition that a fiduciary relationship is essential before property can be followed in equity. Lord Dunedin did not mention fiduciary relationship and apparently thought it irrelevant. Only Lord Parker,[65] and possibly Lord Haldane,[66] thought such a relationship necessary; and Lord Parker apparently discovered the relationship as existing between the *ultra vires* depositors and the directors of the Society. This was a surprising discovery since the money had not passed through the directors' hands; moreover it is not easy to see how directors, who are never in a fiduciary relationship to their shareholders, can be in a fiduciary relationship to *ultra vires* depositors.[67] As the Court of Appeal frankly admitted in *Re Diplock*,[68] the speeches in *Sinclair* v. *Brougham* are "in many respects not only difficult to follow out but difficult to reconcile with one another."[69]

---

[58] He held, however, following *Re Guardian Permanent Benefit Building Society* (1882) 23 Ch.D. 440, that the assets should be applied, first, in paying the costs of liquidation; next in paying off the outside creditors; then in paying the shareholders; the balance to be divided rateably among the depositors. The Court of Appeal affirmed his decision, but not without hesitation: [1912] 2 Ch. 183, 230–233, *per* Buckley L.J.

[59] [1912] 2 Ch. 183. Fletcher Moulton L.J. dissented.

[60] (1880) 13 Ch.D. 696: see below, p. 87.

[61] [1914] A.C. 398, 404.

[62] *Cf. Re Diplock* [1948] Ch. 465, 539: see below, p. 90.

[63] The general creditors had been paid off first by agreement: *cf.* above, n. 56.

[64] There may, however, be circumstances where a debt is created at law but a fiduciary relationship nonetheless is deemed to exist in equity: see *Barclays Bank Ltd.* v. *Quistclose Investments Ltd.* [1970] A.C. 567; and *cf. Re Kayford (in liquidation)* [1975] 1 W.L.R. 279; *Carreras Rothmans Ltd.* v. *Freeman Mathews Treasure Ltd.* [1985] Ch. 207.

[65] [1914] A.C. 398, 441–442.

[66] [1914] A.C. 398, 421.

[67] It appears that the Society was unincorporated (see [1914] A.C. 398, 439, *per* Lord Parker). But it does not follow that the directors were, therefore, the fiduciaries of the borrowers although the rules apparently gave them the power (which was *ultra vires*) to borrow.

[68] [1948] Ch. 465, 518.

[69] For another interpretation of the case, see Birks, *Introduction*, pp. 380–387, 396–400.

Yet in *Re Diplock*[70] the Court of Appeal held, purporting to follow *Sinclair* v. *Brougham*, that a fiduciary relationship was essential. It was enough, however, that there was a fiduciary relationship between the claimant and a third party through whose hands the property had passed; it was not necessary that it should exist between the claimant and the defendant.[71] Consequently the next-of-kin could trace into the hands of the charities the money which had been paid to them under mistake by the executors.[72]

It would be surprising if the House of Lords were to confirm that a fiduciary relationship is a prerequisite of tracing in equity.[73] In any event, the class of fiduciaries has always been a very wide one,[74] and may include even persons who have entered into a commercial agreement with each other.[75] The courts have always been ready "to discover" a fiduciary relationship in order to enable a plaintiff to trace. For example, if A pays money to B under a mistake of fact, A is said to retain "an equitable property in it [the money] and the conscience of that other [B] is subjected to a fiduciary duty to respect his proprietary right."[76] To have refused an equitable proprietary claim because there was no fiduciary

---

[70] [1948] Ch. 465, 532. The question did not arise in the House of Lords: [1951] A.C. 251.

[71] It has been argued ((1976) 40 Conv. 277 [Pearce]) that the Court's observations in *Re Diplock* must be read against the facts of that case. In particular a fiduciary relationship may have been necessary on the facts of *Re Diplock* because the next-of-kin had no equitable interest in the money: see *Commissioner of Stamp Duties (Queensland)* v. *Livingstone* [1965] A.C. 694. This ingenious rationalisation was not, however, we think, in the mind of the Court of Appeal.

[72] *Aluminium Industrie Vaasen B.V.* v. *Romalpa Aluminium Ltd.* [1976] 1 W.L.R. 676; *Agip (Africa) Ltd.* v. *Jackson* [1991] Ch. 547, 566–567, *per* Fox L.J.

[73] *United Scientific Holdings Ltd.* v. *Burnley B.C.* [1978] A.C. 904, H.L. *Cf. Lipkin Gorman (A Firm)* v. *Karpnale Ltd.* [1991] 2 A.C. 548, 579–582, *per* Lord Goff; *Nelson* v. *Larholt* [1948] 1 K.B. 339 [Denning J.].

[74] The following persons may be fiduciaries: trustees (*Price* v. *Blakemore* (1843) 6 Beav. 507); personal representatives (*Re Diplock* [1948] Ch. 465); company directors (*Sinclair* v. *Brougham* [1914] A.C. 398); mortgagees (*Thorne* v. *Heard* [1894] 1 Ch. 599, [1895] A.C. 495 (a limitation case)); co-owners (*Betiemann* v. *Betiemann* [1895] 2 Ch. 474 (a limitation case)); solicitors (*Re Hallett's Estate* (1880) 13 Ch.D. 696, *cf. Dooby* v. *Watson* (1888) 39 Ch.D. 178; *Moore* v. *Knight* [1891] 1 Ch. 547; [1893] A.C. 282); bailees (*Re Hallett's Estate* (1880) 13 Ch.D. 696; *Aluminium Industrie Vaasen B.V.* v. *Romalpa Aluminium Ltd.* [1976] 1 W.L.R. 676); and agents who are in a fiduciary relationship with their principals (*Kirkham* v. *Peel* (1880) 43 L.T. 171, 172, *per* Jessel M.R., limiting his own judgment in *Hallett's* case, where he used language wide enough to cover any agent, whether a fiduciary or not; *Aluminium Industrie Vaasen B.V.* v. *Romalpa Aluminium Ltd.* [1976] 1 W.L.R. 677).

It is particularly difficult to define precisely who is a fiduciary agent, although the authorities on the statutes of limitation afford a valuable, if limited, analogy. They suggest that much depends on whether the agent is under a duty to keep separate his own money from his principal's money; see Brunyate, *Limitation of Actions in Equity*, p. 91; Preston and Newsom, *Limitation of Actions*, pp. 174–177; and *cf. Bowstead on Agency*, pp. 191–193. If he is under no such duty, he is not a fiduciary agent; *Burdick* v. *Garrick* (1870) L.R. 5 Ch. 233, 240, *per* Lord Hatherley; see also *Piddocke* v. *Burke* [1894] 1 Ch. 343, 346, *per* Chitty J.; *Henry* v. *Hammond* [1913] 2 K.B. 515, 521, *per* Channell J. *Cf. Watson* v. *Woodman* (1875) L.R. 20 Eq. 721, 731, *per* Hall V.-C. This is a useful, pragmatic yardstick, which seems to meet the majority of cases: but see the wider dicta in *Re Tidd* [1893] 3 Ch. 154, 157, *per* North J.; and below pp. 93–94.

[75] *Cf. LAC Minerals Ltd.* v. *International Corona Resources Ltd.* [1989] 2 S.C.R. 574 (S.Ct. of Canada): see below, p. 644.

[76] *Chase-Manhattan Bank* v. *Israel-British Bank (London) Ltd.* [1981] 1 Ch. 105, 119, *per* Goulding J. But see Birks, *Introduction*, pp. 383–385 for another view.

relationship would have produced the unjust and anomalous result that a person who pays money under mistake would never have a proprietary claim. Again, it is inconceivable that an English court would not allow a plaintiff, whose money had been stolen, to trace in equity into the bank account of the thief.[77] In our view the courts should not hesitate to hold that a person who is legally and beneficially entitled to property should be able to trace in equity into a mixed fund; and the authorities,[78] including *Banque Belge pour l'Etranger* v. *Hambrouck*[78a] support this conclusion.

Identifying the Plaintiff's Property

The "tracing" rules and presumptions

The identity of fungibles is easily lost if mixed with other fungibles. In equity, as as law, it appears that different rules apply to identify fungibles depending on the nature of the fungibles.

If a trustee mixes fungibles (other than money) with other fungibles, then in equity the beneficiary can treat that aggregate mass as belonging to the trust save to the extent that the trustee can distinguish his own property.[79] But identification of money in a mixed fund seems to be made in accordance with different principles,[80] which are highly technical and often irrational. The scope of the beneficiary's claim will depend on the nature of the mixed fund, how it arises and how it has been employed. Equity, like common law, does not regard the bank as in itself a barrier to a beneficiary's claim to follow money. "The claim is a claim of substance, founded in equity which fastens on the conscience of the recipient."[81] Consequently it will not be defeated "by the incidental legal relationships that arise in the course of [the] passage"[82] of money through different bank accounts.

The equitable rules of tracing into a mixed fund can be formulated in the following propositions:

(1) If the trustee has used the beneficiary's money to buy property, the beneficiary can "elect either to take the property purchased, or to hold it as security for the amount of trust money laid out in the purchase." But if the trustee has mixed the beneficiary's money with his own money in one fund and uses that fund to buy other property, then the beneficiary is entitled either to a beneficial interest proportionate to his contribution, or to a charge or lien "on the property purchased, for the amount of the trust money laid out in the

---

[77] *Bankers Trust Co.* v. *Shapiro* [1980] 1 W.L.R. 1274, 1280, 1282, *per* Lord Denning M.R. *Cf.* Att.-Gen.'s Reference (No. 4 of 1979) [1981] 1 W.L.R. 667, 670, C.A.

[78] Such as *Re Hallett's Estate* (1880) 13 Ch.D. 696: see below, p. 73. A. J. Oakley discusses the authorities in (1975) 28 *Current Legal Problems* 64, 69–73. *Cf. Chase-Manhattan Bank* v. *British-Israel Bank (London) Ltd.* [1981] Ch. 105 (see below, p. 130).

[78a] See above, p. 79.

[79] *Lupton* v. *White* (1808) 14 Ves. 432; *Cooke* v. *Addison* (1869) L.R. 7 Eq. 466.

[80] *Cf. Re Pumfrey* (1882) 22 Ch.D. 255, 260–261, *per* Kay J.

[81] *Selangor United Rubber Estates Ltd.* v. *Cradock (No. 3)* [1968] 1 W.L.R. 1555, 1615, *per* Ungoed-Thomas J.

[82] *Ibid.*

purchase."[83] He cannot elect to take the property, because it has not been bought with the trust money "simply and purely."[84]

A mixed fund may be used to buy an investment which increases in value. If the mixed fund consists of the trustee's own money and the trust money, then there is authority that the trustee and the trust will enjoy rateably, in accordance with their contributions, the investment.[85] A similar rule should apply if the fund consists of the trustee's money and the money of an innocent volunteer. If the mixed fund consists of the moneys of two different trusts or of trust money and the money of an innocent volunteer, then any increase in the fund should also be enjoyed rateably.

(2) A trustee mixes his own money with the trust money. Subsequently he makes a withdrawal from the mixed fund and dissipates the money which he has taken out. It was established in *Re Hallett's Estate*[86] that the fiduciary is presumed to have an honest intention and to draw out his own money first. Consequently the beneficiaries of the trust are entitled to a charge on that part of the mixed fund which remains for the amount of the trust money. In *Re Oatway*[87] a mechanical application of this presumption would have defeated the claims of the beneficiaries of the trust. In that case the trustee withdrew money from the mixed fund and placed it in certain investments; subsequently he withdrew the remainder of the fund and dissipated it. Counsel for the trustee's trustee in bankruptcy relied on *Re Hallett's Estate* and argued that the money which he had drawn out first was his own. Joyce J. rejected this argument and held that the investments belonged to the beneficiaries of the trust.[88] The beneficiaries' claim must be satisfied from any identifiable part of the fund before the fiduciary could get anything.[89]

Exceptionally it may be possible for a trustee to show that the money which he withdrew from the mixed fund was his own money and not money belonging to the trust.[90] In *Re Oatway* Joyce J. concluded that the trustee in bankruptcy was not entitled to claim that the money which had been withdrawn was free of the trust "unless or until the trust money paid into the account had been first restored, and the trust fund reinstated by due investment of the money in the joint names of the proper trustees."[91] So, in the American case of *Carey* v. *Safe Deposit & Trust Co.*,[92] a trustee deposited trust

---

[83] *Re Hallett's Estate* (1879) 13 Ch.D. 696, 709, *per* Sir George Jessel M.R.

[84] *Ibid.*

[85] *Re Tilley's W.T.* [1967] Ch. 1179, 1189, following *Scott* v. *Scott* (1964) 37 A.L.J. R. 345. *Cf. Re Hallett's Estate* (*ibid.*), fund decreased in value.

[86] (1879) 13 Ch.D. 696.

[87] [1903] 2 Ch. 356.

[88] At pp. 360–361. The judge held that the principle of *Lupton* v. *White* (1808) 15 Ves. 432 (see above, p. 86, n. 70) only applied if it was impossible to apportion the parties' respective shares: *Cf.* the common law position; see above, p. 76, n. 23; (1963) 79 L.Q.R. 388, 394 [McConville].

[89] *Cf. Primeau* v. *Granfield*, 184 F. 480, 484, *per* Judge Learned Hand (1911).

[90] *Ex p. Kingston* (1871) 6 Ch.App. 632; *Re Hallett's Estate* (1879) 13 Ch.D. 696, 738, *per* Baggallay L.J.; *Re Diplock* [1948] Ch. 465, 551–554; see also *Re Cozens* [1913] 2 Ch. 478, 486.

[91] [1903] 2 Ch. 356, 361.

[92] 168 Md. 501, 178 A.242 (1935).

funds in the account of a firm of lawyers of which he was a member. He had no intention of defrauding the trust and at all times the amount of money on deposit exceeded the trust funds deposited in the account. On his death his administrator withdrew the trust funds and deposited them in a separate trust account in the same bank. The bank later failed. The Supreme Court of Maryland held that the trustee's estate was not subject to any liability. Although there had been a breach of trust, "the error of co-mingling was cured by the unscrambling of the trust funds."[93]

(3) A trustee mixes his own money with trust money; he withdraws money from the mixed fund, dissipates some of it and then deposits more money into the mixed fund. Subsequent deposits of the fiduciary into the mixed fund are not presumed to be impressed with the trusts in favour of the beneficiary.[94] Consequently if the trustee is insolvent, that part of the mixed fund, equal to the amount paid in, will normally pass to the trustee's general creditors. The beneficiary will be entitled to additions to the mixed fund only if he can prove that thereby the trustee intended to make restitution to the trust. It follows that the trust is entitled only to the lowest intermediate balance of the mixed fund. So, if the fund is wholly dissipated before any additions are made to it, the interest of the trust in the mixed fund is extinguished. Professor Scott has justified this result on the ground that "the real reason for allowing the claimant to reach the balance [of the mixed fund] is that he has an equitable interest in the mingled fund which the wrongdoer cannot destroy as long as any part of the fund remains; but there is no reason for subjecting other property of the wrongdoer to the claimant's claim any more than to the claims of other creditors merely because the money happens to be put in the same place where the claimant's money formerly was, unless the wrongdoer actually intended to make restitution to the claimant."[95]

(4) A trustee is a trustee of two different trusts. In breach of trust he mixes the trust funds of the two different trusts in one fund and then subsequently withdraws part of the fund. How is the loss to be borne as between the two trust funds? It appears that the answer will depend upon whether the mixed fund is, or is not, in an active, unbroken banking account.

If the mixed fund is in an active, unbroken banking account, such as a current (but not a deposit) account at a bank, then any withdrawals from the mixed fund will be borne between the two main trusts in accordance with the rule in *Clayton's* case,[96] namely first in, first out.[97] For example a trustee pays £500 from trust fund A into his bank account, which contains no other money,

---

[93] *Scott on Trusts* (3rd ed.), p. 3632. But see the sensible decision in *Re Tilley's Will Trusts* [1967] Ch. 1179 which is, however, difficult to reconcile with *Re Oatway* [1903] 2 Ch. 356: above, n. 91.

[94] *Roscoe* v. *Winder* [1915] 1 Ch. 62, 69, *per* Sargant J.

[95] *Scott on Trusts* (3rd ed.) § 518.1, p. 3638; but see below, pp. 99 *et seq.*

[96] (1817) 1 Mer. 572.

[97] *Pennell* v. *Duffell* (1853) 4 De G.M.G. 372; *Re Hallett's Estate* (1879) 13 Ch.D. 696, 700, *per* Fry J. (the point did not arise in the Court of Appeal); *Hancock* v. *Smith* (1889) 41 Ch.D. 456, 461,

on January 1; two days later he pays £500 from trust fund B into the same account. On February 1, he withdraws £500. In accordance with the rule in *Clayton's* case the loss is wholly borne by trust fund A. The result is capricious and arbitrary. As Judge Learned Hand once said: "when the law attempts a fiction, it is, or at least it should be, for some purpose of justice. To adopt [the fiction of first in, first out] . . . is to apportion a common misfortune through a test which has no relation whatever to the justice of the case."[98]

If the mixed fund is not in an active, unbroken banking account, any loss is borne *pari passu* so that the parties recover proportionately in relation to their contributions. In the example just given, both trust funds would then bear the loss equally.

The scope of the rule in *Clayton's* case was recently considered by the Court of Appeal in *Barlow Clowes International Ltd. (in liq.) v. Vaughan*.[99] The authority of *Pennell* v. *Duffell* and *Re Diplock* compelled the Court to conclude that the rule prima facie governed the competing claims of beneficiaries of different trusts and those of beneficiaries of a trust and innocent volunteers, whose moneys have been wrongfully mixed in a single current account. The Court also concluded that, on the particular facts, the "North American" solution (namely, that "credits to a bank account made at different times and from different sources [are treated] as a blend or cocktail with the result that when a withdrawal is made from the account it is treated as a withdrawal in the same proportions as the different interests in the account (here of the investors) bear to each other at the moment before the withdrawal is made"[1] was, on the particular facts, impracticable, although "manifestly fairer." However, the rule in *Clayton's* case should not be applied if it would be impracticable or result in injustice between the parties, such as investors whose moneys are to be paid into a common pool. It is a "mere rule of evidence, and not an invariable rule of law . . . "[2] If there was a "shared misfortune, the investors will be presumed to have intended the rule not to apply."[3] The fund should then be shared rateably in proportion to the amount due to the different parties who had contributed to the mixed fund. There is, however, one significant *caveat* to that rule. It is this: the investor's claim is to the lowest intermediate balance in the fund. Consequently, if it can be shown that his money was deposited in a fund which had been exhausted, he has manifestly no claim to sums subsequently deposited by other investors.

---

per Lord Halsbury L.C.; *Re Stenning* [1895] 2 Ch. 433; *Mutton* v. *Peat* [1899] 2 Ch. 556; *Re Diplock* [1948] Ch. 465.

[98] *Re Walter J. Schmidt & Co.*, 298 F. 314, 316 (1923). But precedent compelled the judge to apply the rule to the facts. See (1950) 36 Cornell L.Q. 176 [Chaffee]. The fiction of *Clayton's* case has now been rejected by the New Zealand Court of Appeal in *Re Registered Securities Ltd.* [1991] 1 N.Z.L.R. 545.

[99] [1992] 4 All E.R. 22.

[1] At p. 35, *per* Woolf L.J.

[2] *Re British Red Cross Balkan Fund, British Red Cross Society* v. *Johnson* [1914] 2 Ch. 419, 421, *per* Astbury J.

[3] At p. 42, *per* Woolf L.J.

The decision in *Barlow Clowes* is a welcome relaxation of the rule in *Clayton's* case. Both Woolf and Leggatt L.JJ. regretted that *Clayton's* case was binding on the Court of Appeal. The "fairness of rateable division is obvious." Dillon L.J. was less sure that it was unfair to adopt the "first in, first out" rule; later investors might well be aggrieved if their claims were to rank *pari passu* with those of earlier investors.[4]

(5) The principles set out in the preceding section (d) also apply where the mixed fund consists of trust money and the money of an innocent volunteer. In *Re Diplock*[5] money was mistakenly distributed by executors to charities under a will which was later held to be void for uncertainty. The charities mixed this money with their own money in current and deposit accounts. The Court of Appeal[6] held that the next-of-kin could recover the money from the charities by a direct personal action in equity. But the court went on to say that the next-of-kin could also follow their money in equity.[7] Withdrawals from the current account had to be debited to the next-of-kin and to the charities in accordance with the principle in *Clayton's* case, first in, first out.[8] Those from the deposit accounts were, however, to be debited rateably, even though the mixing was the act of the charities and not of the executors. The analogy of *Sinclair* v. *Brougham*[9] persuaded the Court that the next-of-kin could trace into the hands of the volunteers, the charities, but that both parties must recognise each other's claims to the mixed fund.

> "It would be inequitable for the volunteer to claim priority for the reason that he is a volunteer: it would be equally inequitable for the true owner of the money to claim priority over the volunteer for the reason that the volunteer is innocent and cannot be said to act unconscionably if he claims equal treatment for himself. The mutual recognition of one another's rights is what equity insists upon as a condition of giving relief."[10]

(6) As the law now stands, the right to trace property in equity is lost, either in whole or in part, in the following circumstances:

(a) if the property reaches the hands of a bona fide purchaser;

(b) if it would be inequitable to allow the plaintiff to trace. This limitation on the right to trace was recognised in *Re Diplock*. The Court of Appeal instanced two cases where it would be inequitable to allow the plaintiff to trace in equity.[11] In the last edition of this book we described them as an emasculated application of the defence of change of position. Now that the House of Lords

---

[4] *Cf.* Legatt L.J. (at p. 44) and Dillon L.J. (at p. 32).
[5] [1948] Ch. 465; [1951] A.C. 251.
[6] Affirmed *sub nom. Ministry of Health* v. *Simpson* [1951] A.C. 251, H.L.: see below, Chap. 29.
[7] This question did not arise in the House of Lords.
[8] See above, pp. 88–89.
[9] [1914] A.C. 398.
[10] [1948] Ch. 465, 539.
[11] [1948] Ch. 465, 546–547.

has recognised the defence as a general defence to all restitutionary claims,[12] the two examples, which we shall now discuss, should be seen as two possible illustrations of change of position.

In the view of the Court of Appeal, the equitable proprietary claim will fail if an innocent volunteer improves his land: the land may not have necessarily increased in value, the property to which a lien could attach may be uncertain, and it would be inequitable to require the sale of the property subject to the charge. These may be persuasive reasons on the facts of *Re Diplock*; there the innocent volunteers were hospitals, one of which had used the Diplock money to build a new ward. But on other facts it may not be inequitable to impose a lien. For example, the innocent volunteer may be a rich banker who has used the money wisely to increase the value of his country house; and he has, furthermore, ample liquid assets to discharge any lien imposed over it.

The second illustration given by the Court of Appeal was of the innocent volunteer who used the Diplock money to pay off his debts. The creditor who grants the discharge is, of course, a bona fide purchaser.[13] But if he was a secured creditor, should the plaintiff be allowed to step into his shoes and enjoy the priority which he once enjoyed? The Court of Appeal thought not.[14] But, on other facts, this may be an unattractive conclusion since it may give the general creditors of an insolvent volunteer a windfall at the expense of the plaintiff who did not take the risk of the innocent volunteer's insolvency.[15]

The defence of change of position should not be narrowly defined, and should be allowed to grow in a flexible and pragmatic fashion. In each case it is a question of fact whether it is inequitable, given the change of position, to reject the particular restitutionary claim.[16] It should not necessarily be a defence that the defendant is an innocent volunteer who has improved land or paid off a secured debt;

(c) if the claimant's property disappears, as will be the case if the defendant buys wine with the trust money and drinks it.[17] The right to trace is also lost if the claimant's property is mixed by the defendant with his own property of a different kind, thereby forming a new product.[18] (We shall argue that, even though the plaintiff's money can no longer be identified, in accordance with equity's traditional rules, it may be just, *in some circumstances*, to impose a lien over the defendant's unsecured assets if, for example, it is necessary to ensure his priority over the defendant's general creditors[19]);

(d) if, in claims arising from the administration of an estate, the claimants have already recovered in an action against the executors for *devastavit*. In *Re*

---

[12] *Lipkin Gorman (A Firm)* v. *Karpnale Ltd.* [1991] 2 A.C. 548.

[13] Unless he knew, an unlikely event, of the executor's mistake.

[14] [1991] 2 A.C. 548 at p. 549.

[15] *Cf. Space Investments Ltd.* v. *Canadian Imperial Bank of Commerce Ltd.* [1986] 1 W.L.R. 1072: see below, p. 98.

[16] *Lipkin Gorman (A Firm)* v. *Karpnale Ltd.* [1991] 2 A.C. 548, 579–580, *per* Lord Goff: see above, Chap. 40.

[17] *Re Diplock* [1948] Ch. 465, 521.

[18] *Borden (U.K.) Ltd.* v. *Scottish Timber Products Ltd.* [1981] Ch. 25, C.A.

[19] See below, pp. 98–99.

Diplock[20] the Court of Appeal held that before the next-of-kin could bring a personal action against the charities they must first sue the executors, who had mistakenly paid the money; and any sums recovered from the executors should be credited rateably among the charities. The Court added that, "prima facie and subject to discussion,"[21] the next-of-kin's proprietary claim should be similarly reduced. The limitation may be peculiar to claims arising from the administration of an estate, but it may also be applicable to claims arising under *inter vivos* trusts.[22] If it is accepted, the amount which a wrongly paid volunteer must disgorge is directly dependent on how much money can be extracted from the executors. In our view the next-of-kin's proprietary claim against volunteers should not be reduced or destroyed by the sums recoverable from the executors. If they are able to identify their property in the hands of a volunteer they should be able to recover that property and it should be no defence to the volunteer that the next-of-kin have recovered *in personam* against the executors. The executors should then be subrogated, as is an insurer in comparable circumstances, to that part of the next-of-kin's fund which represents the difference between the total of the sums recovered from the executors and the volunteer and the loss suffered by the next-of-kin.[23] But the most practical and sensible rule, which has been adopted by statute in New Zealand and Western Australia,[24] is to require the claimant to sue the volunteer before suing the executors who should be liable only for any amount which the claimant has failed to recover from the volunteer. The volunteer would enjoy the usual defences.

Equity's rules and presumptions enable the beneficiaries of the trust to identify their property in the hands of the trustee or an innocent volunteer. But when does the beneficial title to an asset vest in them when there are multiple transactions? For example, there is a mixed fund, consisting of £3,000 of trust money and £3,000 of the trustee's own money. The trustee withdraws £3,000 and uses the money to buy a painting from D, who knows of the breach of trust. At the date of the purchase the painting is worth £6,000; it is now worth £8,000. The beneficiaries can proceed either against the trustee or D; they have an election to look to D, who is a constructive trustee, to make restitution of £3,000 or to claim the painting in the trustee's hands. Seemingly, they cannot recover both the painting and the £3,000. On these facts they will take the painting; their election would be very different if the painting is now worth only £2,000. The beneficial interest in the painting will probably vest in them at the date of their election, and not before. But there is slender authority to

---

[20] [1948] Ch. 465; see below, Chap. 29, for a further criticism of this principle.

[21] [1948] Ch. 465, 556. See also *John* v. *Dodwell & Co.* [1918] A.C. 563, 575.

[22] See below, pp. 585–587.

[23] *Cf.* below, p. 601; and *cf. Lord Napier and Ettrick* v. *R. F. Kershaw Ltd.* [1993] 1 All E.R. 385.

[24] New Zealand Administration Act 1952, s.30B(5), added in 1960; Western Australia Trustee Act 1962, s.65(7).

support this conclusion[25-26]; although there is also the analogy of the case law which holds that the right to have a deed set aside on account of fraud or undue influence is a "mere equity."[27]

3. CONSTRUCTIVE TRUSTS, LIENS AND SUBROGATION AS EQUITABLE REMEDIES CREATED AND IMPOSED BY THE COURTS[28]

As has been seen, to enable a plaintiff to trace property in equity a court has to find either that the defendant was his fiduciary or that there was a fiduciary relationship between him and a third party through whose hands trust property passed on its way to the defendant. If there is an existing fiduciary relationship, then if the person who is entitled to the equitable interest can identify his asset in the defendant's hand, he can, subject to defences, claim it as his own.

There may be no existing fiduciary relationship between the parties, and yet it may be desirable to impose a trust or lien over assets, or to subrogate the plaintiff to a third party's lien over assets. Indeed it may also be necessary to create a fund over which a trust or lien can be imposed. It should not necessarily follow that courts should adopt the same rules and presumptions to identify that fund if the equitable interest of the claimant is created and imposed by the court; here the court is not enforcing an existing equitable interest.

(a) *The Necessity for a Fiduciary Relationship?*

At times a court has discovered, indeed invented, a fiduciary relationship to enable a plaintiff to follow *his* property. In *Sinclair* v. *Brougham*[29] the directors were said to be in a fiduciary relationship to the *ultra vires* depositors; and in *Chase Manhattan Bank N.A.* v. *Israel-British Bank (London) Ltd.*[30] a company which had received money paid under a mistake was the fiduciary of the mistaken payer. There are dicta that a person who has been defrauded is entitled to trace in equity[31]; in such a case he may also rescind any transfer.[32] Such decisions demonstrate that a fiduciary relationship is a condition which is

---

[25-26] *Cf. Re R and J Leslie Engineering Co. Ltd.* [1976] 1 W.L.R. 292; *Lipkin Gorman (A Firm)* v. *Karpnale Ltd.* [1991] A.C. 548, 573, *per* Lord Goff.

[27] Megarry and Wade, *The Law of Real Property*, pp. 145–147, who discuss the relevant authorities.

[28] See, generally, Birks, *op. cit.* Chap. XI; Goode, *Essays* (ed. Burrows), pp. 215 *et seq.*; (1989) 39 Univ. of Toronto L.R. 258, 328 [Stevens]; Maddaugh and McCamus, *op. cit.* pp. 77–158; Elias, *op. cit.*, pp. 16–26.

[29] [1914] A.C. 398: see above, p. 83.

[30] [1981] Ch. 105: see above, p. 86 and below, p. 130. See also *Elders' Pastoral Ltd.* v. *The Bank of New Zealand* [1989] 2 N.Z.L.R. 180, C.A.; (affirmed on different grounds: [1990] 1 W.L.R. 1478 (P.C.).

[31] *Bankers Trust Co.* v. *Shapira* [1980] 1 W.L.R. 1274, 1280, 1282, *per* Lord Denning M.R. *Cf. Att.-Gen's Reference (No. 4 of 1979)* [1981] 1 W.L.R. 667, 670, C.A.

[32] *Cf. El Ajou* v. *Dollar Land Holdings plc* (unrep.), *per* Millett J.; see below, pp. 99–100.

easily satisfied and which conceals the conclusion that the particular plaintiff should be granted an equitable proprietary remedy.[33] As Bingham J. once said: "the receiving of money [or any property] which consistently with conscience cannot be retained is, in equity, sufficient to raise a trust in favour of the party for whom or in whose account it was received."[34]

It is probable that the House of Lords will not require there to be a fiduciary relationship before a plaintiff can trace in equity.[35] But it is only open to the House to do so. The Court of Appeal is bound so to hold.[36]

(b) The Ground and Scope of the Plaintiff's Claim

A person who confers a benefit, normally a money payment, under mistake, compulsion, necessity, or in consequence of another's wrongful act or unconscionable conduct will be *deemed* to have retained the equitable title in the money paid.[36a] In many cases the recipient will be insolvent, and the plaintiff will be seeking to gain priority over his general creditors. If he can identify his money, his claim will normally prevail. Unlike the general creditors he has not taken the risk of the recipient's insolvency. In contrast, if he had paid money under an ineffective contract, intending to advance credit to the defendant, then his proprietary claim should, in principle, normally fail.[37]

The ground of the restitutionary claim should then be of critical importance. But it should also be seen in the context of the facts of the particular case. The

---

[33] *Cf. Agip (Africa) Ltd.* v. *Jackson* [1990] Ch. 265, 290, *per* Millett J. (but contrast below, n. 36; *Bannister* v. *Bannister* [1948] 2 All E.R. 133, following *Rochefoucauld* v. *Boustead* [1897] 1 Ch. 196 (breach of an undertaking to hold land for the benefit of another). *Cf.* the cases where a landowner has stood by while another improved his land (see below, Chap. 5).

[34] *Neste Oy* v. *Lloyds Bank plc* [1983] 2 Lloyd's Rep. 658, 665–666, citing Joseph Story's *Commentaries on Equity Jurisprudence* (2nd ed., 1893), Vol. II, section 1225.
See also *Metall und Rohstoff* v. *Donaldson Inc.* [1990] 1 Q.B. 391, 479, *per* Slade L.J., accepting that there was a "good arguable case" that there may be circumstances in which a court will be prepared to "impose a constructive trust de novo as a foundation for the grant of equitable remedy by way of account or otherwise . . . for want of a better description [we] will refer to a constructive trust of this nature as a remedial constructive trust." *Cf. Hospital Products Ltd.* v. *United Surgical Corp.* (1984) 156 C.L.R. 41, 121–125, *per* Deane J.

[35] *Cf. United Scientific Holdings Ltd.* v. *Burnley Borough Council* [1978] A.C. 904, H.L.; *Lipkin Gorman (A Firm)* v. *Karpnale Ltd.* [1991] 2 A.C. 548, 579–580, *per* Lord Goff and *Tinsley* v. *Milligan* [1993] 3 All E.R. 65, 86, *per* Lord Browne-Wilkinson.

[36] C.A. insisted on the existence of a fiduciary relationship: see *Agip (Africa) Ltd.* v. *Jackson* [1991] Ch. 547, 566–567, *per* Fox L.J. Not surprisingly given earlier precedents (see above, pp. 83–86). Contrast *LAC Minerals Ltd.* v. *International Corona Resources Ltd.* [1989] 2 S.C.R. 574; and *Hospital Products Ltd.* v. *United States Surgical Corp.* (1984) 156 C.L.R. 41, 121–125, *per* Deane J.

[36a] If there is a subsisting fiduciary relationship, the court will most certainly hold that "the dominant factor appears to be that an equitable interest in moneys was regarded as not having been relinquished . . . in others it appears to have been unconscionability in retaining moneys against claimants": *Liggett* v. *Kensington* [1993] 1 N.Z.L.R. 257, 281, *per* Gault J. (See also his observations at p. 293, citing and following *Elders' Pastoral Ltd.* v. *Bank of New Zealand* [1989] 2 N.Z.L.R. 180, C.A.) The judge added (at p. 281) that: "In this developing field which is one in which the principles of law and equity are being melded in many jurisdictions, it would be unwise and conducive of inflexibility to attempt any general formulation."

[37] But *cf. Lord Napier and Ettrick* v. *R. F. Kershaw Ltd.* [1993] 1 All E.R. 385, H.L., where insurer contractually bound to indemnify the assured: see above, p. 24 and below, p. 100.

defendant may or may not know the facts which form the basis of the particular restitutionary claim. Moreover, he may or may not be solvent. If the plaintiff's claim is grounded on his equitable title, as at present it appears to be, then, subject to such defences as bona fide purchase and change of position, the remedy which the court will grant will not be dependent upon whether the defendant knew or did not know the facts which ground the claim, or upon whether he is insolvent or solvent. This is a regrettable conclusion,[38] and one which the court should not be compelled to reach if it is accepted that a constructive trust may be imposed *de novo*.[39]

The relevance of the factors of knowledge and solvency

(1) *If the defendant did not know the facts which form the basis of the plaintiff's restitutionary claim and is solvent*

For example, the defendant may receive money under mistake, not knowing of the plaintiff's mistake; he may innocently trespass on the defendant's land; he may unwittingly betray confidence; or he may in perfect good faith allow his self-interest to conflict with his fiduciary duty of loyalty to his principal. If the litigation is between the plaintiff and a solvent defendant, then there is much to be said for the view that the plaintiff's restitutionary claim should be limited to the value, at the date of its receipt, of the benefit gained by the defendant at his expense.[40] He should be granted, if he so elects, a lien over an identifiable asset to secure that sum. So, a bona fide defendant who receives £3,000 under a mistake of fact and invests the money in a painting now worth £30,000 should be liable to repay £3,000 but should, subject to any lien to secure the payment of £3,000, be allowed to retain the painting. Indeed, in a comparable situation the Court of Appeal has held that a confidant who innocently exploited another's trade secret was not required to account for his profits but did have to pay the market value of the secret.[41] Exceptionally, the relationship between the parties may be so sensitive that a court may hold that even an honest defendant should be deemed to be a constructive trustee of all the profits gained at the plaintiff's expense. That was the fate of Mr. Boardman, a

---

[38] But contrast Birks, *op. cit.* Chap. XI and Goode, *op. cit. Essays* (ed. Burrows), pp. 215 *et seq.* who insist that the plaintiff's claim should have a proprietary base. *Cf.* Elias, *op. cit.*, pp. 16–26. In Burrows' view restitutionary proprietary remedies, designed to reverse enrichment, are "triggered by pre-existing equitable ownership"; and tracing is the bridge between that ownership and restitutionary remedies. Constructive trusts and resulting trusts are substantive institutions. However, if the restitutionary claim is based on a wrong, the constructive trust is a restitutionary remedy: The Law of Restitution, pp. 35–45, 369–375.
[39] See above, p. 74.
[40] In *Boardman* v. *Phipps* [1967] 2 A.C. 67, the H.L. required B to account for his profits. But trial judge, Wilberforce J., held he was a constructive trustee of a percentage of the shares acquired in breach of trust: [1964] 2 All E.R. 187. See below, pp. 663–665.
[41] *Seager* v. *Copydex Ltd.* [1967] 1 W.L.R. 293, C.A.: see below, p. 692. This was admittedly a personal claim.

self-appointed agent, who had acted in the trust's best interests in circumstances where the trustees had no power, means or desire to acquire the benefit
which he was deemed to have gained in breach of his trust.[42]

(2) *If the defendant did not know the facts which form the basis of the plaintiff's
restitutionary claim and is insolvent*

The contest is then not between the plaintiff and the defendant. It is between
him and the defendant's general creditors who have advanced credit and are
equally innocent. It is true that they have taken the risk of the debtor's
insolvency. But equally the plaintiff should not receive a windfall at their
expense; for example, £27,000 in the above example. In our view, he should be
granted only a lien over an identifiable asset to secure the value, at the date of
its receipt, of the benefit which he conferred.[43]

These are admittedly radical conclusions. In both these circumstances the
defendant may rely upon any relevant defence and, in particular, that of
change of position. Even if *knowledge* is said to embrace *constructive notice*, a
person who does not have actual knowledge or does not wilfully close his eyes
to the facts is arguably one who acts in good faith and can therefore invoke the
defence of change of position.[44]

It is also an open question whether a defendant can be said to have *knowledge*
in this context if he knew the facts but did not appreciate their legal significance. Beneficiaries of a trust have not been allowed to say that they did not
realise that they were concurring in a breach of trust.[45] But, in those cases, the
question was whether the beneficiaries could recover from the trustees any loss
arising from a breach of trust if they had instigated, requested or consented to
the breach of trust. A court may confine this somewhat harsh rule to these
particular facts.

(3) *If the defendant knew the facts which form the basis of the plaintiff's
restitutionary claim and is solvent*

We have seen that a cynical wrongdoer's personal liability may be greater than
that of an innocent defendant.[46] Similarly, the fact that he knew that he was not
entitled to the benefit conferred may persuade the court that he should not be
allowed to retain any gain. Consequently, if D knew that P had paid £3,000 to
him under a mistake of fact, he should be held to be a constructive trustee of
any asset, say a painting now worth £30,000, bought with that money. We

---

[42] *Boardman* v. *Phipps* [1967] 2 A.C. 67, following *Regal (Hastings) Ltd.* v. *Gulliver* [1942] 1 All
E.R. 378: see below, p. 663 and for a suggestion that the fiduciary's liability should only be, on
these facts, a personal liability.
[43] *Cf.* Professor Goode *op. cit.* p. 74, n. 13, pp. 240–244.
[44] See below, pp. 670–672.
[45] *Re Pauling's S.T.* [1961] 3 All E.R. 713, 729–730, *per* Wilberforce J., following *Evans* v. *Benyon*
(1887) 37 Ch.D. 329, C.A.
[46] See above, pp. 31–35.

discuss elsewhere whether he should be granted any allowance for his contribution, financial or otherwise, made to its purchase.[47]

(4) *If the defendant knew the facts which form the basis of the plaintiff's restitutionary claim and is insolvent*

Here the contest is between the plaintiff and the defendant's general creditors. Even though the defendant may have been guilty of wrongdoing, the plaintiff should be granted a lien over identifiable assets, but only to secure a sum which represents the value, at the date of its receipt, of the benefits conferred; for example, the £3,000, but not the painting now worth £30,000.[48] In our view, to grant him a proprietary remedy, such as a constructive trust over an asset whose value is now greater than the cost of its acquisition, would give him a windfall at the expense of the defendant's general creditors. The English case law does not support this conclusion. But in the United States there is some authority which suggests that the plaintiff should recover no more than he lost even if it can be demonstrated that *his* money had been used by a wrongdoer, who embezzled trust money, to acquire an asset whose value was, at the date of the suit, greater than the purchase price.[49]

In our view these principles should provide sure guidelines for exercise of the court's discretion; they take into account the ground of the plaintiff's claim, the defendant's knowledge of the facts which form its basis, and the factor of the defendant's solvency or insolvency.

Some writers have expressed fears that, if the constructive trust and equitable lien are seen to be remedies created and imposed by the courts, the remedy may be imposed retrospectively; for example, to the date when a particular asset was acquired, thereby threatening the priority of secured creditors. But these are unreal fears. As the United States Circuit Court of Appeals for the Fourth Circuit once said, "a constructive trust is not a title to or lien upon property but a mere remedy to which equity resorts in granting relief against fraud; and it does not exist so as to affect the property held by a wrongdoer until it is declared by a court of equity as a means of affording relief."[50] The court is then in a position to protect the interests of creditors, who have lent money before the court's declaration, on the security of specific assets.

Finally, it may be said that to grant the court such a discretion to impose a trust or a lien will breed undesirable uncertainty. We are not so persuaded. The proposed discretion is not unbridled. Certainty of principle is a much-

---

[47] See above, pp. 32–35.

[48] *Cf.* p. 96.

[49] See Palmer, *op. cit.* Vol. I, § 2.14, citing the case of fiduciaries who had used trust funds to pay premiums on policies on their lives; the insurance proceeds on death were greater than the embezzled trust funds. The beneficiaries were granted a lien, to secure the repayment of the trust funds, over the proceeds. For another example, see *Haskell Engineering and Supply Co.* v. *Harford Accident & Indemnity Co.*, 78 Cal.App. 3d 371, 144 Cal.Reptr. 189 (1978).

[50] *International Refugee Organisation* v. *Maryland Drydock Co.*, 179 F. 2d 284 (4th Cir. 1949). See also *Rawluk* v. *Rawluk* [1990] 1 S.C.R. 70, 103, *per* McLachlin J. *Cf. Constructive Trusts In Bankruptcy* [1989] 2 Univ. of Ill.L.R. 297 [Sherwin].

prized virtue, and properly so in commercial transactions. But it is less seductive in the context of restitutionary claims which are, for example, based on another's mistake, compulsion, necessity, or wrongdoing.

(c) *The Identification of Assets*

Equity's rules and presumptions may enable a plaintiff to identify an asset in the defendant's hands. Most of the cases have involved beneficiaries who sought security over a bankrupt trustee's assets in order to recover what they had lost. As the law stands the asset belongs to him in equity, although in the preceding section we suggest that a plaintiff, who can so identify an asset, should not necessarily be able to capture it or its value.

There is the converse situation, namely, where equity's traditional rules and presumptions cannot identify a fund, but where it is just that the plaintiff should be granted a proprietary remedy. Take the facts of *Chase Manhattan Bank N.A.* v. *Israel-British Bank (London) Ltd.*[51] Millions of pounds flowed into the accounts of the Israel-British Bank between the day it received Chase's mistaken payment and its liquidation. Equity's rules and presumptions, conceived in the horse-and-buggy world of trifling sums paid into relatively passive banking accounts, cannot identify Chase's money.

Equity's notion of a *fund* over which a lien can be imposed has always been a flexible one, as *Re Hallett's Estate*[52] and *Re Oatway*[53] demonstrate.[54] In *Space Investments Ltd.* v. *Canadian Imperial Bank of Commerce Trust Co.*,[55] Lord Templeman, giving the advice of the Privy Council, was prepared to refine equity's rules in order to prefer a particular claimant. In his judgment he discussed the hypothetical question whether beneficiaries of a trust should be allowed to trace their money into the hands of a bank, now in liquidation, which had agreed to hold that money on trust for the beneficiaries but had failed to segregate the trust money in a separate fund. He concluded that they would be entitled to an equitable charge over the bank's assets, "in priority to any payment of customers' deposits and other unsecured debts." In his view[56]:

> "This priority is conferred because the customers and other unsecured creditors voluntarily accept the risk that the trustee bank might become

---

[51] [1981] Ch. 105: see above, p. 130.

[52] (1979) 3 Ch.D. 696: see above, p. 87.

[53] [1903] 2 Ch. 356: see above, p. 87. *Cf. Republic Supply Co.* v. *Richfield Oil Co.*, 79 F.2d 375 (9th Cir., 1935).

[54] For examples of the converse situation, where the court limited the plaintiff's claim in order to do justice to the defendant, see *Roscoe* v. *Winder* [1915] 1 Ch. 62 (see above, p. 88 and *cf.* Maitland, *Equity* (revised by J. Brunyate), Lecture XIV, pp. 220 *et seq.*); *Re Diplock* [1948] Ch. 465, 547–550, C.A. (see above, p. 90) and *Borden (U.K.) Ltd.* v. *Scottish Timber Products Ltd.* [1981] Ch. 25, C.A.

[55] [1986] 1 W.L.R. 1072. *Cf.* the American cases of *State* v. *McKinley County Bank*, 252 P. 980 (1927); *Re Erie Trust Co.* 191 A. 613 (1937); *Re Teltronics*, 649 F.2d 1236 (1981). And see (1906) Harv.L.R. 511, 521 [Ames].

[56] At p. 1074.

insolvent and unable to discharge its obligations in full. On the other hand, the settlor of the trust and the beneficiaries interested under the trust, never accept any risks involved in the possible insolvency of the trustee bank. On the contrary the settlor could be certain that if the trusts were lawfully administered, the trustee bank could never make use of trust money for its own purposes and would always be obliged to segregate trust money and trust property in the manner authorised by law and by the trust instrument free from any risks involved in the possible insolvency of the trustee bank. It is therefore equitable that where the trustee bank has unlawfully misappropriated trust money by treating the trust money as though it belonged to the bank beneficially, merely acknowledging and recording the amount in a trust deposit account with the bank, then the claims of the beneficiaries should be paid in full out of the assets of the trustee bank in priority to the claims of customers and other unsecured creditors of the bank. . . . Where a bank trustee is insolvent, trust money wrongfully treated as being on deposit with a bank must be repaid in full so far as may be out of the assets of the bank in priority to any payment of customers' deposits and other unsecured debts."

Such reasoning would lead to the conclusion that Chase Manhattan would have priority over the Israel-British Bank's unsecured creditors. Lord Templeman did not suggest that the beneficiaries of the trust should gain priority over secured creditors,[57] although the New Zealand Court of Appeal, adopting his dicta, has now held that the claims of the plaintiffs, whose position was not dissimilar to that of beneficiaries of a trust, should take priority over that of a bank who, as a debenture holder, held a floating charge over the assets of a company now in liquidation.[57a] Moreover, it is not clear whether Lord Templeman would be prepared to grant a lien if it could be demonstrated that the bank had dissipated the beneficiaries' assets.[58] But if a court concludes that the beneficiaries' claim should prevail over that of the bank's general creditors, it may also possibly conclude that a lien should be imposed over the bank's assets even on these facts.[59]

In *El Ajou* v. *Dollar Land Holdings plc*[60] the plaintiff had been induced by the fraudulent misrepresentations of third parties to part with his money. The

---

[57] Similarly, the beneficiaries could not trace into the hands of creditors whose debts have been paid with their money: cf. *Magenta Finance and Trading Co.* v. *Savings & Investment Bank* 1985 F.S.R. 237 (Isle of Man High Court).

[57a] *Liggett* v. *Kensington* [1993] 1 N.Z.L.R. 257, C.A. But contrast *Re London Wine Co (Shippers) Ltd.* [1986] PCC 121, 166, *per* Oliver J.

[58] In principle the burden of proof should be on the recipient of the mistaken payment.

[59] See above, p. 94. Lord Templeman's dicta go only *some way* to adopting the "swollen assets" theory which many American courts accepted in the 1930s. But Prof. Scott's influence was such that they later abandoned it and insisted that assets should be "identifiable." See *Scott on Trusts*, para. 521; and 39 Col.L.R. 172 (1939) [Taft]. For a defence of "swollen assets" see (1983) 68 Cornell L.R. 176, 189, n. 33 [Oesterle] and [1989] 2 Univ. of Illinois L.R. 297 [Sherwin]. The C.A. would seemingly reject the swollen asset theory: see *Barlow Clowes Int. Ltd.* v. *Vaughan* [1992] 4 All E.R. 22: see above, pp. 88–89.

[60] June 12, 1992, unrep.

money was mixed with moneys of other victims of a share fraud in a series of foreign bank accounts. It was alleged that some of the plaintiff's money had been invested in land in Battersea and that the defendants, who had bought that land pursuant to a joint venture agreement with the third parties, received the money knowing of the fraud. This claim failed. Millett J. held that they had no such knowledge. But in principle the judge was prepared to impose a lien over each of the recipient's bank accounts even though the plaintiff's money had been mixed with other moneys and could not now be identified as "theirs". He justified this conclusion thus:

> "If the money in an account subject to a charge is afterwards paid out of the account and into a number of different accounts, the victims can claim a similar charge over each of the recipient's accounts. They are not bound to choose between them. Whatever may be the position between the victims *inter se*, as against the wrongdoer his victims are not required to appropriate debits to credits in order to identify the particular account into which their money has been paid. Equity's power to charge a mixed fund with the repayment of trust moneys (a power not shared by the common law) enables the claimants to follow the money, not because it is theirs, but because it is derived from a fund which is treated as if it were subject to a charge in ther favour."

The lien is then imposed by the court. Millett J., like Lord Templeman, was not deterred by the fact that equity's traditional rules and presumptions could not identify the plaintiff's money. It was because the plaintiff was the victim of the fraud, just as, in Lord Templeman's hypothetical situation, the beneficiaries were the victims of the trustees' breach of trust, that the judge was prepared to impose a lien over assets in the recipient's hands.

Another example of equity's readiness to impose a lien over a fund because of the attraction of the plaintiff's claim is *Lord Napier and Ettrick* v. *R. F. Kershaw Ltd.*[61] In that case the House of Lords held that an insurer, who had indemnified the assured, could be subrogated to the assured's right over a fund, in the hands of the assured's agents, which represented settlement damages recovered by the assured from a third party. The House concluded that precedent, dating from Lord Mansfield's court, supported this conclusion. In Lord Templeman's view "it would be unconscionable for the names [the assured] to take their share of the damages without providing for the sums due to the stop loss insurers to be paid out of the damages".[62] He would have so held even if the assured had been insolvent. The plaintiff's claim should prevail over the claims of the general creditors of the assured.[63]

It has been said that the imposition of an equitable lien may circumvent the provisions of the insolvency legislation which provides that all unsecured claimants should have equal priority on a person's bankruptcy. But, for

---

[61] [1993] 1 All E.R. 385.
[62] At pp. 397–398.
[63] It is debatable whether the insurer should be so preferred: see below pp. 618–619.

example, to impose an equitable lien over the unsecured assets of a bank trustee, which has failed to segregate trust assets, is to do no more than what the courts have done in the past when they formulated their equitable rules and presumptions to identify trust property.[64]

It is doubtful whether an English court will go further and find a causal nexus between the plaintiff's asset, which the fiduciary improperly sold, and another asset which cannot be identified by applying equity's traditional rules and presumptions as the product of the sale but which is similar in character to the asset sold. This problem arose in the New York case of *Simonds* v. *Simonds*.[65] A separation agreement required the husband, H, to maintain an existing life insurance policy, to the value of $7,000, for the benefit of his then wife, the plaintiff in the suit. The agreement, later embodied into a divorce decree, expressly provided for a change in policies and that the plaintiff's right should then attach to the new policies. H later remarried. He allowed the original insurance policies to lapse and took out new policies for the benefit of his new wife, the defendant and his children by her. The New York Court of Appeals held that a constructive trust should be imposed over the insurance proceeds, in the defendant's hands, to secure the payment of $7,000. H had been in a fiduciary relationship to the plaintiff. Consequently, the separation agreement vested in the plaintiff an equitable interest in the insurance policies then in force, and that interest was superior to that of the defendant, a mere volunteer. There was no finding that the new policies were "quid pro quo replacements for the original policies." But the separation agreement "provides nexus between plaintiff's rights and the later acquired policies."[66]

This reasoning is not without its difficulties but may possibly be justified on the ground that the second policies were a "replacement of another asset of known value" in circumstances where the plaintiff could have specifically enforced the agreement to maintain the policies in her favour.[67]

(d) *Some Tentative Conclusions*

It is our view that:

(1) it should no longer be necessary to find a fiduciary relationship between the parties;

(2) if the claim is *not* based on an existing equitable title, it is the ground of the plaintiff's claim which should be of paramount importance;

(3) the scope of the proprietary remedy should also depend on such factors as whether the contest is between the plaintiff and a solvent or an insolvent defendant and whether that defendant knows, or does not know, the facts which form the basis of the restitutionary claim;

---

[64] See [1989] 2 Univ. of Ill.L.R. 297 [Sherwin]; (1989) 68 Can. 315 [Paciocco].

[65] 380 N.E. 2d 189 (1978), followed, *inter alia*, in *Rogers* v. *Rogers* 473 N.E. 2d 226 (1984).

[66] At p. 193, *per* Breitel Chief Judge.

[67] *Cf. Restatement of Restitution 2d, Tentative Draft*, section 33(2). This section, and the preceding section, are discussed in *Tracing Claims in the Modern World*, *King's Counsel* (1988/89), No. 17, p. 15 [Jones].

(4) the plaintiff's claim to a lien over a fund should not necessarily fail simply because equity's traditional rules and presumptions cannnot identify the plaintiff's money in the defendant's hands;

(5) the plaintiff's claim should be subject to defences such as bona fide purchase and change of position. Change of position may protect the honest recipient, whether a purchaser or a volunteer, even if the plaintiff is able to identify his property in the recipient's hands.[68]

---

[68] See below, p. 745.

PART II

THE RIGHT TO RESTITUTION

The principal section of Part II, **The Right to Restitution**, deals with the situation where the defendant has acquired a benefit from or by the act of the plaintiff. Exceptionally, however, the benefit has been acquired from a third party but nonetheless is deemed in law to have been gained at the plaintiff's expense. In both cases the defendant's gain is commensurate with the plaintiff's loss.

The plaintiff's ground of recovery may be that he was mistaken, that he was compelled to do what he did, that he acted out of necessity, that the consideration for his payment had wholly failed, or that the defendant had freely accepted the services which he had rendered or the goods which he had delivered. Exceptionally, he may succeed because he intervened in an emergency to assist the defendant.

In many of the situations here discussed the restitutionary claim is all-important for the plaintiff may have no claim for loss suffered. For example, he may have wrongfully repudiated a contract under which the money has been paid; the contract may be void or voidable; or contractual negotiations may have collapsed in circumstances where he has conferred a benefit on the defendant. Even if he has a claim for loss suffered, it may be more advantageous for him to bring a restitutionary claim; he may have made a losing contract, he may not be able to prove the loss which he has suffered or his reliance loss may be real but not recoverable in law, while the benefit gained by the defendant is demonstrably measurable.[1]

The final section of Part II deals with benefits acquired by wrongdoers at the plaintiff's expense. In this situation there may be little coincidence between loss suffered and benefit gained. Nonetheless the wrongdoer is compelled to make restitution.[2] The benefit gained by him may consist of expenses which he has saved or profits which he has gained. A defendant may be characterised as a wrongdoer even though he acted innocently; but innocence may be critical in determining the value of the benefit which he has gained at the plaintiff's expense and whether a lien should be imposed over identifiable assets.[3]

---

[1] See particularly below, pp. 400 *et seq.*
[2] See below, pp. 641 *et seq.* on who is a wrongdoer.
[3] See above, pp. 31–35.

WHERE THE DEFENDANT HAS ACQUIRED A BENEFIT FROM OR BY THE ACT OF THE PLAINTIFF

A. MISTAKE

CHAPTER 3

RECOVERY OF MONEY PAID UNDER A MISTAKE OF FACT

(a) *The Kind of Mistake that will Ground Recovery*[1]

Mistake and ignorance

IN this section we shall inquire what kind of mistake will ground recovery if money is paid under a mistake of fact.[2] In our view, the case law is authority for the simple proposition that the plaintiff will succeed if he can show that he would not have made the payment if he had not been mistaken. Before discussing the extensive case law, we wish to refer to Professor Birks' proposition in his *Introduction*,[2a] that restitution for mistake "does not involve the proof of any wrong . . . total ignorance is *a fortiori* from the most fundamental mistake. Hence a system which believes in restitution for mistake cannot but believe in restitution for ignorance, quite independently of any wrong incidentally committed." We nevertheless doubt whether ignorance can properly be of itself the ground of a restitutionary claim.[3]

---

[1] There are certain equitable actions, analogous to the action for money had and received, by means of which money paid mistakenly by a trustee or executor to the wrong person may be recovered from the recipient by the person beneficially entitled thereto. These actions are discussed separately: see below, Chap. 29. Cases concerning recovery of benefits conferred under contracts void for mistake are also considered: see below, Chap. 21.

[2] In recent years it has been argued that this body of law is best rationalised in terms of the concept of total failure of consideration, "that is, failure of the basis or condition on, or purpose for, which the payment was made": Butler, *Mistaken Payments, Change of Position and Restitution*, in *Essays on Restitution*, (ed. Finn) Chap. 4. (*Cf.* [1980] N.L.J. 587 [Matthews], cited in *National Mutual Life Association* v. *Walsh* (1987) 8 N.S.W.L.R. 585.) In his view the concept also unites the case law on mistake of fact and mistake of law. Given the precedents, we are not persuaded by these arguments. English courts continue to formulate the principles governing the payment of money under mistake in different terms from those governing total failure of consideration: see, *e.g. Rover International Ltd.* v. *Cannon Film Sales Ltd.* [1989] 1 W.L.R. 912, C.A., discussed, below, pp. 543–544. But it is possible that, as the law of restitution matures, general principles, uniting hitherto disparate bodies of law, will crystallise. The question was left open in *David Securities Pty. Ltd.* v. *Commonwealth Bank of Australia* (1992) 66 A.L.J.R. 768, 778. As has been seen, it has also been argued that the total failure of consideration more happily explains those cases which are, in this text, taken as illustrations of the application of the principle of free acceptance: (1988) 104 L.Q.R. 576 [Burrows]; see above, pp. 18–22.

[2a] pp. 140–146. See also Burrows, *The Law of Restitution*, Chap. 4.

[3] See *Mistake of Law* (1943) 59 L.Q.R. 327 [Winfield], cited in *David Securities Pty. Ltd.* v. *Commonwealth Bank of Australia* (1992) 66 A.L.J.R. 768, 773, 775.

It is desirable first to consider the case in which the plaintiff transfers a benefit to the defendant in a state of ignorance, and secondly the case where an asset of the plaintiff comes into the hands of the defendant without the knowledge of the plaintiff and without any act of transfer by him. In the former case, the transfer by the plaintiff in ignorance will inevitably involve some error on his part. Indeed, most if not all cases of mistake can also be classified as cases of ignorance, because the plaintiff's mistake will result from his ignorance of the true state of affairs.[4] In cases of transfer under a mistake it is therefore very difficult to see how any separate role can be assigned to ignorance. Even where the plaintiff is totally unaware of the fact of transfer, as in the case of his handing over money to the defendant without knowledge that he is doing so, it can sensibly and properly be said that he is making the payment under a mistake. The same can be said even in the case of some mechanical error, for example a payment through the malfunction of a computer, for in such a case the payer or his agent or employee may have caused the computer to make the payment, at least in the sense of failing to stop it doing so, in the mistaken belief that the computer is functioning correctly.[5]

If we turn from the case of transfer by the plaintiff to the case where an asset of the plaintiff comes into the hands of the defendant without any transfer by or on behalf of the plaintiff, the fact of the plaintiff's ignorance of the event (if that be the case) may or may not be relevant, but it cannot in our opinion constitute of itself a ground of recovery. For even where the plaintiff is ignorant of what is happening, recovery of the asset or its value must depend upon some specific ground of recovery, relating the plaintiff to the asset and rendering it unjust for the defendant to retain it.[6]

For these reasons, we do not treat ignorance as a ground of recovery.

The Ground of Recovery

For a long time it was thought that the only type of mistake which would ground recovery of money paid under a mistake of fact was a mistake which was essential to liability.[7] A dictum of Bramwell B. in *Aiken* v. *Short*[8] was frequently cited and was particularly influential. In that case he said: "In order to entitle a person to recover back money paid under a mistake of fact, the mistake must be as to a fact which, if true, would make the person paying liable to pay the money; not where, if true, it would merely make it desirable that he should pay the money."

---

[4] See below, pp. 113 *et seq.*
[5] *Avon County Council* v. *Howlett* [1983] 1 W.L.R. 605, C.A.
[6] *Cf. Lipkin Gorman (A Firm)* v. *Karpnale Ltd.* [1991] 2 A.C. 548: see above, pp. 82–83.
[7] For a valuable comparative law survey see, Ishak England, *Restitution of Benefits Conferred Without Obligation*, Vol. X of *Restitution—Unjust Enrichment and Negotiorum Gestio* of the *International Encyclopedia of Comparative Law.*
[8] (1856) 1 H. & N. 210, 215; see also *Kelly* v. *Solari* (1854) 9 M. & W. 54, 58, *per* Parke B; *Deutsche Bank* v. *Beriro & Co. Ltd.* (1895) 1 Com.Cas. 255, 259, *per* Lindley L.J.; *Re Bodega Co.* [1904] 1 Ch. 276; see (1968) 6 Melb. U.L.R. 308, 311–312 [Luntz].

In the majority of cases, the mistake relied upon falls within this category. For, as Scott L.J. once said:

> "In human affairs the vast majority of payments made without any fresh consideration are made to perform an obligation or discharge a liability. . . . For this reason of human nature, that proposition [of Bramwell B.] is very often—and perhaps usually—a crucial test of the question whether the payment was in truth made by reason of a mistake or was merely voluntary and therefore irrecoverable."[9]

A common example is where there is a valid contract subsisting between the parties, and one of them mistakenly forms the impression that events have occurred which render him liable to pay money to the other under the contract.[10]

During this century, however, judges have seriously challenged the suggestion that recovery will only be allowed if the mistake is a mistake as to liability.[11] There are cases in the reports where it has been recognised that recovery should be granted even though the mistake was not such that the payer thought he was liable to pay; for example, a bank may recover money paid to a payee under mistake, having overlooked a stop order,[12] and a donor may recover a gift of money paid under a mistake as to the identity of the recipient.[13] At one time it was fashionable to look for a broader test which would embrace both the kind of mistake which will ground recovery of money in an action for money had and received and also the kind of mistake which will be sufficient to avoid a contract or will prevent the passing of property in goods. Some statements of this test are in extremely general terms. For example, it has been said that "the mistake must be in some respect or another fundamental to the transaction,"[14] or that the mistake must have destroyed the intention of the payer to pay the money.[15] Perhaps the most comprehensive statement is that of Lord Wright:

---

[9] *Morgan* v. *Ashcroft* [1938] 1 K.B. 49, 74.

[10] Contrast *Rover International Ltd.* v. *Cannon Film Sales Ltd.* [1989] 1 W.L.R. 912, C.A. (payments made in the mistaken belief that they were due under a valid contract; the contract was, however, ineffective): see below, pp. 543–544.

[11] *Kleinwort, Sons & Co.* v. *Dunlop Rubber Co.* (1907) 97 L.T. 263; *Kerrison* v. *Glyn, Mills, Currie & Co.* (1911) 81 L.J.Q.B. 465; *R. E. Jones Ltd.* v. *Waring and Gillow Ltd.* [1926] A.C. 870; *Morgan* v. *Ashcroft* [1938] 1 K.B. 49, 64–67, *per* Greene M.R., 71–74, *per* Scott L.J. See also *Larner* v. *L.C.C.* [1949] 2 K.B. 683; *Barclays Bank Ltd.* v. *W. J. Simms (Southern) Ltd.* [1980] Q.B. 677.

[12] *Barclays Bank Ltd.* v. *W. J. Simms (Southern) Ltd.* [1980] Q.B. 677.

[13] *Morgan* v. *Ashcroft* [1938] 1 K.B. 49, 66–67, *per* Greene M.R.: see below, p. 119.

[14] *Morgan* v. *Ashcroft* [1938] 1 K.B. 49, 77, *per* Scott L.J.

[15] *R. E. Jones Ltd.* v. *Waring & Gillow Ltd.* [1926] A.C. 670, 696, *per* Lord Sumner. See also *Sinclair* v. *Brougham* [1914] A.C. 398, 431, *per* Lord Dunedin; *Morgan* v. *Ashcroft* [1938] 1 K.B. 49, 64–67, *per* Greene M.R. *Cf. Legal and General Assurance Society* v. *Vogue Café Holdings* [1949] 1 W.W.R. 269.

"The facts which were misconceived were those which were essential to liability and were of such a nature that on well-established principles any agreement concluded under such mistake was void in law, so that any payment made under such mistake was recoverable. The mistake, being of the character that it was, prevented there being that intention which the common law regards as essential to the making of an agreement or the transfer of money or property."[16]

And again, on the same occasion:

"It is true that in general the test of intention in the formation of contracts and the transfer of property is objective; that is, intention is to be ascertained from what the parties said or did. But proof of mistake affirmatively excludes intention. It is, however, essential that the mistake relied on should be of such a nature that it can be properly described as a mistake in respect of the underlying assumption of the contract or transaction or as being fundamental or basic."[17]

In our view these dicta also fail to provide the lawyer with a practical test for deciding whether a specific mistake is sufficient to ground recovery of money. A claim to recover money paid under mistake is essentially different from a claim to avoid or set aside a contract for mistake. To avoid a contract, the mistake "must be basic enough to overcome the pressures favouring finality of contract,"[18] hence the condition in cases of mutual or shared mistake that the mistake must be fundamental.[19] A fundamental mistake in the sense used in contract law will, of course, enable money paid under such a mistake of fact to be recovered,[20] whether the money was paid under a supposed liability or as a gift.[21] But the test of mistake in restitution should be broader. The only transaction that needs to be set aside is the payment.[21a] A restitutionary claim "does not destroy expectations created by a previous bargain,"[22] it merely seeks to prevent the defendant's unjust enrichment.

The authorities since *Aiken* v. *Short*[23] reject the proposition that money can be recovered only if the payer mistakenly thinks he was liable to pay. Indeed,

---

[16] *Norwich Union Fire Insurance Society* v. *Price* [1934] A.C. 455, 461–462.

[17] *Ibid.* 463.

[18] G. E. Palmer, *Mistake and Unjust Enrichment*, p. 25.

[19] *Bell* v. *Lever Bros* [1932] A.C. 761; distinguished in *Sybron Corp.* v. *Rochem Ltd.* [1984] Ch. 112.

[20] *A fortiori* if the mistake frustrates the transfer of property.

[21] *e.g.* if the payer is mistaken as to the identity of the payee; see also *Restatement of Restitution*, §§ 18–22.

[21a] *David Securities Pty. Ltd.* v. *Commonwealth Bank of Australia* (1992) 66 A.L.J.R. 768 (H. Ct. of Aust.): below p. 122, n. 5a.

[22] G. E. Palmer, *Mistake and Unjust Enrichment*, p. 8; pp. 21–22 (see also 11 Colum.L.Rev. 197, 303–325 (1911) [Foulke], where a similar argument is advanced); *Citibank N.A.* v. *Brown Shipley & Co.* [1991] 2 All E.R. 690, 700–701, *per* Waller J.

[23] Luntz points out that the words "liable to pay" do not appear in the report of this case in 11 L.J.(N.S.) Ex. 10, 13: (1968) Univ. of Melb. L.R. 308, 311–312.

three decisions of the House of Lords[24] and one of the Privy Council[25] provide formidable authority for the simple principle that "if a person pays money to another under a mistake of fact which caused him to make the payment, he is prima facie entitled to recover it as money paid under a mistake of fact."[26]

The recognition of this principle, which is the only one capable of reconciling the majority of the cases, should not produce greater uncertainty. The burden will always be on the payer to prove that he was mistaken and that his mistake caused[27] him to make the payment. Moreover, it should be irrelevant to inquire whether the mistake is or is not "fundamental" in a contractual sense; what is critical is whether the payer has been mistaken as to some assumption of fact which proved false and which caused him to make the payment.[28] Equally it should be irrelevant whether the defendant shared the plaintiff's mistake. It is the mistake of the payer which is important.

The acceptance of this wider principle makes it essential to protect the payee who has no notice of the payer's mistake and who may have changed his position in consequence of the receipt. In the old case of *Brisbane* v. *Dacres*[29] Gibbs J. recognised how vulnerable the recipient is. He said:

> "He who receives it has a right to consider it his without dispute: he spends it in confidence that it is his; and it would be most mischievous and unjust, if he who has acquiesced in that right by such voluntary payment, should be at liberty, at any time within the statute of limitations, to rip up the matter, and recover back the money. He who has received it is not in the same condition. He has spent it in the confidence that it was his, and perhaps has no means of repayment."

But the payer's right to recover his money has never been an absolute one. English law has always recognised that he will be denied restitution if he has paid the money voluntarily, in submission to an honest claim.[30] Most importantly, the House of Lords has now recognised a general defence of change of position, which will be allowed to develop pragmatically over the years.[31] It will enable the court to protect the innocent recipient of the mistaken payment,

---

[24] *Kleinwort Sons & Co.* v. *Dunlop Rubber Co.* (1907) 97 L.T. 263 (see below, p. 115); *Kerrison* v. *Glyn, Mills, Currie & Co.* (1911) 81 L.J.K.B. 465 (see below, p. 114); *R. E. Jones Ltd.* v. *Waring & Gillow Ltd.* [1926] A.C. 870 (see below, p. 115).

[25] *Colonial Bank* v. *Exchange Bank of Yarmouth, Nova Scotia* (1885) 11 App.Cas. 84: see below, p. 115.

[26] *Barclays Bank Ltd.* v. *W. J. Simms (Southern) Ltd.* [1980] Q.B. 677, 695, *per* Robert Goff J.; *David Securities Pty. Ltd.* v. *Commonwealth Bank of Australia* (1992) 66 A.J.L.R. 768 (H. Ct. of Aust.).

[27] See below, p. 122.

[28] *Barclays Bank Ltd.* v. *W. J. Simms (Southern) Ltd.* [1980] Q.B. 677; *David Securities Pty Ltd.* v. *Commonwealth Bank of Australia* (1992) 66 A.J.L.R. 768 (II. Ct. of Aust.): see below, pp. 122–123. *Cf.* (1979) 12 Univ. of Brit.Col.L.R. 159 [Needham], where a similar principle is formulated; and contrast Birks, *Introduction*, pp. 156 *et seq.*

[29] (1815) 5 Taunt. 143, 152.

[30] See below, Chap. 40.

[31] *Lipkin Gorman (A Firm)* v. *Karpnale Ltd.* [1991] 2 A.C. 548.

to the extent that it is inequitable to require him to repay.[32] But it is not a defence which is limited to claims based on mistake; later in this book we discuss the defence of change of position as a general defence to restitutionary claims.[33]

Cases where restitution has been granted

(1) *Where money is paid under a mistaken belief that there is a present liability*

"The vast majority of payments"[34] held to be recoverable are those where the payer is led erroneously to believe that he is under a liability to pay the money to the payee. The leading authority is *Kelly* v. *Solari*.[35] The directors of an insurance company paid to the defendant, the executrix of the assured, money under an insurance policy on the life of the assured, recently deceased. They paid the money in entire forgetfulness of the fact that the policy had lapsed because of non-payment of premiums by the assured.[36] The Court of Exchequer held that the money could be recovered in an action for money had and received. Parke B. stated the principle in these terms:

> "I think that where money is paid to another under the influence of a mistake, that is, under the supposition that a specific fact is true, which would entitle the other to the money, but which fact is untrue, and the money would not have been paid if it had been known to the payer that the fact was untrue, an action will lie to recover it back, and it is against conscience to retain it. . . ."[37]

A similar case is *Norwich Union Fire Insurance Society Ltd.* v. *Wm. H. Price Ltd.*[38] The appellant insurance company insured a shipment of lemons on a voyage from Messina to Sydney. On the voyage the vessel struck a submerged object and, after survey at Gibraltar, was ordered to proceed to Holland for repairs. The lemons were ripening, and were sold by the shipowners at Gibraltar for the best available price. The appellants, from information received, mistakenly concluded that the lemons had been damaged by a peril insured against and had been sold on that account. They therefore paid the insured value of the lemons to the assured. On discovering their mistake, they brought an action to recover the money as paid under a mistake of fact, and the Privy Council held that they were entitled to recover.[39]

---

[32] See below, pp. 740–741.
[33] See below, Chap. 40.
[34] *Morgan* v. *Ashcroft* [1938] 1 K.B. 49, 74, *per* Scott L.J., cited above, p. 109.
[35] (1841) 9 M. & W. 54.
[36] *Cf. R. E. Jones Ltd.* v. *Waring & Gillow Ltd.* [1926] A.C. 670, 696, *per* Lord Sumner.
[37] (1841) 9 M. & W. 54, 58.
[38] [1934] A.C. 455.
[39] Contrast [1989] L.M.C.L.Q. 431 [Andrews]; and [1987] N.Z. Recent Law Review 277, 287. [McLauchlan and Rickett]. We are not persuaded that our description of the facts of the case are "inadequate": see [1934] A.C. at pp. 458 and 467.

For similar reasons restitution should be allowed where the contract calls for payment according to a certain formula and where the payer has overpaid because he has mistakenly applied that formula.[40]

In all these cases the payer thought he was under a contractual liability to make the payment. But the supposed liability may include any type of legal liability. Where a trustee pays money under a mistake of fact which leads him to believe that he is doing so in the course of his fiduciary duty *qua* trustee,[41] he can recover the money. And in *Baylis* v. *Bishop of London*[42] the Court of Appeal held that, where the plaintiffs had paid a rentcharge to the sequestrator of a benefice under a mistake of fact, thinking that a lease was in force when it had in fact expired, they were entitled to recover the money.

These are representative of a large number of cases.[43] To succeed the plaintiff must be able to point to a specific fact as to which he was mistaken. It has therefore been held that he cannot recover if he knows the money is not due but pays because he has lost the defendant's receipt.[44] "The subsequent discovery of evidence to prove a fact, known to the party when he makes the payment, cannot authorise a recovery back of the money."[45] Nor is it enough for the plaintiff to say that he is merely mistaken as to the final upshot, liability

---

[40] See, *e.g. Smart* v. *Valencia*, 50 Nev. 359, 261 P. 655 (1927). For other cases, see Palmer, *op. cit.* § 14.8.

[41] *Re Horne* [1905] 1 Ch. 76, 80, *per* Warrington J. A personal representative should be in a similar position; see *Whittaker* v. *Kershaw* (1890) 45 Ch.D. 320, 325, *per* Cotton L.J. *Cf.* below, pp. 154–155 (mistake of law).

[42] [1913] 1 Ch. 127. See also *Durrant* v. *Ecclesiastical Commissioners for England and Wales* (1880) 6 Q.B.D. 234. *Cf. County of Carleton* v. *City of Ottawa* (1965) 52 D.L.R. (2d) 220, discussed below, p. 177.

[43] The action dates from the 17th century: see *Bonnel* v. *Foulke* (1657) 2 Sid. 4; *Tomkins* v. *Bernet* (1693) Salk. 22; *Att.-Gen.* v. *Perry* (1733) 2 Com.Rep. 481. The later cases include: *Buller* v. *Harrison* (1777) 2 Cowp. 565; *De Hahn* v. *Hartley* (1786) 1 T.R. 343, 2 T.R. 186; *Anderson* v. *Pitcher* (1800) 2 Bos. & P. 164; *Jones* v. *Ryde* (1814) 5 Taunt. 488; *Bruce* v. *Bruce* (1814) 5 Taunt. 495; *Martin* v. *Morgan* (1819) 3 Moo.C.P. 635; *Wilkinson* v. *Johnson* (1824) 3 B. & C. 428; *Milnes* v. *Duncan* (1827) 6 B. & C. 671; *Dupen* v. *Keeling* (1829) 4 C. & P. 102; *Newsome* v. *Graham* (1829) 10 B. & C. 234 (*cf. Finck* v. *Tranter* [1905] 1 K.B. 427); *Lucas* v. *Worswick* (1833) 1 M. & R. 293; *Kelly* v. *Solari* (1841) 9 M. & W. 54; *Standish* v. *Ross* (1849) 3 Ex. 527; *Barber* v. *Brown* (1856) 1 C.B.(N.S.) 121; *Townsend* v. *Crowdy* (1860) 8 C.B.(N.S.) 477; *Newall* v. *Tomlinson* (1871) L.R. 6 C.P. 405; *Durrant* v. *Ecclesiastical Commissioners for England and Wales* (1880) 6 Q.B.D. 234; *Leeds & County Bank Ltd.* v. *Walker* (1883) 11 Q.B.D. 84; *King* v. *Stewart* (1892) 66 L.T. 339; *Imperial Bank of Canada* v. *Bank of Hamilton* [1903] A.C. 49; *Re The Bodega Co. Ltd.* [1904] 1 Ch. 276; *Continental Caoutchouc & Gutta Percha Co.* v. *Kleinwort, Sons & Co.* (1904) 90 L.T. 474; *Meadows* v. *Grand Junction Waterworks Co.* (1905) 69 J.P. 244; *Kleinwort, Sons & Co.* v. *Dunlop Rubber Co.* (1907) 97 L.T. 263; *Kerrison* v. *Glyn, Mills, Currie & Co.* (1911) 81 L.J.K.B. 465; *Baylis* v. *Bishop of London* [1913] 1 Ch. 127; *Scottish Metropolitan Assurance Co.* v. *P. Samuel & Co.* [1923] 1 K.B. 348; *R. E. Jones Ltd.* v. *Waring & Gillow Ltd.* [1926] A.C. 670; *Anglo-Scottish Beet Sugar Corporation Ltd.* v. *Spalding U.D.C.* [1937] 2 K.B. 607; *Weld-Blundell* v. *Synott* [1940] 2 K.B. 107; *Larner* v. *L.C.C.* [1949] 2 K.B. 683; *T. Place & Sons Ltd.* v. *Turner* (1951) 101 L.J. News, 93; *Turvey* v. *Dentons* (1923) *Ltd.* [1953] 1 Q.B. 218. See also *Bize* v. *Dickason* (1786) 1 T.R. 285; *Bank Russo-Iran* v. *Gordon, Woodroffe & Co., The Times*, October 4, 1972, cited in *Edward Owen* v. *Barclays Bank International Ltd.* [1978] Q.B. 159, 169.

[44] *Marriot* v. *Hampton* (1797) 7 T.R. 269; *Freeman* v. *Jeffries* (1869) L.R. 4 Ex. 189.

[45] *Windbiel* v. *Carroll*, 16 Hun. 101 (N.Y. 1878).

or non-liability, if this is necessary to decide whether his mistake was one of law or fact.[46]

(2) *Where money is paid under a mistaken belief that a liability will accrue in the future*

In the great majority of the examples of supposed liability, the payer's mistake led him to believe that he was under a *present liability* to the defendant to pay the money. There are other cases, where recovery has been allowed, in which the payer's mistake was not of this character, and where the payer could not be said to have thought that he was presently liable to make the payment.

In *Kerrison* v. *Glyn, Mills, Currie & Co.*,[47] the House of Lords held that the payer could recover in such circumstances. The appellant was the manager in England of a Mexican mine. There was an arrangement whereby certain New York bankers would honour drafts drawn by the manager of the mine in Mexico and the appellant was bound to reimburse them by placing money with the respondent bankers to the credit of the New York bankers. In anticipation of such future liabilities, the appellant placed £500 with the respondents; but, unknown to him, the New York bankers had at the time committed an act of bankruptcy, and he therefore claimed to recover the money from the respondents as having been paid under a mistake of fact. The respondents, to whom the New York bankers were substantially indebted, resisted the claim. The House of Lords held that he was entitled to recover, although it is clear that his mistake did not lead him to believe that he was under any liability existing at the time of payment. As Lord Shaw of Dunfermline said[48]: "The money was paid . . . under a mistake of fact—which was material, and was indeed the only reason for payment—that [the New York bankers] could perform their obligations."

(3) *Where the payer mistakenly thought that he was authorised by or under a duty to a third party to make the payment to the payee*

Such a case would arise if a bank clerk were to pay a cheque, overlooking the drawer's instructions to cancel it; or if an agent were to pay money to a third party, mistakenly believing that he had his principal's authority to do so.

It has been said that the money cannot be recovered in such circumstances because the mistake is not one "as between" plaintiff and defendant, or is one "with which the defendant has nothing to do." These obscure phrases have been interpreted to mean that the mistake is not such "that, if the mistaken

---

[46] *Maskell* v. *Horner* [1915] 3 K.B. 106, 110, *per* Rowlatt J.; *Home and Colonial Insurance Co. Ltd.* v. *London Guarantee & Accident Co. Ltd.* (1928) 45 T.L.R. 134. *Cf. Avon County Council* v. *Howlett* [1982] 1 W.L.R. 605, 620, *per* Slade L.J.

[47] (1911) 81 L.J.K.B. 465, 17 Com.Cas. 41; *Aiken* v. *Short* (1856) 1 H. & N. 210 is not cited in the reported judgments. (See also *York Air Conditioning & Refrigeration (A/Sia) Pty. Ltd.* v. *The Commonwealth* (1949) 80 C.L.R. 11, 31, *per* Williams J.) Query if the mistake in *Kerrison* was a misprediction, a mistake as to future events: see *Bethune* v. *R.* [1912] 4 D.L.R. 229; Birks, *Introduction*, p. 147; n. 21.

[48] (1911) 81 L.J.K.B. 465, 471. See also Lord Atkinson (at p. 470) and Lord Mersey (at p. 472).

assumption of the payer had been true, there would have been a legal right in the payee to demand, and a legal obligation in the payer to pay, the money in question."[49] On this basis it has been held, in a few decisions at first instance, that money so paid is irrecoverable.[50]

Such statements amount to no more than dogmatic denials of the plaintiff's right to recover in restitution.[51] In principle, recovery should be allowed in such cases because it is the payer's mistake which alone should be relevant; and there can be no doubt that the payer who mistakenly thought that he owed a duty to a third party to pay the defendant would not have made the payment if he had known the true position. To invoke "privity" to defeat his claim is to insist once more on an "implied contract" between the parties. Since the House of Lords decision in *United Australia Ltd.* v. *Barclays Bank Ltd.*[52] this view of the basis of the action can no longer be supported.[53]

Moreover, there are decisions of the House of Lords and the Privy Council which reject any such limitation on the right of recovery.[54] In *Colonial Bank* v. *Exchange Bank of Yarmouth, Nova Scotia,*[55] the firm of B. Rogers & Son instructed the plaintiff bank to remit money to a bank at Halifax, Nova Scotia; but, owing to a mistake of the agents of the plaintiff bank, the money was paid to the defendants. The plaintiffs sought to recover the money from the defendants; but the firm of Rogers was indebted to the defendants, who accordingly refused to repay the money to the plaintiffs. The Supreme Court of Nova Scotia denied recovery to the plaintiffs on the ground that they were "not the parties to recover." The Privy Council reversed the decision of the Supreme Court. Lord Hobhouse said[56]:

> "Then it is said that the plaintiffs have no interest to recover the fund because they were originally set in motion by Rogers who paid them. But if it were only to relieve themselves from all questions about the mistake

---

[49] *R. E. Jones Ltd.* v. *Waring & Gillow Ltd.* [1925] 2 K.B. 612, 632, *per* Pollock M.R., reversed [1926] A.C. 670: see below, p. 116; *Weld-Blundell* v. *Synott* [1940] 2 K.B. 107, 112, *per* Asquith J.; *Porter* v. *Latec Finance (Qld.) Pty. Ltd.* (1964) 11 C.L.R. 177, 204, *per* Windeyer J. *Cf. The Deutsche Bank (London Agency)* v. *Beriro & Co.* (1895) 1 Com.Cas. 123, 128–129, *per* Mathew J.

[50] *Barclay & Co.* v. *Malcolm & Co.* (1925) 133 L.T. 512, where, however, Roche J.'s judgment on this point is very briefly reported, and the case was also decided on the grounds of ratification. See also *Weld-Blundell* v. *Synott* [1940] 2 K.B. 107; *Commonwealth Trading Co.* v. *Reno Auto Sales Ltd.* [1967] V.L.R. 790, 798, *per* Gillard J.; *Royal Bank of Canada* v. *Boyce* (1966) 57 D.L.R. (2d) 683.
  In *Barclays Bank Ltd.* v. *W. J. Simms (Southern) Ltd.* [1980] Q.B. 677, 694–695, Robert Goff J. concluded that the reasoning, if not the decision, in *Barclay & Co. Ltd.* v. *Malcolm & Co.* could not be reconciled with the decision of the House of Lords in *R. E. Jones Ltd.* v. *Waring & Gillow Ltd.* [1926] A.C. 670, on which see below, p. 116.

[51] *Cf. Thomas* v. *Houston Corbett & Co.* [1969] N.Z.L.R. 151, 161–162, 166–167, 174.

[52] [1941] A.C. 1.

[53] See above, pp. 5 *et seq.*

[54] See also, *Australia & New Zealand Banking Group Ltd.* v. *Westpac Banking Corp.* (1988) 62 A.L.J.R. 292, 295–296 (H.Ct. of Aust.).

[55] (1885) 11 App.Cas. 84. See also *Stevenson* v. *Mortimer* (1778) 2 Cowp. 805, 806, *per* Lord Mansfield; *Walter* v. *James* (1871) L.R. 6 Ex. 124, 127, *per* Kelly C.B.

[56] At pp. 90–91.

that their agents made in New York, and to relieve themselves from liability to be sued for the whole consequences proceeding from that mistake, the plaintiffs would have an interest to recover the money. They were told to convey the money to a certain quarter. They, through their agents, were the authors of the mistake by which it went to another quarter. It seems a perfectly untenable position to say that an agent in that position has not got an interest to recall the money, so that it may be put into the right channel."

In *Kleinwort, Sons & Co.* v. *Dunlop Rubber Co.*,[57] a customer directed the respondents to make a payment to a third person; they mistakenly paid it to the appellants who received the money in good faith. The House of Lords held that the respondents could recover the payment,[58] and yet they never believed they were liable to pay the appellants. Similarly, in *R. E. Jones Ltd.* v. *Waring and Gillow Ltd.*,[59] the plaintiffs were led by a third party's fraudulent misrepresentations to make payments to the defendants whom they mistakenly thought to be nominees of a company whose representative the third party was. The House of Lords allowed the plaintiffs to recover and did not suggest that this was because they mistakenly believed that they were liable to make the payment. Indeed it appears from Lord Sumner's statement of the facts that he concluded that the payer mistakenly thought that he was discharging an obligation to the company and not to the defendants.[60]

This "formidable line of authority" led Robert Goff J. in *Barclays Bank Ltd.* v. *W. J. Simms Son & Cooke (Southern) Ltd.*[61] to hold that a bank could recover money which it paid, when the defendant presented a cheque for payment, having overlooked the drawer's instructions to stop the cheque. The mistake had caused the bank to make the payment. In his view the decisions of the House of Lords in *Kleinwort, Sons & Co.* v. *Dunlop Rubber Co.*,[62] *Kerrison* v. *Glynn, Mills, Currie & Co.*[63] and *R. E. Jones Ltd.* v. *Waring and Gillow Ltd.*[64] and that of the Privy Council in *Colonial Bank* v. *Exchange Bank of Yarmouth, Nova Scotia*[65] authoritatively rejected the proposition that a payer could recover only if his mistake was "as between the payer and payee," in the sense of a mistake, shared by both parties, that the payer was liable to the defendant to make the payment.[66] The payer mistakenly thought that he owed a duty to

---

[57] (1907) 97 L.T. 263. The principal question in the case was whether the appellants could rely on a defence of change of position, on which see below, Chap. 40.

[58] *Cf.* the broad language of Lord Loreburn L.C., at p. 264.

[59] [1926] A.C. 670: see below, pp. 135–137.

[60] At pp. 691–692. See *Barclays Bank Ltd.* v. *W. J. Simms (Southern) Ltd.* [1980] Q.B. 677, 693–694, *per* Robert Goff J.

[61] [1980] Q.B. 677; followed in *Bank of New South Wales* v. *Murphett* [1983] 1 V.R. 489.

[62] (1907) 97 L.T. 263: see above, n. 57.

[63] (1911) 81 L.J.Q.B. 465: see above, p. 115.

[64] [1926] A.C. 870: see above, n. 59.

[65] (1885) 11 App.Cas. 84: see above, p. 115.

[66] *Cf. Commercial Bank of Australia* v. *Younis* [1979 1 N.S.W.L.R. 444.

another to make the payment; it was this mistake which led him to pay, and that was sufficient to ground recovery.[67]

Moreover, in our view, the principle underlying these decisions is also consistent with the advice of the Privy Council in *Imperial Bank of Canada* v. *Bank of Hamilton*,[68] namely, that if a bank pays the holder of a marked cheque, which has been fraudulently increased in value, it may recover the excess from the holder even though it would not have been liable to the holder if the facts had been as it supposed.

Again, an agent (A), who pays money to a third party (T), his principal's (P's) creditor, in the mistaken belief that he has P's authority to do so, should likewise have a good ground for recovery.[69] An unauthorised payment by A will not, without ratification, discharge P's debt,[70] and so T can still proceed against P for the debt. If P does not ratify the payment, T should be required to refund the money to A because the consideration for A's payment has failed.[71] A has not received his expected return, namely, the discharge of his principal's liability,[72] and this discharge should have enabled him to obtain an indemnity from his principal. This may not strictly be a case of supposed liability; yet it is similar to such cases for the consideration for A's payment has totally failed.

Finally, it is well settled that where T pays money to A, for transmission to A's principal, P, under a mistake of fact which leads T to believe that he owes the money to P, T can recover that money from A if he claims it from A before A has paid the money over to P or done anything equivalent thereto.[73] Yet the mistake is not one which leads T to think that A is entitled to the money: it is a mistake "as between" T and P.

It is our view therefore that, on principle and in accordance with the great weight of authority, a person should be entitled to recover money paid by him to the defendant in the mistaken belief that he was authorised by, or under a duty to, a third party to make that payment.[74]

(4) *Where the payer mistakenly believed that he was under a moral obligation to make the payment*

There are authorities, in England and the United States, which suggest that in some circumstances recovery may be allowed where the plaintiff mistakenly

---

[67] [1980] Q.B. 677, 694; cited with approval in *Australia & New Zealand Banking Group Ltd.* v. *Westpac Banking Corp.* (1988) 62 A.L.J.R. 292, 294, (H.Ct. of Aust.).

[68] [1903] A.C. 49.

[69] *Restatement of Restitution*, § 23.

[70] See *Simpson* v. *Eggington* (1855) 10 Exch. 845, 847, *per* Parke B., and cases there cited: see above, p. 17, n. 2; and *cf.* below, p. 135, nn. 98–99.

[71] See *Walter* v. *James* (1871) L.R. 6 Ex. 124, 127, *per* Kelly C.B.: see above, p. 17, n. 2.

[72] If the payment did discharge P's debt a claim for recovery should fail, for T will have given consideration for the payment.

[73] See, generally, below, pp. 750–753.

[74] Subject to any relevant defences, the plaintiff's claim will not be defeated even though the defendant was owed money by the third party: see *T. Place & Sons Ltd.* v. *Turner* (1951) 101 L.J. News. 93; but *cf. Aiken* v. *Short* (1856) 1 H. & N. 210: see below, p. 135.

believed that he was under a moral obligation to make the payment. Particularly important is the decision of the Court of Appeal in *Larner* v. *L.C.C.*[75] The Council had resolved to pay all their employees, who entered the Services during the Second World War, the difference between their war service pay and their civil pay. Each employee was asked to keep the Council informed of changes in his war service pay so that the Council could make consequent adjustments in their pay. Larner was an ambulance driver, employed by the Council, who was called up and joined the Royal Air Force. He failed to keep the Council informed of changes in his service pay and the Council consequently overpaid him. The Court of Appeal held that the Council was entitled to recover from him the amount so overpaid, as having been paid under a mistake of fact. Denning L.J., who delivered the judgment of the court, pointed out that Bramwell B.'s dictum[76] should no longer be regarded as an exhaustive statement of the law. He said[77]:

> "London County Council, by their resolution, for good reasons of national policy, made a promise to the men which they were in honour bound to fulfil. The payments made under that promise were not mere gratuities. They were made as a matter of duty: see *National Association of Local Government Officers* v. *Bolton Corporation*[78] . . . It is not necessary to inquire whether there was any consideration for the promise so as to enable it to be enforced in a court of law. It may be that, because the men were legally bound to go to the war, there was in strictness no consideration for the promise. But that does not matter. It is not a question here of enforcing the promise by action. It is a question of recovering overpayments made in the belief that they were due under the promise, but in fact not due."

It follows from this decision that it is not necessary that the mistake should lead the payer to believe that he is legally bound to pay the money. It is enough that the payment is made not as a mere gratuity, but "as a matter of duty." In *Larner* v. *L.C.C.*, the duty was "to give reasonable effect to the national policy, which is to encourage men to engage in war service and to relieve them from pecuniary anxieties if they do so."[79] A conception of duty which includes such an obligation as this is a vague one. On the other hand, the decision in *Larner* v. *L.C.C.* is just, and any system of law unfettered by the doctrine of consideration would have held that the Council's promise to make up their employees' pay was legally binding.[80]

---

[75] [1949] 2 K.B. 683; see also *Wilkinson* v. *Johnson* (1824) 3 B. & C. 428.
[76] *Aiken* v. *Short* (1856) 1 H. & N. 210, 215: see above, p. 135.
[77] At p. 688.
[78] [1943] A.C. 166.
[79] *National Association of Local Government Officers* v. *Bolton Corporation* [1943] A.C. 166, 186–187, *per* Lord Wright.
[80] Possibly, the moral duty of a promisor to keep his word is valuable consideration: (1978) 12 Univ. of Brit.Col.L.R. 159, 168–169 [Needham].

It may be that in some cases where the payer claims that the payment was paid because of his mistaken sense of moral obligation a court may conclude that the payment was irrecoverable because it was made in settlement of an honest claim. The American case of *Lowe* v. *Wells Fargo & Co. Express*[81] demonstrates how difficult it may be to determine whether a bona fide settlement has been reached. The plaintiff's son was employed by the defendants as an express messenger. In the course of his duties he received from a train a package containing over $400. Thereafter no trace of it could be found. The plaintiff, in the belief that his son had dropped the package and lost it between the station and the defendants' office, paid the value of the contents to the defendants to protect his son's reputation. In fact, his son had safely delivered the package at the defendants' office, but had neglected to obtain a receipt for it. Another employee, Davis, had stolen it and squandered the proceeds. Davis was a man of straw, and the defendants resisted the plaintiff's claim for refund of the money. Although it was clear that on neither the real nor the supposed state of facts was the plaintiff under any liability to pay the money to the defendants, the Supreme Court of Kansas held that he could recover it as paid under a mistake of fact; if he had known the true facts he would not have made the payment.

Lowe v. *Wells Fargo & Co. Express* goes significantly further than *Larner* v. *L.C.C.* In *Larner*, the recipient must have known of the L.C.C.'s mistake; indeed he was responsible for it since he failed to keep the L.C.C. informed of the changes in his service pay.[82] In *Lowe* the defendants honestly thought that the plaintiff's son had lost the package; but the plaintiff paid, not apparently to settle the defendants' claim, but to protect his son's reputation. *Lowe* v. *Wells Fargo & Co. Express* is a finely balanced decision[83] which can if necessary be supported on the ground that the money was mistakenly paid under a sense of paternal duty.[84]

(5) *Mistake in gifts*

Although the courts have allowed recovery of a gift on the ground of the payer's mistake, it is not wholly clear from the authorities when recovery will be allowed and when denied.

In *Morgan* v. *Ashcroft*[85] the respondent, a bookmaker, claimed that his clerk had mistakenly credited the appellants twice over with the sum of £24 2s 1d. The county court judge held that the money was recoverable, having been paid under a mistake of fact. But the Court of Appeal held, on two distinct grounds, that the money could not be recovered. First, the court could not, by reason of the Gaming Act 1845, examine the state of account between the parties in order

---

[81] 78 Kans. 105, 96 P. 74 (1908).
[82] See above, p. 118.
[83] The plaintiff had, arguably, compromised an honest claim: *cf.* below, pp. 127–130.
[84] *Cf. Deskovick* v. *Porzio*, 187 A.2d 610 (1963), where money was paid, under a mistaken moral obligation, to a third party to the defendant's use.
[85] [1938] 1 K.B. 49.

to determine whether there had indeed been an overpayment. Secondly, the money was, in any event, not recoverable as having been paid under a mistake of fact; the payment was voluntary because "the law prevents the plaintiff from saying that he intended anything but a present."[86] Sir Wilfred Greene M.R. concluded that "a person who intended to make a voluntary payment and thinks that he is making one kind of voluntary payment whereas upon the true facts he is making another kind of voluntary payment does not make the payment under a mistake of fact which can be described as fundamental or basic."[87] He then gave two contrasting examples:

> "If a father, believing that his son has suffered a financial loss, gives him a sum of money, he surely could not claim repayment if he afterwards discovered that no such loss had occurred. . . . To hold the contrary would almost amount to saying that motive not mistake was the decisive factor. . . . If A makes a voluntary payment of money to B under the mistaken belief that he is C, it may well be that A can recover it. . . . If we are to be guided by the analogous case of contract, where mistake as to the person contracted with negatives the intention to contract, the mistake in the case which I have mentioned ought to be held to negative the intention to pay the money and the money should be recoverable."

In our view Greene M.R.'s antithesis is not convincing. For reasons already explained,[88] the analogy of contract law should not be persuasive. If adopted, it might be interpreted to restrict recovery to cases where the plaintiff makes a mistake as to identity of the donee.[89] But it should not be necessary to ground recovery in restitution that the mistake should be fundamental in the sense that it would have negatived an intention to contract. This seems an inappropriate enquiry when the question is whether a mistaken gift should be recoverable. Likewise, it should not be necessary to find that the payer thought that he was liable to make the payment[90]; otherwise a gift made under mistake could normally not be recovered. What should be critical is whether the mistake has caused the payer to make the payment. Was the donor mistaken as to some assumption which proved false and which caused him to make the gift?[91]

---

[86] [1938] 1 K.B. 49, 77, *per* Scott L.J. See also *Barclays Bank Ltd.* v. *W. J. Simms (Southern) Ltd.* [1980] 1 Q.B. 677, 696–698, *per* Robert Goff J.

[87] At p. 66.

[88] See above, p. 110.

[89] Indeed, in some circumstances, a mistake of identity cannot be sufficiently fundamental to ground recovery: see, *e.g. Porter* v. *Latec Finance (Qld.) Pty. Ltd.* (1964) 38 A.L.J.R. 184, 186–187, *per* Barwick C.J.

[90] As Greene M.R. apparently thought: at pp. 66–67. But Scott L.J. did not accept Bramwell B.'s dictum (see above, p. 108) as authoritative: see pp. 73–74. See also *Larner* v. *L.C.C.* [1949] 2 K.B. 683, 688, *per* Denning L.J., declining to follow Greene M.R.: see above, p. 118.

[91] *Cf. Restatement of Restitution*, § 26, comment c: "a mistake which entails the substantial frustration of the donor's purpose entitles him to restitution. No more definite general statement can profitably be made as to what constitutes a basic mistake in the making of a gift."

The line between mistake and motive is admittedly a thin one.[91a] The reluctance of the courts to entertain a plea that a gift was made under mistake is understandable; a donor who has had second thoughts should not be encouraged to revoke his gift. Nevertheless this danger can be met by imposing on the donor the burden of proving that he would not have made the gift if he had not been mistaken about a particular fact. If a father can demonstrate that he would not have given £10,000 to his son if he had not been given false information by a third party that his son was on the verge of financial ruin, it is difficult to see why he should not be able to recover his payment. His gift was made on the basis of an assumption which proved false. Whether this burden of proof is discharged will depend on the particular facts, including such factors as the amount of the gift and the relationship of the parties.[92] There appears to be no reason why a gift, like any other transaction,[93] should not be set aside in these circumstances. Indeed, it is arguable that courts ought to impose a less stringent burden of proof on the payer who claims that he made a gift under mistake than in other cases. The recipient of a mistaken gift is a mere volunteer and, as long as he is "afforded some protection for his reliance or change of position as a result of the gift, there is little to be said for allowing him to keep the property."[94]

It is significant that courts of equity have adopted a more generous test in determining whether voluntary instruments should be set aside for mistake. As Lindley L.J. said in *Ogilvie* v. *Littleboy*[95]: "In the absence of all such circumstances of suspicion[96] a donor can only obtain back property which he has given away by showing that he was under some mistake of so serious a character as to render it unjust on the part of the donee to retain the property given to him." So where a gift has been made by deed, the deed may be rescinded on the grounds of the donor's error even though the error would apparently not fall within the test proposed by Greene M.R. In *Lady Hood of Avalon* v. *Mackinnon*[97] the plaintiff made an appointment of £8,600 to her younger daughter, and later, anxious to put her elder daughter in an equally advantageous position, made a similar appointment to her by deed poll. There had been an earlier appointment to the elder daughter of an even larger amount, which the plaintiff had entirely forgotten. Eve J. rescinded the second

---

[91a] *e.g.* take the case of the father who gives his son £1,000 in the belief, not induced by his son's misrepresentation, that his son has achieved straight As in his mock examination. When his reports arrived on the door step, he discovered that his son had got straight Ds.

[92] *Cf. Clelland* v. *Clelland* [1944] 4 D.L.R. 703.

[93] *Cf. Norwich Union London Fire Insurance Society Ltd.* v. *Wm. H. Price Ltd.* [1934] A.C. 455, 461–462, 463, *per* Lord Wright.

[94] 58 Mich.L.Rev. 90, 92 (1959) [Parker].

[95] (1897) 13 T.L.R. 399, 400; approved on appeal (1899) 15 T.L.R. 294, 295, *per* Lord Halsbury.

[96] The "circumstances of suspicion" include fraud, undue influence, misrepresentation, and breach of fiduciary relationship.

[97] [1909] 1 Ch. 476.

appointment on the ground of the plaintiff's mistake. There are other cases[98] which:

> "show that, wherever there is a voluntary transaction by which one party intends to confer a bounty upon another, the deed will be set aside if the court is satisfied that the disponor did not intend the transaction to have the effect which it did. It will be set aside whether the mistake is of law or of fact, so long as the mistake is as to the effect of the transaction itself and not merely as to its consequences or the advantages to be gained by entering into it."[99]

It would be unfortunate if such a mistake should result in rescission of a deed, and yet should not be sufficient to ground recovery of money. It is to be hoped that recovery of gifts under mistake will not be restricted in the manner suggested by Greene M.R. in *Morgan* v. *Ashcroft*.[1] In our view, it is open to the courts to grant restitution if the donor is mistaken as to some assumption which proves false and which caused him to make the payment.[2]

(b) *The Mistake must have Caused[3] the Plaintiff to Make the Payment*

The burden is on the plaintiff to show from the facts that he would not have made the payment but for his mistaken assumption of fact. The courts have approached the problem by asking themselves this question: if the payer had known the true facts, would he have paid the money? If he would have done so, he cannot recover; if he would not, he can.[4] This burden of proof should not normally present him with any difficulty but on occasion it may do so.[5] In any event it should not be necessary to demonstrate that the mistake was "fundamental".[5a]

---

[98] See *Meadows* v. *Meadows* (1853) 16 Beav. 401; *Walker* v. *Armstrong* (1856) 8 De G.M. & G. 531; *Phillipson* v. *Kerry* (1863) 11 W.R. 1034; *Ellis* v. *Ellis* (1909) 26 T.L.R. 166; *Re Walton's Settlement* [1922] 2 Ch. 509.

[99] *Gibbon* v. *Mitchell* [1990] 3 All E.R. 338, 343, *per* Millett J.: see below, p. 222.

[1] See above, pp. 120.

[2] *Cf.* above, pp. 110–111.

[3] *Holt* v. *Markham* [1923] 1 K.B. 504; *Home & Colonial Insurance Co. Ltd.* v. *London Guarantee & Accident Co. Ltd.* (1928) 45 T.L.R. 134. See also *Trigge* v. *Lavallee* (1862) 15 Moo.P.C. 270, 299, *per* Lord Kingsdown; *Bernard & Shaw Ltd.* v. *Shaw* [1951] 2 All E.R. 267; *cf. Elder* v. *Auerbach* [1950] 1 K.B. 359, 375, *per* Devlin J.

[4] *Barclays Bank Ltd.* v. *W. J. Simms (Southern) Ltd.* [1980] 1 Q.B. 677; *David Securities Pty. Ltd.* v. *Commonwealth Bank of Australia* (1992) 66 A.L.J.R. 768 (H. Ct. of Aust.).

[5] *Cf.* below, p. 127–130.

[5a] This view, which we have always held, has now been accepted by the High Court of Australia in *David Securities Pty Ltd.* v. *Commonwealth Bank of Australia* (1992) 66 A.L.J.R. 768, 777: "The requirement that mistake be fundamental as well as causative is not as restrictive as the liability approach considered above but it has been suggested that the requirement is still a worthwhile precaution against a potential flood of claims and consequent insecurity of receipts (Birks. *Introduction*, p. 159). The notion of fundamentality is, however, extremely vague and

Exceptionally, the facts may demonstrate that the mistake was *a* reason, as distinct from *the* reason, why the plaintiff made the payment; the analogy of the cases on duress to the person[6] suggests that, in these circumstances, his claim should nonetheless succeed. In principle this conclusion is correct.[7] His claim to restitution should succeed if he can prove that he would not have made the payment but for his mistake. Whether he has done so is in each case a question of fact.

Special problems may arise if the plaintiff was labouring under a mistake of fact or a mistake of law. In such a case it may be necessary to decide whether he made the payment under a mistake of fact[8]; for a mistake of law will not generally ground recovery. The burden will be on the payer "to satisfy the court that, on the balance of probabilities in all the circumstances of the case, it was a mistake of fact which gave rise to the overpayment."[9]

(c) *Mistake Induced by Fraud*

Money paid under a mistake induced by fraud can be recovered as money had and received.[10] Since the establishment of a separate tort of deceit,[11] recovery of money so paid may also be regarded as an example of waiver of the tort.[12] If a mistake is induced by fraud, it is enough that the plaintiff mistakenly relies upon the misstatement and is thereby induced to pay the money to the defendant.[13] Fraud will also ground recovery of a payment made under a compromise or in final settlement of a claim, though such a payment could not be recovered on the ground of a unilateral mistake of fact alone.[14] The plaintiff takes the risk of being mistaken when he made the compromise but not the risk that the defendant has acted fraudulently. There are a number of examples in the reports of the exercise of this right of recovery, in cases of both active

---

would seem to add little, if anything, to the requirement that the mistake caused the payment . . . insistence upon that factor would only serve to focus attention in a non-specific way on the nature of the mistake, rather than the fact of enrichment".

[6] In particular *Barton* v. *Armstrong* [1976] A.C. 104; see below, p. 234.

[7] *Cf. Essays* (ed. Burrows), pp. 53–54 [Burrows]; Birks, *Introduction* p. 158.

[8] *Holt* v. *Markham* [1923] 1 K.B. 504; *Avon County Council* v. *Howlett* [1983] 1 W.L.R. 605, 618–620, *per* Slade L.J.

[9] *Avon County Council* v. *Howlett* [1983] 1 W.L.R. 605, 620, *per* Slade L.J.

[10] *Edward Owen* v. *Barclays Bank International Ltd.* [1978] Q.B. 159, 169–170, *per* Lord Denning M.R., citing *Bank Russo-Iran* v. *Gordon, Woodroffe & Co. Ltd., The Times*, October 4, 1972.

[11] *Pasley* v. *Freeman* (1789) 3 T.R. 51.

[12] On waiver of tort, see below, Chap. 38. Historically, the right of recovery in *indebitatus assumpsit* is more ancient: see *Tomkins* v. *Bernet* (1693) Salk. 22; *Astley* v. *Reynolds* (1731) 2 Str. 915, 916, *per curiam; Att.-Gen.* v. *Perry* (1733) 2 Com.Rep., 481, 491, *per curiam*. See Jackson, *History*, pp. 58–61, 73–75; (1985) 100 L.Q.R. 653, 661 [Hedley].

[13] It has also been suggested that, in some cases at least, the action should be available to the plaintiff even where the fraudulent misrepresentation is not one of fact but of law. *West London Commercial Bank* v. *Kitson* (1884) 13 Q.B.D. 360, 362–363, *per* Bowen L.J.: see below, p. 187.

[14] *Brooke* v. *Mostyn* (1864) 2 De G.J. & Sm. 373; *Holsworthy U.D.C.* v. *Holsworthy R.D.C.* [1907] 2 Ch. 62.

fraudulent misrepresentation[15] and of fraudulent suppression of facts.[16] Today, however, it is more usual to bring an action for damages in tort.[17]

(d) *Problems Concerning Principal and Agent*

Action by principal or agent

Where an agent pays money under a mistake of fact on his principal's behalf, the proper person to sue for its recovery is generally the principal, even though he is an undisclosed principal.[18] But where the agent pays money under a mistake which leads him to think that he has his principal's authority to pay, and the principal repudiates his action, the agent may, as has been seen,[19] be entitled to recover from the recipient.

The question has arisen whether knowledge on the part of the principal or of another agent of the facts as to which the paying agent was mistaken will preclude recovery by the principal. It is now established that, if the paying agent was mistaken, the principal can recover, provided that neither he nor any responsible agent of his knew of the paying agent's mistake even though they knew the true facts. This was established in *Anglo-Scottish Beet Sugar Corporation Ltd.* v. *Spalding U.D.C.*[20] The plaintiff company, whose head office was at Glasgow, contracted with the defendants for the supply of water to their branch factory at Spalding. Originally the minimum quarterly payment for this supply was £375, but in 1927, by a new contract, that payment was reduced to £100. This new contract, negotiated by the plaintiffs' managing director at Glasgow, was not, by mistake, made known either to their factory

---

[15] *Madden* v. *Kempster* (1807) 1 Camp. 12; *Crockford* v. *Winter* (1807) 1 Camp. 124; *Refuge Assurance Co. Ltd.* v. *Kettlewell* [1908] 1 K.B. 545, [1909] A.C. 243; *Edmeads* v. *Newman* (1823) 1 B. & C. 418; *Andrews* v. *Hawley* (1857) 26 L.J.Ex. 323. See also *Hill* v. *Perrott* (1810) 3 Taunt. 274; *Abbotts* v. *Barry* (1820) 2 B. & B. 369; and *Cf. Read* v. *Hutchinson* (1813) 3 Camp. 352; *Biddle & Loyd* v. *Levy* (1815) 1 Stark. 20; *Pope* v. *Wray* (1838) 4 M. & W. 451, 453. See, generally, Jackson, *History*, pp. 74–75.

[16] *Billing* v. *Ries* (1841) Car. & M. 26; see also *Martin* v. *Morgan* (1819) 3 Moo.P.C. 635.

[17] *Cf.* below, Chap. 38.

[18] *Duke of Norfolk* v. *Worthy* (1808) 1 Camp. 337. Where the defendant has fraudulently obtained money from an agent, either principal or agent can sue for its recovery: see *Holt* v. *Ely* (1853) 1 E. & B. 795, applying *Stevenson* v. *Mortimer* (1778) 2 Cowp. 805. See also *Marsh* v. *Keating* (1834) 1 Bing.N.C. 198.

[19] See above, p. 117.

[20] [1937] 2 K.B. 607, followed in *Turvey* v. *Dentons (1923) Ltd.* [1953] 1 Q.B. 218; *Saronic Shipping Co. Ltd.* v. *Huron Liberian Co.* [1979] 1 Lloyds 341, 363, *per* Mocatta J.; and *Royal Municipality of Storthoaks* v. *Mobil Oil Canada Ltd.* (1975) 55 D.L.R. (3d) 1 (Sup.Ct. of Canada). See also *London County Freehold & Leasehold Properties Ltd.* v. *Berkeley Property & Investment Co. Ltd.* [1936] 2 All E.R. 1039, and in particular the judgment of Mark Romer L.J. in that case, in which he might be thought to have expressed the view that a representation made innocently by one agent of a company, which was untrue as to certain facts known to another agent of the company, would amount to a fraudulent misrepresentation by the company. Atkinson J. in the *Anglo-Scottish Beet Sugar* case took the view that the judgment disclosed no such statement. But in *Armstrong* v. *Strain* [1951] T.L.R. 856, affd. [1952] 1 K.B. 232, Devlin J. and Charles Romer L.J. were of opinion that Mark Romer L.J.'s judgment did disclose such a statement and that it was wrong; Singleton and Birkett L.JJ. shared the view of Atkinson J. See (1937) 53 L.Q.R. 344, 363 [P. Devlin].

manager at Spalding or to their commercial manager at Nottingham. The defendants continued to be paid at the old rate, by cheques drawn by the commercial manager on notification by the factory manager, and signed by the managing director on his fortnightly visits to the area, the cheques being signed along with a very large number of other cheques purely as a matter of routine. Atkinson J. held that the plaintiffs were entitled to recover these overpayments as paid under a mistake of fact. The knowledge of the managing director as to the existence of the new contract was immaterial, since he was unaware at the time of payment that it was not being acted upon.

Action against principal or agent

Where the plaintiff had paid money under a mistake of fact to the agent of a third party, he is entitled to proceed against the principal even though he has no proof that the agent has accounted to him.[21] He may not, however, wish to sue the principal, as, for example, where the latter is insolvent; and if the agent still retains the money, there is nothing to prevent him from proceeding against the agent.[22] But if the agent has paid over the money to his principal, or done something equivalent thereto, he is generally immune from such proceedings and the plaintiff is restricted to his rights against the principal.[23]

(e) *Demand before Action*

It has been suggested that a demand before action is a prerequisite of an action to recover money paid under a mistake of fact. In *Freeman* v. *Jeffries*,[24] the amount which the incoming tenant of a farm was to pay the outgoing tenant was referred to two valuers for valuation, and the incoming tenant gave the outgoing tenant a promissory note for the amount so found due, which he subsequently paid. He later discovered that certain errors had been made in the valuation, and that he had, therefore, paid too much. Without giving the outgoing tenant any information as to the nature of his complaint, he sought to recover from him the alleged overpayment. The Court of Exchequer gave judgment for the defendant on various grounds, one of which[25] was that the plaintiff had made no demand before action. Martin B. considered that the plaintiff could not recover the money unless the arrangement between the

---

[21] *Duke of Norfolk* v. *Worthy* (1808) 1 Camp. 337. Similarly if the money was obtained through the fraudulent misrepresentation of an agent without authority: see *Crockford* v. *Winter* (1807) 1 Camp. 124, 127, *per* Lord Ellenborough; *Refuge Assurance Co. Ltd.* v. *Kettlewell* [1908] 1 K.B. 545, [1909] A.C. 243.

[22] See, *e.g. Buller* v. *Harrison* (1977) 2 Cowp. 565. No action can be brought by a third person against an agent under s.2(1) of the Misrepresentation Act 1967, although the agent may owe a duty of care at common law to that third person: see *Resolute Maritime Inc.* v. *Nippon Kaiji Kyokai* [1983] 1 W.L.R. 857.

[23] See below, pp. 750–755.

[24] (1869) L.R. 4 Ex. 189. See also *Kelly* v. *Solari* (1841) 9 M. & W. 54, 58, *per* Parke B.; Keener, pp. 141–152; Woodward, pp. 49–51.

[25] Martin and Bramwell BB., but not Kelly C.B. and Pigott B., held for the defendant on this ground.

parties was rescinded and this could not be achieved "unless some communication has been made by the plaintiff."[26] Bramwell B. relied on the analogy of trover and on the authority of *Wilkinson* v. *Godefroy*.[27] In trover, however, demand and refusal are only evidence that the tort has been committed; and *Wilkinson* v. *Godefroy* was concerned with recovery of money from a stakeholder to whom it had been entrusted, when a demand is necessary to throw upon the depositee a duty to repay.

It is difficult to see why a demand should be necessary before an action can be maintained to recover money paid under a mistake of fact. The duty to repay does not arise because the defendant has refused to return the money. It arises from the date of the receipt of the money, because the defendant has received money which he never ought to have received. "It is not a case in which a consideration, which has once existed, fails by subsequent election or other act of either party, or of a third person; but there is never, at any stage of the transaction, any consideration for the payment."[28]

It has been said that, in cases of mistake shared by both parties, "it is just that he [the payee] should have an opportunity to correct the mistake, innocently committed on both sides, before being subjected to the risks and expenses of a litigation."[29] But service of the writ and certainly delivery of the pleadings should be sufficient notice of the claim; any failure to give notice before action can always be taken into account in awarding costs.[30]

Notice of action may, however, sometimes be made necessary by statute.[31]

(f) *The Effect of Negligence*

In the leading case of *Kelly* v. *Solari*,[32] the Court of Exchequer held that money

---

[26] At p. 200.

[27] (1839) 9 A. & E. 536.

[28] *Leather Manufacturers' Bank* v. *Merchants' Bank*, 128 U.S. 26, 35, *per* Gray C.J. (1888).

[29] *Sharkey* v. *Mansfield*, 90 N.Y. 227, 229 (1882), *per* Finch J.

[30] In *Baker* v. *Courage & Co.* [1910] 1 K.B. 56, Hamilton J. held that no demand was necessary where the money was paid under a mistake shared by both parties. If, however, a demand is ever necessary, then it should be in such a case rather than where the payer alone is mistaken. Hamilton J. considered (see pp. 65–66) that *Freeman* v. *Jeffries*, above, could be distinguished on the ground that the mistake was there unilateral. But if any action could have been maintained in that case on the ground of mistake, such mistake must have been shared by the payee.

Atkinson J. in *Anglo-Scottish Beet Sugar Corporation* v. *Spalding U.D.C.* [1937] 2 K.B. 607, 609, *arguendo*, considered that, where it is the payee's own fault that he does not know of the mistake, he cannot be heard to say that he ought to have had notice. *A fortiori* must that be the case where he was aware of the mistake at the time of the payment or has become aware of it before action was brought, or possibly where he was responsible, *e.g.* by misrepresentation, for the plaintiff's mistake.

[31] See, *e.g.* *Midland Ry.* v. *Withington Local Board* (1883) 11 Q.B.D. 788, construing Public Health Act 1875, s.264, now repealed.

[32] (1841) 9 M. & W. 54, disapproving *Milnes* v. *Duncan* (1827) 6 B. & C. 671, 677, *per* Bayley J. The principal case, *Kelly* v. *Solari*, together with *Lucas* v. *Worswick* (1833) 1 M. & R. 293, is strongly criticised in 2 *Smith's Leading Cases* at p. 407, but it was approved in *Brownlie* v. *Campbell* (1880) 5 App.Cas. 925, 952, *per* Lord Blackburn, and was applied in *Bell* v. *Gardiner* (1842) 4 Man. & G. 11; *Townsend* v. *Crowdy* (1860) 8 C.B.(N.S.) 477; *Imperial Bank of Canada* v. *Bank of Hamilton* [1903] A.C. 49; *R. E. Jones Ltd.* v. *Waring & Gillow Ltd.* [1926] A.C. 670;

paid by directors of an insurance company on a policy which had lapsed by reason of non-payment of premiums could be recovered even though the means of knowing that the policy had so lapsed was available to the plaintiffs. Parke B. said[33] that if money "is paid under the impression of the truth of a fact which is untrue, it may, generally speaking, be recovered back, however careless the party paying may have been, in omitting to use due diligence to inquire into the fact."

This is now the general rule,[34] but there is said to be one exception. In *Byles on Bills*[35] this passage appears:

> "If the drawee discovers, after payment, that the bill or cheque is a forgery he may in general, by giving notice on the same day, or within a reasonable time, recover back the money. So, too, if a forged note is discounted, the transferee, on discovery of the forgery within a reasonable time, may recover back the money paid, the imagined consideration totally failing. But any fault or negligence on the part of him who pays the money on the note will disable him from recovering."

The authorities cited by Byles are, however, unconvincing. The cases mentioned are *Price* v. *Neal*[36] and *Smith* v. *Mercer*.[37] In both cases some reliance was placed on the plaintiff's negligence; but not only were they decided before *Kelly* v. *Solari*, but in *London & River Plate Bank* v. *Bank of Liverpool*,[38] Mathew J. considered that the principle underlying both the decisions cited by Byles was that, if the plaintiff "so conducted himself as to lead the holder of the bill to believe that he considered the signature genuine, he could not afterwards withdraw from that position," a principle independent of negligence. We therefore suggest that the rule in *Kelly* v. *Solari* applies to bills of exchange.

(g) *Voluntary Payment: Submission to an Honest Claim*

In this context,[39] as elsewhere,[40] a payment made in submission to an honest

---

Anglo-Scottish Beet Sugar Corporation v. Spalding U.D.C. [1937] 2 K.B. 607 (which in its turn was applied in *Turvey* v. *Dentons (1923) Ltd.* [1953] 1 Q.B. 218); and see *Dails* v. *Lloyd* (1848) 12 Q.B. 531.
The decision has been accepted as authoritative in the U.S.A. and Canada; see *inter alia, Simms* v. *Vick* 151 N.C. 78 (1909); *Chicago M. & St. P.R.Co.* v. *Malleable Iron Range Co.*, 187 Wis. 93 (1925); *Royal Bank of Canada* v. *R.* [1931] 1 W.W.R. 709; *Purity Dairy Co.* v. *Collinson* (1967) 58 D.L.R. (2d) 67; and see also the South African case of *Union Government* v. *National Bank of South Africa* [1921] A.D. 121.
[33] At p. 59.
[34] See cases cited above, n. 32; *cf. Milnes* v. *Duncan* (1827) 6 B. & C. 671; *Bramston* v. *Robins* (1826) 4 Bing. 11.
[35] 26th ed., p. 146.
[36] (1762) 3 Burr. 1354.
[37] (1815) 6 Taunt. 76.
[38] [1896] 1 Q.B. 10–11: see below, pp. 757–758. See also *Place* v. *Turner* (1951) 101 L.J. News. 93.
[39] *Beevor* v. *Marler* (1898) 14 T.L.R. 289.
[40] See above, pp. 58–60.

claim is irrecoverable.[40a] The payer has, in these circumstances, assumed the risk of his mistake.[41] In *Kelly* v. *Solari*, Parke B. said[42]:

> "If, indeed, the money is intentionally paid, without reference to the truth or falsehood of the fact, the plaintiff meaning to waive all inquiry into it, and that the person receiving shall have the money at all events, whether the fact be true or false, the latter is certainly entitled to retain it."

And in the same case, Lord Abinger C.B. commented[43]: "There may also be cases in which, although [the payer] might by investigation learn the state of facts more accurately, he declines to do so, and chooses to pay the money notwithstanding; in that case there can be no doubt that he is . . . bound."

It appears that a payer may be deemed *in law* to intend to "pay the money notwithstanding," even though he did not *in fact* intend to do so. In *Morgan* v. *Ashcroft*[44] a bookmaker claimed that he had mistakenly credited twice over the defendant with a sum of £24 2s. 1d. The Court of Appeal held that he was not entitled to recover. The Gaming Act 1845 was an insuperable barrier to an examination of the state of accounts. Moreover, the money was not recoverable as having been paid under a mistake of fact. It is not easy to discern the *ratio decidendi* of this part of the case. But:

> "it may well be found in the opinion of both judges [Greene M.R. and Scott L.J.] that an overpayment of betting debts by a bookmaker is not made under a mistake of fact sufficiently fundamental to ground recovery, apparently on the basis that the payment is in any event intended to be a purely voluntary gift, 'because the law prevents the plaintiff from saying that he intended anything but a present.'"[45]

Consequently the payer's claim may fail, not only when he intends that the payee shall have the money at all events, but when he "is deemed in law so to intend."

In the United States, the principle that a voluntary payment is irrecoverable has sometimes been invoked where insurance companies have paid claims under policies. So, in *New York Life Assurance Co.* v. *Chittenden*,[46] the defen-

---

[40a] *Cf.* Burrows, *The Law of Restitution*, pp. 101–103.

[41] Some doubt as to the facts will not prevent recovery: see *Charfield* v. *Paxton* (1799) 2 East 471 n. (a), *per* Ashurst J. For an elaborate discussion of the nature and effect of doubt and suspicion in this context, see *Restatement of Restitution*, § 10; and *cf.* Palmer, *op. cit.* Vol. III, pp. 170–172; *Burrows, op cit.*, p. 102.

[42] (1841) 9 M. & W. 54, 59. See also *Townsend* v. *Crowdy* (1860) 8 C.B.(N.S.) 477, 490, *per* Willes J., 494, *per* Williams J.

[43] At p. 58.

[44] [1938] 1 Q.B. 49: see above, p. 109.

[45] *Barclays Bank Ltd.* v. *W. J. Simms (Southern) Ltd.* [1980] 1 Q.B. 677, 698, *per* Robert Goff J., citing *Morgan* v. *Ashcroft* [1938] 1 Q.B. 49, 77, *per* Scott L.J. *Cf. Lipkin Gorman (A Firm)* v. *Karpnale Ltd.* [1991] 2 A.C. 548, 577, *per* Lord Goff.

[46] 134 Iowa 613, 112 N.W. 96 (1907); see also *Meeme Mutual Home Protection Fire Insurance Co.* v. *Lorfeld*, 194 Wis. 322, 216 N.W. 507 (1927). See, generally, Palmer, *op. cit.* Vol. III, § 14.11. For the application of this principle in cases other than insurance: see *Carter* v. *Iowa State Business Men's Building & Loan Association*, 135 Iowa L.Rev. 368, 112 N.W. 828 (1907);

dants were assignees of a policy issued by the plaintiff company on the life of a man named Jarvis. Jarvis disappeared from his home and, after he had been absent and his whereabouts had remained unknown for over seven years, the defendants claimed payment of the policies, threatening if necessary to bring legal proceedings. The company at first only agreed to pay if the defendants gave a bond of indemnity for return of the money if Jarvis was not dead. The defendants refused, and the company gave way and paid up. Jarvis was in fact alive at the time of payment. The company sought to recover the money they had so paid. The Supreme Court of Iowa held that they were precluded from recovery, for this was a voluntary payment made for the purpose of avoiding litigation, analogous to a compromise of a doubtful claim. The question whether Jarvis was dead was within the contemplation of both parties at the time of the payment.

But other jurisdictions in the United States have rejected the argument that an insurance company which makes such a payment inevitably assumes the risk of a mistake. As the Kentucky court said in *Phoenix Indemnity Co.* v. *Steiden Stores*[47]:

> "In applying the 'assumption of risk' theory the courts actually have been making a judicial determination that the insurer and the recipient of the payment have entered into a compromise, where no real compromise has been made. The fact that the insurer pays the full amount of the claim, plus the fact that the insurer is ignorant of the mistake, is evidentiary of a lack of any intention to compromise the claim. In our opinion, should we adopt 'the assumption of risk' theory, insurance companies would be inclined to delay payment of claims, thus forcing the beneficiary to resort to litigation."

Much depends on the circumstances in which the payment was made; for example, whether it was made in response to a claim by the payee, or whether the payer has waived any or any further investigation of the facts.[48] A factor of peculiar importance is whether the payee has threatened to bring legal proceedings against the payer in respect of the money claimed. In English law, money paid under compulsion of legal process cannot be recovered on the grounds of mistake.[49] The plaintiff cannot choose his own time for litigation. If he is sued, he must fight or submit; if he chooses to submit, his submission cannot be revoked on the ground that he was then mistaken.[50]

Remington Arms Co. v. *Feeney Tool Co.*, 97 Conn, 129, 115 A. 629 (1921); *Restatement of Restitution, Reporter's Notes*, p. 3. This line of cases is criticised in 7 Okla.L.Rev. 251, 271 (1954) [Seavey]. But it is significant that in the *New York Life Insurance* case the assured had threatened legal proceedings.

[47] 267 S.W. 2d 733, 735 (1954), *per* Waddill C. See also *Pilot Insurance* v. *Cudd*, 36 S.E.2d 860 (1945) (S.Ct. of South Carolina).

[48] See above, pp. 58–60.

[49] *Moore* v. *Vestry of Fulham* [1895] 1 Q.B. 399.

[50] See above, pp. 50–54.

Closely analogous are those cases where the payment has been made under a binding compromise. It has long been the law that a compromise of a disputed claim made in good faith is binding on the parties thereto, even though the claim in dispute was without foundation.[51] A payment made under such a compromise cannot in the absence of misrepresentation, duress, undue influence or lack of good faith,[52] be recovered on grounds of mistake of fact,[53] unless it can be shown that it was an express or implied term of the agreement that, in the event of the parties being mistaken as to that fact in question, the money should be repaid,[54] or unless the agreement can be shown to have been entered into on the basis of a mistake shared by both parties as to some fact of fundamental importance.[55]

But even where an honest claim has been settled or a compromise reached, the plaintiff's claim based on his mistaken belief will not necessarily fail. If he can demonstrate that he would not have made the payment but for that mistaken belief, he should be granted restitution.[56] It is only if he assumed the risk that he might be mistaken, and paid or agreed to pay to resolve that question, that his claim should be denied.[57]

(h) Proprietary Claims

The question whether a person who has paid money under a mistake of fact should be granted a restitutionary proprietary remedy can arise in a number of contexts. It will be most important when the payee is insolvent and the payer seeks to gain priority over the payee's general creditors. Such were the facts of *Chase Manhattan Bank N.A.* v. *Israel-British Bank (London) Ltd.*[58] The plaintiffs were incorporated in New York, the defendants in London. By mistake on July 3, 1974, the plaintiffs paid the defendants some $2 million. Two days later the defendants learned of the mistake but made no attempt to correct it.[59] On August 2, 1974, the defendants petitioned the court for a winding-up order, which was made on December 2, 1974. In the action the plaintiffs sought to trace and recover in equity the sum they had paid under mistake. Goulding J. held that there was no conflict between New York and English law. Both under New York law and English law the defendants were constructive trustees of the money which had been paid under mistake. In English law it was necessary to

---

[51] *Callisher* v. *Bischoffsheim* (1870) L.R. 5 Q.B. 449: see above, pp. 50–54.

[52] *Ward & Co.* v. *Wallis* [1900] 1 Q.B. 675, 678, *per* Kennedy J.; *The Siboen and the Sibotre* [1976] 1 Lloyd's Rep. 293, 335–336, *per* Kerr J.: see below, p. 258.

[53] *Da Costa* v. *Firth* (1766) 4 Burr. 1966; *Cumming* v. *Bedborough* (1846) 15 M. & W. 438, 443, *per* Parke B.; *Holmes* v. *Payne* [1930] 2 K.B. 301. *Cf. Huddersfield Banking Co. Ltd.* v. *Henry Lister & Son* [1895] 2 Ch. 273: see below, p. 214.

[54] *Holmes* v. *Payne* [1930] 2 K.B. 301, *semble*.

[55] *Lawton* v. *Campion* (1854) 18 Beav. 87; *Holmes* v. *Payne* [1930] 2 K.B. 301, *semble. Cf. Lucas* v. *Worswick* (1833) 1 Moo. & Rob. 293.

[56] *Cf. Kelly* v. *Solari* (1841) 9 M. & W. 54: see above, pp. 110 *et seq.*

[57] See Palmer, *op. cit.* Vol. III, pp. 166 *et seq.*; *Essays* (ed. Burrows) pp. 22–23 [Arrowsmith].

[58] [1981] Ch. 105. *Cf. Royal Products* v. *Midland Bank* [1981] 2 Lloyd's Rep. 194, 210 (no mistake found); followed in *Liggett* v. *Kensington* [1993] 1 N.Z.L.R. 257, 268, *per* Cooke P.

[59] At p. 115.

find that there was a fiduciary relationship between the payer and the recipient.[60] There was such a relationship. "A person who pays money to another under a factual mistake retains an equitable property in it and the conscience of that other is subjected to a fiduciary duty to respect his proprietary right."[61]

It is not surprising that a judge at first instance should have felt bound to "discover" a fiduciary relationship between the plaintiffs and the defendants.[62] Consequently it was necessary for Goulding J. to conclude, unrealistically, that a fiduciary relationship arises from the fact that a mistaken payment was made by one commercial competitor to another. "In reality this dispenses with the requirement of such a relationship."[63] It is to be regretted that Goulding J. was not free to ask the critical question, namely, whether it was just, given the ground of the plaintiff's claim, to grant him priority over the defendant's general creditors.[64]

The equities of the plaintiffs' claim in *Chase Manhattan* are appealing.[65] The mistake was discovered within two days, when the defendants were still trading, and the defendants made no attempt to return the money. Unlike the defendants' general creditors, the plaintiffs did not advance credit to the defendants and did not take the risk of the defendants' insolvency. In these circumstances the defendants' general creditors may receive a windfall if a lien were not imposed. This is not to say that a lien should necessarily be imposed in every case where a payer mistakenly makes a payment to a recipient who subsequently becomes insolvent; for example, if general creditors have subsequently been induced to grant or extend credit because the recipient's assets were materially swollen by the mistaken payment, a court may be persuaded that the payer should not be granted priority over them.

There is, however, another difficult question which must be answered before a plaintiff in the position of *Chase Manhattan* can succeed. Can its money be identified in the defendant's hands?[66] In *Re Berry*[67] the United States Court of Appeals for the Second Circuit applied the rule in *Re Hallett's Estate*[68]

---

[60] *Sinclair* v. *Brougham* [1914] A.C. 398, as interpreted in *Re Diplock* [1948] Ch. 465: see above, pp. 83–85.

[61] At p. 119. There was much discussion in the case whether New York law would characterise the constructive trust as a remedy or whether it formed part of its substantive law. Having heard expert evidence, the judge concluded that it was part of its substantive law. Not every American lawyer would agree with that finding: Palmer, *op. cit.* Vol. I, 1992 Supplement, § 1.4. Professor Palmer was an expert witness for the defendants.

[62] See above, pp. 83 *et seq.*

[63] Palmer, *op. cit.* Vol. I, 1992 Supplement, § 1.3.

[64] For a defence of the judge's reasoning, see Birks, *Introduction*, pp. 377 *et seq.*

[65] In *Barclays Bank Ltd.* v. *W. J. Simms (Southern) Ltd.* [1980] Q.B. 677 (see below, pp. 139), the money which had been paid under mistake was placed by the receiver of the defendant company in a separate account, pending the resolution of the question whether the paying bank could recover the payment. It was seemingly assumed that if its claim succeeded, as it did, the money belonged to the bank.

[66] See above, Chap. 2, for a general discussion.

[67] 147 F. 696 (1906). See also *Knight Newspapers Inc.* v. *C.I.R.*, 143 F. 2d 1007 (1944); contrast *Re Archer, Hervey & Co.*, 289 F. 267, 277 (1923) where it was said that *Re Berry* "seems to have gone as far as the rule can be carried."

[68] (1880) 13 Ch.D. 696: see above, pp. 87–88.

in order to determine what was the lowest intermediate balance in the defendant's hands. But in *Chase Manhattan* Goulding J. left this question open, declining counsel's invitation to state that an English court would apply a different rule.[69] Equity's tracing rules, such as those embodied in *Re Hallett's Estate*, were generally formulated in the context of a beneficiary's claim that he was entitled to priority over the general creditors of a bankrupt trustee. In the formative English cases, the sums involved were relatively modest so that the identification of the plaintiff's assets in the mixed fund did not present insurmountable problems and could be solved through the application of artificial presumptions.[70] Similarly, in *Re Berry*, only $1500 had been paid by mistake into the defendant's bank account the day before the defendant made a general assignment for the benefit of its creditors; and the lowest intermediate balance in that account never fell below that figure. In contrast, in *Chase Manhattan*, over $2 million was paid into the account of a bank with substantial assets; millions of pounds probably passed through its accounts daily and the bank continued trading for almost a month after the receipt of the mistaken payment. It is difficult to perceive how Chase Manhattan's money could be identified through the application of traditional tracing rules.

The rules which the court will formulate to identify money paid under a mistake of fact will reflect the readiness of the court to grant the plaintiff priority over the defendant's general creditors in the event of the defendant's insolvency. At one time, for example, some American jurisdictions adopted the "swollen assets" theory.[71] This theory tacitly recognised that, because the rules of tracing are so artificial, it is better to accept frankly that plaintiffs in the position of *Chase Manhattan* should gain priority over unsecured creditors simply because they can demonstrate that their mistaken payments went to swell the defendant's assets. In England there are influential dicta[72] which suggest that the plaintiff's claim to a proprietary remedy may be so attractive that a court may impose a lien over an insolvent defendant's unencumbered assets. Their rationalisation is that a mistaken payer does not take the risk of his recipient's insolvency, while general creditors do. It is doubtful whether such a claim will succeed if it is shown that the recipient must have dissipated the mistaken payment. If this is a defence,[73] the burden should be on the recipient to prove that fact.

---

[69] At p, 120. Seemingly he assumed that English law, as the *lex fori*, should determine what tracing rules are applicable.

[70] See above, pp. 83 *et seq.*

[71] Most American States have rejected the theory: see above, p. 99, n. 59. And see *Simonds* v. *Simonds*, 408 N.Y.S. 2d 359 (1978), (above p. 101), cited in *Chase Manhattan*; and *Restatement of Restitution* 2d. Tentative Draft, §§ 34 *et seq.* Tracing, so interpreted, has obvious similarities to the principles underlying the common law action for money had and received: see above, pp. 75 *et seq.*

[72] *Space Investments Ltd.* v. *Canadian Imperial Bank of Commerce Trust Co. (Bahamas) Ltd.* [1986] 3 All E.R. 75, 77, *per* Lord Templeman, P.C.: see above, p. 98.

[73] *Sed quaere*: see above, p. 99.

(i) *Defences*

Change of position

In *Lipkin Gorman (A Firm)* v. *Karpnale Ltd.*[74] the House of Lords held that it is a defence, complete or *pro tanto*, to a restitutionary claim that, where "an innocent defendant's position is so changed that he will suffer an injustice if called upon to repay or to repay in full, the injustice of requiring him so to repay outweighs the injustice of denying the plaintiff restitution."[75]

We discuss this defence, as a general defence to restitutionary claims, later in this book.[76] The defence will be particularly important in the context of payments made under mistake. Its existence will protect the innocent defendant who has no knowledge of the plaintiff's mistake, and should encourage the courts to affirm the wide principle that *any* mistake is a ground for restitution provided that the payer can prove that he would not have made the payment but for the mistake.[77] In *Lipkin Gorman* the House of Lords accepted that it "would be unwise to attempt to define its scope in abstract terms, but better to allow the law on the subject to develop on a case-by-case basis."[78] What is clear is that a recipient who, when he changes his position, has actual knowledge that the payer was mistaken, will not be able to invoke the defence. He will have changed his position in bad faith, for he has knowledge of the facts entitling the plaintiff to restitution.[79]

In contrast, it is an open question whether the defendant who is found not to have actual knowledge of the mistake but ought to have known that the payer was mistaken should be able to defend himself successfully on the ground that he had changed his position. In this situation the recipient must repay unless he can establish this defence. In contrast, in trust law,[80] the hitherto accepted view is that a stranger who purchases trust property will be deemed to be *liable* as a constructive trustee of the property transferred if he knew or ought to have known that it was transferred in breach of trust.[81] But it should not necessarily follow that he or a recipient of money, who ought to have known of the payer's mistake, has acted *in bad faith* and is precluded from successfully pleading change of position. He is honest if foolish. We are of the tentative view that the defence should then be open to him. This conclusion derives some support from an admittedly slender line of authority which holds that an innocent

---

[74] [1991] 2 A.C. 548.
[75] At p. 579, *per* Lord Goff.
[76] Chap. 40.
[77] See above, pp. 110 *et seq.*
[78] At p. 558, *per* Lord Bridge.
[79] At p. 580, *per* Lord Goff.
[80] See below, pp. 670–672.
[81] See below, pp. 672–673.

volunteer who received trust property should be *personally* liable as a constructive trustee only if he acted with a want of probity, but not otherwise.[82] We discuss these difficult problems at greater length in the Chapter on Change of Position.[83]

The defence applies to both personal and proprietary claims. A plaintiff's proprietary claim will, as the law now stands, normally be grounded on his equitable title. If the plaintiff is able to identify his property in the defendant's hands, then the defendant will be held to be a trustee of, or a lien will be imposed over, that property.[84] In such a case, normally a defendant cannot successfully plead that it would be inequitable for him to hand back what does not belong to him. But on occasions he may. For example, A mistakenly pays £30,000 to an honest B, who pays that money into his Barclays Bank account at Cambridge. B then decides to take a trip to Alaska, which costs him £5,000; he would not have taken it but for the mistaken payment. But he pays for it with money withdrawn from his Oxford Midland Bank. The defence should defeat *pro tanto* A's proprietary claim to the fund in the Cambridge bank.[85]

Money paid in discharge of a debt owed to the defendant

The plaintiff makes a payment under a mistake of fact. It may be made in discharge of a debt owed by him to the defendant,[86] or it may be made in discharge of a debt owed to the defendant by a third party or in discharge of the defendant's lien over the property of a third party.[87] In these circumstances his claim to recover his payment will normally fail.

But it is not clear from the decided cases why it does so. The mistake certainly caused him to make the payment.[88] Arguably his claim will fail because the defendant has given valuable consideration for the payment. But a defence of bona fide purchase is normally a defence only to a claim based on the plaintiff's legal or equitable title,[89] and the plaintiff's claim, as the facts of the cases discussed in this Chapter demonstrate, is normally a personal claim based on his mistaken payment. Today the defence that the defendant has released the debt may be seen as a particular illustration of the defence of change of position. In the cases to which we now turn it is, if it is a defence, a complete defence; for the sum which the defendant received was the face value of the debt which was released.[90]

---

[82] See, for example, *Re Montagu's Settlement Trusts* [1987] Ch. 264: see below, p. 672.
[83] Chap. 40.
[84] See above, pp. 86 *et seq.*
[85] See below, p. 745.
[86] *Bize* v. *Dickason* (1786) 1 T.R. 285.
[87] See below, p. 135.
[88] See below, p. 135.
[89] See below, Chap. 41.
[90] *Cf. Citibank NA* v. *Brown Shipley & Co.* [1991] 2 All E.R. 690, where P was tricked into paying bankers' drafts to D who then paid the amount of the drafts to the rogue. P's claim, based on the submission that P's mistake prevented the passing of title to D, failed. But Waller J. (at pp. 701–702) was prepared to hold that if P's restitutionary claim had been that the drafts had been delivered under a mistake of fact (which was not pleaded), it would have been met by D's defence that it had changed its position in good faith.

In *Aiken* v. *Short*[91] the plaintiff, a banker, sought to recover from the defendant a sum of over £200, which the plaintiff, as transferee from one Carter of an inheritance supposedly due to him, had paid to the defendant. The payment was made in discharge of a debt owed to the defendant by Carter and secured by an equitable mortgage of Carter's supposed inheritance. In fact Carter had no inheritance. The plaintiff sought to recover the money so paid to the defendant as money paid under a mistake of fact, but the Court of Exchequer held that he could not recover. Bramwell B.[92] thought that his mistake was not sufficiently fundamental. But there is much to be said for the view that the mistake as to the existence of the inheritance was in fact basic to the transaction, in the sense that the plaintiff would not have made the payment if he had been aware of the true facts.[93] It is significant that both Pollock C.B.[94] and Platt B.[95] based their judgments on another ground, namely that the "money which the defendant got from her debtor was actually due to her, and there can be no[96] obligation to refund it."[97] Both these judges stressed the fact that the plaintiff paid the money as Carter's agent. If the money had not been so paid and the payment had not been ratified by Carter, the debtor would not have been discharged.[98-99]

However, in the difficult case of *R.E. Jones Ltd.* v. *Waring and Gillow Ltd.*,[1] the appellants' claim succeeded on facts which are significantly different, in one respect, from those in *Aiken* v. *Short*. In that case a rogue, named Bodenham, obtained from the respondents furniture and other goods, worth nearly £14,000, under a hire-purchase agreement in accordance with which he gave a cheque for £5,000 and promised to pay a monthly sum thereafter. The cheque was dishonoured, and the respondents sued him on the cheque and took back the furniture. The impecunious but ingenious Bodenham then went

---

[91] (1856) 1 H. & N. 210. See also *Steam Saw Mills Co. Ltd.* v. *Baring Bros. & Co. Ltd.* [1922] 1 Ch. 244; *Porter* v. *Latec Finance (Qld.) Pty. Ltd.* (1964) 111 C.L.R. 177. *Cf. Rahim* v. *Minister of Justice*, 1964 (4) S.A. 630, A.D.; (1965) 82 S.A.L.J. 144 [Wouter de Vos]. And contrast *R. E. Jones Ltd.* v. *Waring & Gillow Ltd.* [1926] A.C. 670: see below, pp. 745–748.

[92] At p. 215: see above, p. 108.

[93] *Barclays Bank Ltd.* v. *W. J. Simms (Southern) Ltd.* [1980] Q.B. 677, 687, *per* Robert Goff J.

[94] At p. 214.

[95] At p. 215.

[96] The English Reports omit this word.

[97] At p, 215, *per* Platt B.

[98-99] *Simpson* v. *Eggington* (1855) 10 Ex. 845, 847, *per* Parke B.: see above, p. 17, n. 2. See also *Restatement of Restitution*, § 14.

A similar but distinct problem arises if a debtor pays the assignee of his creditor. He subsequently discovers that the debt is tainted in some way (*e.g.* for fraud) so that if he had paid the assignor, not the assignee, he could have recovered the payment from the assignor. In the U.S.A. there is authority which suggests that the debtor's claim will fail since the assignee cannot be said to be "unjustly enriched when he receives payment of a claim for which he had previously given value": see Palmer, *op. cit.* Vol. III, p. 483. It is unlikely that an English court would accept this conclusion since an assignee can be in no better position than his assignor and takes subject to equities having priority over the right of the assignee: see *Government of Newfoundland* v. *Newfoundland Railway* (1888) 13 App.Cas. 199; *Lawrence* v. *Hayes* [1927] 2 K.B. 111. But contrast *Stoddard* v. *Union Trust Ltd.* [1921] 1 K.B. 181.

[1] [1926] A.C. 670, H.L., reversing the C.A., [1925] 2 K.B. 612, C.A.

to the appellants and falsely represented to them that he acted for a firm of motor manufacturers which was putting a new car on the market. Neither the firm nor the car existed, but the appellants were persuaded by Bodenham to sign an agency agreement by which they purported to be appointed the agents for the sale of the new car and agreed to buy 500 cars, for which they were to pay £5,000 at once by way of deposit. They did not like paying so much money to Bodenham or the supposed motor manufacturers, neither of whom they knew, but Bodenham said that "the people who were financing the thing" were the respondents. Accordingly the appellants gave him two cheques made out to the respondents for £2,000 and £3,000 respectively. Bodenham passed on these cheques to the respondents as having been received by him under some valuable contracts. The respondents noticed that the cheques had been signed by only one director, but in a telephone conversation with the appellants, in which nothing was said about the reason for the payment, arranged for them to be replaced by one cheque for £5,000 in the proper form. That cheque they received and cashed; and on the faith of the payment they released the furniture to Bodenham and let him have some more furniture. Later the fraud was exposed. The respondents retook the furniture, which had, however, depreciated in value. The appellants claimed to recover the money from the respondents as paid under a mistake of fact; the respondents pleaded *inter alia*, estoppel.

The Court of Appeal dismissed the plaintiff company's claim to recover £5,000. Both Scrutton and Sargant L.JJ. held that where "the defendant had received the plaintiff's money from a third party bona fide and under a binding contract, he is not accountable for it to the plaintiff"[2]; he was not party to the mistake and did not contribute to it. The House of Lords held that this defence could not succeed because the rogue was not the plaintiff company's agent in making the payments to the defendant company.[3] Consequently, the House concluded that the money was recoverable, having been paid under a mistake of fact.[4] It is true that the defendant company believed throughout that the plaintiff company was discharging a debt which was owed to it. But, unlike the defendant in *Aiken* v. *Short*, the defendant company did not receive the money in discharge of the debt which the rogue owed it. Moreover, the plaintiff company was not estopped by its conduct; there was no sufficient representation of fact which led the defendant company to act to its detriment. There is no doubt, however, that the defendant company had changed its position, at least *pro tanto*, for it had released the furniture to the rogue and had let him

---

[2] [1925] 2 K.B. 612, 637, *per* Scrutton L.J. Pollock M.R. held that the plaintiffs must fail since their mistake was that they thought the rogue was honest when he was not; that mistake did not cause him to make the payment: at pp. 630–631. It is not easy to support this reasoning.

[3] For a discussion of this aspect of the decision, see above, p. 748, and *Barclays Bank Ltd.* v. *W.J. Simms (Southern) Ltd.* [1980] Q.B. 677, below, p. 139.

[4] As it was in *Watson* v. *Russell* (1862) 3 B. & S. 34 and (1864) 5 B. & S. 968, which was said to be the foundation of Scrutton L.J.'s principle: see pp. 681–682, *per* Viscount Cave; pp. 687–690, *per* Lord Shaw; p. 695, *per* Lord Sumner; p. 700, *per* Lord Carson. This is not, in our view, a fair reading of his judgment.

have more furniture. It did resume possession of the furniture, but it is likely that the furniture had depreciated in value.[5] However, the extent of that depreciation was, on the facts, speculative.[6] Today the defendant company would be able to plead the defence of change of position, which, if established, would now defeat *pro tanto* the plaintiff company's claim.

In *Aiken* v. *Short* a debt was due to the defendant and the plaintiff's mistake was as to the value of a security.[7] But other common law jurisdictions have distinguished those facts from the following situation, which has not yet arisen in England. T impersonates the owner of real property, X. He obtains a loan from D, giving as security a forged mortgage which is purported to be executed by X. T repeats the impersonation and obtains a larger loan from P, giving as security another forged mortgage, also purported to be executed by X. T directs P to hand (or P hands) part of the proceeds of the loan to D, to discharge the purported mortgage in D's favour. On such facts, in *National Shawmut Bank of Boston* v. *Fidelity Mutual Life Insurance Co.*[8] the Supreme Judicial Court of Massachusetts allowed P to recover his payment from D. Since D has no lien or claim against the "supposed debtor [X] or against anyone, except its claim against [T] for the forgery[9] D had nothing to lose or to surrender. D had not, therefore, given consideration for P's payment. The cancellation of the supposed mortgage was no consideration because there was no valid mortgage in favour of D. Moreover there was no evidence that D had released or surrendered any right of action against the forger, T.[10] It has also been suggested that P should recover on a different ground. The contract between P and D was void because of "common and fundamental mistake as to the existence of a subject matter"[11]; both parties mistakenly thought that D was a creditor of X, the real owner, and that his debt was secured by a valid mortgage.

Other common law jurisdictions, however, have rejected any distinction between *Aiken* v. *Short* and the case of the impersonator who raises money from P and D on the security of a forged mortgage, though a variety of reasons have been given for this conclusion. In *Porter* v. *Latec Finance (Qld.) Pty. Ltd.*,[12] the High Court of Australia, Kitto and Windeyer JJ. dissenting, denied P recovery because the money, having been paid on behalf of T, "was paid in discharge and did discharge a debt actually owing to [D] by [T] under the name

---

[5] At p. 683, *per* Viscount Cave.
[6] *Cf. Citibank NA* v. *Brown Shipley & Co.* [1991] 2 All E.R. 690, 703, *per* Waller J.
[7] It would have been a different matter if there was no obligation to discharge. *Cf. British American Continental Bank* v. *British Bank for Foreign Trade* [1926] 1 K.B. 328 (money paid to the principal's agents in ignorance of fact that the principal had repudiated the contract: recovery allowed).
[8] 318 Mass. 142, 61 N.E. (2d) 18 (1945).
[9] 61 N.E. 201, 18, 21, *per* Lummus J.
[10] *Ibid.* 23, *per* Lummus J.
[11] *Porter* v. *Latec Finance (Qld.) Pty. Ltd.* (1964) 111 C.L.R. 177, 204, *per* Windeyer J.; *cf.* pp. 189–190, *per* Kitto J. Both judges were dissenting.
[12] (1964) 111 C.L.R. 177.

of [X]."[13] But some United States courts, and the *Restatement of Restitution*, find for D because he has given consideration for P's payment in that "he surrenders a claim against the forger [T]."[14] The payee has, therefore, surrendered something of value in law.

The law is then in a state of confusion. The problem is the perennial one of which of two innocent parties shall bear a loss caused by the fraudulent acts of a third party; and the common law's refusal to apportion loss has led, here as elsewhere, to the development of technical learning. We incline to the view that, if the question should arise in England, P should be denied recovery on the ground that his payment was accepted by D in discharge of a debt owing to him. It is irrelevant that the contract between D and T may have been void, for T would in any event have been indebted to D in quasi-contract. Money was therefore owed by T to D; and P paid D, at T's request, to discharge T's obligation to D in that sum.[15] Moreover, this situation has the merit that it produces a result consistent with *Aiken* v. *Short*.[16]

Payments by banks

Acting under a mistake, a bank pays a cheque drawn upon it which has been presented for payment by or on behalf of the payee. In what circumstances, if at all, can the bank recover from the payee? In particular, is the payee able successfully to plead that he has changed his position by the surrender of the cheque to the bank?

The balance of authority in the Commonwealth supports the conclusion that a drawee bank which pays money overlooking an order countermanding payment can recover the money from the payee.[17] In contrast, in the United States of America, both at common law and under the Uniform Commercial Code, the drawee bank is denied restitution.[18]

---

[13] *Ibid.* pp. 187–188, *per* Barwick C.J. The majority, except the Chief Justice, thought it critical that P had paid money to D on T's behalf: see 111 C.L.R. 177, 186, 198, 208. *Semble* only then would D's debt be discharged: *cf.* above, p. 17.

[14] *Restatement of Restitution, Reporter's Notes*, p. 9; but two of the advisers would have reached a different conclusion. See generally, *Restatement of Restitution*, § 14, ill. 6 and ill. 7, and *Notes*, pp. 7–10, where the authorities are collected.

[15] But what if the defendant knew when he received the payment from the plaintiff that T's security was worthless? He could not then be said to have acted in good faith. Arguably he should not be allowed this defence which may be regarded as one manifestation of the general defence of change of position: see Chap. 40. See, generally, *Martin* v. *Morgan* (1819) 1 Bodr. & B. 289, 293, *per* Burrough J.; *Ward & Co.* v. *Wallis* [1900] 1 Q.B. 675, 689, *per* Kennedy J.; *Barclays Bank Ltd.* v. *W. J. Simms (Southern) Ltd.* [1980] Q.B. 677, 695, *per* Robert Goff J. *Cf. Thompson* v. *J. Barke & Co.*, 1975 S.L.T. 67 (Ct. Sess.O.H.); *Royal Bank of Canada* v. *Huber* (1972) 23 D.L.R. (3d) 209.

[16] See above, p. 135.

[17] The earlier cases are collected in *The Bank's Right to Recover on Cheques paid by Mistake* (1968) 6 Melbourne Univ. L.R. 308 [Luntz]. A leading Australian case is *Bank of New South Wales* v. *Murphett* [1983] V.R. 489). For the Canadian cases, which are not consistent, see Maddaugh and McCamus, *op. cit.* pp. 240–243: see below, p. 139, n. 19.

[18] Palmer, *op. cit.* Vol. III, pp. 300 *et seq.*, who discusses the authorities.

Until relatively recently there was little English authority on this point. In 1979, in *Barclays Bank Ltd.* v. *W. J. Simms (Southern) Ltd.*,[19] the question arose directly for the first time. The bank made the payment to the defendant company in liquidation, overlooking the fact that its customer, the drawer, had countermanded payment. Robert Goff J. held that the bank could recover the payment. Its mistake had caused it to make the payment,[20] which was made without its customer's mandate.[21] Consequently "the bank cannot debit its customer's account, nor will its payment be effective to discharge the obligation (if any) of the customer on the cheque, because the bank has no authority to discharge such obligation." The defendant company did not invoke the defence of change of position, which had not then been recognised in English law.[22] The judge distinguished the facts before him from the case where a customer draws a cheque on his bank without funds or agreed overdraft facilities. This is in essence a request to the bank to provide sufficient overdraft facilities to meet the cheque. If the bank pays, even though it mistakenly thinks its customer has sufficient funds, it accepts the request.[23] The payment is then made with the customer's authority and so discharges the customer's obligation to the payee on the cheque. The bank cannot then recover from the payee but can debit the customer's account.[24]

The conclusion in *Barclays Bank Ltd.* v. *W. J. Simms (Southern) Ltd.* has been criticised on the ground that the payee suffered a detrimental change of position in that he was no longer able to sue upon the cheque but was thrown back on any right arising from his contract with the drawer; for that reason it is said that the bank's claim should have failed.[25] The payee suffers a detriment in

---

[19] [1980] Q.B. 677; followed in *Bank of New South Wales* v. *Murphett* [1983] V.R. 489, and *Royal Bank of Canada* v. *LVG Auctions Ltd.* (1983) 43 O.R. (2d) 582, (1985) 12 D.L.R. (4th) 768.

[20] See above, p. 122.

[21] Nor had the customer subsequently ratified the payment.

[22] [1980] Q.B. 677, 699.

[23] [1980] Q.B. 677, 800. The judge also held that the principle in *Cocks* v. *Masterman* (1829) 9 B. & C. 902 (see below, p. 756), namely, that notice of dishonour must be given to the holder of a bill on the same day he receives payment, had no application. It could not apply where notice of dishonour is not required; and no notice is required in the case of an unindorsed cheque which has been countermanded: Bills of Exchange Act 1882, s.40(2)(c).

[24] *Cf. Chambers* v. *Miller* (1862) 13 C.B.N.S. 125, as interpreted by Goff J. in [1980] Q.B. 688–689, 700. American case law reaches similar conclusions, see Palmer, *op. cit.* § 14–24(d). It is difficult, if not impossible, to reconcile the *Barclays Bank* case with Roche J.'s decision in *Barclay & Co. Ltd.* v. *Malcolm & Co.* (1925) 133 L.T. 512, where the plaintiff bank's claim failed on the ground that the mistake was not between the payer and the payee. As Robert Goff J. pointed out in the later *Barclays Bank* case, this reasoning is inconsistent with the decision of the House of Lords in *R. E. Jones Ltd.* v. *Waring & Gillow Ltd.* [1926] A.C. 670 where this argument was rejected: see above, pp. 135–137.

[25] The bank did not rely on its legal title, grounding its claim on mistake of fact. Contrast (1981) 97 L.Q.R. 254 [Goode]; (1983) 99 L.Q.R. 534, 551–554 [Friedmann]. Professor Goode also argues that Barclays had the apparent authority of the drawer to make the payment so that the payment was effective to discharge the drawer's liability on the cheque. We know of no case in which this argument has been advanced; and we doubt whether it can be right that the drawer held out the bank as having authority to make the payment so as to preclude him from asserting that the bank did not have the authority to do so: see *Freeman & Lockyer* v. *Buckhurst Park Properties (Mangal) Ltd.* [1964] 2 Q.B. 480. Moreover, the payee simply relies on the bank's willingness to pay the

not being able to sue upon the cheque because only in exceptional circumstances will the court, under Ord. 14, r. 3, exercise its discretion to give the drawer leave to defend or to stay execution until a counterclaim is heard.[26]

But under section 63(3) of the Bills of Exchange Act 1882 a cancellation of a negotiable instrument under a mistake is inoperative,[27] in which event it might be possible for the bank to restore the cheque to the payee to enable him to take proceedings upon it against the drawer.[28] Even if that is not right, it by no means follows that the payee can rely upon a defence of change of position. The detriment he suffers must be weighed against the injustice of denying the bank's restitutionary claim. To deny the bank a right of restitution must result in the unjust enrichment of either the payee or the drawer, depending on the merits of the payee's claim against the drawer. Article 4–407 of the Uniform Commercial Code accepts this to be so, and therefore subrogates the drawee both to the rights of the payee against the drawer either on the cheque or on the transaction out of which it arose *and* to the rights of the drawer against the payee with respect to such transaction. In our view, however, it is not evident that a statutory or common law right of subrogation would solve the problem. The bank will have no knowledge of the nature of the dispute between the drawer and the payee, or of where the merits lie. In such a case it will not know whether it should be subrogated to the drawer or to the payee; and if it seeks to be subrogated to both parties, then it will be liable to pay the costs of the party who emerges victorious.[29]

Moreover, if the bank is subrogated to the payee, whose underlying claim is good, the effect is in practice that the bank can render the drawer liable as if he had not stopped the cheque; and if the drawer is not liable under the underlying obligation, he will normally have no right to which the bank can be subrogated. Stripped of its legal technicalities, the true dispute is between the

---

cheque when he takes the money and not upon any apparent authority of the bank to discharge the drawer's obligation on the cheque. Neither the submission in this footnote nor that discussed in the text above was put to the judge in the case.

[26] *Nova (Jersey) Knit Ltd.* v. *Kammgarn Spinnerei GmbH* [1977] 1 W.L.R. 713, 726, *per* Lord Salmon, H.L. "The rule of practice is thus, in effect, pay on the bill of exchange first and pursue claims later": *Cebora S.N.C.* v. *S.I.P. (Industrial Products) Ltd.* [1976] 1 Lloyd's Rep. 271, 279, *per* Sir Eric Sachs, cited in [1978] C.L.J. 236 [Thornely].

[27] It is the custom of the City of London to return the bill with the words "cancelled in error" on it: *Byles on Bills*, pp. 145–146. *Semble* the payee can then sue on the cheque; *cf. Bank of New South Wales* v. *Murphett* [1983] V.R. 489. *Cf.* also Bills of Exchange Act 1882, s.69 (holder's right to duplicate of lost bill); and s.70 (action on lost bill).

[28] This is the solution preferred by Luntz in (1968) 6 Melbourne Univ.L.R. 308.

[29] In *Shapera* v. *Toronto-Dominion Bank* (1971) 17 D.L.R. (3d) 122, the Manitoba court held that the bank was entitled in equity to debit its customer's account because its payment had discharged a genuine liability of its customer. It is difficult to accept that an agent who has ignored his principal's instructions should, in these circumstances, be entitled to be indemnified by him. In other Canadian cases (see Maddaugh and McCamus, *op. cit.* p. 243), where the bank's claim has been against the payee, whether the bank will succeed has turned on whether its payment does or does not discharge a legitimate liability of the customer to the payee. If it does do so, the bank's claim will fail. The bank would in English law be denied any claim against its customer.

drawer and the payee, and to allow the bank to recover its mistaken payment means that that dispute can be ventilated and resolved on its merits.[30]

(j) *Estoppel*

Before the recognition of a general defence of change of position, a defendant had to rely on the defence of estoppel. For a number of reasons, however, estoppel does not provide an adequate defence to a claim to money paid under a mistake. The defendant has to show that the plaintiff had made a representation of fact, and a mere payment of money cannot be so described; or he has to show that the payment was made in breach of a duty which he owed to the defendant.[31] With the recognition of the more generous defence of change of position, it would be improbable, so it might be thought, that a defendant who has received money paid under a mistake of fact would seek to rely on the defence of estoppel. However, in one situation, he may be anxious to do so. For in *Avon County Council* v. *Howlett*[32] the Court of Appeal held that an estoppel by representation cannot operate *pro tanto*. So, a defendant who has spent only some of the money paid under mistake has a complete defence. In contrast, the House of Lords held in *Lipkin Gorman (A Firm)* v. *Karpnale Ltd.*[33] that the defence of change of position does operate *pro tanto*. Given this tension, the courts may hold that a defendant should make restitution of any sums which he has not spent; it would be inequitable, in these circumstances, for him to retain that money.[34]

---

[30] It is a distinct question whether the payee can rely on any defence of change of position if he knew, at the date he presented the cheque, that the drawer had stopped it. In the U.S.A., the bank, whose claim is normally rejected, can then recover; the payee knows of the bank's mistake and cannot therefore be said to have acted in good faith: see Palmer, *op. cit.* pp. 303–304.

[31] See below, pp. 747–750.

[32] [1983] 1 W.L.R. 605: see below, p. 749.

[33] [1991] 2 A.C. 548, 579–580, *per* Lord Goff: see below, pp. 740–741.

[34] See below, Chap. 40 for a fuller discussion.

CHAPTER 4

RECOVERY OF MONEY PAID UNDER A MISTAKE OF LAW

INTRODUCTION

FEW subjects are more confused than recovery of money paid under a mistake of law. At the root of this confusion lies Lord Ellenborough's judgment in *Bilbie* v. *Lumley*,[1] a decision which has frequently been claimed to have established the broad proposition that all payments made under a mistake of law are irrecoverable.

Bilbie v. *Lumley* was first heard at the York Assizes. The defendants were the assured under a policy underwritten by the plaintiff, and the trial judge, Rooke J., held that they had, at the date of the policy, failed to disclose to the plaintiff certain material facts. Subsequently, the defendants made a claim under the policy. The plaintiff did not appreciate that he could have repudiated liability on the grounds of non-disclosure, and settled the claim. On discovering his mistake, he sought to recover the payment from the defendants in an action for money had and received. The defendants pleaded that the plaintiff had paid their claim with full knowledge or means of knowledge of the circumstances. The plaintiff contended that this was irrelevant. He argued that recovery should be permitted simply because the money had been paid under a mistake of law, an argument which Rooke J. accepted. A rule nisi was granted for setting aside the verdict and for a new trial.

The same submissions were made before the Court of King's Bench. The plaintiff's argument clearly startled Lord Ellenborough, who inquired of Mr. Wood, later Baron Wood and at that time a practitioner of experience, whether he knew of any case in which a voluntary payment under a mere mistake of law had been recovered. Mr. Wood's silence encouraged the Chief Justice to say, in a tersely reported judgment, that "every man must be taken to be cognisant of the law; otherwise there is no saying to what extent the excuse of ignorance might not be carried. It would be urged in almost every case."[2] The rule was accordingly made absolute.

---

[1] (1802) 2 East 469. See also *Lowrey* v. *Bourdieu* (1780) Doug. 467, 468, *per* Buller J.; and see below, n. 5.

[2] At p. 472.

Bilbie v. *Lumley* was immediately accepted both in England and the United States,[3] and it is said to be still authoritative in England.[4] At the end of the last century, its principle was challenged by Keener who lamented that Baron Wood's own *ignorantia juris* has resulted in a rule as novel as it was unfortunate.[5] There is general agreement that the application of the maxim *ignorantia juris non excusat* has often resulted in the unjust enrichment of the payee[6-7] and that a payer should be denied restitution only if "he would not have been so entitled had the mistake been one of fact."[8]

Much of the difficulty in assessing the force of these criticisms springs from the fact that the rationale of the rule in *Bilbie* v. *Lumley* has often been misunderstood. In so far as it lays down that a payment made to close a transaction in settlement of an honest claim is irrecoverable, it embodies a sound rule of policy.[9] Such settlements should not be lightly set aside. The payer has had his opportunity to dispute his legal liability in court and has chosen to forgo it. As Singleton J. said in *Bullingdon R.D.C.* v. *The Oxford Corporation*,[10] the paramount consideration is that settlements and compromises made and accepted by both parties should be honoured.[11] This is a well-established and sound principle; a simple demand for money is legitimate pressure, which does not amount in law to duress.

In our view the principle in *Bilbie* v. *Lumley* should only preclude recovery of money which was paid in settlement of an honest claim. Any other payment made under a mistake of law should be recoverable if it would have been

---

[3] Within 14 years it had been approved in the U.S.A.: see *Shotwell* v. *Murray*, 1 Johns Ch.R.N.Y. 512, 516 (1815), *per* Chancellor Kent.

[4] See below, p. 146.

[5] Keener, pp. 85–86; see also Woodward, pp. 57–58. It is doubtful whether Keener was correct to describe *Bilbie* v. *Lumley* as historically anomalous. *Munt* v. *Stokes* (1792) 4 T.R. 561 provides some support for the decision in *Bilbie* v. *Lumley*. Other earlier cases are inconclusive. In one of the earliest, *Bonnel* v. *Foulke* (1657) 2 Sid. 4, it is not certain whether the plaintiff paid money because of a mistake of law or because it was demanded under compulsion *colore officii*, the defendant being the Mayor of London. *Hewer* v. *Bartholomew* (1598) Cro.Eliz. 614 is peculiarly obscure as the mistake could have been mutual or induced by the defendant. There are a number of dicta in favour of Keener's view, but they are in general terms: see *Lansdown* v. *Lansdown* (1730) Mos. 364, 365, *per* Lord King C.; *Farmer* v. *Arundel* (1772) 2 Wm.Bl. 824, 825–825, *per* De Grey C.J.; *Bize* v. *Dickason* (1786) 1 T.R. 285, 286–287, *per* Lord Mansfield; *Butler* v. *Harrison* (1772) 2 Cowp. 565, 566, *per* Lord Mansfield. See, generally, Ames, *Lectures*, pp. 160–164; Jackson, *History*, pp. 57–59; *Tomkins* v. *Bernet* (1693) Salk. 22; *Att.-Gen.* v. *Perry* (1733) 2 Comyns 481, 491, *per curiam*; (1943) 59 L.Q.R. 327, 333, n. 41 [Winfield].

[6-7] *Cf.* the Reporters' *Notes* to § 44 of the *Restatement of Restitution*.

[8] See the provisional recommendations of the Law Commission: Consultation Paper No. 120, *Restitution of Payments Made Under a Mistake of Law* (hereinafter cited in this Chapter as Law Commission, Consultation Paper, No. 120), paras. 2.36–2.37; and below pp. 144 *et seq.*

[9] *Woolwich Equitable Building Society* v. *Commissioners of Inland Revenue* [1993] A.C. 70, 165, 173, *per* Lord Goff; *Hydro Electric Commission of the Township of Nepean* v. *Ontario Hydro* (1982) 132 D.L.R. (3d.) 193, 206–207, *per* Dickson J., dissenting; see below, pp. 50 *et seq.*

[10] [1936] 3 All E.R. 875, 883. See also *Martindale* v. *Falkner* (1846) 2 C.B. 706, 719, *per* Maule J.; *R.* v. *Mayor of Tewkesbury* (1868) L.R. 3 Q.B. 629, *per* Blackburn J.

[11] *Cf. Woolwich Equitable Building Society* v. *Commissioners of Inland Revenue* [1993] A.C. 70, 165, 173, *per* Lord Goff: see below, Chap. 24.

recoverable had the mistake been one of fact.[12] The essential difference between a restitutionary claim arising from a mistake of law rather than of fact is
that the limiting principle, that benefits conferred in submission to an honest
claim are irrecoverable, assumes significant importance if the payer's mistake
is one of law. But it is only in rare cases that a plaintiff's claim is defeated
because he has voluntarily assumed the risk of his own mistake of fact.[13]

Many of the English cases where recovery has been denied because of
mistake of law are examples of payments to close transactions in settlement of
honest claims. But judges have not usually given that reason for dismissing the
plaintiff's action. At times they have been content simply to reiterate that
ignorantia juris non excusat.[14] On other occasions, in order to grant restitution
and to escape from the supposed rule in *Bilbie* v. *Lumley*, what might well have
been categorised as a mistake of law has been treated as a mistake of fact.[15] And
in cases where equitable relief has been sought, an unreal distinction has been
drawn between a mistake of "general law" and a mistake as to "private rights"
which is characterised as a mistake of fact.[16] The courts have not therefore
always addressed themselves to the key question: did the payer make his
payment in submission to an honest claim?[17] It is to be hoped that in the future
the courts will have regard to this underlying principle rather than simply
apply the maxim *ignorantia juris non excusat*. As Latham C.J. once said in the
High Court of Australia,[17a] in dismissing a claim to recover sales tax on
second-hand goods which had been held in independent litigation not to be
subject to that tax:

> "If a person instead of contesting a claim elects to pay the money in order
> to discharge it, he cannot, thereafter, because he finds out that he might
> have successfully contested the claim, recover the money which he so paid
> merely on the ground that he made a mistake of law."

The future?

As long ago as 1948 the Privy Council held that the common law rule of

---

[12] *Hydro Electric Commission of the Township of Nepean* v. *Ontario Hydro* (1982) 132 D.L.R. (3d)
193, 206–207, *per* Dickson J., dissenting, whose dissent was subsequently adopted by the
majority of the Supreme Court of Canada in *Air Canada and Pacific Western Airlines Ltd.* v. *R. in
Right of British Columbia* [1989] 4 W.W.R. 97.

[13] See above, pp. 127–130.

[14] *e.g. Sawyer and Vincent* v. *Window Brace Ltd.* [1943] 1 K.B. 32.

[15] *e.g. George (Porky) Jacobs Enterprises Ltd.* v. *City of Regina*, 1964 S.C.R. 326. The burden of
demonstrating that the mistake is one of fact is on the person who asserts that the mistake was of
fact not law: *Avon County Council* v. *Howlett* [1983] 1 W.L.R. 605, 620, *per* Slade L.J.

[16] *e.g. Stanley Brothers Ltd.* v. *Corporation of Nuneaton* (1912) 107 L.T. 760; *cf Hunter* v. *Bradford
Property Trust*, 1970 S.L.T. 173. See also *Stone* v. *Stone*, 29 N.W. 2d 271 (1947). The distinction
was originally drawn by Lord Westbury in *Cooper* v. *Phibbs* (1867) L.R. 2 H.L. 149, 170;
discussed further below, p. 213.

[17] *Cf. Restatement of Restitution*, § 45.

[17a] *Werrin* v. *The Commonwealth* (1938) 59 C.L.R. 150, 159. See also *David Securities Pty. Ltd.* v.
Commonwealth Bank of Australia (1992) 66 A.L.J.R. 786, 775.

non-recovery of moneys paid under a mistake of law must give way to the clear language of the Indian Contract Act.[18] More and more common law jurisdictions have enacted legislation which provides in essence that relief shall not be denied merely because the mistake was one of law rather than fact.[19] The English Law Commission[20] and Commonwealth Law Commissions[21] unite in their condemnation of the non-recovery rule. The majority of the Supreme Court of Canada has not waited for Canadian legislatures to act. It now accepts that "the distinction between mistake of fact and law should play no part in the law of restitution."[22] More recently, both the High Court of Australia and the Appellate Division of the Supreme Court of South Africa have reached a similar conclusion.[22a] Whether Parliament will ever enact any proposals which may be made by the English Law Commission is, given the pressures on Parliamentary time and the sensitivity of Whitehall, problematical.

---

[18] *Shiba Prasad Singh* v. *Srish Chandra Nandi* 1948 A.I.R.P.C. 297, interpreting s.72 of the Act which reads as follows: "a person to whom money has been paid, or anything delivered, by mistake or coercion must repay or return it."

[19] Including New York (Civil Practice Act, amended 1942, para. 112f.); New Zealand (Judicature Amendment Act 1958, s.94A, on which see R.J. Sutton, *The A. G. Davis Essays*, p. 218), and Western Australia (Law Reform (Property, Perpetuities and Succession) Act 1962, s.23, interpreted in *Bell Bros.* v. *Shire of Serpentine-Jarrahdale* [1969] W.A.R. 104, [1969] W.A.R. 155, C.A.; rev'd on different grounds (1969) 121 C.L.R. 137 (Aust.H.Ct.)). Connecticut and Kentucky will allow recovery even if the mistake is a mistake of law provided that the "recipient had no right in good conscience to retain the money": see, for example, *Scott* v. *The Board of Trustees of Newcastle*, 116 S.W. 788 (1909). California, Montana, Oklahoma, North Dakota and South Dakota have adopted the provisions of the Field Code which also allow recovery in certain circumstances if the payer acted under a mistake of law. The interpretation of this legislation has, however, not been startling. Oklahoma and North Dakota (*Chrysler Light & Power Co.* v. *City of Belfield*, 58 N.D. 39 (1929); (1935) 4 *Fordham Law Rerview* 468, n. 17) have held that the Code provisions do not exclude the common law rule in *Bilbie* v. *Lumley*, while California has held that recovery will be permitted only if the payment is involuntary; see *Gregory* v. *Cladbrough's Executors*, 129 Cal. 475 (1900); Cal. Civil Code, 1949, §§ 1576, 1578. The approach of the New York courts is also cautious; see New York Civil Practice Act, para. 112f; Report of New York Law Revision Commission, Leg.Doc (1942) No. 65(B) at p. 5; *Mercury Machine Importing Corp.* v. *City of New York*, 144 N.E. 2d 400 (1957).
See generally Palmer, *op. cit.* Vol. III, § 14.27; (1979) 10 Man. L.J. 23, 42–47 [Knutson]; (1980) Osgoode Hall L.J. 428, 465–477 [Lange].
Cf. article 1047 of the Quebec Civil Code. For a discussion of the Continental law, see Zweigert and Kötz, *op. cit.* pp. 606 *et seq.*

[20] Law Commission, Consultation Paper, No. 120.

[21] Law Reform Commission of British Columbia, "Report on Benefits conferred under a Mistake of Law" (Vancouver 1981); Law Reform Committee of South Australia, "Report Relating to the Recoverability of Benefits Obtained by Reason of Mistake of Law" (1984); New South Wales Law Reform Commission, "Restitution of Benefits Conferred Under Mistake of Law" (Sydney 1987).

[22] *Air Canada* v. *British Columbia* [1989] 4 W.W.R. 97, 126–130, *per* La Forest J. (Lamer and L'Heureux-Dube JJ. concurring), following the dissenting judgment of Dickson J. in *Nepean Hydro Electric Comm.* v. *Ontario Hydro* [1982] 1 S.C.R. 347, 362 *et seq.* Wilson J., who dissented, also thought that no distinction should be drawn between a mistake of fact and law. Beetz and McIntyre JJ. decided the case on other grounds.

[22a] *David Securities Pty. Ltd.* v. *Commonwealth Bank of Australia* (1992) 68 A.L.J.R. 768; *Willis Faber Enthoven (Pty.) Ltd.* v. *Receiver of Revenue* 1992 (4) S.A. 202. Both cases are discussed in [1993] C.L.J. 225 [Jones].

In *R.* v. *Tower Hamlets London Borough Council, ex p. Chetnik Developments Ltd.*,[23] it was assumed[24] that money paid under mistake of law is generally irrecoverable and that Chetnik could recover payments made to the rating authority only if it could bring itself within one of the exceptions to the rule in *Bilbie* v. *Lumley*; seemingly, counsel did not invite the House to reject the rule. Whether it will do so is conjectural. In *Woolwich Equitable Building Society* v. *Commissioners of Inland Revenue*,[25] Lord Keith was of the opinion that the rule was "too deeply embedded in English jurisprudence to be uprooted judicially." But Lord Slynn thought that it was open to review by the House of Lords[26] and the other law Lords did not suggest otherwise.[26a] It is to be hoped that such a review would, where appropriate, be undertaken. Any judicial reform must necessarily be cautiously pragmatic. But the principle that money paid under mistake, whether of fact or law, is recoverable is manifestly a desirable one. It is admittedly a generous principle. However, the payer's claim for repayment should fail if the recipient can demonstrate that the payment was the product of a compromise, made in settlement of an honest claim[27] or (as a general rule) was paid in consequence of threatened or actual legal proceedings for its recovery.[28] The recipient will also have his defences: in particular, the defence of change of position.[29] Moreover, the plaintiff's restitutionary claim should in any event fail if the payment was made in reliance on a judicial decision which is subsequently overruled by statute or in independent litigation brought by a third party.[29a]

The application of the "rule" in Bilbie v. Lumley

Although many cases where a payer failed to recover a payment made under a mistake of law are consistent with the principle that a payment made in submission to an honest claim cannot be recovered, some claims have, regrettably, failed when a comparable claim, based on a mistake of fact and not law, would have succeeded. As will be seen,[30] the severity of the rule in *Bilbie* v. *Lumley* has from time to time been mitigated; and equity grants its remedies, such as rectification, even though a donor acted under a mistake of law. The cases fall into four main groups:

(a) where the "rule" in *Bilbie* v. *Lumley* has been invoked to preclude recovery of money paid under a mistake of law;

(b) where money paid under a mistake of law may be recoverable because the payment was not a voluntary payment;

---

[23] [1988] A.C. 858: see below, p. 156.
[24] At pp. 876–877, *per* Lord Bridge.
[25] [1993] A.C. 70, 154.
[26] At p. 199.
[26a] *Cf.* at p. 164, *per* Lord Goff.
[27] See above, pp. 50–54.
[28] *Ibid.*
[29] Chap. 40.
[29a] See below, pp. 148–149; and [1993] C.L.J. 225 [Jones].
[30] See below, pp. 150 *et seq.*

(c) where recovery of money paid under a mistake of law has been allowed for special reasons;

(d) where gifts have been made under a mistake of law.

We shall now discuss the case law under these four heads.

(a) *Cases where the "Rule" in Bilbie v. Lumley has been Invoked to Preclude Recovery of Money Paid under a Mistake of Law*

The following groups of cases, although not comprehensive,[31] illustrate some of the more common instances where recovery has been denied under the principle in *Bilbie* v. *Lumley*.

Money paid in consequence of the mistaken construction of a statute

In *Woolwich Equitable Building Society* v. *Commissioners of Inland Revenue*[32] the House of Lords held, Lord Keith and Lord Jauncey dissenting, that the plaintiff could recover, with interest, payments made, not under mistake but under protest, in pursuance of an *ultra vires* demand by the Revenue.[33] The authority of the rule in *Bilbie* v. *Lumley* was not therefore before the House. However, there are cautious dicta which suggest that a taxpayer should likewise be entitled to recover any payment made to satisfy the demand of the Revenue or any public authority[34] if the demand was based on the misconstruction of an *intra vires* statute or statutory regulation.[35] It should be immaterial that the taxpayer shared the Revenue's or public authority's mistake[36] or paid under protest. The Supreme Court of Canada has reached a similar conclusion.[37]

The dicta are confined to this one situation. It may well be that it will unfortunately be necessary to distinguish those cases where the demand for payment is made by the Revenue or a public authority from those where the demand for payment is made by a private citizen. It is uncertain whether *National Pari-Mutuel Association Ltd.* v. *R.*,[38] where the Court of Appeal held that the suppliant company could not recover betting duty mistakenly paid as a result of their misconstruction of the Finance Act 1926, would now be decided in the same way. However, in *Woolwich* no member of the House suggested

---

[31] For a case where the payer discharges another's liability under a mistake of law, see *Hydro Electric Commission of the Township of Nepean* v. *Ontario Hydro* (1982) 132 D.L.R. (3d) 193.

[32] [1993] A.C. 70.

[33] See below, Chap. 24 for a full discussion.

[34] On the distinction, see below, pp. 549–550.

[35] [1993] A.C. 70, 177, *per* Lord Goff, 205, *per* Lord Slynn.

[36] There are dicta in the *Woolwich* case which lead to the conclusion that if the taxpayer had paid under a mistake of law he should nonetheless be able to recover the payments with interest: [1993] A.C. 70, 205, *per* Lord Slynn.

[37] In *Air Canada* v. *British Columbia* [1989] 4 W.W.R. 137.

[38] (1930) 47 T.L.R. 110. Overpayments of tax under mistake may now be recoverable: see below, pp. 161–162.

that this, and comparable decisions,[39] were wrongly decided.[40] It is possible that, on similar facts, the plaintiff's claim may still fail but on grounds other than that of mistake of law. For example, *Whiteley Ltd.* v. *R.*,[41] where Walton J. held that the plaintiff's claim failed, *inter alia*, on the ground of mistake of law, can now be seen as an illustration of the principle that a voluntary payment, made to close a transaction, is irrecoverable.[42]

The other group of cases, where the demand was made by a private citizen, is represented by such decisions as *Sharp Bros. & Knight* v. *Chant*.[43] A tenant paid his landlord's increased demand for rent in ignorance of the fact that this increase was beyond the standard rent permitted under the Increase of Rent and Mortgage Interest (War Restrictions) Act 1915. It was held that the landlord's demand was not illegal and the tenant's claim for repayment must fail, his payment being in law a voluntary payment.

It is sound principle that payments made to close a transaction and to settle an honest claim are irrecoverable. It should also be a sound principle that money paid under mistake is recoverable. If the mistake is one of law, then there may be a tension between the two principles. Decisions such as *Sharp Bros. & Knight* v. *Chant* are, arguably, erroneous applications of the former principle, for the tenant was in all probability not aware, at the time of the payment, that there was any question that the defendant was not entitled to make his demand.

Money paid in reliance on judicial decisions subsequently overruled by statute or in independent litigation brought by a third party[43a]

The courts have denied recovery of money paid in reliance on a judicial decision which is subsequently overruled. In *Henderson* v. *The Folkestone Waterworks Co. Ltd.*[44] a divisional court refused relief to the plaintiff who had paid the defendants' charges on the faith of a Court of Appeal decision, later overruled in the House of Lords. "Can it be," inquired Lord Coleridge C.J. in the course of argument, "that every reversal of a decision may give rise to hundreds of actions to recover back money previously paid?"[45] Lord Greene

---

[39] *Slater* v. *The Mayor of Burnley* (1988) 59 L.T. 636; *Stanley Bros.* v. *Nuneaton Corp.* (1913) 108 L.T. 986.

[40] [1993] A.C. 70, 158, *per* Lord Keith, 165, *per* Lord Goff.

[41] (1909) 26 T.L.R. 19.

[42] See [1993] A.C. 70, 157, *per* Lord Keith, 165, *per* Lord Goff, 183–184, *per* Lord Jauncey, 204, *per* Lord Slynn.

[43] [1917] 1 K.B. 771. See also *Finck* v. *Tranter* [1905] 1 K.B. 427; *Andrew* v. *Bridgman* [1908] 1 K.B. 596; *Hill* v. *Kirshenstein* [1920] 3 K.B. 556; *Aktieselskabet Dampskibs Steinstad* v. *W. Pearson Hall Co. Ltd.* (1924) 43 T.L.R. 531.

[43a] *Cf.* below p. 165.

[44] (1885) 1 T.L.R. 329; see also *Platt* v. *Bromage* (1854) 24 L.J.Ex. 63; *R.* v. *Blenkinsop* [1892] 1 Q.B. 43; *Cushen* v. *Hamilton Corp.* (1920) 4 Ont.L.R. 265; *Julian* v. *Auckland Corp.* [1927] N.Z.L.R. 453; *Werrin* v. *The Commonwealth* (1938) 59 C.L.R. 150.

[45] At p. 329.

put the matter as forcibly in *Derrick* v. *Williams*,[46] where a settlement had been reached on the basis that damages could not be recovered for the loss of expectation of life, a proposition which the House of Lords later rejected.[47] He said:

> "It would be an intolerable hardship on successful litigants if, in circumstances such as these, their opponents were entitled to harass them with further litigation because their view of the law had turned out to be wrong."[48]

Money paid under covenants which have been misconstrued

English courts have consistently refused restitution to those who have sought to recover payments which were made in consequence of a mistaken construction of a particular deed.[49] Covenantors who are led by a mistake of law to misconstrue their covenants have been denied recovery of any consequential overpayments. So, in *Re Hatch*,[50] a husband covenanted to pay his wife £200 per annum instead of permanent alimony. He paid the annuity without exercising his right to deduct tax. Sargant J. held that the overpayments could neither be recovered as a debt nor deducted from future payments of the annuity.[51] The court did not attempt to determine whether the payee did or did not make an honest claim on the payer.[52] The *Restatement of Restitution* has sought to explain comparable decisions on the ground that the payee "is entitled to retain what he has received if, because of a mistake of law, he does not know when he learns of the transfer and for what it was given, that he was not entitled to it"[53]; it is not essential that he demand performance. This rationalisation gains some support from the English cases. But it is not convincing. The recipient is fully protected by the defence of change of position, which the House of Lords has now recognised.[54] It is unfortunate that English

---

[46] [1939] 2 All E.R. 559.

[47] In *Rose* v. *Ford* [1937] A.C. 826.

[48] At p. 565. Even those jurisdictions which have apparently rejected the principle of *ignorantia juris non excusat* have accepted that money paid in consequence of the mistaken construction of a statute or in reliance on a judicial decision subsequently reversed or overruled cannot be recovered. The plaintiff's action has been dismissed on one of three grounds: that he, knowing of the doubtful validity of the defendant's demand, nonetheless paid; that it would be against public policy to allow recovery; or that he was not mistaken at all. Some jurisdictions have been equally unsympathetic to claims to recover taxes paid under mistake of law: *e.g.* see *Mercury Machine Importing Corp.* v. *City of New York*, 144 N.E. 2d 400 (1957); Palmer, *op. cit.* Vol. II, §14.27(g); and see above, n. 9.

[49] The line of authority (which dates from the 18th century) is not, however, very substantial. The earlier cases are reported cursorily: see *Atwood* v. *Lamprey* (1719), cited in a note to *East* v. *Thornbury* (1734) 3 P.Wms. 127; *Warren* v. *Warren* (1895) 72 L.T. 628; *Shrewsbury* v. *Shrewsbury* (1906) 23 T.L.R. 100.

[50] [1919] 1 Ch. 351. See also *Ord* v. *Ord* [1923] 2 K.B. 432.

[51] For the right of a trustee who overpays a beneficiary, see below, pp. 154–155.

[52] *e.g.* in *Re Hatch*, a leading decision, counsel's *admission* that the money was irrecoverable was said by Sargant J. to be correct: [1919] 1 Ch. 351, 354, 356.

[53] *Restatement of Restitution*, p. 186.

[54] *Lipkin Gorman (A Firm)* v. *Karpnale Ltd.* [1991] 2 A.C. 548, see Chaps. 2 and 40.

judges have not sought to distinguish between "a genuine *compromise*, the parties knowing that they may be surrendering legal rights, and a settlement made 'under the name of a compromise' but really in total and unconscious ignorance that any possible legal right is yielded."[55]

When granting equitable relief Chancery judges have been more ready to circumvent the authority of *Bilbie* v. *Lumley*, for example, by characterising a mistake as to "private rights" as a mistake of fact.[56] They have also been sensitive to the distinction between conscious and unconscious ignorance of the law.[57] But the "reason of the doctrine" that "litigation is not to be multiplied," by disputing again demands which have been given up or compromised, "applies equally to suits [in equity]."[58] As Sir John Leach V.-C said in *Naylor* v. *Winch*[59]:

> "If a party, acting in ignorance of a plain and settled principle of law, is induced to give up a portion of his indisputable property to another under the name of a compromise, a Court of Equity will relieve him from the effect of his mistake. But where a doubtful question arises ... it is extremely reasonable that parties should terminate their differences by dividing the stake between them, in the proportions which may be agreed upon."

Equity has not therefore attempted to impugn the authority of those common law decisions which deny a plaintiff the right to recover money paid under a mistake of law, arising from the mistaken construction of a statute or from reliance on a judicial decision subsequently reversed or overruled or from the misconstruction of a covenant.[60] But next-of-kin have been allowed to recover money paid to a charity because of the mistake of law of their executors.[61]

(b) *Cases where Money Paid under a Mistake of Law may be Recoverable because the Payment was not a Voluntary Payment*

If the money has been paid under a mistake of law induced by the payee's fraud, oppression,[62] undue influence or breach of fiduciary relationship, or if

---

[55] Woodward, *op. cit.*, p. 68. The application of this distinction may admittedly not always be easy; *e.g.* the payee may be a minor who is incapable in law of making a demand.

[56] *Cooper* v. *Phibbs* (1867) L.R. 2 H.L. 149. See, generally, (1943) 59 L.Q.R. 327, 328–329 [Winfield].

[57] *Cf. Naylor* v. *Winch* (1824) 1 Sim. & St. 555.

[58] *Goodman* v. *Sayers* (1820) 2 J. & W. 249, 263, *per* Sir Thomas Plumer M.R.

[59] (1824) 1 Sim. & St. 555, 564–565; see also *Rogers* v. *Ingham* (1876) 3 Ch.D. 351, 355, *per* James L.J.

[60] *Nicholls* v. *Leeson* (1747) 3 Atk. 573, 575, *per* Lord Hardwicke L.C.

[61] *Re Diplock* [1948] Ch. 465, [1951] A.C. 251; see below, pp. 85–86.

[62] *Rogers* v. *Ingham* (1876) 3 Ch.D. 351, 355–356, *per* James L.J. A simple demand for payment by the Revenue or some other public authority does not amount in law to illegitimate pressure. In exceptional cases such a payment may be voluntary, if, despite the oppression, there is a real intention to close the transaction: see *Maskell* v. *Horner* [1915] 3 K.B. 106, 118, *per* Lord Reading C.L.; see below, pp. 268 *et seq.*

the money has been received by the payee in bad faith, it may be recoverable. A payee may act in bad faith if he knows that the payer made the payment under mistake of law.[63]

Even if the payment is made under an illegal contract, the payer can recover if he was not *in pari delicto* with the payee.[64] In *Kiriri Cotton Co. Ltd.* v. *Ranchoddas Keshavji Dewani*,[65] the appellants had let a flat to the respondents. In consideration for the lease they had obtained from the respondents, contrary to the provisions of the Uganda Rent Restriction Ordinance 1949, a premium of 10,000 shillings. At the time of the demand and payment neither party realised that the demand was illegal. The respondents, who had occupied the flat, claimed that the premium was money received by the appellants to their use, a claim which the Court of Appeal for Eastern Africa upheld. In their argument before the Judicial Committee of the Privy Council, the appellants claimed that the payments were voluntary and therefore irrecoverable. Lord Denning, who delivered the advice of the Board, accepted the general principle, stated by Littledale J. in *Hastelow* v. *Jackson*,[66] that "if two parties enter into an illegal contract, and money is paid upon it by one to the other, that may be recovered back before the execution of the contract, but not afterwards." But he held that, even if the contract was executed, as it was, the payer was entitled to recover provided that he was not *in pari delicto* with the payee; though if the parties were on equal terms, the plaintiff could not recover merely because he mistook the law.[67] Here the parties were not *in pari delicto*. The Rent Restriction Ordinance was passed with the object of protecting the tenant and the duty of observing the law was placed by that legislation on the shoulders of the landlord. The tenant was, therefore, entitled to recover his premium in an action for money had and received.[68] As Lord Denning said:

> "It is not correct to say that everyone is presumed to know the law. The true proposition is that no man can excuse himself from doing his duty by saying that he did not know the law on the matter. *Ignorantia juris neminem excusat.* Nor is it correct to say that money paid under a mistake of law can never be recovered back. The true proposition is that money paid under a mistake of law, by itself and without more, cannot be recovered

---

[63] *Ward & Co.* v. *Wallis* [1900] 1 Q.B. 675, 678, *per* Kennedy J.; see also *Nicholls* v. *Leeson* (1747) 3 Atk. 573, 575, *per* Lord Hardwicke.

[64] *Smith* v. *Bromley* (1760) 2 Doug. K.B. 696: see below, pp. 506–507, for a full discussion.

[65] [1960] A.C. 192; see also *Amar Singh* v. *Kulubya* [1964] A.C. 142; *Rogers* v. *Louth C.C.*: [1981] I.R. 268. And *cf. Shelley* v. *Paddock* [1980] Q.B. 348 (parties not *in pari delicto*; damages for fraud).

[66] (1828) 8 B. & C. 221, 226.

[67] [1960] A.C. 192, 204.

[68] In some cases, a payer may recover his money by virtue of an implied right of action arising under the statute which has rendered the payment illegal. This question was discussed in *Green* v. *Portsmouth Stadium Ltd.* [1953] 2 Q.B. 190; see below, pp. 508–509 for a discussion and a reconciliation of this case with *Kiriri's* case.

back. . . .[69] If there is something more in addition to a mistake of law—if there is something in the defendant's conduct which shows that, of the two of them, he is the one primarily responsible for the mistake—then it may be recovered back. Thus, if as between the two of them the duty of observing the law is placed on the shoulders of the one rather than the other—it being imposed on him specially for the protection of the other— then they are not *in pari delicto* and the money can be recovered back. . . .[70] Likewise, if the responsibility for the mistake lies more on the one than the other—because he has misled the other when he ought to know better—then again they are not *in pari delicto* and the money can be recovered back."[71]

In *Eadie* v. *Township of Brantford*[72] the Supreme Court of Canada adopted and extended Lord Denning's observations in the *Kiriri Cotton* case. The appellant owned a large parcel of land in the respondent township. He had wanted to subdivide and sell it but had abandoned the plan when told of the township's conditions for planning permission. Because of prolonged illness he was, however, forced to sell. He gave instructions to put through a severance application to subdivide the land and did not object to the township's terms, which were a fee of $400 per lot and a certain footage of land for improved highway works. A year later the by-laws, under which these demands were made, were declared invalid in litigation brought by another landowner. The appellant then sought to recover what he had paid and to annul the transfer of the land. The Supreme Court of Canada, Judson and Ritchie JJ. dissenting, held that the appellant could succeed. The payments and conveyance were made under practical compulsion.[73] Moreover, because the parties were not *in pari delicto*, it was not fatal that they were made under a mistake of law:

> "the clerk-treasurer [of the Township] was under a duty towards the appellant and other taxpayers of the municipality. When [he] demands payment of a sum of money on the basis of an illegal by-law despite the fact that he does not then know of its illegality, he is not *in pari delicto* with the taxpayer who is required to pay that sum."[74]

This was a novel extension of *Kiriri Cotton*, for the transaction in *Eadie* could hardly be described as illegal or unlawful.[75] In *Hydro Electric Commission of the*

---

[69] Citing *Rogers* v. *Ingham* (1876) 3 Ch.D. 351, 355, *per* James L.J.

[70] Citing *Browning* v. *Morris* (1778) 2 Cowp. 790, 792, *per* Lord Mansfield.

[71] Citing *Harse* v. *Pearl Life Assurance Co.* [1904] 1 K.B. 558, 564, *per* Romer L.J.

[72] (1967) 63 D.L.R. (2d) 561; criticised in (1967) 17 U. Toronto L.J. 344, 352–354 [Crawford].

[73] See below, p. 246. Contrast *G. Gordon Foster Developments* v. *Township of Langley* (1979) 102 D.L.R. (3d) 730 (British Columbia Sup. Ct.)

[74] (1967) 63 D.L.R. (2d) 561, 572, *per* Spence J., citing *Kiriri Cotton Co.* v. *Dewani* [1960] A.C. 192, 204, *per* Lord Denning: see above, p. 151.

[75] *Cf. Andrew* v. *Bridgeman* [1908] 1 K.B. 596; *Sharp Bros. & Knight* v. *Chant* [1917] 1 K.B. 771.

Township of Nepean v. *Ontario Hydro*[76] Estey J., giving the judgment of the Supreme Court of Canada, doubted[77] whether this was a proper application of the *in pari delicto* principle. In his view, in *Eadie* "the presence of mistake of law in the parties to a transaction was superfluous as the entitlement to recovery arose on the finding of payment under practical compulsion."[78]

Kiriri Cotton Co. v. *Dewani* may also be contrasted with the decision of the Court of Appeal in *Harse* v. *The Pearl Life Assurance Co.*[79] The agent of the defendant company had honestly represented to the plaintiff that an insurance effected by the plaintiff on the life of his mother would be a valid insurance. The plaintiff, relying on his representation, took out the policy and, on discovering that it was illegal, sued the defendant company to recover the premiums. The Court of Appeal held that the premiums were irrecoverable. Collins M.R. said that the payer was "in the position of a person, who has made an illegal contract and has sustained a loss in consequence of a misstatement of law, and must submit to that loss."[80] There was no fraud, oppression, duress "or difference in the position of the parties which created a fiduciary relationship to the plaintiff so as to make it inequitable for the defendants to insist on the bargain that they had made with the plaintiff."[81] *Harse's* case is clearly a hard decision and it is debatable whether the Court of Appeal was right to conclude[82] that the agents of insurance companies are under no greater obligation to know the law than the persons they approach.

Whether damages are now recoverable in such a case under the Misrepresentation Act 1967 is open to doubt, since section 2(1) of that Act, which creates a new statutory liability in damages for misrepresentation, can be construed as referring only to misrepresentations of fact.[83]

---

[76] (1982) 132 D.L.R. (3d) 193.

[77] For a suggestion, now supported by *R.* v. *Tower Hamlets L.B.C., ex p. Chetnik Developments Ltd.* [1988] A.C. 858 (see below, p. 156), that the rule in *ex p. James* (payments made to officers of the court and to public bodies may be recoverable) would support the Court's decision; see Maddaugh and McCamus, *op. cit.* pp. 268–269.

[78] At p. 241. For Estey J.'s interpretation of *Kiriri Cotton*, see pp. 226–229; he clearly found some difficulty in reconciling this case with *Green* v. *Portsmouth Stadium Ltd.* [1953] 2 Q.B. 190: see below, p. 508–509. But contrast Dickson J., at p. 211, dissenting on this point.

[79] [1904] 1 K.B. 558; followed in *Evanson* v. *Crooks* (1911) 106 L.T. 264. See Lord Denning's comment on *Harse's* case in *Kiriri Cotton Co.* v. *Dewani* [1960] A.C. 192, 204.

[80] At p. 563.

[81] At p. 563.

[82] *Cf. The British Workmen's and General Assurance Co. Ltd.* v. *Cunliffe* (1902) 18 T.L.R. 502, which Collins M.R. distinguished in *Harse's* case on the ground that there the representation was fraudulent; see also *Hughes* v. *Liverpool Victoria Legal Friendly Society* [1916] 2 K.B. 482, 486, *per* Swinfen Eady L.J., 491, *per* Phillimore L.J., 495, *per* Bankes L.J. But in the *British Workmen's* case, Lord Alverstone C.J. had expressly denied there was any fraud: see (1902) 18 T.L.R. 425.

[83] For s.2(1) provides that the person making the representation can escape liability if he proves that he has reasonable grounds to believe and did believe that "the *facts* represented were true." (Italics supplied).

(c) *Where Recovery of Money Paid under a Mistake of Law has been Allowed for Special Reasons*

Payments made by personal representatives and trustees

After some early hesitation[84] it is now well established that the courts will allow a trustee or a personal representative to deduct sums overpaid under a mistake of law from future instalments due to the overpaid beneficiary. In *Dibbs* v. *Goren*[85] Lord Langdale M.R. permitted a trustee to deduct such sums from other funds due to a legatee; and in *Re Musgrave*[86] a trustee who had failed through a mistake of law to deduct income tax from payments of annuities, was allowed to deduct from future payments the amount of the tax which he had failed to deduct from previous payments.[87] Indeed a trustee will have a lien over the trust fund for this purpose, and his claim will therefore prevail over the creditors of an insolvent beneficiary.[87a] The court will always correct, in the administration of a trust, errors of account between trustees and beneficiaries. Only if the trustee is himself a beneficiary and inadvertently underpays himself and overpays his fellow beneficiaries will the court deny restitution. "Any equity that he might have had in his character of beneficiary is displaced by the fact that he is himself responsible for the mistake which has been made."[88]

The authority for this limitation is the decision of Warrington J. in *Re Horne*[89] which, though commented upon in later cases, has been neither followed nor challenged. *Re Horne* is a hard case. Innocent trustees acting bona fide should not be treated with the severity of former days,[90] and there is much to be said for allowing a trustee-beneficiary to adjust accounts by deducting the overpayments from future payments due to overpaid beneficiaries, subject to the beneficiaries being able to invoke any special defences which may be open to them.[91]

There seems to be no English[92] case, however, where a trustee or personal representative has directly recovered from the recipient money paid under a

---

[84] See *Currie* v. *Goold* (1817) 2 Madd. 163, where *Bilbie* v. *Lumley* (1802) 2 East 469, was cited.

[85] (1849) 11 Beav. 483, 484; see also *Livesy* v. *Livesy* (1827) 3 Russ. 287.

[86] [1916] 2 Ch. 417; *Re Robinson* [1911] 1 Ch. 502.

[87] See *Re Ainsworth* [1915] 2 Ch. 96; *Re Reading* [1916] W.N. 262 (distribution of residue); *Re Wooldridge* [1920] W.N. 78 (payment of balance due). *Cf. Re Sharp* [1906] 1 Ch. 793. In the context of a claim to recover overpayments of rates, it has been said that there is "no general principle that money paid under a mistake of law which is irrecoverable may nevertheless found a defence of equitable set off", and that it is anomalous to allow recovery by way of set-off when there is no direct right of recovery: see *R.* v. *Tower Hamlets L.B.C.*, *ex p. Chetnik Developments Ltd.* [1988] A.C. 858, 876–877, *per* Lord Bridge.

[87a] *Dibbs* v. *Goren* (1849) 11 Beav. 483; *Williams* v. *Allen (No. 2)* (1863) 32 Beav. 650.

[88] *Re Horne* [1905] 1 Ch. 76, 81, *per* Warrington J.; see also *Re Reading* [1916] W.N. 262.

[89] [1905] 1 Ch. 76.

[90] *Re Ainsworth* [1915] 2 Ch. 96, 105, *per* Joyce J.

[91] In principle the beneficiaries would, we suggest, have a good defence if they have changed their position in good faith in consequence of the overpayment: see below, Chaps. 29 and 40.

[92] But *cf. Old Colony Trust Co.* v. *Wood*, 321 Mass. 519 (1947); *Roach* v. *Underwood*, 192 Tenn. 378 (1950); *contra* cases cited in 147 A.L.R. 121 (1943).

mistake of law. It is generally assumed[93] that at law such a claim must fail because "the rule that the mistake...must be a mistake of fact is...of completely general application.[94] In equity there is no reported example of a successful action by a trustee or personal representative against a wrongly paid recipient. Nonetheless, in our view, a trustee or a personal representative should be entitled, as he is in the United States,[95] to recover payments made under a mistake of law, unless the recipient can rely on change of position or estoppel,[96] or the payment was made in satisfaction of an honest claim.[97] To deny recovery in such cases may result in considerable hardship to the trustee or personal representative[98] and in the unjust enrichment of the recipient.[99]

In *Re Robinson*[99a] there are dicta which suggest that a beneficiary can maintain a suit in equity against a co-beneficiary who has been over-paid; but it is a condition precedent of such a claim that he joins the trustee as a party to the action. Moreover, it is established that next of kin, legatees, or creditors, in claims arising out of the administration of an estate, may recover against a volunteer who has been wrongly paid as a result of the executors' mistake of law.[1] Whether a beneficiary of an *inter vivos* trust can recover in comparable circumstances is an open question.[2]

Where there is a contract for repayment

The payer may protect his position by exacting from the payee an undertaking that, in the event of the payment proving to be not legally due, it shall be repaid.[3]

---

[93] See, *e.g.* the argument in *Re Sharp* [1906] 1 Ch. 793, 795.

[94] *Re Diplock* [1947] Ch. 716, 725–726, *per* Wynn-Parry J.; see also [1948] Ch. 465, 479–480, *per curiam. Cf. Hunter's Trustees* v. *Hunter* (1894) 21 R. 949; *Rowan's Trustees* v. *Rowan*, 1940 S.L.T. 34.

[95] *Cf. Scott on Trusts*, pp. 2185–2186; *Old Colony Trust Co.* v. *Wood*, 74 N.E. 2d 141 (1947).

[96] See below, Chap. 40.

[97] See above, pp. 50–54.

[98] See below, Chap. 30.

[99] If the beneficiary induced the payment by consciously misrepresenting the law, the trustee should, even if the analogy of the American cases is rejected, be allowed to recover.

[99a] [1911] 1 Ch. 502, 507–508, *per* Warrington J.; see also *Re Mason* [1928] Ch. 385, 391–392, *per* Romer J. See generally, Harpum, *Knowing Assistance and Knowing Receipt: the Basis of Equitable Liability*, as yet unpublished.

[1] *Ministry of Health* v. *Simpson* [1951] A.C. 251: see below, Chap. 29.

[2] These questions are discussed below, Chap. 29.

[3] *Sebel Products Ltd.* v. *Commissioners of Customs and Excise* [1949] Ch. 409.
In *Woolwich Equitable Building Society* v. *Commissioners of Inland Revenue* [1993] A.C. 70, it was held that no such contract could be implied. Lord Goff accepted that in *Sebel Products* such an undertaking was given "(although the legal basis upon which Vaisey J. there inferred the existence of such an agreement may be open to criticism). On the other hand, the mere fact that money is paid under protest will not give rise of itself to the inference of such an agreement; though it may form part of the evidence from which it may be inferred that the payee did not intend to close the transaction": at pp. 165–166, citing *Maskell* v. *Horner* [1915] 3 K.B. 106, 120, *per* Lord Reading C.J.: see below pp. 268 *et seq.*

Payments made to officers of the court and to public bodies

(1) *The principle underlying the authorities*

There is a line of authority, the limits of which are by no means firmly drawn, which establishes that money paid to an officer of the court is recoverable even though paid under a mistake of law. In *Ex p. James*[4] it was debated whether a trustee in bankruptcy should be compelled to repay money obtained from an execution creditor who paid money to the trustee in the mistaken belief that he was entitled to the payment. James L.J. recognised that the principle of voluntary payment must "not be pressed too far." The trustee in bankruptcy was an officer of the court and the "court, then, finding that he has in his hands money which in equity belongs to someone else, ought to set an example to the world by paying it to the person really entitled to it. In my opinion the Court of Bankruptcy ought to be as honest as other people."[5]

In *R. v. Tower Hamlets L.B.C., ex p. Chetnik Developments Ltd.*[6] Lord Bridge concluded that the equity, to which James L.J. referred, is "not to an *equity* enforceable in a suit or action, but to a moral principle, which the court could expect to be observed by a public body such as a rating authority." The principle underlying the authorities is that:

> "... the retention of money known to have been paid under a mistake of law, although it is a course permitted to an ordinary litigant, is not regarded by the courts as a 'high-minded thing' to do, but rather as a 'shabby thing' or a 'dirty trick' and hence is a course which the court will not allow one of its own officers, such as a trustee in bankruptcy to take."[7]

Applying this principle, the House of Lords held that the rating authorities' statutory discretion to refuse to pay overpaid rates was not unfettered and had to be exercised in accordance with the statutory intention. In exercising that discretion the authorities should act in the same high-principled way expected by the court of its own officers. It ought not, therefore, to retain moneys paid under a mistake of law.

The *Tower Hamlets* case is then important for two reasons. First, it states unequivocally and authoritatively the principle underlying the authorities. Secondly, it is now clear that public bodies are expected to behave, in exercising a statutory decision to make repayments, in the same high-principled way as officers of the court.

(2) *The application of the rule in Ex parte James*

In *Re Carnac, ex p. Simmonds*,[8] where settlement trustees had paid under mistake of law surplus income to the trustee in bankruptcy of a debtor, Lord

---

[4] (1874) L.R. 9 Ch.App. 609; see also *Re Opera Ltd.* [1891] 2 Ch. 154, 161, *per* Kekewich J., reversed on other grounds, [1891] 3 Ch. 260.
[5] At p. 614.
[6] [1988] A.C. 858.
[7] At pp. 876–877.
[8] (1885) 16 Q.B.D. 308.

Esher emphasised that the rule is not confined to the Court of Bankruptcy. He said[9]:

> "If money had by a mistake of law come into the hands of an officer of a Court of Common Law, the court would order him to repay it so soon as the mistake was discovered. Of course, as between the litigant parties, even a Court of Equity would not prevent a litigant from doing a shabby thing. But I cannot help thinking that, if money had come into the hands of a receiver appointed by a Court of Equity through a mistake of law, the court would, when the mistake was discovered, order him to repay it."

The Court of Appeal, therefore, ordered the trustee in bankruptcy to refund the money if still in his hands and, to the extent that it had been applied in the payment of dividends, to repay it from other moneys subsequently coming into his hands and applicable to the payment of dividends. "The funds applicable to the payment of dividends to creditors have been erroneously increased by means of that payment to the trustee, and the question is whether the sum thus paid in error ought not to be repaid out of those funds."[10]

It is not necessary to invoke the principle in *Ex p. James* to prove that the officer acquired the money "by unworthy means." The question is whether it is "dishonourable for the officer of the Court, knowing the full facts, to use the money to pay [the debtor's] creditors."[11] Moreover, it is only the acts of the officer of the court, and not the acts of third parties, which are critical in determining whether it is a "shabby thing" to retain the money paid under mistake.[12] As Younger L.J. emphasised in *Re Wigzell*,[13] it is essential to distinguish transactions initiated by the bankrupt himself from those initiated by the trustee or the court.

> "[I]n considering the extent of this particular jurisdiction it is quite vital to distinguish between a trustee not insisting or the Court not permitting him to insist on all the legal consequences of, on the one hand, a transaction initiated by himself or by the Court in the interests of the general body of creditors and on the other hand a transaction initiated by the bankrupt. In the first case the creditors are the constituents of the trustee throughout, and they are entitled to benefit by the transaction, so it does not seem to be wrong to say that they shall take it as it honourably is no

---

[9] (1885) 16 Q.B.D. 308, 312. See also *Re Brown* (1886) 32 Ch.D. 597; *Re Rhoades* [1899] 2 Q.B. 347; *Marshall Shipping Co.* v. *Board of Trade* [1923] 2 K.B. 343; *Re Tyler* [1907] 1 K.B. 865, 873, *per* Buckley L.J.; *Re Thellusson* [1919] 2 K.B. 735, 760–762, *per* Atkin L.J. *Quaere*, if a solicitor is an officer of the court for the purposes of this rule: *cf.* the Canadian case of *London Guarantee & Accident Co.* v. *Henderson, McWilliams* (1915) 8 W.W.R. 1260.

[10] At p. 313, *per* Cotton L.J. For the American cases, see Palmer, *op. cit.* Vol. III, § 14. 27(d).

[11] *Re Thellusson* [1919] 2 K.B. 735, 764, *per* Atkin L.J.

[12] *Re Thellusson* [1919] 2 K.B. 735, 749, *per* Warrington L.J.

[13] [1921] 2 K.B. 835, 869. In *Re Wigzell* the Court of Appeal confined *Re Thellusson* [1919] 2 K.B. 735 to its own special facts. See, generally, *Williams and Muir Hunter on Bankruptcy*, pp. 249–254.

more and no less. But in the second case the bankrupt has no consti-
tuents—that is to say, the transaction is initiated by him presumably in his
own interests alone—and it is not obvious that a creditor with whom that
transaction has been carried out and is complete, even one who in relation
to it may have been tricked by the bankrupt, has any equity at all as
against the other creditors of the same bankrupt, who may all have been
equally tricked, merely because in his case the proceeds of the transaction
cannot be traced amongst the bankrupt's assets, and in the other cases
they cannot . . .

[T]he general extension of this principle to transactions initiated by the
bankrupt as distinct from transactions initiated by the trustee is one which
in future cases will have to be very jealously guarded . . ."

For these reasons it was held not to be unconscionable for a trustee in
bankruptcy to reclaim from a bank sums paid in by the bankrupt between the
date of the receiving order and the date of the gazetting of the bankruptcy
without giving credit for sums paid out by the bank to the bankrupt.[14]

More recently, in *Re Byfield*,[15] Goulding J. applied Younger L.J.'s observations to defeat a bank's claim to recover money paid after its customer's
bankruptcy had been gazetted. The customer instructed the bank to transfer
£19,500 to her mother's account at another bank. The bank, in good faith and
without notice of the publication of the receiving order, did so and the mother
used £12,356 to pay off some of the bankrupt's creditors. The bank, having
repaid the trustee in bankruptcy, lodged a proof of debt on the ground that it
was entitled to be treated as an unpaid creditor because it would be unjust for
the trustee in bankruptcy (and the bankrupt's creditors) to benefit from its
payments. The judge held that the rule in *Ex p. James* had no application; for
the trustee in bankruptcy did not initiate the payment, it was the customer who
did so. In the judge's view, "there is nothing offensive either to commercial or
general morality in the general body of creditors receiving a benefit, a windfall,
if you will, from the bank's unfortunate payment."[16] The judge also rejected
the bank's claim to be subrogated to the rights of creditors paid off from the
bank's payment. The Bankruptcy (Amendment) Act 1926, s.4, protected
persons in the position of the bank only when the bankrupt's money was paid
after the date of the receiving order but before it had been gazetted.[17] Goulding
J. could not see why "good conscience and equity" should demand further
relief "beyond that which the statute has so marked out."[18] Consequently he
stopped his "ears to the siren song of unjust enrichment."[19] It is not easy to

---

[14] See now Insolvency Act 1986, s.284(5) and 307(4).

[15] [1982] Ch. 267.

[16] At p. 271.

[17] Thereby reversing *Re Wigzell* [1921] 2 K.B. 835; see above. But see now Insolvency Act 1986,
s.284(5): see above, p. 157.

[18] At p. 276. The judge emphasised that the bank had not made the payment for the express
purpose of paying off the creditors. *Sed quaere* if this would have affected his decision.

[19] At p. 276. But *cf.* above, p. 67.

accept that it is just to deny the bank's claim to be subrogated to the general creditors which it had paid off. The bankrupt's estate, and hence the creditors, obtained, in the judge's own words, a windfall. Moreover the policy underlying s.4 would arguably not have been frustrated if subrogation had been allowed.[20]

As *Re Byfield* demonstrates, the principle in *Ex p. James* is not restricted to payments made under mistake of law[21] though it assumes particular importance in this context because of the rule in *Bilbie* v. *Lumley*. But it is limited to payments made to officers of the court and does not therefore apply to payments to an executor or private trustee.[22]

This group of decisions is remarkable for more than one reason. In some of the cases the payer was allowed to recover money paid under mistake of law despite an honest claim by the trustee in bankruptcy.[23] In others the payer was in no position to submit an ordinary proof of a debt and yet the officer of the court was required to repay as he had "in his hands money which in equity belongs to someone else."[24] The money mistakenly paid is not deemed to constitute assets available for distribution among the bankrupt's general creditors, and the payer is therefore given priority over the general creditors because the court considers it just to do so.[25] It is not surprising that some judges have treated with reserve a principle which gives the court a "discretionary jurisdiction to disregard legal right . . . wherever the enforcement of legal right would, in the opinion of the Court, be contrary to natural justice"[26] and have said that it should be "applied with the greatest caution."[27]

In *Government of India* v. *Taylor*,[28] Lord Keith of Avenholm emphasised that the discretionary power of the court to compel repayment "appears to have been exercised only in cases where there has been some form of enrichment of the assets of a bankrupt or insolvent company at the expense of the person seeking recoupment"; and then, as Walton J. later said, only "to the extent necessary to nullify the enrichment of the estate."[29] But, in this context, benefit gained at another's expense has been restrictively and arguably too

---

[20] See above, p. 67. Contrast the approach of Oliver J. in *Taylor Fashions Ltd.* v. *Liverpool Trustees Co.* (1978) [1982] Q.B. 133: see below, pp. 169–170.

[21] See, *e.g. Re Tyler* [1907] 1 K.B. 865.

[22] *Re Sandiford (No. 2)* [1935] Ch. 681, 691, *per* Clauson J.; see also *Re London County Commercial Reinsurance Office Ltd.* [1992] 2 Ch. 67. But *cf. Eadie* v. *Township of Brantford* (1967) 62 D.L.R. (2d) 561, 570, *per* Spence J., who thought that there was much to be said for the view of the trial judge, that the position of a treasurer of a township was like that of a "highly placed Civil Servant . . . or an officer of the Court." See also *Re Hall* [1907] 1 K.B. 875. But see above, p. 153.

[23] See *Re Carnac* (1885) 16 Q.B.D. 308.

[24] *Re Tyler* [1907] 1 K.B. 865, 869, *per* Vaughan Williams L.J. See *Re Clark (a bankrupt)* [1975] 1 W.L.R. 559: see below, p. 160, n. 33.

[25] See above, Chap. 2.

[26] *Re Wigzell* [1921] 2 K.B. 835, 845, *per* Salter J. Scrutton L.J. was, predictably, one of their number: *Re Wigzell* [1921] 2 K.B. 385, 859.

[27] *Re Sandiford (No. 2)* [1935] Ch. 681, 691, *per* Clauson J.

[28] [1955] A.C. 491, 512–513. For exceptions, see *Re Clark (a bankrupt)* [1975] 1 W.L.R. 559, 563–564.

[29] *Re Clark (a bankrupt)* [1975] 1 W.L.R. 559, 564.

narrowly interpreted[30]; and the court's discretion has not been exercised "where there has been no enrichment of one party with corresponding loss to the other."[31] Consequently the court will not order repayment if the payments had not increased the bankrupt's assets but had simply diminished the number of claims on his estate. For that reason, in *Re Hall*[32] the mortgagees' claim failed since they had simply paid off the bankrupt's creditors in a composition in the mistaken belief that they were entitled under the mortgage to add the money so paid to their security.

As Clauson J. remarked in *Re Sandiford (No. 2)*[33] the reported cases go no further than this: "that where the trustee in bankruptcy, *during the bankruptcy*, has received certain moneys which in the view of the Court it is not honest for him to hold, the Court will, under certain circumstances, make him refund them." It has never been applied "so as to order the trustee in bankruptcy to return money, which *before the bankruptcy* had become indistinguishably mixed with the rest of the bankrupt's property." Consistently with this view the court will refuse to order creditors, to whom money has already been distributed, to refund what they have received.[34] The power to require an officer of the court to return money paid under mistake "should not be used unless the result of enforcing the law is such that, in the opinion of the Court, it would be pronounced to be obviously unjust by all right-minded men."[35]

Public moneys paid without legal authority

"No money can be taken out of the Consolidated Fund into which the revenues of the State have been paid, excepting under a distinct authorisation from Parliament itself. The days are long gone by in which the Crown, or its servants, apart from Parliament could give such an authorisation or ratify an improper payment. Any payment out of the Consolidated Fund made without Parliamentary authority is simply illegal and *ultra vires* and may be recovered by the Government if it can . . . be traced."[36] This right, which has never been

---

[30] *Cf.* above, Chap. 1.

[31] [1955] A.C. 491, 513, *per* Lord Keith of Avenholm. There is no necessity to point to an identifiable fund: see *Re Clark (a bankrupt)* [1975] 1 W.L.R. 559, 564, *per* Walton J. And *cf. Re Wyvern Developments Ltd.* [1974] 1 W.L.R. 1097, 1105, *per* Templeman J. For cases where the mistake of law did not enrich the trustee in bankruptcy, see *Re Gozzett* [1936] 1 All E.R. 79; *Re M.C.C. Precision Products Ltd.* (1972) 27 D.L.R. (3d) 4.

[32] [1907] 1 K.B. 875. The mortgagee had not made any payment to an officer of the court: see above, n. 22.

[33] [1935] Ch. 681, 691–692; italics supplied. Consequently the rule does not generally apply where the claimant can submit an ordinary proof of debt: *Re Clark (a bankrupt)* [1975] 1 W.L.R. 559, 563–564.

[34] *Ex p. Simmonds* (1885) 16 Q.B.D. 308, 314, *per* Lindley L.J.

[35] *Re Wigzell* [1921] 2 K.B. 835, 845, *per* Salter J.

[36] *Auckland Harbour Board* v. *R.* [1924] A.C. 318, 326–327, *per* Viscount Haldane. This was one of the "particular reasons" which led Lord Goff to conclude, in *Woolwich Equitable Building Society* v. *Commissioners of Inland Revenue* [1993] A.C. 70, 177, that the taxpayer was entitled to his repayments with interest.
The statement that the moneys can be *traced* is puzzling. In *Woolwich Equitable Building Society* v. *Commissioners of Inland Revenue* [1993] A.C. 70, 177, Lord Goff thought that Lord Haldane

questioned in any common law jurisdiction,[37] is so extensive that the recipient cannot plead that he changed his position in reliance on any representation that he was entitled to the money. For a "party cannot be assumed by the doctrine of estoppel to have lawfully done that which the law says he shall not do."[38]

Payment by the court

If the court pays out money under a mistake of law, it is recoverable. In *Re Birkbeck Permanent Benefit Building Society*[39] a contest arose, on the liquidation of the Society, between shareholders and other claimants who had deposited money with the Society under contracts which were *ultra vires* the Society.[40] The Official Receiver paid the shareholders in full before he received notice of the depositors' appeal to the House of Lords.[41] This appeal was partially successful and, on the application of the liquidator, the shareholders were ordered to repay the amount by which they had been overpaid. "The court has the right, and ought ... to make an order that the money, which has been overpaid by an official of the court, should be refunded."[42]

Mistake of foreign law

A mistake of foreign law is treated as a mistake of fact.[43] It is difficult to support this distinction between English and foreign law. Its only merit is that a plaintiff who makes a payment under a mistake of foreign law may recover his payment within the limits previously discussed.[44]

Recovery of tax from the Revenue

Special provision has been made in the Taxes Management Act 1970[45] for the determination of any application for relief from the payment of tax overpaid by the taxpayer to the Revenue, which has been charged under an assessment which was excessive by reason of some error or mistake in the return or statement made by him for the purposes of the assessment. The Board is directed to "give by way of repayment such relief ... in respect of the error or

---

meant that the claim was "proprietary in nature". In contrast, in *Commonwealth of Australia* v. *Burns* [1971] V.R. 825, 828, Newton J., sitting in the Supreme Court of Victoria, concluded that Lord Haldane was referring to *tracing* the "identity of the recipient of the money" for the facts do not suggest that the moneys were identifiable in his hands.

[37] *Wisconsin Central Railroad* v. *U.S.*, 164 U.S. 190 (1896); *U.S.* v. *Wurts*, 303 U.S. 414 (1938); *R.* v. *Toronto Terminals Railway Co.* [1948] Can.Rep.Ex. 563.
[38] *The Commonwealth* v. *Burns* [1971] V.R. 825, 830, *per* Newton J.
[39] [1915] 1 Ch. 91.
[40] See above, pp. 83 *et seq.*
[41] *Sub nom. Sinclair* v. *Brougham* [1914] A.C. 398: see above, pp. 83 *et seq.*
[42] [1915] 1 Ch. 91, 93, *per* Neville J.
[43] *Lazard Bros. & Co.* v. *Midland Bank Ltd.* [1933] A.C. 289.
[44] See above, Chap. 3.
[45] Taxes Management Act 1970, s.33(1), on which see 1989 B.T.R. 151 [Stopforth].

mistake as is reasonable and just,"[46] having regard to all the relevant circumstances of the case, and, in particular, to the consideration whether the granting of relief would result in the exclusion from charge to tax of any part of the profits[47] of the taxpayer, not only for the year of the application but for any other year.[48] Relief may apparently be given even though the taxpayer's mistake is one of law.[49] But no relief is given where the return is made on the basis of, or in accordance with, the Revenue practice generally prevailing at the time of the return, but which has subsequently been shown to be wrong in law.[50]

(d) *Mistake of Law and Gifts*

There is very little authority relating to gifts made under mistake of law. But there is no reason to think that the foregoing principles should not be similarly applicable. As the authorities[51] now stand, a donor who overpays a donee because he misconstrues the legal effect of a voluntary covenant cannot recover, even though his donee made no claim on him.[52]

Gifts may, however, be made under a mistake of law although no deed of covenant has been executed. Suppose, for example, that a donor makes a gift of £1,000 to a social club in the belief, induced by a mistake of law, that the club is a legal charity. He would not have made the gift if he had known that the club was not a charity. On discovering his mistake, he immediately writes to the secretary of the club and asks for a return of the gift. If he can establish that his mistake caused him to make the payment, the donor should be entitled to recover his money. The rationale of *Re Hatch*[53] cannot apply, for the donee was in no position to make any claim against the donor. The principle that voluntary payments are irrecoverable should, therefore, have no application and should not preclude recovery. In such circumstances it should be irrelevant that the payment was made under a mistake of law.

Certainly, the courts are more ready to grant equitable relief, at least in the context of a suit to set aside or to rectify a deed of gift which was executed under

---

[46] See s.33(2). Applications for relief must be made to the Commissioners within six years of the end of the year within which the assessment was made: and the High Court cannot review the decision of the Special Commissioners, sitting on appeal from the Board, on the question whether the relief was just and reasonable: s.33(4).

[47] By s.33(5) "profits" means income in relation to income tax; chargeable gains, in relation to capital gains tax; profits, as computed for the purposes of corporation tax.

[48] See s.33(3); *cf. Carrimore Six Wheelers Ltd.* v. *I.R.C.* (1944) 26 T.C. 301.

[49] *Cf. Heastie* v. *Veitch & Co.* [1934] 1 K.B. 535, 18 T.C. 305; *Barlow* v. *I.R.C.* (1937) 21 T.C. 354.

[50] s.33(2). What is the "prevailing practice" is a question of fact: see *Rose, Smith & Co. Ltd.* v. *I.R.C.* (1933) 17 T.C. 586. *Aliter* if the assessment is *ultra vires*. The assessment is then a nullity, and the taxpayer is not eligible for statutory relief and must rely on his common law rights: see *Woolwich Equitable Building Society* v. *Commissioners of Inland Revenue* [1993] A.C. 70, where the taxpayer recovered his payment with interest: see Chap. 24 for a full discussion.

[51] See above, pp. 149–150.

[52] *Re Hatch* [1919] 1 Ch. 351: see above, p. 149.

[53] [1919] 1 Ch. 351: see above, p. 149.

mistake. In *Gibbon* v. *Mitchell* Millett J. accepted that the "proposition that equity will never relieve against mistakes of law is clearly too widely stated."[54] The true principle is, in his view, that:

> "the deed will be set aside if the court is satisfied that the disponer did not intend the transaction to have the effect it did. It will be set aside for mistake whether the mistake is a mistake of law or of fact, so long as the mistake is as to the effect of the transaction itself and not merely as to its consequences or the advantages to be gained by entering into it."[55]

In that case the plaintiff had executed the deed in the clear belief that it vested the entire beneficial interest of the assets in his children; contrary to his intention and instructions it had the entirely different effect of creating a discretionary trust of income during his lifetime and a trust of capital after his death. The deed was therefore set aside.

(e) *Proprietary Claims*

We have already discussed the circumstances which the court may take into account in determining whether to grant a restitutionary proprietary claim if money has been paid under a mistake of fact.[56] Similar principles should be applicable where money paid under mistake of law is recoverable.

(f) *Defences*

Only if the plaintiff can claim restitution from the recipient does the question of the relevance and scope of any defence arise. In this section we will deal with aspects of those defences which are of particular relevance to restitutionary claims based on mistake of law.

Submission to an honest claim and bona fide compromises

Whether this is described as a defence or a limit on the right of restitution, it is clear that if the recipient can prove that the payer has submitted to an honest claim, then the restitutionary claim must fail. A similar fate awaits the payer who, having had an opportunity of contesting liability in proceedings, does not do so, and pays.[57]

Change of position

The House of Lords has now recognised a general defence of change of position.[58] Restitution will be denied "where an innocent defendant's position is so changed that he will suffer an injustice if called upon to repay or to repay in

---

[54] [1990] 1 W.L.R. 1304, 1309.
[55] *Ibid.*
[56] See above, Chap. 2.
[57] See above, pp. 50–54.
[58] *Lipkin Gorman (A Firm)* v. *Karpnale Ltd.* [1991] 2 A.C. 548. For a full discussion of the defence see Chap. 40.

full, the injustice of requiring him so to repay outweighs the injustice of denying the plaintiff restitution."[59] A recipient of money paid under a mistake of law may change his position in many different ways, for example, he may determine to live more luxuriously or he may give money to a charity. We discuss these general questions in the Chapter on Change of Position.[60]

In the *Tower Hamlets* case,[61] the ratepayer paid rates under a mistake of law. The House of Lords was troubled by the argument that the rating authority should not be required to make restitution because it no longer had the ratepayer's money "in hand." In particular, a substantial part of the money had been paid over to meet precepts issued to it by the Greater London Council. Moreover, the rating authority, having no money in hand, would be required to look to its ratepayers to reimburse the plaintiffs who had paid under mistake of law[62]; and, if it were required to do so, it would impose the burden of repayment on a body of ratepayers different from those who had enjoyed the benefit of the mistaken payments. This was essentially a submission that its change of position was such as to render it inequitable to require the rating authority to make restitution.[63] The House of Lords, however, never reached this question, for it held that to allow this defence would frustrate the intention of Parliament in enacting section 9 of the General Rate Act 1967, which conferred on the authority a discretionary power to refund amounts mistakenly paid in respect of rates.

The defence that it would cause "fiscal chaos" if repayment were ordered is one known to, and has been accepted by, American and Canadian courts.[64] For example, in *Air Canada* v. *British Columbia*,[65] the Supreme Court of Canada held that it was a defence to the plaintiff's claim to recover money paid pursuant to a demand based upon an *ultra vires* statute.[66] The financial implications for the Province of British Columbia were said to be dire if the restitutionary claim were allowed. The Court was moved by the vision of corporations, with large potential claims, waiting in the wings. "Fiscal chaos" is an evocative phrase. It would be preferable for an English court to affirm that restitution will be denied, wholly or in part, if it would be inequitable, in all the circumstances of the case, to compel the recipient to repay.[67] However, in each case it is a question of fact whether a defendant has changed his position. In principle the burden should be on him to prove that fact.[68]

---

[59] [1991] 2 A.C. 548, 579, *per* Lord Goff.
[60] See below, Chap. 40.
[61] [1988] A.C. 858: see above, p. 156.
[62] At pp. 879–880, *per* Lord Bridge.
[63] At p. 882, *per* Lord Goff. But see below, p. 741, n. 18a.
[64] For a full discussion see Jones, *Restitution in Public and Private Law*, Chap. 1; and see below, p. 552.
[65] [1989] 4 W.W.R. 97.
[66] See below, Chap. 24.
[67] See above, n. 59.
[68] But see *Air Canada* v. *British Columbia* [1989] 4 W.W.R. 97, 133, *per* La Forest J., who assumed that the burden of proof was on the claimant.

Passing on the burden of the payment to others

P pays a tax to D pursuant to a demand from D. P passes on the tax to his customers. It is later held that P paid the tax under a mistake of law. Is his claim defeated on the ground that he has suffered no loss? Has D been enriched, if enriched at all, at the expense of P's customers and not P? These questions have never arisen in England. As a matter of convenience we discuss these questions further in the Chapter entitled Money paid to a Public Authority pursuant to an Ultra Vires Demand.[69]

As the High Court of Australia recognised in *David Securities Pty. Ltd.* v. *Commonwealth Bank of Australia*,[70] the defences, just discussed, may defeat a restitutionary claim even if Parliament or the House of Lords were to conclude, as did the High Court, that money paid under mistake of law is recoverable. Indeed, it may be necessary to recognise new defences; for example many jurisdictions which allow recovery of money paid under a mistake of law hold that the payer's claim will fail if the payment was made in reliance on a judicial decision subsequently overruled by statute or in independent litigation brought by a third party.[71]

---

[69] At p. 552–553.

[70] (1992) 66 A.L.J.R. 768.

[71] Above p. 148. See also Law Commission: Consultation Paper No. 120, paras. 2.57–2.65, which discusses the various Commonwealth statutory provisions and proposals for reform: *cf.* Taxes Management Act 1970, s. 33(2): above p. 161.

In South Africa restitution is denied if the conduct of the payer is "inexcusably slack", a defence which the Appellate Division thought it neither possible nor prudent to define: see *Willis Faber Enthoven (Pty.) Ltd.* v. *Receiver of Revenue* 1992 (4) S.A. 202. It is to be hoped that the House of Lords will not be tempted to adopt this inherently vague defence: see [1993] C.L.J. 225 [Jones].

CHAPTER 5

RESTITUTION IN RESPECT OF SERVICES RENDERED UNDER A MISTAKE

1. INTRODUCTION

A PERSON who renders services to another, who has neither requested them nor freely accepted them,[1] has generally no right to recover from the recipient remuneration for the work so done or recompense in respect of any benefits, however great, conferred thereby.[2] Such a person is in a different position from the payer of money under a mistake. The receipt of money incontrovertibly benefits the recipient. But the receipt of services is not necessarily advantageous, and, unlike money, services, once rendered, cannot be restored.[3] Consequently, it is not enough that the plaintiff should have rendered the services under a mistake; in principle, he must go further and show that the services were requested or freely accepted by the defendant.

This is the general rule but, as has been seen,[4] the courts are now ready to accept that a restitutionary claim may lie, even in the absence of a free acceptance, if it can be shown that the defendant has been incontrovertibly benefited by the services which have been rendered. It is only in recent years that English courts have recognised the principle of incontrovertible benefit. Moreover, it is not, as the law now stands, of general application. A person who mistakenly improves another's land cannot claim the benefit of that principle. Historically, the law of real property has developed very differently from the law of personal property. As will be seen, English law has denied the mistaken improver, whose improvements have become attached to the land, any remedy, if the land owner has not acted unconscionably.[5] Other common law

---

[1] On *free acceptance*, see above pp. 18 *et seq.*
[2] *Falcke* v. *Scottish Imperial Insurance Co.* (1886) 34 Ch.D. 234, 248, *per* Bowen L.J.; *Macclesfield Corporation* v. *Great Central Ry.* [1911] 2 K.B. 528. See below, pp. 369–371 for a discussion of *Falcke's* case.
[3] *Taylor* v. *Laird* (1856) 25 L.J.Ex. 329, 332, *per* Pollock C.B.; see above, p. 18.
[4] See above, pp. 22 *et seq.*
[5] *Appleby* v. *Myers* (1867) L.R. 2 C.P. 651, 659–660, *per* Blackburn J.; *Reynolds* v. *Ashby & Son* [1909] A.C. 466, 475, *per* Lord Atkinson. The genesis of the rule is medieval: see 42 Edw. III f. 6, pl. 9; 21 Hen. VIII, f. 13, pl. 24. Exceptionally, a statute may give relief: see, *e.g.* Matrimonial Proceedings and Property Act 1970, s.37.

jurisdictions,[6] as well as civil law countries,[7] have looked with greater sympathy on the good faith improver, although they have recognised that it is not easy to fashion an appropriate remedy if the conduct of the land owner is blameless.[8] It is unlikely that English courts will reject the inheritance of the past.[9] For that reason it is necessary to discuss claims arising from mistaken improvements to land separately from other restitutionary claims arising from services rendered under mistake.[10-11]

2. RESTITUTIONARY CLAIMS ARISING FROM MISTAKEN IMPROVEMENTS TO LAND

The plaintiff improves the defendant's land, mistakenly thinking that he owns it. The defendant did not request the improvements and, given their nature, they cannot be returned.[12] The plaintiff's restitutionary claim will then fail. But what if the defendant knew that the plaintiff was mistaken but made no attempt to disabuse him of his mistake?

In equity there is the doctrine of estoppel by acquiescence or, as it is sometimes confusingly called, proprietary estoppel. In the leading case of *Ramsden* v. *Dyson*,[13] Lord Cranworth L.C. described the estoppel as precluding a "person, who stands by and allows another to incur expenditure or otherwise act on the basis of a mistaken belief as to his rights, from thereafter asserting rights inconsistent with that mistaken belief."[14] In contrast, Lord Kingsdown concluded that the doctrine protected the improver's expectation,

---

[6] The misfortune of the bona fide but mistaken improver of land has enlisted the sympathy of some common law jurisdictions, which have, to a limited extent, modified the strict rule of law. Many of the states of the U.S.A. (see (1942) 137 A.L.R. 1078) recognised at a very early date that some compensation should be given to the mistaken improver. Betterment statutes were enacted with this object in view, and still remain in force, having withstood attacks on their constitutionality: Woodard, *op. cit.*, pp. 301–304; Keener, *op. cit.* pp. 377–387; (1959) 11 Stan.L.R. 456 [Merryman]; *Restatement of Restitution*, §§ 39–42. For the Canadian statutes see Maddaugh and McCamus, *op. cit.*, pp. 291–301. For other legislation see Gray, *Elements of Land Law*, p. 397, n. 8.

[7] For example, German Civil Code, §§ 951 and 994, which allows a *quantum valebat* claim if the improver is in possession of the land and what is done is necessary or at least useful. (We are grateful to Horst Eidenmüller for this reference). *Cf.* French Civil Code, Art. 554–555; Italian Civil Code, Art. 936.

[8] *Cf.* see below, n. 11.

[9] But English courts have not been wholly consistent. A purchaser, who improves land under a contract which both vendor and purchaser believe to be valid but which is void for uncertainty, can obtain relief: see below, pp. 486–487. Indeed a trustee, who improperly buys trust property and improves it, has been granted equitable relief when the sale is subsequently set aside: see below, p. 652.

[10-11] See generally, Gray, *Elements of Land Law*, Chap. 13, a most comprehensive analysis; and R. J. Sutton, *What Should be Done for Mistaken Improvers?*, in *Essays on Restitution* (ed. Finn), Chap. 8, who suggests that something can and should be done: see below, p. 171 n. 39.

[12] See above, p. 18.

[13] (1866) L.R. 1, H.L. 129.

[14] *Ibid.* at pp. 140–141, as explained in *Amalgamated Investment & Property Co. Ltd. (in liquidation)* v. *Texas Commerce International Bank Ltd.* [1982] 1 Q.B. 84, 103, *per* Robert Goff J.

generated by the owner's encouragement or representation that he would be entitled to an interest in or over the plaintiff's land, which he had consequently improved.[15] It is Lord Cranworth's conception of the doctrine of acquiescence which is, in this particular context, the equitable analogue of free acceptance,[16] although more recent authorities reject any rigid classification into exclusive and defined categories.[17]

In *Ramsden* v. *Dyson* the defendant had improved the plaintiff's land in the belief that, if he did so, he would be granted a long lease. The plaintiff, his landlord, was not aware of that belief. As that decision demonstrates, the mere fact that an improver was mistaken does not give him any right against the owner. The House of Lords held that there was no equitable jurisdiction either to enjoin the landlord from ejecting him or to grant him compensation for the value of his improvements which must have benefited the landlord.

Only if the owner has "acquiesced" in the improver doing what he did is the improver entitled to relief in equity. When, therefore, is he deemed to have acquiesced? When, in Lord Cranworth's words, is it "dishonest in me to remain wilfully passive . . . in order afterwards to profit by the mistake which I might have prevented"?[18] Or, in a more recent formulation, when is it *unconscionable* for the owner to rely on his legal rights?[19]

In *Willmott* v. *Barber*[20] Fry J., in a much cited judgment, answered these questions by formulating five conditions which a defendant must satisfy before equity would grant him a remedy. He said:

> "It has been said that the acquiescence which will deprive a man of his legal rights must amount to fraud, and in my view that is an abbreviated statement of a very true proposition. A man is not to be deprived of his legal rights unless he has acted in such a way as would make it fraudulent for him to set up those rights. What, then, are the elements or requisites necessary to constitute fraud of that description? In the first place the plaintiff must have made a mistake as to his legal rights. Secondly, the plaintiff must have expended some money or must have done some act (not necessarily upon the defendant's land) on the faith of his mistaken belief. Thirdly, the defendant, the possessor of the legal right, must know of the existence of his own right which is inconsistent with the right

---

[15] (1866) L.R. 1, H.L. 129, at pp. 170–171.

[16] On which, see above, p. 167.

[17] *Taylor Fashions Ltd.* v. *Liverpool Victoria Trustees Co. Ltd.* (1979) [1982] Q.B. 133n: see also the decisions cited below, n. 19.

[18] *Ramsden* v. *Dyson* (1866) L.R. 1, H.L. 129, 140–141.

[19] *Taylor Fashions Ltd.* v. *Liverpool Victoria Trustees Co. Ltd.* (1979) [1982] Q.B. 133n.; *Amalgamated Investment & Property Co. Ltd.* v. *Texas Bank Ltd.* [1982] 1 Q.B. 84; and two decisions of the High Court of Australia, *Walton Stores (Interstate) Ltd.* v. *Maher* (1988) 76 A.L.J.R. 513 and *Commonwealth of Australia* v. *Verwayen* (1990) 95 A.L.J.R. 321.

[20] (1880) 15 Ch.D. 96, 105–106 (italics supplied), developing the reasoning of Lord Cranworth L.C. and Lord Kingsdown in *Ramsden* v. *Dyson* (1866) L.R. 1, H.L. 129, see above, nn. 13–14, see also *Lala Beni Ram* v. *Kundan Ral* (1899) 15 T.L.R. 258, 259, *per* Lord Macnaghten (for Lord Watson).

claimed by the plaintiff. If he does not know of it he is in the same position as the plaintiff, and the doctrine of acquiescence is founded upon conduct with a knowledge of your legal rights. Fourthly, the defendant, the possessor of the legal right, must know of the plaintiff's mistaken belief of his rights. If he does not, there is nothing which calls upon him to assert his own rights. Lastly, the defendant, the possessor of the legal right, must have encouraged the plaintiff in his expenditure of money or in the other acts which he has done, *either directly or by abstaining from asserting his legal right.* Where all these elements exist, there is fraud of such a nature as will entitle the court to restrain the possessor of the legal right from exercising it, but, in my judgment, nothing short of this will do."

This statement of the law must be qualified. First, it is clear that the plaintiff need not be mistaken as to an existing fact. It is enough that he mistakenly thought that he would be granted an interest in the land.[21] Moreover, the improver may obtain relief even if his mistake is one of law.[22]

Secondly, it "may well be"[23] that these five probanda must be satisfied if the owner "stood by without protest while his rights have been infringed"; but if he encouraged the improver to act as he did, it is immaterial that he knew or did not know that the improver was mistaken. The proper inquiry is whether "in [the] particular individual circumstances, it would be unconscionable for a party to be permitted to deny that which, knowingly or unknowingly, he has allowed or encouraged another to assume to his detriment" rather than "whether the circumstances can be fitted within the confines of some pre-conceived formula serving as a universal yardstick for every form of uncon-scionable behaviour."[24]

So, in *Taylor Fashions Ltd.* v. *Liverpool Victoria Trustees Ltd.*,[24a] both parties mistakenly thought than an option to renew a lease was not registrable as an estate contract and, in that belief, the tenants, the second plaintiffs, had made substantial improvements. Oliver J. held that the defendants, the landlords, were estopped from denying that the tenants had not effectively exercised their

---

[21] *Plimmer* v. *Wellington Corp.* (1884) 9 App.Cas. 699, 710 (P.C.); *Commonwealth of Australia* v. *Verwayen* (1990) 95 A.L.J.R. 321, 331, *per* Mason C.J., and authorities there cited.

[22] *Taylor Fashions Ltd.* v. *Liverpool Victoria Trustees Co. Ltd.* (1979) [1982] Q.B. 133n., 150–151, *per* Oliver J.; *Commonwealth of Australia* v. *Verwayen* (1990) 95 A.L.J.R. 321, 333, *per* Mason C.J., citing, *inter alia*, *Sarat Chunder Dey* v. *Gopal Chunder Laha* (1892) L.R. 19 Ind.App. 203 (P.C.) (representation as to the legal effect of a document can give rise to an estoppel).

[23] *Taylor Fashions Ltd.* v. *Liverpool Victoria Trustees Co. Ltd.* (1979) [1982] Q.B. 133n. 147, *per* Oliver J. But the judge added that he thought that "this must now be considered open to doubt." *Cf. E. & L. Berg Homes Ltd.* v. *Grey* (1979) 253 E.G. 473, C.A.

[24] (1979) [1982] Q.B. 133, n. 151–152, *per* Oliver J., relying on *Inwards* v. *Baker* [1965] 2 Q.B. 29 and *E. R. Ives Investment Ltd.* v. *High* [1967] 2 Q.B. 379. See also *Shaw* v. *Applegate* [1978] 1 All E.R. 123, 130, *per* Buckley L.J., 132, *per* Goff L.J.; *Amalgamated Investment & Property Co. Ltd.* v. *Texas Commerce International Bank Ltd.* [1982] Q.B. 84, 104, *per* Robert Goff J., 122, *per* Lord Denning M.R. (*cf.* Brandon L.J. at pp. 130–131, citing Spencer Bower & Turner, *Estoppel by Representation*, p. 157. See also, the decisions cited above, p. 168.

[24a] (1979) [1982] Q.B. 133n.

opinion. It is not then necessary for the defendant's encouragement to be "knowing" encouragement; *a fortiori*, it should be unconscionable for the owner to deny that he did not know of the plaintiff's mistake if he ought to have known that the plaintiff was acting under a mistaken belief that he was acquiring some interest in, or over, land.[25]

Thirdly, there has been some controversy as to the character of the equitable doctrine, which has reflected itself in how different judges have described it at different times: an equity, an equity created by estoppel, equitable estoppel, estoppel by acquiescence, proprietary estoppel.[26] This semantic confusion has at times led courts mistakenly to equate the doctrines of estoppel by representation or conduct with estoppel by acquiescence.[27] Historically, the equitable doctrine is distinct from common law estoppel.[28] It is not dependent on any representation. Most importantly, it enables the mistaken improver to bring an action in equity against the owner who acquiesced.[29] It is often said that estoppel is a shield but not a sword. But that is a misleading metaphor. As Brandon L.J. once said[30]: "while a party cannot in terms found a cause of action on an estoppel, he may, as a result of being able to rely on an estoppel, succeed on a cause of action on which, without being able to rely on that estoppel, he would necessarily have failed."

Finally, what principles determine which is the appropriate remedy? It is said that "the court must look at the circumstances in each case to decide in what way the equity can be satisfied"[31]; and that "there must be proportionality between the remedy and the detriment which is its purpose to avoid. It would be wholly inequitable and unjust to insist upon a disproportionate making good of the relevant assumption."[32] "Of all doctrines, equitable estop-

---

[25] See, *e.g. Salvation Army Trustee Co. Ltd.* v. *West Yorkshire Metropolitan County Council* (1981) 41 P. & C.R. 179 at 194, 196, *per* Woolf J.; *Swallow Securities Ltd.* v. *Isenberg* (1985) 274 E.G. 1028, 1030, *per* Cumming-Bruce L.J.; *Watson* v. *Goldsbrough* [1986] 1 E.G.L.R. 265, 266–267: cited in Gray, *op. cit.* p. 402 n. 11.

[26] *Cf. Crabb* v. *Arun District Council* [1976] Ch. 179, 187–188, *per* Lord Denning M.R., 193–194, *per* Scarman L.J.; *Inwards* v. *Baker* [1965] 2 Q.B. 29, 38, *per* Danckwerts L.J.

[27] In *De Bussche* v. *Alt* (1878) 8 Ch.D. 286, 314; *per* Thesiger L.J. See also *Proctor* v. *Bennis* (1887) 36 Ch.D. 740, 766, *per* Fry L.J.; *Commonwealth of Australia* v. *A. E. Goodwin Ltd.* [1962] S.R.(N.S.W.) 315, 322, *per* Brereton J.; *Inwards* v. *Baker* [1965] 2 Q.B. 29, 38, *per* Danckwerts L.J.

[28] See the Chancery petition E.96/59 (c. 1486), cited in C. M. Gray, *Copyhold, Equity and the Common Law*, p. 157; *Paterson* v. *Hickman*, cited in *Earl of Oxford's* case (1815) 1 Ch.Rep. 1, 5.

[29] *Ramsden* v. *Dyson* (1866) L.R. 1, H.L. 129, 140, *per* Lord Cranworth, 168, *per* Lord Wensleydale; *Plimmer* v. *Wellington Corp.* (1884) 9 App.Cas. 699; *Crabb* v. *Arun D.C.* [1976] Ch. 179, 187, *per* Lord Denning M.R.; *Pascoe* v. *Turner* [1979] 1 W.L.R. 431, 436, *per* Cumming-Bruce L.J.

[30] *Amalgamated Investment & Property Co. Ltd.* v. *Texas Commerce International Bank Ltd.* [1982] Q.B. 84, 131–132.

[31] *Plimmer* v. *Wellington Corp.* (1884) 9 App.Cas. 699, 714 (P.C.); see also *Chalmers* v. *Pardoe* [1963] 1 W.L.R. 677, 682 (P.C.).

[32] *Commonwealth of Australia* v. *Verwayen* (1990) 95 A.L.J.R. 321, 333, *per* Mason C.J.

pel is surely one of the most flexible"[33]; but it should go "no further than is necessary to prevent unconscionable conduct."[34]

Given these general principles, if the owner has been incontrovertibly benefited by the improvements, the benefit which he has gained should be the market value of the services or the increased value of the land.[35] If he has encouraged the improver to act as he did, the improver should be entitled to the higher of those two figures; the owner's conduct, in acting as he did, is unconscionable. Indeed, in our view, that should be the proper measure of his enrichment if he has simply stood by without protest; his conduct is similarly unconscionable.[36] It is a distinct question whether the court should also grant the improver a lien over the land to secure that sum. That may depend on a number of factors, such as whether the land is already encumbered or whether the owner is insolvent. The improver's position is not very different from that of the person who pays money under mistake, and prima facie he should enjoy priority over the general, but not the secured, creditors of the recipient.[37]

However, in a number of cases the courts have gone further and protected the improver's expectation interest.[38] The equitable doctrine is flexible, and that flexibility is to be welcomed. But, in protecting the expectation interest, the courts may well have, in some situations, gone further than was necessary to prevent unconscionable conduct.[39]

---

[33] *Amalgamated Investment & Property Co. Ltd.* v. *Texas Bank Ltd.* [1982] Q.B. 84, 103, *per* Robert Goff J.

[34] *Walton Stores (Interstate) Ltd.* v. *Maher* (1988) 76 A.L.J.R. 513, 535, *per* Brennan J.

[35] In contrast, the land owner may have stood by or encouraged the plaintiff's expenditures but may not have benefited from his inaction or action. Nonetheless, a plaintiff may be reimbursed his reliance loss: see, *e.g. Walton Stores (Interstate) Ltd.* v. *Maher* (1988) 76 A.L.J.R. 513. Contrast *Crab* v. *Arun R.D.C.* [1976] Ch. 179, where the defendant had gained no benefit.

[36] *Cf.* above pp. 168–169.

[37] See above pp. 130–132. *Cf. Unity Joint Stock Mutual Banking Association* v. *King* (1858) 25 Beav. 72. In our view, the improver should never gain priority over secured creditors, even if they became creditors after the date of the improvements unless they had knowledge of the improver's mistake and the owner's acquiescence—a most unlikely finding of fact. Consequently the lien should be imposed at the date of judgment. Contrast, on very different facts, *Re Sharpe (A Bankrupt)* [1980] 1 W.L.R. 219, 225, *per* Browne-Wilkinson J.

It is another question whether the plaintiff's right based on the estoppel by acquiescence is a registrable interest. If the land is not registered land, it has been held that it is not registrable as a *lis pendens*: see *Haslemere Estates Ltd.* v. *Baker* [1982] 1 W.L.R. 1109, 1119–1120, *per* Megarry V.-C. If the land is registered and the plaintiff is in actual occupation, query whether he can claim to have an overriding interest within s.70(1)(g) of the Land Registration Act 1925.

[38] See, *e.g. Huning* v. *Ferrers* (1711) Gilb. 85; *Unity Joint-Stock Mutual Banking Association* v. *King* (1858) 25 Beav. 72; *Dillwyn* v. *Llewelyn* (1866) 4 De G. F. & J. 517; *Inwards* v. *Baker* [1965] 2 Q.B. 29.

[39] *Cf.* the difficult case of *Hussey* v. *Palmer* [1972] 1 W.L.R. 1286, where the plaintiff was content to accept what she had spent in building an extension to her son-in-law's house: discussed in Birks, *Introduction*, pp. 285–286 and 292–293.

It is, of course, another and difficult question whether English law should grant a mistaken improver a restitutionary claim in circumstances where the owner cannot be said to have "acquiesced". But it is not easy to fashion a remedy which would balance the interests both of the mistaken improver and the innocent owner who may find it burdensome to discharge a lien over his land, even if he is given a period of years so to do: See Sutton, *op. cit.* p. 167 nn. 10–11 and the text below, n. 6 for the various common law and civilian solutions.

3. OTHER RESTITUTIONARY CLAIMS

P renders services to D under mistake. The mistake which leads him to do so may take many forms. Indeed, the nature of the mistake may determine the principles governing the restitutionary claim.

(1) *P rendered services under mistake to D in circumstances when D knew of his mistake*

The analogy of the cases on improvement to land[40] suggests that if D encouraged P to act, or stood by, allowing P to render services, then he will be considered to have freely accepted the services. In such a case his unconscionable conduct has enabled him to make a gain at P's expense. As a general rule, that benefit should be taken to be the market value of P's services; but it may be the increased value of D's assets, if that is the greater sum. As will be seen,[41] the courts have reached a similar conclusion in the context of claims arising out of ineffective contracts.

(2) *P rendered services to D under mistake, in circumstances in which D did not know of his mistake*

D should be required to make restitution only if P can prove that D has been incontrovertibly benefited by the receipt of the services. D will be incontrovertibly benefited if P can show that he has gained a financial benefit, readily realisable without detriment to himself, or has been saved a necessary expense. In such circumstances the equities of the plaintiff's claim are normally more compelling than the defendant's plea that he did not request or freely accept services which he is now in no position to return.[42] His ground of recovery is his mistake.

We turn now to discuss two particular situations, which illustrate the application of the principle of incontrovertible benefit. These are the improvement of chattels and the discharge of another's statutory or contractual duty.[43]

(a) *Improvements of Chattels*

The judgment of Lord Denning M.R. in *Greenwood* v. *Bennett*[44] suggests that one illustration of the principle of incontrovertible benefit may arise where the plaintiff, thinking that he owns a chattel, improves it in circumstances where

---

[40] See above, pp. 167 *et seq.*

[41] See below, Chaps. 19 *et seq.*

[42] See above, pp. 18 *et seq.* Contrast Palmer, *op. cit.* Vol. III, pp. 211 *et seq.*

[43] Another possible illustration of the principle is where a person provides necessary services under mistake. *E.g.* a nephew supports a miserly aunt, mistakenly thinking that she is destitute. She has no reason to be aware that he is mistaken. She dies, leaving a substantial estate. It is not easy to conclude that she freely accepted the services; yet she has received an incontrovertible benefit. *Cf. Re Agnew's Will*, 230 N.Y.S. 519 (1928); and *Descovick* v. *Porzio*, 187 A. 2d 60 (1963).

[44] [1973] 1 Q.B. 195, 201–202.

the true owner is unaware that the improvements have been made.[45] In that case B a car dealer, entrusted S with a car, worth some £400–£500, for the purpose of carrying out £85 worth of repairs. S took the car out on a frolic of his own and extensively damaged it in a collision with another vehicle. S then sold the car to H, a garage owner, for £75. H, acting in good faith, put the car in good order, spending about £226 on labour and materials, and then sold it to a finance company which let it on hire-purchase to P for £450. In the meantime B had informed the police that the car was not in S's possession. The police found it with P and took possession of it. Eventually the dispute "resolved itself into a contest" between B and H. The police took out interpleader proceedings in the county court to determine the question of the parties' rights. The county court judge held that B was entitled to the car and that H was not entitled to any allowance. H appealed from this judgment. B then sold the car for £400. The Court of Appeal allowed the appeal. The judge ought not to have released the car except on condition that B paid H £226 in respect of the improvements. Since B now had the car, the court ordered B to pay H £226.

Each member of the court gave a different reason for his decision. Lord Denning M.R.'s judgment is the most radical. B "should not be allowed to enrich [himself] at [H's] expense. The court will order [B] if they recover the car, or its improved value, to recompense the innocent purchaser for the work he has done to it. No matter whether they recover it with the aid of the courts, or without it, the innocent purchaser will recover the value of the improvements he has done to it."[46] The Master of the Rolls would, therefore, have allowed the innocent improver a direct cause of action to recover the cost of his work from the true owner. Otherwise "you would get the very odd result that by suing [P, the person in possession,] in detinue, [B] could—by this indirect means—recover from [H] more than [B] could by suing him directly in conversion,"[47] namely £75, being the value of the car at the date of the conversion by sale to H. Phillimore L.J. thought that the county court judge had treated the facts as giving rise to an application for specific restitution; since specific restitution should have been refused "on equitable principles," H should be given credit for his materials and labour.[48] Cairns L.J. considered that, in interpleader proceedings, "similar considerations come into play as those which would affect an action for detinue"; and, in an action for detinue, H would have been allowed his expenditure. But he considered that, if the car had reached B's hands, "it is difficult to see that [H] could have had any claim against him for the expenditure that he was put to in making the repairs to it."[49]

---

[45] In the past, other common law jurisdictions have generally rejected the possibility of a claim for restitution in these circumstances: see, *e.g.* *Ings* v. *Industrial Acceptance Corp.* (1962) 32 D.L.R. 2d 611 (Ontario); *Cahill* v. *Hall*, 37 N.E. 573 (1894) (Mass.). But contrast *Mayne* v. *Kidd* [1951] 2 D.L.R. 651 (Sask., C.A.), cited in Maddaugh and McCamus, *op. cit.* p. 302.

[46] At p. 202; *cf.* Birks, *Introduction*, p. 124.

[47] At p. 201. This point is now met by the Torts (Interference with Goods) Act 1977, see below, p. 174.

[48] At p. 202.

[49] At p. 203.

The Court of Appeal awarded, therefore, an innocent H what he spent on repairing the car. But it should not follow that he should have recovered what he had spent. This award would have been proper if B had freely accepted the services rendered. Given that he had no idea what H was doing to the car, such a conclusion cannot be supported. The appropriate award should have been the value of B's incontrovertible benefit in consequence of what H had done. How should that be measured?[50] It is true that the car was worth £400 to £500 when B entrusted the car to S. However, in litigation between B and an innocent H it should not be open to B to deny that its value was £75 when H bought it, given that it was B who had entrusted S with the car. B's incontrovertible benefit is the difference between the market value of the car when B regained possession and £75.[50a] But the improver should never recover from the innocent owner more than the amount which he spent on repairs. That is the ceiling of any award. Otherwise he would, albeit innocent, be allowed to profit from his own tort.

Parliament has now accepted that the mistaken improver should be granted an allowance and that the extent of that allowance should be the incontrovertible benefit which the owner has gained at the improver's expense. The Torts (Interference with Goods) Act 1977 creates a new statutory tort, called "wrongful interference" or "wrongful interference with goods"[51] which embraces the common law tort of conversion[52] but not detinue, which is "abolished."[53] Section 6(1) gives the improver, who acts in the mistaken but honest belief that he had good title to the goods, "an allowance . . . for the extent to which, at the time as at which the goods fall to be valued in assessing damages, the value of the goods is attributable to the improvement."[54]

The statute gives no direct guidance on how "the value of the goods . . . attributable to the improvement" should be determined. In principle, the defendant's incontrovertible benefit should be the difference between the improved and unimproved value of the chattel. But if the reasonable value of the services rendered is less than that sum, then the improver should be awarded the lesser figure.[55]

Again, what is the relevant date for assessing the value of the goods? The statute is silent. Seemingly, the common law still applies; and, in conversion, value is assessed as at the date of the conversion.[56] Any increase in value through the improvement would normally, therefore, be excluded from the

---

[50] See above, p. 22.
[50a] It is B's inconvertible benefit which is critical: see Burrows, *The Law of Restitution*, pp. 10 and 121.
[51] s.1.
[52] s.1. It also "means" trespass to goods; negligence, resulting in damage to goods; and "any other tort"; (subject to s.2, see below, n. 53) resulting in damage to goods.
[53] s.2(1).
[54] *Cf.* above, pp. 34–36.
[55] *Cf.* pp. 22 *et seq.*
[56] *Green* v. *Farmer* (1768) 4 Burr. 2214; *Reid* v. *Fairbanks* (1853) 13 C.B.(N.S.) 692; *Caxton Publishing Co.* v. *Sutherland Publishing Co.* [1939] A.C. 178, 192–193, *per* Lord Roche.

award of damages[57]; and in such a case at common law the improver, who is neither mistaken nor honest, will be indirectly compensated for the work he has done. But section 6(1) will be important if the improver commits a fresh act of conversion, for example, by selling the goods so improved, and the true owner relies on the subsequent sale.[58] It is doubtful, however, whether the improver is entitled to the statutory allowance if the owner recaps the goods; for "the allowance shall be made" only in "proceedings for wrongful interference" against the improver. In such a case the improver may still have to rely on the authority of Lord Denning's judgment in *Greenwood* v. *Bennett*.[59] The burden should, at common law, be upon him to demonstrate what is the value attributable to the improvement.

Section 6 is not happily drafted. At common law there was authority which suggested that even if the improver knew that the plaintiff was disputing his title, he nonetheless could claim an allowance.[60] Under the Act the improver would no longer have a claim. The statutory claim is clearly limited to improvements made by a person who acts in the mistaken but honest belief that he had good title to the goods. But the Act does not say what is an improvement, who has the burden of proving that the goods have been improved or what value is attributable to the improvement. These questions will become particularly important if the owner's claim is against a bona fide purchaser from the improver, who is given an allowance similar to that given to the improver.[61] Seemingly, the burden of proof must be on the defendant. But it is an open question, for example, whether the cost of preserving a chattel can be taken into account in determining the value attributable to the improvement[62]; and if the reasonable value of the improver's services is less than the net increase in value of the chattel attributable to the improvement, then in principle he should be awarded that lesser sum.[63]

There is then a recognition, both by statute and at common law, that a bona fide improver of chattels should, in some situations, be granted restitution. It is true that the statutory allowance is granted only if he sues for wrongful interference. Moreover, the judgments of Phillimore and Cairns L.JJ. do not suggest that a mistaken improver enjoys a common law restitutionary right to recover from the owner the value of the benefit conferred. In contrast, Lord Denning M.R. would allow the improver to recover directly against the owner. There may be some logic in granting an allowance but denying a direct restitutionary claim; for the claim, if it succeeds, may compel the owner to sell

---

[57] Since the act of conversion will generally occur when the improver initially acquired the goods.
[58] Even in such a case the honest improver may have had an allowance at common law. *Greenwood* v. *Bennett* [1973] 1 Q.B. 195 assumed so; but *cf*. (1955) 71 L.Q.R. 346 [Gordon], which discusses the earlier authorities; and (1977) 93 L.Q.R. at 288–289 [Jones].
[59] See above, pp. 172–173.
[60] *Munro* v. *Wilmott* [1949] 1 K.B. 295.
[61] s.6(2).
[62] See *McGregor on Damages*, § 1357 *et seq*.
[63] See above, pp. 22 *et seq*.

the car; it is then "a form of realisation in money."[64] But, in our view, it is enough that the benefit is realisable by the sale of the chattel. We are persuaded that it is normally just and reasonable to require the owner of a chattel, which is not unique, who has benefited from another's services rendered under mistake, to sell his chattel if that is the only way he can make restitution.[65] In the past the common law has taken the position that an owner should never be required to pay for improvements which he did not want or request. But the merits of that defence must be balanced against the claim of the honest and mistaken improver. In our view the equities of his claim are more appealing.[66]

The position of the improver of a chattel who mistakenly thinks that he owns it is different from that of the improver who carries out repairs on the instructions of a person whom he mistakenly believes to be the owner. For example, a garage which repairs a stolen car at the request of a thief has no common law lien for the value of the repairs made to the car.[67] In such a case there is, to paraphrase Holmes J., "little ground for charging [the owner] on a fictitious or quasi-contract. The [garage] furnished [its] services under a valid contract with the [thief] and must look to him [for reimbursement]."[68] In *Greenwood* v. *Bennett* there was a contract between the rogue S and the improver H; but it was a contract for sale, and H's restitutionary claim against the owner, B, for the value of the repairs was independent of, and not governed by, the contract of sale. In contrast, a garage which has specifically contracted with the thief to carry out the repairs must look to that contract for its remedies, just as the sub-contractor must normally look to the main contractor and not to the owner of the improved land[69]; in both these cases the owner has merely been incidentally benefited from another's performance of his contract with a third party.[70] It is generally[71] unwise to cut across contractual bound-

---

[64] See Birks, *Introduction* pp. 122–123, who points out that B had sold the car.

[65] If the chattel is unique, the hardship in requiring a sale of the chattel may persuade a court to deny any restitutionary claim. In contrast under the Torts (Interference with Goods) Act 1977, s.6, the improver is entitled to an allowance even though it would be unreasonable to require the owner to sell the goods to pay for the improvements (*e.g.* they may be unique and the owner has no free funds to pay for the improvement). It is arguable that in such a case there should be no allowance and a restitutionary claim should be denied.

[66] For another view, see [1981] C.L.J. 340 [Matthews], who argues that Lord Denning's judgment cannot be reconciled with *Falcke* v. *Scottish Imperial Insurance Co.* (1886) 34 Ch.D. 234, C.A., on which see below, pp. 369 *et seq.*

[67] *Tappenden* v. *Artus* [1964] 2 Q.B. 185, C.A.

[68] *Cahill* v. *Hall*, 37 N.E. 573 (1894) (where a horse was broken in by the plaintiff at the request of a person who was not the owner); see also *Winney* v. *Leuci,* 74 N.Y.S. 2d 285 (1947) and *Express Coach Finishers* v. *Caulfield* 1968 S.L.T. (Sh.Ct.) 11. But *cf. Hertford Fire Insurance* v. *Allertson*, 298 N.Y.S. 2d 321 (1969) and the South African cases of *New Club Garage* v. *Milborrow & Son* (1931) G.W.L. 86; *Klug and Klug* v. *Perkin* [1932] C.P.D. 401; *Charnock* v. *Liverpool Corp.* [1968] 1 W.L.R. 1498.

[69] *Cf. Thomson, Jackson, Gourlay, Taylor* v. *Lochhead* (1889) 16 R. 373.

[70] Contrast *Mason* v. *Burningham* [1949] 2 K.B. 545, where the seller sold a typewriter to which he had no title; the buyer recovered damages for the value of improvements which it was reasonably foreseeable he would make.

[71] In our view s.6(4) of the Torts (Interference with Goods) Act 1977 has not amended the common law, as stated in the text above. But see above, p. 56, for a possible exception: *cf.* Sutton, *op. cit.* p. 167, nn. 10–11, pp. 290–292.

aries and, through the grant of a restitutionary claim, to redistribute to a stranger, such as the owner of the car, the burden of risks which the garage has assumed under its contract with the rogue.[72]

(b) *Discharge of Another's Statutory or Contractual Duty*

A striking illustration of a claim based on services mistakenly rendered is where a plaintiff mistakenly discharges, without the defendant's knowledge, the defendant's contractual or statutory duty to a third party. The defendant has not requested or freely accepted these services. Yet liabilities would not be forced upon him if he were required to recompense the plaintiff for the reasonable value of his services or the value of the benefit conferred upon him, that is, the expense which he has saved, whichever is the less. These facts are, in our view, stronger than those in *Greenwood* v. *Bennett*, since the terms of the defendant's contract or statutory duty, which the plaintiff has unofficiously discharged or helped to discharge, demonstrate that the defendant has incontrovertibly benefited from the services rendered.[73] The decisions of other common law jurisdictions support the view that a person who mistakenly discharges another's contractual or statutory duty should be granted a restitutionary claim. The most important of these is the Supreme Court of Canada's decision in *County of Carleton* v. *City of Ottawa*,[74] where the appellant municipality discharged the respondent's duty to provide board, lodging and medical assistance to an indigent who was thought to be resident within its boundaries but was in fact resident within the respondent's. Hall J., who delivered the judgment of the Court,[75] adopted Cartwright J.'s observation in *Deglman* v. *Guaranty Trust Co. of Canada*[76] that "any civilised system of law is bound to provide remedies for cases of what has been called unjust enrichment or unjust benefit." The appellant municipality was allowed to recover the amount it had paid to a third party to board the indigent and also the cost of maintaining the indigent which it had itself incurred.[77]

---

[72] See "The Self-Serving Intermeddler," 87 Harv.L.Rev. 1409 [Dawson].

[73] For that reason it has been suggested that a distinction should be drawn between these facts and those of *Greenwood* v. *Bennett*; that is, a distinction should be drawn between *irrefutable* and *incontrovertible* benefits: Klippert, *Unjust Enrichment*, pp. 58–60, 95–98.

[74] (1965) 52 D.L.R. (2d) 220 on which see Maddaugh and McCamus, *op. cit.* pp. 731 *et seq.* *Cf.* *Arnett & Wemsley Ltd.* v. *Good* (1967) 64 D.L.R. (2d) 81. Other cases where restitution has been granted include: *McClary* v. *Michigan Central Ry. Co.*, 60 N.W. 695 (1894); *Blowers* v. *Southern Ry. Co.*, 54 S.E. 368 (1906); *Blackwood* v. *Southern Ry. Co.*, 100 S.E. 610 (1919); *Presby* v. *Bethlehem Village Dist.*, 416 A. 2d 1382 (1980); *cf.* the South African case of *Jamieson* v. *Dunne* (1898) 50 O.R. 186. But restitution was denied in *Rohr* v. *Baker*, 10 P. 627 (1886) and *Johnson* v. *Boston & Maine Ry. Co.*, 38 A. 267 (1897); and see the Scottish case of *The Lawrence Building Co. Ltd.* v. *Lanarkshire C.C.* (1977) S.L.T. 110 (O.H.).

[75] At p. 224.

[76] [1954] 3 D.L.R. 785.

[77] In our view the plaintiffs should have recovered this sum or the amount which the defendant saved as a result of the plaintiff's intervention, whichever is the less. *Cf.* the cases on services rendered under contracts void for mistake (see below, Chap. 21) and under contracts void for want of authority (see below, Chap. 20).

It is not difficult to conceive of other cases where a person may be said to have received an incontrovertible benefit from services rendered by another under mistake.[78] The general principle should be that restitution should always be granted when, as a result of the plaintiff's services, the defendant has gained a financial benefit readily realisable without detriment to himself or has been saved expense which he inevitably must have incurred.

---

[78] An intriguing case, where it is debatable whether a restitutionary claim should have succeeded, is *Upton R.D.C.* v. *Powell* [1942] 1 All E.R. 220. The defendant's house caught fire, so he called the Upton police and asked for the "fire brigade." The police called the Upton fire brigade, believing that the defendant was in their area; and the Upton fire brigade, which arrived on the scene, shared this belief for a time. In fact the defendant was in the Pershore fire brigade's district. The Court of Appeal held that the Upton fire brigade could recover against the defendant in contract. But it is difficult to support the decision on that ground since Upton did not intend to charge and the defendant thought he was entitled to the services free. Moreover, it is most doubtful whether the plaintiff could have succeeded in restitution: the defendant had not freely accepted the services, knowing that he had to pay for them; *cf. Merritt* v. *American Dock & Trust Co.*, 13 N.Y.S. 234 (1891) where the plaintiff intended to charge for his services but his claim nonetheless failed. And it is not easy to see that he has been incontrovertibly benefited since he was entitled to Pershore's services free. (Contrast Birks, *Introduction*, p. 120). For the latter reason it is no solution to subrogate Upton to Pershore's claim against the defendant. But perhaps Pershore received an incontrovertible benefit, in that Upton, acting under mistake, had discharged Pershore's duty to the defendant. If so, Upton should then have recovered from Pershore the expense which Pershore saved in not having to come to the scene of the fire. Some expense must have been saved even though the Pershore fire brigade did eventually arrive on the scene the next day. There is one further complication. Some six hours after the Upton brigade had arrived, it was told by a Pershore officer that "it was a Pershore fire." "But the Upton fire brigade continued rendering services until the next day." It is doubtful, however, whether Upton's conduct thereafter could be characterised as officious simply because it continued to act until Pershore arrived. *Cf.* Burrows. *The Law of Restitution*, pp. 124–125: *Town of Durham* v. *Carlisle* (1975) 63 D.L.R. (3d) 88.

CHAPTER 6

RESTITUTION IN RESPECT OF CHATTELS (OTHER THAN MONEY) TRANSFERRED UNDER A MISTAKE

IF a person transfers a chattel, other than money, to another under a mistake, his right to recover that chattel, or its value, will depend on whether his mistake is such that it vitiates his intention to pass the property in the chattel to the transferee.

If the mistake does vitiate his intention to pass the property to the transferee, for example, if the transferor is mistaken as to the identity of the transferee,[1] the transferor has his remedies in tort.[2]

More difficult problems arise, however, if the mistake of the transferor does not vitiate his intention to pass the property in the chattel to the transferee. Although in such a case the transferor cannot sue in tort, he may be able to sue on a *quantum valebat* for its value. In the parallel case of *quantum meruit* claims[3] the courts will impose liability to pay, although no actual request has been made by the defendant, provided that the defendant, knowing that the services were not rendered gratuitously, has freely accepted the benefit of them. The analogy of these authorities should, in our view, persuade the courts to impose liability on the transferee of goods where he has freely accepted them, knowing of the transferor's mistake,[4] or even where he has accepted the goods, in ignorance of the mistake, but has learned of it before he has consumed the goods.

The following hypothetical situation[5] exemplifies the type of problem that might arise:

> A, in accordance with the terms of his contract with B, delivers to B 125 tins of fruit. B accepts the tins but, having counted them, mistakenly concludes that A had sent 130 tins of fruit. Thereupon he redelivers to A five tins of fruit.

---

[1] Or, in some cases, if the mistake is as to the identity of the chattel. *Cf. Lancs & Yorks Ry.* v. *MacNicoll* (1918) 118 L.T. 596; *The Nordburg* [1939] P. 121, 126, *per curiam*.

[2] *Cundy* v. *Lindsay* (1878) 3 App.Cas. 459.

[3] *Craven-Ellis* v. *Canons Ltd.* [1936] 2 K.B. 403, see below, pp. 478–479; see also *Wm. Lacey (Hounslow)* v. *Davis* [1957] 1 W.L.R. 932, below, p. 555, *Société Franco Tunisienne d'Armement* v. *Sidermar S.P.A.* [1961] 2 Q.B. 278 (overruled on other grounds in *Ocean Tramp Tankers Corp.* v. *V/O Sovfracht ("The Eugenia")* [1964] 2 Q.B. 226).

[4] *Cf.* above, Chap. 5.

[5] *Cf. Restatement of Restitution*, § 39, ill. 3.

If B's mistake vitiated his intention to pass property in the tins, he will have his remedy in conversion. But if it did not, his only remedy will be in restitution. If A accepts the five tins, knowing of B's mistake, he should be liable on a *quantum valebat* to make restitution for the value of the tins. Similarly, A should be liable if, having the tins still in his possession when B informs him of B's mistake, he subsequently refuses to return them to B. In these cases A should at least be liable for a proper proportion of the contract price. It is a more difficult question whether B should be entitled to the reasonable value of the tins (for example, the market value), if that exceeds the contract price. If A has freely accepted the goods then prima facie B should be entitled to recover their market value at the date of acceptance.[6] In this situation the contract price should not be the ceiling of any award; for B has title to the five tins at the date of redelivery. It is a more difficult question if the market price at that time is less than the contract price. B has paid for the goods, and, acting in good faith, redelivered them to A. These facts may well persuade a court to award him a proportion of the contract price.[7]

There are circumstances where a transferee may be liable on a *quantum valebat* for goods which have been delivered without his request and which were consumed without his knowledge that they were to be paid for. For the delivery of the goods may have incontrovertibly benefited the transferee, in the sense that, as a result, he may have saved himself an inevitable expense. He should then be liable to pay the transferor the reasonable price of the goods or, if it is less, the value of the goods to him. For example, Esso delivers oil to the defendant's house, mistakenly believing that it is delivering oil to his neighbour's. The defendant consumes the oil believing that it has been delivered by Texaco, its normal supplier, with whom the defendant has a regular contract. Esso should, in our view, recover the market price which it normally charges to its consumers or, if it is less, the contract price which the defendant agreed to pay Texaco.

---

[6] What if he has eaten the fruit before he learns of the mistake? He may, depending on the facts, then be said to be incontrovertibly benefited: see text accompanying notes 7 and 8, below: And *cf. Boulton* v. *Jones* (1857) 2 H. & N. 564: see below, pp. 488–489.

[7] See above, pp. 22 *et seq.*

CHAPTER 7

RECOVERY OF LAND TRANSFERRED UNDER A MISTAKE

ACTING under a mistake, a transferor may contract to sell or may convey land[1] different from, or more extensive than, the land which he intended to sell or convey. In such a case the transferor may be able to obtain an order for rescission or rectification of the contract or the conveyance. Nowadays a conveyance may be rescinded even though it was induced by an innocent misrepresentation.[2] The conditions under which contracts and conveyances may be rescinded or rectified are discussed in a later Chapter.[3]

There are, however, special statutory provisions governing rectification where the title to the land has been registered under the Land Registration Act 1925. In such cases a transferor may apply for rectification of the land register,[4] and rectification may be granted, *inter alia*, where "by reason of any error or omission in the register, or by reason of any entry made under a mistake, it may be deemed just to rectify the register."[5] It is, however, provided that[6]:

Rectification may only take place against a proprietor in possession if:

(1) it is to give effect to an overriding interest, or an order of the court; or
(2) he has caused or substantially contributed to the error or omission by fraud or lack of care; or
(3) for any reason, it would be unjust not to rectify the register against him.

An innocent purchaser who has suffered loss by reason of rectification of the register[7] or by reason of an error or omission in the register which is not rectified,[8] is entitled to be indemnified from a State indemnity fund. The State

---

[1] In English law title to land can only be transferred in accordance with certain formalities: see, *e.g.* Law of Property Act 1925, ss.40, 52.
[2] Misrepresentation Act 1967, s.1(*b*); see below, p. 185, n. 25.
[3] See below, Chap. 8.
[4] Land Registration Act 1925, s.82, as amended by the Administration of Justice Act 1977, s.24.
[5] Land Registration Act 1925, s.82(1)(*h*). *Cf. Orakpo* v. *Manson Investments Ltd.* [1977] 1 W.L.R. 347, 360, *per* Buckley L.J., 370, *per* Goff L.J., C.A., reversed [1978] A.C. 95; see above, p. 66, below, pp. 595–596.
[6] Land Registration Act 1925, s.82(3).
[7] Land Registration Act 1925, s.83(1) as amended.
[8] Land Registration Act 1925, s.83(2) as amended.

guarantees the title of the registered proprietor,[9] so that claims for rectification of the register and indemnity from the fund are complementary.[10]

---

[9] See, generally, Gray, *Elements of Land Law*, pp. 194 *et seq.*

[10] *Chowood Ltd.* v. *Lyall* (*No. 2*) [1930] 1 Ch. 426, 2 Ch. 156; *Re Chowood's Registered Land* [1933] Ch. 574; *Re 139 Deptford High St., ex p. British Transport Commission* [1951] Ch. 884; *Orakpo* v. *Manson Investments Ltd.* [1977] 1 W.L.R. 347, rvs'd. on other grounds [1978] A.C. 95 (see above, p. 351).

For the recommendations of the Law Commission, see Law Commission Report No. 158 H.C. 269.

CHAPTER 8

RELIEF FROM TRANSACTIONS ENTERED INTO UNDER A MISTAKE

IN this Chapter, we shall consider the various ways in which a party may be relieved from transactions entered into under a mistake. The most important form of relief is *rescission*. Usually, to ground a claim for rescission, the mistake must have been induced by a misrepresentation; exceptionally, however, equity may rescind a transaction on grounds of mistake which has not been so induced.[1] The greater part of this Chapter will be occupied with a discussion of the right to rescind. But we shall also consider two other forms of relief, namely, *rectification* and *reopening accounts*.

1. RESCISSION

(a) *Rescission of Contracts Induced by Misrepresentation*[2]

Introductory

"A representation is a statement or assertion, made by one party to the other, before or at the time of the contract, of some matter or circumstance relating to it. Though it is sometimes contained in a written instrument, it is not an integral part of the contract; and consequently the contract is not broken though the representation proves untrue."[3] A mere representation is to be distinguished, therefore, from a statement which is intended by the parties to have the force of a contractual term. If the statement is false and is a term of the contract between the parties, the innocent party will be able to recover damages for breach of contract; but he will only be entitled to bring the contract to an end[4] if the term is sufficiently important to constitute a breach of condition,[5] as opposed to a breach of warranty[6] which only sounds in damages, or if the other party's breach is such that it will give rise "to an event which will deprive

---

[1] See below, pp. 212 *et seq. Cf.* the power of the court to set aside compromises made by counsel or solicitors if it considers it just to do so: see *Neale* v. *Gordon-Lennox* [1902] A.C. 465; *Shepherd* v. *Robinson* [1919] 1 K.B. 474; Corderey, *op. cit.*, pp. 89–91.
[2] See, generally, Cartwright, *Unequal Bargaining*, Part II. For a valuable comparative law survey see, Izhak England, *Restitution of Benefits Conferred Without Obligation* Vol. X of *Restitution—Unjust Enrichment and Negotiorum Gestio* of the *International Encyclopedia of Comparative Law.*
[3] *Behn* v. *Burness* (1863) 3 B. & S. 751, 753, *per* Williams J.
[4] See below, pp. 412 *et seq.* for a full discussion of the consequences of breach.
[5] Sale of Goods Act 1979, s.11(3).
[6] *Ibid.* ss.11(3) and 61(1).

the party not in default of substantially the whole benefit which it was intended that he should obtain from the contract."[7]

If the statement does not constitute a term of the contract, but is a mere representation, the representee may nevertheless have been induced by the representation to enter into the contract.[8] If so, and the representation proves to be false, the rights of the representee will depend on whether the misrepresentation was innocent, negligent, or fraudulent.

A fraudulent misrepresentation is one which is made "knowingly, or without belief in its truth, or recklessly, careless whether it be true or false."[9] A party who has been induced to enter into a contract by a fraudulent misrepresentation is entitled at common law to rescind the contract, and, whether or not he elects to rescind, to recover damages in tort for deceit.[10] The representee can rescind the contract without having recourse to an action for rescission; but he can, if necessary, bring such an action, as he may wish to do if the representor contests his right to rescind. If, however, *restitutio in integrum* is impossible,[11] or if third party rights intervene,[12] or if the representee affirms the contract with knowledge of his legal rights and the material facts rendering the representation false,[13] or if there is an undue lapse of time,[14] the right to rescind will be lost.

At common law, the victim of an innocent misrepresentation, not embodied in the contract, had originally no remedy,[15] though nowadays he may be able to recover damages from the representor in negligence.[16] The Misrepresentation Act 1967,[17] has also enlarged the remedies available to the representee by providing him, in certain circumstances, with a remedy in damages against a representor who has induced him to enter into a contract through a negligent misrepresentation of fact.

---

[7] *Hong Kong Fir Shipping Co. Ltd.* v. *Kawasaki Kisen Kaisha Ltd.* [1962] 2 Q.B. 26, 70, *per* Diplock L.J. *Cf. A/S Awilco of Oslo* v. *Fulvia S.p.A di Navigazione of Cagliari* [1981] 1 W.L.R. 314.

[8] Formerly, if the representation had been embodied in the contract, it became merged in the "higher contractual right," so that the representee's only remedy was for breach of the term of the contract; he could not therefore have treated it as a mere representation and have sought rescission in equity for misrepresentation: see *Pennsylvania Shipping Co.* v. *Compagnie Nationale de Navigation* [1936] 2 All E.R. 1167. But see now Misrepresentation Act 1967, s.1(a), see below, p. 185, n. 25.

[9] *Derry* v. *Peek* (1887) 14 App.Cas. 337, 374, *per* Lord Herschell; see also *Akerhielm* v. *De Mare* [1959] A.C. 789. *Semble* a deliberate concealment of a change of facts is fraudulent: *Incledon* v. *Watson* (1862) 2 F. & F. 841; but *cf. Arkwright* v. *Newbold* (1887) 17 Ch.D. 301, 325, *per* Cotton L.J., 329, *per* James L.J. For contracts *uberrimae fidei*, see *London Insurance* v. *Mansel* (1879) 11 Ch.D. 363, 368, *per* Jessel M.R. See generally (1969) 85 L.Q.R. 524 [Hudson].

[10] *Newbigging* v. *Adam* (1887) 34 Ch.D. 582, 592, *per* Bowen L.J.

[11] See below, pp. 198–201.

[12] See below, pp. 201–203.

[13] See below, pp. 203–206.

[14] See below, pp. 206–208.

[15] *Hopkins* v. *Tanqueray* (1854) 15 C.B. 130; *Behn* v. *Burness* (1863) 3 B. & S. 751.

[16] *Hedley Byrne & Co. Ltd.* v. *Heller & Partners Ltd.* [1964] A.C. 465; *Esso Petroleum Co.* v. *Mardon* [1975] Q.B. 819; *McInerny* v. *Lloyds Bank Ltd.* [1974] 1 Lloyd's Rep. 246.

[17] s.2(1): see below, p. 190.

Since the middle of the nineteenth century,[18] equity has been prepared to order rescission of a contract induced by innocent misrepresentation.[19] If rescission is granted the courts are ready to award restitution of benefits conferred by the representee on the representor under the rescinded contract, and, in particular, may order the representor to indemnify the representee against liabilities undertaken by the representee under the contract.[20] Wherever the court has power to order rescission for innocent or negligent misrepresentation, it now may "declare the contract subsisting" and award damages instead, if it considers it "equitable to do so, having regard to the nature of the misrepresentation and the loss that would be caused by it if the contract were upheld, as well as to the loss that rescission would cause to the other party."[21] This right to rescind may also be lost on the same grounds as in cases of fraud, namely, if *restitutio in integrum* is impossible,[22] or if third party rights have intervened,[23] or if the representee has affirmed the contract,[24] or if there has been an undue lapse of time.[25]

A contract which is liable to rescission for misrepresentation is, therefore, within certain limits, voidable by the representee. Such a contract should be distinguished from a contract which is void, for example, for fundamental mistake, though occasionally a misrepresentation may induce a fundamental mistake, in which case the effect of the misrepresentation will be to render the contract void.[26] A voidable contract should also be distinguished from one which can be determined or brought to an end,[27] as in some cases of breach of contract. A contract which is voidable for misrepresentation is intermediate between one which is void *ab initio* and one which is liable to be brought to an end; for a contract voidable for misrepresentation stands until some action is taken by the innocent party to bring it to an end, though once that action is successfully taken, the contract is not simply determined but is avoided *ab initio*.

In this section we are concerned with rescission for misrepresentation as a form of restitutionary relief. The rules which we shall discuss relate to rescission for fraudulent, negligent and innocent misrepresentation. We shall first

---

[18] *Cooper* v. *Joel* (1859) 1 De G.F. & J. 240; *Re Liverpool Borough Bank* (1858) 26 Beav. 268.
[19] See below, n. 25.
[20] See below, pp. 210 *et seq.* for a full discussion.
[21] Misrepresentation Act 1967, s.2(2); see below, pp. 208–209.
[22] See below, pp. 198–201.
[23] See below, pp. 201–203.
[24] See below, pp. 203–206.
[25] See below, pp. 206–208. By s.1(*a*) of the Misrepresentation Act 1967, a right to rescind for innocent misrepresentation is no longer lost merely because the representation is subsequently incorporated into the contract as a term of the contract (see above, n. 7). S.1(*b*) abrogates the common law restriction that executed contracts (including contracts for the sale of land) could not be rescinded for innocent misrepresentation.
[26] See, for example, *Cundy* v. *Lindsay* (1878) L.R. 3 App.Cas. 459.
[27] See below, pp. 412 *et seq.*

consider the conditions necessary for rescission; secondly, the limits to rescission; and finally, the recovery of benefits conferred under contracts so rescinded.

The conditions necessary for rescission

To render the contract voidable the representee must establish that the representor[28] made a misrepresentation of fact which induced him to enter into the contract. We shall now analyse the constituent parts of this principle.

(1) There must be a representation

A representation may be made expressly, or may be implied from a person's conduct. An express representation may be found in any written document, including a map[29] or photograph[30]; or it can be oral, through the spoken word, or even a gesture, such as a "nod or a wink, or a shake of a head or a smile."[31]

Representations by conduct may also arise in any number of ways. A buyer of goods at an auction "must be taken to have made an implied representation that he intended to pay for them."[32] And in the celebrated case of Gill v. M'Dowell[33] the sending of a hermaphrodite beast to a sale of bullocks and heifers was held to be an implied representation that the animal was either a bullock or a heifer—in these circumstances, at least, a hermaphrodite was deemed to be a "sort of living lie."[34]

(2) The representation must be false

The representation, which induced the representee to enter into the contract, must have been false. However, a mere representation is "not like a warranty; it is not necessary [that] it should be strictly construed or strictly complied with; it is enough if it is substantially true; it is enough if it is substantially complied with."[35] If the representor can show that what he said is substantially correct, his statement cannot be described as a misrepresentation. Conversely, if the natural result of his acts or language is to convey a false impression, the representation is false.[36]

---

[28] Where a party has entered into a contract with an agent acting for an undisclosed principal, the contract may be rescinded if the undisclosed principal has induced that party to enter into the contract by a fraudulent misrepresentation, even though the agent is innocent of the fraud: *Garnac Grain Co. Inc.* v. *H.M.F. Faure & Fairclough Ltd. and Bunge Corp.* [1968] A.C. 1130. *Sed quaere*, where the undisclosed principal's misrepresentation is innocent: see [1966] 1 Q.B. 650, 684–686, *per* Diplock L.J.

[29] *Re the Mount Morgan (West) Gold Mine Ltd.* (1887) 56 L.T. 622.

[30] *Newman* v. *Pinto* (1887) 57 L.T. 31.

[31] *Walters* v. *Morgan* (1861) 3 De G.F. & J. 718, 724, *per* Lord Campbell L.C.

[32] *Re Shackleton* (1875) 10 Ch.App. 446, 449, *per* Mellish L.J.

[33] [1903] 2 I.R. 463.

[34] [1903] 2 I.R. 463, 469, *per* Gibson J.; see also *Ajello* v. *Worsley* [1898] 1 Ch. 274.

[35] *With* v. *O'Flanagan* [1936] Ch. 575, 581, *per* Lord Wright M.R.

[36] *Arnison* v. *Smith* (1889) 41 Ch.D. 348; *Aaron's Reefs Ltd.* v. *Twiss* [1896] A.C. 273, 281, *per* Lord Halsbury L.C.; *Charles Hunt Ltd.* v. *Palmer* [1931] 2 Ch. 287; *Laurence* v. *Lexcourt Holdings Ltd.* [1978] 1 W.L.R. 1128.

The critical date for determining whether a representation is false is the date when the representee alters his position on the faith of the representation.[37] If, therefore, the representation is false when made but true when acted upon, the representee will not be able to obtain rescission of the contract which he has been induced to enter into as a result of the representation.[38]

(3) *The representation must be of fact*

"The misrepresentation . . . must be a misrepresentation of a matter of fact."[39] The courts have not formulated for the purpose of this rule any general definition of what is a "matter of fact." They have held, however, that it is different from a misrepresentation of law, a statement of opinion and a promise.[40]

A contract entered into under a mistake, induced by an innocent misrepresentation of pure law, cannot be rescinded.[41] But the representee can obtain relief if he can show that the representation was not of pure law but of mixed law and fact and induced a mistake on his part as to private rights, such as rights of ownership.[42] If, however, the representation of law was fraudulent, the court will grant rescission of a contract induced by it even though the misrepresentation was one of pure law. No man who wilfully misrepresents the law should "be allowed in equity to retain any benefit he got by such misrepresentation."[43] Not only is this a just rule but it is consistent with principle, for a representation of law necessarily implies a representation of fact, namely, that the representor has an honest belief that his representation of law is correct.[44]

[37] *Briess* v. *Woolley* [1954] A.C. 333.

[38] *Ship* v. *Crosskill* (1870) L.R. 10 Eq. 73. But if the representation is true when made, and subsequently becomes false, the representor is under a duty to inform the representee of the true facts before the making of the contract: see *With* v. *O'Flanagan* [1936] Ch. 575, see below, p. 190.

[39] *Eaglesfield* v. *The Marquis of Londonderry* (1876) 4 Ch.D. 693, 709, *per* James L.J. See also *Smith* v. *Chadwick* (1884) 9 App.Cas. 187; *Lynde* v. *Anglo-Italian Hemp Spinning Co.* [1896] 1 Ch. 178, 183–184, *per* Romer J.

[40] *Cf. Walker* v. *Boyle* [1982] 1 W.L.R. 495, 501, *per* Dillon J. (a warning in reply to the purchaser's preliminary enquiries that accuracy is not guaranteed does not prevent subsequent replies from being representations of fact).

[41] *Directors of Midland Great Western Ry. of Ireland* v. *Johnson* (1858) 6 H.L. 798, 811, *per* Lord Chelmsford; *Eaglesfield* v. *The Marquis of Londonderry* (1876) 4 Ch.D. 693, 708, 709, *per* James L.J.

[42] *Cooper* v. *Phibbs* (1867) L.R. 2 H.L. 149; *Hirschfeld* v. *The London, Brighton & South Coast Ry.* (1876) 2 Q.B.D. 1; *West London Commercial Bank* v. *Kitson* (1884) 13 Q.B.D. 360.

[43] *West London Commercial Bank Ltd.* v. *Kitson* (1884) 13 Q.B.D. 360, 363, *per* Bowen L.J.

[44] *Cf. Edgington* v. *Fitzmaurice* (1885) 29 Ch.D. 459. But the grounds on which the courts have granted relief to a representee induced to enter into a contract by a misrepresentation of law have been varied: see *Harse* v. *Pearl Life Assurance Co.* [1904] 1 K.B. 558, 563, *per* Collins M.R., 564, *per* Romer L.J.; *Kettlewell* v. *Refuge Assurance Co.* [1908] 1 K.B. 545, 550, *per* Lord Alverstone, 551, *per* Gorrell Barnes P., 552, *per* Buckley L.J.; *Hughes* v. *The Liverpool Victoria Legal Friendly Society* [1916] 2 K.B. 482, 492, *per* Phillimore L.J., 495, *per* Bankes L.J.; and see above, pp. 150–153.

The courts have also distinguished a representation of fact from a representation of opinion.[45] Thus, in *Bisset* v. *Wilkinson*,[46] a statement that certain land had a carrying capacity of 2,000 sheep was held on the facts of the case[47] to be a statement of opinion, for the particular land had never been a sheep farm so that the representee was just as able as the representor to form an equal judgment on the carrying capacity of the land. A statement of opinion may, however, imply a representation of fact. As Bowen L.J. once said[48]:

> "In a case where the facts are equally well known to both parties, what one of them says to the other is frequently nothing but an expression of opinion. The statement of such opinion is in a sense a statement of fact, about the condition of the man's own mind, but only of an irrelevant fact, for it is of no consequence what the opinion is. But if the facts are not equally known to both sides, then a statement of opinion by the one who knows the facts best involves very often a statement of a material fact, for he impliedly states that he knows facts which justify his opinion."

Thus, an estate agent who tells a prospective customer that any building society will lend £1,200 on a particular bungalow, the purchase price of which is £2,400, impliedly represents that the value of the bungalow substantially exceeds £1,200.[49] Similarly if, in the particulars of sale of an absolute reversionary interest in a trust fund on the death of an annuitant, there is a statement by the vendor's solicitor that the annuitant had no aggregable estate, it may be assumed by the purchaser that the solicitor had reasonable grounds for his statement, for as between the vendor and purchaser this was a "case where the vendor's knowledge or means of knowledge is far superior to that of the purchaser."[50]

Just as a statement of description may "for some purposes be a statement of opinion, and, for others, a statement of fact,"[51] so also that which is in form a promise may be in another aspect a representation. A promise, or any statement of intention, may involve a statement of the existing state of mind of the representor, and such a statement is a representation of fact.[52] So, in *Edgington* v. *Fitzmaurice*,[53] a prospectus, inviting subscriptions for certain debentures, stated that the objects of the issue were *inter alia* to complete certain building operations and to develop the company's trade. In fact, the real object of the issue was to enable the directors of the company to pay off certain pressing

---

[45] See, *e.g. Jennings* v. *Broughton* (1853) 5 De G.M. & G. 126.
[46] [1927] A.C. 177.
[47] [1927] A.C. 177, 183–184.
[48] In *Smith* v. *Land & House Property Corp.* (1884) 28 Ch.D. 7, 15.
[49] *Armstrong* v. *Strain* [1951] 1 K.B. 232; see also *Leyland* v. *Illingworth* (1860) 2 De G.F. & J. 248; *Bellairs* v. *Tucker* (1884) 13 Q.B.D. 562, particularly at 573, *per* Denman J.
[50] *Brown* v. *Raphael* [1958] Ch. 636, 643, *per* Evershed M.R.
[51] *Armstrong* v. *Strain* [1951] 1 T.L.R. 856, 860, *per* Devlin J.
[52] *Donner's Motors Ltd.* v. *Kufinya*, 1968 (1) S.A. 434; but *cf. Wales* v. *Wadham* [1977] 1 W.L.R. 199.
[53] (1885) 29 Ch.D. 459. *Cf. Smith Kline & French Laboratories Ltd.* v. *Long* [1989] 1 W.L.R. 1; *Kleinwort Benson Ltd.* v. *Malaysia Mining Corp. Berhad* [1989] 1 W.L.R. 379.

liabilities. The Court of Appeal held that the statement in the prospectus was a statement of fact and not a statement of intention. The directors never had any intention of doing what they said they were going to do, and a "misrepresentation as to the state of a man's mind is . . . a misstatement of fact."[54] The fact that a person does not carry out his intention or does not fulfil his promise does not *ipso facto* mean that his representation is false, although it may provide some evidence that he never intended to do what he promised to do.[55]

Non-disclosure

A party's failure to disclose any fact exclusively within his knowledge to the other contracting party does not generally amount to a misrepresentation, even though he is aware that the knowledge of the fact might "reasonably be expected to influence the price of the subject to be sold. Simple reticence does not amount to legal fraud, however it may be viewed by moralists."[56] Thus, in the well-known case of *Smith* v. *Hughes*,[57] where a buyer bought new oats thinking that he was buying old oats, it was held that it was not incumbent on the seller, even though aware of the buyer's mistake, to inform him that the oats were new, provided that the mistake had not been induced by the seller.[58] The general rule is that the breach by a party to a contract *uberrimae fidei* of his obligation of disclosure does not give rise to an action for damages; the aggrieved party's only right is rescission. As Slade L.J. said in *Banque Keyser Ullmann S.A.* v. *Skandia (U.K.) Insurance Co. Ltd.*:

> "[i]f the bank's right to full disclosure of material facts is founded neither on tort nor on contract nor on the existence of a fiduciary duty nor on statute we [the Court of Appeal] find it difficult to see how as a matter of legal analysis it can be said to be found a claim for damages."[59]

The general rule that silence does not ground an action in damages can be harsh, and the courts have, not surprisingly, kept it within strict limits. A half-truth is not equivalent to complete silence and may amount to a misrepresentation of fact; a representor cannot choose to speak to some facts and colour them by suppressing others.[60] If the representation is a continuing representation, which is true when made but which is, to the representor's knowledge, false when acted upon by the representee, the representor is under a duty to correct the misrepresentation and inform the representee of the true

---

[54] (1885) 29 Ch.D. 459, 483, *per* Bowen L.J.
[55] *Clydesdale Bank Ltd.* v. *Paton* [1896] A.C. 381.
[56] *Walters* v. *Morgan* (1861) 3 De G.F. & J. 718, 723–724, *per* Lord Campbell L.C.; see also *Horsfall* v. *Thomas* (1862) 1 H. & C. 90, 99–100, *per* Bramwell B.
[57] (1871) L.R. 6 Q.B. 597.
[58] (1871) L.R. 6 Q.B. 597, 605, *per* Cockburn C.J. *Aliter*, if the buyer had bought the oats under the mistaken impression that the seller had contracted that they were old; in that case the contract would be void. On this point, there was a misdirection by the county court judge in *Smith* v. *Hughes*, and a new trial was ordered.
[59] [1990] 1 Q.B. 665, 776. Slade L.J.'s judgment was, on this point, adopted by Lord Templeman in the House of Lords: [1991] A.C. 249, 280.
[60] *Tapp* v. *Lee* (1803) 3 Bos. & Pul. 367; *Foster* v. *Charles* (1830) 6 Bing. 396.

facts. Any "representation made as a matter of inducement to enter into a contract is to be treated as a continuing representation,"[61] so that if the "representation relates to an existing state of things, the representor is deemed to be repeating his representation at every successive moment during the interval, unless he withdraws or modifies it by timely notice to the representee in the meantime."[62] Thus, in *With* v. *O'Flanagan*,[63] the vendor, in January 1934, correctly represented to the potential purchaser of his medical practice that its takings were at the rate of £2,000 per annum. When the contract was signed in May 1934 the takings had dropped off to such an extent that in the last weeks of April the average takings were only £5 per week. The vendor did not tell the purchaser about this drop in takings. The Court of Appeal held that the purchaser could rescind the contract.[64] A somewhat similar principle was applied in *Briess* v. *Woolley*,[65] where the House of Lords held that the defendant's agent, who made a fraudulent misrepresentation to the plaintiff before his agency commenced, but allowed it to go uncorrected after the commencement of his agency in the knowledge that it would be acted upon by the representee, was under a duty to correct the misrepresentation. The agent had not done so, and the representee could accordingly rescind a contract, which, induced by the misrepresentation, he had entered into with the agent's principal. It is an open question whether a representation which is true when made but which is subsequently falsified without the representor's knowledge amounts in law to an innocent misrepresentation.[66]

It is possible that the Misrepresentation Act 1967, s.2(1), has not affected the common law of non-disclosure for the Act only applies to "misrepresentations made"[67] by a representor, which seems to embrace continuing representations and half-truths but not, perhaps, simple non-disclosure.

In exceptional cases, the common law imposes upon a party the duty to speak and to disclose all the material facts within his knowledge. Thus, if there

---

[61] *With* v. *O'Flanagan* [1936] Ch. 575, 584, *per* Lord Wright M.R.; see also *Smith* v. *Kay* (1859) 7 H.L.C. 750, 769, *per* Lord Cranworth; *Brownlie* v. *Campbell* (1880) L.R. 5 App.Cas. 925, 950, *per* Lord Blackburn; *Briess* v. *Woolley* [1954] A.C. 333, 358, *per* Lord Cohen.

[62] Halsbury, *Laws* (3rd ed.), Vol. 26, p. 843, cited with approval in *Briess* v. *Woolley* [1954] A.C. 333, 354, *per* Lord Tucker. (*Cf. Laws* (4th ed.), Vol. 31, § 1056, which retains the identical language.) In *With* v. *O'Flanagan* [1936] Ch. 575, 586, Romer L.J. described a similar statement as "obviously consistent with the plainest principles of equity."

[63] [1936] Ch. 575.

[64] *Ibid.* at p. 587.

[65] [1954] A.C. 333.

[66] (1969) 85 L.Q.R. 524, 525 [Hudson]: It is also an open question whether the principle in *With* v. *O'Flanagan* applies if one party to the contract represents to the other party his intention to do something but by the time of the making of the contract he has changed his mind: see *Wales* v. *Wadham* [1977] 1 W.L.R. 199, approved in *Livesey* v. *Jenkins* [1985] A.C. 424, 438 (it does not) and *Trail* v. *Baring* (1864) 4 De G.J. & S. 318 (it does), cited in Cartwright, *op. cit.* n. 2, pp. 84–88.

[67] *Cf. London General Omnibus Co.* v. *Holloway* [1912] 2 K.B. 72, 77, *per* Vaughan Williams L.J. See P. S. Atiyah and G. H. Treitel, "Misrepresentation Act 1967" (1967) 30 M.L.R. 369; and *cf.* (1969) 85 L.Q.R. at pp. 526–527 [Hudson]; see above, p. 184. *Banque Keyser Ullmann S.A.* v. *Skandia (U.K.) Insurance Co. Ltd.* [1990] 1 Q.B. 665, 789–790, affirmed [1991] 2 A.C. 249, H.L.: see below, p. 195.

is a fiduciary relationship between the parties, equity has always insisted that there should be a full and frank disclosure by the fiduciary to the beneficiary of all the facts within the fiduciary's knowledge.[68] Similarly, family compromises, as distinct from contracts between spouses,[69] may be set aside in equity if either party to the compromise conceals material facts from the other.[70]

Contracts uberrimae fidei

There are other contracts where common law or statute[71] insist on a full disclosure of all material facts. The principal examples at common law[72] of such contracts are contracts of insurance and salvage agreements. Their common factor is "that, from the very necessity of the case, only one party possesses knowledge of all the material facts."[73]

The most important example of the so-called contract *uberrimae fidei* is the *contract of insurance.* A contract of insurance, whether marine or non-marine,[74] is a contract of the utmost good faith, "and if the utmost good faith be not observed by either party, the contract may be avoided by the other party."[75] Consequently, the assured is under a duty to disclose to the insurer every "material circumstance"[76] which is known to him. Indeed the obligation to disclose material facts is "a mutual one, imposing reciprocal duties on insurer and insured."[77]

(1) *Non-disclosure by the assured*

The question of materiality is one of fact.[78] A circumstance is material if it would influence the mind and judgment of a prudent[79] insurer, governing

---

[68] *Cf. Esso Petroleum Co.* v. *Mardon* [1975] Q.B. 819.
[69] *Wales* v. *Wadham* [1977] 1 W.L.R. 199.
[70] *Greenwood* v. *Greenwood* (1863) 3 De G.J. & Sm. 28. Other compromises and settled claims may be reopened for want of good faith: see above, pp. 53–54.
[71] *e.g.* under the Financial Services Act 1986, s.146 and Social Security Act 1986, s.53.
[72] *Chitty on Contracts*, Vol. I, §§ 490–491, discusses contracts for the sale of land and of guarantee in this context; but these do not seem to be genuine examples of contracts *uberrimae fidei*.
[73] *Wales* v. *Wadham* [1977] 1 W.L.R. 199, 215, *per* Tudor Evans J.
[74] In relation to non-disclosure, the principles of law are *generally* similar in both classes of insurance: see *London Assurance* v. *Mansel* (1879) 11 Ch.D. 363, 367, *per* Jessel M.R.; *Joel* v. *Law Union Insurance Co.* [1908] 2 K.B. 863, 878, *per* Vaughan Williams L.J. But see below, n. 82.
[75] Marine Insurance Act 1906, s.17; *Mackender* v. *Feldia A.G.* [1966] 2 Lloyd's Rep. 449, 455, *per* Lord Denning M.R.; *Container Transport International Inc.* v. *Oceanus Mutual Underwriting Association (Bermuda) Ltd.* [1984] 1 Lloyd's Rep. 476, 492–493, *per* Kerr L.J.
[76] Marine Insurance Act 1906, s.18(1), (2); *London Assurance* v. *Mansel* (1879) 11 Ch.D. 363. In this context the term "circumstance" includes any communication made to, or information received by, the assured: see Marine Insurance Act 1906, s.18(5). And *cf. Anglo-African Merchants Ltd.* v. *Bayley* [1970] 1 Q.B. 311.
[77] *Banque Keyser Ullmann S.A.* v. *Skandia (UK) Insurance Co. Ltd.* (1990) 1 Q.B. 665, 769–770, *per* Slade L.J., citing *Carter* v. *Boehm* (1766) 3 Burr. 1905, 1909, *per* Lord Mansfield C.J.; see below, p. 195.
[78] *Hoare* v. *Bremridge* (1872) L.R. 8 Ch.App. 22: *Inversiones Mannia S.A.* v. *Sphere Drake Ins. Co. plc* [1989] 1 Lloyd's Rep. 69. Marine Insurance Act 1906, s.18(4).
[79] Or "reasonable." Both words appear to mean the same thing: *cf. Associated Oil Carriers* v. *Union Insurance of Canton* [1917] 2 K.B. 184, 192, *per* Atkin J. But the standard is of a prudent or

himself by the principles on which insurers in practice act, in determining whether he will take the risk or in fixing the premium if he consents to take the risk.[80] The Court of Appeal has held[81] that there is no obvious reason why the rule should be different in marine and non-marine insurance.[82] If the assured fails to make a disclosure the insurer may avoid the policy even though the assured suppressed the material circumstance quite innocently[83] or the loss has arisen from a cause totally unconnected with the fact not disclosed.[84]

"Avoidance of the policy . . . results in it being set aside *ab initio*, the repayment of any losses, and the return of any premiums paid under it."[85] The losses are repayable as money paid under a mistake of fact[86]; the premiums are recoverable because the insurers have never been at risk and hence there has been a total failure of consideration.[87]

The duty of disclosure is common to all classes of insurance, although certain facts may be material in marine but not in non-marine insurance, and vice versa. In marine insurance, for example, it has been held not to be a material circumstance that the assured had been refused cover by another insurer[88]; but in other classes of insurance a previous refusal ought to be disclosed. Thus a fire insurance policy was set aside because the assured had not disclosed that he had been previously refused motor insurance.[89]

---

reasonable insurer, not the *particular* insurer; *Container Transport International Group Inc.* v. *Oceanus Mutual (Underwriting) Association (Bermuda) Ltd.* [1984] 1 Lloyd's Rep. 476, C.A.; *cf.* see below, n. 82.

[80] Marine Insurance Act 1906, s.18(2); Road Traffic Act 1972, s.149(5); *Ionides* v. *Pender* (1874) L.R. 9 Q.B. 531; *Piper* v. *Royal Exchange Assurance* (1932) 44 Ll.L.R. 103; *Container Transport International Inc.* v. *Oceanus Mutual Underwriting Association (Bermuda) Ltd.* [1984] 1 Lloyd's Rep. 476, C.A. (where the argument that, an insurer can succeed only if he can show that a prudent insurer would have declined the risk or demanded a higher premium, was rejected).

[81] *Lambert* v. *Co-operative Insurance Society Ltd.* [1975] 2 Lloyd's Rep. 485, following *Mutual Life Assurance Co. of New York* v. *Ontario Metal Products Company Ltd.* [1925] A.C. 344 (P.C.).

[82] There is authority which suggests that in life assurance the test may be different: should a reasonable man in the assured's position and with knowledge of the facts in dispute have realised that the circumstances were material to the risk?: see *Godfrey* v. *Britannic Assurance Co.* [1963] 2 Lloyd's Rep. 515, which was not cited in *Lambert's* case (see above, n. 72). This test was first formulated in *Life Association of Scotland* v. *Foster* (1873) 11 M. 351, also not cited. For a criticism of the prudent insurer test, see below, p. 195, n. 8.

[83] *Hewitt Bros.* v. *Wilson* [1914] 3 K.B. 1131, [1915] 2 K.B. 739; *Lambert* v. *Co-operative Insurance Company Ltd.* [1975] 2 Lloyd's Rep. 485, 492, *per* Cairns L.J. But *cf.* (1969) 32 M.L.R. 615, 616–617 [Hasson].

[84] *Lynch* v. *Hamilton* (1810) 3 Taunt. 37.

[85] *Cornhill Insurance Co.* v. *Assenheim* (1937) 58 Ll.L.R. 27, 31, *per* MacKinnon J. *Cf.* MacGillivray and Parkington *on Insurance Law*, § 685–686, distinguishing Lord Denning M.R.'s dictum to the contrary in *Mackender* v. *Feldia A.G.* [1966] 2 Lloyd's Rep. 449, 455.

[86] *Cf.* see above, Chap. 3.

[87] *Feise* v. *Parkinson* (1812) 4 Taunt. 640; *Anderson* v. *Thornton* (1853) 8 Ex. 425; Marine Insurance Act 1906, s.84(3)(a); see below, Chap. 18.

[88] *Glasgow Assurance* v. *Symondson* (1911) 104 L.T. 254, 257, *per* Scrutton J.

[89] *Locker & Woolf Ltd.* v. *Western Australia Insurance Co. Ltd.* [1936] 1 K.B. 408.

There are many cases where policies have been avoided for non-disclosure by the assured.[90] In one case, for example, a marine insurance policy was set aside because the assured did not disclose that the covered goods were excessively valued[91]; this is a material circumstance affecting the risk, for it tends to make the assured less careful in selecting his ship and captain, and might diminish his efforts to reduce any loss he might suffer in case of disaster. A fire insurance policy on a warehouse was avoided because the assured failed to disclose that a fire had very recently broken out in adjoining premises, even though the assured was under the impression, when he made his proposal, that the fire had been extinguished.[92] An insurer may, however, waive the assured's failure to disclose a material fact.[93]

If, however, the assured can show that the fact not disclosed would not have influenced the mind of a prudent insurer in taking the risk or fixing the premium, then the policy will not be avoided for non-disclosure. A striking example of such a case is *Associated Oil Carriers Ltd.* v. *Union Insurance Society of Canton Ltd.*[94] In July 1914 the plaintiff shipowners effected an insurance against war risks with the defendants upon freight on a voyage to Romania and back, but they did not disclose to the defendants that the charterers were of German nationality. A few days later war broke out between Great Britain and Germany and the charterparty was determined by supervening illegality. The plaintiffs claimed under the policy for the value of their lost freight, and the defendants pleaded that the plaintiffs had failed to disclose what they alleged to be the material circumstances of the charterers' nationality. Atkin J. allowed the plaintiffs' claim. He held that their non-disclosure did not vitiate the contract, since it had been conclusively established in evidence that at the time the policy was effected no prudent insurer would have been influenced by the nationality of the charterer in determining whether he would take the risk or in adjusting the premium.

Generally an assured is under no duty to disclose facts of which he is not aware. In *Joel* v. *Law Union Assurance Co.*,[95] Fletcher Moulton L.J. stated the law as follows:

"The duty is a duty to disclose, and you cannot disclose what you do not know. The obligation to disclose, therefore, necessarily depends on the knowledge you possess. I must not be misunderstood. Your opinion of the materiality of that knowledge is of no moment. If a reasonable man would

---

[90] See generally Arnould, *Law of Marine Insurance and Average*, §§ 609 *et seq.*; MacGillivray and Parkington on *Insurance Law*, §§ 634 *et seq.* The questions put by the insurers on the proposal forms may limit the applicant's duty of disclosure: see MacGillivray and Parkington, § 644.

[91] *Ionides* v. *Pender* (1874) L.R. 5 Q.B. 531. *Cf. Berger* v. *Pollock* [1973] 2 Lloyd's Rep. 442.

[92] *Bufe* v. *Turner* (1815) 6 Taunt. 338. See also *Arterial Caravans Ltd.* v. *Yorkshire Insurance Co. Ltd.* [1973] 1 Lloyd's Rep. 169.

[93] MacGillivray and Parkington on *Insurance Law*, §§ 711 *et seq.* See generally *Haynes Barlas* v. *Beer* (1946) 78 Ll.L.R. 337; *De Maurier* v. *Bastion* [1967] 2 Lloyd's Rep. 550.

[94] [1917] 2 K.B. 184; *cf. Roselodge Ltd.* v. *Castle* [1966] 2 Lloyd's Rep. 113.

[95] [1908] 2 K.B. 863, 884.

have recognised that it was material to disclose the knowledge in question, it is no excuse that you did not recognise it to be so. But the question always is, Was the knowledge you possessed such that you ought to have disclosed it?"

Insurers often try to circumvent this rule by inserting in the proposal form a declaration to be completed by the proposer that he warrants the accuracy as well as the truthfulness of his statements. The courts, however, tend to construe such a provision strictly against the insurer.[96] But the assured is deemed to know everything, which, in the ordinary course of his business, ought to be known by him.[97] This caveat has received statutory recognition in cases of marine insurance[98]; but it is not clear whether it applies equally to non-marine insurance.[99]

There are certain matters which the assured need not disclose. These include any circumstance known or presumed to be known to the insurer[1]; any circumstance which diminishes the risk[2]; any circumstance as to which information is waived by the insurer[3]; and any circumstance which it is superfluous to disclose because of an express or implied warranty.[4] There is no presumption that matters not in the proposal form are immaterial,[5] although a failure to ask a question relating to a particular fact may be evidence that a prudent insurer would not regard it as a material circumstance.[6]

The assured's duty of disclosure ceases to exist as soon as the contract is concluded, that is, when the proposal of the assured is accepted by the insurer.[7]

From time to time criticisms have been made of the strict rule of full disclosure. It has been suggested that the law should be brought into line with the majority of American jurisdictions which allow a policy to be avoided only

---

[96] *Bond Air Services Ltd.* v. *Hill* [1955] 2 Q.B. 417.

[97] *Joel* v. *Law Union Insurance Co.* [1908] 2 K.B. 863, 884–885, *per* Fletcher Moulton L.J.

[98] Marine Insurance Act 1906, s.18(1).

[99] MacGillivray and Parkington on *Insurance Law*, §§ 639–640, 837; *Cf.* Halsbury's *Laws* (4th ed.), Vol. 25, § 373, which states that s.18(1) represents a "general principle" of insurance law; and *Australia and New Zealand Bank* v. *Colonial Wharves, Boag (Third Party)* [1960] 2 Lloyd's Rep. 241.

[1] *Bates* v. *Hewitt* (1867) L.R. 2 Q.B. 595; *Cantiere Meccanico Brindisino* v. *Janson* [1912] 3 K.B. 452; Marine Insurance Act 1906, s.18(3)(*b*), which further provides that the insurer is presumed to know matters of common notoriety or knowledge, and matters which an insurer, in the ordinary course of his business, ought to know.

[2] *Carter* v. *Boehm* (1766) 3 Burr. 1905; Marine Insurance Act 1906, s.18(3)(*a*).

[3] *Beckwith* v. *Sydebotham* (1807) 1 Camp. 116; *Greenhill* v. *Federal Insurance Co. Ltd.* [1927] 1 K.B. 65; *Anglo-African Merchants* v. *Bayley* [1969] 1 Lloyd's Rep. 268; *Arterial Caravans Ltd.* v. *Yorkshire Insurance Co.* [1973] 1 Lloyd's Rep. 169; Marine Insurance Act 1906, s.18(3)(*c*).

[4] Marine Insurance Act 1906, s.18(3)(*d*).

[5] *Schoolman* v. *Hall* [1951] 1 Lloyd's Rep. 139, particularly at 142, *per* Cohen L.J.

[6] *Joel* v. *Law Union Insurance Co.* [1908] 2 K.B. 863, 878, *per* Vaughan Williams L.J.; *Newsholme Bros.* v. *Road Transport & General Insurance Co. Ltd.* [1929] 2 K.B. 356, 362–363, *per* Scrutton L.J.

[7] Marine Insurance Act 1906, s.21; *Lishman* v. *Northern Maritime Insurance Co.* (1873) L.R. 8 C.P. 216, 10 C.P. 179; *Whitwell* v. *Autocar Fire and Accident Insurance Co.* (1927) 27 Ll.L.R. 418; *Looker* v. *Law Union Assurance* [1928] 1 K.B. 554.

if the assured wilfully conceals a material fact; alternatively, that a policy should only be avoided if a reasonable person in the position of the assured would have disclosed the fact.[8]

(2) *Non-disclosure by the insurer*

No decision has held an insurer liable for failing to disclose a material fact, although there is no doubt that, in an appropriate case, he may be so liable.[9] One example of a material fact, posited by Lord Mansfield, is if an insurer, who had insured a ship for a voyage, knew that she had already arrived.[10]

> "Another example would be the insurance against fire of a house which the insurer knew had been demolished. In these cases the undisclosed information would have had a material and direct effect upon the risk against which the insured was seeking to protect himself. Indeed, the assured would have said that the risk no longer existed."[11]

In contrast, the House of Lords has held that an insurer was not obliged to disclose the fact that it knew of the earlier misconduct of the assured's agent, even though if the assured had known that fact it would not have made a loan, now irrecoverable, to a third party.[12-16]

An agreement to render salvage services may likewise be avoided for non-disclosure of a material fact.[17] So, for example, a salvage agreement has been avoided for failure to disclose damage to the vessel in danger which might have rendered towage longer and more arduous.[18] On the other hand, it has been held that the value of property in peril is not, in this context, a material fact which must be disclosed.[19-20]

---

[8] See generally Law Reform Committee, *Conditions and Exceptions in Insurance Policies*, Cmnd. 62 (1957); Law Commission, *Report* No. 104: *Non Disclosure and Breach of Warranty* Cmnd. 8064 (1980); (1969) 32 M.L.R. 615, 632–637 [R. A. Hasson]; MacGillivray and Parkington on *Insurance Law* §§ 724–726, who question, as do the Law Commission, the adequacy of the insurance industry's Statements of Insurance Practice.

[9] *Banque Keyser Ullmann S.A.* v. *Scandia (U.K.) Insurance Co. Ltd.* [1991] 2 A.C. 249.

[10] *Carter* v. *Boehm* (1766) 3 Burr. 1905, 1909.

[11] *Banque Keyser Ullmann S.A.* v. *Skandia (U.K.) Insurance Co. Ltd.* [1991] 2 A.C. 249, 282, *per* Lord Jauncey; *Cf.* [1990] 1 Q.B. 665, 772, *per* Slade L.J. ("[T]he duty falling upon the insurer must at least extend to disclosing all facts known to him which are material either to the nature of the risk sought to be covered or the recoverability of a claim under the policy which a prudent insured would take into account in deciding whether or not to place the risk for which he seeks cover with that insurer.")

[12-16] *Ibid.*

[17] *The Kingalock* (1854) 1 Spinks E. & A. 263, esp. at 265, *per* Dr. Lushington; see also *The Canova* (1866) L.R. 1 A. & E. 54, 56, *per* Dr. Lushington.

[18] *The Kingalock* (1854) 1 Spinks E. & A. 263.

[19-20] *The Henry* (1851) 15 Jur. 183, criticised in Kennedy, *Civil Salvage*, p. 344.

The misrepresentation must have induced the representee to enter into the contract

It is a question of fact in each particular case whether the representee has been induced to enter into a contract by the misrepresentation of the representor. Though the representee does not have to show that the representation was made to him directly, he must establish that the representor intended him to act upon that representation.[21] "It is sufficient if the representation is made to a third person to be communicated to the plaintiff, or to be communicated to a class of persons of whom the plaintiff is one, or even if it is made to the public generally with a view to its being acted on and the plaintiff, as one of the public, acts on it and suffers damage thereby."[22] Conversely, if the representation is not made to the plaintiff or to a third party to be communicated to him, the plaintiff cannot rescind the transaction.[23]

The misrepresentation need not be the only matter which induced the representee to enter into the contract. Provided that it "materially contributed to his so acting,"[24] it is irrelevant that the representee was influenced by other matters.[25] So, in *Edgington* v. *Fitzmaurice*,[26] the plaintiff was induced to make a contract partly through the defendants' fraudulent misrepresentations and partly through his own mistaken belief that the debentures, for which he was applying, would give him a charge on the company's property. The Court of Appeal rescinded the contract. If the plaintiff's mind was "disturbed by the misstatement of the defendants, and such disturbance was in part the cause of what he did, the mere fact of his also making a mistake himself could make no difference."[27]

It is moreover, immaterial that the representee failed to take an available opportunity to investigate the truth of the representor's statements.[28] The effect of a deceitful representation is not dispelled by the fact that the represen-

---

[21] *Smith* v. *Chadwick* (1884) 9 App.Cas. 187; *Lynde* v. *Anglo-Italian Hemp Spinning Co.* [1896].1 Ch. 178, and cases cited, see below, p. 198, n. 37.

[22] *Swift* v. *Winterbotham* (1873) L.R. 8 Q.B. 244, 253, *per curiam*, cited by Blackburn J. in *Richardson* v. *Silvester* (1873) L.R. 9 Q.B. 34, 36; *Re Ambrose Lake Tin & Copper Mining Co.* (1880) 14 Ch.D. 390. Similarly, it is enough if the representation is made to a third person in circumstances where the representor should, as a reasonable person, anticipate that it would be communicated to the plaintiff: *Smith* v. *Eric S. Bush* [1990] 1 A.C. 831.

[23] *Gross* v. *Lewis Hillman Ltd.* [1970] Ch. 445, 457, *per* Cross L.J., citing *Edinburgh United Breweries Ltd.* v. *Molleson* [1894] A.C. 96. See also *Peek* v. *Gurney* (1873) L.R. 6 H.L. 377, 411, *per* Lord Cairns.

[24] *Edgington* v. *Fitzmaurice* (1885) 29 Ch.D. 459, 482, *per* Bowen L.J.; *cf.* Burrows, *The Law of Restitution*, p. 26. Salesmen's puffs are not deemed to contribute materially to the representee's conduct, for *simplex commendatio non nocet*: see *Dimmock* v. *Hallett* (1866) L.R. 2 Ch. 21; *cf. Central Ry. Co. of Venezuela* v. *Kisch* (1867) L.R. 2 H.L. 99, 113, *per* Lord Chelmsford L.C.

[25] *Cf. Barton* v. *Armstrong* (1973) [1976] A.C. 104; see below, p. 234 (duress).

[26] (1885) 29 Ch.D. 459; see also *Clermont* v. *Tasburgh* (1819) 1 J. & W. 112; *Hallows* v. *Fernie* (1867) L.R. 3 Ch. 467.

[27] (1885) 29 Ch.D. 459, 483, *per* Bowen L.J.

[28] *Redgrave* v. *Hurd* (1881) 20 Ch.D. 1; *cf. Charles Hunt Ltd.* v. *Palmer* [1931] 2 Ch. 287; *Laurence* v. *Lexcourt Holdings Ltd.* [1978] 1 W.L.R. 1128, 1136–1137: *per* Brian Dillon Q.C. (Deputy Judge.)

tee was negligent in failing to discover the falsity of the representation. If, however, the misrepresentation did not in any way induce the representee to act, or influence him[29] in acting, as he did, the representor can successfully resist an action for rescission. But where the misrepresentation is of such a kind as to induce a reasonable man to enter into the contract, the onus of proving that the representee was not so induced is firmly on the representor. As Sir George Jessel M.R. said in *Redgrave* v. *Hurd*[30]:

> "If it is a material misrepresentation calculated to induce him to enter into a contract, it is an inference of law that he was induced by the representa-tion to enter into it, and in order to take away his title to be relieved from the contract on the ground that the representation was untrue, it must be shown either that he had knowledge of the facts contrary to the represen-tation, or that he stated in terms, or showed clearly by his conduct, that he did not rely on the representation."

If, in such a case, the representor can prove that the representee was ignorant of the misrepresentation,[31] or that the representee knew it to be untrue but, nevertheless, decided to enter into the contract,[32] or that the representee did not allow the misrepresentation to affect his decision to contract,[33] the contract will not be rescinded. Thus, in *Atwood* v. *Small*,[34] the plaintiffs employed their own agents to verify the truth of the defendant's representations concerning the earning capacity of a mine, which they were proposing to buy from him. The plaintiffs' agents reported to them that these statements were substantially true and they concluded the contract. The defendant's representations were not in fact true; but the House of Lords held that the plaintiffs could not rescind. For they had not relied on the defendant's representations but had caused their own agents to test their accuracy, and had only decided to go ahead on the faith of their agents' reports.

The relevance of "materiality"

It is commonly said[35] that a plaintiff can only rescind if he can establish, in addition to the requirements of misrepresentation and inducement, that the

---

[29] *Amalgamated Investment & Property Co. Ltd. (in liquidation)* v. *Texas Commerce International Bank Ltd.* [1982] Q.B. 84, 108, *per* Robert Goff J., 120, *per* Lord Denning M.R. *Aliter* if the representation was merely negligent and it was reasonable to assume that the representee would take the opportunity to discover the truth: *Cf. Smith* v. *Eric S. Bush* [1990] 1 A.C. 831 (where the misrepresentation was negligent).

[30] (1881) 20 Ch.D. 1, 21.

[31] *Horsfall* v. *Thomas* (1862) 1 H. & C. 90.

[32] *Dyer* v. *Hargrave* (1805) 10 Ves. 505; *Bawden* v. *London, Edinburgh & Glasgow Assurance Co.* [1892] 2 Q.B. 534.

[33] *Smith* v. *Chadwick* (1884) 9 App.Cas. 187.

[34] (1838) 6 Cl. & F. 232. *Cf. Cooper* v. *Tamms* [1988] 1 E.G.L.R. 257; *The Morning Watch* [1990] 1 Lloyd's Rep. 547, 556.

[35] See, *e.g.* Halsbury's *Laws* (4th ed.), Vol. 31, §§ 1075–1078; Treitel, *op. cit.*, pp. 301–302. But *cf.* Chitty *on Contracts* (26th ed.), Vol. I, § 427; Cartwright, *op. cit.*, pp. 81–84; and (1950) 13 M.L.R. 362, 366 [Gower].

particular misrepresentation was material. It is true that the courts have often used language which suggests that the representation must be material. But in cases other than those dealing with the avoidance of policies for non-disclosure, where the element of materiality is relevant for special reasons[36] they have tended to treat materiality as synonymous with inducement. Jessel M.R.'s observations in *Mathias* v. *Yetts*[37] are not untypical. He said: "It must be no doubt a material misstatement, and the other party must have been induced to act upon it. As it was sometimes said, it must be material to the inducing of the contract, but it need not be the only inducement."

In our view any misrepresentation which induces a person to enter into a contract should be a ground for rescission of that contract.[38] If the misrepresentation would have induced a reasonable person to enter into the contract, then the court will, as we have seen, presume that the representee was so induced, and the onus will be on the representor to show that the representee did not rely on the misrepresentation either wholly or in part. If, however, the misrepresentation would not have induced a reasonable person to contract, the onus will be on the representee to show that the misrepresentation induced him to act as he did.[39] But these considerations relate to the question of onus of proof. To disguise them under the cloak of "materiality" is misleading and unnecessary.[40]

Limits to claims for rescission

(1) *Where restitutio in integrum is impossible*

"It is, I think, clear on principles of general justice, that as a condition to a rescission there must be a *restitutio in integrum*. The parties must be put *in statu quo*. . . . It is a doctrine which has often been acted upon both at law and in equity."[41] But the application of the doctrine was once much more strict at common law. For whereas equity could order an account of profits and make any necessary allowances for deterioration of property transferred under the contract, the courts of common law had no machinery at their command for this purpose.[42] At law, if precise restitution was impossible, the defrauded

---

[36] See above, pp. 190 *et seq.*

[37] (1882) 46 L.T. 497, 502; see the same judge's statement of the law in *Smith* v. *Chadwick* (1882) 20 Ch.D. 27, 44–45; and see also *Flinn* v. *Headlam* (1829) 9 B. & C. 693, 696, *per* Tenterden C.J.; *Traill* v. *Baring* (1864) 4 De G.J. & Sm. 318, 326, *per* Bowen L.J.; *Root* v. *Badley* [1960] N.Z.L.R. 756.

[38] *Museprime Properties Ltd.* v. *Adhill Properties Ltd.* [1990] 2 E.G.L.R. 196. But contrast *Cantiere Meccanico Brindisino* v. *Janson* [1912] 3 K.B. 452, 460, *per* Vaughan Williams L.J., interpreting Scrutton J. in the court below at [1912] 2 K.B. 112, 116; and *Bell* v. *Lever Bros.* [1932] A.C. 161, 234, *per* Lord Thankerton. *Cf. Root* v. *Badley* [1960] N.Z.L.R. 756, 760, *per* McGregor J.; and above p. 122 (a mistake of fact need not be *fundamental*).

[39] *Cf. Moens* v. *Heyworth* (1842) 10 M. & W. 147, 158–159, *per* Alderson B.; *Mathias* v. *Yetts* (1882) 46 L.T. 497, 507, *per* Lindley L.J.

[40] *Cf.* Hart and Honoré, *Causation in the Law*, pp. 90, 301.

[41] *Erlanger* v. *New Sombrero Phosphate Co.* (1878) 3 App.Cas. 1218, 1278, *per* Lord Blackburn.

[42] *Erlanger* v. *New Sombrero Phosphate Co.* (1878) 3 App.Cas. 1218, 1278–1279, *per* Lord Blackburn; see also *Spence* v. *Crawford* [1939] 3 All E.R. 271, 290, *per* Lord Wright.

party had to fall back on his action for damages for deceit. Today, however, all divisions of the High Court are endowed with the powers of the old Court of Chancery. In whichever division the action is brought, therefore, it is enough that

> "the situation is such that, by the exercise of its powers, including the power to take accounts of profits and to direct inquiries as to allowances proper to be made for deterioration, [the court] can do what is practically just between the parties, and by so doing restore them substantially to the *status quo*."[43]

The principle is easier to state than to apply in practice. It has been held that if the character of property transferred under the contract has been completely altered, or if the property itself has disappeared, *restitutio in integrum* is impossible and rescission will not be allowed. Thus in *Clarke* v. *Dickson*[44] the plaintiff was refused rescission of a contract to buy shares in a partnership on the ground that in the meanwhile the partnership had been converted into a limited liability company. The plaintiff bought "shares in a partnership with others. He cannot return those.... Still stronger, he has changed their nature."[45] It appears, too, that a party may not succeed in an action for rescission if he has received a benefit under the contract which of its very nature cannot be restored,[46] or which he has consumed[47] or disposed of,[48] as where the purchaser of a mine seeks to rescind the contract of purchase after the mine has been worked out.[49] But it is, we suggest, consistent with principle[50] that it should be sufficient for the party who has received a benefit under the contract to compensate the other party by paying him the value of that

---

[43] *Alati* v. *Kruger* (1955) 94 C.L.R. 216, 223–224, *per* Dixon C.J., Webb, Kitto and Taylor JJ.; *O'Sullivan* v. *Management Agency and Music Ltd.* [1985] Q.B. 428 (a case of undue influence: see below, p. 284). See *Erlanger* v. *New Sombrero Phosphate Co.* (1878) 3 App.Cas. 1218, 1278–1279, *per* Lord Blackburn; *Hulton* v. *Hulton* [1917] 1 K.B. 813; *Senanayake* v. *Cheng* [1966] A.C. 63. *Cf. South Western Mineral Water Co.* v. *Ashmore* [1967] 1 W.L.R. 1110.

[44] (1858) E.B. & E. 148 (a decision at law); see also *Western Bank of Scotland* v. *Addie* (1867) L.R. 1 Sc. & Div. 145.

[45] (1858) E.B. & E. 148, 154–155, *per* Crompton J.

[46] *Boyd & Forrest* v. *Glasgow & South Western Ry.* 1915 S.C., H.L. 20 (services rendered).

[47] *Clarke* v. *Dickson* (1858) E.B. & E. 148, 155, *per* Crompton J. If the property transferred is perishable, the transferee is *in statu quo* until no duty to preserve it *in statu quo* until the hearing; but he is bound to abstain from touching it after proceedings have been commenced, and probably he ought to warn the other party of any circumstances which would tend to depreciate the value of the property, leaving him to pursue whatever course he thinks fit: see *Maturin* v. *Tredinnick* (1864) 4 New Rep. 15, 17, *per* Wood V.-C.

[48] *Ladywell Mining Co.* v. *Brookes* (1887) 35 Ch.D. 400, 414, *per* Lindley L.J. If the contract is severable, it may be rescinded as to a severable part of the property still in the hands of the plaintiff: see *Maturin* v. *Tredinnick* (1864) 4 New Rep. 15.

[49] *Vigers* v. *Pike* (1842) 8 Cl. & F. 562, *semble*; see also *Atwood* v. *Small* (1838) 6 Cl. & F. 232. Other cases where *restitutio in integrum* was impossible are *Sheffield Nickel and Silver Plating Co. Ltd.* v. *Unwin* (1877) 2 Q.B.D. 214; *Thorpe* v. *Fasey* [1949] Ch. 649. But *cf. Hulton* v. *Hulton* [1917] 1 K.B. 813.

[50] As stated by Lord Blackburn in *Erlanger* v. *New Sombrero Phosphate Co.* (1878) 3 App.Cas. 1218, 1278–1279.

benefit,[51] unless the benefit consists of a chattel which is non-fungible in nature (in which event it must be restored subject to compensation for depreciation), or he was unable to restore the benefit at the time when he learned of the facts giving rise to his right to rescind and did not do so.[52]

It is clear, however, that rescission will not be barred merely because a contract is executed[53] or property transferred under the contract has deteriorated or depreciated in value. "To hold otherwise would be to say that where a losing and insolvent business is sold by means of the representation that it is solvent and profitable, rescission could never be obtained if the loss were increased prior to the discovery of the true state of affairs."[54] Depreciation which would have occurred in any event has, therefore, been disregarded: thus in *Armstrong* v. *Jackson*[55] a contract for the purchase of shares was set aside, despite a substantial intervening fall in their value. In other cases, compensation may be ordered. "Where compensation can be made for any deterioration of the property, such deterioration shall be no bar to rescission, but only a ground for compensation."[56] Thus, in the Canadian case of *Wiebe* v. *Butchart's Motors Ltd.*,[57] where a contract for the sale of a motor-car was induced by a misrepresentation by the seller, the buyer was held to be entitled to rescind the contract on paying the seller $600 for the deterioration of the car, which had been used continuously since the sale. Moreover, if the property is improved as a result of bona fide expenditure of the party who, if rescission takes place, will have to restore it, rescission may be ordered on the terms that such expenditure is to be repaid by the other party.[58]

Where a contract has been induced by fraud, the courts are particularly ready to grant rescission at the suit of the innocent party. Thus, in the Scottish case of *Spence* v. *Crawford*,[59] a purchaser of shares attempted to resist the vendor's action for reduction of the contract, which had been induced by the purchaser's fraudulent misrepresentation, on the grounds that *restitutio in integrum* was impossible. For pursuant to the contract of purchase the vendor

---

[51] *Cf. O'Sullivan* v. *Management Agency and Music Ltd.* [1985] Q.B. 428 (contract executed under undue influence; defendants ordered to account for profits); see below, p. 284.

[52] *Hulton* v. *Hulton* [1917] 1 K.B. 813; *Compagnie Française des Chemins de Fer Paris-Orleans* v. *Leeston Shipping Co. Ltd.* (1919) 1 Ll.L. 235; *Restatement of Restitution*, §§ 65, 66.

[53] *O'Sullivan* v. *Management Agency and Music Ltd.* [1985] Q.B. 428.

[54] *Adam* v. *Newbigging* (1888) 13 App.Cas. 308, 330, *per* Lord Herschell.

[55] [1917] 2 K.B. 822; see also the authorities cited by McCardie J. at pp. 829–830; *cf. O'Sullivan* v. *Management Agency and Music Ltd.* [1985] Q.B. 428, 449 *et seq.*, *per* Dunn L.J.

[56] *Lagunas Nitrate Co.* v. *Lagunas Syndicate* [1899] 2 Ch. 392, 456, *per* Rigby L.J.; see also *Erlanger* v. *New Sombrero Phosphate Co.* (1878) 3 App.Cas. 1218, 1278–1279, *per* Lord Blackburn.

[57] [1949] 4 D.L.R. (N.S.) 838; see also *Addison* v. *Ottawa Auto and Taxi Co.* (1914) 16 D.L.R. (1st) 318.

[58] *Bellamy* v. *Sabine* (1847) 2 Ph. 425; *Davey* v. *Durrant* (1857) 1 De G. & J. 535; *Stepney* v. *Biddulph* (1865) 13 W.R. 576; *Cf. Greenwood* v. *Bennett* [1973] Q.B. 195; Torts (Interference with Goods) Act 1977, s.6(1): see above, p. 174.

[59] [1939] 3 All E.R. 271: see also *Hulton* v. *Hulton* [1917] 1 K.B. 813; *Lagunas Nitrate Co.* v. *Lagunas Syndicate* [1899] 2 Ch. 392, 433–434., *per* Lindley M.R.; see also *Root* v. *Badley* [1960] N.Z.L.R. 756: *O'Sullivan* v. *Management Agency and Music Ltd.* [1985] Q.B. 428, 451, 454, *per* Dunn L.J.

had, at the purchaser's expense, been discharged from a guarantee of the company's debt and had had restored to him certain securities which secured that guarantee; moreover, the company's constitution had been altered, and there had been some change in the individual shareholdings in the company, including that of the purchaser. But the House of Lords rejected these submissions and allowed reduction on terms. Lord Wright said[60]:

> "A case of innocent misrepresentation may be regarded rather as one of misfortune than as one of moral obliquity. There is no deceit or intention to defraud. The court will be less ready to pull a transaction to pieces where the defendant is innocent, whereas in the case of fraud the court will exercise its jurisdiction to the full in order, if possible, to prevent the defendant from enjoying the benefit of his fraud at the expense of the innocent plaintiff. Restoration, however, is essential to the idea of restitution. . . . The court can go a long way in ordering restitution if the substantial identity of the subject-matter of the contract remains."

(2) Third-party rights

The right to rescind a contract will generally be lost if, before rescission, a third party acquires, for value and without notice of the defect with which the contract is tainted, an interest in the subject-matter of the contract.[61]

Thus if a purchaser fraudulently induces another to sell goods to him, and then resells the goods to an innocent third party, it will be too late for the vendor to revest the title to the goods in himself by rescission of the voidable contract of sale.[62] *Phillips* v. *Brooks Ltd.*[63] provides a useful example. A man named North entered the shop of the plaintiff, a jeweller, and, by fraudulently pretending that he was Sir George Bullough and giving a cheque that was subsequently dishonoured, obtained possession of a ring valued at £450. He immediately pledged the ring with the defendants, who in good faith without notice of the fraud advanced him £350 upon it. Horridge J. held, first, that the plaintiff's contract with North, though voidable for fraud, was not void on grounds of mistaken identity, because he contracted to sell and deliver the ring to the person who came into his shop; and secondly, that in the circumstances the property in the ring had so passed to North as to enable him to give a good title to the defendants. Since the defendants had acted in good faith and had given value for the ring, the plaintiff could no longer rescind his contract with

---

[60] [1939] 3 All E.R. 271, 288–289. See also *Kupchak* v. *Dayson Holdings Co. Ltd.* (1965) 53 D.L.R. (2d) 482.

[61] *Clough* v. *London & North Western Ry.* (1871) L.R. 7 Ex. 26, 35, *per curiam*; *Scholefield* v. *Templer* (1859) 4 De G. & J. 429, 433–434, *per* Lord Campbell. See also *Re L. G. Clarke* [1967] Ch. 1121. If the contract has already been rescinded before the transfer, the third party will acquire no title, unless he can invoke ss.2 or 9 of the Factors Act 1889 (see *Newtons of Wembley Ltd.* v. *Williams* [1964] 1 W.L.R. 1028, affd. [1965] 1 Q.B. 560).

[62] *Parker* v. *Patrick* (1793) 5 T.R. 175; *White* v. *Garden* (1851) 10 C.B. 919; *Babcock* v. *Lawson* (1879) 4 Q.B.D. 394, (1880) 5 Q.B.D. 284; *Phillips* v. *Brooks Ltd.* [1919] 2 K.B. 243. See also Sale of Goods Act 1979, s.23.

[63] [1919] 2 K.B. 243.

North. He, therefore, failed in his action against the defendants for the return of the ring or its value and for damages for its detention.

If, however, the third party is a volunteer, or is aware of the defect in his transferor's title, his acquisition of an interest in the subject-matter of the contract will provide no obstacle to rescission.[64] Moreover, if the effect of the misrepresentation is to induce a fundamental mistake which renders the contract void, no title will pass to the transferee or to any third party to whom he purports to give title, and rescission of the contract will be unnecessary to enable the transferor to reclaim his goods, or damages for their conversion, from the third party.[65] Again, third-party rights will only bar rescission if the third party has acquired an interest in the subject-matter of the contract; they will not do so if the third party has only taken an assignment of the contractual rights of one of the contracting parties.[66] The assignee takes the assignment subject to equities having priority over his right. Hence, even if the assignee has given value for the assignment and has no notice of any such equities, rescission of the contract will be possible after the assignment,[67] and the assignee's remedy (if any) will lie against the assignor. Where, however, the assignment takes the form of negotiation of a bill of exchange to a holder in due course, "he holds the bill free from any defect of title of prior parties, as well as from mere personal defences available to prior parties among themselves, and may enforce payment against all parties liable on the bill."[68]

The decision of the House of Lords in *Oakes* v. *Turquand and Harding*[69] was also based on the need to protect third parties. In that case it was held that a shareholder could not repudiate his shares in a company after proceedings had been commenced for the winding-up of the company. Considerable reliance was placed on the following passage from Lord Campbell's judgment in *Henderson* v. *The Royal British Bank*[70]:

> "It would be monstrous to say that, he having become a partner and a shareholder, and having held himself out to the world as such, and having so remained until the concern stopped payment, could, by repudiating the shares on the ground that he had been defrauded, make himself no longer a shareholder, and thus get rid of his liability to the creditors of the Bank, who had given credit to it on the faith that he was a shareholder."

---

[64] *Clough* v. *London & North Western Ry.* (1871) L.R. 7 Ex. 26, 35, *per curiam*; *Scholefield* v. *Templer* (1859) 4 De G. & J. 429, 433–434, *per* Lord Campbell.

[65] *Hardman* v. *Booth* (1863) 1 H. & C. 803; *Cundy* v. *Lindsay* (1878) 3 App.Cas. 459; *Ingram* v. *Little* [1961] 1 Q.B. 31.

[66] *Cf.* above, p. 135, nn. 98–99.

[67] *Graham* v. *Johnson* (1869) L.R. 8 Eq. 36; see also *Abram Steamship Co. Ltd.* v. *Westville Shipping Co. Ltd.* [1923] A.C. 773, and Marshall, *Assignment of Choses in Action*, pp. 182–184, and cases cited.

[68] Bills of Exchange Act 1882, s.38(2).

[69] (1867) L.R. 2 H.L. 325.

[70] (1857) 7 E. & B. 356, 364.

Rescission was barred, therefore, because third parties might have acted on the basis that the party claiming rescission was a shareholder in the company.[71]

(3) Affirmation of the contract

If a party who has a right to rescind a contract elects, with knowledge of his legal rights[72] as well as all the facts giving him that right, to affirm the contract, his election is final. He cannot subsequently change his mind and rescind the contract instead.[73] Conversely, "the party defrauded may keep the question open so long as he does nothing to affirm the contract."[74] The burden is on the representor to demonstrate that the representee has affirmed the contract.[75]

"An affirmation of voidable contract may be established by any conduct which unequivocally manifests an intention to affirm it by the party who has the right to affirm or disaffirm."[76] Thus, in *Sharply v. Louth and East Coast Ry.*,[77] the plaintiff sought to set aside on grounds of misrepresentation a contract to take shares in the defendant company. After learning of the untruth of the defendant company's representations, he had continued to act as a shareholder of the company, attending meetings, moving resolutions and applying for further shares. The Court of Appeal held that he could not rescind, for his conduct clearly evinced an intention to affirm the contract. A useful contrast is provided by *Watson v. Burton*,[78] although it is a case of specific performance. The plaintiff claimed specific performance of a contract to sell certain freehold premises to the defendant. The plaintiff had, however, innocently misrepresented to the defendant the acreage of the land in question. After he had learned the true facts, the defendant wrote to the plaintiff asking for some repairs to be done, did some repairs himself and paid the balance of the deposit which was due. The defendant stated in evidence that he had acted in this way because at the time he was prepared to go on with the contract provided that he received a reasonable rebate for the acreage which the plaintiff had misrepresented as being included in the sale; and the defendant's evidence was supported by the fact that he had claimed such a rebate from the plaintiff

---

[71] See (1867) L.R. 2 H.L. 325, 348, *per* Lord Chelmsford, 361–362, *per* Lord Cranworth. *Cf.* the equitable rule that a shareholder must exercise his right of repudiation with extreme promptness: see below, pp. 207–208; and contrast *MacKenzie v. Royal Bank of Canada* [1934] A.C. 648.

[72] *Cf. Peyman* v. *Lanjani* [1985] Ch. 457, C.A., following *Coastal Estates Pty. Ltd.* v. *Melevende* [1965] V.R. 433. (In that case the representation was deceitful.)

[73] *Clough* v. *London and North Western Ry.* (1871) L.R. 7 Ex. 26, 34, *per curiam.*

[74] *Clough* v. *London and North Western Ry.* (1871) L.R. 7 Ex. 26, 34, *per curiam* (Mellor J.). See also *Aaron's Reefs Ltd.* v. *Twiss* [1896] A.C. 273, 294, *per* Lord Davey; *Allen* v. *Robles* [1969] 1 W.L.R. 1193.

[75] *Halsbury's Laws of England* (4th ed.), Vol. 31, § 1128. No authority is cited; but in principle this statement of the law must be correct, and it was accepted in *Fenton v. Kenny* [1969] N.Z.L.R. 552, [1971] N.Z.L.R. 1. See also *Coastal Estates Pty. Ltd.* v. *Melevende* [1965] V.R. 433, where this was assumed.

[76] *Car and Universal Finance Co. Ltd.* v. *Caldwell* [1965] 1 Q.B. 525, 550, *per* Sellers L.J.; see also *Peyman* v. *Lanjani* [1985] Ch. 457, 488, *per* Stephenson L.J.

[77] (1876) 2 Ch.D. 663. See also *Vigers* v. *Pike* (1842) 8 Cl. & F. 562; *Re Hop and Malt Exchange and Warehouse Co.* (1866) L.R. 1 Eq. 483; *Re Peruvian Ry.* (1869) L.R. 4 Ch. 322.

[78] [1957] 1 W.L.R. 19.

and the matter had been left open between the parties. Wynn-Parry J. accepted that the defendant's conduct was consistent with an intention to negotiate his way out of the difficulties arising from the plaintiff's misrepresentation, and that it did not evince an intention to affirm the contract.[79] He accordingly refused to order specific performance.

If a party who has a right to rescind elects to rescind the contract, his election, to be effective, must be exercised "in the plainest and most open manner competent."[80] It follows that he must, in the ordinary course, communicate his intention to rescind to the other party.[81] But the rescinding party may sometimes be relieved of the necessity of communication. He will be relieved, for example, where he retakes possession of a chattel which forms the subject-matter of the contract.[82] It has also been held that he will be relieved where the other party, by absconding, deliberately puts it out of his power to communicate his intention to rescind, which the other party knows he will almost certainly want to do[83]; for "to hold otherwise would be to allow a fraudulent contracting party by his very fraud to prevent the innocent party from exercising his undoubted right."[84] But this is rough justice for it may effectively undermine the title of an innocent purchaser. The Law Reform Committee has therefore recommended[85] that an innocent purchaser under a voidable contract should acquire title unless notice of rescission has been communicated by one contracting party to the other. Although the purchaser will rarely be in a position to know whether any notice has or had not been communicated,[86] he will, if this recommendation is adopted, generally acquire title since the original owner will normally be in no position to communicate with the fraudulent party.

It appears, however, that affirmation of a contract need not be communicated to the other party,[87] for "a contract may be more readily approved and accepted than it can be terminated where a unilateral right to affirm or disaffirm arises."[88] The reason why an intention to rescind must generally be

---

[79] *Ibid.* at p. 30.
[80] *Reese River Silver Mining Co.* v. *Smith* (1869) L.R. 4 H.L. 64, 74, *per* Lord Hatherley L.C.
[81] *Scarf* v. *Jardine* (1882) 7 App.Cas. 345, 361, *per* Lord Blackburn; *Car and Universal Finance Co. Ltd.* v. *Caldwell* [1965] 1 Q.B. 525, 554, *per* Upjohn L.J.; *Tenax S.S. Co. Ltd.* v. *The Brimnes (Owners)* [1975] Q.B. 929, 945–946, *per* Edmund Davies L.J.
[82] *Re Eastgate* [1905] 1 K.B. 465; *Car and Universal Finance Co. Ltd.* v. *Caldwell* [1965] 1 Q.B. 525, 551, *per* Sellers L.J.
[83] *Car and Universal Finance Co. Ltd.* v. *Caldwell* [1965] 1 Q.B. 525, applied in *Newtons of Wembley Ltd.* v. *Williams* [1965] 1 Q.B. 560. It is doubtful whether communication of intention to rescind is necessary in a case of innocent misrepresentation, where the respresentor innocently so acts that the representee cannot find him to communicate his intention to rescind. This point was left open in *Car and Universal Finance Co. Ltd.* v. *Caldwell* (see 552, *per* Sellers L.J. and 555, *per* Upjohn L.J.).
[84] *Car and Universal Finance Co. Ltd.* v. *Caldwell* [1965] 1 Q.B. 525, 555, *per* Upjohn L.J. But *cf. Macleod* v. *Kerr*, 1965 S.C. 253.
[85] 12th Report, Cmnd. 2958 (1966), § 16. The recommendation has not been implemented.
[86] *Cf.* the position of the purchaser whose title is voidable for duress: see below, p. 230.
[87] *Re Hop and Malt Exchange and Warehouse Co.* (1866) L.R. 1 Eq. 483; *Car and Universal Finance Co. Ltd.* v. *Caldwell* [1965] 1 Q.B. 525, 550, *per* Sellers L.J.
[88] *Car and Universal Finance Co. Ltd.* v. *Caldwell* [1965] 1 Q.B. 525, 550, *per* Sellers L.J.

communicated is that "the other party is entitled to treat the contractual nexus as continuing until he is made aware of the intention of the other to exercise his option to rescind."[89]

It has been held,[90] in cases of sale of goods, that a claim to rescind for innocent misrepresentation[91] is barred when a right to reject for breach of condition is barred. Under section 11(1)(c) of the Sale of Goods act 1893, a purchaser under a contract for the sale of specific goods used to lose his right to reject when the property in those goods passed to him. If the contract was an unconditional contract for the sale of specific goods in a deliverable state the property passed when the contract was made. At that time he lost therefore both his right to rescind and to reject. It was long recognised that this result was a harsh one.[92] Section 35 of the Sale of Goods Act 1979 has now changed the law.[93] The effect of that Act is that a buyer will now lose his right to reject only if he has accepted the goods. A buyer is deemed to have accepted goods if he intimates his acceptance or when, after the lapse of a reasonable time, he retains the goods without intimating rejection. He will also be deemed to have accepted the goods if, when they have been delivered to him, he does an act inconsistent with the seller's ownership. But a buyer is noit deemed to have acted inconsistently with the seller's ownership in respect of goods which he has not previously examined unless and until he has had a reasonable opportunity to examine them. He may, of course, nonetheless lose his right to reject on other grounds; for example, if he is no longer in a position to return the goods because he has sold them to another. Consequently it will now "usually be plain that the buyer's right to reject will be lost at the same time as his right to rescind for misrepresentation."[94]

Lapse of time without rescinding may furnish evidence that the representee has elected to affirm the contract.[95] The effect of lapse of time on the right to rescind is, however, considered in the next section.[96]

A party to a contract, having discovered the existence of one misrepresentation, may affirm the contract and then discover the existence of another misrepresentation of which he was ignorant at the date of his affirmation. In such a case the representee is not "precluded from raising a case upon the

---

[89] *Car and Universal Finance Co. Ltd.* v. *Caldwell* [1965] 1 Q.B. 525, 554, *per* Upjohn L.J. And *cf.* below, p. 230.

[90] *Leaf* v. *International Galleries* [1950] 2 K.B. 86, 90–91, *per* Denning L.J. (this was the basis of Denning L.J.'s judgment); *Long* v. *Lloyd* [1958] 1 W.L.R. 753. But see Treitel, *op. cit.*, pp. 344–345.

[91] It is assumed, in the English cases, that the Sale of Goods Act 1979 does not exclude a right to rescind contracts of sale for innocent misrepresentation. *Cf. Riddiford* v. *Warren* (1901) 20 N.Z.L.R. 572; see Atiyah, *The Sale of Goods* (8th ed. 1990), pp. 520–521; (1953) 16 M.L.R. 174, 190–194 [S. J. Stoljar].

[92] See, *e.g. Long* v. *Lloyd* [1958] 1 W.L.R. 753.

[93] The section embodies the proposal of the Law Reform Committee's 10th Report (1962), Cmnd. 1782, § 8, originally enacted in the Misrepresentation Act 1967, s.4(1).

[94] (1967) 30 M.L.R. 369, 387 [Atiyah and Treitel.]

[95] *Clough* v. *London and North Western Ry.* (1871) L.R 7 Ex. 26, 35, *per curiam*; *Aaron's Reefs Ltd.* v. *Twiss* [1896] A.C. 273, 294, *per* Lord Davey. *Cf. Allen* v. *Robles* [1969] 1 W.L.R. 1193.

[96] See below, pp. 206–208.

second misrepresentation,"[97] unless his affirmation was of such a kind that he must be taken to have given up his right to rescind not only in respect of the misrepresentation of which he was aware but also of other "points of discrepancy" upon which he might have been able to rely.[98] This may depend "on the reasons for his decision and the influence which full knowledge might have had as a reason for deciding differently. . . . [A] party who is ignorant of his right to elect, although he knows the facts which would in law afford a ground for rescission, cannot, because he failed to avail himself in due time of the first ground, be precluded from relying on a second ground of rescission, which he was then unaware of but afterwards discovers."[99]

(4) Lapse of time

It is usually said, that, where a party has a right to rescind a contract for misrepresentation, innocent, negligent or fraudulent, his election to rescind, to be effective, must be made within a reasonable time.[1] But the basis of this rule is not altogether clear. In cases at common law, which are necessarily concerned with fraud, lapse of time is said to constitute evidence of affirmation. In such cases, "lapse of time without rescinding will furnish evidence that [the representee] has determined to affirm the contract; and when the lapse of time is great, it probably would in practice be treated as conclusive evidence to show that he has so determined."[2] In equity, in a case of innocent misrepresentation, it has been said[3] that "laches or lapse of time is treated as a defence" to a claim to rescind,[4] and courts of equity would presumably have given effect to a similar defence in cases of fraud.[5] But the judgment of Jenkins L.J. in *Leaf v. International Galleries*[6] indicates that, in the context of sale of goods at least, lapse of time may be a defence although the representee has not

---

[97] *Re The London and Provincial Electric Lighting and Power Co. Ltd.* (1886) 55 L.T. 670, 671, *per* Chitty J.

[98] *Re Russian (Vyksounsky) Ironworks Co.* (1867) L.R. 3 Eq. 790; *Law v. Law* [1905] 1 Ch. 140.

[99] *Elder's Trustee* v. *Commonwealth Home and Investment Co. Ltd.* (1941) 65 C.L.R. 603, 617, *per curiam*.

[1] See, *e.g. Car and Universal Finance Co. Ltd.* v. *Caldwell* [1965] 1 Q.B. 525, 554, *per* Upjohn L.J. In this context if the analogy of the Statute of Limitations is adopted "reasonable time" begins to run from the time when the representee, acting with "reasonable diligence," learned of his right to rescind: *cf.* below, Chap. 43.

[2] *Clough* v. *London and North Western Ry.* (1871) L.R. 7 Ex. 26, 35, *per curiam*; *cf. Mitchell* v. *Homfray* (1882) 8 Q.B.D. 587.

[3] *Aaron's Reefs Ltd.* v. *Twiss* [1896] A.C. 273, 295, *per* Lord Davey; see also *Lindsay Petroleum Co.* v. *Hurd* (1874) L.R. 5 P.C. 221, 239–241, *per* Sir Barnes Peacock; *Erlanger* v. *New Sombrero Phosphate Co.* (1878) 3 App.Cas. 1218, 1247, *per* Lord Hatherley.

[4] *Leaf* v. *International Galleries* [1950] 2 K.B. 86. *Cf. Peco Arts Inc.* v. *Hazlitt Gallery Ltd.* [1983] 1 W.L.R. 1315, 1323–1324, *per* Webster J.: see below, pp. 769–770.

[5] In cases of fraud, where "it is only a question of the remedy," a court of equity will, in any event, act "by analogy to the Statute of Limitations, and will not allow the plaintiff to succeed if his action is brought more than six years after knowledge of the facts has been acquired by him which justify his coming to the court": see *Molloy* v. *Mutual Reserve Life Insurance Co.* (1906) 94 L.T. 756, 762, *per* Romer L.J., applied in *Oelkers* v. *Ellis* [1914] 2 K.B. 139. See also *Armstrong* v. *Jackson* [1917] 2 K.B. 822, 830–831, *per* McCardie J.

[6] [1950] 2 K.B. 86. See also *Oscar Chess Ltd.* v. *Williams* [1957] 1 W.L.R. 370, 373–374, *per* Denning L.J.

been guilty of laches. In that case, the purchaser of a picture sought to rescind the contract five years later on the ground that the seller had innocently misrepresented the picture to have been painted by Constable. The Court of Appeal affirmed the decision of the county court judge dismissing the claim, and Jenkins L.J. founded his judgment on the time which had lapsed between the contract and the claim to rescind. He said[7]:

"It is perfectly true that the county court judge held that there had been no laches, and, of course, it may be said that the plaintiff had no occasion to obtain any further evidence as to the authorship of the picture until he wanted to sell; but in my judgment contracts such as this cannot be kept open and subject to the possibility of rescission indefinitely. Assuming that completion is not fatal to his claim, I think that, at all events, it behoves the purchaser either to verify or, as the case may be, to disprove the representation within a reasonable time, or else stand or fall by it. If he is allowed to wait 5, 10, or 20 years and then reopen the bargain, there can be no finality at all."

Whatever may be the true basis of the defence, it is clear that what constitutes a reasonable time depends on the circumstances of the case. Thus, "when a person has contracted to take shares in a company and his name has been placed on the register, it has always been said that he must exercise his right of repudiation with extreme promptness after the discovery of the fraud or misrepresentation for this reason; the presence of his name on the register may have induced other persons to give credit to the company or to become members of it."[8] In other cases, the passing of as much as 15 months may not affect the right to rescind[9]; moreover, the representee must normally have acquired knowledge of the falsity of the representation before his claim can be barred by any lapse of time.[10] Again, it has been said that a change of position on the part of the representor, even if his representation was fraudulent, may lead a court to bar a claim on grounds of lapse of time.[11] The cases indicate, therefore, that the availability of the defence of lapse of time is likely to coincide with some other bar to rescission, either affirmation of the contract by the representee, or impossibility of putting the representor *in statu quo*, or the intervention of third-party rights; but this need not necessarily be the case.[12]

---

[7] [1950] 2 K.B. 86, 92.
[8] *Aaron's Reefs Ltd.* v. *Twiss* [1896] A.C. 273, 294, *per* Lord Davey; see also *Scholey* v. *Central Ry. of Venezuela* (1868) L.R. 9 Eq. 266n., 267, *per* Lord Cairns L.C.; *Re Scottish Petroleum Co.* (1883) 23 Ch.D. 413, 434, *per* Baggallay L.J. (who thought that a delay of a fortnight might be too long in the case of a going concern); *First National Reinsurance Co. Ltd.* v. *Greenfield* [1921] 2 K.B. 260.
[9] *Lindsay Petroleum Co.* v. *Hurd* (1874) L.R. 5 P.C. 221.
[10] *Ibid.* at p. 241, *per* Sir Barnes Peacock; *Erlanger* v. *New Sombrero Phosphate Co.* (1878) 3 App.Cas. 1218, 1279, *per* Lord Blackburn. *Cf. Leaf* v. *International Galleries* [1950] 2 K.B. 86.
[11] *Clough* v. *London and North Western Ry.* (1871) L.R. 7 Ex. 26, 35, *per curiam*; *Morrison* v. *The Universal Marine Insurance Co.* (1873) L.R. 8 Ex. 197, 205–206, *per curiam*.
[12] *Leaf* v. *International Galleries* [1950] 2 K.B. 86.

It is a distinct question whether in these circumstances a person's claim is time-barred by statute or by the operation of the equitable doctrine of laches. We discuss this question below.[13]

(5) *Where the court exercises its discretionary power to award damages instead of rescission*

Section 2(2) of the Misrepresentation Act 1967[14] gives the court a discretion to award damages in lieu of rescission where a representee has been induced to enter into a contract because of an innocent misrepresentation whether that representation was made negligently or not. The scope of section 2(2) is far from clear. It reads as follows:

> "Where a person has entered into a contract after misrepresentation has been made to him otherwise than fraudulently, and he would be entitled, by reason of the misrepresentation, to rescind the contract, then, if it is claimed, in any proceedings arising out of the contract, that the contract ought to be or has been rescinded, the court or arbitrator may declare the contract subsisting and award damages in lieu of rescission, if of opinion that it would be equitable to do so, having regard to the nature of the misrepresentation and the loss that would be caused by it if the contract were upheld, as well as to the loss that rescission would cause to the other party."

This subsection does not affect any common law right to claim damages for breach of contract. But before the subsection can apply, a person must claim to have "entered" into a contract after a misrepresentation."[15] There must also be a claim that the contract "ought to be or has been rescinded." Consequently the court's discretion can be exercised only if the representee has not lost the right to rescind the contract at the date of the action.[16] If the right to rescission has been lost it would seem that the court has no jurisdiction to award damages under this subsection; for the subsection speaks of the representee being *entitled* to rescind. In our view it cannot mean *entitled at any time* to rescind; if this is correct, the court has no power to award damages under the subsection when a representee could have at one time rescinded but has now lost that right.

It is also not certain whether the court has a discretionary power to award damages in lieu of rescission in every case where a misrepresentation has been incorporated into the contract as a term of it. The answer may depend on whether it has been incorporated as a condition or a warranty. If the representation is a warranty, then section 2(2) seems applicable. But if it is a condition,

---

[13] See Chap. 43.
[14] See Law Reform Committee, Cmnd. 1782 (1962), §§ 11–13.
[15] Cases of non-disclosure are therefore outside s.2(2): *Ramphal* v. *Toole* (unrep.) March 17, 1989, C.A.; *cf. Banque Keyser Ullmann S.A.* v. *Skandia (U.K.) Insurance Co. Ltd.* [1990] 1 Q.B. 665; [1991] 2 A.C. 249 (on which see above, p. 195).
[16] *Atlantic Lines & Navigation Co. Inc.* v. *Hallam Ltd.*; *The Lucy* [1983] 1 Lloyd's Rep. 188, 201–202, *per* Mustill J.

section 2(2) may be excluded; for the representee's right arising from the breach of the condition is, strictly speaking, *to determine* the contract for breach rather than to claim that the contract ought to be, or has been, *rescinded* for misrepresentation.[17] It is unlikely that the courts will accept this refined argument, when so much confusion has always surrounded the meaning of the term "rescission."[18]

In exercising its discretion the court is directed to take into account the nature of the misrepresentation and the loss that would be caused by it if the contract were upheld as well as the loss that rescission would cause to the other party.[19]

(6) *Where the right to rescind has been excluded by contract*

At common law the right to rescind can be excluded by a provision of the contract, provided that it is unequivocal and reasonable steps have been taken to draw it to the notice of the other party.[20] But section 8 of the Unfair Contract Terms Act 1977 has significantly restricted that right. It amends the Misrepresentation Act 1967[21] as follows:

> "(1) In the Misrepresentation Act 1967, the following is substituted for section 3—
>
> 3. If a contract contains a term which would exclude or restrict—
> (*a*) any liability to which a party to a contract may be subject by reason of any misrepresentation made by him before the contract was made; or
> (*b*) any remedy available to another party to the contract by reason of such misrepresentation,
>
> that term shall be of no effect except in so far as it satisfies the requirement of reasonableness as stated in section 11(1) of the Unfair Contract Terms Act 1977; and it is for those claiming that the term satisfies that requirement to show that it does."[22]

By section 11(1):

> "in relation to a contract term, the requirement of reasonableness for the purposes of this Part of this Act, section 3 of the Misrepresentation Act 1967 and section 3 of the Misrepresentation Act (Northern Ireland) 1967 is that the term shall have been a fair and reasonable one to be included having regard to the circumstances which were, or ought reasonably to

---

[17] *Cf.* Treitel, *op. cit.* p. 337.
[18] See below, pp. 407–409.
[19] s.2(2). See below, p. 212 on how damages may be calculated.
[20] *Walker* v. *Boyle* [1982] 1 W.L.R. 495, 501, *per* Dillon J. (a vendor's warning in small print that his replies are believed to be correct but accuracy is not guaranteed cannot prevent those replies from being representations of fact.)
[21] On which see (1967) 30 M.L.R. 369.
[22] Seemingly s.3 cannot be avoided by means of a contract term to the effect that statements are not to be construed as assertions of fact: *Crendean Properties Ltd.* v. *Nash* (1977) 244 E.G. 547; *Southwestern General Property Ltd.* v. *Marton* (1982) 263 E.G. 290.

have been, known to or in the contemplation of the parties when the contract was made."

Walker v. *Boyle*[23] was the first case where a court was required, in this context, to consider this section. A vendor had made an innocent misrepresentation which induced the defendant to contract to buy the property; he had represented that there were no boundary disputes when, as he ought reasonably to have known, there were. The vendor resisted the claim for rescission and for the return of the deposit by relying on Condition 17 of the National Conditions of Sale ("no error, mistatement or omission in any preliminary answer concerning the property ... shall annul the sale"). Dillon J. held that such a clause would not, in equity, preclude a purchaser from claiming rescission and the return of his deposit.[24] Moreover, whatever the position might be in equity, Condition 17 did not satisfy the "requirement of reasonableness" imposed by section 11 of the 1977 Act. The requirement of reasonableness was not satisfied simply because the parties were legally represented; for it is not a solicitor's duty to go through the small print of the National Conditions with a tooth-comb when he advises a purchaser. It was critical that this was a common-form clause which was not the product of arm's-length negotiations between the parties. The judge did not say why he thought condition 17 unreasonable. Seemingly it was the same reason which led equity judges in the past to grant rescission; to enforce the condition "would be nothing short of a direct encouragement to fraud."[25]

Recovery of benefits conferred under contracts thereafter rescinded[26]

We have already seen that an important limit to rescission is that there must be *restitutio in integrum*.[27] The effect of this principle is that the plaintiff must "be in a position to offer and must formally tender *restitutio in integrum*"[28]; but the court will also, when rescinding the contract, order the restoration to the plaintiff of benefits received by the defendant from him under the contract. There ought to be "a giving back and a taking back on both sides."[29]

---

[23] [1982] 1 W.L.R. 495.

[24] Following *Nottingham Patent Brick and Tile Co.* v. *Butler* (1885) 15 Q.B.D. 261, (1886) 16 Q.B.D. 778 and *Charles Hunt Ltd.* v. *Palmer* [1931] 2 Ch. 287. See also *Faruqi* v. *English Real Estates Ltd.* [1979] 1 W.L.R. 963.

[25] *Nottingham Patent Brick and Tile Co.* v. *Butler* (1885) 15 Q.B.D. 261, 271, *per* Wills J.

[26] Logically, this subject should be considered in the section concerned with recovery of benefits conferred under ineffective transactions (see below, pp. 400 *et seq.*); but it is thought more convenient to deal with it at this stage.

[27] See above, pp. 198 *et seq.*; *Erlanger* v. *New Sombrero Phosphate Co.* (1878) 3 App.Cas. 1218, 1278–1279, *per* Lord Blackburn.

[28] *Steedman* v. *Frigidaire Corporation* [1932] W.N. 248, P.C., *per* Lord Macmillan. See also *Western Bank of Scotland* v. *Addie* (1867) L.R. 1 Sc. & Div. 145; *Glasgow and South Western Ry.* v. *Boyd & Forrest* [1915] A.C. 526, 1915 S.C. 20. The court has "power to make all just allowances": see *Hulton* v. *Hulton* [1917] 1 K.B. 813, 821, *per* Swinfen-Eady J.

[29] *Newbigging* v. *Adam* (1886) 34 Ch.D. 582, 595; *per* Bowen L.J., discussed in *The Glasgow and South Western Ry.* v. *Boyd and Forrest*, 1915 S.C., H.L. 20, 31, 37.

The plaintiff is not only entitled to have restored to him property transferred and money paid by him to the defendant under the contract,[30] but his right is broader and may, for example, include a right to indemnity against liabilities incurred. In *Newbigging* v. *Adam*,[31] the plaintiff was induced to enter into a contract of partnership by misrepresentations of the defendant as to the state of the partnership business. The plaintiff was entitled to rescission of the contract and to repayment of the money which he had put into the partnership, namely, £9,700 in cash and £324 applied by him in payment of partnership debts, less some £750 which he had received from the partnership. He also claimed, however, to be indemnified by the defendant against all outstanding debts and liabilities of the partnership, which he had or might become liable to pay, on account of partnership transactions. The Court of Appeal held that he was entitled to this indemnity,[32] but there was some conflict of view between the Lords Justices as to the nature of this relief. Cotton L.J. considered that it could not be said that the plaintiff was put back into his old position unless he was "relieved from the consequences and obligations which are the result of the contract which is set aside."[33] Fry L.J. said that the plaintiff was "entitled to an indemnity in respect of all obligations entered into under the contract when those obligations are within the necessary or reasonable expectation of both of the contracting parties at the time of the contract."[34] Bowen L.J. took a more limited view of the scope of the equitable relief. He said:

> "It seems to me that when you are dealing with innocent misrepresenta-tion you must understand that proposition that he is to be replaced *in statu quo* with this limitation—that he is not to be replaced in exactly the same position in all respects, otherwise he would be entitled to recover dam-ages, but is to be replaced in this position so far as regards the rights and obligations which have been created by the contract into which he has been induced to enter."[35]

In our view, Bowen L.J.'s statement of the law is to be preferred[36] to those of Cotton and Fry L.JJ. The plaintiff is entitled to restitution, but not to damages. It does not follow that he will be entirely restored to his previous position, for he should be able to recover only the advantages the defendant has

---

[30] See, *e.g. Redgrave* v. *Hurd* (1881) 20 Ch.D. 1; *Newbigging* v. *Adam* (1886) 34 Ch.D. 582; *Whittington* v. *Seale-Hayne* (1900) 82 L.T. 49, 16 T.L.R. 181. Property in goods conveyed under the contract will, in appropriate cases, revest in the transferor upon rescission of the contract.

[31] (1886) 34 Ch.D. 582. *Cf. Rawlins* v. *Wickham* (1858) 3 De. G. & J. 304.

[32] The order made by the Court of Appeal was slightly varied on appeal by the House of Lords: (1888) 13 App.Cas. 308.

[33] (1886) 34 Ch.D. 582, at p. 589.

[34] At p. 596.

[35] At pp. 592–593.

[36] It was accepted by Farwell J. in *Whittington* v. *Seale-Hayne* (1900) 82 L.T. 49, 51.

obtained from him by the contract.[37] In *Newbigging* v. *Adam*[38] one of the advantages which the defendant had received was that, by entering into the contract of partnership, the plaintiff had assumed liability for certain partnership debts. As part of their obligation to make restitution, therefore, the defendant was required to give up this particular advantage created by the contract by indemnifying the plaintiff against such liability.[39]

Where, however, services have been rendered under a contract induced by an innocent misrepresentation, the court will not rescind the contract because the services cannot be returned.[40] Restitution is then impossible. There is much to be said for the view that so strict an application of *restitutio in integrum* is undesirable and may be productive of injustice.[41]

Since the Misrepresentation Act 1967, the power of the court to award restitution of benefits conferred under a contract which a person is entitled to rescind may become of less importance. Under section 2(1) damages for negligent misrepresentation may be awarded; and by section 2(2) the court now has jurisdiction to award damages in lieu of rescission where a contract has been induced by innocent or negligent misrepresentation. But section 2(2) gives no indication how the damages should be calculated and, in particular, whether a plaintiff can recover damages for "loss of bargain" on whether damages should be assessed on a tortious basis.[42] Whether the courts will limit still further the award by giving damages only to the extent that it is necessary to indemnify[43-44] the representee is also conjectural. If damages are awarded *in lieu of* rescission it would seem reasonable to do so; for an award of damages would then come close to achieving the same result as a decree for rescission.

(b) *Rescission of Contracts entered into under a Mistake not Induced by Misrepresentation*

The jurisdiction of the Court of Chancery to set aside[45] transactions entered

---

[37] *Compagnie des Chemins de Fer Paris-Orleans* v. *Leeston Shipping Co.* (1919) 36 T.L.R. 68, 69, *per* Roche J.; *Gilchester Properties Ltd.* v. *Gomm* [1948] 1 All E.R. 493, 497, *per* Romer J.

[38] (1886) 34 Ch.D. 582.

[39] In our view, it is misleading in this context to draw a contrast between indemnity and damages (see, *e.g.* Cheshire and Fifoot, (12th ed.) 1991, pp. 289–290). The true contrast is between restitution and damages. In restitution, the measure of recovery is generally what the defendant has received; in damages, it is what the plaintiff has lost. In some cases of restitution, however, the defendant may be required to give an indemnity against certain liabilities, as in *Newbigging* v. *Adam*.

[40] *Glasgow and South Western Ry.* v. *Boyd and Forrest*, 1915 S.C., H.L. 20.

[41] *Cf. Restatement of Restitution*, §§ 65 and 66.

[42] But *cf.* s.2(1), on which see *Watts* v. *Spence* [1976] Ch. 165, 178 (loss of bargain); and contrast *F & H Entertainments Ltd.* v. *Leisure Enterprises Ltd.* (1976) 120 S.J. 331; *Andre* v. *Ets. Michel Blanc* [1977] 2 Lloyd's Rep. 166, 181, *per* Ackner J.; and *Sharneyford Supplies Ltd.* v. *Edge* [1985] 3 W.L.R. 1 (damages on a tortious basis).

[43-44] *Cf. Newbigging* v. *Adam* (1886) 34 Ch.D. 582: see above, pp. 181–182.

[45] We, however, have used "set aside" and "rescind" interchangeably, following Bucknill, Denning and Jenkins L.JJ. in *Solle* v. *Butcher* [1950] 1 K.B. 671, 687–689, 695, 702–703. On the confusion surrounding the words "rescission" and "rescind," see *Johnson* v. *Agnew* [1980] A.C. 367: see below, pp. 407–409.

into under a mistake is of respectable antiquity. An early case was *Landsdown* v. *Landsdown*,[46] where there was a dispute between two brothers about title to certain lands. The question was referred to their neighbour and schoolmaster who, having consulted *The Clerk's Remembrancer*, decided in favour of the younger brother. Lord King L.C. cancelled the deeds which had been executed in pursuance of the schoolmaster's decision; they had been obtained by "mistake and misrepresentation." Eighteen years later, Lord Hardwicke, in *Bingham* v. *Bingham*,[47] rescinded an agreement under which the plaintiff had "purchased" his own property, believing the defendant owned it, and, in *Cocking* v. *Pratt*,[48] Sir John Strange M.R., in Lord Hardwicke's absence, set aside an agreement between a minor and her mother concerning the distribution of personal estate, on the ground that the estate was much greater than was known to the minor at the date of the agreement.

These cases, and the nineteenth-century decisions which followed them,[49] are scarcely satisfactory. No coherent equitable doctrine of mistake can be spelt from them, and all too often the existence of a misrepresentation or the presence of undue influence was instrumental in persuading the Chancellor to set aside the agreement.[50] Nevertheless, in *Cooper* v. *Phibbs*[51] Lord Westbury treated them as authority for the general proposition that, "if parties contract under a mutual mistake and misapprehension as to their relative and respective rights, the result is, that that agreement is liable to be set aside as having proceeded upon a common mistake."[52] Such a mistake occurred in *Cooper* v. *Phibbs* itself. Both parties believed that the respondent was legally and beneficially entitled to a fishery. In that belief the respondent agreed to lease the fishery and certain other property to the appellant. It was later determined that the appellant was beneficially entitled to the fishery which the respondent had from time to time improved. Because the agreement was valid at common law, the appellant was compelled to go to equity to seek its cancellation and to restrain the respondent from suing on the agreement at law.[53] The House of Lords held that the agreement was "liable to be set aside" on terms.[54] Although

---

[46] (1730) Mos. 364.

[47] (1748) 1 Ves.Sen. 126, Ves.Sen.Supp. 79.

[48] (1749–1750) 1 Ves.Sen. 400; see also *Evans* v. *Llewellin* (1787) 1 Cox 333; *Colyer* v. *Clay* (1843) 7 Beav. 188.

[49] *M'Carthy* v. *Decaix* (1831) 2 Russ. & M. 614; *Sturge* v. *Sturge* (1849) 12 Beav. 229; *Cochrane* v. *Willis* (1865) L.R. 1 Ch. 58.

[50] Even though the conveyance has been executed: see Sugden, *Vendors and Purchasers* (14th ed.), p. 245; *cf.* above, p. 185, n. 25.

[51] [1867] L.R. 2 H.L. 149.

[52] (1867) L.R. 2 H.L. 149, 170: see below, p. 219.

[53] See (1989) 105 L.Q.R. 599 [Matthews] for the history of the litigation.

[54] One of the terms was that the appellant had to compensate the respondent, *qua* trustee, for the improvements. Another was that he should pay rent for the other property which had been conveyed to him and to which he was not beneficially entitled. It is not entirely clear what was the basis of the jurisdiction to impose terms. Because this was a suit in Chancery, the House may well have been exercising its equitable jurisdiction and imposed terms in order to prevent the appellant's unjust enrichment. For another view, arguing that the trustee was *entitled* to these sums, see (1989) 105 L.Q.R. 599, 605–606 [Matthews].

Lord Cranworth, who delivered the only other speech,[55] based his decision partly on other grounds, he too recognised, with Lord Westbury, the power of the Court of Chancery to set aside a contract on grounds of "mutual mistake and misapprehension" as to their rights.[56]

In *Earl Beauchamp* v. *Winn*[57] Lord Chelmsford was prepared to adopt a test similar to Lord Westbury's. He said[58]:

> "The cases in which equity interferes to set aside contracts are those in which either there has been mutual mistake or ignorance in both parties affecting the essence of the contracts, or a fact is known to one party and unknown to the other, and there is some fraud or surprise upon the ignorant party."

The facts of most of these decisions are not dissimilar,[59] for the mistake generally concerned title to land. Yet the principle underlying them is not so limited, as *Huddersfield Banking Co. Ltd.* v. *Henry Lister & Son Ltd.*[60] illustrates. In 1889 Henry Lister, a manufacturer, mortgaged to the plaintiff bank certain mills, together with fixed plant and machinery. A year later the business was transferred to the defendant company, which went into liquidation in 1892. The bank claimed to be entitled as mortgagee to a number of looms, but on inspection of the premises its representatives agreed that the looms were not fixtures and were not, therefore, within the terms of the mortgage deed. In fact the looms had been detached by some independent person. The bank brought an action to have the agreement set aside on the ground of "common mistake," a claim which was upheld by both Vaughan Williams J.[61] and the Court of Appeal. Kay L.J.[62] said:

> "It seems to me that, both on principle and authority, when once the court finds that an agreement has been come to between parties who were under a common mistake of a material fact, the court may set it aside, and the court has ample jurisdiction to set aside the order founded upon that agreement."[63]

Kay L.J. recognised that complications would have occurred if, for example, third-party rights had intervened. But the remedy, being equitable,

---

[55] (1867) L.R. 2 H.L. 149, 164.

[56] See above, p. 213.

[57] (1873) L.R. 6 H.L. 223, 233.

[58] These observations were *obiter* since the House of Lords held that there was in fact no mistake.

[59] *Cf. Hitchcock* v. *Giddings* (1817) 4 Pr. 135; *Colyer* v. *Clay* (1843) 7 Beav. 188.

[60] [1895] 2 Ch. 273; see also *Scott* v. *Coulson* [1903] 1 Ch. 453, [1903] 2 Ch. 249. An independent valuation may also be set aside for mistake of law if it is a "speaking valuation" which gives reasons for the valuer's decision. In contrast a "non-speaking valuation" may not, in the absence of fraud or collusion: see *Campbell* v. *Edwards* [1976] 1 W.L.R. 403 and *Burgess* v. *Purchase & Sons (Farms) Ltd.* [1983] Ch. 216, and authorities there cited.

[61] See [1895] 2 Ch. 273, 275.

[62] [1895] 2 Ch. 273, 284; and see p. 276, *per* Vaughan Williams J. See also *Wilding* v. *Sanderson* [1897] 2 Ch. 534, applied in *Faraday* v. *Tamworth Union* (1916) 86 L.J.Ch. 436.

[63] But *cf.* Lindley L.J. (at p. 281).

was discretionary[64] so that, if necessary, terms could have been imposed, as they were in *Cooper* v. *Phibbs*,[65] where the House of Lords gave the respondent a lien over the fishery for the value of her improvements, and also required the appellant to pay rent for the property which he did not beneficially own. In *Solle* v. *Butcher*[66-67] the equities of the parties were also balanced by the court. In that case the defendant let a flat to the plaintiff for seven years at a rent of £250 per annum. Although the flat had been let in 1938 for £140 per annum, both parties believed that, on account of bomb damage and reconstruction, the Rent Acts did not apply, so that the defendant was entitled to charge a higher rent. Subsequently, the plaintiff contended that the flat had not been decontrolled and brought an action claiming recovery of rent paid above the standard rent of £140 per annum. The defendant pleaded, *inter alia*, that the lease was entered into under a common mistake and asked for its rescission. The Court of Appeal upheld the plaintiff's contention that the Rent Acts were applicable, but set aside the lease on terms. Bucknill and Denning L.JJ. regarded the parties' mistake as one of fact. Bucknill L.J. quoted Lord Westbury's observations in *Cooper* v. *Phibbs*[68] and concluded that the mistake was a mutual mistake as to their private rights and was of "fundamental importance," being "as to the identity of the flat with the dwelling-house previously let at a standard rent of £140 a year."[69] Denning L.J. agreed that the parties had executed the lease under a fundamental mistake shared by both of them, since each had thought that the flat was not subject to a controlled rent. The Court of Appeal[70] held that:

> "the lease should only be set aside if the defendant is prepared to give an undertaking that he will permit the plaintiff to be a licensee of the premises pending the grant of a new lease. Then, whilst the plaintiff is a licensee, the defendant will in law be in possession of the premises, and will be able to serve on the plaintiff, as prospective tenant, a notice under section 7, subsection 4, of the Act of 1938, increasing the rent to the full permitted amount."[71]

The principal interest of the case lies in Denning L.J.'s analysis of equity's power to set aside a contract for mistake and of the relationship between the

---

[64] *Erlanger* v. *New Sombrero Phosphate Co.* (1878) 3 App.Cas. 1218, 1278–1279, *per* Lord Blackburn.

[65] (1867) L.R. 2 H.L. 223: see above, p. 184. And *cf. National Presto Industries Inc.* v. *The United States*, 338 F.2d 99 (1964).

[66-67] [1950] 1 K.B. 671.

[68] (1867) L.R. 2 H.L. 223: see above, p. 213.

[69] [1950] 1 K.B. 671, 686.

[70] Jenkins L.J. dissented on this point. He considered that the mistake was one of law and that relief was therefore impossible.

[71] [1950] 1 K.B. 671, 697. Bucknill L.J. agreed with these terms proposed by Denning L.J. *Cf.* [1949] 2 All E.R. 1107, 1128, where a different form of order is given. For a comment on the nature of the relief granted, see Birks, *Introduction*, p. 163.

common law and equitable doctrines of mistake. His observations were novel and radical. He said[72]:

"It is now clear that a contract will be set aside if the mistake of the one party has been induced by a material misrepresentation of the other, even though it was not fraudulent or fundamental; or if one party, knowing that the other is mistaken about the terms of the offer, or the identity of the person by whom it is made, lets him remain under his delusion and concludes a contract on the mistaken terms instead of pointing out the mistake. . . . A contract is also liable in equity to be set aside if the parties were under a common misapprehension either as to facts or as to their relative and respective rights, provided that the misapprehension was fundamental and that the party seeking to set it aside was not himself at fault."

The authority of these remarks has been challenged.[73] It is said that they are inconsistent with cases such as *Bell* v. *Lever Bros.*,[74] where the House of Lords considered the scope of the decisions in equity and where some of their Lordships expressed the view that the rules of common law and equity on this topic were identical.[75] There is much force in these criticisms. Moreover, the earlier equity cases[76] do not disclose a jurisdiction of the breadth claimed by Denning L.J., and it is difficult to glean from them, and the few subsequent decisions[77] which have followed *Solle* v. *Butcher*, the limits of equity's doctrine of mistake.

It is still open to the House of Lords to conclude that there is no independent doctrine of mistake in equity. On balance it would be regrettable if the House did so, for equity's intervention has given the courts a valuable and flexible power to grant relief from the consequences of mistake.[78] The trend of the present authorities suggests that, despite the relative novelty and uncertainty of Lord Denning's formulation of the equitable doctrine, the courts are ready to accept the existence of an independent equitable jurisdiction to set aside a

---

[72] [1950] 1 K.B. 671, 692–693; see also his observations in *Frederick E. Rose (London) Ltd.* v. *William H. Pim, Jnr. & Co. Ltd.* [1953] 2 Q.B. 450, 460–461: see below, p. 223. But *cf.* the more guarded comments of Bucknill L.J. [1950] 1 K.B. 671, 685–689.

[73] (1954) 70 L.Q.R. 385, 403, 407 [C. J. Slade]; (1961) 24 M.L.R. 421 [Atiyah and Bennion]. For an argument "that interference by the courts in contracts should be limited to those situations where either there is a failure of consideration or there is an imbalance, built into the transaction by virtue of the conduct or position of one party *vis-à-vis* the other party, at the time when the contract was made," see (1987) 103 L.Q.R. 594 [Cartwright].

[74] [1932] A.C. 161. In *Associated Japanese Bank (International) Ltd.* v. *Credit du Nord SA* [1988] 3 All E.R. 902, 911, Steyn J. concluded that the principles enunciated in *Bell* v. *Lever Bros.* "clearly still govern mistake at common law."

[75] [1932] A.C. 161, 200, *per* Lord Blanesburgh, 210, *per* Lord Warrington (dissenting).

[76] *Cf. Hickman* v. *Berens* [1895] 2 Ch. 638, 646–647, *per* Lindley L.J.; *Wilding* v. *Sanderson* [1897] 2 Ch. 534, 550, *per* Lindley L.J., 552, *per* Chitty L.J.

[77] *e.g. Grist* v. *Bailey* [1967] Ch. 532; *Magee* v. *Pennine Insurance Co. Ltd.* [1969] 2 Q.B. 507: see below, p. 218; *Laurence* v. *Lexcourt Holdings* [1978] 1 W.L.R. 1128: see below, p. 218.

[78] *Cf. Associated Japanese Bank (International) Ltd.* v. *Credit du Nord SA* [1988] 3 All E.R. 902, 912, where Steyn J. concluded that it was "sensible and satisfactory" that the narrow common law doctrine should be supplemented by the more flexible doctrine of mistake in equity.

contract for mistake. What is conjectural are the conditions under which this jurisdiction will be exercised. The following propositions are therefore tentatively advanced.

(1) The cases before *Solle* v. *Butcher* suggest that equity would only set aside a contract if a mistake as to some underlying fact was shared by both the parties. Unilateral mistake apparently provided no ground for relief unless "induced by the other party."[79] Lord Thurlow, in *Calverley* v. *Williams*,[80] asked whether it was the "common purpose" of both parties to have conveyed the land in dispute; equity will not impeach a written contract "simply because one of the parties to it put an erroneous construction on the words in which the contract is expressed."[81] Thus, in *Stewart* v. *Kennedy*,[82] the appellant made the respondent an offer of his entailed estate at a certain price, subject to the stipulation that the sale was to be made "with the ratification of the court." The appellant misunderstood the legal meaning of this offer. He did not appreciate that it constituted an unconditional offer of sale. The House of Lords dismissed his plea that the contract should be set aside. Lord Herschell thought that to allow it would be mischievous, for the appellant was seeking to "reduce the contract simply on the ground that the appellant did not intend to make the offer which the courts have held that he did make."[83] As Lord Chelmsford remarked in the earlier case of *Midland G.W. Ry. of Ireland* v. *Johnson and Kinder*[84]: "if a party acts upon a mistaken view of his rights under a contract, he is no more entitled to relief in equity than he would be in law."

(2) The Chancery decisions contain little discussion of the question of how fundamental or basic the mistake of the parties must be before any relief can be given. They do not appear to go so far as to support Denning L.J.'s opinion that the court has a power to set aside a contract, valid at law, "whenever it [is] of opinion that it [is] unconscientious for the other party to avail himself of the legal advantage which he [has] obtained."[85] As the authorities[86] now stand, it seems that the courts have an equitable jurisdiction to set aside contracts where the parties' mistake is substantial but not so fundamental as to render the contract void at law. But it is not clear how substantial the mistake must be before relief is granted in equity. The cases provide few clues. In *Grist* v.

---

[79] *Wilding* v. *Sanderson* [1897] 2 Ch. 534, 550, *per* Lindley L.J.
[80] (1790) 1 Ves.Jun. 210, 211.
[81] *Wilding* v. *Sanderson* [1897] 2 Ch. 534, 550, *per* Lindley L.J.
[82] (1890) 15 App.Cas. 108.
[83] *Ibid.*
[84] (1858) 6 H.L.C. 799, 811. In *Solle* v. *Butcher* [1950] 1 K.B. 671, see above, p. 215, Denning L.J. cited, in support of his proposition that equity will grant relief even though the mistake is unilateral, *Paget* v. *Marshall* (1884) 28 Ch.D. 255; *Torrance* v. *Bolton* (1872) L.R. 8 Ch.App. 118; *Garrard* v. *Frankel* (1862) 30 Beav. 455. But the Court of Appeal has now limited their authority: see *Riverplate Properties Ltd.* v. *Paul* [1975] Ch. 133, see below, p. 225.
[85] *Solle* v. *Butcher* [1950] 1 K.B. 671, 692.
[86] See, *inter alia*, *Colyer* v. *Clay* (1843) 7 Beav. 188; *Bettyes* v. *Maynard* (1882) 46 L.T. 766, 768, *per* Kay J.; *Debenham* v. *Sawbridge* [1901] 2 Ch. 98; *Solle* v. *Butcher* [1950] 1 K.B. 671: see above, p. 215; *Frederick E. Rose (London) Ltd.* v. *William H. Pim, Jr. & Co. Ltd.* [1953] 2 Q.B. 450, 460–461, *per* Denning L.J.

Bailey,[87] Goff J. held that a contract for the sale of a house, "subject to the existing tenancy," which both parties thought was a protected tenancy when it was not, was not void at law but could be set aside in equity on the terms that the vendor entered into a fresh contract at a proper vacant possession price.[88] Similarly, in *Laurence* v. *Lexcourt Holdings Ltd.*[89] it was held that where both parties mistakenly believed that planning permission was available for the use of the premises as offices, they both acted under a fundamental mistake; it did not matter that the mistake was as to the legal suitability of the land for particular use rather than its physical description. And, in *Magee* v. *Pennine Insurance Co. Ltd.*,[90] the Court of Appeal set aside an insurance company's compromise of a claim which had been entered into in the belief, shared by the assured, that the policy was binding when it was voidable for innocent misrepresentation. Lord Denning M.R. invoked equity's jurisdiction to set aside the compromise because of mistake. He dismissed *Bell* v. *Lever Bros.*[91] with the observation that "a common mistake, even on a most fundamental matter, does not make a contract void at law; but it makes it voidable in equity."[92] Fenton Atkinson L.J. concurred with Lord Denning's conclusions; but it is not clear whether he did so on the ground that the contract was voidable in equity or because it was void at law.[93] It was only Winn L.J., dissenting, who found any difficulty in reconciling the common law of *Bell* v. *Lever Bros.* with the equitable principles of *Solle* v. *Butcher.* In his view, although there was a "misapprehension as to rights . . . [there] was no misapprehension whatsoever as to the subject matter of the contract, namely, the settlement of the rights of the assured with regard to the accident that happened."[94] Neither *Grist* v. *Bailey* nor *Magee* v. *Pennine Insurance* can be said to have clarified the principles which govern equity's jurisdiction to set aside contracts for mistake. In particular, the question of how substantial the mistake must be remains unanswered. But it may well be that the only clarification will come from the pragmatic development of the case law.

If, however, the mistake is so fundamental that the contract is void at law,[95] it is difficult to see how equity can intervene since there is no contract to set

---

[87] [1967] Ch. 532.

[88] The vendor had agreed to this condition: [1967] Ch. 432, 543. *Cf. Peters* v. *Batchelor* (1950) 100 L.J. News, 718 (where the parties thought that leased premises had only been used for business purposes when they had been used for residential purposes and were therefore subject to the Rent Acts: the lease was set aside).

[89] [1978] 1 W.L.R. 1128. But contrast *Amalgamated Investment & Property Co. Ltd.* v. *John Walker & Sons Ltd.* [1977] 1 W.L.R. 164 (where the mistake was that the parties expected that the property could be developed; the building was later listed; relief was denied).

[90] [1969] 2 Q.B. 507; followed in *Toronto Dominion Bank* v. *Fortin* (1978) 5 W.W.R. 302.

[91] [1932] A.C. 161.

[92] [1969] 2 Q.B. 507, 514. In *Associated Japanese Bank (International) Ltd.* v. *Credit du Nord SA* [1988] 3 All E.R. 902, 911, Steyn J. described this observation as an "individual opinion" which does not do "justice to the speeches of the majority."

[93] *Ibid.* 517.

[94] *Ibid.* 516.

[95] *Ingram* v. *Little* [1961] 1 Q.B. 31, 62, *per* Pearce L.J.

aside.[96] But there are some indications in the cases that relief may, nevertheless, be granted.[97]

(3) If both parties contracted under the same mistaken view of *general* law, it is sometimes said that they cannot rescind the contract.[98] *Bilbie* v. *Lumley*[99] has persuaded Chancery judges that no equitable relief can be obtained in these circumstances.[1] This was an unfortunate and unnecessary conclusion. The principle which underlies that case, namely, that a payment made in settlement of an honest claim, under a mistake of law, is irrecoverable, should not, in our opinion, be invoked in cases where parties contract under a mistake of law, unless the contract itself embodies an honest settlement or compromise of claims.[2] Before *Bilbie* v. *Lumley*,[3] equity's power to rescind contracts made under a mistake of law shared by both parties had not been disputed; and in *Lansdown* v. *Lansdown*,[4] King L.C. had said that the maxim *ignorantia juris* did not hold "in civil cases." Nevertheless, in *Cooper* v. *Phibbs*,[5] Lord Westbury, in order to escape the consequences of *Bilbie* v. *Lumley*,[6] formulated a distinction whose only merit has been said to be "that it enables a court of equity to give relief in a majority of cases where the parties to a transaction assumed as a basis for it a certain legal situation."[7] Lord Westbury said[8]:

" '*Ignorantia juris haud excusat*'; but in that maxim the word '*jus*' is used in the sense of denoting general law, the ordinary law of the country. But when the word '*jus*' is used in the sense of denoting a private right, that maxim has no application. Private right of ownership is a matter of fact: it may be the result also of matter of law: but if parties contract under a mutual mistake and misapprehension as to their relative and respective rights, the result is, that that agreement is liable to be set aside as having proceeded upon a common mistake."

In *Earl Beauchamp* v. *Winn*,[9] Lord Chelmsford developed this distinction in the following words:

---

[96] Save perhaps to adjust rights and restore the status quo.
[97] In all the cases where the question has arisen, the parties prayed for equitable relief; there was no plea that the contract was void at law. See generally *Cooper* v. *Phibbs* (1867) L.R. 2 H.L. 149; *Solle* v. *Butcher* [1950] 1 K.B. 671, 692–693, *per* Denning L.J.; *Oscar Chess Ltd.* v. *Williams* [1957] 1 W.L.R. 370, 373, *per* Denning L.J.; *Magee* v. *Pennine Insurance Co. Ltd.* [1969] 2 Q.B. 507; *Laurence* v. *Lexcourt Holdings Ltd.* [1978] 1 W.L.R. 1128.
[98] But contrast *Gibbon* v. *Mitchell* [1990] 3 All E.R. 338 (below p. 222).
[99] (1802) 2 East 469: see above, Chap. 4.
[1] *Cooper* v. *Phibbs* (1867) L.R. 2 H.L. 149; *Earl of Beauchamp* v. *Winn* (1873) L.R. 6 H.L. 223.
[2] See above, Chap. 4.
[3] (1802) 2 East 469.
[4] (1730) Mos. 364; see also *Stone* v. *Godfrey* (1854) 5 De G.M. & G. 76, 90, *per* Turner L.J.
[5] (1867) L.R. 2 H.L. 149.
[6] (1802) 2 East 469.
[7] Williston, *Contracts*, § 1589.
[8] *Cooper* v. *Phibbs* (1876) L.R. 2 H.L. 149, 170.
[9] (1873) L.R. 6 H.L. 223, 234; see also *Allcard* v. *Walker* [1896] 2 Ch. 369, 381–382, *per* Stirling J.; *Maskell* v. *Horner* [1915] 3 K.B. 106, 118, *per* Lord Reading C.J. *Cf.* below, pp. 221–222.

" . . . The ignorance imputable to the party was of a matter of law arising upon the doubtful construction of a grant. This is very different from the ignorance of a well known rule of law. And there are many cases to be found in which equity, upon a mere mistake of law, without the admixture of other circumstances, has given relief to a party who has dealt with his property under the influence of such mistake. Therefore, although when a certain construction has been put by a court of law upon a deed, it must be taken that the legal construction was clear, yet the ignorance, before the decision, of what was the true construction, cannot, in my opinion, be pressed to the extent of depriving a person of relief on the ground that he was bound himself to have known beforehand how the grant must be construed."

These dicta have been repeatedly approved. They enable the courts to grant relief even though the parties acted under a mistake of law[10]; and, in this context, that is justification enough.

(4) In *Solle* v. *Butcher*[11] Denning L.J. expressed the view that in equity a party could not seek to take advantage of the mistake if he himself was at fault. But "Denning L.J. did not develop that at all, and it is not . . . absolutely clear what it comprehends. Clearly, there must be some degree of blameworthiness beyond the mere fault of having made a mistake; but the question is, how much, or in what way? Each case must depend on its own facts . . . "[12] This condition, if accepted, would make the scope of equity's jurisdiction even more uncertain.[13]

(5) There is little guidance in the cases as to the limits within which contracts may be rescinded in equity on grounds of mistake. In principle they should be the same as those which prevent rescission for innocent misrepresentation,[14] although section 2(2) of the Misrepresentation Act 1967 can have no application.[15] These limits are: impossibility of making *restitutio in integrum*[16]; intervention of third-party rights; affirmation of the transaction by the party claiming rescission; and lapse of time.

(6) The court's power to set aside the contract is discretionary, and in the exercise of that discretion it may impose terms on the party who is seeking to set aside the agreement.[17]

---

[10] But *cf.* the curious case of *British Homophone Ltd.* v. *Kunz* (1935) 152 L.T. 589, where *Cooper* v. *Phibbs* was not cited and where the mistake of law was fatal.

[11] [1950] 1 K.B. 671, 693.

[12] *Grist* v. *Bailey* [1967] Ch. 532, 542, *per* Goff J.

[13] See, *e.g. Laurence* v. *Lexcourt Holdings Ltd.* [1979] 1 W.L.R. 1128 (given the representation, the defendant was not "at fault" in entering into possession without the usual searches).

[14] See above, pp. 198 *et seq.* However, execution of a transaction was never a bar at common law.

[15] See above, pp. 208–209.

[16] *Cf. Campbell* v. *Edwards* [1976] 1 W.L.R. 403, 407, *per* Lord Denning M.R.

[17] See, *e.g. Cooper* v. *Phibbs* (1867) L.R. 2 H.L. 149 (see above, p. 213); *Grist* v. *Bailey* [1967] Ch. 532 (see above, pp. 217–218).

(c) *Rescission of Voluntary Settlements*

In the absence of fraudulent, negligent or innocent misrepresentations,[18] undue influence, or a fiduciary relationship between the parties, it is not easy to succeed in a claim for rescission of a voluntary settlement.

> "Where there is no fraud, no undue influence, no fiduciary relation between donor and donee, no mistake induced by those who derive any benefit by it, a gift, whether by mere delivery or by deed is binding on the donor. . . . In the absence of all such circumstances of suspicion a donor can only obtain back property which he has given away by showing that he was under some mistake of so serious a character as to render it unjust on the part of the donee to retain the property given to him."[19]

Only in comparatively rare circumstances will this *onus probandi* be discharged.[20] Such a case was *Lady Hood of Avalon* v. *Mackinnon*,[21] where an appointment by deed poll, made in "utter forgetfulness" of an earlier appointment, was set aside. Again, settlements have been successfully challenged on the ground that they did not contain a power of revocation. In *Wollaston* v. *Tribe*,[22] for example, a voluntary settlement was set aside because the settlor was unaware of the omission of such a power; but in that case the settlor "never had fully explained to her the peculiar nature of the settlement which she executed, and she was really in the hands of persons who would derive a benefit from the settlement."[23]

There is authority that a mistake of law may be good grounds for rescission. In *Lister* v. *Hodgson*,[24] Lord Romilly ordered that a deed, which was inconsistent with an earlier prior agreement and which had been executed by the settlor in ignorance of its legal effect, should be delivered up and cancelled. And it appears that rescission can be obtained if the mistake of law embodied in the voluntary instrument results in the frustration of the settlor's objects. Thus, in *Perrott* v. *Perrott*,[25] Lord Ellenborough C.J. set aside the revocation of a power of appointment, where the revocation had been made in the belief that a subsequent will would operate as an appointment. The testator had mistaken either the contents of the will (a question of fact) or its legal effect (a question of law).

---

[18] *Re Glubb* [1900] 1 Ch. 354.

[19] *Ogilvie* v. *Littleboy* (1897) 13 T.L.R. 399, 400, *per* Lindley L.J. See also *Cann* v. *Cann* (1721) 1 P.Wms. 723.

[20] See generally, *Dutton* v. *Thompson* (1883) 23 Ch.D. 278, 281, *per* Jessel M.R., 283, *per* Cotton L.J.

[21] [1909] 1 Ch. 476; see also *Re Isaacs* [1955] 1 D.L.R. 327; *Rowse* v. *Harris* (1963) 39 D.L.R. 2d 29; and *cf. Rosenblum* v. *Manufacturers' Trust Co.*, 270 N.Y. 78, 200 N.E. 587 (1936).

[22] (1869) L.R. 9 Eq. 44; but see *Tucker* v. *Bennett* (1887) 38 Ch.D. 1, 15, *per* Cotton L.J.; *Henry* v. *Armstrong* (1881) 18 Ch.D. 668.

[23] (1869) L.R. 9 Eq. 44, 50, *per* Lord Romilly M.R.

[24] (1867) L.R. 4 Eq. 30.

[25] (1811) 14 East 423; see also *Broughton* v. *Hutt* (1858) 3 De G. & J. 501; *Re Saxon Life Assurance* (1862) 2 J. & H. 408, 412, *per* Page Wood V.-C.

"In either case we think the mistake annulled the cancellation. *Onions* v. *Tyrer*[26] is a strong authority that a mistake in point of law may destroy the effect of a cancellation. And when once it is established, as it clearly is, that a mistake in point of fact may also destroy it, it seems difficult upon principle to say that a mistake in point of law, clearly evidenced by what occurs at the time of cancelling, should not have the same operation."[27]

Moreover, Millett J. recently held in *Gibbon* v. *Mitchell* that[28]:

"wherever there is a voluntary transaction by which one party intends to confer a bounty on another, the deed will be set aside if the court is satisfied that the disponer did not intend the transaction to have the effect which it did. It will be set aside for mistake whether the mistake is a mistake of law or of fact, so long as the mistake is as to the effect of the transaction itself and not merely as to its consequences or the advantages to be gained by entering into it."

In that case the plaintiff had executed the deed with the intention that it should vest the beneficial interest in certain trust funds in his children absolutely. This was not the effect of the deed which created a discretionary trust of income and a capital trust for his children after his death. The deed was set aside.

The limits to these claims are presumably similar to the limits to other claims for rescission for mistake not induced by misrepresentation.[29]

2. Rectification

The object of a suit for rectification is to bring a document which was intended to give effect to a prior agreement into harmony with that prior agreement.[30] The circumstances in which equity will grant rectification are as follows:

---

[26] (1716) 1 P.Wms. 342.

[27] At p. 440. *Cf.* the probate doctrine of dependent relative revocation: see *Stamford* v. *White* [1901] P. 46; *In the Estate of Southerden* [1925] P. 177.

[28] [1990] 3 All E.R. 338, 343. See also *Re Colebrook's Conveyances* [1972] 1 W.L.R. 1397; *Re Slocock's Will Trusts* [1979] 1 All E.R. 358.

[29] For the limits to such claims for rescission, see above, pp. 198 *et seq.*

[30] Where a conveyance is rectified, the effect may be to revest in the transferor the legal title in the land mistakenly conveyed to the transferee: see *Beale* v. *Kyte* [1907] 1 Ch. 564. For the statutory jurisdiction to rectify conveyances of land, the title to which is registered under the provisions of the Land Registration Act 1925, see above, Chap. 7; and *Scott* v. *Frank F. Scott (London) Ltd.* [1940] Ch. 794.

There is now, under the Administration of Justice Act 1982, s.20, a limited jurisdiction to rectify a will if the court is satisfied that the will fails to carry out the testator's intentions "in consequence—(a) of a clerical error; or (b) of a failure to understand his instructions." An application shall not be made, except with the court's permission, after six months from the date on which representation is first taken out. The personal representatives are not liable if they have distributed any part of the estate after the six months' period; but this does not prejudice any right to recover any part of the estate so distributed.

On the meaning of clerical error, see *Wordingham* v. *Royal Exchange Trust Co. Ltd.* [1992] 3 All E.R. 204.

(1) The antecedent agreement must be clear and unequivocal and must have continued unchanged until the execution of the final document. It must, therefore, be proved[31] that the final document did not carry out the parties' earlier, and unchanged, agreement.[32]

(2) There are dicta which suggest that a party cannot obtain rectification of a written instrument save to accord with "an actual concluded contract antecedent to the instrument which is sought to be rectified."[33] The Court of Appeal has now firmly rejected their authority, and has affirmed that it is enough that, if, "in regard to a particular point, the parties were in agreement up to the moment when they executed their formal instrument, and the formal instrument does not conform with that agreement, then the court had jurisdiction to rectify, although it may be that there was, until the formal agreement was executed, no concluded and binding contract between the parties."[34]

If the formal instrument does not, therefore, carry out the parties' earlier and unchanged agreement in this wide sense there can be rectification. But what if the parties entered into that earlier agreement under a mistake shared by both of them? In such a case, the Court of Appeal's decision in *Frederick E. Rose (London) Ltd.* v. *Pim, Jnr. & Co. Ltd.*[35] would suggest that rectification will be denied. The plaintiffs received an order from a third party for "Moroccan horse-beans described here as feveroles." They asked the defendants what they were; the defendants replied that they were just horse-beans and that they could supply them. Negotiations accordingly took place between the plaintiffs and defendants on this basis. The parties agreed to buy and sell horse-beans, and that agreement was embodied in a written contract. The defendants delivered horse-beans to the plaintiffs who in turn delivered them to the third party who, having accepted them, successfully claimed damages on the ground that they were not feveroles. The plaintiffs claimed rectification of the written contract with the defendants, so that it was for the supply of "feveroles." The Court of Appeal denied the plaintiffs' claim for rectification. Denning L.J. said[36]:

---

[31] On which see below, p. 224. Where the purpose of a suit for rectification is to reduce the claimant's liability to pay tax, the court will hesitate before ordering rectification (see *Van der Linde* v. *Van der Linde* [1947] Ch. 306, 311, *per* Evershed J.); but rectification will be ordered in such a case where there is convincing evidence of an antecedent agreement to which the instrument failed to give effect: see *Burroughs* v. *Abbott* [1922] 1 Ch. 86; *Jervis* v. *Howle & Talke Colliery Co. Ltd.* [1937] 1 Ch. 67; *Gibbon* v. *Mitchell* [1990] 3 All E.R. 338 (see below, p. 222).

[32] *Tucker* v. *Bennett* (1887) 38 Ch.D. 1; *Rhodian River Shipping Co. S.A.* v. *Halla Maritime Corp.* [1984] Lloyd's Rep. 373.

[33] *Mackenzie* v. *Coulson* (1869) L.R. 8 Eq. 368, 375, *per* James V.-C.; *Frederick E. Rose (London) Ltd.* v. *Pim, Jnr. & Co. Ltd.* [1953] 2 Q.B. 450, 461–461: see below, n. 35. *Cf. Hooker and Town Developments Property Ltd.* v. *The Director of War Service Homes* (1973) 47 A.L.J.R. 320.

[34] *Joscelyne* v. *Nissen* [1970] 2 Q.B. 86, adopting *Crane* v. *Hegeman-Harris Co. Inc.* [1939] 1 All E.R. 662, 664–665, *per* Simonds J., [1939] 4 All E.R. 68, C.A. See also *Lloyd* v. *Stanbury* [1971] 1 W.L.R. 535, 542–543, *per* Brightman J.

[35] [1953] 2 Q.B. 450. *Cf. Pukallus* v. *Cameron* (1983) 34 A.L.J.R. 243 (H. Ct. of Australia). See generally Palmer, *op. cit.* Vol. III, § 13.4.

[36] At pp. 461–462.

"Formalities apart, there must have been a concluded contract. There is a passage in *Crane* v. *Hegeman-Harris Co. Inc.*[37] which suggests that a continuing common intention alone will suffice; but I am clearly of the opinion that a continuing common intention is not sufficient unless it has found expression in outward agreement."

The court therefore refused to "look into the inner minds of the parties or into their intentions."[38]

In so far as *Rose* v. *Pim* turns on the need for an antecedent contract it cannot now be supported.[39] But it was approved in *Joscelyne* v. *Nissen*[40] on the ground that "prior accord on a term or the meaning of a phrase to be used must have been outwardly expressed or communicated between the parties." A continuing, common intention must still be objectively determined. Yet *Rose* v. *Pim* is a hard case. The mistake had arisen from the defendants' innocent misrepresentation that feveroles were "just horse-beans"[41]; and the court could have concluded on the facts, in the light of the defendants' misrepresentation, that the parties did have a continuing, common intention which was manifested in an outward agreement to buy and sell feveroles.[42]

(3) The burden of proof on a party seeking rectification is "the civil standard of balance of probability."[43] However, it has also been said that the court's jurisdiction should be exercised only "upon convincing proof that the concluded instrument does not represent the common intention of the parties,"[44] since "the alleged common intention *ex hypothesi* contradicts the written instrument."[45] This is a particularly important principle now that it has been established that an antecedent, concluded contract need not be established before rectification may be granted.

(4) Generally,[46] the mistake made in reducing the prior agreement must be shared by both parties; in the absence of grounds such as fraud, there can be no rectification if one party is mistaken and the other has no actual knowledge of

---

[37] [1939] 1 All E.R. 662, 664.

[38] [1953] 2 Q.B. 450, 461, *per* Denning L.J.

[39] See *Joscelyne* v. *Nissen* [1970] 2 Q.B. 86, C.A.: see above, p. 223.

[40] [1970] 2 Q.B. 86, 97, *per* Russell L.J., approving counsel's argument at first instance in *Rose* v. *Pim* [1953] 2 Q.B. at 457; but criticised in (1971) 87 L.Q.R. 532 [Bromley].

[41] But the plaintiffs' right to rescind was lost because of the resale.

[42] Indeed the trial judge, Pilcher J., had concluded that the parties had orally agreed to deal in horse-beans of the feverole type: [1953] 1 Lloyd's Rep. 84. *Cf. Earl* v. *Hector Whaling Ltd.* [1961] 1 Lloyd's Rep. 459, 470, *per* Harman L.J.; *London Weekend Television* v. *Paris and Griffith* (1969) 113 S.J. 222. For a case where a party's intention was never disclosed in the negotiations, see *Re Streamline Fashions Property Ltd.* [1965] V.R. 418.

[43] *Thomas Bates & Sons Ltd.* v. *Wyndham's (Lingerie) Ltd.* [1981] 1 W.L.R. 505, 521, *per* Brightman L.J.; *Agip S.p.A.* v. *Navigazione Alta Italia S.p.A.* [1984] 1 Lloyd's Rep. 353, 359, *per* Slade L.J.

[44] *Crane* v. *Hegeman-Harris Co. Inc.* [1939] 1 All E.R. 662, 664–665, *per* Simonds J., approved in *Joscelyne* v. *Nissen* [1970] 2 Q.B. 86. See also *Ernest Scragg & Sons* v. *Perseverance Banking and Trust Co. Ltd.* [1973] 2 Lloyd's Rep. 101. But *cf. Bercokici* v. *Palmer* (1966) 59 D.L.R. (2d) 513.

[45] *Thomas Bates & Sons Ltd.* v. *Wyndham's (Lingerie) Ltd.* [1981] 1 W.L.R. 505, 521, *per* Brightman L.J.; *cf.* Buckley L.J. at p. 519.

[46] For the principles governing voluntary settlements, see below, p. 228.

his mistake.[47] It may, however, be that one of the parties is aware that the document does not accurately represent that prior agreement. The fact that the mistake is in this sense unilateral may not prevent rectification. Such a case was *A. Roberts & Co. Ltd.* v. *Leicestershire C.C.*[48] The plaintiffs submitted a tender for certain works, but the completion date was left blank. The defendants agreed to accept the tender subject to renegotiation about the price. A revised tender was submitted which specified the period of completion as 78 weeks from the date when instructions were given to proceed. Two of the defendants' officials decided that the period of completion should be considerably longer and instructed their solicitor to prepare a draft contract with a completion date of 30 months. When the defendants forwarded the draft contract and when later meetings were held between the parties, they made no mention of the change, though there was a direct relationship between the period of completion and the price. The plaintiffs then signed the draft contract.

Pennycuick J. held that there was no mistake common to both parties. Nevertheless, he granted rectification and inserted the earlier date as the date of completion. For if a party to a contract concludes that contract with the omission or variation of a contractual term, knowing[49] that the other party believed that term to be included or to be unvaried, the court will rectify the contract to restore the term or to restore it in its unvaried form, as the case may be: *a fortiori*, if the knowing party was in a fiduciary position to the other or was fraudulent.[50] The principle of the case seems closely linked to that of equitable estoppel, but the judge thought its "exact basis" to be a matter of some doubt, and that it could be either such an estoppel or fraud.[51]

Subsequently the Court of Appeal has said that rectification should be permitted only if the defendant's conduct is such as to involve him "in a degree of sharp practice."[52] But more recently Buckley, Eveleigh and Brightman L.JJ. have rejected the view that sharp practice must be shown.[53] It is enough, in Buckley L.J.'s view, that "the mistake [was] calculated to benefit" the party not labouring under mistake.[54] In contrast, in Eveleigh L.J.'s opinion, it is sufficient that the instrument as drafted was detrimental to the interests of the

---

[47] *Agip S.p.A.* v. *Navigazione Alta Italia S.p.A.* [1984] 1 Lloyd's Rep. 353.

[48] [1961] Ch. 555; *cf. Pittsburg Lumber Co.* v. *Shell*, 136 Tenn. 466 (1916).

[49] *Semble* knowledge means "actual knowledge": see *Agip S.p.A.* v. *Navigazione Alta Italia S.p.A.* [1984] 1 Lloyd's Rep. 353, 362, 365, *per* Slade L.J.

[50] [1961] Ch. 555, 570; *cf. Caird* v. *Moss* (1886) 33 Ch.D. 22; *Crane* v. *Hegeman-Harris Co. Inc.* [1939] 1 All E.R. 662, [1939] 4 All E.R. 68.

[51] The decision is, in our view, justifiable only on the grounds of estoppel. The defendants must have been precluded from denying that it had been agreed that the period of completion was 78 weeks; for if there had been no agreement on this point, there could have been no rectification: see *Smith* v. *Hughes* (1871) L.R. 6 Q.B. 597, and *cf. Russell* v. *Shell Petroleum Co.*, 66 F.2d 864 (1933), discussed in Palmer, *Mistake and Unjust Enrichment*, pp. 75–78.

[52] *Riverplate Properties Ltd.* v. *Paul* [1975] Ch. 133, 140 *per curiam* (Russell L.J.), followed in *Saanich Police Association* v. *District of Saanich Police Board* (1983) 43 B.C.L.R. 132.

[53] *Thomas Bates & Sons Ltd.* v. *Wyndham's (Lingerie) Ltd.* [1981] 1 W.L.R. 505.

[54] *Ibid.* 515–516.

mistaken party.[55] If, as we believe,[56] the principle embodied in the *Roberts* case is akin to that of equitable estoppel, it should be sufficient simply to demonstrate that one party sought, in the circumstances of the case, to take unfair advantage of another's mistake.[57]

At one time it was thought, on the basis of certain nineteenth-century cases, that equity had jurisdiction to grant rectification where the defendant had accepted an offer which did not express the plaintiff's real intention and where there was present neither a mistake shared by both parties in reducing the agreement to writing nor conduct on behalf of the defendant which was fraudulent[58] or could give rise to an estoppel. *Paget* v. *Marshall*[59] may be taken as representative of these cases. The plaintiff had written a letter to the defendant offering to lease him certain floors of three houses. The defendant accepted the offer, and the plaintiff then alleged that one of the floors of the houses had been included in the offer by mistake; he had always intended to reserve it for his own use. The defendant denied that he accepted the offer knowing of the plaintiff's mistake. Bacon V.-C. held that on the evidence "common mistake" was not sufficiently proved. But, he continued, "if there was not a common mistake it is plain and palpable that the plaintiff was mistaken, and that he had no intention of letting his own shop. . . . Upon that ground, therefore, I must say that the contract ought to be annulled."[60] He then gave the defendant the option of cancellation or rectification. *Paget* v. *Marshall* and its predecessors were severely criticised in other decisions.[61] And in *Riverplate Properties Ltd.* v. *Paul*[62] the Court of Appeal finally limited their authority and affirmed that, in the absence of fraud or sharp practice, mere unilateral mistake was not a ground for "rescission . . . either with or without the option to the [defendant] to accept rectification to cure the [plaintiff's] mistake."[63]

Since the object of rectification is simply to ensure that the written instrument embodies the previously concluded agreement, it should be irrelevant to consider whether the parties' mistake was shared or unilateral.[64] The sole question should be, does the written instrument embody the previously concluded and objectively determined agreement between the parties?

---

[55] *Ibid.* at 520–521. Brightman L.J. expressed no view on this question.

[56] See above, n. 51.

[57] *Cf. Agip S.p.A.* v. *Navigazione Alta Italia S.p.A.* [1984] 1 Lloyd's Rep. 353, 364–365, *per* Slade L.J. (proffering a draft may amount to a representation that it gives effect to an "accord" already reached); and the cases cited above, pp. 223–224.

[58] *Cf. May* v. *Platt* [1900] 1 Ch. 616, 623, *per* Farwell J.

[59] (1884) 28 Ch.D. 255. See also *Garrard* v. *Frankel* (1862) 30 Beav. 455; and *Harris* v. *Pepperell* (1867) L.R. 5 Eq. 1.

[60] (1884) 28 Ch.D. 255, 266.

[61] *Bloomer* v. *Spittle* (1872) L.R. 13 Eq. 427; *Paget* v. *Marshall* (1884) 28 Ch.D. 255, 260 (where counsel quoted criticisms of Jessel M.R.); *May* v. *Platt* [1900] 1 Ch. 616, 618, 623; *Beale* v. *Kyte* [1907] 1 Ch. 564, 565–566; *Blay* v. *Pollard and Morris* [1930] 1 K.B. 628, 633.

[62] [1975] Ch. 133.

[63] At p. 145, *per curiam.*

[64] *Thomas Bates & Sons Ltd.* v. *Wyndham's (Lingerie) Ltd.* [1981] 1 W.L.R. 505, 521, *per* Brightman L.J.

(5) The mistake must generally be a mistake of fact. But in certain cases the court will give relief even if the mistake is one of law. In *Whiteside* v. *Whiteside*[65] Harman J. adopted this statement of law in Kerr on *Fraud and Mistake*[66]:

"... Though the court will rectify an instrument which fails through some mistake of the draftsman in point of law to carry out the real agreement between the parties, it is not sufficient in order to create an equity for rectification that there has been a mistake as to the legal construction or the legal consequences of an instrument."

When the case came before the Court of Appeal, however, Lord Evershed M.R. qualified the passage in the following way[67]:

"I do not read that passage as meaning that if the mistake made is in using language to perfect an agreement which in law has some result different from the common intention, that is not a case in which there can be rectification. I do not read the passage as so stating, and I think, as at present advised, that if it did it would be too wide. I think it may well be that if the mistake has arisen from the legal effect of the language used that may provide a ground for the exercise of the court's reforming power. Subject, however, to that qualification, I think that the passage cited is correct."[68]

(6) Judges have shown themselves to be cautious of rectifying voluntary settlements, especially where evidence of the settlor's intention rests upon his own statement.[69–70] It is the settlor's intention which is crucial and not, for example, the intention of the trustees of the voluntary settlement which the settlor has executed, although the court will take into account whether the trustees oppose or support rectification in exercising its discretion to grant relief.[71] It is generally enough that it is proved that the settlor intended something different from what is expressed in the instrument. But that instrument will not be rectified without his consent.[72] If he does not consent to rectification the instrument can only be set aside[73]; a volunteer cannot perfect a voluntary instrument against a living donor.[74] In a proper case, rectification is "available not only in a case where particular words must have been added,

---

[65] [1949] Ch. 448, 455; see also *Stone* v. *Godfrey* (1854) 5 De G.M. & G. 76; *Napier* v. *Williams* [1911] 1 Ch. 361; *Burroughes* v. *Abott* [1922] 1 Ch. 86.
[66] 6th ed., at p. 620.
[67] [1950] Ch. 65, 74; see also *Powell* v. *Smith* (1872) L.R. 14 Eq. 85, 90–91, *per* Lord Romilly M.R.; *Haymen* v. *Gover* (1872) 25 L.T. 903, 905, *per* Cockburn C.J.
[68] *Cf. Meadows* v. *Meadows* (1853) 16 Beav. 401; *Re Walton's Settlement* [1922] Ch. 509, cited in *Gibbon* v. *Mitchell* [1990] 3 All E.R. 388 (see above, p. 222).
[69–70] *Bonhote* v. *Henderson* [1895] 1 Ch. 742, affd. [1895] 2 Ch. 202. *Cf.* above, p. 162.
[71] *Re Butlin's Settlement* [1976] Ch. 251. It is another matter if the settlor and the trustees have made a bargain with each other.
[72] *Tucker* v. *Bennett* (1887) 38 Ch.D. 1, 15, *per* Cotton L.J.; see also *Rake* v. *Hooper* (1900) 83 L.T. 669; *Cf. Gibbon* v. *Mitchell* [1990] 3 All E.R. 338 (see above, p. 222).
[73] *Phillipson* v. *Kerry* (1863) 32 Beav. 628, 637–638, *per* Romilly M.R.; *Turner* v. *Collins* (1871) 7 Ch.App. 329, 342, *per* Lord Hatherley L.C.: see above, pp. 221–222.
[74] *Cf.* see below, Chap. 30.

omitted or wrongly written as a result of careless copying or the like. It is also available where the words of the document were purposely used but it was mistakenly considered that they bore a different meaning from their correct meaning as a matter of true construction."[75] Exceptionally, however, a voluntary settlement may be rectified after the death of the settlor. In *Lister* v. *Hodgson*,[76] Lord Romilly suggested that equity might perfect an imperfect gift if the donor had died having donated money on trusts different from those that he intended. In such a case, the gift would presumably be perfected in favour of the "intended" donee. This question is more fully discussed in a later Chapter.[77]

(7) Rectification is an equitable remedy so that the court may refuse relief if it thinks it just to do so. To refuse relief will mean that the parties are bound by the document in its uncorrected form. The equity of rectification will not be enforced against a bona fide purchaser without notice of the facts giving rise to the suit for rectification.[78] The court may also refuse to rectify an instrument if there has been laches, if the plaintiff has led the defendant to rely on the uncorrected document, if *restitutio in integrum*[79] is impossible, or if the party claiming rectification has affirmed the instrument with knowledge of the error contained in it, or if there has been undue lapse of time.

3. Reopening Accounts

Where it can be shown that accounts have been drawn up under a mistake, the courts may either reopen the accounts altogether or give liberty to surcharge and falsify. Lord Cottenham L.C., in *Coleman* v. *Mellersh*,[80] explained the relevant principles in the following words:

> "There is a material difference in the principle on which the court deals with settled accounts with reference to those two kinds of decrees, as there undoubtedly is in the effect in working them out. A settled account, otherwise unimpeachable, in which an error is proved to exist, may be subjected to a decree to surcharge and falsify, upon the supposition that the error having been proved others may be expected upon investigation to be discovered; but if the relative situation of the parties, or the manner in which the settlement took place, or the nature of the error proved, show that the alleged settlement ought not to be considered as an act binding upon the party signing, and that it would be inequitable for the accounting party to take advantage of it, the court is not content with enabling the

---

[75] *Re Butlin's Settlement* [1976] Ch. 251, 260, *per* Brightman J.
[76] (1867) L.R. 4 Eq. 30, 34–35; see also *Thompson* v. *Whitmore* (1860) 1 J. & H. 268, 273, *per* Page Wood V.-C.; *M'Mechan* v. *Warburton* [1896] 1 I.R. 435, 431, *per* Chatterton V.-C.; and see below, Chap. 30. *Cf. Weir* v. *Van Tromp* (1900) 16 T.L.R. 531, *per* Byrne J.
[77] See below, Chap. 30.
[78] *Smith* v. *Jones* [1954] 1 W.L.R. 1089, 1091–1093, *per* Upjohn J.
[79] For the meaning of *restitutio in integrum*, see above, pp. 198–200.
[80] (1850) 2 Mac. & G. 309, 314–315.

party to surcharge and falsify an account which never ought to have been so settled, but directs the taking of an open account."

Thus accounts may be reopened if the mistake is shared by both parties as a result of which too little was accepted or too much admitted.[81] In *Daniell* v. *Sinclair*[82] the Judicial Committee reopened a mortgage account which had been settled on the footing of compound interest with half-yearly rests, both plaintiff and defendant wrongly understanding the mortgage deed to require such interest. It is immaterial that the parties' mistake is one of law, at least if it is a mistake shared by both of them as to their respective rights.[83]

The courts are traditionally suspicious of accounts drawn up between fiduciaries and their beneficiaries. Sir George Jessel M.R., in *Williamson* v. *Barbour*,[84] recognised that "a less amount of error will justify the court in opening the account"[85] where such a relationship exists than where it does not. But a single, important error can be sufficient[86] even if there is no fiduciary relationship between the parties, although in these circumstances it would be more usual, in the absence of fraud, to surcharge and falsify.[87] If there is fraud or undue influence, the court will reopen accounts[88] even though only one item is fraudulent[89] and a substantial time has elapsed since the accounts were settled.[90]

---

[81] *Thomas* v. *Hawkes* (1841) 8 M. & W. 140; *Perry* v. *Attwood and Attwood* (1856) 6 El. & Bl. 691; *Dails* v. *Lloyd and Price* (1848) 12 Q.B. 531, 545, *per* Lord Denman C.J.

[82] (1881) 6 App.Cas. 181.

[83] *Daniell* v. *Sinclair* (1881) 6 App.Cas. 181, 190–191, *per curiam* (Sir Robert Collier). For facts, which were said to be "strongly analogous" but where subsequent events invalidated assumptions made by the parties, see *Davis* v. *Richards & Wallington Industries Ltd.* [1991] 2 All E.R. 563, 594, *per* Scott J.

[84] (1877) 9 Ch.D. 529; see also *Lewes* v. *Morgan* (1817) 5 Pri. 42; *Re Webb* [1894] 1 Ch. 73; *Cheese* v. *Keen* [1908] 1 Ch. 245.

[85] (1877) 9 Ch.D. 529.

[86] *Taylor* v. *Haylin* (1783) 2 Bro.C.C. 310; *Pritt* v. *Clay* (1843) 6 Beav. 503, as explained in *Gething* v. *Keighley* (1878) 9 Ch.D. 547, 550, *per* Jessel M.R.

[87] *Gething* v. *Keighley* (1878) 9 Ch.D. 547. If the errors are considerble, the accounts will, of course, be reopened; see *Perry* v. *Attwood and Attwood* (1856) 6 El. & Bl. 691; *Stainton* v. *The Carron Company* (1857) 24 Beav. 346; *Dails* v. *Lloyd and Price* (1848) 12 Q.B. 531; *Phillips-Higgins* v. *Harper* [1954] 1 Q.B. 411 (discussed below, p. 169).

[88] *Waters* v. *Taylor* (1837) 2 My. & Cr. 526; *Morgan* v. *Higgins* (1859) 1 Gif. 270.

[89] *Coleman* v. *Mellersh* (1850) 2 Mac. & G. 309; *Cheese* v. *Keen* [1908] 1 Ch. 245, 251, *per* Neville J.

[90] *Allfrey* v. *Allfrey* (1849) 1 Mac. & G. 87. But where there is no fraud, the court is, after a considerable lapse of time, reluctant to reopen accounts: see *Brownwell* v. *Brownwell* (1786) 2 Bro.C.C. 62.

B. COMPULSION

CHAPTER 9

RECOVERY OF BENEFITS CONFERRED UNDER DURESS[1]

1. INTRODUCTION

A PERSON confers a benefit on another under duress. If the benefit is money, it is recoverable in restitution[2] in an action for money had and received either on the grounds of "duress or possibly of failure of consideration[3];" if it is services, a claim for services rendered (*quantum meruit*) will lie[4]; if it is a chattel, the property will normally remain in the transferor who will have his remedies in tort,[5] otherwise there will be a claim[6] for goods delivered (*quantum valebat*). Deeds or contracts may be avoided for duress at the instance of the coerced party,[7] but duress renders the document void if the coerced party can prove that "it is not his," *non est factum*.[8] Exceptionally the coerced party may have been required to confer the benefit on a third party who is not party to, and has no knowledge of, the duress.[9] Whether the third party must then make restitution may depend on the nature of the benefit conferred. The analogy of

---

[1] For a valuable comparative law survey see Izhak Englard, *Restitution of Benefits Conferred without Obligation*, Vol. X of *Restitution—Unjust Enrichment and Negotiorum Gestio* of the *International Encyclopedia of Comparative Law*.

[2] *Dimskal Shipping Co. S.A.* v. *International Transport Workers' Federation, The Evia Luck* [1992] 2 A.C. 152, 165, *per* Lord Goff.

[3] Above n. 2. For a historical discussion, see Jackson, *History*, pp. 64–66.

[4] See above, pp. 3–4.

[5] See above, pp. 3–4.

[6] See above, pp. 3–4.

[7] *Pau On* v. *Lau Yiu Long* [1980] A.C. 614, 634, 636, *per* Lord Scarman; *Universe Tankships Inc. of Monrovia* v. *International Transport Workers Federation, The Universe Sentinel* [1983] 1 A.C. 366, 383, *per* Lord Diplock, 400, *per* Lord Scarman, *Dimskal Shipping Co. S.A.* v. *International Transport Workers' Federation, The Evia Luck* [1992] 2 A.C. 152, 168, *per* Lord Goff. *Cf. Lynch* v. *D.P.P. of Northern Ireland* [1975] A.C. 653, 695, *per* Lord Morris. But the contract may be affirmed after the duress has been removed: *North Ocean Shipping Co. Ltd.* v. *Hyundai Construction Co. Ltd.* [1979] Q.B. 705, see below, p. 256.

It is an open question how far the principles governing fraudulent misrepresentation apply where the contract is sought to be rescinded for duress. In *Barton* v. *Armstrong* (1973) [1976] A.C. 104, the Privy Council suggested that their analogy should determine whether a transaction, which has been induced by duress, can be rescinded; *semble* the principle in *Car and Universal Finance Co.* v. *Caldwell* [1965] Q.B. 525 (see above, p. 203) would then apply.

[8] *Cf. Lloyds Bank plc* v. *Waterhouse* [1991] Fam. Law 23, *per* Purchas L.J. (undue influence); and see Williston, § 1624. For an argument that no distinction can be drawn between such a case and a chattel transferred under a contract made under duress; see (1969) 29 M.L.R. 615 [Lanham].

[9] If he is privy to the duress, he can be in no better position than the person who exercises the duress; *cf. Barton* v. *Armstrong* [1976] A.C. 104, 108, *arguendo*.

the cases of money paid under mistake of fact suggest that money, which has been paid to the third party, may be recovered,[10] subject to defences, in particular, change of position[11] for he has been unjustly enriched at the plaintiff's expense.[12] The transferor's title to chattels will generally be protected; and a restitutionary claim for services will succeed if the third party has freely accepted them or has been incontrovertibly benefited by their receipt.[13]

We shall primarily be concerned with money claims against persons exercising duress since these are the claims which arise most frequently in practice. But the categories of duress are common to all restitutionary claims for duress. In the past this was said not to be so and that, to affect the validity of a contract, the duress must be exercised on the person and that duress of goods was not enough.[14] This distinction is unjustifiable in principle and is firmly rejected by recent authority.[15]

The chapter begins with an examination of the established categories of duress. These are actual or threatened violence to the person; improper application of legal process; duress of goods; and refusal by those in a public or quasi-public position to fulfil their duty. But recent case law demonstrates that duress is not restricted to these categories.[16] Any pressure, which the law "does not regard as legitimate,"[17] is wrongful and amounts to duress; for the common law, "under the influence of equity, has developed from the old common law conception of duress—threat to life and limb—and it has arrived at the modern generalisation expressed by Holmes J.—'subjected to an improper motive for action'."[18]

A wrongful act should include, but should not be limited to any illegal act, such as a criminal act. It also embraces a tortious act.[19] It may, in some

---

[10] See above, pp. 235–236. *Cf.* the cases on undue influence: see below, Chap. 10; and *Smith* v. *Weldon* (1924) 34 C.L.R. 29, 34.

[11] *Lipkin Gorman (A Firm)* v. *Karpnale Ltd.* [1991] 2 A.C. 548 see below, Chap. 40.

[12] *Cf.* the facts of *Dimskal Shipping Co. S.A.* v. *International Transport Workers' Federation, The Evia Luck* [1992] 2 A.C. 152.

[13] See above, pp. 18 *et seq. cf. Wilgross Investments Ltd.* v. *Goldshlager* (1974) 51 D.L.R. (3d) 343.

[14] *Skeate* v. *Beale* (1841) 11 A. & E. 983, see below, pp. 240–241.

[15] *Dimskal Shipping Co. S.A.* v. *International Transport Workers' Federation, The Evia Luck* [1992] 2 A.C. 152, 165, *per* Lord Goff. *The Siboen and the Sibotre* [1976] 1 Lloyd's Rep. 293. See below, pp. 240 *et seq.*, for a full discussion.

[16] *e.g. Smith* v. *Cuff* (1817) 6 M. & S. 160; *Kendal* v. *Wood* (1871) L.R. 6 Ex. 243; see also *Smith* v. *Bromley* (1760) 2 Doug. 696n.

[17] *Barton* v. *Armstrong* (1973) [1976] A.C. 104 (P.C.), 121, *per* Lord Wilberforce and Lord Simon of Glaisdale, dissenting. Their Lordships' dissent was on the application of these principles to the facts of the case; *cf.* p. 118, *per* Lord Cross.

[18] *Barton* v. *Armstrong* (1973) [1976] A.C. 104, 121, *per* Lord Wilberforce and Lord Simon of Glaisdale, dissenting. The quotation from Holmes J., which was also cited by the majority (see Lord Cross, at p. 118,) is from *Fairbanks* v. *Snow*, 13 N.E. 568, 598 (1887). Holmes J. was than a Justice of the Supreme Judicial Court of Massachusetts.

[19] It has been said that such examples as fall outside the established categories can be classified as waiver of tort: see Winfield, *Quasi-Contracts*, pp. 97–98. But the governing precedent, *Morgan* v. *Palmer* (1824) 2 B. & C. 729, was not a case of waiver of tort and in many cases no tort had been committed: see, *e.g. Steele* v. *Williams* (1853) 8 Ex. 625 and see below, p. 246. Moreover, intimidation is only tortious if it is a threat to do an act which is itself illegal: see *Rookes* v.

circumstances, be duress to refuse to pay a debt or to carry out a contractual obligation owed to the plaintiff.[20] Indeed in some circumstances it may be wrongful to threaten to do what one is entitled to do.[21] For example, it may be duress[22] to threaten to "do an act, which is not unlawful, but which is calculated seriously to injure another."[23] In many cases, such a threat will be made to obtain a benefit to which the person who made the threat is not entitled. It may also amount in law to duress if a benefit to which a person is entitled has been obtained by an improper threat (for example, if a creditor gains payment of a debt by threatening to tell the debtor's wife of the debtor's adulterous relationship).[24] But it is not always easy to tell when a threat will be characterised as one which a person is not entitled to make.[25] Finally, it is possible that a threat may amount to duress if the court concludes that a person's threat to exercise power over another was immoral or unconscionable.[26]

Most of the old cases have concerned either duress of goods or duress exercised by a person in a public or quasi-public position. But recently English courts have been confronted with the analogous claim that the defendant, who was not in a public or quasi-public position, wrongfully gained a benefit by exerting improper economic pressure on the plaintiff; and they have been required to determine what commercial pressure is legitimate and what pres-

---

Barnard [1964] A.C. 1129. In *Marshall Shipping Co.* v. *Board of Trade* [1923] 2 K.B. 243 and *Brocklebank Ltd.* v. *R.* [1925] 1 K.B. 52 (see below, p. 246, n. 30, the Court of Appeal regarded extortion *colore officii* as a tort; but it is difficult to see what tort had been committed. Moreover it appears that blackmail, which is a crime, may not be a tort; see below, pp. 265–266. In *Universe Tankships Inc. of Monrovia* v. *International Transport Workers' Federation* [1983] 1 A.C. 366, 385, Lord Diplock was of the opinion that "economic duress is not a tort *per se*." Contrast Lord Scarman at p. 400: see below, p. 252; and *Dimskal Shipping Co. S.A.* v. *International Transport Workers' Federation, The Evia Luck* [1952] 2 A.C. 152, 169, *per* Lord Goff.

[20] See below, pp. 260 *et seq.* for a discussion of the cases.

[21] See below, p. 266.

[22] *Universe Tankships Inc. of Monrovia* v. *International Transport Workers' Federation, The Universe Sentinel* [1983] 1 A.C. 388, 401, *per* Lord Scarman. (His Lordship was dissenting; but on a different point). See also *Silsbee* v. *Webber*, 50 N.E. 555 (1898) (an influential opinion of Holmes J., in the Supreme Judicial Court of Massachusetts).

[23] *Thorne* v. *Motor Trade Association* [1937] A.C. 797, 822–823, *per* Lord Wright. (Lord Wright was speaking of blackmail.)

[24] This may well be an academic question. The debtor may succeed on his claim in restitution but the creditor, who made the improper threat, will still have a counter-claim for the debt; *cf.* *Wilbur* v. *Blanchard* 126 P. 1069 (1912). *Aliter* if the debt is a gaming debt: see *Norreys* v. *Zeffert* [1939] 2 All E.R. 187, 189–190, where Atkinson J., following *Thorne* v. *Motor Trade Association* [1937] A.C. 797, concluded that a threat to report the gaming debtor to Tattersalls was one which the creditor was entitled to make; but threats to tell members of a social club or a trade protection association were not legitimate.

[25] *Thorne* v. *Motor Trade Association* [1937] A.C. 797, where there was a threat to put the plaintiff on the "stop list," (which is proper if it is "for some legitimate purpose other than the mere acquisition of money", see p. 807 *per* Lord Atkin); *Norreys* v. *Zeffert* [1939] 2 All E.R. 187; see above, n. 24. See Beatson, *The Use and Abuse of Unjust Enrichment*, Chap. 5, pp. 129–134; and *cf.* Birks, *Introduction* pp. 177–179.

[26] See below, p. 266, *cf.* *Lloyds Bank Ltd.* v. *Bundy* [1975] 1 Q.B. 326, 339, *per* Lord Denning M.R. See below, p. 290, and contrast *National Westminster Bank* v. *Morgan* [1985] A.C. 686, H.L.

sure is illegitimate.[27] As the law now stands, such an inquiry is essential because English courts will not generally set aside a bargain or order restitution of benefits conferred thereunder simply because its terms appear to be unconscionable,[28] although terms which appear to be unconscionable may lead a court to conclude that a person has obtained the benefit of them by illegitimate pressure.[29]

It is often said that duress "must amount to a coercion of will, which vitiates consent."[29a] As Justice Holmes said, in *Union Pacific R.R.* v. *Public Service Commission*[29b]: "It always is for the interest of a party under duress to choose the lesser of two evils. But the fact that a choice was made according to interest does not exclude duress. It is the characteristic of duress properly so called". We agree with Professor Palmer's conclusion that "the test that a party's will must be overcome is not useful except as it expresses an indispensable element of causation: in order to obtain relief the coercion must have caused a party to do something he otherwise would not have done."[29c]

---

[27] See cases cited in n. 29b, see below; for a full discussion, see pp. 250 *et seq.*

[28] See below, Chap. 11. *Cf.* the claim in *Burmah Oil Co.* v. *Bank of England* [1980] A.C. 1090, 1115, 1119–1120.

[29] *Lloyds Bank Ltd.* v. *Bundy* [1975] 1 Q.B. 326, 339, *per* Lord Denning M.R. But *cf. National Westminster Bank* v. *Morgan* [1985] A.C. 686, H.L.; see below, p. 290. Dawson has suggested that in the United States, as in England, undue attention has been paid to the requirement of wrongfulness when the real question should be whether the exchange is unequal and the consequence of the exercise of disproportionate economic power; see (1947) 45 Mich. L.R. 253, particularly at p. 289. See also (1981) 26 McGill L.J. 289 [Ogilvie]. It is doubtful whether the American courts have as yet moved this far. *Cf. Restatement of Contracts 2d*, § 176 (particularly (2)), which may, however, persuade them to do so. § 176 reads as follows:

§ 176 WHEN A THREAT IS IMPROPER
  (1) A threat is improper if
    (a) what is threatened is a crime or a tort, or the threat itself would be a crime or a tort if it resulted in the obtaining of property, or
    (b) what is threatened is a criminal prosecution, or
    (c) what is threatened is the use of civil process and the threat is made in bad faith, or
    (d) the threat is a breach of the duty of good faith and fair dealing under a contract with the recipient.
  (2) A threat is improper if the resulting exchange is not on fair terms, and
    (a) the threatened act would harm the recipient and would not significantly benefit the party making the threat,
    (b) the effectiveness of the threat in inducing the manifestation of assent is significantly increased by prior unfair dealing by the party making the threat, or
    (c) what is threatened is otherwise a use of power for illegitimate ends.

[29a] See, *e.g. North Ocean Shipping Co. Ltd.* v. *Hyundai Construction Co. Ltd.* [1979] Q.B. 705; *Pao On* v. *Lau Yiu Long* [1980] A.C. 614, 635–636, *per* Lord Scarman (P.C.); *The Proodos C* [1981] 3 All E.R. 189, 192, *per* Lloyd J.; *Universe Tankships Inc. of Monrovia* v. *International Transport Workers' Federation* [1983] 1 A.C. 366, 383, *per* Lord Diplock, 400, *per* Lord Scarman; *B. & S. Contracts and Design Ltd.* v. *Victor Green Publications Ltd.* [1984] I.C.R. 419 C.A.; *Hennessy* v. *Craigmyle & Co. Ltd.* [1986] I.C.R. 461, 468, *per* Sir John Donaldson M.R.

[29b] 248 U.S. 67, 70 (1918); and *cf. Universe Tankships Inc. of Monrovia* v. *International Transport Workers' Federation, The Universe Sentinel* [1983] 1 A.C. 366, 400, *per* Lord Scarman; *Dimskal Shipping Co. S.A.* v. *International Transport Workers' Federation, The Evia Luck* [1992] 2 A.C. 152, 166, *per* Lord Goff. See also *Lynch* v. *D.P.P. of Northern Ireland* [1975] A.C. 653, discussed in (1982) 98 L.Q.R. 197 [Atiyah]; and Beatson, *op. cit.*, n. 25, pp. 113–117.

[29c] Palmer, *op. cit.* Vol. II, p. 247. See also (1931) 40 Yale L.J. 704, 728 [Llewellyn]; (1980) 26 McGill L.J. 289 [Ogilvie].

2. THE ESTABLISHED CATEGORIES OF DURESS

(a) *Actual or Threatened Violence to the Person*

It has long been settled[30] that actual or threatened violence to the person[31] constitutes duress. Although the violence must generally be directed against the plaintiff[32] it is also sufficient if it is directed against his wife, child or other near relative.[33] Any deed, contract or transaction entered into under duress of this kind is voidable by the person coerced.[34] It is enough that the threats were only *a* reason as distinct from *the* predominant reason, for the plaintiff entering into the transaction. He "is entitled to relief even though he might well have entered into the contract if [the defendant] had uttered no threats to induce him to do so."[35-36] Presumably there is also a right to recover money paid under such duress, but there is no direct authority on the point.[37] This is hardly surprising. For duress to the person will normally constitute both a crime and a tort, in which case the plaintiff will have other remedies for the recovery of his money.[38] But, in principle, a quasi-contractual action should be available.

(b) *Improper Application of Legal Process*

The proper use of legal process does not constitute duress. Everyone is free to invoke the aid of the law in a proper case; and where a settlement is made or a payment exacted under such pressure as the law allows and provides, there is

---

[30] For ancient authority, see Bracton, f. 16b; Pollock and Maitland, *History of English Law* (2nd ed.), Vol. II, pp. 535–536, and cases from Bracton's *Notebook* there cited; Y.B. 21 Edw. 4, f. 13, pls, 4 and 22; *Thoroughgood's Case* (1584) 2 Co. at f. 9b; 2 Co. Inst. 483; 1 Roll. Abr. 688; 1 Bl. Comm. 131.

[31] *Scott* v. *Sebright* (1886) 12 P.D. 21; *Hussein* v. *Hussein* [1938] P. 159. Such duress includes false imprisonment: see *The Earl of Northumberland's Case* (1583) 4 Leo. 91.

[32] *Cf. Huscombe* v. *Standing* (1607) Cro.Jac. 187 (duress against a principal debtor is no defence to a surety); 1 Roll. Abr. 687, pl. 7.

[33] The categories may be wider: see *Kaufman* v. *Gerson* [1904] 1 K.B. 591; *Williams* v. *Bayley* (1866) L.R. 1 H.L. 200.

[34] 2 Co. Inst. 483; *Scott* v. *Sebright* (1886) 12 P.D. 21; and the authorities cited see above, p. 230, n. 7.

[35-36] *Barton* v. *Armstrong* [1976] A.C. 104, 119, *per* Lord Cross; *cf.* p. 121, *per* Lord Wilberforce and Lord Simon of Glaisdale dissenting. *Cf. Universe Tankships Inc. of Monrovia* v. *International Transport Workers' Federation* [1983] 1 A.C. 366, 387, *per* Lord Diplock, 391, *per* Lord Cross; *Dimskal Shipping Co. S.A.* v. *International Transport Workers' Federation, The Evia Luck* [1992] 2 A.C. 152, 165, *per* Lord Goff (economic pressure), see below, p. 730).

[37] See above, p. 230.

[38] The injured person may have his property refunded to him in the course of criminal proceedings, for under the Theft Act 1968, s.28, the court may make an order for the restoration of the stolen property if the offender is convicted: see *R.* v. *Thibeault* [1983] Crim. L.R. 102, C.A. The "court may order that a sum not exceeding the value of those goods shall be paid to the applicant out of any money of the person convicted which was taken out of his possession on his apprehension." Even where the wrongdoer is not convicted, courts of summary jurisdiction have power to restore to the rightful owner property which has come into the hands of the police "in connection with any criminal charge": see Police (Property) Act 1897, s.1, as amended. The injured party may also, if he considers it worth his while, sue in conversion; or he may waive the tort and bring an action for money had and received (see below, Chap. 38).

no reason for the law to interfere to upset the transaction. Thus it is well settled that to threaten or to institute a civil action in good faith does not constitute duress.[39] Money paid cannot be recovered and a settlement cannot be set aside on that ground.[40] This appears to be the case even though the civil action may result in the imprisonment of the defendant, as in the case of imprisonment for debt. Nor probably did a threat or commencement of bankruptcy proceedings, made in good faith, amount to duress; nor even, in a proper case, a bona fide threat or commencement of criminal prosecution.[41] The same rule applies to lawful arrest, imprisonment,[42] or threat of imprisonment.[43] In each of these cases the aid of the law is being invoked to bring pressure to bear on a person; but provided that the proceedings are regular, that they are lawfully invoked in good faith and are not abused, duress cannot be said to have been exercised on the person against whom they have been brought.

Where, however, pressure has been brought to bear by the improper application of legal process, this will amount to duress. A transaction induced by this means will be set aside, and money paid under such duress can be recovered.[44] A clear example is where there is some irregularity of procedure. Thus, where a person is arrested on an irregular warrant, not only may he have a right of action in tort against the judicial officer responsible,[45] but he may recover money paid to obtain his release, even though the money is lawfully due.[46] But where the payment has been made not to those responsible for the irregular arrest but to a third party, no action is available against the former for recovery of the money, for the good reason that they have not received it. Thus in *O'Connor* v. *Isaacs*,[47] the defendant magistrates made an order in good faith that the plaintiff should pay his wife maintenance. This order was on its face bad for want of jurisdiction. The plaintiff fell into arrears with the payments, and consequently was imprisoned on three occasions. When he learnt that the order was bad, he brought an action against the magistrates, claiming damages for false imprisonment and for damages for acts done by the defendants while sitting as magistrates. Diplock J., whose judgment was affirmed by the Court of Appeal, held that the plaintiff's action of trespass was in the circumstances barred by section 21 of the Limitation Act 1939, and that no action lay against

---

[39] *Hamlet* v. *Richardson* (1833) 9 Bing. 644; *Powell* v. *Hoyland* (1851) 6 Exch. 67, 71, *per* Parke B.; *William Whiteley Ltd.* v. *R.* (1910) 101 L.T. 741. 745, *per* Walton J.: *cf. Moore* v. *Vestry of Fulham* [1895] 1 Q.B. 399; *Self* v. *Hove Commissioners* [1895] 1 Q.B. 685, 690, *per* Wright J.; *Sawyer & Vincent* v. *Window Brace Ltd.* [1943] K.B. 32.
[40] *Cf. Restatement of Restitution,* § 71.
[41] See below, pp. 236–239; *Ward* v. *Lloyd* (1843) 6 Man. & G. 785; *Flower* v. *Sadler* (1883) 10 Q.B.D. 572; *Fisher & Co.* v. *Apollinaris Co.* (1875) L.R. 10 Ch. 297. See also *Goodall* v. *Lowndes* (1844) 6 Q.B. 464.
[42] *Anon.* (1662) 1 Lev. 68; *Smith* v. *Monteith* (1884) 13 M. & W. 427.
[43] *Biffin* v. *Bignell* (1862) 7 H. & N. 877, though in that case there was not even a threat of imprisonment, only a warning.
[44] *Newdigate* v. *Davy* (1692) 1 Ld.Raym. 742.
[45] *Clark* v. *Woods* (1848) 2 Exch. 395; *cf. O'Connor* v. *Issacs* [1956] 2 Q.B. 288.
[46] *Clark* v. *Woods* (1848) 2 Exch. 395; see also *Pitt* v. *Coomes* (1835) 2 A. & E. 459.
[47] [1956] 2 Q.B. 288.

the magistrates in respect of the money which he had paid, for the money had not been paid to them but to their collecting officer to the use of the wife.[48]

Again, an agreement entered into under pressure of wrongful arrest will not be enforced,[49] and money paid under such pressure is recoverable.[50] Similarly, the institution of proceedings in bad faith without reasonable and probable cause amounts to duress.[51] and money so paid can be recovered. In *The Duke de Cadaval* v. *Collins*,[52] the duke was arrested for £10,000 by Collins at Falmouth, shortly after his arrival in England, although Collins knew that he had no legal claim on him. The duke paid £500 to obtain his release, and the writ was later set aside. It was held that he could recover the money in an action for money had and received, for "the arrest was fraudulent; and the money was parted with under the arrest, to get rid of the pressure."[53]

It has also been held that, if a person takes advantage of legal proceedings to apply pressure on the defendant in a matter unconnected with the subject-matter of the process, money paid under such pressure by the defendant to the proceedings so brought is recoverable,[54] for there has been an abuse of legal process.

A similar problem arises if a person promises to confer, or does confer, a benefit on another because of a threat that, if he does not do so, either he or a third party will be criminally prosecuted. The general principle is that any agreement to compromise criminal proceedings is illegal and any benefits conferred thereunder may be recoverable either because the coerced party is not *in pari delicto*[55] or because he acted under duress. Money paid in consequence of the threat is recoverable at law; and agreements, bills or securities may be cancelled in equity.[56] At one time English law distinguished between felonies and misdemeanours. Felonies could never be compounded. Whether misdemeanours could be compounded was more uncertain, for there was a suggestion in *Fisher & Co.* v. *Appollinaris*[57] that, where a person had a choice between a civil and a criminal remedy, he could enter into a compromise. But the better view was that misdemeanours of a public nature could not be stifled

---

[48] The plaintiff could not sue his wife because of an undertaking he had given to the Divisional Court: see [1956] 2 Q.B. 288, 292, 312–313, *per* Diplock J.

[49] *Bromley* v. *Norton* (1872) 27 L.T. 478, *semble*; see also *Pitt* v. *Coomes* (1835) 2 Ad. & El. 459 and *Cumming* v. *Ince* (1847–1848) 11 Q.B. 112.

[50] *De Mesnil* v. *Dakin* (1867) L.R. 3 Q.B. 18, 23–24, *per* Cockburn C.J.; and see *Oughton* v. *Seppings* (1830) 1 B. & Ad. 241.

[51] Or, *semble*, a mala fide threat to institute proceedings: see *Scott* v. *Sebright* (1866) 12 P.D. 21.

[52] (1836) 4 A. & E. 858.

[53] At p. 864, *per* Lord Denman C.J.

[54] *Unwin* v. *Leaper* (1840) 1 Man. & G. 747, approved in *Goodall* v. *Lowndes* (1844) 6 Q.B. 464, 467, *per* Lord Denman C.J.

[55] *Davies* v. *London and Provincial Marine Insurance Co.* (1878) 8 Ch.D. 469, 477, *per* Fry L.J.; see below, p. 237.

[56] A leading case is *Williams* v. *Bayley* (1866) L.R. 1 H.L. 200; (see below, pp. 237–238). See also *Kaufman* v. *Gerson* [1904] 1 K.B. 591; *Mutual Finance Ltd.* v. *John Wetton & Sons Ltd.* [1937] 2 K.B. 389; see below, p. 238.

[57] (1875) L.R. 10 Ch.App. 297, 302, *per* James L.J., 303, *per* Mellish L.J.

even though a civil remedy was available.[58] The Criminal Law Act 1967[59] now provides that "on all matters on which a distinction has previously been made between felony and misdemeanour ... the law and practice in relation to all offences cognisable under the law of England and Wales ... shall be the law and practice applicable at the commencement of this Act in relation to mis-demeanour." It would appear, therefore, that the only criminal proceedings which can now be compromised are proceedings relating to what before 1967 were described as non-public misdemeanours, namely, assault, criminal libel, and the infringement of trade marks.[60] It is most unlikely[61] that section 5 of the Criminal Law Act 1967 has changed the law and validated some compromises which were previously illegal. That section provides that the compounding of an offence is itself an offence where a person "accepts or agrees to accept for not disclosing ... information [to secure the prosecution or conviction of an offender] any consideration other than the making good of loss or injury caused by the offence, or the making of reasonable compensation for that loss or injury. . . ." But there is nothing in section 5 to suggest that an agreement not to prosecute, in consideration of a promise to make reasonable compensation, is necessarily binding. Indeed, if such an agreement was to be upheld, criminal proceedings of a serious nature could be compromised. This would be a most undesirable result which the legislature surely could not have intended to effect by implication.

It is a distinct but related question whether an agreement induced by threats of criminal prosecution can be set aside for duress. A threat to prosecute may constitute duress if it enables a person to gain a benefit through an improper application of legal process. However, in practice the two questions, whether an agreement to stifle prosecution is illegal or whether it is voidable for duress, shade into one another.[62] In most cases where the courts have held the agreement to be illegal, they have also held there was duress.[63] The coerced party may then recover the benefits transferred under the agreement; he is not *in pari delicto*[64] and the benefit has been conferred in consequence of a wrongful

---

[58] *Keir* v. *Leeman* (1846) 9 Q.B. 371, 394–395, *per* Tindal C.J.; *Clubb* v. *Hutson* (1865) 18 C.B.(N.S.) 414; *Windhill Local Board of Health* v. *Vint* (1890) 45 Ch.D. 351; [1959] Crim. L.R. 822, 828–829 [C. Howard]; G. L. Williams, *Criminal Law*, pp. 770–771.

[59] s.1(2).

[60] *Keir* v. *Leeman* (1846) 9 Q.B. 371, 395, *per* Tindal C.J. (assault); *Jones* v. *Merionethshire Permanent B.S.* [1892] 1 Ch. 173, 184, *per* Bowen L.J.; *Fisher* v. *Appollinaris Co.* (1875) 10 Ch.App. 297, 303, *per* Mellish L.J. (libel); *Fisher* v. *Appollinaris Co.* (1875) 10 Ch.App. 297 (trade marks).

[61] See generally (1974) 3 Anglo-American L.R. 472 [Buckley]; *Chitty on Contracts*, § 1157; (1980) 43 M.L.R. 532 [Hudson].

[62] *Fisher* v. *Appollinaris & Co.* (1875) 10 Ch.App. 297, 303, *per* Mellish L.J. See also *Smith* v. *Monteith* (1844) 13 M. & W. 427. *Cf. Société des Hotels Reunis* v. *Hawker* (1913) 29 T.L.R. 578, 579, *per* Scrutton J.

[63] *Williams* v. *Bayley* (1866) L.R. 1 H.L. 200; *Société des Hotels Réunis* v. *Hawker* (1913) 29 T.L.R. 578, *Cf. Kesarmal s/o Letchman Das* v. *N.K.V. Valliappa Chettiar s/o Nagappa Chettiar* [1954] 1 W.L.R. 380, 385, *per curiam* (L.M.D. de Silva).

[64] *Davies* v. *London and Provincial Marine Insurance Co.* (1878) 8 Ch.D. 469, 477, *per* Fry J., following *Williams* v. *Bayley* (1866) L.R. 1 H.L. 200.

threat. Exceptionally the agreement not to prosecute may be legal but still voidable for duress.[65] Generally, however, if the court finds that there was a lawful compromise, it will also conclude that it was not entered into under duress. So in *Flower* v. *Sadler*[66] it was alleged[67] that the plaintiffs had threatened to prosecute their rent collector, Maynard, for embezzlement. Subsequently Maynard indorsed to the plaintiffs bills of exchange drawn on and accepted by the defendant. The plaintiffs sued on the bills and recovered. The Court of Appeal found that the plaintiffs' threats to prosecute Maynard did not mean that they had agreed not to prosecute him if he made good the defalcation. "A creditor may use strong expressions and even threats ... strong language is not conclusive evidence of an agreement to compound a felony or stifle a prosecution."[68] Moreover, Brett and Cotton L.JJ. were prepared to hold that "because a debt was due from Maynard ... there is nothing illegal in a creditor endeavouring to obtain payment of his debt ... even although there may have been a threat by the creditor of criminal proceedings."[69]

The line between the honest compromise and the improper threat, which is a thin one, is essentially one of fact. A threat to prosecute may often be coupled with an implied promise that there will be no prosecution if money is paid to the person making the threat. The threat may be made to a debtor, such as Maynard in *Flower* v. *Sadler*, or to a third party, such as the debtor's relative or friend. In the latter case the court may be more ready to find that there was an agreement which was illegal and voidable for duress. Such a case was *Williams* v. *Bayley*,[70] where the plaintiff had assigned securities to the defendant in consequence of a threat that, if he did not do so, his son would be prosecuted for forgery. The House of Lords held that the securities should be delivered up and cancelled.

As Porter J. said in the later case of *Mutual Finance Ltd.* v. *John Wetton & Sons Ltd.*,[71] no direct threat is necessary, no promise need be given to abstain from prosecution. "It is enough if the undertaking were given owing to a desire to prevent a prosecution and that desire were known to those to whom the undertaking was given. In such a case one may imply ... a term in the contract that no prosecution should take place."[72]

Consequently, a compromise will be upheld only if it is evident that a person is settling a civil claim against another and that the settlement has not been reached by any express or implied promise that, if there is no settlement, the

---

[65] *Kaufman* v. *Gerson* [1904] 1 K.B. 591 (where the agreement not to prosecute was valid by French law).
[66] (1882) 10 Q.B.D. 572; see also *Re Mapleback* (1874) 4 Ch.D. 150.
[67] There was some doubt whether there was in fact such a threat: see p. 575, *per* Brett L.J.
[68] At p. 573, *per* Lord Coleridge C.J.
[69] At p. 575, *per* Brett L.J.; see also at p. 576, *per* Cotton L.J., following *Ward* v. *Lloyd* (1843) 6 M. & G. 785. See too *Mutual Finance Ltd.* v. *John Wetton & Sons Ltd.* [1937] 2 K.B. 389, 396, *per* Porter J.
[70] (1866) L.R. 1 H.L. 200.
[71] [1937] 2 K.B. 389.
[72] At p. 395, citing *Jones* v. *Merionethshire Permanent Benefit Building Society* [1892] 1 Ch. 173.

matter will be reported to the police or that the threatened person or some third person will be prosecuted.

(c) *Duress of Goods*

Recovery of money

"The extension of duress into the field of economic pressure began in the eighteenth century. The situation which inspired the development involved a relatively simple and clear-cut type of oppression—the wrongful seizure or detention of personal property."[73] It was soon established that money paid under duress of goods could be recovered in an action at law provided the plaintiff could show that he owned[74] or was entitled to possession of[75] the goods. In the leading case of *Astley* v. *Reynolds*,[76] the plaintiff pawned plate to the defendant for £20. At the end of three years he went to redeem it, but the defendant insisted on £10 interest. The plaintiff tendered £4 knowing that to be more than the legal interest allowed, but the defendant refused to take it; so later the plaintiff paid the £10 and recovered his plate. The Court of King's Bench held that the plaintiff was entitled to recover the surplus over and above the legal rate of interest in an action for money had and received. The court said[77]:

> ". . . This is a payment by compulsion; the plaintiff might have such an immediate want of his goods, that an action of trover would not do his business: where the rule *volenti non fit injuria* is applied, it must be where the party had his freedom of exercising his will, which this man had not: we must take it he paid the money relying on his legal remedy to get it back again."[78]

No distinction is drawn in this context between actual seizure and threatened seizure; each amounts to duress of goods.[79] So, money paid to prevent a threatened, wrongful sale of goods is also recoverable as paid under duress.[80]

---

[73] Dawson, "Economic Duress: An Essay in Perspective," 45 Mich.L.Rev. 253, 255 (1947).
[74] An equitable proprietary interest was enough: see *Close* v. *Phipps* (1844) 7 Man. & G. 586; *Frazer* v. *Pendlebury* (1861) 31 L.J.C.P. 1, 2, *per* Erle C.J.
[75] *Fell* v. *Whittaker* (1871) L.R. 7 Q.B. 120: see below, p. 242.
[76] (1731) 2 Str. 915.
[77] (1731) 2 Str. 915, 916.
[78] See also *Ashmole* v. *Wainwright* (1842) 2 Q.B. 837; *Irving* v. *Wilson* (1791) 4 T.R. 485; *D. Owen & Co.* v. *Cronk* [1895] 1 Q.B. 265, 271, *per* Lord Esher M.R.
[79] *Snowdon* v. *Davis* (1808) 1 Taunt. 359; *Maskell* v. *Horner* [1915] 3 K.B. 106, 120, *per* Lord Reading C.J.
[80] *Valpy* v. *Manley* (1845) 1 C.B. 594, 602, *per* Tindal C.J.

These principles have been applied to various types of goods: insurance policies[81]; deeds[82]; and, in the United States, to bonds and negotiable instruments.[83] Money paid to prevent a wrongful sale by a mortgagee with power of sale may also be recovered in this way,[84] and a similar principle has been applied in two appeals from India concerned with wrongful seizure of real property.[85] Many of the cases are concerned with claims to liens. For example, in *Somes* v. *British Empire Shipping Co.*,[86] the defendants held the plaintiffs' ship under a lien for money due for repairs to the ship, and then wrongfully claimed to add a charge for the occupation of their graving dock by the ship during the period of time while they so held it. The plaintiffs paid this extra sum under protest simply to recover possession of the ship. The House of Lords held that they were entitled to recover their money.[87]

(1) *Setting aside contracts*[88]

Although it is well established that money paid under duress of goods is recoverable, in all the books a curious distinction was at one time drawn between contracts and money payments; for it was stated that the rule of common law is that for duress to render a contract voidable it must be duress of person and not duress of goods. The authority cited for this proposition was *Skeate* v. *Beale*.[89] The plaintiff distrained for arrears of rent, and the defendant agreed that if the plaintiff would withdraw the distress he would pay the arrears demanded. The distress was withdrawn, but the defendant only paid a smaller part of the agreed sum. The plaintiff sued for the outstanding amount; the defendant pleaded that the seizure was unlawful and that he had only entered

---

[81] *Shaw* v. *Woodcock* (1827) 7 B. & C. 73.

[82] *Pratt* v. *Vizard* (1833) 5 B. & Ad. 808; *Smith* v. *Sleap* (1844) 12 M. & W. 585; *Wakefield* v. *Newbon* (1844) 6 Q.B. 276; *Oates* v. *Hudson* (1851) 6 Ex. 346; *Gibbon* v. *Gibbon* (1853) 13 C.B. 205; *Fraser* v. *Pendlebury* (1861) 31 L.J.C.P. 1. See also *Re Llewellin* [1891] 3 Ch. 145. By this means money paid under duress of land can be recovered.

[83] See cases cited in Palmer, *op. cit.* Vol. II, § 9.6.

[84] *Close* v. *Phipps* (1844) 7 Man. & G. 586. In *North Ocean Shipping Co. Ltd.* v. *Hyundai Construction Co. Ltd.* [1979] Q.B. 705, 716–717, (see below, p. 256) counsel and Mocatta J. thought that, on the facts of *Close* v. *Phipps*, the duress was a threatened breach of contract. But the court treated the threat as akin to duress of goods: "the plaintiff was obliged either to pay it or suffer her estate to be sold."

[85] *Dooli Chand* v. *Ram Kishen Singh* (1881) L.R. 8 Ind.App. 93; *Kanhaya Lal* v. *National Bank of India* (1913) 29 T.L.R. 314.

[86] (1860) 8 H.L.C. 338. The court held that the defendants, who were lienors, were not entitled to claim the expenses incurred in maintaining the value of goods as security for the owners' indebtedness: see *China-Pacific S.A.* v. *The Corporation of India* [1982] A.C. 939, 962–963, *per* Lord Diplock.

[87] In *Huth* v. *Lamport* (1886) 16 Q.B.D. 735 the Court of Appeal left open the question whether the ship-owners, who had a lien on the cargo to secure payment of general average, could refuse the cargo owner's offer of reasonable security. If the ship's master "requires security he cannot impose unreasonable terms": at p. 738, *per* Lindley L.J.

[88] See, generally Beatson, *op. cit.* pp. 99–109.

[89] (1841) 11 Ad. & E. 983. See also *Sumner* v. *Ferryman* (1708) 11 Mod. 201 (where the bond was a civil bond); *Atlee* v. *Backhouse* (1838) 3 M. & W. 633, 650, *per* Parke B.; *Liverpool Marine Credit* v. *Hunter* (1868) 3 Ch.App. 479, 487–488, *per* Lord Chelmsford L.C.; *Willoughby* v. *Backhouse* (1824) 3 B. & C. 821.

into the agreement to prevent the plaintiff carrying out his threat to sell the goods. The Court of King's Bench held, however, that the agreement could not be set aside because duress of goods was no ground for rescinding an agreement, and that the full sum was therefore payable.[90]

There is little to be said for so dogmatic a rule, which was based largely on ancient precedent[91] and decided in disregard of some authority to the contrary.[92] Since money paid under duress of goods may be recovered, there is an apparent conflict between *Astley* v. *Reynolds* and *Skeate* v. *Beale*, as the following examples show:

(1) A demands a sum of money from B under duress of goods. B pays the money. He can recover it.

(2) A extracts from B under similar duress a promise to pay a sum of money. Provided there is some consideration for the promise, B is bound to pay the money.

It is very difficult to support a distinction of this kind since there must have been a *scintilla temporis* when A must have agreed to pay before making the payment.[93] In *Skeate* v. *Beale* Lord Denman C.J. justified the rule on the ground that, whereas duress of person is "a constraining force," "the fear that goods may be taken or injured does not deprive anyone of his free agency who possesses that ordinary degree of firmness which the law requires all to exert."[94] But this requirement of bravery has surely now been abandoned.[95] In fact, the rule in *Skeate* v. *Beale* is in direct conflict with the modern view of duress, namely, that where a transaction has been entered into as a result of illegitimate pressure, consent has not been freely given and the transaction is voidable.[96] The test whether consent has been freely given is subjective, not objective; and this is as true of duress of goods as it is of duress of person. As Kerr J. said in *The Siboen and the Sibotre*[97]: "The true question is ultimately whether or not an agreement in question is to be regarded as having been

---

[90] See Beatson, *op. cit.* pp. 103–105 for an argument that the true ground of the decision was that the plaintiff had settled the defendant's honest claim; see also below, p. 242, n. 1.

[91] 2 Co. Inst. 483; Sheppard's *Touchstone*, p. 61; 1 Bl.Comm. 131. The reason stated for the distinction is that, in the case of threatened distress of goods, should the threat be carried out, a man may have satisfaction by recovering damages; but no suitable atonement can be made for loss of life or limb. This reasoning was, however, rejected in *Astley* v. *Reynolds* (1731) 2 Str. 915, where it was pointed out that the man might have such immediate want of his goods that the remedy of trover would be insufficient; and see, generally, see below, pp. 272–274. *Sumner* v. *Ferryman* (1708) 11 Mod. 201 was cited to the court in *Astley* v. *Reynolds* and apparently disregarded.

[92] See 1 Roll.Abr. 687; Vin.Abr., Duress (B) 3; Bacon, *Maxims, Regula* 18.

[93] Beatson, *op. cit.* p. 107.

[94] (1841) 11 Ad. & E. 983, 990; *cf. Wakefield* v. *Newbon* (1844) 6 Q.B. 276, 280–281, *per* Lord Denman C.J.

[95] *Scott* v. *Sebright* (1886) 12 P.D. 21, 24, *per* Butt J.

[96] *Astley* v. *Reynolds* (1731) 2 Str. 915, 916, *per curiam*; *Scott* v. *Sebright* (1886) 12 P.D. 21, 24, *per* Butt J.; *Kaufman* v. *Gerson* [1903] 2 K.B. 114, 119, *per* Wright J., [1904] 1 K.B. 691, 697, *per* Collins M.R.; *Barton* v. *Armstrong* [1976] A.C. 104, 118, 121; see above, p. 234.

[97] [1976] 1 Lloyd's Rep. 293. *Cf. Fell* v. *Whitaker* [1871] L.R. 7 Q.B. 120; *Tamvaco* v. *Simpson* (1866) L.R. 1 C.P. 363.

concluded voluntarily."[98] *Skeate* v. *Beale* is no longer good law.[99] An agreement induced by duress of goods is voidable at the instance of the coerced party, so that any money paid thereunder will be recoverable in restitution.[99a]

A further ground of the decision in *Skeate* v. *Beale* was that, on the case as pleaded, there was consideration for the defendant's promise, in that the defendant had been benefited by the withdrawal of the distress. Yet on the facts it appears that the distress might well have been excessive and, therefore, unlawful. A promise to pay money to obtain the release of goods unlawfully detained is likely to be unsupported by consideration and so unenforceable.[1] Agreements of this kind will often, therefore, be unenforceable for want of consideration.[2] However, for reasons already stated, such an agreement should, in our view, be voidable even where there is consideration for that agreement.[3]

(2) *Exceptional cases*

Usually the duress has been exercised on goods which belong to the plaintiff. But this was not the case in *Fell* v. *Whittaker*.[4] A tenant allowed his rent to fall into arrears by £9. The landlord distrained for £18 and costs, and seized goods worth £100 which were vested in a trustee on trust for the tenant's wife. The rent actually due was tendered but refused, and before the distress was withdrawn the tenant was forced to give an undertaking to pay the full £18, and he paid a part of that sum. It was held that he was entitled to succeed in an action for excessive distress and on the money counts, though he was neither the legal nor equitable owner of the goods seized; it was sufficient that he had the possession and enjoyment of them. On the other hand, where money has been paid by B under duress of A's goods, A is not entitled to recover that money in an action for money had and received since it was not his money which was paid over,[5] unless the money has been paid on A's behalf under an agreement of loan.[6]

---

[98] At p. 335. The judge cited *Kaufman* v. *Gerson* [1904] 1 K.B. 591 (see above, p. 236); and *D. & C. Builders* v. *Rees* [1966] 2 Q.B. 617, discussed see below, p. 261.

[99] *Cf. Dimskal Shipping Co. S.A.* v. *International Transport Workers' Federation, The Evia Luck* [1992] 2 A.C. 152, 165, *per* Lord Goff. *North Ocean Shipping Co. Ltd.* v. *Hyundai Construction Co. Ltd.* [1979] Q.B. 705, 717–719 *per* Mocatta J.; *Pao On* v. *Lau Yiu Long* [1980] A.C. 614 (P.C.): see below, p. 262. See also *Hills* v. *Street* (1828) 5 Bing. 37.

[99a] *Cf.* Burrows. *The Law of Restitution*, p. 167 n. 3.

[1] *Longridge* v. *Dorville* (1821) 5 B. & Ald. 117; *Callisher* v. *Bischoffsheim* (1870) L.R. 5 Q.B. 449; *Re Blythe* (1881) 17 Ch.D. 480. If there is consideration, then there is probably a compromise of a disputed claim. It is significant that in *Wakefield* v. *Newbon* (1844) 6 Q.B. 276, 280–281, Lord Denman C.J. hinted that *Skeate* v. *Beale* was a case "where the parties had come to a voluntary settlement of their concerns"; and that in *Valpy* v. *Manley* (1845) 1 C.B. 594, 605, Cresswell J. said that *Atlee* v. *Backhouse* (1838) 3 M. & W. 633 was a case "where money paid for the settlement of a doubtful claim was held not to be recoverable back."

[2] See below, p. 236.

[3] See above, p. 241.

[4] (1871) L.R. 7 Q.B. 120; *cf. Scarfe* v. *Hallifax* (1840) 7 M. & W. 288.

[5] *Scarfe* v. *Hallifax* (1840) 7 M. & W. 288.

[6] *Fraser* v. *Pendlebury* (1861) 31 L.J.C.P. 1, following *Close* v. *Phipps* (1844) 7 M. & G. 586.

Some of the cases are complicated by the relationship of principal and agent. Suppose that a person has paid money under duress of goods to the agent of another: can he recover the money from the agent, or must he proceed directly against the principal? It seems that he can always recover the money from the agent himself,[7] except where the agent, having received the money in good faith unaware of the duress, for the use of his principal, has accounted for it to his principal.[8] But if the agent is party to the wrong,[9] he is liable to make restitution, and it is then no defence that he has paid the money over to his principal.[10]

(d) *Money Paid to Obtain the Fulfilment of a Duty*[11]: *A Demand Colore Officii*

Where money has been paid to a public officer to obtain performance by him of a duty which he is bound to carry out for nothing or for less than the sum paid, such money or, where some money is due, the excess is recoverable in the language of the old pleaders as money had and received. For the duty is a "public duty imposed by law; and for the execution of that he had no right to any payment."[12] It is "not necessary to show that the defendant acted in bad faith. . . . Nevertheless the phrase [*colore officii*] bears an imputation of imposition by a person in authority upon another person ignorant of his rights."[13]

The Implications of Woolwich Equitable Building Society v. Commissioners of Inland Revenue

The *colore officii* line of cases, which are discussed in the following section of the book, figure prominently both in the submissions of counsel and the judgments of the House of Lords in *Woolwich Equitable Building Society* v. *Commissioners of Inland Revenue*.[14] In that case the House of Lords held that the plaintiffs could recover payments, with interest, made in pursuance of a demand for tax which was subsequently held to be *ultra vires*. The payments were recoverable on that ground. In Lord Browne-Wilkinson's view, they had also been paid "without consideration." The House considered that the Revenue had not exercised any illegitimate pressure; "since the possibility of distraint by the revenue was very remote, the concept of compulsion would have to be stretched to the utmost to embrace the circumstances of such a case as this."[15]

By way of contrast, in the *colore officii* cases the plaintiff's success depended upon him proving duress; the mere fact that the person making the demand

---

[7] *Smith* v. *Sleap* (1844) 12 M. & W. 585; *Wakefield* v. *Newbon* (1844) 6 Q.B. 276; *Oates* v. *Hudson* (1851) 6 Ex. 346; *T.D. Keegan Ltd.* v. *Palmer* [1961] 2 Lloyd's Rep. 449, 459, *per* Barry J.
[8] *D. Owen & Co.* v. *Cronk* [1895] 1 Q.B. 265; see below, p. 755.
[9] Bowstead, *op. cit.* pp. 481–483.
[10] *Steele* v. *Williams* (1853) 8 Ex. 625; and cases cited below in n. 30.
[11] For the history of this subject, see *Mason* v. *The State of New South Wales* (1959) 102 C.L.R. 108, 139–142, *per* Windeyer J.
[12] *Morgan* v. *Palmer* (1824) 2 B. & C. 729, 737, *per* Littledale J.
[13] *Mason* v. *The State of New South Wales* (1959) 102 C.L.R. 108, 141, *per* Windeyer J.
[14] [1993] A.C. 70. See below, Chap. 24.
[15] [1993] A.C. 70; 173, *per* Lord Goff.

held some official position did not elevate that demand into a coercive demand. As Windeyer J. said, in *Mason* v. *The State of New South Wales*,[16] "extortion by colour of office occurs when a public officer demands and is paid money he is not entitled to, or more than he is entitled to, for the performance of his public duty." Whether the *colore officii* cases are now subsumed within the *Woolwich* common law principle, namely, that money paid in consequence of an *ultra vires* demand is recoverable, is open to question. Lord Browne-Wilkinson thought that:

> "as a matter of principle the *colore officii* cases are merely examples of a wider principle, *viz.* that where the parties are on an unequal footing so that money is paid by way of tax or other impost in pursuance of a demand by some public officer, these moneys are recoverable since the citizen is, in practice, unable to resist the payment save at the risk of breaking the law or exposing himself to penalties or other disadvantages."[17]

Lord Slynn was equally cautious. In his view, "although . . . the facts do not fit easily into the existing category of duress or of claims *colore officii*, they shade into them".[18]

In some of the *colore officii* cases the public officer was often entitled to make a demand but was not entitled to the particular fee which he demanded; in others he was not entitled to make the demand. Before *Woolwich* it was assumed that the two situations were indistinguishable. A leading and difficult case is *Mason* v. *The State of New South Wales*.[19] The High Court of Australia held that the plaintiffs were entitled to recover payments which had been made to enable them to carry on their trade as inter-State carriers. The statute under which the defendants had purported to act was *ultra vires*. The majority of the Court[20] found that the payments had been made in consequence of the defendants' wrongful, implicit threat to exercise their statutory powers, which included that of seizure of vehicles. Menzies J.[21] appears to have thought that the demand was a demand *colore officii*. But Windeyer J.[22] held that there was no such demand but nonetheless, the demand was wrongful. The majority held that it was not sufficient to ground recovery that the demand was *ultra vires*.

The other Law Lords in *Woolwich* did not suggest that the *colore officii* cases are "merely examples" of the *Woolwich* principle. Lord Keith, and Jauncey, who dissented, adopted the reasoning of the majority of the H.C. in *Mason's*

---

[16] (1959) 102 C.L.R. 108, 140, followed by Lord Keith and Lord Jauncey in the *Woolwich Equitable Building Society* case at p. 162 and pp. 189–191 respectively. Their Lordships were dissenting, but they were, in these passages, explaining the *colore officii* cases: see below, pp. 244–245.

[17] [1993] A.C. 70, 198. *Cf. Atchison, Topeka and Santa Fe Rly. Co.* v. *O'Connor*, 223 U.S. 280, 285–286 (1911), *per* Holmes J. (cited below, p. 548) and *Mason* v. *The State of New South Wales* (1959) 102 C.L.R. 108, 116–117, *per* Dixon C.J., 126, 129, *per* Kitto J.

[18] [1993] A.C. 70, 204.

[19] (1959) 102 C.L.R. 108.

[20] Fullagar, Taylor, Menzies and Windeyer JJ.

[21] At pp. 132–133, *cf.* at pp. 123–124, *per* Fullagar J., and at pp. 129–130, *per* Taylor J.

[22] At pp. 140–142. Contrast *Bell Bros. Pty. Ltd.* v. *Serpentine-Jarrahdale Shire* (1969) 121 C.L.R. 137.

case, and Lord Goff and Lord Keith did not question it.[22a] The *colore officii* line of cases may well then retain their independent existence. There are significant distinctions between the facts of *Woolwich* and some of the *colore officii* cases.

If the *colore officii* line of cases still enjoys its own independent existence and authority, then significant distinctions exist between it and cases based on the *Woolwich* common law principle. First, in the *colore officii* cases illegitimate pressure was exerted by a public officer, who had to make a demand for payment in return for the performance of a duty which he was bound to perform for nothing or for less than the sum paid.

Secondly, some of the officers who have been compelled to make restitution can only with generosity be described as *public* officers.[23] It is debatable whether their position is akin to that of the Revenue or some other public authority.

Thirdly, the plaintiff may have received from the public officer part of the consideration for which he had bargained. In such a case his payment cannot be said to have been made "without consideration", *viz.* there has been no total failure of consideration.[23a]

Fourthly, it is not clear whether a payment to a public officer made under a mistake of law is recoverable. In contrast, dicta in the *Woolwich* case suggest that a payment to the Revenue or to any public authority under a mistake of law, pursuant to an *ultra vires* demand, is recoverable.

Finally, there is some authority that a defendant who has exerted illegitimate pressure on the plaintiff is not entitled to defend himself on the ground that the plaintiff has suffered no loss since he passed on the tax demanded to third parties, for example, its customers.[24] That defence is not open to a wrongdoer. The question did not arise in the *Woolwich* case. The Revenue can hardly be said to be a *wrongdoer*. In other jurisdictions public authorities have successfully relied on the defence of *passing on*.[25]

This branch of the law of restitution is then in a state of flux. It may well be that a plaintiff will be able to rely on the *Woolwich* common law principle if there is an *ultra vires* demand by a public officer. But, since it is not at all clear what is the present authority of the *colore officii* line of cases, we have decided to retain our discussion of this topic.

The Colore Officii Cases

A leading decision is *Piggott's Case*.[26] The steward of a manor made an extravagant charge for providing some deeds and court rolls at a trial. It was

---

[22a] [1993] A.C. 70, 164–165, *per* Lord Goff.

[23] *e.g.* arbitrators and umpires as well as common carriers: see below, pp. 247–249.

[23a] See above p. 147; and *cf. R.* v. *Tower Hamlets* London B.C., *ex parte Chetnik Developments Ltd.* [1988] A.C. 858, above p. 156.

[24] *Mason* v. *The State of New South Wales* (1959) 102 C.L.R. 108, 146, *per* Windeyer J.: see above, p. 244.

[25] See below, p. 552.

[26] Cited in *Cartwright* v. *Rowley* (1799) 2 Esp. 723.

held that the person charged could recover his money, because he could not do without the deeds and so the money was paid "through necessity and the urgency of the case."[27] And in *Steele* v. *Williams*[28] it was held that an action for money had and received would lie against a parish clerk who illegally charged the plaintiff for taking extracts from the parish register. Parke B. said[29]: "I think that, upon the true construction of the evidence, the payment in this case was not voluntary, because, in effect, the defendant told the plaintiff's clerk, that if he did not pay for certificates when he wanted to make extracts, he could not be permitted to search." There are many other cases.[30]

In the past it has been usual to speak of such payments as being demanded *colore officii*.[31] The right of recovery has, however, been extended to include all cases where the defendant is in a quasi-public or monopolistic position and

---

[27] (1799) 2 Esp. 723, 724 (Lord Kenyon's *post hoc* comment).

[28] (1853) 8 Ex. 625 (a strong case, since the plaintiff was not required to pay until after he made the abstract, although he knew of the fees before he began). *cf.* Woodward, pp. 351–352; [1980] C.L.P. 191, 200–205 [Birks].

[29] At p. 630.

[30] *Empson* v. *Bathurst* (1620) Hut. 52 (excessive fees paid to sheriff); *Irving* v. *Wilson* (1791) 4 T.R. 485 (carts seized by a revenue collector); *Jons* v. *Perchard* (1796) 2 Esp. 507 (excessive fees paid to sheriff's bailiff when giving bail); *Lovell* v. *Simpson* (1800) 3 Esp. 153 (excessive charge paid to sheriff's officer on arrest); *Parsons* v. *Blandy* (1810) Wight. 22 (payment of extra toll); *Longdill* v. *Jones* (1816) 1 Stark. 345 (retention of money by sheriff after executing *fi.fa.* at plaintiff's suit); *Umphelby* v. *M'lean* (1817) 1 B. & Ald. 42 (excessive charge by collector of taxes on a distress of plaintiff's property); *Dew* v. *Parsons* (1819) 2 B. & Ald. 562 (payment of excessive fee to sheriff); *Morgan* v. *Palmer* (1824) 2 B. & C. 729 (illegal fee paid to mayor for renewal of licence); *Traherne* v. *Gardner* (1856) 5 E. & B. 913 (steward of copyhold court refused to admit except on payment of fines and fees which were not due); *Hooper* v. *Exeter Corporation* (1887) 56 L.J.Q.B. 457 (recovery of harbour dues on limestone); *Martin* v. *Tomkinson* [1893] 2 Q.B. 121 (plaintiff entitled to recover from returning officer, out of his deposit, half the amount of the officer's charges which had been disallowed at the instance of the other candidate); *Queen of the River Steamship Co.* v. *The Conservators of the River Thames* (1899) 15 T.L.R. 474 (recovery of tolls on a ship); *Malkin* v. *R.* [1906] 2 K.B. 886 (suppliant entitled to recover in petition of right money paid under protest to the Commissioners of Inland Revenue, which he was not liable to pay, and which was demanded in circumstances in which he was compelled to pay it); *Eadie* v. *Township of Brantford* (1967) 63 D.L.R. (2d) 561 (taxpayers entitled to recover excessive levies, see above, p. 152; *cf. Campbell* v. *Hall* (1774) 1 Cowp. 204. See also *Lewis* v. *Hammond* (1818) 2 B. & Ald. 206; *R. & W. Paul, Ltd.* v. *The Wheat Commission* [1937] A.C. 139; and, for an early dictum, *Anon.* (1697) Comb. 446, 447, *per* Holt C.J.

In two cases attempts were made to recover money which had been paid in 1919 to the Shipping Controller, purporting to act under the authority of the Defence of the Realm Regulations and receiving the money on behalf of the Exchequer, as a condition for a licence to sell a ship. In the first case, *Marshall Shipping Co.* v. *Board of Trade* [1923] 2 K.B. 343, the action failed on a technicality; in the second, *Brocklebank Ltd.* v. *R.* [1925] 1 K.B. 52, it was held that, although the payment was not voluntary, the right to recover was barred by the Indemnity Act 1920. In both these cases, the Court of Appeal treated an action to recover money extorted *colore officii* as being a case of waiver of tort; but it is difficult to see what tort had been committed (see below, Chap. 38). See also *George (Porky) Jacobs Enterprises Ltd.* v. *City of Regina* (1964) 47 W.W.R. 305; *Eadie* v. *Township of Brantford* [1967] S.C.R. 573; *Bell Bros. Pty. Ltd.* v. *Shire of Serpentine—Jarrahdale* (1969) 44 A.L.J.R. 26. In some cases actions failed because the plaintiff failed to give the required notice to a public officer before commencing his action: see *Waterhouse* v. *Keen* (1825) 4 B. & C. 200; *Selmes* v. *Judge* (1871) L.R. 6 Q.B. 724.

[31] In *Woolwich Equitable Building Society* v. *Commissioners of Inland Revenue* [1993] A.C. 70, 81, Glidewell L.J. dismissed this description as "archaic", "at best vague and at worst almost meaningless at the present day [and] . . . unhelpful."

demands a money payment, to which he is not entitled, for the fulfilment of a duty owed by him. It is irrelevant that no protest was made or question raised at the time of payment[32] by the plaintiff. The principal cases can be classified as follows:

(1) If a public officer takes advantage of his official situation to exact money for the fulfilment of his duty, such exaction being for his own benefit rather than for the public funds, he is not making the charge *colore officii*, and yet the money is recoverable. This is the case even though, for example, the public officer had a discretion to refuse the grant of a licence and thought he was entitled to demand payment for a licence. So, in *Morgan* v. *Palmer*[33] money was paid to a mayor for the renewal of a licence, the mayor mistakenly believing that he had a right to exact such a fee for his own benefit. It was held that the licensee was entitled to recover the money, though the charge was not made *colore officii*.[34]

Moreover, it is not every charge wrongfully exacted by a public officer, or other such person, which can be recovered in this way. The charge must have been paid by the plaintiff to obtain performance of the public officer's duty which he wrongfully refused to perform.[35]

(2) It has been held that, where an arbitrator or umpire fixes his own fee in a case where he has no jurisdiction to do so,[36] or where he charges an exorbitant fee,[37] a party who pays the fee in order to take up the award is entitled to recover the money paid.[38] In such cases, the party taking up the award has been prevented by a person in a quasi-public position from obtaining something to which he was entitled without paying the money demanded of him. Nowadays, by section 19 of the Arbitration Act 1950, a simpler and less expensive procedure is available to the party imposed on in this way. Under this section the High Court can, on application, order that the arbitrator or umpire shall "deliver the award to the applicant on payment into court by the applicant of the fees demanded, and further that the fees demanded shall be taxed by the taxing officer and that out of the money paid into court there shall be paid out to the arbitrator or umpire by way of fees such sum as may be found reasonable

---

[32] But see below, p. 271.

[33] (1824) 2 B. & C. 729. See also *Steele* v. *Williams* (1853) 8 Ex. 625; *Hooper* v. *Exeter Corp.* (1887) 56 L.J.Q.B. 457. But *cf. Bell Bros.* v. *Shire of Serpentine-Jarrahdale* (1969) 44 A.J.L.R. 26, 29, *per* Kitto J.

[34] If the payment was a bribe, the payer cannot recover; for he has not been compelled to pay the money to get what he is entitled to have.

[35] See above, p. 243, n. 12.

[36] *Re Coombs and Freshfield and Fernley* (1850) 4 Ex. 839, 841, *per* Parke B., 843, *per* Alderson B. *Cf. Woolwich Equitable Building Society* v. *Commissioners of Inland Revenue* [1993] A.C. 70.

[37] *Fernley* v. *Branson* (1851) 20 L.J.Q.B. 178; *Barnes* v. *Hayward* (1857) 1 H. & N. 742, 743, *per* Pollock C.B.; *Barnes* v. *Braithwaite* (1857) 2 H. & N. 569; *Roberts* v. *Eberhardt* (1858) 28 L.J.C.P. 74, 75, *per* Watson B. See also *Canadian Northern Ry.* v. *Ousley* [1918] 2 W.W.R. 1005.

[38] Generally an arbitrator only delivers his award when he has been paid; indeed he has a lien on the award for his reasonable costs: see Mustill and Boyd, *Commercial Arbitration in England*, 2nd ed., 1989, pp. 234–235.

on taxation and that the balance of the money, if any, shall be paid out to the applicant."[39]

(3) There is a group of cases where the person or body who makes an excessive demand is in a monopolistic position and where the plaintiff pays because he is not able to obtain the services or goods elsewhere. For that reason the common law imposed upon the common carrier an obligation "to accept and carry all goods delivered to him for carriage according to his profession (unless he had some reasonable excuse for not doing so) on being paid a *reasonable* compensation for so doing; and if the carrier refused to accept such goods, an action lay against him for so refusing; and if the customer, in order to induce the carrier to perform his duty, paid, under protest, a larger sum than was reasonable, he might recover back the surplus beyond what the carrier was entitled to receive, in an action for money had and received as being money extorted from him."[40]

Again, under the Railways Clauses Consolidation Act 1845, section 90, and other statutory provisions,[41] the railways used to be required to make an equal charge on all persons in respect of passengers or goods of the same description passing over the same part of a line in the same circumstances. This was a different obligation from that imposed on the common carrier. "There was nothing in the common law to hinder a carrier from carrying for favoured individuals at an unreasonably low rate, or even *gratis*. All that the law required was, that he should not charge any more than was reasonable. . . . "[42] But if, in contravention of section 90 of the 1845 Act or of some similar statutory provision, a railway made a practice of charging one person less than another in respect of the same service, the second person had the same remedies as one upon whom a common carrier had levied an unreasonable charge; in particular, he would be entitled to recover back the excess over and above the lower charge.[43] These provisions were thought necessary because of the monopolistic position of the railway companies, which were not subject to the ordinary restrictions of competition. However, since the denationalisation of long-distance road transport, it has been thought that the railways are and should be subject to competition from the road transport concerns, and that these and other similar statutory provisions are no longer necessary or desirable. They have, therefore, been repealed.[44]

---

[39] Subsection (1).

[40] *Great Western Ry.* v. *Sutton* (1868–1869) L.R. 4 H.L. 226, 237, *per* Blackburn J.; *Woolwich Equitable Building Society* v. *Commissioners of Inland Revenue* [1993] A.C.70, 165, *per* Lord Goff.

[41] See Kahn-Freund, *Law of Inland Transport*, App. 1.

[42] *Great Western Ry.* v. *Sutton* (1868–1869) L.R. 4 H.L. 226, 237, *per* Blackburn J.

[43] The availability of the action in these circumstances was expressly approved by the House of Lords in *Great Western Ry.* v. *Sutton* (1868–1869) L.R. 4 H.L. 226. There is a large body of case law on the matter. See also Railway and Canal Traffic Act 1854, s.2, discussed in *Lancashire & Yorkshire Ry.* v. *Greenwood* (1888) 21 Q.B.D. 215.

[44] Transport Charges, etc. (Miscellaneous Provisions) Act 1954, s.14 and Second Sched., Pt. II. The Transport Act 1962, 8th Sched., repeals Transport Act 1953, s.22, which had established a special procedure if the charge was thought unreasonable.

A more recent illustration of an excessive demand by a monopolistic supplier is *South of Scotland Electricity Board* v. *British Oxygen Co. Ltd. (No. 2)*.[45] The respondents were supplied with electricity at high voltage by the appellants. Electricity at high voltage was less costly to supply than electricity at low voltage, and the respondents paid for their electricity according to tariffs under which they were charged less than low voltage consumers. In this action the respondents sought to attack the tariffs on the grounds of "undue discrimination" against high voltage consumers in the position of the respondents, in that the tariffs did not fairly differentiate between high and low voltage consumers. Such discrimination was, they alleged, contrary to statute.[46] They also claimed repayment of the overcharges made because of "undue discrimination." The House of Lords, affirming the decision of the Second Division of the Court of Session, held that there should be proof before answer on the question of "undue discrimination," because there could be held to be such discrimination although the price charged to the respondents was lower than that charged to low voltage consumers. Moreover, although no right of recovery was specifically conferred by statute, an action would lie to recover the overcharges. For, in the words of Willes J. in *Great Western Ry.* v. *Sutton*[47]:

> "when a man pays more than he is bound to do by law for the performance of a duty which the law says is owed to him for nothing, or for less than he has paid, there is a compulsion or concussion in respect of which he is entitled to recover the excess by *condictio indebiti*, or action for money had and received."

This principle is potentially one of great importance,[48] as can be seen from the United States cases in which the courts have allowed plaintiffs to recover excessive payments to public utility companies. As the Supreme Court of Michigan said in *Saginaw* v. *Consumers Power Co.*[49]: "To deny recovery would mean depriving consumers of gas until by the institution of legal proceedings they could establish the fact that the charges were illegal. This would be a 'kind of execution in advance of judgment.' "

In such circumstances it seems that recovery will be allowed even though no actual threat was made to cut off an essential service. As was said in the same

---

[45] [1959] 1 W.L.R. 587; the earlier action is reported in [1956] 1 W.L.R. 1069. For an analysis of the *South of Scotland* case, see *Woolwich Equitable Building Society* v. *Commissioners of Inland Revenue* [1993] A.C. 70, 133–134 per Ralph Gibson L.J.

[46] Electricity Act 1947, s.37(8); Hydro-Electric Development (Scotland) Act 1943, s.10A(5). See now Electricity (Scotland) Act 1979.

[47] (1868–1869) L.R. 4 H.L. 226, 249, cited with approval. [1959] 1 W.L.R. 587, 607, *per* Lord Merriman. See also Viscount Kilmuir L.C. at p. 596.

[48] D. Cuthbertson, *The Principle of Voluntary Payment in Quasi-Contract* (1965–1967) 5 University of Queensland L.J. 288, 313.

[49] 8 N.W. 2d 149, 153 (1943), *per* Butzel J. There are many such cases; but it appears that a plaintiff must first exhaust any administrative remedy that he may have: see, generally, Palmer, *op. cit.* Vol. II, § 9.15. For a comparable Australian decision, see *Criterion Theatres Ltd.* v. *Melbourne and Metropolitan Board of Works* [1945] V.R. 267; *cf. South Australian Cold Stores Ltd.* v. *Electricity Trust of South Australia* (1957) 98 C.L.R. 65.

case, the "latent threat that the gas company would shut off the gas was constantly before the consumer."[50]

Three minor points remain to be mentioned. As in other cases of duress, the plaintiff is not necessarily entitled to recover all the money he has paid, but only the surplus over and above the legal charge.[51] Secondly, the action will not lie to recover money paid, but also to recover money retained as an excessive charge for services to which the plaintiff is entitled for less.[52] And thirdly, the plaintiff is entitled to recover from a public officer or other such person even though the latter is acting as agent for a superior and has paid the money over into public funds,[53] though probably the superior is liable if he has received the money so paid.[54]

(e) Economic Duress

Closely allied with the examples of duress of goods are those cases where a person obtains a benefit from another by exerting economic or commercial pressure[55] on him. This may take many forms. For example, D refuses to deliver a crane unless P pays him £1,000 above the contract price; or P promises D to accept £500 as a total payment for a debt of £1,500, D having refused to pay the whole debt, with the knowledge that P is in financial difficulties; or D refuses to enter into a new contract with P unless P admits liability for defective workmanship under an existing contract.[56]

It has long been accepted in the United States that, in certain circumstances, a contract may be set aside and restitution obtained if the contract has been made or benefits have been conferred in consequence of the exercise of illegitimate economic pressure, which is characterised as economic duress.[57] In recent years English courts have also recognised that commercial pressure *may* be illegitimate and constitute duress."[58] It is "now accepted that economic

---

[50] 8 N.W.2d 149, 152 (1943), *per* Butzel J. *Cf.* [1980] C.L.P. 191, 203 [Birks]; see above, p. 245.
[51] *Lovell* v. *Simpson* (1800) 3 Esp. 153; *Dew* v. *Parsons* (1819) 2 B. & Ald. 562.
[52] *Longdill* v. *Jones* (1816) 1 Stark 345.
[53] *Steele* v. *Williams* (1853) 8 Exch. 625; see above, p. 246.
[54] *Brocklebank Ltd.* v. *R.* [1925] 1 K.B. 52, 68, *per* Scrutton L.J.; see above, p. 246. Contrast the decisions on duress of goods: see above, p. 239.
[55] This topic is discussed in the books under many headings; "economic duress" and "business compulsion" are among the most popular.
[56] But it has been said that only in exceptional circumstances will economic duress be successfully alleged in employment law: *Hennessy* v. *Craigmyle & Co. Ltd.* [1986] I.C.R. 461.
[57] The American cases are conveniently collected by John Dalzell, "Duress by Economic Pressure," 20 N.C.L.R. 237, 341 (1942). For later cases, see Palmer, *op. cit.* Vol. II, § 9.12. See also Dawson, "Economic Duress—an Essay in Perspective," 45 Mich.L.R. 253 (1947), which is a most stimulating survey; and R. J. Sutton, "Economic Duress" (1974) 20 McGill L.J. 554; M. H. Ogilvie, Economic Duress, Inequality of Bargaining Power and Threatened Breach of Contract, (1981) 26 McGill L.J. 289.
[58] *The Siboen and the Sibotre* [1976] 1 Lloyds Rep. 293; *North Ocean Shipping Company Ltd.* v. *Hyundai Construction Company Ltd.* [1979] A.C. 704; *Pao On* v. *Lau Yiu Long* [1980] A.C. 614; *Burmah Oil Co.* v. *Bank of England* [1980] A.C. 1090, 1140, *per* Lord Scarman; *Universe Tankships Inc. of Monrovia* v. *International Transport Workers' Federation* [1983] 1 A.C. 366, 383–384, *per* Lord Diplock, 400–401, *per* Lord Scarman; *Dimskal Shipping Co. S.A.* v.

pressure may be sufficient to amount to duress, . . . provided at least that the economic pressure may be characterised as illegitimate and has constituted a significant cause inducing the plaintiff to enter into the relevant contract"[59] or to make a payment. However, "[c]ommercial pressure, in some degree, exists wherever one party to a commercial transaction is in a stronger bargaining position than the other party"[60]; so that economic duress should not, therefore, be found lightly.[61] The critical questions are, when is commercial pressure illegitimate and when will illegitimate pressure be actionable? The cases now provide some clues to the answer.[62]

What is an Illegitimate Threat?

Most important is the nature of the threat or pressure. "The law regards the threat of unlawful action as illegitimate, whatever the demand."[63] Indeed a threat to break a contract may be characterised as illegitimate. Such may be[64] the case if the person making the threat knew that he would be in breach of contract if it were implemented.[65] But what if the person who made the threat believed that it was commercially reasonable for him to ask for a variation of an existing contract? In the United States, some jurisdictions have upheld agreements which were subsequently varied, without fresh consideration, when unexpected difficulties, physical or economic, made one party's performance unduly onerous, in circumstances when it could not be said that the contract was discharged by impossibility or frustration.[66] The *Restatement of Contracts 2d* accepts that such a variation, even if induced by the threat of non-performance, is binding in the absence of consideration if it is "fair and equitable."[67]

It is not surprising that lower English courts have not been confronted with such a submission. The pre-existing duty rule has hitherto been an insurmountable barrier. In any event, it is debatable whether a court is in the best position

---

International Transport Workers' Federation, The Evia Luck [1992] 2 A.C. 152, 165, *per* Lord Goff.

[59] *Dimskal Shipping Co. S.A. v. International Transport Workers' Federation, The Evia Luck* [1992] 2 A.C. 152, 165 *per* Lord Goff. Contrast the case law on duress to the person (see above, p. 234), where it is enough that it is "*a*" reason for the plaintiff acting as he did.

[60] *Universe Tankships Inc. of Monrovia* v. *International Transport Workers' Federation, The Universe Sentinel* [1983] 1 A.C. 366, 384, *per* Lord Diplock.

[61] *Moyes & Groves Ltd.* v. *Radiation New Zealand Ltd.* [1982] 1 N.Z.L.R. 368 (N.Z.C.A.).

[62] In *Universe Tankships Inc. of Monrovia* v. *International Transport Workers' Federation, The Universe Sentinel* [1983] 1 A.C. 366, 383–384, *per* Lord Diplock.

[63] *Ibid.* [1983] 1 A.C. 366, 401, *per* Lord Scarman. Lord Scarman was dissenting: see below, p. 252.

[64] *B & S Contracts and Design Ltd.* v. *Victor Green Publications* [1984] I.C.R. 419, 428, *per* Kerr L.J.; see below, p. 255, for instances where duress was not found.

[65] *B & S Contracts and Designs Ltd.* v. *Victor Green Publications* [1984] I.C.R. 419, C.A.; *North Ocean Shipping Co. Ltd.* v. *Hyundai Construction Co. Ltd.* [1979] Q.B. 704, 719, *per* Mocatta J., see below, p. 256; *Dimskal Shipping Co. S.A.* v. *International Transport Workers' Federation, The Evia Luck*, [1992] 2 A.C. 152, 166, 168, *per* Lord Goff.

[66] The cases are collected in *Contracts*, § 4.22. Professor Farnsworth is the Reporter of the *Restatement of Contracts 2d.*

[67] § 176, comment e; see above, p. 233, n. 29. *Cf.* the duty of dealing in good faith, imposed under the Uniform Commercial Code, Section 2–103 ("honesty in fact and observance of reasonable commercial standards of fair dealing in the trade").

to determine whether a variation is "fair and equitable" and whether it is wise to shift commercial risks which a party originally undertook.[68-69]

Yet a builder who finds hidden horrors in the sub-soil, while digging the foundations of a building, may not think it unreasonable to demand more money if he is to complete the work. If he threatens not to perform unless he is paid more, it is most unlikely that his action on the defendant's promise to pay will succeed. But exceptionally it may if the court finds that he did not exert any illegitimate pressure; for example, if it is the promisor who takes the initiative and offers him the extra douceur.[70]

A more difficult question arises if the person who made the threat thought he was entitled in law to make it and did not believe that the threat, if carried out, would be a breach of contract. In such circumstances, the position of the "coerced" party does not change. The pressure on him is just the same whatever the threatener believes. But it is then open to the court to conclude that the threat was not a "significant cause" inducing the plaintiff to act, and that the parties had entered into a compromise of a genuine dispute.[71] On the other hand, finding that the party who made a threat believed that in law he was entitled to make it is not conclusive that there was no operative duress,[72] for the court may find that the threatened party gave in because of the threat and not because he wished to compromise a claim.[73]

In *Universe Tankships Inc. of Monrovia* v. *International Transport Workers' Federation, The Universe Sentinel*[74] the House of Lords concluded that a threat to black a ship would be legitimate if it was an act done in contemplation or furtherance of a trade dispute. But the House held[75] that a threat to black the ship unless the owners paid, *inter alia*, $6480 to the I.T.W.'s Welfare Fund was a threat which was not made in furtherance or contemplation of a trade dispute and was not therefore legitimate.[76] Consequently the owner could recover that sum; to allow recovery would not circumvent legislative policy. In the view of Lord Diplock, the sections of the Trade Union and Labour Relations Act

---

[68-69] *Cf.* Beatson, *op. cit.* pp. 126–129. *Cf.* (1991) 107 L.Q.R. 649, 661–664 [Halson].

[70] *Cf.* See *William Bros.* v. *Roffey Bros. & Nicholls (Contractors) Ltd.* [1991] 1 Q.B. 1: see below, p. 261. *Cf. North Ocean Shipping Company Ltd.* v. *Hyundai Construction Company Ltd.* [1979] Q.B. 705, see below p. 256; *Pao On* v. *Lau Yiu Long* [1980] A.C. 614, see below, p. 262. But see *T.A. Sundell & Sons Pty.* v. *Emm Yannoulatos (Overseas) Pty. Ltd.* (1956) 56 S.R. (N.S.W.) 323.

[71] *Dimskal Shipping Co. S.A.* v. *International Transport Workers' Federation, The Evia Luck,* [1992] 2 A.C. 152, 165, *per* Lord Goff. For one illustration see *Moyes & Groves Ltd.* v. *Radiation New Zealand Ltd.* [1982] N.Z.L.R. 368, C.A.

[72] Contrast *Woodar Investment Development Ltd.* v. *Wimpey Construction UK Ltd.* [1980] 1 W.L.R. 277: unjustified rescission, erroneously relying on the exercise of a contractual term, did not amount to an act of repudiation. Query if unjustified rescission may nevertheless amount to a wrongful act: (1985) 48 M.L.R. 106 [Palmer and Catchpole].

[73] *Mason* v. *The State of New South Wales* [1959] 102 C.L.R. 108; see below, p. 271.

[74] [1983] 1 A.C. 366.

[75] Lord Scarman and Lord Brandon dissented on this point. The House unanimously held that the payment to the Welfare Fund was not impressed with a resulting trust for the owner.

[76] Lord Diplock (at p. 395) thought that "economic duress is not a tort *per se*" (*contra* Lord Scarman at p. 400); *cf. Dimskal Shipping Co. S.A.* v. *International Transport Workers' Federation, The Evia Luck* [1992] A.C. 152, 165–167 *per* Lord Goff below, p. 730. See, generally, [1983] J.B.L. 218, 224 [Carty and Evans].

1974,[77] which gave immunities from liability in tort, "are not directly applicable to the shipowners' cause of action for money had and received. Nevertheless, these sections, together with the definition of trade dispute in section 29, afford an indication, which your Lordships should respect, of where public policy requires that the line should be drawn between what kind of commercial pressure by a trade union upon an employer in the field of industrial relations ought to be treated as legitimised despite the fact that the will of the employer is thereby coerced, and what kind of commercial pressure in that field does amount to economic duress that entitles the employer victim to restitutionary remedies."[78]

These statutory provisions recognise that, as the law then stood,[79] it was desirable to protect a trade union from tortious claims which could cripple its legitimate activities. But it does not follow that because it is wise to enact that a trade union should be insulated from tortious claims for *loss* suffered that it should be allowed to retain an enrichment which was gained from an act which was at common law wrongful, if not necessarily tortious.[80] For that reason it was debatable whether the concession that payments of backpay were irrecoverable, being sums paid in furtherance of a trade dispute, was a wise one. It is true that such a claim against the defendants may have failed for a very different reason, namely, that it was the seamen, not the Federation, which had been enriched at the plaintiff's expense (*cf.* above, pp. 235–236). And a claim against an individual seaman would not have been worth pursuing even though he may have accepted his money with the knowledge that it was the product of the Federation's wrongful act.[81]

The Absence of Choice: Was the Threat a "Significant Cause"?

A threat may be wrongful but the court may nonetheless conclude that the illegitimate threat was not a "significant cause" in inducing the plaintiff to do what he did.[82]

In *The Universe Sentinel*[83] Lord Scarman concluded that the classic case of duress is "the victim's intentional submission arising from the realization that there is no other practical choice open to him. . . . The absence of choice can be proved in various ways, *e.g.* by protest, by the absence of independent advice, or by a declaration of intention to go to law to recover the money paid or the

---

[77] ss.13, 14 and 29.
[78] [1983] 1 A.C. 366, 385. See also Lord Scarman at p. 401; and *cf.* [1983] C.L.J. 43, 47 [Jones].
[79] See now Employment Act 1980, s.17.
[80] However, in *Dimskal Shipping Co. S.A.* v. *International Transport Workers' Federation, The Evia Luck* [1992] 2 A.C. 152, both Lord Templeman (at pp. 160–161) and Lord Goff (at p. 166–167) appeared to accept *obiter* Lord Diplock's reasoning and conclusion.
[81] See above, pp. 230–231.
[82] *Dimskal Shipping Co. S.A.* v. *International Transport Workers' Federation, The Evia Luck* [1992] 2 A.C. 152, 165, *per* Lord Goff. See below, p. 730.
[83] [1983] 1 A.C. 366, 400. *Cf.* his observations in *Pao On* v. *Lau Yiu Long* [1980] A.C. 614, 635–635. See also *Maskell* v. *Horner* [1915] 3 K.B. 106 (see below, p. 268), and see above, p. 233 for a criticism of this test of "absence of choice."

property transferred." The consequences of a refusal must be "serious and immediate so that there is no reasonable alternative open, such as by legal redress."[84] The absence of an effective adequate remedy is said to be most significant.[85] So, in *The Universe Sentinel* the plaintiffs' ship was blacked; the plaintiffs' acceded to the defendants demand for payments of backpay and contribution to a welfare fund because it was a matter of "most urgent commercial necessity" that they should regain the ship; and they "were advised that their prospects of obtaining an injunction [to prevent the blacking] were minimal."[86] Moreover, "they [had] sought recovery of the money with sufficient speed once the duress had terminated."[87]

The shipowner chose the lesser of two evils. So does the plaintiff who has contracted with the defendant for the supply of goods or for his skilled labour and is met with the threat not to perform unless he is paid more than the contract price. He will only do so if he cannot get the goods or the labour as cheaply or expeditiously in the market.[88] Economic or personal necessity characterises the case law which we shall now discuss.

The Modern Case Law

The law on economic duress is still in the course of development; whether or not economic duress is found to exist will turn on the facts, as has been seen, of each case.[89] We have sought to analyse the topic further under the following headings:

(1). Where P confers some benefit upon D because of D's threat that otherwise he will not carry out his obligations under a contract;

(2). Where P promises to confer some benefit on D in order to make D perform his obligations under a contract;

(3). Where P confers a benefit on D because D threatens to interfere with P's business relations with T;

(4). Where P confers some benefit on, or contracts with, D because of D's threat that he will not contract with him in the future or that he will exercise some legal privilege to P's detriment.

---

[84] *B & S Contracts and Design Ltd.* v. *Victoria Green Publications Ltd.* [1984] I.C.R. 419, 428, *per* Kerr L.J., see below, p. 255.

[85] For an argument that this condition is not evidential, but that it is a "prerequisite to a finding of duress," see Beatson, *op. cit.* pp. 122 *et seq.*

[86] [1981] I.C.R. 129, 143, *per* Parker J., cited in [1983] A.C. 366, 400, *per* Lord Scarman. See also "*The Alev*" [1989] 1 Lloyd's Rep. 138, 146–147, *per* Hobhouse J. (no other practical choice); *Alec Lobb (Garages) Ltd.* v. *Total Oil G.B. Ltd.* [1983] 1 W.L.R. 87, 93, *per* Millett Q.C., Deputy Judge ("no realistic alternative but to submit"). Contrast the facts of *Pao On* v. *Lau Yiu Long* [1980] A.C. 614, see below, p. 263.

[87] See above, p. 252.

[88] See below, p. 233.
For a further discussion of the relevance of the principle of "adequacy of remedy," see *post*, pp. 272–274.

[89] *B & S Contracts and Design Ltd.* v. *Victor Green Publications Ltd.* [1984] I.C.R. 419, 425, *per* Griffiths L.J.

Some of these problems have been solved through the application of well established common law principles, for example, that D gave no consideration for P's promise to confer on him an additional benefit.[90] In others a court has held that P submitted to D's honest claim. This may be a particularly troublesome question, for it is not always easy to determine whether there has been a compromise or whether the benefits have been conferred under duress.[91] Again, he may have subsequently affirmed the contract.[92]

(1) *P confers a benefit upon D because of D's threat that otherwise he will not carry out his obligations under a contract*

Whether P can recover money paid or obtain recompense for other benefits conferred in consequence of such threats may depend, as has been seen, on a number of factors.

If D threatens not to perform his part of the contract, knowing that this will amount to a breach of the contract, the threat may be characterised as an illegitimate or wrongful act, which amounts in law to duress. To take one example. In *B & S Contracts and Design Ltd.* v. *Victor Green Publications Ltd.*,[93] the plaintiffs agreed to erect exhibition stands for the defendants at Olympia, under a contract with a *force majeure* clause. The plaintiffs decided to use for the work employees who had already been given redundancy notices. On arriving at Olympia they threatened to strike unless they were paid £9000 severance pay, to which they were not entitled; subsequently they rejected the plaintiffs' offer of £4500. The plaintiffs informed the defendants about the employees' threat, and the defendants offered the balance of £4500 "on account." The plaintiffs refused that offer and told the defendants, "if you will give us £4500 we will complete the contract." The defendants paid because, in the words of their director, they were "over the barrel." In this action the plaintiffs sued to recover the £4500 which the defendants subsequently deducted from the contract sums due to them. The Court of Appeal agreed with the trial judge that the plaintiffs had made a "veiled threat," that they would walk off the job unless the defendants paid the £4500. The threatened breach of contract amounted to duress for the defendants had been influenced against their will "to pay money under the threat of unlawful damage to [their] economic interest."[94] They were faced with no alternative course of action but to pay the sum demanded of them."[95] It could not be said that the plaintiffs' threat was lawful. They could not have taken advantage of the *force majeure* clause to cancel the contract; it would have been reasonable for them to have paid the £9000 demanded, there being no evidence that they could not have

---

[90] See above, p. 242.
[91] See above, pp. 53–54.
[92] See above, pp. 256–257.
[93] [1984] I.C.R. 419. See also *The Alev* [1989] 1 Lloyd's Rep. 138; *Atlas Express Ltd.* v. *Kapco (Importers and Distributors) Ltd.* [1989] Q.B. 833.
[94] At pp. 423–424, *per* Eveleigh L.J.
[95] At p. 426, *per* Griffiths L.J.

afforded to have done so. Consequently, the defendants were entitled to make the deduction which they had made.

A more difficult case is *T. A. Sundell & Sons Pty. Ltd.* v. *Emm Yannoulatos (Overseas) Pty. Ltd.*,[96] for the appellant might well have thought that he was acting reasonably in making the particular demand. The appellant, an importer, had agreed to sell galvanised iron to the respondent at £104.15s. a ton. The iron was to come from France. Subsequently there was a sharp rise in the world price of zinc which led the appellant to demand an extra £31 a ton. The respondent increased his letter of credit, reserving his rights under the original contract,[97] because of the appellant's threat that if he failed to do so "no iron at all would be delivered." The appellant delivered the iron and had recourse in full to the letter of credit. The respondent, who has sub-contracted to sell to a third party, sued to recover the amount paid in excess of the original contract price. The Supreme Court of New South Wales found that the respondent had not willingly agreed to pay the increased price. Even if he had, the promise was not binding since the appellant had provided no fresh consideration. The Court accepted[98] that a "compulsive threat ... to refrain from performing merely a contractual duty" may amount in law to duress and rejected the argument that duress embraced only "a threat to refrain from performing a statutory duty or a threat to interfere with a proprietary right of the payer."

In *Sundell* the appellant believed that he was entitled to pass on the price increase to the respondent; indeed he offered to assist the respondent, by giving him access to his files, to pass on the increase to the sub-purchaser. The Court did not consider these factors to be conclusive.[99] As a matter of law the appellant's threat could amount to duress, and the trial judge had found duress. It would not interfere with his conclusion that the appellant had paid under practical compulsion. It may be open to the court, on comparable facts, to hold that the defendant had made no threat but had simply pointed out that he could not perform his side of the bargain in the changed economic circumstances.[1] But the line between an implicit threat and a statement of "my position" is inevitably a very thin one.

In *North Ocean Shipping Co. Ltd.* v. *Hyundai Construction Co. Ltd.*,[2] Mocatta J. also accepted that the threat not to carry out a contract amounted to duress, but held that the plaintiffs had nonetheless affirmed the contract. In this case the defendant shipyard had contracted with the plaintiffs to build a tanker for a fixed price in U.S. dollars, payable in five instalments. After the plaintiffs had paid the first instalment, the dollar was devalued by 10 per cent. The defen-

---

[96] (1956) 56 S.R.(N.S.W.) 323. See also *Carr* v. *Gilsenan* [1946] S.R. (Qd) 44.

[97] The appellant had stated that the respondent knew that it could not deliver at the contract price. The respondent continued to assert that its increase of the letter of credit was without prejudice.

[98] At p. 328, *per curiam.*

[99] *Cf.* above, pp. 251–252.

[1] *Cf. Williams* v. *Roffey Bros. & Nicholls (Contractors) Ltd.* [1991] 1 Q.B. 1, C.A.: see below, p. 261; Beatson, *op. cit.* pp. 126–129.

[2] [1979] Q.B. 705.

dant shipyard then demanded that the plaintiffs increase their remaining instalments by 10 per cent. The plaintiffs realized that the yard would not accept anything other than the unqualified agreement to the increase. At that time the plaintiffs were negotiating with Shell a very lucrative time-charter of the tanker, a contract which was later finalised. Consequently they agreed to make the payments "without prejudice to our rights" because they did not wish to default in the performance of their profitable time-charter with Shell. In turn the defendant shipyard agreed, at the plaintiffs' request, to a corresponding increase in letters of credit which had been provided as security for any default in their performance. The remaining instalments were paid without protest; the plaintiffs took delivery of the tanker, again without protest, and took no further action for seven months, when they made a formal claim for the return of the excess payments. Mocatta J. held that, although the defendant shipyard had given consideration for the varied agreement by increasing their letters of credit[3] that agreement was voidable for duress. It has been induced by a threat to break the contract which amounted to economic duress.[4] Nonetheless, the judge dismissed the plaintiffs' claim. Their conduct amounted to an affirmation of the varied agreement to pay the extra 10 per cent. At the time of taking delivery of the tanker they had made no protest when there was no danger at that time that the shipyard would refuse to deliver if they had done so; and the final instalment payments were made "without qualification" and were followed by a delay of seven months before the plaintiffs made their claim.[5] Here is a rare example of a situation where a party fully realises that he has been coerced into paying more than he had agreed to pay but went on with the contract, as varied, because it was in his best economic interests so to do.[6]

In *North Ocean Shipping Co. Ltd.* v. *Hyundai Construction Co. Ltd.*[7] the defendant shipyard knew that its threat, if carried out, would be a breach of its contractual obligations. But in *The Siboen and the Sibotre*[8] counsel argued that the

"defence of duress is made out whenever one party to a contract threatens [whether in good faith or not] to commit a breach of it and the other party agrees to vary or cancel the contract under this threat because it has no effective legal remedy in respect of the threatened breach. . . . Duress must *a fortiori* be a defence when the party threatening to break the

---

[3] He reached this decision with considerable hesitation. Contrast *The Siboen and the Sibotre* [1976] 1 Lloyd's Rep. 293, 336, where Kerr J. suggested that it should make no difference, in considering the validity of a settlement made under duress, that the defendants "had also insisted on some purely nominal but legally sufficient consideration; and *"The Alev"* [1989] 1 Lloyd's Rep. 138, 147, *per* Hobhouse J.
[4] [1979] Q.B. 705, 719.
[5] [1979] Q.B. 705, 720.
[6] *Cf.* below, p. 263.
[7] [1979] Q.B. 705.
[8] [1976] 1 Lloyd's Rep. 293.

contract is putting forward some justification for doing so without any bona fides."[9]

Kerr J. thought this proposition "much too wide," probably because it implied that an honest settlement, made with the intention of settling a claim, could subsequently be avoided, even if the party making the threat was acting in good faith or, if not, the other party was aware of his lack of bona fides but still wished to dispose of the matter by settlement.[10] In *The Siboen and the Sibotre* the owner had agreed to vary the charter rates because of the charterers' representation that they would go bankrupt if this were not done, so that the owner would be without any commercial redress. The charterers' representation was found to be fraudulent and the case was ultimately decided on that ground.[11] But it was argued that, even if there were no misrepresentation, the charter agreement, as varied, was voidable for duress. There was a threatened breach of the charter, and "if the charterers were liable to go bankrupt if the owners did not reduce their rates, then the owners would be left without any effective legal remedy in the face of these threatened breaches."[12] Kerr J. rejected that argument. The owner had voluntarily agreed to vary the terms of the charter; there had been no protest and the owner had later sought to uphold the varied charter by subsequent arbitration. The owner "was acting under great pressure, but only commercial pressure, and not under anything which could in law be regarded as a coercion of his will so as to vitiate his consent."[13]

A bona fide compromise which is entered into with the intention of closing a transaction is binding on the parties.[14] Conversely, as has been seen,[15] money paid because of a "compulsive threat . . . to refrain from performing merely a contractual duty"[16] may amount to duress. A finding that both parties acted in good faith should not, however, lead to an inevitable conclusion that they had agreed to compromise a claim; indeed in the other categories of duress, such as duress of goods it is "not necessary to show that the defendant acted in bad faith."[17] A compromise is upheld because it is proper to threaten litigation if bona fide demands are not met and because it is desirable to uphold settlements made in consequence of such a threat.[18] But a compromise can be set aside for duress.[19] Was the benefit exacted by the mere threat of legal proceedings, or was it exacted by illegitimate pressure which went beyond the threat of legal

---

[9] At p. 334.
[10] This is to be inferred from Kerr J.'s judgment.
[11] At pp. 321 *et seq.*
[12] At p. 334.
[13] At p. 336. For other facts which gave rise to a genuine variation, see *Moyse & Groves Ltd.* v. *Radiation New Zealand Ltd.* [1982] 1 N.Z.L.R. 368 (N.Z.C.A.).
[14] See below, pp. 263–264.
[15] See above, p. 256.
[16] *Sundell & Sons* v. *Emm Yannoulatos (Overseas) Pty. Ltd.* (1956) 46 S.R.(N.S.W.) 323, 328.
[17] *Mason* v. *The State of New South Wales* (1959) 102 C.L.R. 108, 141, *per* Windeyer J.
[18] See above, pp. 50–54.
[19] *Deacon* v. *Transport Regulation Board* [1958] V.R. 458, 459–460, *per* Lowe J.; see above p. 230.

proceedings?[20] This is often a difficult question to answer when the defendant honestly believes that he was entitled to refuse to perform his part of the contract. In Australia it has arisen in the context of disputes between vendors and purchasers,[21] where one of the parties has maintained that he is not liable under the contract to bear certain charges, such as a water rate. The purchaser protests but capitulates when the vendor honestly, but as it is later determined without right, threatens not to complete. The courts have held that it is not conclusive that the "vendor honestly believed that he was legally entitled . . . to the price which he asked. . . . The withholding of another's legal right [to completion] is . . . itself treated as 'a practical compulsion.' "[22] The purchaser could not then be said to have acted voluntarily, with the intention of closing the transaction. On the contrary, he was "endeavouring to the utmost of [his] ability to preserve [his] legal rights as regards the question in issue so far as [he] could without jeopardising [his] rights under the contract as against the [vendor]. . . ."[23] It is true that the equitable title to land had passed to the purchaser when the contract was made, so that there was also present a threat of an unauthorised interference with property as well as a threat to withhold "another's legal right." But the Australian cases suggest that the refusal to complete the contract, even though the vendor acted in good faith, may be, in some circumstances, "practical compulsion"[24] if it caused the coerced party to act as he did.[25]

In the United States, the courts have also found that a bona fide threat not to perform a contract may amount to duress provided that there were present other facts which suggested that the plaintiff did not intend to compromise the defendant's claim; for example that his legal and equitable remedies were inadequate, that he had special need for the services or goods; or that he was in a distressed financial position. If these facts were known to the defendant, the court is more likely to hold that the plaintiff was coerced into making the payment.[26]

In determining whether there is a voluntary settlement of an honest claim, it may also be significant to inquire whether the defendant has relied on contractual or statutory provisions which impose a penalty or a forfeiture of property. The problem may arise if an insurance company claims that a premium is due

---

[20] *Cf. Re Hooper and Grass' Contract* [1949] V.R. 269.

[21] See, *e.g. Nixon* v. *Furphy* (1925) 25 N.S.W.(S.R.) 151; *Re Hooper and Grass' Contract* [1949] V.R. 269; see generally (1974) 20 McGill L.J. 554 [Sutton]. *Cf. Knutson* v. *The Bourkes Syndicate* [1941] S.C.R. 419.

[22] *Re Hooper and Grass' Contract* [1949] V.R. 269, 272, *per* Fullagar J.

[23] *Nixon* v. *Furphy* (1925) 25 N.S.W.(S.R.) 151, 158, *per* Long Innes J. Other Australian cases include *White Rose Flour Milling Co. Pty.* v. *Australian Wheat Board* (1944) 18 A.L.J.R. 324; *Carr* v. *Gilsenan* [1946] S.R. (Qd.) 44.

[24] See *Re Hooper and Grass' Contract* [1949] V.R. 269, 272, *per* Fullagar J.; *Sundell & Sons* v. *Emm Yannoulatos (Overseas) Pty. Ltd.* (1956) S.R.(N.S.W.) 323.

[25] Contrast *Peter Kiewit Sons' Co. of Canada Ltd.* v. *Eakins Construction Ltd.* [1960] S.C.R. 361 (S. Ct. of Canada); and see below, n. 29.

[26] The cases are collected in Palmer, *op. cit.* Vol. II, § 9.12, *Cf. Pao On* v. *Lau Yiu Long* [1980] A.C. 614 (see below, p. 263).

under a personal injury policy; the assured asserts that he is totally disabled, in which case he is not bound, under the terms of the policy, to pay a premium. But he pays under protest because he realises that if he fails to do so and he is not totally disabled the policy will lapse. This question has not yet arisen in an English reported case. But in the United States, where it frequently has, the jurisdictions are divided, some allowing and some denying recovery.[27] Possibly an English court might treat the assured's payment as having been made as a precautionary measure pending the resolution of the dispute,[28] although such a convenient interpretation would be impossible if the insurance company has refused to accept it on those terms. Then the court may have to decide whether the assured made the payment intending to close the transaction or whether a penal provision in the contract of assurance, that the policy would lapse if the premium was not paid promptly, led the assured to make the payment.[29] The decision of the High Court of Australia in *Mason* v. *The State of New South Wales*[30] suggests that the existence of a provision, providing for penalties and forfeitures, may be enough to persuade a court to find that a payment was then not made voluntarily, but under compulsion, although in *Mason's* case the penalty provisions were embodied in a statute rather than a contract.[31] In *Mason's* case the plaintiff paid for a statutory licence because he knew that, if he did not do so, he could not carry on as an inter-state carrier; for the statute would impose on him severe penalties, including the seizure of his vehicles and books of account, if he attempted to work without a licence. The statute was held, in independent litigation, to be *ultra vires*. The High Court of Australia allowed the plaintiff to recover. The majority of the Court held that the payments had been made under duress."[32]

(2) Where P promises to confer some benefit on D in order to make D perform his obligations under a contract

It has been an established principle of the common law,[33] which has stood for hundreds of years, that a promise made by one contracting party to the other contracting party to fulfil his existing contractual obligation is not a promise supported by valuable consideration. The principle has been much criticised,[34]

---

[27] *Cf. Still* v. *The Equitable Life Assurance*, 54 S.W.2d (1932), where recovery was allowed and which represents the majority view, with *Rossenfeld* v. *Boston Mutual Life Ins. Co.*, 110N.E. 304 (1915).

[28] *Cf. Sebel Products Ltd.* v. *The Commissioners for Customs and Excise* [1949] Ch. 409; see above, p. 155. In practice payments are made under similar conditions if there is a dispute as to the liability to pay instalments under a time-charter.

[29] Contrast the much criticised case of *Peter Kiewet Sons' Co. of Canada Ltd.* v. *Eakins Construction Ltd.* [1960] S.C.R. 361. But see now B.C.Misc. Statutes Amendment Act (No. 1) 1987, s.51.

[30] (1959) 102 C.L.R. 108.

[31] See below, Chap. 24.

[32] See below, pp. 243–245. Contrast *Atchison Topeka and Santa Fe Rly. Co.* v. *O'Connor*, 223, U.S. 280, 285–286, *per* Holmes J. (see below, p. 548), and the judgment of Dixon C.J. and Kitto J. in the principal case.

[33] *Harris* v. *Watson* (1791) Peake 102; *Stilk* v. *Meyrick* (1809(2 Camp. 317.

[34] *Cf.* Lord Blackburn's famous, but tantalising dissent in *Foakes* v. *Beer* (1884) 9 App.Cas. 605, 622.

but it has been justified on the ground that it enables the court to protect one contracting party from the illegitimate demands made on him by the other. If that is its justification, it operates capriciously and may result in the court refusing to uphold a contractual variation which has been freely entered into between the parties.

Recently, in *Williams* v. *Roffey Bros. & Nicholls (Contractors) Ltd.*,[35] the Court of Appeal recognised this to be so, and enforced a promise to pay more than the promisor, a contractor, was contractually bound to pay. The promisee, his sub-contractor, was said to have conferred a benefit on the promisor, *viz.* the performance of the existing contract, for the promisor did not have to find another sub-contractor and also avoided the payment of penalties for delay under the main contract. These distinctions are, given the precedents, hardly persuasive.[36] But the decision in *Williams* v. *Roffey Bros.* is appealing, and the Court's concern to uphold the promise is readily understandable. For there was no suggestion that the promisee had made an illegitimate threat; indeed it was the promisor who had made the offer to pay a larger sum to induce the promisee to go on with the contract. If the existing duty rule was rejected, and only the House of Lords is free to do so, the Court would be free to uphold a genuine variation, which is not the product of illegitimate pressure, and yet protect a contracting party from such pressure through the development of the law of duress.

In *D. & C. Builders Ltd.* v. *Rees*,[37] Lord Denning M.R., possibly realising the strength of the authorities, relied on a concept more akin to that of equitable estoppel or the civilian concept of abuse of rights. But in 1965 when that case was decided economic duress was still a concept which lurked unrecognised in the case law.

The defendant owed the plaintiffs £482 odd for work done. The plaintiffs pressed the defendant for months to settle the bill. The defendant's wife knew that the plaintiffs were in financial difficulties and offered £300 in final settlement, saying that if this was not accepted nothing would be paid. The plaintiffs accepted her cheque and gave a receipt "in completion of the account." The plaintiffs then sued for the balance of £182 odd. The Court of Appeal held that the plaintiffs could recover. Lord Denning M.R., with whose judgment Danckwerts L.J. agreed, found the solution in the equitable doctrine that a party will not be allowed to enforce his legal rights under a contract "where it would be inequitable, having regard to the dealings which have taken place between the parties,"[38] to do so. The defendant's wife was "putting undue pressure on the creditor. She was making a threat to break the contract (by paying nothing) and she was doing it so as to compel the creditor to do what

---

[35] [1991] 1 Q.B. 1, C.A.
[36] See above, p. 260, n. 33.
[37] [1966] 2 Q.B. 617. *Cf. Ormes* v. *Beadel* (1860) 2 Giff. 166, revsd. 2 De G.F. & J. 333.
[38] At p. 624, quoting Lord Cairns in *Hughes* v. *The Metropolitan Rly. Co.* (1877) 2 App.Cas. 439, 448.

he was unwilling to do."[39] Winn L.J. decided the case on the more orthodox ground that the accord was not binding in law, for it was neither under seal nor supported by consideration.[40]

Pao On v. *Lau Yiu Long*[41] suggests that the courts may be, as yet, unwilling whole-heartedly to accept Lord Denning M.R.'s flexible and unorthodox principle. For in that case where the court found that there was no duress, the Privy Council rejected the argument that public policy may "invalidate the consideration if there has been a threat to repudiate a pre-existing contractual obligation or an unfair use of a dominating bargaining position. . . . Where businessmen are negotiating at arms' length it is unnecessary for the achievement of justice, and unhelpful in the development of the law, to invoke such a rule of public policy."[42] Businessmen should be held to their bargains in the absence of fraud, mistake or duress. The uncertainty inherent in the adoption of a defence of public policy was said to be most undesirable. Moreover to accept that the consideration was illegal, as being against public policy, would "create unacceptable anomaly"; "[it] would be strange if conduct less than duress could render a contract void, whereas duress does no more than render a contract voidable."[43]

In other cases, however, D may give fresh consideration for P's agreement to vary the contract.[44] For example, P and D agree to cancel their original contract and to release each other from their executory obligations under it. Do their mutual promises supply the necessary consideration for the variation? While a genuine variation of contractual terms will undoubtedly be upheld, a variation which is induced simply by one party's claim to an extra payment or by his threat not to perform the contract may be entered into under pressure which amounts in law to duress. It is then voidable at the election of the injured party.[45]

It is not always easy to determine whether a person willingly agreed to a variation supported by fresh consideration and whether that variation was the product of illegitimate pressure. Certainly it is not conclusive that a party provides "some purely nominal but legally sufficient consideration."[46] But, as

---

[39] At p. 625. The Master of the Rolls considered that this was "a case of intimidation," citing *Rookes* v. *Barnard* [1964] A.C. 1129, which was not, however, a case where P threatened to break his contract with D, but where D induced T to dismiss P. See (1966) 82 L.Q.R. 165 [Winder].

[40] At pp. 627 *et seq.*

[41] [1980] A.C. 614. Lord Scarman delivered the advice of the Privy Council.

[42] [1980] A.C. 614, 634. But query if the parties in *D. & C. Builders* v. *Rees* were negotiating "at arms' length."

[43] At p. 634. Contrast *Harris* v. *Watson* (1791) Peake 102 with *Stilk* v. *Meyrick* (1809) 6 Esp. 129, 2 Camp. 317: see Lord Scarman's comments, at pp. 632–633.

[44] For a doubtful illustration of this principle, see *North Ocean Shipping Co. Ltd.* v. *Hyundai Construction Co. Ltd.* [1979] Q.B. 705; see above, p. 257.

[45] *Cf.* see above, pp. 230 and 242.

[46] *The Siboen and the Sibotre* [1976] 1 Lloyd's Rep. 293, 336, *per* Kerr J.; see above, p. 257, n. 3. *Cf.* (1966) 29 M.L.R. 428 [W. R. Cornish]. But contrast *"The Alev"* [1989] 1 Lloyd's Rep. 138, 147, *per* Hobhouse J.

the history of the litigation in *Pao On* v. *Lau Yiu Long*[47] illustrates, judges may disagree on whether there is any real consideration to support a variation and whether it was voluntarily entered into. The plaintiffs agreed ("the main agreement") with the FC Co. to sell their shares in the SO Co. to FCC. In exchange the plaintiffs were to receive shares in FC. The plaintiffs also agreed not to sell 60 per cent. of these shares for a year or so, in order to prevent the market price of FC shares from being depressed by the plaintiffs' sale of their shares. In consideration for that promise the defendants, who were the majority shareholders in FC agreed ("the subsidiary agreement") to buy back the shares at the end of the year for $2.50 a share which was their deemed value at the date of the agreement. On reflection, the plaintiffs formed the view that the subsidiary agreement was a commercial blunder since they anticipated that the price of a FC share would worth more than $2.50 in a year's time. So they refused to complete the main agreement unless and until the subsidiary agreement was varied so as to guarantee them, by way of indemnity, the price of $2.50 if the market price was less than that figure. The defendants yielded. They were not prepared to tolerate the delay which would follow if they sued for specific performance, although they were advised that the plaintiffs had no defence to such a claim; and they were afraid that the public would lose confidence in FC if the news broke that the plaintiffs had refused to complete the main agreement. Moreover, they thought that the risk which they were now required to bear was more academic than real since everyone expected FC shares to continue to rise over the year. In fact they did not; and at the end of the year FC shares had fallen to 36 cents. The plaintiffs sued on the subsidiary agreement as varied. The defendants contended that neither the original subsidiary agreement nor the subsidiary agreement as varied had any legal effect. The Privy Council, reversing the Hong Kong Court of Appeal, held that the subsidiary agreement as varied was enforceable. Lord Scarman described the defendants' argument as "remarkable." If it were accepted it would mean that the plaintiffs, having accepted, at the defendants' request, restrictions on their power to sell FC shares, would have not been safeguarded in the event of a fall in the market. "If the law really compels such a conclusion, one may be forgiven for thinking that the time has come to reconsider it."[48] The law did not compel such a conclusion. There was valuable consideration to support the subsidiary agreement as varied; it was not past consideration. The defendants' promise of an indemnity was not independent of the plaintiffs' antecedent promise to FC not to sell the shares for a year or so.[49] Extrinsic evidence was admissible to show that the real consideration for the defendants' promise was the plaintiffs' promise to the defendants to complete their contract with FC,

---

[47] [1980] A.C. 614.
[48] At p. 628.
[49] *Lampleigh* v. *Braithwait* (1615) Hobart 105; *Re Casey's Patents* [1892] 1 Ch. 104, 115–116, *per* Bowen L.J.

and that consideration was valuable in law.[50] Moreover the plaintiffs' threats did not amount to economic duress. There was commercial pressure but no improper coercion. As the trial judge had found,[51] the defendants "considered the matter thoroughly, chose to avoid litigation, and formed the opinion that the risk in giving the guarantee was more apparent than real.[52]

Here is yet another case[53] where economic duress was not found to exist even though the plaintiffs must have known that they could not have resisted an action on the main agreement if they refused to complete. Unlike the Hong Kong Court of Appeal, the Privy Council was not prepared to strike down a subsidiary agreement which was commercially reasonable, and which formed part of a bargain which had been made for the defendants' benefit.

(3) *Where P confers a benefit on D because D threatens to interfere with P's business relations with T*[54]

If P confers a benefit on D because D threatens[55] to persuade T to break his contract with P, that threat should, in our view, be characterised as an illegitimate act and amount in law to duress, even if the defendant's conduct is not tortious.[56] Moreover it should be irrelevant that D thought he was justified in so acting.

(4) *Where P confers some benefit on, or contracts with, D because of D's threat that he will not contract with him in the future or that he will exercise some legal privilege to P's detriment*

A person who obtains a benefit from another by threatening not to contract with him in the future is generally not liable to restore that benefit. His threat is not illegitimate. As a general rule, he may contract with whom he pleases and upon what terms he pleases; it cannot be said that the benefit has been obtained through a wrongful act.[57] Consequently if the plaintiff enters into a contract with the defendant because "there was no one else with whom he could contract for the supply of the particular commodity he required," he cannot escape its provisions.[58] As Singleton L.J. said in *Eric Gnapp Ltd.* v. *Petroleum Board*[59]: "there is here no question of force or threat of force or fear of personal suffering or abuse of legal proceedings. None of the essential elements of duress is present. . . ." Today, however, the courts may be prepared to scruti-

---

[50] A promise by P to D to carry out his contract with T is given for valuable consideration: *New Zealand Shipping Co. Ltd. A. M. Satterthwaite & Co. Ltd.* [1975] A.C. 154 (P.C.).

[51] Cited at pp. 634–635.

[52] At p. 635.

[53] *Cf. The Siboen and The Sibotre* [1976] 1 Lloyd's Rep. 293; see above, pp. 257–258.

[54] If D knowingly induces T to break his contract with P, D's conduct will be tortious: *cf. Ramp Buildings Corp.* v. *Northwest Building Co.* 4 P.2d 507 (1931).

[55] Such a threat may be implicit: see *Ross Systems* v. *Linden Deri-Delite Inc.* 173 A 2d 258 (1961).

[56] *Cf. Ellis* v. *Barke* (1871) 40 L.J.Ch. 603, L.R. 2 Ch. 104. Such a threat, even if made in bad faith, may not be tortious: see [1964] C.L.J. 225, 226–227 [Weir].

[57] See below, Chap. 11 for a discussion of unconscionable bargains.

[58] *Eric Gnapp Ltd.* v. *Petroleum Board* [1949] 1 All E.R. 980, 986, *per* Singleton L.J.

[59] *Ibid.*

nise the terms of some standard form contracts, at least if they involve a restraint of trade, to determine if they are unconscionable.[60] And the Unfair Contract Terms Act 1977[61] now limits the extent to which parties are free to exclude or restrict their liability for breach of contract.[62]

Other common law jurisdictions have also reached the conclusion that a threat not to enter into a contract with another is generally not an illegitimate act. In the Australian case of *Smith* v. *William Charlick Ltd.*[63] the Australian Wheat Harvest Board sold and delivered wheat to the respondents, some at 5s. and some at 6s 6d. per bushel. Having found at a later date that the respondents had a large amount of this wheat still in their possession, it demanded from them a further sum of money, calling it a surcharge. "The demand was made, admittedly, not by reason of any legal obligation, but on the ground that, as the controlled price of flour was increased in correspondence with the higher price of wheat, the wheat-growers were morally entitled to the advanced price, inasmuch as the wheat had originally been sold for weekly requirements only, and the actual retention of wheat or flour proved overstatement of requirements at the time.[64] The Board threatened not to do any further business with the respondents unless the demand was met. Having paid £1,952 under protest, the respondents sued for its recovery. The High Court of Australia dismissed their claim. There was no mistake and no wrongful threat. The payment was made with "full knowledge of all material facts. . . . It was paid, not in order to have that done which the Board was legally bound to do, but in order to induce the Board to do that which it was under no legal obligation to do."[65] The respondents had simply chosen to pay a "further sum for wheat already sold to them rather than to be shut out from further trade with the mandatary of the owners of wheat."[66]

In contrast, in the view of the *Restatement of Contracts 2d*,[67] exceptionally a threat not to contract may amount to duress. For example, A intentionally misleads B into thinking that he will deliver goods at the "usual price," as he has done in the past. B does not attempt to buy them elsewhere. A then refuses to deliver unless B pays a price greatly in excess of the price usually charged. B has urgent need of the goods and makes the contract. "If the court concludes that the effectiveness of A's threat in inducing B to make the contract was significantly increased by A's prior unfair dealing, A's threat is improper and

---

[60] *Schroeder Music Publishing Co. Ltd.* v. *Macaulay* [1974] 1 W.L.R. 1308, 1315–1316, *per* Lord Diplock see below, p. 290.

[61] See below, p. 294.

[62] See below, p. 290, n. 22, on the possible influence of the statute outside its statutory provisions.

[63] (1924) 34 C.L.R. 38, Cf. *Paul* v. *Wheat Commission* [1937] A.C. 139 (where the restitutionary claim was statute barred).

[64] At pp. 51–52, *per* Isaacs J.

[65] At p. 51, *per* Knox C.J.

[66] At p. 70, *per* Starke J. Cf. *Morton Construction Ltd.* v. *City of Hamilton* (1961) 31 D.L.R. (2d) 323.

[67] § 176, illustration 13. There is some support for this principle in the cases. The Reporter collects the cases in his note, at pp. 489–490.

the contract is voidable by B." Abuse of a long-standing commercial relation-ship may be characterised as an illegitimate or wrongful act.[68]

Whether a threat to do what one is entitled to do is improper depends on the nature of the threat.[69] So, it has been held that a party may properly threaten another that his membership of a trade association will be terminated unless a fine is paid.[70] But some threats to exercise a privilege may amount in law to blackmail[71]; and any criminal threat must be illegitimate for the purpose of the law of restitution.[72] Indeed a threat may not amount in law to blackmail but may nevertheless amount in law to duress because it is made for an illegitimate purpose. In the New Jersey case of *Wolf* v. *Marlton Corporation*,[73] the purchas-ers, having contracted to buy a house, demanded the return of their deposit, accompanying the demand with a threat that otherwise they would resell the property to a "purchaser who would be undesirable in our tract, and that the [vendors] would not be happy with the results." The Superior Court of New Jersey held that the threat amounted in law to duress, in that it involved an abuse of legal remedies, and was also wrongful in a moral sense. The threat was malicious and unconscionable and "fundamental fairness requires the conclu-sion that his conduct in making this threat be deemed 'wrongful'."[74] The doctrine of abuse of rights is not known to the English common law, and the defendant's threat may not be tortious in England.[75] Nevertheless an English court may conclude that such a threat is illegitimate,[76] and that the deposit may be recovered by the vendor.

Conclusions

English courts have recently come to recognise that in certain circumstances commercial pressure may constitute duress. The nature of the threat is critical. A threat of unlawful action is always illegitimate, whatever the nature of the demand.[77] So, a threat to commit a crime or a tort is an illegitimate (or wrongful) threat.

A person puts commercial pressure on another, by threatening not to perform an existing contractual obligation, or by threatening not to enter into a contract with the other person except on certain terms. Whether that threat amounts to duress depends on a number of factors.[78]

---

[68] *Lloyds Bank Ltd.* v. *Bundy* [1975] 1 Q.B. 326, 339, *per* Lord Denning M.R.; see below, p. 290. *Cf.* (1974) 20 McGill L.J. 554, 583 [Sutton].
[69] See above, p. 232 for a fuller discussion.
[70] *Cf. Hardie and Lane Ltd.* v. *Chilton* [1928] 2 K.B. 306; but contrast *Fuerest* v. *Musical Mutual Protective Union*, 95 N.Y.S. 155 (1905).
[71] Theft Act 1968, s.21.
[72] *Cf. Universe Tankships of Monrovia* v. *International Transport Workers' Federation, The Universe Sentinel* [1983] 1 A.C. 366, 401, *per* Lord Scarman.
[73] 154 A.2d 625 (1959).
[74] At p. 630, *per* Freund, J.A.D.
[75] *Cf.* see above, p. 252, n. 76.
[76] See above, pp. 231–232.
[77] *Ibid.*
[78] See above, pp. 250 *et seq.*

(1) A threat which a person knows he is not entitled in law to make, where he refuses to perform his side of a bargain, will normally be characterised as illegitimate.[78a] But whether it is found as a fact to have been a significant cause which induced the threatened person to confer a benefit upon the threatener may depend on a number of factors[79]: for example, the existence of a vigorous protest; the absence of independent advice; the inadequacy of an alternative legal or equitable remedy (whether the threatened person had "no realistic alternative but to submit to the defendant's demands"[80]); the threatener's knowledge of the other party's financial or personal circumstances; the prompt repudiation of the transaction as soon as the pressure of the threat is removed.

As the law now stands it appears that an English court may not be ready to accept as legitimate a threat which was made in the belief that it was commercially reasonable for the threatener to make a new demand (for example, to vary the terms of an existing contract).[81]

(2) A person makes a threat not to perform his side of the bargain, believing that he is entitled in law not to do so. The other party gives in and makes an additional payment because he does not want to contest that honest claim; he cannot then obtain restitution. But a court may hold that a threat is illegitimate even if it is made in the honest belief that the person is entitled to make it. The other party may have given in because of that threat and not because he wished to enter into a compromise; whether it is found *as a fact* that the threat was coercive may depend on the presence of factors such as those outlined in the previous sub-paragraph.

(3) Special problems are presented if the consequence of P's threat not to perform a contract or pay a debt is simply the variation of the terms of an existing contract or debt. If D's promise to confer an additional benefit on P is not supported by fresh consideration, then P will not be able to enforce that promise.[82–83] Even if it is, the contract, as varied, may be voidable because a court may conclude that P's threat not to perform his side of the bargain was illegitimate and wrongful.[84] Whether a court will conclude that the threat was in fact coercive may

---

[78a] Burrows in *The Law of Restitution*, pp. 179–181, argues that it is "hard to tell what motivates a threatening party." But judges frequently make such a judgment, as the case law demonstrates. He invokes what is arguably a more nebulous test, namely bad faith.

[79] See above, p. 251. This catalogue is not, of course, exhaustive.

[80] *Alec Lobb (Garages) Ltd.* v. *Total Oil G.B. Ltd.* [1983] 1 W.L.R. 87, 93, *per* Millett Q.C., Deputy Judge (reversed in part, [1985] 1 All E.R. 944). *Cf. Maskell* v. *Horner* [1915] 3 K.B. 106, 118, *per* Lord Reading C.J., quoted below, p. 269.

[81] See above, pp. 251–252.

[82–83] See above, pp. 260–264. But he may be able to do so if there is no finding that the promisee made an illegitimate threat. See above, p. 261.

[84] See above, pp. 261–262.

depend on the presence of such factors as those outlined in the preceding sub-paragraphs, (a) and (b).

(4) As a general principle, it is legitimate for a person to take advantage of his position of economic strength to force a hard bargain on another. English courts have refused to rewrite contracts between the strong and the weak, although by statute they now have power to do so in certain circumstances.[85] Statutory jurisdiction apart, it has long been recognised that there may be exceptional circumstances where a contract may be set aside because its terms are unconscionable. We discuss this question later in this book.[86] It is sufficient here to emphasise that English courts have wisely not accepted any general principle that a threat not to contract with another, except on certain terms, may amount in law to duress.[87]

3. DURESS AND SUBMISSION TO HONEST CLAIMS

We have already seen[88] that difficult questions may arise in determining whether there has been a compromise when one of the parties, acting bona fide, refuses to do what he is contractually bound to do. This is just one aspect of the general problem which arises when A makes a claim on B, in good faith but in fact without right, and supports his claim with an illegitimate threat. B submits to the claim and pays the money. Can he subsequently recover the money so paid?

The question was considered in *Maskell* v. *Horner*,[89] where the duress was duress of goods. The plaintiff carried on business as a dealer in produce in the neighbourhood of Spitalfields Market. As soon as he started dealing there, the defendant claimed tolls from him. The plaintiff objected on the grounds that he was not in the market, whereupon the defendant threatened to seize his goods and even to force him to close down his business. On one occasion actual seizure of goods took place. The plaintiff then consulted his solicitor; and acting under his advice and discovering that all the other dealers outside the market were paying tolls, he paid the tolls under protest. He continued to pay the tolls, always under protest; indeed the protests were so regular that they became a joke. Whenever there was a dispute, there was a seizure or threatened seizure of the plaintiff's goods.

It later appeared[90] that the tolls were demanded without right, and the plaintiff brought an action to recover such tolls as he had paid during the preceding six years as paid either under a mistake of fact or under pressure of seizure of goods. In the court of first instance, Rowlatt J. dismissed the claim. First, he held that the plaintiff was not mistaken. The plaintiff paid because he

---

[85] See below, Chap. 11.
[86] *Ibid.*
[87] *National Westminster Bank* v. *Morgan* [1985] A.C. 686, H.L.; see below, p. 290.
[88] See above, pp. 258–260.
[89] [1915] 3 K.B. 106.
[90] From the decision in *Att.-Gen.* v. *Horner (No. 2)* [1913] 2 Ch. 140.

did not wish to be involved in litigation and because the other dealers were paying tolls, not because he mistakenly thought that the defendant had a good right to them.[91] Secondly, Rowlatt J. held that the plaintiff could not recover on the ground that the payments were made under pressure of seizure of goods. He said[92]:

"... The protests passing into a standing joke passed out of the sphere of effective protests; they came to indicate a grumbling acquiescence and were not what they must be to satisfy the rule that there must be a declaration that the transaction was not closed but that the payment, which was only made for the relief of a deadlock, was to be reclaimed.... I can only conclude that the transaction was regarded as closed and payments acquiesced in."

On this second point Rowlatt J. was reversed by the Court of Appeal, which held that the plaintiff had not acquiesced in the defendant's claim but had paid the money under pressure of seizure of goods. Lord Reading C.J. delivered the leading judgment. He said[93]:

"If a person with knowledge of the facts pays money, which he is not in law bound to pay, and in circumstances implying that he is paying it voluntarily to close the transaction, he cannot recover it. Such a payment is in law like a gift, and the transaction cannot be reopened. If a person pays money, which he is not bound to pay, under the compulsion of urgent and pressing necessity or of seizure, actual or threatened, of his goods he can recover it as money had and received. The money is paid not under duress in the strict sense of the term, that implies duress of the person, but under the pressure of seizure or detention of goods which is analogous to that of duress.... The payment is made for the purpose of averting a threatened evil and is made not with the intention of giving up a right but under immediate necessity and with the intention of preserving the right to dispute the legality of the demand."

It was into this latter category that the plaintiff's payments were held to fall.

The Court of Appeal, however, recognised that, even if there is duress, a person may submit to a claim which he knows to be unfounded, simply because he cannot be bothered to dispute it; or, as other decisions demonstrate, because he cannot produce the evidence necessary to unmask its falsehood[94] or perhaps because he thinks it commercially realistic to do so.[95] "It is certainly not impossible that the person from whom the sum is so demanded

---

[91] On this point, the Court of Appeal affirmed his decision.
[92] [1915] 3 K.B. 106, 111.
[93] [1915] 3 K.B. 106, 118. Cf. *Woolwich Equitable Building Society* v. *Commissioners of Inland Revenue* [1993] A.C. 70, 128–129, *per* Ralph Gibson L.J., 165–166, *per* Lord Goff.
[94] See, *e.g. Spragg* v. *Hammond* (1820) 2 Brod. & B. 59, 62, *per* Dallas C.J.; *Slater* v. *Burnley Corporation* (1888) 59 L.T. 636.
[95] Cf. *The Siboen and the Sibotre* [1976] 1 Lloyd's Rep. 293: see above, pp. 257–258.

may pay the sum to avoid the inconvenience attendant on disputing the demand and to put an end to the matter."[96]

But this principle should not be carried too far. An extreme case is *Twyford* v. *Manchester Corporation*.[97] The plaintiff, a monumental mason, paid to the defendants, under protest, fees for permission to enter their cemetery and re-cut, re-paint or re-gild inscriptions on monuments. He made these payments over a number of years, and then brought an action to recover them, asserting that the defendants had no statutory authority[98] to make the charges. Romer J. held that, although the defendants were not entitled to charge the fees, the plaintiff could not recover the money he had paid. The defendants had made no threats and the fact that the plaintiff had protested at the time of payment did not assist him. "If he wished to challenge the validity of the registrar's demand, his best course was to refuse to pay and to test the matter by inviting the corporation to sue him."[99]

This decision is, in our view, open to criticism. It is doubtful whether the plaintiff truly submitted to the claim of the Corporation. *Twyford's* case marks a departure from the early cases, which were apparently based on the inequality of the position of the two parties. Thus, in *Steele* v. *Williams*,[1] the plaintiff was entitled to recover his money even though he had not paid until after he had taken the extracts from the parish register. But in *Twyford's* case, where the payments were always made under protest and it was surely probable that if the plaintiff did not pay the corporation would have excluded him from working in the cemetery in future, it is very difficult to see why he should not have been entitled to recover his money as paid under duress. Certainly there is nothing in the earlier cases to show that it is a prerequisite of recovery that the threat must in fact have been made.[2] *Twyford's* case alone stands in the way of the proposition that it is sufficient to ground recovery that the plaintiff should have realised that, if he did not make the payment, he would in all probability be excluded by the defendants from some benefit to which he was entitled without payment of the money demanded.[3]

---

[96] *Deacon* v. *Transport Regulation Board* [1958] V.R. 458, 460, *per* Lowe J.; see also *Mason* v. *The State of New South Wales* (1959) 102 C.L.R. 108, 143, *per* Windeyer J. (quoted below, p. 271; *Woolwich Equitable Building Society* v. *Commissioners of Inland Revenue* [1993] A.C. 70, 98–99, *per* Glidewell L.J.; 165 *per* Lord Goff.

[97] [1946] Ch. 236.

[98] Under the Burial Act 1852.

[99] [1946] Ch. 236, 242.

[1] (1853) 8 Ex. 625, 633, *per* Martin B.: see above, p. 246. See also the remarks of Best J. in *Dew* v. *Parsons* (1819) 2 B. & Ald. 562, 568, which seem to indicate that one idea underlying the early doctrine was that the public officer was in a better position to know the law than the plaintiff. *Cf.* the decision of the Supreme Court of Canada in *Eadie* v. *The Township of Brantford* (1967) 63 D.L.R. (2d) 561, where the treasurer of the municipality was deemed to be under such a duty to the taxpayer. Yet the treasurer acted in good faith since he was entitled to make the demand.

[2] See above, p. 246, n. 30 and p. 271, n. 7; and *cf.* the cases on economic duress, see above. pp. 250 *et seq.*

[3] *Liverpool Corp.* v. *Arthur Maiden Ltd.* [1938] 4 All E.R. 200, 207, *per* Croom-Johnson J.: [1980] C.L.P. 191, 193 [Birks] But *cf.* [1974] C.L.J. 96, 111–112 [Beatson].

The Court of Appeal's decision in *Maskell* v. *Horner* presents a further problem. If a person submits, even under protest, to claims repeated at frequent intervals and accompanied by duress, and does not take the opportunity in the meanwhile to contest the claimant's right in the courts, should he later be precluded from recovering the money he has paid? It seems to follow from the decision of the Court of Appeal[4] in *Maskell* v. *Horner* that recovery is not denied in these circumstances. Each case must, however, be viewed on its own facts. Indeed, on the facts of *Maskell* v. *Horner* itself, there is much to be said for the view that, in this sense, the plaintiff had submitted to the defendant's claim. In the words of Rowlatt J.[5]: "This has been left to sleep for twelve years. . . . The plaintiff did not want to challenge the defendant's right, though he was ready enough to claim his money back when someone else had shown that the money was wrongly claimed."

A plaintiff who sits on his rights for 12 years is surely guilty of a quite unnecessary delay, and his conduct may be regarded as evidence of acquiescence in the claim.

In some of the old cases the fact that the plaintiff has protested at the time of his payment is stressed by the court as though it were a necessary and integral part of the plaintiff's case.[6] But, as was pointed out in *Maskell* v. *Horner*,[7] a protest is simply "some evidence, when accompanied by other circumstances, that the payment was not voluntarily made to end the matter." In the High Court of Australia, Windeyer J. has affirmed that:

> "there is no magic in a protest; for a protest may accompany a voluntary payment or be absent from one compelled. . . . Moreover the word 'protest' is itself equivocal. It may mean the serious assertion of a right or it may mean no more than a statement that payment is grudgingly made."[8]

The situation may be such that protest would obviously be fruitless; if so, the absence of a protest should be irrelevant. So, in *Universe Tankships Inc. of Monrovia* v. *International Transport Workers' Federation; The Universe Sentinel*,[9] the House of Lords held that a shipowner could recover a sum paid to the respondents' Welfare Fund in consequence of a threat to black a ship. They

---

[4] See particularly [1915] 3 K.B. 106, 125, *per* Buckley L.J.

[5] [1915] 3 K.B. 106, 111–112.

[6] *Pratt* v. *Vizard* (1833) 5 B. & Ad. 808, 812, *per* Parke J.; *Valpy* v. *Manley* (1845) 1 C.B. 594, 603, *per* Tindal C.J.

[7] [1915] 3 K.B. 106, 120, *per* Lord Reading C.J., see also 124–125, *per* Buckley L.J.; *Pao On* v. *Lau Yiu Long* [1980] A.C. 614, 635, *per* Lord Scarman; but *cf.* text accompanying n. 11, below. There was apparently no protest in *Astley* v. *Reynolds* (1731) 2 Str. 915 or *Irving* v. *Wilson* (1791) 4 T.R. 485: see also *The Siboen and the Sibotre* [1976] 1 Lloyd's Rep. 293.

[8] *Mason* v. *The State of New South Wales* (1959) 102 C.L.R. 108, 143: see also *Brocklebank Ltd.* v. *R.* [1925] 1 K.B. 52, 62, *per* Bankes L.J.; *Knutson* v. *The Bourkes Syndicate* [1941] S.C.R. 419.

[9] [1983] A.C. 366; see above, p. 253.

did not protest but paid because it was "a matter of the most urgent commercial necessity"[10] that they should regain the use of the vessel.[11]

4. THE EFFECT ON RECOVERY OF AN ALTERNATIVE REMEDY

In many of the old books it is said that the threatened harm must be such that a person of ordinary courage would yield to it.[12] But this requirement, which suggests an objective assessment of duress,[13] has most probably been abandoned. The modern view of duress is that a transaction will be set aside when one party capitulates because of illegitimate pressure.[14]

In the past there have been suggestions that a person has no right to avoid a contract or recover money paid under duress where he had an adequate legal remedy to recover compensation for the threatened harm.[15] Such a rule can only be justified on the ground that a person of reasonable courage would not be coerced by such duress.[16] This justification is hardly tenable, and indeed there is doubt whether the rule exists. In some, but not all, of the cases on duress, it is accepted that the mere existence of a remedy at law for compensation would not give adequate protection to the person under pressure. Thus, in *Astley* v. *Reynolds*,[17] recovery was allowed of money paid under duress of goods even though the plaintiff could, instead of paying the money, have brought an action of trover, because "the plaintiff might have such an immediate want of his goods, that an action of trover would not do his business."[18] Indeed the delay, expense and uncertainty of legal process would prevent practically any legal remedy from being called adequate in this context. In any case, as Williston has pointed out, "so far as it would require a person threatened with injury necessarily to endure the injury because the law provides a remedy for it, [the rule] cannot be accepted."[19]

In the law of distress, in particular, statements are to be found in the old cases to the effect that where the plaintiff has a remedy at law he cannot pay the

---

[10] [1981] I.C.R. 129, 143, *per* Parker J.

[11] See particularly on this point Lord Scarman, who was dissenting, at p. 400. *Cf. Dimskal Shipping Co. S.A.* v. *International Transport Workers' Federation, The Evia Luck* [1992] 2 A.C. 152, H.L.: see below, pp. 730–731.

[12] *Bracton,* 48.21.1; Co.2 Inst. 483; 1 Bl. Comm. 131.

[13] *Skeate* v. *Beale* (1841) 11 A. & E. 983, 990, *per* Lord Denman C.J.

[14] *Scott* v. *Sebright* (1886) 12 P.D. 21, 24, *per* Butt J.; *Kaufman* v. *Gerson* [1903] 2 K.B. 114, 119, *per* Wright J.; [1904] 1 K.B. 591, 597, *per* Collins M.R.; *H.* v. *H.* [1954] P. 258, 266, *per* Karminski J.; *The Siboen and The Sibotre* [1976] 1 Lloyd's Rep. 296, 336, *per* Kerr J. See also *Astley* v. *Reynolds* (1731) 2 Str. 915, 916, *per curiam*: "where the rule *volenti non fit injuria* is applied, it must be where the party had his freedom of exercising his will. . . ."

[15] See 2 Co. Inst. 483; 1 Bl.Comm. 131; *Ashmole* v. *Wainwright* (1842) 2 Q.B. 837, 845, *per* Lord Denman. This rule was used by older writers to justify the distinction between duress of person and duress of goods in relation to setting aside contracts (see above, pp. 239 and 241).

[16] See *Williston on Contracts,* § 1620.

[17] (1731) 2 Str. 915: see above, p. 239.

[18] At p. 916; see also *Close* v. *Phipps* (1844) 7 Man. & G. 586, 590, *per* Tindal C.J.

[19] *Williston on Contracts,* § 1620.

money and afterwards recover it in an action for money had and received.[20] There is considerable doubt, however, whether these cases can now be said to represent the law.[21] The principal objection to allowing an action for money had and received was that the defendant "might be surprised at the trial . . . ; he could not tell what sort of right of common or other justification the plaintiff might set up."[22] But this objection applies equally in other cases where the action is allowed, and it can be met today by the defendant's right to apply for particulars of the plaintiff's claim. Moreover, the mere existence of a remedy which will enable the plaintiff to claim compensation for the threatened wrong will not normally affect his right to bring an action for money had and received.[23] It is true that, in these cases, replevin may be available and that it is a more summary remedy than many others. Nevertheless, it still suffers from sufficient doubts and delays to make it more efficacious for the plaintiff to recover his goods by the simple expedient of payment and reservation of rights, seeking later to recover the money in an action at law. In our view, the action for money had and received should be available in these cases; and the later authorities support this view.[24]

The central question is whether a particular threat coerced a person to act as he did; for example, to agree to vary the terms of a contract or to make a payment.[25] As has just been seen, when an owner's goods are seized, there appears to be an almost irrebuttable presumption that "the owner can only release them from seizure by payment,"[26] and that it was this illegitimate seizure which compelled him to pay. But if the duress takes other forms no such presumption can seemingly be made. In recent years, whether a plaintiff had or had not an adequate legal remedy has been said to be a relevant factor in determining whether the pressure was illegitimate and coercive, amounting to economic duress.[27] So in *North Ocean Shipping Co. Ltd.* v. *Hyundai Construction Co. Ltd.*,[28] Mocatta J., in determining whether the shipowners acted under compulsion, concluded that it would be "unreasonable" to hold that they

---

[20] *Lindon* v. *Hooper* (1776) 1 Cowp. 414, 418, *per* Lord Mansfield; *Anscomb* v. *Shore* (1808) 1 Camp. 285; *Gulliver* v. *Cosens* (1845) 1 C.B. 788. *Cf. Hills* v. *Street* (1828) 5 Bing. 37; and see G. L. Williams, *Animals*, pp. 115–118. A similar rule was laid down in old cases on distress of rent: see *Knibbs* v. *Hall* (1794) 1 Esp. 84; *Glynn* v. *Thomas* (1856) 11 Ex. 870.

[21] See Bullen, *Distress* (2nd ed.), pp. 223–224.

[22] *Lindon* v. *Hooper* (1776) 1 Cowp. 414, 418, *per* Lord Mansfield.

[23] An action in restitution is frequently alternative to an action in tort or in contract: see above, Chap. 38.

[24] *Loring* v. *Warburton* (1858) El.B. & El. 507; *Green* v. *Duckett* (1883) 11 Q.B.D. 275, 279, *per* Denman J.; *Maskell* v. *Horner* [1915] 3 K.B. 106, 122, *per* Lord Reading C.J. See generally (1944) 60 L.Q.R. 344 [Winfield].

[25] See above, pp. 234 and 253 *et seq.*

[26] *Maskell* v. *Horner* [1915] 3 K.B. 106, 122, *per* Lord Reading C.J.

[27] *The Siboen and the Sibotre* [1976] 1 Lloyd's Rep. 293, see above. p. 257, *Pao On* v. *Lau Yiu Long* [1980] A.C. 614, 635: see above, p. 263; *Universe Tankships Inc. of Monrovia* v. *International Transport Workers' Federation, The Universe Sentinal,* [1983] 1 A.C. 366, 400, *per* Lord Scarman: see above, p. 252; *"The Alev"* [1989] 1 Lloyd's Rep. 138, 146–147, *per* Hobhouse J. *Cf. Dimskal Shipping Co.S.A.* v. *International Transport Workers' Federation, The Evia Luck* [1992] 2 A.C. 152.

[28] [1979] Q.B. 705, 719; see above, p. 256.

should have claimed damages against the defendant shipyard,[29] given the existence of their profitable time-charter with Shell. And in *Universal Tankships Inc. of Monrovia* v. *International Transport Workers' Federation, The Universe Sentinel*[30] the plaintiffs had been advised that their prospects of obtaining an injunction to prevent the blacking of their ship were minimal. Conversely, if a person did have an adequate alternative remedy but nonetheless did not invoke it, this will provide some evidence that he gave in not because of the illegitimate pressure which was imposed on him but for other reasons.[31]

5. FAILURE TO TENDER AMENDS

It may be a bar to recovery that the plaintiff did not at the time make a proper tender of amends (in the case of distress damage feasant) or of arrears (in the case of distress for rent). Such a question cannot arise where the distress is wrongful,[32] but only where the distrainor is demanding an excessive amount. The effect of a proper tender of amends or arrears, if made before impounding, is to render it illegal to proceed any further with the distress; and in the case of distress for rent, if the tender is made before the distress, the distress itself is illegal. But to ground recovery it should not be necessary to show that the distress is illegal; it should be enough that money not due has been paid under duress of goods. A proper tender of amends or arrears should, therefore, be irrelevant, at least in those cases where the excess extorted by the defendant was so great that clearly a tender of the proper amount would have been ineffective. But in *Gulliver* v. *Cosens*[33] it was said that a proper tender of amends was necessary as "the risk of determining the real amount of damage is not by law imposed upon the defendant."[34] More recently the question was incidentally considered in *Sorrell* v. *Paget.*[35] The defendant had impounded a heifer in his barn. The plaintiff's servant claimed the heifer but made no tender, and the defendant refused to deliver it up. The plaintiff then brought an action in conversion and detinue. The Court of Appeal held, following the earlier authorities, that it made no difference in principle that the demand of the defendant for "salvage" and keep was excessive.[36] Until the plaintiff tendered the money, whatever the nature of the defendant's demands, the

---

[29] Citing *Astley* v. *Reynolds* (1731) 2 Str. 915; see above, p. 289.

[30] See the judgment of the trial judge, Parker J., in [1981] I.C.R. 129, 143: *cf.* see above, p. 254, n. 86.

[31] The duress may be *one* of the reasons why he succumbed. In that case it will, nevertheless, be open to the court to find that he acted under duress: *cf. Barton* v. *Armstrong* [1976] A.C. 104; see above, p. 234.

[32] *Fell* v. *Whittaker* (1871) L.R. 7 Q.B. 120.

[33] (1845) 1 C.B. 788.

[34] At p. 796, *per* Tindal C.J.; *Glynn* v. *Thomas* (1856) 11 Ex. 870, 878, *per* Coleridge J. But *cf. Loring* v. *Warburton* (1858) El.B. & El. 507.

[35] [1950] 1 K.B. 252.

[36] The court held it to be immaterial that the defendant was not entitled to "salvage."

detention was lawful.[37] In *Sorrell* v. *Paget* there was no claim in quasi-contract, for the plaintiff had made no repayment. But Cohen L.J. made this comment:

> "Had the plaintiff paid the amount demanded and sought to recover it as money had and received, the fact that there was an excessive demand in quality might have afforded a ground, notwithstanding the decision in *Gulliver* v. *Cosens*, on which he would have been entitled to recover the amount paid as money had and received."[38]

In our view, for reasons already stated, money paid under duress[39] should be recoverable though no tender of amends has been made. In any event it is clear that no tender is necessary if the defendant is the only person who could know the proper charge.[40]

6. PROPRIETARY CLAIMS

There is no authority on the question whether a person who pays money or confers some other benefit under duress has, in addition to a personal claim, a restitutionary proprietary claim. In our view the courts should grant the coerced person such a claim and should not be inhibited from doing so by the absence of any fiduciary relationship.[41] Subject to the general principles discussed in Chapter 2 of this text, it would not normally be just to allow, on an insolvency, the general creditors of the person exercising duress to share in the fund, obtained by their debtor, as a result of the debtor's illegitimate pressure exercised on the claimant. As the law now stands, a court will deem the equitable title[42] to remain in the plaintiff.

---

[37] Provided, of course, the original taking was lawful.

[38] [1950] 1 K.B. 252, 264. He then quoted G. L. Williams, *Animals*, p. 116, to the effect that an action for money had and received might lie, and added: "but there is nothing to suggest that *in so far* as the case laid down that the onus of making a proper tender was on the plaintiff, it was not still the law" (italics supplied). Bucknill L.J. did not deal with this point. Asquith L.J. seems to have regarded *Gulliver* v. *Cosens* as authority for the wider view that a tender was necessary even in an action for money had and received, although he admitted that the rule was "harsh, and, it may be, unreasonable" (at pp. 265–266).

[39] See *Green* v. *Duckett* (1883) 11 Q.B.D. 275, 279, *per* Denman J.; *Campbell* v. *Halverson* (1919) 49 D.L.R. 463; *McCrae* v. *Lyons* [1921] 2 W.W.R. 490 (Sask.), *Jolin* v. *White* (1922) 65 D.L.R. 643; G. L. Williams, *Animals*, pp. 114–117.

[40] *Ashmole* v. *Wainwright* (1842) 2 Q.B. 837.

[41] See above, Chap. 2.

[42] *Cf. Chase Manhatten Bank N.A. Ltd.* v. *Israel-British Bank (London) Ltd.* [1981] Ch. 105: see below, p. 130.

CHAPTER 10

RECOVERY OF BENEFITS CONFERRED UNDER UNDUE INFLUENCE

1. GENERAL PRINCIPLES

THE Court of Chancery had always been conscious that the common law conception of duress was so limited that substantial injustice could result. A person could be imposed upon and influenced by subtle methods which lay outside the scope of duress.[1] For example, he could be persuaded by one standing in an intimate relationship with him to pursue a course of conduct to his detriment and to the other's advantage. The Chancellor, therefore, formulated the equitable doctrine of "undue influence," whereby transactions could be set aside in equity and money paid or property transferred thereunder recovered. The credit for its formulation is usually given to Lord Hardwicke,[2] but it is possible that its origins are older.[3]

Undue influence is an expression of "ambiguous purport."[4] Probate as well as Chancery judges have frequently used it, but identity of language conceals here a diversity of meaning. The probate doctrine is distinct from equity's, and more circumscribed.[5] In probate law, the undue influence must "amount to force and coercion destroying free agency—it must not be the influence of affection and attachment—it must not be the mere desire of gratifying the wishes of another; for that would be a very strong ground in support of a testamentary act."[6] The equitable doctrine, which is limited to the setting aside of transactions *inter vivos*, was created, as Lindley L.J. said in *Allcard* v. *Skinner*,[7] "to protect people from being forced, tricked or misled in any way by others into parting with their property." In the same case, Cotton L.J. concluded that Chancery judges had distinguished between two distinct classes of influence[8]:

---

[1] *Cf. Restatement of Restitution*, § 70.

[2] In *Morris* v. *Burroughs* (1737) 1 Atk. 398.

[3] *Blunden & Hester* v. *Barker* (1720) 1 P.Wms. 634, 639–640, *per* Lord Macclesfield; see Ashburner, *Principles of Equity*, pp. 303–305.

[4] *Bullock* v. *Lloyds Bank* [1955] Ch. 317, 324, *per* Vaisey J.

[5] *Boyse* v. *Rossborough* (1857) 6 H.L.C. 2, 48–49; *Hindson* v. *Weatherill* (1854) 5 De G.M. & G. 301; *Parfitt* v. *Lawless* (1872) L.R. 2 P. & D. 462; *Baudains* v. *Richardson* [1906] A.C. 169.

[6] *Williams* v. *Goude* (1828) 1 Hag.Ecc. 577, 581, *per* Sir John Nicholl. *Cf.* (1939–1940) 3 M.L.R. 97 [Winder]; and see *Wintle* v. *Nye* [1959] 1 W.L.R. 284, 291, *per* Viscount Simonds, 295–296, *per* Lord Reid.

[7] (1887) 36 Ch.D. 145, 183.

[8] At p. 171.

276

"First, where the court has been satisfied that the gift was the result of influence expressly used by the donee for the purpose; second, where the relations between the donor and donee have at or shortly before the execution of the gift been such as to raise a presumption that the donee had influence over the donor. In such a case the court sets aside the voluntary gift, unless it is proved that in fact the gift was the spontaneous act of the donor acting under circumstances which enabled him to exercise an independent will and which justifies the court in holding that the gift was the result of a free exercise of the donor's will. The first class of cases may be considered as depending on the principle that no one shall be allowed to retain any benefit arising from his own fraud or wrongful act. In the second class of cases, the court interferes, not on the ground that any wrongful act has in fact been committed by the donee, but on the ground of public policy, and to prevent the relations which existed between the parties and the influence arising therefrom being abused."

We shall now consider these two categories of cases in which equity may give relief. They are not, however, mutually exclusive[9]; in a particular case there may be a presumption of undue influence as well as undue influence in fact.[10]

(a) *Where a Relationship between the Parties Gives Rise to a Presumption of Undue Influence*

The advantages of bringing one's case within Cotton L.J.'s second class are clear from his statement of the law. Once the presumption is raised, the onus of proof is on the other party to show that the transferor acted with an independent mind and will. If the presumption is not rebutted, the transaction is set aside even though there is no actual proof of undue influence. The "underlying purpose of the courts of equity, in raising a presumption of undue influence in certain cases, is to prevent victimisation by influence over the mind of another in circumstances where proof of the exercise of such influence may be impossible, and that they do so by requiring proof of the removal of that influence."[11]

The courts have always been "careful not to fetter this useful jurisdiction by defining the exact limits of its exercise."[12] The Court of Appeal held, in *Re Coomber*,[13] that it is not every confidential relationship between settlor and recipient which gives rise to the presumption against the validity of the transaction, but the Court provided little guidance for identifying the relationships to which the presumption applies. Fletcher Moulton L.J. was content to say that "the nature of the fiduciary relation must be such that it justifies the

---

[9] *Morley* v. *Loughnan* [1893] 1 Ch. 736; *Lancashire Loans Ltd.* v. *Black* [1934] 1 K.B. 380.
[10] *Re Craig* [1971] Ch. 95.
[11] *Re Craig* [1971] Ch. 95, 104, *per* Ungoed-Thomas J.
[12] *Tate* v. *Williamson* (1886) 2 Ch.App. 55, 61, *per* Lord Chelmsford; *Lloyds Bank* v. *Bundy* [1975] 1 Q.B. 326, 342, *per* Sir Eric Sachs.
[13] [1911] 1 Ch. 723, 726–727, *per* Cozens-Hardy M.R.

interference."[14] In *National Westminster Bank plc* v. *Morgan*,[15] Lord Scarman concluded that the presumption arises if one person exercised a "dominating influence" over another. Subsequently Nourse L.J. went further and suggested that the principle is that:

> "the degree of trust and confidence is such that the party in whom it is reposed, either because he is or has become an adviser of the other or because he has been entrusted with the management of his affairs or every-day needs or for some other reason, is in a position to influence him into effecting the transaction of which complaint is later made."[16]

It is not necessary for one to *dominate* the other, "in any sense in which that word is generally understood."[17]

The cases indicate that the courts may presume that undue influence was exercised by a parent over a minor child[18]; (possibly) by a parent over a very ill adult child[19]; by a well-educated adult child over less well-educated and elderly parents[20]; but no longer by a husband over his wife,[21] although that relationship "has never been divested completely of what may be called equitable presumptions of an invalidating tendency"[21a]; by a solicitor over his client[22]; by a doctor over his patient[23]; by spiritual advisers over their followers[24]; by a

---

[14] At p. 729, cited and applied in *Re Craig* [1971] Ch. 95, 103. See also *Re Brocklehurst's Estate* [1978] Ch. 14.

[15] [1985] A.C. 686, 707 (with the added condition that the transaction must be to the manifest disadvantage of the other: see below, p. 279).

[16] *Goldsworthy* v. *Brickell* [1987] Ch. 378, 401, *per* Nourse L.J.

[17] *Ibid.* at p. 401 and cases there cited. *Cf. Lloyds Bank* v. *Bundy* [1975] 1 Q.B. 326, 341, *per* Sir Eric Sachs.

[18] *Archer* v. *Hudson* (1844) 7 Beav. 551; *Wright* v. *Vanderplank* (1855) 2 K. & J. 1; *Bainbrigge* v. *Browne* (1881) 18 Ch.D. 188; *Berdoe* v. *Dawson* (1865) 34 Beav. 603; *Re Pauling's Settlement Trusts* [1964] Ch. 303, 336, *per curiam*; *cf. Dimsdale* v. *Dimsdale* (1856) 3 Dr. 556.

[19] *Cf. Re T* (Refusal of Treatment), [1992] 3 W.L.R. 782 (C.A.).

[20] *Cf. Avon Finance Co. Ltd.* v. *Bridger* (1979) [1985] 2 All E.R. 281; *Coldunell Ltd.* v. *Gallon* [1986] 2 W.L.R. 466, C.A.

[21] *Howes* v. *Bishop* [1909] 2 K.B. 390; *Bank of Montreal* v. *Stuart* [1911] A.C. 120, 137, *per* Lord Macnaghten (P.C.); *National Westminster Bank* v. *Morgan* [1985] A.C. 686, 703, *per* Lord Scarman; *Kings North Trust Ltd.* v. *Bell* [1986] 1 W.L.R. 119, 123, *per* Dillon L.J.; *Midland Bank* v. *Shephard* [1988] 3 All E.R. 17, 21, *per* Neill L.J.; contrast pp. 284–286. And *cf.* below p. 285.

[21a] *Yerkey* v. *Jones* (1939) 63 C.L.R. 649, 675, *per* Dixon J., cited with approval in *Barclays Bank plc* v. *O'Brien* [1992] 4 All E.R. 983, 996, *per* Scott L.J. See below, p. 285.

[22] *Tomson* v. *Judge* (1855) 3 Dr. 306; *Wright* v. *Carter* [1903] 1 Ch. 27; *cf. Welles* v. *Middleton* (1784) 1 Cox 112; L. A. Sheridan, *Fraud in Equity*, pp. 90–92. For gifts to solicitors in wills, see *Hindson* v. *Weatherill* (1854) 5 De G.M. & G. 301; *Wintle* v. *Nye* [1959] 1 W.L.R. 284.

[23] *Ahearne* v. *Hogan* (1844) Dr.t.Sug. 310; *cf. Re Craig* [1971] Ch. 95; *Nelson* v. *Dodge*, 68 A.2d 51 (1949).

[24] *Huguenin* v. *Baseley* (1807) 14 Ves. 273; *Lyon* v. *Home* (1868) L.R. 6 Eq. 655; *Allcard* v. *Skinner* (1887) 36 Ch.D. 145. *Cf. Roche* v. *Sherrington* [1982] 2 All E.R. 426 (arguably even if the defendant is an unincorporated association). In *Slovchenko* v. *Toronto-Dominion Bank and Mereshko* (1963) 42 D.L.R. (2d) 484, the Ontario High Court held that, in such a case, the presumption only applies to *inter vivos*, and not to death-bed, gifts.

trustee over the beneficiary[25]; by guardians over wards[26]; by a step-parent over a step-child[27]; by a manager over a young and inexperienced entertainer.[28]

But a presumption of undue influence may arise between other persons. While it is wrong to work backwards from an unconscionable bargain and to conclude from its terms that there existed a sufficient fiduciary relationship,[29] it is open to the parties to prove the existence of such a relationship in any particular case.[30] The courts have, in the past,[31] found such a relationship to exist between a secretary companion and her elderly employer[32]; a lodger and his old landlady[33]; an employer's insurers and an employee[34]; (exceptionally) even a bank manager and customer[35]; and a publishing house and a young entertainer.[36]

The presumption is perfected only if two conditions are satisfied. First, the complaining party must show that the transaction is "wrongful", in the sense that the victim must be "victimised" and "forced, tricked or misled in any way by others into parting with their property."[37] Secondly, the transaction must be to the manifest disadvantage of the person influenced and is explicable only on the basis that undue influence has been exercised to procure it.[38] Whether a transaction is manifestly disadvantageous "must depend on the balance of two factors, namely, (a) the seriousness of the risk of enforcement to the giver, in practical terms; and (b) the benefits gained by the giver in accepting the risk."[39] A "disadvantage would be a manifest disadvantage if it would be obvious as such to any independent and reasonable persons who considered the

---

[25] *Plowright* v. *Lambert* (1885) 52 L.T. 646; but see (1940) 4 *Conveyancer* (N.S.) 274, 287–288 [Winder], on the question whether the presumption applies to gifts as distinct from purchases.
[26] *Hylton* v. *Hylton* (1754) 2 Ves.Sen. 547; *Hatch* v. *Hatch* (1804) 9 Ves. 292.
[27] *Powell* v. *Powell* [1900] 1 Ch. 243.
[28] *O'Sullivan* v. *Management Agency and Music Ltd.* [1985] Q.B. 428, see below, p. 284, n. 79.
[29] *Tufton* v. *Sperni* [1952] 2 T.L.R. 516, 530, *per* Jenkins L.J.
[30] *Morley* v. *Loughnan* [1893] 1 Ch. 736; *Tufton* v. *Sperni* [1952] 2 T.L.R. 516; *Antony* v. *Weerasekera* [1953] 1 W.L.R. 1007. *Re Craig* [1971] Ch. 95, 104–105, *per* Ungoed-Thomas L.J.; *Lloyds Bank* v. *Bundy* [1975] 1 Q.B. 326, 341, *per* Sir Eric Sachs: *Re Brocklehurst's Estate* [1978] Ch. 14, 41–42, *per* Bridge L.J.
[31] But a court may be reluctant to follow uncritically earlier authorities. So, in *Zamet* v. *Hyman* [1961] 1 W.L.R. 1442, 1445–1446, Lord Evershed M.R., concluded that given the position of women in modern society, the court may infer a fiduciary relationship not only "in the man towards the woman but in the woman towards the man"; but see above, n. 21a.
[32] *Re Craig* [1971] Ch. 95.
[33] *Hodgson* v. *Marks* [1971] Ch. 892, 906, *per* Ungoed-Thomas J., 929, *per curiam*, C.A.
[34] *Horry* v. *Tate and Lyle Refineries Ltd.* [1982] 2 Lloyds Rep. 416 [release set aside].
[35] *National Westminster Bank* v. *Morgan* [1985] A.C. 686, 707, H.L., commenting on *Lloyds Bank* v. *Bundy* [1975] 1 Q.B. 326. See also *Cornish* v. *Midland Bank p.l.c.* [1985] 3 All E.R. 513.
[36] *O'Sullivan* v. *Management Agency and Music Ltd.* [1985] Q.B. 428; see below, p. 284.
[37] *National Westminster Bank* v. *Morgan* [1985] A.C. 686, 705, *per* Lord Scarman, citing *Allcard* v. *Skinner* (1887) 36 Ch.D. 145 at pp. 182–183, *per* Lindley L.J.
[38] *National Westminster Bank* v. *Morgan* [1985] A.C. 686. Contrast *Geffen* v. *Goodman Estate* [1991] 2 S.C.R. 353.
[39] *Bank of Credit and Commerce International S.A.* v. *Aboody* [1990] 1 Q.B. 923, 965, *per curiam*. (In this case there was no presumption of undue influence, which was proved as a fact: see below, p. 282).

transaction at the time with knowledge of all the relevant facts."[40] It is surprising that the courts should insist on the transaction being for the manifest disadvantage of the party influenced. Certainly, no such condition is imposed on a party who seeks to recover a benefit, or set aside a transaction, for duress or misrepresentation. In principle, once undue influence is presumed or found to exist, the transaction should, subject to defences, be set aside.[41]

Once the presumption is perfected, the onus of proof is on the other party to show that the grantor or donor exercised an independent will which justifies "the court in holding that the gift or transaction was the result of a free exercise of his will."[42] For example, the fact that the gift was small[43] may persuade the court that it was intended to be an act of bounty. Conversely, "if the gift is so large as not to be reasonably accounted for on the ground of friendship, relationship, charity or other ordinary motives on which ordinary men act, the burden is upon the donee to support the gift."[44]

The fact that the recipient has not had independent advice to enable him to form an independent and informed judgment[45] is an important[46] factor in determining whether undue influence existed, and in many circumstances it is a prudent course that the other party should strongly recommend that it be sought.[47] In the case of a gift "the rule applied by the Court of Equity may be more stringent, is more absolute, than the rule that is applied in the case of a bargain or a contract."[48] In *Wright* v. *Carter*, Vaughan Williams L.J. was not prepared to lay down that, in every case of purchase, competent independent advice is necessary as distinguished from the advice of the purchasing solicitor. "It may be," he continued, "that a particular transaction of purchase appears to be so manifestly fair that independent advice is not necessary."[49] If the client was fully informed, and the transaction was in all respects fair and proper, that may be enough.[50]

In contrast, gifts are scrutinised much more carefully to see if the donor's intention to give was freely formed. In *Re Coomber*,[51] Fletcher Moulton L.J.

---

[40] *Ibid.* citing the trial judge. See also at pp. 960–961.

[41] *Goldsworthy* v. *Brickell* [1987] Ch. 378, 401, *per* Nourse L.J.

[42] See below, p. 282.

[43] *Allcard* v. *Skinner* (1887) 36 Ch.D. 145, 185, *per* Lindley L.J.; see also *Rhodes* v. *Bate* (1866) L.R. 1 Ch. 252.

[44] *Allcard* v. *Skinner* (1887) 36 Ch.D. 145, 185, *per* Lindley L.J.

[45] *Re Coomber* [1911] 1 Ch. 723; *Zamet* v. *Hyman* [1961] 1 W.L.R. 1442, 1446, *per* Lord Evershed M.R.; *Lloyds Bank* v. *Bundy* [1975] 1 Q.B. 326, 342, *per* Sir Eric Sachs.

[46] *Re Brocklehurst's Estate* [1978] Ch. 14.

[47] *National Westminster Bank* v. *Morgan* [1983] 3 All E.R. 85, 93, *per* Slade L.J. (The decision was reversed in [1985] A.C. 686; but this dictum was not questioned.); *Kings North Trust Ltd.* v. *Bell* [1986] 1 W.L.R. 119, 123–125, *per* Dillon L.J.; *Coldunell Ltd.* v. *Gallon* [1986] Q.B. 1184, 1199–1200, *per* Oliver L.J. see below, p. 285.

[48] *Wright* v. *Carter* [1903] 1 Ch. 27, 50, *per* Vaughan Williams L.J.; see also *Kingsland* v. *Barnewall* (1706) 4 Bro.P.C. 154; *Hunter* v. *Atkins* (1834) 3 My. & K. 113; *Pisani* v. *Att.-Gen. for Gibraltar* (1874) L.R. 5 P.C. 516.

[49] [1903] 1 Ch. 27, 54–55.

[50] *Cf. Coldunell Ltd.* v. *Gallon* [1986] Q.B. 1184. See below, p. 285.

[51] [1911] 1 Ch. 723, 727–730.

thought the donor should be advised as to the nature and consequence of his act by an independent person; but it is not essential to prove either that the advice was given by a lawyer or that it was taken. It is enough, said Lord Hailsham in *Inche Noriah* v. *Shaik Allie Bin Omar*,[52] that the

> "gift was the result of the free exercise of independent will. The most obvious way to prove this is by establishing that the gift was made after the nature and effect of the transaction had been fully explained to the donor by some independent and qualified person so completely as to satisfy the court that the donor was acting independently of any influence from the donee and with the full appreciation of what he was doing."

In that case the Privy Council was not prepared[53] to accept the decision of Farwell J. in *Powell* v. *Powell*,[54] in which he held that independent advice is not sufficient unless acted upon. *Powell* v. *Powell* appears to be an anomalous exception, whose authority should, at best, be confined to cases involving young persons, minors or those who have just attained their majority.[55] Equity has always been peculiarly concerned to protect their interests, as can be seen from the more recent case of *Bullock* v. *Lloyds Bank Ltd*.[56] There the plaintiff, on coming of age, was persuaded by her father to settle property on certain trusts, which were peculiar in that they gave her no general power of appointment and prevented her dealing with the capital. She received no advice other than from her father and his solicitor. Vaisey J. set aside the settlement, even though he accepted that the father's motives were to benefit his daughter. But such settlements will be upheld,

> "if executed under the advice of a competent adviser capable of surveying the whole field with an absolutely independent outlook, and who explains to the intending settlor, first, that she could do exactly as she pleased, and secondly, that the scheme put before her was not one to be accepted or rejected out of hand but to be discussed, point by point, with a full understanding of the various alternative possibilities."[57]

(b) *Where There is no Special Relationship*

In the absence of a sufficient fiduciary relationship,[58] undue influence must be

---

[52] [1929] A.C. 127, 135; applied in *Re Brocklehurst's Estate* [1978] Ch. 14. See also *Antony* v. *Weerasekera* [1953] 1 W.L.R. 1007, 1011, *per* L. M. de Silva (P.C.); *Armstrong* v. *Armstrong* (1873) I.R. 8 Eq. 1; *cf. National Westminster Bank* v. *Morgan* [1983] 3 All E.R. 85, 93, *per* Slade L.J. (see n. 47, above).

[53] [1929] A.C. 127, 134–135.

[54] [1900] 1 Ch. 243, 245–246; *cf. Howes* v. *Bishop* [1909] 2 K.B. 390, C.A.

[55] *Cf. Lancashire Loans Ltd*. v. *Black* [1934] 1 K.B. 380, 404, *per* Scrutton L.J., who described this case as the "high water mark."

[56] [1955] Ch. 317.

[57] *Ibid.* 326; see below, Chap. 11, for unconscionable bargains.

[58] Common lawyers are inclined "to rely more on individual proof than on general presumption": see *Lancashire Loans Ltd*. v. *Black* [1934] 1 K.B. 380, 404, *per* Scrutton L.J.; *cf. Zamet* v. *Hyman* [1961] 1 W.L.R. 1442, 1452, *per* Donovan L.J.

proved to exist,[59] and the burden of proof is on the complaining party to show the existence of the influence.[60] In the view of the Court of Appeal in *BCCI* v. *Aboody*[61]:

> "Leaving aside proof of manifest disadvantage, we think that a person relying on a plea of actual undue influence must show that: (a) the other party to the transaction (or someone who induced the transaction for his own benefit) had the capacity to influence the complainant; (b) the influence was exercised; (c) its exercise was undue; (d) its exercise brought about the transaction."

If, on the balance of probabilities, the party influenced would have entered into the transaction in any event, it will not be set aside.[62] There are dicta which suggest that the burden of proving undue influence is less heavy if the recipient is a donee and not a purchaser for value.[63]

In *BCCI* v. *Aboody*[64] the Court of Appeal held that even if it can be demonstrated that there had been actual undue influence, nevertheless the transaction would only be set aside if it was manifestly disadvantageous[65] to the party who had been subjected to the undue influence. No distinction should be drawn, therefore, between presumed and actual undue influence.[66] The Court acknowledged that the party, who had been unduly influenced, might have objected to the bargain, even though it was not to his manifest disadvantage, for example, "for strong conscientious or sentimental reasons."[67] But the Court found solace in the law of abuse of confidence, which is independent of the existence of undue influence. Where there is such abuse, commercial transactions may be set aside even though no manifest disadvantage has been shown; the onus is then on the other party to establish the fairness of the transaction. But the principle of abuse of confidence is, as the Court recognised, of limited application, being confined to "the relationship of trustee and beneficiary, principal and agent and solicitor and client, or of persons in similar positions."[68] Certainly, it is not applicable, concluded the Court, as between husband and wife. So, the relationship between the parties, whether it is characterised as fiduciary or non-fiduciary, will determine whether the transaction may or may not be upheld. This is not a happy distinction. Again, to insist on the condition that the transaction must be to the manifest disadvantage of the party influenced is in principle strange. Certainly

---

[59] See Cartwright, *op. cit.*, pp. 171–174.
[60] *Lancashire Loans Ltd.* v. *Black* [1934] 1 K.B. 380; *Goldsworthy* v. *Brickell* [1987] Ch. 378, 400, *per* Nourse L.J. cited above, p. 278.
[61] [1990] 1 Q.B. 923, 967.
[62] At pp. 970–971.
[63] *Blackie* v. *Clark* (1852) 15 Beav. 595, 601, *per* Romilly M.R.; *Wright* v. *Carter* [1903] 1 Ch. 27, 50, *per* Vaughan Williams L.J. *Cf.* see above, p. 280.
[64] [1990] 1 Q.B. 923.
[65] See above, pp. 279–280 on the meaning of "manifestly disadvantageous."
[66] Interpreting *National Westminster Bank* v. *Morgan* [1985] A.C. 686.
[67] At p. 962, *per curiam*.
[68] At pp. 962–964.

it is unique to the law of undue influence, and will result in counsel seeking to persuade the court that the party influenced had been coerced or had been induced to act by the other's misrepresentation.[68a]

In bargaining transactions, where it is alleged that one contracting party has been unduly influenced by the other, there is no obligation on a party to insist that the other receive independent advice, still less to satisfy himself that the advice has been followed. That would impose an unreasonable burden on him; if imposed it would severely inhibit commercial transactions.[69] To this general principle there may be one significant exception. Married women who guarantee their husband's debts may be treated as a specially protected class. In such a case, the spousal relationship between the debtor and the surety, which is known to the creditor, may put the creditor, because of that knowledge, under an obligation to see that she obtains independent legal advice or, if she declines to do so, to offer a fair explanation of the guaranty document before she signs it. This is an exception which, if upheld, should not be of general application.[70] Some wives may need this special protection, but others may not.

In contrast, a donative transaction may only be affirmed if it can be shown that the donor received independent legal advice.[71]

2. LIMITS TO RELIEF

The circumstances in which a plaintiff may lose his right to set aside a transaction on the ground of undue influence are similar to those which may bar a claim for rescission or rectification.[72] Consequently, his right is lost if he affirms the transaction,[73] if the status quo ante cannot be restored, or if he is guilty of laches or acquiescence.

In *Allcard* v. *Skinner* it was said[74] that the party influenced must object within a reasonable time; if he does not, he is deemed to have affirmed the transaction. In *Mutual Finance Ltd.* v. *Wetton*[75] the critical time was said to be the date when the influence ceased to operate. The reconciliation of these dicta may well be found in the principle that a transaction will not be set aside if it

---

[68a] See above, Chap. 8.
[69] *Coldunell Ltd.* v. *Gallon* [1986] Q.B. 1184, 1201, *per* Oliver L.J. *Cf.* above, p. 280.
[70] *Barclays Bank plc* v. *O'Brien*, [1992] 4 All E.R. 983, C.A. Scott L.J. discerned two conflicting lines of authority. In one line, which he refused to follow, the creditor would not be able to enforce the guarantee if it were found that the husband, who exercised the undue influence, was its agent: see, *e.g. BCCI* v. *Aboody* [1990] 1 Q.B. 923: see below p. 285 and above p. 282. The second line, represented by *Turnbull Co.* v. *Duval* [1902] A.C. 429, was authority for the principle which he adopted. See (1992) 108 L.Q.R. 534 [Cretney].
[71] *Cf.* above, pp. 198 *et seq.*
[72] But the Misrepresentation Act 1967, s.2(2) has no application: see above, pp. 198 *et seq.*
[73] *Mitchell* v. *Homfray* (1882) 8 Q.B.D. 587. It appears from this case that independent advice is not a necessary prerequisite of affirmation. Moreover, no positive act is necessary to show that a donor had elected to abide by his gift. All that is required is "proof of a fixed, deliberate and unbiased determination that the transaction should not be impeached"; see at p. 592, *per* Lord Selborne L.C. See also *Coldunell Ltd.* v. *Gallon* [1986] Q.B. 1184, C.A.
[74] (1887) 36 Ch.D. 145, 187.
[75] [1937] 2 K.B. 389, 397.

would be inequitable to allow the influenced party to set aside the transaction.[76]

Again, as a general rule, a voidable agreement will not be set aside if restitution is impossible. But the court has long had the power to do "what is practically just between the parties, and by so doing restore them substantially to the status quo."[77] In *O'Sullivan* v. *Management Agency and Music Ltd.*[78] the Court of Appeal compelled the defendants to disgorge profits made from contracts which had been wholly performed but which had been obtained by undue influence, through, an abuse of personal trust and confidence.[79] Such transactions could be set aside even though it was impossible to place the parties precisely in the position in which they were before, provided that the court could achieve "practical justice" between the parties.[80] To achieve this practical justice, the defendants were granted reasonable remuneration, which included a profit element.[81]

Laches and acquiescence are well established equitable defences. Laches is often taken to mean undue delay in making a claim. But it may be used "to mean acquiescence in its proper sense, which involves standing by so as to induce the other party to believe that the wrong is assented to."[82] A person may be said to have acquiesced even though he was ignorant of his legal rights; the test is whether it is just in all the circumstances that the plaintiff should succeed.[83]

3. Third Party Rights

It is a defence to a claim based on equitable title that the defendant is a bona fide purchaser without notice of the plaintiff's equitable interest. Notice embraces not only actual notice but also constructive and imputed notice. A person will be deemed to have constructive notice if he knew all the facts constituting the undue influence.[84]

In recent years the courts have frequently been confronted with transactions entered into by banks with wives who had been induced by their husbands to

---

[76] *Goldsworthy* v. *Brickell* [1987] Ch. 378, 416.

[77] *Alati* v. *Kruger* (1955) 94 C.L.R. 216, 223–224; see above, p. 199 for a fuller discussion.

[78] [1985] Q.B. 428.

[79] The plaintiff was at the time of the making of the contracts a young, inexperienced entertainer who subsequently made his fame and fortune. The third defendant was his manager upon whose judgment he relied and who was a substantial shareholder in the defendant companies, with whom the plaintiff contracted. The third defendant was held to be in a fiduciary relationship with the plaintiff; "accordingly undue influence was to be presumed."

[80] At p. 458, *per* Dunn L.J.

[81] Query if this part of the decision is still good law: see *Guinness plc* v. *Saunders* [1990] 2 A.C. 663: see below, pp. 32–35.

[82] *Goldsworthy* v. *Brickell* [1987] Ch. 378, 410, *per* Nourse L.J., who points out that, though there are analogies with equitable estoppel, there are also important differences so that the two doctrines cannot be equated.

[83] *Ibid.* at pp. 411–412, citing the unreported case of *John* v. *James* (1985) and analogous authorities in trust law.

[84] *Lancashire Loans Ltd.* v. *Black* [1934] 1 K.B. 380, C.A.

guarantee the banks' loans, often by executing charges over the matrimonial homes; in each case the wife's defence was that the loan transaction should be set aside on the ground of undue influence exerted over the wife by the husband. There is another line of cases, where the defendants were elderly parents who claimed to have entered into the transaction because of their son's undue influence. In what circumstances can the bank, who acts in good faith, enforce the guaranty, assuming that undue influence is established and that the transaction is to the manifest disadvantage of the wife and parents respectively?

The case law, emanating from the Court of Appeal, is in a state of considerable confusion. There is some authority to the effect that "the authorities which demonstrate the voidability of such transactions against third parties are all based on the concept of the person exercising the influence having acted as the agent of the third party [the creditor] in procuring the transaction."[85] In other cases the court's reasoning is not dependent upon a finding of "agency"; indeed such a finding was recently condemned as "highly artificial."[86]

There is a significant group of cases which suggests that wives (query elderly parents) should be treated "differently and more tenderly"[87] than other defendants who plead that they were the victims of undue influence. The creditor should be obliged to take reasonable steps to attempt to ensure that the surety has an adequate understanding of the nature and effect of the guarantee which she is giving and that her consent is a "true and informed one." In contrast, there are other cases which hold that the same rules should be applied whether the surety and the debtor are or are not in a special relationship to each other. Equity's special protection of the married woman is "now of only historical interest . . . Third party security taken by creditors would be impeachable on account of misrepresentation or undue influence by the debtor only if the creditor had knowledge of the relevant facts or if the debtor had been acting as the agent of the creditor." The creditor is not under a duty to ensure that the surety fully understands what the surety is taking on; the "surety would have to look after himself or herself, as most sureties have always had to do."[88]

Contracts of guarantee are transactions of everyday occurrence, and to impose on banks and other lenders the burden of explaining the consequences of the contract of guarantee is an onerous one.[89] Moreover, there are wives and wives, elderly parents and elderly parents. Baroness Thatcher would not think

---

[85] See, *e.g. Coldunell Ltd.* v. *Gallon* [1986] Q.B. 1184 (son taking advantage of elderly parents); *cf. Avon Finance Co. Ltd.* v. *Bridger* [1985] 2 All E.R. 281.

[86] *Barclays Bank plc* v. *O'Brien* [1992] 4 All E.R. 983, 1007 (wife).

[87] *Ibid.* at p. 1008, *per* Scott L.J., who cites *Turnbull* v. *Duval* [1902] A.C. 429 as the *fons et origo* of this line of authority. His judgment contains a comprehensive review of the authorities.

[88] *Ibid.*, at pp. 1007–1008, explaining *Midland Bank* v. *Perry* (1987) 56 P. & C.R. 202; *Bank of Baroda* v. *Shah* [1988] 3 All E.R. 24; and *Bank of Credit and Commerce International S.A.* v. *Aboody* [1990] 1 Q.B. 923. See also *Barclays Bank* v. *Khaira*, C.A., April 30, 1992 (C.A. Transcript No. 92/405) and *Contractors Bonding Ltd.* v. *Snee* [1992] N.Z.L.R. 137, discussed in (1993) 108 L.Q.R. 534, 536 [Cretney].

[89] *Cf. Coldunell Ltd.* v. *Gallon* [1986] Q.B. 1184, 1201, *per* Oliver L.J.

of herself as a person within a class who needs special protection. Each case should turn on its own facts. There is much to be said for the view that whether a bank can enforce the guarantee should depend upon whether it is equitable, in all the circumstances of the particular case, so to do. In the absence of any presumption of undue influence, the bank should have "notice of the circumstances alleged to constitute the actual exercise of the undue influence."[90]

In contrast, third party volunteers must always disgorge any benefits acquired by undue influence, unless they receive those benefits from or through a bona fide purchaser.[91]

4. Proprietary Claims

A person who can establish undue influence will undoubtedly be in a position to show the existence of a fiduciary relationship. He may be able to identify *his* property through the application of traditional equitable principles. Even if he cannot do so, the court may hold, in the context of litigation between him and the general creditors of the defendant, that it is just and equitable to impose a lien over the unencumbered assets of the defendant who had exercised the undue influence. It will be generally proper to do so.[92]

---

[90] *Bank of Credit and Commerce International S.A.* v. *Aboody* [1990] 1 Q.B. 923, 973, *per* Slade L.J.; *cf. CIBC Mortgages plc* v. *Pitt* (1993) T.L.R. 209. If undue influence is presumed, the creditor should know of the circumstances giving rise to the presumption: below pp. 277–281.

[91] See *Bridgeman* v. *Green* (1757) Wilm. 58, 65, *per* Lord Commissioner Wilmot; *Goddard* v. *Carlisle* (1821) 9 Price 169; *Morley* v. *Loughnan* [1893] 1 Ch. 736, 757, *per* Wright J.; *Bullock* v. *Lloyds Bank* [1955] Ch. 317, 324, *per* Vaisey J. *Cf. Re Pauling's Settlement Trusts* [1964] Ch. 303. The right of a party to set aside a transaction for undue influence is assignable and devisable: see *Dickinson* v. *Burrell* (1866) L.R. 1 Eq. 337.

[92] For the general principles determining whether a plaintiff should be granted a proprietary remedy, see above, Chap. 2.

CHAPTER 11

RELIEF FROM UNCONSCIONABLE BARGAINS

1. IN EQUITY

"THERE is hardly any older head of equity than that described by Lord Hardwicke in *Earl of Chesterfield* v. *Janssen*[1] as relieving against the fraud 'which infects catching bargains with heirs, reversioners, or expectants in the life of the father.' "[2]

The basis of equity's intervention in these cases is very similar to that underlying the relief granted in cases of undue influence.[3] But it is a distinct equitable jurisdiction which does not depend on the existence of any relationship of confidence and trust between the parties or on any proof that the dominant party actually induced the payment through the influence he had unfairly obtained. A bargain may, therefore, be set aside as unconscionable even though there is no presumed or actual abuse of an existing relationship of confidence.[4] In unconscionable bargains, "there is always fraud presumed or inferred from the circumstances or conditions of the parties contracting: weakness on one side, usury on the other, or extortion or advantage taken of that weakness. There has always been an appearance of fraud from the nature of the bargain."[5]

> " 'Fraud' in an equitable context does not mean, or is not confined to, deceit: 'it means an unconscientious use of the power arising out of these circumstances and conditions' of the contracting parties . . . It is a victimisation, which can consist either of the active extortion of a benefit or the passive acceptance of a benefit in unconscionable circumstances."[6]

Equity presumes bargains with expectants[7] to be unconscionable. The person claiming the benefit of the bargain can rebut the presumption by

---

[1] (1751) 2 Ves.Sen. 125, 157.
[2] *Earl of Aylesford* v. *Morris* (1873) 8 L.R.Ch. 484, 489, *per* Lord Selborne.
[3] See above, pp. 276 *et seq.*
[4] *Morrison* v. *Coast Finance Ltd.* (1966) 54 W.W.R. 257, 259, *per* Davey J.A. But the line between pure inequality of bargaining power and a relationship of confidence, which has been abused, may be thin: see *Mutual Finance Ltd.* v. *John Wetton & Sons Ltd.* [1937] 2 K.B. 389.
[5] *Earl of Chesterfield* v. *Janssen* (1751) 2 Ves.Sen. 125, 157, *per* Lord Hardwicke.
[6] *Hart* v. *O'Connor* [1985] A.C. 1000, 1024, *per* Lord Brightman, P.C., citing *Earl of Aylesford* v. *Morris* (1873) L.R. 8 Ch.App. 484, 491. For a somewhat critical comment, see *Nichols* v. *Jessup* [1986] 1 N.Z.L.R. 226, 228, *per* Cooke P.
[7] Expectants include not only heirs apparent and presumptive, but those who have either a vested or a contingent remainder or any reversionary interest. Relief has been granted against usurious

showing that it is fair, just and reasonable. The *onus probandi* is a heavy one and will not easily be discharged; for example, it is not enough to show that the father, or other person on whose death the expectancy was to mature, was a party to the bargain.[8] Independent professional advice[9] is important evidence of fairness, as is adequacy of the consideration.[10] Since the bargain is voidable, it can be affirmed expressly or impliedly by the expectant party after coming into his inheritance.[11]

It is not only bargains with expectants that equity may presume to be unconscionable. Equity will intervene to prevent any "unconscientious use of power," when there is weakness on the one side and extortion on the other, and will set aside improvident bargains, made with any "poor or ignorant person acting without independent advice, which cannot be shown to be a fair and reasonable transaction."[12] In *Alec Lobb Ltd.* v. *Total Oil GB Ltd.*[13] Peter Millett Q.C., sitting as a Deputy Judge of the High Court, concluded that:

> "It is probably not possible to reconcile all the authorities, some of which are of great antiquity, on this head of equitable relief, which came into greater prominence with the repeal of the usury laws in the nineteenth century. But if the cases are examined, it will be seen that three elements have almost invariably been present before the court has interfered. First, one party has been at a serious disadvantage to the other, whether through poverty, or ignorance, or lack of advice, or otherwise, so that circumstances existed of which unfair advantage could be taken: see, for example, *Blomley* v. *Ryan* (1954) 99 C.L.R. 362, where, to the knowledge of one party, the other was by reason of his intoxication in no condition to negotiate intelligently. Second, this weakness of the one party has been exploited by the other in some morally culpable manner: see, for example, *Clark* v. *Malpas* (1862) 4 De G.F. & J. 401, 25 E.R. 1238, where a poor and illiterate man was induced to enter into a transaction of an unusual nature, without proper independent advice, and in great haste. And third, the resulting transaction has been, not merely hard or improvident, but overreaching and oppressive. Where there has been a sale at an undervalue, the undervalue has almost always been substantial, so that it calls for an explanation, and is in itself indicative of the presence of some fraud,

---

loans: see *Benyon* v. *Cooke* (1875) L.R. 10 Ch. 389, 391, *per* Jessel M.R. (This jurisdiction is independent of statute, on which see below, pp. 291 *et seq.*).

[8] *King* v. *Hamlet* (1834) 2 Myl. & K. 456, 473–475, *per* Lord Brougham; *Savery* v. *King* (1856) 5 H.L.C. 627; *Talbot* v. *Staniforth* (1861) 1 J. & H. 484.

[9] *O'Rorke* v. *Bolingbroke* (1877) 2 App.Cas. 814; *Fry* v. *Lane* (1888) 40 Ch.D. 312. *Cf.* see above, pp. 280–281, 282–283.

[10] *Shelly* v. *Nash* (1818) 3 Madd. 232; *Perfect* v. *Lane* (1861) 3 De G.F. & J. 369.

[11] *Cf. Levin* v. *Roth* [1950] 1 All E.R. 698n.

[12] *Hart* v. *O'Connor* [1985] A.C. 1000, 1023–1024, *per* Lord Brightman, P.C.

[13] [1983] 1 W.L.R. 87, 94–95, reversed in part, [1985] 1 W.L.R. 173, C.A. See also *Hart* v. *O'Connor* [1985] A.C. 1000, 1023–1024 (P.C.); and *cf. Multiservice Bookbinding Ltd.* v. *Morden* [1979] Ch. 84, 110, *per* Browne-Wilkinson J.

undue influence, or other such feature. In short, there must, in my judgment, be some impropriety, both in the conduct of the stronger party and in the terms of the transaction itself (though the former may often be inferred from the latter in the absence of an innocent explanation) which in the traditional phrase 'shocks the conscience of the court', and makes it against equity and good conscience for the stronger party to retain the benefit of a transaction he has unfairly obtained."[14-15]

There are many illustrations in the cases where bargains have been set aside on these grounds: bargains with the feeble-minded, drunkards, the seriously ill, the old, the eccentric, the illiterate, the ill-educated, the impoverished,[16] and (perhaps) persons unfamiliar with the English language.[17]

But in these cases it appears that the party seeking to take advantage of the bargain knew that he was dealing with a "poor or ignorant person." But what if he did not know, or ought not as a reasonable person to have known, this fact? In *Hart* v. *O'Connor*[18] the Privy Council held that the validity of a contract entered into by a lunatic but who is ostensibly sane, acting without independent advice, is to be "judged by the same standards as a contract by a person of sound mind and is not voidable by the lunatic or his representatives by reason of 'unfairness' unless such unfairness amounts to equitable fraud which would have enabled the complaining party to avoid the contract even if he had been sane." Seemingly, the same principle should determine whether a contract entered by any other poor or ignorant person should be set aside. In *Hart* it was clear that no reasonable person standing in Mr Hart's position could have known that he was entering into a contract with a person of unsound mind. Subsequently, in *Nichols* v. *Jessup*[19] the New Zealand Court of Appeal held that accepting the benefit of an improvident bargain made by an ignorant person acting without independent advice may be unconscionable if the circumstances are such that a reasonable person would have adverted to the possibility of the existence of his disability or disadvantage. Such a conclusion is consistent with the principle enunciated by the Privy Council.

[14-15] See also *Cresswell* v. *Potter* (1968) [1978] 1 W.L.R. 255 and *Watkin* v. *Watson-Smith, The Times,* July 3, 1986, and *cf. Commercial Bank of Australia* v. *Amadio* (1983) 57 A.L.J.R. 358, 363–364, *per* Mason J.

[16] *Evans* v. *Llewellin* (1787) 1 Cox 333; *Clark* v. *Malpas* (1862) 4 De G.F. & J. 401; *O'Rorke* v. *Bolingbroke* (1877) 2 App.Cas. 814; *Morrison* v. *Coast Finance Ltd.* (1966) 54 W.W.R. 257; *Black* v. *Wilcox* (1976) 70 D.L.R. (2d) 192; *Backhouse* v. *Backhouse* [1978] 1 W.L.R. 243; *Creswell* v. *Potter* [1978] 1 W.L.R. 255; *Harry* v. *Kreutziger* (1978) 95 D.L.R. (3d) 231; *Commonwealth Bank of Australia* v. *Amadio* (1983) 57 A.L.J.R. 358 (H.Ct. of Aust.). In *Mountford* v. *Scott* [1974] 1 All E.R. 248, 252–253, Brightman J. is reported to have said that the "court would not permit the educated person to take advantage of the illiteracy of the other." This dictum is not reported in [1975] Ch. 258, which also reports the judgment of the Court of Appeal. The Court of Appeal reversed his decision on other grounds.

[17] *Cf. Commonwealth Bank of Australia* v. *Amadio* (1983) 57 A.L.J.R. 358, 375, *per* Dawson J.

[18] [1985] A.C. 1000, 1027, *per* Lord Brightman, P.C.

[19] [1986] 1 N.Z.L.R. 226.

In *Lloyds Bank Ltd.* v. *Bundy*,[20] Lord Denning M.R. was prepared to set aside a "poor gentleman's" guarantee of his son's loan to the plaintiff bank, even though he knew what he was doing; in his view the case law impliedly recognised that a bargain could be set aside because of "inequality of bargaining power." However Lord Scarman, in *National Provincial Bank* v. *Morgan*,[21] doubted whether it was necessary to create any "general principle of relief against inequality of bargaining power" and suggested that it was a legislative task to impose "restrictions on freedom of contract."[22] In our view, in this area of the law, judicial restraint is a wise policy in the absence of any evidence of any wrongful conduct on the part of one of the contracting parties.[23] At the same time it should be recognised, as it has been, that relief may be granted in exceptional circumstances. So, equity may grant relief against forfeiture, may relieve against penalties and may exceptionally order the return of earnest payments.[24] And in *Schroeder Music Publishing Co. Ltd.* v. *Macauley*[25] Lord Diplock contemplated that standard form contracts in restraint of trade, where the terms were not the product of arm's-length negotiations, could be set aside and declared to be unconscionable.[26]

In our opinion it is undesirable for the courts to enjoy an unfettered power to rewrite contracts simply because the substantive terms *appear* to be unfair.[27] To create and to exercise such power will involve the courts in the solution of problems which litigation *inter partes* is not equipped to solve.[28]

---

[20] [1975] 1 Q.B. 326, 331; applied in *McKenzie* v. *Bank of Montreal* (1976) 70 D.L.R. (3d) 113. *Cf. Harry* v. *Kreutziger* (1978) 95 D.L.R. (3d) 231, 241, *per* Lambert J.A. (Is the transaction "seen as a whole . . . sufficiently divergent from community standards of commercial morality that it should be rescinded"?)

[21] [1985] A.C. 686. *Cf.* his observations in *Pao On* v. *Lau Yiu Long* [1980] A.C. 614, 634: see above, p. 263.

[22] At p. 708. The other members of the House of Lords agreed with Lord Scarman. The facts, which were similar to *Lloyds Bank Ltd.* v. *Bundy*, gave rise to a claim of undue influence: see above, p. 279. See also *Hart* v. *O'Connor* [1985] A.C. 1000, 1023–1024, P.C. But *cf.* Lord Diplock's observations in *Erven Warnick Besloten Vennootschap* v. *J. Townend & Sons (Hull) Ltd.* [1979] A.C. 731, 743: "where over a period of years there can be discerned a steady trend in legislation which reflects the view of successive Parliaments as to what the public interest demands in a particular field of law, development of the common law in that part of the same field which has been left to it ought to proceed upon a parallel rather than a diverging course." *Cf.* Birks, *Introduction*, p. 178.

[23] *Cf.* see above, p. 268.

[24] *Cf. Stockloser* v. *Johnson* [1954] 1 Q.B. 476, 490, 492, *per* Denning L.J.; *The Scaptrade* [1983] 2 A.C. 694, 702, *per* Lord Diplock; *Sport International Bussum BV* v. *Inter-Footwear Ltd.* [1984] 1 W.L.R. 777; *BICC p.l.c.* v. *Burndy Corp.* [1985] Ch. 232, discussed below, p. 437.

[25] [1974] 1 W.L.R. 1308, 1326, applauded by Lord Denning M.R. in *Clifford Davis Management Ltd.* v. *W.E.A. Records Ltd.* [1975] 1 W.L.R. 61, 64.

[26] [1974] 1 W.L.R. 1308, 1315; *cf.* [1974] 1 All E.R. 171, 181, C.A. and see (1974) 90 L.Q.R. 460–463 [Dawson].
Releases by an injured party of his claim to damages may also be set aside on the grounds of unconscionability: *Saunders* v. *Ford Motor Co.* [1974] 1 Lloyd's Rep. 379; *Arrale* v. *Costain Civil Engineering* [1976] 1 Lloyd's Rep. 98, 102, *per* Lord Denning M.R.

[27] *Cf. Shiloh Spinners Ltd.* v. *Harding* [1973] A.C. 691, 723, *per* Lord Wilberforce; and see (1976) 39 M.L.R. 369 [Waddams].

[28] *Cf. Pao On* v. *Lau Yiu Long* [1980] A.C. 614, 634, *per* Lord Scarman ("it would render the law uncertain"); *Alec Lobb Ltd.* v. *Total Oil GB Ltd.* [1985] 1 W.L.R. 87; see above, p. 288.

Unconscionability and inequality of bargaining power are elusive and mercurial concepts which mean different things to different people.[29] It is "seldom in any negotiation that the bargaining powers of the parties are absolutely equal." It should not be enough to show that a contractual provision "is objectively unreasonable."[29a] It is a distinct question whether there has been impropriety or unfairness in the bargaining process (so-called procedural unconscionability), although a conclusion that the bargaining process was unfair may conceal a conclusion that the contractual terms are substantively unconscionable.[30]

If the court sets aside a bargain as unconscionable, it will do so on equitable terms.[31] Generally the principal sum must be repaid with interest[32] and costs[33] may be awarded to the defendant.[34]

2. By Statute

(a) *The Moneylenders Acts 1900 and 1927*[35]: *Moneylending at an Excessive Rate of Interest*

Parts of these statutes are still in force, although the Consumer Credit Act 1974 has given power to the Secretary of State to order by statutory instrument their repeal[36]; however, any repeal "shall have effect only as provided by an order so made."[37]

A borrower who is charged an excessive rate of interest[38] may be granted relief if he satisfies the court that the borrowing transaction is either harsh and unconscionable, or is otherwise such that equity should give relief.[39] The

---

[29] See *The Doctrine of Inequality of Bargaining Power, Post-Benthamite Economics in the House of Lords* (1976) 26 Univ. of Toronto L.J. 359 [Trebilcock].

[29a] *Alec Lobb Ltd.* v. *Total Oil GB Ltd.* [1985] 1 W.L.R. 173, 183, *per* Dillon L.J.

[30] *Cf.* (1988) 8 Oxford Jo.L.S. 17 [Thal] for an argument that procedural impropriety (unfair bargaining) should lead the court to inquire into the adequacy of the contractual consideration. The article then goes on to discuss "what sort of bargaining situations are unfair": *cf.* (1986) 6 Oxford Jo.L.S. 123 [Beale].

[31] *Cf. Instone* v. *A. Schroeder Music Publishing Co. Ltd.* [1974] 1 All E.R. 171, 181, *per curiam*; *Lloyds Bank Ltd.* v. *Bundy* [1975] 1 Q.B. 326.

[32] *Gwynne* v. *Heaton* (1778) 1 Bro.C.C. 1; *St. Albyn* v. *Harding* (1857) 27 Beav. 11.

[33] Unless the defendant's conduct has been sharp and tricky: see *Gowland* v. *De Faria* (1810) 17 Ves. 20; *Tyler* v. *Yates* (1871) L.R. 6 Ch. 665.

[34] In exceptional circumstances a court may not order the repayment of the principal sum. Such a case was *Morrison* v. *Coast Finance Ltd.* (1966) 54 W.W.R. 257, 262, *per* Davey J.A., where the lender was in collusion with a third party, to whom the borrower had, in turn, lent the loan money; the loan money was then used to repay the third party's debt to the lender.

[35] See, generally, Meston's *Law Relating to Moneylenders*.

[36] *e.g.* s.6 of the Moneylenders Act 1900 (definition of money-lender) has been repealed: see Consumer Credit Act 1974, s.192(3)(*b*), Sched. 5, Pt. I; S.I. 1983 No. 1551.

[37] Consumer Credit Act 1974, s.192(4).

[38] Or where "the amounts charged for expenses, inquiries, fines, bonus, premiums, renewals or any other charges are excessive": Moneylenders Act 1900, s.1.

[39] Moneylenders Act 1900, s.1.

court's powers, which are conferred by statute,[40] are generous, and the nature of the relief which can be awarded is of the widest kind.

Whether an interest rate is excessive is a question of fact.[41] There is, however, a statutory presumption that, unless the contrary is proved[42] the rate of interest is excessive if it exceeds 48 per cent. per annum.[43] If the rate is excessive, the court has a power to create a fresh bargain between the parties, to reopen any accounts between them and to ascertain what sum is fairly due for principal and interest, having regard to the presumption against interest in excess of 48 per cent.,[44] the risk taken by the moneylender, and all the circumstances of the case. If the interest is still unpaid, the borrower may be granted relief from the payment of anything in excess of a reasonable sum[45]; if the interest has been paid, the creditor may be directed to repay the excess over a reasonable sum.[46]

This statutory jurisdiction is therefore different from the ordinary jurisdiction of courts of equity to set aside unconscionable bargains. It is a "new jurisdiction."[47] Courts of equity have never remodelled bargains with expectant heirs[48]; but under the Moneylenders Acts the courts have, as has been seen, power to create a new agreement between the parties.

(b) *The Consumer Credit Act 1974: Reopening of Credit Agreements*

The Consumer Credit Act 1974 confers far wider powers on the court to reopen credit agreements and to create new bargains in order to do justice between the parties.[49]

Section 137(1) of the 1974 Act provides that "if the court finds a credit bargain extortionate it may reopen the credit agreement so as to do justice between the parties.[50] This key subsection is circumspectly drafted. What may be reopened is the credit *agreement*; but to do so the court must look to the credit *bargain*, which includes not only the credit agreement but also "other transactions" which must be "taken into account in computing the total charge for credit."[51] A " 'credit agreement' means any agreement between an indivi-

---

[40] Moneylenders Act 1900; Moneylenders Act 1927.

[41] See, *e.g. Hanyet Securities Ltd.* v. *Mallet* [1968] 1 W.L.R. 18, 29, *per* Pennycuick J. (rate of 45% on an unsecured loan not excessive).

[42] *Reading Trust Ltd.* v. *Spero* [1930] 1 K.B. 492.

[43] Moneylenders Act 1900, s.1; Moneylenders Act 1927, s10(1).

[44] Moneylenders Act 1927, s.10(1).

[45] See, *e.g. Collings* v. *Charles Bradbury Ltd.* [1936] 3 All E.R. 369.

[46] Moneylenders Act 1900, s.1.

[47] *Samuel* v. *Newbold* [1906] A.C. 461, 476, *per* Lord Atkinson: see also 468, *per* Lord Macnaghten.

[48] *Samuel* v. *Newbold* [1906] A.C. 461, 468–469, *per* Lord Macnaghten. (But *cf. Stockloser* v. *Johnson* [1954] 1 Q.B. 476; see below, pp. 433 *et seq.*) If the bargain was held unconscionable, then, on the plaintiff repaying the loan, the court set aside the transaction and ordered the securities impeached to stand security for the money actually advanced with interest.

[49] See, generally, R. M. Goode, *Consumer Credit Law* (London, 1989).

[50] Whether an agreement is extortionate is determined by looking at the facts at the time of the agreement; any conclusion should not be coloured by subsequent events.

[51] s.137(2)(*b*)(ii).

dual ('the debtor') and any other person ('the creditor') by which the creditor provides the debtor with credit of any amount."[52] The Act makes separate provision for hiring agreements.[53]

An extortionate credit bargain is defined as follows[54]: "A credit bargain is extortionate if it—(a) requires the debtor or a relative of his to make payments (whether unconditionally, or on certain contingencies) which are grossly exorbitant, or (b) otherwise grossly contravenes ordinary principles of fair dealing." In determining whether the credit bargain is extortionate, "regard shall be had to such evidence as is adduced concerning—(a) interest rates prevailing at the time it was made, (b) the factors mentioned in subsections (3) to (5), and (c) any other relevant considerations."[55]

The factors which are mentioned in subsection (3), as applicable to the debtor, include[56]: "(a) his age, experience, business capacity and state of health; and (b) the degree to which, at the time of the making of the credit bargain, he was under financial pressure, and the nature of that pressure." Similarly, the factors applicable to the creditor include[57]:

(1) the degree of risk accepted by him, having regard to the value of any security provided;
(2) his relationship to the debtor; and
(3) whether or not a colourable cash price was quoted for any goods or services included in the credit bargain.[58]

In *A. Ketley Ltd.* v. *Scott*[59] it was held that an actual interest rate of 48 per cent. was not extortionate given the fact that little security was offered and that the loan was for the purchase of a heavily mortgaged property.

Section 171(7) further strengthens the hand of the debtor by providing that if a debtor or surety alleges[60] that any credit bargain is extortionate, it is for the creditor to prove the contrary.[61]

---

[52] s.137(2)(*b*)(i).
[53] See s.132.
[54] s.138(1). See *Multiservice Bookbinding Ltd.* v. *Marden* [1979] Ch. 84, 110, *per* Browne-Wilkinson J.; *Davies* v. *Direct Loans Ltd.* [1986] 2 All E.R. 783 (the statutory definition is comprehensive), not following a dictum to the contrary in *Castle Phillips Finance Co. Ltd.* v. *Khan* [1980] C.C.L.R. 1, 3, C.A.
[55] Query the effect of the lender's failure to explain to the borrower the effect of the transaction. This was fatal under the Moneylenders Acts: see *Halsey* v. *Wolfe* [1915] 2 Ch. 330. But the 1974 Act makes independent, elaborate provisions for the imparting of information. If these are satisfied, are the lender's duties discharged?
[56] s.138(3).
[57] s.138(4), (5), deals with the so-called linked transactions, defined in ss.19(1) and 189(1).
[58] *Avon Finance Co. Ltd.* v. *Bridge* (1979) [1985] 2 All E.R. 281, 286–287; *Coldunell Ltd.* v. *Gallon* [1986] 2 W.L.R. 466, 481, *per* Oliver L.J.; *Davies* v. *Directloans Ltd.* [1986] 1 W.L.R. 823.
[59] [1981] I.C.R. 241. And *cf. Woodstead Finance Ltd.* v. *Petrou* [1986] New L.J. 188 (42.5% per annum not unconscionable).
[60] But the evidential burden of adducing sufficient evidence *to raise* the issue probably rests initially on the debtor or surety.
[61] [1975] C.L.J. 79, 121.

The Act confers on the court a wide range of remedies which it may grant in favour of the debtor or his surety.[62] The court may:

"(a) direct accounts to be taken . . .
 (b) set aside the whole or part of any obligation imposed on the debtor or a surety by the credit bargain or any related agreement,
 (c) require the creditor to repay the whole or part of any sum paid under the credit bargain or any related agreement by the debtor or a surety, whether paid to the creditor or any other person,
 (d) direct the return to the surety of any property provided for the purposes of the security, or
 (e) alter the terms of the credit agreement or any security instrument."

An order may be made by the court "notwithstanding that its effect is to place a burden on the creditor in respect of an advantage unfairly enjoyed by another person who is a party to a linked transaction."[63] This is a wide power which enables a court to require a creditor to refund to a debtor premiums which the creditor has paid to a third party, such as an insurance company.[64]

(c) The Unfair Contract Terms Act 1977

The Act[65] makes wholly ineffective any attempt to exclude or restrict a person's business liability[66] for, or in respect of: "death or personal injury resulting from negligence"[67]; certain guarantees in the case of goods ordinarily supplied for private use or consumption[68]; as against a consumer,[69] the statutory implied

---

[62] s.139(2).

[63] s.139(3).

[64] Query whether the creditor can obtain an indemnity from the third party in these circumstances. The Civil Liability (Contribution) Act 1978 appears to have no application since the Act only applies where persons are liable in respect of *damage suffered*; and at common law contribution (or indemnity) will normally be available only if the parties are subject to a common demand, which the creditor and the third party are not. See below, Chap. 13 for a full discussion of contribution claims. And *cf.* R. M. Goode, [1975] C.L.J. 79, 122, n. 45.

[65] We have discussed only in outline the statutory provisions. For a more detailed discussion, see the standard texts on the law of contract.

[66] s.1(3) reads
"In the case of both contract and tort, sections 2 to 7 apply (except where the contrary is stated in section 6(4)) only to business liability, that is liability for breach of obligations or duties arising—
 (a) from things done or to be done by a person in the course of a business (whether his own business or another's); or
 (b) from the occupation of premises used for business purposes of the occupier;
 and references to liability are to be read accordingly."
See also ss.12 and 14.

[67] s.2(1); *Johnstone* v. *Bloomsbury Health Authority* [1991] 2 All E.R. 294.

[68] s.5.

[69] s.12 reads:
"(1) A party to a contract 'deals as consumer' in relation to another party if—
 (a) he neither makes the contract in the course of a business nor holds himself out as doing so; and
 (b) the other party does make the contract in the course of a business; and

terms relating to conformity of goods with description or sample, quality or fitness for a particular purpose, in contracts for the sale or hire of goods and other such contracts where possession or ownership passes.[70] The statutory implied terms as to title can never be excluded.[71]

The Act also provides that certain exemption clauses, excluding or restricting liability, are invalid except in so far as they satisfy the statute's requirement of reasonableness.[72] These include:

(1) Where one party deals as consumer or on the other's written standard terms of business as against that party, the other cannot by reference to any contract term exclude or restrict any liability in respect of the breach; or "claim to be entitled—
   (i) to render a contractual performance substantially different from that which was reasonably expected of him, or
   (ii) in respect of the whole or any part of his contractual obligation, to render no performance at all."[73]

(2) As against a person dealing otherwise than as consumer, liability cannot be excluded or restricted by reference to terms in contracts for sale, hire-purchase or other contracts for the supply of goods which seek to exclude liability for the breach of the statutory implied terms relating to correspondence with description or sample or quality and fitness for a particular purpose.[74]

(3) Any term excluding or restricting liability for negligence[75] (but terms purporting to exclude or restrict liability for death or personal injury are wholly ineffective[76]).

(4) A person who deals as a consumer cannot be made to indemnify another (whether a party to the contract or not) in respect of a business liability incurred by that other for negligence or breach of contract.[77]

(c) in the case of a contract governed by the law of sale of goods or hire-purchase, or by section 7 of this Act, the goods passing under or in pursuance of the contract are of a type ordinarily supplied for private use or consumption."
See *R & B Customs Brokers Co. Ltd.* v. *United Dominions Trust Ltd.* [1988] 1 All E.R. 847, C.A.
[70] ss.6(2), 7(2), as amended by the Supply of Goods and Services Act 1982, s.17.
[71] s.6(1). Note that s.6(4) provides: "The liabilities referred to in this section are not only the business liabilities defined by section 1(3) [see above, n. 66], but include those arising under any contract of sale of goods or hire-purchase agreement."
[72] On which see below, p. 296.
[73] s.3., extended by s.13(1), on which see *Stewart Gill Ltd.* v. *Horatio Myer & Co. Ltd.* [1992] 2 All E.R. 257, C.A. But *cf. Micklefield* v. *SAC Technology Ltd.* [1991] 1 All E.R. 275 (no application to share options).
[74] ss.6(2)(3) and 7(2)(3), as amended by the Supply of Goods and Services Act 1982, s.17.
[75] s.2(2). S.2(2) applies if a duty of care already existed or if the disclaimer was effective to prevent a duty of care from arising. All exclusion notices must satisfy the requirements of reasonableness. *Cf. Smith* v. *Eric S. Bush (a firm)* [1990] 1 A.C. 831, 858–859, *per* Lord Griffiths, who factors which the court should take into account in determining whether a valuer's disclaimer of liability is reasonable.
[76] s.2(1) protects the victim of negligence. Any arrangement made by the wrongdoer with any other person to share or bear the burden of compensating the injured party is not caught by the sub-section: see *Thompson* v. *T Lohan (Plant Hire) Ltd.* [1987] 2 All E.R. 631, C.A.
[77] s.4; see (1993) 109 L.Q.R. 41 [Brown and Chandler].

The Act has also amended section 3 of the Misrepresentation Act 1967.[78]

There are specific statutory provisions relating to the requirement of *reasonableness*[79]:

(1) The person claiming that the contract term satisfies the requirement of reasonableness must prove its reasonableness.[80]

(2) Whether the requirement of reasonableness is satisfied is determined when the contract is made.[81] Whether a contract term satisfies the test of reasonableness, has to be determined by considering the term as a whole, and not merely a part of it.[82]

(3) "Where by reference to a contract term or notice a person seeks to restrict liability to a specified sum of money, and the question arises (under this or any other Act) whether the term or notice satisfies the requirement of reasonableness, regard shall be had in particular (but without prejudice to subsection (2) . . . [see paragraph 4 below] in the case of contract terms) to:–

(i) the resources which he could expect to be available to him for the purpose of meeting the liability should it arise; and

(ii) how far it was open to him to cover himself by insurance."[83]

(4) Further guidelines are provided to determine for the purposes of sections 6 and 7 of the Act whether a contract term satisfies the requirement of reasonableness.[84] These are:–[85]

"Guidelines" for application of reasonableness test

The matters to which regard is to be had in particular for the purposes of sections 6(3), 7(3) and (4), 20 and 21 are any of the following which appear to be relevant—

(1) the strength of the bargaining positions of the parties relative to each other, taking into account (among other things) alternative means by which the customer's requirements could have been met;

(2) whether the customer received an inducement to agree to the term, or in accepting it had an opportunity of entering into a similar contract with other persons, but without having to accept a similar term;

(3) whether the customer knew or ought reasonably to have known of the existence and extent of the term (having regard, among other things,

---

[78] s.8; see above, p. 209 for a full discussion.

[79] For a discussion of the recent case law, see (1985) 82 L.S. Gaz., p. 2393 [Lawson].

[80] s.11(5).

[81] s.11(1).

[82] *Stewart Gill Ltd.* v. *Horatio Myer & Co. Ltd.* [1992] 2 All E.R. 257, C.A.

[83] s.11(4). *Cf.* s.24(3) (other contracts for the sale of goods). See also s.9: (requirement of reasonableness must be satisfied, though contract terminated or subsequently affirmed by a party entitled to repudiate).

[84] s.11(2).

[85] Sched. 2.

to any custom of the trade and any previous course of dealing between the parties);

(4) in cases where the term excludes or restricts any relevant liability if some condition is not complied with, whether it was reasonable at the time of the contract to expect that compliance with that condition would be practicable;

(5) whether the goods were manufactured, processed or adapted to the special order of the customer.

There are other provisions which are designed to prevent the evasion of these statutory provisions by means of a "secondary contract"[86] or through a choice of law clause designed wholly or mainly to evade the Act.[87] Certain contracts are specifically excepted from some of these statutory provisions.[88]

The provisions of the Unfair Contract Terms Act 1977 are therefore technical and limited in scope. Whether their existence and example will persuade the courts to extend their equitable jurisdiction to set aside contracts on the grounds of unconscionability is conjectural.[89] The most recent decision of the House of Lords[90] suggests not, and that it is rather the legislature's task to impose further restrictions on freedom to contract.

3. IN ADMIRALTY

Salvage agreements are liable to be set aside if the court regards their terms as inequitable. In *Akerblom* v. *Price, Potter, Walker & Co.* Brett L.J. stated the "fundamental rule" to be as follows[91]:

> "The fundamental rule of administration of maritime law in all courts of maritime jurisdiction is that, whenever the court is called upon to decide between contending parties, upon claims arising with regard to the infinite number of marine casualties, which are generally of so urgent a character that the parties cannot be truly said to be on equal terms as to any agreement they may make with regard to them, the court will try to discover what in the widest sense of the terms is under the particular circumstances of the particular case fair and just between the parties. If the parties have made no agreement, the court will decide primarily what is fair and just. . . . If the parties have made an agreement, the court will enforce it, unless it be manifestly unfair and unjust; but if it be manifestly unfair and unjust, the court will disregard it and decree what is fair and just."

---

[86] s.23.
[87] s.27.
[88] Sched. I.
[89] *Cf. Erven Warnick Besloten Venootschap* v. *J. Townend & Sons (Hull) Ltd.* [1979] A.C. 731, 741, *per* Lord Diplock, cited above, p. 290, n. 22.
[90] *National Westminster Bank* v. *Morgan* [1985] A.C. 686, H.L. see above, p. 291.
[91] (1881) 7 Q.B.D. 129, 132–133.

In the majority of cases where salvage agreements have been set aside, it has been because the reward stipulated for by the salvor in the agreement has been exorbitantly high. The court will be particularly ready to set aside such an agreement if the circumstances of the case and the conduct of the salvor were such as to give the owner of the salved property or his representative no option but to enter into the agreement. Thus, in *The Port Caledonia and The Anna,*[92] a vessel in difficulty requested assistance from a tug, and the tugmaster's terms were: £1,000, or no rope. The master of the vessel in difficulty had no option but to accept. The agreement was set aside, and the tug was awarded £200.

But it is not only in cases of compulsion, such as these, that agreements are liable to be set aside. As appears from the passage from Brett L.J.'s judgment, quoted above, salvage agreements will be set aside whenever they are manifestly unfair and unjust.[93] Thus an agreement to render salvage services for a sum which is extravagantly small has been set aside as inequitable,[94] even when the agreement constituted a settlement made after the services had been rendered.[95] Again, agreements relating to the apportionment of a salvage reward among salvors may also be set aside if they are inequitable.[96]

It is, however, no part of the court's duty to set aside an agreement merely because it disagrees with the reward fixed by that agreement. Only if the amount stipulated is so exorbitantly large or so extravagantly small that, in all the circumstances of the case, the agreement must be regarded as inequitable, will the court interfere. Moreover, an agreement will not be set aside merely because the service agreed to be performed proved to be more arduous than was expected[97]; an agreement "cannot become fair or unfair by reason of circumstances which happened afterwards."[98]

---

[92] [1903] P. 184.
[93] *The Mark Lane* (1890) 15 P.D. 135.
[94] *The Phantom* (1866) L.R. 1 A. & E. 58 (£10 substituted for 8s. 6d.).
[95] *The Case of Silver Bullion* (1854) 2 E. & A. 70 (£50 substituted for 11s.).
[96] *The Enchantress* (1860) Lush. 93.
[97] *The True Blue* (1843) 2 W.Rob. 176.
[98] *The Strathgarry* [1895] P. 264, 271, *per* Bruce J.

CHAPTER 12

THE RIGHT TO CONTRIBUTION OR RECOUPMENT

GENERAL INTRODUCTION

IT is an established, if anomalous, principle of English law that a person who makes a voluntary payment, intending to discharge another's debt, will only discharge that debt if he acts with that other's authority or if that other subsequently ratified the payment.[1] Consequently, if he pays the creditor without authority and if his payment is not subsequently ratified, he has in general no direct[2] redress against the debtor; for the debt has not been discharged by the payment. A similar principle applies if a person makes a voluntary payment to an injured person, intending to indemnify him for the loss which he suffered in consequence of another's alleged negligent act.[3] In these circumstances it would appear that the creditor and he who has been indemnified continue to have vested in them their rights of action against the debtor and the alleged tortfeasor respectively.[4]

There is, however, an important if limited exception to these general principles. It is this: if a payment has been made under *compulsion of law*, then the payer will have a right to contribution or recoupment from the person who has been benefited by his payment. The compulsion must be of law. It is not enough that the payer was contractually bound to a third party to make the payment to the recipient.[5]

Compulsion of law embraces a complex body of case law which falls into two groups. There are claims to contribution which are discussed in Chapter 13 under the heading, "The Right to Contribution." At common law and in equity such a right would only arise if the claimant discharged more than his proportionate share of a common obligation which he and another owed to a third party. There must then be liability for "the *same* debt resting on the plaintiff and defendant [which] the plaintiff has been legally compelled to

---

[1] See above, p. 17, n. 2.

[2] Query whether he can be subrogated to the rights of the creditor who has accepted his payment: see *Owen* v. *Tate* [1976] 1 Q.B. 402, which suggests that subrogation is not possible but which is criticised below, pp. 597–598.

[3] *Esso Petroleum Co. Ltd.* v. *Hall, Russell & Co. Ltd., The Esso Bernicia* [1989] A.C. 643, H.L. This was an appeal from the First Division of the Inner House of the Court of Session. But the House of Lords assumed that there was no material difference between Scottish and English law: see below, p. 344 for a fuller discussion.

[4] At pp. 662–663, *per* Lord Goff; see below, p. 345.

[5] *The Esso Bernicia* [1989] A.C. 643, H.L.

pay."[6] Co-obligors, being *aequali jure*, must share equally the burden of payment. Today the right to contribution has been enlarged. The Civil Liability (Contribution) Act 1968 provides that "any person liable in respect of any damage suffered by another may recover from any other person liable in respect of the same damage (whether jointly with him or otherwise)."[7] The court has power to assess the contribution as is "just and equitable having regard to the extent of that person's responsibility for the damage in question."[8]

The second group of cases concern a situation where the plaintiff is compelled by law to pay money which the defendant was primarily liable to pay. So, in *Exall* v. *Partridge*,[9] the plaintiff's goods, which were on land leased to the defendant, were seized by the landlord in distress of rent. The plaintiff, having paid the rent to obtain the release of the goods, obtained recoupment[10] from the defendants for he had satisfied the defendants' liability to the landlord.[11] It is, therefore, enough that the plaintiff is compelled *by law* to pay a debt owed by the defendant to a third party; it does not matter that there is no common liability to be sued. These cases are discussed in Chapter 14 under the heading, "The Right to Recoupment; Compulsory Discharge of Another's Liability."

At common law and in equity, therefore, a person may claim contribution from another if there is liability *in solidum*. Under the Civil Liability (Contribution) Act 1978, he may claim contribution, "in respect of any damage suffered by another," from any person liable in respect of the same damage. Consequently, no contribution claim can generally succeed if the plaintiff and defendant owe separate debts to a third person.

Compulsion of law apart, it is still therefore a real question whether contribution or recoupment will be allowed if the parties are liable in debt but are not liable *in solidum*.[12] It is true that general average contribution requires parties to a common maritime adventure to contribute towards losses incurred for preservation of ship or cargo. But such claims owe their origin to the Rhodian sea law and have always been regarded as *sui generis*.[13] Whether contribution or recoupment will otherwise be allowed if the defendant's liability to a third

---

[6] *Brook's Wharf & Bull Wharf Ltd.* v. *Goodman Bros.* [1937] 1 K.B. 534, 544, *per* Lord Wright M.R.; italics supplied.

[7] s.1(1).

[8] s.2(1). The Act, which came into force on January 1, 1979, enables *any person* to recover contribution. So tortfeasors, trustees, directors, partners, and contractors may claim contribution under the Act: see below, Chap. 13.

[9] (1799) 8 T.R. 308; see below, pp. 346 *et seq.*; see also *Whitham* v. *Bullock* [1939] 2 K.B. 81; see below, p. 356.

[10] This is Vaughan Williams L.J.'s phrase in *Bonner* v. *Tottenham and Edmonton Permanent Investment Building Society* [1899] 1 Q.B. 161, 175; we have adopted it because it reflects the true nature of the plaintiff's claim, which is for reimbursement for the benefit gained by the defendant rather than for an indemnity for loss incurred by him. But *cf. Owen* v. *Tate* [1976] 1 Q.B. 402, 409, *per* Scarman L.J.

[11] (1799) 8 T.R. 308, 311, *per* Lawrence J.; see below, p. 346.

[12] *Cf. The Esso Bernicia* [1989] A.C. 643, H.L. see below, p. 344.

[13] See below, pp. 333 *et seq.*

party has not been discharged is most doubtful. In *Porteous* v. *Watney*,[14] Thesiger L.J. said that a bill of lading holder would have a defence in equity to an action for demurrage by the shipowner when "all demurrage due under the charterparty has been paid to the shipowner [by another bill of lading holder]."[15] It would appear to follow, therefore, that the bill of lading holder who had paid the demurrage should obtain contribution from other bill of lading holders whose obligations had thereby been discharged in equity. But Brett L.J., in the same case, denied the possibility of a contribution claim, for the bill of lading holders were not severally liable for a common debt[16]; and Thesiger L.J.'s dictum has never been followed. Subsequently Vaughan Williams L.J., in *Bonner* v. *Tottenham and Edmonton Permanent Investment Building Society*,[17] expressed the view that in equity a claim for contribution or recoupment will lie if there is "community of interest in the subject matter to which the burden is attached, which has been enforced against the plaintiff alone, coupled with benefit to the defendant, even though there is no common liability to be sued."[18] This principle is very similar to that underlying general average claims.[19] But there appears to be no single case, general average apart, where it has been applied to allow a claim for contribution or recoupment which would otherwise have failed.[20] Indeed, in *Bonner's* case itself, the Court of Appeal held that a lessee, who had paid the head rent, could not claim recoupment in equity from an underlessee of an assignee; there was no "community of interest" between them since "the covenant in accordance with which a lessee pays rent or expends money in repairs is a covenant in a lease in which the underlessee has no interest."[21]

However, a principle similar to that of "community of interest"[22] underlies contribution claims between landowners, where there is a common encumbrance over different parcels of land.[23] For example, A acquires Blackacre and Whiteacre both subject to a mortgage in favour of M. A sells Whiteacre to B. M later satisfies his debt from Whiteacre. B is entitled to contribution from A,

---

[14] (1878) 3 Q.B.D. 534.

[15] At p. 540.

[16] At p. 544. Contribution was indeed denied in *Leer* v. *Yates* (1811) 3 Taunt. 387, which was, however, criticised in *Rogers* v. *Hunter* (1827) M. & M. 63 and *Dobson* v. *Droop* (1830) M. & M. 44 but accepted as sound in *Straker* v. *Kidd* (1878) 3 Q.B.D. 223, 227, *per* Lush J. and *Porteous* v. *Watney* (1878) 3 Q.B.D. 534, 542–544, *per* Brett L.J. If Brett L.J. is correct, then *semble* the shipowner can recover demurrage in full from each bill of lading holder.

[17] [1899] 1 Q.B. 161.

[18] At p. 174.

[19] See below, pp. 333 *et seq.*

[20] *Cf. Whitham* v. *Bullock* [1939] 2 K.B. 81, 89, *per curiam.*

[21] [1899] 1 Q.B. 161, 176; and *cf. Whitham* v. *Bullock* [1939] 2 K.B. 81; see below, p. 356. Professor Sutton suggests that a claim for recoupment should succeed even though there is no privity of contract or estate; in his view, which has much to commend it, the basis of the equity should simply be part ownership of the burdened leasehold property: see *Essays* (ed. Burrows), pp. 101–103.

[22] For a discussion of the authorities, see (1991) 107 L.Q.R. 126, 151, 153 *et seq*, and particularly n. 24 [Derham]. See also below, pp. 321–322.

[23] See below, p. 302; *cf. Essays* (ed. Burrows), pp. 101–103 [Sutton]; see above, n. 21; see below, p. 302.

and the amount of the contribution is seemingly determined by reference to the proportionate values of the respective properties. And yet there is no common liability to be sued.[24]

If a restitutionary claim were granted, it is conceivable that a defendant might be made to pay twice over or to pay when he had a defence to a third party's claim. The potential dangers can be illustrated by an analysis of the claim by one sub-lessee against other sub-lessees for contribution. A landlord leases land to L who executes separate sub-leases to P, D1 and D2. P pays the head rent to the landlord under compulsion of law, for example, under a threat of forfeiture, and then (because L is insolvent) seeks to recover contribution from the other two sub-lessees, D1 and D2. The balance of authority suggests that P's claim will fail because his payment has not discharged any liability owed by D1 or D2 to the landlord; there is neither privity of estate nor privity of contract between lessor and sub-lessee.[25-26] This may seem a harsh conclusion, for D1 and D2 may have gained a benefit from P's payment; for example, their estates may have thereby been relieved of the potential threat of forfeiture or distress. But sub-lessees are not *in aequali jure*; they may hold their leases from L on different terms and on different covenants. D1 may have already paid his rent to L, the lessee; and D2 may have a defence to L's claim on the ground that L was in breach of his covenants to him. There is also the practical difficulty of determining what sums D1 and D2 should contribute when the sub-leases may be of different durations, when the properties sub-leased may of different values, when the rents may be of substantially different amounts (reflecting the swings and roundabouts of the property market), and when the sub-lessees may have distinct defences.[27] It may be possible to find a solution to this particular problem through subrogation. P may seek to be subrogated to the landlord's rights against the lessee, L. But if L is insolvent, P will want to be subrogated to L's rights against D1 and D2, to the extent that it is necessary to indemnify him and to prevent their unjust enrichment.[28] Such a conclusion

---

[24] (1991) 107 L.Q.R. 126, 148 *et seq.* [Derham]. From this analogy Dr. Derham argues that if A is owed two debts by X, one of which he assigns to P and the other to D, P can claim contribution from D if X employs a cross-claim or set off against P, thereby releasing D from the possibility that X would seek to enforce the same cross-claim or set off against him. "The ratio of contributions presumably would be ascertained by reference to the value of each of the assigned debts." But D may be insolvent. So, his preferred solution is to subrogate P to D's rights on the second debt when the second debt becomes payable.

[25-26] *Hunter v. Hunt* (1845) 1 C.B. 300, 305, *per* Tindal C.J.; *cf. Johnson v. Wild* (1890) 44 Ch.D. 146 and *Bonner v. Tottenham and Edmonton Permanent Investment Building Society* [1899] 1 Q.B. 161. But see (*contra*) *Webber v. Smith* (1689) 2 Vern. 103 and *Allison v. Jenkins* [1904] 1 I.R. 341, 348, *per* Porter M.R.; and *cf. Chatham Empire Theatre (1955) Ltd. v. Ultrans Ltd.* [1961] 1 W.L.R. 817. For a general discussion, see (1967) 31 *Conveyancer* 38 [Langan].

[27] Contrast text accompanying nn. 23 and 24, below: *cf. The Albazero* [1977] A.C. 774, 847–848, *per* Lord Diplock and see below, p. 312, n. 58.

[28] *Bonner v. Tottenham and Edmonton Permanent Investment Building Society* [1899] 1 Q.B. 161, 178–179, *per* Vaughan Williams L.J. *Semble* P can also recoup his payment by deducting any payment from rent due to L: see *Carter v. Carter* (1829) 5 Bing. 406 (see below, p. 361, n. 24).

is attractive. P's payment to the landlord must have discharged L's, the lessee's, debt to the landlord so that L should reimburse P to the extent of the payment made[29]; and "a right of reimbursement carries with it the right of subrogation."[30]

It would seem, however, desirable, given the uncertain state of the law, to extend the provisions of the Civil Liability (Contribution) Act 1978 so as to enable the court to order contribution, as is just and equitable, between such persons as bill of lading holders and sub-lessees, as well as between persons who are jointly liable for the same debt.[31]

---

[29] It is a distinct question, however, whether P should be preferred to L's general creditors in the event of L's insolvency.

[30] *Re Downer Enterprises Ltd.* [1974] 1 W.L.R. 1460, 1468, *per* Pennycuick V.-C., citing *Duncan, Fox & Co.* v. *North and South Wales Bank* (1880) 6 App.Cas. 1, 10–11, *per* Lord Selborne L.C. Although there is an affinity, recoupment and subrogation are distinct. As Sholl J. said, in *Dawson* v. *Bankers & Traders Insurance Co. Ltd.* [1957] V.R. 491, 503, a case on indemnity insurance: "in the pleadings in a contribution action, the rights litigated are the rights of the insurer-parties themselves; in the pleadings in a subrogation action, they are those of the insured."

[31] The Law Commission Report, No. 79: "Law of Contract; Report on Contribution" (March 9, 1977), pp. 8–9, rejected this last proposal on grounds which we do not find convincing. To give the court this discretion should not result in undesirable uncertainty.

CHAPTER 13

THE RIGHT TO CONTRIBUTION

1. INTRODUCTION

IT has long been held that at law and in equity, sureties, joint-contractors, trustees, directors, partners, insurers, mortgagors and co-owners can generally claim contribution from their co-obligors if they satisfy more than their proper share of the common debt.[1] But contribution claims were and are not limited to these familiar situations. Any obligor who owes with another a duty to a third party and is liable with that other to a *common demand* should be able to claim contribution.[2] So a plaintiff who is jointly responsible with the defendant for maintaining a party wall can obtain contribution if he has to bear the expense of pulling down the wall which has been condemned as a dangerous structure.[3] In all these cases the basis of the right to contribution is unjust enrichment. As Eyre C.B. once said[4]: "If a view is taken of the cases, it will appear the bottom of contribution is a fixed principle of justice, and is not founded in contract. . . . " There could be no contribution if there was no liability to a common demand. Consequently, there was no contribution if tortfeasors independently caused damage to a third party, or if the liability of contractors to a third person arose from separate and independent contracts. The Law Reform (Married Women and Tortfeasors) Act 1935, s.6, however, gave tortfeasors a limited right of contribution. The Civil Liability (Contribution) Act 1978 has now repealed that section, but has extended the statutory right of contribution, enacting that "any person liable in respect of any damage suffered by another person may recover contribution from any other person liable in respect of the same damage (whether jointly with him or not)."[5]

The new statutory right of contribution is not all-embracing. First, the statutory provisions are only prospective; they have no application if the damage occurred before the date when the Act came into force (January 1, 1979), or if a party's liability is "based on breach of any obligation assumed by

---

[1] It was in the surety cases that the right to contribution was first fully analysed: see *Deering* v. *The Earl of Winchelsea* (1787) 2 Bos. & Pul. 270: see below, p. 309.

[2] *Cf. Muschinski* v. *Dodds* (1985) 160 C.L.R. 583, 596–597, *per* Gibbs C.J.

[3] *Spiers & Son* v. *Troup* (1915) 84 L.J.Q.B. 1986, 1992, *per* Scrutton L.J.; and *cf. Re Downer Enterprises Ltd.* [1974] 1 W.L.R. 1460: see below, p. 601.

[4] *Deering* v. *The Earl of Winchelsea* (1787) 2 Bos. & Pul. 270, 272.

[5] The "proportions in which, as between themselves, the defendant must meet the plaintiff's claim do not have any direct relationship to the extent to which the total damages have been reduced by the contributory negligence": *Fitzgerald* v. *Lane* [1989] A.C. 328, 339, *per* Lord Ackner, H.L.

him" before that date.[6] Secondly, the statutory right of contribution arises only if there is liability in respect of "*any damage*" suffered.[7] The Law Commission, on whose *Report* the statute is largely based,[8] regrettably rejected a proposal that the statutory right should embrace a situation where persons are jointly liable for the same debt.[9] Consequently the equitable principle still survives and applies if there is liability of debtors *in solidum*, and the co-obligors, being *aequali jure*, must bear any loss equally.[10] In contrast, the 1978 Act gives the court power to assess the amount of contribution for damage suffered as is "just and equitable having regard to the extent of that person's responsibility for the damage in question"[11] Thirdly, the Maritime Conventions Act 1911 has not been repealed. It allows contribution claims between vessels responsible for a collision at sea resulting in loss of life or personal injuries suffered by any person on board.[12] Finally, there is general average contribution whose origins lie in the Rhodian sea law.[13] This body of law is *sui generis*, although its existence was influential in establishing the equitable right of contribution.[14] The parties to a maritime adventure are compelled to contribute not because of any common liability but because of their interest in a common adventure. "Natural justice requires that all should contribute to indemnify for loss of property which is sacrificed by one that the whole adventure may be saved."[15]

This diverse body of law presents formidable problems of classification. To complicate matters further the same co-obligors may be liable, depending on the facts, either in debt or for damages; for example, partners are jointly liable for the firm's *debts* and a partner may be liable to third parties for *damages* suffered in consequence of the acts of his fellow partners done during the course of partnership business. There is also the unresolved question of the extent to which the old cases in equity will influence the exercise of the statutory discretion to assess the amount of contribution; for example, in determining whether one trustee must indemnify another for the loss suffered by the trust from a breach of trust.

---

[6] s.71(1)(2); the provisions of the 1935 Act (on which, see the second edition of this work, pp. 232–235) may conceivably still be important: see, *e.g. Harper* v. *Gray and Walker (a firm)* [1985] 1 W.L.R. 1196, 1202, *per* Judge Newey Q.C. ("It would not be right to construe the 1935 Act by reference to a subsequent [1978] Act."); and *Southern Water Authority* v. *Carey* [1985] 2 All E.R. 1077, interpreting the words, "who is, or would if sued have been, liable" within s.6(1)(*c*) of the 1935 Act.
[7] See *Société Commerciale de Réassurance* v. *Eras International* [1992] 1 Lloyd's Rep. 570, C.A. (A contribution claim may nonetheless succeed if D is liable both in contract and tort, while T is liable only in tort.) Contrast s.3 (the effect of judgment against persons liable in respect of any debt or damage) which speaks of any person "liable in respect of *any debt or damage*."
[8] The Law Commission Report No. 79: *Law of Contract, Report on Contribution*, March 9, 1977. (Hereinafter cited as *Report*).
[9] See below, p. 323.
[10] See below, p. 306. For the position if there is no liability *in solidum*, see above, Chap. 12.
[11] s.2(1), following the 1935 Act.
[12] See below, p. 333.
[13] See below, p. 333.
[14] See below, p. 307.
[15] *Burton* v. *English* (1883) Q.B.D. 218, 221 *per* Brett M.R.

With these considerations in mind we have adopted the following classification:

(A) *Contribution Claims at Common Law and in Equity; Liability in Debt.* The most important categories are co-sureties; insurers; mortgagors; joint tenants; joint contractors.

(B) *Contribution Claims under the Civil Liability (Contribution) Act 1978; Liability in Damages.* The most important categories are independent contractors; tortfeasors; trustees; directors.

(C) *Contribution Claims between Obligors which may arise either at Common Law and in Equity, or under the Civil Liability (Contribution) Act 1978, depending on the nature of the claim:* partners.[16]

(D) *Contribution Claims under the Maritime Conventions Act 1911.*

(E) *General Average Contribution.*

2. PARTICULAR CONTRIBUTION CLAIMS

(A) Contribution Claims at Common Law and in Equity: Liability in Debt

As has been seen, the general principle is that co-obligors are only liable to make contribution if there is liability to a common demand. From this simple principle four propositions flow:

(1) Prima facie all contributing parties are *aequali jure* and must bear any loss equally.

(2) Although the right of contribution is based on the principle of unjust enrichment, the liability of co-obligors can be varied *inter se* by contract.

(3) The amount of an obligor's contribution is prima facie assessed by dividing the amount of the common debt by the number of solvent co-obligors still bound at the date of the contribution action.

(4) The right to contribution arises as soon as (i) an obligor has paid a sum which he is liable to pay and is more than his share of the common debt, *or* (ii) judgment has been obtained against an obligor for more than his share, *or* (iii) a claim has been allowed against the estate of a deceased obligor for more than his share.

The right to contribution was first established in the surety cases; and their analogy has been influential outside the boundaries of suretyship in determining whether a contribution claim should lie between other co-obligors. Accord-

---

[16] See below, p. 331, n. 98.

ingly it is appropriate to begin with a discussion of contribution claims between co-sureties.

(a) *Co-Sureties*[17]

The basis of the right to contribution

It is doubtful whether common law allowed any contribution between co-sureties before the beginning of the nineteenth century. The early cases, which are reported in a cursory fashion, reject such a claim, apparently on the ground that to allow it would have been "a great cause of suits."[18] Even when this uncompromising position was abandoned, the claim of a surety to contribution from each of his co-sureties was limited to the total amount owed by the principal debtor, divided by the number of sureties.[19] No adjustment was made if one of the sureties was unable to pay his share because of insolvency. Little hardship was caused by this conservative rule of law, for from the early seventeenth century it had been established in equity that sureties "who *can* pay must not only contribute their own shares, but they must also make good the shares of those who are unable to furnish their own contribution."[20] This conflict of law and equity was resolved in 1873 in favour of the rules of equity,[21] and the modern law is based on the principles of equity governing the contribution of sureties *inter se*.[22] The appropriate cause of action is, therefore, an action for contribution in the Chancery Division,[23] when the rights of all the parties will be settled in the same inquiry. It is still possible to bring an action for money paid to the use of the co-surety, but since 1873 the common law action in this context appears to have fallen into disuse.[24]

---

[17] A contract of suretyship is a contract of guarantee, "to answer for the debt, default or miscarriage of another who is to be primarily liable to the promisee": *Yeoman Credit Ltd.* v. *Latter* [1961] 1 W.L.R. 828, 831, *per* Holroyd Pearce L.J.

[18] See *Wormleigton* v. *Hunter* (1614) Godb. 243; *cf. Offley and Johnson's Case* (1584) 2 Leon 166.

[19] *Cowell* v. *Edwards* (1800) 2 Bos. & Pul. 268; *Browne* v. *Lee* (1827) 6 B. & C. 689; *Batard* v. *Hawes* (1853) 2 E. & B. 287; *Re a Debtor* [1937] Ch. 156.

[20] *Lowe & Sons* v. *Dixon & Sons* (1885) 16 Q.B.D. 455, 458, *per* Lopes J.; see also *Peter* v. *Rich* (1629/1630) 1 Chan.Rep. 34; *Morgan* v. *Seymour* (1637/1638) 1 Chan.Rep. 120; *Herle* v. *Harrison* (1674–1675) 73 Selden Society 138.

[21] Judicature Act 1873, s.25(11); see now Supreme Court Act 1981, s.49.

[22] *Lowe & Sons* v. *Dixon & Sons* (1885) 16 Q.B.D. 455.

[23] *Hay* v. *Carter* [1935] Ch. 397; *Kent* v. *Abrahams* [1928] W.N. 266, which gives the form of the appropriate order.

[24] *Cf.* Winfield, *Province*, p. 163; Keener, pp. 401–403. Common law judges reconciled satisfactorily to their own minds the principles of contribution with the theory of implied contract; see, for example, *Collins* v. *Prosser* (1823) 1 B. & C. 682; *Cowell* v. *Edwards* (1800) 2 Bos. & Pul. 268; *Batard* v. *Hawes* (1853) 2 E. & B. 287. Lord Eldon L.C., in *Craythorne* v. *Swinburne* (1807) 14 Ves. 160, 164, 169, sought to reconcile the equitable doctrine and implied contract thus: "that, the principle of equity being in its operation established, a contract may be inferred upon the implied knowledge of that [equitable] principle by all persons, and it must be upon such a ground, of implied assumpsit, that in modern times courts of law have assumed a jurisdiction upon this subject. . . . And Sir Samuel Romilly has very ably put, what is consistent with every idea, that, after that principle of equity has been universally acknowledged, then persons, acting under circumstances, to which it applies, may properly be said to act under the head of contract, implied from the universality of that principle." See Woodward's comment, *op. cit.* pp. 398–401.

The first reported statement of the rationale of the equitable doctrine is to be found in the decision of the Equity Side of the Exchequer in *Deering* v. *The Earl of Winchelsea* in 1787.[25] In that case, Eyre C.B. said[26]:

> "Contribution was considered as following the accident on a general principle of equity in the Court in which we are now sitting. In the particular case of sureties, it is admitted that one surety may compel another to contribute to the debt for which they are jointly bound. On what principle? Can it be because they are jointly bound? What if they are jointly and severally bound? What if severally bound by the same or different instruments? In every one of those cases sureties have a common interest and a common burthen. They are bound as effectually *quoad* contribution, as if bound in one instrument, with this difference only that the sums in each instrument ascertain the proportions, whereas if they were joined in the same engagement, they must all contribute equally."

Thus, between themselves, co-sureties prima facie are *aequali jure*,[27] although they can agree to be bound for different sums. It is, therefore, immaterial that they are bound jointly, jointly and severally or simply severally[27a]; that they are bound by the same or different instruments; that they are ignorant of each other's existence[28]; or that the first surety agreed to become a surety before the second surety had even been approached[29]: provided that they are co-sureties for the same principal and guarantee the same debt.[30] As Eyre C.B.'s statement of the law in *Deering* v. *The Earl of Winchelsea* indicates, not every surety can claim contribution from other sureties of the same debtor in equity. In particular:

(1) A surety cannot obtain contribution from another if they have guaranteed different debts of the same principal debtor.[31] The fact that the instruments entered into by the sureties are separate is a valuable, though not a conclusive, indication that they are not sureties for the same principal sum. On

---

[25] (1787) 2 Bos. & Pul. 270; 1 Cox 318.

[26] (1787) 2 Bos. & Pul. 270, 273; see also *Hunt* v. *Amidon*, 4 Hill N.Y. 345, 347, *per* Walworth Ch. (1842).

[27] *Stirling* v. *Forrester* (1821) 3 Bli. 575, 590, *per* Lord Redesdale: *Spottiswoode's Case* (1855) 6 De G.M. & G. 345, 372, *per* Turner L.J. Lord Eldon L.C., who was one of the counsel in *Deering* v. *The Earl of Winchelsea*, stated that the case was at first thought to be contrary to the accepted view of Westminster Hall, but he had later become convinced of its correctness; see *Coope* v. *Twynam* (1823) 1 T. & R. 426, 429.

[27a] Contrast *Owen* v. *Tate* [1976] Q.B. 402 (see below pp. 351–352), and Burrows, *The Law of Restitution*, pp. 215–216.

[28] But an instrument may show on its face that other joint and several sureties are intended to be parties; a surety is then bound only on the footing that his co-sureties have also agreed to be bound: *Evans* v. *Bembridge* (1855) 25 L.J. Ch. 102, (1856) 25 L.J.Ch. 334. For the effect of a forged signature, see *James Graham & Co. (Timber) Ltd.* v. *Southgate-Sands* [1986] Q.B. 80.

[29] For a more recent decision applying these established principles, see *Scholefield Goodman & Sons Ltd.* v. *Zyngier* [1986] A.C. 562, P.C.

[30] See below, p. 312, n. 58.

[31] *Coope* v. *Twynam* (1823) 1 T. & R. 426, 429, *per* Lord Eldon; *cf. Deering* v. *The Earl of Winchelsea* (1787) 2 Bos. & Pul. 270. See also *Ellis* v. *Emmanuel* (1876) 1 Ex.D. 157, 162, *per* Blackburn J.

occasion, the court may be convinced to the contrary, in which case the form of the transaction is wholly disregarded.[32]

(2) A party may be a surety for a surety. If the principal surety is compelled to pay the creditor, he cannot demand contribution from his surety, for they are not subject to a common demand.[33]

(3) In *Turner* v. *Davies*,[34] Lord Kenyon suggested that there is no right to contribution if a surety becomes a surety at the request and instance of his fellow surety: "there is no pretence for saying that he shall be liable to be called upon by the person at whose request he entered into the surety."[35] It is difficult to justify in principle this bald statement of law. In each case it should be a question of fact whether both parties have undertaken the risk of the principal debtor's insolvency and have become subject to a common demand for the same debt. If they have so agreed, it should be irrelevant that one became a surety at the invitation of the other.

Although the right to contribution is based on equitable principles, it may be modified by, or indeed excluded by, contract.[36] Hutton J., in *Swain* v. *Wall*,[37] accepted the submission of the plaintiff that by the terms of the bond the parties had agreed to pay only their respective parts of the principal debt, even in the event of the insolvency of one of their number. The principle of this case has been repeatedly accepted.[38] Any agreement to vary a surety's rights *inter se* may, however, be set aside if there is fraud[39] or fraudulent concealment,[40] or if any necessary condition has not been observed.[41]

When does the right to contribution arise?

Before a surety can claim contribution from a co-surety he must first show that the principal debtor is either insolvent or that he is joined as a party to the action. This sensible rule seeks to avoid multiplicity of suits. The primary liability is the principal debtor's, and a surety is expected to enforce his right of indemnity against him before he seeks contribution.

---

[32] *Reynolds* v. *Wheeler* (1861) 10 C.B.(N.S.) 561; see also *Davies* v. *Humphreys* (1840) 6 M. & W. 153.

[33] *Craythorne* v. *Swinburne* (1807) 14 Ves. 160; *Re Denton's Estate* [1904] 2 Ch. 178, 192–193, *per* Stirling L.J., 195, *per* Cozens-Hardy L.J.

[34] (1796) 2 Esp. 478.

[35] At p. 479.

[36] *Scholefield Goodman & Sons Ltd.* v. *Zyngier* [1986] A.C. 562, 574–575, P.C.

[37] (1641) 1 Rep. Ch. 149. Richard Hutton, who is reported to have decided this case, died in 1638 or 1639. He was a judge of the Court of Common Pleas, and the reports of his decisions were published posthumously. It was not unusual for common law judges to hear Chancery disputes but, if Hutton did decide this case, then the date of the report must be erroneous.

[38] See *Pendlebury* v. *Walker* (1841) 4 Y. & C.Ex. 424, 441–442, *per* Alderson B.; *Re Ennis* [1893] 3 Ch. 238.

[39] *Pendlebury* v. *Walker* (1841) 4 Y. & C.Ex. 424.

[40] *Mackreth* v. *Walmesley* (1884) 51 L.T. 19, 20, *per* Kay J.

[41] *Arcedeckne* v. *Lord Howard* (1875) L.J.Ch. 622, H.L.; *Barry* v. *Moroney* (1873) I.R. 8 Ch. 554. Such an agreement may presumably be also set aside for innocent misrepresentation or undue influence.

This rule was considered by the Court of Appeal in *Hay* v. *Carter*.[42] The plaintiff and three fellow directors had given guarantees to a bank guaranteeing their company's account. In 1933 the bank demanded from the guarantors £1,195, the amount of the company's overddraft, and the plaintiff paid £384. The bank, not satisfied with this contribution, recovered judgment against the plaintiff for the balance. Finally, the plaintiff paid the balance when a bankruptcy petition was served on him. He then sued the defendants, his co-sureties, for contribution. The defendants pleaded that, since the principal debtor was not a party to the action and since its insolvency had not been proved, the court had no jurisdiction to deal with the matter. Farwell J., relying on the old case of *Lawson* v. *Wright*,[43] where Lord Kenyon "had some doubts whether it was not absolutely necessary to prove the insolvency of the principal,"[44] upheld this submissioin. The Court of Appeal reversed his decision. Their analysis of previous authority, and particularly Eyre C.B.'s dicta in *Deering* v. *The Earl of Winchelsea*,[45] led them to the conclusion that the rule in *Lawson* v. *Wright* "does not lay down a condition precedent, but deals with matter of form, and a departure from it may be made it if is proved or if it becomes plain to the court that there is sufficient revealed in the facts before the court, to justify the inference that the principal debtor is insolvent."[46] On the facts of *Hay* v. *Carter* itself there was "strong prima facie ground for thinking that the presence of the company would have been perfectly useless and would only have led to an increase in the costs."[47] The only proper inference was that the company itself was insolvent and unable to pay.

The surety, having satisfied the court on this preliminary point, can claim contribution in the following alternative circumstances:

(1) A surety can claim contribution if he has paid more than his proportion of the debt for which he stood surety.[48] Lord Eldon L.C., in *Ex p. Gifford*,[49] recognised that if one surety "pays more than his proportion, there shall be a contribution for a proportion of the excess beyond the proportion, which in all events he is to pay." If he has paid more than his share, he can get contribution even though the creditor, at the date of payment, had not obtained judgment or even issued a writ against him.[50]

---

[42] [1935] Ch. 397.

[43] (1786) 1 Cox 275; see also *Stirling* v. *Burdett* [1911] 2 Ch. 418; *Ex p. Snowdon* (1881) 17 Ch.D. 44.

[44] (1786) 1 Cox 275.

[45] (1787) 1 Cox 318, 323; "but in substance the insolvency of Mr. Deering may be collected from the whole proceedings, which strongly imply it." This remark is not reported in 2 Bos. & Pul. 270.

[46] [1935] Ch. 397, 405–406, *per* Lord Hanworth M.R.; see also Romer L.J., at p. 408, and Maugham L.J., at pp. 411–412.

[47] *Per* Maugham L.J. at p. 411.

[48] But see below, p. 313, for the exceptional case where a creditor accepts a surety's share of the common debt in full payment of the debt.

[49] (1802) 6 Ves. 805, 808; see also *Holmes* v. *Williamson* (1817) 6 M. & S. 158; *Davies* v. *Humphreys* (1840) 6 M. & W. 153, 168; *Reynolds* v. *Wheeler* (1861) 30 L.J.(C.P.) 350; *Ex p. Snowdon* (1881) 17 Ch.D. 44.

[50] *Pitt* v. *Purssord* (1841) 8 M. & W. 538; *Restatement of Restitution*, § 81, comment h.

Instalment debts create special difficulties. The mere payment of more than his share of an instalment of a debt does not enable the surety to claim contribution unless each instalment can be regarded as a separate debt. The cases were analysed by Warrington J. in *Stirling* v. *Burdell*.[51] In that case, the plaintiffs and the defendants had executed a deed whereby they jointly and severally guaranteed repayment of £15,000 advanced on mortgage. At the date of the action the plaintiffs had paid more than their proportion of the total interest and premiums already paid, but had not yet paid their proportion of the entire debt. Warrington J. rejected the plaintiff's claim; for there can be no contribution until the payer, by paying more than his own proportionate share, has relieved a co-surety from a payment the latter should bear. "It is possible," he said,[52] "that if the co-sureties are now ordered to contribute to the payments of the plaintiffs they may ultimately be required to pay a larger sum than the amount of the limit because the payment to the co-sureties would be no answer to the claim" of the creditor. He construed the particular contract before him as one and indivisible so that the payment of each instalment of the debt could not be regarded as the payment of a separate debt.[53] He therefore rejected the claim for contribution. Strong indications in the contract will be required to persuade a court to come to a contrary conclusion.

(2) Alternatively, a surety is entitled to a declaration of his right to contribution from his co-surety if the creditor has obtained judgment or something equivalent to a judgment against him. In *Wolmershausen* v. *Gullick*,[54] the plaintiff was the executrix of the deceased, who, with four others, was surety for the debt of a company to a bank. The bank put in a claim against the estate for the whole amount of the debt, and the plaintiff, who had paid nothing at the date of the action, claimed contribution from the co-sureties, who contended that the plaintiff could not maintain the action until she had paid more than her share. The question posed was this: had the plaintiff to wait until she actually sustained a loss or would relief be given if the loss was imminent? R. S. Wright J. granted a declaration that the plaintiff would be entitled to contribution "whenever she has paid any sum beyond her share." He said[55]:

> "I think that, if the plaintiff had made the creditor a defendant to the present action, I ought to have held that the allowance of the principal creditor's claim in the administration action was equivalent to a judgment against the plaintiff for the whole amount of the guarantee, and that on the precedents of *Morgan* v. *Seymour* and *Deering* v. *The Earl of Winchelsea*, the plaintiff would have been entitled to a declaration of her right to contribution and to an order upon the solvent co-surety to pay his proportion to the principal creditor. The principal creditor, not being a party, I

---

[51] [1911] 2 Ch. 418.
[52] At p. 423.
[53] *Cf. Re Macdonald* [1881] W.N. 130, C.A.
[54] [1893] 2 Ch. 514.
[55] At pp. 528–529.

think that I cannot order payment to him or directly prevent him from enforcing his judgment against the plaintiff alone. Nor can I at present order the co-surety to pay his half to the plaintiff, for the plaintiff cannot give him a discharge as against the principal creditor. . . . But I think I can declare the plaintiff's right, and make a prospective order under which, whenever she has paid any sum beyond her share, she can get it back. . . . "

There are indications in this decision that the principle is wider, and that judgment, or its equivalent, is unnecessary if the creditor has a right to immediate payment from the surety.[56] The scope of this principle is uncertain. Possibly it is enough that the creditor threatens to make the surety liable for more than his share.[57]

The amount recoverable by way of contribution

Unless the sureties have made an agreement *inter se* varying their liability, each solvent surety must contribute equally to the common debt.[58] Thus, if A, B and C are sureties for a debt of £600 and both the debtor and A become insolvent, then C and B are liable to contribute equally; so that if C pays the whole debt, he can recover £300 from B on proof of the debtor's and A's insolvency. If, however, A, B and C had agreed to bear the debt in the ratios 1 to 2 to 1, then C will be able to recover from B £400, that is B's own share, £300, plus two-thirds of A's share (£150), £100.[59] Similar consequences should follow if a surety dies and his death discharges him from liability.[60]

Each surety, moreover, must bring into hotchpot any benefits, such as securities, recovered from the principal debtor[61] or even from an insolvent

---

[56] See his apparent approval, at pp. 527–528, of a passage in *Lindley on Partnership* (5th ed.), p. 374, which reaches a somewhat similar conclusion.

[57] *Cf.* Rowlatt, *Principal and Surety*, p. 159.

[58] *Deering* v. *The Earl of Winchelsea* (1787) 2 Bos. & Pul. 270; *Ellesmere Brewery Co.* v. *Cooper* [1896] 1 Q.B. 75. See, generally, Williston, § 1279. For the position at law, which is no longer relevant since 1873, see above, p. 307.
Difficult questions arise if the sureties guarantee different amounts, *e.g.* if A guarantees £300, B, £400 and C £500. The initial question is to determine whether the sureties are sureties for different debts or whether their guarantee is for the same debt. Only in the latter case is there any question of contribution. In *Ellis* v. *Emmanuel* (1876) 1 Ex.D. 157, 162, Blackburn J. was of the opinion that "the limits put on the amounts which could be recovered from the sureties respectively would affect the amount which each was to contribute." But he did not indicate how the contribution claim would be affected. Assume that the principal debt was £600 but the creditor had accepted £500 from C in discharge of the debt. What can C recover from A and B, who had guaranteed £300 and £400 respectively? Under the maximum liability principle (see below, p. 318) it is three-twelfths and four-twelfths respectively of £500: see *Re McDonough* (1876) 10 Ir.Rep. 269; and *cf. Cornfoot* v. *Holdenson* [1931] A.L.R. 376. But in *Commercial Union Assurance Co. Ltd.* v. *Hayden* [1977] Q.B. 804, 815, Cairns L.J. emphasised that there was no authority binding on the Court of Appeal: see below, pp. 318–319 for a fuller discussion. See also Burrows, *The Law of Restitution*, p. 221.

[59] *Pendlebury* v. *Walker* (1841) 4 Y. & C.Ex. 424; *Ellesmere Brewery* v. *Cooper* [1896] 1 Q.B. 75, 81, *per* Lord Russell C.J. *Cf. Naumann* v. *Northcote* (February 7, 1978, C.A. Transcript No. 7835), cited in Rowlatt, *op.cit.* p. 156.

[60] For the effect of death of a surety, see below, p. 316.

[61] *Ex p. Crisp* (1744) 1 Atk. 133, 135, *per* Lord Hardwicke; *Berridge* v. *Berridge* (1890) 44 Ch.D. 168. A surety who has paid a creditor's debt has a statutory right under the Mercantile Law

co-surety.[62] On a similar principle, Pearson J. held in *Re Arcedeckne*[63] that, before claiming contribution, a surety had to bring into hotchpot policies on the life of the debtor, originally taken out by the creditor and assigned by him, on payment of the debt, to the surety. For the surety must be deemed to have "purchased those rights at the time . . . not for the benefit of himself only, but for the benefit of his co-sureties"[64]; the solvent co-sureties were, therefore, entitled to the benefit of the proceeds of the policies.[65]

These principles have, in some cases, been modified to prevent injustice. For example, a surety may pay only his share of a common debt, but the creditor may accept that payment in full settlement of the debt: the surety can claim only a rateable contribution from his co-sureties.[66] Again, the principal debtor may make a payment to his creditor in relief of his sureties; each surety will then be liable only for his share less a rateable proportion of the debtor's contribution.[67]

Loss of the right to contribution

(1) *By the act of the creditor*

A creditor who releases the principal debtor thereby discharges the debtor's sureties. The effect of the release is to discharge the debt and the sureties are

---

Amendment Act 1856, s.5, to the benefit of every judgment or other security held by the creditor in respect of the debt; see *Duncan, Fox & Co.* v. *North and South Wales Bank* (1880) 6 App.Cas. 1, 19, *per* Lord Blackburn. Indeed, he may use all remedies to compel contribution; see *Stirling* v. *Forrester* (1821) 3 Bli. 575, 590, *per* Lord Redesdale; *Re Parker* [1894] 3 Ch. 400, C.A.

[62] *Duncan, Fox & Co.* v. *North and South Wales Bank* (1880) 6 App.Cas. 1, 19, *per* Lord Blackburn, impliedly dissenting from Jessel M.R. in the Court of Appeal in that case at (1879) 11 Ch.D. 88, 96. His conclusion is, in our view, supported by the terms of the Mercantile Law Amendment Act 1856, s.5. Cf. *Restatement of Restitution*, § 85. But *semble* a surety should not be entitled to securities given to the creditor by a stranger: see *Chatterton* v. *Maclean* [1951] 1 All E.R. 761, 766–767, *per* Parker J.; *Goodman* v. *Keel* [1923] 4 D.L.R. 468. But *cf. Sherwin* v. *McWilliams* (1921) 17 Tasm.L.R. 16, 94.

[63] (1883) 24 Ch.D. 709; see also *Steel* v. *Dixon* (1881) 17 Ch.D. 825; *Re Albert Life Assurance Co.* (1870) L.R. 11 Eq. 164.

[64] At p. 716 (an allowance was given for premiums paid by the assignee for the upkeep of the policies); see also *Aldrich* v. *Cooper* (1803) 8 Ves. 382, 385, *per* Lord Eldon.

[65] In the absence of any contract between them, it is doubtful whether a surety can recover from his co-surety the costs of defending an action brought against him by the creditor, even where the defence was, in the circumstances, reasonable. The surety decisions are not conclusive, though they suggest that costs are recoverable if there is a contract between the sureties: see generally, *Holmes* v. *Williamson* (1817) 6 M. & S. 158; *Gillett* v. *Rippon* (1829) M. & M. 406; *Kemp* v. *Finden* (1844) 12 M. & W. 421; *Smith* v. *Howell* (1851) 6 Ex. 730; *Wolmerhausen* v. *Gullick* [1893] 2 Ch. 514, 529–530, *per* R. S. Wright J.; *Shepheard* v. *Bray* [1906] 2 Ch. 235, 254, *per* Warrington J.; *cf. Knight* v. *Hughes* (1828) 3 Car. & P. 467; *Roach* v. *Thompson* (1830) 4 Car. & P. 194. In principle the surety should, in the absence of a contract with his co-surety, be reimbursed only to the extent that his payment has benefited the co-surety. A similar problem has arisen in trust law and in compulsory discharge of another's liability: see below, p. 330, n. 83, pp. 348–349, 361–362.

[66] *Ex p. Snowden* (1881) 17 Ch.D. 44, 47, *per* James L.J.; see also *Davies* v. *Humphreys* (1840) 6 M. & W. 153; *Walker* v. *Bowry* (1924) 35 C.L.R. 48.

[67] *Stirling* v. *Forrester* (1821) 3 Bli. 575, 590, *per* Lord Redesdale. See, generally, G. L. Williams, *Joint Obligations*, pp. 167–168.

thus freed from their guarantee.[68] But a creditor who covenants not to sue a principal debtor and reserves his rights against the sureties[69] does not release them.

The giving of time by the creditor to the principal debtor also discharges the debtor's sureties. The justification for this rule is not easily apparent. In *Philpot* v. *Briant*,[70] Best C.J. gave the following rationalisation:

> "A creditor by giving further time for payment, undertakes that he will not, during the time given, receive the debt from any surety of the debtor, for the instant that a surety paid the debt he would have a right to recover it against his principal. . . . If to prevent the surety from suing the principal, the creditor refuses to receive the debt from the surety until the time given to the debtor for payment by the new agreement, the surety must be altogether discharged, otherwise he might be in a situation worse than he was by his contract of suretyship. If he be allowed to pay the debt at the time when he undertook that it should be paid, the principal debtor might have the means of repaying him. Before the expiration of the extended period of payment the principal debtor might have become insolvent. A creditor, by giving time to the principal debtor, in equity, destroys the obligation of the sureties. . . . "

This reasoning is based on the surety's right to pay off the creditor and to sue the debtor in the creditor's name. But Blackburn J. was "not aware of any instance in which a surety ever in practice exercised this right."[71] And though he thought the rule "consistent neither with justice nor common sense," he admitted that "it has been so long firmly established that it can only be altered by the legislature."[72]

A surety who has paid more than his share before the creditor's release of the principal debtor cannot recover the excess from the creditor; he still has his action against the principal debtor. In *Reade* v. *Lowndes*[73] Romilly M.R. pointed out that the "right of action against the principal debtor" (or, *semble*,

---

[68] *Nisbet* v. *Smith* (1789) 2 Bro.C.C. 579; *Samuell* v. *Howarth* (1817) 3 Mer. 272; *Commercial Bank of Tasmania* v. *Jones* [1893] A.C. 313.

[69] There is much confusion in the books whether a creditor who covenants not to sue, as distinct from one who releases a debtor, discharges the sureties. The real antithesis appears to be between an absolute release and a release which reserves rights against sureties, often called a covenant not to sue. As Brett J. said in *Bateson* v. *Gosling* (1871) 7 L.R.C.P. 9, 17, "the proviso reserving the rights of creditors having security has the effect of reducing it to a covenant not to sue, the debt is not gone, and the remedy of the creditor against the surety remains," See also *Walmesley* v. *Cooper* (1839) 11 A. & E. 216; *Kearsley* v. *Cole* (1846) 16 M. & W. 128; *Price* v. *Barker* (1855) 4 E. & B. 760; *Bailey* v. *Edwards* (1864) 4 B. & S. 761; *Solly* v. *Forbes* (1820) 2 B. & B. 38; *cf. Ex p. Smith* (1789) 3 Bro.C.C.1. These are archaic distinctions (see *Bryanston Finance* v. *de Vries* [1975] Q.B. 703, 723, *per* Lord Denning M.R.), but they survive.

[70] (1828) 4 Bing. 717, 719. See also *Nisbet* v. *Smith* (1789) 2 Bro.C.C. 579, 582, *per* Lord Thurlow L.C.; *English* v. *Darley* (1800) 2 Bos. & Pul. 61, 62, *per* Lord Eldon C.J.; *Bailey* v. *Edwards* (1864) 4 B. & S. 761.

[71] *Swire* v. *Redman* (1876) 1 Q.B.D. 536, 541.

[72] *Ibid.* at p. 542; see also *Legal and General Assurance Society Ltd.* v. *Drake Insurance Co. Ltd.* [1992] 1 All E.R. 283, 293–294, *per* Ralph Gibson L.J., dissenting.

[73] (1857) 23 Beav. 361, 368.

any fellow surety) "had accrued to the surety as soon as he paid to the creditor the amount required from him and he is alone to blame if he does not enforce his demand."

On the other hand a creditor's release of a surety only discharges the remaining sureties if their liability is joint or joint and several,[74] or if it is an express condition that they may be released in that event.[75] The position of a several surety was considered in *Ward* v. *The National Bank of New Zealand Ltd.*[76] Sir Robert Collier, who delivered the advice of the Judicial Committee of the Privy Council, pointed out that:

> "the claim of a several surety to be released upon the creditor releasing another surety, arises not from the creditor having broken his contract, but from his having deprived the surety of his remedy for contribution in equity. The surety, therefore, in order to support his claim, must show that he had a right to contribution, and that that right has been taken away or injuriously affected."[77]

In such a case, the co-surety's release should be limited to the extent of the contribution he could have claimed from the released surety.

A creditor who agrees to give time to a surety does not thereby discharge the remaining sureties.[78] Such an agreement must be for the eventual benefit of all the sureties since it postpones a claim for contribution and gives the principal debtor more time to pay. But the position may be different if the creditor agrees with the principal debtor to give a surety time to pay.[79]

A secured creditor does not owe his surety any duty of care to exercise at any particular time or at all the power of sale, conferred by the debtor's mortgage, over assets deposited to secure the principal debt. The tort of negligence "does not supplant the principles of equity or contradict contractual promises or complement the remedy of judicial review or supplement statutory rights."[80] In contrast:

> "if the person guaranteed does any act injurious to the surety, or inconsistent with his rights, or if he omits to do any act which his duty enjoins him to do, and the omission proves injurious to the surety, the latter will be

---

[74] The discharge of a joint debtor discharges all: see *Bonser* v. *Cox* (1841) 4 Beav. 379; *Nicholson* v. *Revill* (1836) 4 A. & E. 675. Contrast Civil Liability (Contribution) Act 1978, s.3 (judgment against any person liable in respect of any debt or damage shall not bar an action against any other person jointly liable).

[75] *Ellesmere Brewery Co.* v. *Cooper* [1893] 1 Q.B. 75.

[76] (1883) L.R. 8 App.Cas. 755; applied in *Walker* v. *Bowry* (1924) 35 C.L.R. 48.

[77] At p. 766.

[78] *Dunn* v. *Slee* (1817) 1 Moo.C.P. 2; see also *Ex p. Smith* (1713) 1 P.Wms. 237, 238, *per* Lord Harcourt.

[79] *Oriental Financial Corporation* v. *Overend, Gurney & Co.* (1871) 7 Ch.App. 142, 152, *per* Lord Hatherley L.C.; see, generally, G. L. Williams, *Joint Obligations*, pp. 121–127.

[80] *China and South Sea Bank Ltd.* v. *Tan* [1990] 1 A.C. 536, 543–544, *per* Lord Templeman, P.C.

discharged . . . the rights of a surety depend rather on principles of equity than upon the actual contract."[81]

(2) *By the act of the surety*

It is doubtful whether time given to a principal debtor by a surety, who has become the principal creditor, discharges a co-surety from his duty to contribute.[82] It is equally doubtful whether a surety's release of a co-surety discharges any remaining sureties from contributing such a proportion of the debt as they would have recovered from the released surety.[83] If and when these points arise for decision, the principle underlying the Judicial Committee's decision in *Ward* v. *The National Bank of New Zealand Ltd.*[84] should, in our view, be followed: namely, did the release of the co-surety or the giving of time to the principal debtor take away or injuriously affect the remaining sureties' right to contribution?[85] An analogous problem arises where a surety pays the principal creditor without giving any notice to his co-surety, who considers that there was a valid defence to the creditor's claim. In *Smith* v. *Compton*,[86] Lord Tenterden C.J. considered that the only effect of want of notice to a defendant was to allow the latter to show that a compromise, made by the plaintiff with the creditor, was improvident and could have been struck on better terms. Therefore, if a co-surety can prove that the demand for payment might have been resisted, he may be able to show that the compromise was improvident and that he "might have obtained better terms if the opportunity had been given him."[87] If so, he should be released.[88]

(3) *Death*

The death of a surety does not of necessity release his estate from its duty to contribute to the payment of the common debt. If the sureties are bound severally, the estate of any deceased surety must contribute,[89] although the amount of the contribution will depend in equity on the number of solvent

---

[81] *Watts* v. *Shuttleworth* (1860) 5 H.& N. 235, 247–248, *per* Pollock C.B., adopted by Lord Templeman in *China and South Sea Bank Ltd.* v. *Tan* [1990] 1 A.C. 536. See above, n. 80. See also *Wulf* v. *Jay* (1872) L.R. 7 Q.B. 756. For instance where the creditors claim failed, see *Burns* v. *Trade Credits Ltd.* [1981] 1 W.L.R. 805, P.C. (creditors' substantial alteration of mortgage terms, guarantor discharged); *National Westminster Bank* v. *Riley* [1986] F.L.R. 213, C.A. (distinguishing repudiatory from non-repudiatory breach by the creditor); *Westpac Securities* v. *Dickie* [1991] 1 N.Z.L.R. 657, C.A. (creditors' non-disclosure). Contrast *James Graham & Co. (Timber) Ltd.* v. *Southgate-Sands* [1986] Q.B. 80 (contract of guarantee not binding, signature of one of the sureties forged). See, generally, [1990] J.B.L. 325 [Phillips].

[82] *Greenwood* v. *Francis* [1899] 1 Q.B. 312, 320–322, *per* A. L. Smith L.J.; *cf. Way* v. *Hearne* (1862) 11 C.B.(N.S.) 774.

[83] See *Fletcher* v. *Grover*, 11 N.H. 368 (1840).

[84] (1883) L.R. 8 App.Cas. 755. And see *Molsons Bank* v. *Kovinsky* [1924] 4 D.L.R. 330.

[85] *Cf. Griffith* v. *Wade* (1966) 60 D.L.R. (2d) 62, 70, *per* Johnson J.A.

[86] (1832) 3 B. & Ad. 407, (an indemnity case), doubted, on grounds not affecting the principle stated in the text, in *Great Western Ry.* v. *Fisher* [1905] 1 Ch. 316, 324, *per* Buckley J.

[87] At p. 408.

[88] *Ibid.*

[89] *Cf. Restatement of Restitution*, § 83.

sureties.[90] It is doubtful whether death releases joint sureties. Although a creditor's rights against a joint surety cease on that surety's death, it does not follow that the living surety's right to seek contribution from the deceased surety's estate also ends, for it may be said that the right to contribution depends not on a present common obligation but on a common obligation which existed at some time in the past.[91] The cases are not conclusive and those which have allowed a contribution claim in these circumstances have been decided on the ground that the liability to contribute survived because of an implied contract between the sureties.[92] But, in principle, a contribution claim in equity should lie.

(b) *Insurers*[93]

Non-marine insurance

An assured person cannot recover more than the loss he has suffered, even though he is covered by more than one policy of insurance.[94] He may proceed against one insurer for the whole amount. If he does, the insurer, who has paid more than his share of the common debt, may recover contribution from the other insurers liable *in solidum*.[95] The right of contribution between insurers is independent of contract.[96] But it may be modified and limited by contract; so, one insurer may agree to pay only a certain percentage of the loss, to pay up to a fixed sum, or to pay only if another insurer does not meet his obligations.[97] What is the "rateable proportion" of the loss which each insurer must bear is dependent upon the construction of the particular clause in the particular policy.[98] In such circumstances, there appears to be two principal methods of apportioning liability. There is the "maximum liability" basis, which apportions liability according to the maximum liability for which each insurer agrees to make himself liable under its policy. Then there is the "independent liability" basis, under which it is first ascertained "what would have been the liability of each insurer if it had been the only insurer and the total liability to

---

[90] See Rowlatt, *op. cit.* p. 157.

[91] The position was different at law: see *Batard* v. *Hawes* (1853) 2 E. & Bl. 287.

[92] G. L. Williams, pp. 165–166; *cf.* Rowlatt, pp. 157–158 and *Cunningham-Reid* v. *Public Trustee* [1944] K.B. 602.

[93] See, generally, Clarke, *The Law of Insurance Contracts* (1989) pp. 586 *et seq.*

[94] *Godin* v. *London Assurance Co.* (1758) 1 Burr. 489, 492, *per* Lord Mansfield (a marine insurance case, but the principles are similar).

[95] *North British and Mercantile Insurance Co.* v. *London, Liverpool and Globe Insurance Co.* (1876) 5 Ch.D. 569, 581, *per* James L.J.

[96] The equitable right arises because the parties are co-insurers; it is not acquired from or through the insured: *Legal and General Assurance Co. Ltd.* v. *Drake Insurance Co. Ltd.* [1992] 1 Q.B. 877, C.A.: see below, p. 319.

[97] But see *Gale* v. *Motor Union Insurance Co.* [1928] K.B. 359.

[98] It is not uncommon for a policy to contain a contribution clause which effectively compels the claimant to distribute the loss himself. Consequently the clause limits the liability of the insurer to a rateable proportion of the loss. "So the basis on which the co-insurers' contribution is to be rated or calculated ... has become important to the assured" as well as to the insurer: see *Commercial Union Assurance Co. Ltd.* v. *Hayden* [1977] Q.B. 804, 819, *per* Stephenson L.J.

the assured should be divided in proportion to those independent liabilities."[99]
The maximum liability basis appears to follow the analogy of the cases on
suretyship, where each surety seemingly contributes "proportionately to the
amount for which each is surety."[1]

It is possible that the maximum liability basis determines apportionment
claims between property insurers[2]; but in practice most domestic policies
"contain *pro rata* average clauses . . . when the independent liability basis is
used."[3] Claims between liability insurers, where each policy states that the
insurer "shall not be liable for more than its rateable proportion thereof" and
where the insurance policies cover the same risk, are, however, determined on
an independent liability basis. In *Commercial Union Assurance Co. Ltd.* v.
Hayden,[4] the Court of Appeal was not persuaded that "the same basis should
apply to liability insurance as to property insurance, nor that the analogy with
co-sureties is a reliable guide."[5] The independent liability basis is said to
produce, in liability insurance, a more realistic result which fulfils the expectations of, and fairly distributes the burdens between, the insurers.[6] An insurer
may not know that there will be double insurance; and the purpose of imposing
a limit in liability insurance is to protect the insurer against exceptionally large
claims. Premiums under the two types of insurance policies are differently
assessed; unlike premiums on property insurance, liability insurance premiums are not calculated on a percentage of the sum or value insured.
Moreover, the maximum liability principle is unworkable if one policy has a
limit on liability and the other does not. Consequently, in liability insurance,
there is an equal division of liability up to the lower limit assumed by one of the
insurers; but on a claim above that limit the burden would "fall on the insurer
who had accepted the higher limit."[7] For example, if insurer A's maximum
liability was £1,000,000 and B's £10,000, and the assured's claim was for
£10,000, apportionment would be in the ratio of 1:1. But if the claim was for
£40,000, apportionment would be in the ratio of 4:1.[8] In *Commercial Union*

---

[99] *Commercial Union Assurance Co. Ltd.* v. *Hayden* [1977] Q.B. 804, 811, *per* Cairns L.J.

[1] *Pendlebury* v. *Walker* (1841) 4 Y. & C. 429, 441, *per* Alderson B.; see above, p. 312, and n. 58.
But *cf.* Cairns L.J. in the *Commercial Union* case at p. 815.

[2] See below, text accompanying nn. 4–12; and *cf.* Marine Insurance Act 1906, s.80(1), and the
comments on this section in *Commercial Union Assurance Co. Ltd.* v. *Hayden* [1977] Q.B. 804,
813, 819: but see below, p. 319.

[3] *Commercial Union Assurance Co. Ltd.* v. *Hayden* [1977] Q.B. 804, 811–812, *per* Cairns L.J. But
Cairns L.J. and Lawton L.J. left open the question of the proper basis of apportionment in
property assurance: see above, n. 90. *Cf. Commercial Union Insurance Co. of New York* v. *The
Farmers Mutual Fire Insurance Co. of St. Louis County*, 457 S.W. (2d) 224, (1970). (Paid the
whole of the fire loss without knowing that another insurer, D, had also provided insurance
against that loss. The Missouri court denied contribution; the contracts of insurance were
independent of each other and had *pro rata* clauses: there was, therefore, no common liability.)

[4] [1977] Q.B. 804.

[5] At p. 814, *per* Cairns L.J. See also Lawton L.J. at p. 822.

[6] At p. 816, *per* Cairns L.J.

[7] At p. 822, *per* Lawton L.J.

[8] Seemingly this is the appropriate ratio: at pp. 806–807, *arguendo*.

Assurance this result was described as a just one. Once established it may persuade the courts to conclude that the independent liability principle should also apply to property insurance.[9]

Each policy must be in force at the time of the loss.[9a] But what if the insurer is in a position to repudiate liability on the ground that the assured has broken a condition? For example, the assured may have entered into policies (both of which contain "rateable proportion" clauses) with two different insurers and insurer A, having fully indemnified the assured, seeks contribution from insurer B, to be met by the defence that the assured had failed to notify B of his potential claim under the policy. In *Legal and General Assurance Society Ltd.* v. *Drake Insurance Co. Ltd.*[10] the Court of Appeal held, Ralph Gibson L.J. dissenting, that insurer A's right of contribution was not defeated even though the requirement to give notice was a condition precedent to insurer B's liability. It was said that there is a "sharp distinction between steps required to enforce a valid claim under a policy in force at the time of the loss, and a claim which never was valid, and never could be enforced," for example, if the insurer has a good defence based on the assured's misrepresentation or non-disclosure.[11] Consequently, a co-insurer will, subject to any defences, be required to make contribution even though the assured had failed to give a valid notice of claim within the time stipulated in the policy; the co-insurer is then *potentially* liable. To deny "contribution in such a case would be to place the equity [the equitable right to contribution] at the whim of the insured."[12]

However, in *Eagle Star Insurance Co. Ltd.* v. *Provincial Insurance plc*,[12a] the Privy Council doubted whether, as a matter of principle, the distinction drawn in the *Legal and General Assurance* case was justified. The facts of that case were different from *Legal and General Assurance* in that it was a third party who was injured. Neither insurer had therefore any contractual relationship with him; their liability arose under statute.[12b] But Lord Woolf, who delivered the Board's advice, concluded that the distinction in the source of liability was not material, but that the rate of contribution between the insurers should nonetheless be determined by their separate contracts of insurance if those contracts were in force at the date of the loss. In *Eagle Star* insurer A had cancelled the defendant assured's policy before the accident but had failed to take steps to obtain its surrender. In contrast, insurer B would have been able to avoid its liability to the assured because it had not been given notice of the accident within the time specified in the policy. But "looking at the issue from the

---

[9] See above, n. 2. See also [1977] C.L.J. 231 [Harpum], cited in *MacGillivray & Parkington on Insurance Law*, § 1747.

[9a] *Monksfield* v. *Vehicle and General Insurance Co. Ltd.* [1971] 1 Lloyd's Rep. 139: see below, n. 12c.

[10] [1992] Q.B. 887.

[11] *Legal and General Assurance Society Ltd.* v. *Drake Insurance Co. Ltd.* [1992] Q.B. 887, 891–897, *per* Lloyd L.J.

[12] *Ibid.*: [1989] 3 All E.R. 923, 925, *per* Roger Buckley Q.C., sitting as a Deputy Judge of the High Court.

[12a] [1993] 3 All E.R. 1.

[12b] Bahamas Road Traffic Act, s.12.

insurer's and the insured's standpoint, it makes no difference if an insurer defeats a claim by relying on action taken before or after the loss occurred." There could then be no justification for determining the parties' liability to make contribution by looking to their potential liability at the date of the loss. If both insurers had been liable in part to the assured, then they should contribute to their statutory liability in accordance with their respective liability under their contracts to the assured. But, on the facts, since neither insurer was liable to the assured, they should share their statutory liability equally, "irrespective of the date upon which they repudiated liability."[12c] The Privy Council was aware that this conclusion meant that "the action of a person insured in relation to one insurer can affect the rights of contribution of the other insurer." But the Board took comfort from the fact that "it is unlikely that the existence of the other insurer would have been known at the time the contract of assurance was made."[12d] The claim for contribution will fail if the insurer's payment is a voluntary payment; and it is a voluntary payment if the insurer is not obliged to make the payment to the assured. It follows, therefore, that if both policies contain rateable proportion clauses and the insurer pays a claim in full, with full knowledge that a co-insurer has covered the same loss, his contribution claim[13] will be excluded in respect of any payment made voluntarily in excess of the rateable proportion.

For a contribution claim to succeed, there must be a common peril and the policies must cover the same interest in the same property; if the interests are different the contribution claim will fail, as *North British and Mercantile Insurance Co. Ltd.* v. *London, Liverpool and Globe Insurance Co. Ltd.* demonstrates. In that case wharfingers, whose liability against loss was strict, took out several insurance policies against loss or damage to goods by fire; every policy contained a contribution clause limiting each insurer's liability to an *aliquot* share of the loss. Some grain which they were storing was owned by a merchant who had also insured it with different insurers on similar terms. Fire destroyed the grain and the wharfingers' claims were met by their insurers, who then claimed contribution from the insurers of the merchant. The Court of Appeal, affirming Jessel M.R., held that the merchant's insurers were not liable to contribute.[14] For the merchant's policies had been entered into for his own benefit as an additional security. Although there was a common peril, the policies protected different interests in the same property.[15]

[12c] At p. 8. Hence *Monksfield* v. *Vehicle and General Insurance Co. Ltd.* [1971] 1 Lloyd's Rep. 139, which the majority of the Court of Appeal in *Legal and General* did not follow, was correctly decided.

[12d] *Ibid.*

[13] *Legal and General Assurance Society Ltd.* v. *Drake Insurance Co. Ltd.* [1992] Q.B. 887, C.A., applying s.149(4) of the Road Traffic Act 1972, which enables the insurer to recover the excess over its net liability from the assured.

[14] See also *Portavon Cinema Co. Ltd.* v. *Price and Century Insurance Co. Ltd.* [1939] 4 All E.R. 601; and see the surety and mortgage cases, above, pp. 310–311 and below, pp. 321–322.

[15] It appears that the principle of this case is in practice disregarded: see *MacGillivray and Parkington on Insurance Law*, § 1750.

Marine insurance

The conditions governing contribution claims by marine insurers are similar to those just discussed.[16] In marine insurance, however, the law has been codified in the Marine Insurance Act 1906. Section 32(2) of that Act allows the assured in cases of double assurance to claim against the insurers in any order he thinks fit; this rule is subject to a contrary intention expressed in a particular policy.[17] Section 80(1) requires each insurer to contribute rateably to the loss in proportion to the amount of his liability under the contract of insurance. In *Commercial Union Assurance Co. Ltd.* v. *Hayden*[18] it was said that section 80(1) was ambiguous and may mean "either the amount of the insurance or the actual liability in the particular case." There appears to be no authority whether the maximum or independent liability method governs contribution claims between marine insurers. It is to be hoped that the courts will adopt the independent liability method.[19] Certainly the maximum liability method cannot be easily applied if one policy is valued and the other unvalued, or if the policies cover different risks only some of which overlap.[20]

(c) *Mortgagors*

Claims of this nature, which are rare, generally arise in the following circumstances. A owns land subject to a charge. He transfers part of the land to B and retains the remainder of the land. He then pays off the charge on the whole land. Can he claim contribution from B?

Whether A can claim contribution from B in these circumstances depends on principles akin to those laid down in the surety cases. He must show that he has an equity to call upon B to contribute to the debt. Prima facie he has, for the "original principle of the Common Law was *equality*, that is to say contribution in the *ratio* of value, wholly irrespective of priority of dates of purchase."[21] But this equity can be displaced if it is evident that either A or B was intended to bear the primary liability. So if, as in *Re Dunlop*,[22] A's property is subject to a specific charge and B's to a general lien for the same debt, and A pays the debt, A cannot claim contribution from B towards his payment; "the special incumbrance creates a primary charge, and the property included in it is primarily liable..."[23] But if A conveys part of mortgaged land to B, subject to the mortgage, and retains the remainder, he can claim contribution from B in

---

[16] *Newby* v. *Reed* (1763) 1 Wm.Bl. 416.

[17] *American Surety Co. of New York* v. *Wrightson* (1910) 16 Com.Cas. 37, 54, *per* Hamilton J.

[18] [1977] Q.B. 804, *per* Cairns L.J., citing *Ivamy on General Principles of Insurance Law*, p. 469.

[19] See above, pp. 317–319.

[20] *Arnould on Marine Insurance*, §§ 434–438 for a full discussion.

[21] *Ker* v. *Ker* (1869) 4 I.R. Eq. 15, 28 *per* Christian L.J., paraphrasing the conclusions of the court in *Harbert's Case* (1584) 3 Co. 11b.

[22] (1882) 21 Ch.D. 583.

[23] At p. 592, *per* Jessel M.R.

proportion to the respective value of A's and B's land.[24] To throw the burden completely on to B, A must prove that B expressly agreed to indemnify him against the whole mortgage debt.[25] Again, if A has personally covenanted to pay the mortgage debt, the principle of casting proportionate parts of the debt on different properties is displaced. It is equitable that he who is "under a personal obligation to pay the debt should bear it."[26]

It follows, therefore, that a contribution claim is only likely to arise today where A's property is originally subject to a paramount charge, that is, a charge not created by himself, and where A's property and the property conveyed to B are subject to a common liability of the same degree.[27] But if A has created the mortgage, he will have personally covenanted to pay the mortgage debt; he will not then be able to claim contribution.[28]

(d) Joint Tenants

Before 1926 contribution claims between joint tenants were not uncommon, and Fitzherbert[29] gives a precedent for a writ of contribution, which "lieth where there are tenants ... who jointly hold a mill *pro indiviso* ... "[30] Claims arose because one joint tenant had incurred expense on behalf of them all. But since the 1925 property legislation such claims are not likely to recur.[31] The property will normally be held on trust for sale, and any expenses will have been incurred by the trustees for sale.[32]

(e) Joint Contractors

A joint contractor who is called upon to perform more than his proper share of a common liability under a contract can recover contribution from his fellow joint contractors.[33] A principle similar to that of *Deering* v. *The Earl of Winchelsea*[34] still governs these claims, which arise, therefore, "not from any notion of implied contract, but as an equitable right springing from the

---

[24] *Re Mainwaring's Settlement Trusts* [1937] Ch. 96. There is some uncertainty as to the date when the properties should be valued: see pp. 105–106, *per* Romer L.J.

[25] *Waring* v. *Ward* (1802) 7 Ves. 332, 337, *per* Lord Eldon.

[26] *Re Best* [1924] 1 Ch. 42, 45, *per* Tomlin J.

[27] *Ker* v. *Ker* (1869) I.R. 4 Eq. 15.

[28] *Re Darby's Estate* [1907] 1 Ch. 465.

[29] *F.N.B.* 162 and 127; see also Co.Litt. 200.

[30] *F.N.B.* 162. In the writ, partially quoted in the text, Fitzherbert envisages that a contribution claim would arise even between tenants in common (but see *Leigh* v. *Dickeson* (1884) 15 Q.B.D. 60, where the Court of Appeal rejected such a claim and restricted the writ, which governed claims arising from titles to realty, to joint tenants).
In *Davitt* v. *Titcumb* [1989] 3 All E.R. 417, Scott J. was prepared to allow a contribution claim where one tenant in common had discharged a common debt in most unusual circumstances. Contrast *Re Leslie* (1883) 23 Ch.D. 552.

[31] *Cf. Cunningham-Reid* v. *Public Trustee* [1944] K.B. 602.

[32] Megarry and Wade, *op. cit.* Chap. 9.

[33] In the 19th century, the courts were often asked to consider whether a party was a partner or a contractor: see below, pp. 331–333.

[34] (1787) 2 Bos. & Pul. 270: see above, pp. 307 *et seq.*

relations of the parties as persons liable for the same debt."[35] It has been suggested that the courts should have power to "make an apportionment that takes into account the part played by each defendant in the circumstances giving rise to the claim."[36] But the Civil Liability (Contribution) Act 1978, which gives the court a power to assess the amount of contribution on just and equitable grounds, has no application since the contractors are not liable in respect of any damage suffered. Consequently, the burden falls equally on joint contractors unless they have agreed to vary their liability *inter se*.[37]

Only in two rather special instances has the analogy of the surety cases been rejected. First, as we have seen, it is established that a creditor who covenants not to sue the principal debtor releases the sureties of the debtor unless he reserves his rights against them.[38] But the covenant of a creditor not to sue one joint contractor does not of itself release other joint contractors, who remain liable for the debt.[39] Secondly, the courts have refused to extend to joint contractors the curious rule that a creditor who gives time to a principal debtor discharges the debtor's sureties.[40] In our view, this shows a proper reticence. The rule is anomalous and the perpetuation of anomaly is never welcome.

(B) Contribution Claims under the Civil Liability (Contribution) Act 1978: Liability in Damages

(a) *General Principles*

Section 1(1) of the Civil Liability (Contribution) Act 1978 provides that: "Subject to the following provisions of this section, any person liable in respect of any damage suffered by another person may recover contribution from any other person liable in respect of the same damage (whether jointly with him or otherwise)." And by section 6(1):

> "A person is liable in respect of any damage for the purposes of this Act if the person who suffered it (or anyone representing his estate or dependants) is entitled to recover compensation from him in respect of that damage (whatever the legal basis of his liability, whether tort, breach of contract, breach of trust or otherwise)."[41]

It would appear from section 1(2) and (3) that a person's liability arises when the damage to "another" person occurs.[42] The Act does not apply where the

---

[35] *Shepheard* v. *Bray* [1906] 2 Ch. 235, 253, *per* Warrington J.; see also *Boulter* v. *Peplow* (1850) 9 C.B. 493, 507, *per* Maule J.

[36] Law Commission, Working Paper, No. 59, p. 26; see also § 20.

[37] See above, p. 309.

[38] See above, pp. 313–314.

[39] *Lacy* v. *Kynaston* (1701) 2 Salk. 575; *Hutton* v. *Eyre* (1815) 6 Taunt. 289, 294–296, *per* Gibbs J.; *Walmesley* v. *Cooper* (1839) 11 A. & E. 216, 221–222, *per* Denman C.J. See G. L. Williams, *Joint Obligations*, para. 52.

[40] See above, p. 315, *Swire* v. *Redman* (1876) 1 Q.B.D. 536, 542, *per* Cockburn C.J.

[41] On which see *Frydman Properties* v. *Bejam Group* [1987] C.L.Y. 1841.

[42] s.1(1) is silent on this point. See below, pp. 325–326 for a discussion when the right to contribution arises.

debt or damage in question occurred before 1979: section 7(1). Again, a person is not entitled to recover contribution, or to be liable to make contribution, "by reference to any liability based on breach of any obligation assumed by him" before 1979: section 7(2). In *Lampitt* v. *Poole Borough Council*,[43] the Court of Appeal held that the verb assumed was apt to cover a situation in which there is a consensual acceptance of obligations, for example, by a contractor or trustee, but was not apt to cover that where a duty, for example, a duty of care in tort, was "thrust" upon another.

These provisions are much wider than section 6 of the Law Reform (Married Women and Tortfeasors) Act 1935, which is now repealed. The phrase *any person* can include not only tortfeasors, but trustees, directors, partners and independent contractors, whose acts cause damage "to another person."

In these circumstances the court has power to assess the amount of contribution as is "just and equitable having regard to that person's responsibility for the damage in question."[44]

The effect of cesser of liability

There are specific statutory provisions which deal with the problem of the liability of a person to make contribution where he has ceased to be liable to "another person" at the date of that other's claim to contribution. Section 1(2) provides that:

> A person shall be entitled to recover contribution by virtue of subsection (1) above notwithstanding that he has ceased to be liable in respect of the damage in question since the time when the damage occurred, provided that he was so liable immediately before he made or was ordered or agreed to make the payment in respect of which the contribution is sought.

So D1 may recover contribution from D2 even though D1's liability has now ceased, provided that he was liable immediately before he made or was ordered or agreed to make the payment "in respect of which the contribution is sought."

Section 1(3) deals with the converse situation, where D2 has ceased to be liable. It should be read in conjunction with section 1(5). They provide as follows:

> (3) A person shall be liable to make contribution by virtue of subsection (1) above notwithstanding that he has ceased to be liable in respect of the damage in question since the time when the damage occurred, unless he ceased to be liable by virtue of the expiry of a period of limitation or prescription which extinguished the right on which the claim against him in respect of the damage was based.
>
> (5) A judgment given in any action brought in any part of the United Kingdom by or on behalf of the person who suffered the damage in

---

[43] [1991] 2 Q.B. 545.
[44] s.2(1): see below, p. 326.

question against any person from whom contribution is sought under this section shall be conclusive in the proceedings for contribution as to any issue determined by that judgment in favour of the person from whom the contribution is sought.

Section 1(3)[45] was enacted with the object of reversing the decision of the House of Lords in *Geo. Wimpey and Co. Ltd.* v. *B.O.A.C.*[45a] D1 may now claim contribution from D2[46] even though D2 has ceased to be liable to "another person" because of the running of the Statute of Limitation, unless (1) D1's right of contribution is statute-barred[47]; *or* (2) D2 has obtained a favourable judgment against "another person" in a hearing on the merits.

Bona fide settlement or compromise

D1 may now claim contribution from D2 when he has made a payment[48] in bona fide settlement or compromise with "another person" provided that the factual basis of the claim against him can be established. It is no longer necessary for D1 to demonstrate that he would have been liable if sued to judgment.[49] Section 1(4) reads as follows:

> (4) A person who has made or agreed to make any payment in bona fide settlement or compromise of any claim made against him in respect of any damage (including a payment into court which has been accepted) shall be entitled to recover contribution in accordance with this section without regard to whether or not he himself is or ever was liable in respect of the damage, provided, however, that he would have been liable assuming that the factual basis of the claim against him could be established.

---

[45] In *Logan* v. *Uttlesford District Council and Hammond* [1984] C.A.T. 263, it was argued that a joint wrongdoer would rarely settle with a plaintiff if it remained open to the plaintiff to claim further damages from the wrongdoer by the indirect route of suing the other wrongdoer and leaving it to that wrongdoer to collect a contribution from the wrongdoer who had settled with the plaintiff. It was further argued and there should be a purposive construction of s.1(3) as follows: "A person shall be liable to make a contribution by virtue of subs. (1) above, notwithstanding that he had ceased to be liable in respect of the damage in question since the time when the damage occurred *otherwise than by a judgment on the merits or by reason of a bona fide settlement*, unless he ceased to be liable . . . " The Court of Appeal rejected those arguments on the ground that subss. 2 and 3 were quite unambiguous and there could be no justification for judicial amendment of them.

[45a] [1955] A.C. 169, interpreting the different language of s.6(1)(*c*) of the 1935 Act. *Cf. Nottingham Health Authority* v. *Nottingham City Council* [1988] 1 W.L.R. 903, C.A. (Contrast *Hart* v. *Hall & Pickles Ltd.* [1969] 1 Q.B. 405). See Law Commission *Report*, No. 79, §§ 60–67.

[46] The *liability* of a tortfeasor to make contribution is purely a question of substantive law. It does not need to be procedurally enforceable as a current and subsisting liability: *R. A. Lister Ltd.* v. *E. G. Thomson (Shipping) Ltd.* [1987] 1 W.L.R. 1614 (Hobhouse J.), construing s.1(6) of the Act. Moreover, claims are not limited to liabilities which occur in England and Wales: *The Kapetan Georgis* [1988] 1 Lloyd's Rep. 352 (Hirst J.).

[47] The limitation period is two years; Limitation Act 1980, s.10: see below, pp. 771–773.

[48] If the settlement takes the form of something other than a payment, then seemingly s.1(4) has no application: see (1979) 42 M.L.R. 182, 185 [Dugdale].

[49] See *Stott* v. *West Yorkshire Road Car Co. Ltd.* [1971] 1 Q.B. 651.

Section 1(4) only applies, therefore, if the settlement or compromise is bona fide. The Act is silent on the question on whom rests the burden of demonstrating that the settlement or compromise is bona fide. In principle it should be on him who challenges it. The amount of the settlement, the relationship of the parties to the settlement and the circumstances surrounding the settlement are all relevant factors.[50] In practice, it may not be easy for D2 to demonstrate that the settlement is collusive.[51]

The proviso to the subsection limits the contribution claim to settlements made in circumstances where it is doubtful *on the facts* whether a person is or is not liable to another. A person who settles when it is doubtful whether he is legally liable cannot then claim contribution.[52]

The burden will be on D1 to prove that D2 would have been liable if D2 had been sued by the injured person.[53] It is open to D2 to challenge the amount of the compromise, which will, however, serve as a maximum limit of the amount recoverable by D1.

The discretion of the court

Section 2(1) follows precisely the language of the 1935 Act.[54]

> "Subject to subsection (3) below, in any proceedings for contribution under section 1 above the amount of the contribution recoverable from any person shall be such as may be found by the court to be just and equitable having regard to the extent of that person's responsibility for the damage in question."

Decisions interpreting the 1935 Act had held that such factors as the relevant culpability[55] of the parties and causation[56] should be taken into account in determining the amount of contribution; and in *Madden* v. *Quirk*[57] Simon Brown J. held, interpreting section 2(1) of the 1978 Act, that in determining *responsibility* for the damage a court should take into account such considerations as "blameworthiness" and "causative potency."

Section 2(3) deals with the situation where D2's liability is subject to a limit or where P's damages from D2 have been, or might have been, reduced because of P's contributory negligence.

> "Where the amount of the damages which have or might have been awarded in respect of the damage in question in any action brought in

---

[50] *Cf.* Law Commission, *Report*, No. 79, §§ 55–57.
[51] *Cf.* the Memorandum of the Senate of the Inns of Court and the Bar to the Law Commission on this point.
[52] (1979) 42 M.L.R. 182, 184 [Dugdale].
[53] On the question of the multiplicity of proceedings, see Law Commission, *Report*, No. 79, § 49.
[54] s.6(2).
[55] *Smith* v. *Bray* (1939) 59 T.L.R. 200; *Collins* v. *Hertfordshire C.C.* [1947] K.B. 598; *Weaver* v. *Commercial Press* (1947) 63 T.L.R. 466.
[56] *Randolph* v. *Tuck* [1962] 1 Q.B. 175; *The Miraflores and the Abadesa* [1967] 1 A.C. 826, 845, *per* Lord Pearce.
[57] [1989] 1 W.L.R. 702, 707.

England and Wales by or on behalf of the person who suffered it against
the person from whom the contribution is sought was or would have been
subject to—

(a) any limit imposed by or under any enactment or by any agreement
made before the damage occurred;

(b) any reduction by virtue of section 1 of the Law Reform (Contributory
Negligence) Act 1945 or section 5 of the Fatal Accidents Act 1976; or

(c) any corresponding limit or reduction under the law of a country
outside England and Wales;

the person from whom the contribution is sought shall not by virtue of any
contribution awarded under section 1 above be required to pay in respect
of the damage a greater amount than the amount of those damages as so
limited or reduced."

The Law Commission, upon whose recommendations section 2(3) is based,
would have preferred to have allowed D2 to plead contributory negligence as a
partial defence but felt that this could only be implemented in the context of a
consideration of the reform of contributory negligence.[58]

Accrual of the cause of action

Any person entitled to claim contribution must pursue his claim to contribution within "two years from the date on which the right accrued"[59] to him. The
right to contribution shall be deemed to accrue from the date when any
judgment is given in any civil proceedings or any arbitral award is handed
down[60]; or, where:

"the person in question makes or agrees to make any payment to one or
more persons in compensation for that damage (whether he admits any
liability in respect of that damage or not) . . . the earliest date on which the
amount to be paid is agreed between him . . . and the person . . . to whom
the payment is to be made."[61]

The Limitation Act 1980 should not limit the exercise of the court's discretion
to award contribution.[62]

We shall now discuss the more important contribution claims which are
likely to arise under the 1978 Act.

(b) *Independent Contractors and Tortfeasors*

The plight of independent contractors was one of the main reasons for the

---

[58] Law Commission *Report*, No. 79, §§ 30–31, 75–79.

[59] Limitation Act 1980, s.10(1): see below, p. 772.

[60] s.10(3).

[61] s.10(4).

[62] *Cf. Scott* v. *West Yorkshire Road Car Co.* [1971] 2 Q.B. 651, 659, *per* Salmon L.J. who was
speaking of the Limitation Act 1963 and the Law Reform (Married Women and Tortfeasors)
Act 1935, s.6. The Limitation Act 1980 is a consolidating statute, so that there is presumed to be
no change in the law.

enactment of the Civil Liability (Contribution) Act 1978. A typical case arose when P, seeking to build a house, contracted with D1 to be his architect and with D2 to be his builder. The house was poorly constructed and both D1 and D2 were found to be in breach of their separate contracts. P sued D1 and recovered the whole loss from him. At common law D1's claim for contribution from D2 would have failed[63]; there was no liability *in solidum*. Today D1 can claim contribution under the 1978 Act.

Tortfeasors will be, in practice, the most likely persons to invoke this statutory right. As has been seen, the court may take into account culpability and causation in determining the amount of contribution which is just and equitable having regard to his responsibility for the damage in question.[64]

(c) *Trustees*

Trustees, who are subject to a common obligation in equity, are jointly and severally liable[65-66] to the trust estate for any loss resulting from their breach of trust.[67] Each trustee is, therefore, individually responsible to the beneficiaries for the whole of the damage to the trust estate. But to deny him a right of contribution "leaving one party, who has paid the whole, without remedy, would be the greatest injustice."[68] A trustee's right to contribution will normally arise when his liability for the breach of trust is ascertained, for example, from the date of judgment in an action for breach of trust.[69] The death of a trustee does not exonerate his estate from contributing to losses incurred while he was a trustee.[70]

In equity the courts had been reluctant, in the absence of any agreement, to apportion the guilt of trustees *inter se*, and to compel one trustee to contribute more than another.[71] The passive trustee was equally liable with the active trustee whom he had allowed to administer the trust. To give him an indemnity would "act as an opiate upon the conscience of trustees."[72] This was a harsh

---

[63] See *McConnell* v. *Lynch-Robinson* [1957] N.I. 70; Law Commission, *Report*, No. 79, §§ 5–7. But *cf.* above, Chap. 12.

[64] See above, p. 326.

[65-66] See *Jackson* v. *Dickinson* [1903] 1 Ch. 947, 952, *per* Swinfen Eady J., following *Ashhurst* v. *Mason* (1875) L.R. 20 Eq. 225, 233, *per* Bacon V.-C.; *cf. Smith* v. *Cock* [1911] A.C. 317.

[67] It is true that at common law trustees are liable only for their own acts or omissions; but they are liable for failing to take reasonable care in supervising their co-trustees. The better view is that this duty is not affected by the Trustee Act 1925, s.30. But *cf. Re Vickery* [1931] 1 Ch. 572, criticised in (1959) 22 M.L.R. 381 [Jones]. And see *Re Lucking's W.T.* [1968] 1 W.L.R. 866.

[68] *Lingard* v. *Bromley* (1812) 1 V. & B. 115, 117, *per* Sir Samuel Romilly, *arguendo*; see also *Baynard* v. *Woolley* (1855) 20 Beav. 583.

[69] Limitation Act 1980, s.10(3), (4): see above, p. 772; *Robinson* v. *Harkin* [1896] 2 Ch. 415, 426, *per* Stirling J.; following *Wolmerhausen* v. *Gullick* [1893] 2 Ch. 514, above, p. 311 and granting trustees the benefits of the Mercantile Law Amendment Act 1856, s.5.

[70] *Jackson* v. *Dickinson* [1903] 1 Ch. 947, *cf. Robinson* v. *Evans* (1843) 7 Jur. 738; *Blyth* v. *Fladgate* [1891] 1 Ch. 337, 366, *per* Stirling J.

[71] The principles of the surety cases (see above, pp. 307 *et seq.*) were adopted: see *Bacon* v. *Camphausen* (1888) 55 L.T. 851, 852; *Robinson* v. *Harkin* [1896] 2 Ch. 415, 426, *per* Stirling J.

[72] *Bahin* v. *Hughes* (1886) 31 Ch.D. 390, 398, *per* Fry L.J.

rule which may not have survived the Civil Liability (Contribution) Act 1978. Under that statute the amount of contribution which is recoverable is that which the court considers to be "just and equitable, having regard to the extent of [the trustee's] responsibility for the damage in question."[73] So the court may now, if it thinks it just and equitable, treat an active trustee more harshly than a passive trustee, or a professionally paid trustee more rigorously than the old family friend who kindly undertook the burden of trusteeship.

It is an open question whether the courts will be guided, in the exercise of their statutory discretion, by the principles which formerly governed the exercise of the equitable right of contribution. For example, it was said at one time that a fraudulent trustee has no right of contribution against a co-trustee who is also fraudulent.[74] Contribution should certainly be refused if such a claim requires the court to enforce an illegal transaction[75]; but the courts may now be persuaded to order contribution if there is no question of the enforcement of such a transaction. Again, in equity a trustee was ordered to indemnify his co-trustees against the whole loss caused by the breach of trust in the following special circumstances.

(1) The right of indemnity may arise under contract. Such contracts of indemnity are not void. In *Warwick* v. *Richardson*,[76] Alderson B. was quite clear that, in a court of law at least, there was nothing "illegal or wrong in the conduct of a trustee who has been a party to such an arrangement."[77] Moreover, the 1978 Act does not affect the validity of any "express or implied contractual or other right to indemnity."[78]

(2) Even where there is no express contract, equity implied a right of indemnity in the following circumstances: (i) Where one trustee applied the trust fund solely to his own use.[79] (ii) Where a trustee did not actively participate in the breach of trust[80] and committed the breach merely because of the advice of a solicitor trustee. Here the lay trustee was entitled to an indemnity from the solicitor trustee.[81] As Warrington J. said in *Re Linsley*,[82] the lay trustee looks to the solicitor trustee to do what a solicitor acting in a reasonable and proper manner would do. Accordingly, in that case, the solicitor trustee was required to indemnify his co-trustee against costs incurred by his negligent management of the trust, in that he unreasonably resisted a

---

[73] s.2(1): see above, p. 326.
[74] *Charitable Corporation* v. *Sutton* (1742) 2 Atk. 400, 406, *per* Lord Hardwicke; *Att.-Gen.* v. *Wilson* (1840) Cr. & Ph. 1, 28, *per* Lord Cottenham L.C. (The trustees were directors of joint stock companies.)
[75] *Cf.* below, Chap. 22.
[76] (1842) 10 M. & W. 284.
[77] At p. 295.
[78] s.7(3).
[79] *Wynne* v. *Tempest* [1897] 1 Ch. 110; see also *Bahin* v. *Hughes* (1886) 31 Ch.D. 390, 395, *per* Cotton L.J.
[80] *Head* v. *Gould* [1898] 2 Ch. 250.
[81] There are many authorities; see, *inter alia*, *Lockhart* v. *Reilly* (1856) 25 L.J.Ch. 697, (1857) 27 L.J.Ch. 54; *Wilson* v. *Thomson* (1875) L.R. 20 Eq. 459; *Re Turner* [1897] 1 Ch. 536.
[82] [1904] 2 Ch. 785.

suit by a beneficiary of the trust.[83] (iii) Where a trustee was a beneficiary under the trust, he was under an obligation to indemnify his co-trustee for a breach of trust, for which they were both liable, out of and to the extent of his beneficial interest.[84] "But except so far as it is thus neutralised his right of contribution will remain."[85] In *Chillingworth* v. *Chambers*,[86] in which this principle was established, the trustee-beneficiary alone had actually benefited, since the object of his breach was to increase the income of the trust fund. Thus viewed, the decision is not remarkable; but there are dicta which suggest that the case is authority for the wider and more doubtful proposition that at common law a trustee-beneficiary must indemnify his fellow trustee even though the trustee-beneficiary might not himself have sought or derived any benefit from the breach of trust.[87]

(d) *Directors*

Directors who enter into an *ultra vires* transaction are liable to indemnify the company against any loss caused by their breach of duty.[88] If one of the directors pays more, is held liable to pay more, or agrees to pay more than his share of the loss, he can claim contribution from the other directors.[89] Today the courts have power under the Civil Liability (Contribution) Act 1978 to apportion the loss as is just and equitable having regard to the individual director's responsibility for the damage in question.

It is conjectural to what extent the court will be influenced by the old common law of equity in determining how to exercise its statutory discretion. At common law the right to contribution depended not on contract but on the general principle of equity enunciated in *Deering* v. *The Earl of Winchelsea*[90]: "they must bear equally the burthens consequent upon their acts."[91] But if the breach of trust benefited only one director, that director could not claim contribution from his fellow directors, even though they had previously con-

---

[83] *Sed quaere* if a trustee can generally recover, in a contribution action, a proportion of his costs in resisting reasonably an action by a *cestui que trust* for breach of trust: see *Lingard* v. *Bromley* (1812) 1 V. & B. 114, 116–117, *per* Grant M.R.; *Prince* v. *Hine* (1859) 27 Beav. 345; *Birks* v. *Micklethwait* (1864) 33 Beav. 409, 411–412, *per* Romilly M.R. see above, pp. 313, n. 65; see below, pp. 348–349 and 361–362.

[84] *Chillingworth* v. *Chambers* [1896] 1 Ch. 685; but *cf.* Underhill, *Trusts and Trustees* (14th ed., 1987), p. 799 quoting an unreported point in *Re Fountaine* [1909] 2 Ch. 382, that a trustee-beneficiary, who is subsequently appointed and who fails to repair a breach, does not fall within the main rule.

[85] At p. 698, *per* Lindley L.J. The rule applies even though the trustee subsequently becomes a beneficiary: see *Evans* v. *Benyon* (1887) 37 Ch.D. 329.

[86] [1896] 1 Ch. 685.

[87] At p. 700, *per* Lindley L.J.; *cf.* Kay L.J. at p. 707.

[88] It is a nice question how far a director is a trustee. Certainly, in this context, he is deemed to act *qua* trustee; *Charitable Corporation* v. *Sutton* (1742) 2 Atk. 400. See, generally, [1967] C.L.J. 83 [Sealy].

[89] The appropriate limitation period is two years: Limitation Act 1980, s.10(3), (4): see below, p. 772.

[90] (1787) 2 Bos. & Pul. 270: see above, pp. 307–308.

[91] *Spotiswoode's Case* (155) 6 De G.M. & G. 345; 372, *per* Turner L.J. See also *Ramskill* v. *Edwards* (1885) 31 Ch.D. 100, 110, *per* Pearson J.

sented to the breach.[92] Indeed, a director could not normally claim contribution from another if the conduct of the other was such that there was no equity to make him contribute.[93] Unlike a trustee, "an individual director is not a necessary party to a transaction involving the company's property."[94] While trustees must act jointly, a director must accept the decision of the majority of his colleagues. A distinction was therefore properly drawn between those directors who did not attend a meeting where the *ultra vires* transaction was authorised, who need not contribute, and those who attended and neglected or omitted to perform a duty "which ought to have been performed at those meetings,"[95] who had to contribute. Consistently a director who did attend but dissented was not held liable for the acts or omissions of his fellow directors.[96] Third parties who took property with notice of an *ultra vires* act acquired no greater rights than directors who committed the act. Thus, in *Moxham* v. *Grant*,[97] a shareholder who knew that a certain distribution was *ultra vires* was deemed to be a constructive trustee and was liable to the extent of his share of that distribution to indemnify the directors who had performed the *ultra vires* act.

(C) Contribution Claims between Obligors which may arise either at Common Law and Equity, or under the Civil Liability (Contribution) Act 1978, depending on the Nature of the Claim

Partners

Partners are in a special relationship to each other. Each partner is jointly liable with his fellow partners for all partnership debts and obligations incurred while he is a partner.[98] A claim for contribution by a partner who has satisfied more than his share of the partnership debt is still governed by equitable principles.[99] Since they are liable to a common demand, partners are entitled to

---

[92] *Walsh* v. *Bardsley* (1931) 47 T.L.R. 564.
[93] *Ramskill* v. *Edwards* (1885) 31 Ch.D. 100, 110, *per* Pearson J.
[94] [1967] C.L.J. 83, 87 [Sealy].
[95] *Marquis of Bute's Case* [1892] 2 Ch. 100, 109, *per* Stirling J. See also *Perry's Case* (1876) 34 L.T. 716; *Cargill* v. *Bower* (1878) 10 Ch.D. 502; *Re Denham & Co.* (1883) 25 Ch.D. 752. And *cf.* *Davies's Case* (1890) 45 Ch.D. 537; *Land Credit Co. of Ireland* v. *Lord Fermoy* (1870) 5 Ch.App. 763. *Sed quaere* if the non-attendance is continuous: see *Charitable Corporation* v. *Sutton* (1742) 2 Atk. 400, 405, *per* Lord Hardwicke.
[96] See generally on this topic Palmer's *Company Law*, §§ 8.403 *et seq.*
[97] [1900] 1 Q.B. 88, 93, *per* Collins L.J., 95, *per* Vaughan Williams L.J.
[98] Apart from partners, a trustee may possibly seek contribution in equity against co-trustees. Such a case could arise if one trustee incurred debts to third parties while properly carrying on the business of the trust and the trust estate had no funds available to indemnify him. There is no reported instance of such a claim, which will be so rare that it has not persuaded us to depart from the classification adopted in the text.
A director may act as an agent of his company, and, in the capacity, incur debts on the company's behalf. Again there is no case where he had sought contribution from a co-director. Such a claim should arguably fail since the director's liability has been incurred *qua* agent and not *qua* director; and there is no authority to suggest that one agent can claim contribution from another in these circumstances.
[99] See above, pp. 306 *et seq.*

claim contribution *inter se*. Lord Cranworth L.C. in *Re the Royal Bank of Australia, Robinson's Executors*[1] stated the law in the following terms:

> "Every shareholder, as a partner, is liable to every creditor to the full amount of his demand ... The solvent shareholders are bound to make up this sum [the aggregate demand of all the creditors], not by virtue of any engagement contained in the deed, but because by the general rules of law every partner is liable to the whole of the demands on the partnership ... When, indeed, the money has been raised and the demands on the partnership have been liquidated, the shareholder who has paid a sum exceeding his rateable proportion, calculated on the number of his shares, will have a right of contribution against the other shareholders, and the extent of that right must be measured according to the provisions contained [in the particular deed of partnership]."

When a partnership is a going concern, the right of contribution is enforceable only in an action for a general partnership account.[2] On the taking of accounts, the amount of each partner's contribution will depend upon the terms of the partnership agreement.[3] In the absence of any contrary intention, it is presumed that the partners intend to share equally the profits and contribute equally to the losses[4]; if the benefits are shared unequally, it is presumed that partners intend to contribute to the losses in the same proportion.[5]

A partner may be prevented from claiming contribution because of illegality. The cases have carefully distinguished two situations. If the partnership is illegal and a partner discharges more than his share of the partnership debt, he cannot claim contribution, for the court will not assist in the execution of an illegal contract.[6] But if the partnership is legal, the fact that one partner has been guilty of illegal acts in the conduct of the partnership business does not make the partnership itself illegal,[7] and does not prevent the innocent partner[8] from claiming contribution.

Unless otherwise agreed, both the right of contribution and duty to contribute survive the death of the partner entitled or liable to make contribution.[9]

---

[1] (1856) 6 De G.M. & G. 572, 587–588. This right of contribution is independent of a partner's right to be indemnified out of the firm's assets; *cf.* Partnership Act 1890, s.24(2).

[2] *Boulter* v. *Peplow* (1850) 9 C.B. 493; *Sedgwick* v. *Daniell* (1857) 2 H. & N. 319; see *Restatement of Restitution*, p. 361.

[3] *Gillan* v. *Morrison* (1847) 1 De G. & Sm. 421; *Re Worcester Corn Exchange Co.* (1853) 3 De G.M. & G. 180. *Cf. Oaldaker* v. *Lavender* (1833) 6 Sim. 239; *Cruickshank* v. *McVicar* (1844) 8 Beav. 106.

[4] Partnership Act 1890, s.24(1).

[5] *Ibid.*, s.44.

[6] *Canhen* v. *Boyce* (1819) 3 B. & Ad. 179; *De Begnis* v. *Armistead* (1833) 10 Bing. 107; *Sykes* v. *Beadon* (1879) 11 Ch.D. 170, 193, 196, *per* Jessel M.R.; *Foster* v. *Driscoll* [1929] 1 K.B. 470.

[7] *Campbell* v. *Campbell* (1840) 7 Cl. & F. 166; see also *Sharpe* v. *Taylor* (1849) 2 Ph. 801.

[8] But not the guilty partner: see *Thomas* v. *Atherton* (1879) 10 Ch.D. 179.

[9] *Simpson* v. *Ingham* (1823) 2 B. & C. 65, 72, *per* Bayley J.; *In the Matter of the Northern Coal Mining Co.* (1852) 3 Mac. & G. 726; *Re Agriculturist Cattle Insurance Company, Baird's Case* (1870) 5 Ch.App. 725; *Mathews* v. *Ruggles-Brise* [1911] 1 Ch. 194. The partners cannot claim

However, a partner is also liable for the wrongful acts of his fellow partners done in the course of partnership business during the period when he was a partner. If these acts cause damage to another person and one partner satisfies that other's claim, then he can claim contribution from his co-partners.[10] The contribution claim will then be governed by the Civil Liability (Contribution) Act 1978. The amount of contribution shall be such as the court considers to be just and equitable "having regard to the extent of [the co-partner's] responsibility for the damage in question."[11]

(D) Contribution Claims under the Maritime Conventions Act 1911

This statute allows contribution between vessels responsible for a collision at sea resulting in "loss of life or personal injuries . . . suffered by any person on board."[12] It provides that the vessels so responsible are jointly and severally liable,[13] and allows a contribution claim *inter se* for the amount that the damages recovered against a vessel "exceeds the proportion in which she was in fault."[14] "The liability of each vessel involved must be assessed by comparison of her fault with the fault of each of the other vessels involved individually, separately, and in no way conjunctively."[15] But a claim by a vessel to contribution is defeated to the extent that the other vessel is exempt from liability to the injured person, whether that exemption is conferred by statute, contract or for any other reason.[16] For damage to vessels or cargo, however, the Act states that each vessel is only liable in proportion to its fault,[17] so that questions of contribution cannot generally arise in this context.[18]

(E) General Average Contribution

The basis of the right to contribution

The principle of general average contribution,[19] which requires parties to a

---

contribution from any purchaser of partnership property, even though he bought with notice: see *Re Langmead's Trusts* (1855) 20 Beav. 20, 27, *per* Romilly M.R.; *cf. Moxham* v. *Grant* [1900] 1 Q.B. 88; see above, p. 331.

[10] Partnership Act 1890, ss.9–12. See, generally, *Lindley on Partnership*, Chap. 12. But losses incurred by the unauthorised, culpably negligent or fraudulent conduct of one partner must be borne by him alone: *Thomas* v. *Atherton* (1879) 10 Ch.D. 185, 199, *per curiam*. See also *Bury* v. *Allen* (1845) 1 Coll. 604; but *cf. Cragg* v. *Ford* (1842) 1 Y. & C.C.C. 285.

[11] s.2(1): see above, p. 326.

[12] s.2.

[13] *Ibid.*

[14] s.3.

[15] *The Miraflores and the Abadesa* [1967] 1 A.C. 826, 847, *per* Lord Pearce. For the meaning of "fault," see *The Cairnbahn* [1914] P. 25, C.A.; *The Norwhale* [1975] Q.B. 589.

[16] Proviso to s.3; *The Cedric* [1920] P. 193, discussed in G. L. Williams, *Joint and Torts Contributory Negligence*, pp. 112–113. *Cf.* Civil Liability (Contribution) Act 1978, s.2(3)(*a*); see above, pp. 326–327.

[17] s.1. On which see, *The Anneliese* [1969] 2 Lloyd's Rep. 78, [1970] 1 Lloyd's Rep. 355, C.A.; and *The Calliope* [1970] 1 Lloyd's Rep. 84.

[18] But see *The Cairnbahn* [1914] P. 25, and *cf. The Miraflores and the Abadesa* [1967] 1 A.C. 826.

[19] See, generally, Lowndes & Rudolf's *General Average* (10th ed.); *Arnould on Marine Insurance* (16th ed.), Chap. 26; Carver's *Carriage by Sea* (13th ed.), Chap. 14; *Scrutton on Charterparties*

common maritime adventure to contribute towards losses incurred for preservation of ship or cargo, has as old a history as any part of the law.[20] Its origin lies in the Rhodian sea law, later embodied in the Digest of Justinian under the title *De Lege Rhodia de Iactu*,[21] which governed mercantile transactions in the Mediterranean and the Adriatic for a millennium before the advent of Christianity. The extant Admiralty records suggest that that court adopted the principles of Rhodian sea law, and compelled parties to maritime adventures to contribute "towards the losses or damages susteyned"[22]; and the English common lawyers, having pirated from the Admiralty much of its mercantile jurisdiction, were content to adopt these principles. In one of the earliest and most influential cases at law, *Birkley* v. *Presgrave*,[23] Lawrence J. propounded a definition of general average loss which closely followed ancient precedent.[24] This definition, which has provided the foundations of the modern English law of general average, runs as follows: "All loss which arises in consequence of extraordinary sacrifices made or expenses incurred for the preservation of the ship and cargo come within general average, and must be borne proportionately by all those who are interested."

The Rhodian law, the Digest of Justinian, the Court of Admiralty and the majority of common law judges have all accepted that general average contribution is based upon "common principles of justice."[25] "Natural justice requires that all should contribute to indemnify for the loss of property which is sacrificed by one in order that the whole adventure may be saved,[26] for one interested party should not be unjustly enriched at the expense of another. Thus, though the principle has a unique origin in the maritime lore of the Mediterranean, its rationale is similar to that of the rule which enables one surety to obtain contribution from his co-surety; indeed, in *Deering* v. *The Earl*

(19th ed.); pp. 276–288. General average (loss to be shared by all) should be distinguished from particular average (loss to be borne by a particular interest).

[20] For the history of general average, see Lowndes & Rudolf, Chap. 1.

[21] See R. G. Marsden, *Select Pleas in the Court of Admiralty*, Vols. 1 and 2; (1892) 6 Selden Society 95 (citing *Whitefield* v. *Garrarde* (1540), and (1897) 11 Selden Society 39 (citing *The Elizabeth* (1575)). But *cf.* G. O. Sayles, *Select Cases in the Court of King's Bench*, 55 Selden Society, pp. 156–157, citing a case decided in 1285.

[22] Holdsworth, *History of English Law*, Vol. 1, pp. 553 *et seq.*

[23] (1801) 1 East 220, 228–229. *Cf.* the definition of the Marine Insurance Act 1906, s.66(1), and that of rule A of the York-Antwerp Rules 1974. S.66(1) reads: "A general average loss is a loss caused by or directly consequential on a general average act. It includes a general average expenditure as well as a general average sacrifice." In *Austin Friars SS Co.* v. *Spillers & Bakers Ltd.* [1915] 1 K.B. 833, 835, Bailhache J. suggested that the definition in s.66(1) of the Marine Insurance Act 1906 would now prevail for all purposes, but this is doubtfully correct since the Act is only concerned with marine insurance.

Rule A of the York-Antwerp Rules reads as follows: "There is a general average act when, and only when, any extraordinary sacrifice or expenditure is intentionally and reasonably made or incurred for the common safety for the purposes of preserving from peril the property involved in a common maritime adventure" (§ 556). And see below, p. 336.

[24] *Cf.* the Ordonnance of Louis XIV, quoted in Lowndes & Rudolf, p. 11.

[25] *Birkley* v. *Presgrave* (1801) 1 East 220, 227, *per* Lord Kenyon C.J., 229, *per* Le Blanc J.

[26] *Burton* v. *English* (1883) 12 Q.B.D. 218, 221, *per* Brett M.R. See also the declaration in *The Elizabeth* (1575), (1897) 11 Selden Society 39 ("ought by lawe and equitye to make contribution").

of Winchelsea,[27] Eyre C.B. invoked the analogy of general average to establish the surety's right to contribution on an equitable basis. It was unfortunate, therefore, though perhaps inevitable in the prevailing intellectual climate, that attempts should have been made at the end of the nineteenth century to rationalise general average contribution in terms of implied contract.[28] This rationalisation has been rejected by many judges,[29] although it is accepted that, here as elsewhere, a right of contribution may always be modified by contract between the parties.[30]

Sacrifice and expenditure

A general average loss may result from either extraordinary sacrifice or extraordinary expenditure. The sacrifice may consist of loss of or damage to ship, including her stores, furniture and tackle; or loss of or damage to cargo, or loss of freight which would otherwise have been earned by the shipowner. Familiar examples of sacrifice are the jettison of cargo or ship's stores; damage to ship or cargo in extinguishing a fire; use of ship's stores as fuel; cutting away the ship's mast or cables. Liability incurred under an indemnity clause in a towage contract may be held to be a general average loss.[31] An accident subsequent to the general average act, such as the breaking of a tow-line and the subsequent liability to tug-owners under the indemnity clause, does not break the chain of causation if at the time of the general average act that accident was foreseeable.[32] Consequently, those losses, damages or expenses which ought reasonably to have been foreseen as flowing from the general average act constitute "a general average loss . . . caused by and directly consequential on a general average act."[33]

The expenditure is normally incurred in the first instance by the ship. Important examples of general average expenditure are port of refuge expenses and the cost of salvage operations.[34]

---

[27] (1787) 2 Bos. & Pul. 270, 274; see also *Stirling* v. *Forrester* (1821) 3 Bl. 575, 590, *per* Lord Redesdale.

[28] *Wright* v. *Marwood* (1881) 7 Q.B.D. 62, 67, *per* Bramwell L.J. In *Strang, Steel & Co.* v. *A. Scott & Co.* (1889) 14 App.Cas. 601, 608, Lord Watson left the point open.

[29] See, *e.g. Burton* v. *English* (1883) 12 Q.B.D. 218, 220–221, *per* Brett M.R.; *Price* v. *Middle Dock Co.* (1881) 44 L.T. 426, 428, *per* Williams J.; *Milburn & Co.* v. *Jamaica Fruit Transporting and Trading Co. of London* [1900] 2 Q.B. 540, 546, *per* A. L. Smith L.J., and 550, *per* Vaughan Williams L.J.

[30] *Union of India* v. *E. B. Aaby's Rederi A/S* [1975] A.C. 797; *Alma Shipping Corp.* v. *Union of India* [1971] 2 Lloyd's Rep. 494, 501, *per* Roskill J. See generally Lowndes & Rudolf, pp. 21 *et seq.*

[31] But see *The Beauregard* [1977] 2 Lloyd's Rep. 84 (C.C.A., 2nd Circuit).

[32] *Australian Coastal Shipping Commission* v. *Green* [1971] 1 Q.B. 456.

[33] Within the Marine Insurance Act 1906, s.66(1): *Australian Coastal Commission* v. *Green* [1971] 1 Q.B. 456, 481, *per* Lord Denning M.R. See also *Federal Commerce & Navigation Ltd.* v. *Eisenerz G.m.b.H.* [1970] 2 Lloyd's Rep. 332, [1975] 1 Lloyd's Rep. 105; Lowndes & Rudolf, §§ 570 *et seq.*

[34] Prima facie, expenditure on salvage operations gives rise to no right to contribution, because each interest benefited is liable only for its own proportion of such expenditure. But where such expenditure is incurred under a salvage agreement, the ship may be liable for the full amount of the expenditure under the agreement; and, in any event, by rule 44A of the rules of practice of

The burden is on the plaintiff to demonstrate that the damage was the direct consequence of a general average act.[35]

The York-Antwerp Rules

Although trading nations throughout the world have generally adopted the principle of general average contribution as part of their municipal law, important differences have developed in the application of the principle in various countries. In particular, there are marked divergences between the law of England and the law applicable in the United States on this subject.[36] Since the middle of the last century, efforts have been made to eliminate these differences.[37] Proposals have varied from a universally adopted code to the total abolition of general average contribution.[38] Neither of these extremes has as yet found acceptance. Instead, a series of rules has been developed with the purpose of resolving differences and, more recently, of reaching agreement on matters of principle. These are known as the York-Antwerp Rules, the most recent edition of which was drawn up in 1974. They have no statutory force, but have found wide acceptance among shipowning and mercantile interests, and are very frequently incorporated into contracts of affreightment by standard clauses which usually also provide for the place of adjustment, often London or New York. In practice, therefore, the rules are of great importance. They are divided into a rule of construction, seven lettered rules (A–G) which are concerned with matters of principle, and 22 numbered rules (I–XXII) which deal with more specific matters.[39]

Rules of practice of the Association of Average Adjusters

When a general average act has been committed, the loss has to be adjusted between the contributing interests. The adjustment is performed by an average adjuster, who sets out his information, calculations, etc., in a document, often of formidable dimensions, called a general average statement. Since the decided cases in this field leave wide gaps uncovered by authority, the Association of Average Adjusters in this country, as in the United States, has established a number of rules of practice[40] which will automatically be applied by their members when adjusting averages. These rules of practice do not, however, have the force of law. They can be challenged in the courts and, if found to be contrary to legal principle, will be rejected. Since, however, they

---

the Association of Average Adjusters' expenses for salvage services rendered by or accepted under agreement are in practice treated as general average, provided they were incurred for the common safety within the meaning of Rule A of the York-Antwerp Rules. See Lowndes & Rudolf, p. 300; see below, pp. 398–399.

[35] *The Alpha* [1991] 2 Lloyd's Rep. 515.

[36] See Lowndes & Rudolf, *passim*.

[37] *Ibid.*, Chap. 10.

[38] *Ibid.*

[39] The rules are set out in Lowndes & Rudolf, App. 1. Custom cannot override the Rules: see *Marida Ltd.* v. *Oswal Steel* [1992] 1 Lloyd's Rep. 636.

[40] The text of the rules of practice may be found in Lowndes & Rudolf, App. 2.

represent established mercantile practice, they will not be lightly overturned[41] and in cases of doubt they are likely to be upheld.[42]

Conditions of the right to contribution

(1) *The right is only applicable to a maritime adventure in the nature of a voyage*

The nature of the principle's origin, and its place in the maritime law, have led judges and jurists to assert that it applies only to maritime adventures.[43] It clearly has no application to sacrifice or expenditure on land; but the scope of the term "maritime adventure" remains doubtful. Thus it may be that the principle is applicable to voyages on inland waters, such as rivers or canals[44] or lakes, or to voyages within the confines of a port. It is consistent with the definition of Lawrence J. in *Birkley* v. *Presgrave*,[45] and with that in section 66 of the Marine Insurance Act 1906,[46] that the principle should apply in such cases, but the point must be regarded as still open.

It has also been asserted,[47] with considerable force, that the adventure must be in the nature of a voyage. Accordingly cases concerned with ships used as floating warehouses should fall outside the ambit of the principle.

(2) *The sacrifice or expenditure must be extraordinary*

If they are not extraordinary, they will fall within the "ordinary duties and ordinary expenses of the navigation to which the shipowner is bound by the nature of the contract between himself and the freighter, and for which he is to be remunerated by the freight."[48] In *Robinson* v. *Price*[49] a ship sailed with a reasonable supply of coal for her donkey engine, but she ran into such continuously bad weather that she sprang a leak and the consequent pumping exhausted the donkey engine's coal supply. It was held that the use of spare spars and of part of the cargo as fuel for the engine to work the pumps constituted an extraordinary sacrifice and did not arise from any failure to take on board sufficient fuel. On the other hand, in *Société Nouvelle d'Armement* v. *Spillers & Bakers Ltd.*,[50] Sankey J. held that expenditure incurred in employing a tug to tow a vessel from Queenstown to Sharpness in 1915 in order to

---

[41] *Svendsen* v. *Wallace* (1885) 10 App.Cas. 404, 416, *per* Lord Blackburn.
[42] But see *Union of India* v. *E. B. Aaby's Rederi A/S* [1975] A.C. 797.
[43] *Falcke* v. *Scottish Imperial Insurance Co.* (1886) 34 Ch.D. 234, 248, *per* Bowen L.J.; Lowndes & Rudolf, pp. 26–27. See also rule A of the York-Antwerp Rules 1974.
[44] Lowndes & Rudolf, pp. 66–67. *Cf. Apollinaris Co.* v. *Nord Deutsche Insurance Co.* [1904] 1 K.B. 252; *Whitteridge* v. *Norris* 6 Mass. 125 (1809). Contrast the law of maritime salvage: see *The Goring* [1988] A.C. 831; see below, Chap. 16.
[45] (1801) 1 East 220, 228, see above, p. 335.
[46] See above, p. 335, n. 33.
[47] Lowndes & Rudolf, pp. 26–27.
[48] Arnould, § 920 and see *Corfu Navigation Co.* v. *Mobil Shipping Co. Ltd.* [1991] 2 Lloyd's Rep. 515.
[49] (1876) 2 Q.B.D. 91, 295.
[50] [1917] 1 K.B. 865.

minimise the danger from submarines did not constitute extraordinary expenditure, for a risk of submarine attack was not extraordinary on such a voyage in wartime.

(3) The sacrifice or expenditure must be intentional and reasonable[51]

There is little guidance on these requirements, which are similar to those of rule A of the York-Antwerp Rules 1974.

(4) The sacrifice or expenditure must be made or incurred in time of peril

This has been said[52] to include not only danger to ship, freight, or cargo, but also danger to life.

Although it is not necessary to show that disaster was imminent, the peril must be shown to have been imminent and real. In *Société Nouvelle d'Armement* v. *Spillers & Bakers Ltd.*[53] the risk of submarine attack was not considered to have been sufficiently imminent to render expenditure incurred in minimising it general average expenditure. Moreover, it is not enough that the master should have mistakenly believed a peril to exist. In *Joseph Watson & Son Ltd.* v. *Firemen's Fund Insurance Co. of San Francisco*,[54] a master, who mistakenly believed that a fire had broken out, turned steam into the hold to extinguish it. Rowlatt J. held[55] that this was not a general average act, because there had never been a peril as required by section 66(2) of the Marine Insurance Act 1906. The rule imposes a heavy burden on the master.[56] It is doubtful whether the York-Antwerp Rules have affected it.[57]

(5) The sacrifice or expenditure must have been made or incurred for the purposes of preserving the interest imperilled in the common adventure

From this proposition it follows, first, that the contributing interests must have been involved in a common adventure. Cargo laden on a ship is necessarily involved in a common adventure with both the ship and other cargo laden on the same ship; but it is difficult to conceive of circumstances in which cargo laden on different ships, or in which ship A and cargo laden on ship B, would be held to be involved in a common adventure.[58] Secondly, different interests

---

[51] On the interpretation of these words, see *The Seapool* [1934] P.53, 64, *per* Langton J.; *Athel Line Ltd.* v. *Liverpool & London War Risks Association Ltd.* [1944] K.B. 87. For the special case of voluntary stranding, see Lowndes & Rudolf, pp. 114–119, and rule V of the York-Antwerp Rules 1974.

[52] *Montgomery* v. *Indemnity Mutual Marine Assurance Co.* [1902] 1 K.B. 734, 740, *per* Vaughan Williams L.J.; *cf.* Marine Insurance Act 1906, s.66(2).

[53] [1917] 1 K.B. 865.

[54] [1922] 2 K.B. 355; *cf. M'Call* v. *Houlder Bros.* (1897) 2 Com.Cas. 129.

[55] *Semble*, however, if there had in fact been a peril, then the court would have been more ready to accept the "view of the captain formed at the time the peril existed as to what would be the outcome of that peril"; see [1922] K.B. 355, 358, *per* Rowlatt J.

[56] See Lowndes & Rudolf, pp. 28–31.

[57] See *Vlassopoulos* v. *British & Foreign Marine Insurance Co.* [1929] 1 K.B. 187; *The Seapool* [1934] P. 53; *Daniolos* v. *Bunge & Co. Ltd.* (1937) 59 Ll.L.R. 175.

[58] See *Dabney* v. *New England Co.*, 14 Allen 300 (1867); *The J. P. Donaldson*, 167 U.S. 599 (1897). Cargo in ship A which has to pay a general average contribution to ship A, in respect of a collision between ship A and ship B, may, however, be able to recover from ship B a proportion of such

must have been imperilled; they must have been exposed to a common danger of damage.[59] It appears that more than one interest must be imperilled before there can be a general average act[60]; though the fact that different interests, for example, ship and cargo, are in the same ownership, and that accordingly there is no contribution between them, does not prevent the act from being a general average act for purposes of insurance law.[61] Thirdly, the sacrifice or expenditure must have been made for the purpose of preserving the imperilled interests. Moreover, it must to some extent result in preservation. For if the property of a particular party to the adventure is lost or so damaged that it loses all value, that party cannot be called on to contribute in general average; the adjustment is made on the basis of values at the port of destination, and if an interest has then no value, there is no basis for its contribution.[62]

(6) *Must the act have been ordered or authorised by the master?*

It is an open question whether the act must have been ordered or authorised by the master before it can be said to constitute an average act. In two nineteenth century cases general average contribution was allowed in circumstances in which it appears that the act was ordered by a stranger to the adventure, but neither case can be said to provide clear authority. In the earlier case,[63] an act of jettison was ordered by a prize master, but the vessel's mate was on board and participated in the act; in the later case,[64] the act was ordered by the captain of a port, but Mathew J. took the view that the master had sanctioned what was done.[65] There is much to be said for the view[66] that, provided the other conditions of general average are fulfilled, a sacrifice ordered by a stranger to the adventure should be sufficient as having been made for the common good in a time of common danger. This is consistent with the York-Antwerp Rules, and can be justified on the basis that the stranger should be regarded as being in the position of a necessitous intervener.[67] The contrary has, however, been decided[68] by the Supreme Court of the United States.

---

[59] contribution, calculated with reference to the blame attaching to ship B for the collision: see *Morrison S.S. Co.* v. *Greystoke Castle (Cargo Owners)* [1974] A.C. 265.

[59] Carver, §§ 1354–1355.

[60] *Kemp* v. *Halliday* (1865) 34 L.J.Q.B. 233, 242, *per* Blackburn J.; Marine Insurance Act 1906, s.66; Lowndes & Rudolf, pp. 47–48; *cf. Potter* v. *Ocean Assurance Co.*, 216 Fed. 303 (1837).

[61] *Montgomery* v. *Indemnity Mutual Marine Insurance Co.* [1902] 1 K.B. 734.

[62] *Chellew* v. *Royal Commission on Sugar Supply* [1921] 2 K.B. 627; Carver, pp. 786–790; Lowndes & Rudolf, pp. 195 *et seq.* In *Chellew's* case, the Court of Appeal affirmed the decision of Sankey J. on the basis of the York-Antwerp Rules, but declined to express a view on the common law position: see [1922] 1 K.B. 12.

[63] *Price* v. *Noble* (1811) 4 Taunt. 123.

[64] *Papayanni & Jeronica* v. *Grampian S.S. Co. Ltd.* (1896) 1 Com.Cas. 448.

[65] In *Athel Line Ltd.* v. *Liverpool & London War Risks Ins. Assocn. Ltd.* [1944] K.B. 87, 96, Tucker J. considered there was no clear authority on the point.

[66] Lowndes & Rudolf, pp. 32–35. But an employer may be entitled to call in the master's discretion and make the decision himself: see *Australian Coastal Shipping Commission* v. *Green* [1971] 1 Q.B. 456.

[67] See below, Chap. 16.

[68] *Ralli* v. *Troop*, 157 U.S. 386 (1894).

(7) The right to contribution is lost if the peril which occasioned the sacrifice or expenditure arose from the actionable fault of the claimant

This qualification to the principle of general average contribution was established in *Schloss* v. *Heriot*.[69] Two reasons were given[70] for the rule: first, that the claimant should have no claim to contribution to a loss of which he has himself been the cause,[71] and, secondly, that the defendant, having a cross-claim in damages, should have a defence to the claimant's claim to contribution to avoid circuity of action. The fact that one party is thereby deprived of contribution does not, however, prevent the act from being a general average act; accordingly other parties who are not at fault are entitled to recover contribution in the ordinary way.[72]

A party's claim to contribution will only be barred by this rule if his fault is actionable.[73] It follows that if the peril is occasioned by the fault of a party who has, by the appropriate exception, contracted out of liability, he will not be debarred from claiming general average contribution[74]; and the same applies where he is relieved by statute from liability for such fault.[75] Where, however, the effect of the provision is, as in the case of section 503 of the Merchant Shipping Act 1894,[76] not to discharge him but merely to limit his liability, his fault remains actionable and he loses the right to contribution.[77]

Rule D of the York-Antwerp Rules 1974, provides that: "Rights to contribution in general average shall not be affected, though the event which gave rise to the sacrifice or expenditure may have been due to the fault of one of the parties to the adventure; but this shall not prejudice any remedies which may be open against that party for such fault." The effect of this rule was considered in *Goulandris Brothers Ltd.* v. *B. Goldman & Sons Ltd.*[78] In that case, a shipowner claimed general average contribution from cargo in respect of expenditure occasioned by the vessel's unseaworthiness. The bill of lading in question was subject to the Hague Rules, and the shipowner contended that his fault was no longer actionable because over a year had passed since the delivery

---

[69] (1863) 14 C.B.(N.S.) 59.

[70] (1863) 14 C.B.(N.S.) 59, 64, *per* Erle C.J.

[71] *Cf.* salvage, where it is doubtful whether a similar defence exists; see below, pp. 392–393, and *The Beaverford* v. *The Kafiristan* [1938] A.C. 136.

[72] *Strang, Steel & Co.* v. *Scott & Co.* (1889) 14 App.Cas. 601.

[73] *Cf. The Evje (No. 2)* [1978] 1 Lloyd's Rep. 351, C.A.

[74] *The Carron Park* (1890) 15 P.D. 203; *Milburn* v. *Jamaica Fruit Importing Co.* [1900] 2 Q.B. 540. *Cf.* see above, pp. 323 *et seq.*, for the position of tortfeasors under the Civil Liability (Contribution) Act 1978. See also *State Trading Co. of India* v. *Doyle Carriers Inc.* [1991] 2 Lloyd's Rep. 55.

[75] *Louis Dreyfus & Co.* v. *Tempus Shipping Co.* [1931] A.C. 726 (concerned with the Merchant Shipping Act 1894, s.502). For the development of the law in the United States which has resulted in the incorporation of the "New Jason Clause" in many contracts of affreightment, see Lowndes & Rudolf, pp. 44–46.

[76] As amended by the Merchant Shipping Acts 1981, s.1, and 1984, s.12.

[77] *The Ettrick* (1881) L.R. 6 P.D. 127. This case was in fact concerned with the Merchant Shipping Act 1862, s.54, a precursor of s.503 of the Merchant Shipping Act 1894. See also *The Evje (No. 2)* [1976] 2 Lloyd's Rep. 714.

[78] [1958] 1 Q.B. 74. *Cf. Smith, Hogg & Co. Ltd.* v. *Black Sea & Baltic General Insurance Co.* (1939) 64 Ll.L.R. 87, 89, *per* MacKinnon L.J.

of the goods and accordingly, he argued, his liability to any cross-claim by cargo had been discharged by Article III, rule 6, of the Hague Rules.[79] This contention was rejected by Pearson J., who considered that it was contrary to "the evident objects of rule D, which are to keep the whole question of alleged fault outside the average adjustment and to leave the legal 'remedies' in respect of fault unimpaired."[80] He accordingly construed the word "remedies" in rule D to include defences as well as cross-claims, and held that cargo was protected by the defence that the shipowner could not claim in respect of the consequences of his own wrong. He also held that, on a true construction, Article III, rule 6, of the Hague Rules did not discharge the shipowner from liability to a cross-claim in respect of general average contribution; cargo was, therefore, also protected by the rule avoiding circuity of action. The shipowner's claim to contribution accordingly failed.

Adjustment and contributory values

The common law rule is that, when the voyage is completed, the adjustment is to be made at and in accordance with the law of the port of destination; but where the voyage is broken, it is to be made at and in accordance with the law of the place where it is broken. Frequently, however, the contract of affreightment makes express provision for these matters.

It is also the common law rule that the sacrifice is to be valued in accordance with its assumed value as at the date of the termination of the adventure, so that the owner of the thing lost or damaged may be put in the same position as he would have been in if the sacrifice had not been made. A similar rule has been applied to expenditure,[81] but this has been questioned.[82] Rule G of the York-Antwerp Rules 1974, provides that the loss shall be valued "at the time and place when and where the adventure ends."

The contributing interests may include ship, cargo, freight and the property sacrificed. Freight will be included unless it has been absolutely prepaid or is payable irrespective of completion of the voyage; for except in such cases the shipowner will have reaped a benefit in freight from the sacrifice or expenditure. The property sacrificed is included because the owner of such property must bear his proportion of the loss in common with the other parties to the adventure.

At common law the contributing interests, like the amount to be made good, are valued as at the date of the termination of the adventure; the same principle is applied by rule G of the York-Antwerp Rules 1974. Detailed provisions for valuation of the contributing interests and the amount to be made good are to

---

[79] Article III, rule 6, provides that " ... the carrier and the ship shall be discharged from all liability in respect of loss or damage unless suit is brought within one year after delivery of the goods or the date when the goods should have been delivered."
[80] [1958] 1 Q.B. 74, 100.
[81] *Chellew* v. *Royal Commission on Sugar Supply* [1921] 2 K.B. 627.
[82] See Lowndes & Rudolf, pp. 195 *et seq.*

be found in the York-Antwerp Rules[83] and in the rules of practice.[84] Once the various values have been ascertained, each interest contributes a part of the amount to be made good proportionate to its contributory value, the property sacrificed bearing its proportionate part of the loss.

Remedies

An action for contribution may be brought either by ship against cargo, or by cargo against ship or against other cargo.

In addition to his right of action, the shipowner has a lien[85] on the cargo for general average contribution. In practice, this means that cargo will be delivered against an average bond together with cash deposit or guarantee. The shipowner is bound to exercise his lien so as to obtain adequate security for the benefit of those cargo-owners who have suffered general average loss; if he does not do so, he will be liable in damages to such cargo-owners,[86] who have, therefore, an indirect lien for the protection of their rights.[87]

---

[83] rr. XVI, XVII and XVIII.
[84] rr. 30, 31 and 32.
[85] The lien is in origin a common law lien, but has been statutorily extended by the Merchant Shipping Act 1894, ss.492–501.
[86] *Crooks* v. *Allen* (1879) 5 Q.B.D. 38; *Strang Steel & Co.* v. *Scott & Co.* (1889) 14 App.Cas. 601; *Nobel's Explosives Co.* v. *Rea* [1896] 2 Q.B. 326.
[87] *Cf. The Corinthian Glory* [1977] 2 Lloyd's Rep. 280 (charterers' waiver of cesser clause).

CHAPTER 14

THE RIGHT TO RECOUPMENT: COMPULSORY DISCHARGE OF ANOTHER'S LIABILITY[1]

IN general, anybody who has under compulsion of law made a payment whereby he has discharged the primary liability of another is entitled to be reimbursed by that other. In the great majority of the cases discussed in this Chapter, that other was liable to pay a debt or other liquidated sum.[2] Consequently the Civil Liability (Contribution) Act 1978 will have no application and the common law will still govern.

The classic statement of the common law principle is to be found in a passage from the first edition of *Leake on Contracts*, which was quoted by Cockburn C.J. in *Moule* v. *Garrett*[3] in 1872:

> "Where the plaintiff has been compelled by law to pay, or being compellable by law, has paid money which the defendant was ultimately liable to pay, so that the latter obtains the benefit of the payment by the discharge of his liability; under such circumstances the defendant is held indebted to the plaintiff in the amount."

The basis of this right is similar to that which underlies the right to contribution.[4] The plaintiff is allowed to recover because he has been compelled by law[5] to make a payment which has discharged the defendant's liability to another. Whereas in contribution, the plaintiff seeks to recover only a proportionate

---

[1] Professor Sutton, in his essay entitled, *Payments of Debts Charged upon Property*, in *Essays* (ed. Burrows), Chap. 4, argues that the cases on compulsory discharge are one illustration of cases "where the debt can be charged upon, or enforced . . . against property. The critical question is not whether the payment is a compulsory one (since the doctrine also applies in the case of mistake), or even, indeed, whether the payment is 'involuntary' in a strict restitutionary sense. It is whether the payer is a part-owner of the property against which the debt is liable to be enforced. Such people have something 'in common', a 'community of interest' with those whose debts are secured, or whose interests are affected by, the same lien or other charge, and are therefore outside the general principles stated in the *Ruabon* [see above, p. 56 of this text] and *Cleadon* [see below, p. 662 of this text] cases": see pp. 78–79; and see above, Chap. 12 and below, p. 355. In our view, this statement is not supported by the authorities.
[2] Conceivably, this may arise from the discharge of a tortious obligation: *cf.* see below, pp. 357–358.
[3] (1872) L.R. 7 Ex. 101, 104. See also *Johnson* v. *Royal Mail Steam Packet Co.* (1867) L.R. 3 C.P. 38, 43, *per* Willes J.
[4] See *Edmunds* v. *Wallingford* (1885) 14 Q.B.D. 811, 814–815, *per* Lindley L.J.; *Bonner* v. *Tottenham and Edmonton Permanent Investment Building Society* [1899] 1 Q.B. 161, 178, *per* Vaughan Williams L.J.; see above, Chap. 12.
[5] Compulsion by a foreign system of law is sufficient: *Liberian Insurance Agency Inc.* v. *Mosse* [1977] 2 Lloyd's Rep. 560.

share of his payment, in the cases discussed in this Chapter he claims to be recouped the whole of the payment since the defendant is primarily liable to pay it. He may also seek relief by subrogation.[6]

To succeed in his claim for recoupment, the plaintiff must satisfy certain conditions. He must show:

(1) that he has been compelled, or was compellable, by law to make the payment;
(2) that he did not officiously expose himself to the liability to make the payment; and
(3) that his payment discharged a *liability* of the defendant.[7]

The plaintiff enforces his right to reimbursement by recovering his money as paid to the defendant's use.[8] But in certain cases[9] the plaintiff is given a right to deduct a sum equal to his payment from money which he owes the defendant. He may also become entitled, on making the payment, to the benefit of securities deposited with the creditor by the defendant to secure the debt paid by the plaintiff.[10]

1. THE PLAINTIFF'S PAYMENT MUST HAVE BEEN COMPULSORY

Compulsion is strictly defined. As appears from Leake's statement of the law, the compulsion must be a compulsion of law. The plaintiff need not have been sued for the money. It is enough that he, "being compellable by law, has paid money which the defendant was ultimately liable to pay."[11]

A payment is not compulsory within the meaning of that statement if it is made because the plaintiff thought he was morally obliged to make it.[12] Similarly, it is not a compulsory payment if it was made because the payer and his co-contractors had contractually bound themselves to make that payment to third parties. That was the fate of Esso in *The Esso Bernicia*.[13] Esso had entered into an agreement with other tanker owners and bareboat charterers to assume liability for pollution damage caused by oil which escaped or was discharged from any vessel owned by the participating parties. Pursuant to that agreement, Esso paid over half a million pounds to crofters in respect of damage to sheep due to the pollution of the foreshore from the discharge of oil

---

[6] See Chap. 31, *Re Downer Enterprises Ltd.* [1974] 1 W.L.R. 1460; see above, p. 303.

[7] *Liberian Insurance Agency Inc.* v. *Mosse* [1977] 2 Lloyd's Rep. 560; see below, pp. 355 *et seq.*

[8] See above, p. 3.

[9] See below, pp. 361–362.

[10] *Duncan Fox & Co.* v. *North & South Wales Bank* (1880) 6 App.Cas. 1. The case is concerned with the rights of an indorser of a bill of exchange but in some respects the speech of Lord Selborne L.C. is broad enough in its terms to cover the rights of any person who has been compelled to discharge another's liability: see below, pp. 605–606. Contrast *Scholefield Goodman & Sons* v. *Zyngier* [1985] 3 W.L.R. 953 [P.C.].

[11] See above, p. 343, n. 3.

[12] But contrast below, pp. 596–599 (on subrogation, suggesting that such a payment may not always be officious).

[13] [1989] A.C. 643.

from *The Esso Bernicia*. It was averred that the damage was the consequence of the negligence of the tug builders, Hall Russell. The House of Lords rejected Esso's submission that it was entitled to be subrogated to the crofters' claim in tort against Hall Russell.[14] In Lord Goff's view, assuming that the payment was to indemnify the crofters in respect of their loss, its payment did not have the effect of discharging Hall Russell's liability to them. Hall Russell had not then been unjustly enriched at Esso's expense. If "anybody has been enriched, it is the crofters, to the extent that they have been indemnified by Esso and yet continue to have vested in them rights of action against Hall Russell in respect of the loss or damage which was the subject matter of Esso's payment to them."[15] If the crofters did recover substantial damages from Hall Russell, the crofters would indeed be unjustly enriched.[16] If Esso were to seek reimbursement from the crofters, its claim would probably fail[17]; its payments would be characterised as voluntary or gratuitous. Indeed, it was for that reason that Esso's payments were not recoverable from Hall Russell as economic loss directly flowing from the damage to the tanker.[18]

The cases, where a restitutionary claim has succeeded, fall into three main groups: relief of property from distress, assignment of leases and abatement of nuisances. But these categories are not exclusive. The general principle is that a plaintiff should recover in restitution whenever he made, under legal compulsion, a payment which has discharged the defendant's liability to a third party.[19] Consequently, other cases can arise outside the established categories. An important example is *Brook's Wharf & Bull Wharf Ltd.* v. *Goodman Bros.*[20] The defendants were a firm of furriers who had imported a consignment of squirrel skins from Russia. They stored 10 packages of the skins in the plaintiff's bonded warehouse. While they were so stored, the packages were stolen, but the theft was held not to have been due to any negligence on the part of the plaintiffs. As bonded warehousemen, the plaintiffs were compelled, by statute,[21] to pay the duties on these packages out of their own moneys on the demand of the customs. The Court of Appeal held, applying the principle enunciated by Cockburn C.J. in *Moule* v. *Garrett*,[22] that the plaintiffs were entitled to be reimbursed by the defendants, because they had been compelled by law to pay duty which the defendants were primarily liable to pay.[23]

---

[14] On subrogation, see below, pp. 596 *et seq.*

[15] At p. 663. For a comment on the case, see Jones, *Restitution in Public and Private Law* (1991), pp. 131–133.

[16] Query whether the crofters could then successfully plead that Esso's payment was *res inter alios acta*.

[17] If the crofters do recover substantial damages, do they hold the damage award on trust for Esso?: *cf.* below p. 598. It is not easy to conclude that the position of Esso is akin to that of an insurer; *e.g.*, what if it was Esso's negligence which caused the pollution?

[18] For a critical comment, see [1989] L.M.C.L.Q. 1 [Weir].

[19] See above, Chap. 12.

[20] [1937] 1 K.B. 534.

[21] Customs Consolidation Act 1876, s.85.

[22] See above, p. 348.

[23] See [1937] 1 K.B. 534, 544, *per* Lord Wright M.R., quoted below, p. 355.

Another illustration of this principle is *Edmunds* v. *Wallingford*.[24] The defendant bought in his own name an ironmonger's business for his two sons. Although the business was thereafter carried on by the sons as partners, it was on premises of which the lease was in the defendant's name. The defendant also kept the firm's banking account and signed the business cheques in the firm's name. A third party obtained a judgment against the defendant, and some goods belonging to the sons were seized by the sheriff. Upon an inter-pleader summons taken out by the sheriff, a claim by the sons to the goods was barred. The goods were sold for £1,300, and that sum was paid into court in the action by the third party against the defendant. The sons were later adjud-icated bankrupt, and the plaintiff was appointed their trustee. The Court of Appeal held that the plaintiff was entitled to recover from the defendant £1,200, which he was prepared to accept instead of the sum of £1,300 which the goods realised, on the grounds that the sons' goods had been lawfully taken in execution for the defendant's debt.

Most of the cases fall, however, within the three main categories, which we shall now discuss.

(a) *Relief of the Plaintiff's Property from Distress or a Lien Lawfully Exercised Thereon*

This is the earliest and most familiar example of compulsory discharge of another's liability. The first case was *Exall* v. *Partridge*,[25] decided in 1799. There were three defendants in the action, Partridge and two others, who were lessees of certain premises from Welch. Two of the defendants with the plaintiff's knowledge assigned their interest to Partridge, who was a coach-maker. Thereafter, the plaintiff placed his carriage on the premises, presum-ably for work to be done on it by Partridge; and while there it was seized by Welch as distress for rent.[26] To redeem his carriage, the plaintiff was forced to pay Welch the rent due to him, and he then sued all three defendants to recover from them the sum he had so paid. At the trial before Lord Kenyon, the plaintiff was nonsuited on the ground that the action should have been brought against Partridge alone, he being, with the plaintiff's knowledge, in sole possession of the premises at the time when the plaintiff entrusted his carriage to him. The Court of King's Bench, however, set aside the nonsuit, because all three defendants were liable to Welch for the rent, and the plaintiff had been compelled to discharge that liability. Even though he had "put his goods on the premises, knowing the interests of the defendants, and thereby placed himself

---

[24] (1885) 14 Q.B.D. 811. See also *Jeffreys* v. *Gurr* (1831) 2 B. & Ad. 833; *Cross* v. *Cheshire* (1851) 7 Ex. 43.

[25] (1799) 8 T.R. 308, see below, p. 354. *Cf. Re Button* [1907] 2 K.B. 180; and see also *Dawson* v. *Linton* (1822) 5 B. & Ald. 521; *Ex p. Elliott* (1838) 3 Deac. 343 (*cf. Jones* v. *Simmons* (1881) 45 J.P. 666); *Johnson* v. *Skafte* (1869) L.R. 4 Q.B. 700.

[26] The landlord's common law right to distrain for rent on goods of a third party has been restricted by the Law of Distress Amendment Act 1908. The scope of the Act is, however, very limited: see Halsbury, *Laws*, Vol. 13, §§ 254 *et seq.*

in a situation where he was liable to pay this money, without the concurrence of two of the defendants, he could not be said to have been a volunteer *vis-à-vis* those defendants,"[27] and so was entitled to recover from all three. Again, in *Johnson* v. *Royal Mail Steam Packet Co.*,[28] a shipowner mortgaged two of his ships to the plaintiffs. With their acquiescence, he later entered into an agreement with the defendants whereby the defendants were to work the ships, paying the expenses and taking the profits, subject to an indemnity from the shipowner against any loss which they might incur. A few months later, the plaintiffs gave notice to the defendants of their mortgage and called upon them to deliver up the ships to the plaintiff's agent in Sydney. The defendants delivered up the ships as requested; but at the time of delivery more than £5,000 was due from the defendants to the officers and crews of the ships for their wages. For this sum the officers and crews were entitled to their maritime lien on the vessels, and on their taking proceedings in the Vice-Admiralty Court in Sydney the officers of the court seized the vessels. The money was not forthcoming from the defendants, and the vessels were detained for some months until ultimately the plaintiffs paid the sum claimed in order to obtain possession of the ships. The Court of Common Pleas held that the plaintiffs were entitled to recover from the defendants the sum which they had so been compelled to pay.

Compulsion of a similar kind has also been exercised in a number of cases in which a tenant has been compelled, by distress of goods or by threat of distress, to make payment to a ground landlord or to some other person having a claim paramount to his immediate landlord. In such cases the tenant has a right over against his immediate landlord, but it is usually a right to deduct the money he has so paid from the rent then due or accruing due. These cases are discussed later.[29] It may, however, be that the person so compelled to pay money, although lawfully in possession of the land, does not strictly hold it under a tenancy,[30] or does not pay any rent.[31] In such circumstances, he will have no right of deduction, and should be entitled to claim reimbursement from his immediate landlord.

(b) *Cases Concerned with Assignment of Leases*

If the assignor of a lease is the original lessee, he may find himself compelled to pay rent or damages for breach of covenant, although the rent has accrued due or the breach has been committed after he has assigned away his term. Very often he has taken an express covenant, or nowadays has received, by virtue of

---

[27] (1799) 8 T.R. 308, 310, *per* Lord Kenyon C.J.; see also *Bevan* v. *Waters* (1828) 3 C.P. 520 and *cf. Johnson* v. *Royal Mail Steam Packet Co.* (1867) L.R. 3 C.P. 38, 45, *per* Willes J.
[28] (1867) L.R. 3 C.P. 38; applied in *The Orchis* (1890) 15 P.D. 38; *cf. Walker* v. *Duncombe* (1824) 2 L.J.(o.s.) K.B. 80; *The Ripon City* [1898] P. 78; *The Heather Bell* [1901] P. 143, 272.
[29] See below, pp. 361–362.
[30] *Ryan* v. *Byrne* (1883) 17 Ir.L.T. 102. See also *Gregory* v. *Stanway* (1860) 2 F. & F. 309, *per* Martin B.
[31] *Murphy* v. *Davey* (1884) 14 L.R.(Ir.) 28. *Cf. Crouch* v. *Tregonning* (1872) L.R. 7 Ex. 88, 91, *per* Bramwell B.

section 77 of the Law of Property Act 1925, an implied covenant from the assignee to indemnify him against breaches of covenant.[32] But even where the assignor has received no such express or implied covenant from his immediate assignee, he can recover from him any sum in respect of rent[33] or damages for breach of covenant[34] which he has had to pay to the lessor, provided that such rent has accrued due or such breach has been committed during the period of the assignee's interest. In these cases, the obligation to indemnify should properly be regarded as contractual, being an obligation implied by virtue of the assignor having, at the request of the assignee, assigned to him the term in question. In the leading case of *Moule* v. *Garrett*,[35] however, the Court of Exchequer Chamber held that the original lessee can also proceed against subsequent assignees of the term, his right being unaffected by the fact that each assignee may have covenanted to indemnify his immediate assignor against all subsequent breaches. Here there is no contractual relationship between the parties, and the right of the original lessee to reimbursement is quasi-contractual.

Where the original lessee has received a covenant, express or implied, from his assignee, he may be entitled on the terms of such covenant to recover from the assignee not only payments made in respect of rent or breaches of covenant, but also his costs.[36] But where the assignor is relying upon his quasi-contrac-

---

[32] The extent of the liability will then depend on the terms of the particular covenant: see *Staines* v. *Morris* (1812) 1 V. & B. 8; *Gooch* v. *Clutterbuck* (1899) 2 Q.B. 148; *cf. Hawkins* v. *Sherman* (1828) 3 C. & P. 459. On express covenants, see *Wolveridge* v. *Steward* (1833) 1 C. & M. 644; *Groom* v. *Bluck* (1841) 2 Man. & G. 567; *Smith* v. *White* (1866) L.R. 1 Eq. 626; *Hardy* v. *Fothergill* (1888) 13 App.Cas. 351; *Harris* v. *Boots Cash Chemists (Southern) Ltd.* [1904] 2 Ch. 376; *Butler Estates Co. Ltd.* v. *Bean* [1942] 1 K.B. 1; see also *M'Creery* v. *Luttrell* (1852) 2 I.C.L.R. 289.

[33] *Wolveridge* v. *Steward* (1833) 1 C. & M. 644, 659–660, *per* Denman C.J. But payment of the rent gives the assignor only a right to recover the amount of such payment from the assignee. It does not give him a lien on the term; he cannot, therefore, be prejudiced by its subsequent assignment: *Re Russell* (1885) 29 Ch.D. 254. Where the assignment was invalid and the "assignee" was not accepted by the lessor as tenant, it was held that the "assignee" was not liable to indemnify the assignor in respect of rent which had accrued during the term purportedly assigned but which was not due until after the "assignee" had ceased to occupy the premises: see *Crouch* v. *Tregonning* (1872) L.R. 7 Ex. 88. In that case, Bramwell B. further suggested (at p. 91) that the "assignee" was not liable to indemnify the assignor even in respect of rent accrued due during his occupation because there was no common liability of the two parties to the lessor. *Aliter*, however, if the parties expressly or impliedly agree to the contrary; see *Willson* v. *Leonard* (1840) 3 Beav. 373.

[34] *Burnett* v. *Lynch* (1826) 5 B. & C. 589; *Smith* v. *Peat* (1853) 9 Ex. 161. The assignor can only claim payment in respect of breaches already committed; see *Lloyd* v. *Dimmack* (1877) 7 Ch.D. 398.

[35] (1872) L.R. 5 Ex. 132; 7 Ex. 101. For the position where the intermediate assignee is bankrupt, see *Re Parkins* [1898] 2 Ch. 182. *Cf.* the position of an equitable assignee: see *Close* v. *Wilberforce* (1838) 1 Beav. 112; *Nokes* v. *Fish* (1857) 3 Drew. 735, 742–743, *per* Kindersley V.-C.

[36] If the assignee has covenanted to indemnify the assignor, the assignor is entitled to recover all costs necessarily incurred by him, in particular costs properly incurred for the purpose of ascertaining the amount of the assignee's liability: see *Smith* v. *Howell* (1851) 6 Ex. 730; *Howard* v. *Lovegrove* (1870) L.R. 6 Ex. 43; *Murrell* v. *Fysh* (1883) Cab. & Ell. 80; *Re Russell* (1885) 29 Ch.D. 254. But if the assignee has simply covenanted to perform the covenants in the lease, the assignor will have to show that he incurred costs as a necessary consequence of the assignee failing to perform those covenants: see *Willson* v. *Leonard* (1840) 3 Beav. 373; *Penley* v. *Watts* (1841) 7 M. & W. 601; *Walker* v. *Hatton* (1842) 10 M. & W. 249.

tual right to reimbursement by a subsequent assignee, the measure of recovery may be different. Here the right is not a right to indemnity against the assignor's reasonable expenditure. It is a right to reimbursement in respect of a compulsory payment to the extent to which that payment has conferred a benefit upon the assignee. On principle, therefore, the assignee's liability should be limited to the amount by which his liability to the landlord has been discharged, and he should not be held liable to pay any part of the assignor's costs.[37]

(c) Abatement of Nuisances

In these cases,[38] health authorities served notices on occupiers, calling upon them under various Health Acts to abate nuisances, and the occupiers thereupon caused work to be carried out for which, as it later appeared, they were not in fact responsible. If in such circumstances the occupier can show that he was compelled to incur the cost of such work, he can recover the cost from the person responsible, whether the health authority itself or some other person. Thus, in *Gebhardt* v. *Saunders*,[39] the plaintiff was tenant of the defendant's house in London, in which a nuisance had been created by a stoppage in the drains. The health authority served a statutory notice at the premises, directed to the owner or occupier and requiring the nuisance to be abated and imposing a penalty on default. The health authority served no notice on the defendant, the owner, and it was impossible at the time to tell whether the nuisance was due to improper use by the plaintiff, for which he was responsible, or to a structural defect, which was the defendant's responsibility. The plaintiff carried out the work, in the course of which it was found that the stoppage had been caused by a structural defect. He therefore claimed from the defendant the costs and expenses which he had incurred in abating the nuisance. A divisional court held that he was entitled to recover under the relative Act; but Charles J. stated that, apart from the statute, the plaintiff was entitled to recover at common law on the grounds that he had "been legally compelled to expend money on what another man ought to have done."[40] "Common sense and the necessity of the case"[41] require that, in situations of this kind, the plaintiff should abate the nuisance. He is compelled to do so by the service of the statutory notice, carrying with it penalties on default,[42] and by the necessity for immediate action.[43] If either of these elements is absent, he cannot establish

---

[37] *Cf.* above, p. 330, n. 83 for contribution claims; and see below, pp. 361–362 for a further discussion.

[38] The cases were considered by Sir James Campbell C.J. in *Hackett* v. *Smith* [1917] 2 I.R. 508.

[39] [1892] 2 Q.B. 452.

[40] [1892] 2 Q.B. 452, 458.

[41] *Gebhardt* v. *Saunders* [1892] 2 Q.B. 452, 456, *per* Day J.

[42] It has been said that the person upon whom the notice is served is prima facie liable to the penalty, unless he can show that he is not responsible for the work: see *Andrew* v. *St. Olave's Board of Works* [1898] 1 Q.B. 775, 781, *per* Lord Russell C.J.

[43] *Gebhardt* v. *Saunders* [1892] 2 Q.B. 452, 456, *per* Day J.; *Andrew* v. *St. Olave's Board of Works* [1898] 1 Q.B. 775, 781, *per* Lord Russell C.J.; *North* v. *Walthamstow U.D.C.* (1898) 67

compulsion. So, if an authority merely warns him[44] or recommends that certain work should be done,[45] without actual or implicit[46] threat of legal proceedings,[47] the work, if done, will not be regarded as having been done under compulsion. Similarly, if there is no necessity for the work to be done at once, the plaintiff is not under sufficient compulsion to claim recovery.[48]

There may be exceptional cases where, despite the compulsion, the plaintiff accepted such full responsibility for the work that he will not be allowed to reopen the matter and claim the cost of the work from the person legally responsible.[49] It is as if he has made a voluntary payment.[50] His submission to the authority's claim that he is the person responsible renders his expenditure voluntary and, therefore, irrecoverable.

2. THE PLAINTIFF MUST NOT HAVE OFFICIOUSLY EXPOSED HIMSELF TO THE LIABILITY TO MAKE THE PAYMENT

In the first section of this Chapter we considered compulsion in relation to the plaintiff's act of payment. It may be,[51] however, that the plaintiff by his own act has put himself in the position where he was compelled to make the payment.[52] In such circumstances the question arises whether he can claim that his money was paid to the defendant's use.[53]

L.J.Q.B. 972, 974, *per* Channell J.; *Rhymney Iron Co.* v. *Gelligaer District Council* [1917] 1 K.B. 589, 594, *per* Viscount Reading C.J.

[44] An "intimation" notice was held to be a mere warning in *Thompson and Norris Manufacturing Co.* v. *Hawes* (1895) 73 L.T. 369; *Harris* v. *Hickman* [1904] 1 K.B. 13. See also *Oliver* v. *Camberwell B.C.* (1904) 90 L.T. 285. But *cf. Proctor* v. *Islington B.C.* (1903) 67 J.P. 164; *North* v. *Walthamstow U.D.C.* (1898) 67 L.J.Q.B. 972. But in later cases Channell J. distinguished a tenant fulfilling his landlord's duty from an occupier fulfilling the health authority's; in the case of the former it was necessary to show real compulsion: see *Haedicke* v. *Friern Barnet U.D.C.* [1904] 2 K.B. 807, 814–815 (reversed, on a different point, [1905] 1 K.B. 110); *Wilson's Music and General Printing Co.* v. *Finsbury B.C.* [1908] 1 K.B. 563, 569–570.

[45] *Silles* v. *Fulham B.C.* [1903] 1 K.B. 829.

[46] *Cf. North* v. *Walthamstow U.D.C.* (1898) 67 L.J.Q.B. 972.

[47] *Ellis* v. *Bromley R.D.C.* (1899) 81 L.T. 224.

[48] *Ibid.* at p. 225, *per* Ridley J.

[49] *Self* v. *Hove Commissioners* [1895] 1 Q.B. 685, 689–690, *per* Wills J.; *North* v. *Walthamstow U.D.C.* (1898) 67 L.J.Q.B. 972, 974, *per* Channell J. *Cf. Andrew* v. *St. Olave's Board of Works* [1898] 1 Q.B. 775, which has been cogently criticised on the ground that the plaintiff could have successfully resisted the defendant's notice: see *Hackett* v. *Smith* [1917] 2 I.R. 508, 524, *per* Campbell C.J.; see also *Butcher* v. *Ruth* (1887) 22 L.R.Ir. 380; and *cf. Maskell* v. *Horner* [1915] 3 K.B. 106, discussed above, p. 268.

[50] See above, pp. 58–60.

[51] But *cf. Moule* v. *Garrett* (1872) L.R. 5 Ex. 132, 7 Ex. 101.

[52] *Exall* v. *Partridge* (1799) 8 T.R. 308, 310, *per* Lord Kenyon. But *cf. Restatement of Restitution,* § 103, ill. 3, which *semble* would allow recovery even if the payer officiously exposes himself to liability. *Quaere*, if this solution is reconcilable with § 2 of the *Restatement*, which denies recovery to the officious stranger.

[53] *Cf.* the similar problem that arises in the context of the adoption of the benefit of unauthorised transactions: see *Re Cleadon Trust* [1939] Ch. 286, see below, pp. 622–623.

Nineteenth century lawyers would no doubt have sought the solution to this problem in the notion of request. A request was a necessary prerequisite to the action for money paid, and if the plaintiff had officiously exposed himself to the liability, it could not be said that the defendant had requested him to make the payment. But the formal language of request, which was, as we have seen,[54] artificially extended to include cases where the plaintiff had acted under compulsion, concealed the true grounds on which the courts granted or refused relief. Today it is more realistic to solve the problem by reference to the concept of officiousness.[55]

The plaintiff's payment will not be officious if he has exposed himself to liability at the true request, express or tacit, of the defendant,[56] or if he has been forced to place himself in the position which rendered him liable to make the payment, or, perhaps, if he has intervened as a matter of necessity.[57] In such cases if, in consequence of his intervention, he finds himself compelled to make the payment, he should be entitled to reimbursement. But if, in other circumstances, he freely and without request[58] undertakes the risk of liability, he generally has no right to any direct reimbursement, even though he is compelled to make the payment. In some cases,[59] where the defendant has incontrovertibly benefited from the plaintiff's intervention, this limiting principle[60] has arguably been too generously interpreted in order to deny a plaintiff restitution.

The problem may be illustrated by reference to three situations concerned respectively with suretyship, bills of exchange, and relief of goods from distress.

(1) Where a person guarantees the debt of another, he cannot claim a direct right of indemnity against that other if the guarantee has been given officiously or purely at the request of the creditor. Consequently, in *Owen* v. *Tate*[61] the Court of Appeal held that the plaintiff, who had become a surety in place of another surety without the debtor's consent or subsequent ratification, was not entitled to be reimbursed by the debtor after paying the creditor. It was not "reasonably necessary in the interests of the volunteer [the plaintiff] or the

---

[54] See above, pp. 3–4.

[55] If it is still necessary to cling to the old language of request, it should, in our view, be recognised that no request will be implied if the plaintiff officiously exposes himself to liability; see above, pp. 58–60.

[56] *Moule* v. *Garrett* (1872) L.R. 5 Ex. 132, 138, *per* Channell B., 7 Ex. 101, 104, *per* Cockburn C.J.

[57] *Owen* v. *Tate* [1976] 1 Q.B. 402, 412–413, *per* Stephenson L.J.; see also at pp. 409–410, *per* Scarman L.J.; *Power* v. *Nash*, 37 Maine (2 Heath) 322 (1853).

[58] *The Esso Bernicia* [1989] A.C. 643, H.L.: see above, p. 344. 19th century lawyers also sought to solve the problem by invoking the conception of privity. If the plaintiff's act was unofficious, it could generally be referred to some relationship or "privity" between him and the defendant; if the act was officious, there was *a fortiori* no privity: see *Exall* v. *Partridge* (1799) 8 T.R. 308; *England* v. *Marsden* (1866) L.R. 1 C.P. 539. Privity was, therefore, used in an artificial sense: see *Moule* v. *Garrett* (1872) 7 Ex. 101, 104, *per* Cockburn C.J.; *Edmunds* v. *Wallingford* (1885) 14 Q.B.D. 811, 815, *per* Lindley L.J.

[59] See below, pp. 351–352.

[60] See above, pp. 22 *et seq.*; see below, p. 352.

[61] [1976] 1 Q.B. 402. For a fuller discussion of this case, see pp. 596–599.

person for whom the payment was made, or both, that the payment should be made."[62] Indeed the court found it difficult to imagine any situation,[63] other than necessity,[64] when it could be "reasonably necessary" for a volunteer to assume the burden of suretyship without the debtor's consent. In such a case the volunteer cannot confer an incontrovertible benefit on the debtor since the debt cannot be discharged without the debtor's authority. But he will generally be able to recover his payment from the creditor, for there will have been a total failure of consideration since the payment was made to discharge a debt which has not been discharged.[65] The facts of *Owen* v. *Tate* were however exceptional. The volunteer's claim against the creditor, a bank, would have failed, for the bank had given consideration to the volunteer in that it had released another surety at the volunteer's instigation. Yet the volunteer should not necessarily have been without a remedy. There would be no objection to him deriving any rights against the debtor through and from the creditor by assignment. Even if the creditor has not expressly assigned his claim to the volunteer, it is arguable that he should be subrogated to the creditor who has accepted his suretyship and his payment.[66] His conduct may be condemned as officious *vis-à-vis* the debtor but it cannot be so condemned *vis-à-vis* the creditor who accepted his payment *qua* surety.[67]

(2) It was decided in the leading case of *Jones* v. *Broadhurst*[68] that, where a drawer or indorser pays a bill of exchange, the acceptor is not discharged but remains liable to the holder of the bill. Any sum which the holder may thereafter recover from the acceptor is, however, held on trust by him for the drawer or indorser to the extent of the latter's payment of the bill. It is now provided by section 59(2) of the Bills of Exchange Act 1882 that payment of a bill by a drawer or indorser does not discharge the bill, unless the bill is an accommodation bill and is paid in due course by the party accommodated.[69]

No doubt bills of exchange are subject to special considerations. Nevertheless, on general principle there is much to be said against the rule so estab-

---

[62] At pp. 409–410, *per* Scarman L.J.

[63] At p. 414, *per* Ormrod L.J.

[64] At p. 412, *per* Stephenson L.J., citing *Re A Debtor* [1937] Ch. 156, 166, *per* Greene L.J., and *Anson* v. *Anson* [1953] Q.B. 636, 642–643, *per* Pearson J. See above, n. 57, and *cf.* below, Chap. 15.

[65] *Walter* v. *James* (1871) L.R. 6 Ex. 124, 127, *per* Kelly C.B.; see above, p. 17. Contrast (1983) 99 L.Q.R. 534 [Friedmann]; *The Esso Bernicia* [1989] A.C. 643 (see above, p. 344 and below, p. 596).

[66] For an attempted reconciliation of this decision, where the obligation of suretyship was voluntarily assumed but where the payment was compulsory, with the *Exall* v. *Partridge* line of cases (above), see *Essays* (ed. Burrows), pp. 100–101 [Sutton].

[67] For a further discussion, see below, pp. 596–599. Contrast Birks, *Introduction*, pp. 191–192, 311–312 who argues that it would be more honest to recognise that the officious surety should, in these circumstances, have a claim against the debtor.

[68] (1850) 9 C.B. 173. See also *Agra & Masterman's Bank Ltd.* v. *Leighton* (1866) L.R. 2 Ex. 56.

[69] Bills of Exchange Act 1882, s.59(3). An accommodation party to a bill of exchange is a surety for the person on whose behalf he has become a party to the bill. His rights over against such person are, therefore, the same as a surety's rights over against his principal debtor: see *Oriental Financial Corporation* v. *Overend Gurney & Co.* (1871) L.R. 7 Ch.App. 142, (1874) L.R. 7 H.L. 348; and Rowlatt, *op. cit.* pp. 214–215.

lished.[70] It is true that the indorser of a bill of exchange is not, strictly, a surety; nor has he, strictly speaking, indorsed the bill at the request of the acceptor. Yet the primary liability rests upon the acceptor, that of the indorser being "only secondary"[71]; and it is certainly within the contemplation of acceptors of bills of exchange that others will indorse the bills and so render themselves liable thereon.[72] It is difficult to see, therefore, why the payment of a drawer or indorser should not operate to discharge the acceptor, *pro tanto*, if the payment is partial, and completely, if the payment is in full. The indorser is not an officious intervener and he should be entitled to recover the amount of any such payment from the acceptor. This was tacitly recognised by the Court of Appeal in *Ex p. Bishop*,[73] a case concerned with bill brokers. Bill brokers do not generally indorse over to bankers, who advance money to them, every bill they discount. They customarily give to the bankers a general guarantee to pay any discounted bill as it falls due. The court held that, if a bill broker has to pay a bill to his banker, he is entitled, despite the absence of indorsement, to sue the acceptor for reimbursement. For the acceptor must be taken to have had knowledge of this well-established practice of the City of London and to have authorised the bill broker to rediscount the bill in the ordinary way of business by giving the necessary guarantee to his banker. In our view, an acceptor of a bill should equally be liable to reimburse any person who subsequently indorses the bill. Indeed the result of *Ex p. Bishop* appears to be that one who has not indorsed the bill may find himself in a stronger position *vis-à-vis* the acceptor than one who has. Again, in *Pownal* v. *Ferrand*,[74] an indorser who paid part of the amount due on a bill to the holder was held entitled to recover from the acceptor the amount so paid as money paid to the acceptor's use. The indorser paid the holder £40 on account of the bill which had been accepted for £350. Thereafter the holder obtained a judgment against the acceptor for the full amount of the bill, but only levied for the balance, giving credit for the £40 which the indorser had paid. The court held that, since the indorser might be unable to sue on the bill on which the holder had obtained judgment in full, and since the acceptor had had the benefit of the indorser's payment, the indorser could recover £40 from the acceptor as money paid to his use. It is difficult to see how this case can be reconciled with *Jones* v. *Broadhurst*,[75] or, indeed, with section 59(2) of the Bills of Exchange Act 1882, except on the rather doubtful ground that the acceptor should be taken to have ratified the

---

[70] See the criticisms in *Cook* v. *Lister* (1863) 13 C.B.(N.S.) 543.
[71] *Tindal* v. *Brown* (1786) 1 T.R. 167, 170, *per* Buller J.
[72] *Ex p. Bishop* (1880) 15 Ch.D. 400, 416, *per* Cotton L.J.; see also *Duncan, Fox & Co.* v. *North & South Wales Bank* (1880) 6 App.Cas. 1, 14, *per* Lord Selborne L.C. But it is surely not correct to say with Lord Selborne that the acceptor is under a duty to *indemnify* every indorser, since there is normally no contract between the acceptor and indorser of a bill of exchange.
[73] (1880) 15 Ch.D. 400.
[74] (1827) 6 B. & C. 439.
[75] (1850) 9 C.B. 173.

indorser's payment.[76] Nowadays, the only safe course is for the indorser to pursue his remedies through the holder.[77]

(3) Where a person has officiously exposed his goods to the risk of seizure, by placing them without authority on land in the occupation of a tenant, and the goods are later seized by the landlord in distress for the tenant's rent, the trespasser should not be entitled to reimbursement by the tenant if he pays the rent to the landlord to redeem his goods. But where he has placed his goods on the land with the authority of the tenant, the tenant cannot be heard to say that the owner of the goods acted officiously in placing them there. If, therefore, his goods are seized by the landlord by way of distress and he has to redeem them by paying the tenant's rent, he should be entitled to be reimbursed by the tenant. Thus, in *Exall* v. *Partridge*,[78] there had originally been three lessees of a plot of land, two of whom had assigned their interests to the third, Partridge. Thereafter the plaintiff placed his goods on the land with the authority of Partridge only. When the plaintiff's goods were seized as distress for rent, which the plaintiff was compelled to pay in order to redeem his goods, it was held that he was entitled to reimbursement, not only as against Partridge, but also against the two other lessees. Lord Kenyon was obviously concerned that the two other lessees had not authorised the plaintiff to place his goods on the land.[79] But by assigning their interests to Partridge, they must be taken to have given to him the sole power of authorising others to come onto the land, and therefore through Partridge to have authorised Exall to place his goods thereon.[80]

Again, in *England* v. *Marsden*,[81] the plaintiff, under a bill of sale, seized "all the household furniture, goods, etc.," on the defendant's premises, and then left them there. The jury found that the plaintiff had no express authority from the defendant to leave the goods; but undoubtedly the defendant knew they were there, and probably he raised no objection. The goods were later taken in distress for rent, which the plaintiff paid to relieve the goods, and he sought to recover from the defendant the amount so paid. The Court of Common Pleas held that he was not entitled to recover, on the grounds that he had "by his own

---

[76] The holder can prove in an acceptor's bankruptcy only for so much of the bill as remains unpaid: see *Cooper* v. *Pepys* (1741) 1 Atk. 107; *Ex p. Wyldman* (1750) 2 Ves.Sen. 113; *Ex p. Tayler* (1857) 1 De G. & J. 302; *Ex p. Maxoudoff* (1868) L.R. 6 Eq. 582. This appears to be the law despite the Bills of Exchange Act 1882, s.59(2).

[77] If the indorser pays the bill in full, he can require the holder to deliver it up and can then sue the acceptor: see *Duncan, Fox & Co.* v. *North & South Wales Bank* (1880) 6 App.Cas. 1, 18, *per* Lord Blackburn; Bills of Exchange Act 1882, s.59(2)(*b*); see below, pp. 605–606. If he only pays part, he must persuade the holder to recover from the acceptor the full amount, and the holder will then hold in trust for the indorser a sum equal to the amount of his payment: see *Jones* v. *Broadhurst* (1850) 9 C.B. 173; *Cook* v. *Lister* (1863) 13 C.B.(N.S.) 543, 597, *per* Willes J.; *cf. Duncan, Fox & Co.* v. *North & South Wales Bank* (1880) 6 App.Cas. 1; see below, p. 605.

[78] (1799) 8 T.R. 308; see above, p. 346, see below, p. 356.

[79] (1799) 8 T.R. 308, 310.

[80] So in *Ex p. Bishop* (1880) 15 Ch.D. 400, it was held that the acceptor of the bills had impliedly authorised the drawers to have the bills discounted in the ordinary course of business; see above, p. 353.

[81] (1866) L.R. 1 C.P. 529.

voluntary act, and without any request of the defendant, express or implied, placed his goods in a position to enable the landlord to seize them."[82] But the goods must have been on the premises with the tacit authority of the defendant; and, after some strong criticism,[83] it was later stated in the Court of Appeal[84] that the decision was one which ought not to be followed.

3. The Plaintiff's Payment must have Discharged a Liability of the Defendant

Compulsion is not enough in itself to enable a plaintiff to recover. He must also, by reason of the compulsion, have paid money which the defendant was primarily liable to pay, *so that the latter obtained the benefit of the payment by the discharge of his liability.*[85]

At first sight it is puzzling that the plaintiff's payment should be capable of discharging the defendant's liability in these cases, for a stranger cannot discharge the debt of another without that other's authority.[86] The present cases can only be explained on the ground that the *law* compels the plaintiff to make the payment and therefore enables him, although a stranger, to discharge the liability of the defendant. It is for this reason, we suggest, that the doctrine is limited to those cases where the plaintiff has been compelled by law to make the payment; if he were not, for example, if his goods had been wrongfully taken in distress for rent, it appears that his payment would not of itself discharge the liability of the person primarily liable to pay.

It is therefore critical that the payment discharged the defendant's *liability* to a third party, who will normally be the person exercising the compulsion. The liability will generally be a debt. There is no doubt that the defendant's liability will be discharged if both he and the plaintiff are liable *in solidum* for the same debt. There are many such cases. Prominent among them is *Brook's Wharf Ltd.* v. *Goodman Bros.*,[87] where bonded warehousemen who had been compelled by statute to pay custom duties owed by their customers, were allowed to recoup their payments from the customers. In the words of Lord Wright M.R.[88]:

> "The essence of the rule is that there is liability for the same debt resting on the plaintiff and the defendant and the plaintiff has been legally compelled to pay, but the defendant gets the benefit of the payment because his debt is discharged either entirely or *pro tanto*, whereas the defendant is primarily liable to pay as between himself and the plaintiff."

---

[82] (1866) L.R. 1 C.P. 529, 533, *per* Montague Smith J.
[83] *Ex p. Bishop* (1885) 15 Ch.D. 400, 417, *per* Thesiger L.J.
[84] *Edmunds* v. *Wallingford* (1885) 14 Q.B.D. 811, 816, *per* Lindley L.J.
[85] *Moule* v. *Garrett* (1872) L.R. 7 Ex. 101, 104, *per* Cockburn C.J., quoting a passage from *Leake on Contracts* (1st ed.); see also *The Ripon City* [1898] P. 78, 85–86, *per* Sir F. H. Jeune P.; *Liberian Insurance Agency Inc.* v. *Mosse* [1977] 2 Lloyd's Rep. 560.
[86] See above, p. 17, n. 2.
[87] [1937] 1 K.B. 534.
[88] At p. 544; see above, p. 345.

But the plaintiff's payment, if compelled by law, may discharge another's liability even though the parties are not subject to a common demand. In the leading case of *Exall* v. *Partridge*[89] the plaintiff paid the rent to the landlord to secure the release of his goods which had been placed on land leased to the defendants and which had been seized by the landlord in distress. The three "defendants were liable to the landlord for the rent in the first instance, and as by this payment made by the plaintiff, all three were released from the demand of the rent. . . . This action may be supported against all of them."[90] A similar case, where the claim succeeded in equity, is *Witham* v. *Bullock*.[91] There an assignee of part of the demised land, who had paid the whole of the head rent under the threat of distress, was allowed to recover from an assignee of another part of the demised land the proportionate share of the rent owed by him. It was not fatal that the plaintiff could not have been sued for the whole of the head rent. His claim for recoupment succeeded because he had paid the defendant's share of the rent under the stress of legal process and because the defendant was liable to be sued by the landlord for his share of the rent.[92] The Court of Appeal did not consider whether the defendant's liability at law to the landlord was discharged by the plaintiff's payment. But, in our view, it must have assumed that it was. For the court expressly cited the analogy of *Exall* v. *Partridge*[93] and distinguished such cases as *Johnson* v. *Wild*[94] and *Bonner* v. *Tottenham and Edmonton Permanent Investment Building Society*.[95] In both *Johnson's* case and *Bonner's* case the head landlord had compelled the lessee, the plaintiff, to pay the rent. Nevertheless the plaintiff's claim for recoupment from the defendant failed because the defendant, "being a sub-lessee [of an assignee] could not be sued for the sum which the plaintiff . . . had been forced to pay."[96] In these cases, unlike *Witham* v. *Bullock*, there was no debt which the plaintiff's payment had discharged.

There are dicta which suggest that similar principles will determine whether the plaintiff's payment has discharged his and the defendant's common con-

---

[89] (1799) 8 T.R. 308; see above, pp. 346–347.

[90] At p. 311, *per* Lawrence J.

[91] [1939] 2 K.B. 81.

[92] [1939] 2 K.B. 81, 88 *per curiam*. In our view he would also have succeeded at law. But the court invoked Vaughan Williams L.J.'s principle, in *Bonner's* case [1899] 1 Q.B. 161, 174 (see above, pp. 301, 343) that there was here "community of interest in the subject matter to which the burden was attached which had been enforced against the plaintiff alone, coupled with benefit to the defendant."

[93] (1799) 8 T.R. 308.

[94] (1890) 44 Ch.D. 146.

[95] [1899] 1 Q.B. 161.

[96] *Witham* v. *Bullock* [1939] 2 K.B. 81, 88, *per curiam*. See also *Penley* v. *Watts* (1841) 7 M. & W. 601; *Walker* v. *Hatton* (1842) 10 M. & W. 249; *Moule* v. *Garrett* (1872) L.R. 7 Ex. 101, 102, *per* Blackburn J. (*arguendo*). But the plaintiff should, in these circumstances, be subrogated to the rights of a third party (such as an assignee of the lease) against the defendant: *cf. Bonner's* case [1899] 1 Q.B. 161, 178–179, *per* Vaughan Williams L.J.; see above, pp. 301, 343.

tractual or tortious obligation.[97] The obligation must be a common obligation. If it is not, the defendant's liability is not discharged. It is for this reason that Esso's claim against Hall Russell, whose negligence, it was alleged, was responsible for the damage to its tanker, failed in *The Esso Bernicia*.[98] Esso and other tanker owners had agreed to assume liability for pollution damage. Oil from its tanker was discharged, causing widespread pollution. Esso, in discharge of its contractual obligation, paid over half a million pounds to the crofters. The House of Lords held that the payments did not discharge the alleged tortfeasor's liability to the crofters. Its claim based on its right to be subrogated to their rights against the alleged tortfeasor therefore failed. Moreover, its payment to the crofters was said to be gratuitous and was not recoverable from the alleged tortfeasor as economic loss directly flowing from the damage to its tanker.

There have been other situations where the plaintiff has been denied recovery because there was no liability which his payment could discharge. This was the crucial factor in a group of cases where the defendant had negligently injured a policeman while he was on duty, in consequence of which the policeman had been disabled from performing his duties for a considerable period of time. The police authority concerned was required by statute to continue to pay the policeman so injured, even though he was prevented by his injury from carrying out his duties. Having so paid him, the authority sought to recover from the defendant the amount paid to the policeman.

In the first case, *Receiver for the Metropolitan Police District v. Tatum*,[99] Atkinson J. took the view that "the real legal liability for the payment of this money rests on the defendant, because his negligence was the cause of the Receiver being compelled to pay."[1] He therefore held that the police authority had, by its payment, discharged the defendant's liability and was accordingly entitled to reimbursement. Slade J. adopted a similar approach in *Receiver for the Metropolitan Police District v. Croydon Corporation*.[2] The judge concluded that the policeman who had been injured could "recover what he has lost in respect of wages if he has not been paid either from the Receiver or from the tortfeasor whose negligence injures him, and is entitled to elect which of the two he will sue."[3] On this basis, the defendants were bound to reimburse the police authority who had paid money which the defendants, as tortfeasors, were primarily liable to pay.

In the third case, *Monmouthshire County Council v. Smith*,[4] Lynskey J. declined to follow these two earlier decisions. He pointed out that the police

---

[97] *Monmouthshire County Council v. Smith* [1956] 1 W.L.R. 1132, 1141, *per* Lynskey J.; *Receiver for Metropolitan Police District v. Croydon Corp.* [1956] 1 W.L.R. 1113, 1122, *per* Slade J. (reversed [1957] 2 Q.B. 154).

[98] [1989] A.C. 643: see above, p. 344.

[99] [1948] 2 K.B. 68.

[1] At p. 73.

[2] [1956] 1 W.L.R. 1113.

[3] At p. 1123.

[4] [1956] 1 W.L.R. 1132.

authority was bound to pay the wages of the policeman, notwithstanding his incapacity, and it followed that the policeman had not lost any wages. Accordingly, the policeman was not in a position to recover any damages from the defendant in respect of lost wages, because he had lost none.[5] The defendant was never liable to the policeman for any lost wages, and the police authority, in paying the policeman's wages during the period of his incapacity, never discharged any liability of the defendant. Lynskey J. therefore held that the police authority was unable to obtain reimbursement from the defendant. Its action was nothing more than a disguised claim for loss of services.[6] An appeal from this decision was heard[7] at the same time as an appeal from Slade J.'s contrary decision in the *Croydon Corporation* case; and Lynskey J.'s view was vindicated in the Court of Appeal. The police authority had lost not the payment to the policeman, but the policeman's services. The defendant had in no way been enriched by the payment to the policeman, but had reaped an incidental benefit in that his liability to the policeman for damages had been reduced by the application of the statutory rule requiring the police authority to continue paying the policeman despite his incapacity. As Morris L.J. said[8]:

> "It is said that the defendants have benefited. It seems to me that the answer to that is that they have not benefited. It is said that their obligation to Bowman [the policeman] was reduced *pro tanto*; again it seems to me the answer to that is that their obligation has not been reduced at all. Their obligation was to pay what Bowman lost, and they have been adjudged to pay what they were liable to pay. It seems to me, therefore, that the real position in this case is that what has been lost, probably not by the plaintiff but by someone else, is the benefit of the services that the police officer would have rendered during the time when he was incapacitated. It can be said with some force that the wrongdoer has been fortunate in that he has injured someone who must be paid whether he is injured or not, whereas those entitled to his services are during the period of his incapacity denied those services. It might be said that a case could be put forward for consideration as to whether there might be some change in the law in regard to this matter so as to permit of the recovery of wages payable and paid in reference to a period of incapacity caused by a wrongdoer. But it does not seem to me that the defendants have in this case benefited or received an advantage."

Morris L.J.'s suggestion that some change in the law may be desirable is attractive. It is unjust that the defendant should be under no responsibility either for the policeman's wages during the period of his incapacity, or for the services which his employer has lost during that period, though this injustice is

---

[5] At pp. 1149–1150.
[6] This action could not lie: see *Att.-Gen. for New South Wales* v. *Perpetual Trustee Co. Ltd.* [1955] A.C. 457.
[7] [1957] 2 Q.B. 154.
[8] [1957] 2 Q.B. 154, 166.

due not to the application of the rules of quasi-contract but to the statutory rules relating to the payment of the police. A majority of the Law Reform Committee has accepted that an employer should have a remedy. It has recommended[9] that an employer, who is required[10] to pay an employee during a period of incapacity caused by the wrongful act of any person, should have a direct action against such person for reimbursement.[11] This proposal has not been implemented.[11a]

If no liability has been discharged, it is irrelevant that the plaintiff, in the performance of a duty or otherwise, has incidentally conferred some benefit on the defendant by his payment. For it is a limiting principle of restitution that the mere conferring of some incidental benefit, while discharging an obligation to another, does not in itself give rise to any right to be recouped.[12] An extreme example of this principle is to be found in *Re Nott and Cardiff Corporation*.[13] In that case, Nott was a contractor who was employed by Cardiff Corporation to "take over" a railway and put it in repair; but nothing was said in the contract about who was liable to pay the rates on the railway during the period when it was so taken over. Nott was placed on the rate-book as the person bound to pay the rates. He disputed his liability, but paid the rates and sought to recover them from the Cardiff Corporation. The Court of Appeal accepted the arbitrator's finding that Nott was not the occupier and so had been wrongfully placed on the rate-book.[14] Nevertheless the Court held that, since Nott was liable to pay rates so long as his name was on the rate-book, he could not recover from the Cardiff Corporation the rates he had paid. Cardiff Corporation were not liable for the rates while his name was on the book. His proper course, therefore was to have refused payment and to have taken steps to have his name taken off the rate-book.[15]

4. THE QUASI-CONTRACTUAL RIGHT IS A RIGHT TO REIMBURSEMENT NOT TO INDEMNITY

It is important to draw a distinction between cases in which the plaintiff has a contractual right of indemnity, and cases in which he has a quasi-contractual right to reimbursement. Typical examples of a contractual right of indemnity are the right of the surety who has given a guarantee at the request of the

---

[9] 11th Report, Cmnd. 2017.

[10] By statute, contract, or settled practice; see paras. 7, 8.

[11] Paras. 5, 24(3); see also paras. 8 and 9.

[11a] But see the Social Security Act 1989, s.2 and Sched. 4, which allows the state which has paid social security benefits to an injured party to recoup the payments from the tortfeasor whose liability had been reduced by not having to reimburse the injured party.

[12] See above, pp. 55–58.

[13] [1918] 2 K.B. 146 (reversed on a different point in the House of Lords [1919] A.C. 337). *Cf. Jeffreys* v. *Gurr* (1831) 2 B. & Ald. 833; *Eastwood* v. *McNab* [1914] 2 K.B. 361.

[14] [1918] 2 K.B. 146.

[15] The problem of *Nott's* case can still be a real one; see *London Borough of Camden* v. *Herwald* [1978] Q.B. 626, C.A.

principal debtor, and the right of the agent who has incurred expenditure at his principal's request. In these cases, the plaintiff's right of recovery is not limited to the benefit, if any, conferred on the defendant by the plaintiff's payment. The plaintiff will be entitled to be indemnified against his expenditure, even though his payment may have conferred no benefit on the defendant, by discharging a liability or otherwise.[16-17] Where, however, the plaintiff's claim is quasi-contractual, his right is not to indemnity but to reimbursement to the extent that his payment has conferred a benefit on the defendant.[18] Consequently, as has been seen,[19] a lessee cannot recover from an assignee, other than his immediate assignee, his reasonable costs of resisting the lessor's claim[20] to rent or damages for which the assignee is primarily responsible.

There are some cases in which a quasi-contractual right to reimbursement has been enforced, although there was in fact a contractual relationship between the parties on the basis of which the plaintiff might have claimed a right to indemnity. For example, in *Exall* v. *Partridge*,[21] it might have been said that the defendants by virtue of having received the plaintiff's goods on to their land, had impliedly undertaken to indemnify the plaintiff against any expenditure reasonably incurred because of the seizure of his goods in distress for rent while on the defendants' land.[22] In these cases it was not necessary for the payer to claim any more than his quasi-contractual right to reimbursement. In other cases, a plaintiff in similar circumstances may find it necessary to go further and claim a right to indemnity, if some or all of his expenditure has in fact conferred no benefit on the defendant. Provided there is a contractual relationship between the parties which is capable of giving rise to a right of indemnity there is, in principle, no reason why he should not do so. Thus there may be cases in which the quasi-contractual right to reimbursement may be merged in the contractual right of indemnity. It is only in rare cases that a payer is compelled to rely exclusively on his quasi-contractual rights. One example is, as we have seen, *Moule* v. *Garrett*.[23] Another would, no doubt, be where the defendant had seized the plaintiff's goods without his consent and the goods were thereafter taken from the defendant's land as distress for rent.

[16-17] *Brittain* v. *Lloyd* (1845) 14 M. & W. 762; see also *Warlow* v. *Harrison* (1858) 1 E. & E. 295, 317.

[18] *Cf. Restatement of Restitution*, § 80 comment c.: "he [a volunteer surety] is not entitled to expenses which he may have incurred in defending an action brought against him by the creditor, since the benefits accruing to the other from such defence are merely incidental."

[19] See above, pp. 347–349. See also above, pp. 330, 349.

[20] *Cf.* cases on the agent's right of indemnity, such as *The James Seddon* (1866) L.R. 1 A. & E. 62; *Re Wells & Croft* (1895) 72 L.T. 359; *Williams* v. *Lister* (1913) 109 L.T. 699. And see above, pp. 347–349.

[21] (1799) 8 T.R. 308; see above, p. 346.

[22] See also *Brook's Wharf and Bull Wharf Ltd.* v. *Goodman Bros.* [1937] 1 K.B. 534; see above, pp. 345, 355.

[23] (1872) L.R. 5 Ex. 132, 7 Ex. 101; see above, pp. 345, 348.

5. CASES IN WHICH THE PLAINTIFF HAS A RIGHT OF DEDUCTION

Where a person has been compelled to make a payment for which, as between himself and another, the other is primarily responsible, his usual remedy is to claim the money as paid to the other's use. He may, however, be able to recoup himself by deducting the amount of such payment from money due from him to that other.[24] So a tenant, who has been compelled, for example, by distress of goods or by threat of distress,[25] to make payments to a ground landlord for which as between himself and his immediate landlord the latter is primarily responsible, has been held entitled to deduct the amount of such payments from rent then due or accruing due to his immediate landlord.[26] The tenant cannot, however, make such a deduction from rent which, at the time of his payment, is not yet accrued or accruing due.[27]

The payment by the tenant is generally[28] regarded as a payment of rent.[29] But it has been said that, if the payment exceeds the rent due from him to his landlord, the tenant may recover the excess from him as money paid to his use.[30] In certain cases, where the duty of payment is thrown primarily upon the

---

[24] *Sapsford* v. *Fletcher* (1792) 4 T.R. 511 (payment of ground rent to head landlord); *Taylor* v. *Zamira* (1816) 6 Taunt. 524 (payment of annuity to annuitant having first charge on the land); *Carter* v. *Carter* (1829) 5 Bing. 406 (payment of ground rent); *Johnson* v. *Jones* (1839) 9 A. & E. 809 (payment to mortgagee); *Baker* v. *Greenhill* (1842) 3 Q.B. 148 (payment of rate for repairs of bridge for which landlord liable *rationae tenurae*); *Jones* v. *Morris* (1849) 3 Ex. 742 (payment of arrears to prior incumbrancer); *Underhay* v. *Read* (1887) 20 Q.B.D. 209 (payment to mortgagee). See also *Williamson* v. *Cawood* (1797) 3 Aust. 903; *Sturgess* v. *Farrington* (1812) 4 Taunt. 614; *Dyer* v. *Bowley* (1824) 2 Bing. 94; *Pope* v. *Biggs* (1829) 9 B. & C. 245; *Waller* v. *Andrews* (1838) 3 M. & W. 312; *Davies* v. *Stacey* (1840) 12 A. & E. 506; *Franklin* v. *Carter* (1845) 1 C.B. 750; *O'Donoghue* v. *The Coalbrook and Broadoak Co.* (1872) 26 L.T. 806; *Lamb* v. *Brewster* (1879) 4 Q.B.D. 220, 607. At one time, by the Income Tax Act 1952, s.173, a tenant who had paid Schedule A tax could deduct it from rent accrued or accruing due at the time when such payment was demanded of him. Such cases can no longer arise: see below, n. 31.

[25] In *Carter* v. *Carter* (1829) 5 Bing. 406, the tenant was called on to pay ground rent to the head landlord, and was given six weeks to pay, after which he paid. This was held to be a compulsory payment; for he "knew that he was liable to distress, though not actually distrained on; and a payment under such circumstances is no more voluntary, than a donation to a beggar who presents a pistol" (at p. 409, *per* Best C.J.).

[26] *Sapsford* v. *Fletcher* (1792) 4 T.R. 511; *Carter* v. *Carter* (1829) 5 Bing. 406.

[27] *Stubbs* v. *Parsons* (1820) 3 B. & Ald. 516; *Boodle* v. *Campbell* (1844) 7 Man. & G. 386; *Graham* v. *Allsopp* (1848) 3 Ex. 186; *Cumming* v. *Bedborough* (1846) 15 M. & W. 438; *Vestry of Mile End Old Town* v. *Whitby* (1898) 78 L.T. 80. But if the payment by the tenant exceeds the amount of rent accrued or accruing due, it may be that the tenant can deduct the excess from future rent: see Smith's *Leading Cases*, Vol. I, pp. 172–173. *Cf. Taylor* v. *Taylor* [1938] 1 K.B. 320.

[28] *Graham* v. *Allsopp* (1848) 3 Ex. 186, 198, *per* Rolfe B., delivering the judgment of the Court of Exchequer.

[29] And may be pleaded by way of payment. See Smith's *Leading Cases*, Vol. I, pp. 170–171, for a discussion of the distinction between the pleas of payment and set-off.

[30] *Taylor* v. *Zamira* (1816) 6 Taunt. 524, 529, *per* Burroughs J.; see also *Earle* v. *Maugham* (1863) 14 C.B.(N.S.) 626, 633, *per* Byles J. *Cf. Dawson* v. *Linton* (1822) 5 B. & Ald. 521, and cases where a sub-letting was made contrary to the terms of the head lease and so no sub-tenancy was created; *Ryan* v. *Byrne* (1883) 17 Ir.L.T. 102, where the sub-tenant who paid the rent to the head landlord to prevent eviction was able to recover from the "mesne landlord" in an action for money paid; see, too, *Gregory* v. *Stanway* (1860) 2 F. & F. 309; *cf. Crouch* v. *Tregonning* (1872) L.R. 7 Ex. 88, 91, *per* Bramwell B.

tenant as occupier but he is granted a statutory right to deduct such payment from his rent, he is limited to his right of deduction and cannot proceed against his landlord for money paid, for the payment has not been made to the use of the landlord.[31]

---

[31] *Dawes* v. *Thomas* [1892] 1 Q.B. 414.

Under the old Schedule A, tax was charged on the occupier. The tax was regarded as the tenant's debt and was not therefore paid on behalf of the landlord. But the tenant did have a statutory right of deduction: see the Income Tax Act 1952, s.173, now repealed by the Finance Act 1963, Sched. XIII. The right of deduction was from his first subsequent payment of rent or, if the rent had fallen into arrears, when the arrears were paid: see *Kirk* v. *Cunningham* [1921] 3 K.B. 637. But it was suggested in *Hill* v. *Kirschenstein* [1920] 3 K.B. 556, 565, *per* Warrington J., that "if there is no future payment from which deduction may be made, the sum which might be deducted may be recovered as a debt." *Sed quaere*: *cf. Cumming* v. *Bedborough* (1846) 15 M. & W. 438.

Nowadays these problems cannot arise. Under the new Schedule A tax, the Revenue first looks to payment to the person, not in occupation, who is entitled to the rents and profits. If he fails to pay the tax, then the Revenue may require any lessee of the land to make payment of such sums necessary to pay the tax. But the liability of the lessee is limited to the rent and other payments due from him to the person, not in occupation, who is in default. The lessee is entitled "to deduct that sum [paid to the Revenue] from any subsequent payment" due to the person in default; when he does he "shall be acquitted and discharged of the amount so deducted." Special provision is made if a demand is made on an assignee who then makes a deduction from the amount payable to the lessee, his lessor. The lessee can then make a similar deduction from the amount due to the head lessor. If that amount is insufficient to cover the deduction, he may recover any deficiency from the Revenue: see Income and Corporation Taxes Act 1970, s.70, as amended by the Finance Act 1980, s.115.

C. NECESSITY

CHAPTER 15

RESTITUTION AT COMMON LAW

IN Roman law a stranger who intervened to carry on the affairs of another was entitled in certain circumstances to recover from that other his reasonable expenses.[1] Similarly in the modern civil law systems of Western Europe, he will be described as " 'the manager of another's affairs' and the impulse will be both to praise and reward him."[2] But the great majority of common law jurisdictions, including England, appear to have rejected any notion of *negotiorum gestio*, and "to have done their best to discourage good Samaritans"[3] by denying the stranger restitution no matter how grave the emergency which prompted his intervention. For "liabilities are not to be forced upon people behind their backs any more than you can confer a benefit upon a man against his will."[4]

There are, however, cases where English law has recognised the rights of a person who intervenes in an emergency to help another. The authorities fall into two groups. In the first group, there has been a pre-existing relationship between the parties, normally that of principal and agent, and the agent has gone beyond his authority by intervening on his principal's behalf in an emergency. Here the courts have been ready to regularise the agent's position and to treat him as though he had had the necessary authority. An agent of this kind is known as an agent of necessity. In the second group, there is no such pre-existing relationship. The intervener is a stranger. English courts have been generally reluctant to assist him, although there are some instances[5] when the necessity for the intervention and the public interest in encouraging it have persuaded them to allow a restitutionary claim.

In our view the line between these two groups of cases has been too firmly drawn, for the rationale of the agency of necessity cases is similar to that which underlies those exceptional instances where a person who has intervened in an emergency has been granted restitution. But it is convenient to discuss them

---

[1] Buckland, *Text Book*, 537; (1928) 13 Cornell L.Q. 190 [Lorenzen]. Roman law has influenced the more liberal Scottish, French and German developments: see *S.M.T. Sales and Service Co.* v. *Motor and General Finance Co.*, 1954 S.L.T. 107; D. M. Walker, *Principles of Scottish Private Law*, Book IV (4th ed., 1988), pp. 513 *et seq.*; T. B. Smith, *Scotland (British Commonwealth, Laws and Constitution*, Vol. 11), pp. 631–632; (1962) 36 *Tulane Law Review* 605, 618 *et seq.* [J. K. B. M. Nicholas]; (1960–1961) 74 Harv.L.Rev. 817, 1073 [J. P. Dawson].
[2] J. P. Dawson, *Rewards for the Rescue of Human Life?, Essays presented to Hans Yntema*, p. 142.
[3] *Ibid.*
[4] *Falcke* v. *Scottish Imperial Insurance Co.* (1886) 34 Ch.D. 234, 248, *per* Bowen L.J.
[5] See below, pp. 369 *et seq.*

separately. We shall also attempt to assess whether it is desirable to recognise a restitutionary claim for services rendered in an emergency or whether it is preferable to affirm that altruism should be its own reward.[6]

1. AGENCY OF NECESSITY[7]

Where there is a contractual or other pre-existing legal relationship[8] between two parties, P and A, and there occurs an emergency under the stress of which A, acting outside the scope of his authority, reasonably intervenes on P's behalf, A will be treated as P's agent for the purposes of the intervention, provided that it was impracticable at the time for A to communicate with P, and the action was taken by A, bona fide, in the interests of P. In particular A will be entitled to be reimbursed by P in respect of his reasonable expenses.[9]

The origin of this doctrine is to be found in the power available in an emergency[10] to the master of a ship to deal with the ship or her cargo outside the ordinary scope of his authority.[11] For example, a master may, to preserve the ship or the remainder of the cargo, dispose of part, and sometimes even the whole, of the cargo in various ways: he may jettison the goods to lighten the ship[12]; he may sell[13] part, or hypothecate[14] part or even the whole of the cargo to raise money to pay for such repairs as are necessary to enable the ship to continue her voyage; and he may enter into a salvage agreement on the part of the cargo owner.[15] The master also has an extensive power in cases of necessity to deal with the ship herself.[16] But in all these cases, whether he is dealing with

---

[6] For an argument that the claim of unjust sacrifice should be recognised as a cause of action, see Muir, *Unjust Sacrifice and the Officious Intervener* in *Essays* (ed. Finn), Chap. 9; and *cf.* Stoljar, *Unjust Enrichment and Unjust Sacrifice* (1987) 50 M.L.R. 603.

[7] See, generally, (1945) 22 Can. Bar Rev. 492 [W. B. Williston]; *Bowstead on Agency*, pp. 84–90. The expression "agent of necessity" has also been used to describe a wife who, living apart from her husband, pledges his credit. With this type of agency of necessity, which is now abolished (see below, p. 381, n. 48), we are not concerned.

[8] Such as a bailment: *cf. The Winson* [1982] A.C. 939 (where a salvor rendered services after the termination of the original bailment which was for valuable consideration; the services were then rendered as a gratuitous bailee); see above, p. 24.

[9] *Tetley* v. *British Trade Corp.* (1922) 10 Ll.L.R. 678; *The Argos* (1873) L.R. 5 P.C. 134, 165, *per* Sir Montague Smith. *Cf. The Winson* [1982] A.C. 939, 958, *per* Lord Diplock, who distinguishes the question of whether A has the power to create contractual rights between P and T from the question whether A should be indemnified by P for expenses incurred where there is no question of the liability *inter se* of P and T. Lord Diplock would limit the use of the phrase "agency of necessity" to the former situation; for different conditions should determine whether A has the power to create a contract between P and T as distinct from whether A is authorised to dispose of P's property or should be reimbursed or recompensed for saving P's property.

[10] There must be a true necessity: see *Industrie Chimiche Italia Centrale and Cerealfin S.A.* v. *Tsavliris (Alexander G.) Maritime Co.* [1990] 1 Lloyd's Rep. 516, C.A.

[11] For historical background, see Holdsworth, viii, pp. 248 *et seq.* And *cf.* J. Story, *Agency* (1839 ed.), paras. 93 *et seq.* See, generally, Carver, *Carriage by Sea*, §§ 752 *et seq.*

[12] *The Gratitudine* (1801) 3 Ch.Rob. 240, 258, *per* Lord Stowell.

[13] *Gunn* v. *Roberts* (1874) L.R. 9 C.P. 331, 337, *per* Brett J.

[14] *The Gratitudine* (1801) 3 Ch.Rob. 240.

[15] *The Winson* [1982] A.C. 939; see above, p. 24.

[16] *Robertson* v. *Carruthers* (1819) 2 Stark. 571.

the ship or with her cargo, it is essential for the master, if he wishes to establish that he acted as agent of necessity, to show not only that there was a necessity[17] at the time which forced him to act in the way he did, but also that his action was wise and prudent in the circumstances and that it was impracticable for him to communicate with the owner of the ship or her cargo as the case may be. Where he can establish these things, he is entitled to charge the owners with expenses properly incurred by him.[18]

At first, attempts were made to restrict the doctine to carriage by sea and to the special case of the acceptance of a bill of exchange for the honour of the drawer.[19] These did not succeed. The doctrine of agency of necessity was subsequently applied to carriage of goods by land[20]; to an agent who employed a substitute in "unforeseen emergencies"[21]; and to an agent who removed goods to another country, without the authority of his principal, to prevent their loss in a local disturbance.[22] Moreover, there are examples of its application where the agent intervened to fulfil his principal's duty to a third party.[23] In all these cases, the agent should be entitled to recover his reasonable expenses from his principal.[24]

In 1924 McCardie J., in *Prager v. Blatspiel, Stamp and Heacock Ltd.*,[25] pointed out that the doctrine had already expanded to such an extent that it could no longer be restricted to cases of carriage of goods by sea and acceptance of bills of exchange for honour. He considered[26] that it applied to cases where an agent who is unable to communicate with his principal intervenes in an emergency bona fide in the interests of the parties concerned. Three years later Scrutton L.J. expressed[27] the fear that McCardie J.'s remarks would extend the doctrine to cases where there was no pre-existing agency between the

---

[17] *Atlantic Mutual Insurance Co.* v. *Huth* (1880) 16 Ch.D. 474.

[18] *The Argos* (1873) L.R. 5 P.C. 134, 165, *per* Sir Montague Smith; *Notara* v. *Henderson* (1872) L.R. 7 Q.B. 225; *Hingston* v. *Vent* (1876) 1 Q.B.D. 367.

[19] *Hawtayne* v. *Bourne* (1841) 7 M. & W. 595, 599, *per* Parke B., 600, *per* Alderson B.; *Gwilliam* v. *Twist* [1895] 2 Q.B. 84, 87, *per* Lord Esher. See, generally, S. J. Stoljar, *Law of Agency*, pp. 154–155; (1954) 3 Western Australia L.R. 1 [G. H. Treitel]. On acceptance of bills of exchange for honour, see below, pp. 378–379.

[20] *Great Northern Ry.* v. *Swaffield* (1874) L.R. 9 Ex. 132; *Sims* v. *Midland Ry.* [1913] 1 K.B. 103, 112, *per* Scrutton J., approved in *Soringer* v. *G.W. Ry.* [1921] 1 K.B. 257, 265, *per* Bankes L.J.; see also *Notara* v. *Henderson* (1872) L.R. 7 Q.B. 225; *The Winson* [1982] A.C. 939, 960–961, *per* Lord Diplock; and *Garriock* v. *Walker* (1873) 1 R. 100 (Ct. of Sess.) (see above, p. 25).

[21] *De Bussche* v. *Alt* (1878) 8 Ch.D. 286, 310–311, *per* Thesiger L.J.; *cf. Harris* v. *Fiat Motors Ltd.* (1906) 22 T.L.R. 556.

[22] *Tetley* v. *British Trade Corp.* (1922) 10 Ll.L.R. 678. In *Prager* v. *Blatspiel, Stamp and Heacock Ltd.* [1924] 1 K.B. 566, 571, McCardie J. said that "a like ruling has been given, on substantially similar facts, in other cases (unreported) in the King's Bench Division." For another development of the doctrine, see *Montaignac* v. *Shitta* (1890) 15 App.Cas. 357.

[23] *Walker* v. *G.W. Ry.* (1867) L.R. 2 Ex. 228; *Langan* v. *G.W. Ry.* (1873) 30 L.T. 173. *Cf. Cox* v. *Midland Counties Ry.* (1849) 3 Ex. 268, doubted in *Langan's* case, but followed in *Houghton* v. *Pilkington* [1912] 3 K.B. 308, where apparently *Langan's* case was not cited.

[24] *Great Northern Ry.* v. *Swaffield* (1874) L.R. 9 Ex. 132, 138, *per* Pollock B.

[25] [1924] 1 K.B. 566. See also his earlier decision in *Transoceania Società Italiana di Navigazione* v. *H. S. Shipton & Sons* [1923] 1 K.B. 31, 42–43.

[26] At pp. 571–573.

[27] In *Jebara* v. *Ottoman Bank* [1927] 2 K.B. 254, 270–271.

parties.[28] He did not, however, deny that the doctrine could apply where there was such a relationship, and in the same year, the Court of Appeal held that "a servant has implied authority upon an emergency to endeavour to protect his master's property if he sees it in danger or has reasonable grounds for thinking that he sees it in danger."[29] Some very similar doctrine seems to have been applied by the Privy Council in a case where it was held that a firm of commission agents had implied authority in an emergency to grant credit to a debtor who was financially embarrassed.[30]

The doctrine has also been invoked by persons who have undertaken to store another's goods and who, unable to get in touch with the owner, claim after a long period of time to have implied authority to dispose of the goods. In *Sachs* v. *Miklos*[31] the defendant was sued for damages for conversion of the plaintiff's furniture, which the defendant had stored for the plaintiff at his home as an act of kindness. Some considerable time later, the defendant needed the space. He could not trace the plaintiff by any reasonable means, so he sold the furniture, and claimed that he had done so as agent of necessity. The Court of Appeal held that there was no emergency to justify such a contention, and in any case the defendant could hardly be said to have acted bona fide in the interests of the owner. Lord Goddard C.J. also said[32] that he knew of no case of the doctrine being applied to carriers by land to enable them to sell their principal's goods except where the goods were either perishable or livestock.[33] Today, by statute[34] a bailee of uncollected goods is entitled, subject to conditions, to sell them provided that he has given the bailor notice of his intention to sell or has failed to trace the bailor having taken reasonable steps to do so.

Conditions Necessary to Create an Agency of Necessity

The cases do not, it seems, preclude further extension of the doctrine of agency of necessity. But they suggest that four conditions must always be fulfilled[35] before a plaintiff can bring himself within the doctrine.[36]

(1) The agent must not have been able to obtain his principal's instructions. This does not necessarily mean that it must be impossible for him to communicate with his principal; "it must be practically impossible to get the owner's

---

[28] See also *Re Banque des Marchands de Moscou (Koupetschesky)* [1952] 1 All E.R. 1269, 1278, *per* Vaisey J.

[29] *Poland* v. *John Parr & Sons* [1927] 1 K.B. 236, 240, *per* Bankes L.J.; see also at p. 244, *per* Scrutton L.J.

[30] *Firm of Gokal Chand-Jagan Nath* v. *Firm of Nand Ram Das-Atma Ram* [1939] A.C. 106; (1939–1940) 3 M.L.R. 272, 277 [R. F. T. Chorley].

[31] [1948] 2 K.B. 23; see also *Munro* v. *Willmott* [1949] 1 K.B. 295.

[32] [1948] 2 K.B. 23, 35.

[33] *Cf. Kemp* v. *Pryor* (1812) 7 Ves. 237, 247, *per* Lord Eldon L.C.

[34] Torts (Interference with Goods) Act 1977, ss. 12, 13 and Sched. 1.

[35] See, generally, *Prager* v. *Blatspiel, Stamp and Heacock Ltd.* [1924] 1 K.B. 566, 571–573, *per* McCardie J.

[36] The onus of proof is heavy; see *The Glasgow* (1856) Swab. 145; *The Australia* (1859) Swab. 480.

instructions in time as to what shall be done."[37] It is apparently enough if the agent asked his principal for instructions but the principal "failed to give any instructions when apprised."[38]

(2) There must have been a necessity for the agent to have acted in the way he did. It is difficult to define the concept of "necessity" in this context.[39] Some form of emergency may give rise to a necessity to act in the principal's interests,[40] but the agent is not required to establish such an emergency as would compel him to take a certain course of action. In the words of Sir Montague Smith[41]:

"... The word 'necessity' when applied to mercantile affairs, where the judgment must, in the nature of things, be exercised, cannot, of course, mean an irresistible compelling power—what is meant by it in such cases is, the force of circumstances which determines the course a man ought to take. Thus, when by the force of circumstances, a man has a duty cast on him of taking some action for another, and, under that obligation, adopts the course which, to the judgment of a wise and prudent man, is apparently the best for the interest of the persons for whom he acts in a given emergency, it may properly be said of the course so taken, that it was, in a mercantile sense, necessary to take it."

The relevant time for determining whether there is a necessity is the time when the emergency becomes apparent.[42]

(3) The agent must "satisfy the court that he was acting bona fide in the interests of the parties concerned."[43]

(4) The action taken by the agent must have been reasonable and prudent in the circumstances[44] and must be taken to protect the interests of the principal.[45]

Agency of necessity is traditionally regarded as part of the law of contract. The agent is said to have his principal's implied authority to act as he has

---

[37] Sims v. Midland Ry. [1913] 1 K.B. 103, 107, per Scrutton J. A good example of failure by an agent to communicate is Springer v. G.W. Ry. [1921] 1 K.B. 257.

[38] The Winson [1982] A.C. 939, 961, per Lord Diplock. Cf. Birks, Introduction, p. 201, who argues that the test is now whether the steps taken to preserve the goods were reasonable; and the "possibility of communication is only one element." See also Firm of Gokal v. Firm of Nand Ram [1939] A.C. 106.

[39] See The Victor (1865) 13 L.T. 21.

[40] Cf. Re F. (Mental Patient: Sterilisation) [1990] 2 A.C. 1, 75, per Lord Goff; and Re T. (Adult: Medical Treatment) [1992] 3 W.L.R. 782, C.A.

[41] In Australasian Steam Navigation Co. v. Morse (1872) L.R. 4 P.C. 222, 230; see also Phelps, James & Co. v. Hill [1891] 1 Q.B. 605, 610, per Lindley L.J.; John Koch Ltd. v. C. & H. Products Ltd. [1956] 2 Lloyd's Rep. 59, 69, per Romer L.J.

[42] The Winson [1982] A.C. 939, 965, per Lord Simon of Glaisdale, approving the Court of Appeal: [1981] 1 Q.B. 403, 424.

[43] Prager v. Blatspiel, Stamp and Heacock Ltd. [1924] 1 K.B. 566, 572, per McCardie J. Semble this must mean the interests of the parties concerned at the time of the intervention. Cf. The Winson [1982] A.C. 939, 965, per Lord Simon of Glaisdale.

[44] See Broom v. Hall (1859) 7 C.B.(n.s.) 503; The Australia (1859) Swab. 480; (1945) 22 Can. Bar Rev. 492, 501 [W. B. Williston].

[45] The Winson [1982] A.C. 939.

done.[46] But this explanation is not entirely satisfactory. First, the relationship to which the authority is referred may not be contractual: for example, it is possible that it may arise for a mere gratuitous bailment.[47] Secondly, a pre-existing contractual relationship between the parties may be brought to an end by impossibility or illegality or some other cause.[48] The agent may find himself with his principal's goods on his hands, and some pressing emergency, indeed the very one which rendered the contract with his principal illegal or impossible, may compel him to deal with the goods in some way in the best interests of his principal.[49] In such cases, his contract of agency will have been terminated. Will he, therefore, be denied reimbursement of expenses incurred in performing these services? May he even find himself paying damages for conversion? Scrutton L.J. seemed to think that the agent would find himself in such a quandary.[50] But there is much to be said against this view.[51] For the agent has simply acted as a wise and prudent agent would have done in the circumstances. His situation is fundamentally different from that of an agent whose principal protests that he does not want him to intervene,[52] or one whose principal has ceased to exist.[53]

Contract is not, therefore, a satisfactory basis for the doctrine of agency of necessity. But it is difficult to suggest an alternative explanation other than one based upon the necessity for intervention. The principle of necessitous intervention is not entirely unknown to English law and there are certain groups of cases where the rights of a stranger, who has intervened in an emergency, have been recognised on this very ground. The rationale of the agency of necessity cases is, in our view, similar to that which underlies these "exceptional" cases, which will now be discussed.[54]

From this body of law:

> "can be derived the basic requirements, applicable in these cases of necessity, that, to fall within the principle, not only (1) must there be a necessity to act when it is not practicable to communicate with the assisted person, but also (2) the action taken must be such as a reasonable person

---

[46] Cf. Gaudet v. Brown, Cargo ex Argos (1893) L.R. 5 P.C. 134; Notara v. Henderson (1872) L.R. 7 Q.B. 225. See also Buckland and McNair, Roman Law and Common Law, p. 336.

[47] Cf. The Winson [1982] A.C. 939; Sachs v. Miklos [1948] 2 K.B. 23; Munro v. Willmott [1949] 1 K.B. 295, semble.

[48] Jebara v. Ottoman Bank [1927] 2 K.B. 254, 271, per Scrutton L.J.

[49] It is possible that, in Prager's Case [1924] 1 K.B. 566, the pre-existing contract had been avoided by illegality because of the outbreak of war.

[50] Jebara v. Ottoman Bank [1927] 2 K.B. 254, 271; see also Re Banque des Marchands de Moscou (Koupetschesky) [1952] 1 All E.R. 1269, 1278, per Vaisey J.

[51] See Re Bryant's Estate, 180 Pa. 192, 36 Atl. 738 (1897).

[52] Stokes v. Lewis (1785) 1 T.R. 20; Howard v. Tucker (1831) 1 B. & Ad. 712. But see Great Northern Ry. v. Swaffield (1874) L.R. 9 Ex. 132, which suggests that an agent may recover his reasonable expenses, despite the fact that he acted contrary to his principal's instructions, if his act was necessary in the public interest. Cf. Garriock v. Walker (1873) 1 R. 100 (Ct. of Sess.): see above, p. 25.

[53] Re Banque des Marchands de Moscou (Koupetschesky) [1952] 1 All E.R. 1269.

[54] See below, pp. 369 et seq.

would in all the circumstances take, acting in the best interests of the assisted person."[55]

2. NECESSITOUS INTERVENTION BY A STRANGER[56]

We turn now to discuss the few situations where English law has recognised a restitutionary claim based upon the plaintiff's necessitous intervention. It is not clear whether English law will recognise other claims. It is possible that it may; for example, there are dicta which suggest that a surety who had assumed his suretyship out of necessity would be entitled to restitution from the debtor whose debt he had discharged.[56a]

(a) *Preservation of the Property, Life, Health, Credit or other Interests of Another Person*

Preservation of property

There is a body of dicta which has always been understood to deny the right of a person who intervenes to preserve another's property to remuneration or even reimbursement. The most commonly quoted statement is that of Bowen L.J. in *Falcke* v. *Scottish Imperial Insurance Co.*[57]:

> "The general principle is, beyond all question, that work or labour done or money expended by one man to preserve or benefit the property of another do not according to English law create any lien upon the property saved or benefited, nor even, if standing alone,[58] create any obligation to

---

[55] *Re F. (Mental Patient: Sterilisation)* [1990] 2 A.C. 1, 75, *per* Lord Goff; see below, p. 376.

[56] See generally, (1929–30) 15 Cornell L.Q. 25, 205 [Hope], and *Essays* (ed. Finn), pp. 256–261 [Sutton]. For an economic analysis in terms of efficiency, see (1978) 8 *Journal of Legal Studies* 83 [Landes and Posner]. Contrast (1973) 2 *Journal of Legal Studies* 151, 202–203 [Epstein].

[56a] *Owen* v. *Tate* [1976] Q.B. 404, 409, 411–412, *per* Scarman L.J., applied in *"The Zuhal K"* [1987] 1 Lloyd's Rep. 151. In the latter case, insurers had given, to the knowledge of the owner's agent, a bond guarantee to secure the release of his vessel arrested by the cargo-owners—"it was reasonably necessary in the interests of the shipowners that the guarantee should be given" (at p. 156).

See too *Re Berkeley Applegate (Investment Consultants) Ltd.* [1989] Ch. 32, where a liquidator was remunerated and reimbursed out of the company's own assets and assets which it held on trust for others. If "the liquidator had not done this work, it is inevitable that the work, or at all events a great deal of it, would have had to be done by someone else"; this statement echoes Greer L.J.'s words in *Craven-Ellis* v. *Canons Ltd.* [1936] 2 K.B. 403, 412, (which was not cited, below, p. 478) and that of Wilberforce J. in *Phipps* v. *Boardman* [1964] 1 W.L.R. 993, 1018 (which was cited, at p. 47). But it is doubtful whether these facts can be characterised as an example of necessitous intervention. The court has an inherent jurisdiction to remunerate and reimburse a trustee and a liquidator for costs incurred and skill and labour expended in connection with the administration of property: *Re Duke of Norfolk's Settlement Trusts* [1982] Ch. 61.

[57] (1886) 34 Ch.D. 234, 248–249. But *cf.* the old case of *Waters* v. *Weigall* (1795) 2 Anst. 575 see below, p. 372, n. 79a, and see the unusual decision of *White J.D.* v. *Troups Transport* (1976) C.L.Y. 33 (Cty.Ct.): see below, p. 372, n. 79a. In America the development of the intervener's right to reimbursement in such cases was preceded by restrictive dicta similar to those of Bowen L.J.; see, *e.g. Mason* v. *Ship Blaireau*, 2 Cranch. 239, 265 (1804), *per* Marshall C.J.

[58] The report in the *Law Reports* places the comma between "nor" and "even," and so runs "nor, even if standing alone, create any obligation to repay the expenditure." This does not make sense, as it appears to indicate that if the intervention stood alone, such an obligation might more

repay the expenditure. Liabilities are not to be forced on people behind their backs any more than you can confer a benefit upon a man against his will.

There is an exception to this proposition in the maritime law. . . . The maritime law, for the purposes of public policy and for the advantage of trade, imposes in these cases a liability upon the thing saved, a liability which is a special consequence arising out of the character of mercantile enterprises, the nature of sea perils, and the fact that the thing saved was saved under great stress and exceptional circumstances. No similar doctrine applies to things lost upon land, nor to anything except ships or goods in peril at sea."

This statement involves three propositions. First, it denies that the common law grants to a stranger any lien upon the property of another which he has preserved. Secondly, it appears to deny that, in cases of salvage at sea, the common law gives any right to recompense, the only available remedies being those granted in Admiralty. And thirdly, it denies that intervention on land to preserve another's property, if such intervention stands alone, gives the stranger any right to reimbursement or remuneration for his services.

Both the first and second propositions are established by authority. Apart from the exceptional instance of the possessory lien in the case of maritime salvage,[59] a stranger who intervenes to preserve another's property has no lien at common law for his services. In *Nicholson* v. *Chapman*,[60] Eyre C.J. stressed the great inconvenience of holding that a lien should be available in such a case; the owner's position would be impossible since it would compel him to "make a tender of sufficient recompense."[61] Again there is no claim at common law[62] for recompense for salvage at sea; common law will not interfere with what is regarded as exclusively Admiralty jurisdiction.[63]

---

probably have been imposed on the owner of the property saved. It seems virtually certain, therefore, that there must be a printer's error here and that the comma should have been placed between "even" and "if," as we have placed it; this is borne out by the report in 56 L.T. 220, 224. 56 L.J.Ch. 707, 713 omits "even" but puts the comma after "nor."

[59] *Hartford* v. *Jones* (1698) 1 Ld.Ray. 393.

[60] (1793) 2 H.Bl. 254, following *Binstead* v. *Buck* (1777) 2 Wm.Bl. 1117; see also *Sorrell* v. *Paget* [1950] 1 K.B. 252. *Cf. Robinson* v. *Walter* (1616) 3 Bulst. 269; and *Hingston* v. *Wendt* (1876) 1 Q.B.D. 367.

[61] (1793) 2 H.Bl. 254, 259.

[62] In the 19th century some authorities thought such an action possible. Abbott's *Merchant Shipping* (3rd ed., 1808), p. 383, after referring to the possessory lien available to the salvor at common law, said of the salvor's compensation that, "if the parties cannot agree upon it, it may, by the same law, be ascertained by a jury in an action brought by the salvor against the proprietor of the goods." This sentence was still retained in the 14th ed., p. 961, but see note (*e*) on that page. See also *A Raft of Timber* (1844) 2 W.Rob. 251, 255, *per* Dr. Lushington.

[63] *Lipson* v. *Harrison* (1853) 2 W.R. 10, 11, *per* Lord Campbell C.J.; *Atkinson* v. *Woodall* (1862) 1 H. & C. 170, 172–173, *per* Wilde B.; *cf. Newman* v. *Walters* (1804) 3 Bos. & Pul. 612, 616–617, *per* Holt J.; *The Elton* [1891] P. 265, 270, *per* Sir F. Jeune. See also *Castellain* v. *Thompson* (1862) 13 C.B.(N.S.) 105.

In contrast, there is no decided case which supports Bowen L.J.'s third proposition.[64] *Nicholson* v. *Chapman*[65] concerned a claim for a lien,[66] as did *Falcke's* case[67] itself. In *Falcke's* case a mortgagor of a life insurance policy paid a year's premium to keep the policy alive. He appears to have made this payment under the belief that there existed a contract between himself and one of the mortgagees for the purchase by him of that mortgagee's interest in the policy; but it was held by the court that there was no such contract.[68] The policy was subsequently sold by the mortgagee's representatives to enforce the security. The mortgagor was held to have no lien.[69] As Cotton L.J. said[70]: "It would be strange indeed if a mortgagor expending money on the mortgaged property could establish a charge in respect of that expenditure in priority to the mortgagee." Nor was he entitled to be paid out of the proceeds of sale the year's premium which he had supplied. He had paid the premium to protect his own interests in the property saved.[71] Bowen L.J.'s observations, which deny a stranger who intervenes to preserve another's property, reimbursement, were therefore purely *obiter*. But his view has been frequently reiterated and accepted as authoritative.[72]

In other branches of the law the stranger is in a more favourable position. For example, if he commits what is prima facie a trespass on another's

---

[64] There is Irish authority to the contrary: see *Re Pike* (1888) 23 L.R.(Ir.) 9; *Allison* v. *Jenkins* [1904] 1 I.R. 341, 348, *per* Sir Andrew Porter M.R.

[65] (1793) 2 H.Bl. 254. *Cf. Macclesfield Corp.* v. *The Great Central Ry.* [1911] 2 K.B. 528, where the plaintiffs acted officiously.

[66] There is a great difference between claims for a lien and for reimbursement: see *Peruvian Guano Co.* v. *Dreyfus Bros. & Co.* (1887) [1892] A.C. 166, 177, *per* Lord Macnaghten.

[67] (1886) 34 Ch.D. 234, *Cf. Lee-Parker* v. *Izzet* [1971] 1 W.L.R. 1688, 1694–1695, *per* Goff J.

[68] For a discussion of the insurance cases, see *Essays* (ed. Burrows), pp. 86–96 [Sutton], who supports the actual decision in *Falcke's* case on the ground that it was consistent with those authorities which establish that a mortgagor was not permitted to assert a lien which would take precedence over a second mortgage; but see below, n. 71.

[69] *Cf.* Birks, *Introduction*, pp. 194–195.

[70] At p. 243; see also Fry L.J. at p. 254.

[71] *Cf. Brooke* v. *Stone* (1865) 34 L.J.Ch. 251; *Landowners West of England, etc.* v. *Ashford* (1889) 16 Ch.D. 411, 433, *per* Fry J. It is arguable that the mortgagor should have recovered the year's premium. The payments were not made voluntarily but under mistake. The defendants had gained an incontrovertible benefit and that benefit could, moreover, have been restored. The analogy of the mistaken improver of the land, who is denied restitution, should not therefore have been persuasive.

Cotton L.J., who was the only judge prepared to accept that the mortgagor might have been mistaken, would nonetheless deny recovery; his was an apparent and not a real title to the property. Relief should be granted only if the owner stood by, knowing of the mortgagor's estate. For an argument that this conclusion is inconsistent with later case law, such as *Chetwynd* v. *Allen* [1899] 1 Ch. 353 and *Butler* v. *Rice* [1910] 2 Ch. 277 (see below, p. 621), and that the mistaken mortgagor should be subrogated to the mortgagee, see *Essays* (ed. Burrows), pp. 96–99 [Sutton]. Contrast (1976) 92 L.Q.R. 188, 205–206 [Birks and Beatson].

[72] See, *e.g. Re Cleadon Trust Ltd.* [1939] Ch. 286, 322, *per* Clauson L.J.; *Sorrell* v. *Paget* [1950] 1 K.B. 252, 260, *per* Buckmill L.J. See [1981] C.L.J. 340 [Matthews].

property, he will, nevertheless, be exempted from liability if he can show that his intervention was reasonably necessary for the protection of the property of the person whose rights have been infringed,[73] though "voluntary and capricious interference should be altogether forbidden,"[74] and will amount to a trespass. There is a similar rule in the case of involuntary bailments.[75] In such cases, if the involuntary bailee deals reasonably with the goods in an emergency, his act will not be tortious,[76] even if he disposes of the goods.[77] On the other hand, if there is no emergency and, therefore, no necessity for intervention, interference on the part of the involuntary bailee is officious and is carried out at his peril.[78]

Similarly, if a stranger assists a person in an emergency, there is no reason to doubt the lawfulness of his action. "[I]t is the necessity itself which provides the justification for the intervention."[79]

There is much to be said for the view that in English law an intervener should not only be exempted from tortious liability but should, in appropriate cases, be granted a restitutionary claim.[79a] A few American states, following

---

[73] See *The Tithe Case* (1506) Y.B.21 Hen. 7 f. 27, pl. 5, *per* Kingsmill J.; *Kirk* v. *Gregory* (1876) 1 Ex.D. 55; *Carter* v. *Thomas* [1893] 1 Q.B. 673, 678–679, *per* Kennedy J.; *Cope* v. *Sharpe* (*No. 2*) [1912] 1 K.B. 496, 508–509, *per* Kennedy L.J. The same rule applies if the intervention is necessary in the public interest: see *Maleverer* v. *Spinke* (1538) Dy. 35b; *Dewey* v. *White* (1827) Moo. & M. 56.

[74] *Kirk* v. *Gregory* (1876) 1 Ex.D. 55, 59, *per* Cleasby B.

[75] *Elvin & Powell Ltd.* v. *Plummer Roddis Ltd.* (1933) 50 T.L.R. 158, 159, *per* Hawke J.

[76] *Elvin & Powell Ltd.* v. *Plummer Roddis Ltd.* (1933) 50 T.L.R. 158; see also *Heugh* v. *L.N.W. Ry.* (1870) L.R. 5 Exch. 51; *M'Kean* v. *M'Ivor* (1870) L.R. 6 Ex. 36. *Cf. Howard* v. *Harris* (1884) C. & E. 253, where the involuntary bailee who intervened did not exercise reasonable care; but see also *Grimoldby* v. *Wells* (1875) L.R. 10 C.P. 391.

[77] *Kemp* v. *Pryor* (1812) 7 Ves. 237, 247, *per* Lord Eldon. If the reasonable course for the involuntary bailee to take is, for example, to warehouse the goods then he should be able to recover the expense of such warehousing; see *Restatement of Restitution*, § 117, example i. The right to reimbursement seems at least to have been contemplated in *Heugh* v. *L.N.W. Ry.* (1870) L.R. 5 Exch. 51, 56, where Kelly C.B. referred with apparent approval to the practice of the railway company, "when goods are refused at the address to which they are consigned, to deposit the goods in safety, and to send an advice note to the consignees, informing them that the goods remain at their risk *and charges*, and requesting them to give instructions for their delivery . . . " (italics supplied). *Cf. The Winson* [1982] A.C. 839: see above, p. 24.

[78] He may then be liable in conversion: see *Hiort* v. *Bott* (1874) L.R. 9 Exch. 86; Paton, 116; (1922) 35 Harv.L.Rev. 873; (1960) 76 L.Q.R. 364 (H. W. Burnett); Torts (Interference with Goods) Act 1977, ss.12, 13 and Sched. I. But *cf. The Winson* [1982] A.C. 939: see above, pp. 24, 364; and the position of the innocent convertor, who improves the chattel after the conversion: see above, pp. 172 *et seq.*

[79] *Re F.* (*Mental Patient: Sterilisation*) [1990] 2 A.C. 1, 78, *per* Lord Goff.

[79a] Indeed some such claim appears to have been admitted in *Waters* v. *Weigall* (1795) 2 Anst. 575, where a tenant was allowed to deduct from his rent the cost of repairing the damage to the demised property caused by a tempest: "it is money paid to [the landlord's] use; and may be set off against the demand of rent." And *cf. White* (*J.D.*) v. *Troups Transport* [1976] C.L.Y. 33 (Cty.Ct.), where a crane hire firm, which had been called in by the police, recovered a reasonable fee from the owner of a lorry, jammed under a bridge, because it was an agent of necessity. There was no pre-existing relationship between the parties. [We are grateful to D. N. Spark Esq., Solicitor, for information about this case.]

the *Restatement of Restitution*,[80] have allowed restitution.[81] The limits of any restitutionary claim should, however, be carefully defined; and the nature of these limitations will inevitably reflect the extent to which courts wish to encourage strangers to intervene in an emergency. However, in accepting the desirability of such a claim, there is a danger that the court may impose too great a burden on the owner of the land who has neither requested nor freely accepted the intervention.[82]

(1) *The limits of the restitutionary claim*

(a) Necessity must have compelled the intervention. The emergency must be so pressing as to compel intervention without the property owner's authority. The analogy of maritime law suggests that there was an emergency if there was "no immediate risk, no immediate danger; but there was a possible contingency that serious consequences might have ensued."[83] If the agency cases are followed, the relevant time for determining whether intervention was necessary should be the time when the emergency became apparent.[84]

(b) The intervener must demonstrate that he acted reasonably and in the best interests of the owner.[85]

(c) The intervener must not have been able to obtain his principal's instructions. The agency cases suggest that it must be "practically impossible", as distinct from impossible, to do so and that it is sufficient that he asked for instructions and only acted when no reply was received.[86]

However, in *The Goring* [1987] Q.B. 687, 708, Ralph Gibson L.J. was of the view that the common law's reluctance "has not rested . . . only on the lack of prior authority and the fear of innovations but can be supported by reasons." He found these reasons in the judgment of Eyre C.J. in *Nicholson* v. *Chapman* (1793) 2 H.Bl. 254, 259 (which was a claim for a lien over the property salvaged: see above, p. 371): it would encourage "wilful attempts of ill designing people to turn . . . floats and vessels adrift, in order that they may be paid for finding them." But the claim in *The Goring* was for a reward and not one for expenses incurred or loss suffered. If the restitutionary award is as limited as we suggest in the text (see below, p. 374), it will hardly encourage officious intervention.
See also (1929–1930) 15 Cornell L.Q. 25, 36, where Professor Hope dismisses the argument, that to admit a restitutionary claim would "breed overnight a nation of busy-bodies anxious to perform useless and meddlesome services for others", as fanciful.

[80] § 117.
[81] *Berry* v. *Barbour*, 279 P. 2d 335 (1954), where the plaintiff, a roofing contractor, did necessary repairs to the defendant's roof "to prevent further damage by the elements." The Supreme Court of Oklahoma held that the defendant, who could not be contacted, must reimburse the plaintiff for the cost of his materials and labour. See Palmer, *op. cit.* Vol. II, pp. 371–372.
[82] Some of the dangers are described by Dawson, "Rewards for the Loss of Human Life," *Essays Presented to Hans Yntema*, p. 142; see below, p. 375.
[83] *The Elia Constance* (1864) 33 L.J.Adm. 189, 193, *per* Dr. Lushington. A cautious court may well conclude that the contingency should be *probable* rather than *possible*.
[84] See above, p. 367.
[85] *Cf.* above, p. 367 (analogy of agency of necessity).
[86] *The Winson* [1982] A.C. 939, 961–962, *per* Lord Diplock: see above, p. 364.

(d) There is some authority to suggest that the intervener must demonstrate that he intended to charge for his services.[87] But the intervener's claim is appealing because he acted from moral compulsion. In our view it is illogical to conclude that if it is good public policy to encourage intervention that this burden should be imposed on the intervener; the assisted person should be required to prove that the intervener intended to act gratuitously.[88] However, as will be seen, we consider that only if the intervener is a professional performing a professional service should he be remunerated for what he has done.[89]

The intervener's claim should be defeated if the intervener knows that there was a more suitable person who was ready and able to act or if the owner would not have welcomed his intervention.[90] A restitutionary claim should also be denied if the predominant reason for the intervention was to protect the intervener's own personal interests.[91]

(2) *Remedies*

How is the extent of the benefit gained by the defendant through the plaintiff's intervention to be measured? *A priori* there are a number of possible solutions. The court may choose to reward, remunerate or simply reimburse the stranger. The maritime salvor is rewarded in order to provide a real and positive incentive to "seafaring folk to take risks for the purpose of saving property,"[92] but he is rewarded only if his services are successful.[93] To reward the land salvor would only be justifiable if the courts considered that the land salvor should be given a similar incentive. In our view there is no justification for doing so. It is essential to encourage individuals to salvage property on the high seas. There is not the same urgency to do so on land.

Whether the stranger should be remunerated for his services is more debatable.[93a] The analogy of the few authorities on the preservation of life[94] suggests that remuneration should be awarded if the stranger is a "professional," such as a roofing contractor who undertook repairs in an emergency, for example, after a disastrous fire. We are not convinced, however, that it is desirable to remunerate all strangers; such an award would be realistic only if the stranger were a professional doing a professional job.[95]

---

[87] *Re Rhodes* (1884) 44 Ch.D. 94; see *Restatement of Restitution* § 117(d), below, p. 380.
[88] *Cf.* the Ulpian text D.3.5.4: *nisi donandi animo fideiussit.*
[89] See below, p. 377.
[90] But the answer of the court may depend on whether it considers that the public interest in the preservation of property is so great that the owner's interest should be overridden.
[91] *Cf. Warfel* v. *Vondersmith*, 101 A. 2d 736 (1954).
[92] *The Sandefjord* [1953] 2 Lloyd's Rep. 557, 561, *per* Willmer J.
[93] See below, pp. 391 *et seq.*
[93a] And see above, p. 374(d).
[94] See below, p. 377.
[95] *Cf. White (J.D.)* v. *Troups Transport* [1976] C.L.Y. 33: see above, n. 79a. Contrast *The Goring* [1987] Q.B. 687, 708, *per* Ralph Gibson L.J.

As a general rule we would limit the stranger's claim to the sums which he has expended, including the materials which have been used in his attempt to preserve the property. He should recover these expenses even if his intervention is unsuccessful; for it is proper to assume that the defendant would have authorised this expenditure if he had been given the opportunity of doing so.[96] But the courts should only reimburse the stranger's expenses which were reasonably incurred in, and which contributed to, the attempts to preserve the property in an emergency. They should not reimburse his expenses, which no reasonable person would have incurred. Nor should they compensate him, through the guise of a restitutionary claim, for any damage which he has suffered through his intervention. A roofing contractor may recover the cost of materials used for repairing the roof, but not compensation for the loss of an arm broken while doing so.[97]

Preservation of life or health

A man dives into a river to save a drowning child. A doctor gives medical attention to a man rendered unconscious by an accident. A reward is, we consider, inappropriate. But is the intervener entitled to remuneration for his services or reimbursement of his expenses?

It is not surprising that there are few cases on this point. Those who render services do not generally intend to charge for them; and if they do, the assisted person may well be willing to pay.[98] If a person who unofficiously supplies

---

[96] Consequently, some commentators have argued that this body of law is best explained as an illustration of the application of the principle of *undue sacrifice* rather than unjust enrichment: see *Essays* (ed. Finn) 297 [Muir]; *Negotiorum Gestio* in the *International Encyclopaedia of Comparative Law* (1984) Vol. 10, Chap. 17 [Stoljar]. Contrast (1989) 9 Oxford Jo.L.S. 167 [Rose].

[97] These conclusions should in no way be affected by the fact that the defendant was insured against the risk that the property might be damaged or destroyed. "As a general proposition it has not . . . been questioned for nearly 200 years that in determining the rights *inter se* of A and B the fact that one or other of them is insured is to be disregarded": see *Lister* v. *Romford Ice and Cold Storage Co. Ltd.* [1957] A.C. 555, 576–577, *per* Lord Simonds. The assured should be able to recover under the policy any sums which he is required to pay to the intervener. For example, under a standard fire policy any losses incurred in attempting to check the progress of a fire are accepted to be within the risk assured against, at least if the assured or his agent had acted in good faith and had taken reasonable steps to extinguish the fire: see *Stanley* v. *Western Insurance Co.* (1868) L.R. 3 Ex. 71, 74, *per* Kelly C.B. It would be unreasonable to allow an insurer to deny liability on the ground that the intervener was not the plaintiff's agent. If necessary, the intervener should be subrogated to the assured claim. More difficult questions arise if the assured is now insolvent: *semble* the intervener would then come in as a general creditor.

[98] In a few common law jurisdictions (*e.g.*, Vermont and Minnesota) a person who fails to come to another's rescue may be punished by imprisonment or a fine: see Vermont Stat.Ann.tit. para. 519 (Supp. 1971); Min.Stat.Ann. para. 604–605 (1) (West 1983 Supp.); and, generally, 25 Stanford L.R. 51 (1972) [Franklin]. The statutory provisions have not yet persuaded a court to impose a civil duty of care.
Similarly, there is no German decision which permits "this translation of criminal into civil liability": (1961) 74 Harv.L.R. 1207 [Dawson].
In the United States services rendered in an emergency may constitute sufficient moral consideration to support a subsequent promise to pay for them: see E. A. Farnsworth, *Contracts*, para. 2.8, for the authorities.

necessaries to a lunatic is entitled to reimbursement,[99] there is much to be said for the general principle that an intervener who intervenes in an emergency to save life or health should at least be entitled to be reimbursed his reasonable expenses. A professional, rendering professional services, should be entitled to reasonable remuneration.[1]

(1) *The limits of the restitutionary claim*

(a) There must be an emergency which is "simply a frequent origin of the necessity which impels intervention."[2] The central question should be: is the need great enough and immediate enough to justify the plaintiff's intervention?[3] The intervention should be justified if there is a possible contingency that serious consequences might otherwise have ensued[4]; and the relevant time for determining whether there is an emergency should be the time when the emergency became apparent.[5]

(b) The "overriding consideration is that [the intervener] should act in the best interests of the [assisted person]."[6]

(c) In the very few cases where a restitutionary claim has succeeded it was assumed that the intervener must prove an intent to charge[7]; but, since he was a doctor carrying out medical duties, that intent could be presumed. In our view, the burden should be on the assisted person to demonstrate that the intervener intended to render the services gratuitously, although a failure to discharge this burden would not necessarily lead to the conclusion that the intervener should be remunerated for his services as distinct from being reimbursed his expenses.[8]

(d) It must not be practicable to communicate rationally with the assisted person.[9]

The restitutionary claim should not then be defeated on the ground that the assisted person was not in a position to consent to the intervention. In an

---

[99] *Cf. Re Rhodes* (1890) 44 Ch.D. 94 (where the claim failed because there was no intention to charge); see below, p. 380.

[1] Professor Friedmann, in *Essays* (ed. Burrows), pp. 255–256, posits the situation of the guest who falls ill while staying with his host. He argues persuasively that any duty to summon a doctor should not include an obligation *vis-à-vis* the patient to cover the costs of the intervention.

[2] *Re F. (Mental Patient: Sterilisation)* [1990] 2 A.C. 1, 75, *per* Lord Goff (an operation on a patient suffering from a serious mental disability could be carried out even though she could not consent to it).

[3] *Cf.* Palmer *op. cit.* Vol. II, p. 381.

[4] *Cf.* above, p. 373.

[5] *Re T. (Adult: Medical Treatment)* [1992] 3 W.L.R. 782, C.A.

[6] *Re F. (Mental Patient: Sterilisation)* [1990] 2 A.C. 1, 78, *per* Lord Goff.

[7] *Re F. (Mental Patient: Sterilisation)* [1990] 2 A.C. 1, 75, *per* Lord Goff.

[8] *Cotnam* v. *Wisdom* (1907) 104 S.W. 164; *Matheson* v. *Smiley* [1932] 2 D.L.R. 787 (Manitoba Court of Appeal); *Greenspan* v. *Slate* (1953) 12 N.J. 426. See also *Re Rhodes* (1890) 44 Ch.D. 94 (where a claim based on the supply of necessaries to a mentally incompetent failed on the ground that the intervener did not intend to charge: see below, p. 380).

[9] See above, p. 373.

analogous situation it has been held that to require persons suffering from a severe mental disorder to consent to medical treatment would mean that they "would in some circumstances at least, be deprived of the benefit of medical treatment which adults competent to give consent would enjoy."[10] For similar reasons, in an Arkansas case, a surgeon was allowed to recover for services rendered by him to an unconscious patient.[11] It is a more difficult question if the intervener knew or ought to have known that the assisted person would not welcome his intervention. It may be critical to know why this is so. For example, the position of the attempted suicide[12] may be distinguishable from that of the Christian Scientist. The attempted suicide may possibly be as incompetent as the mentally disordered person, but the devout Christian Scientist cannot be so described,[12a] and should be entitled to refuse treatment.

The Court of Appeal has recently concluded,[13] in giving guidance to hospitals and doctors, that if a patient is deprived of his capacity by long term mental incapacity, retarded development or by temporary factors such as unconsciousness or confusion or the effect of shock, fatigue, pain or drugs, and if the patient did not have capacity at the date of the purported refusal and still did not have that capacity to decide at the date the doctors' decision was made, then the duty of the doctors is to treat him in the way they consider to be in his best interests.

Public policy demands that every effort should be made to save human life. For that reason, if the intervention was reasonable, it should not be relevant that the services rendered were unavailing.[14]

(2) Remedies

There is no suggestion in the case law of any jurisdiction that the intervener should be rewarded for his efforts in saving life.[15] However, an intervener who is a professional should be remunerated for his professional services; in the United States and Canada, doctors have been remunerated for their professional services.[16] In contrast, there is no reasonable yardstick which determines the remuneration of the intervener who is not a professional; for example, what remuneration do you award the pure mathematician who saves the life of a business tycoon?

However, all interveners should be reimbursed their reasonable expenses. There is some authority to support this modest conclusion; a person who discharged another's obligation to bury a corpse recovered the reasonable

---

[10] Re F. (Mental Patient: Sterilisation) [1990] 2 A.C. 1, 68.
[11] Cotnam v. Wisdom (1907) 104 S.W. 164.
[12] Or an anorexic teenager?: see above, n. 10.
[12a] Cf. Malette v. Shulman (1990) 67 D.L.R. (4th) 321.
[13] See generally, (1929–1930) 15 Cornell L.Q. 25, 47–53 [Hope]. Cf. Re T. (Adult: Medical Treatment) [1992] 3 W.L.R. 782, C.A. (Jehovah's Witness, whose belief was shallow, could not consent, being under the influence of her mother, a devout adherent).
[14] Matheson v. Smiley [1932] 2 D.L.R. 787: see particularly at p. 789, per Robson J.A.
[15] Cf. above, p. 374.
[16] See above, n. 7.

expenses of burial, suitable to the situation in life of the deceased.[17] But the courts should not be tempted to extend this principle in order to compensate the intervener for any injury or loss suffered in the act of rescue. If the assisted person has not negligently created the emergency which prompted the intervention, he should not have imposed upon him this burden which could be, as Professor Dawson demonstrated from his analysis of German and Swiss law, financially crippling.[18]

Preservation of credit[19]

A third party may accept a bill of exchange for the honour of the drawer.[20] But his acceptance can only be made after a protest for non-acceptance[21] and it is subject to the consent of the holder of the bill,[22] for the latter may wish to exercise his right of recourse which arises on non-acceptance.

The acceptor for honour undertakes that he will, "on due presentment, pay the bill according to the tenor of his acceptance, if it is not paid by the drawee, provided it has been duly presented for payment, and protested for non-payment, and that he receives notice of these facts."[23] If the bill is so paid, the payer for honour is subrogated to, and succeeds to both the rights and duties of, the holder as regards the party for whose honour he pays, and all parties liable to that party.[24]

This appears to be another manifestation of necessitous intervention.[25] The stranger's intervention takes the form of fulfilment of the contractual duty of the person assisted; and since his action preserves the latter's commercial credit which would otherwise be endangered, he is entitled to reimbursement in respect of his expenditure. However, the mere payment of another's debt will not generally, of itself, discharge the debt[26] or give a right to

---

[17] *Cf.* below, p. 382. See also *Shallcross* v. *Wright* (1850) 12 Beav. 558, 562, *per* Lord Langdale. *Cf.* the agency of necessity cases: above, pp. 368–369.

[18] *Rewards for the Loss of Human Life?, Essays presented to Hans Yntema*, pp. 142–158; (1961) 74 Harv.L.R. 1073 [Dawson].

[19] See *Byles on Bills*, pp. 123–124, 155–156, 259–260.

[20] Bills of Exchange Act 1882, s.65(1). On notice of dishonour, see *Eaglehill Ltd.* v. *J. Needham Builders Ltd.* [1973] A.C. 992.

[21] *Vandewall* v. *Tyrrell* (1827) M. & M. 87; *Geralopulo* v. *Wieler* (1851) 10 C.B. 690; Bills of Exchange Act 1882, s.65(1).

[22] *Mitford* v. *Wallicot* (1700) 12 Mod. 410; Bills of Exchange Act 1882, s.65(1).

[23] Bills of Exchange Act 1882, s.66(1).

[24] *Ibid.*, s.68(5).

[25] See *Restatement of Restitution*, § 117(2). In *Hawtayne* v. *Bourne* (1841) 7 M. & W. 595, 599, see above, p. 365 Parke B., although he took a most restricted view of the rights of the necessitous intervener, accepted the link between the rights of the acceptor for honour and of the master of a ship who deals with the ship or cargo in an emergency.

[26] *James* v. *Isaacs* (1852) 12 C.B. 791; *Simpson* v. *Eggington* (1855) 10 Ex. 844; *Lucas* v. *Wilkinson* (1856) 1 H. & N. 420; *Re Rowe* [1904] 2 K.B. 483; *Smith* v. *Cox* [1940] 2 K.B. 558. See also *M'Intyre* v. *Miller* (1845) 13 M. & W. 725; *Jones* v. *Broadhurst* (1850) 9 C.B. 173; *Belshaw* v. *Bush* (1851) 11 C.B. 191; *Kemp* v. *Balls* (1854) 10 Ex. 607; *Purcell* v. *Henderson* (1885) 16 L.R.(Ir.) 213; see above, p. 17, n. 2. In the cases on vicarious performance, *e.g. British Waggon Co.* v. *Lea* (1880) 5 Q.B.D. 149, the performance by another is authorised by the person actually bound to perform.

reimbursement.[27] This strict and perhaps illogical rule should not usually cause hardship, for an intervener who pays another's debt in an emergency should be able to protect himself in other ways,[28] such as assignment or, possibly, subrogation.[29] However, there are dicta which suggest that the courts may now be ready to recognise a direct restitutionary action against a debtor whose debt has been discharged by another in an emergency.[30]

The supply of necessaries to persons suffering from legal incapacity

Generally, persons suffering from such incapacity can contract for the supply of necessaries. Moreover, if a person suffering from incapacity enters into a contract for the supply of necessaries, and the contract is for some reason ineffective, his liability to pay for necessaries received, though it may be quasi-contractual, will not be based on any concept of necessitous intervention; it will be founded on his request.[31]

Exceptionally, however, necessaries may be supplied to a person in an emergency and without request. It is with these cases that we are concerned in this Chapter. In a Welfare State, examples of necessitous intervention in such circumstances may be few and far between, but those that do exist show that the courts are prepared to reimburse a stranger if he intervenes in such an emergency.

(1) *Mentally disordered persons*[32]

In *Williams* v. *Wentworth*[33] it was suggested that:

> "however beneficial to the lunatic, the expenditure may have been, yet, as the lunatic was incapable of contracting, no debt could be constituted; but I am of opinion, that in the case of money expended for the necessary protection of the person and estate of the lunatic, the law will raise an implied contract, and give a valid demand or debt, against the lunatic or his estate. . . ."

Before a supplier can obtain payment for necessaries supplied to a mentally disordered person in a case of necessitous intervention, he must satisfy the following conditions. He must show that there was some necessity, which may be done by proving that he supplied necessaries; that he was a suitable person

---

[27] *Tappin* v. *Broster* (1823) 1 C. & P. 112; *Re National Motor Mail-Coach Co. Ltd.* [1908] 2 Ch. 228.

[28] *e.g.* he may obtain an assignment of the debt; or the debtor may so act that it could be said that he ratified the payment. If the debtor repudiates the payment, the payer may be able to recover from the recipient on grounds of total failure of consideration: see *Walter* v. *James* (1671) L.R. 6 Ex. 124, 127, *per* Kelly C.B.; see above, p. 17, n. 2.

[29] See below, pp. 596 *et seq.*

[30] *Cf. Owen* v. *Tate* [1976] 1 Q.B. 402, 409–410, *per* Scarman L.J., 412, *per* Stephenson L.J.; see above, p. 351. See also *Re a Debtor* [1937] Ch. 156, 166, *per* Greene L.J.; *Anson* v. *Anson* [1953] Q.B. 636, 642–643, *per* Pearson J.

[31] See below, pp. 525 *et seq.*

[32] Mental Health Act 1983, s.1(1), (2). At common law such persons were called "lunatics."

[33] (1842) 5 Beav. 325, 329, *per* Lord Langdale M.R. The doctrine has been invoked on a number of occasions: see *Wentworth* v. *Tubb* (1841) 1 Y. & C.C.C. 171; *Nelson* v. *Duncombe* (1846) 9 Beav. 211; see also *Howard* v. *Earl Digby* (1834) 2 Cl. & F. 634; *Re E.G.* [1914] 1 Ch. 927.

to intervene (such as, for example, a relation),[34] and that he intervened bona fide in the interests of the mentally disordered person.[35] Moreover, he must intend to charge, and it has been said that the onus is on him to prove such an intention. In *Re Rhodes*,[36] a woman of unsound mind was confined in a private asylum. Her brother, and, after his death, his son, received her income and applied it towards the payment of the asylum's charges; but as it was not sufficient, they made up the deficiency, the brother out of his own pocket, and the nephew partly out of his own pocket and partly by means of contributions from his brothers and sisters. They made no claim against her during her life, nor did they keep an account of any claim they might have against her. On her death, the Court of Appeal held that the nephew, her administrator, was not allowed to retain out of the estate, as against her next-of-kin, the sums so paid by his father, himself and his brothers and sisters. The court had no doubt that in a proper case such a claim might be sustained.[37] But here the claimant failed because there was no evidence of intention to charge for the necessaries supplied; indeed, the absence of accounts and the fact that no claim was made in the lifetime of the deceased pointed the other way.[38]

It appears to have been the opinion of the Court of Appeal in *Re Rhodes* that the onus is on the supplier to show an intention to charge. But there is much to be said for the view that the onus should be on the defendant to show that the supplier had no intention to charge.[39] A stranger should be in no different position from an agent of necessity, who, like other agents, should be entitled to his expenses unless the defendant can show that he intended them to be a gift.[40] It may well be that, in *Re Rhodes*, even if the onus had been on the defendant, the supplier would have failed since no accounts were kept and no claim was made in the lunatic's lifetime.

(2) *Drunkards*

We know of no case of a stranger's intervention on behalf of a drunkard. This is hardly surprising. The condition of drunkenness is usually of a temporary nature. If it becomes permanent, as in the case of *delirium tremens*, it is more

---

[34] The intervener must not disregard or anticipate the rights of those who have a better right to intervene and are ready, able and willing to do so; see *Re Rhodes* (1890) 44 Ch.D. 94, 107, *per* Lindley L.J.; (1929–30) 15 Cornell L.R. 25, 43 [Hope].

[35] It should be irrelevant that the lunatic told the intervener that he did not require the necessaries; see *Carr* v. *Anderson*, 154 Minn. 162 (1923), and the cases on preservation of life; see above, p. 375.

[36] (1890) 44 Ch.D. 94. See also *Carter* v. *Beard* (1839) 10 Sim. 7 (which was, however, doubted, *arguendo*, in *Re Rhodes* (1898) 44 Ch.D. 94, 103–104, *per* Cotton and Lopes L.JJ.); *Wentworth* v. *Tubb* (1841) 1 Y. & C.C.C. 171, 173–174, *per* Knight Bruce V.-C. *Cf. Re Gibson* (1871) L.R. 7 Ch.App. 52; *Re Weaver* (1882) 21 Ch.D. 615; *Samilo et al.* v. *Phillips* (1968) 69 D.L.R. (2d) 411.

[37] (1890) 44 Ch.D. 94, 108, *per* Lindley L.J.

[38] (1890) 44 Ch.D. 94, 107, *per* Lindley L.J.

[39] *Cf.* D.3.5.4., cited above, p. 374, n. 88.

[40] See above, p. 374.

akin to madness. The reports provide at least one successful claim[41] of necessitous intervention on behalf of such a sufferer.

(3) Minors[42]

Under certain conditions, a minor who has attained the age of understanding is capable of making a valid contract for necessaries.[43] Even if the purported contract is not enforceable against the minor,[44] necessaries supplied thereunder must generally be paid for, because the necessaries have been supplied at the minor's request.[45] Therefore, the doctrine of necessitous intervention can rarely be invoked in this context. It can only be relevant where necessaries are supplied to minors, who have not reached the age of understanding and who cannot contract.[46] But such cases are highly improbable.[47]

(b) Fulfilment of the Duty of Another, of which the Public Interest Requires Immediate Performance

The parents' duty to support their children[48]

At common law it was often stated that to make a father liable for goods, necessaries or otherwise, delivered to his minor children, it was essential to

---

[41] *West Ham Union* v. *Pearson* (1890) 62 L.T. 638; but *cf. Gore* v. *Gibson* (1845) 13 M. & W. 623, 626, *per* Parke B., 627, *per* Alderson B.

[42] They *may* now be called *minors*; Family Law Reform Act 1969, s.12.

[43] See below, pp. 525 *et seq.*

[44] *Ibid.*

[45] In the case of goods sold and delivered, the claim is now statutory; see Sale of Goods Act 1979, s.3(2); see below, p. 525.

[46] See below, p. 524.

[47] But see *Re Clabbon* [1904] 2 Ch. 465; *Pontypridd Union* v. *Drew* [1927] 1 K.B. 214, 220, *per* Scrutton L.J.

[48] At common law and by statute a husband was under a duty to support his wife; and if he neglected to support her she generally had an irrevocable agency to pledge his credit for necessaries. This right was abolished in 1970 by the Matrimonial Proceedings Property Act 1970, s.41 (now repealed, but the common law has not been revived): see below, p. 627, n. 83. For an unusual example of a restitutionary claim arising from the plaintiff's fulfilment of the husband's common law duty, see *Carr* v. *Anderson*, 191 N.W. 407 (1923), with which contrast *Chipp* v. *Murray*, 379 P. 2d 297 (1963).
The problem could also arise under the old poor law, where parishes were liable to supply medical attention and other necessaries to poor persons settled in the parish. Sometimes, however, a poor person fell ill or met with an accident in such circumstances that somebody other than the officers of the parish in which he was settled supplied the medical attention; was such a person entitled to reimbursement by the parish in which the pauper was settled?
The usual case was where the poor person fell ill or was injured in some parish other than that in which he was settled, and the officers of the former parish supplied the assistance. Here, however, the rule was that in such a case the parish responsible for him was the parish in which the illness or injury occurred (see *Tomlinson* v. *Bentall* (1826) 5 B. & C. 738; *Atkins* v. *Banwell* (1802) 2 East 505), and not the parish in which he was settled, unless the latter parish adopted or otherwise accepted responsibility for the cost (*Watson* v. *Turner* (1767) Buller N.P. 147; *Atkins* v. *Banwell* (1802) 2 East 505; *Wing* v. *Mill* (1817) 1 B. & Ald. 104; *Paynter* v. *Williams* (1833) 1 C. & M. 810). Hence in this type of case there was no room for necessitous intervention. But apart from that special case, it seems that a necessitous intervener might recover. Thus, in *Simmons* v. *Wilmott* (1800) 3 Esp. 91, it was held by Lord Eldon that a stranger who arranged for

prove some sort of contract between the father and the person who supplied the goods.[49] But on the occasions when these statements have been made, the plaintiff has alleged that there was something resembling a contract between him and the father. Probably he thought he had to do so, for there is authority that at common law there was no more than a moral obligation on the father to maintain his children.[50] A person who intervened to fulfil the father's duty had, therefore, to overcome the special obstacle of proving that he was entitled to recover even when the duty fulfilled was not one binding in law. There is no decided case which rejects such an intervener's claim. The question was mooted and left open in *Urmston* v. *Newcomen* in 1836.[51]

Today, parents are under a statutory duty to maintain their children until they attain the age of 16.[52] While it is arguable that the doctrine of necessitous intervention could be invoked in this connection, the contingency is most unlikely to arise in view of modern conditions and the number of statutes under which parents may be compelled to provide maintenance for their children.[53]

In the United States, a doctor has recovered his professional fees for services rendered in an emergency when the parents had failed to provide medical care for their child.[54]

Fulfilment of another's duty to bury the dead

The personal representatives of the deceased are primarily responsible for his burial[55]; and for this expenditure they will be reimbursed out of the estate before all other claims.[56] Two special cases require mention. Before 1883 a husband was responsible, at common law, for the burial of his wife.[57] This responsibility now[58] falls on her personal representatives, who are entitled to

---

the provision of medical assistance to a poor person "under the pressure of immediate want" might be reimbursed by the parish responsible.

[49] *Seaborne* v. *Maddy* (1840) 9 C. & P. 497, 498, *per* Parke B. See also *Blackburn* v. *Mackey* (1823) 1 C. & P. 1; *Rolfe* v. *Abbott* (1833) 6 C. & P. 286; *Mortimore* v. *Wright* (1840) 6 M. & W. 482; *Shelton* v. *Springett* (1851) 11 C.B. 452.

[50] *Mortimore* v. *Wright* (1840) 6 M. & W. 482; *Coldingham Parish Council* v. *Smith* [1918] 2 K.B. 90. But see *contra Nichole* v. *Allen* (1827) 3 C. & P. 36, 37, *per* Lord Tenterden C.J. The point was left open in *Urmston* v. *Newcomen* (1836) 4 A. & E. 899; and see *Bazeley* v. *Forder* (1868) L.R. 3 Q.B. 559, 564, *per* Blackburn J.

[51] (1836) 4 A. & E. 899.

[52] Social Security Act 1986, s.26(3), as amended.

[53] See, generally, Cretney and Masson, *Family Law*, pp. 339 *et seq.*

[54] *Greenspan* v. *Slade*, 97 A. 2d 390 (1953) (on its facts, perhaps, a doubtful case); *Restatement of Restitution*, § 113.

[55] 2 Bl.Com. 508. How far this duty is enforceable at law is uncertain; see *Rogers* v. *Price* (1829) 3 Y. & J. 28, 35–36, *per* Hullock B.

[56] Administration of Estates Act 1925, ss.33(2), 34(3), Sched. I, Pt. I; see also *Edwards* v. *Edwards* (1834) 2 C. & M. 612, 615, *per* Parke B.

[57] *Jenkins* v. *Tucker* (1788) 1 H.Bl. 90. This was so even where she had a separate estate. Equity would not allow a husband to throw on to that estate the expense of burial: see *Bertie* v. *Chesterfield* (1722) 9 Mod. 31; *Gregory* v. *Lockyer* (1821) 6 Madd. 90.

[58] *Rees* v. *Hughes* [1946] K.B. 517.

be reimbursed out of her estate before all other claims.[59] Presumably, if she does not leave a sufficient estate, her husband is responsible under the old common law rule. Secondly, a parent is probably responsible for the burial of a deceased child,[60] at least if the parent has sufficient means.

Apart from these primary rules, it has been suggested that at common law any householder under whose roof the body lies is responsible for the decent burial of that body.[61] But under modern legislation, it is the duty of local authorities to bury or cremate the body of any person found dead in their area, if it appears that no suitable arrangements for the disposal of the body are being made.[62]

In the past, cases have occurred where those primarily responsible have not carried out their duty to bury the deceased, and others have intervened to carry out this task. It may not be known in time who are the personal representatives, or the husband of a deceased woman may be abroad or otherwise inaccessible. In these circumstances, it has generally been held that the stranger may recover his reasonable expenses from the person primarily responsible for the burial. The cases form a common pattern.[63] From them the elements of necessitous intervention plainly emerge. The stranger is justified by the necessity of prompt action, the public interest in the disposal of the body and the impracticability of communicating with the person on whom lies the primary responsibility to bury the body. He must not act officiously; for example, he must not intervene knowing that a more suitable person is ready, able and willing to act.[64] It has been said that the burial cases are exceptional,[65]

---

[59] *Re M'Myn* (1886) 33 Ch.D. 575; *Rees* v. *Hughes* [1946] K.B. 517.

[60] *R.* v. *Vann* (1851) 2 Den. 325; *Clarke* v. *London General Omnibus Co.* [1906] 2 K.B. 648, 659, *per* Lord Alverstone C.J.; *cf.* Farewell L.J. at p. 663.

[61] *R.* v. *Stewart* (1840) 12 A. & E. 773, 778, *per* Lord Denman C.J.

[62] Public Health (Control of Disease) Act 1984, ss.46–48; see also *Davey* v. *Cornwallis* (1931) 2 D.L.R. 80.

[63] An early discussion is in *Besfich* v. *Coggil* (1628) 1 Palm. 559; *cf. Church* v. *Church*, cited in T.Raym. 260, and Vin.Abr. Executors B. a 24. (In cases of necessity a stranger may direct the funeral, and defray the expenses out of the deceased's effects, without rendering himself liable as executor de son tort). Later decisions include *Jenkins* v. *Tucker* (1788) 1 H.Bl. 90, 93, *per* Lord Loughborough; *Ambrose* v. *Kerrison* (1851) 10 C.B. 776; *Tugwell* v. *Heyman* (1812) 3 Camp. 298; *Rogers* v. *Price* (1829) 3 Y. & J. 28; *Green* v. *Salmon* (1838) 8 A. & E. 348. For a more recent dictum, see *Croskery* v. *Gee* [1957] N.Z.L.R. 586, 588–589. But *cf. Bradshaw* v. *Beard* (1862) 12 C.B.(n.s.) 344; *Cunningham* v. *Reardon*, 98 Mass. 538 (1868).

[64] In *Patterson* v. *Patterson*, 17 American Repts. 384, 392, (N.Y.) (1875) Folger J., speaking of the executor's duty to bury the deceased, said: "From this duty springs a legal obligation, and from the obligation the law implies a promise to him, who in the absence or neglect of the executor, not officiously, but in the necessity of the case directs a burial and incurs and pays such expenses thereof as is reasonable." See also *Quinn* v. *Hill* 4 Dem.N.Y. 69 (1886); *Cape Girardeau Bell Telephone Co.* v. *Hamil*, 160 Mo.App. 521 (1911). Other American cases are cited in 35 A.L.R. 2d., 1399 (1954); see also (1929–1930) 15 Cornell L.Q. 25, 44 [Hope]; *Davey* v. *Cornwallis* [1931] 2 D.L.R. 80, 83, *per* Robson J.A.

[65] Winfield, *Province*, 173–174; (1944) 60 L.Q.R. 341, 354; Buckland and McNair, *Roman Law and Common Law*, p. 335. *Cf. Rees* v. *Hughes* (1946) 1 K.B. 517, 528, *per* Tucker L.J., where it was said that the "law will imply a request on the part of the husband [or executor] to do that which it is his legal and moral obligation to perform." There is no mention of "implied request" in the earlier cases, and such an implication, in our view, is a transparent fiction.

but the judges[66] did not treat them as so and spoke in terms of general principle.[67]

3. CONCLUSION

Bowen L.J.'s dicta in *Falcke's* case, which have been endorsed on numerous occasions, have hitherto prevented the development of any general doctrine of necessitous intervention. This is, in our view, regrettable, for it is sound legal policy to recognise a restitutionary claim in these circumstances. It is true that the boundaries of the restitutionary claim must be carefully defined; and the limits which a particular jurisdiction imposes may reflect how anxiously it wishes to encourage or discourage such intervention. We have suggested that an intervener should be required to show that there was an emergency and that he did not act officiously but in the defendant's best interests. It is not, in our view, reasonable to impose upon him the burden of showing that he intended to charge for his services; but his claim should be defeated if the defendant proves that he intended to provide his services gratuitously. To allow him to recover the expenses which he has reasonably incurred, and exceptionally his remuneration, is not to impose on the defendant a penal liability.

These requirements are substantially the same as those which determine the success or failure of a claim by an agent of necessity, though there the presence of a pre-existing relationship ensures that the agent was a suitable person to intervene. The courts, however, have sought to analyse agency of necessity in the language of contract. But contract, as we have seen, does not provide the whole answer.[68] In our view, both agency of necessity, and the comparatively rare cases in English law where necessitous intervention by a stranger has been recognised, are united by the same principle, whereby one who intervenes on another's behalf in an emergency should, within the limits indicated, be treated as though he had the authority of that person to intervene.

It is still open to the English courts modestly to extend the principle of necessitous intervention. It is to be hoped that they will do so and that they will generalise the nascent English development into a coherent and rational doctrine.

---

[66] See, *e.g. Jenkins* v. *Tucker* (1788) 1 H.Bl. 90, 93, *per* Lord Loughborough; *Ambrose* v. *Kerrison* (1851) 10 C.B. 776, 779, *per* Jervis C.J.

[67] With the cases discussed in this section may be contrasted those where the plaintiff discharges the defendant's contractual duty to supply necessaries to a third party, the defendant having failed to do so. The problem has not directly arisen in England; but *cf. Gregg* v. *Coates* (1856) 23 Beav. 33, 38, *per* Romilly M.R.; *Re Williams* (1885) 54 L.T. 105. (See also *Gill* v. *Gill* (1921) 21 S.R. (N.S.W.) 400.) It has, however, frequently arisen in the United States; some, but not all, states, allow recovery. There are also American cases which have allowed a plaintiff to recover when he discharged the statutory duty of a public authority which had failed to act when it should have done. The American cases are discussed in Palmer, *op. cit.* Vol. II, § 10.4.

[68] See above, p. 367 *et seq.*

CHAPTER 16

MARITIME SALVAGE

1. The Nature of the Right

A SALVAGE service may be briefly described as a necessary service voluntarily rendered which assists in saving a recognised subject of salvage from danger at sea.[1] The salvor's right to reward for such a service has long been enforced in the Court of Admiralty as part of the maritime law; but the right has, in modern times, been extended by statute.[2]

By maritime law, the only property which could be the subject of salvage was a ship, her apparel and cargo, the wreck of these, and freight at risk.[3] Statute has, however, extended the law of salvage to cover aircraft, and to include the salvage of lives as well as property.[4] Salvage services may take many forms. Common examples are towing or piloting a ship in peril; raising a sunken ship or cargo; rescuing cargo or passengers from a ship in peril; and refloating a ship which has been stranded. The classes of salvage service are, however, by no means closed, and new categories are recognised from time to time.[5]

Although the parties may, if they wish, regulate the rendering of salvage services by agreement,[6] the right to reward for salvage services is not, in origin, contractual. The Admiralty judges have successfully resisted the temptation to invoke the fiction of "implied contract" as a basis of the right. In the words of Sir Francis Jeune P.[7]

> "To rest the jurisdiction of the Admiralty Court upon an implied request from the owner of the property in danger to the salvors, or on an implied contract between the salvors and owner with the relinquishment of the *res* for consideration, is, I think, to confuse two different systems of law and to resort to a misleading analogy. The true view is, I think, that the law of Admiralty imposes on the owner of property saved an obligation to pay

---

[1] This is a description of civil salvage, with which we are here concerned. Civil salvage should be distinguished from military salvage, which is the rescue of property from an enemy in wartime and which gives rise to a claim for reward in a prize court. On civil salvage generally, see *Kennedy on Civil Salvage*; Carver, *Carriage by Sea*, Chap. 13; Brice, *Maritime Law of Salvage*.
[2] See below, pp. 388–389.
[3] *Cf. The Silia* [1981] 2 Lloyd's Rep. 534 (bunker oil, part of the ship).
[4] See below, p. 388.
[5] A list of the principal classes of salvage service is set out in Kennedy, pp. 6–9.
[6] Nowadays, salvage services are more frequently rendered under agreement than not, and usually Lloyd's standard form of agreement is used: see generally, Brice, *op. cit.* Chap. 5, who also discusses proposals for reform including the CMI Draft Convention on Salvage.
[7] *The Cargo ex Port Victor* [1901] P. 243, 249.

the person who saves it simply because in the view of that system of law it is just he should. . . . "

The court does not, therefore, usually[8] inquire whether the services have been requested by the master of the salved vessel,[9] indeed salvage may be awarded even where the services have been accepted under protest.[10] It is, however, essential that the services should have been of such a kind and rendered in such circumstances that a reasonably prudent owner would have accepted them.[11] It is this requirement which, coupled with the further requirement that the subject of salvage must have been in danger, indicates that the foundation of salvage is necessity and demonstrates the connection between maritime salvage and the limited common law right to reimbursement (and, sometimes, remuneration) in respect of services rendered in an emergency without request.[12] The basis of both is necessity; but the law of maritime salvage is, within its limited scope of necessity arising from peril at sea, more generalised and, moreover, gives rise to a right to reward which goes beyond the common law right to reimbursement or remuneration.

This right to reward, rather than remuneration, is a consequence of the fact that salvage is, what Story J. called, a mixed question of private right and public policy.[13] The purpose of a salvage award is not merely to compensate the salvor for the benefit he has received by the salvage. It is also to provide a positive incentive to "seafaring folk to take risks for the purpose of saving property."[14] This public policy results in substantial awards. Liberality is particularly encouraged in the case of services rendered by tugs specially maintained for purposes of salvage,[15] and in the case of salvage of passenger

---

[8] Exceptionally, the fact that the services have been requested may be relevant. Thus, if the services have been rendered at the request of the master of the salved vessel, the salvor may be entitled to a reward even though the vessel is salved through some other cause (see *The Undaunted* (1860) Lush. 90); and if such services are not completed because they are stopped or prevented by the master of the salved vessel, the salvor may be entitled not only to a reward for services he has rendered but also to some compensation for having lost the opportunity of completing his services and, therefore, of reaping a greater reward (see *The Maude* (1876) 3 Asp.Mar. Law Cas. 338; *The Hassel* [1959] 2 Lloyd's Rep. 82). These cases should not, however, be rationalised as being akin to common law claims on a *quantum meruit* basis; for part, at least, of the property in danger must in fact be saved, and the right is to reward not to remuneration, though the grant of the reward is a recognition of the fact that "if men are engaged by a ship in distress . . . they are to be paid according to their efforts made, even though the labour and services may not prove beneficial to the vessel" (see *The Undaunted* (1860) Lush. 90, 92, *per* Dr. Lushington; *The Orelia* [1958] 1 Lloyd's Rep. 441).

[9] *The Vandyck* (1881) 7 P.D. 42.

[10] Provided that the master of the salved vessel would have acted unreasonably with regard to the safety of his ship and the other property in his charge if he had not accepted the services: see *The Kangaroo* [1918] P. 327. *Cf.* the cases at common law where services are rendered against the will of the defendant, and yet there is a right to reimbursement: see *Great Northern Ry.* v. *Swaffield* (1874) L.R. 9 Ex. 132; *Matheson* v. *Smiley* [1932] 2 D.L.R. 787; see above, pp. 373, 377.

[11] *The Emilie Galline* [1903] P. 106.

[12] See above, Chap. 15.

[13] Cited in *The Albion* (1861) Lush. 282, 284, *per* Dr. Lushington.

[14] *The Sandefjord* [1953] 2 Lloyd's Rep. 557, 561, *per* Willmer J. For that reason its basis cannot be "moral compulsion": *cf.* Birks, *Introduction*, p. 304.

[15] See, *e.g. The Glengyle* [1898] A.C. 519.

vessels.[16] In the words of Sir John Nicholl, the principle underlying this element of public policy is "to encourage enterprise, reward exertion, and to be liberal in all that is due to the general interests of commerce, and the general benefit of owners and underwriters, even though the reward may fall upon an individual owner with some severity."[17] It is a concomitant to the rule that a salvor receives a reward, rather than remuneration, for his services, that the services must have been successful before any reward is given.[18] They need not have been completely successful, but part at least of the property must have been saved. In assessing the amount of the reward, the court will remember that in other cases great efforts, though undeservedly unsuccessful, may reap no reward at all.[19] There may, however, be exceptional cases. By special agreement, remuneration may be payable even though the services are unsuccessful; and where services are rendered at the specific request of the vessel in distress, a reward will be payable in respect of such services irrespective of their success.[20]

Where salvage services have ended with the successful preservation of the cargo, the salvors will be entitled to recover further expenditure subsequently incurred in preserving the goods for the benefit of an owner who refused to give them further instructions.[21]

Although the origin of salvage is not contractual, in most cases nowadays salvage is regulated by a salvage agreement, which is frequently in Lloyd's standard form.[22] Since, however, salvage is based on principles of equity, the court has power to set aside a salvage agreement on the grounds that it is fraudulent, or induced by misrepresentation or non-disclosure,[23] or even because the court considers its terms to be "manifestly unfair and unjust."[24] In particular, an agreement is likely to be regarded as inequitable if it stipulates for an exorbitant reward which the master was forced to agree to on account of the necessitous position in which he found himself to be placed.[25] An agreement may, however, also be set aside on the grounds that the agreed sum was far too small.[26]

---

[16] *The Ardincaple* (1834) 3 Hag.Adm. 151, 153, *per* Sir John Nicholl.
[17] *The Industry* (1835) 3 Hag.Adm. 203, 204.
[18] See below, pp. 391–392.
[19] *The City of Chester* (1884) 9 P.D. 182, 202, *per* Lindley L.J.
[20] Provided some part of the property in danger is saved, as it may be through the efforts of some other salving vessel; see above, p. 386, n. 8. and *The Undaunted* (1860) Lush. 90. If this condition is fulfilled, a reward may be given for requested services even though such services have been of no benefit to the salved vessel: see *The Undaunted* (above) and; *The Orelia* [1958] 1 Lloyd's Rep. 441.
[21] *Cf. The Winson* [1982] A.C. 939 (where there was no necessity): see above, pp. 24, 364.
[22] The form is set out in Kennedy, *op. cit.* at pp. 292–299.
[23] See above, p. 195.
[24] *Akerblom* v. *Price, Potter, Walker & Co.* (1881) 7 Q.B.D. 129, 132–133, *per* Brett L.J.
[25] See, *e.g. The Port Caledonia and The Anna* [1903] P. 184; see above, p. 297.
[26] See, *e.g. The Phantom* (1886) L.R. 1 A. & E. 58; see above, pp. 297–298.

2. CONDITIONS OF THE RIGHT TO SALVAGE REWARD

(a) *The Salvage Services must have been Rendered on the High Seas or at a Place within the Statutory Limits*

By maritime law, salvage was only awarded for services rendered on the high seas. The court has no jurisdiction to award salvage for services to vessels in non-tidal waters.[27] Various statutes were, however, enacted which gave rights to reward for salvage services rendered within the body of a county. Today,[28] apart from the ordinary case of services rendered on the high seas, the limits within which salvage services may be rendered are set out in section 546 of the Merchant Shipping Act 1894, which provides as follows:

> Where any vessel is wrecked, stranded, or in distress at any place on or near the coasts of the United Kingdom or any tidal water within the limits of the United Kingdom, and services are rendered by any person in assisting that vessel or saving the cargo or apparel of that vessel or any part thereof, and where services are rendered by any person other than a receiver in saving any wreck,[29] there shall be payable to the salvor by the owner of the vessel, cargo, apparel, or wreck, a reasonable amount of salvage to be determined in case of dispute in manner hereinafter mentioned.

The provisions of this section have since been rendered applicable to aircraft.[30]

(b) *The Thing Saved must be a Recognised Subject of Salvage*

It was the rule of maritime law that the only property which could be the subject of salvage was a ship, her apparel and cargo, the wreck of these, and freight at risk.[31] The law of salvage has, however, been extended by statute[32] to cover aircraft, their apparel and cargo, and the wreck of these.

Traditionally, the true subject of salvage has been property, not lives. Some concession was made by the maritime law under which those who salved lives as well as property could expect a greater reward for their services; but those who salved lives alone received no reward at all. This paradoxical situation has been largely remedied by statute. Life salvage from aircraft is now an accepted subject of salvage[33]; life salvage from ships is so when lives are salved from a

---

[27] *The Goring* [1988] A.C. 831. For the meaning of a harbour, see s.742 of the 1894 Act and *Powstaniec Wielkopolski* [1989] Q.B. 279.

[28] Administration of Justice Act 1956, ss.1(1) and (3), as amended by Merchant Shipping Act 1974, s.6.

[29] s.510 of the 1894 Act provides that the expression "wreck" includes jetsam, flotsam, lagan and derelict found in or on the shores of the sea or any tidal water.

[30] Civil Aviation Act 1982, s.87.

[31] *The Gas Float Whitton (No. 2)* [1896] P. 42, affd. [1897] A.C. 337.

[32] See above, n. 30.

[33] Civil Aviation Act 1982, s.87.

British ship anywhere, or from a foreign ship in British waters.[34] Life salvage is payable by the owner of the aircraft or vessel from which the lives were salved.

(c) *The Claimant must Fall within One of the Recognised Categories of Salvors*

There are two recognised categories of salvors, namely, those who are entitled to reward by reason of their ownership of the salving vessel, and those who are so entitled by having personally rendered salvage services. The first category is not limited to the true owner or owners of the salving vessel; for sometimes a charterer is *pro hac vice* owner in respect of salvage, in which event it will be he, and not the true owner, who is entitled to the reward. A charterer is, however, only *pro hac vice* owner where he is rendered so by the terms of the charter,[35] or where the charter is by demise.[36] In the second category of salvors, the usual claimants are the master and crew of the salving vessel; but anybody who has personally rendered salvage services may claim.

No claim can, however, be made by the owner of the salving vessel against a salved vessel of which he is also owner; though he can claim against cargo carried on his own vessel, unless he would, but for the salvage services, have been liable to the cargo for loss or damage which would have been caused by the danger so averted.[37] The crew of a salving vessel can claim salvage against a salved vessel in the ownership of their employers,[38] unless their services were such that they were bound to perform them under their contract of employment.[39]

(d) *The Services must have been Rendered Voluntarily*

In the context of salvage, the requirement of voluntariness means that the salvor's actions must neither fall within the scope of a pre-existing duty owed by him to the owner of the salved property, nor have been undertaken for his own self-preservation. A person bound by duty should not, and a person in personal danger will not, need the bait of a prospective award to induce him to intervene; and nobody deserves any special reward merely for carrying out his own duty or for performing actions for his own benefit which incidentally have benefited another.

The pre-existing duty may have been undertaken by contract, or it may have fallen within the salvor's official duties, or have been imposed by general law[40] or by custom. The general principle is that, where the salvor acted under any such pre-existing duty, he is only entitled to receive a salvage award if his

---

[34] Merchant Shipping Act 1894, s.544(1).
[35] *The Scout* (1872) L.R. 3 A. & E. 512, 515, *per* Sir Robert Phillimore.
[36] *Elliott Steam Tug Co.* v. *Admiralty Commissioners* [1921] 1 A.C. 137.
[37] *The Glenfruin* (1885) 10 P.D. 103; *cf.* see below, pp. 392–393.
[38] *The Sappho* (1871) L.R. 3 P.C. 690.
[39] *The Maria Jane* (1850) 14 Jur. 857.
[40] Certain statutory duties, which require masters of vessels to go to the assistance of other vessels in distress, exceptionally do not affect the right to salvage; see Merchant Shipping Act 1894, s.422, as amended; Maritime Conventions Act 1911, s.6; Merchant Shipping (Safety Convention) Act 1949, s.22.

services went beyond the ordinary scope of his duty. So, for example, to entitle a pilot on board the salved vessel to receive a salvage reward, he must show that the vessel was in such distress as to "call upon him to run such unusual danger, or incur such unusual responsibility, or exercise such unusual skill, or perform such an unusual kind of service, as to make it unfair and unjust that he should be paid otherwise than upon the terms of salvage reward."[41] Similarly, where there is a pre-existing towage contract, an award of salvage will be justified "if the services rendered are beyond what can be reasonably supposed to have been contemplated by the parties entering into such a contract."[42] This principle has been applied to many different classes of people,[43] including foyboatmen,[44] harbourmasters,[45] and various officials. One effect of the principle is that the crew of the salved vessel are debarred from recovering salvage, unless they rendered salvage services after their contracts of service had already been determined[46]; for the crew of a ship "are to be taken as pledging the last ounce of strength and service to their ship when they sign their articles and enter upon the voyage."[47] Officers and men of the Royal Navy can recover no reward for matters within their ordinary duties, such as, for example, repressing mutinies on vessels,[48] or protecting ships or cargo from pirates[49]; moreover, the final adjudication of any salvage to the commander or crew or part of the crew of any of Her Majesty's ships is subject to the consent of the Admiralty to the prosecution of the claim.[50] The crews of lifeboats, which are provided by the Royal National Life-Boat Institution for the saving of life, are only permitted by the Institution's regulations to intervene to salve property if other craft are not available or, if available, are inadequate for the purpose. If a salvage award is made in favour of a lifeboat crew, the Institution will have a first charge on the award for expenses involved in launching the boat, etc., in the cost of stores used, and in any repairs rendered necessary by the intervention.[51]

A person who has rendered salvage services for his own preservation will ordinarily have been on board the salved ship. If he was a member of the crew of that ship, he will have no right to salvage because he was under a duty to

---

[41] *Akerblom* v. *Price, Potter, Walker & Co.* (1881) 7 Q.B.D. 129, 135, *per* Brett L.J.; see also *The Driade* [1959] 2 Lloyd's Rep. 311.

[42] *Five Steel Barges* (1890) 15 P.D. 142, 144, *per* Sir James Hannen.

[43] Its application in the case of ships' agents has been unusually lenient; see Kennedy, *op. cit.* pp. 66–74, and cases there cited.

[44] *The Macgregor Laird* [1953] 2 Lloyd's Rep. 259; *The Southwark* [1962] 2 Lloyd's Rep. 62.

[45] *The Corcrest* (1946) 80 Ll.L.R. 78.

[46] *e.g.* by being discharged by the master (see *The Warrior* (1862) Lush. 476), or by the proper abandonment of the ship at sea (see *The Florence* (1852) 16 Jur. 572).

[47] *The Albionic* (1941) 70 Ll.L.R. 257, 263, *per* Langton J.

[48] *The Francis and Eliza* (1816) 2 Dods. 115.

[49] *The Cargo ex Ulysses* (1888) 13 P.D. 205, 208, *per* Sir James Hannen.

[50] Merchant Shipping Act 1894, s.557(1). Where salvage services have been rendered by or on behalf of the Crown, the Crown is entitled to claim salvage in respect of those services to the same extent as any other salvor; see the Crown Proceedings Act 1947, s.8(2).

[51] For examples of awards to lifeboatmen, see *The Harold Brown and The S.H.M.I.* [1959] 2 Lloyd's Rep. 187, and *The Boston Lincoln* [1980] 1 Lloyd's Rep. 481.

assist. If he was a passenger, he will not be entitled to a reward[52] unless he rendered some exceptional service.[53]

(e) *There must have been a Danger at Sea from which the Salved Property or Lives were Saved*

It is this element of danger which gives rise to the necessity which is the foundation of all salvage claims. But in the context of salvage the test of what constitutes danger is probably not so stringent as in general average.[54] Salvage will be awarded in a case "in which there was no immediate risk, no immediate danger; but there was a possible contingency that serious consequences might have ensued."[55] It has been suggested that an appropriate test is that the danger must have been:

> "so much a just cause of present apprehension, that, in order to escape out of it or to avoid it (as the case may be) no reasonably prudent and skilful seaman [or person in charge of an aircraft] in charge of the venture would refuse the salvor's help if it were offered to him upon the condition of his paying for it the salvor's reward."[56]

As in general average, however, the danger must have in fact existed; a supposed, but non-existent, danger will not found a salvage award.[57]

(f) *The Services Must have Achieved some Success*

It is essential to an award of salvage that some part at least of the property in danger should in fact be saved.[58] The salvor, who takes the risk that he will receive nothing if nothing is saved, has the corresponding opportunity of gaining a substantial reward if his efforts are successful. This reward is payable by the owner of the salved property because he has been benefited by the salvor's services. In the words of Dr. Lushington[59]:

> "I apprehend that, upon general principles, a mere attempt to save the vessel and cargo, however meritorious that attempt may be, or whatever degree of risk or danger may have been incurred, if unsuccessful, can

---

[52] *The Branston* (1826) 2 Hag.Adm.3n.; *The Vrede* (1861) Lush. 322.

[53] *Newman* v. *Walters* (1804) 3 Bos. & P. 612.

[54] For the test in general average, see above, p. 337. Nonetheless there must be a true necessity: see *Industrie Chimiche Italia Centrale and Cerealfin S.A.* v. *Tsavliris (Alexander G.) Maritime Co.* [1990] 1 Lloyd's Rep. 516, C.A.

[55] *The Ella Constance* (1864) 33 L.J.Adm. 189, 193, *per* Dr. Lushington. A particularly generous view is taken in cases of towage; see *Troilus (Cargo Owners)* v. *Glenogle (Owners, Master and Crew)* [1951] A.C. 820.

[56] Kennedy, *op. cit.* p. 14. See also Brice, *op. cit.* §§ 15 *et seq.*

[57] *The British Inventor* (1933) 45 Ll.L.R. 263.

[58] *The Renpor* (1883) 8 P.D. 115. To save a vessel from one danger only to leave her exposed to another equivalent danger does not, however, constitute success in this context: see *The Melanie (Owners)* v. *The San Onofre (Owners)* [1925] A.C. 246.

[59] *The Zephyrus* (1842) 1 W.Rob. 329, 330–331.

never be considered in this court as furnishing any title to a salvage reward. The reason is obvious, *viz.* that salvage reward is for benefits actually conferred, not for a service attempted to be rendered."

If, however, some part of the property in danger is saved, every person who contributed to the saving of the property will be entitled to receive a reward, even though his own efforts would not, without assistance from others, have been successful.[60]

(g) *The Claimant Must not have been at Fault*

Where the salvage services were made necessary by the claimant's fault

It has been held that, where salvage services to ship A were made necessary by the fault of ship B, not merely those members of the crew of ship B who were actually at fault, but also the remaining members of the crew[61] and, indeed, the owners of ship B[62] are precluded from recovering reward for salvage services rendered to ship A by them or their vessel consequent upon the faulty action. The foundation of this rule has been said to be the principle that no man should profit from his own wrong[63]; and the owners of the vessel at fault have been held to be precluded from recovering any reward because the fault was committed by persons for whom they were vicariously responsible.[64]

Nevertheless, in the leading case of *Beaverford* v. *The Kafiristan*,[65] the House of Lords held that the fact that salvage services to ship A were rendered necessary by the fault of ship B would not prevent the owners of ship C, which had rendered salvage services, from recovering reward, even though the owners of ship C were also the owners of ship B. It is obviously difficult, on principle, to reconcile this decision with the earlier cases in which owners were unable to recover because of their vicarious responsibility for those at fault; for the owners of ship C must have been vicariously responsible for the fault of their servants on ship B, and yet were able to recover. Moreover, the manner in which Lord Wright, who delivered the principal speech, approached the problem indicated that he had serious doubts as to the correctness of the earlier cases. He said[66]:

> "... The maritime law of salvage is based on principles of equity. There does not seem to be any reason in equity why the salved vessel ... should not pay the appropriate salvage remuneration merely because the salving vessel belongs to the same owners as the other colliding vessel. That fact seems to be irrelevant so far as concerns the usefulness and meritorious character of the actual services rendered.

---

[60] *The Jonge Bastiaan* (1804) 5 C.Rob. 322.
[61] *The Duc d'Aumale (No. 2)* [1904] P. 60.
[62] *Ibid.*
[63] *The Cargo ex Capella* (1867) L.R. 1 A. & E. 356, 357, *per* Dr. Lushington.
[64] *The Duc d'Aumale (No. 2)* [1904] P. 60.
[65] [1938] A.C. 136, applying *The Glengaber* (1872) L.R. 3 A. & E. 534.
[66] [1938] A.C. 136, 147–149.

... The rubric 'that no man can profit by his own wrong' ... in my opinion is wholly inapplicable. The claim to salvage is not based on the fact that the *Empress of Britain* was guilty of negligent navigation. It is based on a separate fact, that the *Beaverford* rendered salvage services. It is for these meritorious services and not for the negligence of the crew of the *Empress of Britain* that the appellants claim the right to have salvage awarded. They are not seeking to profit by their own wrong, for which in the final account they will make the appropriate compensation by, among other things, bearing their proper share of the salvage award."

He went on to declare[67] that, even "if the rule laid down in *Cargo ex Capella*[68] is at all sound, it is at any rate excluded where the ship which is the instrument of the salvage is a different ship from that which is the instrument of the negligent collision."

It follows that, in the light of Lord Wright's reasoning, the earlier cases may yet be overruled, despite the long period for which they have been accepted as good law. Moreover, despite the parallel with general average,[69] it cannot, at least in ordinary cases, be accepted that the claimant's claim should be barred on principles of circuity of action, even where the claimant vessel was solely to blame.[70] Circuity of action "can only be pleaded when the rights of the litigants are such that the defendants would be entitled to recover back from the plaintiffs the same amount of damages which the plaintiffs sought to recover from the defendants"[71]; and where, as will usually be the case, the wrongdoing vessel is able to limit her liability for her wrongdoing,[72] the principle of circuity of action cannot have the effect of altogether defeating that vessel's claim to salvage.

Where the salvors were guilty of fault after rendering the salvage services

Where, after rendering the salvage services, the salvors have been guilty of wilful or criminal misconduct, as, for example, where they have stolen part of the salved property,[73] or where they have wrongfully prevented the master and crew of the salved vessel from returning on board,[74] they will be deprived of any right to reward.[75] They may also lose their right to reward if, by their subsequent gross negligence, they bring the salved vessel into danger at least as great as that she was saved from[76]; but where the salvors' negligence or

---

[67] [1938] A.C. 136, 149.
[68] [1867] L.R. 1 A. & E. 356; see above, n. 63.
[69] *Cf.* see above, pp. 340–341.
[70] *The Susan V. Luckenbach* v. *Admiralty Commissioners* [1951] P. 197.
[71] *The Kafiriston* [1937] P. 63, 69, *per* Bucknill J., cited with approval by the Court of Appeal in *The Susan V. Luckenbach* v. *Admiralty Commissioners* [1951] P. 197, 203.
[72] Under s.503 of the Merchant Shipping Act 1894.
[73] *The Kedah* (1948) 81 Ll.L.R. 217.
[74] *The Capella* [1892] P. 70.
[75] They may also be deprived of their right to reward if they have wrongfully dispossessed earlier salvors; see Kennedy, *op. cit.* pp. 145–148, and cases there cited, and Brice, *op. cit.* §§ 176 *et seq.*
[76] *The Duke of Manchester* (1846) 2 W.Rob. 470; affd. (1847) 6 Moo.P.C. 90.

misconduct is not of a serious nature, they will not be deprived of all right to reward,[77] unless the loss arising from the negligence or misconduct is equal to or exceeds the potential loss from which the salved property was rescued.[78] Moreover, the owners are entitled to maintain an action for negligence against the salvors by way of counter-claim and are not restricted to setting off their loss against the amount of any salvage award.[79]

In *The St. Blane*,[80] Brandon J. formulated the following principles as governing "the general approach of the Court to charges of negligence against persons who render or try to render assistance at sea":

> "As to this, it is well established that the Court takes a lenient view of the conduct of salvors and would-be salvors, and is slow to find that those who try their best, in good faith, to save life or property in peril at sea, and make mistakes or errors of judgment in doing so, have been guilty of negligence. Nevertheless it is not in doubt that the Court may, in a proper case, after making all allowances, find negligence against salvors and, having done so, award damages against them in respect of it. *The Alenquer*, [1955] 1 Lloyd's Rep. 101; [1955] 1 W.L.R. 263; *The Tojo Maru*, [1972] A.C. 242; [1971] 1 Lloyd's Rep. 341. In deciding such matters the Court looks at all the circumstances of the case, including the status of the salvors—whether amateur or professional—and the question whether they have acted at request or on their own initiative. This principle of the lenient approach to mistakes is an important one. It derives from the basic policy of the law relating to salvage services, which is always to encourage, rather than discourage, the rendering of such services. The principle is especially important in cases involving life salvage, where its application demands that salvors should not in general be criticised if, faced with an actual or potential conflict between saving life on the one hand, and preserving property on the other, they err on the side of the former at the expense of the latter. I approach the charges of negligence in this case in the light of the principle of leniency stated above."

(h) *The Services Must not have been Rendered Against the Owner's Will*

The services must not have been rendered against the will of the owner of the thing in danger, or of his representative (usually the master of the ship in danger),[81] unless the owner or his representative is guilty of unreasonable disregard to the safety of the ship or other property in his charge.[82]

---

[77] *The Atlas* (1862) Lush. 518, 528, *per* Sir John Coleridge. The authorities are fully discussed in *The Tojo Maru* [1972] A.C. 242.

[78] *The Yan-Yean* (1883) 8 P.D. 147.

[79] *The Tojo Maru* [1972] A.C. 242.

[80] [1974] 1 Lloyd's Rep. 557, 560–561.

[81] *The Black Boy* (1837) 3 Hag.Adm. 386n.; *The Barefoot* (1850) 14 Jur. 841; *The Samuel* (1851) 15 Jur. 407.

[82] *The Kangaroo* [1918] P. 327. *Cf.* the cases at common law where services are rendered against the will of the defendant, and yet there is a right to reimbursement; see above, pp. 376 *et seq.*

3. THE AWARD

(a) *Assessment of the Award*

The amount of the salvage award[83] may be fixed by agreement. Such an agreement may, however, be set aside on the grounds that it is inequitable,[84] and it may be inequitable either because the agreed sum is exorbitantly high or because it is inadequate. But the agreement will, if it is not inequitable or otherwise liable to be avoided,[85] be enforced; the mere fact that the court might have awarded a rather different sum, whether higher or lower, than the sum agreed will not prevent the court from upholding the agreement.[86]

Where there is no enforceable agreement as to the amount of the salvage award, assessment of the award is a matter for the court's discretion. In the words of Dr. Lushington[87]: "The amount of salvage reward due is not to be determined by any rules; it is a matter of discretion, and probably in this, or in any other case, no two tribunals would agree."

In exercising this discretion, the court is not concerned to calculate reasonable remuneration for work done, as is done in *quantum meruit* claims. The court's task is to assess the amount of a reward which will, in the interests of public policy, encourage others to act as salvors, but which at the same time will not bear too harshly on the owners of the salved property. In *The Telemachus*, Willmer J. stated "the underlying principle upon which all awards of salvage must be based" as follows[88]:

> "I have to arrive at such an award as will fairly compensate the master and crew of the salving vessel, without injustice to the salved interests, and such an award as will, in the interests of public policy, encourage other mariners in like circumstances to perform like services."

It is usually said that an award will not be made of more than half the value of the property salved. Generally, this is true, and on occasions the award may be much less than half. But there are circumstances in which an award of more than half may be made,[89] as, for example, where the property is derelict; or where the salvors have rendered services which are particularly deserving of high reward; or where the value of the salved property is very low. Thus, in *The Boiler Ex Elephant*,[90] five men found a derelict marine boiler from the *S.S. Elephant* (which had been lost with all hands five years before) floating on the

---

[83] See *The Teh Hu* [1970] P. 106; but *cf. Jugoslovenska Oceanska Plovidba* v. *Castle Investment Co. Inc.* [1974] Q.B. 292.

[84] See above, pp. 297–298.

[85] *e.g.* for misrepresentation or non-disclosure. For non-disclosure avoiding salvage agreements, see above, p. 195.

[86] *The Africa* (1880) 5 P.D. 192, 196, *per* Sir Robert Phillimore.

[87] *The Cuba* (1860) Lush. 14, 15.

[88] [1957] P. 47, 49.

[89] Until the turn of the 19th century, the salvor's only remedy was *in rem* against the vessel saved. "This itself disabled him from recovering more than its value": *The Tojo Maru* [1972] A.C. 242, 293, *per* Lord Diplock.

[90] (1891) 64 L.T. 543.

high seas about three miles off Eastbourne. With some difficulty they succeeded in towing it ashore and, with the aid of men and horses, for whose
assistance they paid £10, they hauled it up the beach above the high-water
mark. The proceeds of sale of the boiler were only £58 3s. 4d. and the five
salvors were awarded a sum of £50 with costs. It is significant that, in that case,
nobody appeared to defend the action, which is another factor tending to
increase the amount of the award. But the court will never make an award
amounting to the whole value of the salved property, unless the parties fix in
advance a sum of salvage remuneration greater than the salvaged fund.[91]

The circumstances which are material to the assessment of a salvage award
are classified as follows in *Kennedy on Civil Salvage*[92]:

> "A. As regards the salved property:
>> (1) The degree of danger, if any, to human life.
>> (2) The degree of danger to the property.
>> (3) The value of the property as salved.
>
> B. As regards the salvors:
>> (1) The degree of danger, if any, to human life.
>> (2) The salvors' (a) classification, (b) skill and (c) conduct.
>> (3) The degree of danger, if any, to property employed in the salvage
>>   service and its value.
>> (4) The (a) time occupied and (b) work done in the performance of the
>>   salvage service.
>> (5) Responsibilities incurred in the performance of the salvage service,
>>   such, *e.g.* as risk to the insurance, and liability to passengers or
>>   freighters through deviation or delay.
>> (6) Loss or expense incurred in the performance of the salvage service,
>>   such, *e.g.* as detention, loss of profitable trade, repair of damage
>>   caused to ship, boats, or gear, fuel consumed, etc."

But, as Kennedy goes on to observe,[93] there has been considerable difference of
opinion as to the weight to be given to these various circumstances. It is,
however, at least "clear that the court is . . . bound to take into special consideration the salvation of human life, and to give a corresponding award"[94]; and the
same applies where lives on board the salving vessel are endangered.[95]

A case examplifying the problems which may face a court when assessing a
salvage award is *The Queen Elizabeth*.[96] In that case Willmer J. had to assess an

---

[91] *The Lyrma (No. 2)* [1978] 2 Lloyd's Rep. 30, 33, *per* Brandon J. But see above p. 395.
[92] At pp. 458–459. This classification received the judicial approval of Lord Merriman P. in *The
Bosworth (No. 1)* [1959] 2 Lloyd's Rep. 511, 526. There is a conflict of judicial opinion whether
the incidence of taxation should be taken into account when assessing an award: see *The
Telemachus* [1957] P. 47; *The Makedonia* [1958] 1 Q.B. 365; *The Frisia* [1960] 1 Lloyd's Rep. 90.
In practice it is not: see Brice, *op. cit.* § 155.
[93] At pp. 174–176.
[94] *The Bartley* (1857) Swab. 198, 199, *per* Dr. Lushington.
[95] *The Thomas Fielden* (1862) 32 L.J.Adm. 61, 62, *per* Dr. Lushington.
[96] (1949) 82 Ll.L.R. 803. For other awards, see *The Orelia* [1958] 1 Lloyd's Rep. 441 (towage); *The
Amity* [1959] 1 Lloyd's Rep. 328 (towage); *The Bosworth (No. 1)* [1960] 1 Lloyd's Rep. 163

award for services rendered by tugs to a very large ship of exceptional value. The services were rendered when *The Queen Elizabeth* went aground outside Southampton Water. The sound value of the vessel was £6,000,000; making allowance for the cost of repairs and for the value of cargo on board, the salved value of ship and cargo was £6,208,000. Willmer J. made an award of £43,500 in all, in respect of the 12 tugs represented before him. He took into account matters such as that, although the services only lasted about a day, they were skilfully and efficiently rendered; that the danger to the ship was continuous and increasing, and there was a chance, though very remote, of total loss; and that it was essential to the owners of the ship that she should be refloated as soon as possible. On the exceptionally high value of the salved property, he had this to say[97]:

> "I am not saying that you can measure salvage awards as sums in arithmetical proportion in relation to the salved property when you have values of the magnitude that you have in this case, but equally it would not, I think, be right to say that, where you have a value of this size, the addition of a few millions or the subtraction of a few millions would make no difference whatsoever. So long as even an outside chance of anything in the nature of total loss remains, then I think that the increase of value must involve some, although possibly not great, increase in the salved award over and above what might have been awarded had the value been much smaller."

The court has power to award interest on a salvage award. A claim for salvage is a claim for the recovery of a debt within the Law Reform (Miscellaneous Provisions) Act 1934, section 3(1).[98]

(b) *Apportionment of the Award among Salvors*

Like the amount of the award, the apportionment of the award among the salvors can be regulated by agreement,[99] though again such an agreement may be set aside if it is inequitable.[1] If, however, no valid agreement regulating apportionment has been entered into, the court has power to apportion the award.[2] Section 556 of the Merchant Shipping Act 1894 provides as follows:

(vessel listing, crew taken off and vessel towed into port); *The Santa Alicia and the Gorm* [1961] 2 Lloyd's Rep. 20 (towage); and *The Southwark* [1962] 2 Lloyd's Rep. 62 (vessel drifting, towed into berth); *The Evaine* [1966] 2 Lloyd's Rep. 413 (yacht on fire, award increased on appeal); *The Boston Lincoln* [1980] 1 Lloyd's Rep. 481 (lifeboat refloats the casualty).

[97] (1949) 82 Ll.L.Rep. 803, 821.

[98] *The Aldora* [1975] Q.B. 748; *The Rilland* [1979] 1 Lloyd's Rep. 455; *The Ilo* [1982] 1 Lloyd's Rep. 39; *The Helenus and Montagua* [1982] 2 Lloyd's Rep. 261.

[99] See Brice, *op. cit.* Chap. 5.

[1] *The Enchantress* (1860) Lush. 93; see above, pp. 297–298.

[2] For examples, see *The New Australia* [1958] 2 Lloyd's Rep. 35; *The Driade* [1959] 2 Lloyd's Rep. 311; *The Frisia* [1960] 1 Lloyd's Rep. 90. The court will take into account the fact that the salvage services may have removed the prospect of the owner of the salvaged property being subject to the claims of third parties: see Brice, *op. cit.* §§ 314–318.

Whenever the aggregate amount of salvage payable in respect of salvage services rendered in the United Kingdom has been finally ascertained, and exceeds two hundred pounds, and whenever the aggregate amount of salvage payable in respect of salvage services rendered elsewhere has been finally ascertained, whatever that amount may be, then, if any delay or dispute arises as to the apportionment thereof, any court having Admiralty jurisdiction may cause the same to be apportioned amongst the persons entitled thereto in such manner as it thinks just. . . .

It is clear from the wording of the section that apportionment is a matter for the court's discretion. Nevertheless, there are certain accepted methods of apportionment which are generally acted upon. Thus, as between owner, master and crew of the salving vessel, it is usual to award three-quarters to the owner; to award one-third of what remains to the master; and to divide the remainder rateably among the crew.[3] If more than one salving vessel is involved, then in apportioning the award between them the court will pay regard to much the same circumstances as it considers when assessing the amount of the award[4]; but the ship which was first on the scene may receive a more generous award than one which arrived later.

(c) *Contribution to Payment of the Award by Those Interested in the Salved Property*

The liability to pay salvage falls on every person interested in the property benefited by the salvage services[5]; but in the case of life salvage, the reward is payable not by those whose lives have been saved but by the owners of the vessel, cargo or apparel preserved.[6]

Each interest, therefore, contributes rateably towards the payment of the reward, the amount of each interest's contribution being dependent on the value of the property saved.[7] In the absence of agreement to the contrary, no one interest is liable for more than its rateable proportion of the reward.[8] Accordingly, if a salvor proceeds only against one of the salved interests, he can recover from that interest only the proportion of the salvage reward for which it is liable.[9]

The ship may, however, undertake by contract an obligation to the salvor to pay the reward in full. Indeed, if the owner or the master of the ship enters into a valid salvage agreement in which the amount of the reward is fixed, the ship will become liable to the salvor for the whole reward so fixed.[10] If the ship is

---

[3] There is no "general rule" that the master is entitled to a third; he may be awarded more: *The Golden Falcon* [1990] 2 Lloyd's Rep. 366.

[4] See above, pp. 395–397.

[5] *The Fusilier* (1865) B. & L. 341, 352, *per* Lord Chelmsford; *Five Steel Barges* (1890) 15 P.D. 142.

[6] Merchant Shipping Act 1894, s.544(1).

[7] *The Longford* (1881) 6 P.D. 60.

[8] If there is no such agreement, the rule should not be departed from: see *The M. Vatan* [1990] 1 Lloyd's Rep. 336.

[9] *The Mary Pleasants* (1857) Swab. 224.

[10] *The Cumbrian* (1887) 6 Asp.Mar.Law Cas. 151.

liable for the whole reward, and the expenditure is incurred for the common safety of ship and other interests, the ship should be entitled to recover from those other interests their share of the salvage reward by way of general average contribution,[11] and the shipowners can exercise their lien on the cargo to secure payment of its contribution.[12] But the master of a ship has no implied authority to bind cargo by contract; accordingly, if a contract entered into by the master with salvors after the ship has been brought to safety specifies the salvage reward, that sum is not binding on the cargo-owners as the sum to which they must contribute in general average.[13] In any event, the ship's claim to general average contribution may be barred, as, for example, where the salvage services were rendered necessary by the actionable fault of the shipowner or of those for whom he is responsible,[14] or where the cargo, although saved, is not benefited thereby, as may occur if the freight payable at the destination is greater than the value of the cargo saved.[15]

4. REMEDIES

A salvor's usual and most effective remedy is his maritime lien on the property salved, including freight if this has been saved. The lien arises as soon as the salvage services have been rendered, and ranks before all previous liens on the property salved. In furtherance of this lien, the court has power to arrest the property and, if necessary, sell it to raise the funds needed to satisfy the award; but often an arrest is avoided by an undertaking by those interested in the property to give security.[16]

In addition to his lien, a salvor has the right to proceed *in personam*,[17] which he may wish to do if the salved property has not been available for arrest within the jurisdiction.[18] A salvor may also seek a "Mareva" injunction against the assets within the jurisdiction of the owner of the salved property.[19]

---

[11] By r. 44A of the Rules of Practice of the Association of Average Adjusters, expenses for salvage services rendered by or accepted under agreement shall in practice be treated as general average, provided that such expenses were incurred for the common safety within the meaning of r. A of the York-Antwerp Rules. In the absence of a right to a general average contribution, or of express authority from cargo to incur the expenditure, a ship which pays cargo's share of salvage reward should, in principle, have no right to contribution from cargo, because ship and cargo are not liable *in solidum*: see above, Chap. 12. But see Kennedy, *op. cit.* pp. 272–273; *The Makedonia* [1962] 1 Lloyd's Rep. 316, 341, *per* Hewson J.

[12] *The Prinz Helrich* (1888) 13 P.D. 31, 34, *per* Butt J.

[13] *Anderson Tritton & Co.* v. *Ocean S.S. Co.* (1884) 10 App.Cas. 107.

[14] *The Ettrick* (1881) 6 P.D. 127; see above, pp. 392–393.

[15] *Cox* v. *May* (1815) 4 M. & S. 152.

[16] See also *The Span Terza* [1982] 1 Lloyd's Rep. 225, (C.A.); [1984] 1 W.L.R. 27, (H.L.).

[17] *Five Steel Barges* (1890) 15 P.D. 142. For limitations on the right to proceed in *personam*, see Brice, *op. cit.* §§ 93, 101.

[18] By s.3(4) of the Administration of Justice Act 1956 (as amended) other ships in the same ownership as the salved vessel may be arrested in order to found jurisdiction and obtain security.

[19] Supreme Court Act 1981, s.37.

D. INEFFECTIVE TRANSACTIONS

CHAPTER 17

INTRODUCTION[1]

IN this Part we shall consider the circumstances in which restitution may be granted in respect of benefits conferred under ineffective transactions.

Transactions may be or become ineffective for a variety of reasons. But the reason why the courts will award restitution is in each case fundamentally the same, namely, that the plaintiff's expectations have not been fulfilled.[2] In certain cases, however, special rules apply, particularly in cases where benefits have been conferred under contracts or trusts rendered ineffective by illegality, or under contracts rendered ineffective by incapacity. Sometimes the position is affected by statute: indeed, the law relating to the recovery of benefits conferred under contracts thereafter frustrated is, subject to specified exceptions, now governed by the Law Reform (Frustrated Contracts) Act 1943.

In cases of ineffective contracts, the applicable restitutionary principles may depend on whether the benefit conferred takes the form of money, or of services or goods. The legacy of the old forms of action is that different juristic concepts determine whether a restitutionary claim should succeed. The receipt of money is an enrichment; the receipt of services may or may not be so. In a money claim the payer claims the payment of a sum paid under the ineffective contract; in a claim for services rendered, which cannot be restored, he claims not the return of the benefit but payment for it. The principles governing claims for goods delivered are generally similar to those governing claims for services rendered.[3-4] The nature of the benefit may also determine the ground of the restitutionary claim.

Money paid

If money has been paid under a contract which is or becomes ineffective, the recipient is evidently enriched. It is a distinct question whether that enrichment is an *unjust* enrichment. In some of the situations discussed in this Part the basis of the restitutionary claim is that money has been paid under a

---

[1] For a valuable comparative law survey, see Izhak Englard, *Restitution of Benefits Conferred Without Obligation, Restitution—Unjust Enrichment and Negotiorum Gestio*, Vol. X of the *International Encyclopedia of Comparative Law.*

[2] *Re Ames' Settlement* [1946] Ch. 217, where a settlement was made in consideration of a marriage, subsequently declared void, Vaisey J. (at p. 223) described the case as "a simple case of money paid on a consideration which failed,": see below, Chap. 26, p. 565.

[3-4] But see *Free Acceptance and the Law of Restitution* (1988) 104 L.Q.R. 576 [Burrows].

mistake, for example, both the payer and the recipient mistakenly thinking that a valid contract was in existence or would come into existence.

In most of the situations, however, the ground of recovery is that the expected return for the payment, or consideration, as it is confusingly called, has failed. The rule at common law is that the plaintiff can only recover his money if the consideration for his payment has totally failed.[5] In this context, "when one is considering the law of failure of consideration and of the quasi-contractual right to recover money on that ground, it is, generally speaking, not the promise which is referred to as the consideration, but the performance of the promise. The money was paid to secure performance and, if performance fails, the inducement which brought about the payment is not fulfilled."[6] Where the payment is made under a contract, therefore, a distinction must be drawn between the consideration which moved from the defendant to support the plaintiff's contractual promise, and the consideration which the plaintiff expected to receive for his contractual performance, though these may coincide in the case of a contract founded upon an executed consideration.

The court looks to the terms of the contract to determine whether a party has or has not received from the other party any part of the bargained for performance. If the contract is ineffective the inquiry is critical, for the payer's only claim may be in restitution. In such a case, if it is held that there is no total failure of consideration, he may be without any remedy. This may persuade a court to construe an agreement narrowly. For example, in *Rover International Ltd.* v. *Cannon Film Sales Ltd.*,[7] the defendants had delivered films to the plaintiffs who had agreed to dub and distribute them. The plaintiffs made up front payments. The Court of Appeal held that the contract was void[8] and that the plaintiffs could recover these payments. In Kerr L.J.'s view, the agreed performance, the consideration, was the plaintiffs' opportunity to earn a substantial share of the receipts; and this consideration had totally failed.[9]

---

[5] *Fibrosa Spolka Akcyjna* v. *Fairbairn Lawson Combe Barbour Ltd.* [1943] A.C. 32, 49–50, *per* Viscount Simon, 54–55, *per* Lord Atkin: see below, pp. 408–409.

[6] *Fibrosa Spolka Akcyjna* v. *Fairbairn Lawson Combe Barbour Ltd.* [1943] A.C. 32, 48, *per* Viscount Simon: *The Julia* [1949] A.C. 293, 316, *per* Lord Simonds, 322–323, *per* Lord MacDermott. Cf. *McDonald* v. *Dennys Lascelles Ltd.* (1933) 48 C.L.R. 457, 477, *per* Dixon J. who explains the concept in terms of a payment which is conditional on the defendant performing his side of the bargain; see below, p. 430.

[7] [1989] 1 W.L.R. 912, C.A.: see below, pp. 542–544 for a full discussion.

[8] Rover was not incorporated at the date of the agreement: see below, p. 523.

[9] Both he and Dillon L.J. held that the money was recoverable, having been paid under a mistake of fact: see above Chap. 3 and see below p. 523. Dillon L.J. did not consider the question whether the money could be recovered on the ground that the consideration had wholly failed.

It is an over-simplification to say[10] that there can only be a total failure of consideration if the payer has received no benefit in return for his payment.[11] If the defendant is ready to perform his promise, then the consideration for the plaintiff's payment has not failed even though the contract is unenforceable by action and the plaintiff has not yet received any part of the defendant's bargained for performance.[11a] Again, there are cases where the payer has received a benefit under the ineffective contract, and yet has recovered his money on this ground.[12] Thus, where a buyer determines a contract of sale of goods in consequence of a defect in the seller's title, he can recover the price on grounds of total failure of consideration despite the benefit he has derived from the intermediate use of the chattel.[13] The principle underlying a case of this kind appears to be that, in such circumstances, the defect in the seller's title relieves the buyer from any obligation to restore the goods to the seller or to account to him for their use. In other cases, if the benefit received by the plaintiff under an ineffective transaction is of such a kind that he can and does restore it to the defendant, the plaintiff should be entitled to recover money paid by him under the transaction on the ground of total failure of consideration. Moreover, "[i]n circumstances where both parties have impliedly acknowledged that the consideration can be 'broken up' or apportioned in this way

---

[10] See, generally, below, pp. 420–422. In the anomalous case of *Linz* v. *Electric Wire Co. of Palestine Ltd.* [1948] A.C. 371, the Privy Council held that the purchaser of preference shares, the issue of which was alleged to have been *ultra vires* the defendant company, was unable, after she had parted with the shares to a third party for value, to "challenge the validity of the issue and, succeeding in that challenge, then claim that she received something of no value and that there was a total failure of consideration" (at p. 377, *per* Lord Simonds). But the fact that she had received value from a third party was surely irrelevant to the question whether she had received any consideration from the defendant company. In our view, unless the plaintiff had had some substantial intermediate enjoyment out of the shares which she could not restore, this was, assuming the issue to have been invalid, a clear case of total failure of consideration. It is, however, a different question whether the defendant company could have taken advantage of the payment which the plaintiff had received on the resale of the shares. If the plaintiff was not bound to restore that payment to the third party who had purchased the shares from her, the defendant company should, upon reimbursing the plaintiff, have been subrogated to the benefit of the resale price in the plaintiff's hands. If, on the other hand, the plaintiff was obliged to refund the resale price to the third party, and the defendant company (as appears to have been the case) had reimbursed the third party as a holder of the invalid shares, the defendant company should then have been subrogated to the benefit of the third party's right of action against the plaintiff, or should have taken an assignment of that right as a condition of reimbursement. *Cf. Re Bank of Hindustan* (1873) L.R. 15 Eq. 394; see below, p. 495.

[11] For an early example, see *Dutch* v. *Warren* (1720) 1 Str. 406 (and the fuller account given by Lord Mansfield in 2 Burr. at 1011).

[11a] *Thomas* v. *Brown* (1876) 1 Q.B.D. 714 (where the vendor was in breach, see below p. 474), discussed in Burrows, *The Law of Restitution*, pp. 257–258.

[12] *Towers* v. *Barrett* (1786) 1 T.R. 133, *semble*. But where the plaintiff has received all that he has contracted for, he should not be entitled to reopen the transaction and recover his money; see above, pp. 61–62.

[13] *Rowland* v. *Divall* [1923] 2 K.B. 500; see below, pp. 421–422; and *Rover International Ltd.* v. *Cannon Film Sales Ltd.* [1989] 1 W.L.R. 912, C.A.: see below, pp. 543–544.

[for example, where a loan agreement was severable], any rationale for adhering to the traditional rule requiring *total* failure of consideration disappears."[13a]

However, the benefit received by the plaintiff may be incapable of restoration. For even where the benefit received from the defendant consists of a thing, such as a chattel or land, which itself could be restored, the plaintiff is likely to have had some intermediate enjoyment or use of the thing and this he cannot restore.[14] Matters of this kind could easily have been dealt with if the common law had been prepared to make allowances and give credit to the defendant for things which could not be restored to him; but here, as elsewhere, the common law has set its face against apportionment.[15] This is regrettable, for the plaintiff may have no action on the contract or may recover only nominal damages for breach of contract.[16] To mitigate this strict common law rule, the legislature has on occasions, as in the case of frustration,[17] given the courts power to adjust the situation between the parties where there has been a partial failure of consideration.

Money is therefore recoverable only if there is a *total failure of consideration*. However it must be remembered that other principles of restitution must be observed. In particular, when money has been paid under a contract which was originally effective, that contract must be determined before the money is recoverable in restitution; if the contract is not brought to an end, the payer is restricted to his remedies under the contract which continues to govern the situation.[18] At one time, indeed, it was thought necessary that the contract should be rescinded *ab initio* before the payer could recover his money in restitution.[19] But harsh results followed, particularly in cases of frustrated contracts, where rescission *ab initio* was impossible; for there the payer had

---

[13a] *David Securities Pty. Ltd.* v. *Commonwealth Bank of Australia* (1992) 66 A.L.J.R. 768, 780. Similarly: if "counter-restitution is relatively simple . . . , insistence on total failure of consideration can be misleading or confusing": at p. 779.

[14] *Hunt* v. *Silk* (1804) 5 East 449; discussed see below, p. 420.

[15] *Fibrosa Spolka Akcyjna* v. *Fairbairn Lawson Combe Barbour Ltd.* [1943] A.C. 32, 49–50, *per* Viscount Simon; see below, pp. 408–409.

[16] The Law Commission, (*Report* No. 121, *Law of Contract; Pecuniary Restitution on Breach of Contract*, §§ 3.8–3.9), rejects its original tentative proposal (*Working Paper*, No. 65, §§ 51–56, 79(2)(9)) that a payer should be entitled to restitution of money paid, in excess of the value of the benefit which has been conferred on him by the party in breach. For a criticism of the Law Commission's second thoughts, see above, p. 40 and (1984) 47 M.L.R. 76 [Burrows]; Birks, *Introduction* pp. 259–264. See below, pp. 408–409, 417 *et seq.* for a further discussion. Both American and Canadian courts allow recovery if there has been a partial failure of consideration. The payer must, however, give credit for benefits received: see below p. 420, n. 93a.

[17] Law Reform (Frustrated Contracts) Act 1943; see below, p. 450.

[18] *Lipkin Gorman (A Firm)* v. *Karpnale Ltd.* [1991] 2 A.C. 548, 579, *per* Lord Goff; see below, Chap. 40. But where the contract is unenforceable, the plaintiff can have recourse to restitution (see *Scott* v. *Pattison* [1923] 2 K.B. 723; *Souch* v. *Strawbridge* (1846) 2 C.B. 808, 814–815, *per* Tindal C.J.); *Pavey & Matthews Pty. Ltd.* v. *Paul* (1987) 69 A.L.R. 577 (see above, p. 65 and below, p. 475); provided such recourse is not contrary to the policy of the statute which renders the contract unenforceable: see above, pp. 62 *et seq.*

[19] *Hunt* v. *Silk* (1804) 5 East 449; *Chandler* v. *Webster* [1904] 1 K.B. 493; *Rowland* v. *Divall* [1923] 2 K.B. 500, 503, *per* Bankes L.J.; see below, pp. 418 *et seq.*

usually no claim in damages, and if he could not recover his money in restitution he was left without a remedy. Today, however, it is accepted that money paid under an ineffective contract which has been brought to an end may be recoverable in restitution, even though the contract has not been rescinded *ab initio*.[20]

Services rendered

To obtain restitution for services rendered under an ineffective contract, the defendant must have gained a benefit, at the plaintiff's expense, which it is unjust for him to retain.

If the services have been conferred at the defendant's request or have been freely accepted by him, then he cannot deny that he has received a benefit.[21] The value of the benefit is normally the market price of the services rendered.[22] Such request or acceptance is usually present in cases of benefits conferred under ineffective contracts. But it may be lacking where benefits have been conferred under contracts void for mistake or for want of authority, or in anticipation of a contract which does not materialise. Nevertheless, the defendant may have been incontrovertibly benefited by the services which have been rendered.[23] The value of his incontrovertible benefit will depend on the particular facts.[24] For example, it may be the market value of the services or what he normally pays a third party to perform comparable services or the increased value of the property improved by the services.[25]

It is a distinct question whether, given that the defendant has gained a benefit, an enrichment, it would be *unjust* to require him to make restitution. In some of the situations discussed in this Part, the basis of the restitutionary claim will be that the plaintiff was mistaken. In others, the defendant will have freely accepted the services, with the knowledge that the plaintiff expected to be paid for them and in circumstances when it could not be said that he had acted officiously. But on occasions a restitutionary claim for services rendered has succeeded in circumstances where a plaintiff was not mistaken and where it was not possible, on the particular facts, to conclude that there had been a free acceptance of services. Such situations are exceptional. The courts have simply assumed that it was just that the defendant should make restitution.[26] Today

---

[20] *Fibrosa Spolka Akcynja* v. *Fairbairn Lawson Combe Barbour Ltd.* [1943] A.C. 32; *cf. Johnson* v. *Agnew* [1980] A.C. 367; *Hyundai Shipbuilding and Heavy Industries Ltd.* v. *Papadopoulos* [1980] 1 W.L.R. 1129; see below, p. 430.

[21] See above, pp. 18–22. The basis of this principle is that ordinarily, in the absence of request or acceptance of this kind, it would be unjust to impose liability on the recipient of services or goods which he had no opportunity to return.

[22] See above, p. 424. In some situations the contract price may form the ceiling of any award: see above, pp. 29–30. For problems arising under the Law Reform (Frustrated Contracts) Act 1943, see below, pp. 458–459.

[23] See above, pp. 22 *et seq.*

[24] See above, p. 30, n. 24.

[25] See above, p. 30, n. 25.

[26] *e.g.* see *Craven-Ellis* v. *Canons Ltd.* [1936] 2 K.B. 403; below, p. 478 for a full discussion.

the ground of the restitutionary claim may possibly be necessity, the unconscionability of the defendant's conduct or even failure of consideration.

There are limiting principles which may determine the success or failure of the restitutionary claim. If the benefit was conferred under a contract which was originally effective, that contract must be determined before the plaintiff can proceed in restitution.[27] Indeed, if he has an accrued right to payment under the contract, his appropriate course is to proceed on the contract for the sum due rather than to determine the contract and claim in restitution.[28] However, in cases concerned with services, as opposed to money, if the plaintiff has received any payment, it should only bar his claim in restitution if it constitutes payment in full, if it has been received by the plaintiff in full satisfaction of his claim, or if, by accepting it, he has waived his right to determine the contract and proceed in restitution.

Goods supplied

If the property in the goods has not passed to the recipient, the plaintiff should have recourse to the law of property for his remedies. Consequently, in cases of goods supplied, a restitutionary claim should be appropriate only if the property in the goods has passed to the recipient. In the case of ineffective transactions, the property in goods delivered will generally have passed to the recipient. If he has requested or freely accepted[29] the goods, then he has undoubtedly been benefited[30]; in the absence of a request or free acceptance, he may have been incontrovertibly benefited.[31]

The ground of the restitutionary claim will normally be, if goods have been delivered under an ineffective contract, mistake or free acceptance. Exceptionally, it may possibly be necessity, the unconscionability of the defendant's conduct or even failure of consideration.[32]

The plaintiff's claim may be defeated, however, by the application of limiting principles similar to those which govern restitutionary claims for services rendered.

A restitutionary claim for money paid, services rendered or goods delivered under an ineffective contract should normally be in principle, personal rather than proprietary. Under an ineffective contract the plaintiff will generally[33] be the defendant's unsecured creditor. For that reason he should not be granted a

---

[27] See above, pp. 45–46.
[28] See below, pp. 45–46.
[29] See above, pp. 26–27.
[30] In some cases his claim may be subject to the ceiling of the contract price: see above, pp. 29–30. For problems arising under the Law Reform (Frustrated Contracts) Act 1943: see below, pp. 458–459.
[31] See above, p. 22.
[32] See above, pp. 43–44.
[33] But in some cases property may not have passed because of the transferor's mistake as to the identity of the transferee; the transferor may then bring a pure proprietary claim: see above, Chap. 2.

proprietary claim[34]; otherwise he would be in a better position than the general creditors of the defendant who have likewise given him credit.[35]

Most of the restitutionary claims which are discussed in this Part arise from bargaining transactions which are or have become ineffective. Two Chapters concern restitutionary claims which cannot be so characterised. The subject-matter of Chapter 24 is claims against the Revenue or some other public authority arising from payments made in pursuance of an *ultra vires* demand, and that of Chapter 26 is the restitution of benefits conferred under trusts which fail wholly or in part.

We do not suggest that we have considered every kind of ineffective transaction. There may be other cases. For example, where goods are supplied under contracts of sale or return, the buyer may, if he decides in due time not to accept the goods, return them and recover from the seller any advance payment he has made[36]; and a vendor, who forfeits a purchaser's deposit because of the latter's default, may be required to pay his agent reasonable remuneration for services rendered even though the agent has no contractual claim to the commission.[37] Again, transactions may be determined by agreement, though here the parties will usually make express provision for restoration of benefits; but if necessary, restitution may, consistently with the agreement to determine the transaction, be awarded in respect of benefits conferred thereunder. Indeed, whenever money has been paid for a purpose which had not been fulfilled, it should be recoverable on grounds of total failure of consideration. This principle is wide enough to cover a situation where money is paid under an arrangement which is not a contract, where the parties did not intend to create a legal relationship and the payer did not receive his expected return.[38]

A more important omission is of the cases concerned with restitution of benefits conferred under contracts rescinded or set aside for mistake, misrepresentation, duress, or undue influence. As a matter of convenience, however, the principles upon which such benefits will be restored are considered elsewhere,[39] in the sections concerned with the circumstances under which contracts will be rescinded or set aside on these grounds. Such cases apart, however, we shall in this section consider the more important categories of ineffective transactions, and particularly those where special restitutionary problems are likely to arise. To these categories we will now turn.

---

[34] See above, p. 94.

[35] But see *Sinclair* v. *Brougham* [1914] A.C. 398, criticised above, pp. 84–85.

[36] *Towers* v. *Barrett* (1786) 1 T.R. 133. And *cf. Rose & Frank Co.* v. *J. R. Crompton & Bros. Ltd.* [1925] A.C. 445, *semble*; *Cam & Sons Pty. Ltd.* v. *Ramsay* (1960) 104 C.L.R. 247, 263, *per* McTiernan J.

[37] *Boots* v. *E. Christopher & Co.* [1952] 1 Q.B. 89, 98–99, *per* Denning L.J.

[38] See, *e.g.* the terms of the arrangement in *Jones* v. *Vernon's Pools Ltd.* [1938] 2 All E.R. 626; and see below, Chap. 17.

[39] See above, Chaps. 8–10.

CHAPTER 18

CONTRACTS DISCHARGED THROUGH BREACH OR FRUSTRATION

At common law the principles governing the restitution of benefits conferred under contracts discharged through frustration or breach were fundamentally similar. In cases of frustration, however, they have been modified and largely superseded by the Law Reform (Frustrated Contracts) Act 1943.[1] In cases of breach they still apply, as they do in the few cases of frustration excepted from the scope of the 1943 Act. To understand the modern law, however, it is first necessary to outline the common law principles which formerly applied to both groups of cases.

1. The Common Law Background

(a) *The Recovery of Money*

A party to a contract who brings it to an end on the grounds of the other party's breach can recover money paid thereunder only if he can show that there has been a total failure of consideration; so that if he receives any part of the benefit under the contract which he cannot restore he has no remedy in quasi-contract.[2] He can, however, always fall back on his alternative remedy in damages. The party in breach has generally neither power to determine the contract nor a right to recover damages, though he may have a right under the contract to recover a prepayment[3]; and, possibly, even a deposit made as a guarantee of performance.[4]

In cases of frustration, however, it was at one time held that money paid under the contract was irrecoverable in any event and that the loss must lie where it fell. This, the so-called rule in *Chandler* v. *Webster*,[5] rested on the misconception that there could be no total failure of consideration unless the

---

[1] Hereinafter referred to as the 1943 Act.
[2] For a full discussion of these common law principles, see above, Chap. 17 and below, pp. 407 *et seq.*
[3] *Dies* v. *British and International Mining and Finance Corporation* [1939] 1 K.B. 724: see below, p. 429.
[4] There is a very limited equitable jurisdiction to relieve against forfeiture: see below, pp. 433 *et seq.*
[5] [1904] Q.K.B. 493. The rule was first established in *Blakeley* v. *Muller & Co.* [1903] 2 K.B. 760n. See also *Civil Service Co-operative Society Ltd.* v. *General Steam Navigation Co.* [1903] 2 K.B. 756; *Krell* v. *Henry* [1903] 2 K.B. 740; *French Marine* v. *Compagnie Napolitaine* [1921] 2 A.C. 494. *Cf. Elliott* v. *Crutchley* [1904] 1 K.B. 565.

contract was void *ab initio*. Severely criticised by judge and jurist,[6] the fallacy underlying *Chandler* v. *Webster* was exposed in *Fibrosa Spolka Akcyjna* v. *Fairbairn Lawson Combe Barbour Ltd.*,[7] where the House of Lords overruled *Chandler* v. *Webster*, despite the fact that it had stood for 38 years and had previously received some measure of acceptance by the House.[8] In the *Fibrosa* case, the respondents in England had contracted in July 1939, to sell to the appellants in Poland a quantity of machinery for a sum of £4,800, of which the appellants made an advance payment of £1,000. The contract was frustrated by the outbreak of war before any of the machinery had been supplied. The appellants claimed to recover the £1,000 which they had paid in advance. The House of Lords held that they were entitled to recover the money as having been paid for a consideration which had wholly failed. As Viscount Simon said[9]:

> "... in the law relating to the formation of contract, the promise to do a thing may often be the consideration, but when one is considering the law of failure of consideration and of the quasi-contractual right to recover money on that ground, it is, generally speaking, not the promise which is referred to as the consideration, but the performance of the promise.... If this were not so, there could never be any recovery of money, for failure of consideration, by the payer of the money in return for a promise of future performance, yet there are endless examples which show that money can be recovered, as for a complete failure of consideration, in cases where the promise was given but could not be fulfilled."

The effect of the *Fibrosa* case was, therefore, that money paid under a contract thereafter frustrated was recoverable, though only if the consideration for the payment had wholly failed.[10] As we shall see,[11] however, the 1943 Act has allowed recovery in cases of partial failure of consideration.

---

[6] *Lloyd Royal Belge S.A.* v. *Stathatos* (1917) 33 T.L.R. 390, 392, *per* Atkin J.; *Russkoe* v. *Stirk* (1922) 10 Ll.L.R. 214, 217, *per* Atkin J.; *Cantiare Sane Rocco S.A.* v. *Clyde Shipbuilding & Engineering Co.* [1924] A.C. 236, 248, *per* Lord Dunedin, 258–259, *per* Lord Shaw; (1933) 46 Harv.L.R. 1281 [W. W. Buckland]; (1941) 5 M.L.R. 1, 7–9 [G. L. Williams]. The rule also conflicted with earlier authority: see *Knowles* v. *Bovill* (1870) 22 L.T. 70.

[7] [1943] A.C. 32.

[8] See *French Marine* v. *Compagnie Napolitaine* [1921] 2 A.C. 494.

[9] At p. 48. Viscount Simon here referred to Bullen & Leake's *Precedents of Pleading* (9th ed.), p. 263, and *Rugg* v. *Minett* (1809) 11 East 210. See also *Giles* v. *Edwards* (1797) 7 T.R. 181; *Nockels* v. *Crosby* (1825) 2 B. & C. 814; *Asphitel* v. *Sercombe* (1850) 5 Ex. 147; *Devaux* v. *Conolly* (1849) 8 C.B. 640; *Johnson* v. *Goslett* (1857) 3 C.B.(n.s.) 569; *Knowles* v. *Bovill* (1870) 22 L.T. 70; *Wilson* v. *Church* (1879) 13 Ch.D. 1; *National Bolivian Navigation Co.* v. *Wilson* (1880) 5 App.Cas. 176.

[10] *Cf.* an early group of frustration cases concerning apprentices and articled clerks, who sought to recover premiums in part or in full on the death or bankruptcy of their masters. After their period of apprenticeship or clerkship had begun, it was held that there could be no total failure of consideration, and therefore no recovery: see *Whincup* v. *Hughes* (1871) L.R. 6 C.P. 78; *Learoyd* v. *Brook* [1891] 1 Q.B. 431; see also *Anglo-Egyptian Navigation Co.* v. *Rennie* (1875) L.R. 10 C.P. 271; *Lumsden* v. *Barton & Co.* (1902) 19 T.L.R. 53; G. L. Williams, *Law Reform (Frustrated Contracts) Act 1943*, pp. 12–16.

[11] See below, pp. 447 *et seq.*

The decision in the *Fibrosa* case did not affect[12] a principle of mercantile law, akin to the rule in *Chandler* v. *Webster*, namely, that "an advance on account of freight to be earned . . . is, in the absence of any stipulation to the contrary, an irrevocable payment at the risk of the shipper of the goods."[13] Moreover, freight payable in advance remains payable although the voyage has been frustrated after it has fallen due.[14] This rule, precluding recovery of advanced freight, is of respectable antiquity,[15] hallowed by practice and strictly applied.[16] But it is open to the same criticisms as *Chandler* v. *Webster* and to the practical objection that, as a rule affecting international commerce, it is contrary to the law of other trading nations.[17] Nevertheless, as we shall see, it has been allowed to survive the 1943 Act.

(b) *Recompense for Services Rendered and Goods Supplied*

The discharge of a contract through breach or frustration will not in itself prevent the passing of property in goods transferred under the contract. Goods so delivered or, indeed, services rendered under the contract will, however, have been requested by the recipient who should therefore be liable, in principle, to pay for the benefit received. Nevertheless, a serious obstacle at common law to claims to payment for goods delivered or services rendered is the doctrine of entire contracts. Although in cases of frustration the doctrine has been restricted by the 1943 Act, it remains widely applicable in cases of breach. Accordingly, it is necessary to examine its scope in some detail.

An entire contract is one which provides expressly or impliedly that a party must perform his part in full before he can recover any part of the price or other consideration due to him under the contract; in particular, in the absence of anything to the contrary, a contract is held impliedly so to provide where the consideration is a lump sum or is otherwise unapportioned, or where the payment of the consideration is postponed until completion of the work. In such cases a long line of authority has established that the party who has contracted to perform his part on such terms "can recover nothing unless the work be done, or it can be shown that it was the defendant's fault that the work

---

[12] See [1943] A.C. 32, 64, *per* Lord Wright, 74, *per* Lord Roche, 79, *per* Lord Porter.
[13] *Allison* v. *Brisol Marine Insurance Co.* (1876) 1 App.Cas. 209, 253, *per* Lord Selborne. See also: *Anon.* (1682) 2 Shower 283; *De Silvale* v. *Kendall* (1815) 4 M. & S. 37; *Saunders* v. *Drew* (1832) 3 B. & Ad. 445; *Greeves* v. *West Indian & Pacific S.S. Co.* (1870) 22 L.T. 615; *Byrne* v. *Schiller* (1871) L.R. 6 Ex. 20, 319. *Cf. Ex p. Nyholm* (1873) 29 L.T. 634. See also *Civil Service Co-operative Society* v. *General Steam Navigaion Co.* [1903] 2 K.B. 756.
[14] *Andrew* v. *Moorhouse* (1814) 5 Taunt. 435; *Byrne* v. *Schiller* (1871) L.R. 6 Ex. 20, 319; *Oriental S.S. Co.* v. *Taylor* [1893] 2 Q.B. 518; *A. Coker & Co.* v. *Limerick S.S. Co.* (1918) 87 L.J.K.B. 767.
[15] *Anon.* (1682) 2 Shower K.B. 283. No reasons are given in the report. *Cf.* the sentence to the contrary in the Admiralty case of *Le Buck* v. *Van Voisdonck* (1554) in (1897) 11 Selden Society 93, where advance freight was recovered. The case in Shower is a manifestation of Admiralty's decline in the 17th century.
[16] *Coker & Co.* v. *Limerick S.S. Co.* (1918) 87 L.J.K.B. 767.
[17] *Byrne* v. *Schiller* (1871) L.R. 6 Ex. 319, 325, *per* Cockburn C.J.; *Watson & Co.* v. *Shankland* (1871) 10 Ct.Sess. (3rd Series), 142, 153, *per* Lord President Inglis.

was incomplete, or that there is something to justify the conclusion that the parties have entered into a fresh contract."[18]

These contractual principles have inhibited the development of restitutionary rights. It is true that a party may contract out[19] of his right to restitution; but it has been assumed that a contractual condition which demands complete performance before there can be recovery under the contract *necessarily* excludes all right to recompense for benefits conferred on the other party in part performance of the contract. Thus servants who were engaged at a specified sum for a definite period of time could recover nothing unless they completed their period of service.[20] It was immaterial whether their failure to perform was due to their own breach[21] or to frustration. This development is sometimes traced back, though in our view unjustifiably, to the leading case of *Cutter* v. *Powell*.[22] Cutter was employed by the defendant as second mate on a voyage from Jamaica to Liverpool, and took a promissory note from the defendant in the following terms:

> "Ten days after the ship 'Governor Parry,' myself master, arrives at Liverpool, I promise to pay Mr. T. Cutter the sum of thirty guineas, provided he proceeds, continues and does his duty as second mate, in the said ship from hence to the port of Liverpool. Kingston, July 31st, 1793."

The ship sailed from Jamaica on August 2, 1793, and arrived at Liverpool just over two months later, on October 9. But on September 20, Cutter died on the voyage. There was evidence that a voyage of this kind usually took about two months, and that the usual monthly wage for a second mate upon such a voyage was about £4 per month. The Court of King's Bench held that, on the particular facts and in the absence of any contrary usage, the contract was entire and that the plaintiff, Cutter's administratrix, was not entitled to recover upon a *quantum meruit* in respect of the services which he had rendered before his death. The court, impressed by the unusually high rate of remuneration and by the express terms of the note, concluded that the contract put the risk of non-completion upon Cutter.[23] On these special facts, the conclusion was

---

[18] *Appleby* v. *Myers* (1867) L.R. 2 C.P. 651, 661, *per* Blackburn J. Entire contracts must be distinguished from divisible or serverable contracts, when payment becomes due from time to time as designated parts of the contract are performed. The courts lean in favour of construing obligations as severable. See generally Treitel, *op. cit.* 587–592; G. L. Williams, *Law Reform (Frustrated Contracts) Act* 1943, pp. 2–7, 62–72; s.2(4) of the same Act: see below, pp. 462–464; (1975) 38 M.L.R. 413 [Beck].
[19] See above, pp. 45–48.
[20] A particularly harsh rule, because "a general hiring was a hiring for a year": see *Huttman* v. *Boulnois* (1825) 2 C. & P. 510, 511–512, *per* Abbott C.J.
[21] *Spain* v. *Arnott* (1817) 2 Star. 256; *Huttman* v. *Boulnois* (1825) 2 C. & P. 510; *Turner* v. *Robinson* (1833) 5 B. & Ad. 789; *Ridgway* v. *Hungerford Market Co.* (1835) 3 A. & E. 171; *Lilley* v. *Elwin* (1848) 11 Q.B. 742; *Boston Deep Sea Fishing & Ice Co.* v. *Ansell* (1888) 39 Ch.D. 339. The rule applied even if the servant left his master's service with the latter's consent: see *Lamburn* v. *Cruden* (1841) 2 Man. & G. 253.
[22] (1795) 6 T.R. 320, on which see (1987) 8 J.L.H. 48 [Barton].
[23] (1795) 6 T.R. 320, 324, *per* Lord Kenyon.

justifiable. But the doctrine of entire contracts was later to be invoked in cases where there was no such evidence that the servant had taken the risk of incomplete performance. In some cases the position has, however, since been rectified by statute.[24]

There are other cases in which the operation of the doctrine of entire contracts has affected parties' restitutionary rights. For example, if a contract for work and materials is entire, common law did not award recompense for partial performance if the contract had been discharged by frustration,[25] and only in very limited circumstances does it do so if the contract is discharged through the claimant's breach.[26] But nowadays, in cases of frustration, recompense for partial performance may be awarded under the provisions of the 1943 Act.

Similarly, it is settled law[27] that a contract to carry goods by sea for freight to be paid upon delivery of the goods at the port of discharge is an entire contract.[28] It is a condition precedent to the shipowner's right to recover such freight that he shall have delivered, or at least be ready to deliver, the goods at the agreed destination. The shipowner may be deprived of freight even though his inability to deliver was due to some event beyond his control.[29] It will not necessarily assist him in his claim for freight if the cargo owner has received delivery of goods at an intermediate port and has thereby gained some advantage[30]; for such mere receipt will not of itself give rise to the inference that the cargo owner has dispensed with fulfilment of the condition precedent or has agreed to pay freight *pro rata*.[31] These cases are open to the same objection as the cases on master and servant, and on work and materials. Since the contract is entire, the parties are assumed to intend that no recompense shall be recoverable, even in restitution for partial performance. In carriage of goods by sea, this attitude is peculiarly unfortunate, conflicting as it does with the

---

[24] See the Apportionment Act 1870: below, p. 440. (The Merchant Shipping Act 1970, s.16, does not deal with this question.) But the Apportionment Act 1870 gives way to an express stipulation that there shall be no apportionment: see s.7 and below, p. 440; *Cutter* v. *Powell* would therefore probably be decided today the same way.

[25] *Appleby* v. *Myers* (1867) L.R. 2 C.P. 651; *The Madras* [1898] P. 90; *cf. Menetone* v. *Athawes* (1764) 3 Burr. 1592.

[26] See below, p. 440 *et seq.*

[27] *Metcalfe* v. *Britannia Ironworks Co.* (1877) 2 Q.B.D. 423, 428, *per* Bramwell L.J.

[28] Carver, *op. cit.* Chap. 18.

[29] *Cook* v. *Jennings* (1797) 7 T.R. 381 (wrecked); *Metcalfe* v. *Britannia Ironworks Co.* (1877) 2 Q.B.D. 423 (ice); *Osgood* v. *Groning* (1810) 2 Camp. 466; *Castel & Latta* v. *Trechman* (1886) Cab. & E. 276 (enemy blockade); *St. Enoch Shipping Co.* v. Phosphate Mining Co. [1916] 2 K.B. 624 (illegality).

[30] *Cook* v. *Jennings* (1797) 7 T.R. 981; *Metcalfe* v. *Britannia Ironworks Co.* (1877) 2 Q.B.D. 423. But contrast below, pp. 442–443.

[31] Scrutton, *op. cit.* pp. 343–347 and cases there cited: Carver, *op. cit.* paras. 1685–1690 *et seq. Cf. Sumpter* v. *Hedges* [1898] 1 Q.B.673, discussed below, p. 439. But it is not necessary, subject to any contrary agreement, to deliver *all* the goods before the shipowner can recover freight. There is a distinction between short delivery and failure to complete the voyage; see *Ritchie* v. *Atkinson* (1808) 10 East 295; *Dakin* v. *Oxley* (1864) 15 C.B.(n.s.) 646, 665, *per* Willes J.; *Blanchet* v. *Powell's Llantivit Collieries Co.* (1874) L.R. 9 Ex. 74; *The Norway* (1865) 13 L.T. 50, 52, *per* Sir E. V. Williams.

mercantile laws of other nations,[32] though, in practice, the shipowner insures his freight. Regrettably, however, the rule precluding recovery of freight *pro rata itineris*, like that precluding recovery of advanced freight, has been allowed to continue under the 1943 Act.

2. CONTRACTS DISCHARGED THROUGH BREACH

(a) *Introduction*

A breach of contract may be so fundamental that it deprives the "party who has further undertakings still to perform of substantially the whole benefit which it was the intention of the parties as expressed in the contract that he should obtain as the consideration for performing those undertakings."[33-34] The innocent party has then an election.[35] He may affirm the contract, or he may bring it to an end. In the latter event, if he has paid money to the defendant under the contract, he can, as an alternative to claiming damages, sue for recovery of the money provided that the consideration for the payment has wholly failed; if the consideration has partially failed, his only action is for damages.[36] If he has rendered services or delivered goods under the contract, he can either sue for damages or he can recover their market value at the date when they were effectively rendered or delivered.[37] But if he has performed his obligations under the contract, he has an accrued right of action under the contract and cannot have recourse to an action in restitution; so, if he has done all (or probably substantially all[38]) that he has promised to do, his only action in respect of his contractual performance is an action for the contract price.[39]

The *innocent party's* right to sue in restitution for the value of the benefits conferred is particularly important if he has made a losing contract. If he sues on the contract for loss suffered, he will, of course, recover only nominal damages. But his claim in restitution is for the value of benefits conferred. If he has paid money, he will recover that payment if the consideration for the payment has totally failed. The party in breach is not allowed to deduct the loss which the innocent party would have suffered if he had fully performed the contract; to allow him to do so would be to allow him to profit from his breach

---

[32] *Metcalfe* v. *Britannia Ironworks Co.* (1876) 1 Q.B.D. 613, 626–627, *per* Cockburn C.J. Lord Mansfield, in *Luke* v. *Lyde* (1759) 2 Burr. 882, was inclined to award freight *pro rata itineris*, as did the Admiralty in the 16th century: see R. G. Marsden (1897) 11 Selden Society, lxvi, lxvii. Lord Mansfield's view, of course, did not prevail.

[33-34] *Hong Kong Fir Shipping Co. Ltd.* v. *Kawasaki Kisen Kaisha Ltd.* [1962] 2 Q.B. 26, 66, *per* Diplock L.J.

[35] *Cf. Peyman* v. *Lanjani* [1985] Ch. 457, C.A.: an election is effective only if a person knows his legal rights as well as the facts giving rise to those rights: see above, p. 203.

[36] There is no legislation amending the common law akin to that of the Law Reform (Frustrated Contracts) Act 1943: see above, Chap. 17; see below, pp. 417 *et seq.*

[37] See below, pp. 426 *et seq.* for a critical comment.

[38] See below, p. 424.

[39] He may also recover for any loss suffered from the defendant's failure to carry out his obligations, *e.g.* from failing to deliver materials on time.

of contract.[40] But if the innocent party receives from the party in breach any part of the bargained for performance, which he is not in a position to restore, his claim will fail. Money paid for a consideration which has partially failed is irrecoverable.[41] This distinction, although now accepted by the English Law Commission,[42] is unappealing and productive of injustice. Recovery should be permitted to the extent of the difference between the amount paid and the benefit received. It is not persuasive to conclude that the common law rule must stand because it may be difficult, if not impossible, to value the benefit conferred by the party in breach.[43] This objection has never defeated a claim to rescind a transaction in equity, where each party must be restored to the *status quo ante* and where there may be an accounting on both sides even where *restitutio in integrum* is not strictly possible.[44]

In contrast, this distinction is not relevant to claims based on a *quantum meruit* or a *quantum valebat*. The innocent party then recovers the value of the benefit conferred, which is the market value of the services and goods respectively. However, as in claims for money paid, the contract price is not a ceiling to the plaintiff's claim, although it is evidence of market value.[45]

The *party in breach* who has paid a sum of money to the innocent party, which is not a deposit,[46] can recover the sum so paid if the consideration for the payment has totally failed, although he will be liable in damages for any loss caused by his wrongful repudiation. In contrast, a person who rendered services or delivered goods (which cannot be returned) in pursuance of the terms of an entire contract and who has not performed or substantially performed his side of the bargain is denied a restitutionary claim.[47]

In recent years jurists have criticised the distinction, which is the product of the old common counts,[48] between money claims on the one hand and claims for services rendered and goods delivered on the other.[49] They argue that the proper ground of a restitutionary claim for benefits conferred in performance of a contract, which is or has become ineffective, should be failure of consideration. There is little precedent to support this argument. Moreover, it impli-

---

[40] *Cf.* the Connecticut case of *Bush* v. *Canfield* 2 Conn. 485 (1818). D agreed to deliver 2000 barrels of flour to P at $7 a barrel. P. paid $5000 in advance. D inexplicably failed to deliver even though the market price was then only $5.50. P sued for the $5000 prepayment and recovered. The court rejected the argument that P's recovery should be limited to $2000, since, if the flour had been delivered, he would have to pay an additional $9000 in order to receive flour now worth only $11000. If D's argument had been accepted, he would have been better off in the amount of $3000 whether he was the innocent party or the party in breach: contrast below, pp. 424–426.
[41] See above, Chap. 17 and below, pp. 419 *et seq.*
[42] *Law of Contract: Pecuniary Restitution on Breach of Contract*, Report No. 121 (1983), paras. 3.8–3.9, rejecting its preliminary recommendation in its Working Paper, No. 65, paras. 51–56.
[43] For a cogent criticism, see (1984) 47 M.L.R. 76, 83–86 [Burrows].
[44] See above, pp. 60–62.
[45] See below, p. 413.
[46] See below, pp. 428 *et seq.*
[47] See below, pp. 444–447 which also discuss proposals for the reform of this branch of the law.
[48] See above, pp. 3–5.
[49] See, particularly, (1988) 104 L.Q.R. 576 [Burrows].

citly rejects the common law rules that if the failure of consideration is only partial a restitutionary claim will fail and that a party in breach, who has partially performed his executory obligations under an entire contract by rendering services or goods, which cannot be returned, is without any remedy. In principle there is much to be said for the view that the ground for recovery should be the same whatever the nature of the benefit conferred, and that, subject to an unequivocal agreement to the contrary, even a party in breach should be recompensed to the extent of the value of the benefit conferred.[50] Only the House of Lords is free to adopt these radical, if desirable, proposals.

The legacy of the common counts has meant that restitutionary claims have been limited to actions for money had and received, money paid, services rendered or goods delivered. If a party succeeds, he recovers the value of the benefit which he has conferred. In contrast, an innocent party has never recovered the profits which the party in breach has gained from his breach of contract.[51] Judges and jurists as distinguished as Oliver Wendell Holmes and Richard Posner accept that the promisor should be free to break his contract if he so chooses.[52] Moreover, in Judge Posner's view, it may be desirable to encourage him to do so, for the recognition of a restitutionary claim for profits would deter efficient breaches of contract when it would be economically efficient to encourage such breaches. The innocent party is adequately protected by his action for damages for loss suffered; an award of damages makes him whole.

Other jurists have not been persuaded by such arguments.[53] They believe that *pacta sunt servanda* and that parties should be encouraged to perform their contractual obligations.[54] Moreover, an award of damages may not make the innocent party whole. He does not always recover his true loss; for example, he may not be compensated for the time and money spent (the so-called transaction costs) in seeking to mitigate his loss, and some items of his true loss may be dismissed as too remote in law and hence irrecoverable. Above all, he may be anxious that the other party performs his side of the bargain.

It is not true to say that a claim for profits gained from a breach of contract is without precedent. Certainly it is known to the courts of equity. A fiduciary obligation may arise from a contract between the parties[55]; and it is well established that a fiduciary who is in breach of his duty of loyalty to his

---

[50] It is another and distinct question whether a contracting party has benefited from the acts of the plaintiff: see above, Chap. 1.

[51] See *The Siboen and The Sibotre* [1976] 1 Lloyd's Rep. 293, 337, *per* Kerr J.

[52] O. W. Holmes, *The Common Law* (edited by Mark de Wolfe Howe), pp. 235–236; R. Posner, *Economic Analysis of Law* (4th ed., 1992), pp. 117–120.

[53] For a persuasive critique of the theory of efficient breach, see "The Efficient Breach Fallacy" (1989) 18 Jo. of Legal Studies 1 [Friedmann].

[54] See, *e.g.* Charles Fried, *Contract as Promise*.

[55] It is true that a court is unlikely to find that a party, who is in an arm's-length commercial relationship, owes the other party any fiduciary duty of loyalty. But exceptionally he may: see *LAC Minerals Ltd.* v. *International Corona Resources Ltd.* [1989] 2 S.C.R. 574 (S.Ct. of Canada); and *cf. Hospital Products Ltd.* v. *U.S. Surgical Corp.* (1984) 156 C.L.R. 41, 122–125, *per* Deane J.

principal must account for any profits made thereby.[56] A confidant who consciously breaches another's confidence has been required to account for profits[57]; and a vendor of real property, who sells land to a third party in breach of his contract with the plaintiff, is a constructive trustee of the profits he makes thereby.[58]

No common law court has explicitly recognised such a claim. But a concern to strip the party in breach of his profits may lurk behind an award of damages for breach of contract. For example,[59] in disputes between landlord and tenant, arising out of the breach of repairing covenants, at common law the landlord's loss was measured by the cost of repairs and not by the diminution in the value of the reversion,[60] even though it was known that the landlord intended to demolish the property or that the repairs would not increase its value.[61]

A party in breach may make a handsome profit from a breach of contract; such is the shipowner who wrongfully repudiates a time charter in a rising freight market. He may also have saved himself considerable expense by failing to perform a collateral term of the contract. In more recent years the courts have required the innocent party to prove that he has or will incur economic loss as a result of the defendant's breach; for example, by demonstrating that he will do what the defendant failed to do.[62] A prominent and colourful illustration of the application of this principle is *Tito* v. *Waddell (No. 2)*.[63] The plaintiffs owned small scattered plots of land on Ocean Island in the South Pacific. The defendants were granted licences to mine phosphate and covenanted to replant the land "as nearly as possible to the extent to which it

---

[56] See below, Chap. 33 for the many illustrations of this principle. Indeed, he is a constructive trustee of any identifiable asset.

[57] *Peter Pan Manufacturing Co.* v. *Corsets Silhouette Ltd.* [1964] 1 W.L.R. 96: see below, p. 691.

[58] *Lake* v. *Bayliss* [1974] 1 W.L.R. 1073.

[59] For a full discussion of these cases, see "The Recovery of Benefits from a Breach of Contract" (1983) 99 L.Q.R. 443 [Jones].

[60] *Cf.* among other decisions, *Joyner* v. *Weeks* [1981] 2 Q.B. 31, C.A. and *Conquest* v. *Ebbets* [1896] A.C. 490, H.L. See also *Wrotham Park Estate Co.* v. *Parkside Homes Ltd.* [1974] 1 W.L.R. 798 (breach of restrictive covenant, where no loss was suffered), distinguished and explained in *Stoke-on-Trent C.C.* v. *W. J. Wass Ltd.* [1988] 1 W.L.R. 1406, 1414, *per* Nourse L.J.
In *Surrey County Council* v. *Bredero Homes Ltd.* [1992] 3 All E.R. 302 Ferris J. restrictively distinguished *Wrotham Park* on the ground that it concerned an award of equitable damages only. The defendants had built more houses on the site than under an approved scheme, thereby making extra profit. Although aware of the breach the plaintiffs did not seek equitable relief but waited until the houses were built. The plaintiffs' claim for damages failed; they had suffered no loss. There was no jurisdiction to award equitable damages because at the date of the writ there was no case for equitable relief; it is doubtful whether this conclusion is reconcilable with the decision of the House of Lords in *Johnson* v. *Agnew* [1980] A.C. 367. (The Court of Appeal has now affirmed Ferris J.'s judgment.)

[61] In the U.S.A. the courts have allowed a restitutionary claim for profits made from the tort of inducing a breach of contract, even though the plaintiff had made a losing contract: *Federal Sugar Refining Co.* v. *United States Sugar Equalisation Board*, 268 F. 575 (S.D.N.Y. 1920): see below, p. 724. A court may regard such a decision as providing a persuasive analogy when pressed with argument that a party in breach should disgorge his profits.

[62] *Radford* v. *De Froberville* [1978] 1 All E.R. 33, followed in *Dean* v. *Ainley* [1987] 1 W.L.R. 1729.

[63] [1977] Ch. 106. *Cf. City of New Orleans* v. *Fireman's Charitable Association* 9 So. 486 (1891); discussed in (1983) 99 L.Q.R. 443.

was planted at the start of the commencement of the agreement."[64] They failed to do so, leaving high coral pinnacles adjacent to pits. The evidence was that to replant would involve the construction of 80 miles of roadway and the importation of soil from Australia; all in all it would take five years before planting would begin and 12 to 14 years before any of the planted trees would bear fruit. Sir Robert Megarry V.-C. refused to order specific performance, and awarded the plaintiffs damages based on the diminution in the value of the land in consequence of the breach. He denied them the cost of replanting; for it was clear that, living as they did, 1,500 miles away from Ocean Island, they would never return and therefore would not incur that expense.[65] The question was not one of making the defendant disgorge what he saved by committing the wrong, but one of compensating the plaintiff.

The novelty of a restitutionary claim has compelled counsel, on these and other comparable facts,[66] to frame their claim as one for loss suffered. However, so framed, it invites the court to find that the plaintiff had suffered only minimal or a nominal loss. This may be a harsh conclusion. For example, in *Tito* v. *Waddell* the plaintiffs might have made a different bargain for a greater consideration, perhaps the contractual consideration plus the cost of replanting, if the contract had not contained a provision obliging the defendant to replant. Again, the party in breach may have substituted a cheaper product, for example, inferior electrical wiring, embedded in the concrete structure of the plaintiff's building; the market value of the building is not thereby diminished but the builder saves a significant sum. In such cases the party in breach should account for the expense which he has saved from his breach of contract.[67]

The recognition of a restitutionary claim will not in practice revolutionise the common law. The innocent party will rarely seek an accounting of profits. He will have mitigated his loss, and his loss will normally be the measure of the defendant's gain, from the breach. Only in a volatile market may this not be so.[68] Moreover, the burden will be on the innocent party to demonstrate that the party in breach would not have made his profits but for the breach. Finally, the court will be well aware that an accounting of profits is an equitable remedy and hence discretionary. A court may take into account such factors as the nature of the contract,[69] the nature of the breach, whether it is conscious or not,

---

[64] For the terms of the agreement, see [1977] Ch. 106, 273–274.

[65] [1977] Ch. 106, 332. See also *Surrey County Council* v. *Bredero Homes Ltd.* [1992] 3 All E.R. 302; above n. 60.

[66] *Cf. Stoke-on-Trent City Council* v. *W. J. Wass Ltd.* [1988] 1 W.L.R. 1406, C.A. (see below, p. 722 where the defendant was a tortfeasor); and *Surrey County Council* v. *Bredero Homes Ltd.* [1992] 3 All E.R. 30 (see above, n. 60).

[67] For the academic debate on the desirability of the restitutionary claim, see (1959) 20 Ohio State L.J. 175 [Dawson]; (1980) 80 Col.L.R. 504 [Friedmann]; (1983) 99 L.Q.R. 443 [Jones]; (1985) 94 Yale L.J. 1339 [Farnsworth]; (1989) 2 Jo. of Contract Law 1 [Stoljar] and 74–76 [Beatson]; (1990) 12 *Advocate's Quarterly* 1 (Hon. J. R. Maurice Gautrean); Palmer, *op. cit.* Vol. I, para. 4.9; and Birks, *Introduction*, pp. 334–336.

[68] See below, n. 71.

[69] Palmer would deny the remedy if the contract is one for personal services: *op. cit.* Vol. I, pp. 444–445, followed by Friedmann in (1980) 80 Col.L.R. 504, 519–521. Contrast (1983) 99 L.Q.R. 443, 456 [Jones].

and the laches of the innocent party.[70] For such reasons, which are not exclusive, the court may deny the restitutionary claim.

It is evident from the authorities that it is only open to the House of Lords to hold that a restitutionary claim for profits gained from a breach of contract is, in some circumstances, an appropriate remedy. There is much to be said for the view that it should do so.[71]

We shall now discuss the circumstances in which the innocent party and the party in breach can obtain restitution when a contract has been discharged on account of breach. We shall begin with the position of the innocent party.

(b) *The Position of the Innocent Party*

Recovery of money

If the innocent party has paid money under a contract which has been determined by him in consequence of the other party's breach, he will be entitled to recover his payment if he can show that it was paid for a consideration which has wholly failed.[72] Thus, in *Giles* v. *Edwards*,[73] the defendant had agreed to

---

[70] *Cf. Beard* v. *Turner* (1866) 13 L.T. 746, 750, *per* Page Wood V.-C. (a trade mark owner must sue as soon as he learns of the infringement).

[71] The Israeli Supreme Court has so concluded: see *Adras Ltd.* v. *Harlow & Jones GmbH*, discussed in (1988) 104 L.Q.R. 383 [Friedmann], in Jones, *Restitution in Public and Private Law*, pp. 88–91 and in *Essays on Restitution* (ed. Finn), pp. 8–9 [Jones].
The plaintiffs had suffered no loss from the breach; yet they recovered the defendant's profits. The Israeli market for iron ore, which the defendants had failed to deliver in full, was very volatile, with the outbreak of the Yom Kippur war.

[72] In all the English cases the restitutionary claim is brought by one of the contracting parties against the other. English law does not recognise a *jus quaesitum tertio*, and the attempts to outflank that general rule have by and large failed: see, generally, Treitel, *op. cit.* Chap. 15.
However, in *Trident General Insurance Co. Ltd.* v. *McNiece Bros. Pty. Ltd.* (1988) 165 C.L.R. 107, the High Court of Australia upheld (by a majority of 5 to 2) a claim by a third party who was not a party to a liability insurance policy but for whose benefit the contract had been entered into. Three members of that majority were, at least in the context of a claim arising from a liability insurance policy, prepared to abandon the rule that the common law does not recognise a *jus quaesitum tertio*. However, Gaudron J. (at pp. 174–176) adopted the radical proposition that the promisor, having accepted the agreed consideration, "is unjustly enriched at the expense of the third party to the extent that the promise is unfulfilled and the non-fulfilment does not attract proportional legal consequences" (at p. 176): *cf.* the comments of Deane J., (who found that there was a trust of the promise, at pp. 145–146), where he gives very guarded support to the possibility of a cause of action based upon principles of unjust enrichment.
Gaudron J.'s reasoning has been severely criticised. The promisor has been enriched, but the enrichment was a proportionate part of the premiums received from the promisee, who may well have had a claim against him based on total failure of consideration. The enrichment is not "the extent to which the promise is unfulfilled." Granted that there is an enrichment, it has not been gained at the expense of the third party; it is surely at the expense of the promisee. Again, what is the ground of the third party's restitutionary claim? Disappointed expectations have never been a ground of restitution unless the third party is able to invoke some application of common law or equitable estoppel: on which see above, Chap. 5. Moreover, these expectations can be wholly or partially frustrated if the contracting parties agree. (Gaudron J. conceded that the "obligation of the promisor to the third party will [then] be varied, modified or extinguished": see p. 177).

[73] (1797) 7 T.R. 181. See also *Greville* v. *Da Costa* (1797) Peake 113; *Nockels* v. *Crosby* (1825) 3 B. & C. 814; *Fitt* v. *Cassanet* (1842) 4 Man. & G. 898; *Ashpitel* v. *Sercombe* (1850) 5 Ex. 147; *Johnson* v. *Goslett* (1857) 3 C.B.(n.s.) 569; *Devaux* v. *Conolly* (1849) 8 C.B. 640; *Wilson* v. *Church* (1879) 13 Ch.D. 1.

sell to the plaintiffs all the corded wood growing at Tredgodoer. The defendant cut the wood and corded some of it. The plaintiffs then paid him 20 guineas, which was considerably more than the value of the wood already corded. The defendant, however, neglected to cord the rest of the wood, whereupon the plaintiffs brought an action for money had and received to recover the 20 guineas. The Court of King's Bench upheld the claim. The contract was an entire contract and it was through the defendant's breach of contract that it was not carried into execution. Consequently, "the plaintiffs were at liberty to consider the contract at an end and recover back the money they had paid, the consideration having failed."[74]

It was at one time thought that, before the innocent party could proceed in quasi-contract, he must rescind the contract *ab initio* and that, as a condition of rescission, he must restore to the party in breach all the benefits he had received under the contract.[75] "Where a contract is to be rescinded at all, it must be rescinded *in toto*, and the parties put *in statu quo*."[76] But in cases of breach of contract it is now accepted that, whatever the nature of the contract,[77] where the innocent party determines the contract, he "is thereby absolved from future performance of his obligations under the contract,"[78] but the contract is not wiped out altogether.[79] In *Fibrosa Spolka Akcynja* v. *Fairbairn Lawson Combe Barbour Ltd.*,[80] Lord Atkin, commenting on the argument that a "claim for money paid on consideration which wholly failed could only be made where the contract was wiped out altogether," said that he "knew of no authority for the proposition. It is true," he continued, "that where a party is in a position to rescind a contract he may be able to sue for money which he has paid under the contract now rescinded, but there are numerous cases where there has been no question of rescission where such an action has lain." Both he and Lord Wright emphasised that the position of the innocent party who has determined a contract because of the other party's breach is to this extent no different from that of a party to a contract discharged by frustration. As Lord Wright said[81]:

---

[74] (1797) 7 T.R. 181, 182, *per* Lawrence J., whose decision was affirmed and whose reasoning accepted by the Court of King's Bench.

[75] *Hunt* v. *Silk* (1804) 5 East 449 (see below, p. 420); *Chandler* v. *Webster* [1904] 1 K.B. 493 (overruled in *Fibrosa Spolka Akcyjna* v. *Fairbairn Lawson Combe Barbour Ltd.* [1943] A.C. 32); *Berchem* v. *Wren* (1904) 21 R.P.C. 683; *Thorpe* v. *Fasey* [1949] Ch. 649; *Horsler* v. *Zorro* [1975] Ch. 302; *Williams on Vendor and Purchaser*, p. 1006; see above, pp. 407–408.

[76] *Hunt* v. *Silk* (1804) 5 East 449, 452, *per* Lord Ellenborough.

[77] See above, p. 407.

[78] *Heyman* v. *Darwins Ltd.* [1942] A.C. 356, 399, *per* Lord Porter; *Johnson* v. *Agnew* [1980] A.C. 367, 392, 393, *per* Lord Wilberforce. See also *Johnstone* v. *Milling* (1886) 16 Q.B.D. 460, 467, *per* Lord Esher M.R.; *Boston Deep Sea Fishing & Ice Co.* v. *Ansell* (1888) 39 Ch.D. 339, 364–365, *per* Bowen L.J.

[79] *Johnson* v. *Agnew* [1980] A.C. 367. See also *McDonald* v. *Dennys Lascelles Ltd.* (1933) 48 C.L.R. 459, 476–477, *per* Dixon J.

[80] [1943] A.C. 32, 52.

[81] *Ibid.* at p. 65. This reasoning is consistent with the language of the court in *Giles* v. *Edwards* (1797) 7 T.R. 181.

"The contract is in neither case wiped out, or avoided *ab initio*. The right in such a case to claim repayment of money paid in advance must in principle, in my judgment, attach at the moment of dissolution. The payment was originally conditional. The condition of retaining it is eventual performance. Accordingly, when that condition fails, the right to retain the money must simultaneously fail. It is not like a claim for damages for breach of the contract which would generally differ in measure and amount, nor is it a claim under the contract, It is in theory and is expressed to be a claim to recover money, received to the use of the plaintiff."

Nevertheless, before he can proceed in quasi-contract the innocent party must first bring the contract to an end. If he does not do so, the contract continues to govern the situation, and the plaintiff must seek his remedy on the contract and not in quasi-contract.[82] Moreover if, with knowledge of the breach, the innocent party affirms the contract, he will have lost his right to determine the contract for that breach, unless the breach is of a continuing nature.[83] As Devlin J. said in *Kwei Tek Chao* v. *British Traders & Shippers Ltd.*,[84] a case concerned with a c.i.f. contract of sale:

"If goods have been properly rejected, and the price has already been paid in advance, the proper way of recovering the money back is by an action for money paid for a consideration which has wholly failed, *i.e.*, money had and received; but that form of action is governed by exactly the same rules with regard to affirming or avoiding the transaction as in any other case."

We have already seen[85] that, if the benefit conferred on the defendant takes the form of money, the plaintiff can only recover his money in quasi-contract if the consideration for his payment has wholly failed. It is regrettable[86] that "the English common law does not undertake to apportion a prepaid sum in such circumstances."[87] The result appears to be that if the plaintiff has received a benefit from the defendant's partial performance,[88] he must restore that benefit to the defendant before he can recover his money in quasi-contract.[89] If he

---

[82] *Weston* v. *Downes* (1778) 1 Doug. 23; *Restatement of Restitution*, § 107; 2 Smith's *Leading Cases*, p. 9; see above, pp. 46–48.

[83] *Yeoman Credit Ltd.* v. *Apps* [1962] 2 Q.B. 508: see below, p. 423.

[84] [1954] 2 Q.B. 459, 475. See also *Goodman* v. *Pocock* (1850) 15 Q.B. 576.

[85] See above, Chaps. 17 and 18.

[86] The Law Commission recommended in its Working Paper, No. 65, §§ 51–56, 79(2), that in such a case recovery should be granted, namely a proportion of the payment, in excess of the benefit conferred. But its *Report*, No. 121, § 3.8–3.9 rejects this recommendation. For a criticism see above, pp. 444–447.

[87] *Fibrosa Spolka Akcynja* v. *Fairbairn Lawson Combe Barbour Ltd.* [1943] A.C. 32, 49, *per* Viscount Simon. Contrast Law Commission, Working Paper, No. 65, §§ 51–56.

[88] *Cf. Linz* v. *Electric Wire Co. of Palestine Ltd.* [1948] A.C. 371, where the Privy Council held that the receipt by the plaintiff of a benefit from a third party prevented there being a total failure of consideration. The case is criticised above, p. 402, n. 10.

[89] *Towers* v. *Barrett* (1786) 1 T.R. 133; *Baldry* v. *Marshall* [1925] I. & B. 260.

cannot restore the benefit, he must fall back on his right to damages, unless the circumstances of the case are such as to relieve him from his duty to restore.[90] In other words, even though the innocent party is no longer required to rescind the contract *ab initio*, he may still be required to make *restitutio*. No quasi-contractual claim is then possible if the benefit, for example, services rendered, cannot be restored.[91] Moreover, even where the plaintiff has received a thing, such as land or a chattel, which prima facie he is able to restore, he may have had some intermediate enjoyment of that thing before the contract is determined, and that enjoyment cannot be restored. Difficult questions have been raised by cases concerned with the point whether such enjoyment by the plaintiff will preclude him from recovering his money.[92]

An early case concerned with intermediate enjoyment of land was *Hunt* v. *Silk*.[93] For a consideration of £10, Silk agreed to let a house to Hunt, to carry out certain repairs and execute a lease within 10 days. Hunt went into immediate possession and paid the £10, but Silk failed to do the repairs or execute the lease within the required period. Hunt remained in possession for some days later but, after repeated protestations, he left and gave notice to Silk that he had rescinded the agreement because of his default. The Court of King's Bench held that Hunt was unable to recover his money in an action for money had and received. His intermediate enjoyment of the land prevented the restoration of the *status quo ante*; he could not, therefore, rescind the contract.[93a]

Although the rescission *ab initio* is no longer a necessary prerequisite to a quasi-contractual claim in this context, it is a reasonable inference from *Hunt* v. *Silk* that intermediate enjoyment of this kind may likewise defeat a claim founded on total failure of consideration.[94] But we suggest that the enjoyment should be at least of a reasonably substantial nature to defeat such a claim. It is true that in *Hunt* v. *Silk* the intermediate enjoyment was not substantial. But that case is best explained as an example, perhaps harsh, of the principle of

---

[90] *Rowland* v. *Divall* [1923] 2 K.B. 500: see below, p. 421.

[91] *Harrison* v. *James* (1862) 7 H. & N. 804.

[92] Where the party in breach has been let into occupation of land before the contract is determined, it appears that the innocent party is entitled in equity, on determining the contract, to recover possession and to recover any rents or profits received by the party in breach, but not to charge the party in breach rent for the land occupied by him: see *Williams on Vendor and Purchaser*; p. 1009, and cases cited. Contrast *Lee-Parker* v. *Izett (No. 2)* [1972] 1 W.L.R. 775: see below, p. 486.

[93] (1804) 5 East 449, Smith K.B. 15.

[93a] "From the earliest decisions American courts have ordered restitution of the purchaser's payments of the price after taking into account in some manner the benefit received by him from occupancy of the land": Palmer, *International Encyclopedia of Comparative Law*, Vol. X, Chap. 3, *History of Restitution in Anglo-American Law*, pp. 35–36 and nn. 253–255 which cite the relevant case law.
Canadian courts have arguably also rejected the rule that there must be a *total* failure of consideration before recovery is permitted: see Maddaugh & McCamus, *op. cit.* pp. 424 *et seq.*, citing case law which demonstrates that interim enjoyment of goods will not defeat a claim for money paid.

[94] See *Spence* v. *Crawford* [1939] 3 All E.R. 271, 290, *per* Lord Wright.

affirmation. Hunt was held to have affirmed the contract,[95] because he had remained in possession of the land "some days after" he knew of Silk's breach.[96] Lord Ellenborough said: "He waived his right, and voluntarily paid the money; . . . and afterwards continued in possession notwithstanding the defendant's default."[97] Decisions in which *Hunt* v. *Silk* has been followed[98] may similarly be interpreted as cases of affirmation or waiver. Conversely, in other cases where it has been cited as authority for the proposition that any intermediate enjoyment will automatically bar recovery, *Hunt* v. *Silk* has been distinguished.[99] The mere fact of entry into possession should not, therefore, be regarded as important.[1]

In certain circumstances, however, the plaintiff may be entitled to recover his money on grounds of total failure of consideration despite substantial intermediate enjoyment of a chattel. The leading case is *Rowland* v. *Divall*.[2] The plaintiff bought a car from the defendant in May 1922. He took possession of it at once, and later sold it to a third party. In September 1922, the car was found to be stolen property, and it was seized by the police and returned to its true owner. The plaintiff repaid to the third party the price he had received from him, and brought an action against the defendant to recover, on the ground of total failure of consideration, the price he had originally paid the defendant for the car.[3] For the defendant it was argued, relying on *Hunt* v. *Silk*,[4] that there could be no rescission, for the temporary use of a chattel was a benefit which could not be restored. The Court of Appeal rejected the defendant's submission. Bankes L.J., the only member of the court to refer to *Hunt* v. *Silk*, commented that "it cannot possibly be said that the plaintiff received any portion of what he had agreed to buy."[5] Both Scrutton and Atkin L.JJ. regarded the plaintiff's use of the car as irrelevant, Atkin L.J. said[6]:

> "Under those circumstances can it make any difference that the buyer had used the car before he found out that there was a breach of the condition? To my mind, it makes no difference at all. . . . The buyer has not received

---

[95] Cf. *Root* v. *Bradley* [1960] N.Z.L.R. 756.

[96] Cf. *Farnworth Finance Facilities Ltd.* v. *Attryde* [1970] 1 W.L.R. 1053.

[97] (1804) 5 East 449, 452; and p. 453, *per* Le Blanc J. The report in Smith K.B. confirms that this was the reason why the plaintiff's claim failed. (We are grateful to Brian Davenport Esq., Q.C. for drawing our attention to this fact.) See also *Morley* v. *Attenborough* (1849) 3 Ex. 500; *Eicholz* v. *Bannister* (1864) 17 C.B.(n.s.) 708. Contrast [1988] Convey. 333 [Pottage]. Cf. Burrows, *The Law of Restitution*, p. 264.

[98] *Beed* v. *Blandford* (1828) 2 Y. & J. 278; *Blackburn* v. *Smith* (1848) 2 Ex. 783; *Freeman* v. *Jeffries* (1869) L.R. 4 Ex. 189; *Heilbutt* v. *Hickson* (1872) L.R. 7 C.P. 438, 451, *per* Bovill C.J.

[99] See, *e.g. Spence* v. *Crawford* [1939] 3 All E.R. 271.

[1] *Abram S.S. Co.* v. *Westville Shipping Co.* [1923] A.C. 773, 782, *per* Lord Atkinson (referring to *Lamare* v. *Dixon* (1873) L.R. 6 H.L. 414), with which *cf. Pucjlowski* v. *Johnston's Executors* [1946] W.L.D. 1 (S. Africa).

[2] [1923] 2 K.B. 500, followed, on very different facts, in *Rover International Ltd.* v. *Cannon Film Sales Ltd.* [1989] 1 W.L.R. 912, C.A.: see below, p. 543.

[3] The plaintiff did not, apparently, make a claim for damages.

[4] (1804) 5 East 449.

[5] [1923] 2 K.B. 500, 504.

[6] [1923] 2 K.B. 500, 507.

any part of that which he contracted to receive—namely, the property and right to possession—and, that being so, there has been a total failure of consideration."

The principle in *Rowland* v. *Divall* has been criticised on the ground that the buyer may thereby recover more than he should, since he is not required to bring into account the use which he has had of the car while it was in his possession.[7] Yet the actual decision seems just since the plaintiff had been compelled to settle a claim by the third party and had hardly used the car.[8] However, the application of the principle in that case to other circumstances can lead to apparently extreme results.[9] Thus, in *Butterworth* v. *Kingsway Motors*,[10] the purchase of a motor-car from a seller with a defective title was able to recover the full purchase price on the ground of total failure of consideration, although at the date when he determined the contract he had had the use of the car for several months and its value had considerably fallen, and although, if he had waited one more week before bringing the contract to an end, his seller's and, therefore, his own title would have been made good.[11] A similar case is *Warman* v. *Southern Counties Car Finance Corporation*,[12] where it was held that a hirer under a hire-purchase agreement was entitled to determine the agreement for a defect of title and to recover the whole of his deposit and all his hire-purchase instalments, despite his intermediate use of the chattel. It is undoubtedly true that in both *Butterworth's* case and *Warman's* case the buyer did enjoy part of the bargained-for exchange, namely, the use of the car. But it appears that he did not enjoy that benefit at the seller's expense; the seller had no right to any recompense for the intermediate use of the car because he had not been deprived of the use of a car to which he had title. However, if the true owner, having recovered the car, had successfully sued the seller for the rental value of the car, it is arguable that the buyer's gain would then have been made at the seller's expense. Conversely, if the true owner chose not to sue the seller but chose to sue the buyer, the gain would not be made at the seller's expense. In principle, therefore, the question whether the buyer should be required to make an allowance for the use of the car should arise only if he is not at risk of being sued by the true owner. But it is a question

---

[7] Law Reform Committee, 12th Report, Cmnd. 2958, § 36 (1966). *Cf.* (1967) 30 M.L.R. 139, 145–149 [Treitel]; Atiyah, *Sale of Goods*, pp. 87 *et seq.*; Benjamin's *Sale of Goods* § 4–005.

[8] Moreover, the defendant could not complain that the car had not been returned to him because it was his breach of condition which made it impossible for the plaintiff to do so.

[9] *Cf.* Law Commission Working Paper No. 65, §§ 68–70. (Buyer should only make allowance to seller if the seller has satisfied the claim of the true owner.)

[10] [1954] 1 W.L.R. 1286.

[11] It has been argued that the question whether there has been a total failure of consideration should be considered as at the date of the action, by which time the defect in title may have been cured. But this point was rejected by Pearson J. in *Butterworth* v. *Kingsway Motors* [1954] 1 W.L.R. 1286, 1294 on good grounds. However, Pearson J. did doubt (at p. 1295) whether the buyer would have succeeded if the seller had cured his defective title before the buyer purported to rescind.

[12] [1949] 2 K.B. 576: see below, p. 439.

of considerable difficulty how the value of any benefit gained from the use of the car is to be determined.[13]

On the other hand, where the chattel in question has been consumed[14] by the buyer, he will not have been relieved from having to restore it by a third party's assertion of superior title,[15] and in any event the property in the chattel will have passed to the buyer when he consumed it.[16] The mere fact that the seller's title is defective, therefore, will not entitle the buyer to recover the price on the ground of total failure of consideration.

Moreover, it is only in cases of defective title that the plaintiff is relieved from "restoring" the intermediate enjoyment; in other cases, however defective the defendant's performance, substantial[17] intermediate enjoyment of the subject-matter of the contract will prevent the plaintiff from recovering his money on grounds of total failure of consideration. Thus, in *Yeoman Credit Ltd.* v. *Apps*,[18] the defendant entered into an agreement with the plaintiffs for the hire-purchase of a second-hand car. The agreement excluded all liability for the condition of the car. When delivered, the car was unsafe and unroadworthy but the defendant, though he complained, kept it and paid three instalments of hire. He then defaulted, and the plaintiffs determined the hiring and towed the car away. To the plaintiffs' claim for damages and arrears of instalments, the defendant counterclaimed to recover the deposit and the instalments paid, on the ground of total failure of consideration. The Court of Appeal held that the condition of the car was such that the plaintiffs were in fundamental breach of the contract and so could not rely on the exemption clause.[19] Consequently, the defendant was entitled to reject the car and to bring the contract to an end. But the court held that the defendant could not entirely succeed on his counterclaim because there had been no total failure of consideration:

"This is not a case like *Rowland* v. *Divall* where title was lacking, and the defendant never had lawful possession. Here the defendant had the possession of the car and its use, such as it was. . . . Admittedly, the use

---

[13] For a full discussion of these questions, see Treitel, *op. cit.* pp. 929–932; Atiyah, *op. cit.* pp. 87–92. The Law Commission, Working Paper No. 65, §§ 57–78; Benjamin's *Sale of Goods*, § 4–005.

[14] See the hypothetical example given by Atiyah, *op. cit.* pp. 88–89, "Suppose that A buys a crate of whisky from B. Suppose further that after consuming the whisky A discovers that it never belonged to B but that B had bought it in good faith from a thief. Is it to be said that A can recover the full purchase price on the ground that there has been a total failure of consideration?"

[15] The position would then be akin to that hypothesised in n. 14, above, when *restitutio* becomes impossible because of the plaintiff's own act rather than the failure of the buyer to make title.

[16] By inseparable *accessio*.

[17] What is "substantial" must depend on the facts: see *Farnworth Finance Facilities Ltd.* v. *Attryde* [1970] 1 W.L.R. 1053.

[18] [1962] 2 Q.B. 508; see also *Kelly* v. *Lombard Banking Co.* [1959] 1 W.L.R. 41.

[19] But see now *Photo Production Ltd.* v. *Securicor Transport Ltd.* [1980] A.C. 827 (rejecting the doctrine of fundamental breach).

was of little (if any) value, but . . . that use, coupled with possession, and his continuance of the hiring agreement with the intention of keeping the car and getting Goodbody [the dealers] to pay half the repairs, debars the defendant from saying that there was a total failure of consideration."[20]

The plaintiffs' breach, however, continued; and "in continuing contracts, like hire-purchase . . . the right to reject remains so long as the fundamental breach continues."[21] While he paid the instalments, the defendant had shown an intention to maintain the contract; but, in view of the continuing nature of the breach, his payments did not preclude him from thereafter bringing the contract to an end.

As the law now stands, a plaintiff cannot recover money paid if the failure of consideration is only partial; his only action is then on the contract. We have already given our reasons[22] why we regret that English law does not allow him to recover his payment; this should be conditional on him restoring, or paying the value of, any benefits received.

Recompense for services rendered or goods supplied

If the innocent party has rendered services or has supplied goods under a contract which has been determined by him because of the other party's breach, he may recover the value of the services rendered or the goods supplied, on a *quantum meruit* or a *quantum valebat* respectively rather than sue for damages for loss arising from the breach. The party in breach cannot deny that he has received a benefit.[23] It is said that because the contract is at an end, he cannot keep the innocent party to the contract price.[24] However, there is no English authority to suggest that the innocent party may elect to sue in quasi-contract if he has performed or substantially performed[25] his part of the contract; and in Canada[25a] and the United States "there is no dissent from the view that where the defendant's obligation is to pay money the plaintiff who has fully performed cannot obtain restitution but is limited to recovery of the debt."[26] We consider this conclusion to be historically sound and to be correct in principle. The plaintiff was granted an action in quasi-contract because he could not sue in debt until he had completed his part of the bargain[27]; but if he had completed the contract, he was entitled to sue for the contract price.

---

[20] [1962] 2 Q.B. 508, 521, *per* Pearce L.J.; see also p. 525, *per* Davies L.J.
[21] [1961] C.L.J. 159, 162 [J. W. A. Thornely].
[22] See above, Chap. 17.
[23] See Carter, *Ineffective Transactions*, in *Essays* (ed. Finn) 206, 218 *et seq*. The defendant has prevented performance and is therefore precluded from saying that the plaintiff's performance does not correspond to his requested performance.
[24] See below, pp. 426–428 for a criticism.
[25] If he has substantially performed, his action is on the contract: *cf.* below, p. 441.
[25a] See below, p. 428, n. 51.
[26] 20 Ohio St.L.J. 264, 266 [Palmer]; Palmer, *op. cit.* Vol. I, § 4.3.
[27] Williston, *op. cit.* § 1459, pp. 4076–4077. *Cf.* the pleadings in *Planché* v. *Colburn* (1831) 5 Carr. & P. 58, 59.

Sums recoverable on a *quantum meruit* or *quantum valebat* may be greater than an award of damages for loss suffered, for the value of the services rendered and goods supplied is measured by their market value when they are rendered or supplied, and the "contract price" is regarded only as evidence of that value.[28] If, therefore, an innocent party has entered into a contract which, if it had not been determined, would have been fully performed at a loss, he is likely to elect, if the election is available, to sue in quasi-contract rather than to seek nominal damages.[29] A dramatic illustration of such a situation is the California case of *Boomer* v. *Muir*.[30] Boomer was a sub-contractor of Muir who was engaged in constructing a large dam. By the terms of his contract with Muir, Boomer was to receive monthly progress payments based on an agreed schedule. Friction developed between the parties, culminating in Boomer leaving the site 18 months after the making of the contract. When Boomer left, the dam was nearing completion. The District Court of California found that Boomer was justified in leaving the site since Muir's failure to supply materials as rapidly as Boomer needed them was a fundamental breach of his obligations, which entitled Boomer to put an end to the contract. The court, having taken into account payments already made, awarded Boomer $258,000, which represented the market value of his services and labour, even though only $20,000 was still due under his contract. Yet, if Boomer had performed or substantially performed his contract, his only claim would have been for the balance of the contract price and for any loss suffered because of any breach by the defendant of the terms of the contract.[30a]

England, and other common law jurisdictions, accept these principles, although there is relatively little authority to support them.[31] A leading case is said to be[32] *Planché* v. *Colburn*.[33] The defendant had engaged the plaintiff to write a book on costume and ancient armour for *The Juvenile Library*. The plaintiff wrote part of the book and was ready to complete the whole, but the defendant ceased publication of *The Juvenile Library* and refused to pay him.

---

[28] See below, Chap. 17.
[29] *Cf.* 20 Ohio State L.J. 264, 269–273 [Palmer]; 73 Col.L.R. 1208 [Perillo]; 64 Northwestern Univ.L.R. 433 [Childres and Garamella].
[30] 24 P. 2d 570 (1933).
[30a] See below, p. 424.
[31] *De Bernardy* v. *Harding* (1853) 8 Ex. 822; *Prickett* v. *Badger* (1856) 1 C.B.(n.s.) 296, 360, *per* Crowder J. (distinguished, on grounds not affecting the principles set out in the text, in *Luxor (Eastbourne) Ltd.* v. *Cooper* [1941] A.C. 108); *Bartholomew* v. *Markwick* (1864) 15 C.B.(N.S.) 711; *Lodder* v. *Slowey* [1904] A.C. 442, P.C.; *Hoenig* v. *Isaacs* [1952] 2 All E.R. 176, 180, *per* Somervell L.J. (For a recent decision of the Court of Appeal of New South Wales, affirming this principle: see *Renard Constructions (ME) Pty. Ltd.* v. *Minister of Public Works* [1992] A.C.L. Rep. 325.) See, generally, (1920) 33 Harv.L.R. 376 [Costigan]. *Lodder* v. *Slowey* is an influential decision. But in that case the Privy Council gave no reasons to support the conclusion that the innocent party should have such an election. The New Zealand Court of Appeal, whose judgment was affirmed, allowed the election because the contract has been *rescinded*: see (1902) 20 N.Z.L.R. 321. It is no longer accepted that the contract is wiped out; it is determined prospectively: see above, pp. 407–409.
[32] See below, n. 35.
[33] (1831) 8 Bing. 14, 1 M. & S. 51, 5 Carr. & P. 678. *Cf. Chandler* v. *Boswell* [1904] 1 K.B. 493; *Varney* v. *Lanark Boro.* 1973 S.L.T.(Notes) 82.

The Court of Common Pleas held that, as the jury had found that the contract was abandoned and no new contract had been entered into, "the plaintiff ought not to lose the fruit of his labour"[34]; he could, without tendering his treatise, recover on a *quantum meruit* for the services which he had performed.[35]

Planché v. *Colburn* is also important for its implicit conclusion that a *quantum meruit* claim will lie even though the plaintiff had not delivered or tendered any of the manuscript. Services had nonetheless been requested by, and rendered to, the defendant; the defendant was deemed to have gained a benefit simply because of that request. The contract was not one for sale of goods, in which case it could not be said that the defendant has benefited until delivery.[36] In our view such fine distinctions are unattractive,[37] and a restitutionary claim should lie only if the defendant had, or could have, received an objective benefit which he bargained for.[38] In any event, a restitutionary claim should fail if the plaintiff has only performed acts preparatory to contractual performance.[39] In such a case the innocent party's expenditure should be relevant only in assessing the damages which he is entitled to recover by reason of the defendant's breach of contract.

The restitutionary claim is said to arise because the contract has been determined. The "defendant cannot refuse to abide by his contract and at the same time claim its protection when the other party is not in default,"[40] a proposition which ignores the argument that, at the time of the innocent party's performance, the contract was in full force and effect, and that the breach does not, if treated as a repudiation, avoid the contract *ab initio*. Some common law jurisdictions have concluded that an innocent party's right to elect to claim a reasonable sum for services rendered or goods delivered should be restricted.[41] In the State of Washington it is said that the measure of the plaintiff's recovery should be such proportion of the contract price as the work done bears to the whole work embraced by the terms of the agreement; for it "is difficult to perceive why [the plaintiff] should receive more compensation for the labour performed by him than he would have received for the same services

---

[34] At p. 16, *per* Tindal C.J.

[35] But is doubtful whether *Planché* v. *Colburn* was a claim in quasi-contract, although later authorities have so interpreted it. A *quantum meruit* claim could also lie as a remedy on a special contract. With the cases cited in n. 31, above, *cf.* the pleadings in *Planché* v. *Colburn* (1831) 5 Carr. & P, 58, 59 and in *Hochster* v. *De La Tour* (1853) 2 El. & Bl. 678, 693.

[36] *Cf. Lee* v. *Griffen* (1861) 3 B. & S. 272; *Restatement of Contracts* 2d, § 370 comment.

[37] *Cf.* below, p. 430.

[38] Contrast *Acme Process Equipment Co. Ltd.* v. *U.S.*, 347 F. 2d 509 (1965), reversed on other grounds in 385 U.S. 138 (1966), where the Court of Claims held that the contract was not simply for the supply of goods, thereby enabling a manufacturer who had made a disastrously losing contract to recover on a *quantum meruit* for rifles which he had not delivered. And see below, pp. 427–428.

[39] *Cf. Restatement of Contracts* 2d § 370, comment a.

[40] Williston, *op. cit.* § 1485.

[41] The court may do so by finding that there had been substantial performance of a contract in order to frustrate the possibility of a restitutionary claim: see *Oliver* v. *Campbell*, 273 P. 2d 15 (1954) and see below, p. 441.

had the contract not been broken."[42] And in Oregon[43] while it is accepted that a plaintiff may recover on a *quantum meruit*, it has been held that he may never recover more than the contract price.[44]

The incongruity of the award in such cases as *Boomer* v. *Muir*[45] has led some commentators to question the wisdom of the common law principle. It is of course a truism that the innocent party enjoys an election of remedies. In suing for damages, he seeks to recover the loss suffered. His restitutionary claim seeks to recover the value of the defendant's benefit gained at his expense. However, the decision of the Oregon court that the contract price should be the ceiling of the award does protect the contractual expectations of both parties to the contract[46] in circumstances where it may be quite unclear, until the question is determined by a final appellate court, who is the party in breach.[47] To adopt this principle will admittedly only go some way to meeting the objection that the party in breach would then be allowed to retain part of the profit which should be his only if he fully performed his side of the bargain. It is also true that if the Oregon limitation is accepted, the innocent party who renders services may be in a less favourable position than he who claims the repayment of money on the ground of total failure of consideration; he will recover his money in full.[48] But the innocent party's claim is less favourable if he has received any part of the bargained-for performance which he cannot return.[49] Moreover, in a claim for money paid, is not seeking to ignore the contract price, as he does if his claim is for services rendered.

We have never found the resolution of this question easy, but we have reached the conclusion that the "Oregon" principle has much to commend it.[50]

---

[42] *Noyes* v. *Pugin*, 27 P. 548, 549, *per* Anders C.J. (1891).
Burrows, *The Law of Restitution*, pp. 268–270 supports the view that, unless the defendant has been incontrovertibly benefited, a plaintiff should recover the pro rata contract price on the ground that the defendant can validly argue that he was only willing to pay at the contractual rate: *cf.* Birks, *Essays on the Law of Restitution* (ed. Burrows) pp. 135–137. He describes as "extreme" and "unconvincing" the view that a wrongdoer cannot subjectively devalue. But that is one of the reasons why the courts have refused to allow the party in breach to rely on the contract price. Moreover, we do not consider that the problem is solved by characterising the contract price as a "valuation ceiling" rather than a "contract ceiling."
[43] *Wuchter* v. *Fitzgerald*, 163 P. 819 (1917).
[44] *Cf.* the solution in 20 Ohio State L.J. 264, 281 [Palmer]. (The courts should judge the nature and extent of the breach; the more fundamental the breach, the more ready should the courts be to permit an election of remedy.)
[45] 24 P. 2d 570 (1933): see above, p. 425.
[46] (1989) 2 Jo. of Contract Law 65, 72–74 [Beatson]; Jones, *Restitution in Public and Private Law*, pp. 118–121: see above, pp. 28–31, for a general discussion of the question whether the contract price should be the ceiling of the restitutionary claim.
[47] It is at first sight surprising that a defendant should breach a contract which is, for him, a highly profitable contract. Many of the disputes arise out of building contracts which are later resolved with the wisdom of many years' hindsight and where the party held to be in breach passionately believed that right was wholly on his side.
[48] See above, p. 413, n. 40.
[49] See above, pp. 420 *et seq.*
[50] The innocent party who brings a restitutionary claim for profits gained is not asking the court to value the benefits which he has conferred on the party in breach. The contract price and the market price determine what are the profits gained from the breach: see above pp. 413 *et seq.*

It is difficult to contemplate with equanimity "windfall" awards, such as the award in *Boomer* v. *Muir*, particularly when, if the innocent party has substantially or fully performed, the common law rule is that the contract price is the limit of his recovery, even though the defendant was guilty of breaches of contract.[51]

(c) *The Position of the Party in Breach*[52]

Recovery of money

(1) *By statute*

Section 49(2) of the Law of Property Act 1925 provides that: "Where the court refuses to grant specific performance of a contract, or in any action for the return of a deposit, the court may, if it thinks fit, order the repayment of any deposit."

In recent years the courts have interpreted this subsection generously, concluding that the discretion should be exercised where the justice of the case requires.[53] In Buckley L.J.'s view, "justice" must be "used in a wide sense, indicating that repayment must be ordered in any circumstances which makes this the fairest course between the two parties."[54] The courts have not as yet indicated what are the criteria which determine what is the *fairest course*. There is much to be said for the view that the principles which determine whether penalty payments are recoverable[55] should guide the courts in the exercise of their discretion, namely, the court should order restitution of the whole or part of the deposit if the sum forfeited is out of all proportion to the vendor's loss arising from the purchaser's repudiation.[56]

(2) *At common law*

A party in breach has generally no power to determine a contract which he has broken; only "the injured party may accept the renunciation as a breach going to the root of the whole consideration."[57] Nevertheless, the party in breach may, in certain circumstances, recover payments made by him under the

---

[51] The innocent party then recovers in addition to the contract price, any loss he suffered from the breach of contract. But the burden is on him to prove that loss, and that burden may be difficult to discharge. *Morrison-Knudsen Co. Inc.* v. *British Columbia Hydro and Power Authority* (1978) 85 D.L.R. (3d) 186 (Court of Appeal of British Columbia) is a dramatic illustration of such a situation.

[52] Restitutionary problems do not generally arise if the party has performed but performed badly; see *Corbin on Contracts*, Vol. 5, pp. 465–466.

[53] *Schindler* v. *Pigault* (1975) 30 P. & C.R. 328, 336, *per* Megarry V.-C.

[54] *Universal Corp.* v. *Five Ways Properties Ltd.* [1979] 1 All E.R. 552, 555. See, generally, Jones & Goodhart, *Specific Performance*, pp. 246–248.

[55] Treitel, *op. cit.* pp. 891–892.

[56] *Cf. Stockloser* v. *Johnson* [1954] 1 Q.B. 476, 490–492, *per* Denning L.J., who added that it must also be "unconscionable" for the seller to retain the money, on which see below, p. 433.

[57] *Heyman* v. *Darwins Ltd.* [1942] A.C. 356, 399, *per* Lord Porter. See also *Fitt* v. *Cassanet* (1842) 4 Man. & G. 898, 904, *per* Tindal C.J.; *Stray* v. *Russell* (1859) 1 E. & E. 888, 903–904, *per* Campbell C.J., 911, *per* Hill J.; (1860) 1 E. & E. 916, 917, *per curiam*.

contract. He may recover any money paid if he can demonstrate that it has been paid for a consideration which has totally failed.[58] To this general principle there is one important exception.

A deposit is money paid as a guarantee that the contract shall be performed.[59] Consequently, the general rule is that the innocent party may keep anything that he has received from the party in breach[60]; indeed a deposit which is due is forfeitable even though it has not yet been paid.[61] The common law rule is today of importance in the context of contracts for the sale of goods[62] and contracts for the supply of services.[63]

In *Dies* v. *British and International Mining and Finance Corporation*,[64] where £100,000 out of a contract price of £270,000, for the purchase of rifles and ammunition, had been paid in advance Stable J. drew a distinction between a payment made as a guarantee of performance and a part payment. He allowed the plaintiff, the party in breach, to recover the £100,000 on the ground that:

"[W]here the language used in a contract is neutral, the general rule is that the law confers on the purchaser the right to recover his money, and that to enable the seller to keep it he must be able to point to some language in the contract from which the inference to be drawn is that the parties intended and agreed that he should."[65]

---

[58] *Cf. Rover International Ltd.* v. *Cannon Film Sales Ltd. (No. 3)* [1989] 1 W.L.R. 912, C.A.; see above, p. 401 and see below pp. 543–544.

[59] If there is no concluded contract, then any sums paid as a "deposit" are recoverable on a total failure of consideration: *Chillingworth* v. *Esche* [1924] 1 Ch. 97; *aliter* if the contract is merely unenforceable, see *Monnickendam* v. *Leanse* (1923) 39 T.L.R. 445.

[60] *Howe* v. *Smith* (1884) 27 Ch.D. 89, 92, *per* Cotton L.J., 97, *per* Bowen L.J.; *Mayson* v. *Clouet* [1924] A.C. 980. This is so, even if it is later discovered that the depositee's title to the subject-matter of the contract is defective: *Soper* v. *Arnold* (1889) 14 App.Cas. 429.

[61] *Hinton* v. *Sparkes* (1868) L.R. 3 C.P. 161; *Dewar* v. *Mintoft* [1912] 2 K.B. 373. *Cf. Polloway* v. *Abdullah* [1974] 1 W.L.R. 493 (auctioneer may sue on a cheque which was given as a deposit and subsequently dishonoured); *Millichamp* v. *Jones* [1982] 1 W.L.R. 1422 (vendor must warn if failure to pay is inadvertent); *Damon Cia Naviera S.A.* v. *Hapag-Lloyd International Ltd.* [1985] 1 W.L.R. 435. (*Lowe* v. *Hope* [1970] Ch. 94 cannot be good law since *Johnson* v. *Agnew* [1980] A.C. 367: see *Millichamp* v. *Jones* [1982] 1 W.L.R. 1422, 1430, *per* Warner J.) See also *Ron Engineering & Construction Eastern Ltd.* v. *The Queen* (1979) 98 D.L.R. (3d) 548. *Aliter* if it is a pre-payment (on which see below, p. 430): *McDonald* v. *Dennys Lascelles Ltd.* (1933) 48 C.L.R. 457 (see below, pp. 430).

[62] *Damon Cia Naviero SA* v. *Hapag-Lloyd International SA* [1985] 1 W.L.R. 435; *Bot* v. *Ristavski* [1981] V.R. 120. *Cf. Elson (Inspector of Taxes)* v. *Prices Tailors Ltd.* [1963] 1 W.L.R. 287.

[63] *Cf. Rover International Ltd.* v. *Cannon Film Sales Ltd. (No. 3)* [1989] 1 W.L.R. 912, C.A.; see above, p. 401 and see below, pp. 543–544.

[64] [1939] 1 K.B. 724; see also *McDonald* v. *Dennys Lascelles Ltd.* (1933) 48 C.L.R. 475, see below, n. 67; *Mason* v. *Clouet* [1924] A.C. 980; *Ruddenklau* v. *Charlesworth* [1925] N.Z.L.R. 161; *Reynolds* v. *Fury* [1921] V.R. 14, 17. And see *Laird* v. *Pim* (1841) 7 M. & W. 474, 478, *per* Parke B; *Palmer* v. *Temple* (1839) 9 Ad. & El. 588; *Howe* v. *Smith* (1884) 27 Ch.D. 89, *semble*.

[65] [1939] 1 K.B. 724, 743, *per* Stable J. *Cf. Rover International Ltd.* v. *Cannon Film Sales Ltd. (No. 3)* [1989] 1 W.L.R. 912, 927–928, C.A., following *McDonald* v. *Dennys Lascelles Ltd.* (1933) 48 C.L.R. 457: see above, p. 430.

The innocent party is protected. He has his action on the contract for loss suffered, and can set off that claim against the claim for the return of the purchase price.[66]

In principle, whether a party has the right to retain a part payment should depend on the terms of the contract. As Dixon J. once said, in the High Court of Australia: "a title to retain may not be absolute but conditional upon the subsequent completion of the contract."[67] If there is an express term to that effect, the court will enforce it. If the contract is silent, *Dies* would suggest that the payer has a right to recover his money. But the Court of Appeal and House of Lords have recently suggested that that conclusion may be too simple. Whether a party in breach can recover his part payment may depend on such factors as the nature of the contract, and possibly on the amount of the part payment; the same principles apply whether an instalment has been paid or has fallen due but has not been paid.[68] In *Hyundai Shipbuilding and Heavy Industries Co. Ltd.* v. *Pournaras*[69] and *Hyundai Shipbuilding and Heavy Industries Co. Ltd.* v. *Papadopoulos*,[70] the Court of Appeal and the House of Lords respectively held that guarantors were liable to pay the second instalment of 2.5 per cent. of the contract price, due to the plaintiff shipbuilders under two shipbuilding contracts, which the buyers had failed to pay.[71] In *Papadopoulos*, the House of Lords held unanimously that the plaintiffs could recover from the guarantors the amount due irrespective of the contractual position between the shipbuilders and the buyers. The House also held, Lord Russell and Lord Keith of Kinkel *dubitante*, that the buyers remained liable to pay the second instalment because their liability arose before the plaintiffs exercised their contractual right to cancel the contract. Accordingly the guarantors remained liable on the guarantee; for "rights and obligations which arise from the partial execution of the contract and causes of action which have accrued from its breach alike continue unaffected."[72] Contracts "to build, launch, equip and complete [a vessel] . . . and to deliver and sell her" were not akin to contracts for sale.[73] They were not of "that comparatively simple character."[74] They were more like contracts to perform work or to provide services, such as a

---

[66] At p. 744; see also *Fitt* v. *Cassanet* (1842) 4 Man. & G. 898; *Hyundai Shipbuilding and Heavy Industries Co. Ltd.* v. *Pournaras* [1978] 2 Lloyd's Rep. 502, 507, *per* Roskill L.J.

[67] *McDonald* v. *Dennys Lascelles Ltd.* (1933) 48 C.L.R. 455, 477.

[68] *Cf. Hinton* v. *Sparkes* (1868) L.R. 3 C.P. 161, 166, *per* Willes J; see above, p. 429.

[69] [1978] 2 Lloyd's Rep. 502.

[70] [1980] 1 W.L.R. 1129.

[71] In each case the first instalment had been paid, and the shipbuilders had the right, which they exercised, to cancel the contract, to retain instalments already paid and to sell the ship if the buyer defaulted.

[72] *McDonald* v. *Dennys Lascelles Ltd.* (1933) 48 C.L.R. 457, 476, *per* Dixon J.; cited and approved in *Johnson* v. *Agnew* [1980] A.C. 367, 396, and in *Hyundai Heavy Industries Ltd.* v. *Papadopoulos* [1980] 1 W.L.R. 1129, 1141.

[73] [1980] 1 W.L.R. 1129, 1134, *per* Viscount Dilhorne.

[74] [1980] 1 W.L.R. 1129, 1148, *per* Lord Fraser, *Cf.* J. Beatson, *Discharge for Breach* (1981) 97 L.Q.R. 389, 402–403.

building contract.[75] A contract to design and construct a ship was not the same as a contract to sell a ship.[76] Viscount Dilhorne[77] did not think it necessary to consider whether *Dies*[78] was correctly decided. Lord Edmund-Davies doubted whether *Dies* was reconcilable with earlier authority,[79] and concluded that it was unrealistic to compare a modest instalment of 2.5 per cent. with the £100,000 paid in *Dies*.[80] And Lord Fraser distinguished *Dies* on the ground that it was not a contract which required the vendor to perform any work or to incur any expense. In contrast, it was very likely that in *Papadopoulos* "the increasing proportions of the contract price represented by the five instalments bore some relation to the anticipated rate of [the shipbuilders'] expenditure"[81]; and it must be assumed that the shipbuilders "had carried out their part of the bargain up till the date of cancellation."[82]

It would then appear that if instalments are paid under a contract to do work or perform services, such as a building contract under which the recipient is bound to incur expenses in its performance, these instalments will be irrecoverable, at least if the sums are not penal; if the instalment is due but not yet paid, the obligor will be liable to pay, again, unless the sum is not penal.[83] Conversely, if instalments are paid or due under a contract of sale, they are recoverable unless they are earnest payments. The payer then recovers his pre-payment either because there is deemed to be a total failure of consideration or because it is an implied term of the contract of sale that he should be restored to his pre-contractual position in the event of breach.[84]

---

[75] [1980] 1 W.L.R. 1129, 1148–1149, *per* Lord Fraser, citing *Government of Newfoundland* v. *Newfoundland Railway Co.* (1888) 13 App.Cas. 199. See also Viscount Dilhorne at p. 1134. The House also held that the same principles apply to hire purchase contracts. Contrast *Lee* v. *Griffen* (1861) 1 B. & S. 272; see above, p. 426, n. 36.

[76] For a similar distinction, in the context of a claim by an innocent party for services rendered, see above, p. 426, n. 38. English courts were also at one time compelled to draw this distinction in determining whether a contract was for the sale of goods which should be evidenced in writing; see, *e.g. Robinson* v. *Graves* [1935] 1 K.B. 579, C.A.

[77] [1980] 1 W.L.R. 1129, 1131.

[78] See above, p. 429.

[79] [1980] 1 W.L.R. 1129, 1142–1143. In *Pournaras* the appeal was conducted on the basis that *Dies* was correctly decided. But Roskill L.J. considered that the arguments for the seller in *Dies* "were not without considerable merit": [1978] 2 Lloyd's Rep. 502, 507.

[80] At p. 1142. But the 2.5 per cent. amounted to $357,000.

[81] At p. 1148, *per* Lord Fraser.

[82] *Ibid.*

[83] See below, p. 433.

[84] In *Papadopoulos* Viscount Dilhorne based his decision on the ground that there was no total failure of consideration: the services rendered by the shipbuilder were part of the bargained for performance: see below, p. 432: [1980] 1 W.L.R. at 1135–1136 (and see *Rover International Ltd.* v. *Cannon Film Sales Ltd. (No. 3)* [1989] 1 W.L.R. 912, C.A.; see above, p. 401 and below, p. 543). But *cf.* the more equivocal observations of Lord Fraser at 1148. See generally, (1981) 97 L.Q.R. 389, [Beatson], who discusses the comparative merits of both approaches and concludes that it is more satisfactory to imply a term: a person's reliance will thereby always be protected. Query if the shipbuilders could also have sued on a *quantum meruit* based on the buyer's request: (1981) 97 L.Q.R. at 414–415 [Beatson].

Yet the line between contracts to perform services and a contract for sale can be a very thin one. It is not easy, for example, to distinguish the facts of *Papadopoulos* from the facts of the *Fibrosa* case,[85] where the buyer recovered his pre-payment from the seller who had agreed to supply certain machinery.[86] Again, in *Rover International Ltd.* v. *Cannon Film Sales Ltd.*[87] the contract was to exhibit films on Italian television but was nonetheless said to be akin to the contract in *Dies*; the pre-payment was in the nature of an advance for a consideration to be provided in the future.[88] In Kerr L.J.'s view, the earlier decisions are best explained in terms of failure of consideration[88a]; whether a pre-payment is recoverable should depend on the construction of the contract and, in particular, whether the right to retain the pre-payment is conditional on the completion of the contract. But the inquiry, whether a party to the contract has received any part of the bargained for performance, may require the court to draw the finest of distinctions[89]; and the conclusion may depend on how anxious the court is to grant restitution.[90] The contract may be, as it often is, uninformative. It may then be necessary to presume that "where the language of the contract is neutral, the general rule is that the law confers on the purchaser the right to recover his money."[91] This is, we consider, a sound presumption.

In cases of payment of money, therefore, a distinction is to be drawn between a deposit, which is recognised as being forfeitable on default, and other part payments, which may or may not be retained by the payee. In each case, it should be, in principle, a question of construction of the contract into which category the part payment falls, and whether it is forfeitable.[92] However, it is:

"possible that in a particular contract the parties may use language normally appropriate to deposits properly so called and as to forfeiture which turns out on investigation to be purely colourable and that in such a case the real nature of the transaction might turn out to be the imposition

---

[85] [1943] A.C. 32: see above, pp. 408–409.

[86] See Beatson, *The Use and Abuse of Unjust Enrichment* Chap. 3, who argues that the substance of the *Fibrosa* contract was the sale of the machines (in our view, a debatable conclusion), and that in *Papadopoulos* it was to design and build, which was severable from the obligation to deliver and sell. See also (1989) 105 L.Q.R. 460 [Mead].

[87] [1989] 1 W.L.R. 912: see above, p. 401.

[88] [1939] 1 K.B. 724, 740, 742; see above, p. 429.

[88a] *Sed quaere*: see above, pp. 429–431.

[89] See Jones, *Restitution in Public and Private Law*, pp. 102–106.

[90] See above, Chap. 17.

[91] *Dies* v. *British and International Mining and Finance Corp.* [1939] 1 K.B. 724, 743; see also *McDonald* v. *Dennys Lascelles Ltd.* (1933) 48 C.L.R. 457, 478–479, *per* Dixon J., and see above, pp. 429–430.

[92] If the word "deposit" is used, it is presumed to mean "earnest payment"; see *Elson (Inspector of Taxes)* v. *Prices Tailors Ltd.* [1963] 1 W.L.R. 287; but see *Smyth* v. *Jessup* [1956] V.L.R. 230; and see below, p. 429.

of a penalty, by purporting to render forfeit something which is in truth part payment."[93]

(3) *In equity*

In recent years it has been suggested that a deposit may be recoverable in equity by the party in breach if the forfeiture clause is penal and it is unconscionable for the recipient to retain the money.[93a] In *Stockloser* v. *Johnson*,[94] the plaintiff agreed to buy plant and machinery from the defendant. The contract provided that the purchase price was payable by instalments and that, if there was a default in any of the instalments for a period of more than 28 days, the defendant could rescind, forfeit the instalments already paid, and retake possession of the plant and machinery. The plaintiff brought an action against the defendant for the return of all instalments paid, on the ground that their retention amounted to an exaction of a penalty from which he was entitled to be relieved in equity. On the facts the Court of Appeal refused him relief, though Somervell and Denning L.JJ., but not Romer L.J., thought that in appropriate circumstances relief could be given.

In Somervell and Denning L.JJ.'s view, the plaintiff's readiness and willingness to perform were not essential to obtain relief from forfeiture. They considered that, in a proper case, equity will give relief if two conditions are fulfilled. As Denning L.J. said[95]:

> " . . . First, the forfeiture clause must be of a penal nature, in this sense, that the sum forfeited must be out of all proportion to the damage, and, secondly, it must be unconscionable for the seller to retain the money. . . .
>
> In a proper case there is an equity of restitution which a party in default does not lose simply because he is not able and willing to perform the contract. Nay, that is the very reason why he needs the equity. The equity operates, not because of the plaintiff's default, but because it is in the particular case unconscionable for the seller to retain the money. In short, he ought not unjustly to enrich himself at the plaintiff's expense. The equity of restitution is to be tested, I think, not at the time of the contract but by the conditions existing when it is invoked."

The innocent party will, of course, have his action on the contract for damages.

It is not clear whether these two conditions are distinct conditions, or whether the first, that the sum forfeited must be out of all proportion to the

---

[93] *Linggi Plantations Ltd.* v. *Jagatheesan* [1972] 1 M.L.J. 89, 94, *per* Lord Hailsham of Marylebone L.C.

[93a] In Scotland the court does not have inherent equitable power to grant relief: *Zemhunt (Holdings)* v. *Control Securities* (1991) S.L.T. 653 (O.H.).

[94] [1954] 1 Q.B. 476; see *Pitt* v. *Curotta* (1931) 31 S.R. (N.S.W.) 477; *McDonald* v. *Dennys Lascelles Ltd.* (1933) 48 C.L.R. 457, 475–479, *per* Dixon J.; *Coates* v. *Sarich* [1964] W.A.R. 2.

[95] *Ibid.* at p. 490, 492; see also Somervell L.J. at pp. 485, 486–487. *Cf.* the judicial observations on the scope of the judicial discretion to grant relief under the L.P.A. 1925, s.49(2); above, p. 428; see also *Restatement of Contracts 2d*, § 229.

damage, is simply one manifestation of unconscionable behaviour. Certainly, the first condition cannot be condemned, as some may condemn *unconscionability*, as vague and woolly jurisprudence.

Romer L.J. vigorously dissented. Equity had always granted relief against fraud, undue influence or breach of a fiduciary relationship, but it had never interfered with contracts because they were improvident.[96] Equity would go no further than to give a party time to fulfil his obligations[97] and to grant relief against penalties.[98] In Romer L.J.'s view, there is "nothing inequitable *per se* in a vendor, whose conduct is not open to criticism in other respects, insisting upon his contractual right to retain instalments of purchase-money already paid."[99]

A similar sharp division of view is to be found in *Stern* v. *McArthur*[1] among the Justices of the High Court of Australia. The purchasers had contracted to buy land by monthly instalments, and had paid over half the instalments. They then defaulted and remained in default for over a year. Under the terms of the contract the balance of the purchase price fell immediately due and payable without notice. The vendors terminated the contract and brought proceedings for possession, the purchasers having been allowed to take possession of the land. In answer, the purchasers sought a decree of specific performance and relief against forfeiture. The High Court, Mason C.J. and Brennan J. dissenting, granted specific performance and the relief sought by the purchasers. Deane and Dawson JJ. held that the transaction was in essence akin to a mortgage transaction. But they also went on to consider the scope of equity's inherent jurisdiction to grant relief against forfeiture and, in particular, the submission that it was unconscionable for the vendors to exercise their legal rights under the contract.[2] The classical manifestations of unconscionability were fraud, mistake, accident or surprise. But they concluded that this catalogue was not exhaustive and went on to say:

"The general underlying notion is that which has been long identified as underlying much of equity's traditional jurisdiction to grant relief against

---

[96] [1954] 1 Q.B. 476, 495–496, citing *Mussen* v. *Van Diemen's Land Co.* [1938] Ch. 253; *cf. Bridge* v. *Campbell Discount Co. Ltd.* [1962] A.C. 600, 613–614, *per* Viscount Simonds (where the Privy Council left open the possibility of ordering repayment if it was unconscionable for the vendor to retain the payments).

[97] *Kilmer* v. *British Columbia Orchard Lands Ltd.* [1913] A.C. 319, following *Re Dagenham (Thames) Dock Co.* (1873) L.R. 8 Ch. 1022. *Cf. Barton; Thompson Co. Ltd.* v. *Stapling Machines Co.* [1966] Ch. 499.

[98] *Cf. Starside Properties Ltd.* v. *Mustapha* [1974] 1 W.L.R. 816, 819, *per* Edmund Davies L.J.

[99] [1954] 1 Q.B. 476, 501. The previous authorities were not conclusive: see, in particular, *Steedman* v. *Drinkle* [1916] 1 A.C. 275 (P.C.), cited by Somervell and Denning L.JJ. in [1954] 1 Q.B. 476, 486 and 490, and distinguished by Romer L.J. at p. 501.
In *Workers Trust Bank* v. *Dojap Investments* [1993] 2 W.L.R. 702, P.C., the Privy Council found it unnecessary to decide which of these two views was correct. But the Privy Council held that a 25% deposit was not a true deposit by way of earnest; "the provision for its forfeiture was a plain penalty."

[1] (1988) 165 C.L.R. 489.

[2] But their Honours expressly refused to decide the case on this ground.

unconscientious conduct, namely, that a person should not be permitted to use or insist upon his legal rights to take advantage of another's special vulnerability or misadventure for the unjust enrichment of himself."[3]

This is a generous principle. Their Honours gave it content by stressing that the parties had a common expectation that the purchasers would benefit from any increase in the value of the land over the period of the payment of the instalments; and to refuse relief would result in a "windfall" gain for the vendors.

For the third member of the majority of the High Court, Gaudron J., it was critical that the vendors could have recovered the balance of the purchase price by bringing an action for specific performance. To rely on their legal rights, when the purchasers had built a house on the land which had increased in value and which they had occupied for 10 years and when the payments outstanding were relatively insignificant, was unconscionable. For these reasons, and these reasons alone, her Honour concluded that specific performance should be decreed and relief against forfeiture granted.

Mason C.J. and Brennan J. dissented for reasons which are not dissimilar to those of Romer L.J. in *Stockloser* v. *Johnson*: "to grant relief against forfeiture on the basis of unconscionability on the [vendor's] part would be to drain unconscionability of any meaning."[4] Certainly, courts should not seek to exercise "a power to destroy the rights and obligations which the parties to a contract create."[5] But they accepted that there should be an inherent jurisdiction to grant relief, even if the contract is between commercial men, if the retention of the whole of, or part of, the deposit would be out of proportion to the loss suffered. Such would be the case if a vendor had sold land at a higher price to a third party and the purchaser's payments were substantial.

It is conjectural whether Denning L.J.'s dicta in *Stockloser* v. *Johnson*, now reinforced by the dicta in *Stern* v. *McArthur*, will be accepted as authoritative. Sachs J. had refused to follow them in *Galbraith* v. *Mitchenhall Estates Ltd.*[6] But Lloyd J. in *The Afovos*[7] "attached importance" to the majority judgments in *Stockloser* v. *Johnson*. And in *Shiloh Spinners Ltd.* v. *Harding*,[8] Lord Simon of Glaisdale went so far as to say that equity has an "unlimited and unfettered

---

[3] At pp. 526–527.
[4] At p. 505, *per* Mason C.J.
[5] *Stern* v. *McArthur* (1988) 165 C.L.R. 489, 514, *per* Brennan J., who was, however, prepared to compensate the purchasers for the value of their improvements and possibly to make adjustments in respect of occupation rent. (The vendors had made a late concession that the purchasers should be compensated for the value of the improvements). See, on this point, Waddams in *Essays* (ed. Burrows) at pp. 203–204.
[6] [1965] 2 Q.B. 743. Sachs J. relied on dicta in the Court of Appeal in *Campbell Discount Co. Ltd.* v. *Bridge* [1961] 1 Q.B. 445. But only Harman L.J. can clearly be said to support Romer L.J.'s dissent in *Stockloser* v. *Johnson*.
[7] [1980] 2 Lloyd's Rep. 469, (revs'd) [1982] 1 W.L.R. 848, C.A.; [1983] 1 W.L.R. 195, H.L.); and *cf.* Lord Diplock's comment in *The Scaptrade* [1983] 2 A.C. 694, 702: see below, p. 436.
[8] [1973] A.C. 691, 726–727. *Cf.* the more limited observations of Lord Wilberforce at 723–724, discussed in *The Scaptrade* [1983] 2 A.C. 694, 702.

equity has an "unlimited and unfettered jurisdiction" to relieve against contractual penalties and forfeitures. More recently, in *The Scaptrade*,[9] Lord Diplock dismissed this observation as a "beguiling heresy."[10] In that case, the House of Lords has held that there is no jurisdiction to prevent an owner from exercising his right under a time-charter to withdraw his vessel for non-payment of hire. There are sound practical reasons for denying this form of equitable relief, which if granted, would endanger the certainty of commercial transactions.[11] In reaching this conclusion the House considered the scope of equity's jurisdiction to relieve against forfeiture of property. In Lord Diplock's view it arose historically in the context of contracts involving the transfer of proprietary or possessory rights, where the object of the transaction and of the insertion of the right to forfeit is essentially to secure the payment of money[12]; for example, a forfeiture clause to secure the payment of rent due under lease. But he was prepared to assume that equity's jurisdiction to relieve against forfeiture might be extended, as the majority judgments in *Stockloser* v. *Johnson* suggested,[13] to circumstances where:

> "money already paid by one party to the other under a continuing contract prior to an event which under the terms of the contract entitled that other party to elect to rescind it and to retain the money already paid might be treated as money paid under a penalty clause and recovered to the extent that it exceeded to an unconscionable extent the value of any consideration that had been given for it."[14]

But the court had no jurisdiction to relieve against payments of hire in advance; such a clause was not a penalty but "represents the agreed rate of hire for services already rendered, and not a penny more."[15]

In *Sport International Bussum BV* v. *Inter-Footwear Ltd.*,[16] the courts had a further opportunity to consider the scope of the equitable jurisdiction. Under a consent order, following the settlement of litigation between the parties, the plaintiffs had granted the defendants licences to use certain names and trade-marks in consideration of a payment of £105,000. The money was to be paid in three instalments; the defendants were to provide guarantees for each of the second and third instalments "immediately upon payment" of the previous instalment; and if they failed to do so the whole sum would fall due and the licences be terminated. The defendants failed to provide the second guarantee until 14 days after the payment of the second instalment. The House of Lords, affirming the Court of Appeal, denied them any relief. Lord Templeman, who

---

[9] [1983] 2 A.C. 694, *sub nom. Scandinavian Trading Tanker Co.* v. *Flota Petrolera Ecuatoriana.*
[10] At p. 700.
[11] [1983] Q.B. 529, 540–541, *per* Robert Goff L.J., adopted by Lord Diplock at pp. 703–704.
[12] At p. 702.
[13] See above, pp. 433–434.
[14] At p. 702.
[15] At p. 703. *Cf. Goker* v. *NWS Bank plc, The Times*, May 23, 1990, C.A., jurisdiction to provide relief to hirer of chattels from forfeiture will be exercised only in exceptional circumstances.
[16] [1984] 1 W.L.R. 776, C.A.; [1984] 1 W.L.R. 776, 790, H.L.

gave the only reasoned speech, thought that the case was not a suitable one in which "to define the boundaries of the equitable doctrine of relief against forfeiture."[17] The contract was "unusual," designed to bring hostile litigation to an end. But he accepted that the recognised "equitable boundaries" do not permit claims for relief arising from the termination of contractual licences, and he could see "profound objections to the intervention of equity"[18] in such circumstances. Oliver L.J.'s judgment, in the Court of Appeal, was more conservative.[19] He considered that the court had no jurisdiction to grant relief in ordinary commercial contracts, where the forfeited interests depend only on the contract. Indeed, he doubted whether relief could be granted outside the area of contracts connected with interests in land. In his view, there was no compelling reason to extend equity's jurisdiction to other classes of contracts.[20] But in *BICC plc* v. *Burndy Corporation*,[21] Kerr and Dillon L.JJ. took a wider view, and concluded that the equitable jurisdiction to grant relief against forfeiture exists if what is liable to forfeiture is a proprietary or possessory interest in land, or a similar interest in personal property arising under a commercial agreement. The fact that forfeiture arises under a commercial agreement is, however, highly relevant to the question whether there should be relief against forfeiture, "but does not preclude the jurisdiction to grant relief, if forfeiture of proprietary or possessory rights, as opposed to mere contractual rights, is in question."[22]

The cases suggest therefore that the courts may relieve against the forfeiture of proprietary or possessory interests if the forfeiture can be characterised as unconscionable. But the certainty of commercial transactions would not be endangered if, following Lord Denning in *Stockloser* v. *Johnson*,[23] the courts were to accept a jurisdiction to relieve against the consequence of forfeiture of other instalment payments, even if there was no forfeiture of a proprietary or possessory right, if the forfeiture would in all the circumstances be out of proportion to the loss suffered.[24] Equity already relieves against the payment of penalties,[25] and may raise an estoppel against a person if it would be unconscionable for him to assert his legal rights.[26] It would be regrettable, therefore,

---

[17] [1984] 1 W.L.R. 776, 794.

[18] *Ibid.*

[19] [1984] 1 W.L.R. 776, 787.

[20] For an argument that it is wrong in principle to say that the court may never grant specific performance in these circumstances, see [1984] C.L.J. 134 [Harpum].

[21] [1985] Ch. 232 (where the court granted an extension of time to the defendants to make payments).

[22] [1985] Ch. 232, 251–252, *per* Dillon L.J. *Cf.* at p. 253, *per* Kerr L.J. Dillon L.J. cited the following cases, in support of the principle that relief could be granted to relieve against forfeiture of proprietary or possessory interests in personal property: *Barton Thompson & Co. Ltd.* v. *Stapling Machines Co.* [1966] Ch. 499, 509, approved in *Starsides Property* v. *Mustapha* [1974] 1 W.L.R. 816, 822.

[23] [1954] 1 Q.B. 476, 490, 492, quoted above, p. 433. See also *The Scaptrade* [1983] 2 A.C. 694, 702, *per* Lord Diplock, quoted above, p. 436.

[24] *Stockloser* v. *Johnson* [1954] 1 Q.B. 476, 490, *per* Denning L.J.: see above, p. 433.

[25] *Dunlop Pneumatic Tyre Co. Ltd.* v. *New Garage and Motor Co. Ltd.* [1915] A.C. 79.

[26] See above, Chap. 5; and *cf.* the facts of *BICC plc* v. *Burndy Corp.* [1985] Ch. 232.

to conclude that the courts *never* have jurisdiction to relieve against the forfeiture of such payments, made in the course of the performance of commercial contracts, although it is proper to affirm that relief should be granted only in exceptional circumstances and that the burden should be on the party in breach to demonstrate that the retention of any payment was unconscionable.[27]

In these circumstances, the court should take into account, in determining whether the retention of instalment payments is unconscionable, such factors as whether the sum forfeited is out of all proportion to the damage suffered by the recipient.[28] It is debatable whether it is relevant to inquire whether the breach is "wilful."[29] In the past the wilful nature of the breach has been a factor which the courts have taken into account in determining whether to grant relief against forfeiture of a lease.[30] It may not be easy to determine whether a breach is or is not "wilful"[31]; and both the English Law Commission[32] and the *Restatement of Contracts 2d*[33] have suggested that the wilful as well as the non-wilful contract breaker may in some circumstances be granted restitution for services rendered under an entire contract. We are persuaded that the civil law should not penalise a contracting party who has wrongfully repudiated, for whatever reason, the contract.[34] The wilfulness of the breach should not, in principle, persuade a court to deny relief against forfeiture.

Recompense for services rendered or goods supplied

If the contract is not entire but divisible[35] the party in breach can recover payment under the contract for any divisible part or parts of services rendered

---

[27] *Cf. BICC plc* v. *Burndy Corp.* [1985] Ch. 232.

[28] See above, pp. 433–434. *Linggi Plantations Ltd.* v. *Jagarseathan* [1972] 1 M.L.J. 89 (deposit of 10% not a penalty). In its Working Paper on *Penalty Clauses and Forfeiture of Monies Paid*, No. 61, §§ 61–67 (1975), the Law Commission proposed that the court should also take into account the general practice in transactions of a similar nature, the reasonableness of the sums involved, and the particular circumstances of the case. Deposits made on contracts for the sale of land may therefore be treated differently from deposits made on contracts for the sale of goods.

[29] *Stockloser* v. *Johnson* [1954] 1 Q.B. 476, 490–2; see above, p. 433. In *Re Young and Harston's Contract* (1885) 31 Ch.D. 168, 175, Bowen L.J. said that, in his view, "wilful" "implies nothing blameable, but merely that the person of whose action or default the expression is used, is a free agent, and that what has been done arises from the spontaneous action of his will. It amounts to nothing more than this, that he knows what he is doing, and intends to do what he is doing, and is a free agent."

[30] *Shiloh Spinners Ltd.* v. *Harding* [1973] A.C. 691, 723–724, *per* Lord Wilberforce. *Cf.* Law Commission's Working Paper, No. 61, see above, p. 446.

[31] Although that difficulty may be exaggerated: *cf.* below, p. 446.

[32] Law Commission, Report No. 121, *Law of Contract, Pecuniary Restitution on Breach of Contract* (1983); see below, p. 446.

[33] § 374, see below, p. 446.

[34] *Cf.* below, p. 446.

[35] For this distinction, see above, p. 409.

or goods supplied by him under the contract.[36] But if the contract is entire,[37] the party in breach can generally[38] obtain no recompense for services rendered or goods supplied if the innocent party determines the contract before the contract has been substantially or wholly performed. Thus, in *Sumpter* v. *Hedges*,[39] Sumpter had contracted with the defendant to build on the defendant's land two houses and stables for £565. He did work to the value of £333, receiving part payment of the price. Later he became insolvent and told the defendant he could not go on with the work. The defendant finished the building, using materials which the plaintiff had left behind. On the plaintiff's claim for work done and materials supplied, Bruce J. allowed the plaintiff the value of the materials left on the site but nothing more. The Court of Appeal affirmed his decision. There was no evidence of any fresh contract; certainly, no contract could be implied from the fact that the defendant took the benefit of the work that was done, for he had no choice but to accept it. "The circumstances must be such as to give an option to the defendant to take or not to take the benefit of the work done. It is only where the circumstances are such as to give that option that there is any evidence on which to ground the inference of a new contract."[40]

Similarly, no payment can be recovered by the party in breach for goods supplied under an uncompleted entire contract of labour and materials if the innocent party had no choice whether to accept or to reject the goods, which he can no longer return. Sumpter was unable to recover anything for the materials which, at the time when he abandoned the contract, had already been incorporated into the building on Hedges' land, but he was able to recover payment for materials which he had merely left behind on the land[41] and which were thereafter used by Hedges.

In other cases the party in breach may be unable to recover because he cannot be allowed to make a profit from his own wrong. In *Warman* v. *Southern Counties Car Finance Corporation Ltd.*,[42] the plaintiff entered into an agreement for the hire-purchase of a car from the defendants. After he had signed the

---

[36] He will recover at the contract rate or, if no rate is specified in the contract, on a *quantum meruit* or *quantum valebat*: see *Roberts* v. *Havelock* (1832) 3 B. & Ad. 404; *Hoenig* v. *Isaacs* [1952] 2 All E.R. 176, 180, *per* Denning L.J.; Williams, *Law Reform (Frustrated Contracts) Act* 1943, pp. 66–67.

[37] See above, p. 409.

[38] But if the innocent party has made a pre-payment and has obtained a benefit from the party in breach's part performance, he may be denied recovery of the pre-payment for there has been no total failure of consideration: *cf. Whincup* v. *Hughes* (1871) L.R. 6 C.P. 78; see above, p. 420.

[39] [1898] 1 Q.B. 673; see also *Munro* v. *Butt* (1858) 8 E. 7 B. 738; *Hopper* v. *Burness* (1876) 1 C.P.D. 137; *Whitaker* v. *Dunn* (1887) 3 T.L.R. 602; *Wheeler* v. *Stratton* (1917) 105 L.T. 786; *Bolton* v. *Mahadeva* [1972] 1 W.L.R. 1009.

[40] [1898] 1 Q.B. 673, 676, *per* Collins L.J.; see also *Cutter* v. *Powell* (1795) 6 T.R. 320, see above, p. 410; *Boston Deep Sea Fishing & Ice Co.* v. *Ansell* (1889) 39 Ch.D. 339, 364, 365, *per* Bowen L.J.; *Forman & Co. Proprietary Ltd.* v. *S.S. Liddesdale* [1900] A.C. 190.

[41] See *Laird* v. *Pim* (1841) 7 M. & W. 474, 478, *per* Parke B.; Salmond & Williams, p. 571. *Cf. Oxendale* v. *Wetherell* (1829) 9 B. & C. 386 (see below, p. 442); and *Rugg* v. *Minett* (1809) 11 East 210.

[42] [1949] 2 K.B. 576; see also above, p. 422.

contract he became aware that a third party was claiming title to the car. Nevertheless, he continued to pay the instalments of the hire-purchase price to the defendants and ultimately exercised his option to purchase the car from them. As soon as he had done this, the third party served a writ on him claiming the return of the car, whereupon he surrendered it to the third party. In this action, the plaintiff claimed from the defendants, as damages, the amount of the sums paid under the contract of hire-purchase, and his claim was successful; but the defendants counterclaimed for a reasonable sum for the hire of the car during the period of the plaintiff's possession. The counterclaim failed. The car was never the defendant's property, and, for that reason, the plaintiff had not been enriched at their expense.[43] If the plaintiff was unjustly enriched, he was enriched at the expense of the true owner of the car, but not at the expense of the defendants.

It has long been established that there may be circumstances, albeit exceptional, where a party in breach can obtain recompense for benefits conferred even under an entire contract. Generally, his right of recovery is contractual, but there are three cases where it cannot be so classified.

(1) *Cases where recovery is based on statute or contract*

Apportionment. At common law a servant, who was properly dismissed, could not recover wages already earned but not payable until some date after his dismissal.[44] Section 2 of the Apportionment Act 1870, however, provides that "all rents, annuities, dividends, and other periodical payments in the nature of income . . . shall . . . be considered as accruing from day to day, and shall be apportionable in respect of time accordingly"[45]; and the word "annuities" is deemed to include "salaries and pensions." There is some doubt whether the expression "salaries"[46] includes "wages."[47] And it is also an open question whether the properly dismissed servant is within the section. In *Moriarty* v. *Regent's Garage & Engineering Co.*,[48] Lush J. said that "if something has happened during the service which forfeits the right to the salary it may well be that the servant cannot take advantage of the Act." It is to be hoped that this view will not prevail. For at common law a servant was debarred from claiming his wages not because of any conception of forfeiture but because he had not fully performed his contract.[49]

---

[43] See above, p. 422.

[44] *Boston Deep Sea Fishing & Ice Co.* v. *Ansell* (1888) 39 Ch.D. 339, 364–365, *per* Bowen L.J.

[45] *Sim* v. *Rotherham MBC* [1987] Ch. 216, 255. (*Cutter* v. *Powell* (1795) 6 T.R. 320, see above, p. 410, would, however, probably still be decided the same way.) The Act is subject to a contrary agreement (s.7), and Cutter had contracted to work for a rate much higher than the current rate.

[46] s.5. For an argument restrictively interpreting the meaning of "salaries" see [1982] Jo. of Legal Studies 302 [Matthews].

[47] *Moriarty* v. *Regent's Garage Co.* [1921] 1 K.B. 423; *Re William Porter & Co. Ltd.* [1937] 2 All E.R. 361, 363, *per* Simonds J.

[48] [1921] 1 K.B. 423, 435.

[49] *Cf. Boston Deep Sea Fishing & Ice Co.* v. *Ansell* (1888) 39 Ch.D. 339, 369–370, *per* Cotton L.J.; (1941) 57 L.Q.R. 373, 381–383 [G. L. Williams].

It is a different question if he has not been dismissed but has not properly and fully performed his contract. If he has rendered services under a contract which is not divisible and which has not been performed, it would appear that he is without remedy.[50] There are, however, dicta[51] which suggest that a *quantum meruit* claim may lie if an employee offers to perform some of his duties but not others, and the employer accepts the services, not voluntarily[52] but from necessity. It is difficult to accept their authority. In such a case the contract of employment has not been superseded by any new agreement; and if it has not been terminated, his restitutionary claim should fail.[53]

Substantial performance.   A party in breach may be able to recover if he has substantially performed the contract.[54] After some early doubts,[55] it seems to be now settled that the plaintiff's action is on the contract, for the contract price less the cost of defects and omissions.[56]

(2) Cases where recovery is based on restitution

Free acceptance.   A plaintiff in breach can recover if he can show that the defendant has freely accepted his work or has otherwise "waived" the necessity for complete performance. The scope of this principle is not easy to define. Mere acceptance of the benefits conferred by the plaintiff's partial performance may not be enough.[57] The defendant must have had a reasonable opportunity of accepting or rejecting the part performance. If he had had that opportunity, he should be taken to have freely accepted the benefit.[58] He cannot then deny that he has been enriched,[59] and that he has been unjustly

---

[50] See above, pp. 438 *et seq.*

[51] *Miles* v. *Wakefield M.D.C.* [1987] A.C. 539, 553, *per* Lord Brightman, 561, *per* Lord Templeman; *contra* Lord Bridge (at p. 552). Lord Brandon (at p. 552) and Lord Oliver (at p. 576) left the point open.

[52] But even if he accepts the services voluntarily, he can claim damages for loss suffered unless it is found that he has waived the breach of contract.

[53] See above, pp. 45–47.

[54] *Boone* v. *Eyre* (1779) 1 Hy.Bl. 273n.

[55] *Farnsworth* v. *Garrard* (1807) 1 Camp. 38; *Chapel* v. *Hickes* (1833) 2 C. & M. 214; *Thornton* v. *Place* (1832) 1 Moo. & Rob. 218; *Cutler* v. *Close* (1832) 5 C. & P. 337.

[56] *H. Dakin & Co. Ltd.* v. *Lee* [1916] 1 K.B. 566, 573, *per* Ridley J. 576, *per* Sankey J., affd. on different grounds [1916] 1 K.B. 577 (misfeasance); *Hoenig* v. *Isaacs* [1952] 2 All E.R. 176. It is difficult to glean from the decided cases whether the courts will interpret generously this doctrine: see *Mondel* v. *Steel* (1841) 8 M. & W. 858; *Hoenig* v. *Isaacs* [1952] 2 All E.R. 176, 179–180, *per* Somervell L.J. *Cf. Bolton* v. *Mahadeva* [1972] 1 W.L.R. 1009. And see (1941) 57 L.Q.R. 373, 386–387 [G. L. Williams]; and *Oliver* v. *Campbell*, 273 P. 2d 15 (1954), where the doctrine was invoked to defeat a restitutionary claim (see above, p. 426, n. 41).

[57] *Forman & Co. Proprietary Ltd.* v. *S.S. Liddesdale* [1900] A.C. 190, at p. 204, P.C., *per* Lord Hobhouse, where the plaintiffs had failed to repair according to the contract. The mere fact that defendants took the ship and sold it, thereby making the best use of it they could, did not "give the plaintiffs any additional right." *Cf. Nees* v. *Weaver*, 222 Wis. 492 (1936); and see above, p. 18.

[58] It is difficult to find modern English authority. *Christy* v. *Row* (1808) 1 Taunt. 300 is the case generally cited; but *cf. Munro* v. *Butt* (1858) 8 E. & B. 739. A good illustration from Canada is *Tanenbaum and Downsview Meadows Ltd.* v. *Wright-Winston Ltd.*, 49 D.L.R. (2d) 386 (1965).

[59] See above, pp. 18–22.

enriched.[60] For that reason, in *Sumpter* v. *Hedges*,[61] the innocent party was required to pay for materials which the builder had left on the site and which he had used to complete the building. Conversely, if he had no opportunity of returning the materials, he is, as the law now stands, not liable even though he may have incontrovertibly benefited from their receipt. The plaintiff in breach is then in no better position than the officious volunteer.[62]

Short delivery[63] *under an entire contract for the sale of goods.*   At common law, where a seller delivers less than the quantity contracted for and the purchaser accepts the goods so delivered, the purchaser will be liable to pay a reasonable sum for them.[64] This is consistent with principle if the goods so delivered form a divisible part of a divisible contract, or if the purchaser, on learning of the breach, had an opportunity of returning the goods to the seller but decided to retain them.[65] But if the purchaser has consumed the short delivery, in the expectation of a complete delivery under an entire contract, he is denied this opportunity.[66] It is difficult to see how he can be said in this case to have requested or freely accepted the short delivery. Nevertheless, he must pay a reasonable sum for the goods delivered to him.

The common law rule has been adopted in section 30(1) of the Sale of Goods Act 1979, with the modification that the purchaser shall pay for the goods at "the contract rate."[67]

Freight after a deviation.   A shipowner deviates but delivers goods to the cargo owner at the port of discharge named in the contract. Is he entitled to freight earned? The problem, which can only arise when the cargo owner exercises his right to bring the contract to an end, was discussed in *Hain Steamship Co. Ltd.* v. *Tate & Lyle Ltd.*[68] In the Court of Appeal, Scrutton L.J.[69] was of the opinion that "as a matter of logic" no freight could be earned. He said: "The fact that a volunteer without authority renders services to another man's property does not give him a right to remuneration, or to keep the property unless he gets remuneration."

---

[60] See above, pp. 39 *et seq.*

[61] [1898] 1 Q.B. 673; *cf. Hoenig* v. *Isaacs* [1952] 2 All E.R. 176, 181, *per* Denning L.J., 183, *per* Romer L.J. *Cf.* Law Commission *Report*, No. 121, *Law of Contract; Pecuniary Restitution on Breach of Contract* (1983) § 2.45 (proposing a new statutory remedy (see below, p. 446)).

[62] See below, pp. 444 *et seq.* where there is a critique of this state of the law.

[63] For the common law, if the seller delivers more than the contractual amount, see *Shipton* v. *Casson* (1826) 5 B. & C. 378, 383, *per* Bayley J.

[64] *Oxendale* v. *Wetherell* (1829) 9 B. & C. 386, 387–388, *per* Parke J.; *Chanter* v. *Leese* (1838) 4 M. & W. 295; (1839) 5 M. & W. 698; *Steven* v. *Bromley & Son* [1919] 2 K.B. 722, 728, *per* Atkin L.J. See, generally, *Benjamin's Sale of Goods*, §§ 8–041 *et seq.*

[65] See above, pp. 18–22.

[66] G. L. Williams, *Law Reform (Frustrated Contracts) Act 1943*, p. 5.

[67] See below, p. 447, n. 3 for a further comment.

[68] (1934) 39 Com.Cas. 259, C.A.: (1936) 41 Com.Cas. 350, H.L.

[69] *Ibid.* at pp. 271–272; see also p. 285, *per* Greer L.J., and p. 290, *per* Slesser L.J. On the facts the claim for freight against the bill of lading holders failed in the Court of Appeal and the House of Lords, since the freight was payable by the charterers. All these observations are therefore *obiter.*

The harsh consequences of Scrutton L.J.'s reasoning clearly startled the House of Lords when the case came before them. The House accepted that the innocent party "is not bound by the promise to pay the agreed freight any more than by his other promises,"[70] but did not endorse Scrutton L.J.'s dictum that there could be no *quantum meruit* claim. Lord Maugham was strongly inclined to doubt Scrutton L.J.'s views,[71] and Lord Wright felt that the court would not be "slow to infer an obligation when the goods are received at destination to pay, not indeed the contract freight but a reasonable remuneration."[72]

It is just that, in these circumstances, the court should be prepared to impose an obligation on the cargo owner to remunerate the shipowner for carrying his goods to the port of discharge named in the contract, provided that they are delivered "without injury or substantial delay."[73] It is clear that the cargo owner wanted his goods to be delivered at the port of discharge. In our view, he has benefited at the plaintiff's expense for he cannot deny that he has received the performance which he bargained for. The value of the benefit conferred should be the reasonable value of the services rendered, subject to this *caveat*: that, if the freight market has risen, the shipowner should not recover more than the agreed freight. The shipowner should not be permitted to benefit from his breach of contract.

But what is the ground of the shipowner's claim to recover on a *quantum meruit*? The original contract of affreightment has ceased to exist,[74] and no new contract can be implied from the cargo owner's acceptance of his own goods at the agreed port of discharge. The shipowner's *quantum meruit* claim must therefore be restitutionary.[75] Given his breach of contract, it can hardly be said that the ground of his claim is the innocent party's request or the free acceptance of his own goods.[76] If the party in breach's claim for services could be based, as would a comparable claim for money paid, on the fact that the consideration had totally failed, then the shipowner might succeed; even if he had received some of the agreed freight, this is a benefit which he can restore.[77]

---

[70] (1936) 41 Com.Cas. 350, 355, *per* Lord Atkin.

[71] *Ibid.* at p. 373; see also p. 358, *per* Lord Atkin.

[72] *Ibid.* at p. 368. See also *Joseph Thorley Ltd.* v. *Orchis S.S. Co.* [1907] 1 K.B. 660, 668, *per* Collins M.R., 669, *per* Fletcher Moulton L.J.; *Charles Weis & Co.* v. *Northern Traffic Ltd.* (1919) 1 Ll.L.R. 241; *U.S. Shipping Board* v. *J.J. Masters & Co.* (1922) 10 Ll.L.R. 573, 575, *per* Bankes L.J.; *Atlantic Shipping & Trading Co.* v. *Louis Dreyfus Co.* [1922] 2 A.C. 250, 257, *per* Lord Dunedin.

[73] (1936) 41 Com.Cas. 350, 373, *per* Lord Maugham.

[74] If the contract is not terminated, the shipowner's claim must be in principle on the contract and would therefore fail: but see the *dicta* in *Miles* v. *Wakefield M.D.C.* [1987] A.C. 539, discussed above, pp. 45–46.

[75] *Cf. U.S. Shipping Board* v. *Bunge y Born* (1925) 31 Com.Cas. 118; *Craven-Ellis* v. *Canons Ltd.* [1936] 2 K.B. 403; *Société-Franco Tunisienne d'Armement* v. *Sidermar S.P.A.* [1961] 2 Q.B. 278, 313, *per* Pearson J., overruled on a different ground in *Ocean Tramp Tankers Corp.* v. *V/O Sovfracht* [1964] 2 Q.B. 226. *Cf. Chandris* v. *Isbrandtsen-Moller Co. Inc.* [1951] 1 K.B. 240, 250, *per* Devlin J.

[76] Contrast above, p. 442.

[77] See above, pp. 60–62. If English courts were to accept that a claim for money paid should not be defeated simply because the failure of consideration was only partial, then the shipowner would have to bring the value of the benefit gained into account: see above, Chap. 17.

But, as yet, the courts have not been prepared to accept that restitutionary claims for services rendered and goods delivered can be grounded on that principle.[78] A possible ground which can form the basis of the restitutionary claim is the unconscionability of the cargo owner's conduct, namely, his refusal to pay reasonable freight, the cargo having been delivered at the agreed port of discharge. The analogy of equity's inherent, if uncertain, jurisdiction to grant relief against forfeiture and, in particular, the principle that "the sum [benefit] forfeited must be out of all proportion to the damage"[79] which the innocent party suffers, may be persuasive.

But what if the shipowner delivers the cargo, which the cargo owner accepts, at a port other than the agreed port of discharge? Dicta suggest that the shipowner will be entitled to recover on a *quantum meruit* only if the circumstances reveal that the cargo owner requested their carriage to a new port of discharge.[80] If the cargo owner has made no such request, it may be said that he has nonetheless benefited from the receipt of the cargo; moreover, he has his claim for damages for loss suffered from the failure to carry to the agreed port of discharge. But, in our view, any restitutionary claim must fail for the services rendered were not those which the cargo owner had bargained for; and the cargo owner cannot then be said to act unconscionably in refusing to pay reasonable freight for the carriage of his own goods.[81]

(3) *Conclusions: proposals for reform*

A party in breach, who renders services or supplies goods in part performance of his obligations under an entire contract, is in a precarious position. The doctrine of entire contracts assumes that, because a party has promised to perform in full, if he fails to do so he can obtain no recompense for services rendered or goods supplied to the innocent party under the contract. The courts have been aware of the severity of the doctrine, but their attempts to mitigate its rigour have been tentative and piecemeal in character and, in the limited cases where the courts have granted relief, they have, as we have seen, often found it necessary to ground it on contract.[82]

In our view, the party in breach should be granted a restitutionary claim and should recover the value of the benefits conferred by him on the innocent party, who is protected by his action on the contract for damages for loss suffered.[83] It is true that "wrongdoers" are normally denied any restitutionary

---

[78] See above, Chap. 17.
[79] *Stockloser* v. *Johnson* [1954] 1 Q.B. 476, 490–492, *per* Denning L.J.
[80] *Hopper* v. *Burness* (1876) 1 C.P. D 137; *Hain S.S. Co.* v. *Tate & Lyle Ltd.* (1936) 41 Com.Cas. 350, 368, *per* Lord Wright, 373, *per* Lord Maugham; *cf.* Greer L.J. in the Court of Appeal in (1934) 39 Com.Cas. 259, 285.
[81] *Cf.* pp. 442–443.
[82] Hence the artificial exception of substantial performance.
[83] Admittedly, his action for damages may not make him whole. For this reason we are attracted by the Law Commission's proposal in its Report, *No. 121, Law of Contract: Pecuniary Restitution on Breach of Contract* (1983), (hereafter cited, in this Chapter, as *Report*), that any clause in the contract excluding or restricting the innocent party's right to damages should not be enforced: para. 2.64.

claim. But a party who is held to be in breach of contract should not be treated with the same severity as the tortfeasor or the criminal. The common law has recognised this to be so in the context of claims for money paid; the party in breach can recover any payment (other than a deposit) if he can demonstrate that the consideration for the payment has totally failed.[84] In contrast, the pleading of the *quantum meruit* and *quantum valebat* counts, that the services were rendered or the goods were delivered at the defendant's *request*,[85-86] and the doctrine of entire contracts combine to defeat the plaintiff's restitutionary claim.

Civilian jurisdictions have not been so stern. In Scotland[87] it has long been held that:

> "[If a party] perform a part and then fail in completing the contract. I shall be bound in equity to allow him credit to the extent to which I am *lucratus* by his materials and labour, but no further; and if I am not *lucratus* at all, I shall be entitled to repetition of the whole advance [I have made] however great his expenditure and consequent loss may have been."[88]

Many jurisdictions in the United States, following the *Restatement of Contracts 2d*, now grant a party in breach "restitution for any benefit that he has conferred by way of part performance or reliance in excess of the loss that he has caused by his own breach."[89] The innocent party has benefited at the expense of the party in breach, for he has received part of the performance which he requested.[90] The *Restatement* does not, however, spell out what is the ground of the restitutionary claim. It is difficult to conclude that, given the breach of contract, it is the innocent party's free acceptance of the performance. However, it may be said that the consideration which the party in breach was to receive for the services which he has rendered has failed; and this is a possible ground of his complaint.[91] Alternatively, if precedent precludes this rationalisation, the defendant's reliance on the terms of the contract to deny the plaintiff any recompense may be said to be unconscionable; it is unjust to penalise the party in breach, when the value of the benefit conferred is out of all proportion to the loss which the innocent party suffered.[92-93]

If the restitutionary claim were to be recognised, its limits should be carefully defined. Among the most contentious questions which will have to be answered are these:

---

[84] And, in the ideal common law world, he should recover his payment even if the failure of consideration was partial: see above, Chap. 17.

[85-86] See above, pp. 3–5.

[87] *Watson & Co.* v. *Shankland* (1871) 10 M. 142; *Ramsay & Son* v. *Brand* (1898) 25 R. 1212; *Graham & Co.* v. *United Turkey Red Co.*, 1922 S.C. 533. See also (1962) 37 Tulane L.R. 49, 56–60 [J. K. B. Nicholas].

[88] *Watson & Co.* v. *Shankland* (1871) 10 M. 142, 152, *per* Lord President Inglis.

[89] *Restatement of Contracts 2d*, § 374, comment b.

[90] For the valuation of that benefit, see below, p. 446.

[91] See Burrows, *The Law of Restitution*, pp. 273–274.

[92-93] *Cf.* above, p. 433.

(1) Should the restitutionary claim be denied if the breach of contract is wilful? Both the *Restatement of Contracts 2d*[94] and the English Law Commission's *Report*[95] consider that in principle it should not; moreover, given how vague is the concept of *wilful* breach, it may, in some situations, be difficult if not impossible to distinguish the wilful from the non-wilful breach of contract. The party who has wrongfully repudiated his contract has conferred a benefit upon the innocent party, and the innocent party must disgorge the value of that benefit only if it exceeds his loss. Why he breached his contract cannot inflate or contract the value of the benefit which has been conferred.[95a] And to reject his claim because it is a wilful breach is to penalise the party in breach. We are not persuaded that this is a proper or just conclusion.[96]

(2) What is the value of the benefit conferred? In principle, this should be the incontrovertible benefit gained by the innocent party, and that benefit is prima facie the extent to which the value of his assets has increased in consequence of the part performance of the party in breach. Exceptionally, the innocent party may be said to be benefited when he derived no objective benefit from the party in breach's performance, for example, if services were rendered to a third person at his request.[97]

There should be three important *caveats* to this general principle. First, the party in breach should never recover more than a rateable share of the contract price, otherwise he may profit from his breach. Secondly, if the reasonable value of the benefit conferred (that is, what it would have cost the innocent party to obtain the benefit from another person) is less than the increased value of the innocent party's assets and less than a proportionate part of the contract price, that should be the measure of his recovery.[98] Thirdly, the party in breach should not be awarded any recompense for benefits conferred which were not requested by the innocent party. He then takes the risk that the innocent party will not reimburse him.[99]

---

[94] § 374.

[95] *Report*, paras. 2.58–2.60.

[95a] It is not inconsistent with this conclusion to suggest that the party in breach may, in some circumstances, have to account for the profits made from his breach of contract: see above, pp. 413–417. The innocent party's remedies for breach of contract are in no way diluted by the recognition of this restitutionary claim.

[96] *Cf.* above, p. 429 (money claims, where the nature of the breach is not relevant).

[97] *Cf. Report*, para. 2.47.
The position of a person who partially performs an entire contract is significantly different from that of the mistaken improver of land; see above, Chap. 5. It should be no answer to the claim of the party in breach, who has conferred a benefit on the innocent party, that it would be a hardship to compel the innocent party to dispose of an asset, land or chattel, in order to satisfy that claim, since he has requested the services. It is true that his request was to perform the entire contract. But he has nonetheless requested the services, has agreed to pay for them, and will never be liable to pay more than a rateable part of the contract price. Moreover, the innocent party always has his claim for damages.

[98] *Cf. Restatement of Contracts 2d*, § 371.

[99] *Restatement of Contracts 2d*, § 374 comment b characterises the conduct of a person who renders services which have not been requested as 'officious': see above, p. 58.

The burden of demonstrating that the benefits conferred were those requested should be on the party in breach. The innocent party is best able to prove the extent to which his assets have increased in value, and the burden should fall on him if he asserts that the reasonable value of the benefits conferred is less than that figure.

(3) Should the parties be in a position to agree that a party in breach should not be paid a penny unless he performed in full his contractual obligations? The answer to this question must surely be, yes. Indeed that is the principle which underlies the doctrine of entire contracts. In its *Report* the Law Commission concluded that the restitutionary claim should not be excluded simply because the consideration is expressed as a lump sum or the payment is postponed until the completion of the contract, the traditional hall-marks of an entire contract.[1] The parties "must make it clear" that the risk of failure to perform should unequivocally be placed on the non-performer.[2] If the Law Commission's recommendation is adopted, the ingenuity of lawyers will be tested to the full, to draft the appropriate clause which will be so "clear" that it will convince the court that the restitutionary claim is excluded.

The Law Commission's recommendations have not yet been implemented, and its *Report* is now 10 years old.[3] It may well be that the burden of reform will once more fall, if it is to fall at all, on the Appellate Committee of the House of Lords.

3. CONTRACTS DISCHARGED THROUGH FRUSTRATION

Unjust enrichment provides no easy formula for the solution of the question whether parties should restore to each other benefits conferred under a contract thereafter frustrated. The central problem is to identify the benefit, gained by the defendant by reason of the plaintiff's contractual performance, in respect of which he should make restitution to the plaintiff.[4] If that benefit takes the form of money, the defendant is incontrovertibly benefited. In such a case, subject to such considerations as the effect of inflation or what has been called the time value of money (*i.e.* the benefit arising from the possession of a sum of money over a period of time), and defences such as change of position,[5] the loss suffered by the plaintiff is generally equal to the defendant's gain so that no difficulty arises concerning the amount to be paid.[6]

---

[1] See above, p. 409.
[2] Paras. 2.66–2.69.
[3] The Law Commission, for reasons which we do not find convincing, recommended that its proposal to allow a restitutionary claim should not lie if a party repudiated a contract for the sale of goods (we have argued (see above, p. 442) that the remedy provided by the Sale of Goods Act 1979 is too favourable a remedy) or a contract for the carriage of goods. See paras. 2.85–2.87.
[4] See above, pp. 18–22.
[5] See below, Chap. 40.
[6] *B.P. Exploration Co. (Libya) Ltd.* v. *Hunt (No. 2)* [1979] 1 W.L.R. 783; [1981] 1 W.L.R. 232, C.A.; [1983] 2 A.C. 352. It is hereinafter cited in the footnotes as *B.P.* v. *Hunt.*

But if the defendant receives a benefit other than money, for example services or goods, the matter becomes much more complicated; for services can never be restored and goods may have been consumed or transferred to another. In these circumstances, how is the court to identify the benefit in respect of which the defendant should make restitution?[7] Is it the value of the services or goods themselves? Or is it the actual benefit derived by the defendant from the plaintiff's contractual performance, *i.e.* the extent to which his assets have been increased by what the plaintiff has done? If the former, to what extent should the contract consideration control the award of restitution? The answer to these questions may be critical. The value of the services rendered may have been diminished or destroyed by the frustrating event,[8] or indeed by any other event before the date of frustration; the services rendered at the defendant's request may not have increased the value of his property, for example because of the eccentricity of that request; or the value of the services rendered may be trivial in comparison with the actual benefit gained from their receipt. In principle, restitution should be made in respect of the reasonable value of the services rendered or goods supplied, subject to such defences as change of position. Historically, the plaintiff's claim is on a *quantum meruit* or *quantum valebat* basis. Since the defendant has requested the plaintiff's performance, he should take the benefit of subsequent appreciation in value of that performance and the risk of its subsequent diminution in value. The Law Reform (Frustrated Contracts) Act 1943 appears to reject that principle in favour of the actual benefit gained by the defendant.[9] However it also enacts that the provisions of the contract shall always govern if, upon a true construction, they were intended to apply in the events which have occurred; if intended to apply in the event of frustration, they can have the effect of allocating the risk of loss arising from the frustrating event, or of controlling the measure of recovery in restitution.[10]

The common law did not, as we have seen,[11] deal satisfactorily with these problems. Nor did the Report of the Law Revision Committee, published in 1939.[12] The terms of reference of the Committee were limited to consideration of the rule in *Chandler* v. *Webster*[13] which was, however, overruled in the

---

[7] *Cf.* see above, pp. 16 *et seq.*

[8] *Cf.* Woodward, *op. cit.* pp. 183–184; Williston, *op. cit.* §§ 1975–1976; Corbin, *op. cit.* § 1372; and the American authorities there cited. See also G. L. Williams, *Law Reform (Frustrated Contracts) Act 1943*, pp. 54–55. For a contrary view, see Keener, *op. cit.* pp. 253–258. See *Parson Bros. Ltd.* v. *Shea* (1965) 53 D.L.R. (2d) 86, interpreting the Newfoundland statute. The language of the particular provision is critical. Consequently decisions interpreting Commonwealth and American statutes should be read in their particular statutory context: *cf.* see below, p. 468.

[9] *B.P.* v. *Hunt* [1979] 1 W.L.R. 783, 801–802, *per* Robert Goff J. Contrast the provisions of British Columbia (Frustrated Contracts) Act 1974, s.5(1)(4), and the New South Wales (Frustrated Contracts) Act 1978, ss.9–15.

[10] Law Reform (Frustrated Contracts) Act 1943, s.2(3); see below, p. 462.

[11] See pp. 407 *et seq.* above.

[12] 7th Interim Report, Cmnd. 6009.

[13] [1904] 1 K.B. 493; see above, p. 407.

Fibrosa case,[14] decided in 1943 between the date of the Report and the enactment of the Law Reform (Frustrated Contracts) Act 1943. "The Act's scope is considerably wider than that of the Report."[15] Consequently, it has been said that the Report is of no assistance in interpreting the Act.[16]

In brief, the 1943 Act accepts the principle in the *Fibrosa* case that money paid under a contract thereafter frustrated is recoverable, though it does not limit recovery to cases of total failure of consideration. The court is, however, given a power to allow the other party to retain or recover the whole or part of any sum paid or payable to him up to the limit of his contractual expenditure. The Act also provides that a party who receives a benefit other than money under the contract must pay the other party a just sum, not exceeding the value of the benefit obtained by the defendant. The Act binds the Crown, but does not apply to Scotland, where "the relief, if any, must be sought . . . in the law of recompense."[17] It applies to all contracts, "governed by English law," discharged after July 12, 1943.

The Act does not contemplate the possibility that loss should be apportioned between the parties[18]; consequently, as will be seen, there is only a limited jurisdiction to make to either party any allowance for expenses incurred. Nor is the Act concerned to put the parties in the position in which they would have been if the contract had been performed; or, conversely, to restore the parties to the position they were in before the contract was made. In our view the fundamental principle underlying the Act is, quite simply, the principle of unjust enrichment.[19]

We now turn to a detailed analysis of the Act. It is a striking fact that, although the Act was passed in 1943, there was no decided case under the Act until 1978, when the case of *B.P. Exploration Co. (Libya) Ltd.* v. *Hunt (No. 2)*[20] was decided. That case was concerned with a contract for the exploration and development of an oil concession in Libya which was frustrated when the plaintiffs' interest in the concession was expropriated by the Libyan Government. The claim advanced by the plaintiffs was in respect of a benefit which, for the most part, consisted of services rendered. Awards of restitution under the Act in respect of such benefits are provided for in section 1(3); and, at first instance and in the Court of Appeal, the construction of that subsection was central to the case. But the decision is also important for the light it throws on section 1(2) and section 2(3) of the Act. Section 2(3) is concerned with the

---

[14] *Fibrosa Spolka Akeyjna* v. *Combe Barbour Ltd.* [1943] A.C. 32; see above, p. 450.

[15] *B.P.* v. *Hunt*, [1979] 1 W.L.R. 783, 798, *per* Robert Goff J.

[16] *Ibid.*

[17] (1957) Holdsworth Club Address 20 [Lord Keith].

[18] *B.P.* v. *Hunt* [1979] 1 W.L.R. 783, 799. For another view, arguing that the Act provides a flexible machinery for adjustment of loss, see *Frustration and Restitution* [1984] Jo. of Business Law 207 [Haycroft and Waksman]: see below, p. 468.

[19] In *B.P.* v. *Hunt* this was Robert Goff J.'s conclusion. But the Court of Appeal got "no help from the use of words which are not in the Statute": [1981] 1 W.L.R. 232, 243: see *Frustration, Restitution, and Loss Apportionment* in *Essays* (ed. Burrows) pp. 154–155 [McKendrick].

[20] [1979] 1 W.L.R. 783; [1981] 1 W.L.R. 232, C.A.; [1983] 2 A.C. 352.

effect of the contractual provisions upon an award under the Act; and the argument that the plaintiffs had contracted to take the risk of expropriation was one of the principal grounds of the defendant's appeal in the House of Lords.

We now turn to a detailed analysis of the Act.

The Law Reform (Frustrated Contracts) Act 1943

The Circumstances in which the Act Applies

These are set out in section 1(1), which reads as follows:

Adjustment of rights and liabilities of parties to frustrated contracts

"(1) Where a contract governed by English law has become impossible of performance or been otherwise frustrated, and the parties thereto have for that reason been discharged from the further performance of the contract, the following provisions of this section shall, subject to the provisions of section two of this Act, have effect in relation thereto."

Contracts determined by supervening illegality are probably frustrated-contracts within the Act, but not contracts discharged through breach.[21]

Recovery of money

"1.—(2) All sums paid or payable to any party in pursuance of the contract before the time when the parties were so discharged (in this Act referred to as "the time of discharge") shall, in the case of sums so paid, be recoverable from him as money received by him for the use of the party by whom the sums were paid, and, in the case of sums so payable, cease to be so payable:

Provided that, if the party to whom the sums were so paid or payable incurred expenses before the time of discharge in, or for the purpose of, the performance of the contract, the court may, if it considers it just to do so, having regard to all the circumstances of the case, allow him to retain or, as the case may be, recover the whole or any part of the sums so paid or payable, not being an amount in excess of the expenses so incurred."

Money paid before the time of discharge is therefore recoverable under the subsection; and money then due but unpaid ceases to be due.[22] It is also clear that the right to repayment now extends to cases of partial failure of consideration: section 1(2) provides for the recovery of *all* sums paid in pursuance of the contract before the time of discharge and cases of partial failure of consideration can be catered for by a cross-claim by the defendant under the subsection

---

[21] (1944) 60 L.Q.R. 160, 162–163 [A. D. McNair].

[22] *Fibrosa Spolka Akcyjna* v. *Fairbairn Lawson Combe Barbour Ltd.* [1943] A.C. 32, 54–55, *per* Lord Atkin.

or under section 1(3).[23] The subsection makes no provision for recovery of any payment made after the time of discharge without knowledge of the frustrating event, or without knowledge that such event has operated to discharge the parties from further performance of the contract. The payer should then be entitled to recover the money so paid[24] as money paid under a mistake of fact.[25]

The proviso to this subsection is, together with the parallel provision in section 1(3), one of the more controversial parts of the Act. It provides that the loss of expenditure incurred by a party before the time of discharge "in, or for the purpose of, the performance of the contract" shall not necessarily fall on him. If the other party has paid or has contracted to pay money in advance before the time of discharge, the court has power to allow the party who has incurred the expenditure to retain or recover the whole or part of the sums so paid or payable, not, however, exceeding the amount of such expenditure.[26] This provision follows the recommendation of the Law Revision Committee, which was based on the assumption that in stipulating for pre-payment the payee *always* intends to protect himself against loss under the contract.[27] That assumption is open to criticism. It by no means follows that, where a pre-payment is stipulated for, the parties intend that the payer shall stand the risk of expenditure lost by the payee because of the frustration of the contract. Moreover, it is arguable that, under the proviso, a party who has made an advance payment before the time of discharge which he was *not* bound to make, to that extent stands the risk of the other party's lost expenditure. Such a conclusion cannot have been intended by the Law Revision Committee; but its effect may in practice be alleviated or negatived by the exercise of judicial discretion. It may, however, be that the court's power to make an allowance for expenses incurred in, or for the purpose of, the performance of the contract under which the payment has been made is "best rationalised as a statutory recognition of the defence of change of position."[28] However, the defendant's change of position may not necessarily defeat the plaintiff's claim; for the object of the advance may be to put the payee in funds to continue the contract, or to protect him from loss flowing from the payer's breach or insolvency.[29]

---

[23] *B.P.* v. *Hunt* [1979] 1 W.L.R. 783, 800, *per* Robert Goff J.

[24] *Aliter* if the payment is made under a mistake of law: see above, Chap. 4.

[25] *Cf. Asantewah* v. *Duneport Ltd.*, unreported, Shoreditch Cty. Ct., 1982 (car brought for shipment to Ghana; shipment later made illegal by local decree, before car shipped; price recovered. We are grateful to A. Hughes-Chamberlain Esq., Barrister, for this information.)

[26] The Act does not apply to Scotland. But in *Cantiare San Rocco* v. *Clyde Ship Building and Engineering Co.*, 1923 S.C. (H.L.) 105, 106, the appellants admitted that the respondents were entitled to retain so much as was adequate for their work in preparing the engines. See (1957) Holdsworth Club Address 19 [Lord Keith].

[27] 7th Interim Report. Cmnd. 6009 at p. 7.

[28] *B.P.* v. *Hunt* [1979] 1 W.L.R. 783, 800. Of course, the scope of the defence (on which see below, Chap. 40) is, in this context, restricted by the language of the statute: *cf. Essays* (ed. Burrows), pp. 156–159 [McKendrick].
Cf. Burrows, *The Law of Restitution*, pp. 283–286, arguing that this is too narrow an interpretation of s.1(2) which, in his view, allows the court to apportion reliance expenses.

[29] Mr. Beatson argues that s.2(3) of the Act (see below, p. 462), enables the court to conclude that the Act does not apply in these circumstances: see *Essays* (ed. Burrows), p. 290: *sed quaere.*

"Expenses" in the proviso includes a reasonable sum for overhead expenses and for work or services personally performed.[30] They must have been incurred before the time of discharge, and it is to be presumed that expenses must mean net expenses. Moreover, the expenses must have been incurred in, or for the purpose of, the performance of the contract.[31] Such a test would, of course, exclude expenditure incurred in mere speculation on future contracts, but would include expenditure incurred before the contract is entered into on the reasonable assumption that it will be made. The following hypothetical cases may be contrasted:

> A erects a stand for a procession and sells tickets for seats in the stand. The procession is cancelled, and the contracts to supply seats are frustrated. The ticket holders should be entitled to recover their money; but A should not be entitled to invoke the proviso in respect of expenditure incurred in the erection of the stand.
>
> A and B enter into serious negotiations which, in the light of past experience, A assumes will very likely result in a contract. In anticipation of such contract, A incurs expenditure for the purpose of its performance. The contract is duly made, but is subsequently frustrated. A should be able to recover his expenses.[32]

The party incurring the expenditure has no *right* to retain or recover any sum paid or payable by the other party before the time of discharge; he can only invite the court to exercise its discretion to enable him to do so.[33]

Finally, there is the question whether the court has the power to increase the sum recoverable by the plaintiff, or the amount of expenses to be allowed to the defendant, to allow for the time value of money. The money may have been paid, or the expenses incurred, many years before the date of frustration; but the case of action accrues on that date, and the sum recoverable under the Act as at that date can be no greater than the sum actually paid, though the defendant may have had the use of the money over many years, and indeed may have profited from its use. "There is no scope in this subsection for adding to the sum paid something extra to represent the time value of money."[34] However, the court does have power, under the Law Reform (Miscellaneous Provisions) Act 1934, s.3(1) to award interest on the principal sums from the date of the accrual of the cause of action. The words of that subsection—"in any proceedings tried in any court of record for the recovery of any debt or damages"—are "very wide, so that they cover any sum of money which is recoverable by one party from another either at common law, or in equity or under a statute [such as the Law Reform (Frustrated Contracts) Act 1943] of

---

[30] s.1(4).

[31] *Cf.* Williams, *Law Reform (Frustrated Contracts) Act 1943*, pp. 35–39.

[32] Contrast Benjamin's *Sale of Goods* § 6–058. See below, Chap. 25, for benefits conferred in anticipation of contracts which do not materialise.

[33] Only in exceptional circumstances will an appellate court interfere with the discretion of the trial judge: see below, p. 454.

[34] *B.P.* v. *Hunt* [1981] 1 W.L.R. 232, 244, C.A.

the kind here concerned."[35] An appellate court should not generally interfere with the exercise of the trial judge's discretion to award interest:

> "There cannot be any general rule that, whenever the amount of any debt or damages payable by one party to the action to the other cannot be ascertained until judgment is given, the court should never, in the exercise of its discretion, award interest from a date earlier than the date of such judgment. To apply such a rule would, in my opinion, be plainly inconsistent with the express terms of section 3(1) [of the 1934 Act], and in many cases, for instance in the case of a claim on a *quantum meruit*, work serious injustice on a successful plaintiff."[36]

Consequently, in *B.P. Exploration Co. (Libya) Ltd.* v. *Hunt (No. 2)*, the House of Lords refused to interfere with Robert Goff J.'s order that interest should be paid from June 14, 1974, which was the date when the defendant "first became fully aware of B.P.'s intention to bring a claim against him."[37]

Restitution of benefits other than money

Section 1(3) provides for restitution of benefits other than payments of money. The subsection reads as follows:

> Where any party to the contract has, by reason of anything done by any other party thereto in, or for the purpose of, the performance of the contract, obtained a valuable benefit (other than a payment of money to which the last foregoing subsection applies) before the time of discharge, there shall be recoverable from him by the said other party such sum (if any), not exceeding the value of the said benefit to the party obtaining it, as the court considers just, having regard to all the circumstances of the case and, in particular—
> (a) the amount of any expenses incurred before the time of discharge by the benefited party in, or for the purpose of, the performance of the contract, including any sums paid or payable by him to any other party in pursuance of the contract and retained or recoverable by that party under the last foregoing subsection, and
> (b) the effect, in relation to the said benefit, of the circumstances giving rise to the frustration of the contract.

The interpretation of this subsection and, in particular, what principles determine whether a defendant has benefited, how that benefit is to be valued, and the assessment of the "just sum," was at the centre of the litigation in *B.P. Exploration Co. (Libya) Ltd.* v. *Hunt (No. 2)*. At first instance, Robert Goff J. analysed the subsection at considerable length and concluded that the principle underlying the Act is the prevention of the unjust enrichment of the

---

[35] *B.P.* v. *Hunt* [1983] 2 A.C. 352, 373, *per* Lord Brandon of Oakbrook.
[36] At p. 374, *per* Lord Brandon of Oakbrook.
[37] *Ibid.*

defendant at the plaintiff's expense.[38] But the Court of Appeal got "no help from the use of words which are not in the statute."[39] "What is just is what the trial judge thinks is just."[40] An appellate court should not interfere with his "decision unless it is so plainly wrong that it cannot be just."[41] It "would not be justified in setting aside the judge's way of assessment merely because [it] thought that there were better ways."[42] So, the Court of Appeal upheld the judge's assessment of the just sum; but did not indicate what "better ways" there might be. These questions did not arise in the House of Lords.

It is to be regretted that the Court of Appeal did not indicate in what circumstances the exercise of judicial discretion would be "so plainly wrong that it cannot be just." In our view it would not be right, as the Court of Appeal implicitly accepts, to allow a trial judge an unbridled discretion, which varies with the length of his judicial foot. This is not the normal type of case where a court has a discretionary power. In such a case, the court is normally vested with a discretion because it is required to consider various imponderable factors. Here, on the contrary, the court is given power to award a sum of money. The power to award a just sum should, we consider, be exercised in accordance with explicit principles, which would guide the trial judge and enable an appellate court to determine whether the sum awarded is "just, having regard to all the circumstances of the case. . . ." It would not be acceptable for restitution to be awarded to plaintiff A in accordance with one set of principles, and to plaintiff B in accordance with another. In our view, in determining what these principles should be, a court should derive invaluable help from the application of the principle of unjust enrichment, even though those words do not appear in the statute. Section 1(3) demonstrates that it was the intention of the legislature to require a defendant to make restitution for the benefit which he had gained. The section was couched in general terms because the draftsman was prescient enough to foresee that it was only through the pragmatic development of case law that subsidiary principles, which would provide guidance for judges in the exercise of their power under the Act, would be developed.

Robert Goff J.'s judgment provides then the only extended analysis of section 1(3). His conclusions may be summarised as follows:

(1) *General*

It has to be shown that the defendant has, by reason of something done by the plaintiff in, or for the purpose of, the performance of the contract, obtained a valuable benefit (other than a payment of money) before the time of discharge. The benefit has to be identified, and valued, and such value forms the upper limit of the award. The court may award to the plaintiff such sum, not greater

---

[38] [1979] 1 W.L.R. 783, 799–800.
[39] [1981] 1 W.L.R. 232, 243.
[40] At p. 238.
[41] *Ibid.*
[42] At p. 243.

than the value of such benefit, as it considers just having regard to all the circumstances of the case, including in particular the matters specified in section 1(3)(*a*) and (*b*). The amount to be awarded is the just sum, unless the defendant's benefit is less, in which event the award will be limited to the amount of that benefit.

(2) *Identification of the defendant's benefit*

The judge concluded that, as a matter of construction, "benefit" within the meaning of section 1(3) should be, in an appropriate case, identified as the end product of the services and not the value of the services themselves. He accepted that some commentators would wish to reach the opposite conclusion, since the defendant had requested the services.[43] But, in his view, section 1(3) makes a clear distinction between the plaintiff's performance and the defendant's benefit. Moreover, in his view, section 1(3)(*b*) clearly relates to the product of the plaintiff's performance:

> "Suppose that a contract for work on a building is frustrated by a fire which destroys the building and which therefore also destroys a substantial amount of work already done by the plaintiff. Although it might be thought just to award the plaintiff a sum assessed on a *quantum meruit* basis, probably a rateable part of the contract price, in respect of the work he has done, the effect of section 1(3)(*b*) will be to reduce the award to nil, because of the effect, in relation to the defendant's benefit, of the circumstances giving rise to the frustration of the contract. It is quite plain that, in section 1(3)(*b*), the word benefit is intended to refer, in the example I have given, to the actual improvement to the building, because this is what will be affected by the frustrating event; the subsection therefore contemplates that, in such a case, the benefit is the end product of the plaintiff's services, not the services themselves. This will not be so in every case, since in some cases the services will have no end product; for example, where the service consists of doing such work as surveying, or transporting goods. In each case, it is necessary to ask the question: what benefit has the defendant obtained by reason of the plaintiff's contractual performance? But it must not be forgotten that in section 1(3) the relevance of the value of the benefits is to fix a ceiling to the award. If, for example, in a building contract, the building is only partially completed, the value of the partially completed building (*i.e.* the product of the services) will fix a ceiling for the award; the stage of the work may be such that the uncompleted building may be worth less than the value of the work and materials that have gone into it, particularly as completion by another builder may cost more than completion by the original builder would have cost. In other cases, however, the actual benefit to the defendant may be considerably more than the appropriate or just sum to be awarded to the plaintiff in which event the value of the benefit will not

---

[43] [1979] 1 W.L.R. 783, 802.

in fact determine the *quantum* of the award. I should add however, that in a case of prospecting, it would usually be wrong to identify the discovered mineral as the benefit. In such a case there is always (whether the prospecting is successful or not) the benefit of the prospecting itself, *i.e.* of knowing whether or not the land contains any deposit of the relevant minerals; if the prospecting is successful, the benefit may include also the enhanced value of the land by reason of the discovery; if the prospector's contractual task goes beyond discovery and includes development and production, the benefit will include the further enhancement of the land by reason of the installation of the facilities, and also the benefit of in part transforming a valuable mineral deposit into a marketable commodity."[44]

(3) *Apportioning the benefit*

Where it is appropriate to identify the benefit with an end product and it appears that the defendant has obtained the benefit by reason of work done both by the plaintiff and by himself, the court will have to do its best to apportion that benefit, and to decide what proportion is attributable to the work done by the plaintiff. That proportion will then constitute the relevant benefit for the purposes of section 1(3) of the Act.

(4) *Valuing the benefit*

First, at the stage of valuation of the benefit (as opposed to assessment of the just sum), the task of the court is simply to assess the value of the benefit to the defendant:

> "For example, if a prospector after some very simple prospecting discovers a large and unexpected deposit of a valuable mineral, the benefit to the defendant (*viz.* the enhancement in the value of the land) may be enormous; it must be valued as such, always bearing in mind that the assessment of a just sum may very well lead to a much smaller amount being awarded to the plaintiff. But conversely, the plaintiff may have undertaken building work for a substantial sum which is, objectively speaking, of little or no value—for example, he may commence the redecoration to the defendant's execrable taste of rooms which are in good decorative order. If the contract is frustrated before the work is complete, and the work is unaffected by the frustrating event, it can be argued that the defendant has obtained no benefit because the defendant's property has been reduced in value by the plaintiff's work; but the partial work must be treated as a benefit to the defendant, since he requested it, and valued as such."

Secondly, "section 1(3)(*b*) makes it plain that the plaintiff is to take the risk of depreciation or destruction by the frustrating event. If the effect of the frustrating event upon the value of the benefit is to be measured, it must surely

---

[44] [1979] 1 W.L.R. 783, 801–802.

be measured upon the benefit as at the date of frustration."[45] But in determining the value at that time, no allowance should be made for the "time-value" of money:

> "First, the subsection limits the award to the value of the benefit *obtained* by the defendant; and it does not follow that, because the defendant has had the money over a period of time he has in fact derived any benefit from it. Second, if an allowance was to be made for the time value of the money obtained by the defendant, a comparable allowance should be made in respect of expenses incurred by the defendant, *i.e.* in respect of the period between the date of incurring the expenditure and the date of frustration, and section 1(3)(*a*) only contemplates that the court, in making an allowance for expenses, shall have regard to the 'amount of the expenses.' Third, as I have already indicated, no allowance for the time value of money can be made under section 1(2); and it would be inconsistent to make such an allowance under section 1(3) but not under section 1(2)...."[46]

There is a further problem arising from the valuation of the defendant's benefit as the end product:

> "Section 1(3)(*a*) requires the court to have regard to the amount of any expenditure incurred before the time of discharge by the benefited party in, or for the purpose of, the performance of the contract. The question arises—should this matter be taken into account at the stage of valuation of the benefit, or of assessment of the just sum? Take a simple example. Suppose that the defendant's benefit is valued at £150, that a just sum is assessed at £100, but that there remain to be taken into account defendant's expenses of £75: is the award to be £75 or £25? The clue to this problem lies, in my judgment, in the fact that the allowance for expenses is a statutory recognition of the defence of change of position. Only to the extent that the position of the defendant has so changed that it would be unjust to award restitution, should the court make an allowance for expenses. Suppose that the plaintiff does work for the defendant which produces no valuable end product, or a benefit no greater in value than the just sum to be awarded in respect of the work; there is then no reason why the whole of the relevant expenses should not be set off against the just sum. But suppose that the defendant has reaped a large benefit from the plaintiff's work, far greater in value than the just sum to be awarded for the work. In such circumstances it would be quite wrong to set off the whole of the defendant's expenses against the just sum. The question whether the defendant has suffered a change of position has to be judged in the light of all the circumstances of the case. Accordingly, on the Act as

---

[45] In determining the value at that time, it must be remembered that the services have been requested: [1979] 1 W.L.R. 783, 803.
[46] [1979] 1 W.L.R. 783, 804.

it stands, under section 1(3) the proper course is to deduct the expenses from the value of the benefit, with the effect that only in so far as they reduce the value of the benefit below the amount of the just sum which would otherwise be awarded will they have any practical bearing on the award."[47]

(5) *Assessment of the just sum*

"Where, as in cases under section 1(2), the benefit conferred on the defendant consists of payment of a sum of money, the plaintiff's expense and the defendant's enrichment are generally equal; and, subject to other relevant factors, the award of restitution will consist simply of an order for repayment of a like sum of money. But where the benefit does not consist of money, then the defendant's enrichment will rarely be equal to the plaintiff's expense. In such cases, where (as in the case of a benefit conferred under a contract thereafter frustrated), the benefit has been requested by the defendant, the basic measure of recovery in restitution is the reasonable value of the plaintiff's performance—in a case of services, a *quantum meruit* or reasonable remuneration, and in a case of goods, a quantum valebat or reasonable price. Such cases are to be contrasted with cases where such a benefit has not been requested by the defendant. In the latter class of case, recovery is rare in restitution; but if the sole basis of recovery was that the defendant had been incontrovertibly benefited, it might be legitimate to limit recovery to the defendant's actual benefit—a limit which has (perhaps inappropriately) been imported by the legislature into section 1(3) of the Act. However, under section 1(3) as it stands, if the defendant's actual benefit is less than the just or reasonable sum which would otherwise to be awarded to the plaintiff, the award must be reduced to a sum equal to the amount of the defendant's benefit.

A crucial question, upon which the Act is surprisingly silent, is this: what bearing do the terms of the contract, under which the plaintiff has acted, have upon the assessment of the just sum? First, the terms upon which the work was done may serve to indicate the full scope of the work done, and so be relevant to the sum awarded in respect of such work. . . . Secondly, the contract consideration is always relevant as providing some evidence of what will be a reasonable sum to be awarded in respect of the plaintiff's work. . . . Thirdly, however, the contract consideration, or a rateable part of it, may provide a limit to the sum to be awarded. To take a fairly extreme example, a poor householder or a small businessman may obtain a contract for building work to be done to his premises at considerably less than the market price, on the basis that he cannot afford to pay more. In such a case, the court may consider it just to limit the award to a rateable part of the contract price, on the ground that it was the under-

---

[47] [1979] 1 W.L.R. 783, 804. There is no comparable language in s.1(2); see above, pp. 450 *et seq.*, on which see Birks, *Introduction*, p. 257. On change of position, see below, Chap. 40.

standing of the parties that in no circumstances (including the circumstances of the contract being frustrated) should the plaintiff recover more
than the contract price or a rateable part of it."[48]

The judge's construction of the statute was based then on the premise that
the fundamental principle underlying the statute was that of unjust enrichment. This conclusion has been criticised on the ground that this ignores the
plain language of the statute which creates "a flexible machinery for the
adjustment of loss."[49] It is true that the task of the court is to determine what is
the just sum.[50] But to do so it is first necessary to identify the "benefit" gained
by the contracting party, for the benefit is the ceiling of any award under the
Act. In our view, the benefit must be the defendant's enrichment, however it is
measured.

The judge's conclusion that the benefit gained by the defendant, within the
meaning of section 1(3), was his net benefit rather than the value of the services
rendered was based on his construction of section 1(3) and, in particular, on
the antithesis between the words "performance" and "benefit" in section
1(3)(b).[51] The judge recognised that there must be exceptions; for example, if
the requested services resulted in no end value or were objectively speaking of
little or no value.[52] In these cases the defendant has benefited nonetheless,
because he requested the services. Another interpretation has been suggested.
The benefit gained by the defendant is the market value of the services when
rendered, on the basis that that is the "valuable benefit" obtained "*before* the
time of discharge."[53] If that interpretation is accepted, the landowners in
Appleby v. *Myers*[54] would have been benefited to that extent before the partially
built house was destroyed by the frustrating event. The circumstances set out
in section 1(3)(a) and (b) should be treated, it is suggested, as no more than
guidelines, which the court must take into account in determining what is the
just sum. So, on that basis, even if a building is destroyed, the court would then
have discretion to make some award under the Act.[55] But this construction

---

[48] At pp. 805–806.
[49] [1984] Jo. of B.L. 207, 225 [Haycroft and Waksman], who argue that it will generally be just to
divide the loss between the parties.
[50] A frustrating event may discharge a plaintiff from perfoming what would have been a losing
contract. In such a case it may be improper to ignore the terms of the contract and reallocate
risks which the parties had agreed to bear. So, if in *B.P. Exploration Co. (Libya) Ltd.* v. *Hunt
(No. 2)* the plaintiff had made a losing contract, the loss which would have been suffered by him
if the contract had been performed might be taken into account in determining what is a just
sum.
[51] *Essays* (ed. Burrows), pp. 161–163 [McKendrick], who accepts with hesitation the judge's
construction. Contrast the different language of the British Columbia (Frustrated Contracts)
Act 1974, s.5(1)(4) and the New South Wales (Frustrated Contracts) Act 1978, ss.9–15: see
below, p. 468.
[52] [1979] 1 W.L.R. 783, 801–802.
[53] Emphasis supplied.
[54] (1867) L.R. 2 C.P. 651.
[55] Treitel, *op. cit.* pp. 811–812; Birks, *Introduction*, pp. 249–258. In Burrow's view, *The Law of
Restitution*, pp. 287–292, the critical distinction is between the receipt of services and the end
product of those services. The "defendant's benefit comprises his saving of expense in paying

creates great problems as to how such a "discretion" should be exercised in any particular case, and the reasons why the judge in *B.P. Exploration Co. (Libya) Ltd. (No. 2)* v. *Hunt* preferred a different solution are to be found in the passages from his judgment quoted in the text. If his construction of the Act was wrong, the Court of Appeal could, and should, have interfered with his award.

In *B.P. Exploration Co. (Libya) Ltd. (No. 2)* v. *Hunt* it was, as will be seen, an academic question whether the benefit gained was the end-product or the value of the services rendered. In that case, Mr. Hunt was the owner of an oil concession in Libya. He entered into a "farm-in agreement" with the plaintiffs (whom we shall refer to as BP), under which BP received a half-share in the concession, and agreed (a) to transfer to Mr. Hunt certain farm-in contributions in cash and in oil, and (b) to undertake (subject to the terms of the contract) exploration of the concession and, if oil was found, the development of the field and the production of oil from the field. BP was to provide all the necessary finance until the field came on stream; but once the field came on stream, BP was to receive, not only one-half of all oil produced from the field, but also "reimbursement oil," which consisted of three-eighths of Mr. Hunt's share of production, until BP had received in reimbursement oil 125 per cent. of their farm-in contributions and of one-half of the money expended by them in the exploration and development of the field. After the field came on stream, the costs of production and future development of the field were to be borne equally by BP and Mr. Hunt. The effect of the agreement was therefore that not only were BP advancing all necessary finance before the field came on stream, but also they were taking the risk of oil being found in commercial quantities. A giant oilfield was discovered by BP, the discovery well being drilled in November 1961. The appraisal and development of the field, and the construction of production facilities (including a pipeline over 500 km long from the field to a newly constructed terminal near Tobruk), were completed by the end of 1966, and the field came on stream in January 1967. During the next five years, substantial quantities of oil were produced from the field. In December 1971, as a reprisal for the annexation by Iran of three small islands in the Persian Gulf, the Libyan Government enacted a law purporting to expropriate BP's interest in the concession, and thereafter effectively excluded BP and its personnel from the concession and production facilities. Following the expropriation of BP's interest, Mr. Hunt continued to export some oil from the field for his own account, with the consent of BP, under conditions of increasing difficulty; in June 1973 his interest was also expropriated. At the time of the expropriation of BP's interest in December 1971, BP had received some but not all of the reimbursement oil to which they were entitled. BP and Mr. Hunt in turn claimed that the expropriation of their interests by the Libyan Government was unlawful; later, after the expropriation of Mr. Hunt's

---

for the services producing that end product." But in *B.P.* v. *Hunt* the purpose of the contract was to produce an end product.

interest, each entered into a separate settlement with the Libyan Government, under which the Libyan Government paid compensation based upon the book value of the claimant's interest in the facilities in Libya.

BP commenced proceedings against Mr. Hunt in England, claiming a declaration that the contract had been frustrated, and the award of a just sum under section 1(3) of the 1943 Act. Mr. Hunt contended that the contract was not governed by English law and that it had not been frustrated, and that therefore the Act did not apply; in the alternative, he opposed the award of any sum to BP under the Act, and he in his turn advanced a cross-claim under section 1(3). Robert Goff J. held (following Kerr J. on this point) that the contract was governed by English law; and he further held that the contract had been frustrated when the plaintiffs' interest in the concession was expropriated. He went on to award to BP under section 1(3) a sum which he assessed at $10,801,534 and £5,666,399. The judge held that he had power to award interest under section 3 of the Law Reform (Miscellaneous) Provisions Act 1934, and that interest accrued from the date when Mr. Hunt became fully aware of BP's intention to bring a claim against him.[56] He rejected Mr. Hunt's cross-claim. The Court of Appeal concluded that the judge had properly exercised his discretion and affirmed the award. Mr. Hunt did not attempt to challenge the *quantum* of the award in the House of Lords but chose to rely on the argument that the parties had agreed that BP should bear the risk of expropriation if the contract were frustrated by the events which occurred.[57] The House rejected the argument and dismissed the appeal.

The award to BP was made up as follows. First, Robert Goff J. identified the benefit obtained by Mr. Hunt by reason of BP's contractual performance as being the enhancement in the value of his share of the concession. However that benefit was greatly reduced by the effect of the circumstances giving rise to the frustration of the contract, and was therefore held to be limited to the benefit of the oil obtained by Mr. Hunt from the concession and the benefit of his settlement with the Libyan Government. Furthermore the judge, making a rough apportionment, held that only half of that benefit derived from BP's contractual performance, the other half deriving from Mr. Hunt's contribution to the joint enterprise, namely the concession itself. No allowance was made for the time value of money, because the Act gave the court no power to make any such allowance.[58] On this basis, the judge valued Mr. Hunt's benefit at $84,951,000 (net of reimbursement oil). He then went on to assess the just sum to be awarded to BP in respect of their contractual performance.

That sum was made up of the expenditure incurred by BP for Mr. Hunt before and after the field came on stream, plus farm-in payments in cash and oil. From that sum was to be deducted reimbursement oil, received by BP and valued at the date of delivery. This was the benefit directly conferred on Mr.

---

[56] See above, p. 448.
[57] See below, pp. 462–463.
[58] See above, p. 457.

Hunt. Following *Despina R and The Folias*[59] he concluded that "the award of restitution should be made in the currency in which the defendant's benefit can be most fairly and appropriately valued."[60] The farm-in oil and farm-in payments were therefore valued in dollars since the dollar was the currency most closely linked with oil. This sum came to $10,801,534. But BP's other expenditure was valued in sterling since it was an English company keeping its accounts in sterling and operating under a contract governed by English law; this sum amounted to £5,666,399. Interest was also awarded. The total award, being considerably less than the benefit received by Mr. Hunt, was the amount of the award to BP on their claim under the Act. The Court of Appeal upheld the award,[61] and the House of Lords affirmed its judgment.[62]

In assessing the just sum to be awarded to BP, the judge referred to the contract as providing evidence of a reasonable level of remuneration for the services which BP had rendered, and accordingly made his award on the basis that BP should receive a sum equal to the aggregate of the expenditure they had incurred for Mr. Hunt's account and the value of their farm-in contributions. But in two respects he did not follow the contract. First, the contract had provided that BP's reimbursement, in the form of reimbursement oil, should be of 125 per cent. of their expenditure and farm-in contributions, no doubt to allow for the lapse of time between payment and reimbursement; the judge made no such allowance, since he did not consider it open to him under the Act to make any allowance for the time value of money. Secondly, in 1967 the parties had entered into a variation of the contract whereby they agreed that the amount of reimbursement oil in respect of BP's expenditure on Mr. Hunt's account before the field came on stream, and their farm-in contributions, should be fixed at 50 million barrels of oil, irrespective of any variation in the price of oil. This agreement put the parties at the mercy of fluctuations in the oil price, which in fact increased substantially so that the agreement proved to be a very poor bargain for Mr. Hunt. The judge disregarded the variation as being too speculative to provide any useful evidence of the value of BP's services and not of sufficient weight to displace sterling as the currency by which the value of BP's services was to be measured.

Mr. Hunt's cross-claim under the Act was dismissed, on the ground that, although BP had derived an actual benefit from Mr. Hunt's contractual performance (*i.e.* the transfer by him to them of a half share in the concession valued at $27,600,000), nevertheless Mr. Hunt had already received full recompense by reason of BP's performance under the contract.

Contracting out

Section 2(3) of the Act provides as follows:

---

[59] [1979] A.C. 685.
[60] [1979] 1 W.L.R. 783, 840.
[61] [1981] 1 W.L.R. 232.
[62] [1983] 2 A.C. 352.

Where any contract to which this Act applies contains any provision which, upon the true construction of the contract, is intended to have effect in the event of circumstances arising which operate, or would but for the said provision operate, to frustrate the contract, or is intended to have effect whether such circumstances arise or not, the court shall give effect to the said provision and shall only give effect to the foregoing section of this Act to such extent, if any, as appears to the court to be consistent with the said provision.[63]

There is no difficulty if there is a clear indication in the contract that the parties intended the clause to be applicable in the event of frustration. So, it is open to the parties to enter into an express agreement that the plaintiff shall not be paid until the occurrence of an event; if the event does not occur because of the frustration of the contract the plaintiff must then bear the loss. The parties may impliedly make such an agreement; for example, the plaintiff may, by insuring against the consequences of the frustrating event, agree to bear the risk of its occurrence. "The Court should not act inconsistently with the contractual intention of the parties applicable in the events which have occurred."[64] But if there is no clear indication, the court should be "very careful before it draws the inference that the clause was intended to be applicable in such radically changed circumstances."[65] The mere fact that the contract which is frustrated is an entire contract should not preclude an award under the 1943 Act. Under section 1(2) the plaintiff appears to be entitled in this situation, the proviso apart, to the return of his money; and it would be strange if an award under section 1(3) should be automatically precluded simply because the contract was construed as an entire contract. There would surely be an express provision in the statute "if it was the intention that so fundamental a qualification was to be imposed on the power of the court under this subsection."[66]

In the House of Lords in *BP Exploration Co. (Libya) Ltd.* v. *Hunt (No. 2)*, the defendant's principal ground of appeal was that clause 6 of the contract demonstrated that the plaintiffs had taken the risk of the expropriation of the oil concession. Clause 6 provided that Mr. Hunt should have:

"no personal liability to repay the sums . . . to be advanced by BP for Mr. Hunt's account or paid to Mr. Hunt, but BP's right to recover any such sums which BP is required to pay or advance for Mr. Hunt's account shall be limited to recovery solely out of three-eighths of Mr. Hunt's half of the production, and in the manner specified [in the contract] if, as and when produced, saved and delivered at the Libyan sea terminal."

---

[63] s.2(4) governs divisible contracts.
[64] [1979] 1 W.L.R. 783, 807, *per* Robert Goff J.
[65] [1979] 1 W.L.R. 783, 829.
[66] At p. 807.

The House of Lords rejected this argument. In the words of Lord Brandon of Oakbrook[67]:

> " . . . There is nothing in the terms of the contract between the parties, or in the circumstances surrounding the making of it, as found by Robert Goff J., to indicate expressly or by necessary implication, that the parties when they made their contract in 1960, had in contemplation political risks, such as the expropriation of the concession in whole or in part by the Libyan government, which would operate to frustrate the contract; or, that having had such risks in contemplation, they included in the contract any provision, which expressly or by necessary implication, was to take affect in the event of such risks materialising."

The relevance to a claim under the Act of a prior breach by the plaintiff

In *BP Exploration Co. (Libya) Ltd.* v. *Hunt (No. 2)*, it was submitted by Mr. Hunt that BP had committed certain breaches of contract in developing the field, as a result of which he had obtained less oil from the field than he should have received. In the alternative, he submitted that another operator, acting prudently, could have developed the field more rapidly than BP. The trial judge rejected these submissions on the facts. In doing so, he made the following comments on the relevance of such an allegation, if proved, to an award under the Act.[68]

> "If the plaintiff in an action in which he claims an award of restitution under the Act has committed a breach of the relevant contract prior to frustration, the only relevance of such breach is that, since the defendant will have an accrued right to damages, the defendant's claim to damages may be the subject of a set-off or counterclaim in the action. I cannot see that the breach of contract can have any other relevance. It certainly cannot otherwise affect a claim for repayment of money under section 1(2), since the court has (subject to an allowance for expenses, or a cross claim or set-off) no option but to order repayment in an appropriate case. Nor, in my judgment, can any such breach of contract have any other relevance to the award of a just sum under section 1(3); the basis of such an award is that the defendant has been unjustly enriched at the plaintiff's expense, and the mere fact that the plaintiff has committed a prior breach of contract does not affect the question whether the defendant has been unjustly enriched, which depends upon the quite separate question whether he has received a benefit in respect of which he ought, in justice, to make restitution. The appropriate way of enforcing a claim for damages for breach of contract is by an action for damages or (where appropriate) by a counterclaim or set-off; such proceedings are, of course, subject to the ordinary rules relating to limitation of actions. If a defendant allows

---

[67] [1983] 2 A.C. 352, 372.
[68] [1979] 1 W.L.R 783, 808.

such a claim to become time-barred, I cannot see why he should be able to revive his claim by the back door by inviting a court to take it into account when assessing a just sum to be awarded to the other party under section 1(3) of the Act. *A fortiori*, I cannot see any possible justification for the award of a just sum under section 1(3) being reduced on the ground that the plaintiff, acting reasonably, might have acted in a manner more favourable to the defendant; quite apart from the fact that such action might have enhanced the benefit received by the defendant (and so have raised the limit to an award to the plaintiff), I cannot see how any such matter can have the slightest bearing on the question whether the defendant has, in the events which occurred, been unjustly enriched at the plaintiff's expense."

Excepted cases

Section 2(5) sets out the cases to which the Act does not apply. They are as follows:

> (*a*) to any charterparty, except a time charterparty or a charterparty by way of demise, or to any contract (other than a charterparty) for the carriage of goods by sea.

At common law there are two special limits on the right to restitution affecting the recovery of benefits conferred under frustrated contracts of affreightment. First, there is the rule,[69] akin to the rule in *Chandler* v. *Webster*[70] whereby freight due in advance will remain due and payable although the voyage may be frustrated after such freight has fallen due. Secondly, a shipowner cannot recover freight *pro rata itineris*[71] because a contract for carriage of goods by sea for freight to be paid on delivery is an entire contract. However, despite the overruling of *Chandler* v. *Webster* and the restriction of the doctrine of entire contracts, these two rules have, though criticised, been preserved by the 1943 Act. This is perhaps regrettable.

The practical consequence of the exception contained in section 2(5)(*a*), is that the Act has no application to voyage charters or to ordinary bill of lading contracts.[72] So limited, the Act is of very little consequence in the field of carriage of goods by sea, because time charters, which are within the Act, ordinarily provide for payment of hire on a periodical, usually a monthly or

---

[69] See above, p. 409.
[70] [1904] 1 K.B. 493: see above, p. 407.
[71] See above, p. 409.
[72] *Cf. Société Franco-Tunisienne d'Armement* v. *Sidermar S.P.A.* [1961] 2 Q.B. 278, where a *quantum meruit* claim was allowed for services rendered although the contract was frustrated; see p. 313. Pearson J. followed *Craven-Ellis* v. *Canons Ltd.* [1936] 2 K.B. 403 and dicta in *Hain Steamship Co. Ltd.* v. *Tate and Lyle Ltd.* [1936] 2 All E.R. 597, 612–613, *per* Lord Wright, 616 *per* Lord Maugham: see above, p. 24. The case was later overruled on the ground that the contracted was not frustrated: see *Ocean Tramp Tankers Corp.* v. *Vl O Sovfracht* [1964] 2 Q.B. 226. But no doubt was cast on Pearson J.'s decision that a *quantum meruit* claim would lie, if the contract had been frustrated.

semi-monthly, basis.[73] Where, however, a time charter is entered into for a lump sum, the owner may have to have recourse to the Act to recover hire for uncompleted service.

> (b) to any contract of insurance, save as is provided by subsection (5) of the foregoing section.

At common law,[74] as soon as the risk has started to run, the whole of the premium for that risk is treated as having been earned by the insurer.[75] If the premium has been paid to him, he is entitled to retain it; if it has not, he can recover it in full. Accordingly, even if the contract is frustrated during the currency of the risk, no part of the premium can be recovered by the assured.[76] For, in the absence of any contrary provision, the risk is construed as an entire risk; once, therefore, it has attached, the premium is regarded as earned in full.

Logically there was no reason why the 1943 Act should not have empowered the courts to apportion the premium. The desirability of any such change in the law does not appear to have been considered. So fundamental a change would require careful consideration before it was effected.

> (c) to any contract to which section seven of the Sale of Goods Act [1979] (which voids contracts for the sale of specific goods which perish before the risk has passed to the buyer) applies, or to any other contract for the sale, or for the sale and delivery, of specific goods, where the contract is frustrated by reason of the fact that the goods have perished.[77]

Contracts for the sale of goods are generally immune from the doctrine of frustration. Upon the passing of the property to the buyer, an event which frequently occurs when the contract is made, the risk will generally also pass. Thereafter the buyer will remain liable to pay the price for the goods even though some supervening event may cause their damage or destruction, though, of course, the seller will, if they are destroyed, be relieved from his duty to make delivery.

---

[73] If the hire paid in advance had not fallen due, it would have been recoverable at common law: see *Gibbon* v. *Mendez* (1818) 2 B. & Ald. 17; and *cf. C. A. Stewart & Co.* v. *PHS Van Ommeren (London)* [1918] 2 K.B. 560.

If, however, the hire so paid was due, there was authority that such hire could not be recovered whether the period of hire had or had not commenced to run at the time of frustration; see *Civil Service Co-operative Society* v. *General Steam Navigation Co.* [1903] 2 K.B. 756; *Lloyd Royal Belge* v. *Stathatos* (1917) 33 T.L.R. 390; *French Marine* v. *Compagnie Napolitaine* [1921] 2 A.C. 494. These decisions, which are supportable in so far as they deny recovery at law if the period has begun to run, have propably survived the *Fibrosa* case, although they were decided on grounds similar to *Chandler* v. *Webster*. The charterer may now invoke the Act in such a case, unless, as is probable, the contract has provided for adjustment of hire in the event of its premature determination.

[74] See above, pp. 493–494.

[75] *Tyrie* v. *Fletcher* (1777) 2 Cowp. 666; *Bermon* v. *Woodbridge* (1781) 2 Doug. 781. For the modern statutory position with regard to the recovery of premiums paid under policies of marine insurance, see Marine Insurance Act 1906, ss.82–84, on which see above, p. 494.

[76] *Furtado* v. *Rogers* (1802) 3 B. 7 P. 191, *semble*.

[77] As amended by Sale of Goods Act 1979, s.63 and Sched. 2(2).

Before the risk has passed to the buyer, however, it is possible for a contract for the sale of goods to be frustrated. This possibility is recognised by section 7 of the Sale of Goods Act 1979.[78] Section 2(5)(c) of the 1943 Act provides that that Act shall not apply to any contract to which section 7 of the Sale of Goods Act 1979 applies, or to "any other contract for the sale, or for the sale and delivery, of specific goods, where the contract is frustrated by reason of the fact that the goods have perished." It is, however, difficult to see to what contracts this last sentence of the subsection was intended to refer[79]; it appears to have been inserted out of caution.

Therefore, the practical effect of the subsection is to exclude frustrated contracts for the sale of goods from the 1943 Act if (a) the goods contracted for are specific, and (b) the frustration is due to the perishing of the goods. It is possible to conceive of cases of frustrated contracts for the sale of goods which could fall within the 1943 Act. For example, a contract for the sale of generic goods, contracted to come from a certain defined source of supply, may be frustrated if that source of supply fails.[80] Again, a contract for the sale of specific goods may be frustrated without their perishing, by requisitioning or by the subsequent illegality of the contract of sale.[81]

It has long been the law that a pre-payment in part or in full of the purchase price can, if the contract of sale is frustrated, be recovered back by the buyer, provided that the consideration for such payment has wholly failed.[82] Where the 1943 Act applies, a part of the pre-paid price may be recoverable by the buyer even though there has been only a partial failure of consideration,[83] subject to the court's discretion to let the seller retain the whole or part in respect of expenses incurred by the seller before the time of discharge.[84] This appears to be the only difference between cases at common law and cases under the Act. It is difficult to see why the Act should not be made applicable to all

---

[78] s.7 reads as follows: "Where there is an agreement to sell specific goods, and subsequently the goods, without any fault on the part of the seller or buyer, perish before the risk passes to the buyer, the agreement is thereby avoided."

[79] It cannot refer to agreements to sell, which are within the Sale of Goods Act 1979, s.7, unless the goods have perished by the fault of the seller or buyer. The party in default will then have probably committed a breach of contract. In sales, risk will generally pass with the property, so that the doctrine of frustration, and the 1943 Act, can have no application.

[80] *Howell* v. *Coupland* (1876) 1 Q.B.D. 258; *Re Badische Co.* [1921] 2 Ch. 331. *Cf. Hayward Bros. Ltd.* v. *James Daniel & Son* (1904) 91 L.T. 319; *Monkland* v. *Jack Barclay Ltd.* [1951] 2 K.B. 252, 258, *per curiam*. The better view is that these cases do not fall within s.7: see *Re Wait* [1927] 1 Ch. 606, 630–631, *per* Atkin L.J.; *Sainsbury Ltd.* v. *Street* [1972] 1 W.L.R. 834; *Benjamin's Sale of Goods* § 6–031; Chalmers, *Sale of Goods*, p. 100.

[81] *Re an Arbitration between Shipton, Anderson & Co. and Harrison Bros. & Co.* [1915] 3 K.B. 676.

[82] *Rugg* v. *Minett* (1809) 11 East 210; see also *Logan* v. *Le Mesurier* (1847) 6 Moo.P.C. 116; *Taylor* v. *Caldwell* (1863) 3 B. & S. 826, 837, *per* Blackburn J. These cases survived *Chandler* v. *Webster*, and the right was recognised in the *Fibrosa* case [1943] A.C. 32, 48–49, *per* Viscount Simon L.C., 52–53, *per* Lord Atkin.

[83] *e.g.* where the property in one of a number of different, but specific, goods passed before frustration. *Sed quaere* if recovery was possible at common law on "a total failure of consideration as to part"; see *Devaux* v. *Conolly* (1849) 8 C.B. 640; *Ebrahim Dawood Ltd.* v. *Heath (Est. 1927) Ltd.* [1961] 2 Lloyd's Rep. 512.

[84] s.1(2).

frustrated contracts for the sale of goods. Section 2(5)c) in its present form is open to the serious criticism that it draws as unnecessary distinction. In our view, it should be repealed.

Conclusion

It is clear from this discussion that the 1943 Act can hardly be described as perfect legislation. Indeed the Law Reform Commission of British Columbia roundly condemned many sections of the Statute as not "well thought out or well drafted."[85] The legislation which the Province subsequently enacted,[86] and which has in substance been followed in other Commonwealth juris-dictions,[87] adopts the principle that losses which are the product of the frustra-tion of the contract should be apportioned between the parties.[88] In England there has been little impetus to consider the merits of such a principle; one decision, interpreting the Act, in 50 years does not suggest that its provisions present problems which are pressing or are ones which trouble the commercial community. If the English Law Commission were to consider the desirability of recommending new legislation, then, as the Law Reform Commission of British Columbia said,[89] there are:

> "three matters to be considered—
> 1. The problem of restitution for obligations performed;
> 2. The problem of relief from liability for obligations unperformed but which were due to be performed prior to the time of frustration; and
> 3. The question of apportionment of loss."

Apportionment of loss suffered in consequence of an unforeseen event is superficially a seductive principle. But to direct a court to apportion loss is to initiate an inquiry of considerable complexity.[90] At least it can be said that the 1943 Act, with all its defects, significantly mitigates the rigour of the common law, in particular, in rejecting the common law principle that money paid can be recovered only if the consideration for that payment has totally failed.[91]

---

[85] *Report on the Need for Frustrated Contracts Legislation in British Columbia (Project No. 8)* p. 7.
[86] Frustrated Contracts Act 1974 (B.C.).
[87] Such as South Australia and New South Wales. For a discussion of the statutory provisions, and a perceptive analysis of the various statutory solutions, see *Essays* (ed. Burrows), pp. 165–170 [McKendrick].
[88] *Op. cit.* n. 85, p. 28.
[89] *Cf.* Beatson, *The Use and Abuse of Unjust Enrichment*, pp. 81–85.
[90] See the American experience, discussed in 58 North Western U.L.R. 750 (1964) [Coons] and 69 Yale L.J. 1054 (1969) [Weiss]. *Cf.* Beatson, *op. cit.* pp. 39–42.
[91] See above, Chap. 17. It is most unlikely that the courts will regard the statutory provision as a green light to jettison, in other areas of the law of restitution, the common law principle: *cf. Essays* (ed. Burrows), *op. cit.* pp. 169–170 [McKendrick].

CHAPTER 19

CONTRACTS FOR THE SALE OR DISPOSITION OF LAND WHICH ARE VOID FOR LACK OF WRITING: AND VOID BILLS OF SALE

1. CONTRACTS FOR THE SALE OF LAND

(A) Contracts Made After September 26, 1989

SECTION 40 of the Law of Property Act 1925 required a contract for the sale or other disposition of land or any interest in land to be evidenced in writing.[1] If the contract was not evidenced in writing, it was unenforceable by action. Section 40 has now been repealed. Section 2(1) of the Law of Property (Miscellaneous Provisions) Act 1989, which governs contracts made after September 26, 1989,[2] provides that: "A contract for the sale or other disposition of an interest in land can only be made in writing and only by incorporating all the terms which the parties have expressly agreed in one document or, where contracts are exchanged, in each."

An oral contract is a void contract. The doctrine of part performance is, therefore, a relic of the past: to invoke that doctrine to perform specifically an oral contract would make nonsense of a statutory provision which requires the contract to be in writing.

It is predictable that the courts will still be confronted with the purchaser who has acted to his detriment in reliance on an oral contract with his vendor, and will be required to consider:

(a) whether there are any circumstances in which the courts will compel the vendor to convey the property to, or will declare him to be a trustee of the property for the benefit of, the purchaser;
(b) whether the purchaser has any restitutionary claim against the vendor, to recompense him for benefits conferred in reliance on the oral contract; and
(c) whether the court will enforce an oral promise to hold land on trust for the benefit of another.

---

[1] For the full text, see below, p. 474.
[2] s.5(3), (4).

(a) *Whether the Court will Compel the Conveyance of, or Impose a Trust Over, the Property*

A question which the statute leaves unanswered is whether it is legitimate, in the light of the statutory provision, for the court, by invoking the equitable doctrine of estoppel by acquiescence,[3] to compel the vendor to convey the land to, or declare him a trustee of the land for, the purchaser. Few vendors may behave more unconscionably than Giles in *Van den Berg* v. *Giles*.[4] The plaintiff leased a house from the defendant. On the clear understanding that he would eventually be able to buy it, he spent over $22,000 on renovations. It was found as a fact that the defendant had "deliberately misled and inveigled the plaintiff into spending very considerable sums of money on her property, and used as the enticement for this work to be done that he would be the ultimate owner."[5] Jeffries J. held that the plaintiff was entitled to recover the increase in the value of the house in consequence of his improvements to it, some $20,500.[6]

If today an English vendor orally agreed to sell[7] a house to a purchaser and had behaved as unconscionably as Giles, would the courts specifically enforce the oral agreement?[8] It is said that the court "must look to the circumstances in each case to decide in what way the [plaintiff's] equity can be satisfied"[9] and that there must be "proportionality between the remedy and the detriment which it is its [the equity's] purpose to avoid."[10] But, in this context, the principle which is of overriding importance is that the court should not grant a remedy which would subvert the policy which underlies a particular statute or a rule of the common law.[11]

It would appear from the *Report* of the Law Commission, which led to the enactment of the 1989 Act, that the statutory purpose was the attainment of certainty.[12] If the contract is not in writing, it is void. To compel the vendor to convey the property to, or to declare that he holds the property as a trustee for, the purchaser would appear to frustrate the policy underlying the section.

However, the courts will also have to take into account section 2(5) of the statute, which provides that: "nothing in this section shall affect the creation or operation of resulting, implied or constructive trusts."[13] English courts have never allowed a statutory provision, such as sections 53 and 54 of the Law of Property Act 1925, to stand in the way of their equitable jurisdiction to grant

---

[3] On which see above, Chap. 5.

[4] [1979] 2 N.Z.L.R. 111.

[5] [1979] 2 N.Z.L.R. 111, 120, *per* Jeffries J.

[6] Query if this is the proper measure of the defendant's enrichment: see above, pp. 28 *et seq.*

[7] In the New Zealand case there was no concluded contract; the parties had not agreed a price.

[8] See *Informal dealings with land after section 2* (1990) 10 *Legal Studies* 325 [Bently and Coughlan], who introduced us to Ms. Giles.

[9] *Plimmer* v. *Wellington Corporation* (1884) 9 App.Cas. 699, 714: see above, Chap. 5.

[10] *Commonwealth of Australia* v. *Verwayen* (1990) 64 A.L.J.R. 540, 546, *per* Mason C.J.

[11] See above, pp. 62–68.

[12] *The Transfer of Land: Formalities for Contracts for Sale or other Dispositions of an Interest in Land* (Law Com. No. 164. 1987).

[13] s.2(5).

relief in the case of a plain, clear and deliberate fraud. The case law, arising from a contracting party's attempt to invoke section 53(1)(*b*) of the Law of Property Act 1925, is clear authority for the principle that it is fraudulent conduct to repudiate an oral undertaking to hold land on trust for another.[14] When the plea of equitable fraud was successfully invoked, the promisor's oral agreement to hold land on trust for the promisee or a third party[15] was specifically enforced; the promisor was said to be a constructive trustee of the land for the benefit of the promisee or the third party.[16] But in these cases the land had been conveyed to the promisor, and the imposition of a constructive trust did not enforce a void contract; the contract was unenforceable by action.[17] Consequently, we reach the tentative conclusion that, even if the purchaser can demonstrate that the vendor's conduct was so unconscionable that it would be inequitable for him to rely on the absence of writing, to order the conveyance of, or to declare him a trustee of, the property is an inappropriate remedy in that it frustrates the policy underlying section 2(1) of the 1989 Act.[18] However, the purchaser should not be denied other relief.[18a]

If the courts refuse to perform specifically an oral contract between a dishonest vendor and an honest purchaser, they will certainly deny that remedy to a purchaser who cannot prove that his vendor behaved unconscionably.

(b) *What is the Appropriate Remedy?*

The appropriate remedy will depend on the conduct of the parties and on the scope of the rule that a plaintiff will be denied restitution if he has conferred a benefit under a mistake of law: *ignorantia juris non excusat.*

The vendor who behaves unconscionably

If the vendor's conduct is unconscionable,[19] the purchaser's restitutionary

---

[14] See, *e.g. Rochefoucauld* v. *Boustead* [1897] 1 Ch. 196, C.A.; *Bannister* v. *Bannister* [1948] 2 All E.R. 133, C.A.; see below, p. 473.

[15] See the discussion in Oakley, *Constructive Trusts* pp. 30–47 and Hayton and Marshall, *Cases and Commentaries on the Law of Trusts*, pp. 55–58.

[16] *Cf.* the cases where the purchaser buys land with notice of another's contractual interest or licence. In one of the early cases, *Binions* v. *Evans* [1972] Ch. 359, 368–369, Lord Denning M.R. thought it would be "utterly inequitable" to allow the purchaser to rely on the absence of writing or indeed on the legal rights conferred on him by statute. See now, *Ashburn Anstalt* v. *Arnold* [1989] Ch. 1, C.A.: see below, p. 473.

[17] See below, p. 472 for a fuller discussion.

[18] But contrast *Taylor Fashions Ltd.* v. *Liverpool Trustees Ltd.* (1979) [1982] Q.B. 133n.
As will be seen, the courts have on occasion held that a defendant is estopped from denying that he and the plaintiff have entered into a binding contract: see below, Chap. 25. But in these cases the defendant's conduct led the plaintiff to believe that he would enter into a contract in circumstances where the enforcement of the contract did not conflict with any statutory provision which required the observance of certain formalities.

[18a] See below, pp. 471–472.

[19] Of course if his conduct amounts to deceit at law, then the purchaser can sue for loss suffered.

claim should not be barred because he acted under a mistake of law. A court may conclude that he had behaved unconscionably if he had entered into an oral contract with the purchaser knowing that the contract was void because it was not in writing, in circumstances where the purchaser believed that the parties had made a valid contract. As Lord Denning once said, in the context of a claim to recover money paid under mistake: "If there is something more in addition to a mistake of law—if there is something in the defendant's conduct which shows that, of the two of them, he is the one primarily responsible for the mistake—then it may be recovered back."[20]

So, money paid is recoverable if the consideration for the payment has totally failed. But if the purchaser has entered into possession of the land, his intermediate enjoyment, at least if it is not insubstantial, may be fatal; he will then have received part of the consideration which he is unable to restore.[21] In such circumstances it is possible that a court may nonetheless order the vendor to repay the purchase money, although he should be allowed to deduct the fair rental value of the land for the period of the purchaser's possession. He may be estopped from denying that it would be unconscionable to repay that sum.

If the purchaser has improved the land, he should recover the value of the benefit conferred. In this context the value of the benefit should be what he has spent in improving the land or, if it is a greater figure, possibly the increased value of the land.[22] In these circumstances the defendant cannot deny that he has freely accepted the services.[23] Indeed a court may well, on these facts, indemnify the purchaser in respect of his expenditure which did not benefit the defendant and which he incurred in reliance on the completion of the oral contract.[24]

If both parties contracted under a mistake of law

In our view, the case law on proprietary estoppel suggests that even if both parties are so mistaken, the purchaser should be granted relief. The vendor should be estopped from denying that he has benefited[24a] from the purchaser's improvements but not from denying, given the mischief which the 1989 Act was designed to suppress, that the contract of sale is void.[25] However, as the law now stands, money paid under a mistake of law will not normally be recoverable even if it was paid for a consideration which had totally failed.[25a]

---

[20] *Kiriri Cotton Co. Ltd.* v. *Ranchoddas Keshavji Dewani* [1960] A.C. 192, 204; see above, p. 151.
[21] *Hunt* v. *Silk* (1804) 5 East 449: see above, p. 420.
[22] *Cf.* above, pp. 28–30.
[23] *Ibid. Cf. Walton Stores (Interstate) Ltd.* v. *Maher* (1988) 76 A.L.J.R. 513: see below, p. 561.
[24] See below, Chap. 25; and *cf. Planche* v. *Colburn* (1831) 8 Bing. 14: see above, pp. 425–426.
[24a] Query whether he can recover, in these circumstances, his reliance expenses which have not benefited a vendor who is not "at fault": *cf.* below, Chap. 25.
[25] See above, p. 471 and n. 18 and, generally, Chap. 5.
[25a] See above, Chap. 4.

(c) *Agreements to Hold Land on Trust*

In the preceding sections we discussed the situation where P agrees to sell land to D and that agreement is embodied in an oral contract, which is a void contract. A distinct situation arises if P voluntarily conveyed land to D in consideration of D's oral promise to hold land on trust for P or a stranger, T. There is an ancient and consistent line of authority which holds that a defendant who pleaded the absence of a written memorandum in an attempt to defeat a trust, was deemed to hold the property as constructive trustee for the beneficiary or beneficiaries under that trust. As early as 1737, Lord Hardwicke[26] allowed evidence to be introduced of an oral agreement by the defendant to hold a leasehold estate, which had been absolutely conveyed to him, on trust for the plaintiff in certain events which had occurred; and the courts have never permitted a defendant to retain an estate, which had *ex facie* been conveyed to him absolutely but which he had orally agreed to hold as mortgagee.[27] In the words of Lindley L.J. in *Rochefoucauld* v. *Boustead*[28]: "It is a fraud on the part of a person to whom land is conveyed as trustee, and who knows it was so conveyed, to deny the trust and claim the land himself."

A more recent example of the application of these principles is *Bannister* v. *Bannister*.[29] The defendant had agreed to sell the plaintiff certain properties, on the plaintiff's oral promise that the defendant could live rent free in a particular cottage for as long as she liked. After the conveyance had been executed, disagreement arose between the parties and the plaintiff claimed possession of the cottage. The defendant pleaded the oral agreement, and the plaintiff relied on sections 53 and 54 of the Law of Property Act 1925, which require declarations of trust affecting land to be evidenced in writing. The Court of Appeal held, *inter alia*, that it was fraudulent conduct on the plaintiff's part to insist on the absolute nature of the conveyance so as to defeat the defendant's beneficial interests. Accordingly, he was a constructive trustee of the property for the defendant on the trusts of the oral agreement.[30] "The test ... is whether the owner of the property has so conducted himself that it would be inequitable to allow him to deny the claimant an interest in the property."[31] "The court will not impose a constructive trust unless it is satisfied that the conscience of the estate owner is affected,"[32] but the mere fact that he has notice of another's contractual rights does not necessarily imply that his conscience is affected.[33] But if his conscience is affected it would be "utterly inequitable"[34] to allow him

---

[26] *Hitchins* v. *Lee* (1737) 1 Atk. 447, 448; see also *Davies* v. *Otty (No. 2)* (1865) 35 Beav. 208.
[27] *Lincoln* v. *Wright* (1859) 4 De G. & J. 16, 22, *per* Turner L.J.; *Rochefoucauld* v. *Boustead* [1897] 1 Ch. 196.
[28] [1897] 1 Ch. 196, 206.
[29] [1948] 2 All E.R. 133.
[30] At p. 136, *per* Scott L.J. See s.53(2): s.53 does not affect the creation or operation of resulting, implied or constructive trusts.
[31] *Ashburn Anstalt* v. *Arnold* [1989] Ch. 1, 22, *per curiam*, C.A.
[32] *Ibid.* at p. 25. *Cf. Binions* v. *Evans* [1972] Ch. 359; *D.H.N. Food Distributors Ltd.* v. *Tower Hamlets L.B.C.* [1976] 1 W.L.R. 852; *Lyus* v. *Prowsa Developments Ltd.* [1982] 1 W.L.R. 1044.
[33] *Ashburn Anstalt* v. *Arnold* [1989] Ch. 1, 25.
[34] *Binions* v. *Evans* [1972] Ch. 368–369, *per* Lord Denning M.R.

to rely on the absence of writing or indeed on legal rights conferred on him by an Act of Parliament.[35] A statute should not be used as an instrument of fraud.[36]

The question may arise whether a court should follow these decisions.[37] The land had been conveyed by P to D. What was in issue was whether an oral but valid agreement to hold the land on trust would be specifically enforced even though it was unenforceable by action. Sections 53 and 54 of the Law of Property Act 1925 have not been repealed. Section 2(1) of the Law of Property (Miscellaneous Provisions) Act 1989 should not be construed so widely as to embrace such an oral agreement. This was not the mischief which section 2(1) was designed to suppress.

(B) A Note on the Old Law: Contracts Made Before September 27, 1989

Section 40 of the Law of Property Act 1925 provides that:

> "no action may be brought upon any contract for the sale or other disposition of land, unless the agreement upon which such action is brought, or some memorandum or note thereof, is in writing, and signed by the party to be charged or by some other person thereunto by him lawfully authorised."

An oral contract was therefore unenforceable by action. This statute still governs contracts made before September 27, 1989; similarly worded statutes are in force in other common law jurisdictions.

In the past, English courts were required to consider whether a restitutionary claim, arising from an oral contract for the disposition of land, should succeed. Where a vendor was unwilling or unready to perform the contract, the purchaser was entitled to recover his deposit on the ground of total failure of consideration, even though the contract was unenforceable.[38-39] The analogy of decisions on the Statute of Frauds suggested that if the plaintiff had rendered services under a contract which was unenforceable by action and which the vendor had wrongfully repudiated, then the plaintiff, having determined the contract, could recover reasonable remuneration for the services

---

[35] Such as the Land Registration Act 1925, s.20, which provides that the registration of the transferee of a freehold title is to confer an absolute title subject to entries on the register and overriding interests, but "free from all other estates and interests whatsoever ..."

[36] The decisions before *Ashburn Anstalt* cited in n. 32, have been severely criticised (see [1983] C.L.J. 54 [Harpum]; [1983] Conveyancer 64 [Jackson]). It should never be "fraudulent" to rely on legal rights conferred by statute (*cf. Midland Bank Ltd. v. Green* [1981] A.C. 513, and that the imposition of a constructive trust might give a litigant an unjustified preference on another's insolvency (on the dangers of which, see above, pp. 95 *et seq.*).

[37] See p. 473.

[38-39] *Gosbell* v. *Archer* (1835) 2 A. & E. 500; *Pulbrook* v. *Lawes* (1876) 1 Q.B.D. 284, 289, *per* Blackburn J., 290, *per* Lush J.; *Thomas* v. *Brown* (1876) 1 Q.B.D. 714. *Cf. Foran* v. *Wright* (1989) 64 A.L.J.R. 1 (High Ct. of Australia).

rendered.[40] In Canada, the Supreme Court, interpreting legislation akin to section 40, concluded that, if the defendant failed or refused to perform his part of the bargain, the plaintiff could recover reasonable remuneration for the services which he had rendered.[41] What the Court refused to do was to enforce the letter of the contract.

On occasions courts have properly considered whether the grant of the restitutionary claim would frustrate the policy of the particular statute which rendered the contract unenforceable.[42] This was often a task of great difficulty, given that a court could normally look only to the bald language of the statute itself.[43] It is never a happy conclusion to hold that a defendant would be unjustly enriched if the plaintiff's restitutionary claim were denied but that the policy embodied in the statute was an effective bar to a restitutionary claim. It is one which should be reached only with reluctance, when it is clearly demonstrated that to allow the plaintiff's restitutionary claim would frustrate the policy of the particular legislation.

If the defendant's conduct was characterised as fraudulent in equity, then the courts would specifically enforce any oral promise to hold land on trust for the promisor or a third party.[44]

2. VOID BILLS OF SALE

A bill of sale which is not made in accordance with the statutory form is void,[45] and it follows that any agreement contained in it for repayment of principal or interest falls with the bill of sale and is also void.[46] In *Bradford Advance Co.* v. *Ayers*[47] a divisional court held, however, that money advanced under a void bill of sale can be recovered by the lender, together with interest at a reasonable rate. This decision has been applied where the bill of sale was held to be void for non-registration.[48]

In contrast, the courts have denied recovery of loans made under contracts void for *ultra vires*[49] or unenforceable under the Moneylenders Act 1927.[50] To grant a direct quasi-contractual remedy in these cases has been held to result in

---

[40] *Scarisbrick* v. *Parkinson* (1869) 20 L.T. 175; *Pulbrook* v. *Lawes* (1876) 1 Q.B.D. 284; *James* v. *Thomas H. Kent & Co. Ltd.* [1951] 1 K.B. 551, 556, *per* Denning L.J.

[41] *Deglman* v. *Guaranty Trust Co. of Canada and Constantineau* [1954] 3 D.L.R. 785 is the leading case.

[42] See above, pp. 62–68.

[43] *Cf.* the important decision of the High Court of Australia in *Pavey & Matthews Pty Ltd.* v. *Paul* (1987) 61 A.L.J.R. 151: see above, p. 65.

[44] See above, p. 474.

[45] Bills of Sale Act (1878) Amendment Act 1882, s.9.

[46] *Davies* v. *Rees* (1886) 17 Q.B.D. 408; *Smith* v. *Whiteman* [1909] 2 K.B. 437.

[47] [1924] W.N. 152.

[48] *North Central Wagon Finance Co.* v. *Brailsford* [1962] 1 W.L.R. 1288.

[49] *Sinclair* v. *Brougham* [1914] A.C. 398; see above, p. 83.

[50] *Orakpo* v. *Manson Investments Ltd.* [1978] A.C. 95; see above, pp. 66–67. But *cf.* minors' contracts where, although a direct restitutionary claim is denied, subrogation to the rights of third parties was permitted in certain circumstances: see above, pp. 62–68.

the indirect enforcement of the principal obligation under the contract which the law has refused to enforce. But, in the case of security bills of sale, the principal purpose of the bill is not simply to bind the borrower by a personal obligation to repay the loan; it is to secure that obligation by a mortgage of personal chattels. To allow recovery of money lent under the void bill of sale will not, therefore, amount to indirect enforcement of the principal purpose of the bill.[51]

---

[51] *Cf.* the cases where recovery was allowed of benefits conferred under contracts unenforceable for want of corporate seal (*Lawford* v. *Billericay R.D.C.* [1903] 1 K.B. 772) and unenforceable under the Statute of Frauds, 1677 (*Souch* v. *Strawbridge* (1846) 2 C.B. 808, 813–814, *per* Tindal C.J.; *Scott* v. *Pattison* [1923] 2 K.B. 723.

CHAPTER 20

CONTRACTS VOID FOR WANT OF AUTHORITY

A THIRD party (T) may be induced by an "agent" (A) to enter into a supposed contract with A's "principal" (P), which is void because A had no authority to bind P to such a contract. In such a case, if T has acted to his detriment on the faith of A's false representation that he had the necessary authority, he can sue A for damages for breach of warranty of authority or seek restitution from A of any benefit retained by him.[1] If, however, T has conferred some benefit on P under the supposed contract, he may be entitled to restitution from P in respect of the benefit so conferred.

1. WHERE T PAYS MONEY TO P OR TO A

If T paid the money directly to P, retention of the money by P may well be evidence that he has ratified A's act.[2] If there is no ratification and P has given no consideration for the payment, T should be entitled to recover the money from him for the consideration for the payment has totally failed. It is more likely, however, that the money will have been paid to A. If so, T can recover it from him, subject to the usual defences. It is an open question whether A can plead the special defence, akin to change of position, which applies if A has paid the money over to P or otherwise altered his position in relation to P on the faith of the payment.[3] In principle he should be permitted to do so if he has acted in good faith, not knowing of his want of authority.[4]

If A has borrowed money from T on P's behalf but without his authority, and has applied that money in the discharge of legal liabilities of P which he had authority to discharge, or possibly in some other authorised manner on P's behalf, T can proceed directly against P in equity and recover from him a sum equal to such part of his money as has been so applied.[5]

2. WHERE T TRANSFERS GOODS TO P OR TO A

The mere fact that T has transferred goods to P will not of itself impose any

---

[1] *Collen* v. *Wright* (1857) 8 E. & B. 647. If A's representation was fraudulent, T can proceed against A for damages for fraud; see *Polhill* v. *Walter* (1832) 3 B. & Ad. 114.
[2] *Jacobs* v. *Morris* [1902] 1 Ch. 816, 832, *per* Vaughan Williams L.J.
[3] See below, Chap. 40.
[4] *Cf.* above, p. 243 (agent ignorant of duress).
[5] *Bannatyne* v. *D. & C. MacIver* [1906] 1 K.B. 103; *Reversion Fund & Insurance Co. Ltd.* v. *Maison Cosway Ltd.* [1913] 1 K.B. 364; *Rolled Steel Products (Holdings) Ltd.* v. *British Steel Corp.* [1986] Ch. 246, 300, 307, C.A.; see below, pp. 629–631, for a discussion of these cases.

liability on P. When P discovers the true position, he may be able to return the goods *in specie*. If he does not do so, he may be taken to have purchased the goods from T and will be liable for their reasonable price on a *quantum valebat*.

On the other hand, P may have already consumed the goods. If he has consumed them in the belief that he would not be required to pay for them, he should not, in our view, be liable to T in conversion because the property in the goods will have passed to him. But it is a distinct question whether he should be liable in restitution on a *quantum valebat*. In such a case he cannot be said to have requested or freely accepted the goods.[6] But exceptionally a *quantum valebat* claim should lie if P has incontrovertibly benefited from their delivery; the ground of T's restitutionary claim is mistake, induced by A's false representation.[7] One such case may arise where T supplies P with necessary goods under a contract void for want of authority. There is then "room for the supposition that [P] might either have accepted [T's] goods . . . or have obtained similar goods [elsewhere]."[8] The benefit gained by P should be measured, in such a situation, by the reasonable price of the goods delivered, the "supposed" contract price or the price which P would normally have paid for such necessary goods, whichever is the least.

If A still has the goods in his possession, he must restore them or pay their reasonable value.[9]

3. Where T Renders Services to P or to A

Similar principles apply where T has rendered services to P under a supposed contract of this kind. The mere rendering of the services cannot of itself impose any liability upon P to pay for them,[10] because, as in all claims for services, the general rule is that either the services must have been rendered at the defendant's request or they must have been freely accepted by the defendant.[11] On occasions, however, P has been held liable to make restitution even though he did not request or freely accept the services.

The important decision of the Court of Appeal in *Craven-Ellis* v. *Canons Ltd.*[12] illustrates the difficulties which may arise in determining whether a restitution claim should lie in respect of services, which have been rendered under a contract void for want of authority. The plaintiff was appointed managing director of the defendant company, under an agreement to which

---

[6] See above, pp. 18–22, and *cf. Boulton* v. *Jones* (1857) 27 L.J.Exch. 117, 2 H. & N. 564, see below, pp. 488–491. It is possible, however, that T may, in certain circumstances, be subrogated to benefits in P's hands, *e.g.* to a fund which represents the proceeds of a resale by P of the goods: see below, p. 390.

[7] See above, pp. 22 *et seq.*

[8] Woodward, *op. cit.* p. 94; cited below, p. 491. And see *Craven-Ellis* v. *Canons, Ltd.* [1936] 2 K.B. 403, 412, *per* Greer L.J.; see below, p. 478.

[9] See above, pp. 26–27.

[10] *Schmaling* v. *Thomlinson* (1815) 6 Taunt. 147.

[11] See above, pp. 18–22.

[12] [1936] 2 K.B. 403. See also *Van Deusen* v. *Blum*, 18 Pick. (Mass.) 229 (1836); and *Campbell* v. *Tennessee Valley Authority*, 421 F.2d 293 (1969).

the company's seal was affixed pursuant to a resolution of directors who were unqualified so to act because they had failed to take up their qualification shares. Moreover, the directors had power to appoint only one of their own number as managing director, and the plaintiff was unqualified to be a director as he held no shares. The agreement was therefore void. The plaintiff, however, rendered services to the company under this void agreement, both parties to the agreement believing that there was a valid agreement,[13] and claimed remuneration for those services from the company. The Court of Appeal held that he was entitled to recover on a *quantum meruit*. Greer L.J. said:

> "The defendants seem to me to be in a dilemma. If the contract was an effective contract by the company, they would be bound to pay the remuneration provided for in the contract. If, on the other hand, the contract was a nullity and not binding either on the plaintiff or the defendants, there would be nothing to prevent the inference which the law draws from the performance by the plaintiff of services to the company, and the company's acceptance of such services, which, if they had not been performed by the plaintiff, they would have had to get some other agent to carry out."[14]

The company had been incontrovertibly benefited.[15] But Greer L.J. had no doubt that the *quantum meruit* claim, based on "the company's acceptance" was quasi-contractual rather than contractual. He said[16]:

> "In my judgment, the obligation to pay reasonable remuneration for the work done when there is no binding contract between the parties is imposed by a rule of law, and not by an inference of that arising from the acceptance of services or goods. It is one of the cases referred to in books on contracts as obligations arising *quasi ex contractu*. . . . "

However, in *Craven-Ellis* v. *Canons Ltd.*, it is difficult to see how the company could be said to have freely accepted the services in the knowledge that they were to be paid for. There were no qualified directors "at any material time who could act for the company, who could acquire knowledge for the company, who could receive notices for the company, who could make requests for the company, or who could enter into any contract, express or

---

[13] At p. 414, *per* Greene L.J.
[14] [1936] 2 K.B. 403, 412. *Cf. Re Berkeley Applegate (Investment Consultants) Ltd.* [1989] Ch. 32.
[15] It is a distinct question of how the value of that benefit is measured. Seemingly it is the reasonable value of the services at the date when they were rendered. However, Craven-Ellis must have had a "contract" which should form the ceiling of any award (see above, pp. 29–30); and the contract price, having been agreed by the parties, is on these facts a proper measure of what is the reasonable value of the services rendered: *cf.* below, p. 30.
[16] [1936] 2 K.B. 403, 412.

implied."[17] Lord Denning, writing in the *Law Quarterly Review*[18] soon after the case was decided, concluded "that the acceptance must have been by the whole body of shareholders. . . . It is well established that the assent or acquiescence or ratification of the whole body of the shareholders on a matter *intra vires* the company is equivalent to the assent or acquiscence or ratification of the company."[19] The rationalisation is ingenious, but it does not find any support from the facts or the judgments of the Court of Appeal. What is clear is that the court was not prepared to allow the plaintiff's claim to founder on the technicalities of company law, when it was apparent that the company had incontrovertibly benefited from the services of a plaintiff who had acted unofficiously.

Today a court may, on comparable facts, find that the plaintiff's claim is grounded on mistake, for both parties thought that they had entered into a valid contract. But the Court of Appeal did not consider mistake, particularly the plaintiff's mistake, to be relevant. In the absence of any free acceptance or mistake, what is the basis of the restitutionary claim? There is necessity,[20] for Craven-Ellis's services were necessary services since the company "would have had to get some other agent to carry [them] out."[21] But English law recognises such a claim only in the most exceptional circumstances.[22] Again, it may be said that Craven-Ellis had rendered his services for a consideration which had totally failed; attractive as this rationalisation may be,[23] English courts have not yet accepted that it is an appropriate principle to determine the success of a *quantum meruit* or a *quantum valebat* claim. Finally, the defendant company's conduct, in refusing to reimburse Craven-Ellis, having incontrovertibly benefited from his necessary services, may properly be described as unconscionable conduct,[24-25] and consequently is a possible ground of his restitutionary claim.[26]

In *Guinness plc v. Saunders*[27] Mr. Ward was a director of Guinness. It was assumed that he had acted honestly and had rendered services which, it was further assumed, had benefited Guinness. These services were rendered in performance of an oral contract which had been authorised by the board's sub-committee, of which Mr. Ward was a member, but which had not been disclosed to the full board of directors, as required by the company's articles of association. The House of Lords held that the contract was void for want of

---

[17] [1936] 2 All E.R. 1066, 1069, *per* Croom Johnson K.C., *arguendo*. (The passage does not appear in [1936] 2 K.B. 403.)

[18] (1939) 55 L.Q.R. 54 [A. T. Denning].

[19] At p. 54. See also *Monks v. Poynice Pty Ltd.* (1987) 8 N.S.W.L.R. 662 (S.Ct.).

[20] Birks, *op. cit.* pp. 118–119.

[21] See above, n. 14.

[22] See above, Chap. 15.

[23] See above, Chaps. 15–16.

[24-25] See the observations of Oliver J., cited above, pp. 169–170, in *Taylor Fashions Ltd. v. Liverpool Victoria Trustees Co. Ltd.* [1982] Q.B. 133n, 151–152.

[26] However, if the plaintiff knew the company had no authority to enter into a contract with him, it may then be said, in the absence of any representation by the company's agents, that he has taken the risk that the company might not reimburse him for his services.

[27] [1990] 2 A.C. 663: see above, p. 33 and see below p. 664.

authority. Nonetheless, Mr. Ward was not entitled to claim remuneration on a *quantum meruit*. Furthermore, he was not entitled to an equitable allowance for his services. Mr. Ward had put himself in a position in which his interests were "in stark conflict with his duty as a director."[28]

It was only Lord Templeman who discussed *Craven-Ellis* v. *Canons Ltd*. In his view it was clearly distinguishable.

> "In *Craven-Ellis's* case the plaintiff was not a director, there was no conflict between his claim to remuneration and the equitable doctrine which debars a director from profiting from his fiduciary duty, and there was no obstacle to the implication of a contract between the company and the plaintiff entitling the plaintiff to claim reasonable remuneration as of right by an action in law."[29]

But *Craven-Ellis* thought that he was the managing director, and, even though he was not, he was, like Mr. Ward, the company's fiduciary being a self-appointed agent of the company. On the assumptions which the House of Lords made, that Mr. Ward had acted in good faith, that his remuneration was reasonable and that his services had benefited the company, the denial of remuneration is a stringent application of equity's draconian principles.[30]

In *Craven-Ellis* v. *Canons Ltd.*, the fact that the work had been done in pursuance of an express contract which proved to be void did not prevent the imposition of this quasi-contractual obligation. However, the situation will be different if the circumstances which have vitiated the contract have also vitiated the acceptance by the recipient of the services rendered to him[31] and frustrated any presumption that the defendant has incontrovertibly benefited from the receipt of the services. For these reasons the restitutionary claim did not succeed in *Re Allison*.[32] In that case a liquidator, who had been appointed under a winding-up resolution which was invalid *ab initio*, failed in his claim in respect of services rendered in connection with the liquidation of the company. As Greene L.J. said in *Craven-Ellis* v. *Canons Ltd.*,[33] when commenting on *Re Allison*:

> "I do not see how any request could in any circumstances be implied when the whole assumption upon which the work was done, and the only assumption upon which it would have been of any use to the company,

---

[28] At p. 702, *per* Lord Goff; see above, p. 33.

[29] At p. 693.

[30] *Ibid*. On the fiction of the implied contract, see above, p. 5. Lord Templeman found a further distinction between the facts of the two cases, namely, that the agreement was sanctioned by all the directors. But the directors who resolved to appoint Craven-Ellis were not qualified so to act: see above, p. 479.

[31] On this point, the Court of Appeal questioned a dictum to the contrary of Kennedy J. in *Re Allison* (1904) 2 K.B. 327, 330.

[32] [1904] 2 K.B. 327. Similarly, it has never been questioned that a person who does work for an *unformed* company cannot recover: *cf. Kepong Prospecting Ltd.* v. *Schmidt* [1968] A.C. 810 (P.C.).

[33] [1936] 2 K.B. 403, 415.

namely, that a valid liquidation was in progress, turned out to be ill-founded."

Similarly, if the circumstances which vitiated the contract led the defendant to believe that he was under no obligation to pay for the services, no *quantum meruit* claim should lie unless the services were necessary services which the defendant would have had to obtain elsewhere.[34] However, if the services were rendered voluntarily, with the intention of making a gift, a *quantum meruit* claim should fail; the defendant's enrichment would not then be unjust.[35]

It may be the case that T has rendered services to A, and not to P, in pursuance of a contract which is void for want of authority. There is some authority[36] to suggest that if T rendered services to A but intended to give credit to P alone, he cannot proceed against A on a *quantum meruit*. It was never intended that A should pay for the services and A did not receive them knowing that he must pay for them. T must look to P for any remedy. If his contract with P is void, he cannot turn around and claim against A since credit was extended to P alone.

---

[34] *Cf.* above, pp. 22 *et seq.*
[35] *Brown & Green Ltd.* v. *Hayes* (1920) 36 T.L.R. 330; see above, p. 44.
[36] *Smouth* v. *Ilberry* (1842) 10 M. & W. 1; *cf. White* v. *Cuyler* (1795) 6 T.R. 176.

CHAPTER 21

CONTRACTS VOID FOR MISTAKE OR UNCERTAINTY

IN this Chapter we shall consider the extent to which benefits conferred under contracts which are void for mistake or uncertainty may be recovered from the recipient. We shall consider the cases under the following heads:

(1) Where there is held to be no contract because of some unresolved ambiguity in, or incompleteness of, the contractual terms.
(2) Where there is no objective correspondence of offer and acceptance.
(3) Where there has been a failure of some condition precedent or other essential term of the contract.

The principles which determine whether a plaintiff can recover the value of benefits conferred should be the same in all these three cases. If money has been paid, recovery will be permitted if there has been a total failure of consideration.[1] The success of a *quantum meruit* or *quantum valebat* claim will generally depend on whether the services or goods respectively have been requested or freely accepted[2]; in other situations, the ground of recovery is the plaintiff's mistake.[3]

There is another case, which we shall briefly consider. It is:

(4) Where there has been a successful plea of *non est factum*.

1. WHERE THERE IS HELD TO BE NO CONTRACT BECAUSE OF SOME UNRESOLVED AMBIGUITY IN, OR INCOMPLETENESS OF, THE CONTRACTUAL TERMS

Where money has been paid under such a contract, it can be recovered provided that the consideration for the payment has wholly failed. If the contract under which the money was paid was a void contract of loan, the money can be recovered as money lent. Thus, in *Re Vince*,[4] where the appellant had lent money to a trader who became bankrupt, under an agreement which was unintelligible and was, therefore, treated as void, the Court of Appeal held that he was entitled to prove for the unpaid balance of the loan simply as for money lent.

---

[1] See above, pp. 28 *et seq.*
[2] See above, pp. 18–22.
[3] See above, pp. 39–40.
[4] [1892] 2 Q.B. 478.

Where the plaintiff has rendered services or supplied goods under such a contract, he will be entitled to recover upon a *quantum meruit* or *quantum valebat*, as the case may be, provided that the services or goods were requested or freely accepted by the defendant.

The American case of *Turner* v. *Webster*[5] provides a useful example of a case where the defendant freely accepted the services rendered. The plaintiff directed the sheriff to employ the defendant to watch a certain mill, pending attachment proceedings. The sheriff asked the defendant what he would undertake the job for, and he replied, one dollar and a half a day, and nights the same. He was duly employed on that basis; but the sheriff and the plaintiff had understood the defendant to mean a dollar and a half for each day of 24 hours, whereas the defendant meant a dollar and a half for a day of 12 hours, and the same amount for each night. The court refused to resolve the ambiguity in favour of either party, but held that the defendant was entitled to reasonable remuneration from the plaintiff for the work which he had done in pursuance of the void contract.[6]

The conclusion of the court in *Turner* v. *Webster* was, in our view, a sensible one, given that both parties were mistaken. However, it has been argued that the sum that the plaintiff thought that he was obliged to pay, a dollar and a half a day for a day of 24 hours, should be the ceiling of his liability to make restitution; to award the defendant a reasonable sum if that is more than the plaintiff's ceiling is to impose upon him a liability which he did not agree to bear.[7] But it is equally true that the defendant would never have done the work if he had known what the plaintiff intended to pay. The award of a reasonable sum was a just conclusion since both parties had acted under mistake.

In *Way* v. *Latilla*[8] the appellant and the respondent had also not agreed on the remuneration to be paid to the appellant for services rendered. The appellant had, at the respondent's request, obtained for him certain valuable information and concessions relating to gold mines in West Africa. The appellant maintained that these services had been rendered by him pursuant to a binding agreement, whereby the respondent had agreed to give him a share in the concessions and to pay him for the information so supplied. The respondent had paid him nothing. The appellant, therefore, claimed damages for breach of the agreement, with an alternative claim upon a *quantum meruit* which, he maintained, should be computed with regard to the profit which the respondent had made, a profit which was said to be in the region of £1,000,000.

---

[5] (1880) 24 Kan. 38, 36 Am.Rep. 251. See also *Meeme Haskins Coal Corp.* v. *Pratt*, (1945) 187 S.W.2d 435.

[6] For a similar case see *Shapiro* v. *Solomon*, (1956) 126 A.2d 654. And *cf. Vickery* v. *Ritchie*, (1909) 88 N.E. 835: see below, p. 491.

[7] (1989) 9 J.L.S. 121, 131–132 [Arrowsmith]; *Essays on Restitution* (ed. Burrows), pp. 129, 136–137 [Birks].

[8] [1937] 3 All E.R. 759. *Cf. Taylor* v. *Brewer* (1813) 1 M. & S. 290; *Roberts* v. *Smith* (1859) 4 H. & N. 315; *Loftus* v. *Roberts* (1902) 18 T.L.R. 532; *Gross Fine & Kreiger Chalfen* v. *Clifton* (1974) 232 E.G. 837; *John Meacock & Co.* v. *Abrahams* [1956] 1 W.L.R. 1463; *Peter Lind* v. *Mersey Docks and Harbour Board* [1972] 2 Lloyd's Rep. 234.

The House of Lords held that there was no concluded contract between the parties as alleged by the appellant, because they had never reached agreement about an essential term, namely, the amount of the share in the concessions which the appellant was to receive. Nevertheless, the appellant was held to be entitled to remuneration upon a *quantum meruit* basis.[9] Lord Wright said[10]:

> " . . . the work was done by the appellant and accepted by the respondent on the basis that some remuneration was to be paid to the appellant by the respondent. There was thus an implied promise by the respondent to pay on a *quantum meruit*, that is, to pay what the services were worth."

It was further held that, in computing the amount of such remuneration, the House was entitled to have regard to what had passed between the parties,[11] which showed that it was their intention that "the appellant was employed on the basis of receiving a remuneration depending on results."[12] On that basis, the appellant was awarded a sum of £5,000.[13]

If the defendant has freely accepted the plaintiff's services, the court should award the plaintiff the reasonable value of his services.[14]

> "The basis of [the court's] implication is that the services have been requested and have been performed by the plaintiff in the known expectation that he would receive compensation, and neither the extent nor the presence of benefit to the defendant from their performance is of controlling significance."[15]

In *Turner* v. *Webster* and *Way* v. *Latilla*, there was no doubt that one party had requested the other's services; moreover, the mistake did not vitiate his acceptance of those services although it did lead to problems of the valuation of the enrichment gained.[16] But in other cases the mistake which avoids the contract may prevent any inference that the defendant freely accepted the

---

[9] Lord Atkin concluded that, although there was no concluded contract between the parties as to the amount of the share which the appellant was to receive, nevertheless, there was "a contract of employment" between the parties (see [1937] 3 All E.R. 759, 763). Since, however, the parties had proceeded on the basis that the appellant was to be remunerated by receiving a share in the concession, and no agreement was reached as to the amount of such share and "the court could not supply the figure," the original contract must have been void because the parties had failed to reach agreement as to an essential term: see Birks, *Introduction*, p. 272. Whether, when services are tendered and accepted under such a void agreement, the right to remuneration is contractual or quasi-contractual is doubtful: see *Jewry* v. *Busk* (1814) 5 Taunt. 302; *Bryant* v. *Flight* (1839) 5 M. & W. 114; *Broome* v. *Speake* [1903] 1 Ch. 586, *Cf.* cases on sale of goods: see below, p. 494. Although there are difficulties, it is open to a court to hold that a fresh contract is to be inferred from the conduct of the parties, and that such a contract incorporates those terms in the original void contract which were agreed; so that either party can sue the other for damages for defective performance contrary to those terms.

[10] At p. 765.

[11] *Cf. Scarisbrick* v. *Parkinson* (1869) 20 L.T. 175.

[12] [1937] 3 All E.R. 759, 766, *per* Lord Wright.

[13] *Cf. Faraday* v. *Tamworth Union* (1917) 86 L.J. (Ch.) 436, on the assessment of remuneration.

[14] We suggest that this should be subject to a ceiling of the contract price: *cf.* above, pp. 28–30.

[15] *Kearns* v. *Andree* (1928) 139 A. 695, 697, *per* Maltbie J.

[16] See above, p. 28.

services rendered. In the Canadian case of *Estok* v. *Heguy*,[17] the plaintiff had signed a contract to buy land from the defendant. Before completion he went into possession of the land and deposited a substantial amount of manure on it, with the object of changing it from pasture to arable soil. This cost him $350. In fact the parties were never *ad idem* so that there was no contract between them. The defendant re-entered and declared his intention to use the land for property development. Nevertheless, the Supreme Court of British Columbia held that the plaintiff could succeed in restitution and that he could recover the $350 which he had spent. In our view the plaintiff's claim should have failed. The nature of the mistake prevented any inference that the defendant, who must have allowed the plaintiff into possession at the plaintiff's request,[18] had freely accepted the services. Moreover the defendant had not incontrovertibly benefited from those services[19]; he had been a dairy farmer but was now going to be a property developer so that the manuring of the land was of no benefit to him.

It would have been another matter if, in *Estok* v. *Heguy*, the defendant had intended to be an arable farmer; he could not then have denied that he had been incontrovertibly benefited. In *Lee-Parker* v. *Izett (No. 2)*,[20] a purchaser, having contracted to buy land, went into possession and made certain improvements, which were of value to the vendor. The contract of sale was subsequently held void for uncertainty. Goulding J. was prepared to allow the purchaser reasonable compensation for her expenditure; and he assumed that the proper remedy was a lien to secure the sums so spent.[21] In the authorities[22] cited to him, the defendant had stood by and had allowed the plaintiff to make improvements, knowing that the plaintiff was acting under a mistake; the defendant could then be said to have freely accepted the service.[23] But in *Lee-Parker's* case, both the plaintiff and defendant acted in good faith, mistakenly believing that the contract was valid. In such circumstances the plaintiff should have recovered the reasonable value of his services only if that sum was less than the difference between the improved and unimproved value of the land. But the vendor had the right to set off the reasonable value of the use of the land while in the purchaser's possession.[24] In *Lee-Parker* v. *Izett (No.*

---

[17] (1963) 40 D.L.R. (2d) 88. (The decision is criticised in (1964) 42 Can.B.R. 318 (Crawford), but was followed in *T. & E. Development Ltd.* v. *Hoornaert* (1977) 78 D.L.R. (3d) 606.

[18] This is most probable, although there is no specific finding of fact on this point.

[19] Difficult questions may arise in determining the time when the benefit to the defendant is to be measured: is it the date when the services were rendered, the date of surrender of possession on discovery of the mistake, or the date of the judgment? Arguably it should be the date when the services were rendered.

[20] [1972] 1 W.L.R. 775. *Cf.* the position of the mistaken improver: see above, Chap. 5.

[21] At pp. 780–781. The ideal solution, "to complete the purchase on the terms supposed to have been in force," was not open on the facts.

[22] *Plimmer* v. *Wellington Corp.* (1884) 9 App.Cas. 699; *Willmott* v. *Barber* (1881) 15 Ch.D. 96; see above, Chap. 5. But *cf. Cooper* v. *Phibbs* (1867) L.R. 2 H.L. 149 (see above, p. 213), which was not cited.

[23] See above, p. 171 where the argument is developed. *Cf. Preeper* v. *Preeper* (1978) 84 D.L.R. (3d) 74.

[24] [1974] 1 W.L.R. 775, 781; *cf. Wlaschin* v. *Affleck*, 93 N.W. 2d 186 (1958).

2), the value of that use was greater than the reasonable value of the services rendered, so that the plaintiff's claim failed.[25]

Just as a contract for services may be void for failure to agree on an essential term, so may a contract for the sale of goods. The question has arisen whether failure to agree on the price prevents the formation of a binding contract. The test, which is equally applicable to a contract to render services,[26] appears to be this: is it consistent with the intention of the parties that a reasonable price should be paid?[27] If a term can be implied to that effect, there is a binding contract.[28] If it cannot, for example, because it is clear that the parties intended the contract to be binding only if they reached agreement as to the price,[29] then there is no binding contract. Nevertheless, even if there is no such binding contract, if the goods are supplied at the request of the recipient, or if they are freely accepted by him,[30] he will be bound to pay a reasonable price[31] for them. Whether such an obligation is to be referred to a fresh contract arising from the conduct of the parties or to a quasi-contractual obligation imposed by law is, in the present context, generally academic if the goods have been requested or freely accepted by the defendant. Only a reasonable sum can be recovered in either case. Since, however, *ex hypothesi* the goods have then been accepted, the courts are likely to conclude that the parties were from the beginning content that a reasonable price should be paid[32] or that a fresh contract is to be inferred from the conduct of the parties.[33-34] These solutions have the advantage that the buyer receives the benefit of the various terms implied by the Sale of Goods Act 1979, relating to such matters as title and quality.

2. WHERE THE CONTRACT IS VOID BECAUSE THERE HAS BEEN NO OBJECTIVE CORRESPONDENCE OF OFFER AND ACCEPTANCE

This section is concerned with cases where A makes an offer to B concerning a certain subject-matter, and either:

(1) B purports to accept the offer on different terms[35]; or accepts, thinking he is buying a different subject-matter[36]; or C, a third party, intervenes and purports to accept the offer[37]; or

---

[25] *Cf. Lee-Parker* v. *Izett* [1971] 1 W.L.R. 1688, 1694–1696, *per* Goff J.
[26] See the cases cited above, n. 9.
[27] *Foley* v. *Classique Coaches Ltd.* [1934] 2 K.B. 1, 11–12, *per* Greer L.J.; *British Steel Corp.* v. *Cleveland Bridge and Engineering Co. Ltd.* [1984] 1 All E.R. 504, 511, *per* Robert Goff J.
[28] *Valpy* v. *Gibson* (1847) 4 C.B. 837; *Foley* v. *Classique Coaches Ltd.* [1934] 2 K.B. 1; see also *W. N. Hillas & Co.* v. *Arcos Ltd.* (1932) 38 Com.Cas. 23; *F. & G. Sykes (Wessex) Ltd.* v. *Fine Fare Ltd.* [1967] 1 Lloyd's Rep. 53.
[29] *May & Butcher* v. *R.* (1929) [1934] 2 K.B. 17n.
[30] See above, pp. 18–22.
[31] Sale of Goods Act 1979, s.8(2).
[32] *Acebal* v. *Levy* (1834) 10 Bing. 376, 382, *per* Tindal C.J.
[33-34] See above, p. 485, n. 9.
[35] This is, strictly, no more than a counter-offer.
[36] *Thornton* v. *Kempster* (1814) 5 Taunt. 786.
[37] *Boulton* v. *Jones* (1857) 27 L.J.Ex. 117, 2 H. & N. 564.

(2) B, who knows or ought to know that A's offer does not express A's true intention, in that it was not intended to be made to him[38] or to relate to the subject-matter referred to or to be in the terms specified,[39] nevertheless purports to accept such offer.

Where money has been paid under a void contract of this kind, it is recoverable[40] provided the consideration for the payment has wholly failed. But where goods have been supplied or services rendered in pursuance of such void contracts, it may be unjust to compel the defendant to pay for goods or services which he cannot return *in specie* and which, had he known the true circumstances, he might never have ordered or accepted.[41]

The courts will allow a plaintiff to recover the reasonable value of services rendered or goods supplied if the defendant has requested the goods or services or freely accepted them. This may be the case if, for example, the defendant knew or ought reasonably to have known that the plaintiff was acting under a mistake.[42-43] However, it may be clear that the mistake which has vitiated the contract in pursuance of which goods have been delivered has also destroyed the intention of the transferor to pass the property in the goods to the transferee, as when the mistake is as to the identity of the transferee. In such circumstances, the transferor can usually recoup his loss by means of an action for damages for conversion, brought either against the transferee or some subsequent holder of the goods.[44]

The mistake which prevents the formation of the contract may preclude any inference that the defendant has freely accepted the goods or services. This may arise if the mistake relates to the identity of the parties but does not prevent the passing of property in the goods. The problem is illustrated by the well-known case of *Boulton* v. *Jones*.[45] The defendant had been accustomed to deal with Brocklehurst, against whom he had a set-off. One day he sent an order to Brocklehurst for some hose-pipe; but, unknown to him, Brocklehurst had that very day sold and transferred his business to his ex-foreman, the plaintiff. The plaintiff executed the order and supplied the goods to the defendant, who was not informed of the change of ownership in the business until after he had "consumed" the goods. The Court of Exchequer held that the plaintiff was not entitled to recover from the defendant in an action for the price of goods sold and delivered. The all-important factor was the existence of the set-off. For since, as may reasonably be inferred,[46] the plaintiff as Brocklehurst's ex-foreman should have known of the set-off, he should also have

---

[38] *Hill* v. *Gray* (1816) 1 Stark. 434; *Cundy* v. *Lindsay* (1878) 3 App.Cas. 459.

[39] *Smith* v. *Hughes* (1871) L.R. 6 Q.B. 597; *Hartog* v. *Colin & Shields* [1939] 3 All E.R. 566.

[40] *Fowler* v. *Scottish Equitable Life Insurance Society* (1858) 4 Jur.(N.S.) 1169; *cf. Mowatt* v. *Provident Savings Life Assurance Society* (1902) 32 S.C.R. 147.

[41] *Cf.* the cases of services rendered under a mistake, discussed above, Chap. 5.

[42-43] See, *e.g. Stamford Finance Co.* v. *Gandy* [1957] C.L.Y., § 597.

[44] *Cundy* v. *Lindsay* (1878) 3 App.Cas. 459.

[45] (1857) 27 L.J.Exch. 117, 2 H. & N. 564; discussed in (1945) 23 C.B.R. 380, 383–391 [G. J. Williams]. *Cf. Barnes* v. *Shoemaker*, 112 Ind. 512, 14 N.E. 367 (1887).

[46] See below, p. 491.

realised that the offer was intended for Brocklehurst personally and not for the owner of the business whoever he might be. The contract was, therefore, void, and the action failed It is, moreover, to be inferred from the judgment that the court believed the plaintiff to be without any remedy against the defendant.[47] Bramwell B. said[48]:

> "When any one makes a contract in which the personality, so to speak, of the particular party contracted with is important, for any reason, whether because it is to write a book or paint a picture, or do any work of personal skill, or whether because there is a set-off due from that party, no one else is at liberty to step in and maintain that he is the party contracted with, that he has written the book or painted the picture, or supplied the goods; and that he is entitled to sue, although, had the party really contracted with sued, the defendant would have had the benefit of his personal skill, or of a set-off due from him. As to the difficulty suggested, that if the plaintiff cannot sue for the price of the goods, no one else can, I do not feel pressed by it any more than I did in such a case as I may suppose, of work being done to my house, for instance, by a party different from the one with whom I had contracted to do it. The defendant has, it is true, had the goods; but it is also true that he has consumed them and cannot return them. And that is no reason why he should pay money to the plaintiff which he never contracted to pay, but upon some contract which he never made, and the substitution of which for that which he did make would be to his prejudice, and involve a pecuniary loss by depriving him of a set-off."

If the defendant had learnt of the identity of the supplier of the goods before he had consumed them, the situation would have been different. His proper course would have been to return them to the supplier, or to ask him to remove them. If he did not do so but instead retained them and used them, he would have been taken to have accepted the supplier's "offer" to sell them, and would have been bound to pay for them as goods sold and delivered.[49] This was not, however, the case in *Boulton* v. *Jones*.

The difficulties which stand in the plaintiff's way in cases of this kind are, therefore, most formidable. They are further illustrated by the controversial

---

[47] See below, pp. 490–491. Historically, an action for the price of goods sold and delivered was the appropriate form of action whether the claim was in contract or quasi-contract: see Bullen & Leake, *Pleadings* (1863), pp. 31–32, 210–212. Strictly speaking, therefore, the judgment in *Boulton* v. *Jones* also barred any claim in quasi-contract. Trover would have been inappropriate since the property would have passed to the defendants: *Stocks* v. *Wilson* [1913] 2 K.B. 235, 246–247, *per* Lush J.; *Singh* v. *Ali* [1960] A.C. 167. But *cf. Greer* v. *Downs Supply Co.* [1927] 2 K.B. 28, 35, *per* Scrutton L.J., who left the point open. And see *Burton Lumber Co.* v. *Wilder*, 18 So. 552 (1895); *Great Western Smelting & Ref. Co.* v. *Evening News Association*, 102 N.W. 286 (1905).

[48] (1857) 27 L.J.Exch. 117, 119.

[49] *Mitchell* v. *Lapage* (1816) Holt N.P. 253; *Mill & Logging Supply Co. Inc.* v. *West Tenino Lumber Co. Inc.*, 265 P. 2d 807 (1954); *Laws Holding Pty. Ltd.* v. *Short* (1972) 46 A.L.J.R. 563.

American case of *Boston Ice Co.* v. *Potter*.[50] The defendant had in the past ordered from the plaintiffs, and had received from them, regular supplies of ice. He had, however, become dissatisfied with their service, and had terminated his contract with them. Instead, he placed an order for ice with the Citizens' Ice Co. This latter company then sold their business to the plaintiffs, together the the privilege of selling ice to their customers. For a year thereafter the plaintiffs again supplied ice daily at the defendant's house, the amount delivered each day being regulated by orders received from the defendant's servants. In an action brought by the plaintiffs for the price of the ice so delivered, the trial judge found that the defendant had no notice of the change of business until all the ice had been delivered, and that there was no contract of sale between the parties except such as was to be implied from the delivery of the ice and its use by the defendant. The defendant had, he considered, the right to assume that the ice was being delivered by the Citizens' Ice Co. Upon the plaintiffs alleging exceptions, it was held that they were not entitled to recover. Endicott J. said[51]:

> "There was no privity of contract established between the plaintiffs and the defendant, and without such privity the possession and use of the property will not support an implied *assumpsit*. . . . And no presumption of assent can be implied from the reception and use of the ice, because the defendant had no knowledge that it was furnished by the plaintiffs but supposed that he received it under the contract made with the Citizens' Ice Company. Of this change he was entitled to be informed.
>
> A party has a right to select and determine with whom he will contract, and cannot have another person thrust upon him without his consent. It may be of importance to him who performs the contract, as when he contracts with another to paint a picture, or write a book, or furnish articles of a particular kind, or when he relies upon the character or qualities of an individual, or has, as in this case, reasons why he does not wish to deal with a particular party. In all these cases, as he may contract with whom he pleases, the sufficiency of his reasons for so doing cannot be inquired into."[52]

In restitution, the factors which Endicott J. emphasised in this passage are subsumed in the limiting principle that restitution will be denied if benefits have been officiously conferred on another.[53] A person who renders services or supplies goods to another in the knowledge that that other does not wish to contract with him may be said to have acted officiously.[54] Such must have been the case in *Boston Ice Co.* v. *Potter*. Boston Ice's restitutionary claim should then fail even though it can be shown that the defendant had received an

---

[50] 123 Mass. 28 (1877).
[51] At pp. 29–30.
[52] *Cf.* (1907) 7 Columbia L.R. 32 [Costigan]. See also (1904) 18 Harv.L.Rev. 23, 26 [Woodward].
[53] See above, pp. 58 *et seq.*
[54] *Ibid.*

incontrovertible benefit.[55] It is not possible to accept Woodward's argument that:

> "... where there is room for the supposition that the defendant might either have accepted the plaintiff's goods or services, or have obtained similar goods or services elsewhere, had he known that he would have to pay for them, there is ground for requiring him to make restitution. Thus, he should be compelled to pay for goods in the nature of necessaries for his family or his business received and consumed by him in the reasonable belief that compensation was not expected.[56]

In contrast, on the facts of *Boulton* v. *Jones*,[57] it would be admittedly harsh to conclude that Boulton should be denied any restitutionary claim if Boulton had acted honestly, if unreasonably, not appreciating that Jones would only contract with Brocklehurst.[58] An honest person cannot normally be said to have acted officiously.[59] Jones had requested the goods and certainly he could not deny that he benefited from their receipt if he would otherwise have obtained similar goods elsewhere. Jones, having "consumed" the hose-pipe, still enjoyed his right of set-off against Brocklehurst; and to that extent he had been incontrovertibly benefited even if the hose-pipe was not "in the nature of necessaries."[60] For that reason, a court may be persuaded, on comparable facts, to subrogate a mistaken and honest plaintiff to the defendant's right of set-off against a third party, to the extent of the value of the goods delivered to the defendant.

A comparable problem arises if a rogue cheats both the plaintiff and the defendant, and induces the plaintiff to deliver goods or render services to the defendant under a contract which is subsequently avoided for mistake. Whether a restitutionary claim should succeed will depend on whether the defendant has requested or freely accepted the goods or services. In some cases the mistake will not preclude any presumption of the defendant's free acceptance, although the nature of the mistake may make it difficult to determine the *quantum* of benefit gained by the defendant. The Massachusetts case of *Vickery* v. *Ritchie*[61] provides a good illustration of such a situation. An architect fraudulently induced the defendant to believe that the plaintiff had contracted to build him a Turkish bathhouse for $23,200, and the plaintiff to believe that the defendant had contracted to pay him $33,721 for building it. The fraud was not discovered until after the bathhouse had been built. The Supreme Judicial Court of Massachusetts found that there was no contract between the parties

---

[55] See above, p. 22.
[56] Woodward, *op. cit.* p. 94.
[57] See above, p. 488.
[58] In only one report is the question of Boulton's knowledge of the change of ownership mentioned, when counsel for Jones is reported to have said that Boulton did know that this had taken place: 6 W.R. 107.
[59] See above, p. 58.
[60] See above, n. 56.
[61] 88 N.E. 835 (1909).

since "their minds never met in any agreement about the price." Nevertheless, the court allowed the plaintiff to recover the "fair value" of the work done, $32,950, which was his "total cost,"[62] even though the increase in the market value of the property after the bathhouse had been built was only $22,000.

In *Vickery* v. *Ritchie*, the plaintiff's mistake, the ground of his claim, was as to the amount of the payment due under the contract. It is true that he would not have built the bathhouse if he had known the true facts. But it is equally true that the defendant would not have had it built if he had. It is just to conclude that the defendant had benefited in these circumstances, for he did want a bathhouse. The problem is to measure the benefit gained by him. It has been said that the defendant should never be required to pay more than he thought he was liable to pay; he should only be made to pay what the services are worth to him.[63] But that is a harsh conclusion, given that the plaintiff was also the dupe of the rogue. Another possibility is to apportion the "loss" between the parties. But common lawyers have traditionally been reluctant to accept this solution. If apportionment is rejected, the price which the plaintiff thought he was to get and the price which the defendant thought he was to pay should form respectively the upper and lower limits of any restitutionary award.[64] Again, to measure the defendant's benefit by the extent to which the value of his land has been increased as a result of the improvements is to place a plaintiff at the mercy of a capricious and eccentric defendant who delights in constructing follies. The court's solution, to require the defendant to pay the cost[65] of the services and the goods supplied, is, in our view, a just conclusion. Here is another situation where it is necessary to override the defendant's expectation, albeit to a limited extent, in order to balance the competing claims of two innocent parties.[66]

In contrast, in other cases, the mistake of the parties, induced by a rogue, may preclude any presumption of free acceptance. For example, a rogue who owes the defendant £20 persuades the defendant to buy some timber from him on the terms that the debt should be set off against the price. The rogue then induces his principal to deliver the timber to the defendant who consumes it before the invoice is delivered, in the belief that it has been supplied by the rogue.[67] There is arguably no contract between the parties because the defendant honestly and reasonably believed that he was contracting with the rogue and only with the rogue.[68] The nature of the defendant's mistake makes it

---

[62] This was not as generous as it might appear. What the plaintiff recovered was the cost to him; there was no allowance for the profit element. The market value of the work and labour (including the profit element) was $33,499.30, which did not include the customary charge for supervision.

[63] *Cf.* above, p. 29.

[64] See above, pp. 29–30.

[65] See above, n. 62.

[66] *Cf.* above, pp. 483–484.

[67] See, *e.g. Greer* v. *Downs Supply Co.* [1927] 2 K.B. 28 (where "no case [of the defendant's liability] was made upon any implied contract"); see also *Concord Coal Co.* v. *Ferrin*, 71 N.H. 301 (1901) (where recovery was denied).

[68] *Greer* v. *Downs Supply Co.* [1927] 2 K.B. 28, 35, *per* Scrutton L.J.

impossible to ground a restitutionary claim on the defendant's free acceptance of the timber. But it can be grounded on the plaintiff's mistake. The defendant is, however, enriched only if the plaintiff can prove that the defendant has gained an incontrovertible benefit from the delivery of the timber.[69] Such a situation would arise if the timber was necessary to the defendant's business, in the sense that, if the plaintiff had not supplied it, the defendant would have had to buy similar goods elsewhere.[70] In our view the benefit gained by the defendant should then be the reasonable value of the timber, the "supposed" contract price, or the price which the defendant was normally accustomed to pay for timber, whichever is the least.[71]

3. Where the Contract is Held to be Void by Reason of the Failure of Some Condition Precedent or Other Essential Term

Where money has been paid under a void contract of this kind, it can be recovered if the consideration for the payment has wholly failed. Where goods or services[72] have been supplied, the plaintiff should ordinarily be entitled to recover their reasonable value on a *quantum valebat* or *quantum meruit*, respectively, for the failure of the contract should not preclude him from establishing that the goods or services have been requested or freely accepted by the defendant. In the absence of a request or free acceptance, he may obtain restitution if the defendant has gained an incontrovertible benefit.

The principal cases fall within three groups.

(a) *Recovery of Insurance Premiums*

Where parties have entered into an insurance policy, to insure against a risk which, unknown to either party, does not exist, and a premium has been paid, the premium can be recovered as having been paid for a consideration which has wholly failed.[73] Thus, in *Pritchard* v. *The Merchant's and Tradesman's Mutual Life Assurance Society*,[74] reinsurers of a life policy accepted an overdue premium unconditionally but without either party knowing that the life had dropped two days before the premium was paid. The Court of Common Pleas held that the agreement for renewal of the policy was void and that the premium could be recovered.[75]

---

[69] See above, p. 22.

[70] *Cf.* above, pp. 490–491.

[71] See above, p. 30.

[72] *Craven-Ellis* v. *Canons Ltd.* [1936] 2 K.B. 403, 413, *per* Greene L.J. *Cf. Re Allison* [1904] 2 K.B. 327, as explained in *Craven-Ellis* v. *Canons Ltd.* [1936] 2 K.B. 403, 414–415, *per* Greene L.J.: see above, p. 481.

[73] *Pritchard* v. *Merchant's Life Insurance Co.* (1858) 3 C.B.(n.s.) 622; *Stone* v. *Marine Insurance Co., Ocean Ltd. of Gothenburg* (1876) 1 Ex.D. 81, 86, *per* Bramwell B. See also *Att.-Gen.* v. *Ray* (1874) L.R. 9 Ch.App. 397. *Cf.* above, p. 192 for the situation where a premium is recoverable when the policy is set aside for non-disclosure.

[74] (1858) 3 C.N.(n.s.) 622.

[75] See at p. 645, *per* Byles J.

In cases of marine insurance, the rule was long ago laid down by Lord Mansfield in the following terms.[76]

> "Where the risk has not been run, whether its not having been run was owing to the fault, pleasure or will of the insured, or to any other cause, the premium shall be returned: because a policy of insurance is a contract of indemnity. The underwriter receives a premium for running the risk of idemnifying the insured, and whatever cause it be owing to, if he does not run the risk, the consideration, for which the premium or money was put into his hands, fails, and, therefore, he ought to return it."

The law on this subject is now to be found in sections 82–84 of the codifying Act, the Marine Insurance Act 1906, the provisions of which are generally in accordance with the ordinary principles relating to failure of consideration.[77] In particular, where the risk under the policy is entire, the premium can only be recovered where the failure of consideration is total. Where it is possible to apportion the premium, and there is a total failure of any apportionable part of the consideration for which the premium has been paid, a proportionate part of the premium is recoverable.[78] It is by no means easy to ascertain when a premium can be so apportioned, and the Act provides no direct assistance on this point.[79]

(b) Recovery of Price Paid in Advance for Goods which do not Materialise; and Analogous Cases

There are a number of cases in which it has been held that a price paid for goods, which unknown to either party did not in fact exist at the time of the sale, or which were not at the date of delivery in the same condition as they were in when sold, or which did not correspond with their description in a contract for the sale of goods of that description, could be recovered as having been paid for a consideration which has wholly failed. It is not always clear whether this failure of consideration is due to the contract being void, or to the seller being in breach in failing to deliver the goods which he has contracted to deliver. The distinction is not important, for in either event the buyer is

---

[76] *Tyrie* v. *Fletcher* (1777) 2 Cowp. 666, 668.
[77] For cases where the contract is illegal, see below, p. 514.
[78] s.84(2).
[79] *Cf.* Arnould, *op. cit.* Chap. 32.
Where part of a voyage is contingent upon the happening of a certain event, the risk is regarded as having been divided between that part of the voyage which is so contingent and that which is not: see *Stevenson* v. *Snow* (1761) 3 Burr. 1237, explained in *Tyrie* v. *Fletcher* (1777) 2 Cowp. 666, 669, *per* Lord Mansfield; *Bermon* v. *Woodbridge* (1781) 2 Doug. K.B. 781, 790. See also *Gale* v. *Machell* (1785), *Marshall on Insurance* (4th ed.), p. 529.
Apportionment has also been allowed by usage: see *Tyrie* v. *Fletcher*, above; *Loraine* v. *Thomlinson* (1781) 2 Doug. 585. But in time policies, where the "insurance is for a special term at one entire premium," there can be no apportionment. It is common today to provide expressly for a reduction in the premium if the vessel is not continuously employed during the whole of the specified period: see Arnould, § 1341.

entitled to recover his money. In the majority of cases, however, the failure of consideration appears to have been due to the seller's breach of contract.[80]

Recovery has been allowed on similar grounds in cases which are not concerned with sale of goods. Thus, in *Re Bank of Hindustan, China & Japan*,[81] two companies agreed to amalgamate, and a shareholder in the first company, which was to be wound up, was allotted shares in the second and made a payment for them. The amalgamation was declared *ultra vires* and void, and it was held that the shareholder was entitled to recover the money which he had paid together with interest. James L.J. said[82]:

> "This is a very simple case. . . . The applicant seeks the return of money which he has paid as the price of certain shares which he did not get. There has been on both sides a common mistake of fact as well as of law, but without any fraudulent intention on the part of any one concerned. As it has turned out, there never were in existence any shares such as the company purported to allot to him. That being so, it seems a mere matter of course for him to say, 'Give me back my money; I have received no shares.' "

Similarly, in *Strickland* v. *Turner*,[83] the plaintiff purchased an annuity and paid the purchase price. Three weeks before the sale was completed the annuitant had died. The purchase price was held to be recoverable as having been paid for a consideration which had wholly failed.

(c) *Recovery of Money Paid in Respect of Void Patents*

In an assignment of a patent, or an agreement to assign, there is no implied promise by the assignor that the patent is valid, nor is the payment of the price by the assignee conditional upon its validity. In the absence of any express warranty by the assignor, the assignee generally contracts for the use of the assignor's right, such as it is, without regard to the question whether it can be sustained in litigation or not.[84] This rule has been justified on the ground that it is usually as much within the knowledge of the one party as of the other whether a patent is sound. If, therefore, the patent is defeasible, the assignee

---

[80] *Barr* v. *Gibson* (1838) 3 M. & W. 390, 399–400, *per* Parke B.; *Couturier* v. *Hastie* (1852) 8 Ex. 40, 54, *per* Parke B.; *cf.* Sale of Goods Act 1979, s.13. It was on this ground that it was held in *Gompertz* v. *Bartlett* (1853) 2 E. & B. 849 and in *Gurney* v. *Womersley* (1854) 4 E. & B. 133, that the price paid for a bill of exchange could be recovered: on cases of this kind, see *Bell* v. *Lever Bros.* [1932] A.C. 161, 222, *per* Lord Atkin. *Cf.* Sale of Goods Act 1979, s.6, where a contract for the sale of specific goods, which have perished when the contract is made, is void: *aliter* if the goods have never existed; see *McRae* v. *Commonwealth Disposals Commission* (1950–1951) 84 C.L.R. 377. And *cf. Hamilton Finance Co.* v. *Coverley Westray Finance Co.* [1959] 1 Lloyd's Rep. 53.

[81] (1873) L.R. 15 Eq. 394.

[82] At p. 397.

[83] (1852) 7 Ex. 208. *Cf. Scott* v. *Coulson* [1903] 1 Ch. 453, 2 Ch. 249, in which the contract was set aside in equity and money paid thereunder was ordered to be repaid: see above, pp. 213–214.

[84] *Smith* v. *Neale* (1857) 27 L.J.C.P. 143, 148, *per* Willes J., delivering the judgment of the court.

can neither resist an action for money due in respect of the assignment,[85] nor, if he has paid the money, can he recover it on the grounds of failure of consideration.

Sometimes the assignor has contracted that he has made an invention.[86] If he has made no invention, the assignee may be able to resist an action to enforce the contract, or he may recover money paid by him thereunder. The same consequences follow[87] if the assignor has expressly promised that the patent is valid and it is not.[88]

Again, where a patentee gives a licence to use a patent upon payment of royalties, for the same reasons he does not impliedly promise that the patent is valid.[89] If the licensee subsequently discovers a basis for attacking the validity of the patent, he may, subject to any enforceable term to the contrary, give notice that he is terminating the agreement, thereby challenging the patentee to sue him for infringement. He is not, however, entitled to maintain the licence as a shield against an infringement suit, while at the same time asserting that, because the patent is invalid, he is under no obligation to pay royalties or is able to recover royalties already paid.[90]

In the past, it was common practice to bind a licensee not to challenge the validity of the licensed patent for the duration of the licence.[91] Another quite frequent clause obliged the licensee to pay royalties on production under the licence, whether or not the patent was valid. However, in any agreement which, by reason of its economic significance and geographical impact, becomes subject to the Rules of Competition of the Rome Treaty establishing the European Economic Community, such clauses are no longer generally permissible.[92]

---

[85] *Hall* v. *Conder* (1857) 26 L.J.C.P. 135, 288; *Smith* v. *Neale* (1857) 26 L.J.C.P. 143; *Smith* v. *Buckingham* (1870) 18 W.R. 314. See also *Liardet* v. *Hammond Electric Light & Power Co.* (1883) 31 W.R. 710.

[86] *Hall* v. *Conder* (1857) 26 L.J.C.P. 135, 143, *per* Cresswell J.; *Smith* v. *Buckingham* (1870) 18 W.R. 314, *per* Cockburn C.J. A warranty that the assignor is the original inventor does not amount to a warranty that the patent is valid: *Thompson* v. *Jefferson* (1928) 45 R.P.C. 309, P.C.

[87] *Hazlehurst* v. *Rylands* (1890) 9 R.P.C. 1; *Nadel* v. *Martin* (1903) 20 R.P.C. 721; (1905) 23 R.P.C. 41.

[88] *Berchem* v. *Wren* (1904) 21 R.P.C. 683 suggests that the plaintiff's right to recover his money is dependent upon his ability to *rescind* the contract and, as a prerequisite of rescission, to make *restitutio in integrum*. Nowadays, the plaintiff can bring the contract to an end without rescinding it; but if he does so, he can only recover money paid thereunder if there has been a total failure of consideration. See above, pp. 407 *et seq.*

[89] *Taylor* v. *Hare* (1807) 1 B. & P. (N.R.) 260.

[90] *Lawes* v. *Purser* (1856) 6 E. & B. 930; *Crossley* v. *Dixon* (1863) 10 H.L.C. 293.

[91] In the absence of an express "no challenge" clause, in an exclusive licence there would be an implied warranty that the patent was good: *Chanter* v. *Leese* (1838) 4 M. & W. 295; and see *Bowman* v. *Taylor* (1834) 4 L.J.K.B. 58; *R.H.F. Suhr* v. *Crofts (Engineers) Ltd.* (1932) 49 R.P.C. 359.

[92] Treaty of Rome, 1957, Art. 85; Commission Regulation 2349/84 on the application of Art. 85(3) to certain categories of patent licensing agreements, esp. Art. 3.1, 3.4; *A.O.I.P.* v. *Beyrard* (76/29 EEC) [1976] 1 C.M.L.R. D14; but see *Bayer AG and Maschinen Fabrik Hennecke GmbH* v. *Süllhöfer* (Case 65/86) [1990] 4 C.M.L.R. 182.

4. WHERE THERE HAS BEEN A SUCCESSFUL PLEA OF NON EST FACTUM

In certain cases a person may deny that a written document is his: *non est factum*.[93] To sustain his plea, he must be able to prove that he was mistaken as to the very nature and character of the document; a mistake merely as to the contents of the document will not be sufficient.[94] If the plea is established, then any contract embodied in the written document is void.[95] No title to land or chattels will pass to the transferee, and any money paid under the contract will be recoverable on grounds of total failure of consideration.[96]

---

[93] See, generally, *Thoroughgood's Case* (1582) 2 Co.Rep. 9a.
[94] *Lewis* v. *Clay* (1898) 67 L.J.Q.B. 224; *Bagot* v. *Chapman* [1907] 2 Ch. 222; *Howatson* v. *Webb* [1907] 1 Ch. 537, [1908] 1 Ch. 1, C.A.; *Muskham Finance Ltd.* v. *Howard* [1963] 1 Q.B. 904; *Mercantile Credit Co. Ltd.* v. *Hamblin* [1965] 2 Q.B. 242.
[95] For a generous application of the defence, see *Lloyds Bank plc.* v. *Waterhouse* [1991] Fam. Law 23, *per* Purchas L.J.
[96] The House of Lords reviewed the scope of *non est factum* in *Gallie* v. *Lee, sub nom. Saunders* v. *Anglia B.S.* [1971] A.C. 1004, followed in *Union Dominions Trust Ltd.* v. *Western (B. S. Romanay)* [1976] Q.B. 513. See, generally, (1972) 88 L.Q.R. 190 [Stone].

CHAPTER 22

ILLEGAL CONTRACTS[1]

1. GENERAL PRINCIPLES

AFTER some uncertainty,[2] it was settled towards the end of the eighteenth century that in general money paid under an illegal contract cannot be recovered. Thus illegality may be a defence to an action in quasi-contract as well as to a contractual action. This rule has become epitomised in the oft-quoted maxims, *in pari delicto potior est conditio defendentis, nemo suam turpitudinem allegans audiendus est*, and *ex turpi causa non oritur actio*.[3] The classical statement is Lord Mansfield's[4]:

> "The objection, that the contract is immoral or illegal as between plaintiff and defendant, sounds at all times very ill in the mouth of the defendant. It is not for his sake, however, that the objection is ever allowed; but it is founded in general principles of policy, which the defendant has the advantage of, contrary to the real justice, as between him and the plaintiff,

---

[1] A complex and special body of law determines whether restitutionary claims arising out of illegal contracts should or should not succeed. The defendant's gain is manifestly at the plaintiff's expense and matches his loss. For that reason the subject of illegal contracts is in this Part of the book, and not in Part III which deals with benefits acquired through wrongful acts.

[2] In *Tomkins* v. *Bernet* (1693) 1 Salk. 22, it was held that *indebitatus assumpsit* would not lie to recover money paid on a usurious bond. There are also certain observations which suggest that bribes could not be recovered by this action; but in *Wilkinson* v. *Kitchin* (1697) 1 Ld.Ray. 89, Holt C.J. apparently held that money given by a principal to his agent to spend on bribes and so spent by the agent could, nevertheless, be recovered from him by the principal. Attempts have been made to explain this decision; see Holdsworth, *History of English Law*, Vol. 8, p. 94; Jackson, *History*, p. 89, nn. 3 and 4. By the late 18th century the reasoning of *Wilkinson* v. *Kitchin* was disregarded; see *Pickard* v. *Bonner* (1794) Peake 289; and *cf. Anon* (1695) Comb. 341; *Bosanquet* v. *Dashwood* (1734) Talbot 38.

[3] (1955) 71 L.Q.R. 254, 257 [J. K. Grodecki]. However, a contract may be frustrated, as was the *Fibrosa* contract (on which see above, pp. 408–409), by supervening illegality, in which case the restitutionary claim is governed by the provisions of the Law Reform (Frustrated Contracts) Act 1943: see above, pp. 447 *et seq.*

[4] *Holman* v. *Johnson* (1775) 1 Cowp. 341, 343; see also *Collins* v. *Blantern* (1767) 2 Wils.K.B. 342, 350, *per* Wilmot C.J. Lord Mansfield's first reference to the maxim was in *Smith* v. *Bromley* (1760) 2 Doug. 696n., 697. See also his other statements of the law in *Clarke* v. *Shee* (1774) 1 Cowp. 197, 200; *Browning* v. *Morris* (1778) 2 Cowp. 790, 792; *Lowry* v. *Bourdieu* (1780) 2 Doug. 468, 470, 472: below p. 502. For early American cases, see *Barnard* v. *Crane*, 1 Tyler 457 (1802); *Austin's Administratrix* v. *Winston's Execs.*, 1 Hen. & M. 32 (1806). The courts are prepared to go behind any document to discover if the transaction is tainted by illegality; so a loan is deemed to be illegal if made to discharge an obligation which had arisen under a transaction known to the lender to be illegal: *Cannan* v. *Bryce* (1819) 3 B. & Ald. 179; *Fisher* v. *Bridges* (1854) 3 E. & B. 642; *Spector* v. *Ageda* [1972] Ch. 30.

by accident, if I may say so. The principle of public policy is this: *ex dolo malo non oritur actio*. No court will lend its aid to a man who founds his cause of action upon an immoral or an illegal act. If from the plaintiff's own stating or otherwise, the cause of action appears to arise *ex turpi causa*, or the transgression of a positive law of this country, there the court says he has no right to be assisted. It is upon that ground the court goes; not for the sake of the defendant, but because they will not lend their aid to such a plaintiff. So if the plaintiff and defendant were to change sides, and the defendant was to bring his action against the plaintiff, the latter would not then have the advantage of it; for where both are equally in fault, *potior est conditio defendentis*."[5]

The rule has been consistently applied, and relief has been denied in many cases.[6] Thus, in *Berg* v. *Sadler and Moore*,[7] the plaintiff had formerly been a member of the Tobacco Trade Association, but had been put on the Stop List and so could not get supplies of cigarettes from any member of the Association. A member, Reece, agreed, for a consideration, to obtain cigarettes for the plaintiff from the defendants. Reece ordered the cigarettes and an assistant of the plaintiff, accompanied by a representative of Reece, went to fetch them. The plaintiff's assistant paid for them, but the defendants became suspicious and refused either to deliver the cigarettes or to return the money. The plaintiff then sued the defendants for recovery of the money so paid. The Court of Appeal held that this was an attempt to obtain goods by false pretences. A disclosure of the illegal nature of the transaction was necessary to found the plaintiff's cause of action, so he was not entitled to recover his money.

---

[5] For a comparative view see Zweigert and Kötz, *op. cit.* Vol. II, pp. 407 *et seq.*

[6] Important examples are *Lowry* v. *Bourdieu* (1780) 2 Doug. 468; *Lubbock* v. *Potts* (1806) 7 East 449; *Thistlewood* v. *Cracroft* (1813) 1 M. & S. 500; *Re Scott* (1813) 1 M. & S. 751; *Simpson* v. *Bloss* (1816) 7 Taunt. 246; *Ex p. Brookes* (1822) 1 Bing. 105; *Goodall* v. *Lowndes* (1844) 6 Q.B. 464; *Begbie* v. *Phosphate Sewage Co.* (1875) L.R. 10 Q.B. 491 (affd. C.A. (1876) 1 Q.B.D. 679); *Allkins* v. *Jupe* (1877) 2 C.P.D. 375; *Scott* v. *Brown, Doering, McNab & Co.* [1892] 2 Q.B. 724; *Re Myers* [1908] 1 K.B. 941; *Wild* v. *Simpson* [1919] 2 K.B. 544; *Parkinson* v. *College of Ambulance and Harrison* [1925] 2 K.B. 1; *Re National Benefit Assurance Co.* [1931] 1 Ch. 46; *Berg* v. *Sadler and Moore* [1937] 2 K.B. 158; *J. M. Allan (Merchandising) Ltd.* v. *Cloke & Another* [1963] 2 Q.B. 340; *Shaw* v. *Shaw* [1965] 1 W.L.R. 537; *Ashmore, Benson, Pease & Co. Ltd.* v. *A. W. Dawson* [1973] 1 W.L.R. 828; *Spector* v. *Ageda* [1973] Ch. 30; *United City Merchants (Investments) Ltd.* v. *Royal Bank of Canada* [1983] A.C. 168, applied in *Mansouri* v. *Singh* [1986] 1 W.L.R. 1393. See also *Boissevain* v. *Weil* [1950] A.c. 327. Other cases are mentioned in connection with the exceptions discussed below, pp. 505 *et seq.*
The courts will not enforce an agreement, governed by English law, where the parties intend to perform an act in a friendly foreign state which is illegal by its law; similarly, if they intend to procure a third party to do such an act: see *Foster* v. *Driscoll* [1929] 1 K.B. 470; *Regazzoni* v. *K. C. Sethia (1944) Ltd.* [1958] A.C. 301; and *cf. Lemenda Trading Co. Ltd.* v. *African Middle East Petroleum Co. Ltd.* [1988] Q.B. 448.

[7] [1937] 2 K.B. 158: see (1938) 54 L.Q.R. 201 [C. K. Allen]. For a more recent case where it was held contrary to public policy to enforce a claim under a valid insurance policy, see *Geismar* v. *Sun Alliance and London Insurance Ltd.* [1978] Q.B. 383.

The same rule may similarly preclude recovery of land[8] or chattels[9] transferred under an illegal transaction, though sometimes it is possible to establish a title to them without having recourse to facts which disclose the illegality.[10] Consequently, if the plaintiff, in order to establish his cause of action, must disclose as a necessary part of his claim the illegal nature of the transaction, his claim will necessarily fail.[11] Conversely, if he can recover his property by invoking an independent right not tainted by illegality, he will succeed.[12]

As Lord Browne-Wilkinson recently said[12a]:

"Neither at law nor in equity will the court enforce an illegal contract which has been partially, but not fully performed. However, it does not follow that all acts done under a partially performed contract are of no effect. In particular it is now clearly established that at law (as opposed to in equity), property in goods or land can pass under, or pursuant to, such a contract. If so, the rights of the owner of the legal title thereby acquired will be enforced, provided that the plaintiff can establish such title without pleading or leading evidence of the illegality. It is said that the property lies where it falls, even though legal title to the property was acquired as a result of the property passing under the legal contract itself."

Moreover, "it is irrelevant that the illegality of the underlying agreement was either pleaded or emerged in evidence: if the plaintiff has acquired legal title under the illegal contract that is enough".[12b]

There are many examples in the reports where the plaintiff has succeeded because he was able to invoke an independent legal title which was not tainted by illegality. So, a plaintiff may enter into a contract which is an illegal contract but nonetheless he may have an independent claim in tort based on the defendant's fraudulent conduct[13] or the defendant's conversion of his goods.[14]

---

[8] *Gas Light and Coke Co.* v. *Turner* (1840) 6 Bing. N.C. 324; *Taylor* v. *Bowers* (1876) 1 Q.B.D. 291, 295, *per* Cockburn C.J.; *Alexander* v. *Rayson* [1936] 1 Q.B. 169, 186–187, *per curiam*; *Joe* v. *Young* [1964] N.Z.L.R. 24.

[9] *Taylor* v. *Chester* (1869) L.R. 4 Q.B. 309. See also *Kingsley* v. *Sterling Securities Ltd.* [1967] 2 Q.B. 747. *Cf.* contracts in restraint of trade: see *Instone* v. *A. Schroeder Music Publishing Co. Ltd.* [1974] 1 All E.R. 171, 181, *per curiam*, C.A.

[10] *Ferret* v. *Hill* (1854) 15 C.B. 207; *Taylor* v. *Chester* (1869) L.R. 4 Q.B. 309; *Alexander* v. *Rayson* [1936] 1 K.B. 169; *Bowmakers Ltd.* v. *Barnet Instruments Ltd.* [1945] K.B. 65; *Singh* v. *Ali* [1960] A.C. 167; *Amar Singh* v. *Kulubya* [1964] A.C. 142.

[11] In such a case, if the court becomes aware of the illegality, from the pleadings or some other source, it will be fatal to the plaintiff's case; see generally *Holman* v. *Johnson* (1775) 1 Cowp. 341, 343, *per* Lord Mansfield; *cf. Scott* v. *Brown, Doering, McNab & Co.* [1892] 2 Q.B. 724, 728, *per* Lindley L.J.; *North Western Salt Co.* v. *Electrolytic Alkali Co.* [1914] A.C. 461, 469, *per* Viscount Haldane; *Edler* v. *Auerbach* [1950] 1 K.B. 359, 371–372, *per* Devlin J.; *Thomas Brown & Sons* v. *Fazal Deen* (1962) 108 C.L.R. 391; *Regazzoni* v. *K. C. Sethia (1944) Ltd.* [1958] A.C. 301. But *cf. National Westminster Bank Ltd.* v. *Barclays Bank Ltd.* [1975] Q.B. 654, 665, *per* Kerr J.

[12] See cases cited in n. 10, above. If the plaintiff is relying on the title, it is not necessary for him to show that he has ever taken possession of his property so long as title has passed to him: see *Belvoir Finance Co. Ltd.* v. *Stapleton* [1971] 1 Q.B. 210.

[12a] *Tinsley* v. *Milligan*, [1993] 3 All E.R. 65, 85.

[12b] *Ibid.*

[13] *Saunders* v. *Edwards* [1987] 1 W.L.R. 1116.

[14] *Bowmakers Ltd.* v. *Barnet Instruments Ltd.* [1945] K.B. 65, criticised in (1949) 10 C.L.J. 249 [Hamson]. See also (1947) 95 Univ. of Pa. L.P. 261, 262 [Wade].

In such circumstances he will not have to rely on the illegal contract or plead its illegality, and his tortious claim will normally succeed.

In *Tinsley* v. *Milligan*[15] the House of Lords was recently required to decide whether equity will aid a party to a fraud to assert, establish or enforce an equitable, as opposed to a legal, proprietary interest.[15a] Miss Tinsley and Miss Milligan bought a house. They took out a mortgage and the balance of the purchase money was provided by them in equal shares. But the title to the house was transferred into the sole name of Miss Tinsley so that Miss Milligan could misrepresent to the D.H.S.S. that she had no stake in the house or in the business which the parties ran from it. They quarrelled and Miss Tinsley moved out. She then gave Miss Milligan notice to quit and subsequently claimed possession of, and asserted ownership to, the house. Miss Milligan counterclaimed for an order for sale and a declaration that the property was held by Miss Tinsley upon trust for the two of them in equal shares. The House of Lords,[15b] Lord Keith and Lord Goff dissenting, affirmed the judgment of, but did not endorse the reasoning of, the Court of Appeal, and allowed the counterclaim and granted the declaration. The House of Lords rejected the submission, which the dissenting Law Lords adopted, that Miss Milligan should be denied relief because she did not come to equity with clean hands and consequently was precluded from asserting that she enjoyed an equitable interest in the property. The austere and absolute rule, formulated by Lord Mansfield,[15c] was that equity will never aid a plaintiff who has transferred property to another for an illegal purpose. But the House of Lords concluded that later in the nineteenth century the courts had recognised that there were exceptions to that rule.[16] Moreover, today, as Lord Browne-Wilkinson said[17]:

> "More than 100 years has elapsed since law and equity became fused. The reality of the matter is that, in 1993, English law has one single law of property made up of legal and equitable interests. Although for historical reasons legal estates and equitable estates have differing incidents, the person owning either type of estate has a right of property, a right *in rem* not merely a right *in personam*. If the law is that a party is entitled to enforce a property right acquired under an illegal transaction, in my judgment the same rule ought to apply to any property right so acquired, whether such right is legal or equitable."

---

[15] [1993] 3 All E.R. 65.
[15a] At p. 85, *per* Lord Browne-Wilkinson.
[15b] Lord Jauncey, Lord Lowry and Lord Browne-Wilkinson. Lord Browne-Wilkinson gave the leading speech.
[15c] *e.g.* in *Holman* v. *Johnson* (1775) 1 Cowp. 341.
[16] *e.g. Haigh* v. *Kaye* (1872) L.R. 7 Ch. 469; *Ayers* v. *Jenkins* (1873) L.R. 16 Eq. 275.
[17] [1993] 3 All E.R. 65, 86.

The clean hands rule may be a good reason for denying equitable relief, but arguably not for denying the existence of equitable title.[17a] Miss Milligan had established the resulting trust by demonstrating that she had contributed to the purchase price of the house and that the common understanding of the parties was that they owned the house equally. Her claim was based on the fact that the house was vested in Miss Tinsley alone. The illegality emerged only because Miss Tinsley sought to raise it. Moreover, on the facts of the case, the presumption of advancement had no application; consequently Miss Milligan did not have to rely on her own illegality in order to rebut it.[18]

Both Lord Goff and Lord Browne-Wilkinson rejected the so-called "public conscience test" which had been adopted in earlier Court of Appeal decisions[18a] and by Nicholls L.J. in the Court of Appeal in *Tinsley* v. *Milligan*. This test looked to the plaintiff's conduct. Would it be "an affront to the public conscience if by affording him the relief sought the court would be seen to be indirectly assisting or encouraging the plaintiff in his criminal act"[19] or "encouraging others in similar criminal acts?"[20] Lord Browne-Wilkinson described the appeal to public conscience as an "imponderable factor" which should not determine the consequences of being a party to an illegal transaction. In Lord Goff's view, it was not open to the Court of Appeal, given the authorities binding on it, to apply the public conscience test. This would:

> "constitute a revolution in this branch of the law, under which what is in effect a discretion would become vested in the court to deal with the matter by the process of a balancing operation, in place of a system of rules, ultimately derived from the principle of public policy enunciated by Lord Mansfield C.J. in *Holman* v. *Johnson*, which lies at the root of the law relating to claims which are, in one way or another, tainted by illegality."[21]

If there was to be reform, it must be legislative reform.[22]

Not infrequently a statute will declare illegal and void contracts which do not comply with its provisions. Such a prohibited contract will not be enforced by the courts; and it is immaterial that the contract is express or implied.[23] But it is not always easy to determine whether there is an express prohibition of a

---

[17a] Lord Browne-Wilkinson did not make this point in his speech, although he implicitly rejected the particular application of the clean hands rule.

[18] Endorsing the reasoning of the Ontario Court of Appeal in *Gorog* v. *Kiss* (1977) 78 D.L.R. (3d) 690.

[18a] See below nn. 19 and 20.

[19] *Thackwell* v. *Barclays Bank plc* [1986] 1 All E.R. 676, 678, *per* Hutchison J.

[20] In *Saunders* v. *Edwards* [1987] 1 W.L.R. 1116, 1132, Nicholls L.J. accepted, with this amendment, Hutchison J.'s "affront to the public conscience" principle.

[21] *Ibid.*

[22] *Ibid*; see below pp. 519–522 for a full discussion.

[23] *Archbolds (Freightage) Ltd.* v. *S. Spanglett Ltd. (Randall, third party)* [1961] 1 Q.B. 374, 388, *per* Devlin J.

particular contract.[24] For example, a contract may be held to be illegal even though the particular statute contains no reference to any contract.[25] Conversely, a court may conclude, as a matter of construction, that the statute simply imposed a penalty upon a particular individual and did not prohibit the contract if made with a party "who is innocent of the offence created by the statute."[26] In recent years the litigation has centred around the provisions of the Insurance Companies Act 1974 which provides that it is an offence to carry out certain insurance business without authorisation. The Court of Appeal has now held, in *Phoenix General Insurance Co. of Greece S.A.* v. *Administratia Asigurarilor de Stat*[27] that such contracts are illegal and unenforceable, with the consequence that no assured can enforce, either directly or indirectly, any contract of insurance or reinsurance. Kerr L.J., who gave the only judgment of the Court, recognised that this construction, which was, given the language of the statute,[28] regrettably inevitable, meant that innocent members of the public would suffer "grave inconvenience and injury," leaving them with "the doubtful remedy of seeking to recover [their] premium[s] as money had and received." The Financial Services Act 1986 has now amended the 1974 statute, to enable the assured, but not the insurer, to enforce the insurance contract.[29]

In the *Phoenix General Insurance* case, Kerr L.J. formulated the following presumptions of construction[30]:

(1) "Where a statute prohibits both parties from concluding or performing a contract when both or either of them have no authority to do so, the contract is impliedly prohibited."

(2) If the statute imposes a penalty if one party enters into a contract or prohibits him from entering such a contract without authority, whether the contract is illegal and void "depends on considerations of public policy in the light of the mischief which the statute is designed to prevent, its language, scope and purpose, the consequences for the innocent party, and any other relevant considerations."

These presumptions are necessary if the statute is silent as to the effects of the illegality. The task of the court, to determine what is the *purpose* of the statute, is then a particularly difficult one. Unless the language of the

---

[24] See, *e.g. Bloxsome* v. *Williams* (1824) 3 B.L.C. 232 (statutory prohibition on Sunday trading), doubted by Parker J. in *Bedford Insurance Co. Ltd.* v. *Instituto de Resseguros do Brasil* [1985] Q.B. 966, 984: see Treitel, *op. cit.* p. 431.

[25] *Cope* v. *Rowlands* (1836) 2 M. & W. 149; *Cornelius* v. *Phillips* [1918] A.C. 199.

[26] *Re Mahmoud and Ispahani* [1921] 2 K.B. 716, 731, *per* Atkin L.J. (where the contract was, however, prohibited). A number of leading cases are discussed below, p. 508, where it is emphasised that the imposition of a penalty is not conclusive evidence that the contract is not prohibited.

[27] [1988] Q.B. 216. *Cf.* Financial Services Act 1986, s.132.

[28] The Act embraced the business of "carrying out contracts of insurance": see also *Re Cavalier Insurance Co.* [1989] 2 Lloyd's Rep. 430.

[29] s.132. The statute was enacted on November 7, 1986. Judgment in the *Phoenix Insurance* case was given on October 9, 1986. No mention of the Bill is to be found in Kerr L.J.'s judgment.

[30] [1988] Q.B. 216, 273.

statute is compelling, as it was in the *Phoenix Insurance* case, an important consideration should be whether the "avoidance of the contract would cause grave inconvenience and injury to innocent members of the public without furthering the object of the statute."[31]

In some cases a contract is legal in form but may be performed in an unlawful manner. Then the court must inquire whether the "mode of performance adopted by the party performing the contract was rendered illegal by the statute, even though the contract itself could be performed in a perfectly lawful manner?"[32] "The question whether a statute impliedly prohibits the contract in question is one of public policy."[33] A distinction was at one time drawn between statutes which impose penalties to protect the Revenue and those which impose penalties for the protection of the public[34]; in the former case a plaintiff could recover his payment, in the latter he could not. But this distinction is not now regarded as conclusive of the question whether the manner in which the contract was performed makes it a contract prohibited by the statute.[35] "The correct general approach... [is to] look at the relevant statute or series of statutes *as a whole* and then assess whether the legislature intended to preclude the plaintiff recovering in the action, even when an essential act is under consideration."[36] So, in *St. John Shipping Corporation* v. *Joseph Rank Ltd.*,[37] where the shipowner sought to recover freight, Devlin J. rejected the charterer's defence that the ship was overloaded and had incurred a penalty under the Merchant Shipping (Safety and Load Lines Convention) Act 1932; and in *Shaw* v. *Groom*[38] the Court of Appeal held that a landlord's failure to provide his tenant with a proper rent book, as required by the Landlord and Tenant Act 1962, did not disentitle the landlord from suing for the rent of the premises. In both these cases the illegality in the performance of the contract did not transform the contract into an illegal contract. "The true question is, has the statute impliedly forbidden the contract?"[39] The object of each statute was simply to impose a fine; and the legislature did not intend to impose on the shipowner or the landlord respectively any forfeiture beyond the prescribed penalty. In neither case had the statute forbidden the particular contract.[40]

The general, stringent rule prohibiting recovery is based on public policy. Two reasons are given for the rule. First, the risk of non-recovery will deter the

---

[31] *Archbold (Freightage) Ltd.* v. *S. Spanglett Ltd.* [1961] 1 Q.B. 374, 390, *per* Devlin L.J.
[32] *Shaw* v. *Groom* [1970] 2 Q.B. 504, 516, *per* Harman L.J., citing Atkin L.J. in *Anderson Ltd.* v. *Daniel* [1924] 1 Q.B. 138, 150.
[33] [1970] 2 Q.B. 504, 516, *per* Harman L.J.
[34] *Anderson Ltd.* v. *Daniel* [1924] 1 Q.B. 138; *Shaw* v. *Groom* [1970] 2 Q.B. 504, 520, *per* Sachs L.J.
[35] See *St. John Shipping Corp.* v. *Joseph Rank Ltd.* [1957] 1 Q.B. 267, 283–284, *per* Devlin J. *Cf.* also *Solomons* v. *Gertzenstein Ltd.* [1954] 2 Q.B. 243, 266, *per* Romer L.J.
[36] *Shaw* v. *Groom* [1970] 2 Q.B. 504, 523, *per* Sachs L.J.
[37] [1957] 1 Q.B. 267.
[38] [1970] 2 Q.B. 504.
[39] *Ibid.* at p. 516, *per* Harman L.J. *Cf.* Birks, *Introduction*, p. 429.
[40] [1970] 2 Q.B. 504, 516, *per* Harman L.J. *Cf. Barrett* v. *Smith* [1965] N.Z.L.R. 460; and contrast *Ashmore, Benson, Pease & Co. Ltd.* v. *Dawson Ltd.* [1973] 1 W.L.R. 828.

potential delinquent from illegality. As Ralph Gibson L.J. said in *Tinsley* v. *Milligan*[41]:

> "In so far as the basis of the *ex turpi causa* defence, as founded on public policy, is directed at deterrence it seems to me that the force of the deterrent effect is in the existence of the known rule and in its stern application. Lawyers have long known of the rule and must have advised many people of its existence ... I think that the law has upheld the principle on the simple ground that, ugly though its working may be, it is better than permitting the fraudulent an avenue of escape if the fraud is revealed."

The second reason for the stringent rule is that the plaintiff must come to court with clean hands; moreover, it "is not possible to distinguish between degrees of iniquity."[42]

It is questionable whether this fastidious aloofness is sound public policy and whether reform, if reform there should be, should be left to the legislature.[42a] In any event, as has been seen, "dirty hands" do not defeat the claim of the plaintiff who simply asks the court to protect his existing legal or equitable title to property.[43]

The rule denying recovery is subject to exceptions which we will now discuss.

2. WHERE THE PARTIES ARE NOT IN PARI DELICTO

(a) *Mistake*

Where the plaintiff has paid money to the defendant under an illegal contract, but the illegality is unknown to the plaintiff because of some mistake of fact, he is entitled to recover his money in an action for money had and received, if he has not got what he bargained for. Thus, in *Oom* v. *Bruce*,[44] the plaintiff, as agent for a Russian subject abroad, purported to insure with the defendant goods on board the ship *Elbe*, at and from St. Petersburg to London, and paid a premium under the policy. Unknown to the plaintiff, Russia had commenced hostilities against Great Britain shortly before the insurance was effected, and the policy was therefore illegal. The Court of King's Bench held that the plaintiff was entitled to recover the premium.

---

[41] [1992] Ch. 310, 334: cited with approval by Lord Goff, dissenting, in the House of Lords.
[42] *Tinsley* v. *Milligan*, [1993] 3 All E.R. 65, 79, *per* Lord Goff.
[42a] See below, pp. 519–522.
[43] See above, pp. 500 *et seq.*
[44] (1810) 12 East 224, followed in *Hentig* v. *Staniforth* (1816) 5 M. & S. 122. See also *Siffken* v. *Allnutt* (1813) 1 M. & S. 39; *Branigan* v. *Saba* [1924] N.Z.L.R. 481; and *Adler* v. *C. J. Searles & Co.*, 86 Miss. 406 (1905).

If the payer's mistake is one of law, he can only recover if his payment was involuntary.[45] Accordingly, if there is any "fraud, duress, oppression or difference in the position of the parties which created a fiduciary relationship so as to make it inequitable for the defendants to insist on the bargain,"[46] he can succeed in his claim.[47]

Where parties enter into a contract which can be performed in a legal manner, which the defendant without the plaintiff's knowledge elects to perform illegally, it has been said that the defendant cannot plead its illegality.[48] But, on discovering the illegal performance, the plaintiff is bound to bring the contract to an end,[49] in which event he can recover on a *quantum meruit* the value of services rendered in the performance of his side of the bargain. Thus in *Clay* v. *Yates*,[50] the plaintiff, a printer, agreed to print 500 copies of the defendant's treatise, to which a dedication was to be attached. "He had been furnished with the treatise without the dedication. The dedication was afterwards sent, but he had no opportunity of reading it until after it was printed; he then discovered that it was libellous, and refused to permit the defendant to have it."[51] The Court of Exchequer held that the plaintiff was justified in refusing to complete the printing of the dedication and was entitled to recover for the printing of the treatise without the dedication.

(b) *Fraud and Pressure*

Transactions rendered illegal under laws made for the protection of persons in the plaintiff's position

In *Smith* v. *Bromley*,[52] the plaintiff's brother had committed an act of bankruptcy. But the defendant, his chief creditor, at first refused to sign his certificate of discharge. Later he authorised its signature, but only on condition that the bankrupt, or somebody for him, would pay him £40 and give a note for £20 more. The plaintiff paid the £40 on behalf of her brother, and she

---

[45] *Nash* v. *Stevenson Transport Ltd.* [1936] 2 K.B. 128; *Kiriri Cotton Ltd.* v. *Dewani* [1960] A.C. 192; see above, pp. 150 *et seq.*

[46] *Harse* v. *Pearl Life Assurance Co.* [1904] 1 K.B. 558, 563, *per* Collins M.R. See also *Howard* v. *Refuge Friendly Society* (1886) 54 L.T.(N.S.) 644; *Phillips* v. *Royal London Mutual Insurance Co. Ltd.* (1911) 105 L.T.(N.S.) 136; *Evanson* v. *Crooks* (1911) 106 L.T.(N.S.) 264. And see *Lubbock* v. *Potts* (1806) 7 East 449, 456, *per* Lord Ellenborough C.J.; *Wilkinson* v. *Loudonsack* (1814) 3 M. & S. 118, 126, *per* Lord Ellenborough C.J.

[47] He may also have a right of recovery under the terms of the statute, which makes the transaction illegal: see below, pp. 508–510.

[48] *Re Mahmoud and Ispahani* [1921] 2 K.B. 716, 729, *per* Scrutton L.J.; *Chai Sau Yin* v. *Liew Kwee Sam* [1962] A.C. 304, 311, *per* Lord Hodson; *Dromorne Linen Co. Ltd.* v. *Ward* [1963] N.Z.L.R. 614.

[49] *Cowan* v. *Milbourn* (1867) L.R. 2 Exch. 230.

[50] (1856) 1 H. & N. 73; *cf. Apthorp* v. *Neville & Co.* (1907) 23 T.L.R. 575.

[51] At pp. 78–79, *per* Pollock C.B.

[52] Although decided in 1760, it was not reported until 1781 in 2 Doug. 696n.; *cf. Sievers* v. *Boswell* (1841) 3 M. & G. 524. Other statements of the doctrine by Lord Mansfield are found in *Clarke* v. *Shee* (1774) 1 Cowp. 197, 200; *Browning* v. *Morris* (1778) 2 Cowp. 790, 792; *Lowry* v. *Bourdieu* (1780) 2 Doug. 468, 472.

then sued the defendant for its recovery. Lord Mansfield held that she was entitled to recover. He said:

> "If the act is in itself immoral, or a violation of the general laws of public policy, there, the party paying shall not have this action; for where both parties are equally criminal against such laws ... the rule is, *potior est conditio defendentis*. But there are other laws, which are calculated for the protection of the subject against oppression, extortion, deceit, etc. If such laws are violated, and the defendant takes advantage of the plaintiff's condition or situation, there the plaintiff shall recover."[53]

A plaintiff has been granted relief, on a number of occasions, on similar grounds.[54] An important illustration is *Kiriri Cotton Co.* v. *Ranchhoddas Keshavji Dewani*,[55] in which the Privy Council held that a premium paid contrary to the provisions of the Uganda Rent Restriction Ordinance 1949 was recoverable by the tenant, for the Ordinance was passed for the protection of persons in his position.

There are two possible limits to this right of recovery. The first originated in *Lodge* v. *National Union Investment Co. Ltd.*[56] The plaintiff sought to recover, in equity, policies deposited as security for a loan, the transaction being illegal under the Money-lenders Act 1900. Parker J. held that he was only entitled to recover the securities on repayment of the money advanced to him.

> "I do not think it either *aequum* or *bonum* that the plaintiff, who has had the benefit of the £1,075 and who is relying on the illegality of the contract and the exception enabling him to sue notwithstanding such illegality, should have relief without being put on terms by which both parties may be restored to the position they occupied before the transaction commenced."[57]

The scope of this decision has been the subject of debate. "Its history is one of being distinguished rather than applied."[58] In *Chapman* v. *Michaelson*, the Court of Appeal held that Parker J.'s reasoning only applied if the plaintiff sought true equitable relief,[59] and in *Cohen* v. *Lester (J.) Ltd.*,[60] Tucker J.

---

[53] At p. 697.

[54] *Jacques* v. *Golightly* (1776) 2 W.Bl. 1073; *Jaques* v. *Withy* (1788) 1 H.Bl. 65; *Browning* v. *Morris* (1778) 2 Cowp. 780; *Williams* v. *Hedley* (1807) 8 East 378; *Bloxsome* v. *Williams* (1824) 3 B. & C. 232; *Ray* v. *Johnson*, 7 Gray 162 (Mass.) (1856); *Barclay* v. *Pearson* [1893] 2 Ch. 154.

[55] [1960] A.C. 192; discussed above, p. 151.

[56] [1907] 1 Ch. 300.

[57] At p. 312. It is doubtful how far such a restriction on recovery would be imposed in some actions at common law, *e.g.* trover: see *Fitzroy* v. *Gwillim* (1786) 1 T.R. 153 (doubted in *Tregoning* v. *Attenborough* (1830) 7 Bing. 97, and *Hargreaves* v. *Hutchinson* (1834) 2 A. & E. 12); *Hindle* v. *O'Brien* (1809) 1 Taunt. 413 (distinguished in *Roberts* v. *Goff* (1820) 4 B. & Ald. 92). The matter is discussed at some length by Parker J. in *Lodge's* case, at pp. 307–311, and by Lord Radcliffe in *Kasumu* v. *Baba-Egbe* [1956] A.C. 539, 549.

[58] (1956) 72 L.Q.R. 481 [R.E.M.].

[59] [1909] 1 Ch. 238, 242, *per* Cozens-Hardy M.R. and Fletcher Moulton L.J., 243, *per* Farwell L.J.

[60] [1939] 1 K.B. 504 Cf. *Colin Campbell* v. *Pirie*, 1967 S.L.T. 49.

refused to impose terms when the particular contract was not illegal but simply unenforceable under section 6 of the Moneylenders Act 1927. The point was again reconsidered in *Kasumu* v. *Baba-Egbe*.[61] The respondent had mortgaged land to the appellants, licensed moneylenders, as security for a loan. The transaction was unenforceable under the particular Nigerian ordinance because no book record had been kept. The sole question on the appeal was whether, as a condition of obtaining, *inter alia*, cancellation and delivery up of the mortgage deeds, the respondent should be compelled to repay the outstanding balance of the loan with interest. The Privy Council refused, in granting relief, to impose this condition. The ordinance declared the particular transaction to be unenforceable; and to impose terms, as requested by the appellant, would be to enforce "directly or indirectly, a claim in respect of the transaction."[62] Lord Radcliffe, who delivered the Board's advice, accepted that *Lodge's* case did not establish "any wide general principle that governs the actions of courts in granting relief in moneylending cases."[63] The court would never grant equitable relief on terms if to do so would in effect reverse an Act of Parliament.[64]

The principle of *Lodge's* case has, therefore, been narrowly confined. The claim must be a claim for "true equitable relief," whatever that precisely may mean,[65] and the exercise of the court's discretion must not conflict with the provisions of statutory enactments. Rarely will both these conditions be satisfied.

The second limitation to this head of recovery was laid down in *Green* v. *Portsmouth Stadium Ltd.*[66] In that case, the plaintiff, a bookmaker, alleged that he had, over a long period of time, been overcharged by the defendants each time he went on their course, contrary to section 13(1) of the Betting and Lotteries Act 1934. He sought to recover the charges so paid, in excess of the amount allowed by the statute, as money had and received by the defendants to his use. Parker J. held,[67] following Lord Mansfield in *Browning* v. *Morris*,[68] that the action would lie. The defendants appealed, and the Court of Appeal allowed their appeal. The statute was not a bookmakers' charter, but a law for the regulation of racecourses and other such matters in the interests of the general public, and did not contemplate the bringing of an action for money had and received at the suit of a person in the plaintiff's situation.[69] There was

---

[61] [1956] A.C. 539.

[62] [1956] A.C. 539, 551. *Cf. Sinclair* v. *Brougham* [1914] A.C. 398; see above, pp. 83–85.

[63] [1956] A.C. 539, 549.

[64] *Ibid.*

[65] (1956) 72 L.Q.R. 480–481 [R.E.M.].

[66] [1953] 2 Q.B. 190. For a discussion of the possible impact of the decision of the House of Lords in *Woolwich Equitable Building Society* v. *Inland Revenue Commissioners* [1993] 1 A.C. 70 (discussed below in Chap. 24), see (1993) 109 L.Q.R. 401, 416–417 [Beatson].

[67] [1953] 1 W.L.R. 487.

[68] (1788) 2 Cowp. 790.

[69] The House of Lords had already held that no action for damages would lie for breach of another section of the same statute: see *Cutler* v. *Wandsworth Stadium Ltd.* [1949] A.C. 398. No more, therefore, would an action for money had and received avail the plaintiff here.

"nothing in this statute to authorise such an action."[70] This reasoning makes it difficult to establish this right of recovery today. In Denning L.J.'s view, in modern statutes "one finds that if it is intended that an overcharge shall be recoverable the Act says so."[71] Accordingly, in the absence of such a statutory provision, it will clearly no longer be easy to invoke the principle enunciated in *Smith* v. *Bromley*. In the past, the imposition of a penalty on the defendant but not on the plaintiff was regarded as an indication that the plaintiff was to be protected and hence that he might have an action,[72] though that fact alone was never regarded as conclusive.[73] In *Green's* case, where penalties could have been imposed on the defendants under the Act, Denning L.J. took the view that "the presumption is that where the statute provides those consequences for a breach, no other remedy is available."[74] It may well be, however, that Denning L.J.'s interpretation of Lord Mansfield's judgment in *Smith* v. *Bromley* is too restrictive and that the courts may yet conclude that it is not necessary to find in the statute express provision for a restitutionary action.[75]

This presumption is, in any event, displaced when the statutory provision is enacted specifically for the protection of persons in the plaintiff's position. In *Green* v. *Portsmouth Stadium Ltd.*,[76] the statute was not passed for the protection of people in the position of Green, and there was no oppression. The plaintiff had, therefore, to find his remedy on the statute; since the statute provided no remedy, his action could not succeed. In *Kiriri's* case,[77] where the plaintiff recovered despite the fact that there was no statutory remedy specifically provided, it was held that the plaintiff belonged to that class of persons which the Ordinance was intended to protect.[78] In such circumstances, though the Ordinance gave no remedy, the plaintiff could have an action at common law to recover the money he had paid.[79]

It is clear that where a statute which renders a transaction illegal expressly grants a right of recovery to the plaintiff, he will, of course, be entitled to recover his money in spite of the illegality. Thus a premium paid by a tenant to

---

[70] [1953] 2 Q.B. 190, 196, *per* Denning L.J.
[71] *Green* v. *Portsmouth Stadium Ltd.* [1953] 2 Q.B. 190, 195. *Cf.* the suggestion of Lord du Parcq in *Cutler* v. *Wandsworth Stadium Ltd.* [1949] A.C. 398, 410, that the legislature should always state expressly that a civil action will lie, if that is the intention; this suggestion was approved by Lord Morton of Henryton in the same case at p. 415.
[72] *Browning* v. *Morris* (1788) 2 Cowp. 790, 793, *per* Lord Mansfield.
[73] *Stokes* v. *Twitchen* (1818) 8 Taunt. 492.
[74] [1953] 2 Q.B. 190, 195.
[75] See, in particular, *South Australia Cold Stores Ltd.* v. *Electricity Trust of South Australia* (1966) 115 C.L.R. 247, 257–258, *per* Kitto J.; and *cf. Mistry Amar Singh* v. *Kulubya* [1964] A.C. 142, P.C.
[76] [1953] 2 Q.B. 190, 195, 196.
[77] [1960] A.C. 192: see above, p. 151.
[78] *Cf. Hydro Electric Commission of the Township of Nepean* v. *Ontario Hydro* (1982) 132 D.L.R. (3d) 193, 226–229, *per* Estey J.
[79] Following *Smith* v. *Bromley* (1781) 2 Doug. 696n.: see above, p. 506. But *cf.* (1960) 23 M.L.R. 322 [G. Webber].

a landlord, contrary to the provisions of the Rent Restrictions Acts, may be
recovered by the tenant.[80]

Other illegal transactions where fraud or oppression has been exerted on the plaintiff

There are other cases where there is "introduced the element of fraud, duress,
or oppression or difference in the position of the parties which created a
fiduciary relationship to the plaintiff so as to make it inequitable for the
defendants to insist on the bargain that they have made with the plaintiff."[81] In
such cases, in spite of the illegality, the plaintiff is entitled to recover money
paid under the transaction.

Fraud

In *Hughes* v. *Liverpool Victoria Friendly Society*,[82] the plaintiff took out five
policies of insurance on lives in which she had no insurable interest. She was
induced to do so by the defendant's agent, who fraudulently misrepresented
that, by paying the arrears due on the premiums and keeping them up,
"everything would be all right." The plaintiff later discovered that the policies
were illegal and void,[83] and brought an action against the insurance company to
recover the premiums she had paid. The Court of Appeal held that, although
the contract was illegal, the plaintiff was not *in pari delicto* with the defendants
because she had been induced to enter into the contract by fraudulent misrepresentation. In *Hughes's* case, the representation was one of fact. But relief
may equally be granted if the fraudulent representation was one of law.[84] In all
cases it is essential, however, that the fraud should have concealed from the
plaintiff the illegal nature of the transaction. So, in *Parkinson* v. *College of
Ambulance Ltd. and Harrison*,[85] the plaintiff was induced to make a large
donation to a charity by the secretary's fraudulent representation that he or the
charity could and would obtain a knighthood for the plaintiff. No title was
forthcoming. The plaintiff brought an action against the charity and its secretary to recover his gift as money had and received, or as damages for deceit or
breach of contract. Lush J. held that he could not recover damages as the
contract was illegal and contrary to public policy; nor could he recover his
money as money had and received for, although there had been fraud on the

---

[80] *Gray* v. *Southouse* [1949] 2 All E.R. 1019, 1020, *per* Devlin J.
[81] *Harse* v. *Pearl Life Assurance Co.* [1904] 1 K.B. 558, 563, *per* Collins M.R. See *Drummond* v.
Deey (1794) 1 Esp. 151, 153–154, *per* Lord Kenyon C.J.; *Atkinson* v. *Denby* (1862) 7 H. & N.
934; *Kiriri Cotton Co. Ltd.* v. *Dewani* [1960] A.C. 190, 205, P.C.: see above, p. 151.
[82] [1916] 2 K.B. 482; see also *British Workman's and General Assurance Co. Ltd.* v. *Cunliffe* (1902)
18 T.L.R. 425, 502: see above, p. 153, n. 82; *Refuge Assurance Co. Ltd.* v. *Kettlewell* [1909] A.C.
243; *Byrne* v. *Rudd* [1920] 2 I.R. 12.
[83] By the Assurance Companies Act 1909, ss.23, 36(3).
[84] See above, p. 187.
[85] [1925] 2 K.B. 1. See also *Drummond* v. *Deey* (1794) 1 Esp. 151, 153–154, *per* Lord Kenyon;
Howarth v. *Pioneer Life Assurance Co. Ltd.* (1912) 107 L.T. 155.

part of the secretary, the plaintiff was always aware of the improper nature of the transaction.

There is also jurisdiction in equity to grant relief in cases of fraud.[86]

Oppression

Examples of oppression are few.[87] A well-known case is where a creditor in a composition exacts from the debtor an extra payment as a condition of his acceptance of the composition. In *Smith* v. *Cuff*,[88] the debtor was forced in this way to give one of the creditors promissory notes for the remainder of his debt; the creditor negotiated them and the holder of one of them enforced payment by the debtor. It was held that the debtor could recover the excess of the amount so paid over the amount due under the composition from the creditor in an action for money paid. Lord Ellenborough said:

> "This is not a case of *par delictum*: it is oppression on one side, and submission on the other: it never can be predicated as *par delictum*, when one holds the rod, and the other bows to it. There was an inequality of situation between these parties: one was creditor, the other debtor, who was driven to comply with the terms which the former chose to enforce."[89]

But where a debtor gave the oppressing creditor a bill of exchange and, after the creditor had signed the composition deed, paid him the amount due on the bill, the Court of King's Bench held[90] that he could not recover the money so paid, because although the bill of exchange had been extracted under oppression, the debtor had a good defence to an action by the creditor on the bill. The payment was not made under oppression; it was voluntary and, therefore, irrecoverable.[91] Since, therefore, the payment itself as well as the making of the illegal contract must have been under constraint, cases of recovery are necessarily few.[92]

Equitable relief has been granted in cases where the plaintiff has been induced by pressure, which may be extraneous,[93] to enter into the illegal transaction. In *Williams* v. *Bayley*,[94] a son gave to bankers certain promissory

---

[86] *Reynell* v. *Sprye* (1852) 1 De G.M. & G. 660; reported in the court below, (1849) 8 Hare 222.
[87] *Cf. Andrews* v. *Parker* [1973] Qd.R. 93.
[88] (1817) 6 M. & S. 160. The decision was followed in *Alsager* v. *Spalding* (1838) 4 Bing. (N.C.) 407; *Bradshaw* v. *Bradshaw* (1841) 9 M. & W. 29; *Horton* v. *Riley* (1843) 11 M. & W. 492, 493–494, *per* Parke B.; *Atkinson* v. *Denby* (1861) 6 H. & N. 778, affd. 7 H. & N. 934.
[89] At p. 165.
[90] In *Wilson* v. *Ray* (1839) 10 A. & E. 82. See also *Gibson* v. *Bruce* (1843) 5 Man. & G. 399 and *Viner* v. *Hawkins* (1853) 9 Ex. 266, doubting part of the decision in *Ex p. Hart* (1845) 2 D. & L. 778; *cf. Re Lenzberg's Policy* (1877) 7 Ch.D. 650. Presumably *Turner* v. *Hoole* (1822) Dowl. & Ry. 27 is no longer a good authority.
[91] *Semble* in *Smith* v. *Cuff* (1817) 6 M. & S. 160, it was not suggested that the plaintiff's payment of the note to the holder was voluntary.
[92] *Miller* v. *Aris* (1800) 3 Esp. 231; *Townson* v. *Wilson* (1808) 1 Camp. 396.
[93] *Cf. Kiriri Cotton Co. Ltd.* v. *Dewani* [1960] A.C. 190, 205, *per curiam* (P.C., *per* Lord Denning).
[94] (1866) L.R. 1 H.L. 200: see above, p. 151. *Cf. Re Campbell, ex p. Wolverhampton Banking Co.* (1884) 14 Q.B.D. 32; *Jones* v. *Merionethshire Permanent Benefit Building Society* [1892] 1 Ch. 173; *McClatchie* v. *Haslam* (1891) 65 L.T. 691. See also *Bosanquet* v. *Dashwood* (1734) Tal. 38; *Henkle* v. *Royal Exchange Assurance* (1749) 1 Ves.Sen. 317; *Morris* v. *M'Cullock* (1763) Amb.

notes on which he had forged his father's indorsement. On the discovery of the forgery a meeting was held at which it was made reasonably clear to the father that, if some settlement was not reached, the bankers would prosecute the son. Under this pressure the father agreed in writing that, in consideration for the return of the promissory notes, he would pay the bankers the amount advanced by them on the notes, and deposit with them the title deeds of his colliery as security for this payment. The House of Lords held that the contract was made under duress and was also illegal as an agreement to stifle a prosecution. The House affirmed a decree of Stuart V.-C. that the agreement was invalid and must be cancelled, and that the bankers must deliver up the promissory notes to the father.

3. EXECUTORY CONTRACTS

Another exception to the rule of non-recovery is to be found in executory contracts. Where money has been paid under an illegal contract, the payer is allowed a *locus poenitentiae*; so long as the contract remains wholly, or perhaps even substantially, executory, he may withdraw from his illegal bargain and recover the money he has paid.[95]

This doctrine originated in 1780 in *Lowry* v. *Bourdieu*.[96] Then two distinct lines of authority developed. In the first, a plaintiff who innocently entered into an illegal contract was entitled on discovering the illegality to withdraw and recover the money paid thereunder, provided that the contract was substantially unperformed.[97] The second line was principally concerned with wagers. Here it was held that the plaintiff was allowed to withdraw even though he was aware of the illegality unless the illegality was *malum in se*.[98]

For many years the doctrine was dormant until its revival in 1876 in the controversial case of *Taylor* v. *Bowers*.[99] The plaintiff was in embarrassed circumstances. To prevent his creditors seizing his goods, he made over and delivered all his stock-in-trade to one Alcock. Subsequently, meetings of the plaintiff's creditors were held, but no compromise was reached with them. Alcock then executed a bill of sale of the goods to the defendant, one of the plaintiff's creditors, who had been aware of the original arrangement between the plaintiff and Alcock. The alleged purpose of the bill was to secure the debt

---

432; *Re Lenzberg's Policy* (1877) 7 Ch.D. 650; *Davies* v. *London & Provincial Marine Insurance Co.* (1878) 8 Ch.D. 469; *Whitmore* v. *Farley* (1882) 29 W.R. 825. See (1947) 95 Univ. of Pa.L.R., 276–278 [Wade].

[95] See (1975) 91 L.Q.R. 313 [Beatson]; (1981) 97 L.Q.R. [Merkin]; Birks, *Introduction*, pp. 299–303.

[96] (1780) 2 Doug. 468, 471, *per* Buller J.; *Andree* v. *Fletcher* (1789) 3 T.R. 266. Buller J. first advanced the idea in his *Nisi Prius* (1772 ed.), p. 132.

[97] *Tappenden* v. *Randall* (1801) 2 B. & P. 467; *Stainforth* v. *Staggs* (1808) 1 Camp. 398n.; *cf. Watkins* v. *Hewlett* (1819) 1 Brod. & B. 1; *Clark* v. *Johnson* (1826) 3 Bing. 424; *Chappel* v. *Poles* (1837) 2 M. & W. 867.

[98] *Aubert* v. *Walsh* (1810) 3 Taunt. 277; *Busk* v. *Walsh* (1812) 4 Taunt. 290, 292, *per* Mansfield C.J.; *Hastelow* v. *Jackson* (1828) 8 B. & C. 221, 224–225, *per* Bayley J. See, generally, Jackson, *History*, pp. 91–93.

[99] (1876) 1 Q.B.D. 291.

owing by the plaintiff to the defendant, but the plaintiff did not sanction the bill, nor was he even aware of it. After demand, he sued the defendant for detention of the goods. The Court of Queen's Bench held that he was entitled to recover because, as Cockburn C.J. said, "Where money has been paid, or goods delivered, under an unlawful agreement, but there has been no further performance of it, the party paying the money or delivering the goods may repudiate the transaction, and recover back his money or goods."[1]

The Court of Appeal affirmed this decision; and the judgment of Mellish L.J.,[2] with which Baggallay J.A. agreed, was based on similar reasoning. All these judgments are open to criticism. The arrangement was not wholly executory, for the goods had been handed over by the plaintiff to Alcock with the intention of defrauding his creditors. Moreover, the doctrine was here for the first time applied where there was not only illegality but immorality, of which the plaintiff was aware, to which he was a party and out of which he intended to profit. There is much to be said for the reasoning of the remaining member of the Court of Appeal, James L.J.,[3] who pointed out that the plaintiff could recover because he could prove his title to the goods independently of the fraudulent transaction.

The principle of *Taylor* v. *Bowers* was unsuccessfully invoked in *Kearly* v. *Thomson.*[4] The plaintiff offered to pay a sum of money to the defendants, solicitors to a petitioning creditor, if they undertook neither to appear at the public examination of the bankrupt nor to oppose his order of discharge. This the defendants, with their client's consent, agreed to do, and they received the sum of money. They did not appear at the public examination; but, before any application for discharge had been made, the plaintiff brought an action for the return of the money. His action failed. The contract was illegal as tending to pervert the course of justice; and where, as here, "there has been a partial carrying into effect of an illegal purpose in a substantial manner, it is impossible, though there remains something not performed, that the money paid under that illegal contract can be recovered back."[5] The action therefore failed. Fry L.J., who delivered the unanimous judgment of the Court of Appeal, indicated[6] that the principle enunciated by the majority of the Court of Appeal in *Taylor* v. *Bowers* required consideration by the House of Lords. However, the principle has been invoked and applied in subsequent cases.[7]

---

[1] (1876) 1 Q.B.D. 291, 295.
[2] At p. 297.
[3] At pp. 297–298.
[4] (1890) 24 Q.B.D. 742.
[5] At p. 747, *per curiam.*
[6] At p. 746.
[7] *Wilson* v. *Strugnell* (1881) 7 Q.B.D. 548 (though this case was overruled in *Herman* v. *Jeuchner* (1885) 15 Q.B.D. 561, the particular point was left open); *Hermann* v. *Charlesworth* [1905] 2 K.B. 123, 131, 134, *per* Collins M.R. 136, *per* Mathew L.J.; *Petherpermal Chetty* v. *Muniandy Servai* (1908) 24 T.L.R. 462, 463, *per* Lord Atkinson. *Cf. Symes* v. *Hughes* (1870) L.R. 9 Eq. 475; *South Western Mineral Water Co.* v. *Ashmore* [1967] 1 W.L.R. 1110.
Probably a plaintiff can recover if the ownership of a chattel has been transferred, provided that

In any event, there are important limitations to the right to recover money paid under executory illegal contracts. The first, as has been seen,[8] is that the illegal agreement must not have been substantially carried into effect; "some sort of *restitutio in integrum* on equitable terms"[9] must still be possible. Secondly, there must be genuine repentance on the part of the plaintiff.[10] A distinction is drawn between "repentance cases" where recovery is allowed, and "frustration cases" where it is not. In *Bigos* v. *Bousted*,[11] the defendant wished to send his wife and daughter abroad for the sake of his daughter's health. In those days foreign currency was in short supply. He therefore made an arrangement, illegal by English law, under which the plaintiff agreed to provide Italian currency in Italy and the defendant promised to repay her in English money in England, depositing a share certificate with the plaintiff as security. The defendant's wife and daughter went to Italy but the plaintiff failed to provide the promised currency. Pritchard J. held that the defendant was unable to recover his share certificate from the plaintiff. The defendant had not repented; his scheme had merely been frustrated by events beyond his control. If this limit on the right of recovery is strictly enforced, there will in the future be few cases in which the exception in favour of executory contracts can be successfully invoked.

Thirdly, it is doubtful whether the exception now applies in marine insurance. Section 84 of the Marine Insurance Act 1906 provides that a premium is returnable by the insurer if there is a total failure of consideration[12] and, in particular, "where the policy is void, or is avoided by the insurer as from the commencement of the risk, the premium is returnable, provided that there has been no . . . illegality on the part of the assured."[13] No distinction is drawn between executed and executory contracts although it was accepted at common law before the Act.[14]

Finally, it was suggested in the old case of *Tappenden* v. *Randall*[15] that relief would only be given where the contract was not "too grossly immoral for the

---

he repents and there has been no substantial performance: see cases cited above, p. 512 and *cf.* [1958] C.L.J. 199, 205 [R. N. Gooderson]; (1981) 97 L.Q.R. 420, 433 [Merkin].

[8] *Kearley* v. *Thomson* (1890) 24 Q.B.D. 742, *per* Fry L.J.: see above, pp. 512–513. See also *Symes* v. *Hughes* (1870) L.R. 9 Eq. 475; *Re Great Berlin Steamboat Co.* (1884) 26 Ch.D. 616; *Apthorp* v. *Neville & Co.* (1907) 23 T.L.R. 575; *Re National Benefit Insurance Co.* [1931] 1 Ch. 46. See [1958] C.L.J. 199, 204–207 [R. N. Gooderson].

[9] *South Western Mineral Water Co. Ltd.* v. *Ashmore* [1967] 1 W.L.R. 1110, 1127, *per* Cross J.

[10] *Parkinson* v. *College of Ambulance Ltd. and Harrison* [1925] 2 K.B. 1, 16, *per* Lush J.; *Alexander* v. *Rayson* [1936] 1 K.B. 190, *per curiam*; *Berg* v. *Sadler and Moore* [1937] 2 K.B. 158, 165, *per* Lord Wright M.R.; *Harry Parker* v. *Mason* [1940] 2 K.B. 590, 608–609, *per* Luxmoore L.J.; *Bigos* v. *Bousted* [1951] 1 All E.R. 92, 95, *per* Pritchard J.; *Chettiar* v. *Chettiar* [1962] A.C. 294, 302, *per* Lord Denning. There are hints of some repentance theory in the early Chancery cases: see below, pp. 517–519, and *Birch* v. *Blagrave* (1755) Amb. 264.

[11] [1951] 1 All E.R. 92. (The plaintiff's claim on the loan agreement was abandoned at the commencement of the hearing.) *Cf. United City Merchants (Investments) Ltd.* v. *Royal Bank of Canada* [1982] Q.B. 208, C.A., revs'd. [1983] 1 A.C. 168, H.L.

[12] s.84(2).

[13] s.84(3); see also *Lowry* v. *Bourdieu* (1780) 2 Doug. 468, 471, *per* Buller J.

[14] *Palyart* v. *Leckie* (1817) 6 M. & S. 290.

[15] (1801) 2 B. & P. 467, 471, *per* Heath J.

court to enter into any discussion of it." How far this limitation applies to the doctrine in its modern form is, however, debatable.

4. CASES ON AGENCY

Every agent is under a duty to account to his principal for all money and property received by him on his principal's behalf. This duty to account[16] extends to money and property received by the agent from a third party in furtherance of an illegal contract; the third party by his payment is deemed to have waived the illegality and the agent has no right in conscience or in equity to retain the money or goods.[17] Moreover, it is the better view, though there is no clear authority on the point, that it is irrelevant that the agent has knowledge of or is privy to the illegal contract between the principal and the third party.[18] If the rule were otherwise, the agent "if he be innocent, he shall be answerable in this action; but if he be guilty, he shall be free; his innocence shall work a loss to him, his guilt shall be his indemnity."[19]

Where, however, the contract of agency itself is illegal, the principal cannot recover any money paid to the agent thereunder if the contract has been substantially performed. In *Harry Parker Ltd.* v. *Mason*[20] the defendant, on the faith of certain false representations by the plaintiffs that they could place bets so as not to affect the starting price, employed them to place £12,000 in bets on a certain horse in a race at Nottingham. The horse lost and the defendant paid to the plaintiffs £11,875, which was the £12,000 less a small sum which the plaintiffs owed him. The defendant discovered that the plaintiffs believed that the horse would lose and had not bothered to place the money. In a subsequent action, brought by the plaintiffs, the defendant counterclaimed for the sum of £11,875 as damages for fraudulent misrepresentation, or alternatively as money had and received to the defendants' use. Stable J. dismissed the claim and counterclaim, and the Court of Appeal affirmed his decision. The transaction was illegal[21] and had been substantially performed. Luxmoore and MacKinnon L.JJ. could

> "see no difference in principle between the case of a principal seeking to recover money handed to an agent for an illegal purpose and that of one principal seeking to recover money paid by him to another principal in

[16] See Bowstead, *op. cit.* pp. 193–197.

[17] *Tenant* v. *Elliott* (1797) 1 Bos. & Pul. 3, 4, *per* Eyre C.J.; *Farmer* v. *Russell* (1798) 1 Bos. & Pul. 296, 298, *per* Eyre C.J.; *Bousfield* v. *Wilson* (1846) 16 M. & W. 185, 188–189, *arguendo*; *Bridger* v. *Savage* (1885) 15 Q.B.D. 363; *De Mattos* v. *Benjamin* (1894) 63 L.J.Q.B. 248. See (1947) 95 Univ. of Pa.L.R. 293–295 [Wade].

[18] See *Farmer* v. *Russell* (1798) 1 Bos. & Pul. 296, 298–299, *per* Eyre C.J., 301, *per* Rooke J.

[19] *Farmer* v. *Russell* (1798) 1 Bos. & Pul. 296, 301, *per* Rooke J.; see also 298–299, *per* Eyre C.J.

[20] [1940] 2 K.B. 590. *Cf.* the older partnership cases, *Booth* v. *Hodgson* (1795) 6 T.R. 405; *Catlin* v. *Bell* (1815) 4 Camp. 183; *Knowles* v. *Haughton* (1805) 11 Ves. 168; *Battersby* v. *Smyth* (1818) 3 Madd. 110; *Sykes* v. *Beadon* (1879) 11 Ch.D. 170. See *Restatement of Agency*, 2d, § 412 and note the *caveat* to § 412(2).

[21] It was contrary to the Street Betting Act 1906 and was a conspiracy to make a sham bet with the intention of deceiving the public.

pursuance of an illegal contract . . . for where both are equally at fault *potior est conditio defendentis*."[22]

Du Parcq L.J.,[23] while accepting this proposition of law, thought that if the defendant had had clean hands his claim might possibly have been put "on an equitable ground." But it is difficult to see what this ground could be.

Stakeholders

Stakeholders are in an anomalous position. Where money has been deposited with a stakeholder to abide the result of some illegal transaction, it can be recovered from him by the depositor on giving notice of his demand, unless the stakeholder has already paid the deposit over to another party as winner.[24] Some authorities indicate that the rule depends on the doctrine of executory contracts[25]; others that it stems from the duty of an agent to account to his principal for money in his hands even though it has been received by him as the result of some illegal transaction.[26] If, however, the stakeholder has, before his authority has been countermanded, paid over the money in accordance with directions received from the parties, the depositor will generally have lost his right to recover his stake from either the stakeholder or the person to whom it has been paid.[27]

The Gaming Act 1845, s.18, enacts that "no suit shall be . . . maintained . . . for recovering any sum of money or valuable thing . . . which shall have been deposited in the hands of any person to abide the event on which any wager shall have been made."[28] But this section has been held[29] to "apply only to the non-recovery by the winner of a sum deposited by the other party to abide the event, and not to the right of the depositor to recover back his deposit, if demanded before the money was paid over."[30] This principle was

---

[22] *Per* Luxmoore L.J. at p. 609; see also MacKinnon L.J. at p. 603.

[23] At pp. 613–614.

[24] *Smith* v. *Bickmore* (1812) 4 Taunt. 474; *Bate* v. *Cartwright* (1819) 7 Price 540; *Robinson* v. *Mearns* (1825) 6 D. & R. 26; *Hodson* v. *Terrill* (1833) 1 C. & M. 797. In cases where the stake was deposited on a wager which was valid (before the Act of 1845), it was laid down that the depositor could similarly recover his deposit from the stakeholder: see *Eltham* v. *Kingsman* (1818) 1 B. & Ald. 683, affirmed in *Hampden* v. *Walsh* (1876) 1 Q.B.D. 189, 194–195, in spite of earlier dissent: for primarily the stakeholder is "the agent of the depositor, and can deal with the money deposited so long only as his authority subsists": *Hampden* v. *Walsh*, at p. 915, *per curiam*.

[25] *Hastelow* v. *Jackson* (1828) 8 B.C. 221; *Barclay* v. *Pearson* [1893] 2 Ch. 154, 168–169, *per* Stirling J.; *Hermann* v. *Charlesworth* [1905] 2 K.B. 123.

[26] *Cotton* v. *Thurland* (1793) 5 T.R. 405.

[27] *Howson* v. *Hancock* (1800) 8 T.R. 575. *Aliter* if the stakeholder pays over after the depositor has asked for its return: see *Hampden* v. *Walsh* (1876) 1 Q.B.D. 189, 193, removing earlier doubts. It has also been held that the mere bringing of an action to recover the deposit before it has been paid over is not sufficient notice of a demand on the stakeholder to countermand his authority: see *Gatty* v. *Field* (1846) 9 Q.B. 431. *Cf.* Financial Services Act 1986, s.132.

[28] Applied in *Lipkin Gorman (A Firm)* v. *Karpnale Ltd.* [1991] 2 A.C. 548: see below, p. 82.

[29] *Varney* v. *Hickman* (1847) 5 C.B. 271; *Martin* v. *Hewson* (1855) 10 Ex. 737; *Graham* v. *Thompson* (1867) I.R. 2 C.L. 64. *Cf. Savage* v. *Madder* (1867) 36 L.J.Exch. 178.

[30] *Hampden* v. *Walsh* (1876) 1 Q.B.D. 189, 196, *per curiam*.

accepted as binding in *Hampden* v. *Walsh*.[31] The plaintiff[32] entertained "a strong disbelief in the received opinion as to the convexity of the earth," and in a newspaper advertisement defied "all the philosophers, divines and scientific professors in the United Kingdom to prove the rotundity and revolution of the world, from scripture, from reason, or from fact." The challenge was taken up by a Mr. Wallace, and each party deposited £500 with the defendant, as stakeholder, to abide the event. Mr. Wallace carried out some experiments on the Bedford Level Canal, and after some wrangling it was adjudged that by so doing he had proved his case. The plaintiff, however, objected, and directed the defendant to return his deposit to him. The defendant, nevertheless, paid both sums over to Mr. Wallace. A divisional court held that the plaintiff was entitled to judgment. The Gaming Act 1845 had not affected his right of recovery.[33]

The depositor's right of recovery has also survived[34] the enactment of section 1 of the Gaming Act 1892.[35]

5. SPECIAL EXCEPTIONS IN EQUITY

Equity will generally grant relief where the common law gives a right of recovery.[36] But there are other cases in which equity will intervene, when common law has hesitated to give relief. Lord Eldon stated the principle underlying them as follows: "It will not be an obstacle to the plaintiffs that they do not come with clean hands, for it is settled, that if a transaction be objectionable on grounds of public policy, the parties to it may be relieved; the relief not being given for their sake, but for the sake of the public."[37]

One group of cases, which has been revived this century and which illustrates the scope of equity's intervention, is concerned with marriage brokage contracts.[38] A marriage brokage contract is an agreement by A with B that A

---

[31] (1876) 1 Q.B.D. 189.

[32] Not, as is mistakenly printed in the report at p. 190, the defendant.

[33] See also *Diggle* v. *Higgs* (1877) 2 Ex.D. 422, approved by the Privy Council in *Trimble* v. *Hill* (1879) 5 App.Cas. 342. See also *Batson* v. *Newman* (1876) 1 C.P.D. 573; *Strachen* v. *Universal Stock Exchange* [1895] 2 Q.B. 329, affd. [1896] A.C. 166. All these cases are, in general, unaffected by the decision of the House of Lords in *Hill* v. *William Hill (Park Lane) Ltd.* [1949] A.C. 530; see, *e.g. per* Lord Simonds at p. 550 dissenting from dicta in *Varney* v. *Hickman* (1847) 5 C.B. 271 and in *Diggle* v. *Higgs* (1877) 2 Ex.D. 422.

[34] *O'Sullivan* v. *Thomas* [1895] 1 Q.B. 698, approved by the Court of Appeal in *Burge* v. *Ashley and Smith* [1900] 1 Q.B. 744. And see *Bridger* v. *Savage* (1885) 15 Q.B.D. 363, 367–368, *per* Bowen L.J.; *Shoolbred* v. *Roberts* [1900] 2 Q.B. 497; *Barclay* v. *Pearson* [1893] 2 Ch. 154.

[35] s.1 enacts that "any promise, express or implied, to pay any person any sum of money paid by him under or in respect of any contract or agreement rendered null and void by the Act of 8 & 9 Vict. c. 109 . . . shall be null and void, and no action shall be brought or maintained to recover any such sum of money."

[36] *Cf.* Chap. 2, on proprietary claims.

[37] *The Vauxhall Bridge Co.* v. *The Earl Spencer* (1821) Jac. 64, 67. See also *St. John* v. *St. John* (1803–1805) 11 Ves. 526, 535–536, *per* Lord Eldon; *Reynell* v. *Sprye* (1852) 1 De G.M. & G. 660, 678–679, *per* Knight Bruce L.J.; and Story, *Equity Jurisprudence* (14th ed.), para. 421, citing *Rider* v. *Kidder* (1805) 10 Ves. 360, 366, *per* Lord Eldon.

[38] (1953) 6 *Current Legal Problems*, 254 [R. Powell].

will procure or attempt to procure the marriage of B to another specified or unspecified[39] person, for a reward to be paid to A usually on the successful conclusion of such marriage. These contracts were not originally regarded with disfavour[40]; but in the seventeenth century the Court of Chancery began to grant relief in particular cases, especially where there was an element of fraud[41] or where advantage had been taken of youthful femininity.[42] At the turn of that century it began to be accepted,[43] as it is now settled,[44] that all such agreements are to be relieved against as contrary to public policy.[45] Repayment may be ordered even though the match-maker has incurred expense in bringing about introductions or in other similar matters.[46] In *Hermann* v. *Charlesworth*,[47] the defendant, a marriage advertising agent, undertook to assist the plaintiff to get married by introducing her to gentlemen. She paid him £52 as a "special client's fee" and promised to pay him a further £250 on the successful conclusion of a marriage. The defendant agreed to repay £47 of the £52 if no marriage was concluded within nine months. After four months, although the plaintiff had been given various introductions, she decided to call the matter off and demanded the whole £52 back. The Court of Appeal held that she was entitled to recover the £52, in spite of the introductions supplied and the other work done by the defendant.

Marriage brokage contracts do not supply the only example of the application of Lord Eldon's principle. It has been applied to agreements between husband and wife for future separation[48]; to cases of trafficking in public offices[49]; to frauds on settlements[50]; and to various other cases.[51] How far,

---

[39] *Hermann* v. *Charlesworth* [1905] 2 K.B. 123.
[40] *Grisley* v. *Lother* (1614) Hob. 10; *Law* v. *Law* (1735) 3 P.Wms. 391, 393, *per* Lord Talbot L.C. But *cf. Arleston* v. *Kent* (1619) Tot. 27, and *Arundel* v. *Trevillian* (1635) 1 Rep.Ch. 87.
[41] *Glanvill* v. *Jennings* (1669) 3 Ch.Rep. 31.
[42] *Drury* v. *Hooke* (1686) 2 Chan.Cas. 176.
[43] *Hall* v. *Potter* (1695) Shower 76.
[44] *Cole* v. *Gibson* (1750) 1 Ves.Sen. 503.
[45] *Hermann* v. *Charlesworth* [1905] 2 K.B. 123, 133, *per* Collins M.R.
[46] *Smith* v. *Bruning* (1700) 2 Vern. 392 (see also 1 Eq.Ca.Abr. 89, pl. 4, sub. tit. *Goldsmith* v. *Bruning*); *Hermann* v. *Charlesworth* [1905] 2 K.B. 123.
[47] [1905] 2 K.B. 123. It was also held that relief was available at common law on the ground that the money had been deposited with a stakeholder to abide the result of an event which never occurred; on stakeholders, see above, pp. 516–517.
[48] *St. John* v. *St. John* (1803–1805) 11 Ves. 526; see, especially, at pp. 535–536, *per* Lord Eldon L.C.
[49] *Law* v. *Law* (1735) Cas.*t*.Talb. 140; *Morris* v. *M'Cullock* (1763) Amb. 432; *Hanington* v. *du Châtel* (1781) 1 Bro.C.C. 124; *Whittingham* v. *Burgoyne* (1796) 3 Anst. 900; *Osborne* v. *Williams* (1811) 18 Ves. 379.
[50] *Gay* v. *Wendow* (1687) 2 Freeman 101; *Neville* v. *Wilkinson* (1782) 1 Bro.C.C. 543 (on which see *The Vauxhall Bridge Co.* v. *The Earl Spencer* (1821) Jac. 64, 67, *per* Lord Eldon). See also *Palmer* v. *Neave* (1805) 11 Ves. 165.
[51] *Debenham* v. *Ox* (1749) 1 Ves.Sen. 276 (bond given by plaintiff to defendant's wife, in consideration that she would use influence over plaintiff's grandfather that he should dispose of his whole estate for plaintiff's benefit); *Hatch* v. *Hatch* (1804) 9 Ves. 292 (conveyance by ward to guardian). See also *Woodhouse* v. *Shepley* (1742) 2 Atk. 535 (bond given by lady plaintiff, under penalty of £500, to marry nobody but defendant). Lord Selborne L.C. refused to apply the principle in *Ayerst* v. *Jenkins* (1873) L.R. 16 Eq. 275; *cf. Coulson* v. *Allison* (1860) 2 De G.F. & J.

marriage brokage contracts apart, the principle would be applied today is most doubtful.

There are a few other special cases where equity may grant relief. First, where the court is exercising jurisdiction over one of its own officers, that officer cannot resist a claim by resort to the defence of illegality.[52] Secondly, it has been said that "there is great difficulty in applying that principle [*in pari delicto melior est conditio defendentis*] to a case where money has been placed *in medio*, and where the court must do something with it, or else leave it to be locked up for ever."[53] Thirdly, it seems that relief may be granted where a refusal to grant relief might result in injury to third parties.[54]

6. CRITIQUE

From time to time the rules of English law concerning the recovery of benefits conferred under illegal contracts have been subjected to acute criticism. It has been said that these rules are too harsh; for in our society each day commercial men "flounder in a mass of statutes, orders and regulations governing their daily affairs."[55] Often they have no knowledge of their existence and may innocently infringe them. To deprive them of their remedies is a harsh sanction for innocent transgressions. They may properly feel "that they have not thereby forfeited all right to justice, and may go elsewhere for it if courts of law will not give it to them."[56] "It is, of course, not only commercial men who have to flounder in a mass of statutes, orders and regulations governing their daily affairs. Moreover the average citizen has no opportunity to 'go elsewhere' for what he regards as justice."[57] To nullify bargains because of illegality when the law is unwittingly broken may require a contracting party to forfeit a sum "vastly in excess of any penalty that a criminal court would impose; and the sum forfeited will not go into the public purse but into the pockets of someone who is lucky enough to pick up the windfall or astute enough to have contrived to get it."[58]

Consequently, some judges have regretted the court's inability "to mitigate (upon equitable principles) the serious and often disproportionate effect on

---

521; *Bessey* v. *Windham* (1844) 6 Q.B. 166; *Phillips* v. *Probyn* [1899] 1 Ch. 811. See also *Walker* v. *Chapman* (1773) Lofft. 342.

[52] *Re Thomas* [1894] 1 Q.B. 747.

[53] *Davies* v. *London & Provincial Marine Insurance Co.* (1878) 8 Ch.D. 469, 477, *per* Fry J.; *cf. Re Gurwicz* [1919] 1 K.B. 675.

[54] *Woodhouse* v. *Shepley* (1742) 2 Atk. 535; *Debenham* v. *Ox* (1749) 1 Ves.Sen. 276; *Earl of Chesterfield* v. *Janssen* (1751) 2 Ves.Sen. 125, 156, *per* Lord Hardwicke; *Hatch* v. *Hatch* (1804) 9 Ves. 292, 298; *Ex p. Kirk* (1809) 15 Ves. 464, 469, *per* Lord Eldon; *W.* v. *B.*, *B.* v. *W.* (1863) 32 Beav. 574, 578, *per* Sir John Romilly M.R. See also the interpretation of *Neville* v. *Wilkinson* (1782) 1 Bro.C.C. 543, in *Eastabrook* v. *Scott* (1797) 3 Ves. 456, 461, *per* Arden M.R. *Cf.* the earlier cases, *Drury* v. *Hooke* (1686) 2 Ch.Ca. 176; *Goldsmith* v. *Bruning* (1700) 1 Eq.Ab. 89; *Turton* v. *Benson* (1718) 1 P.Wms. 496.

[55] *Shaw* v. *Groom* [1970] 2 Q.B. 504, 522, *per* Sachs L.J.

[56] *St. John Shipping Corp.* v. *Joseph Rank Ltd.* [1957] 1 Q.B. 267, 289, *per* Devlin J.

[57] *Shaw* v. *Groom* [1970] 2 Q.B. 504, 522, *per* Sachs L.J.

[58] *St. John Shipping Corp.* v. *Joseph Rank Ltd.* [1957] 1 Q.B. 267, 288, *per* Devlin J.

civil rights which so frequently results from a breach of a statutory prohibition or requirement."[59] Jurists have made a number of proposals how such a relaxation could be achieved. One writer has gone so far as to suggest that recovery should be contingent upon the exercise of the court's discretion "to choose such course as would, in practice, best serve the public interest."[60] This test is in the spirit of the American *Restatement of Restitution*, which states simply that "a person may be prevented from obtaining restitution for a benefit because of his criminal or other wrongful conduct in connection with the transaction on which his claim is based."[61] Indeed, as Williston[62] pointed out, some jurisdictions are prepared to allow the plaintiff to recover, if he has not been guilty of serious moral turpitude and the loss which he will suffer by being denied relief is wholly out of proportion to the requirements either of public policy or of appropriate individual punishment.[63] These solutions have been prompted by a desire to prevent the unjust enrichment of the defendant through the capricious application of the maxim *in pari delicto potior est conditio defendentis*, and, nevertheless, to discourage illegal transactions where there is serious moral turpitude. Other writers,[64] however, have suggested that formulae like that of the *Restatement of Restitution* do not in fact properly balance "the policy against allowing an unjust enrichment" against "the policy against extricating a 'bad' man from the coils in which his evil conduct has placed him."[65] They prefer "the rational but perhaps Utopian solution"[66] of Wigmore, who proposed[67] that the plaintiff should be allowed to recover the full extent of his unjust enrichment but that he should suffer a penalty which should be deducted from his award, "taking into consideration the degree of moral turpitude involved, the relative guilt of the parties and the plaintiff's motive in bringing the suit."[68] In a similar vein is the proposal that "the court should be given absolute discretion to apportion the property transferred as between the parties and the State as it thinks fit, taking into account the nature of the illegality, the knowledge and intention of the parties, the amount of performance rendered or money expended and any other relevant matters."[69]

---

[59] *e.g. Cameo Motors Ltd.* v. *Portland Holdings Ltd.* [1965] N.Z.L.R. 109, 116, *per* Richmond J.
[60] (1955) 71 L.Q.R. 254, 273 [Grodecki]. See also (1962) 25 M.L.R. 149, 151–152 [Higgins]; (1981) 97 L.Q.R. 420, 443–444 [Merkin].
[61] § 140. The Reporter lists certain factors which the courts should take into account in the exercising of their discretion; *e.g.* whether the plaintiff was guilty of "serious moral turpitude," or whether a denial of relief would tend to discourage similar illegal transactions.
[62] Contracts, § 1789. *Cf. Restatement of Contracts 2d*, § 199, which proposes a somewhat similar rule.
[63] See Palmer, *op. cit.* Vol. II, § 8.7.
[64] *e.g.* J. W. Wade, (1947) 95 Univ. of Pa.L.R. 261, 302; see also the same writer in (1946) 25 Texas L.R. 31; (1946) 41 Ill.L.R. 487.
[65] (1947) 95 Univ. of Pa.L.R. 261, 302 [Wade].
[66] (1923) 23 Columbia L.R. 665–667.
[67] (1891) 25 "American Law Review," 695, 712.
[68] (1947) 95 Univ. of Pa.L.R. at p. 305 [Wade].
[69] "Restitution by Withdrawal from Executory Illegal Contracts" (1981) 97 L.Q.R. 420, 444 [Merkin].

There is indeed a case for a relaxation of the principle of *ex turpi causa* as presently applied, in particular, as to provide relief for a contracting party who has infringed a statute, statutory regulation or order of which he was wholly ignorant.[70]

It is another question whether relief should be granted if the litigant was party to the illegality, and whether it is possible or desirable "to distinguish between different degrees of iniquity."[70a] In *Tinsley* v. *Milligan* the defendant was allowed to rely on her equitable title. But Lord Goff, who dissented, did not think that:

> "the harsh consequences which will arise from the application of the established principle [*ex turpi causa*[70b]] in a case such as the present provide a satisfactory basis for developing the law in a manner which will open the door to far more unmeritorious cases, especially as the proposed development in the law appears to me contrary to the established principle underlying the authorities."[70c]

In his view, such questions should be left to the legislature. He said[70d]:

> "... if there is to be a reform aimed at substituting a system of discretionary relief for the present rules, the reform is one which should only be instituted by the legislature, after a full enquiry into the matter by the Law Commission, such inquiry to embrace not only the perceived advantages and disadvantages of the present law, but also the likely advantages and disadvantages of a system of discretionary relief, no doubt with particular reference to the New Zealand experience [embodied in the case law interpreting New Zealand Illegal Contracts Act 1970]."[70e]

[70] *Marles* v. *Philip Trant* [1954] 1 Q.B. 29; *Strongman (1945) Ltd.* v. *Sincock* [1955] 2 Q.B. 525; *Chai Sau Yin* v. *Liew Kwee Sam* [1962] A.C. 304. See to *Jamieson* v. *Noble, Watt's Trustee*, 1950 S.C. 265, 279, *per* Lord Jamieson.
[70a] *Tinsley* v. *Milligan* [1993] 3 All E.R. 65, 79, *per* Lord Goff: see above, pp. 501–502.
[70b] See above, p. 501 and n. 15c.
[70c] [1993] 3 All E.R. 68, 79–80. In *Tinsley* both parties were implicated in the same fraud, the fraud was "relatively minor" and Miss Milligan had confessed her wrongdoing and had made amends: see above, pp. 501–503.
[70d] [1993] 3 All E.R. 65, 80.
[70e] Section 6 of that statute provides that "... every illegal contract shall be of no effect and no person shall become entitled to any property under a disposition made by or pursuant to any such contract ...." However, s.7 confers on the court the power to grant relief "by way of restitution, compensation, variation of the contract, validation of the contract in whole or part or for any particular purpose, or otherwise howsoever as the court in its discretion thinks just." The cases interpreting this section include: *Dreadon* v. *Fletcher Development Co.* [1974] 2 N.Z.L.R. 11; *Combined Taxis Co-op Society* v. *Slobbe* [1973] 2 N.Z.L.R. 651; *Barsdell* v. *Kerr* [1979] 2 N.Z.L.R. 731; *Printwell Productions* v. *AA Finance* (1981) 1 D.C.R. 69; which also demonstrate some of the difficulties which that legislation has created; *Cf. Broadlands Rentals Ltd.* v. *R. D. Bull Ltd.* [1976] 2 N.Z.L.R. 595, 600, *per* Cooke J. See also [1971] A.S.C.L. 637–640 [Harris]; 5 N.Z.U.L.R. 151 [Furmston]; (1988) 13 N.Z. Univ. L.R. 160 [Coote], 190 [Asher]; *Essays* (ed. Burrows), pp. 177 *et seq.* [Dickson]. Contrast the Israel Contract Law (General Part) Act 1973, s.31, which grants a party to an illegal contract a right to restitution, subject to the court's discretion to deny it, "if it deems it just to do so." For a discussion of some of the considerations which a court may take into account in exercising its discretion, see (1984) 33 I.C.L.Q. 81 [Friedmann].

It is realistic to conclude that legislation is unlikely, even if the Law Commission so recommends. If the legislature does not intervene, then if the plaintiff is innocent but nonetheless a party to the illegality, the courts should arguably be encouraged to formulate less rigid principles than have hitherto been espoused: to inquire sympathetically, as did Devlin J. in the *St. John Shipping* case, whether the "way in which the contract was performed turned it into the sort of contract that was prohibited by the statute"[71]; to consider invoking the doctrine of waiver[72]; to be more ready to sever the legal from the illegal[73]; to determine whether there is a collateral contract in existence which is untainted by illegality[74]; and to interpret broadly the established exceptions which have been discussed in the text.[75] English courts have not always recognised that the rule "*in pari delicto potior est conditio defendentis* is one that can or ought to be applied in all cases." But the view, long adopted in Roman-Dutch jurisdictions, that, though "the courts will discourage illegal transactions . . . the exceptions show that where it is necessary to prevent injustice or to promote public policy, they will not rigidly enforce the rule,"[76] is not without support in the English case law. As Sachs L.J. said in *Shaw* v. *Groom*[77]:

"If . . . the conclusion [to grant relief] postulates a less rigid policy today than obtained in 1924 [*Anderson Ltd.* v. *Daniel*[78]], so be it. Public policy has been often spoken of as an unruly horse; all the more reason then why its riders should not themselves in these changing times wear blinkers, be oblivious to the scene around, and thus ride for a fall. Sound policy must be flexible enough to take into account the circumstances of its own generation. Today's generation is dominated by that ever-mounting mass of legislative control to which reference has already been made; in support of that control numberless offences have been created each with its appropriate penalty, and it is for the courts to see that this does not result in additional forfeitures and injustices which the legislature cannot have intended."

---

[71] [1957] 1 Q.B. 267, 284.
[72] *Strongman (1945) Ltd.* v. *Sincock* [1955] 2 Q.B. 525.
[73] [1976] Ch. 158; *Carney* v. *Herbert* [1985] A.C. 301, P.C.; *Ailion* v. *Spiekermann* [1976] Ch. 158.
[74] *Townsend (Builders) Ltd.* v. *Cinema News Property Management Ltd.* [1959] 1 W.L.R. 119, 124, *per* Evershed M.R., 126, *per* Lord Cohen.
[75] *Cf. Curragh Investments Ltd.* v. *Cook* [1974] 1 W.L.R. 1559, 1562–1564, *per* Megarry J.; and see *Neider* v. *Carda of Peace River District Ltd.* (1972) 25 D.L.R. (3d) 363.
[76] *Jajbhay* v. *Cassim* [1939] A.C. 537, 550, *per* Watermeyer J. See too *Kelly* v. *Kok* [1948] (3) S.A.L.R. 522; Quebec Civil Code, arts. 989–990; Dennis Lloyd, *Public Policy*, pp. 57–106; (1959) 8 I.C.L.Q. 486, 689 [E. Sabbath].
[77] [1970] 2 Q.B. 504, 523–524.
[78] [1924] 1 K.B. 138.

Chapter 23

CONTRACTS AFFECTED BY INCAPACITY

1. Contracts of the Mentally Disordered[1] and Drunkards

In *Imperial Loan Co.* v. *Stone*[2] Lord Esher M.R. said that a lunatic[3] can only set aside a contract entered into with a person of sound mind in the following circumstances:

> "When a person enters into a contract, and afterwards alleges that he was so insane at the time that he did not know what he was doing, and proves the allegation, the contract is as binding on him in every respect, whether it is executory or executed, as if he had been sane when he made it, unless he can prove further that the person with whom he contracted knew him to be so insane as not to be capable of understanding what he was about."

This principle has been criticised as being too harsh to the mentally disordered person[4]; and in New Zealand it had been held[5] that he could, at his option, set aside a contract if the contract was unfair, even if the other party was not aware, of his incapacity. But the Privy Council, in *Hart* v. *O'Connor*[6] has affirmed Lord Esher's statement of the law and has overruled these decisions. If a mentally disordered person has the right to rescind, he must, of course, be in a position to make *restitutio in integrum*.

It is questionable whether a mentally disordered person is able to make a valid contract for necessaries.[7] There is no binding authority[8] on this point; but

---

[1] The Mental Health Act 1983 now terms such a person as "mentally disordered." The Act does not affect a person's contractual capacity at common law.

[2] [1892] 1 Q.B. 599, 601; see also *Niell* v. *Morley* (1804) 9 Ves. 478, *semble*; *Ball* v. *Mannin* (1829) 3 Bli.(N.S.) 1; *York Glass Co. Ltd.* v. *Jubb* (1925) 134 L.T. 36; *Manches* v. *Trimborn* (1946) 115 L.J.K.B. 305; and *cf. Re Marshall* [1920] 1 Ch. 284; *Re Oppenheim* [1950] Ch. 633.

[3] See above, n. 1.

[4] (1901) 17 L.Q.R. 147 [H. Goudy]; *cf.* (1902) 18 L.Q.R. 21 [R. Wilson].

[5] *Archer* v. *Cutler* [1980] 1 N.Z.L.R. 386, followed by the Court of Appeal of New Zealand in *Hart* v. *O'Connor* [1984] 1 N.Z.L.R. 754.

[6] [1985] A.C. 1000, restrictively interpreting earlier English dicta, on which the New Zealand Court of Appeal had relied; see in particular, *Molton* v. *Camroux* (1848) 2 Ex. 487, 502, 503, *per* Pollock C.B.

[7] For a definition of necessary goods, see Sale of Goods Act 1979, s.3(3).

[8] The point was expressly left open in *Bagster* (or *Baxter*) v. *Earl Portsmouth* (1826) (the fuller report in 7 D. & R. 614–617 is to be preferred to that in 5 B. & C. 170–173). The remarks of the Court of Appeal in *Re Rhodes* (1890) 44 Ch.D. 94 and *Re J.* [1901] 1 Ch. 574 were made in the context of the doctrine of necessitous intervention (see above, p. 380). See also *Howard* v. *Digby* (1834) 2 Cl. & F. 634, 662–663, *per* Lord Brougham L.C., who was counsel in *Bagster* v. *Earl Portsmouth*.

if he can make a binding contract for other things, then *a fortiori* he should be able to make a valid contract for necessaries. The other party can enforce such a contract if he had no knowledge of his disorder. If he did, then his claim on the contract must fail.

By section 3(2) of the Sale of Goods Act 1979 "a person who by reason of mental incapacity . . . is incompetent to contract" must pay a reasonable price for necessary goods sold and delivered to him.[9]

If the property of the mentally disordered person is subject to the control of the court, no contract made without the court's authority disposing of the property binds him, although it binds the other party.[10]

A drunkard, who enters into a contract while drunk, is apparently in the same position as a mentally disordered person.[11]

2. MINORS' CONTRACTS[12]

A minor (in the past, an "infant") is a natural person who has not yet reached the age of 18.[13] There are two classes of minor. A minor who has not yet reached the "age of understanding" probably cannot make a contract at all.[14] But a minor who has reached such an age has a limited contractual capacity; and it is with these minors that the cases are principally concerned.

The general rule at common law was that a contract did not bind a minor unless he ratified it after he came of age.[15] But this rule was subject to certain exceptions. First, contracts for necessaries and certain other cognate transactions imposed some form of liability on minors. There is still considerable dispute whether such liability is contractual or, to use the language of the older cases which are the foundation of the common law, quasi-contractual.[16] Secondly, contracts which conferred on the minor an interest in property and which imposed on him obligations of a continuous or recurring nature, are regarded as binding on the minor unless he repudiated them and disclaimed the property either before or within a reasonable time of coming of age.[17]

Nowadays all other contracts do not, unless ratified, bind the minor although they do bind the other party to the contract.[18]

---

[9] *Semble* he must also pay a reasonable sum for necessary services which have been rendered by the other party.

[10] *Re Marshall* [1920] 1 Ch. 284.

[11] There is very little authority: see *Gore* v. *Gibson* (1845) 13 M. & W. 623; *Moulton* v. *Camroux* (1849) 4 Ex. 17, 19, *per* Patteson J.; *Matthews* v. *Baxter* (1873) L.R. 8 Ex. 132; *Blomley* v. *Ryan* (1956) 99 C.L.R. 362; Sale of Goods Act 1979, s.3(2).

[12] Family Law Reform Act 1969, s.12.

[13] Family Law Reform Act 1969, s.1. By s.9 a person now attains a particular age at the commencement of the relevant anniversary of his or her birth.

[14] See *Johnson* v. *Clark* [1908] 1 Ch. 303, 311–312, *per* Parker J.

[15] *Nash* v. *Inman* [1908] 2 K.B. 1, 12, *per* Buckley L.J.

[16] See below, pp. 525–526.

[17] *North Western Ry.* v. *M'Michael* (1850) 5 Ex. 114; *Lovell & Christmas* v. *Beauchamp* [1894] A.C. 607, 611, *per* Lord Herschell.

[18] Minors' Contracts Act 1987: see below, p. 527.

(a) *The Nature of the Minor's Liability for Necessaries*

A minor is under some liability to pay for necessaries. In the case of necessary goods, as distinct from services, it has often been said that his liability is always quasi-contractual.[19] This is a point of considerable practical importance, because if the minor's liability lies only in quasi-contract, he cannot be bound by an executory contract for necessary goods. Those who argue that his liability is quasi-contractual usually rely upon the following dictum of Fletcher Moulton L.J. in *Nash* v. *Inman*[20]:

> "An infant, like a lunatic,[21] is incapable of making a contract of purchase
> in the strict sense of the words; but if a man satisfies the need of the infant
> or lunatic by supplying to him necessaries, the law will imply an obliga-
> tion to repay him for the services so rendered, and will enforce the
> obligation against the estate of the infant or lunatic. The consequence is
> that the basis of the action is hardly contract. Its real foundation is an
> obligation which the law imposes on the infant to make a fair payment in
> respect of needs satisfied. In other words, the obligation arises *re* and not
> *consensu.*"

Fletcher Moulton L.J.'s dictum apparently derives support from the rule that a minor is only liable to pay a reasonable sum for necessary goods. Section 3(2) of the Sale of Goods Act 1979 reads as follows:

> Where necessaries are sold and delivered to a minor, he must pay a
> reasonable price therefor.

If the basis of his liability is contractual, he should, it is argued, have to pay the contract price. Those rules do not, however, exclude the possibility of liability being contractual rather than quasi-contractual. For it has long been the law that contracts for necessaries only bind a minor if they are for his benefit.[22] If such contracts contain terms onerous to him, they will not bind him unless, in spite of these terms, the contracts are beneficial to him. It follows that a minor will not, in any case, be bound by a contract for necessaries for which more than a reasonable price is charged. Nor does section 3(2) of the Sale of Goods Act affect the position.[23] Its provisions are consistent with the view that a minor may be liable on an executory contract for necessaries provided that the

---

[19] See (1927) 43 L.Q.R. 389 [Sir John Miles]; Cheshire & Fifoot, *op. cit.* pp. 413–414; Keener, *op. cit.* pp. 20–22. Anson, *op. cit.* pp. 197–198, seems to think that this was the law, but that it is now confused by *Roberts* v. *Gray* [1913] 1 K.B. 520. Winfield, though he had moved in this direction ((1944) 58 L.Q.R. 82, 94), had not made up his mind (*Quasi-Contracts*, pp. 108–109).

[20] [1908] 2 K.B. 1, 8; and his dicta in *Re J.* [1909] 1 Ch. 574, 577. See also *Pontypridd Union* v. *Drew* [1927] 1 K.B. 214, 220, *per* Scrutton L.J.

[21] This reference to the lunatic is not altogether happy. It is probable that a lunatic can make a valid contract of purchase; see above, p. 523. *Re Rhodes* (1890) 44 Ch.D. 94, upon which Fletcher Moulton L.J. relies, is a case of necessitous intervention; see above, p. 380.

[22] *Fawcett* v. *Smethurst* (1914) 84 L.J.K.B. 473; *Clements* v. *L. & N.W. Ry.* [1894] 2 Q.B. 482.

[23] It is quoted above.

terms are not onerous to him. A minor's contract to buy necessary goods for less than a reasonable price is surely valid.

The weight of authority is against the view that a minor's liability for necessaries is always quasi-contractual. Apart from two seventeenth century cases, in which it was held that a minor would be liable on an executory contract for necessary goods,[24] in more recent years Buckley L.J. has said[25]:

> "The plaintiff, when he sues the defendant for necessary goods supplied during infancy, is suing him in contract on the footing that the contract was such as the infant, notwithstanding infancy, could make. The defendant, although he was an infant, had a limited capacity to contract. In order to maintain his action the plaintiff must prove that the contract sued on is within that limited capacity. The rule as regards liability for necessaries may, I think, be thus stated: an infant may contract for supply at a reasonable price of articles reasonably necessary for his support in his station in life if he has not already a sufficient supply."

It has also been usual since the time of Coke to speak of beneficial contracts of service together with contracts for necessary goods as contracts for necessaries[26]; and in this century the Court of Appeal has decided[27] that the two types of contract, for necessary services and goods, are similar, and that such contracts, though executory, are binding on a minor provided they are not onerous to him. Thus it is not easy to support a distinction between contracts for necessary goods and for necessary services. To do so, moreover, would introduce an anomaly into the law.[28]

The rule at common law appears, therefore, to be that a contract for necessaries, whether goods or services, will bind a minor provided that it is not on balance onerous to him.[29] If, however, it is burdensome to the minor, it will not bind him, but he will be liable in quasi-contract to pay a reasonable price for necessary goods or services received by him thereunder.[30]

---

[24] *Ive* v. *Charter* (1619) Cro.Jac. 560; *Delavel* v. *Clare* (1652) Latch. 156; see also Y.B. 18 Edw. II f. 2 pl. 7 (debt). The same view seems to have been taken by the court in *Dale* v. *Copping* (1610) 1 Bulst. 39.

[25] *Nash* v. *Inman* [1908] 2 K.B. 1, 12. See also *Stocks* v. *Wilson* [1913] 2 K.B. 235, 242, *per* Lush J.; *Doyle* v. *White City Stadium Ltd.* [1935] 1 K.B. 110, 122–124, *per* Lord Hanworth M.R.

[26] Co.Litt. f. 172a; *Walter* v. *Everard* [1891] 2 Q.B. 369; see also *Mandy* v. *Scott* (1663) 1 Sid. 109, 112, *per curiam*; (1939) 55 L.Q.R. 37, 47 [Holdsworth].

[27] *Roberts* v. *Gray* [1913] 1 K.B. 520; see, particularly, Cozens-Hardy M.R. at pp. 525–526: "as early as Lord Coke . . . it has been held that an infant's contract for necessaries is binding, and it was laid down by him that that doctrine also applied not merely to bread, cheese and clothes, but to education and instruction." *Cf. Chaplin* v. *Leslie Frewin (Publishers) Ltd.* [1966] Ch. 71; see below, p. 529.

[28] (1942) 58 L.Q.R. 82, 95 [Winfield]; *cf. Salmond and Williams, op. cit.* p. 307.

[29] *Doyle* v. *White City Stadium Ltd.* [1935] 1 K.B. 110.

[30] The common law was not affected by the Infants' Relief Act 1874, which has now been repealed: see *Nash* v. *Inman* [1908] 2 K.B. 1, 12, *per* Buckley L.J.; *Roberts* v. *Gray* [1913] 1 K.B. 520.

(b) *Restitution of Benefits Conferred under Contracts Ineffective for Infancy*

Minors' Contracts Act 1987

The Minors' Contracts Act 1987 has repealed the Infants Relief Act 1874. As has been seen[31] at common law certain contracts are voidable at the election of the minor either before, or within a reasonable time of, his attaining his majority. All other contracts, other than contracts for necessary goods, do not bind the minor. Section 3(1) of the 1987 Act provides:

> "Where
> (a) a person ("the plaintiff") has after the commencement of this Act entered into a contract with another ("the defendant"), and
> (b) the contract is unenforceable against the defendant (or he repudiates it) because he was a minor when the contract was made,
> the court may, if it is just and equitable to do so, require the defendant to transfer to the plaintiff any property acquired by the defendant under the contract, or any property representing it."[32]

There is as yet no decided case interpreting section 3(1). It is therefore conjectural whether the courts will interpret generously section 3(1) and, in particular, the words "any *property* acquired by the defendant under the contract, or *any proceeds representing it.*" For example, what if the minor has disposed of the property or "any property representing it?" Must he then make restitution? A literal reading of section 3(1) suggests that he will not be required to do so.[32a] As uncertain are the guidelines which the courts will formulate to determine the exercise of their discretion under section 3(1).[33]

Section 3(2) of the statute provides:

> "Nothing in this section shall be taken to prejudice any other remedy available to the plaintiff."

Consequently, the principles formulated in the cases at common law and in equity are still in force.[34] It may well be that plaintiffs will normally be content to invite the court to exercise its discretion under section 3(1). But a court may refuse to order restitution or may conclude that the facts fall outside the subsection. Again, the minor's liability at law or in equity may conceivably be greater than his statutory liability, given the uncertain factor of the court's discretion.[35] Furthermore, section 3(1) does not govern claims *by* a minor;

---

[31] See above, p. 524.
[32] *Cf.* the happier recommendation of the Latey Committee, Report of the Committee on the Age of Majority Cmnd. 3342 (1967): that a minor should be liable for goods delivered or services rendered, but the court "should be empowered to relieve the infant from his liability to account to such extent as it thinks fit."
[32a] *Cf.* the minor's liability in equity: below p. 533.
[33] *Cf.* (1989) 9 L.S. 307, 317–318 [Arrowsmith].
[34] See above, pp. 524–526; see below, pp. 533 *et seq.*
[35] See below, pp. 528 *et seq.*

their success will also depend on the relevant principles of common law and equity. For these reasons it is necessary to discuss these principles.

Common law and equity

Claims by the minor

It has been held that a minor is only entitled to recover money paid under a contract which he elects to avoid if he can show that the consideration for the payment has totally failed. In *Steinberg* v. *Scala (Leeds) Ltd.*[36] the plaintiff, a minor, was allotted shares in the defendant company, on which she paid the full amount due. Eighteen years later, while still a minor, she repudiated the contract for the purchase of the shares and sought to recover from the defendant company the money she had paid for them. The Court of Appeal held that she was not entitled to recover, because there had been no total failure of consideration.[37]

It is, however, doubtful whether, in such a case, the test of total failure of consideration is appropriate. On principle the question should be whether the minor has made *restitutio in integrum*. A minor who cannot restore the *status quo ante* should be unable to avoid the contract; if he has restored the *status quo*, he should be able to avoid the contract and recover benefits conferred thereunder. Some support for this view is to be found in *Valentini* v. *Canali*[38] where the contract was void under section 1 of the Infants Relief Act 1874. The plaintiff, while a minor, agreed to become the tenant of the defendant's house and to pay £102 for the furniture. He paid £68 on account for the furniture, and occupied the premises and used the furniture for some months. A divisional court held that he was not entitled to recover the £68. Lord Coleridge C.J., with whose judgment Bowen L.J. concurred said[39]:

> "When an infant has paid for something and has consumed or used it, it is contrary to natural justice that he should recover back the money which he has paid. Here the infant plaintiff who claimed to recover back the money which he had paid to the defendant had had the use of a quantity of furniture for some months. He could not give back his benefit or replace the defendant in the position in which he was before the contract."

This passage seems to indicate that a total failure of consideration is not necessary to ground such a claim by the minor, provided that the minor had not used or consumed the goods in such a way as to make *restitutio in integrum* impossible. This approach was not, however, adopted in *Pearce* v. *Brain*,[40]

---

[36] [1923] 2 Ch. 452. See also *Austen* v. *Gervas* (1703) Hob. 77; *Holmes* v. *Blogg* (1818) 8 Taunt. 508; *Re Burrows & Ruddock* (1856) 8 De G.M. & G. 254; *Everett* v. *Wilkins* (1874) 29 L.T. 846.

[37] Cf. *Corpe* v. *Overton* (1833) 10 Bing. 252, 258, *per* Bosanquet J.; *Hamilton* v. *Vaughan-Sherrin Electrical Engineering Co.* [1894] 3 Ch. 589, doubted in *Steinberg* v. *Scala (Leeds) Ltd.* [1923] 2 Ch. 452, 460, *per* Lord Sterndale M.R., 462, *per* Warrington L.J., 465, *per* Younger L.J.

[38] (1889) 24 Q.D.B. 166: see (1957) 73 L.Q.R. 194, 202–205 [Treitel]; (1958) 74 L.Q.R. 97, 101–103 [Atiyah].

[39] At p. 167.

[40] [1929] 2 K.B. 310.

although the court purported to follow *Valentini* v. *Canali*. The plaintiff, a minor, exchanged his motor-cycle and sidecar for the defendant's motor-car. The motor-car only went 70 miles before it broke down. The plaintiff then repudiated the contract on the grounds of his minority and claimed the return of the motor-cycle and sidecar or its value. A divisional court held that the contract of exchange was void under section 1 of the Act, and that, in this context, no distinction could be drawn between recovery of money and recovery of a chattel. In both cases there must be a total failure of consideration before recovery will be allowed; on the facts of the case, however, there was no total failure of consideration, and the plaintiff's action therefore failed.

These cases do not, therefore, formulate any coherent legal principles.[41] Unfortunately, further uncertainty has arisen from the Court of Appeal's decision in *Chaplin* v. *Leslie Frewin (Publishers) Ltd.*[42] A minor contracted with the defendants, who were publishers, to transfer to them the manuscript of his memoirs. Having delivered it, he subsequently regretted his decision. He then sought an interlocutory injunction to restrain the defendants from publishing the manuscript on the ground that the contract was not for his benefit and that the copyright of the manuscript was still vested in him. He succeeded before the trial judge but failed in the Court of Appeal. The Court of Appeal held that the contract was for his benefit and was therefore binding on him[43]; and that, even if it were not, the minor could not recover the copyright transferred under the contract. In Danckwerts L.J.'s opinion, "if an infant revokes a contract, the property and interests which have been previously transferred by him cannot be recovered by the infant. ... The transfers of property made by [the infant] remain effective against him, even if the contract is otherwise revocable."[44] Although Winn L.J. seemed to regard the matter as turning more on the construction of the Copyright Act 1956,[45] he expressed his general agreement with the judgment of Danckwerts L.J.

Lord Denning M.R., who dissented in part, did not regard the particular contract as being for the minor's good. Moreover, he would have allowed the minor to recover the copyright transferred, seemingly on the terms that he returned the money received by him from the defendants.[46] In his view, *Steinberg* v. *Scala (Leeds) Ltd.*, *Valentini* v. *Canali*, and *Pearce* v. *Brain* could

> "have no application to a disposition [such as the transfer of copyright] which requires a deed or writing in order to be effective. They cannot be used so as to nullify the firmly established rule that such a disposition is voidable. For the protection of the young and the foolish, the law holds

---

[41] See (1957) 73 L.Q.R. 194, 202–204 [Treitel]; (1958) 74 L.Q.R. 97, 101–104 [Atiyah].

[42] [1966] Ch. 71. (The case was later compromised: *The Times*, February 16, 1966.)

[43] Lord Denning M.R. dissented on this point. The minor had in fact received some advance royalties; see below, p. 530.

[44] At p. 94, adopting counsel's argument.

[45] ss.36 and 37.

[46] Counsel conceded this point; see p. 86; but the concession is not mentioned in Lord Denning's judgment.

that a disposition by deed or writing can be avoided by the infant at any time before he comes of age. At any rate a disposition is voidable when it is made in pursuance of a contract which is not for the benefit of the infant."[47]

The issue before the Court of Appeal in *Chaplin* v. *Leslie Frewen (Publishers) Ltd.* was whether the trial judge had acted correctly in granting the plaintiff an interlocutory injunction. It is unfortunate that Danckwerts and Winn L.JJ. should have been so ready to determine that the copyright which had been transferred could not have been recovered, even if the minor could have elected to avoid the contract. Lord Denning M.R.'s conclusion that the minor could recover the copyright on terms is, in our view, preferable, although it could have been more happily supported on the ground that the minor had offered to restore, and was capable of restoring, the *status quo ante*. The adoption of the ancient common law rule which requires certain dispositions to be by deed or writing will result in an arbitrary distinction. If accepted, gifts or grants made by a minor by deed or writing will be voidable; in contrast those which may be made by delivery without a deed or writing will not.[48] Moreover, to explain *Steinberg* v. *Scala (Leeds) Ltd.*, *Valentini* v. *Canali* and *Pearce* v. *Brain*[49] as cases where the property in the money or goods, which were handed over by a minor, passed on delivery and "where it is unjust that [the minor] should recover them back"[50] is unconvincing. These cases were not decided on that ground, although they are, as has been suggested, reconcilable with the principle of *restitutio in integrum*.[51]

Claims by the other party

His rights at common law

As has been seen,[52] contracts which conferred on the minor on interest in property and which imposed on him obligations of a continuous or recurring nature are binding on him unless repudiated within a reasonable time of attaining majority. Such repudiation is conditional on the minor's disclaimer of any property received under the contract. Upon such a disclaimer the property then revests in the other party.[53]

All other contracts, save contracts for the supply of necessaries, are not binding on the minor. In all probability, property in goods supplied by the

---

[47] At p. 90.
[48] *Cf.* [1966] C.L.J. 17 [Yale].
[49] For a discussion of these cases see above, pp. 528–530.
[50] [1966] Ch. 71, 90, *per* Lord Denning M.R.
[51] See above, pp. 528–529.
[52] See above, p. 524.
[53] *Cf. Dublin & Wicklow Rly.* v. *Black* (1852) 8 Ex. 181.

other party nonetheless passes to the minor; his intention to pass property in the goods is not vitiated.[54]

The other party may nonetheless seek to recover money paid or lent to the minor, or seek recompense for the value of non-necessary goods or services which he delivered or rendered to him.

It has been held that the other party cannot recover money paid to the minor under the contract even though there has been a total failure of consideration. In *Cowern* v. *Nield*,[55] the defendant, a minor, carried on business as a merchant in hay and straw. The plaintiff ordered some clover and hay from him, and paid him in advance. The clover was delivered, but the plaintiff properly rejected it because it was rotten. The hay was never delivered. The plaintiff, therefore, sued the defendant to recover the money he had paid either as damages for breach of contract or as money paid for a consideration which had wholly failed. The defendant pleaded his minority. A divisional court held that the contract was void against the minor and so the action for damages failed. The court also held that, since the action for money had and received was in form *ex contractu* it, too, must fail, unless it could be shown that there was fraud on the part of the minor[56] and that the action was, therefore, in substance *ex delicto*.[57]

The Court of Appeal reached a similar conclusion a year later in *R. Leslie Ltd.* v. *Sheill*.[58] The defendant, a minor, by fraudulently representing that he was of full age, induced the plaintiff moneylenders to lend him £400. They sued him to recover the money, and he pleaded his minority. The Court of Appeal held that he was not liable to repay the money in an action for money had and received. Lord Sumner said[59]:

"An action for money had and received ... has been sustained, where in substance the cause of action was *ex delicto*: *Bristow* v. *Eastman*,[60] approved before 1874 in *Re Seager*,[61] and cited without disapproval in *Cowern* v. *Nield*. Even this has been doubted, but where the substance of the cause of action is contractual, it is certainly otherwise. To money had

---

[54] *Cf. Stocks* v. *Wilson* [1913] 2 K.B. 235, where it was held that property in goods passed to the minor on delivery even though the underlying contract was void under s.1 of the Infant's Relief Act 1874.

[55] [1912] 2 K.B. 419.

[56] A re-trial was ordered on the issue of fraud.

[57] The court relied on *Bristow* v. *Eastman* (1794) 1 Esp. 172, where Lord Kenyon held that an action for money had and received would lie against a minor to recover money which he had embezzled. In his view, infancy was no defence to the action; that infants were liable to actions "*ex delicto*, though not *ex contractu*; and though the present action was in its form an action of the later description, yet it was of the former in point of substance." The case, therefore, only decides that a minor can be sued in quasi-contract in cases of waiver of tort, and in that sense it was followed in *Re Seager* (1889) 60 L.T. 665. It did not decide that, apart from such a case, no action in quasi-contract would lie against a minor.

[58] [1914] 3 K.B. 607. For a further discussion, see below, p. 536.

[59] At pp. 612–613. See also p. 621, *per* Kennedy L.J., p. 626, *per* A. T. Lawrence J.

[60] (1794) 1 Esp. 172; see above, n. 57.

[61] (1889) 60 L.T. 665.

and received and other *indebitatus* counts infancy was a defence just as to any other action in contract: *Alton* v. *Midland Ry.*, *per* Willes J.[62]; *Re Jones*, *per* Jessel M.R.[63]; *Dicey on Parties*, p. 284; Bullen and Leake's *Precedents of Pleadings* (3rd ed.), p. 605."

In our view, this reasoning, which also underlies *Cowern* v. *Nield*, is unsound. The authorities cited by Lord Sumner in support of his last proposition only go to the length of showing that in some cases a minor may have a defence to an action for money had and received, not that a plea that he is a minor is a bar in every case.[64] If this were so the plea should defeat such an action even where the claim is in substance *ex delicto*: for the argument assumes that all restitutionary actions are founded upon an "implied" contract. This assumption is, in our view, objectionable. It is contrary to earlier authority[65] and allows an antiquated and now discredited[66] pleading fiction to influence substantive rights.

At common law a claim for money lent should fail on the ground that to grant it would lead to the indirect enforcement of the contract of loan which is not binding on the minor.[67] In our view, that is the true *ratio decidendi* of that part of *R. Leslie Ltd.* v. *Sheill* which denied the plaintiff recovery in an action for money had and received—arguably a harsh conclusion.[68]

For similar reasons a restitutionary claim for the value of non-necessary goods[69] or services supplied to a minor, who has refused to pay the contractual price, would be likely to fail, for to allow even a *reasonable* payment in those circumstances would probably be held to undermine the minor's protection.[70] But to award a reasonable sum is simply an attempt to restore the *status quo ante*, in circumstances in which the goods and services cannot themselves be restored. For this reason the rule of policy should not prevent recovery of money paid to a minor under a contract, other than a borrowing contract, where there has been a total failure of consideration; for example, if, as in *Cowern* v. *Nield*, a minor, who contracts to sell goods to an adult fails to deliver them although the adult has paid for them, he should repay the purchase price to the adult contracting party. Here the adult plaintiff does not seek indirectly to enforce the contract, but simply to restore the *status quo ante*. As in the case of an *ultra vires* contract, to which the same rule of policy applies,[71] the money

---

[62] (1865) 34 L.J.C.P. 292, 297–298.
[63] (1881) 18 Ch.D. 109, 118.
[64] See above, pp. 523–524.
[65] *Re Rhodes* (1890) 44 Ch.D. 94, 105, *per* Cotton L.J.
[66] See above, p. 5.
[67] Cf. *Sinclair* v. *Brougham* [1914] A.C. 398; see above, pp. 83–85.
[68] *Jennings* v. *Rundall* (1799) 8 T.R. 335.
[69] *Ex p. Jones* (1881) 18 Ch.D. 109, 120–121, *per* Jessel M.R.; *Stocks* v. *Wilson* [1913] 2 K.B. 235.
[70] Cf. The Law Commission's Report No. 134: *The Law of Contract; Minors Contracts*, (1984) § 4.23.
[71] See above, pp. 62–68.

should be recoverable as money had and received.[72] For these reasons *Cowern* v. *Nield* should, in our view, be overruled.

The common law may therefore be summarised as follows:

(1) A minor will be liable to pay a reasonable price for necessaries supplied to him even where the contract is ineffective because, for example, the price is unreasonably high.

(2) A minor will not be liable at common law to refund money lent to him under a contract of loan. To allow such recovery would indirectly enforce a contract which is not binding on him. The same rule possibly precludes recovery in restitution in respect of non-necessary goods or services supplied to minors.

(3) There is authority that an action for money had and received can never lie against a minor for the recovery of money paid for a consideration which has totally failed. In our view, borrowing contracts apart, such an action should lie, for it does not indirectly enforce a contract which is not binding on him.

(4) Where the minor is a tortfeasor, the plaintiff may sue him in an action in tort provided that the substance of his action is *ex delicto*; and there is authority that, in an appropriate case, he may waive the tort and sue the minor in an action for money had and received.[73]

His rights in equity[74]

If a minor is fraudulent, there is some jurisdiction in equity to grant relief, but, as Knight Bruce V.-C. once said, "in what cases in particular a court of equity will thus exert itself is not easy to determine."[75] There are dicta in general terms: "If an infant is old enough and cunning enough to contrive and carry on a fraud, . . . he ought to make satisfaction for it"[76]. "infancy or coverture shall be no excuse"[77]: "infants have no privilege to cheat men"[78]: "infants are not allowed to take advantage of infancy to support a fraud"[79]: "if there was a fraud, of which the infant was conusant, she would be bound as much as an adult."[80] But the early authorities are conclusive only to this extent, that they show that Chancery judges were prepared to grant some relief, compelling the minor defendant *personally* to disgorge, provided that in so doing equity did

---

[72] *Re Phoenix Life Assurance Co., Burges' & Stock's Case* (1862) 2 J. & H. 441 and the "swap" cases: below, pp. 540–542.
[73] *Bristow* v. *Eastman* (1794) 1 Esp. 172; see below, Chap. 38.
[74] (1959) 22 M.L.R. 273 [P. S. Atiyah].
[75] *Stikeman* v. *Dawson* (1847) 1 De G. & Sm. 90, 110. It is possible that this relief will only be available to the other party after the infant has attained his majority; see, *per* Knight Bruce V.-C. at p. 109.
[76] *Watts* v. *Cresswell* (1714) 2 Eq.Ca.Abr. 515–516, *per* Lord Cowper L.C.
[77] *Savage* v. *Foster* (1722) 9 Mod. 35, 37, *per curiam*.
[78] *Esron* v. *Nicholas, sub nom. Evroy* v. *Nicholas* (1733) 2 Eq.Ca.Abr. 488, 489, *per* Lord King L.C.
[79] *Earl of Buckinghamshire* v. *Drury* (1761) 2 Ed. 60, 71, *per* Lord Hardwicke L.C.
[80] *Beckett* v. *Cordley* (1784) 1 Bro.C.C. 353, 358, *per* Lord Thurlow L.C.

not enforce a contract which was void at common law.[81] So, in *Clarke* v. *Cobley*,[82] the defendant gave the plaintiff his bond for the amount of two notes made to the plaintiff by the defendant's wife, and the plaintiff delivered up the notes. When the bond was put in suit, the defendant pleaded his minority at the time of its execution and the plaintiff filed a bill in equity praying that the defendant might either pay the money or execute a new bond, or return the notes. Sir R. P. Arden M.R. refused to decree payment of the money. He said[83] that he "could only take care that the parties were put in the same situation in which they were at the time of the bond being given, which was done on the principle that an infant shall not take advantage of his own fraud"; and he ordered the notes to be returned to the plaintiff.

In the important case of *Re King*,[84] a minor, by fraudulently stating that he was of full age, obtained a substantial advance from a banking association. He subsequently became bankrupt. It was held that the association was entitled to prove in the bankruptcy for the debt. Both Knight Bruce and Turner L.JJ. expressed their reluctance to come to this decision, believing that they were compelled to do so by the previous course of authority; but, as Lord Sumner subsequently said,[85] "the language of the lords justice is hardly consistent with any other view than that the bankrupt was in equity personally liable to pay the debt in question." Since a view must be implicit in the decision itself, and was expressed by Knight Bruce L.J. in these words[86]: "The question is, whether in the view of a court of equity, according to the sense of decisions not now to be disputed, he has made himself liable to pay the debt, whatever his liability or non-liability at law. In my opinion we are compelled to say that he was." There was no suggestion that the claimant should be given any priority over the general creditors.

The limits of equity's intervention were emphasised in *Levene* v. *Brougham*.[87] The defendant, a minor, by fraudulently representing that he was of full age obtained an advance from the plaintiff, a moneylender, for which he gave a promissory note for £700. The plaintiff sued the defendant on the note, and the defendant pleaded his minority. The Court of Appeal held that the

---

[81] See *Esron* v. *Nicholas* (1733) 2 Eq. Cas. Abr. 488, (*sub nom. Evroy* v. *Nicholas*, see extract from registrar's book set out in 1 De G. & Sm. 118). In *Stikeman* v. *Dawson* (1847) 1 De G. & Sm. 90, 115, Knight Bruce V.-C. concluded that the facts in *Esron* v. *Nicholas* did not support the decree that was made.

[82] (1789) 2 Cox 173; see also *Overton* v. *Banister* (1844) 3 Hare 503; *Wright* v. *Snowe* (1848) 23 De G. & Sm. 321; *Chubb* v. *Griffiths* (1865) 35 Beav. 127; *Woolf* v. *Woolf* [1899] 1 Ch. 343.

[83] (1789) 2 Cox 173, 174.

[84] (1858) 3 De G. & J. 63. See also *Maclean* v. *Dummett* (1869) 22 L.T. 710; *Ex p. Lynch* (1876) 2 Ch.D. 227, which was, however, regarded as anomalous by Lindley J. in *Miller* v. *Blankley* (1878) 38 L.T. 527, 530.

[85] *R. Leslie Ltd.* v. *Sheill* [1914] 3 K.B. 607, 617.

[86] At p. 69. The case was doubted, on grounds which do not affect this statement in the text, in *Ex p. Jones* (1881) 18 Ch.D. 109, 120–121, *per* Jessel M.R., 113, *per* Baggallay L.J. See also *Nelson* v. *Stocker* (1859) 4 De G. & J. 458, 464, *per* Turner L.J.; *Bartlett* v. *Wells* (1862) 1 B. & S. 836, 841, *per* Cockburn C.J., applied in *De Roo* v. *Foster* (1862) 12 C.B.(N.S.) 272; *Miller* v. *Blankley* (1878) 38 L.T. 527.

[87] (1909) 25 T.L.R. 265.

plaintiff could not recover. The contract was void under section 1 of the Infants' Relief Act 1874 and no authority was cited:

> "in which it had been held that a contract which was void under the statute was made good simply because it had been entered into on the faith of a misrepresentation. . . . The most that could be said . . . was . . . that a representation by an infant that he was of full age gave rise to an equitable liability resulting from the fraud. But that did not mean that the contract would be enforced, but that some other remedy would be given."[88]

Equity will not indirectly enforce contracts which are void at law. However, the controversial decision of Lush J. in *Stocks* v. *Wilson*[89] has blurred this principle. The defendant, a minor, by fraudulently representing that he was of full age, induced the plaintiff to sell him on credit non-necessary goods for the price of £300. The defendant then resold some of the goods for £30; and, with the consent of the plaintiff's agent, he granted a bill of sale of the remainder as security for a loan of £100. He failed to pay the price of the goods on the due date. After the defendant had come of age, the plaintiff brought an action against him claiming, *inter alia*, the reasonable value of the goods. Lush J. held that the defendant was liable in equity to account to the plaintiff for the £30 and for the £100 he had obtained as a result of the sale and mortgage respectively. He stated the equitable rules in these terms:

> "What the court of equity has done in cases of this kind is to prevent the infant from retaining the benefit of what he has obtained by reason of his fraud. It has done no more than this, and this is a very different thing from making him liable to pay damages or compensation for the loss of the other party's bargain. If the infant has obtained property by fraud he can be compelled to restore it; if he has obtained money he can be compelled to refund it. If he has not obtained either, but has only purported to bind himself by an obligation to transfer property or to pay money, neither in a court of law nor a court of equity can he be compelled to make good his promise or to make satisfaction for its breach.[90]
>
> The jurisdiction which the court exercises is not only a jurisdiction over the property which the infant has acquired by his fraud, but also over the infant himself to compel him to make satisfaction. . . . If an infant has wrongfully sold the property which he acquired by fraudulent misrepresentation as to his age, he must at all events account for the proceeds to the party he has defrauded. I can see no logical ground on which he can be allowed to resist such a claim in that case, if he is accountable for the money itself in a case where he has obtained money and not goods by means of a like fraud."[91]

---

[88] At p. 265, *per* Lord Alverstone C.J. *Cf. Lemprière* v. *Lange* (1879) 12 Ch.D. 675, 679, *per* Jessel M.R.; *R. Leslie Ltd.* v. *Sheill* [1914] 3 K.B. 607, 614, *per* Lord Sumner.
[89] [1913] 2 K.B. 235.
[90] At pp. 242–243.
[91] At p. 247.

In the following year, however, the Court of Appeal doubted this decision in *R. Leslie Ltd.* v. *Sheill*.[92] In the latter case the defendant, a minor, by fraudulently representing himself to be of full age, induced the plaintiffs, who were moneylenders, to advance to him two sums of £200 each. The plaintiffs sued to recover the sums advanced with interest, either as damages for fraud or as money had and received to their use. The Court of Appeal held:

(1) that the defendant was not liable in tort, because the tort was directly connected with a contract void against the minor under the Infants' Relief Act 1874;

(2) that the defendant was not liable in an action for money had and received[93];

(3) that the defendant was under no personal liability in equity to return the money.

On this last point, the Court of Appeal overruled the decision of Horridge J. Lord Sumner examined the authorities and concluded[94]:

"I think that the whole current of decisions down to 1913, apart from dicta which are inconclusive, went to show that, when an infant obtained an advantage by falsely stating himself to be of full age, equity required him to restore his ill-gotten gains, or to release the party deceived from obligations or acts in law induced by the fraud, but scrupulously stopped short of enforcing against him a contractual obligation, entered into while he was an infant, even by means of a fraud. This applies even to *Re King, ex p. Unity Joint Stock Mutual Banking Association*.[95] Restitution stopped where repayment began; as Kindersley V.-C. put it in *Vaughan* v. *Vanderstegen*,[96] an analogous case, 'you take the property to pay the debt.' "

Lord Sumner considered Lush J.'s statement in *Stocks* v. *Wilson*, that if a minor obtained money by fraud he can be compelled in equity to refund it, was "open to challenge." He continued[97]:

"The learned judge thought that the fundamental principle in *Re King, ex p. Unity Joint Stock Mutual Banking Association* was a liability to account for the money obtained by the fraudulent misrepresentation and that in the case before him there must be a similar liability to account for the proceeds of the sale of the goods obtained by the fraud. If this be his *ratio decidendi*, though I have difficulty in seeing what liability to account there can be (and certainly none is named in *Re King, ex p. Unity Joint Stock Mutual Banking Association*), the decision in *Stocks* v. *Wilson* is distinguishable from the present case and is independent of the above

---

[92] [1914] 2 K.B. 607; applied in *Mahomed Syedol Ariffin* v. *Yeoh Ooi Gark* [1916] 2 A.C. 575.
[93] See above, pp. 531–532.
[94] At p. 618.
[95] (1858) 3 De G. & J. 63; see above, p. 534.
[96] (1854) 2 Dr. 363, 383.
[97] [1914] 3 K.B. 607, 619.

dictum, and I need express no opinion about it. In the present case there is clearly no accounting. There is no fiduciary relation: the money was paid over in order to be used as the defendant's own and he has so used it and, I suppose, spent it. There is no question of tracing it, no possibility of restoring the very thing got by the fraud, nothing but compulsion through a personal judgment to pay an equivalent sum out of his present or future resources, in a word nothing but a judgment in debt to repay the loan. I think this would be nothing but enforcing a void contract. So far as I can find, the court of Chancery never would have enforced any liability under circumstances like the present, any more than a court of law would have done so, and I think that no ground can be found for the present judgment, which would be an answer to the Infants' Relief Act."

It is difficult to say how far *Stocks* v. *Wilson* has survived this onslaught. In our view, the decision is reconcilable with *R. Leslie Ltd.* v. *Sheill*. The basis of the latter decision is, we suggest,[98] the rule of policy that personal remedies in restitution are not to be employed indirectly to enforce contracts which are at law not binding on the minor. This rule of policy overrides the equity whereby a minor would otherwise have to pay for goods obtained by fraud or to repay money obtained fraudulently under a contract of loan. Where a minor has obtained property under a contract (other than a contract for the loan of money) induced by his fraud, he will be compelled in equity to restore such property as is still in his possession[99] and, if he has disposed of the property, to refund the proceeds.[1] Here the rule of policy does not bar recovery. But the minor is under no liability to pay the contract price for the property or even, it seems, a reasonable price[2]; to require him to do so would be indirectly to enforce the contract.[3] Similarly, if he has fraudulently obtained money under a contract of loan, he will not be liable to repay it[4]; but, in the event of his bankruptcy, the person who advanced the money will be entitled to prove as a general creditor in the bankruptcy for the loan.[5]

It has sometimes been suggested that this equity is proprietary rather than personal.[6] But the case law suggests that the other party's right to prove in the minor's bankruptcy is as a simple creditor. He enjoys no priority over other

---

[98] See above, p. 532.

[99] *Clarke* v. *Cobley* (1789) 2 Cox 173; *Bartlett* v. *Wells* (1862) 1 B. & S. 836, 841, *per* Cockburn C.J.; *R. Leslie Ltd.* v. *Sheill* [1914] 3 K.B. 607, 623–624, *per* Kennedy L.J.

[1] It has been argued that a minor's liability to account is only for the actual proceeds in his possession: see, *e.g.* Treitel, *op. cit.* p. 499. But the equity is not proprietary and it is doubtful how far identification of the proceeds is a relevant consideration in this context. The rules of equity have never been adequately developed. *Cf.* see above, Chap. 2.

[2] But see above, p. 532. *Cf.* Minors' Contracts Act 1987, s.3(1); see above, p. 527.

[3] *Stocks* v. *Wilson* [1913] 2 K.B. 235, *semble. Sed quaere* if the minor sues on the contract for damages for breach; *cf.* (1958) 74 L.Q.R. 97, 104 [Treitel].

[4] *R. Leslie Ltd.* v. *Sheill* [1914] 3 K.B. 607.

[5] *Re King* (1858) 3 De G. & J. 63. *Cf. Teynham* v. *Webb* (1751) 2 Ves.Sen. 198, 212, *per* Lord Hardwicke; *Nottingham Permanent Building Society* v. *Thurstan* [1903] A.C. 6.

[6] (1913) 29 L.Q.R. 249; (1914) 30 L.Q.R. 387 [Sir F. Pollock]; and see Salmond and Williams, *Contracts*, p. 318.

creditors.[7] As the law now stands, therefore, it is doubtful whether a restitutionary proprietary claim, to recover from a minor property or its product, obtained by the minor's fraud, will succeed. The property in the goods will have generally passed to the minor[8]; and, in most cases, it may be difficult to spell out a fiduciary relationship, which is still said to be a *sine qua non* of an equitable proprietary claim, although the courts are now astute in finding such a relationship.[9] Subject to the rule of policy that restitutionary remedies should not be employed indirectly to enforce contracts which are void at law, there is, however, much to be said for the view that a proprietary claim should always be available in cases of fraud. If the minor should become bankrupt, his general creditors should not be enabled to benefit from his fraudulent conduct. If it is necessary to do so, the courts should hold that the equitable title to the property remained in the claimant and thereby impose a lien over the minor's property.[10]

So far we have assumed that the equity will only be available to the other party in cases of fraud. But in *Clarke* v. *Cobley*,[11] where equitable relief was granted, there is no indication of fraud in the report. A minor should be compelled to make restitution when he has failed to give consideration whether or not he has been fraudulent. In these cases, equity may regard the retention of the proceeds as fraud in itself; for "it can hardly be denied that ordinarily, one seeking to retain property obtained under a contract while pleading infancy to a claim for the price is acting dishonestly and unconscionably."[12]

3. CONTRACTS MADE BY COMPANIES AND CORPORATIONS

(A) Ultra Vires Contracts

(a) *Ultra Vires Contracts Made by Companies Incorporated Under the Companies Act 1985*

At common law a contract entered into by a company beyond the powers expressly or impliedly conferred upon it by statute or memorandum of association was rendered void. Such is the common law doctrine of *ultra vires*, which the House of Lords firmly endorsed in the leading case of *Ashbury Railway Carriage and Iron Co. Ltd.* v. *Riche*[13] in 1875. In recent years the doctrine of

---

[7] *R. Leslie Ltd.* v. *Sheill* [1914] 3 K.B. 617, 619, *per* Lord Sumner.
[8] *Cf.* (1959) 22 M.L.R. 273, 282–286 [Atiyah].
[9] See above, Chap. 2.
[10] See above, Chap. 2 for the difficulties of "identifying" that property.
[11] (1789) 2 Cox 173; see above, p. 537, n. 99. *Cf.* (1959) 22 M.L.R. 273–276 [Atiyah].
[12] Salmond and Williams, *op. cit.* p. 319.
[13] (1875) L.R. 7 H.L. 653, H.L.

ultra vires has had few admirers. Section 108 of the Companies Act 1989, amending section 35 of the Companies Act 1985, has now given it its virtual quietus, in respect of contracts made by companies incorporated under the 1985 Act.

Section 35 of the 1985 Act, which sought to implement one part of the EEC's first Directive on company law, was infelicitously drafted. It was not all clear how far it did achieve one of the Directive's principal purposes, namely, to "guarantee the security of transactions between companies and those with whom they deal."[14] Sections 35A and 35B are now substituted for it. Their provisions can be summarised as follows:

(1) "The validity of an act done by a company shall not be called into question on the ground of lack of capacity by reason of anything in the company's memorandum" (section 35(1)). It can now no longer be said that a contract is void because of the company's lack of capacity. Moreover, this provision operates both in favour of the company and the person dealing with it.

A member of the company may, however, bring proceedings to restrain an act which would be (but for section 35(1)) beyond the company's capacity. But these proceedings cannot impugn "an act to be done in fulfilment of a legal obligation arising from a previous act of the company" (section 35(2)).

(2) "*In favour of a person dealing with a company in good faith*, the power of the board of directors to bind the company, or authorise others to do so, shall be deemed to be free of any limitation under the company's constitution" (section 35(A)(1)) (emphasis supplied). This subsection is designed to protect such a person if a contract is attacked, not on the ground that the company did not have capacity, but on the ground that it was beyond the powers of the directors to enter into that contract.[15] As the italicised words demonstrate, it confers no rights on the company.

The statute also embodies presumptions designed to protect a person dealing with the company.[16] "A person shall not be regarded as acting in bad faith by reason only of his knowing that an act is beyond the powers of the directors under the company's constitution" (section 35A(2)(*b*)); and "a person shall be presumed to have acted in good faith unless the contrary is proved" (section 35A(2)(*c*)). The burden is therefore on the company to demonstrate a lack of good faith.[17] Furthermore, "a party to a transaction with a company is not bound to inquire as to whether it is permitted by the company's memorandum or as to any limitation on the powers of the board of directors to bind the company or authorise others to do so" (section 35B).

---

[14] See (1973) 89 L.Q.R. 518, 523 [Prentice].

[15] However, s.35(3) imposes a duty on the directors to observe any limitations on their powers imposed by the memorandum of association; a special resolution is necessary to ratify acts which would be (but for s.35(1)) beyond the company's capacity.

[16] "[A] person" deals with "a company if he is a party to any transaction or other act to which the company is a party": s.35A(2)(*a*).

[17] *Cf. International Sales and Agencies Ltd.* v. *Marcus* [1982] 3 All E.R. 551, 560, *per* Lawson J.

Again, a member of the company may restrain acts beyond the directors' powers; however, legal obligations arising from previous acts of the company cannot be questioned in any legal proceedings (section 35A(4)).

The doctrine of *ultra vires* is now, if the company is incorporated under the Companies Act 1985, effectively dead. Only if a person dealing with a company incorporated under the Companies Act 1985 acts in bad faith, within section 35(A), can the question of the relevance of any restitutionary claim arise. Such a case may arise if a company enters into a contract with another which both parties know is beyond the power of the directors to bind the company *and* which is made, in breach of the directors' fiduciary duties, in order to unjustly enrich the contracting parties at the expense of the company.[18] The contract is then *ultra vires* and void. In these circumstances it is inconceivable that the courts would grant either party a restitutionary claim. Indeed the directors and the other party would, in these circumstances, be held to be constructive trustees of any identifiable gain or, if the gain is not identifiable, to account for any profit.[19]

(b) *Companies Incorporated by Special Statute other than under the Companies Act 1985: and Corporations Incorporated by Royal Charter*

The common law is still relevant if the restitutionary claim arises out of a contract entered into by a company which is incorporated by special statute or by a corporation which is incorporated by royal charter but whose powers are circumscribed by a special statute. A prominent and recent illustration of such a claim is that of the banks which had entered into so-called "swap" contracts, with local authorities and which the House of Lords declared to be *ultra vires*.[20] Whether a restitutionary claim arising from these void contracts will be upheld may depend, not only on the terms of the particular contracts, but on whether *Re Phoenix Life Assurance Company, Burges' and Stocks' Case*[21] was correctly decided.

In *Sinclair* v. *Brougham*,[22] the House held that to allow a personal claim based on an *ultra vires* loan contract would "strike at the root of the doctrine of *ultra vires* as established in the jurisprudence of this country."[23] In contrast, in the *Phoenix Life Assurance* case, Sir William Page Wood V.-C. held that the other party who had paid premiums to a company under an *ultra vires* marine insurance contract could prove for the amount of premiums paid. In *Sinclair* v.

---

[18] *Cf.* below, Chap. 33.

[19] *Cf. International Sales and Agencies Ltd.* v. *Marcus* [1982] 3 All E.R. 551. Even if the shareholders unanimously consent to be parties retaining their gains, the transaction may be set aside as amounting to a fraud on creditors: *cf. Aveling Barford Ltd.* v. *Parion Ltd.* [1989] BCLC 626.

[20] *Hazell* v. *Hammersmith and Fulham London Borough Council* [1991] 2 W.L.R. 372.

[21] (1862) 2 J. & H. 441.

[22] [1914] A.C. 398; see above, p. 63, for a suggestion that this was a stringent application of the *ultra vires* doctrine.

[23] *Sinclair* v. *Brougham* [1914] A.C. 398, 414, *per* Viscount Haldane. Nonetheless, the House allowed the *ultra vires* depositors to trace their money into the Society's hands and to share *pari passu* with the shareholders of the building society: see above, pp. 83 *et seq.*

Brougham Lord Parker was careful to point out[24] that none of the cases, which precluded recovery in borrowing contracts,

> "would bind the House, if they were considering whether action would lie in law or in equity to recover money paid under any *ultra vires* contract which was not a contract of borrowing; for example, money paid to a company or association for the purchase of land which the company had no power to sell and the sale of which was therefore void, or money paid to the company or association by way of subscription for shares which it had no power to issue. In such cases the implied promise on which the action for money had and received depends would form no part of, but would be merely collateral to, the *ultra vires* contract."

Although Lord Parker left open the question whether *Re Phoenix Life Assurance* was correctly decided, there is much to be said for the view that, in these and comparable circumstances, the money should be recoverable from the company; to do so would not result in the indirect enforcement of an *ultra vires* contract. Indeed, in two of the "lead" swap actions, *Westdeutsche Landesbank Girozentrale* v. *The Council of the London Borough of Islington* and *Kleinwort Benson Ltd.* v. *The Borough Council of Sandwell*,[24a] Hobhouse J. held that the plaintiffs were entitled to recover the sums "lent" at common law as money had and received by the defendants to the use of the plaintiffs. Moreover, they were entitled to trace their money in equity into the hands of the defendants; their position was indistinguishable from that of the *ultra vires* depositors in *Sinclair* v. *Brougham*.[24b] The ground of the claim, both at law and in equity, was that the defendant had been unjustly enriched at the plaintiffs' expense; they had paid under a purported contract which was, unbeknown to them, void. Consequently, the money had been paid "without consideration."[24c] It was not necessary to demonstrate that there had been a *total* failure of consideration. Indeed, given the fact that there had been some payments both by the plaintiffs to the defendants and vice versa, "on a contractual analysis there was no 'total failure of consideration.' " It is debatable whether the distinction which the judge drew between a payment made *without* consideration and a payment made for a consideration which *totally* failed is a real one. In any event, it would appear that the consideration for each party's payment had totally failed, for both parties could repay the other the *ultra vires* payments which had been made to the other.

In the judge's view the doctrine of *ultra vires* and the decision of the House of Lords in *Sinclair* v. *Brougham* did not bar the restitutionary claim. In that case,

---

[24] At p. 440; *cf.* Viscount Haldane, at p. 416.

[24a] Unreported, February 12, 1993.

[24b] [1914] A.C. 398: above p. 83. However, each party had intended to advance credit to the other. For that reason it is difficult to support the conclusion that they could follow *their* property in equity, although, given the authority of *Sinclair v. Brougham* it may be one which only the House of Lords can reject.

[24c] *Cf. Woolwich Equitable Building Society* v. *Inland Revenue Commissioners* [1993] A.C. 70, 197, *per* Lord Browne-Wilkinson: below, p. 548.

the transaction was a borrowing transaction and a promise to repay could not be implied because of the Building Societies Act. Consequently, its facts were clearly distinguishable from the facts of the present cases, where the banks did not seek directly or indirectly to enforce the *ultra vires* transaction. "Their claims are the reverse of that. They do not allege or need to allege any promise to repay. They simply say that the councils have received their money under void contracts and that they should have it back."

A claim *by the other party* to obtain recompense for goods delivered or services rendered under an *ultra vires* contract is, however, on the very slender English authority,[25] doomed to failure. Canadian courts have interpreted the *ultra vires* doctrine more narrowly and have upheld such a claim, at least where the other party was not aware that the contract was *ultra vires* the company[26]; and this, we consider, is a proper and just conclusion.

The case law, such as it is, suggests that the courts have viewed more sympathetically claims brought *by a company*, arising out of an executed *ultra vires* transaction, against the other party. To allow a restitutionary claim would not undermine the *ultra vires* doctrine; consequently the other party should not be allowed to "take advantage of a doctrine, manifestly for the protection of the shareholders, in order to deprive the company of money which in justice should be paid to it by the [other party]."[27]

(B) Pre-Incorporation Contracts

At common law a company which has not been incorporated does not exist. And if a company does not exist, it cannot enter a binding contract. The rigour of the common law has been mitigated by section 36C of the Companies Act 1985 which provides that:

> "A contract which purports to be made by or on behalf of a company at a time when the company has not yet been formed has effect, subject to any agreement to the contrary, as one made with a person purporting to act for the company or as agent for it, and he is personally liable on the contract accordingly."

But it has been held that the section has no application if the company adopts a new name and enters into a contract before the amended certificate of incorporation has been issued;[28] if it is incorporated outside the United Kingdom[29]; or if, having been incorporated, it had been struck off the register at the

---

[25] *Re Jon Beauforte (London) Ltd.* [1953] Ch. 131.

[26] For the cases, see Maddaugh and McCamus, *op. cit.* pp. 322 *et seq.*

[27] See *Bell Houses Ltd.* v. *City Wall Properties Ltd.* [1966] 2 Q.B. 656, 694, *per* Salmon L.J. and *Re K.L. Tractors Ltd.* (1961) 106 C.L.R. 318, 337–338, *per* Fullagar J. In *Brougham* v. *Dwyer* (1913) 108 L.T. 504 the liquidator of a building society which had carried on an *ultra vires* banking business recovered, in an action for money had and received, the amount of a customer's overdraft.

[28] *Oshkosh B'Gosh Ltd.* v. *Dan Marbel Inc. Ltd.* [1989] BCLC 507.

[29] *Rover International Ltd.* v. *Cannon Film Sales Ltd.* [1987] 1 W.L.R. 1597.

date of entering into the contract.[30] It is true that, if subsequently incorporated, the company can enter into a new contract. But the courts have been reluctant to reach this conclusion; for example, it is not enough that the company's memorandum provides that it shall carry out the pre-incorporation contract,[31] or if it adopts that contract because the directors mistakenly believed that it was contractually bound to do so.[32] Moreover, it cannot ratify the original contract[33]; and the Jenkins' Report's recommendation[34] that it should be granted the power so to do has never been implemented.

In these exceptional circumstances, when section 36C has no application, is a person who has paid money to the "company," incurred expenses on its behalf or rendered services from which it benefited, without remedy? Both Vaughan Williams and Romer L.JJ. expressed, on more than one occasion,[35] the austere view that " . . . [T]here is no binding authority for the proposition that a company, because it has taken the benefit of work done under a contract entered into before the formation of the company, can be made liable in equity under that contract." Consequently, they firmly rejected Mellish L.J.'s earlier dictum[36] that the plaintiff was entitled to an equitable lien over property, which he had improved, to secure payment of the reasonable value of his services.

More recent cases conclude, however, that a restitutionary claim may, in some circumstances, lie. In *Cotronic (U.K.) Ltd.* v. *Dezonie*[37] the company had been incorporated but had been, unbeknown to the parties, struck off the register. Although the Court of Appeal held that section 35C of the Companies Act 1985 had no application, it assumed that the plaintiff which had rendered building services was entitled to bring an action on a *quantum meruit*. Again, in *Rover International Ltd.* v. *Cannon Film Sales Ltd.*[38] the Court of Appeal held that Rover was entitled to recover up front advances which had been paid after its incorporation, in pursuance of a contract entered into before it was incorporated. In the view of the Court the money had been paid under a mistake of fact; both parties mistakenly thought that "there was a contract between them, and [paid] in order to satisfy Rover's obligations under that contract."[39] Kerr L.J. also concluded that the money had been paid for a consideration which had totally failed.[40] Rover had also rendered services, requested by Cannon,

---

[30] *Cotronic (U.K.) Ltd.* v. *Dezonie* [1991] BCLC 721; below, n. 37. See also *Badgerhill Properties Ltd.* v. *Cottrell* [1991] BCLC 805, C.A.

[31] *Melhado* v. *Porto Alegre Rly. Co.* (1874) L.R. 9 C.P. 503.

[32] *Re Northumberland Avenue Hotel Co.* (1886) 33 Ch.D. 16; *Bagot Pneumatic Tyre Co.* v. *Clipper Pneumatic Tyre Co.* [1902] 1 Ch. 146.

[33] *Kelner* v. *Baxter* (1866) L.R. 2 C.P. 174.

[34] Report of the Company Law Committee, Cmnd. 1749 (1962), para. 54(a).

[35] *Re English and Colonial Produce Co. Ltd.* [1906] 2 Ch. 435, 442, 444; see also *Bagot Pneumatic Tyre Co.* v. *Clipper Pneumatic Tyre Co.* [1902] 1 Ch. 146, 156.

[36] *Re Hereford and South Wales Waggon and Engineering Co.* (1876) 2 Ch.D. 621.

[37] [1991] BCLC 721.

[38] [1989] 1 W.L.R. 912, C.A. Section 35C(1) of the Companies Act 1985 was not applicable since Rover was a foreign company: see above, Chap. 17.

[39] At p. 933, *per* Dillon L.J.

[40] At pp. 925 *et seq.* See above, p. 401.

under the ineffective contract. It was conceded by Cannon's counsel that Rover was entitled to recover on a *quantum meruit*, and the Court did not question the propriety of that concession.

In both these cases the plaintiff had conferred a benefit on the defendant company. The receipt of money is manifestly an enrichment.[41] In *Rover International* the Court of Appeal assumed that the services rendered had enriched the defendant company. This attractive conclusion can be supported on the ground that the company had been incontrovertibly benefited by the receipt of the services; the analogy of *Craven-Ellis* v. *Canons Ltd.*[42] is persuasive. Again, in both *Cotronic* and *Rover International* the enrichment had been unjustly gained at the plaintiff's expense. The plaintiffs mistakenly thought that the contract was a valid one; because of that mistake they had paid money and had rendered services.

In *Craven-Ellis* v. *Canons Ltd.*[43] the Court of Appeal held that the plaintiff was entitled to recover on a *quantum meruit* for the services which he had rendered; the company accepted services "which, if they had not been performed by the plaintiff, [the company] would have to get some other agent to carry out." The Court reached this conclusion even though the contract was void for want of authority. There was no finding of fact that the plaintiff was or was not mistaken.[44] This decision may persuade a court to recognise a restitutionary claim even though the plaintiff knew at the time when he conferred the benefit that the company was not incorporated, but had acted as he did in the expectation that he would be paid the sum designated in the agreement. However, in our tentative view, a finding of fact that the defendant had not acted improperly and that the plaintiff had conferred the benefit on the "company" with his eyes open to the true facts is fatal to the success of his claim. He has then taken the risk that the company would not be incorporated and would not pay him for what he had done. In such a case there is the possibility that a plaintiff may be subrogated to the rights of the promoter where the promoter had entered into a new contract, in identical terms, with the company after its incorporation.[45]

---

[41] See above, p. 17.
[42] [1936] 2 K.B. 403, discussed above, p. 478.
[43] *Ibid.*
[44] See above, p. 480.
[45] It is a mere *possibility* which is enshrined in a cautious dictum in Romer L.J.'s judgment in *Bagot Pneumatic Tyre Co.* v. *Clipper Pneumatic Tyre Co.* [1902] 1 Ch. 146.

CHAPTER 24

MONEY PAID TO THE REVENUE OR TO A PUBLIC AUTHORITY PURSUANT TO AN ULTRA VIRES DEMAND

UNTIL the recent decisions of the Court of Appeal and the House of Lords in *Woolwich Equitable Building Society* v. *Commissioners of Inland Revenue*,[1] it appeared to be settled law, at least at the level of the Court of Appeal,[2] that money paid and only paid in consequence of an *ultra vires* demand by a public authority was irrecoverable. To succeed, the taxpayer had to demonstrate that the payment had been made under a mistake of fact[3] (a mistake of law normally defeated his claim)[4] or under compulsion, a concept which embraced payments made in consequence of a demand *colore officii*.

> "Extortion by colour of office occurs when a public officer demands and is paid money he is not entitled to, or more than he is entitled to, for the performance of his public duty. ... The parties were not on an equal footing; and generally the payer paid the sum demanded in ignorance that it was not due."[5]

This statement of principle, pithily summarising a body of case law which dates from the early seventeenth century,[6] "effectively dispose[s] of any suggestion that because the person making the demand holds some official position that of itself amounts to a form of compulsion."[7] Furthermore, even if money is paid under a mistake of fact or under compulsion, the payer's claim will still fail if, having had the opportunity of contesting his liability in proceedings, he gives way and pays, with the intention of closing the transaction.[8]

In *Woolwich Equitable Building Society* v. *Commissioners of Inland Revenue*, Woolwich submitted under protest to the Revenue's demand for taxes, and did

---

[1] [1993] A.C. 70.
[2] [1993] A.C. 70, 164–166, *per* Lord Goff.
[3] See above, Chap. 3.
[4] See above, Chap. 4.
[5] *Mason* v. *The State of New South Wales* (1959) 102 C.L.R. 108, 140, *per* Windeyer J., adopted by Lord Jauncey in *Woolwich Equitable Building Society* v. *Commissioners of Inland Revenue* [1992] A.C. 70, 179.
[6] See above, pp. 243 *et seq.*
[7] *Woolwich Equitable Building Society* v. *Commissioners of Inland Revenue* [1993] A.C. 70, 179, *per* Lord Jauncey; see also *per* Lord Keith, at p. 154–156.
[8] See above, p. 127 and below, p. 551; and see *Woolwich Equitable Building Society* v. *Commissioners of Inland Revenue* [1992] A.C. 70, 165, *per* Lord Goff.

so for a number of sound commercial, financial and legal reasons.[9] Subsequently it challenged by judicial review the validity of the statutory regulations which were the basis of the Revenue's demand. The House of Lords held that the regulations were *ultra vires*.[10] By writ of summons Woolwich then claimed repayment of its payments and interest from the dates of those payments. It was entitled to interest if each payment was a debt due to it from the date when made; only then would the court have power to award interest.[11] The Revenue repaid the payments, but disputed the claim for interest.

Nolan J. dismissed Woolwich's claim. The Court of Appeal upheld it.[12] Woolwich was entitled to repayment as of right.[13] The House of Lords affirmed the judgment of the Court of Appeal. Lord Keith and Lord Jauncey dissented.[14] They concluded that the precedents were clear; the taxpayer could not recover unless he could demonstrate that he made the payment under duress,[15] and there was none.[16] Moreover:

> "[t]o give effect to Woolwich's proposition would, in [Lord Keith's] opinion, amount to a very far reaching exercise of judicial legislation. That would be particularly inappropriate having regard to the considerable number of instances which exist of Parliament having legislated in various fields to define the circumstances under which payments of tax not lawfully due may be recovered, and also in what situations and upon what terms interest on overpayments of tax may be paid."[17]

The majority of the House of Lords, Lord Goff, Lord Browne-Wilkinson and Lord Slynn, accepted that, with the exception of a few if powerful dissenting voices,[18] the precedents lead to the conclusion that Woolwich's claim should fail. At the same time, there was "nothing in the authorities which precludes your Lordship's House from laying down that money paid by way of

---

[9] These are summarised by Nolan J. in [1989] 1 W.L.R. 137, 142–143, cited by Lord Keith [1992] A.C. 70; and see above, p. 147.
[10] *R.* v. *Commissioners of Inland Revenue, ex p. Woolwich Building Society* [1990] 1 W.L.R. 1400.
[11] Under Supreme Court Act 1981, s.35A.
[12] [1993] A.C. 70 (C.A. and H.L.) Ralph Gibson L.J. dissenting.
[13] The Court of Appeal concluded that there were two exceptions to this principle, not applicable on the facts, namely that money was paid under mistake of law or was paid to close the transaction.
[14] But their Lordships were unanimous that there was no implied agreement that the Revenue would repay the sums in issue.
[15] There was no suggestion that the money had been paid under a mistake of fact, which would be another ground of recovery: [1993] A.C. 70, 173, *per* Lord Goff, see above, Chap. 3.
[16] [1993] A.C. 70, 192-193, *per* Lord Jauncey. *Cf.* p. 173, *per* Lord Goff ("the possibility of distraint by the Revenue was very remote").
[17] [1993] A.C. 70, 161. For a comprehensive summary of the legislation, see the Law Commission's Consultation Paper No. 120, *Restitution of Payments Made Under a Mistake of Law*, pp. 74–84.
[18] *e.g. Campbell* v. *Hall* (1774) Cowp. 204, 205, *per* Lord Mansfield; *Steele* v. *Williams* (1853) 8 Ex. 625, 632–633, *per* Martin B.; *Att.-Gen.* v. *Wilts. United Dairy Ltd.* (1921) 37 T.L.R. 884, 887, *per* Atkin L.J.
For the history of the litigation in *Campbell* v. *Hall*, see [1993] A.C. 70, 166.

tax following an ultra vires demand by the Revenue is recoverable."[19] The paramount consideration which persuaded the majority of the House to affirm the decision of the Court of Appeal and to uphold Woolwich's claim was the simple justice of that claim. Faced with the Revenue's demand, which Woolwich was advised was *ultra vires*, it decided to pay first and fight later. It did so because it knew that collection proceedings would be gravely embarrassing, "the more so as it would have been the only building society refusing to pay," and it "feared that if it failed in its legal arguments it might incur penalties."[20] Contemporaneous with its payments Woolwich warned the Revenue that it would challenge the lawfulness of the demand. It did so, and won. The Revenue's response to its claim for repayment with interest, that it was not obliged to repay and that it did so only as a matter of grace, was, in Lord Goff's view:

> "Stated in this stark form, ... as a matter of common justice to be unsustainable; and the injustice is rendered worse by the fact that it involves, as Nolan J. pointed out, the Revenue having the benefit of a massive interest-free loan as the fruit of its unlawful action. I turn then from the particular to the general. Take any tax or duty paid by the citizen pursuant to an unlawful demand. Common justice seems to me to require that tax to be repaid, unless special circumstances or some principle of policy require otherwise; prima facie the taxpayer should be entitled to repayment as of right."[21]

It was not too late to acknowledge that, given article 4 of the Bill of Rights 1689,[22] "retention by the state of taxes unlawfully exacted is particularly obnoxious." A court can only give full effect to the principle enshrined in the Bill of Rights, that taxes should not be levied without the authority of Parliament, "if the return of taxes exacted under an unlawful demand can be enforced as a matter of right."[23] Moreover, it was not too late to recognise, in

---

[19] [1993] A.C. 70, 201, *per* Lord Slynn.
[20] [1989] 1 W.L.R. 137, 142–143, *per* Nolan J., for a fuller statement of all the reasons which led Woolwich to make its payments; see the citations in n. 9.
The Finance Act 1991, s.53, clipped the wings of other building societies which had not been brave enough to challenge the Revenue's demand.
[21] [1992] A.C. 70, 172 *per* Lord Goff.
[22] "That levying money for or to the use of the Crowne by pretence of prerogative without grant of Parliament for longer time or in other manner than the same is or shall be granted is illegal": Art. 4.
[23] [1993] A.C. 70, 172, *per* Lord Goff.
For the particular reasons which led Lord Goff to conclude that Woolwich should recover, see [1993] A.C. 70, 176–178; *inter alia*, it is most unlikely that any government would enact the common law principle; the immediate practical impact of the recognition of the common law principle will be limited; it should give impetus to the Law Commission's deliberations (see above, p. 546, n. 17) on legislative reform; money paid from the consolidated fund without authority is recoverable by the Crown (see above, p. 160)—the comparison with the taxpayer's position is "most unattractive"; and the jurisprudence of the European Court suggests that the taxpayer might recover his payments, on which see below, n. 65.
His Lordship concluded (at p. 171) that, if the Revenue was not contractually bound to repay, any residual discretion it enjoyed to make repayments could only be challenged on "very narrow grounds such as bad faith": *contra* Lord Keith at pp. 150–152.

the words of Holmes J. in *Atchison, Topeka & Santa Fe Railway Company* v. *O'Connor*,[24] which Lord Goff,[25] Lord Browne-Wilkinson[25a] and Lord Slynn[26] endorsed, that:

> "It is reasonable that a man who denies the legality of a tax should have a clear and certain remedy. The rule being established that apart from special circumstances he cannot interfere by injunction with the state's collection of its revenues, an action at law to recover back what he has paid is the alternative left. Of course we are speaking of those cases where the state is not put to an action if the citizen refuses to pay. In these latter he can interpose his objections by way of defence, but, when, as is common, the state has a more summary remedy, such as distress, and the party indicates by protest that he is yielding to what he cannot prevent, courts sometimes perhaps have been a little too slow to recognise the implied duress under which payment is made. But even if the state is driven to an action, if at the same time the citizen is put at a serious disadvantage in the assertion of his legal, and in this case of his constitutional, rights, by defence in the suit, justice may require that he should be at liberty to avoid those disadvantages by paying promptly and bringing suit on his side. He is entitled to assert his supposed right on reasonably equal terms."

In such circumstances the money is, as Lord Mansfield said, paid "without any consideration."[27] Lord Browne-Wilkinson found this approach "attractive: money paid on the footing that there is a legal demand is paid for a reason that does not exist if that demand is a nullity." In his view, there is a "close analogy to the right to recover money paid under a contract the consideration for which has wholly failed."[28]

The majority of the House of Lords were not persuaded that, in allowing Woolwich to recover, the House, sitting in its judicial capacity, would arrogate to itself legislative powers. Lord Slynn did[29]:

---

[24] 223 U.S. 280, 285–286 (1912). *Cf.* Dixon C.J. in *Mason* v. *New South Wales* (1959) 102 C.L.R. 108, 116: see above, p. 244. See generally, "Restitution of Taxes, Levies and other Imposts: Defining the Extent of the Woolwich Principle" (1993) 109 L.Q.R. 401, 411–412 [J. Beatson].

[25] [1993] A.C. 70, 172–173.

[25a] [1993] A.C. 70, 198.

[26] At p. 203.

[27] *Campbell* v. *Hall* (1774) 1 Cowp. 204, 205. The full quotation reads as follows:
"The action is an action for money had and received; and it is brought upon this ground; namely, that the money was paid to the defendant without any consideration; the duty, for which, and in respect of which he received it, not having been imposed by lawful or sufficient authority to warrant the same."
Cf. Steele v. *Williams* (1853) 8 Ex. 625, 632 ("money paid without consideration"); *Queen of the River Steamship Co. Ltd.* v. *Conservators of the River Thames* (1899) 15 T.L.R. 474, cited in [1993] A.C. 70, 197, *per* Lord Browne-Wilkinson.

[28] [1993] A.C. 70, 197. *Semble want* of consideration and *total* failure of consideration are synonymous concepts.

[29] There was, moreover, no statutory provision (in particular s.33 of the Taxes Management Act 1970) upon which Woolwich could rely to reclaim the money and interest: [1993] A.C. 70, 169, *per* Lord Goff, 199 *per* Lord Slynn.

" . . . not consider that the fact that Parliament has legislated extensively in this area means that no principle of recovery at common law can or should at this stage of the development of the law be found to exist. If the principle does exist that tax paid on a demand from the Crown when the tax was the subject of an ultra vires demand can be recovered as money had and received then, in my view, it is for the courts to declare it. In doing so they do not usurp the legislative function. I regard the proper approach as the converse."[29a]

If the legislature were to conclude that the common law right is an "unbridled" right[30] and if it were to determine that the traditional common law defences are inadequate, then it is always open to the legislature to enact its own special defences.[31]

The judgments of the House of Lords in the *Woolwich* case, which reflect the influence of academic writers, particularly Professor Cornish[32] and Professor Birks,[33] on the development of the law of restitution[34] leave unanswered, or at least not unequivocally answered, a number of questions.

First, the *ultra vires* demand in *Woolwich* was made by the Revenue. But both the judgments of Lord Goff and Lord Browne-Wilkinson suggest that "money paid by a citizen to any *public authority* in the form of taxes or other levies paid pursuant to an *ultra vires* demand by the authority is recoverable by the citizen as of right."[35] As Lord Browne-Wilkinson said[36]:

" . . . where the parties are on an unequal footing so that money is paid by way of tax or other impost in pursuance of a demand by some public officer, these moneys are recoverable since the citizen is, in practice, unable to resist the payment save at the risk of breaking the law or exposing himself to penalties or other disadvantages."

[29a] [1993] A.C. 70, 200.

[30] This is Lord Goff's phrase: at p. 174.

[31] [1993] A.C. 70, 174, *per* Lord Goff, who cites the example of the Draconian limitation periods of German law; and at p. 200 *per* Lord Slynn.

[32] "Colour of Office: Restitutionary Redress against Public Authority" (1987) 14 Jo. of Mal. and Comp. Law 41.

[33] "Restitution from the Executive: a Tercentenary Footnote to the Bill of Rights" in *Essays in Restitution* (ed. Finn 1990), pp. 164 *et seq.*

[34] [1993] A.C. 70, 166, *per* Lord Goff.

[35] [1993] A.C. 70, 179, *per* Lord Goff (emphasis supplied).
It is unclear what is a "*public authority*"; for example, are privatised industries and harbour and ferry boards public authorities? For a discussion, see (1993) 109 L.Q.R. 401, 410 *et seq.* [Beatson], who argues that "*public authority*" embraces, not only governmental bodies, but also "other public bodies whose authority to charge is subject to and limited by public law principles, and to other bodies whose authority to charge is solely the product of statute, and thus limited."

[36] At p. 198: see above p. 548 and below p. 551; and *cf.* [1991] 4 All E.R. 577, 583, *per* Glidewell L.J. and 634, *per* Butler-Sloss L.J. But contrast the speech of Lord Slynn who only speaks of "tax."

Moreover, as these quotations demonstrate, the common law principle, enunciated in *Woolwich*, is not, in their view, limited to taxes *strictu sensu*.[36a]

Secondly, Lord Slynn was of the opinion that the *Woolwich* common law principle applied when the money was paid, in consequence of an *ultra vires* demand, under a mistake of law. "That is the situation where the relief is most likely to be needed and if it is excluded not much is left."[37] Lord Goff did not consider that "the principle of recovery should be inapplicable simply because the citizen has paid the money under a mistake of law."[38] In such a case relief is not available under the Taxes Management Act 1970.[39] Consequently, at common law it is no defence to the Revenue, as it would be a defence if an application was made for relief under the statute, that the return of the taxpayer was made on "the basis of or in accordance with the [Revenue] practice generally prevailing at the time when the return was made,"[40] but which was subsequently shown to be wrong in law.

Thirdly, there are cautious dicta in the case which suggest that the *Woolwich* common law principle would apply if the public authority's demand was based on its misconstruction of an *intra vires* statute or statutory regulation.[41] Given the dicta cited in the previous paragraph, it is arguable that the taxpayer would, subject to any appropriate defences,[42] recover his payments even if he shared the Revenue's mistake or even if he paid under protest, having been advised that the Revenue were not entitled in law to make the demand on him. The Supreme Court of Canada has reached a similar conclusion.[43]

Here then is yet another potential exception to the rule in *Bilbie* v. *Lumley*.[44] On these facts, however, the Revenue may enjoy the defence, already discussed, that the taxpayer's return was made in accordance with the Revenue practice generally prevailing at the time of that return.

Fourthly, the House of Lords did not accept or reject the rule in *Bilbie* v. *Lumley*[45]; it was not necessary to consider it. Only Lord Keith considered that it was "too deeply embedded in English jurisprudence to be uprooted judicially."[46] In contrast, Lord Slynn thought it was open to review by the House.[47]

[36a] See the dicta of the Court of Appeal, cited above n.36, suggesting that a tax, customs duty, licence fees or similar imposts paid in consequence of a demand by an officer of central or local government, are recoverable.

[37] At p. 205.

[38] At p. 177.

[39] s.33(1): see above, p. 161. See (1993) 109 L.Q.R. 401, 419, *et seq.* [Beatson] for a full discussion of the statutory provision.

[40] s.33(2), discussed above, pp. 161–162.

[41] [1993] A.C. 70, 177, *per* Lord Goff, 200 *per* Lord Slynn. See also Lord Jauncey at p. 192, doubting whether a payment under a mistake of law can be properly described as a voluntary payment and whether "the distinction between mistake of fact and law can [in this limited context] be justified any longer."

[42] See below, Chaps. 40 *et seq.*

[43] In *Air Canada* v. *British Columbia* [1989] 4 W.W.R. 137: see above, p. 145 and below, p. 551.

[44] (1802) 2 East 469: see above, Chap. 4.

[45] See above, n. 41.

[46] [1993] A.C. 70, 154.

[47] At p. 199. *Cf.* Lord Goff (at p. 174), citing Dickson J.'s dissenting judgment in *Hydro Electric Commission of Township of Nepean* v. *Ontario Hydro* (1982) 132 D.L.R. (3d) 193 and commenting on his "devastating analysis" of the rationale of the mistake of law rule. Dickson J.'s

Such a review would be necessary and critical if the legislature failed to implement proposals which will be doubtless forthcoming from the Law Commission for reform of the law.[48]

Fifthly, it was not necessary for the House to consider whether there were any appropriate defences to the Revenue's claim; the question did not rise. In the *Air Canada* case, Wilson J., in a powerful dissenting judgment,[49] held that where "the payments were made pursuant to an unconstitutional statute, there is no legitimate basis on which they can be retained." It would appear from her judgment that she would not accept any defence to the taxpayer's claim for she peremptorily dismissed such defences as "fiscal chaos will result if restitution is ordered" or the taxpayer had not been enriched in that it had passed on the tax to its customers. But Lord Goff and Lord Slynn do not go so far as to suggest that the public authority may never have a defence to a restitutionary claim,[50] although, in the Court of Appeal, Ralph Gibson L.J. did not reject the logic of Wilson J.'s reasoning.[51] What then are the possible defences open to the Revenue on facts similar to, or comparable to, the *Woolwich* case?

(1) The payment was made *to close the transaction*; this is a voluntary payment.[52] A payment is not normally so made if it is made under protest; however, courts have envisaged that, even if a payment is made under duress, exceptionally it may have been made because the payer cannot be bothered to dispute the defendant's claim.[53]

(2) The payer could have *contested his liability in proceedings and did not do so*. Certainly, this is no defence if the taxpayer paid under protest, warning the Revenue that he intended to take immediate proceedings to recover his payment and did so. These are the facts of *Woolwich*. In the context of claims against the Revenue this defence may manifest itself in the submission that Order 53 of the Rules of the Supreme Court requires the plaintiff to proceed through an application for judicial review,[54] and he is now out of time.[55] There is, however, no provision for joining a claim for restitution, as distinct from damages, with an application for judicial review.[56] It is speculative whether the courts will hold that "damages" within Order 53 embraces a restitutionary claim, or will conclude that a plaintiff may proceed by writ if his claim cannot

---

judgment was subsequently endorsed by the Supreme Court of Canada in *Air Canada* v. *British Columbia* [1989] 4 W.W.R. 97: see above, p. 145.

[48] See above, n. 17.

[49] [1989] 4 W.W.R. 97, 107.

[50] [1992] A.C. 70, 176, *per* Lord Goff (although he found her reasoning "most attractive").

[51] [1991] 3 W.L.R. 790, 836–837. The Lord Justice was dissenting, so this observation was strictly *obiter*.

[52] See above, pp. 50 *et seq.*

[53] See, *e.g. Maskell* v. *Horner* [1915] 3 K.B. 106, 118, *per* Lord Reading: see above, pp. 268–272 for a full discussion.

[54] *O'Reilly* v. *Mackman* [1983] 2 A.C. 237.

[55] By Ord. 53, r. 4, an application for judicial review must be made promptly and in any event within three months from the date when the grounds for the application first arose, unless the court considers that there is good reason for extending the period within which the application shall be made. See also the Supreme Court Act 1981, s.31(6).

[56] *Wandsworth Borough Council* v. *Winder* [1985] A.C. 461, 480, *per* Robert Goff L.J.

be brought under Order 53[57] because it is a genuine private law claim, seeking private law remedies.[58] The *Woolwich* judgments do not address this question directly, But Lord Slynn, in response to the Revenue's argument that Woolwich should have proceeded to challenge the decision not to pay interest by way of judicial review, said[59]:

"If a claim lies for money had and received, judicial review adds nothing. If the money falls in law to be repaid, a direct order for its repayment is more appropriate than a declaration that it should be repaid or an order setting aside a refusal to repay. Moreover, if it is right here that the tax was repaid as a matter of extra-statutory discretion, and interest from the date of Nolan J.'s order was paid on the same basis, it is not clear to me how a review of the discretionary refusal to pay interest which was not due in law can properly be examined by way of judicial review."

(3) The Revenue has *changed its position* and, in consequence of that change, it is inequitable to allow the taxpayer's claim. The House of Lords has now recognised this defence.[60] The submission that to order repayment would cause fiscal chaos is one which has been successfully made in the United States, and was accepted without demur by the Supreme Court of Canada in the *Air Canada* case.[61] It is one manifestation of the defence of change of position. In principle, the burden should be on the Revenue to demonstrate that fiscal chaos would result and consequently that it would be inequitable to compel the State to make restitution. It is unlikely that it will ever be able to discharge that burden of proof. However, if the public authority's assets are more modest, as was Tower Hamlets London Borough Council's, it is possible that it may do so.[62]

(4) The taxpayer has *passed on* the tax to third parties, for example, to his customers. This question did not arise in the *Woolwich* case. But Lord Goff left open the question whether it could apply on other facts, as courts in India and the United States, the Supreme Court of Canada and the European Court of

---

[57] *Cf. Davy* v. *Spelthorpe Borough Council* [1984] A.C. 262, 277–278, *per* Lord Wilberforce. *Wandsworth Borough Council* v. *Winder* [1985] A.C. 461, 480–481, *per* Robert Goff L.J.

[58] See *Doyle* v. *Northumbria Probation Committee* [1991] 1 W.L.R. 1340; *Lonrho plc* v. *Tebbit* [1992] 4 All E.R. 280, C.A., following *Lonrho plc* v. *Fayed* [1992] 1 A.C. 448, 469–470, *per* Lord Bridge and *Roy* v. *Kensington and Chelsea and Westminster Family Practitioner Committee* [1992] 1 A.C. 624. In *Lonrho* the plaintiff was "asserting a private law right, albeit arising out of a background of public law": at p. 288, *per* Dillon L.J. In Sir Michael Kerr's view (*ibid.*), "our law . . . has already suffered too much from the undesirable complexities of this overlegalistic procedural dichotomy."

[59] [1993] A.C. 70, 200.

[60] *Lipkin Gorman (A Firm)* v. *Karpnale Ltd.* [1991] 2 A.C. 548: see above, pp. 82–83; see below, Chap. 40.

[61] See above, n. 47. For a full discussion see Jones, *Restitution in Public and Private Law*, 1991 Chap. 1.

[62] For a more detailed analysis, see above, p. 156, which discusses *R.* v. *Tower Hamlets London Borough Council, ex p. Chetnik Developments Ltd.* [1988] A.C. 858.

Justice have envisaged.[63] The "point is not without its difficulties; and the availability of such a defence may depend upon the nature of the tax or other levy."[64] The mere fact that a tax has been passed on does not mean that the taxpayer has suffered no financial loss. The economic variables are most complex.[65] The burden should, in principle, be on the defendant to show that the plaintiff has suffered no loss.[65a]

Finally, there is the fate of the ancient and elaborate case law on duress *colore officii*.[66] Can it now be jettisoned? In *Woolwich* Lord Browne-Wilkinson appeared ready to do so. He considered that they were merely examples of the wider principle, namely:

> "that where the parties are on an unequal footing so that money is paid by way of tax or other impost in pursuance of a demand by some public officer, these moneys are recoverable since the citizen is, in practice, unable to resist the payment save at the risk of breaking the law or exposing himself to penalties or other disadvantages."[67]

But the other Law Lords did not suggest that they were merely examples of a wider principle.[67a] So, it may be premature to write the obituary notice of the *colore officii* line of cases. Some of the defendants who have been held to have made demands *colore officii* can hardly be described as *public* officers[68]; and the consideration for the plaintiff's payment may not have totally failed since he may have received some of the bargained-for consideration.[69] In the *colore officii* cases, the submission that the taxpayer has passed on the burden of the tax to his customers and has therefore suffered no financial loss, has been rejected.[70] Moreover, a plaintiff who had simply paid money under a mistake of law to a public officer may be denied recovery[71]; however, whether that principle has survived, in this limited context, is debatable.[72]

---

[63] For a full discussion of the case law in these and other jurisdictions, see Jones, *Restitution in Public and Private Law*, Chap. 1.

[64] [1991] A.C. 70, 178, *per* Lord Goff.

[65] *Administrazione delle Finanze dello Stato* v. *San Giorgio SpA* [1985] 2 C.M.L.R. 647, 672, *per* Mancini A.G., discussed in Jones, *op. cit.* n. 61, pp. 32 *et seq.*

[65a] Contrast Finance Act 1989, ss.24(3), 29(3), in an action to recover VAT, excise duty and car tax, it is a defence to the public authority that "repayment of an amount would unjustly enrich the claimant." See also s.29(3) (excise duty and car tax).

[66] See above, pp. 243 *et seq.*

[67] [1993] A.C. 70, 198. *Cf.* at p. 204, *per* Lord Slynn, cited above, p. 245.

[67a] See particularly Lord Jauncey's dicta, cited above, n. 7.

[68] *Cf.* above, pp. 247–250.

[69] See above, p. 548.

[70] *Mason* v. *State of New South Wales* (1958) 102 C.L.R. 108, 143, *per* Windeyer J.

[71] See above, pp. 243–250.

[72] See above, p. 550. In (1993) 109 L.Q.R. 401, 425–431 [1993], Mr. Beatson discusses the question whether further legislation is needed after *Woolwich*.

CHAPTER 25

ANTICIPATED CONTRACTS WHICH DO NOT MATERIALISE

AN offeror may accompany, or quickly follow, his offer with a payment of money or delivery of goods in the confident anticipation that his offer will be accepted by the offeree. Thus, a dealer who has been accustomed to supply goods of a certain description to a customer may, without receiving an order, send an article of that description to the customer in the anticipation that he will accept and pay for it. Conversely, a customer of a shop may accompany an order, which he expects to be fulfilled, with the necessary payment in cash. If the offeree rejects the offer, he should be required to repay the money or deliver up the goods, as the case may be; and the same should apply if the offeror withdraws his offer before it is accepted. The money is recoverable as money had and received, while the court may order specific restitution of the goods or require the offeree to pay their value.[1] However, the simple retention of the goods by the offeree may amount to an acceptance of the offer, especially in the light of a previous course of dealing between the parties.[2]

Where the offeror has rendered services to the offeree, as, for example, by improving his land or chattels, without the knowledge of the offeree[3] so that he has no option "to adopt or decline the benefit,"[4] the offeror will not ordinarily be entitled to recompense.[5] If, however, there has been some course of dealing between the parties, it may be inferred that the recipient has contracted to pay for the services[6]; alternatively, if he freely accepts the services in the knowledge they were to be paid for, he will be bound to make restitution to the plaintiff.[7]

---

[1] See, generally, (1980) 18 Univ. of Western Ontario L.R. 447 [Jones]; (1987) 87 Col.L.R. 217 [Farnsworth]; *Restatement of Restitution*, § 56. The problem is unreal in relation to land.
[2] *Cf. Moss* v. *Sweet* (1851) 16 Q.B. 493; Sale of Goods Act 1979, s.18, r. 4; and see below, n. 6.
[3] See above, Chap. 5 and 6.
[4] *Leigh* v. *Dickeson* (1884) 15 Q.B.D. 60, 64–65, *per* Brett M.R.; and *cf. McClary* v. *Michigan Central Ry.*, 102 Mich. 312 (1894).
[5] See above, p. 18.
[6] *Cf. Canada Steamship Lines Ltd.* v. *Canadian Pacific Ltd.* (1979) 7 B.L.R. 1 (Ont.S.Ct.) ("special relationship from continuous dealings over the years.")
[7] See above, pp. 18–22. Contrast the problems which are the product of the so-called Battle of the Forms, where the parties use their own and conflicting terms of business. See "The Battle of the Forms and the Law of Restitution" (1988) 8 O.J.L.S. 197 [McKendrick], where the author argues that a court should not strain to find that there is a contract between the parties when goods are delivered and accepted, and that the recognition of restitutionary claims can solve some, but not all, of the problems which arise if a court were to conclude that no contract has been concluded: see below, n. 28.

The problem arises most acutely when parties enter into negotiations which they confidently anticipate will mature into a binding contract. The negotiations break down in circumstances where one of the parties has incurred considerable expense, which may or may not have benefited the other. Can he recover all or any of this wasted expenditure? There is, of course, no contract, and consequently no claim for damages for reliance loss arising from its breach. Moreover, English law does not recognise, at least in name,[8] any doctrine of good faith bargaining, *culpa in contrahendo*,[9] as it is known in civilian jurisdictions, which can form the basis of a collateral contract; a gentleman's agreement to pay for services does not bind any gentleman.[10] And it has consistently been held that a contract to negotiate is a contract which is not known to English law.[11]

The relative paucity of the case law provides no clear and consistent answer to the question whether a party can be recompensed for what he has lost. As will be seen, a number of factors may be critical. Prominent among them are whether the expenditure was incurred at the other party's request, whether it benefited the other party, and the reasons why the negotiations collapsed. One of the earliest decisions, which has proved quite influential, is *William Lacey (Hounslow) Ltd.* v. *Davis*.[12]

In that case the defendant was the owner of premises which had been damaged during the war and which he proposed to rebuild. The plaintiffs were one of three builders who submitted tenders for rebuilding. Theirs was the lowest tender, and they were led to believe and thereafter acted on the assumption that they would receive the contract. Subsequently, they did a considerable amount of extra work at the defendant's request, in the form of preparation of calculations and submission of estimates and revised estimates. All of this extra work was held to fall outside the normal work which a builder customarily performs without charge when invited to tender for the erection of a building. Had the contract been concluded, the work would have been paid for under the total price payable under the contract. The contract, however, fell through because the defendant sold the premises. Barry J. held that the plaintiffs were entitled to remuneration from the defendant, on a *quantum meruit* basis, for the work done at his request beyond the original tender. The defendant argued that the common expectation, that a contract would materialise and that the plaintiffs' services would be rewarded by the profits of the

---

[8] See below, p. 559.
[9] On which, see *"Culpa in Contrahendo*, "Bargaining in Good Faith and Freedom of Contract: a Comparative Study" (1964) 77 Harv.L.R. 401 [Kessler and Fine].
[10] Cf. *J. H. Milner & Son* v. *Percy Bilton Ltd.* [1966] 1 W.L.R. 1582, 1586–1587, *per* Fenton Atkinson J.
[11] *Courtney and Fairbairn Ltd.* v. *Tolaini Brothers (Hotels) Ltd.* [1975] 1 W.L.R. 297; see also *Walford* v. *Miles* [1992] 2 W.L.R. 174, H.L.
[12] [1957] 1 W.L.R. 932; *cf. Rogers* v. *Becker-Brainard Milling Machine Co.*, 211 Mass. 559 (1912); *City of Moncton* v. *Stephen* (1956) 5 D.L.R. (2d) 722; *Sinclair* v. *Logan*, 1961 S.L.T. (Sh.Ct.) 10; *Dieterle* v. *Gatton*, 366 F. 2d 386 (1966); *Reynolds* v. *McGregor* [1973] 1 Q.L. 314, *Sabemo Pty. Ltd.* v. *North Sydney Municipal Council* [1977] 2 N.S.W.L.R. 880.

contract, negatived the suggestion that the parties had impliedly agreed that these services should be paid for in any other way. But Barry J. said that *quantum meruit* claims were no longer limited to genuine contractual actions.[13] Relying on *Craven-Ellis* v. *Canons Ltd.*[14] he said[15]:

> "I am unable to see any valid distinction between work done which was to be paid for under the terms of a contract erroneously believed to be in existence, and work done which was to be paid for out of the proceeds of a contract which both parties erroneously believed was about to be made. In neither case was the work to be done gratuitously, and in both cases the party from whom payment was sought requested the work and obtained the benefit of it. In neither case did the parties actually intend to pay for the work otherwise than under the supposed contract, or as part of the total price which would become payable when the expected contract was made. In both cases, when the beliefs of the parties were falsified, the law implied an obligation—and, in this case, I think the law should imply an obligation—to pay a reasonable price for the services which had been obtained."

The calculations and estimates had been requested and received by the defendant; it was proper, therefore, to require him to pay "a reasonable price" for the benefits rendered.

In Barry J.'s view the defendant had requested the work and had benefited from it. The defendant had received a material benefit from the plaintiff's services; he was able to extract a much larger "permissible amount" for the purposes of an award from the War Damage Commission, and this may well have enabled him to obtain a higher price for the building than otherwise might have been the case.[16] But this fact was not central to the judge's decision. The defendant was deemed to have gained a benefit because the defendant had "requested" his services[17]; and the ground of the restitutionary claim also appears to have been that request. The plaintiff was not deemed to have taken the risk that the negotiations might break down; this was not work which was done in the "hope" that the building would be reconstructed. It was "done under a mutual belief and understanding that this building would be reconstructed and that the plaintiff company was obtaining the contract."[18] The

---

[13] *Cf. Turriff Construction Ltd.* v. *Regalia Knitting Mills Ltd.* (1971) 222 E.G. 169.
[14] [1936] 2 K.B. 403: see above, pp. 478–480.
[15] [1957] 1 W.L.R. 932, 939. For a Canadian case, which also followed *Craven-Ellis* v. *Canons Ltd.* [1936] 2 K.B. 403, see *Parklane Private Hospital Ltd.* v. *City of Vancouver* (1974) 47 D.L.R. (3d) 57; but see: *Construction Design & Management* v. *New Brunswick Housing Corp.* (1973) 36 D.L.R. (3d) 458.
[16] [1957] 1 W.L.R. 932, 935.
[17] *Cf. Planché* v. *Colburn* (1831) 8 Bing. 14: see above, p. 425.
[18] [1957] 1 W.L.R. 932, 939. This is a critical finding of fact. However, a court may conclude, as did the New Brunswick Supreme Court, Appeal Division, in *Construction Design and Management Ltd.* v. *New Brunswick Housing Corp.* (1973) 36 D.L.R. (3d) 458, 463, that the "plaintiff had no expectation to be paid otherwise than out of the contract price."

restitutionary claim appears then to be grounded on the defendant's free acceptance of the plaintiff's services.[19]

It is difficult to support the conclusion that in *William Lacey*[20] the defendant had received a *benefit* at the plaintiff's expense.[21] As Chief Justice Traynor once remarked: "[i]f in fact the performance of services has conferred no benefit on the person requesting them, it is pure fiction to base restitution on a benefit conferred."[22] The reality is that the award concealed a claim for loss suffered in anticipation of a contractual agreement which never materialised.[23]

Less troublesome is the situation where the plaintiff's services have manifestly benefited the defendant. In *Brewer Street Investments Ltd.* v. *Barclays Woollen Co. Ltd.*,[24] Romer L.J. said in argument[25]:

> "Suppose that, whilst parties were in negotiation for a lease, the landlords allowed the prospective tenants to go on the land and spend money on it in anticipation of a lease. If the landlords subsequently broke off negotiations for no reason at all they could not get the benefit of the work without paying for it. Equity would give a remedy."

To which Denning L.J. added[26]: "Whether equity would do so or not, the common law, nowadays, would give the prospective tenants the right to recover the value of the work done in an action for restitution."

The plaintiff's case is even stronger if he has rendered services or delivered goods which the defendant requested and accepted. On such facts the court will be anxious to conclude that the parties have entered into a binding contract. But exceptionally the court cannot reach this conclusion. Such were the facts of *British Steel Corporation* v. *Cleveland Bridge and Engineering Co. Ltd.*,[27] where Robert Goff J. followed Barry J.'s judgment in *William Lacey (Hounslow) Ltd.* v. *Davis*.

---

[19] *Cf. Brewer Street Investments Ltd.* v. *Barclays Woollen Co. Ltd.* [1954] 1 Q.B. 428, where landlords had done work at the request of prospective tenants but the negotiations for a lease broke down. Somervell and Romer L.JJ. held that the prospective tenants had agreed to take the risk that negotiations might collapse; it was their fault that the parties had not reached an agreement and they must reimburse the landlords their expenditure. In Denning L.J.'s view, it could not be said that they had contractually bound themselves to pay for the work. Neither party was at fault; and "the proper way to formulate the [landlord's] claim is on a request implied in law, or, as I would prefer to put it in these days, on a claim in restitution": at pp. 435–436. For the relevance of "fault," see below, pp. 558 *et seq.*

[20] See above, p. 555.

[21] See *Sabemo Pty. Ltd.* v. *North Sydney Municipal Council* [1977] 2 N.S.W.L.R. 880, 902–903; discussed in (1980) 18 Univ. of Western Ontario L.R. 447, 456–457 [Jones]; *Essays* (Finn) pp. 228–229 [Carter], pointing out that only by enlarging the concept of benefit to embrace depletion of the plaintiff's assets can this be characterised as an unjust enrichment claim.

[22] *Coleman Engineering Co.* v. *North American Aviation* (1966) 420 P. 2d 713, 729 (dissenting).

[23] For a contrary view, see *Essays* (ed. Burrows) pp. 141–143 [Birks].

[24] [1954] 1 Q.B. 428: see above, n. 19.

[25] At p. 431.

[26] *Ibid.*

[27] [1984] 1 All E.R. 504; see also *Sanders & Forster Ltd.* v. *A. Monk & Co. Ltd.* (1980), C.A. Transcript 35; *OTM Ltd.* v. *Hydranautics* [1981] 2 Lloyd's Rep. 211, 214, *per* Parker J.; and

The plaintiffs delivered to the defendants a variety of cast-steel nodes. They did this at the defendants' request, after they had received from them a letter recording the defendants' intent to enter into the contract. The judge held that no contract had been concluded since the parties had failed to agree on the price and other essential terms but that the plaintiffs could recover on a *quantum meruit.* The law imposes an obligation on the party making the request to pay a reasonable sum for the work done in pursuance of the request. "Consistently with that solution, the party making the request may find himself liable to pay for work which he would not have to pay for as such if the anticipated contract had come into existence, for example, preparatory work which will, if the contract is made, be allowed for in the price of the finished work."[28]

The cases just discussed reject the bald argument of counsel in *William Lacey* that:

> "The existence ... of a common expectation that a contract would ultimately come into being and that the plaintiffs' services would be rewarded by the profits of that contract leaves no room ... and, indeed, wholly negatives any suggestion, that the parties impliedly agreed that these services would be paid for in any other way."[29]

But they only provide some clues as to the principles which should guide the court in determining whether a party to abortive negotiations should recompense the other. One party is said to have taken the risk that the negotiations might fail; and he was "at fault" in that it was he who aborted (without justification?) the negotiations.[30] These are shadowy signposts. "Taking the risk" and "at fault" are not synonymous concepts. You may have taken the risk that the negotiations may fail and have behaved with the utmost propriety, in circumstances when it was the other party who was responsible for the failure of the negotiations. And what is meant by "fault," given that parties should not be inhibited from negotiating and should be free to withdraw from negotiations?

Dickson Elliott Lonergan Ltd. v. *Plumbing World Ltd.* [1988] 2 N.Z.B.L.C. 103, 281. And see above, p. 28 on the valuation of the benefit.

[28] At p. 511. The judge dismissed the defendants' counterclaim for damages for late delivery. There was no contract which could found such a claim; moreover he found that the plaintiffs would have only been willing to contract on their own standard terms. (See generally (1983) 99 L.Q.R. 572 [S. N. Ball], who suggests that to attempt to solve such problems through the recognition of a restitutionary claim may be unjust to a defendant who might have otherwise sought to bargain for some protection against, *e.g.* late delivery; the courts should be more ready to find a contract by filling in the gaps in essential terms.) See also (1988) 8 O.J.L.S. 197, 212–215 [McKendrick], who argues that the court should have taken into account the terms of the request.

[29] [1957] 1 W.L.R. 932, 936, *per* Barry J., paraphrasing counsel's argument: but see above, n.18.

[30] *Jennings and Chapman Ltd.* v. *Woodman, Matthews & Co.* [1952] 2 T.L.R. 409, C.A.; *Brewer Street Investments Ltd.* v. *Barclays Woollen Co. Ltd.* [1954] 1 Q.B. 428; *Sabemo Pty. Ltd.* v. *North Sydney Municipal Council* [1977] 2 N.S.W.L.R. 880.

The Manitoba Court of Appeal, in *MacIver* v. *American Motors (Canada) Ltd.*,[31] concluded that it was the reprehensibility of the defendant's conduct which must be condemned; they had led the plaintiff "to think [that] all was well and lulled him into a false sense of security,"[32] so that the plaintiff did not exercise an option to purchase property and thereby lost a profitable bargain. The Court awarded the plaintiff, *inter alia*, the difference between the price paid by the defendant for the property, over which the plaintiff had the option, and its value at the date of the breakdown of the negotiations. Today an English court may reach the same conclusion as that of the Manitoba Court of Appeal. Recent years have seen the gradual erosion of the historical distinction between common law promissory estoppel and equitable proprietary estoppel (or estoppel by acquiescence).[33] The equitable doctrine has been generously described. In the words of Oliver L.J. in *Taylor Fashions Ltd.* v. *Liverpool Victoria Trustees Co. Ltd.*[34]:

> " . . . the more recent cases indicate, in my judgment, that the application of the *Ramsden* v. *Dyson* principle[35]—whether you call it proprietary estoppel, estoppel by acquiescence or estoppel by encouragement is really immaterial—requires a very much broader approach which is directed to ascertaining whether, in particular individual circumstances, it would be unconscionable for a party to be permitted to deny that which, knowingly or unknowingly, he has allowed or encouraged another to assume to his detriment than to inquiring whether the circumstances can be fitted within the confines of some preconceived formula serving as a universal yardstick for every form of unconscionable behaviour."

Again, in *Amalgamated Investment and Property Co. Ltd. (in liquidation)* v. *Texas Commerce International Bank Ltd.*,[36] Lord Denning M.R. reduced the doctrine of estoppel:

> "into one general principle shorn of limitations. When the parties to a transaction proceed on the basis of an underlying assumption—either of fact or law—whether due to misrepresentation or mistake makes no difference—on which they have conducted the dealings between them—neither of them will be allowed to go back on that assumption when it would be unfair or unjust to allow him to do so."

In *Attorney-General of Hong Kong* v. *Humphreys Estate Ltd.*,[37] the Privy Council approved these observations in the context of litigation arising out of an agreement, which was made subject to contract, to exchange property. The agreement was also made on the basis that it could be varied or withdrawn at

---

[31] (1977) 70 D.L.R. (3d) 473 and *cf. Hoffman* v. *Red Owl Stores*, 133 N.W. 2d. 267 (1965).
[32] At pp. 488–489.
[33] See above, Chap. 5.
[34] [1982] Q.B. 133, 151–152: see above, pp. 169–170.
[35] See above, Chap. 5.
[36] [1982] Q.B. 84, 122.
[37] [1987] A.C. 114.

any time before the formal execution of the transaction and would not be binding on the appellants until that time. The appellants took possession of the respondents' flats, fitted them out and moved civil servants into them, disposing of their previous residences. For their part the respondents, pursuant to the appellants' licence, demolished existing buildings on the appellants' property, and paid the agreed difference between the values of the respective properties belonging to the appellants and the respondents. The respondents withdrew from the transaction, terminated the appellants' licence to occupy the flats, and sought possession of them and other relief.

The Privy Council held that the respondents were not estopped from withdrawing from the transaction. The appellants had acted simply in:

> "the hope that a voluntary agreement in principle expressly made 'subject to contract' and therefore not binding would eventually be followed by the achievement of legal relationships in the form of grants and transfers of property. It is possible but unlikely that in circumstances at present unforeseeable a party to negotiations set out in a document expressed to be 'subject to contract' would be able to satisfy the court that the parties had subsequently agreed to convert the document into a contract, or that some form of estoppel had arisen to prevent both parties from refusing to proceed with the transactions envisaged by the document. But in the present case the government chose to begin and elected to continue on terms that either party might suffer a change of mind and withdraw."[38]

For these reasons the Privy Council affirmed the orders of the trial judge, also affirmed by the Court of Appeal of Hong Kong, which required the appellants to repay the sums which represented the difference in the value between the two properties and to pay mesne profits for wrongful use of the respondents' property, and declared that the respondents were entitled to possession of the flats.

What is significant is, however, that the Privy Council envisaged that there could be circumstances where the doctrine of equitable proprietary estoppel might prevent a defendant who had entered into an agreement, "subject to contract," from which he subsequently withdrew, from denying that a binding agreement had been concluded. Such a case was *Salvation Army Trustee Co. Ltd.* v. *West Yorkshire Metropolitan City Council*,[39] which the Privy Council distinguished but did not suggest was wrongly decided. The defendants had intimated that they intended to acquire the plaintiffs' site and had represented that the plaintiffs would then be entitled to statutory compensation. The plaintiffs agreed in exchange to buy, subject to contract, from the defendants a new site. It was the expectation that they were entitled to compensation which "impelled the Salvation Army, to the knowledge of the city council, to enter

---

[38] At pp. 127–128, *per curiam* (Lord Templeman).
[39] (1980) 41 P. & C.R. 179.

and build on the new site."[40] Woolf J. held that the defendants were bound to acquire the old site and to pay appropriate compensation.

In *Waltons Stores (Interstate) Ltd.* v. *Maher*[41] the majority of the High Court of Australia affirmed that the doctrine of promissory estoppel:

> "extends to the enforcement of voluntary promises on the footing that a departure from the basic assumptions underlying the transaction . . . must be unconscionable. As failure to fulfil a promise does not of itself amount to unconscionable conduct, mere reliance on an executory promise to do something, resulting in the promisee changing his position or suffering detriment, does not bring promissory estoppel into play. Something more would be required. *Humphreys Estate* suggests that this may be found, if at all, in the creation or encouragement by the party estopped in the other party of an assumption that a contract will come into existence or a promise will be performed and that other party relied on that assumption to his detriment to the knowledge of the first party. *Humphreys Estate* referred in terms to an assumption that the plaintiff would not exercise an existing legal right or liberty, the right or liberty to withdraw from negotiations, but as a matter of substance such an assumption is indistinguishable from an assumption that a binding contract would eventuate."[42]

In that case Maher entered into negotiations[43] with Waltons with the intention that he would demolish his building, erect a new one in accordance with Waltons' specifications and then lease the building to Waltons. After detailed negotiations,[44] his solicitors prepared the necessary documents which were signed by him and forwarded their counterparts to Waltons for execution and exchange by Waltons. Waltons, who were having second thoughts, instructed their solicitors to go slow. In contrast Maher, anxious to meet the contemplated deadline for completion, demolished the existing building on his

---

[40] The Privy Council concluded that the Salvation Army, unlike the appellants in *Humphreys Estate*, did not agree to buy the new site because they *hoped* that this agreement, subject to contract, would result in a binding contract. For that reason the facts were distinguishable from those before the Board: [1987] A.C. 114, 127, explaining Woolf J.'s decision.

[41] (1988) 76 A.L.J. 513.

[42] At p. 525, *per* Mason C.J. and Wilson J. who went on to contrast this principle with that formulated in the *Restatement of Contracts* 2d § 90: namely, did the promisor have a reasonable expectation that his promise would induce action or forbearance?
For a more elaborate statement of the relevant principles, see at p. 542, *per* Brennan J.

[43] Deane J. and Gaudron J. agreed that the appeal should be dismissed, but for different reasons. They could not accept that Maher mistakenly believed that an exchange of contracts would take place, as distinct from having taken place. Nonetheless Waltons were estopped.

[44] Maher's solicitors had emphasised that it was necessary to conclude the agreement in the "next day or two" if the work was to be done on time. Thereupon, Waltons' solicitors wrote to them enclosing the documents for the lease and stating that they had not yet received instructions whether certain amendments in the draft lease were acceptable, but that Maher's solicitors would be informed "tomorrow if the amendments were not agreed to." They were never informed.

land and laid the foundations of the new building. Waltons discovered what Maher was doing, but said and did nothing. The High Court of Australia held that Maher was entitled to damages in lieu of specific performance. His equity "was satisfied by avoiding a detriment suffered in reliance on an induced assumption, not by the direct enforcement of the assumption."[45] Waltons' conduct induced Maher to assume that they would exchange contracts. They stood by "in silence when it must have known that the respondents were proceeding on the assumption that they had an agreement and that completion of the exchange was a formality."[46] They had not simply exercised their legal right not to exchange contracts; there was an element of urgency and Maher had executed the counterpart deed which they sat on, knowing that work was proceeding on the site.

The reasoning of the High Court is then consistent with that of the Privy Council in *Humphreys Estate*. Both courts took pains to emphasise that the doctrine of proprietary estoppel should not be used as a device to enforce a gratuitous promise. Hence the concern of the Privy Council to explain the *Salvation Army* case,[47] and of the High Court of Australia to distance itself from the charge that it was specifically enforcing an oral agreement for the disposition of an interest in land.[48] But the principles enunciated, and particularly the elaboration of the concept of unconscionability, should be of significant assistance to future courts when confronted with comparable problems, although, as these two cases demonstrate, the application of those principles to particular facts may never be free from doubt.

There remains one last question to be answered. A party withdraws from negotiations, having incontrovertibly benefited the other party. That other party did not behave unconscionably. Must the other party recompense him? Take the case of the prospective tenant who is allowed at his request into possession of premises and improves them. He then withdraws from the negotiations. It is most probable that a court will hold that his misfortune is of his own doing, and that it is irrelevant that he has incontrovertibly benefited the prospective landlord.[49] Indeed the mistaken improver of land is more to be pitied, but he is denied any remedy if the landowner did not encourage him to act as he did.[50] Similarly, he who fails to perform an entire contract cannot successfully claim that his services have incontrovertibly benefited the other

---

[45] At p. 545, *per* Brennan J. The equity did not arise out of the enforcement of the assumption. "If it did, it would be impossible to distinguish the equity from a contractual right arising out of an oral promise."

[46] At p. 525, *per* Mason C.J. and Wilson J., who posed the quotation as a question.

[47] See above, p. 560.

[48] This would have been ineffective: Conveyancing Act 1919 (NSW), s.54A.

[49] *Cf. Brewer Street Investments Ltd.* v. *Barclays Woollen Co. Ltd.* [1954] 1 Q.B. 428, 434, *per* Somervell L.J., 438, *per* Romer L.J.: see above, p. 557. But in that case the defendant gained little real benefit from what the plaintiff had done; contrast p. 431, *per* Denning L.J., cited in the text at p. 557.

[50] See above, Chap. 5.

party to the contract.[51] But these are harsh decisions which have attracted much criticism and proposals for reform of the law.[52] It is conceivable that a court may be persuaded that "credit should be given in such sum as may be just"[53]; but the balance of authority does not suggest such a conclusion.

---

[51] See above, pp. 438 *et seq.*

[52] See above, pp. 445–447. The Law Commission has recommended that the party in breach of an entire contract be granted some recompense, although, unlike the landlord, the innocent party is protected by his action on the contract for loss suffered: see above, pp. 444 *et seq.*

[53] *Brewer Street Investments* v. *Barclays Woollen Co. Ltd.* [1954] 1 Q.B. 428, 437, *per* Denning L.J.: see above, p. 557.

CHAPTER 26

RESTITUTION OF BENEFITS CONFERRED UNDER TRUSTS WHICH DO NOT EXHAUST THE BENEFICIAL INTEREST OR WHICH FAIL

EQUITY has always distinguished the express trust, which arises because it is evident that the settlor intended to create it, from the resulting, implied and constructive trust.[1] Today an implied trust is, depending on the context in which it is used, either a resulting trust or a constructive trust; it is not a distinct genus. As has been seen,[2] constructive trusts are imposed by the courts, irrespective of the intention of the parties. They arise by operation of law. Resulting trusts may give effect to the intention of a settlor, or may also arise by operation of law. The courts have been asked from time to time to determine whether the transferor of property intended the transferee to take beneficially or to hold that property on trust, and, if on trust, for whom. From an early period, equity created presumptions which were designed for the removal of doubt. For example, A voluntarily transfers pure personalty to B.

"The question is [then] not one of the automatic consequences of a dispositive failure by A, but one of presumption: the property has been carried to B, and from the absence of consideration and any presumption of advancement B is presumed not only to hold the entire interest on trust, but also to hold the beneficial interest for A absolutely. The presumption thus establishes both that B is to take on trust and also what the trust is. Such resulting trusts may be called 'presumed resulting trusts.' "[3]

We shall not discuss presumed resulting trusts for they give effect to the real but unexpressed intention of the parties. But there is a second class of resulting trusts, where A transfers property to B on trust but leaves, for a variety of reasons, all or some of the beneficial interest undisposed of:

"The resulting trust here does not depend on any intentions or presumptions, but is the automatic consequence of A's failure to dispose of what is vested in him. Since *ex hypothesi* the transfer is on trust, the resulting trust does not establish the trust but merely carries back to A the beneficial

---

[1] The distinction has important practical implications, *e.g.* express trusts of land are enforceable only if they are evidenced in writing: see Law of Property Act 1925, s.53(1)(*b*). But this section does not affect the creation or operation of resulting, implied or constructive trusts: see s.53(2) and above, p. 473.

[2] See above, Chap. 2.

[3] *Re Vandervell's Trusts (No. 2)* [1974] Ch. 269, 294. Contrast Law of Property Act 1925, s.60(3), on which see Gray, *op. cit.* p. 247.

interest that has not been disposed of. Such resulting trusts may be called 'automatic resulting trusts.' "[4]

The trustee or the beneficiary is evidently enriched. And equity deems that enrichment to be an unjust enrichment. As Vaisey J. said, in one such case: the settlor has parted with his money "on a consideration which was expressed but which in fact completely failed."[5]

Situations where an Automatic Resulting Trust will be Imposed

If a settlor transfers property to trustees on trusts which do not exhaust the beneficial interest in that property, the trustees will hold the property not effectively disposed of on a resulting trust for the settlor or his estate if he is dead. Thus where S conveys a fee simple interest to T1 and T2 on trust for A for life, T1 and T2 will then hold the reversion on a resulting trust for S.[6] Only very strong evidence will persuade the courts that the settlor intended the trustees to take the property beneficially in such circumstances.[7]

Again, equity implies a resulting trust for the settlor if the beneficial interests under the trust fail. Many of the grounds for the failure of beneficial interests are similar to those which render contracts totally ineffective. For example, the objects of the trust might fail for uncertainty[8]; the beneficiary might renounce his beneficial interests; or the beneficial interests might be conditional on an event, such as the solemnisation of a marriage, which never takes place.[9]

Similarly, a fund may be held on trusts which fail, but there remains a surplus in the fund. There is a body of case law which is the authority for the principle that:

> "Where a trust deed is silent as to the destination of a surplus the law will supply a resulting trust in favour of the provider of the funds in question. That is something which arises outside the trust deed as an implication of law. The trust deed may include a clause which prevents a resulting trust from operating and in that case it will operate according to its terms."[10]

---

[4] *Ibid.*

[5] *Re Ames' Settlement* [1946] Ch. 217, 223, *per* Vaisey J.; see also *Essery* v. *Cowlard* (1884) 26 Ch.D. 191.

[6] *Re West* [1900] 1 Ch. 84; *cf. Re Llanover Settled Estates* [1926] Ch. 626. See, generally, Birks, *Introduction*, pp. 57–64.

[7] The trustees will only take beneficially if they can prove that the property is given to them beneficially, subject to the trusts: see *King* v. *Denison* (1813) 1 V. & B. 260; *Re West* [1900] 1 Ch. 84.

[8] *Re Gillingham Bus Disaster Fund* [1958] Ch. 300, affd. [1959] Ch. 62.

[9] *Re Ames' Settlement* [1946] Ch. 217, 223, *per* Vaisey J.; see also *Essery* v. *Cowlard* (1884) 26 Ch.D. 191.

[10] *Jones* v. *Williams*, *per* Knox J., unrep. March 15, 1988, cited in *Davis* v. *Richard & Wallington Industries Ltd.* [1990] 1 W.L.R. 1511, 1541, *per* Scott J., who adds the gloss that the trust deed may impliedly exclude a resulting trust; below, pp. 566–567.

There are many examples of the application of these principles.[11] But it may not be easy to determine whether the "provider of the funds" for a particular purpose did, or did not, intend to exclude a resulting trust, and that inquiry becomes even more troublesome where there is no trust deed. The questions which the court have to answer are these: is the presumption of the resulting trust rebutted by a finding of fact that the provider of the funds intended to give his money out and out, not intending to retain any beneficial interest in the fund?; and if that was his intention and the purpose for which he subscribed has not been, or cannot be, achieved do the beneficiaries take what remains of the fund beneficially or does it pass to the Crown as *bona vacantia*? The court may be required to construe a deed; a will[12]; or the language of an appeal for a public subscription,[13] the terms of which may be generously, indeed loosely, phrased. Certain canons of construction provide some guidance; for example, if a gross sum, or the whole income of a fund, is given there is a presumption that it is an absolute gift, and the "purpose" is merely the motive for the gift.[14]

Acute problems have arisen on the dissolution of non-charitable unincorporated associations, when it becomes necessary to determine how the surplus funds of the association are to be distributed. These funds may have emanated either from past and present members of the association, from well-wishers or from fund-raising functions, such as the proceeds of entertainments, raffles and sweepstakes. Until very recently it could be said with some confidence that, on these particular facts, a resulting trust never arises. For the only persons interested in the surplus fund, whatever its source, are the surviving members; "save by way of a valid declaration of trust in their [the contributors'] favour, there is no scope for any other person acquiring any rights in the property of the association."[15] Every contributor contributes with the knowledge that the funds of the association shall be distributed on dissolution according to its rules; and in the contract established by the rules is implied a term that on dissolution the society's surplus funds belong equally to the existing members.

The old, and what was thought to be the discredited, view[16] was that surplus funds should prima facie be held on resulting trust for the contributors; if it was demonstrated that they intended to give out and out, then the money passed to the Crown as *bona vacantia*.[17] However, in *Davis* v. *Richard &*

[11] See, *e.g. Re Hobourn Aero Components Ltd.'s Air Raid Distress Fund* [1946] Ch. 194.
[12] See, *e.g. Re Osaba* [1979] 1 W.L.R. 247.
[13] *Re Gillingham Bus Disaster Fund* [1958] Ch. 300.
[14] *Re Andrew's Trust* [1905] 2 Ch. 48, 52–53, *per* Kekewich J.
[15] *Re Bucks Constabulary Widows' and Orphans' Fund Friendly Society (No. 2)* [1979] 1 W.L.R. 936, *per* Walton J. (and authorities cited therein), doubting *Re West Sussex Constabulary's Widows', Children and Benevolent Fund (1930) Trusts* [1971] Ch. 1. The judge recognised that a third party could contract with the trustees of the association and thereby acquire a contractual or proprietary right over its assets.
[16] See above, nn. 11–15 and 16.
[17] *Re Hillier's Trusts* [1954] 1 W.L.R. 9; *Re Gillingham Bus Disaster Fund* [1958] Ch. 300; *Re West Sussex Widows', Children and Constabulary's Benevolent Fund (1930) Trusts* [1971] Ch. 1.

Wallington Industries Ltd.,[18] which concerned the fate of surplus pension funds, Scott J. followed these earlier authorities. The resulting trust should be excluded only when it was absolutely clear, expressly or impliedly, that it was excluded. Adopting this presumption, he concluded that the trustees of the pension fund held a rateable part of the fund, attributable to the contributions of the employers, on resulting trust for them. In contrast, the employees were deemed to have intended to give their contributions out and out. He reached this conclusion, which may well have surprised the employees, because it was impracticable to determine the amount of their beneficial interests for the value of individual benefits would be different for each employee; furthermore, to conclude that a rateable part of their contributions was held on resulting trust would conflict with the legislation which imposed a ceiling on the pension of each employee. The rateable part of the fund attributable to their contributions passed to the Crown as *bona vacantia*. It is, for the very reasons given by the judge, highly artificial to conclude that the employees so *intended*, and it is conjectural whether the decision will be followed. If followed, it may well be confined to the world of pension trusts.

The beneficial interest under a trust may also fail because the object of the trust is illegal.[19] But, in such a case, a resulting trust may not be implied because of the application of the principle *ex turpi causa non oritur actio*. Thus the court may refuse to allow a settlor to set up his own fraud to rebut a presumption that a transfer was intended as a gift and to adduce evidence to show that the transferee held on a resulting trust for his benefit.[20] Consequently a trustee may be allowed to take beneficially where the object of the trust was illegal. Such a case was *Re Great Berlin Steamboat Co.*[21] There, Bowden placed money to the credit of the bankers of the Great Berlin Steamboat Co., so that the company could have a credit balance in the event of inquiries from certain Berlin bankers with whom it was trying to place a number of shares. There was an agreement that the money deposited was not for the general purposes of the company but was to be held on trust for Bowden. The company was wound up without any inquiries having been made from Berlin. The Court of Appeal dismissed Bowden's summons to have the money returned to him. The illegal purpose had been substantially accomplished and it was too late to reclaim the money.

At first sight it is odd that a trustee should thus be allowed to benefit from his trust. But the prohibition against giving relief to a person who has knowingly entered into an illegal transaction is paramount. Nevertheless, the courts are not anxious to provide trustees with a windfall. As in illegal contracts, recovery

---

[18] [1990] 1 W.L.R. 1511.
[19] *Thrupp* v. *Collett* (1858) 26 Beav. 125.
[20] *Curtis* v. *Perry* (1802) 6 Ves. 739; *Groves* v. *Groves* (1829) 3 Y. & J. 163; *Brackenbury* v. *Brackenbury* (1820) 2 Jac. & W. 391; *Gascoigne* v. *Gascoigne* [1918] 1 K.B. 223; *Re Emery's Investment Trusts* [1959] Ch. 410; *Chettiar* v. *Chettiar* [1962] A.C. 294; *Preston* v. *Preston* [1960] N.Z.L.R. 385.
[21] (1884) 26 Ch.D. 616.

is allowed if the parties are not *in pari delicto* or if the object is not substantially executed.[22] All trusts contained in testamentary instruments are deemed to be executory[23]; and if a testamentary trust is illegal, the property will be held on a resulting trust for the testator's estate.

If the trust is a charitable trust, the property may be applied *cy-près* for similar charitable purposes if the purposes of the trust are, or have become, impossible to fulfil.[24]

---

[22] *Davies* v. *Otty (No. 2)* (1865) 35 Beav. 208; *Symes* v. *Hughes* (1870) L.R. 9 Eq. 475, 479, *per* Lord Romilly M.R.; *Re Great Berlin Steamboat Co.* (1884) 26 Ch.D. 616, 620, *per* Cotton and Lindley L.JJ. *Cf. Donaldson* v. *Freeson* (1934) 51 C.L.R. 596.

[23] *Brown* v. *Burdett* (1882) 21 Ch.D. 667, *semble*; *Scott on Trusts* § 422.1.

[24] *Picarda on Charities*, Chaps. 24–30.

WHERE THE DEFENDANT HAS ACQUIRED FROM A THIRD PARTY A BENEFIT FOR WHICH HE MUST ACCOUNT TO THE PLAINTIFF

CHAPTER 27

ATTORNMENT

1. ATTORNMENT IN RESPECT OF MONEY[1]

(a) *The Early Law*

FROM the early years of the seventeenth century, debt and *indebitatus assumpsit* were alternative remedies to account, and all these writs enabled a claimant to proceed against another person who had received money from a third party to the plaintiff's use.[2] In the early cases there is no emphasis on any special or fiduciary relationship as forming the basis of the action. In 1607 Popham C.J. could state[3] quite simply that when the third party "delivered the money to the defendant to deliver to the plaintiff, there was included an agreement of the defendant to deliver it to the plaintiff, which agreement will charge him in *assumpsit* to him who ought to have the money." Not even the defendant's assent to the plaintiff was necessary to give rise to an *assumpsit*. Later cases established that *indebitatus assumpsit*, based on the defendant's receipt of money to the plaintiff's use, was the appropriate remedy[4] and, in *Israel* v. *Douglas* in 1789,[5] the element of "receipt" was widely construed. There the defendant was merely the debtor of the third party, who instructed him to pay the plaintiff the amount of the debt. The defendant agreed to do so, whereupon the plaintiff lent the third party a further sum. The plaintiff recovered the amount of the debt from the defendant on an *indebitatus* count.

Before the beginning of the nineteenth century, therefore, it was unnecessary to show any special relationship between the plaintiff and the defendant, who had received money to the plaintiff's use, or even to show that the defendant had promised to hold the money to the plaintiff's use.[6] In the next century, however, this proposition was to be challenged, and an attempt was to be made to rationalise this type of claim in terms of contract.

---

[1] The historical development of *indebitatus assumpsit* persuades us to treat this topic as part of restitution: see above, p. 71, n. 30.
[2] See above, p. 3.
[3] *Gilbert* v. *Ruddeard*, in a note to (1607) 3 Dy. 272b. Tanfield J. was more cautious.
[4] *Beckingham & Lambert* v. *Vaughan* (1614) 1 Rolle 391; *Ward* v. *Evans* (1703) 6 Mod. 36.
[5] (1789) 1 H.Bl. 239.
[6] The germ of this requirement appears in *Israel* v. *Douglas* (1789) 1 H.Bl. 239, 242, *per* Lord Loughborough; see, too, *Stevens* v. *Hill* (1805) 5 Esp. 247.

(b) *The Modern Law*

The nineteenth century cases have been justly described as "an intractable mass of conflicting authority."[7] It was the hardening of contractual principles, with the consequent emphasis on privity, which first led judges to question the reasoning in the pre-nineteenth century cases. In *Williams* v. *Everett*,[8] one Kelly sent certain bills to the defendants, who were his bankers, instructing them to pay the plaintiffs, his creditors, whom he informed what he had done. The plaintiffs claimed that the defendants held the bills to their use. Lord Ellenborough thought that privity between the parties was necessary and would be satisfied by an "assent express or implied" on the defendants' part. But, on the facts, he found that there was no such assent, nor was there any "engagement entered into by themselves with the person who is the object of the remittance."[9] The claim, therefore, failed. It was now clear that a defendant's assent would no longer be implied simply from receipt of a fund.

Some judges rationalised the situation in terms of agency,[10] others talked the language of "consideration"[11] and yet others invoked estoppel.[12] But all emphasised the necessity for real assent by the defendant to hold to the plaintiff's use. These several explanations were inspired by the judges' concern to analyse in contractual language the situation which arises when A asks B to hold a fund to the use of C, and to distinguish that situation from an assignment of a debt, or a contract made by A with B for the benefit of C. Further confusion was caused when, in the middle of the nineteenth century, the courts turned once again to quasi-contract, and the cases at this time[13] show that the judges were then prepared to "imply" a contract from the mere fact that the defendant had come into possession of a "fund" and had assented to hold it to the plaintiff's use. In 1868, Blackburn J., in *Griffin* v. *Weatherby*,[14] stated the law as follows:

"Ever since the case of *Walker* v. *Rostron*[15] it has been considered as settled law that where a person transfers to a creditor on account of a debt, whether due or not, a fund actually existing or accruing in the hands of a third person, and notifies the transfer to the holder of the fund, although there is no legal obligation on the holder to pay the amount of the debt to

---

[7] Jackson, *History*, p. 99. His analysis has been supplemented in (1959) 75 L.Q.R. 220 [J. D. Davies].

[8] (1811) 14 East 582; see also *Stevens* v. *Hill* (1805) 5 Esp. 247.

[9] At p. 597; see also the cases cited by Jackson, *History*, p. 99, n. 4.

[10] *e.g.* Coleridge J. in *Lilly* v. *Hays* (1836) 5 A. & E. 548, 551. See also the cases cited by Jackson, *History*, p. 100, n. 1.

[11] *Hodgson* v. *Anderson* (1825) 3 B. & C. 842; *Malcolm* v. *Scott* (1850) 5 Exch. 601, 610, *per* Parke, B.; *Wharton* v. *Walker* (1825) 4 B. & C. 163.

[12] *Cobb* v. *Becke* (1845) 6 Q.B. 930, 936, *per* Denman C.J.; *Bower* v. *Hett* [1895] 2 Q.B. 337, 339, *per* Esher M.R.

[13] *Liversidge* v. *Broadbent* (1859) 4 H. & N. 603, 612, *per* Martin B.; *Hamilton* v. *Spottiswoode* (1849) 4 Exch. 200. For a full discussion, see (1959) 75 L.Q.R. 220, 225–230 [J. D. Davies].

[14] (1868) L.R 3 Q.B. 753, 758–759.

[15] (1842) 9 M. & W. 411.

the transferee, yet the holder of the fund may, and if he does promise to pay to the transferee, then that which was merely an equitable right becomes a legal right in the transferee, founded on the promise; and the money becomes a fund received or to be received for and payable to the transferee, and when it has been received an action for money had and received to the use of the transferee lies at his suit against the holder."[16]

On this approach, if A transfers to B a "fund" to hold to the use of C, C can sue B in quasi-contract provided that B had promised C to hold it to C's use. In *Griffin* v. *Weatherby*[17] itself, B, the liquidator of a company, was held liable on his promise to pay C, a creditor of A, who was in turn the creditor of the company.

But the law could not be regarded as settled. Indeed, in *Liversidge* v. *Broadbent*,[18] some nine years before *Griffin* v. *Weatherby*,[19] Martin B. had said that if the defendant held not a "fund" but a mere debt, which he agreed to hold to the plaintiff's use, then the plaintiff had to show consideration, which could not be implied merely from the defendant's assent to hold to the plaintiff's use. In that case the defendant was indebted to William Clapham, who was indebted to the plaintiff on two bills. The plaintiff proposed to Clapham that the defendant should guarantee the bills, whereupon Clapham signed a document authorising the defendant to pay the plaintiff the amount of the bills. The defendant wrote on this document, "acknowledged," and added his signature. The Court of Exchequer held that the plaintiff had no right of action against the defendant. The document purported to be a mere assignment of a chose in action, and, as there was no consideration for the defendant's promise to pay the plaintiff, he could still sue Clapham on the bills.

There have been few cases[20] since *Griffin* v. *Weatherby*. But in 1958 this line of authority was once more revived in *Shamia* v. *Joory*.[21] In that case, the defendant, an Iraqi merchant, was indebted to one Yousuf. Yousuf asked the defendant to pay to the plaintiff part of that debt, namely £500. The defendant agreed. He informed the plaintiff and sent him a cheque for £500, which the plaintiff returned since it was incorrectly drawn. The defendant then refused to pay, and the plaintiff sued him for the £500 as, *inter alia*, money had and received by the defendant to the plaintiff's use. Both counsel accepted the authority of Blackburn J.'s pronouncement in *Griffin* v. *Weatherby*, already quoted,[22] but counsel for the defendant submitted that the money which the

---

[16] *Cf.* his similar observation in *Fleet* v. *Perrins* (1868) L.R. 3 Q.B. 536, 542: the money remained the money of the remittor until the "depositee had by some act attorned" to the claimant.

[17] (1868) L.R. 3 Q.B. 753.

[18] (1859) 4 H. & N. 603.

[19] (1868) L.R. 3 Q.B. 753.

[20] *Greenway* v. *Atkinson* (1881) 29 W.R. 560; *Monkwearmouth Flour Co.* v. *Lightfoot* (1897) 13 T.L.R. 327; *Greenhalgh* v. *Union Bank of Manchester* [1924] 2 K.B. 153, 161, *per* Swift J.; see Winfield, *Province*, p. 137.

[21] [1958] 1 Q.B. 448.

[22] See above, p. 572.

defendant owed Yousuf was not a "fund" in the hands of the defendant. Barry J. rejected this submission. "In my judgment," he said[23]:

> "all that the law requires is that there must be in the hands of or accruing to the third person, either a sum of money or a monetary liability, over which the transferor has a right of disposal. It matters not, I think, from what source the liability arises, and I see no reason why it should not include a debt for money lent, or goods sold, or services rendered or a debt of any other kind; nor do I think that the situation can be altered if the debt is of a temporary nature, which in the ordinary course of things would shortly be extinguished by items of contra account, provided, of course, that the debt still exists at the date of the transfer and of the debtor's promise of payment made to the transferee."

It is difficult to justify the decision in *Shamia* v. *Joory*. It extends *Griffin* v. *Weatherby* and appears to conflict with *Liversidge* v. *Broadbent*, a case not cited in *Shamia* v. *Joory*, where the Court of Exchequer held that the defendant's promise to hold a debt to the plaintiff's use was a *nudum pactum*. Historically, *Shamia* v. *Joory* is unsound since it circumvents the common law's refusal to give effect to assignments of choses in action. Moreover, it is open to the grave objection that it blurs the fundamental distinction between assignment and attornment. Where there is a fund in the hands of the defendant, he can, on the third party's instructions, hold it for the plaintiff, thereby attorning to him. But if the defendant merely agrees to pay a debt to the plaintiff instead of to a third party, there can be no attornment. Attornment requires a right of property[24] in a specific asset[25]; indeed, it is our view that the plaintiff, to whom the holder of a fund as attorned, should have the benefit of an equitable proprietary claim to the fund so as to prevent the general creditors of the holder taking advantage of it in the event of his insolvency.[26] A debt, however, being no more than a chose in action, cannot be the subject of an attornment; it passes, if at all, by assignment.

There are, of course, close similarities between attornment and assignment; for example, both an assignment and an attornment are irrevocable.[27] Nevertheless, they are distinct methods of transferring a "fund" or a "debt" from one person to another.[28] The critical difference is that the consent of the debtor is

---

[23] At p. 459. He, therefore, impliedly disagreed with Romer L.J.'s dictum in *Re Simms* [1934] Ch. 1, which denied the plaintiff a remedy because no contract could be implied in the circumstances: see below, p. 726, n. 94.

[24] The analogy of the bailment cases, where the bailee in possession attorns to a third person, is persuasive: see *Gosling* v. *Birnie* (1831) 7 Bing. 339; *Henderson & Co.* v. *Williams* [1895] 1 Q.B. 521; see below, p. 575.

[25] *Cf. Laurie and Morewood* v. *Dudin & Sons* [1926] 1 K.B. 223: see below, p. 576.

[26] See above, Chap. 2.

[27] *Cf.* the cases on attornment of chattels: see below, p. 575.

[28] In *Shamia* v. *Joory* [1958] 1 Q.B. 448, 460, Barry J. concluded that there was no assignment "if only because there was no evidence that notice of the assignment had been in fact given to him [the plaintiff]. Yousuf's letters certainly gave no hint that he, Yousuf, had assigned to the plaintiff any moneys owing to him by the defendant." It is well established that the assignor

not necessary, though it may be desirable, to perfect an equitable assignment,[29] whereas in cases of attornment it is essential to show that the debtor assented to hold to the plaintiff's use.[30]

The law cannot be regarded as settled. But the following conditions must apparently be satisfied before the plaintiff can succeed in his claim to the money:

(1) There must be a "fund" in the defendant's hands. On the present authorities it is doubtful whether a debt is a "fund" for the purposes of this rule; in our opinion, for reasons already stated, a debt should not, in the present context, be regarded as a fund capable of attornment.

(2) A third party, from whom the defendant received the "fund" or to whose use he held it, must have requested the defendant, either before or after the "fund" reached the defendant's hands, to hold it to the plaintiff's use.

(3) The defendant must have assented to hold the "fund" to the plaintiff's use, and such assent must have been communicated to the plaintiff by the defendant or his authorised agent. In other words, the defendant must have "by some act attorned"[31] to the plaintiff.

2. ATTORNMENT IN RESPECT OF CHATTELS

A bailee, for example, a warehouseman, may have possession of goods which the bailor authorises him to hold on behalf of another person, as may occur if the bailor has sold the goods to that other. If the bailee then admits the other's title, he will become his bailee and will thereafter be estopped from denying his title; it "would be a gross fraud on the plaintiff if, after that, he were not entitled to recover"[32] the goods from the bailee who had so attorned to him. This principle is so stringently applied that it is deemed to be immaterial that the person to whom the defendant has attorned has no title or has a defective title to the goods.[33] Indeed, "a contrary principle would endanger the security of commercial transactions, and destroy that confidence upon which what is called the usual course of trade materially rests."[34] The conditions governing

---

must give notice of the assignment to the assignee; until then, the assignor's instructions to the debtor remain a bare authority to him to pay and will be revocable by the assignor: see *Morrell* v. *Wootton* (1852) 16 Beav. 197, 203, *per* Romilly M.R.; *Re Hamilton* (1921) 124 L.T. 737, 739, *per* Lord Sterndale M.R.; *Curran* v. *Newpart Cinemas Ltd.* [1951] 1 All E.R. 295. *Semble*, therefore, there is not a valid assignment until the assignor tells the assignee of the assignment; it is not enough that the assignee is told by the debtor of the assignor's intention, although in such a case the assignee might succeed in showing that the debtor has "attorned" to him.

[29] *Donaldson* v. *Donaldson* (1854) Kay 711; *cf.* Law of Property Act 1925, s.136.

[30] *Cf. Holl* v. *Griffin* (1833) 10 Bing. 246, 248, *per* Tindal C.J.: see below, p. 571.

[31] *Fleet* v. *Perrins* (1868) L.R. 3 Q.B. 536, 542, *per* Blackburn J.

[32] *Gosling* v. *Bernie* (1831) 7 Bing. 339, 344, *per* Park J. The plaintiff has his action in conversion: see *Henderson & Co.* v. *Williams* [1895] 1 Q.B. 521.

[33] *Woodley* v. *Coventry* (1863) 2 H. & C. 164; see also *Hawes* v. *Watson* (1824) 2 B. & C. 540.

[34] *Henderson & Co.* v. *Williams* [1895] 1 Q.B. 521, 529, *per* Lord Halsbury.

attornment of goods are not dissimilar to those, already discussed, relating to attornment of funds of money. They are as follows:

(1) Though it has been said that "very little will suffice to create an attornment,"[35] it is essential to show some acknowledgment by the defendant of the plaintiff's title. Thus it is not sufficient that a delivery order, in favour of the plaintiff, was brought by a messenger and given to the defendant's clerk, when the defendant neither accepted nor acknowledged the delivery order.[36]

(2) The goods must be in the hands of the defendant. An attornment made by a person out of possession has no immediate application, but when the goods come into his hands "it applies as if made at the time."[37]

(3) The defendant must attorn in respect of a specific chattel, or a chattel which has been specifically appropriated so as to make it specific.[38]

---

[35] *Laurie and Morewood* v. *Dudin & Sons* [1926] 1 K.B. 223, 237, *per* Scrutton L.J.; see also *Dublin City Distillery Ltd.* v. *Doherty* [1914] A.C. 823, 847, *per* Lord Atkinson.

[36] *Laurie and Morewood* v. *Dudin & Sons* [1926] 1 K.B. 223; *cf. Re Savoy Estate Ltd.* [1949] Ch. 622.

[37] *Holl* v. *Griffin* (1833) 10 Bing. 246, 248, *per* Tindal C.J.

[38] *Cf. Knights* v. *Wiffen* (1870) L.R. 5 Q.B. 660.

CHAPTER 28

CASES WHERE THE DEFENDANT WITHOUT RIGHT INTERVENES BETWEEN THE PLAINTIFF AND A THIRD PARTY

1. USURPERS OF OFFICES

OFFICES were originally regarded as a form of property, and the proper remedy for disturbance, and for recovery of profits in the hands of the usurper, was originally novel disseisin.[1] In the seventeenth century, however, case[2] supplanted the possessory assize, and after *Arris* v. *Stukely*[3] in 1677 it was accepted, though sometimes reluctantly, as settled that the action for money had and received also would lie for the profits of a usurped office.[4] It is often said[5] that this is an example of the doctrine of waiver of tort. However, in *Arris* v. *Stukely*, it was held that the action for money had and received was available not because a tort had been committed but because account lay in such circumstances, and whenever account lay *indebitatus assumpsit* would lie. The analogy of the receiver of rents was compelling: "An *indebitatus assumpsit* will lie for rent received by one who pretends a title; for in such case an account will lie. Wherever the plaintiff may have an account, an *indebitatus* will lie."[6]

The application of account in such a case was surprising; for usurpation of an office was, as we have seen, a wrong for which case was available, and account could not generally be brought against a wrongdoer.[7] At the time when it was introduced, therefore, this innovation was viewed with suspicion,[8] for "waiver of tort" had not yet become established. Today, however, though not historically accurate, these cases may be seen as restitutionary claims based on a tortious act.[9] But the plaintiff is only entitled to recover what the defendant has

---

[1] Jackson, *History*, pp. 61–53, and authorities there cited.

[2] *Earl of Shrewsbury's Case* (1610) 9 Co.Rep. 46b, 51a; *Montague* v. *Preston* (1690) 2 Vent. 170.

[3] (1677) 2 Mod. 260. The first case in which an action for money had and received was brought for the profits of an usurped office appears to have been *Woodward* v. *Aston* (1672) 2 Mod. 95.

[4] *Howard* v. *Wood* (1679) 2 Show.K.B. 21; *Bowell* v. *Milbank* (1772) 1 T.R. 399n. The action for money had and received was also used to try title to an office (see *Rains* v. *Commissary of the Diocese of Canterbury* (1703) 7 Mod. 146; *Roberts* v. *Aulton* (1857) 2 H. & N. 432); or to determine whether a person has been rightfully dismissed from an office (*Osgood* v. *Nelson* (1872) L.R. 5 H.L. 636).

[5] Jackson, p. 61; Winfield, *Quasi-Contracts*, pp. 96–97.

[6] *Arris* v. *Stukely* (1677) 2 Mod. 260, 262; see also *Howard* v. *Wood* (1679) 2 Show.K.B. 21, 22.

[7] *Tottenham* v. *Bedingfield* (1572) 3 Leo. 24, *per* Manwood C.B.

[8] *Lamine* v. *Dorrell* (1705) 2 Ld.Raym. 1216, 1217, *per* Holt C.J.; Fifoot, *History and Sources of the Common Law*, p. 365.

[9] See below, Chap. 38.

actually received in the way of profits[10]; the plaintiff cannot recover any greater profits which he might have earned had he been exercising the office.

To succeed in the action the plaintiff must show a full title. In *Bowell* v. *Milbank*,[11] the plaintiff failed to recover the profits of the curacy of Chester-le-Street when it appeared that he had never received his licence from the Bishop. Again, the action can only be brought for fees which accrue to the occupier of the office *qua* office-holder; it will not lie for a salary payable in respect of work which the ousted plaintiff has not performed,[12] nor will it lie for incidental benefits such as gratuities,[13] which depend "entirely on the behaviour and civility" of the person exercising the office, and *"non constat* that anything would have been paid to the plaintiff."[14]

It has been held in the United States[15] that, where the usurper has acted under an apparent right and in good faith, he may deduct his necessary expenditure from the profits for which he is accountable. This is a just and reasonable rule, which should be followed in this country.[16]

Where an office has been usurped, it is of particular importance that the true office-holder should have a remedy against the usurper; for it has long been the rule, for the sake of the public peace, that the acts and grants of a *de facto* occupier of an office are valid and binding upon the true holder.[17] If this is so, then it would appear that, since the *de facto* occupier can give a valid discharge of a debt, the true office-holder loses his right against the debtor, so discharged, and must look to the *de facto* occupier for payment.[18] This possible exception to the general rule,[19] that a stranger cannot discharge a debt without the creditor's consent or subsequent ratification, will cause the creditor hardship if his former debtor is solvent and the usurper insolvent. There is, however, no clear authority which holds that the original debt is discharged.[20]

---

[10] *King* v. *Alston* (1848) 17 L.J.Q.B. 59.

[11] (1772) 1 T.R. 399n.; see also *Brown and Green (Ltd.)* v. *Hays* (1920) 36 T.L.R. 330.

[12] *Lawlor* v. *Alton* (1873) I.R. 8 C.L. 160.

[13] *Boyter* v. *Dodsworth* (1796) 6 T.R. 681.

[14] (1796) 6 T.R. 681, 683, *per* Lawrence J. Damages for loss of such items may, however, be recoverable in tort; see *Lawlor* v. *Alton* (1873) I.R. 8 C.L. 160.

[15] *Mayfield* v. *Moore*, 53 Ill. 428 (1870); *Booker* v. *Donohue*, 95 Va. 359, 28 S.E. 584 (1897); *Albright* v. *Sandoval*, 216 U.S. 331 (1910); *Restatement of Restitution*, § 137 and comment. *Cf. Douglass* v. *The State*, 31 Ind. 429 (1869).

[16] In England a similar rule is applied in the case of an executor *de son tort*: see below, nn. 27–31. See also *O'Sullivan* v. *Management Agency and Music Ltd.* [1985] Q.B. 428; but contrast *Guinness plc.* v. *Saunders* [1990] 2 A.C. 663: see above, pp. 32–34.

[17] Viner Abr. XVI, 114.

[18] It has recently been suggested that these special cases are characterised by the fact that D, in receiving the payments, was authorised to act, or purported to act, on behalf of P; D could not then deny that he had received money to P's use. The corollary of that conclusion should be that T's payment discharged the debt which he owed to P: see [1991] Oxford Jo. L.S. 481 [Lionel Smith].

[19] See above, p. 17, n. 2.

[20] *Cf.* p. 578, n. 18.

"The suit for money had and received avoids circuity of action"[21]; and the true office holder's suit against the *de facto* occupier may be said to be ratification of the debtor's payment.

2. OTHER CASES

It is not surprising to find that there are other cases in which the law has enabled the creditor to proceed directly against the person his debtor has erroneously paid. For "there are many cases in the books where a person has assumed to have authority when in truth he had none. It has always been held that he is accountable just as if he had in fact the authority which he assumed."[22] Perhaps the oldest example of this kind of case occurs where a person intervenes without right to collect another's rents. Such a person is accountable to the person entitled to receive the rents.[23] Account was not, however, available where there had been a disseisin of the land, for there the appropriate remedy lay upon the wrong,[24] and today the plaintiff in such a case should bring not an action for money had and received but an action for mesne profits, in which the measure of his recovery is his loss rather than the defendant's gain.

There are other cases. In *Jacob* v. *Allen*,[25] for example, the plaintiff, as executor, sued the defendant, attorney to one, H, who had acted as administrator of the deceased's estate until a will was found, for money owing to the estate which the defendant had collected on H's behalf. The defendant was held liable in an action for money had and received.[26] The case is analogous to that of a person who has intervened to collect another's rents. Again, an executor *de son tort* is liable to the rightful representative for the assets he has actually received[27]; but from the amount payable by him to the rightful representative he may deduct all payments made in the due course of administration,[28]

---

[21] *Official Custodian for Charities* v. *Mackey (No. 2)* [1985] 1 W.L.R. 1308, 1314–1315, *per* Nourse J.

[22] *Phipps* v. *Boardman* [1965] Ch. 992, 1017, *per* Lord Denning M.R.

[23] Y.B. 4 Hen. VII, 6, pl. 2, *per* Brian C.J.; *Tottenham* v. *Bedingfield* (1572) 3 Leon. 24, *per* Manwood C.B.; *Arris* v. *Stukely* (1677) 2 Mod. 260, 262, *per curiam*; Brooke Abr., tit. *Accompt*, pl. 65; *Lyell* v. *Kennedy* (1889) 14 App.Cas. 437. *Cf. Official Custodian of Charities* v. *Mackey (No. 2)* [1985] Ch. 151: see below, n. 35. A party who intervenes, without authority, to act as bailiff, may also be held accountable: see *Gawton* v. *Lord Dacres* (1590) 1 Leon. 219, 220, *per* Anderson C.J.; see also *English* v. *Dedham Vale Properties Ltd.* [1978] 1 W.L.R. 93 see below, p. 654.

[24] *Tottenham* v. *Bedingfield* (1573) 3 Leo. 24, *per* Manwood C.B.

[25] (1703) 1 Salk. 27. See also *Lamine* v. *Dorrell* (1705) 2 Ld.Ray. 1216, though this case appears to have been treated as a case of waiver of tort; and *Asher* v. *Wallis* (1707) 11 Mod. 146.

[26] The defendant was held liable even though he had, apparently in good faith, paid the money over to his principal; this conclusion was probably wrong even at that time (see *Pond* v. *Underwood* (1705) 2 Ld.Ray. 1210), and recovery would certainly not be allowed in such circumstances today (see below, pp. 750–755).

[27] *Yardley* v. *Arnold* (1842) Car. & M. 434. See also *Stokes* v. *Porter* (1558) 2 Dy. 166b; *Lowry* v. *Fulton* (1839) 9 Sim. 115.

[28] *Padget* v. *Priest* (1787) 2 T.R. 97, *per* Buller J.; *Fyson* v. *Chambers* (1842) 9 M. & W. 460, 468, *per* Lord Abinger C.B.

including funeral expenses,[29] provided at least that he did not act in bad faith.[30-31] The executor *de son tort* has something in common with the usurper of an office, however, for acts done by him in the character of executor will bind the estate. It has also been held that "a lady who took on herself to act as trustee was just as liable as if she were in truth a trustee."[32] This is just one example of the situation which arises when a person becomes liable because he intermeddles in a trust and thereby takes upon himself the burdens of trusteeship.[33]

In the light of these decisions, this category of cases should not be regarded as closed.[34] But it is the

> "essence of all those cases both that there is a contract or some other current obligation between the [debtor] and the [creditor] on which the defendant intervenes and that the [debtor] is indebted to the plaintiff [the creditor] in the precise amount of the sum which he pays to the defendant, so that he cannot claim repayment from the defendant in the face of a claim made against the defendant by the plaintiff."[35]

As has been seen, it is not clear whether the original debt is discharged in these circumstances[36]; but the debtor cannot reclaim repayment from the defendant payee if the creditor has claimed the money from the payee.[37]

---

[29] *Yardley* v. *Arnold* (1842) Car. & M. 434.

[30-31] *Woolley* v. *Clark* (1822) 5 B. & Ald. 744; *Fyson* v. *Chambers* (1842) 9 M. & W. 460, 468, *per* Lord Abinger C.B.; *Thomson* v. *Harding* (1853) 2 E. & B. 630, 635, *per* Lord Campbell C.J. But see above, pp. 32–34.

[32] *Phipps* v. *Boardman* [1965] Ch. 992, 1018, *per* Lord Denning M.R., citing *Rackham* v. *Siddall* (1849) 1 Mac. & G. 607.

[33] *Cf. English* v. *Dedham Vale Properties Ltd.* [1978] 1 W.L.R. 93.

[34] The action can be classified as one of waiver of tort: see, *e.g. Watson* v. *McLean* (1858) E.B. & E. 75. When the defendant has committed the legal wrong of infringement of a patent, copyright or registered trade mark, the plaintiff may, instead of claiming damages at common law, ask for an account in equity of the profits thereby obtained by the defendant: (for patents, see the Patents Act 1977, s.61; for copyright, see the Copyright, Designs and Patents Act 1988, ss.96(1), (2), 97 (plaintiff only entitled to damages if defendant knew, or had reason to believe that there was a breach of copyright); for registered trade marks, see *A. G. Spalding & Bros. Ltd.* v. *A. W. Gamage Ltd.* (1915) 32 R.P.C. 273 (an account will be granted only if defendant knew of the plaintiff's mark)). This accounting is regarded as incidental to the plaintiff's right to an injunction; but where an account is taken, he loses his right to damages—"if you take an account of profits, you condone the infringement" (*Neilson* v. *Betts* (1871) L.R. 5 H.L. 1, 22, *per* Lord Westbury). These cases are, therefore, consistent with the common law cases which have been said to be examples of waiver of tort: see below, pp. 690–692 and Chap. 38.

[35] *Official Custodian of Charities* v. *Mackey (No. 2)* [1985] 1 W.L.R. 1308, 1314, *per* Nourse J., (where the claim by lessors for mesne profits against the receivers and mortgagees of a company in liquidation, the lessees, who were in receipt of rents from sub-lessees, failed.)

[36] This is the probable conclusion: see above, pp. 578–579.

[37] *Cf.* below, pp. 578–579.

3. PROPRIETARY CLAIMS

There appears to be no authority on the question whether the claimant has an equitable proprietary claim to profits in the hands of a usurper or any other person in an analogous position. There is much to be said for the view that such a claim should perhaps lie.[38] Any other result would mean that the general creditors of the usurper or other persons in an analogous position would take the benefit of the profits in the event of his insolvency.

---

[38] *Cf.* above, Chap. 2, p. 93.

CHAPTER 29

CLAIMS UNDER A WILL OR INTESTACY OR UNDER AN INTER VIVOS TRUST

1. PERSONAL CLAIMS

(A) General Principles

IN this Chapter we shall be concerned with personal claims which arise when the beneficiary's money is paid, without his authority or under mistake, to a person who is not a bona fide purchaser[1] and who cannot successfully plead any other appropriate defence, such as change of position.[2]

At common law, as counsel still plead, a fiduciary, F, may seek to recover money paid to D under a mistake of fact in an action for money had and received.[3] D must then make restitution of a like sum. However, if D has paid all or some of that money to T, F's claim against T will fail if D has mixed F's money with his own money in his bank account.[3a] F cannot then show that T has received *his* money. But exceptionally he may still be able to discharge that burden,[4] in which case his claim against T will succeed. It is no defence to D or T that F cannot identify his money in their hands. In an appropriate case, those beneficially entitled (B) can compel F to sue at law.[5] Seemingly F cannot recover from D and T more than the sum mistakenly paid.[5a]

B may wish, however, to proceed directly against D or T; for example, F, a rogue, may have disappeared. If B can prove that D or T received money to which he is entitled in equity, then they should make restitution. They should do so even if (a) the money can no longer be identified in their hands,[6] and (b) they did not know[7] that they had received money paid to them in breach of trust. B may have further remedies. If the money can be identified, B will have a proprietary claim[8]; and if D and T had notice that the money had been paid in breach of trust, then they will be deemed in equity to be constructive trustees.[9]

---

[1] See above, Chap. 41.
[2] Chap. 40.
[3] See below, Chap. 3.
[3a] F's claim against D remains.
[4] See *Banque Belge pour l'Etranger* v. *Hambrouck* [1921] 1 K.B. 321: see above, p. 79.
[5] *Re Robinson* [1911] 1 Ch. 502, 507–508, *per* Warrington J.: below p. 586.
[5a] The question of the liability of D and T *inter se* will arise if D gives T all the money paid by F to him: see above, Chap. 12 (Query: are they liable for the *same* debt?).
[6] See above, pp. 77–78.
[7] See below, pp. 671–672 for a discussion of what is meant by knowledge in this context.
[8] See above, Chap. 2.
[9] It may be advantageous to persuade a court that D and T are constructive trustees. *E.g.* they will not be able to plead change of position as a defence, at least if they did not act in good faith; they

But what if F paid money to D under a mistake of law?[10] The baneful influence of the rule that *ignorantia juris non excusat* and the assumption that F's claim at common law must fail led in *Re Diplock*[11] to the resurrection of a body of law concerning claims arising out of the administration of an estate. As will be seen, the beneficiaries', B's, claim against D will not be defeated by the defence that the money had been paid under a mistake of law.[11a] This is to be welcomed. What is not to be welcomed are the special limitations, which are the product of ancient case law, surrounding this direct equitable action. With the rejection of the *ignorantia juris* rule, this body of law should, in our view, wither away. However, until Parliament or the House of Lords delivers its quietus, it is necessary to discuss the *Diplock* inheritance.

(B) The Diplock Personal Action

(a) *Claims arising out of the Administration of an Estate: Actions by Next-of-Kin, Legatees or Creditors where Personal Representatives have paid Money to Another who is not Entitled to it*

Where personal representatives have paid money from the deceased's estate to a person not entitled to it, the next-of-kin or legatees entitled under the will, or any creditor of the estate,[12] can recover the money from a recipient, other than a bona fide purchaser. The question is likely to arise where the money has been paid under a mistake. If the recipient had notice of the personal representatives' mistake, he will be deemed to be a constructive trustee, for he will then be aware that the money has been transferred to him in breach of trust.[13] More difficult questions arise, however, if the recipient did not know, and could not have known, of the mistake. This was the case in *Re Diplock*,[14] where executors had paid money under a mistake of law to the defendants, certain charities. An action was brought by the next-of-kin to recover the money from the charities. The Court of Appeal,[15] whose judgment was affirmed by the House of Lords,[16] held that the next-of-kin were entitled to succeed in a personal action in equity.

---

cannot plead a defence based on the Statute of Limitations and they may be liable to pay more than simple interest on the money due: see above, p. 73, for a fuller statement of the advantages.

[10] See above, Chap. 4.

[11] See below, n. 12.

[11a] Query whether B can recover from T who has received his money from B: see below, p. 585.

[12] *Re Diplock* [1948] Ch. 465, 502.

[13] *Cf. Re Diplock* [1948] Ch. 465, 477–478, *per curiam*; and cases cited below, pp. 671–672. If the administration of the estate has not been completed, it would appear that the recipient holds on trust for the personal representatives, who in turn hold on behalf of the estate, rather than for the legatees or next-of-kin: *Commissioners of Stamp Duties (Queensland)* v. *Livingstone* [1965] A.C. 694, P.C.

[14] [1947] Ch. 716, [1948] Ch. 465, C.A.; [1951] A.C. 251, H.L. (*sub nom. Ministry of Health* v. *Simpson*).

[15] [1948] Ch. 465.

[16] [1951] A.C. 251.

The origin of the equitable action was held to be distinct from *indebitatus assumpsit*. Accordingly, limitations on that remedy did not necessarily apply to the equitable action; in particular, the limit precluding the recovery of money paid under a mistake of law was inapplicable.[17]

The direct equitable claim arose at a time when the Court of Chancery was seeking to wrest from the ecclesiastical courts control over the administration of the estates of deceased persons[18]; but it may now no longer be confined to such a situation.[19] In any event, there are special limitations on the claimant's right to recover in equity.

First, it is a prerequisite that he must have exhausted his remedies against the personal representatives who made the payment. Any sums recovered thereby must be credited rateably "to all the [recipients] for all purposes."[20] The authorities which persuaded the courts[21] to formulate this qualification are not impressive: two old cases where there was more than a hint of fraud,[22] and a statement by Roper in his book on legacies.[23] The limitation must, for the present, be accepted as law, though, as we have seen,[24] it can result in injustice[25] to the personal representatives if the courts refuse to allow them to recover directly and in full (subject to any relevant defence, such as change of position), from the wrongly paid recipient.[26]

Secondly, the personal claim does not carry interest. This is a curious limitation since most personal claims do.[27]

Thirdly, it is subject to specific defences under the Limitation Act 1980.[28]

Fourthly, if the claimant is an "unsatisfied legatee" who seeks to "maintain a suit against another [legatee] . . . paid by the executor," he cannot compel the satisfied legatee to refund "if the assets be originally sufficient to satisfy all the legacies . . . because the payment was not a devastavit in the executor: and . . .

---

[17] *Bilbie* v. *Lumley* (1802) 2 East. 469: see above, Chap. 4.

[18] [1948] Ch. 465, 481–493.

[19] See below, pp. 585–587.

[20] [1948] Ch. 465, 556. It was further suggested that the proprietary claim was similarly limited; but on principle, this conclusion is open to criticism: see above, pp. 91–92.

[21] *Re Diplock* [1948] Ch. 465, 503–504; [1951] A.C. 251, 267–268.

[22] *Hodges* v. *Waddington* (1684) 2 Vent. 360 and *Orr* v. *Kaines* (1750–1751) 2 Ves.Sen. 194.

[23] (1847 ed.), p. 456, quoted in [1948] Ch. 465 at pp. 483, 503.

[24] See above, pp. 91–92.

[25] This injustice could be avoided by an application of the right of subrogation: see above, p. 92. In New Zealand and Western Australia this problem does not arise, for the claimant is directed to exhaust all other remedies available to him before proceeding against the personal representative or trustee: see New Zealand Administration Act 1952, s.30B(5), (added in 1960); Western Australia Trustee Act 1962, s.65(7); see above, p. 92.

[26] A trustee cannot recover from the recipient money which the trustee has paid to him under a mistake of law: see above, pp. 154–155 where the case law is criticised.

[27] [1948] Ch. 465 at pp. 505–507. *Cf.* the claim *in rem* which, the C.A. held, does carry interest; in principle this is even odder.

[28] See below, Chap. 43.

because the legatee is protected by the principle, that *vigilantibus non dormienti-bus jura subveniunt.*"[29]

Finally, it is doubtful whether the equitable personal claim lies against a third party deriving title through the original recipient.[30] There is no direct authority on this point. The equitable personal claim arose from the Chancellor's power "to regulate assents to legacies so that they shall not be suffered in equity to work a wrong or injustice to a third person [including creditors]."[31] Because the recipient knew that the executor could not assent without assets, he was deemed to have notice of the trust and was "privy to the breach of it."[32] History would suggest, therefore, that the personal claim may lie only against the person to whom an executor has assented. But there are dicta[33] which conclude that any party claiming through such a person will be liable unless he is a bona fide purchaser. If these dicta are accepted, the equitable personal claim will succeed if it can be shown that the defendant had received at one time the assets of the estate, even though those assets were not identifiable in the defendant's hands at the date of the action. The scope of the equitable claim will then be similar to that of the common law action for money had and received.[34]

(b) *Claims other than those Arising out of the Administration of an Estate: Actions by Beneficiaries or Creditors, where a Trustee or some other Fiduciary has paid Money to Another who is not Entitled to it*

In practice this question will become important if trustees of an *inter vivos* trust pay money to another in breach of trust and are unable to repair that breach. The beneficiaries will then seek to recover the money from the recipient. If the recipient has notice[35] that the money had been transferred in breach of trust, he will be a constructive trustee and will be jointly and severally liable with the trustees; conversely, if the recipient is a bona fide purchaser, he will not be liable. But the problem becomes more complex if he is an innocent volunteer

---

[29] Roper, *Legacies* (1847 ed.), p. 456, quoted in *Re Diplock* [1948] Ch. 465, 483–484; see also *Fenwick* v. *Clarke* (1862) 4 De G.F. & J. 240. *Aliter*, however, "if the assets be originally deficient to answer all the legacies": *Peterson* v. *Peterson* (1866) L.R. 3 Eq. 111.

[30] See below, n. 33.

[31] *Chamberlain* v. *Chamberlain* (1675) 79 *Selden Society* (Nottingham's Chancery Cases, Vol. II), p. 202.

[32] *Ibid.* And see *Ministry of Health* v. *Simpson* [1951] A.C. 251, 268, *per* Lord Simonds.

[33] *Nelson* v. *Larholt* [1948] 1 K.B. 339, 342, *per* Denning J.; *Baker (G.L.) Ltd.* v. *Medway Building and Supplies Ltd.* [1958] 1 W.L.R. 1216, 1220–1221, *per* Danckwerts J. (the question was left open in the C.A., [1958] 1 W.L.R. 1216, 1225); *Eddis* v. *Chichester Constable* [1969] 1 W.L.R. 385, 388, where Goff J. left the point open: see below, p. 586.
Contrast *Transvaal & Delagoa Bay Investment Co.* v. *Atkinson* [1944] 1 All E.R. 579 (where the common law claim for money had and received failed, *inter alia*, on the now discredited ground that no contract could be implied between the plaintiff and the defendant); and *Agip (Africa) Ltd.* v. *Jackson* [1990] Ch. 265, 287–289 (where Millett J. concluded that the common law claim could lie against the third party, but only for the value of the money which that party retained: see above, p. 81 which questions whether this conclusion is correct.)

[34] See above, p. 77. *Cf.* Birks, *Introduction*, pp. 441–442.

[35] See below, pp. 671–672 on what is meant by "notice."

who had no notice of the breach of trust. Such a situation may arise if money was transferred to him under mistake. The beneficiaries can, in this case, proceed through the trustees and compel the trustees to exercise any rights at law for their benefit.[36] If the money has been paid under a mistake of fact, the money can then be recovered.[37] Conversely, if the money has been paid under a mistake of law, an action at law must fail.[38] There are, however, dicta which suggest that the beneficiaries may proceed directly in equity against a recipient[39] other than a bona fide purchaser, whatever the nature of the trustees' mistake. The equitable action[40] is based on the defendant's receipt of "trust" money[41]: it is not confined to actions arising out of the administration of estates. But the analogy of *Re Diplock* suggests, however, that before the beneficiaries can sue in equity they must first exhaust their remedies against the trustees and that any sums recovered will reduce *pro tanto* the liability of the innocent volunteer.[42]

In *Butler* v. *Broadhead*[43] there is a suggestion that the equitable action may be available to creditors of a company if a liquidator distributes assets under mistake. In that case, a company conveyed for consideration land to X in 1960. In 1962 the company went into liquidation. Two years later the liquidator, under a mistake of law, sold the same tract of land to P for £825. The liquidator then advertised for claims,[44] paid off the company's debts, and distributed the company's surplus assets among the company's contributories. X dispossessed P, whereupon P brought an action against the contributories, claiming that they had been unjustly enriched at his expense. Templeman J. held that the Companies Act 1948,[45] and the Winding Up Rules[46] made under it, specifically barred P's claim. But he was inclined to the view that, statute apart, "there was a sufficient analogy between the position of an executor and a liquidator to enable equity to intervene in favour of unpaid creditors against overpaid contributories."[47]

---

[36] *Re Robinson* [1911] 1 Ch. 502, 508, *per* Warrington J.; *Re Mason* [1928] Ch. 385, 392, *per* Romer J.; [1929] Ch. 1; *Re Blake* [1932] Ch. 54; *Re Diplock* [1948] Ch. 465, 498–502, [1951] A.C. 251, 273–274, *per curiam*.

[37] See above, Chap. 3.

[38] See above, Chap. 4.

[39] See below, n. 41.

[40] See above, p. 583.

[41] See *Re J. Leslie Engineers Co. Ltd.* [1976] 1 W.L.R. 292, 299, *per* Oliver J.; *Butler* v. *Broadhead* [1975] Ch. 97, 107–108, *per* Templeman J.

[42] See above, p. 584. This was assumed to be so in *Butler* v. *Broadhead* [1975] Ch. 97, 107–108, *per* Templeman J. and in *Re J. Leslie Engineers Co. Ltd.* [1976] 1 W.L.R. 292, 299, *per* Oliver J.

[43] [1975] Ch. 97.

[44] Under Companies (Winding Up) Rules 1949, r. 106, made under Companies Act 1948, s.273(e).

[45] s.264.

[46] Companies (Winding Up) Rules 1949, r. 106.

[47] At p. 108. But see Companies Act 1948, s.272 (now Companies Act 1986, s.566), which was not cited. (We are grateful to Hubert Picarda Esq., Q.C., for drawing our attention to this section.)

The trend of recent authority would suggest, therefore, that the courts are prepared to extend the equitable action to enable beneficiaries and creditors of an *inter vivos* trust, as well as beneficiaries and creditors of other fiduciaries, to proceed directly against the recipients (other than bona fide purchasers) of trust or fiduciary assets. It is an open question whether they can proceed directly against persons, other than the immediate recipient, who have received trust moneys from that recipient.[48]

2. PROPRIETARY CLAIMS

It is now well established that beneficiaries under an *inter vivos* trust, and legatees and next-of-kin, whose claim arises out of the administration of an estate may follow (at least, when administration is complete[49-50]) their property in equity into the hands of recipients other than bona fide purchasers. The conditions under which they may do so have already been considered in an earlier Chapter.[51] An unsecured creditor should not generally be allowed to follow his property in equity[52]; for the essence of a loan transaction is that the creditor parts with legal and equitable property in the money in consideration of the debtor's promise to repay the debt.[53]

---

[48] See above, p. 585, n. 33, for dicta suggesting that they can.
[49-50] See above, n. 13.
[51] See above, Chap. 2.
[52] But see *Sinclair* v. *Brougham* [1914] A.C. 398: see above, p. 83.
[53] But *cf. Barclays Bank Ltd.* v. *Quistclose Investment Co.* [1970] A.C. 567; *Re Kayford (in liquidation)* [1975] 1 W.L.R. 279, (criticised in (1980) 43 M.L.R. 489 [Goodhart and Jones]); and *Carreras Rothmans Ltd.* v. *Freeman Mathews Treasure Ltd. (in liquidation)* [1985] Ch. 207—all cases of "loans" for a specific purpose.

CHAPTER 30

PERFECTION OF IMPERFECT GIFTS IN FAVOUR OF INTENDED DONEES

EQUITY will not generally perfect an imperfect gift in favour of an intended donee. The donor is perfectly free to perfect the gift and will do so if he wishes to do so; if he does not, equity will not compel him to act.[1]

There are, however, dicta,[2] which we do not find convincing,[3] which suggests that equity will assist the intended donee if the donor, having mistakenly given property to the wrong donee, dies or becomes incapacitated before the mistake is discovered. In such a case, it is said that the court is not rectifying a voluntary instrument against the donor, but is perfecting it in his favour.

On the other hand the bequest is imperfect, and to enforce the bequest would arguably frustrate the policy embodied in the Wills Act 1837. However, the Administration of Justice Act 1982, s.20, confers a limited jurisdiction to rectify a will, namely, if the court is satisfied that the will fails to carry out the testator's intentions "in consequence (a) of a clerical error or (b) of a failure to understand his instructions."[4] In such cases the testator's mistake will be rectified. Parliament has determined that only in these circumstances does the court have power to order rectification. It is doubtful, therefore, whether a court will rectify a will if the testator's solicitor or amanuensis did not know or could not have known that the testator was mistaken.[5]

---

[1] *Lister* v. *Hodgson* (1867) L.R. 4 Eq. 30, 34–35, *per* Romilly M.R.; *M'Mechan* v. *Warburton* [1896] 1 I.R. 435.

[2] *M'Mechan* v. *Warburton* [1896] 1 I.R. 435, 439, *per* Chatterton V.-C.; see also *Thompson* v. *Witmore* (1860) 1 J. & H. 268, 273, *per* Page Wood V.-C.; *Rosenblum* v. *Manufacturers Trust Co.*, 270 N.Y. 79, 200 N.E. 587 (1936).

[3] See above, pp. 36–38 for a general discussion.

[4] See above, p. 222, n. 30.

[5] *Cf. Restatement of Restitution*, § 127. But all donees should disgorge if they have fraudulently induced the gift at the expense of the intended donee: see *Restatement of Restitution*, § 133.

CHAPTER 31

SUBROGATION

1. General Principles

THERE are many cases where one person, A, has unofficiously conferred a benefit on another, B, usually in the form of a payment of money, and where it is just, in all the circumstances, that A should be allowed to have the benefit of another's rights or assets in order to prevent B's[1] unjust enrichment. The rights or assets may be B's, or they may be a third party's, C's, to whom B was obligated in some way or other. Consequently B may be compelled to exercise a personal right of action for A's benefit; or A may be allowed to succeed to securities deposited by B with C or to C's lien over B's land; or B may be deemed to be a trustee of assets for the benefit of A. Traditionally English lawyers speak of a *right* of subrogation.[2] But, as these examples show, it is in essence a remedy, fashioned to the particular facts, and designed to ensure "a transfer of rights from one person to another . . . by operation of law,"[3] in order to deprive B of a benefit gained at A's expense.[4]

The origins and the established categories of subrogation

The origins of subrogation are obscure. Some writers find them in Roman law; but the textual evidence is slight.[5] It is conceivable, but unlikely, that Pothier's writings[6] may have influenced the erroneous conclusion that subrogation is possible only if it has been reserved by contract. A contracting party may expressly reserve a right of subrogation[7]; conversely the terms of a particular contract may exclude subrogation or specify that there shall be subrogation

---

[1] Exceptionally it may be C who is *in fact* unjustly enriched: see below, pp. 591, 596.

[2] *Castellain* v. *Preston* (1883) 11 Q.B.D. 380, 390, *per* Brett L.J.; *Page* v. *Scottish Insurance Corp.* (1929) 140 L.T. 571, 575, *per* Scrutton L.J.; *Compania Columbiana de Seguros* v. *Pacific Steam Navigation Co.* [1965] 1 Q.B. 101, 111, *per* Roskill J. But *cf. Orakpo* v. *Manson Investments Ltd.* [1978] A.C. 95, 104, *per* Lord Diplock.

[3] *Orakpo* v. *Manson Investments Ltd.* [1978] A.C. 95, 104, *per* Lord Diplock. *Cf. Restatement of Restitution,* § 162.

[4] *Re T.H. Knitwear (Wholesale) Ltd.* [1988] 1 Ch. 275, 284, C.A.: below pp. 591, 594.

[5] See D. 46.1.17; Schulz, *Classical Roman Law,* pp. 502–505; Buckland, *Text Book,* p. 449; *cf.* Buckland, *Equity in Roman Law,* p. 47. Storey, *Equity Jurisprudence,* § 706, suggests that civil law was influential in the development of equitable subrogation. There is no evidence to support or refute this suggestion, though it may be significant that subrogation developed in the courts of Chancery and Admiralty, which were not insensitive to civilian influences. *Cf.* the Admiralty records in (1897) 11 *Selden Society,* pp. 49 *et seq.* [R. G. Marsden].

[6] *Oeuvres de Pothier,* tit. 20 sec. 5. *Cf.* Story, *Equity Jurisprudence,* § 715.

[7] *Orakpo* v. *Manson Investments Ltd.* [1978] A.C. 95, 119, *per* Lord Keith of Kinkel.

only in certain circumstances.[8] But subrogation was known to the Chancellor in the seventeenth century[9]; and the cases establish that subrogation arises independently of, and "not by force of,"[10] contract and will be granted if it is just and equitable to do so. Subrogation is the "plainest equity that could be"[11]; its basis is a "principle of natural justice."[12] As Buckley L.J. once said: "The doctrine of subrogation does not . . . rest on contract at all. It is an equitable doctrine."[13] Most recently, in *Lord Napier and Ettrick* v. *R.F. Kershaw Ltd.*,[13a] both Lord Goff and Lord Browne-Wilkinson emphasised that equity did not simply supplement the common law. A "principle of subrogation was the subject of a separate development by courts of equity in a line of authority dating from *Randal* v. *Cockran* (1748)"[13b] "Equity itself enforced rights of subrogation against the assured."[13c]

So, a surety who has paid off the principal debt is entitled to any securities deposited by the debtor with the creditor because it would be "against conscience"[14] to allow the debtor to regain them without reimbursing the surety. Indorsees of bills of exchange are, in this respect, in a similar position to sureties[15]; indeed subrogation "applies in any case where there is a primary and secondary liability for the same debt."[16] An insurer is allowed to succeed to the rights of the assured and "has an equity to be recouped"[17] to prevent the possibility of the assured recovering twice over. And business creditors may be subrogated to the right of indemnity of the trustee who has incurred those debts while properly carrying on the trust business, in order to avoid the "injustice of the *cestui que trust* walking off with the assets which have been earned by the use of the property"[18] of the creditors.

Suretyship, bills of exchange, insurance, and trust law are the main areas where English courts have undoubtedly accepted that a person may be subrogated to the rights or assets of another. But there is a fifth, somewhat

---

[8] *Cf. Yorkshire Shipping Co.* v. *Nisbet Shipping Co. Ltd.* [1962] 2 Q.B. 330, 329–340, *per* Diplock J.; *Morris* v. *Ford Motor Co.* [1973] Q.B. 792, 810–812, *per* James L.J.

[9] See the cases cited below, pp. 627 *et seq.*

[10] *Aldrich* v. *Cooper* (1803) 8 Ves. 382, 389, *per* Lord Eldon L.C.

[11] *Randal* v. *Cockran* (1748) 1 Ves.Sen. 98; see also *Burnand* v. *Rodocanachi* (1882) 7 App.Cas. 333, 339, *per* Lord Blackburn.

[12] *Craythorne* v. *Swinburne* (1807) 14 Ves. 160, 162, *per* Sir Samuel Romilly, *arguendo*. See also *Morris* v. *Ford Motor Co.* [1973] Q.B. 792, 800–801, *per* Lord Denning M.R., 807, *per* Stamp L.J.

[13] *Orakpo* v. *Manson Investments Ltd.* [1977] 1 W.L.R. 347, 357; see also at p. 368, *per* Goff L.J.

[13a] [1993] 1 All E.R. 385.

[13b] At p. 400, *per* Lord Goff: see above, n. 11.

[13c] At p. 407, *per* Lord Browne-Wilkinson. But the principle of subrogation in the law of insurance arises in a contractual context: for a further discussion see below, pp. 606–618.

[14] *Aldrich* v. *Cooper* (1803) 8 Ves. 382, 389, *per* Lord Eldon L.C.

[15] See below, p. 605.

[16] *Re Downer Enterprises Ltd.* [1974] 1 W.L.R. 1460, 1468, *per* Pennycuick V.-C.: see below, p. 601.

[17] *Burnand* v. *Rodocanachi* (1882) 7 App.Cas. 333, 339, *per* Lord Blackburn.

[18] *Re Johnson* (1880) 15 Ch.D. 548, 555–556, *per* Jessel M.R.: see below, pp. 619–620.

eclectic, group of cases which provides, in our view, another illustration of the operation of subrogation. Their common factor is that A has lent money to B and the money has been used to discharge a valid liability owed by B to C. The problem whether A can then be subrogated to C arises in two distinct contexts. The first is when A has made a valid loan to B and the money has been applied to discharge B's secured debt to C.[19] In the second, A's loan to B is invalid; but it is used to discharge B's valid liability to C, who may or may not be a secured creditor.[20] Some judges have said that subrogation has "very little, if anything at all, to do"[21] with the relief given to A in the invalid loan cases. In our view this view is not supported by the balance of authority.[22] It is another question whether a more simple and elegant solution would have been to have allowed A to claim in restitution directly from B.

Subrogation in the law of restitution

As has been seen, a restitutionary claim should be granted if it is demonstrable that the defendant has been enriched, that the enrichment has been gained at the plaintiff's expense, and that it would be unjust to allow the defendant to retain the enrichment.[23] Because of the tripartite relationship of the parties, it is not always easy to determine whether it is B or C who has been enriched and why a court should conclude that the enrichment is an *unjust* enrichment, although it may be clear that the enrichment is at A's expense.

In the great majority of cases discussed in this Chapter it is evident that it is B who has been enriched at A's expense; unless A were subrogated to B, B, having been paid by A, would be in a position to sue C and would do so if that were the profitable outcome. Subrogation nips in the bud any ambition to secure a double enrichment.[24] Exceptionally B may have no such ambition even though he has been indemnified by A and can still sue C; it is C who is then in fact enriched. *Re T.H. Knitwear (Wholesale) Ltd.*[25] provides an example of one such case. B had supplied goods to C, a company in liquidation. C had not paid B for the goods. A was then under a statutory obligation to refund to B the VAT element which B had paid A. A did so. But A's claim to be subrogated to B's rights against C failed. B's independent statutory right to prove in C's liquidation for the VAT element was said to be "quite inconsistent" with the existence of a right of A to take over B's right of proof and to

---

[19] See below, pp. 621–622.

[20] See below, pp. 622 *et seq.*

[21] *Re Wrexham, Mold and Connah's Quay Ry.* [1899] 1 Ch. 440, 455, *per* Rigby L.J.

[22] See below, pp. 622 *et seq.* for a full discussion. See, *e.g. Orakpo* v. *Manson Investments Ltd.* [1978] A.C. 95, 104–105, *per* Lord Diplock, 112, *per* Lord Edmund-Davies.

[23] See above, Chap. 1.

[24] *Cf.* equity's rules to police the conduct of fiduciaries, discussed below, Chap. 33.

[25] [1988] Ch. 275. After the company went into liquidation the liquidator found that it had surplus assets: see below, p. 594 for a full account. See also *The Esso Bernicia* [1989] A.C. 643 (see below, p. 596), where it was also most unlikely that B would sue C, having been indemnified by A. B were humble crofters who, having been made whole, would never bring suit against C, the tortfeasor, a powerful company. Here C, a tortfeasor, gained a windfall enrichment.

present it in B's name. If B had exercised his right, and had recovered the VAT element, he would, however, have had to refund the VAT element to A. It may be said that B was enriched in that, having been indemnified by A, he still enjoyed the right to prove in C's liquidation. But it was C's contributories who were in reality enriched since B would in practice never prove in C's liquidation.[25a]

The courts have rarely inquired why it is *just* to subrogate A to another's rights. A and B may have contracted with each other that A should be subrogated to B's rights. But subrogation arises independently of contract.[26] The happiest rationalisation of the case law is that B's conduct would properly be condemned as unconscionable if, having accepted the money payment from A, B were to assert that A cannot be subrogated to his rights against C, rights which, if B's claim were upheld, B would continue to enjoy for his own benefit.[27]

A combination of factors has contributed to the uncertainty which surrounds the role of subrogation in the English law of restitution. The law of subrogation has developed very pragmatically, almost in an insular fashion, within each of these established categories. Although subrogation is an equitable doctrine:

> "the relevant equitable considerations may depend on the nature of the case. They may be different, for example where the basis of subrogation is a contract of indemnity, or where the problem is associated with *ultra vires* borrowings by a company; or where ... a lender lends money which is used for completing a purchase or for paying off an existing mortgage."[28]

Moreover these "equitable considerations" have at times been concealed as implied terms of a contract or have taken the form of misleading analogies with the law of assignment.[29] Metaphor has also contributed to the confusion. Not uncommonly judges talk of a person standing "in the shoes" or "in the place" of another.[30] But the shoes may be those of the unjustly enriched defendant, B, or a third party, C. The insurer, A, is subrogated to the rights of the assured, B, to prevent B's unjust enrichment; but the surety, A, is subrogated to the rights of the creditor, C, to prevent the principal debtor's, B's, unjust enrichment. In insurance A is subrogated to B because A has agreed to indemnify B. In suretyship A is subrogated to C because A has agreed to indemnify C.[31] Indeed in one situation A may seek to be subrogated to C's right of indemnity against B.[32] Subrogation is a tangled web. It should not be assumed that principles

---

[25a] See above, n. 25.

[26] But see above, pp. 589–590.

[27] See above, p. 43.

[28] *Orakpo* v. *Manson Investments Ltd.* [1977] 1 W.L.R. 347, 357, *per* Buckley L.J.

[29] *Jenner* v. *Morris* (1861) 3 De G.F. & J. 45, 51–52, *per* Lord Campbell. And contrast *Orakpo* v. *Manson Investments Ltd.* [1978] A.C. 95, 104, *per* Lord Diplock.

[30] *e.g. Marlow* v. *Pitfeild* (1719) 1 P.Wms. 558; *Re National Permanent Benefit B.S., ex p. Williamson* (1869) 5 Ch.App. 309, 313, *per* Giffard L.J.

[31] See below, pp. 602 *et seq.*

[32] Where business creditors are subrogated to a trustee's right of indemnity from his beneficiaries: see below, pp. 619–620.

which grew up in one area can be transplanted to another.[33] What is critical is to recognise that subrogation is granted in each case to ensure that B disgorges the gain made at the expense of A, and that to achieve this A may be subrogated either to B or C. Subrogation inevitably involves a tripartite relationship.[34] Consequently if B and C are, by chance, the same person, subrogation will not assist A since there is no possible claim against a third party to which he can succeed.[35]

There is a final and inter-related reason why the topic of subrogation is so confused. Some judges have assumed that if A "is subrogated" to C, A must succeed to C's lien or charge over B's property and not to any personal claim which C enjoyed against B.[36] It was natural for common lawyers to take this view since, in most cases, for example, in suretyship, any personal obligation at law owed by B to C was discharged by A's payment to C. But equity should not have been, and is not, so limited.[37] There are many cases, dating from the early eighteenth century, where A, who made an invalid loan to B who used the loan to pay off his valid debt to C, was allowed to stand in C's place and to enforce in equity a personal claim, akin to that discharged at law, against B. So, A, who had lent money to B, an infant, who had used the loan to buy necessaries from C, was allowed to stand in C's shoes.[38] It is unfortunate that in some of the *ultra vires* loan cases[39] subrogation was rejected. These concerned a claim by A, who had made B an *ultra vires* and unsecured loan, to succeed to the rights of C, a secured and *intra vires* creditor, paid off with A's loan money. This claim was indefensible for A would then have been in a better position than if he had made a secured loan. The analogy of other invalid loan cases should have led the court to hold that A should have been subrogated only to C's personal claim against B.[40] But some judges thought that to *subrogate* A to C *must* result in A succeeding to C's security.[41] Consequently, subrogation was dismissed as irrelevant and A was given an independent, equitable right which put him in the same position as any other general creditor. In our view, this distinction was unnecessary and contrary to precedent; moreover, it would inevitably cause, and has caused, confusion as to the scope of equitable subrogation.

Much of the confusion would never have arisen if the courts had accepted the full implications of the principle that subrogation is essentially a remedy, which is fashioned to the facts of the particular case and which is granted in order to prevent the defendant's unjust enrichment. A plaintiff may then be

---

[33] *Orakpo* v. *Manson Investments Ltd.* [1978] A.C. 95, 104, *per* Lord Diplock.
[34] See above, p. 589.
[35] *Simpson* v. *Thompson* (1877) 3 App.Cas. 279, criticised in (1971) 31 M.L.R. 149 [James]. But see Meagher, Gummow and Lehane, *Equity*, §§ 946–949, which is more convincing.
[36] *Thurstan* v. *Nottingham Permanent Benefit B.S.* [1902] 1 Ch. 1, 12, *per* Romer L.J.; *Paul* v. *Speirway Ltd.* [1976] Ch. 220, 227, *per* Oliver J.: see below, p. 622.
[37] *Re Byfield* [1982] CR. 267, 272, *per* Goulding J.: see above, p. 67.
[38] See below, pp. 627–629.
[39] See, in particular, *Re Wrexham, Mold and Connah's Quay Ry.* [1899] 1 Q.B. 440; see below, pp. 637–638 for a full discussion.
[40] See below, pp. 627 *et seq.*
[41] See below, pp. 636–638.

subrogated to a personal claim or another's security interest. Whether subrogation to a security should be permitted should depend on whether a court considers it proper to allow the plaintiff that security and priority; it may be more ready to do so if there is no question of preferring the plaintiff to another's general creditors. As Lord Salmon said[42]: "The test as to whether the courts will apply the doctrine of subrogation to the facts of any particular case is entirely empirical. It is . . . impossible to formulate any narrower principle than that the doctrine will be applied only when the courts are satisfied that reason and justice demand that it should be." In our view the law can only be extended in a coherent and just fashion if this general principle is recognised. It is, of course, a large generalisation which subsequent cases will refine and limit. Some of these limitations can already be observed.

The limits of subrogation

First, subrogation can be excluded or modified by contract.[43]

Secondly, statute or statutory regulations may make it impossible to spell out any transfer of B's rights against C to A. Such was the conclusion of the Court of Appeal in *Re T.H. Knitwear (Wholesale) Ltd.*[44] C, a company, bought goods from B, at a basic price plus VAT. B was statutorily obliged to account for that tax to the Commissioners of Customs and Excise (A), and did so. Subsequently C went into liquidation, apparently hopelessly insolvent. A repaid B the VAT as it was obliged to do. C's liquidator then found, *mirabile dictu*, that it had surplus assets, and consequently applied for directions whether the contributories were entitled to the whole surplus or whether A could be subrogated to B's statutory right, which B, himself, would be most unlikely to exercise,[45] to prove in C's bankruptcy for the VAT element. The Court of Appeal held that, given the statutory VAT regulations, B's right to prove in the liquidation and to receive from the liquidator the proceeds of that proof was "quite inconsistent with the existence of a right in the commissioners [A] to take over the creditor's [B's] right of proof and themselves to present it in his name."[46] Moreover, the statutory regulations made it clear that A's payment to B did not discharge C's liability to pay B the VAT element.[47] As Sir Nicolas Browne-Wilkinson V.-C. recognised,[48] this is a harsh result, given the fact that A was obliged to make the refund and that B would probably never

---

[42] *Orakpo* v. *Manson Investments Ltd.* [1978] A.C. 95, 110; *Re T.H. Knitwear (Wholesale) Ltd.* [1987] 1 W.L.R. 371, 376, *per* Sir Nicolas Browne-Wilkinson V.-C.

[43] See above, p. 589; see below, pp. 607–608.

[44] [1988] Ch. 275. For a discussion of another aspect of this case, see above, p. 591.

[45] If he did so, having already received a refund from A, the statutory regulations required him to repay the fund to A.

[46] At pp. 286–287, *per* Slade L.J.

[47] Contrast *The Esso Bernicia* [1989] 1 A.C. 643: see below, p. 596.

[48] At first instance: [1987] 1 W.L.R. 371, 375.

prove in liquidation, for if he did, he would have to refund the VAT to A.[49] So, the contributories of C received a windfall.

It may well be that the statutory scheme compelled the conclusion that A's claim must fail. And yet if A had contracted with B to indemnify him if C failed to pay a debt owed to B, a court would not hesitate, A having indemnified B, to subrogate A to B's rights against C.[50] Sir Nicolas Browne-Wilkinson V.-C. asked rhetorically,[51] if "the creditor [B] is to continue to have the contractual right against the debtor [C], how can those rights have been transferred by subrogation to another [A]?" The insurer's (A's) payment to the assured (B) does not extinguish B's rights against a third party (C). It is for that reason that A is subrogated to B's rights and that A's suit is always brought in the name of B.

Thirdly, A will not be subrogated to the rights of another if the benefit which he has conferred on B was conferred as a gift.[52]

Fourthly, subrogation will be denied if it will result in the indirect enforcement of a transaction which the law has declared to be ineffective. This may not be easy to determine, as *Thurstan* v. *Nottingham Permanent Benefit Building Society*[53] demonstrates. D, a building society, lent money to P, a minor, not knowing that P was a minor. Contemporaneously P applied the money to buy land from V and secured D's loan by mortgaging that land to D. As soon as D discovered P was a minor, it took possession of the land. P, now of full age, demanded the return of the title deeds and a declaration that the mortgage was void, being a security for a loan which was itself void under the Infants Relief Act 1874. The House of Lords held that the loan was void, but subrogated D to V's unpaid vendor's lien over the land in order to prevent P's unjust enrichment, even though the unpaid vendor's lien had never arisen because V had been paid in full and because D thought it was protected by a valid mortgage. It was said that such real subrogation did not offend against the policy of the Infants Relief Act 1874, which only rendered void loans to minors. This was a generous and ingenious conclusion, undoubtedly inspired by the court's determination to defeat the claim of a less than honest plaintiff. *Thurstan's* case was influential in persuading the Court of Appeal in *Congresbury Motors Ltd.* v. *Anglo-Belge Finance Ltd.*[54] to permit a lender whose secured loan was unenforceable because the formalities required by section 6 of the Moneylenders Act 1927 had not been observed to be subrogated to an unpaid vendor's lien over land which had been bought by the borrower with the money lent. This was not deemed to conflict with the policy underlying the Moneylenders Act 1927.

---

[49] In reality, it is C who has been enriched: contrast the position of B, the crofters, in *The Esso Bernicia* [1989] 1 A.C. 643, discussed below, p. 596.

[50] *Cf.* the contract of insurance.

[51] [1987] 1 W.L.R. 371, 376.

[52] See above, p. 66; see below, pp. 632–634. *Cf. Norton* v. *Haggett* 85 A. 2d 571 (1952): see below, p. 598, n. 80.

[53] [1903] A.C. 6. For a full statement of the facts and a further discussion, see below, pp. 632–634.

[54] [1971] Ch. 81; *cf. London & Harrogate Securities* v. *Pitts* [1976] 1 W.L.R. 1063: and see above, pp. 65–66.

However, in *Orakpo* v. *Manson Investments Ltd.*,[55] the House of Lords over-ruled *Congresbury Motors Ltd.* v. *Anglo-Belge Finance Ltd.* on the ground that subrogation to the lien would frustrate the object of the statute, which required these formalities for the protection of the borrowing public. But the authority of *Thurstan's* case was not questioned. Consequently a lender is in a better position if his loan is declared to be void than if it is unenforceable. This is, in our view, a strange result.[56]

Fifthly, subrogation is granted to prevent another's unjust enrichment *at the plaintiff's expense*. A plaintiff should not, therefore, be allowed to improve his position or to make a profit by succeeding to the rights of another.[57] Sub-rogation should be permitted only so far as it is necessary to enable him to recoup the loss suffered[58]; here the loss suffered is the proper measure of the defendant's benefit, gained at the plaintiff's expense.[59] Consequently, if A makes B an unsecured loan, which proves to be invalid, and the loan is used to discharge C's secured debt, A should be subrogated in equity to C's personal claim against B but not to C's security over B's property; to allow him to succeed to C's security would be to put him in a better position than if his loan had been valid.[60] For similar reasons, if "an unpaid vendor were entitled to a lien in a sum of £5,000 unpaid purchase money and the lender were to advance £3,000 to the purchaser towards the payment of this sum, the balance being found by the purchaser from his own, or other, resources, the lender would only be subrogated to the unpaid vendor's lien to the extent of £3,000."[61] It has also been held that an insurer is entitled to be subrogated to the assured's rights only in so far as it is necessary to recoup the loss suffered, or the expense incurred, in conferring the benefit on the assured, even though the assured gained what is arguably a windfall.[62]

The sixth limitation is the most mercurial: a plaintiff who voluntarily benefits a defendant will not be granted any restitutionary relief.[63] For example, A may be denied subrogation to B's rights against C, who had tortiously injured him, if A indemnified B in pursuance of his contract with a third party, T, so to do. A is deemed to be a mere volunteer. Such were the facts of *The Esso Bernicia*.[64] Esso (A) had entered into a contract with other tanker operators (T) to assume liability for pollution damage caused by oil which had escaped or had been discharged from their tankers. *The Esso*

---

[55] [1978] A.C. 95.

[56] See above, pp. 66–67; see below, p. 633.

[57] *Cf. Boodle Hatfield & Co. (A Firm)* v. *British Films Ltd.* [1986] P.C.C. 176: "subrogation would not be applied where its application would produce an unjust result," *per* Nicholls J.

[58] *Cf. Morris* v. *Ford Motor Co.* [1973] Q.B. 792, 804, *per* Stamp L.J.; C. 8.40.11; *Restatement of Restitution,* § 162(c); *Australasian Conference Association Ltd.* v. *Mainline Construction Pty. Ltd.* (1978) A.L.J.R. 66 (High Ct. of Aust.).

[59] See above, p. 35.

[60] See below, pp. 625–626.

[61] *Orakpo* v. *Manson Investments Ltd.* [1977] 1 W.L.R. 347, 361, *per* Buckley L.J.

[62] *Yorkshire Insurance Co.* v. *Nisbet Shipping Co. Ltd.* [1962] 2 Q.B. 330: see below, p. 613.

[63] See above, pp. 58–60.

[64] *Sub nom. Esso Petroleum Co. Ltd.* v. *Hall Russell & Co. Ltd.* [1989] A.C. 643.

Bernicia collided with a jetty at BP's oil terminal in the Shetlands. A large quantity of oil escaped, causing considerable damage. Pursuant to the tanker operators' agreement, Esso paid, *inter alia*, the crofters (B) £480,000 for their lost sheep. In this suit they claimed these sums[65] from Hall Russell (C) which had designed the tug which had burst into flames, breaking the tow line and causing *The Esso Bernicia* to crash into the jetty. The House of Lords concluded that there was no material difference between Scottish and English law, and held that Esso could not sue Hall Russell in its own name to recover these payments. The rights of action were the crofters', and the crofters' alone. Esso's payments had not been made under a contract of indemnity between Esso and the crofters. If they had been, Esso would have been subrogated to the crofters' claims against Hall Russell. But Esso's payments were voluntary payments. Consequently, Esso could not proceed to enforce the crofters' claims in their own name. "The reason for this is plain. It is that Esso's payment to the crofters does not have the effect of discharging Hall Russell's liability to them."[66] Hall Russell could not then be said to be enriched. If "anybody has been enriched, it is the crofters, to the extent that they have been indemnified by Esso and yet continue to have vested in them rights of action against Hall Russell in respect of the loss or damage which was the subject-matter of Esso's payments to them."[67]

This is a surprising, if inevitable, conclusion, given the common law rule that A's payment to B did not discharge C's liability to B. But to describe A's payment as voluntary and gratuitous, when it was made under an agreement with T to indemnify B against the loss which was suffered, demonstrates how rigid is the common law concept of voluntariness.[68-69]

A similar problem arises if a surety guarantees a debt without the debtor's consent. Can he be subrogated to the creditor whom he later pays? In *Owen* v. *Tate*[70] the Court of Appeal held that the plaintiff had done so voluntarily and could not recover directly from the principal debtor his payment to the creditor.[71] As Scarman L.J. said: "if without an antecedent request a person assumes an obligation or makes a payment for the benefit of another, the law will, as a general rule, refuse him a right of indemnity."[72] But it appears that it was not argued that the surety should be subrogated to the creditor's rights against the debtor. In determining whether there should be an indemnity or

---

[65] There were other claims.
[66] At p. 663, *per* Lord Goff.
[67] *Ibid.*
[68-69] Contrast *Re T.H. Knitwear (Wholesale) Ltd.* [1988] Ch. 275, 286–287, *per* Slade L.J. (See above, pp. 591–592, 594–595), where A was under a statutory obligation to make a refund to B, where B could still claim against C, (but would, like the crofters, though for different reasons, be most unlikely to do so), and where B's right to sue C was founded on a statutory regulation, so that it could not be said that A's payment to B had discharged C's liability to B.
[70] [1976] 1 Q.B. 402. See, generally, "Unrequested Payment of Another's Debt" (1976) 92 L.Q.R. 188 [P. Birks and J. Beatson], Beatson, *The Use and Abuse of Unjust Enrichment*, Chap. 7.
[71] *Cf.* above, pp. 351–352, and *Brown Shipley & Co. Ltd.* v. *Amalgamated Investment (Europe) B.V.* [1979] 1 Lloyd's Rep. 488.
[72] [1976] 1 Q.B. 402, 411–412.

subrogation, a crucial consideration should be whether the surety's unsolicited payment discharged the debt.[73] The Court of Appeal did not consider that question, although Stephenson L.J. assumed that it had done so.[74] And yet in English law a debt can only be discharged with the consent or subsequent ratification of the debtor. If the debt had been discharged by the surety's payment, it can only have been because the debtor has adopted that payment; the plaintiff should have been able to recover from the debtor. However, in *Owen v. Tate*, the Court of Appeal found that the debtor had not adopted the payment, even though "they invited the bank [the creditor] to clear their overdraft by recourse to the plaintiff."[75] It must follow that the debt was not discharged at law. In such circumstances, the plaintiff should normally be able to recover his payment from the creditor on the ground of total failure of consideration.[76] In *Owen v. Tate*, however, it would appear that the bank would have been able to retain its payment, for the bank had released another surety, at the plaintiff's request and in consideration of his guarantee.[77] Moreover it is possible that the bank may still have been able to recover from the debtor since at law the debt was still due.[78] The bank would then be at law in a position to retain the plaintiff's payment and to recover the debt, which is a palpably indefensible result. Conversely, if the bank did not sue for the debt, the debtor would be incontrovertibly benefited. Because the debtor did not seek the plaintiff's guarantee it may have been proper to refuse him an indemnity from the debtor. Yet, though the surety may have been officious *vis-à-vis* the debtor, he had not acted officiously *vis-à-vis* the creditor, the bank, which voluntarily and consciously accepted his suretyship and his payment.[79] For that reason, and to prevent the possibility of the bank's unjust enrichment, the surety should in such circumstances be entitled to be subrogated to the bank.[79a] *Owen v. Tate* is not a case where the creditor accepted the payment, mistakenly thinking that the plaintiff intended to make a gift of the sum represented by the debt to the debtor, in circumstances where the creditor would have refused to assign the debt to the plaintiff.[80] But it is not easy to reconcile this conclusion with *The Esso Bernicia*.[80a]

---

[73] See above, p. 17, n. 2.

[74] At p. 412.

[75] At p. 410, *per*, Scarman L.J.

[76] *Walter v. James* (1871) L.R. 6 Ex. 124, 127, *per* Kelly C.B.: see above, p. 17, n. 2.

[77] At p. 404 and p. 406.

[78] Query whether this would be held to be a fraud on the plaintiff-payer: see *Hirachand Punamchand v. Temple* [1911] 2 K.B. 330. And *cf. Porteous v. Watney* (1873) 3 Q.B.D. 534, 540, *per* Thesiger L.J. (see above, p. 301), who suggests that there may, in these circumstances, be a defence in equity.

[79] It should, however, be a distinct question whether a surety whose guarantee has been accepted by the creditor should succeed to the creditor's lien over securities deposited by the debtor, *cf.* below, p. 604.

[79a] *Cf.* Burrows, *The Law of Restitution*, pp. 82–83, 213–215, arguing that s.5 of the Mercantile Law Amendment Act 1856 (which was not cited) would allow subrogation.

[80] *Norton v. Haggett*, 85 A. 2d 571 (1952).

[80a] However, in *The Esso Bernicia* the plaintiff sued in his own name, not having taken a valid assignment of the crofters' rights of action against Hall Russell: [1989] A.C. 643, 663, 674.

In contrast, he who acts under mistake cannot be said to have acted voluntarily.[81] So, we have argued that, in *Boulton* v. *Jones*,[82] Boulton should have been subrogated to Jones's set-off against Brocklehurst, to the extent of the value of the goods supplied by him to Jones, if he could have shown that he was mistaken in thinking that Jones would be content to buy goods from him as the successor to Brocklehurst's business. Similarly, the North Carolina case of *Boney* v. *Central Mutual Insurance Company of Chicago* suggests that a payment made under moral compulsion is not a voluntary payment.[83] A was an insurance broker who had undertaken to obtain for C, his customer, insurance cover with B, the defendants. A told C that cover had been obtained. However, a dispute arose between A and B as to the amount of premiums due, which led B to repudiate liability under the contract. C made a claim under the policy but B denied that a contract had been entered into. A then settled C's claim in full. B went into liquidation. The receiver, though he admitted that there had been a valid policy between B and C, rejected A's claim against B on the ground that A had acted officiously in paying C. The Supreme Court of North Carolina allowed A to be subrogated to C's rights on the policy against B. The Court was prepared to allow subrogation even though A was not legally bound to make the payment under his contract with C; it was enough that A acted in good faith and believed that he was so liable.[84]

It is then enough that the plaintiff has simply intervened to discharge what he conceives to be a moral duty. If an insurer acknowledges liability to the assured because it thinks it proper to do so, it should not be open to a third party to object that the insurer must show that it is in fact liable under the policy before it can be subrogated to the assured.[85]

It is difficult to predict whether, and in what direction, the boundaries of the English law of subrogation will be extended. It appears that English courts have not concluded that subrogation must be confined to the established categories. Subrogation is the most flexible of remedies. As Lord Edmund-Davies said in *Orakpo* v. *Manson Investments Ltd.*,[85a] "apart from specific agreement and certain well-established cases, it is conjectural how far the right of subrogation will be granted, though in principle there is no reason why it

---

[81] *Cf.* the American cases cited in the Reporters' Notes, *Restatement of Restitution*, p. 199, and *Scott on Trusts*, § 473. Subrogation will not assist A if C has no claim against B. *Cf. County of Carleton* v. *City of Ottawa* (1963) 39 D.L.R. (2d) 11: see above, p. 177.

[82] (1857) 2 H. & N. 564, 27 L.J. (Ex.) 117: see above, pp. 488 *et seq.*

[83] 197 S.E. 122 (1938). *Cf. Alamida* v. *Wilson*, 495 P. 2d 585 (1972) and *Farmers Mutual Auto Ins.* v. *Milwaukee Auto Ins.*, 99 N.W. 2d 746 (1959) (where P erroneously thinking that he was liable in tort paid the injured party; he was subrogated to the latter's rights against the tortfeasor); *King* v. *Victoria Insurance Co.* [1896] A.C. 250; *Prince Albert (City)* v. *Underwood, McLellan and Associates Ltd.* (1968) 3 D.L.R. (3d) 385.

[84] But contrast the law on compulsory discharge: see above, Chap. 14.

[85] *King* v. *Victoria Insurance Co.* [1896] A.C. 250. *Cf. Boney* v. *Central Mutual Insurance Co. of Chicago*, 197 S.E. 122 (1938); *St. John's Hospital* v. *The Town of Capitol*, 220 N.E. 2d 333 (1960). And contrast *Canwest Geophysical Ltd.* v. *Brown* [1972] 3 W.W.R. 23.

[85a] [1978] A.C. 95, 112.

should be confined to the hitherto recognised categories . . . " If English courts are prepared to accept that subrogation is a remedy designed to prevent unjust enrichment, subrogation may solve some of the more intractable problems in the law of restitution. For example, we have suggested that it may resolve the difficulties presented by such diverse decisions as *Bonner* v. *Tottenham and Edmonton Permanent Building Society*,[86] and *Linz* v. *Electric Wire Co. of Palestine Ltd.*[87] It is not difficult to envisage other situations where subrogation may be an appropriate remedy to prevent unjust enrichment. One such case may arise from facts akin to those of *Re Diplock*,[88] where the next-of-kin's money was used by the innocent volunteers, the charities, to pay off their secured debts. The Court of Appeal refused to allow the next-of-kin to be subrogated to the secured creditors; for their debts had been extinguished. In our view it is arguable that the next-of-kin should be preferred to general creditors and that therefore subrogation should have been allowed.[89] The fact that the debt is discharged at law should not be conclusive, as the cases in equity illustrate.[90] Indeed, in *Thurstan's*[91] case, the courts resurrected a vendor's lien to protect the lender.[92] It is true that difficult questions of priority might have arisen if the charities had created new charges after the discharge of the original charges with the *Diplock* money. But these would not have been insoluble; the subsequent chargees should be granted priority over the next-of-kin unless they were fixed with any notice which made it inequitable to grant them priority.

We shall now consider how subrogation has developed in the established categories of suretyship, bills of exchange, insurance, and administration of trusts and estates. The Chapter will conclude with an analysis of the cases where A has lent money to B and the money has been used to discharge a valid liability owed by B to C. In our view, in all these situations, subrogation is granted to prevent another's unjust enrichment, where the plaintiff has acted unofficiously in conferring a benefit on the defendant. We shall see that in some situations, for example, suretyship and insurance, the plaintiff's liability to make the payment is secondary to that of another. In others, such as the cases concerning borrowing transactions,[93] it is not.

---

[86] [1899] 1 Q.B. 161: see above, Chap. 12.

[87] [1948] A.C. 371: see above, p. 402, n. 10.

[88] [1948] Ch. 469, 549 *et seq. Cf.* the situation where P delivers goods to D in circumstances where D reasonably thinks that P intends to give them to him and D subsequently sells them; P may be subrogated, in some circumstances, to the proceeds in D's hands: see above, p. 402, n. 10 (necessitous intervention).

[89] The problem would generally arise on the defendant's insolvency: *cf.* below, pp. 631 *et seq.*

[90] See below, pp. 627 *et seq.*

[91] [1902] 1 Ch. 1; [1903] A.C. 6: see above, p. 595; see below, pp. 632–634.

[92] *Cf.* the loan cases, below, pp. 631 *et seq.*

[93] See below, pp. 621 *et seq.*

2. The Established Categories of Subrogation

It is well established that, in certain circumstances, English law will allow A, a surety (including for this purpose the indorser of a bill of exchange), an insurer, or the creditors of a trust estate, to be subrogated to the rights of another. That other may be a third party, C, or the person who would otherwise be unjustly enriched, B.[94] It is sometimes said that the so-called right of subrogation is dependent on the existence of a contractual or other right of indemnity. But, as Lord Goff recently emphasised in *Lord Napier and Ettrick v. R.F. Kershaw Ltd.*[95]: "I do not see why the mere fact that the purpose of subrogation in this context is to give effect to the principle of indemnity embodied in the contract [of insurance] should preclude recognition of the equitable proprietary right, if justice so requires." As Sir Samuel Romilly put it, subrogation is an equity, based on "a principle of natural justice,"[96] which is granted to prevent unjust enrichment. Whether there is a contractual or other right of indemnity may, however, be important in determining to whom A is to be subrogated, to B or to C, in order to prevent B's unjust enrichment. For example, the surety, A, agrees to indemnify the principal creditor, C; but the insurer, A, agrees to indemnify the assured, B. Consequently, in suretyship, A is subrogated to C because he has indemnified C; in contrast, in insurance, A is subrogated to B because he has indemnified B. However, in trust law, the creditors, A, do not agree to indemnify either B or C. But to prevent the beneficiaries', B's, unjust enrichment it is necessary to subrogate A to the trustee's, C's, right of indemnity from B.

It is also said that a right of recoupment[97] carries with it a right of subrogation; and that this right is "not confined to the case of a guarantee, but applies in any case where there is a primary and secondary liability for the same debt."[98] But it will rarely be advantageous for a guarantor to be subrogated to the rights of the principal debtor who is obliged to recoup him and whose liability to the creditor he has discharged. Occasionally he may wish to do so.[99] But it is much more likely that he will seek to be subrogated to the rights of the third person whom he has indemnified, in order to succeed to his priority. An unusual illustration of such a situation is *Re Downer Enterprises Ltd.*[1] C had let property to A1 for 21 years. A1 assigned the lease to A2, and A2 then assigned the lease to the B Co. B Co. subsequently went into a creditors' voluntary winding-up and thereafter paid no rent. The liquidator of B Co., having been advised that he could not disclaim, disposed of the residue of the lease to M. C

---

[94] See above, p. 591.
[95] [1993] 1 All E.R. 385, 402.
[96] *Craythorne* v. *Swinburne* (1807) 14 Ves. 160, 162, *per* Romilly, *arguendo*: see above, p. 590.
[97] For reasons explained above, Chap. 12, we prefer to describe this right as a right of recoupment rather than reimbursement.
[98] *Re Downer Enterprises Ltd.* [1974] 1 W.L.R. 1460, 1468, *per* Pennycuick V.-C. Contrast *Brown Shipley & Co. Ltd.* v. *Amalgamated Investment (Europe) B.V.* [1979] 1 Lloyd's Rep. 488.
[99] For such a case, see above, pp. 302–303.
[1] [1974] 1 W.L.R. 1460.

recovered the arrears of rent from the winding-up from A1; whereupon A1 recouped from A2, who paid A1 without informing the liquidator. Pennycuick V.-C. held that A2 could be subrogated to C's rights against the B Co. A1, A2 and B Co. were liable for the same debt but, as between them, B Co. was primarily liable to pay the rent. A2 was entitled to be reimbursed by the B Co. and "likewise is entitled to take over by subrogation any securities or rights which the creditor [C] may have against [B Co.]."[2] The judge could see no reason "why such rights should not include the right to be paid rent in full in ... the circumstances of a company in liquidation." Consequently, since B Co.'s debt was an expense which the court would have allowed in the winding-up,[3] A2 was able to gain priority over the general creditors of the B Co.

We shall now turn to discuss in detail the established categories of subrogation, beginning with Sureties.

(a) *Sureties*

The basis of subrogation

A surety[4] who pays off the debt owed by the principal debtor is subrogated to any securities given by the debtor to the creditor as security for the debt.[5] The basis of this right of subrogation enjoyed by the surety is analogous to that underlying his right of contribution from co-sureties.[6] In *Craythorne* v. *Swinburne*,[7] Sir Samuel Romilly described it in the following words, which gained the approval of Lord Eldon.[8] He said:

> " ... a surety will be entitled to every remedy, which the creditor has against the principal debtor; to enforce every security and all means of payment; to stand in the place of the creditor; not only through the medium of contract, but even by means of securities, entered into without the knowledge of the surety; having a right to have those securities transferred to him; though there was no stipulation for that; and to avail himself of all those securities against the debtor. This right of a surety also stands, not upon contract, but upon a principle of natural justice: the

---

[2] At p. 1468. For reasons which do not emerge from the reported facts, A2's claim was for the amount which B Co. gained when it disposed of the lease to M: see [1974] 1 W.L.R. 1460, 1462–1463.

[3] At pp. 1465–1466.

[4] An obligation may be absolute on its face but may be a guarantee: Rowlett, *op. cit.*, pp. 4–5; *Australasian Conference Association Ltd.* v. *Mainline Construction Pty. Ltd. (In liq.)* (1979) 53 A.L. J.R. 68 (High Ct. of Aust.).

[5] *Morgan* v. *Seymour* (1637/1638) 1 Chan.Rep. 120; *Parsons & Cole* v. *Briddock* (1708) 2 Vern. 608; *Ex p. Crisp* (1744) 1 Atk. 133, 135, *per* Lord Hardwicke L.C.; *Greerside* v. *Benson* (1745) 3 Atk. 248. The Roman law principle was similar: see D.46.1.13; C.7.41.21.

[6] See above, pp. 307–317.

[7] (1807) 14 Ves. 160, 162, *arguendo*.

[8] (1807) 14 Ves. 160, 169.

same principle, upon which one surety is entitled to contribution from another."[9]

Subrogation is not then based on contract, for the surety "seldom if ever stipulated for the benefit of the security which the principal debtor has given."[10] Its basis is natural justice; it is against conscience for the debtor to regain the securities from the creditor on the discharge of the debt by the surety, because it is the debtor's obligation to indemnify the surety against any loss he incurs.[11]

The extent of subrogation

The surety's right does not depend on his knowledge of the existence of any security[12]; and, after some doubt, it has now been settled that all the securities held by the creditor as security for the debt must be handed to the surety who pays off the debt, even though they were additional securities given after the contract of guarantee was made, even though they only came into existence after the making of the contract of guarantee,[13] and even though they are deemed to be satisfied by the payment of the debt.[14]

Mortgage securities held by the mortgagee creditor are not *sui generis* and must be transferred to the surety on payment of the debt.[15] Consequently, a surety who pays off a mortgage made by the principal debtor is presumed to keep the mortgage alive for his own benefit.[16]

The surety may be subrogated not only to securities given by the debtor but

---

[9] See too, *Newton* v. *Chorlton* (1853) 10 Hare 646, 648, *per* Page Wood V.-C.; *Aldrich* v. *Cooper* (1803) 8 Ves. 382, 389, *per* Lord Eldon; *Duncan, Fox & Co.* v. *North and South Wales Bank* (1880) 6 App.Cas. 1, 18–19, *per* Lord Blackburn.

[10] *Yonge* v. *Reynell* (1852) 9 Hare 809, 818–819, *per* Turner V.-C.; see also *Duncan, Fox & Co.* v. *North and South Wales Bank* (1880) 6 App.Cas. 1, 13, *per* Lord Selborne.

[11] *Ibid.*

[12] *Aldrich* v. *Cooper* (1803) 8 Ves. 382, 389, *per* Lord Eldon; *Mayhew* v. *Crickett* (1818) 2 Swan. 185, 191, *per* Lord Eldon; *Pearl* v. *Deacon* (1857) 24 Beav. 186, 191, *per* Romilly M.R.; *Newton* v. *Chorlton* (1853) 10 Hare 646, 651, *per* Page Wood V.-C.; *Duncan, Fox & Co.* v. *North and South Wales Bank* (1880) 6 App.Cas. 1; *Leicestershire Banking Co. Ltd.* v. *Hawkins* (1900) 16 T.L.R. 317.

[13] *Lake* v. *Brutton* (1854) 18 Beav. 34; *Campbell* v. *Rothwell* (1877) 38 L.T. 33, 34, *per* Denman J.; *Forbes* v. *Jackson* (1882) 19 Ch.D. 615, 621–622, *per* Hall V.-C., not following Page Wood V.-C. in *Newton* v. *Chorlton* (1853) 10 Hare 646. Indeed, in the later case of *Pledge* v. *Buss* (1860) Johns. 663, 668, Page Wood V.-C. partially recanted. See also *Scott* v. *Knox* (1838) 2 Jon.Ex. 778.

[14] See Mercantile Law Amendment Act 1856, s.5. Before the Mercantile Law Amendment Act 1856, a surety was entitled only to the benefit of those securities which were not discharged or satisfied by the payment to the creditor. It was fatal, therefore, if the debtor and surety had been joined in the same bond; the payment by the surety discharged the debt and he was relegated to the position of a simple contract creditor: see *Copis* v. *Middleton* (1823) 1 T. & R. 224. The earlier authorities, which were somewhat conflicting, are cited in argument at pp. 226–228. S.5 of the 1856 Act reverses this common law rule; the surety is now entitled to all securities held by the creditor whether or not they are deemed to have been satisfied by the payment of the debt.

[15] *Copis* v. *Middleton* (1823) 1 T. & R. 224. *Quaere* if the surety's interest must be registered as a general equitable charge: see Land Charges Act 1972, s.2(4).

[16] *Re Davison's Estate* (1893) 31 L.R.Ir. 249, 255, affd. [1894] 1 I.R. 56. *Cf.* below, pp. 603–604.

to securities given by a co-surety,[17] if the creditor could have been reimbursed out of the co-surety's securities. He is also entitled to securities deposited by a co-surety who has not contributed his due share of the common debt.[18] On the other hand, a person who goes surety for part of a debt cannot take the benefit of any securities which have been given by the debtor to the creditor in respect of another part of the debt not secured by the contract of suretyship, although he is entitled to a *pro rata* share in any securities given as security for the whole debt.

Only when the surety has discharged the whole of the debt can he be subrogated to any securities securing the debt.[19] If he bargains with the creditor and discharges the debt at a discount, then he may be subrogated to the securities, but he cannot enforce the securities to obtain more than he actually paid.[20]

By succeeding to securities in the hands of the creditor, a surety will succeed to the priority enjoyed by the creditor whose debt he has discharged. So, a surety to a judgment creditor[21] or the Crown[22] has been held to be entitled to priority over general creditors in payment out of the assets of a deceased debtor. And, in *Re Lamplugh Iron Ore Co.*,[23] it was held that a surety for a company's rates to the overseers of the poor could stand in the place of the creditors and enforce their priority under the Companies Act. These decisions are the result of section 5 of the Mercantile Law Amendment Act 1856, which allows the surety to have assigned to him "every judgment, specialty or other security held by the creditor."[24] As the law now stands, therefore, a surety may succeed to a creditor's rights even though he did not know that he was the surety of a preferential creditor and even though the securities came into existence after the contract of guarantee.[25] Arguably this places the surety in too favourable a position.[26]

A surety may expressly[27] or impliedly[28] waive his right of subrogation.

---

[17] *Greerside* v. *Benson* (1745) 3 Atk. 248; *Re Kirkwood's Estate* (1878) 1 L.R.Ir. 18; *Duncan, Fox & Co.* v. *North and South Wales Bank* (1880) 6 App.Cas. 1, 19, *per* Lord Blackburn (*cf.* Jessel M.R. in the court below at (1879) 11 Ch.D. 88, 96).

[18] See *Ex p. Crisp* (1744) 1 Atk. 133; *Ex p. Carne* (1868) L.R. 3 Ch. 463, 466, *per* Page Wood V.-C.; *Duncan, Fox & Co.* v. *North and South Wales Bank* (1880) 6 App.Cas. 1, 19, *per* Lord Blackburn, impliedly rejecting Jessel M.R.'s view below: see 11 Ch.D. at p. 96.

[19] *Ewart* v. *Latta* (1865) 4 Marq. 983; *Ferguson* v. *Gibson* (1872) 14 Eq. 379; *Ex p. Turquand* (1876) 3 Ch.D. 445; *Re Howe* (1871) 6 Ch.App. 838, 841, *per* Mellish L.J.

[20] *Reed* v. *Norris* (1837) 2 Myl. & Cr. 361, 375, *per* Lord Cottenham. See also *Ex p. Rushforth* (1804) 10 Ves. 409.

[21] *Re M'Myn* (1886) 33 Ch.D. 174.

[22] *Re Lord Churchill* (1888) 39 Ch.D. 174.

[23] [1927] 1 Ch. 308.

[24] To come within s.5, a plaintiff must be under a *duty* to make the payment. For an unusual case where a director unsuccessfully claimed that he was under such a duty, see *Re M.C.C. Precision Products Ltd.*, 27 D.L.R. (3d) 4 (1972) (Ontario Supreme Court in Bankruptcy); and *cf. Re Major-Way Trailers Ltd.'s Bankruptcy*, 47 D.L.R. (2d) 409 (1964).

[25] See above, p. 603.

[26] *Cf.* above, p. 594.

[27] *Re Fernandes* (1844) 6 H. & N. 717; *Midland Banking Co.* v. *Chambers* (1869) 4 Ch.App. 398.

[28] *Allen* v. *De Lisle* (1857) 5 W.R. 158; *Brandon* v. *Brandon* (1859) 3 De G. & J. 524.

(b) *Indorsers of Bills of Exchange*

Unless the bill is an accommodation bill,[29] payment to the holder by a party other than the acceptor will not operate to discharge the acceptor from his liability on the bill.[30] Accordingly, a drawer or indorser who pays the bill cannot ordinarily proceed against the acceptor in an action for money paid. His rights against the acceptor must be derived from the holder. They are as follows:

First, he is entitled upon paying the bill to the holder in full to require the holder to deliver up the bill to him,[31] and upon gaining possession of the bill he can sue the acceptor on it. His right to sue the acceptor arises, however, from the fact that he himself has become the holder; for "an indorser of a bill is not entitled to sue upon it, unless he becomes the holder."[32] This is consistent with section 59(2)(*b*) of the Bills of Exchange Act 1882, which provides that:

> Where a bill is paid by an indorser, or where a bill payable to drawer's order is paid by the drawer, the party paying it is remitted to his former rights as regards the acceptor or antecedent parties, and he may, if he thinks fit, strike out his own and subsequent indorsements, and again negotiate the bill.

Where, however, he has only paid the bill in part, he cannot compel the holder to surrender the bill to him. In *Pownal* v. *Ferrand*[33] it was held that an indorser who has paid the holder in part can proceed directly against the acceptor in an action for money paid. But that case must now be regarded as of doubtful authority.[34] The best course for an indorser who has paid a bill in part is to persuade the holder to recover the full amount of the bill from the acceptor. The holder will then hold on trust for the indorser an amount equal to the sum which the latter has paid on the bill.[35]

Secondly, the House of Lords held in *Duncan, Fox & Co.* v. *North & South Wales Bank*[36] that the indorser of a bill of exchange who paid the bill was entitled to the benefit of those securities which a member of the firm which accepted the bill had deposited with the holder to cover the bill. Lord Selborne

---

[29] In this section we are not concerned with accommodation parties to bills of exchange. An accommodation party is to all intents and purposes a surety for the person for whom he has become a party to the bill. His rights against that person are the same as the rights of a surety against his principal: see *Oriental Financial Corp.* v. *Overend Gurney Co.* (1871) 7 Ch.App. 142, (1874) L.R. 7 H.L. 348. His subrogation rights are, therefore, discussed in the preceding section on Subrogation of Sureties.

[30] Bills of Exchange Act 1882, s.59(2); *Jones* v. *Broadhurst* (1850) 9 C.B. 173.

[31] *Duncan, Fox & Co.* v. *North and South Wales Bank* (1880) 6 App.Cas. 1, 18, *per* Lord Blackburn.

[32] *Ex p. Bishop, re Fox, Walker & Co.* (1880) 15 Ch.D. 400, 411, *per* James L.J.

[33] (1827) 6 B. & C. 439.

[34] See above, pp. 352–354, for a full discussion.

[35] *Jones* v. *Broadhurst* (1850) 9 C.B. 173.

[36] (1880) 6 App.Cas. 1, applied in *Ispahany* v. *Crisp* (1891) L.R. 19 Ind.App. 24 and extended in *Re Downer Enterprises Ltd.* [1974] 1 W.L.R. 1460. *Cf.* above, p. 601, and contrast *Scholefield Goodman & Sons Ltd.* v. *Zyngier* [1985] 3 W.L.R. 953, P.C.

relied[37] upon the fact that, although the indorser of a bill of exchange could not strictly be called a surety, nevertheless he had some of the characteristics of a surety. In particular, if the holder should without the consent of the indorser discharge or suspend his remedy against the acceptor, the indorser would be discharged. Lord Selborne said[38]:

> "I am unable to conceive any ground on which the principle which prevails in cases of suretyship should go as far as this, in favour of the drawer or the indorser, and not also extend (when the indorser is compelled to pay the bill, and when the question arises between him and the acceptor only) to securities deposited by the acceptor with the holder."

Lord Blackburn invoked the rule established in *Deering* v. *Earl of Winchelsea*,[39] which he stated[40] to be that "where a creditor has a right to come upon more than one person or fund for the payment of a debt, there is an equity between the persons interested in the different funds that each shall bear no more than its due proportion." He went on to say that the indorser of a bill stands in a position sufficiently analogous to that of a surety to bring him within the principle of *Deering* v. *Earl of Winchelsea*; and on that principle he held that, where the holder proceeded against the indorser first, the indorser was entitled to be recouped out of the security deposited by one of the acceptors with the holder to cover the bill.

(c) *Insurers*

The basis of subrogation

The "fundamental rule of insurance law" is "that the contract of insurance contained in a marine or fire policy is a contract of indemnity, and of indemnity only, and this contract means that the assured, in case of a loss against which the policy has been made, shall be fully indemnified, but shall never be more than fully indemnified.[41] An important illustration of this limiting principle is *Lord Napier and Ettrick* v. *R.F. Kershaw Ltd.*[41a] The House of Lords held that:

> "when determining the amount which stop loss insurers are entitled to claim in respect of the Settlement monies [paid by a third party tortfeasor], the stop loss insurers are entitled to be reimbursed any indemnity paid by them to an assured before that assured is fully indemnified by

---

[37] At p. 13.

[38] At p. 14.

[39] (1787) 2 B. & P. 270: see above, Chap. 13.

[40] (1880) 6 App.Cas. 1, 19.

[41] *Castellain* v. *Preston* (1883) 11 Q.B.D. 380, 386, *per* Brett L.J. For an argument that the doctrine of subrogation in insurance law promotes overlapping coverage and wasteful litigation, and substantially undermines the value of an insurance contract, see (1985) 5 O.J.L.S. 416 [Hasson].

[41a] [1993] 1 All E.R. 385: see below, p. 618 for a further discussion.

applying his share of the Settlement monies to a loss occurring below the excess in that assured's policy."[41b]

The rule applies to all insurance contracts which are contracts of indemnity, in particular, fire and marine insurance; it does not, therefore, apply to life insurance[42] contracts for these are not contracts of indemnity. As a corollary to the insurer's duty of indemnity, he is entitled, when he has indemnified the assured against the loss insured, to receive from him by way of subrogation the benefit of all rights of the assured by means of which the loss can be or has been diminished.[43] The same principle applies to contracts of reinsurance.[44]

Although the insurer's "right" of subrogation may be contractual, generally it "does not arise upon any of the terms of the contract of insurance"[45] but from "the very nature of the contract of indemnity itself."[46] Lord Blackburn called it "an equity,"[47] whose basis is the principle of natural justice that, since the insurer is he who bears the loss, he is entitled to all ways and means to lessen it.[48] As Lord Goff said in *Lord Napier and Ettrick* v. *R.F. Kershaw Ltd.*[48a]:

> "Furthermore, it has not been usual to express the principle of subrogation as arising from an implied term in the contract. Even so it has been regarded, both at law and in equity, as giving effect to the underlying nature of a contract of insurance which is that it is intended to provide an indemnity but no more than an indemnity . . . But I do not see why the mere fact that the purpose of subrogation in this context is to give effect to the principle of indemnity embodied in the contract should preclude recognition of the equitable proprietary right, if justice so requires."

However, in *Morris* v. *Ford Motor Co. Ltd.*[49] the Court of Appeal held that subrogation was not an inevitable incident of an insurance contract of indemnity and that, exceptionally, it might be excluded. In that case Cameron had agreed to perform certain cleaning services for Ford and to indemnify it against loss or injury arising therefrom, whether caused by the negligence of Ford or Cameron. The plaintiff, an employee of Cameron, was injured by the admitted

---

[41b] At p. 398, *per* Lord Templeman.
[42] *The Solicitors' and General Life Assurance Society* v. *Lamb* (1864) 2 De G.J. & S. 251.
[43] *Lord Napier and Ettrick* v. *R.F. Kershaw Ltd.* [1993] 1 All E.R. 385; *Castellain* v. *Preston* (1883) 11 Q.B.D. 380, 388, *per* Brett L.J., 404, *per* Bowen L.J. For an analysis of the latter case, see *British Traders' Insurance Co. Ltd.* v. *Monson* (1964) 38 A.L.J.R. 20, 22, *per* Kitto, Taylor and Owen JJ.
[44] Reinsurers are entitled to be subrogated to the rights of the insurer, and those rights include the right to be subrogated to the rights of the assured: *Assicurazioni Generali de Trieste* v. *Empress Assurance Corp. Ltd.* [1907] 2 K.B. 814.
[45] *Castellain* v. *Preston* (1883) 11 Q.B.D. 380, 387, *per* Brett L.J.; *Lord Napier and Ettrick* v. *R.F. Kershaw Ltd.* [1993]. *Cf.* the principle underlying the contribution cases; see above, pp. 317 *et seq.*
[46] *Morris* v. *Ford Motor Co.* [1973] Q.B. 792, 805, *per* Stamp L.J.
[47] *Burnand* v. *Rodocanachi* (1882) 7 App.Cas. 333, 339; *cf. Simpson* v. *Thomson* (1877) 3 App.Cas. 279, 284, *per* Lord Cairns.
[48] *Rankin* v. *Potter* (1873) L.R. 6 H.L. 83, 118, *per* Blackburn J.
[48a] [1993] 1 All E.R. 385, 402: see below, p. 618.
[49] [1973] Q.B. 792.

negligent act of Ford's employee. Ford settled the plaintiff's action and proceeded in third-party proceedings against Cameron on the indemnity clause. Cameron, having agreed to indemnify Ford, then brought in Ford's negligent employee, claiming to be subrogated to Ford's right to recover from its negligent employee the damages and costs for which it was liable. As a matter of practice neither Ford nor Ford's insurer would have enforced this common law right. The Court of Appeal, Stamp L.J. dissenting, held that Cameron was not entitled to be subrogated to Ford's right against its employee. Lord Denning M.R.[50] concluded that it was not "just and equitable" to compel Ford to lend its name in litigation against their employee, knowing that a strike would result and that Cameron had probably insured against the eventuality that it might be liable to Ford. James L.J. was able to find an implied term which excluded the right of subrogation and which sprang "from the nature and terms in the contract between these parties. Their agreement was operative in an industrial setting in which subrogation of the third party to the rights and remedies of the defendants against their employees would be unacceptable and unrealistic."[51] The Court of Appeal therefore limited the right of subrogation in order to circumvent the House of Lords decision in *Lister* v. *Romford Ice & Cold Storage Co. Ltd.*[52] which established the employer's right to claim an indemnity from his negligent employee. One may sympathise with the Court's evident distaste for the principle embodied in *Lister* v. *Romford Ice & Cold Storage Co. Ltd.*, but at the same time remain unconvinced by the reasoning of Lord Denning and James L.J. Subrogation arises because the contract is a contract of indemnity and because it is necessary to prevent the indemnitee's unjust enrichment; to limit that right by invoking a principle of equity or a fictitious implied term will conceal the real questions which were at issue in the case and cause confusion in the future.[53]

Subrogation has been held to be a contingent right which vests in the insurer at the time of entering into the policy[54]; but the right cannot be

---

[50] At pp. 800–801.

[51] At p. 815.

[52] [1957] A.C. 555.

[53] *Cf.* Stamp L.J.'s dissent, which is persuasive.

[54] *Boag* v. *Standard Marine Insurance Co.* [1937] 2 K.B. 113. In that case cargo owners insured their cargo with a company under an agreed value policy. Thereafter the value of the cargo rose, and the cargo owners entered into an increased value policy with underwriters. The cargo became a total loss, and both the company and the underwriters paid up in full. The Court of Appeal held that the company was entitled to be subrogated to the whole of a sum, less than the agreed value paid by them, which cargo had received by way of general average contribution. The subsequent agreement between the assured and the increased value underwriters was not allowed to affect the right of subrogation which was held to have vested in the company when it effected its policy. The decision is, however, questionable because (1) the principle on which the right of subrogation rests, namely, unjust enrichment arising from the insurer's payment, indicates that the right of subrogation does not vest until payment; (2) the decision gives the original underwriters the best of both worlds, because (a) they are entitled to be subrogated in full to the extent of their payment, before the increased value insurers are entitled to any benefits from subrogation, whereas (b) under s.73(1) of the Marine Insurance Act 1906, where the assured is liable for general average contribution and the subject-matter is not insured for its full contributory value, the indemnity payable by the underwriters is reduced in proportion to the

exercised by the insurer until he has paid the loss, partial or total, covered by the policy.[55]

The extent of subrogation

Upon payment, subrogation obtains for the insurer the benefit of all rights of the assured[56] which diminish the loss. These rights may include rights of action against third parties. A common example is a right of action in negligence,[57] as when the insurer of a motorist is subrogated to his assured's right against another motorist who has negligently damaged the other's car by his careless driving. Similarly, the insurer may be subrogated to a right of action in contract, as, for example, when the insurer of a landlord is entitled to the benefit of his tenant's repairing covenant[58]; or to a right of action in restitution, as when cargo underwriters are subrogated to cargo's right to general average contribution from ship or other cargo owners; or to a statutory right, for example, to proceed against a police authority in respect of damage caused by a riot[59]; or to an implied term, which is specifically enforceable, "that the assured will pay the insurer out of the moneys received in reduction of the loss the amount to which the insured is entitled by way of subrogation."[59a]

The rights to which an insurer may be subrogated are, however, not limited to rights of action enforceable against third parties. They include all rights which diminish the loss, including rights which have been exercised by or have accrued to the assured. In *Castellain* v. *Preston*,[60] the Court of Appeal held that, where a house was damaged by fire after the assured had contracted to sell it but before completion and the purchaser thereafter completed and paid the full contract price, the insurers who in ignorance of the sale had paid up on the loss

---

[55] under-insurance; (3) it is just that the original underwriters should recognise the equities of the increased value insurers, for, although the original value may have been agreed between the assured and the original underwriters, this agreement should not have bound the increased value insurers, and the original underwriters should have recognised that an increased value policy might be required (but see [1937] 2 K.B. 113, 129, *per* Scott L.J.). See below, p. 611, n. 70.

[55] *Page* v. *Scottish Insurance Corp.* (1929) 98 L.J.K.B. 308; *Lord Napier and Ettrick* v. *R.F. Kershaw Ltd.* [1993] 1 All E.R. 385, 407, *per* Lord Browne-Wilkinson. The insurer cannot be subrogated to the assured when he has paid a loss under a void policy: see *Edwards & Co.* v. *Motor Union Insurance Co. Ltd.* [1922] 2 K.B. 249. Where, however, an insurer pays a loss in good faith and the payment is accepted by the assured, the payment will be regarded as a payment on the policy, carrying with it the legal incidents of such a payment, including the operation of the doctrine of subrogation, even though it subsequently transpires that the payment was not within the four corners of the policy. Settlements of claims of this kind ought not to be reopened thereafter: see *King* v. *Victoria Insurance Co. Ltd.* [1896] A.C. 250; and see above, p. 599, n. 85.

[56] For the position in the case of a mortgagee's insurance, see *MacGillivray and Parkington on Insurance Law* §§ 1233 *et seq.*

[57] The negligence of the assured (see *Simpson* v. *Thomson* (1877) 3 App.Cas 279) does not of itself entitle the insurer to any right for damages against the assured.

[58] *Andrews* v. *The Patriotic Assurance Co. of Ireland* (1886) 18 L.R.Ir. 355, 369, *per* Palles C.B.

[59] Riot (Damages) Act 1886, s.2(2).

[59a] *Lord Napier and Ettrick* v. *R.F. Kershaw Ltd.* [1993] 1 All E.R. 385, 409, *per* Lord Browne-Wilkinson.

[60] (1883) 11 Q.B.D. 380.

by fire were entitled to recover from the assured a sum equal to the price received by him in diminution of the loss so paid.[61] If, when he pays the loss, the insurer is aware that the assured has received a payment in diminution of the loss, the insurer may deduct the amount of such payment from the sum payable by him to the assured; and if, with such knowledge, he fails to make the appropriate deduction, he may be precluded from recovering thereafter from the assured the amount which he should have deducted if the circumstances are such as to indicate that his failure to deduct constituted a voluntary payment.[62] The assured remains accountable to the insurer for any payments[63] or the value of any other benefits[64] received by him in diminution of the loss after payment of the loss by the insurer. Indeed, such payments or benefits may be held by him on trust for the insurer.[64a]

It is axiomatic that the insurer can only be subrogated to rights which can diminish or have diminished the loss which he has paid. From this proposition certain rules emerge:

(1) If the insurance is a partial insurance, "and the loss is to a much greater extent ... than the aggregate of insurances,"[65] the insurer is not entitled to recover anything from the assured until the latter has been fully indemnified.[66] Until he is fully indemnified, benefits accruing to the assured may be appropriated by him to the fulfilment of his indemnity, and cannot, therefore, be said to diminish the loss insured against.

> "The assured (in case of partial insurance) is not clothed with the full character of trustee *quoad* the insurance companies until he has recovered sufficient from the wrongdoers to fully satisfy all his loss as well as expenses incurred in such recovery. In other words, when the assured is put in as good a position by the recovery from the wrongdoer, as if the damage insured against had not happened, then for any surplus of money or other advantage recovered over and above that, the insurer is entitled to be subrogated into the right to receive that money or advantage to the extent of the amount paid under the insurance policies."[67]

It has, however, been established for nearly a century that in cases of marine insurance the insurer may be entitled to be subrogated to the assured even though the assured is not fully indemnified. Thus, the policy may be a valued policy,[68] and the agreed value may prove to be less than the true value of the thing insured. Nevertheless, upon payment of the agreed value, the insurer

---

[61] *Cf.* Law of Property Act 1925, s.47.

[62] See above, pp. 58–60.

[63] *Darrell* v. *Tibbitts* (1880) 5 Q.B.D. 560.

[64] *West of England Fire Insurance Co.* v. *Isaacs* [1897] 1 Q.B. 226; see also *Phoenix Assurance Co.* v. *Spooner* [1905] 2 K.B. 753.

[64a] *Lord Napier and Ettrick* v. *R.F. Kershaw Ltd.* [1993] 1 All E.R. 385: below p. 618.

[65] *National Fire Insurance Co.* v. *M'Laren* (1886) 12 Ont.L.R. 682, 687, *per* Boyd C.

[66] *Ibid.* at pp. 687–688.

[67] *Ibid.* at p. 688, *per* Boyd C.

[68] On which see *Irving* v. *Manning* (1847) 1 H.L.C. 287; *Steamship "Balmoral" Co. Ltd.* v. *Marten* [1902] A.C. 511; Marine Insurance Act 1906, s.27.

will be entitled to be subrogated to any benefit which may accrue to the assured which diminishes the loss, up to but not exceeding the amount of the insurer's payment. As between the insurer and the assured, the value of the thing insured has been agreed at the value specified in the policy. The assured cannot, therefore, claim to retain part of the benefit received by him on the grounds that it represents the difference between the agreed value and the true value of the thing insured[69]; nor can he claim to apportion the benefit as between himself and the insurer, in accordance with the ratio which the agreed value bears to the true value.[70] In fire insurance, however, it has been suggested that, until the assured is fully indemnified, the insurer is not entitled to be subrogated to the position of the assured.[71]

(2) Until the assured has been fully indemnified, he is entitled to have control as *dominus litis* of any litigation brought in his name.[72] He can proceed to recover the full amount due to him in such litigation, even though his insurers may direct him not to proceed for the amount of their interest,[73] and he can enter into bona fide settlements of such litigation.[74] But in the conduct of the litigation or in the making of the settlement he must always act with due regard to the interests of his insurers. If he does not do so, he may be liable to his insurers for damages for breach of contract.[75] However, if an assured who has been partially indemnified refuses to pursue a claim against a third party, he should be bound to enable his insurer to pursue the claim in the assured's name.[76]

(3) The insurer is not entitled to be subrogated to payments received by the assured which do not diminish the loss. Sometimes, the assured may have received a payment by way of gift. It is a question of fact in each case whether such a gift has or has not been paid in diminution of the loss. Thus, in *Stearns* v.

---

[69] *North of England Iron S.S. Insurance Association* v. *Armstrong* (1870) L.R. 5 Q.B. 244; *Goole & Hull Steam Towing Co.* v. *Ocean Marine Insurance Co.* [1928] 1 K.B. 589.

[70] *Thames & Mersey Marine Insurance Co. Ltd.* v. *British & Chilian S.S. Co. Ltd.* [1915] 2 K.B. 214, affd. [1916] 1 K.B. 30, C.A.; Marine Insurance Act 1906, s.79. This decision, and the decision in *North of England Iron S.S. Insurance Assocation* v. *Armstrong* (1870) L.R. 5 Q.B. 244 (which is said to have been embodied in s.79 of the Marine Insurance Act 1906), are open to criticism. There is much to be said for the view that the agreed valuation is only conclusive in an action on the policy, and should not affect subrogation rights, which do not arise under the policy and which should only give the insurers a right to be subrogated to benefits of the assured which diminish the loss insured against and paid by the insurers; see *Burnand* v. *Rodocanachi* (1882) 7 App.Cas. 33, 342, *per* Lord Blackburn; *Aetna Insurance Co.* v. *United Fruit Co.*, 304 U.S. 430 (1938); *cf. Boag* v. *Standard Marine Insurance Co.* [1937] 2 K.B. 113, criticised above, p. 608, n. 54.

[71] *Re Driscoll* [1918] 1 I.R. 152; and see *Page* v. *Scottish Insurance Corp.* (1929) 140 L.T. 571, 576, *per* Scrutton L.J.

[72] *Commercial Union Assurance Co.* v. *Lister* (1874) L.R. 9 Ch.App. 483.

[73] *Morley* v. *Moore* [1936] 2 K.B. 359.

[74] *Globe & Rutgers Fire Insurance Co.* v. *Truedell* [1927] 2 D.L.R. 659.

[75] *Commercial Union Assurance Co.* v. *Lister* (1874) L.R. 9 Ch.App. 483; *West of England Fire Insurance Co.* v. *Isaacs* [1897] 1 Q.B. 226; *Horse, Carriage & General Insurance Co.* v. *Petch* (1916) 33 T.L.R. 131. See further below, p. 617.

[76] There is no rule that an assured is liable for a mere omission to sue a third party: see *Andrews* v. *Patriotic Assurance Co.* (1886) 18 L.R.Ir. 355.

Village Main Reef Gold Mining Co.[77] gold belonging to the defendant mining company, which had been insured by the plaintiffs, was commandeered by the Transvaal Government shortly before the outbreak of the South African War. Subsequently the Transvaal Government paid the defendant £7,289 odd, in respect of the gold, it being understood between them that as a consequence the defendant's mine would continue operations, with certain benefits to the government. The plaintiff insurers, in ignorance of this payment, paid the defendant the full value of the gold, £21,880. The Court of Appeal held that the understanding between the Government and the defendant did not constitute a binding agreement between them, but that the payment was made in diminution of the loss insured against. The plaintiffs were entitled to recover the sums paid by the Transvaal Government. But the Court of Appeal rejected their claim for interest, "holding that the relationship was one of debtor and creditor not that of trustee and *cestui que trust.*"[77a]

The case may be contrasted with *Burnand* v. *Rodocanachi.*[78] Underwriters insured a cargo under valued policies. Upon its destruction by the Confederate cruiser *Alabama*, the underwriters paid up the agreed value, which was less than the true value of the cargo, as on an actual total loss. After the loss, a compensation fund was created and was distributed under an Act of the United States Congress, and out of this fund a sum was paid to the assured equal to the difference between the true value of the cargo lost and the agreed value paid up by underwriters. The Act of Congress specifically provided that no compensation should be paid for any loss for which the injured party should have received compensation from any insurer. The House of Lords held that the underwriters were not entitled to be subrogated to the sum received by the assured out of the compensation fund. It was clear from the terms of the Act of Congress that the United States Government did not pay it with the intention of reducing the loss insured against. The payment was intended to be solely for the benefit of the assured.[79]

(4) Conversely an insurer, even though he has paid in full upon a total loss, is not entitled to recover by way of subrogation more than the amount of his payment, although he is entitled to be subrogated to any claim of the assured to interest accruing after the date of that payment.[80] However, if the assured is

---

[77] (1905) 10 Com.Cas. 89. See also *Randal* v. *Cockran* (1748) 1 Ves.Sen. 98; *Blaauwpot* v. *Da Costa* (1758) 1 Ed. 130; *Burnand* v. *Rodocanachi* (1882) 7 App.Cas. 333, 337–338, *per* Lord Selborne L.C., 339–340, *per* Lord Blackburn.

[77a] *Lord Napier and Ettrick* v. *R.F. Kershaw Ltd.* [1993] 1 All E.R. 385, 408–409, citing Stirling L.J., *per* Lord Browne-Wilkinson. His Lordship found the "case difficult to understand . . . It was a case of over payment by the insurers under a mistake, not subsequent recovery by the assured from a third party of a fund for which the assured was accountable to the insurers"; See below, p. 618 for a discussion of the circumstances when the assured or his agent is so accountable.

[78] (1882) 7 App.Cas. 333.

[79] In particular, at p. 341, *per* Lord Blackburn; see also *Castellain* v. *Preston* (1883) 11 Q.B.D. 380, 395, *per* Cotton L.J.

[80] Otherwise a wrongdoer would benefit at the insurer's expense: see *H. Cousins & Co. Ltd.* v. *D. & C. Carriers Ltd.* [1971] 2 Q.B. 231. In that case it was stated that, in applying this principle, no

fortunate enough to recover from a third party a sum in excess of his loss, the windfall will be his and not his insurer's; for the insurer's right of subrogation is limited to recovering from the assured an amount equal to the sum he has paid under the policy, plus any claim for interest.[81]

So, in *Yorkshire Insurance Co.* v. *Nisbet Shipping Co. Ltd.*,[82] insurers had paid £72,000 under as policy for the cost of a vessel. Subsequently the assured recovered against a third party damages which, on being transmitted to England and converted into English currency, realised £126,971. The assured repaid the insurers £72,000. But the insurers were not content with the indemnity and brought an action to recover the windfall of £54,971. Diplock J. held that the insurers could not recover the excess for, under the doctrine of subrogation, an insurer was entitled to recover from the assured only to the extent of the payment made to the assured by the insurer under the policy.[83] It has been said[84] that it may not be easy to reconcile this conclusion with dicta in *Castellain* v. *Preston*[85] that the assured shall not be entitled "to retain, as against the insurer, a greater sum than what is shown to be his actual loss." In that case there was no question of the insurer receiving or regaining an excess. Nevertheless, in *L. Lucas Ltd.* v. *Export Credits Guarantee Department*,[86] Megaw L.J. wished to "reserve consideration of certain aspects" of the *Yorkshire Insurance* case, possibly the implication of Diplock J.'s statement[87] that subrogation is, in relation to a contract of marine insurance, "no more than a convenient way of referring to those terms which are to be implied in the contract between the assured and the insurer to give business efficacy to an agreement whereby the assured in the case of a loss against which the policy has been made shall be fully indemnified, and never more than fully indemnified." This analysis of the basis of subrogation, which discounts the many authorities which hold that subrogation is an equitable doctrine[88] could arguably lead to a conclusion

---

distinction can be drawn between marine and non-marine policies; and that the decision of Diplock J. in *Yorkshire Insurance Co. Ltd.* v. *Nisbet Shipping Co. Ltd.* [1962] 2 Q.B. 330 (see below, n. 81) is consistent with this conclusion and "favours the plaintiffs rather than the defendants": at p. 242, *per* Widgery L.J.

[81] *Yorkshire Insurance Co. Ltd.* v. *Nisbet Shipping Co. Ltd.* [1962] 2 Q.B. 330. See also *North of England Iron S.S. Insurance Association* v. *Armstrong* (1870) L.R. 5 Q.B. 244; *Thames & Mersey Marine Insurance Co. Ltd.* v. *British & Chilian S.S. Co. Ltd.* [1915] 2 K.B. 214, affd. [1916] 1 K.B. 30, C.A.; *Glen Line Ltd.* v. *Att.-Gen.* (1930) 36 Com.Cas. 1, 14, *per* Lord Atkin; *Lord Napier and Ettrick* v. *R.F. Kershaw Ltd.* [1993] 1 All E.R. 385, 409, *per* Lord Browne-Wilkinson; *Boag* v. *Standard Marine Insurance Co.* [1937] 2 K.B. 113, 122, *per* Lord Wright M.R.; *Aetna Insurance Co.* v. *United Fruit Co.*, 304 U.S. 430 (1938); and *cf.* Marine Insurance Act 1906, s.79.

[82] [1962] 2 Q.B. 330.

[83] At pp. 340–341.

[84] *L. Lucas Ltd.* v. *Export Credits Guarantee Dept.* [1973] 1 W.L.R. 914, 924, *per* Megaw L.J.

[85] (1883) 11 Q.B.D. 380, 386, *per* Brett L.J.

[86] [1973] 1 W.L.R. 914, 924.

[87] [1962] 2 Q.B. 330, 340.

[88] See above, pp. 590–591.

opposite to that reached in *Yorkshire Insurance*, namely that the insurer should reap the windfall since it is he who has borne the risk.[89]

Abandonment

An assured may in certain circumstances abandon the chattel insured to the insurer. The insurer, as has been seen, is entitled on payment to all rights of the assured which lessen the loss. Accordingly, he is entitled to the article which the assured has abandoned, "on the general principles of equity" that "the person who originally sustains the loss was the owner, but after satisfaction made to him the insurer."[90] In non-marine insurance, the assured rarely exercises his right for he is not generally prejudiced by retaining the uninjured part of the subject-matter of the insurance.[91] But if he does abandon, he need give no notice of abandonment and on payment of the loss in full the salvage is transferred to the insurers.[92]

In marine insurance, however, abandonment is in practice more important. Cases of actual total loss[93] and of partial loss[94] do not in this context create any difficulty. In the latter case, notice of abandonment need not be given,[95] and the assured is entitled to be indemnified in full in respect of the loss insured against; in the former case, no question of abandonment arises. But midway between these two cases lies constructive total loss, which is defined[96] by section 60(1) of the Marine Insurance Act 1906, as follows:

> Subject to any express provision in the policy, there is a constructive total loss where the subject-matter insured is reasonably abandoned on account of its actual total loss appearing to be unavoidable, or because it could not be preserved from actual total loss without an expenditure which would exceed its value when the expenditure has been incurred.

So whereas actual total loss presupposes physical loss of the subject-matter insured, constructive total loss presupposes only its loss as a commercial proposition. The assured is really faced with a choice: he may either treat the loss as a partial loss, or he may abandon the subject-matter to the insurer and treat the loss as if it was an actual total loss.[97] If, however, he elects to take the

---

[89] [1962] 2 Q.B. 330, 344, *arguendo*. For example, what if the assured had later recovered full damages which, on being transmitted, realised only £50,000?

[90] *Rankin* v. *Potter* (1872) L.R. 6 H.L. 83, 118, *per* Blackburn J.; see also *Kaltenbach* v. *Mackenzie* (1878) 3 C.P.D. 467, 470, *per* Brett L.J.

[91] Since most chattels will be covered by a single policy, the damaged chattel is treated as salvage: see Porter, *The Law of Insurance*, p. 231.

[92] *Rankin* v. *Potter* (1873) L.R. 6 H.L. 83.

[93] Marine Insurance Act 1906, s.57(1).

[94] *Ibid.* ss.56, 57.

[95] *Ibid.* s.57(2).

[96] Particular examples are given in s.60(2) of the Marine Insurance Act 1906.

[97] Marine Insurance Act 1906, s.61.

latter course, he must give notice of abandonment to the insurer.[98] Once notice of abandonment has been accepted by the insurer, it cannot be revoked.[99]

Where there is a valid abandonment, it is provided by section 63(1) of the Act that "the insurer is entitled to take over the interest of the assured in whatever may remain of the subject-matter insured, and all proprietary rights incidental thereto."[1]

Abandonment does not, therefore, of itself vest the subject-matter in the insurer. It merely entitles him to acquire it. In some circumstances, he may prefer not to do so. "For it might be a *damnosa hereditas*, whose ownership only imposed liabilities which the underwriters did not want. The owner of a ship wrecked in a harbour might be liable to the harbour authority for the costs of buoying and removing the wreck."[2]

There is some doubt as to who, if anybody, is the owner of the subject-matter after notice of abandonment has been given but before it has been accepted by the insurer. In one case,[3] Bailhache J. seems to have inclined to the view that the subject-matter is in such circumstances a *res nullius*. But the better view is that it remains the property of the assured,[4] for the assured has, by his notice of abandonment, abandoned the subject-matter not to the whole world[5] but only to the insurer. So regarded, abandonment falls into place as part of the doctrine of subrogation, whereby the insurer is entitled to take the benefit of rights of the assured which diminish the loss.[6] It has been said[7] that "the doctrine of notice of abandonment is most difficult to justify upon principle." But it should be remembered that the assured's right to treat as a total loss what is really no more than a very probable total loss is a right which is very favourable to him, releasing him as it does from what might be a highly embarrassing situation.[8] It is not, therefore, wholly unreasonable that in the circumstances he should be required to give notice of abandonment to his insurers if he should desire to take advantage of this right.

---

[98] *Ibid.* s.62(1).

[99] *Ibid.* s.62(6). Though, if between the date of the notice and the date of commencement of legal proceedings there has been a change of circumstances, not brought about by the action of the insurer, in consequence of which the loss is reduced from total to partial, the assured can only recover for a partial loss: see *Sailing Ship "Blairmore" Co.* v. *Macredie* [1898] A.C. 593, 610, *per* Lord Herschell. This is the English doctrine of ademption of loss.

[1] The insurer is also entitled to freight in course of being earned, and which is earned by the ship subsequent to the casualty causing the loss, less the expenses of earning it incurred after the casualty: see Marine Insurance Act 1906, s.63(2).

[2] *Allegmeine Versicherungs-Gesellschaft Helvetia* v. *Administrator of German Property* [1931] 1 K.B. 672, 688, *per* Srutton L.J.

[3] *Boston Corp.* v. *France, Fenwicke & Co.* (1923) 28 Com.Cas. 367, 375–376.

[4] *Occeanic Steam Navigation Co.* v. *Evans* (1934) 40 Com.Cas. 108, 111, *per* Greer L.J.; *Blane Steamships Ltd.* v. *Ministry of Transport* [1951] 2 K.B. 965, 991, *per* Cohen L.J.

[5] At common law and in equity, an owner of property cannot divest himself of his ownership simply by abandoning his property: see *Vandervell* v. *I.R.C.* [1964] T.R. 93, 99, *per* Plowman J.

[6] For a contrary view, see *Page* v. *Scottish Insurance Corp.* (1929) 140 L.T. 571, 575, *per* Scrutton L.J.

[7] *Castellain* v. *Preston* (1883) 11 Q.B.D. 380, 387, *per* Brett L.J.

[8] See Arnould, *op. cit.* para. 1173.

Settlement and release by the assured of claims against third parties

The assured has power to enter into binding agreements for the settlement of claims which he may have against third parties, and even to release third parties from such claims. If an assured enters into a settlement or grants a release in respect of a loss which has not been paid by the insurer, the settlement or release will ordinarily bind the insurer as well as the assured.[9] But if he does so after payment by the insurer of the loss, the insurer will, it appears, only be bound if the third party had no notice of his right of subrogation,[10] for upon payment the right to proceed against the third party became vested in equity in the insurer. Nevertheless, even if the insurer should be bound by such a settlement or release, it does not follow that he will be altogether without a remedy. If the settlement or release was made before the insurance was effected and was not disclosed to the insurer, it may give him grounds for rescinding the contract of insurance. If it was made after the occurrence of a loss insured against but before payment of that loss by the insurer, it will, if prejudicial to the insurer, operate to release him from his duty to make a payment in respect of that loss under the policy.[11] Moreover, a prejudicial settlement or release which is binding on the insurer may, at least if made after payment of the loss, render the assured liable in damages, to the insurer for breach of an implied term of the contract of insurance.[12]

---

[9] *West of England Fire Insurance Co.* v. *Isaacs* [1897] 1 Q.B. 226.

[10] *Ibid.* But *cf. Haigh* v. *Lawford* (1964) 114 L.J. 208 and MacGillivray & Parkington on *Insurance Law* § 1205. The third party may, in these circumstances, be regarded as in the position of a bona fide purchaser.

[11] *Andrews* v. *Patriotic Insurance Co.* (1886) 18 L.R.Ir. 355.

[12] *Commercial Union Assurance Co.* v. *Lister* (1874) L.R. 9 Ch.App. 483; *West of England Fire Insurance Co.* v. *Isaacs* [1897] 1 Q.B. 226; *Horse, Carriage & General Insurance Co.* v. *Petch* (1916) 33 T.L.R. 131; *Boag* v. *Standard Marine Insurance Co.* [1937] 2 K.B. 113, 128, *per* Scott L.J.
It has been said that the basis upon which an insurer may, by a prejudicial settlement or abandonment of a claim by the assured, be released from his liability under the policy is similar to that upon which a surety may be released from his his guarantee by the creditor giving time to the principal debtor: see *Andrews* v. *Patriotic Insurance Co.* (1886) 18 L.R.Ir. 355, 370, *per* Palles C.B.; *Castellain* v. *Preston* (1883) 11 Q.B.D. 380, 403, *per* Bowen L.J. However, the status of insurers and sureties is not similar, nor are they subject to the same rights and duties. Bowen L.J. in *Castellain* v. *Preston* (1883) 11 Q.B.D. 380, 403 put the distinction between a surety and an insurer in this way: "A surety is a person who answers for the default of another, and an insurer is a person who guarantees against loss by an event." It may, of course, be that the event in respect of which the insurer gives his guarantee is the default of another, as in the case of insurance against bad debts. But even in a situation like that, the insurer does not become a surety. He has not undertaken to answer for the default of another, only to guarantee against each loss by such default. The distinction can be of importance. A surety who pays a debt is entitled only to contribution by his co-sureties. But where an insurer makes a payment under a guarantee policy, he is entitled to be subrogated to the insured creditor's rights against the debtor's sureties and to be reimbursed by them in full; see *Parr's Bank Ltd.* v. *Albert Mines Syndicate Ltd.* (1900) 5 Com.Cas. 116; *Page* v. *Scottish Insurance Co.* (1929) 140 L.T. 571, 575, *per* Scrutton L.J. The rights of insurers and sureties differ also in some other respects; see Rowlatt, *op. cit.* pp. 7–8; and below, p. 619, n. 32.

Remedies

In insurance it is commonly said that the insurer has a *right* of subrogation,[13] but that right springs from the court's willingness to allow the insurer to succeed to the assured's rights against third parties.[14] The right of subrogation is normally exercised by the insurer taking action against a third party in the name of the assured.[15] If the assured, after tender by the insurer of indemnity as to costs, refuses to permit the insurer to proceed in the assured's name, the insurer can either bring proceedings in equity to compel him to do so,[16] or he can, since the Judicature Act 1873, more simply bring proceedings in his own name but joining the assured as co-defendant.[17]

It may, however, be that the insurer wishes to recover from the assured money which has already come into the assured's hands. In such a case, the appropriate remedy at law would appear to be an action for money had and received to the use of the insurer.[18] The insurer will not, however, be limited in such circumstances to a personal remedy against the assured. Money received by the assured to which the insurer is entitled to be subrogated may be held by the assured as trustee for the insurer.[19] The insurer should not, therefore, be prejudiced by the bankruptcy of his assured provided that the money can be identified in the hands of the assured.[20] Equity will, moreover, impose a lien over that fund in favour of the insurer. Indeed, in some circumstances, "the imposition of a trust is neither necessary nor desirable; to impose fiduciary liabilities on the assured is commercially undesirable and unnecessary to protect the insurer's interests."[21] There is a danger that the fund may cease to

---

[13] See above, p. 589.

[14] See above, p. 609.

[15] All rights of action against the third party are vested in the assured; his rights to proceed in them are strictly unaffected by the fact that the insurer has paid his loss; see *Bradburn* v. *Great Western Ry.* (1874) L.R. 10 Ex. 1; *The Esso Bernicia* [1989] A.C. 643 (see below, p. 598).

[16] *King* v. *Victoria Insurance Co.* [1896] A.C. 250, 255–256, *per* Lord Hobhouse; *Edwards & Co.* v. *Motor Union Insurance Co.* [1922] 2 K.B. 249, 254, *per* McCardie J.

[17] As in the case of non-statutory assignment, on which see *E. M. Bowden's Patents Syndicate Ltd.* v. *Herbert Smith & Co.* [1904] 2 Ch. 86, 91, *per* Warrington J.

[18] *Assicurazioni Generali de Trieste* v. *Empress Assurance Corp. Ltd.* [1907] 2 K.B. 814. The same form of action appears to have been used in *Castellain* v. *Preston* (1883) 11 Q.B.D. 380 (see in particular at p. 385). But in *Lord Napier and Ettrick* v. *R.F. Kershaw Ltd.* [1993] 1 All E.R. 385, 406 counsel could not find "any reported decision before the fusion of law and equity in which the insurer successfully sued the assured at law for money had and received."

[19] *Lord Napier and Ettrick* v. *R.F. Kershaw Ltd.* [1993] 1 All E.R. 385, H.L., 1 Lloyd's Rep. 10, C.A.; *White* v. *Dobson* (1884) 14 Sim. 273; *Re Miller, Gibb & Co.* [1957] 1 W.L.R. 703. See also *Randal* v. *Cockran* (1748) 1 Ves.Sen. 98, *per* Lord Hardwicke L.C.; *Commercial Union Assurance Co.* v. *Lister* (1874) L.R. 9 Ch.App. 483, 484, *per* Jessel M.R.; *King* v. *Victoria Insurance Co. Ltd.* [1896] A.c. 250, 255, *per* Lord Hobhouse; *Morley* v. *Moore* [1936] 2 K.B. 359, 366, *per* Sir Boyd Merriman P.; *Boag* v. *Standard Marine Insurance Co.* [1937] 2 K.B. 113, 128, *per* Scott L.J. (citing *Bruce* v. *Jones* (1863) 1 H. & C. 769). But *cf. Stearns* v. *Village Main Reef Gold Mining Co.* (1905) 10 Com.Cas 89, 97–98, *per* Stirling L.J., who thought that *ex gratia* payments were not held on trust: above pp. 611–612.

[20] *Cf. Lord Napier and Ettrick* v. *R.F. Kershaw Ltd.* [1993] 1 All E.R. 385, 409, *per* Lord Browne-Wilkinson.

[21] [1993] 1 All E.R. 385, 408, *per* Lord Browne-Wilkinson: see also, to the same effect, at p. 397, *per* Lord Templeman and at pp. 402–403, *per* Lord Goff.

be identifiable. The insurer may wish to safeguard itself against that possibility and may be in a position to do so if the fund is in the hands of a third party, for example, the assured's solicitors. Such were the facts of *Lord Napier and Ettrick v. R.F. Kershaw Ltd.*[22] Stop loss insurers had paid £100,000 to the assured, a name at Lloyd's, under a policy which indemnified the assured for underwriting losses. Subsequently, the managing agent of the name's syndicate compromised the name's claim for negligence for £130,000. This sum was paid to the plaintiff's solicitors who held it as a separate fund. The assured's total loss was £160,000.[23] The House of Lords held that the sum of £95,000 was payable to the stop loss insurer; for the assured had agreed to bear the first £25,000 loss and any loss over £125,000.[24] Moreover, the insurer should not be relegated to a personal claim against the assured. The precedents, dating from *Randal v. Cockran*,[25] demonstrated that the insurer has an enforceable equitable interest in the damages payable by the wrongdoer. The House concluded that a lien over the defined fund, the damages, was the appropriate remedy. To seek to create a trust fund would, on the particular facts, spawn formidable practical difficulties. It left open the question whether the insurers have a pre-existing proprietary interest in the causes of action vested in the assured against third parties, such as the managing agent, which, if enforced, would create a comparable fund.[26]

In Lord Templeman's view, it was just to impose a lien; if the assured were to become insolvent, the unsecured creditors "will benefit by double payment." Indeed, the assured would be guilty of "unconscionable conduct if he does not provide for the insurer to be recouped out of the damages awarded against the wrongdoer."[27] Lord Browne-Wilkinson found the analogy of the law relating to equitable charges and assignments persuasive. In his judgment[28]:

> "the correct analysis is as follows. The contract of insurance contains an implied term that the assured will pay to the insurer out of the moneys received in reduction of the loss the amount to which the insurer is entitled by way of subrogation. That contractual obligation is specifically enforceable in equity against the defined fund (*i.e.* the damages) in just the same way as are other contracts to assign or charge specific property, *e.g.* equitable assignments and equitable charges. Since equity regards as done that which ought to be done under a contract, this specifically

---

[22] [1993] 1 All E.R. 385.

[23] The arguments in the House of Lords were conducted on the assumption that a particular hypothetical name had suffered this loss and recovered this sum from the tortfeasor.

[24] At p. 390, *per* Lord Templeman.

[25] (1748) 1 Ves.Sen. 99, *White v. Dobinson* (1844) 116 L.T.O.S. 233 and *Commercial Union Insurance Co. v. Lister* (1874) 9 Ch.App. 483, 484n, were decisions which their Lordships considered to be convincing illustrations of equity's readiness to grant its remedies.

[26] Lord Templeman thought it should; Lord Browne-Wilkinson had significant reservations: *cf.* pp. 395 with pp. 409–410.

[27] At p. 397, *per* Lord Templeman.

[28] At p. 409.

enforceable right gives rise to an immediate proprietary interest in the moneys recovered from the third party. In my judgment, this proprietary interest is adequately satisfied in the circumstances of subrogation under an insurance contract by granting the insurers a lien over the moneys recovered by the assured from the third party. This lien will be enforceable against the fund so long as it is traceable and has not been acquired by a bona fide purchaser for value without notice. In addition to the equitable lien, the insurer will have a personal right of action at law to recover the amount received by the assured as moneys had and received to the use of the insurer."

The reasons which the House gave for imposing a lien are, on the particular facts, not unpersuasive. There were 246 names, some resident abroad:

"In order to succeed in an action for money had and received stop loss insurers might be obliged to pursue litigation at considerable expense in a country which knows nothing of the action for money had and received or does not recognise the doctrine of subrogation or confines its civil litigation to the tender mercies of juries who are unsympathetic to insurers."[29]

Moreover, the name might not then be in a position to make any repayment.

What is more debatable is the conclusion, specifically endorsed by Lord Templeman,[30] that a lien should be imposed even though the name was insolvent. The unsecured creditors "will benefit by double payment. The stop loss insurers will be in a worse position than an unsecured creditor because the insurers could resist payment under the policy whereas an unsecured creditor may choose whether to advance moneys or not."[31] But it is the case that the stop loss insurers did agree to indemnify the assured, and pursuance to that contract indemnified him. Is their position different from that of the assured's general creditor who promised for consideration to lend money? Do they both not take the risk they may not recover, or recover in full, the loan and the indemnity if the assured becomes insolvent?

(d) *Creditors of a Business Carried on by a Trustee or Personal Representative*

Under certain conditions, where a trustee or personal representative carrying on a business has incurred debts, the business creditors can be subrogated to the right of indemnity which the trustee or personal representative enjoys against the trust estate.

This right of indemnity arises when the trustee or personal representative incurs debts while properly carrying on or continuing the trust business.[32] The

---

[29] Lord Templeman at p. 396.
[30] *Ibid.*
[31] *Ibid.*
[32] *Dowse* v. *Gorton and Others* [1891] A.C. 190, 203–204, 208, *per* Lord Macnaghten. The analogy between this example of subrogation and subrogation of sureties is said to be a close one; see *Yonge* v. *Reynell* (1852) 9 Hare 809, 819, *per* Turner V.-C.

creditors of the business have then not only a personal claim against him,[33] but also have a "right to be put in his place against the assets; that is ... a right to the benefit of indemnity or lien which he has against the assets devoted to the purposes of the trade." Subrogation is "a mere corollary to those numerous cases in equity in which persons are allowed to follow trust assets. The trust assets having been devoted to carrying on the trade, it would not be right that the *cestui que trust* should get the benefit of the trade without paying the liabilities."[34]

The limitations on business creditors' rights of subrogation are those imposed on the trustee's or personal representative's right of indemnity[35]; for the business creditors can be in no better position than the trustee or personal representative.[36] Accordingly, if he has lost his right to be indemnified from the estate because he is in default to the estate, the business creditors have no right of subrogation until the default is made good.[37] There is then no right or asset to which the business creditors can be subrogated. Nor is the trustee or personal representative entitled to an indemnity in priority to the settlor's or testator's original creditors unless the latter have assented to the continuance of the business. Thus, in *Re Oxley*,[38] the Court of Appeal held that, since the original creditors of the testator could not be said to have assented to the carrying on by the executors of the deceased's business merely by standing by and abstaining from interfering, the executors were not entitled to be indemnified out of the estate's assets. Consequently, the business creditors had no right of subrogation and were postponed to the original creditors.[39]

A receiver and manager appointed by the court may also properly incur debts while carrying on a business. The business creditors are entitled to be subrogated to his rights (including his right of indemnity) against the estate given him to manage.[40]

---

[33] *Farhall* v. *Farhall* (1871) 7 Ch.App. 123; *Owen* v. *Delamere* (1872) L.R. 15 Eq. 134.

[34] *Re Johnson* (1880) 14 Ch.D. 548, 552, *per* Jessel M.R. For the position if there is more than one executor, one of whom is in default, see *Re Kidd* (1894) 70 L.T. 648. *Cf.* Burrows, The *Law of Restitution*, p. 84.

[35] *Re Hodges* [1899] 1 I.R. 480.

[36] For an unusual case where a *quantum meruit* claim succeeded even though the fiduciary had no right of indemnity, see *Weldon* v. *Canadian Surety Co.* (1966) 64 D.L.R. (2d) 735.

[37] *Re Johnson* (1880) 15 Ch.D. 549; *cf. Re Kidd* (1894) 70 L.T. 648.

[38] [1914] 1 Ch. 604. And see *Cutbush* v. *Cutbush* (1839) 1 Beav. 184; *cf. Re Frith* [1902] 1 Ch. 342.

[39] For a discussion of the difficulties of enforcing the right of subrogation, see Mr. Justice McPherson in Finn's *Essays in Equity*, 142, 150–151. He properly emphasises the dangers of allowing the creditor to proceed directly against the estate (as suggested in *Re Raybould* [1900] 1 Ch. 199, 201–202, *per* Joyce J.), in particular, that one creditor may then be preferred to another. He concludes that direct payment out of the trust fund has been contemplated or allowed only where the fund is subject to being administered by the court (*Re Evans* (1887) 34 Ch.D. 597) or where the creditor is evidently the sole creditor (*Re Raybould* [1900] 1 Ch. 199).

[40] *Re London United Breweries Ltd.* [1907] 2 Ch. 511; Snell, *op. cit.* p. 692.

3. Authorised Borrowings: The Discharge of the Borrower's
Valid Liabilities

A lends money to B. The money is used to discharge C's mortgage over B's land
or to buy land from C. In what circumstances will A be subrogated to C's
mortgage or to C's unpaid vendor's lien? The problem arises most acutely
when B is insolvent and A is attempting to obtain priority over B's general
creditors.

It has been said that it is not enough for A to show that his money has been
used to pay off B's debt to C.[41] There must be ... something more."[42]
Unfortunately, it is not clear from the case law what that "something more"
must be.[42a] Some judges have regarded the intention of the parties as a matter
of paramount importance. Others have not.[43] It appears that two situations
must be distinguished. First, A pays off C's mortgage without having made
any agreement with B to do so. Here there is a presumption that A intends
"that the mortgage shall be kept alive for his own benefit"[44]; he is, therefore,
subrogated to C's mortgage. Secondly, A lends money to B and the money is
used to pay off C's mortgage or to buy C's land. In this case the real intention of
the parties seems to be critical. If "the true nature of the transaction ...
[between A and B] is simply the creation of an unsecured loan, this in itself will
be sufficient to dispose of any question of subrogation" to C's security.[45]
Conversely, if the parties intended to create a secured loan, then A will succeed
to C's security if no effective security is created by the agreement between A
and B. This will certainly follow if the loan agreement between A and B
expressly provides for a security.[46] But an express agreement for a security is
not essential. "The whole circumstances of the transaction[47] may also indicate
that A intended to take a security over B's property. "The whole circumstances" may include a payment directly by A to C, with B's concurrence,[48] or a
loan to B, accompanied by a direction from A[49] that the money should be used
to discharge C's mortgage or to buy C's land. In resolving the question of A and
B's intention, the allocation of the burden of proof may be critical. The most

---

[41] *Wylie* v. *Carlyon* [1922] 1 Ch. 51, 63, *per* Eve J.

[42] *Paul* v. *Speirway Ltd.* [1976] Ch. 220, 230, *per* Oliver J.

[42a] *Cf.* Burrows, *The Law of Restitution*, p. 86 ("thwarted (actual) common intention").

[43] *Cf. Wylie* v. *Carlyon* [1922] 1 Ch. 51; *Butler* v. *Rice* [1910] 2 Ch. 277 and *Paul* v. *Speirway Ltd.*
[1976] Ch. 220, with *Ghana Commercial Bank* v. *Chandiram* [1960] A.C. 732 and *Burstone
Finance* v. *Speirway Ltd.* [1974] 1 W.L.R. 648.

[44] *Ghana Commercial Bank* v. *Chandiram* [1960] A.C. 732, 745, *per* Lord Jenkins (P.C.). See
Meagher, Gummow and Lehane, *Equity*, §§ 912–913.

[45] *Paul* v. *Speirway Ltd.* [1976] Ch. 220, 232, *per* Oliver J.; *Orakpo* v. *Manson Investments Ltd.*
[1978] A.C. 95, 104–105, *per* Lord Diplock.

[46] *Butler* v. *Rice* [1910] 2 Ch. 277.

[47] *Evandale Estates Pty Ltd.* v. *Keck* [1963] V.R. 647, 652, *per* Hudson J.

[48] *Ibid. Cf. Thurstan* v. *Nottingham Permanent Benefit B.S.* [1903] A.C. 6 and *Congresbury Motors
Ltd.* v. *Anglo-Belge Finance Co. Ltd.* [1971] Ch. 81, cited in *Paul* v. *Speirway Ltd.* [1976] Ch.
220, 229).

[49] An express trust for payment for that purpose would be conclusive evidence of A's intention.

recent decision, *Paul* v. *Speirway Ltd.*[50] suggests that there is a presumption which can be rebutted by contrary evidence that A intended to make a secured loan whenever it can be shown that A's money has been used to discharge C's mortgage or lien over B's property.

4. UNAUTHORISED BORROWINGS: THE DISCHARGE OF THE BORROWER'S VALID LIABILITIES

If A's loan to B is ineffective, being void, unenforceable or *ultra vires*, the question whether A may be subrogated to C, whose valid debt to B has been discharged with the proceeds of the loan, is one of considerable complexity. There are several reasons why this is so.

First, subrogation, like any other restitutionary relief, should not be granted if such relief frustrates the policy underlying the legal rule which has invalidated the loan transaction. A may wish to be subrogated to C's personal claim against B since, the loan being invalid, he will have no action at law against B on the loan contract[51]; or to C's lien over B's property. A must then show that the particular relief which he seeks will not indirectly enforce the invalid loan.[52]

Secondly, before A can be subrogated to C, he must demonstrate that B has adopted the benefit of the invalid loan. He will be able to do this if he can prove that B has used the money to reduce his lawful liabilities, such as paying off his debt to C. But B's valid debt to C will be discharged only if B has authorised the application of the loan for that purpose. Conversely, if the money has been paid to C without B's consent or subsequent ratification, B will not have benefited from the application of the loan money since his debt to C will not have been discharged.[53]

The decision of the Court of Appeal in *Re Cleadon Trust*[54] is an unusual but cogent illustration of this principle. A company had two subsidiaries, the secretary and the two directors of the company being also the secretary and the directors of the subsidiaries. The two subsidiaries were under certain liabilities, which the company had guaranteed and which they were unable to meet. At the request of the secretary and with the approval of the other director, the appellant, one of the two directors, paid money in discharge of these liabilities in the confident expectation that the company, whose liability to pay this money under the guarantee was thereby discharged, would reimburse him. Subsequently, at a meeting of the directors of the company, a resolution was passed which purported to confirm those advances. The Court of Appeal held, however, that the resolution was invalid. The articles required a quorum of two and no director could vote in respect of any contract or arrangement in which he was interested. The appellant was an interested party, so there was no

---

[50] [1976] Ch. 220. But *cf. Orakpo* v. *Manson Investments Ltd.* [1978] A.C. 95, 104, *per* Lord Diplock.
[51] *Cf. Sinclair* v. *Brougham* [1914] A.C. 398; see above, p. 62. If the loan were valid, personal subrogation would be superfluous.
[52] See above, pp. 62 *et seq.*
[53] See above, p. 17; see below, p. 624.
[54] [1939] Ch. 286.

quorum. The company and its subsidiaries went into liquidation and the appellant sought to prove in the company's liquidation for the money he had paid, basing his claim primarily on the equitable right formulated in the invalid loan cases.[55]

The Court of Appeal held, by a majority, that he was not entitled to succeed. Clauson L.J., with whom on this point Scott L.J. substantially agreed, examined the previous cases and was at pains to reconcile them with what he described as the principle in *Falcke* v. *Scottish Imperial Insurance Co.*,[56] namely, that a person who confers an unsought benefit on another does not thereby entitle himself to an equitable right of recoupment by that other. He said[57]:

> "Let it be assumed that A requests B to advance money to C, A being a person who has no authority from C to make the request (whether because C is a company whose powers are limited in such a way as to make it *ultra vires* on C's part to make such a request, or whether because A, though professing to act as C's authorised agent to make the request, has in fact no such authority): let it be further assumed that B, in response to the request, in fact places the money under the control of C or C's agents, and C, or an agent authorised by C to pay off C's debts, uses the money or procures the money to be used in or towards discharge of C's debts. On these assumed facts a court of equity will treat B as entitled to be recouped by C a sum equal to the amount so used in or towards discharging C's debts. . . .
>
> It is to be observed that the equity cannot operate against C (the company or the principal) merely because C has in fact received a benefit from B's action in providing the money; that fact alone, as *Falcke's* case has settled (so far as this court is concerned), would not set up an equity against C. *The equity must, it would seem, arise from the fact that C, by himself or by a person authorised to act, in the matter of payment of C's debts, for C, has used the money so as to obtain a benefit for C.* The benefit has not been an unsought benefit conferred on C behind his back. It is a benefit which C has obtained for himself by using (either himself or by his agent) B's[58] money as his own. It is his conduct in so using B's money which makes it unconscientious that he should retain the benefit while refusing recognition of B's[58a] just claim to recoupment."

It was, therefore, held that the appellant had no equitable right against the company. His application of the money in payment of the debts of the subsidiaries had conferred a benefit on the company by extinguishing *de facto* its liability under the guarantee; but that benefit had been conferred without

---

[55] See below, pp. 627 *et seq.*
[56] (1886) 34 Ch.D. 234. He was in fact referring to the broad dictum of Bowen L.J. at p. 248 in that case, rather than to the *ratio decidendi* of the case itself: see above, p. 369.
[57] [1939] Ch. 286, 322–324 (italics supplied).
[58] The report says A; but it is plainly B whose money has been used to benefit C.
[58a] *Ibid.*

the request, acquiescence, ratification or co-operation of the company. Nor had the company, either by itself or by or with the privity of its authorised agent, made any use of the money: indeed, so far as this particular payment by the appellant was concerned, the company could not take any action, for there was no quorum of directors which was capable of acquiescing in or ratifying the payment. The position was that the appellant had taken the risk of the company's ratifying his act: that risk may at the time have appeared to him slight, but he would have seen it in a different light had he been more closely acquainted with his company's articles of association. He was defeated more by the rules of company law than by any defect in the principles of restitution.

Sir Wilfred Greene M.R. dissented. He pointed out that there were two main points of difference between the case before him and the principle formulated in the agency cases.[59] First, the payment did not operate to discharge the company's debts, but those of its subsidiaries; nevertheless, the payment did operate to discharge the company's liability under the guarantee, and this he regarded as sufficient. Secondly, "the money was not, strictly speaking, borrowed at all in the sense that it went into the coffers of the company. Except in the case of the first cheque, the request was for payment direct"[60] to the creditors of the subsidiaries. In his view, however, this made no difference.

> "I cannot see that it makes any difference whether the agent obtains the money himself from the lender or requests the lender to make the payment direct to the principal's creditor. In each case, if the agent had in fact had authority, the principal would have become liable to the lender, and if the lender is entitled to recover in the one case in spite of the absence of authority, I can see no logical reason why he should not be similarly entitled in the other."[61]

This reasoning ignores, however, the vital requirement that the agent must have had authority to pay off his principal's debts. If he had no such authority, or if his acts were not subsequently ratified, the lender cannot recover whether the payments were made by the agent or by the lender at the agent's request because the principal has not adopted the benefit of the unauthorised borrowing.[62] Greene M.R.'s solution fails to reconcile the equitable right with the rule that the mere payment to another's creditor will not alone entitle a stranger to repayment by the debtor.[63]

---

[59] See below, pp. 629–631.

[60] At p. 303.

[61] *Ibid.*

[62] For a different conclusion, see Birks, *Introduction*, pp. 289–290. (If the company's obligation was not discharged, "the liquidator's own decision to treat the obligation as extinguished would have amounted to a free acceptance of the still imperfect discharge.") See also *Essays* (ed. Finn), pp. 256–261 [Sutton].

[63] *Re Cleadon Trust Ltd.* must cast doubt on the reasoning, if not on the decision, of Wright J. in *B. Liggett (Liverpool) Ltd.* v. *Barclays Bank Ltd.* [1928] 1 K.B. 48. In that case, Liggett, one of the directors of a company, signed cheques which were honoured by the defendant bank, although the regulations of the company required the signature of two directors. As the cheques were

Where A's loan has discharged B's debt to C, B must have adopted the benefit of the unauthorised loan since the debt could only have been discharged with B's authority. To prevent B's unjust enrichment, the courts validate *pro tanto* the invalid loan. It should be irrelevant, therefore, that A did or did not know that the loan to B was invalid, for the basis of his claim is that B has been unjustly enriched because he has used A's loan to discharge his valid liability to C. The *ultra vires* loan cases support this conclusion.[64]

In *Blackburn Benefit Building Society* v. *Cunliffe, Brookes & Co.*,[65] Lord Selborne suggested that A should succeed only if he could establish that B's *liability* to C was discharged. But this observation was made in a case concerned with borrowing by a company beyond its powers; only a reduction in the defendant company's liabilities will then enable a lender to assert a *pro tanto* validation of the loan without infringing the *ultra vires* doctrine.[66] No case has, as yet, arisen where B has used the loan money to benefit himself in another way; for example, B's agent may have used the invalid loan to pay Christmas gratuities to B's employees. In our view, except in the case of *ultra vires* payments where special considerations apply, A should recover to the extent that he can demonstrate that the loan money has been used for any purpose authorised by B.

There is a third reason which makes the invalid loan cases so difficult to analyse. Some judges have said that there is a preponderance of authority for the view that they have nothing to do with subrogation.[67] In our opinion this is not so. There have been many cases where A has succeeded to C's personal claim against B; such were those where A lent money to a married woman, an infant or a lunatic, and the invalid loan money was used to buy necessaries from

---

used to pay the debts of the company, the bank claimed that it was entitled to debit the account of the company, although in fact it was aware that the company's regulations required a second signature. Wright J. upheld the claim of the bank; but on the view of the majority of the Court of Appeal in *Re Cleadon Trust Ltd.*, he was only justified in doing so if Liggett had authority to pay the debts of the company: see [1939] Ch. 286, 316–318, 326–327. Such authority was never held to exist, and was clearly not regarded as important by Wright J.; indeed, it can only be inferred from the fact that Liggett was in reality conducting the company's business at the relevant time. Greene M.R. adopted the reasoning of Wright J.: see [1939] Ch. 286, 303–305; see also (1944) 60 L.Q.R. 341, 355 [Winfield].

[64] *Reversion Fund & Insurance Co. Ltd.* v. *Maison Cosway Ltd.* [1913] 1 K.B. 364, 379–380, *per* Buckley L.J., 384, *per* Kennedy L.J.: see below, p. 634.

[65] (1882) 22 Ch.D. 61, 71.

[66] See below, pp. 634 *et seq.*

[67] *e.g. Re Wrexham, Mold & Connah's Quay Railway Co. Ltd.* [1899] 1 Ch. 440, 455, *per* Rigby L.J. See also *Re National Permanent Benefit Society* (1869) L.R. 5 Ch. 309; *Re Durham County Permanent Investment Land and Building Society* (1871) L.R. 12 Eq. 516; *Re Harris Calculating Machine Co.* [1914] 1 Ch. 920, 925–926, *per* Astbury J.

C.[68] Moreover the House of Lords[69] and the Court of Appeal[70] have independently held that A, who had made an invalid loan to B, who had used that
money to buy land from C, could be subrogated to C's unpaid vendor's lien
over that land. The confusion has arisen from certain observations made in
some of the *ultra vires* loan cases. In the formative decisions where A had made
an *ultra vires* loan to a corporation, B, who had used it to pay off an *intra vires*
creditor, C, C was an unsecured creditor; and the courts allowed A "to be
subrogated" to C's rights against B.[71] But in *Re Wrexham, Mold & Connah's
Quay Railway Co.*[72] C was a secured creditor. The argument of A, who had
made an unsecured but *ultra vires* loan, that he should succeed to C's security
simply because the loan had been used to pay off C was manifestly indefensible. A would then have been in a better position than if he had been an *intra
vires* unsecured creditor. The Court of Appeal, most properly, rejected that
claim. But it was unfortunate that some of its members, particularly Rigby
L.J., should have expressed the view that A could not be *subrogated* to C
because that must mean that A must succeed to C's security and priority.[73] In
order to allow A a personal claim, the court created an independent, personal
claim in equity, akin to C's personal claim against B at law. But, as we have
seen, A may be subrogated either to a personal claim[74] or to a lien.[75] What is the
proper remedy depends on the facts of each case. The real issue is whether it is
just to subrogate A to C's lien or to C's personal claim.[76] A should succeed to
the rights of a secured creditor, C, only if he can show:

(1) that he intended to make a secured loan[77];
(2) that the loan money was used to pay off a secured creditor, C[78]; and
(3) that subrogation to C's rights would not frustrate the policy which had
invalidated the original loan transaction between A and B.

The invalid loan cases are not easy to categorise. For convenience we have
analysed them under the following headings, in an attempt to isolate the real
questions which were at issue in each case:

---

[68] See below, pp. 627 *et seq*. See also the cases where B's agent borrowed money without authority
and the money was used to reduce B's valid liability to C: see below, pp. 629–631. *Cf. Morris* v.
Ford Motor Co. Ltd. [1973] Q.B. 792, 809, *per* James L.J.

[69] *Thurstan* v. *Nottingham Permanent Benefit Building Society* [1903] A.C. 6; see below, pp.
632–633.

[70] *Congresbury Motors Ltd*. v. *Anglo-Belge Finance Co. Ltd*. [1971] 1 Ch. 81. (This decision was
overruled in *Orakpo* v. *Manson Investments Ltd*. [1978] A.C. 95 but on the ground that
subrogation would frustrate the policy of the Moneylenders Act 1927.) See above, pp. 66–67.

[71] *e.g. Re German Mining Co.* (1853) 4 De G.M. & G. 19; *Re Cork and Youghal Ry*. (1869) L.R. 4
Ch. 748; see below, pp. 635 *et seq*., for a discussion.

[72] [1899] 1 Ch. 440.

[73] At p. 455.

[74] See below, pp. 627 *et seq*.

[75] See below, pp. 631 *et seq*.

[76] [1899] 1 Ch. 440, 447, *per* Lindley M.R.

[77] *Cf. Orakpo* v. *Manson Investments Ltd*. [1978] A.c. 95, 105, *per* Lord Diplock.

[78] *Cf.* the unreported New South Wales case of *Hecimovic* v. *Schembri* (1974), discussed in
Meagher, Gummow and Lehane, *Equity* §§ 915 *et seq*. And see *Re Harris Calculating Machine
Co.* [1914] 1 Ch. 920, 925–926.

(i) Where A was subrogated to C's personal claim against B.[79]

(ii) Where A was subrogated to C's lien over B's property.[80]

These are two main categories. The cases on *ultra vires* loans fall within both, because in some of them C was an unsecured creditor and, in others, a secured creditor. But we believe that it will be clearer if we were to treat all the *ultra vires* loan cases together. Hence our third category:

(iii) Where B, a corporation, borrowed money from A. The loan, which was *ultra vires*, was used to pay off B's valid liability to C.[81]

(a) *Where A was Subrogated to C's Personal Claim against B*

(i) Loans to minors and the mentally disordered,[82] used for the purchase of necessaries

At one time a married woman had at common law the power to pledge her husband's credit for necessaries. This authority, however, was abrogated by the Matrimonial Proceedings and Property Act 1970, s.41(1), which was in turn repealed by the Matrimonial Causes Act 1973. Although the common law is not revived[83] it remains influential in determining the application of subrogation in this context.

There was no right in a lender to recover from her husband money lent to her for the purchase of necessaries.[84] The reason given was that "according to the necessary form of action for the recovery of the money, the court of law cannot look behind the advance and enter into the application of the money,[85] which may, therefore, have been applied in some other way than in the purchase of necessaries.[86] Courts of equity, however, intervened to alleviate this hardship and held that where money had been advanced by a stranger to a married woman to enable her to purchase necessaries, in so far as the money has been so applied, the lender was entitled to stand in the shoes of the supplier and sue the husband for the repayment of that part of the loan. This right was first recognised in 1718 in *Harris* v. *Lee*,[87] and was firmly established in *Jenner* v. *Morris* in 1861.[88] In the latter case the defendant sought to set off against a

---

[79] See below, pp. 627 *et seq.*

[80] See below, pp. 631 *et seq.*

[81] See below, pp. 634 *et seq.*

[82] Mental Health Act 1983, s.1.

[83] Interpretation Act 1889, s.38(2)(*a*).

[84] *Earle* v. *Peale* (1711) 1 Salk. 386, 387, *per* Parker C.J.; *cf. Ellis* v. *Ellis* (1698) 1 Ld. Raym. 344; *Biberfeld* v. *Berens* [1952] 2 Q.B. 770, 783, *per* Denning L.J.; Smith's *Leading Cases*, Vol. 2, p. 475, sub tit. *Manby* v. *Scott*. This general view is assumed in the equity cases cited.

[85] *Jenner* v. *Morris* (1861) 3 De G.F. & J. 45, 56, *per* Turner L.J.; see also *Earle* v. *Peale* (1711) 1 Salk. 386, 387, *per* Parker C.J.

[86] The doctrine of necessitous intervention has a very limited role in this context; see above, pp. 379–380.

[87] (1718) 1 P.Wms. 482.

[88] (1861) 3 De G.F. & J. 45, in which *May* v. *Skey* (1849) 16 Sim. 588 was disapproved. *Cf. Deare* v. *Soutten* (1869) L.R. 9 Eq. 151; *Weingarten* v. *Engel* [1947] 1 All E.R. 425. See also *Hutchinson* v. *Standley* (1776) *Annual Register* at p. 117, cited by counsel in *Deare* v. *Soutten* at p. 152.

judgment debt sums which he had paid to the deserted wife of the plaintiff to provide her with necessaries, and which had been so applied. Lord Campbell L.C. and Turner L.J. held that he was entitled to the set-off. Lord Campbell said that no action at law would be available in such a case, and stated the equitable principle in the following terms:

> "It has been laid down from ancient times that a court of equity will allow the party who has advanced the money which is proved to have been actually employed in paying for necessaries furnished to the deserted wife to stand in the shoes of the tradespeople who furnished the necessaries, and to have a remedy for the amount against the husband. I do not find any technical reason given for this; but it may possibly be that equity considers that the tradespeople have for valuable consideration assigned to the party who advanced the money the legal debt which would be due to them from the husband on furnishing the necessaries, and that, although a chose in action cannot be assigned at law, a court of equity recognises the right of the assignee."[89]

Today the principle which is formulated in these cases is only relevant if loans are made to minors and the mentally disordered. A minor is not liable at law to repay money lent to him for the provision of necessaries, even though he may in fact have so applied the money.[90] But in equity he will be liable to the extent that he has applied the money in the purchase of necessaries.[91]

Similarly, a lender who advances money to those responsible for the maintenance of a person who is mentally disordered is entitled in equity to recover from the estate of that person such part of that money as has been expended on necessaries for his support.[92] In *Re Beavan*,[93] a customer of a bank suffered a stroke and became of unsound mind. It was arranged between the bank and the customer's son that the customer's account should be kept open and that the son should be entitled to draw on it for necessary expenditure on the customer's behalf. On the customer's death, the account was overdrawn. Neville J. held that, in so far as the money advanced by the bank had been expended in payment for necessaries for the customer's household and family, and in the protection of his estates, the bank was entitled to stand in the shoes of the creditors who had thereby been paid off and to be paid out of the customer's estate. The bank would only be entitled to interest and commission on the money advanced by means of the overdraft if the creditors were so entitled.

There are therefore authorities, dating from the early eighteenth century, which allow a lender who has made an invalid loan to stand in the shoes of the supplier of necessaries paid off with the proceeds of his loan. Chancery judges

---

[89] At pp. 51–52.
[90] See above, p. 527. *Darby* v. *Boucher* (1693) 1 Salk. 279, *per* Treby C.J.; *Earle* v. *Peale* (1711) 1 Salk. 386; *Probart* v. *Knouth* (1783) 2 Esp. 472n.; but *cf. Ellis* v. *Ellis* (1698) 1 Ld. Raym. 344.
[91] *Marlow* v. *Pitfeild* (1719) 1 P.Wms. 558: see also *Lewis* v. *Alleyne* (1888) 4 T.L.R. 560; *Mercantile Credit Ltd.* v. *Spinks* [1968] Qd. W.N. 32.
[92] *Re Beavan* [1912] 1 Ch. 196.
[93] *Ibid.* followed in *Bank of Nova Scotia* v. *Kelly* (1973) 41 D.L.R. (3d) 273.

were content to allow him to stand in the supplier's shoes without explaining why they did so. Lord Campbell surmised[94] that equity may have considered that the supplier had, for valuable consideration, assigned to the lender his legal debt, even though the chose in action could not have been assigned at law. However, there is no other suggestion in the reports that the lender's equity was based on any fictitious assignment. What is clear is that the lender's equity did arise by operation of law, independently of the parties' intention[95]; and that, in order to prevent the unjust enrichment of the borrower, the lender was allowed to stand in the shoes of the supplier and to be subrogated in equity[96] to the supplier's rights against the borrower. The invalid loan was validated *pro tanto* because it has been used to discharge the borrower's *valid* liability to a third person. Moreover, in cases of loans to minors, subrogation to the personal rights of the supplier did not frustrate the policy of the Infants Relief Act 1874, which only invalidated the loan transaction. The lender was allowed to succeed to the supplier because the contract between the minor and supplier was valid, being a contract for the supply of necessary goods.

There is no direct authority on the question whether the lender must advance money specifically for the supply of necessary goods or whether it is enough that the advanced money has been so applied. Other authorities on invalid loans suggest that it is sufficient that the money has in fact been so applied[97]; and this is, in our view, correct in principle. The lender's equity is based on the fact that the borrower has been unjustly enriched because the money has been used for the reduction of his valid liabilities to third parties. It should, therefore, be irrelevant whether the loan was advanced to buy necessaries or not. The intention of the lender should, however, be critical if he were to claim to succeed to the rights of a secured creditor paid off with his money.[98] Such a claim should only be permitted if the lender both intended to make a secured loan (which proved invalid), and the money so lent was used to pay off a secured creditor who supplied necessaries. The analogy of the cases on valid loans suggests however that, in these circumstances, where the lender's money is used to discharge a secured loan, the presumption is that he intended to make a secured loan.[99]

(ii) Unauthorised acts of agents

In *Bannatyne* v. *D. & C. MacIver*,[1] the money had been borrowed by an agent without authority and applied in discharge of his principal's debts. The

---

[94] *Jenner* v. *Morris* (1861) 3 De G.F. & J. 45, 51–52; see above, p. 627.
[95] *Orakpo* v. *Manson Investments Ltd.* [1978] A.C. 95, 104, *per* Lord Diplock.
[96] *Morris* v. *Ford Motor Co.* [1973] Q.B. 792, 809, *per* James L.J.; *Orakpo* v. *Manson Investments Ltd.* [1978] A.C. 95, 112, *per* Lord Edmund-Davies.
[97] *Reversion Fund & Insurance Co.* v. *Maison Cosway* [1913] 1 K.B. 364; see below, p. 630.
[98] No such case has yet arisen. But see *Orakpo* v. *Manson Investments Ltd.* [1978] A.C. 95, 105, *per* Lord Diplock.
[99] *Paul* v. *Speirway Ltd.* [1976] 1 Ch. 220; see above, pp. 621–622.
[1] [1906] 1 K.B. 103. *Cf. Caledonian Community Credit Union* v. *Haldimand Feed Mill Ltd.*, 45 D.L.R. 3d 676 (1974); *Hazlewood* v. *West Coast Securities Ltd.*, 49 D.L.R. 3d 46 (1974).

London agent of the defendants, a country firm, borrowed money from the plaintiff without authority. The plaintiff was led to believe that the money was for the use of the defendants and he was also under the mistaken impression that the agent had the defendants' authority to borrow money. The Court of Appeal concluded that no distinction could be drawn between these facts and other invalid loan cases, such as *Marlow* v. *Pitfeild*[2] and *Re Cork and Youghal Ry.*[3] Consequently, in so far as the money had been applied in discharge of the defendants' legal liabilities, the plaintiff was entitled in equity to be recouped by them. In the words of Romer L.J.[4]:

> "Where money is borrowed on behalf of a principal by an agent, the lender believing that the agent has authority though it turns out that his act has not been authorised, or ratified, or adopted by the principal, then, though the principal cannot be sued at law,[5] yet in equity, to the extent to which the money borrowed has in fact been applied in paying legal debts and obligations of the principal, the lender is entitled to stand in the same position as if the money had originally been borrowed by the principal."

Romer L.J.'s statement of principle has generally been accepted, though it must be subject to some qualification. For example, his judgment could be read to mean[6] that the lender should have mistakenly believed that the agent had authority to borrow money. A majority of the Court of Appeal rejected this interpretation and held, in *Reversion Fund & Insurance Co. Ltd.* v. *Maison Cosway Ltd.*[7] that the lender can recover from the principal even though he is aware of the agent's lack of authority.[8] In our view this conclusion is correct since the principal has benefited from his adoption of his agent's unauthorised acts.[9]

---

[2] (1719) 1 P.Wms. 558 (invalid loan to an infant): see above, p. 627.

[3] (1869) L.R. 4 Ch.App. 748 (*ultra vires* loan): see below, p. 631.

[4] [1906] 1 K.B. 103, 109: see also p. 108, *per* Collins M.R.

[5] Both Collins M.R. and Romer L.J. thought that the plaintiff had no legal remedy: but see *Reid* v. *Rigby & Co.* [1894] 2 Q.B. 40.

[6] *Reversion Fund & Insurance Co. Ltd.* v. *Maison Cosway Ltd.* [1913] 1 K.B. 364, 379, *per* Buckley L.J.

[7] [1913] 1 K.B. 364. Vaughan Williams L.J. dissented.

[8] To achieve this result, Buckley L.J. (at pp. 379–380) found it necessary to resort to a strained interpretation of the judgments of both Collins M.R. and Romer L.J. in *Bannatyne* v. *D. & C. MacIver*; and his reasoning appears to have been that, since the basis of recovery in the case of *ultra vires* borrowing by a corporation is that in substance there was no borrowing by the corporation, it followed that any question of the lender's knowledge or lack of knowledge of the borrower's power or authority to borrow was irrelevant, both in that case and in the case of unauthorised borrowing by an agent. But this reasoning only reconciles his conclusion with the doctrine of *ultra vires*. If the true basis of equity's intervention is to be found in the adoption of the benefit of the unauthorised transaction by the company or the principal, as we suggest, in principle the lender's knowledge of the company's lack of power or the agent's lack of authority ought to be irrelevant. On that ground the decision in the *Reversion Fund* case can be supported.

[9] This principle was accepted in *Rolled Steel Products (Holdings) Ltd.* v. *British Steel Corp.* [1986] Ch. 246, 300, *per* Slade L.J., 307, *per* Browne-Wilkinson L.J.

In one case some similar equitable right seems to have been applied where the money had not been borrowed by the agent, but had simply been obtained by him by fraud.[10]

(iii) Unauthorised borrowing by partners

The following passage has appeared in *Lindley and Banks on Partnership* through many editions[11]:

> "Where, however, money borrowed by one partner in the name of the firm but without the authority of his co-partners has been applied in paying off debts of the firm, the lender is entitled in equity to repayment by the firm of the amount which he can show to have been so applied, even though he knew that the money was borrowed without authority: and the same rule extends to money bona fide borrowed and applied for any other legitimate purpose of the firm. This doctrine is founded partly on the right of the lender to stand in equity in the place of those creditors of the firm whose claims have been paid off by his money; and partly on the right of the borrowing partner to be indemnified by the firm against liabilities bona fide incurred by him for the legitimate purpose of relieving the firm from its debts or of carrying on its business. The equitable doctrine in question is limited in its application to cases falling under one or other of the principles above indicated."

Of the cases,[12] cited in *Lindley and Banks on Partnership*, only one[13] concerns partners and that does not seem to support his statement of the law.[14] Nevertheless, Lindley and Banks' proposition is consistent with the principle laid down in the agency cases[15] and should, in our view, be followed.[16]

(b) *Where A was Subrogated to C's Lien over B's Property*

A lends money to B and the money is used to buy land from C. The loan proves to be invalid and the mortgage which B has executed in A's favour is also avoided. The question then arises whether, and to what extent, A can be subrogated to C's unpaid vendor's lien against B.[17]

---

[10] *Re the Japanese Curtains and Patent Fabric Co. Ltd.* (1880) 28 W.R. 339.

[11] (16th ed., 1990), at pp. 318–319.

[12] *Re German Mining Co.* (1853–1854) 4 De G.M. & G. 19; *Blackburn Building Society* v. *Cuncliffe, Brooks & Co.* (1884) 9 App.Cas. 857; *Re Cork and Youghal Ry.* (1869) L.R. 4 Ch.App. 748; *Wenlock* v. *River Dee* (1887) 19 Q.B.D. 155; *Bannatyne* v. *D. & C. MacIver* [1906] 1 K.B. 1, 3. The minor and mentally disordered cases are also cited.

[13] *Re German Mining Co.* (1853–1854) 4 De G.M. & G. 19, which concerned a joint stock company, consisting of a large number of partners. But see the New South Wales case of *Turner* v. *Webb* (1941) 42 S.R. (N.S.W.) 68.

[14] *Ibid.*, see particularly, Knight Bruce L.J. at p. 35; see also Turner L.J. at p. 41.

[15] See above, pp. 629–630.

[16] *Quaere* if this equitable right, if invoked, would have produced a different result in cases like *Hawtayne* v. *Bourne* (1841) 7 M. & W. 595; *Burmester* v. *Norris* (1851) 6 Ex. 796. See above, pp. 378–379.

[17] For a recent illustration, see *Boodle Hatfield & Co. (a firm)* v. *British Films Ltd.* [1986] P.C.C. 176.

In *Thurstan* v. *Nottingham Permanent Benefit Building Society*,[18] a building society, A, lent money to a minor, B, not knowing that she was a minor, intending to make her a secured loan. On B's instructions, A paid part of the loan to C, from whom B had contracted to buy certain land. C conveyed the land to B, who contemporaneously executed a legal mortgage to A. Subsequently, A paid B the balance of the loan to pay for improvements which a builder, C2, had made to the purchased land. The Court of Appeal held that the mortgage fell with the invalid loan, but that A could be subrogated to C's unpaid vendor's lien over the land bought by B from C. "The subrogated right of [A] to be repaid the money"[19] did not offend against the policy of the Infants Relief Act 1874, which simply rendered void *loans* to minors. A was refused, however, any relief in respect of the sums advanced to C2 for building; "the Infants Relief Act 1874 is too strong."[20] The House of Lords dismissed A's appeal against that decision; B did not appeal against the decision to subrogate A to C's lien.

Thurstan's case gives rise to as many questions as it answers.[21] There is little discussion in the judgment of the Court of Appeal why it was thought proper that A should be subrogated to C's unpaid vendor's lien. But there was no doubt that A did intend to make B a loan secured on land to be bought from C; hence A paid part of the loan money directly to C.[22] The analogy of the valid loan cases suggests that subrogation to C's lien was in these circumstances appropriate.[23] The Court of Appeal gave no weight to the facts that C's vendor's lien had never arisen since he had been paid in full, or that A did not know that B was a minor when the loan was made. In our view the Court was right not to do so. C's unpaid vendor's lien was resurrected solely to prevent B's unjust enrichment at A's expense. And since B had benefited from the application of the invalid loan, it should be irrelevant that A knew or did not know that B was a minor; dicta in other invalid loan cases support this conclusion.[24]

The Court of Appeal considered that subrogation was appropriate only because A made the payment to C as B's agent. B could not then "adopt the acts of her agents, and claim to have the title deeds and conveyance handed over to her by the building society [A], without repaying to them the purchase money which they paid to obtain the conveyance."[25] It is difficult to accept that this is a condition of subrogation. If it is, then A would not have been subrogated to C

---

[18] [1902] 1 Ch. 1, [1903] A.C. 6.
[19] [1903] A.C. 6, 10, *per* Lord Halsbury L.C. B sought a declaration that the mortgage was void, and the return of the title deed.
[20] [1902] 1 Ch. 1, 12, *per* Romer L.J.
[21] *Cf.* Birks, *Introduction*; pp. 392–393.
[22] See above, pp. 593–594.
[23] See above, pp. 621–622 particularly *Paul* v. *Speirway Ltd.* [1976] Ch. 220, 227, *per* Oliver J.
[24] See above, pp. 629–631, see below, pp. 634–638. *Cf. Boodle Hatfield & Co. (a firm)* v. *British Films Ltd.* [1986] P.C.C. 176.
[25] [1902] 1 Ch. 1, 9, *per* Vaughan Williams L.J.; see also at p. 11, *per* Romer L.J. See too *Orakpo* v. *Manson Investments Ltd.* [1978] A.C. 95, 106–107, *per* Lord Diplock, 113, *per* Lord Keith of Kinkel.

if A had not paid C directly but had lent the money to B who had paid C. The analogy of the cases on authorised loans would suggest that the important factor is not whether A made the payment to C as B's agent but whether A intended to make B a secured loan, which was subsequently used to pay off C's secured valid debt.[26]

Finally, in *Thurstan's* case neither the House of Lords nor the Court of Appeal fully considered whether A should be subrogated to C's or C2's personal claim against B. The conclusion that A could be subrogated to C's unpaid vendor's lien made it unnecessary to decide whether A should be subrogated to C's personal claim against B.[27] But C2 had no lien. The contract between A and B to pay for the building materials supplied by C2 was described as a contract for money lent and was void. There were, however, two quite separate contracts: between A and B and between B and C2, the builder. The contract between A and B was for money lent. The contract between B and C2 was for services rendered or goods supplied, in which case it would also probably have been void under the Infants Relief Act 1874; subrogation to C2 would not, therefore, help A. But Romer L.J. expressed the view that, even if B's contract with C2 "was not one of loan, and might not be void under the statute as a contract for goods supplied . . .[28] it would not help the society [A] in this case, for the builder [C2] had no lien or charge on the land in respect of the building work done."[29] This conclusion is difficult to justify. In so far as it suggests that equity will not subrogate an invalid lender to the personal claim of a third party, it is inconsistent with earlier authority[30] and is wrong in principle. Subrogation to any valid claim which C2 enjoyed against B should be permitted if it is necessary to prevent B's unjust enrichment; to do so would not indirectly enforce the invalid loan contract between A and B.

The problems of *Thurstan's* case arise from a reluctance both to contemplate the possibility of personal as well as real subrogation and the failure to analyse critically whether subrogation to C's or C2's rights against B would indirectly enforce the invalid loan between A and B. Subrogation to an unpaid vendor's lien was, however, at one time,[31] seized upon in an attempt to solve other invalid loan problems, where A's loan to B was not void because of minority but merely unenforceable because the formalities required by the Moneylenders Act 1927 had not been observed. But, in *Orakpo* v. *Manson Investments Ltd.*,[32] the House of Lords held that subrogation to an unpaid vendor's lien would frustrate the policy of the legislation, which was enacted for the protection of the borrowing public, but did not question the authority of *Thurstan's* case.[33]

---

[26] See above, pp. 621–622.
[27] But *cf.* [1902] 1 Ch. 1, 9, *per* Vaughan Williams L.J., 13, *per* Cozens-Hardy L.J.
[28] *Semble* as a contract for the supply of necessary goods.
[29] [1902] 1 Ch. 1, 12.
[30] See above, pp. 627 *et seq.*
[31] *Congresbury Motors Ltd.* v. *Anglo-Belge Finance Co. Ltd.* [1971] 1 Ch. 81.
[32] [1978] A.C. 95.
[33] See above, pp. 65–67 and 595–596 for a critical comment.

In *Thurstan's* case A's security was void. It is a distinct problem whether C's unpaid vendor's lien can co-exist with a security which was valid when granted to A. The balance of authority suggests that it cannot. In *Burston Finance Ltd.* v. *Speirway Ltd.*[34] A lent £413,000 to a company B, to enable it to buy land from C. The loan was secured by a legal mortgage over that land in A's favour. Subsequently B went into a creditors' voluntary liquidation, and the liquidator took the point that A's mortgage was void as against him for lack of registration, by virtue of section 95(1) of the Companies Act 1948.[35] Walton J. refused to follow the earlier decision of *Coptic Ltd.* v. *Bailey*[36] and to allow A to be subrogated to C's unpaid vendor's lien, even though that lien had not been excluded in the contract of sale between B and C. Such a lien could "co-exist with a security which is, from its inception, either wholly void or otherwise completely unenforceable."[37] But A, by taking the valid legal charge, had got what he bargained for.[38] That charge was valid and enforceable when it was created; A was "merely lax in not taking steps to ensure that what [A] bargained for remained good against the world."[39]

In our opinion Walton J.'s conclusion is persuasive and consistent with the Court of Appeal's decision in *Capital Finance Co. Ltd.* v. *Stokes*.[40] The fiction that the unpaid vendor's lien had not been abandoned was acceptable in *Thurstan's* case, because to subrogate A to C's unpaid vendor's lien did not offend against the policy of the Infants Relief Act 1874. To have extended that fiction to the facts of *Burston Finance* would have wholly frustrated the policy underlying section 95 of the Companies Act 1948,[41] which was designed to ensure that holders of unregistered charges should, in a liquidation, be in no more favourable a position than general creditors.

(c) *Where B, a Corporation, borrowed Money from A in Circumstances where the Loan was Ultra Vires, and where B applied the Loan Money to Discharge its Valid Liability to C*

Ultra vires borrowing does not at common law give rise to indebtedness on the part of the corporation. The lender can sue neither on the contract of loan, since it is void, nor by any other personal action at law or in equity to recover the money lent, for this would indirectly enforce the principal obligation under

---

[34] [1974] 1 W.L.R. 1648.

[35] Now, Companies Act 1985, s.395(1), as amended.

[36] [1972] Ch. 446.

[37] At pp. 1652–1653, *per* Walton J. But see *Orakpo* v. *Manson Investments Ltd.* [1978] A.C. 95, 110–111, *per* Lord Salmon, p. 115, *per* Lord Edmund-Davies; *cf.* p. 106, *per* Lord Diplock. (In *Orakpo* the security was unenforceable: see above, pp. 65–67).

[38] *Orakpo* v. *Manson Investments Ltd.* [1978] A.C. 95, 115, *per* Lord Edmund-Davies.

[39] At p. 1657, *per* Walton J.

[40] [1969] 1 Ch. 261. See Lord Edmund-Davies' comment in *Orakpo* v. *Manson Investments Ltd.* [1978] A.C. 95, 115.

[41] See above, n. 35.

the *ultra vires* contract.[42] Such cases will now be rare since the enactment of the Companies Act 1985, s.35, as amended.[43]

If, however, money so borrowed has been applied by or with the privity of an authorised agent of the corporation to reduce the corporation's legal liabilities, then, in so far it has been so applied, the lender can recover in equity that part of his loan from the corporation. This right was first established in 1869 in *Re Cork and Youghal Railway*.[44] The directors of a railway company, who had raised all the money they were entitled to raise by means of shares and borrowing on security, were anxious to borrow more money to complete the construction of their railway. They therefore borrowed large sums from one, Lewis, on securities called Lloyd's bonds. The company was later wound up, and holders of the bonds claimed repayment out of the surplus in the hands of the liquidator. The Court of Appeal in Chancery held that, although the borrowing was *ultra vires* the company, yet so far as the money so lent had been applied to meet the company's legal debts and liabilities, the holders of the bonds were entitled to be repaid. A small part of the money lent had been paid directly to the company's creditors, and to that extent the lenders were clearly entitled to stand in the place of the original creditors. With regard to the rest of the money which had been indirectly so applied, Lord Hatherley L.C. said[45]:

> "The proper course to be taken seems to me to be this: that, so far as the company have adopted the proceedings of their directors by allowing these moneys to be raised by the issue of these debentures, and so far as the money raised on the issue of the debentures has been applied in paying off debts which would not otherwise have been paid off, those who have advanced the moneys ought to stand in the place of those whose debts have been so paid off. It is not simply that the bondholders stand as assignees of the debts, which, no doubt, have not actually been assigned, but it has been represented by the directors that the persons who lent their money on these acknowledgments were lending their money for the purpose of clearing off the debts; in fact, that they were to be put in the position of assignees of the debts."

An inquiry was therefore ordered.

Lord Hatherley relied not only on the application of the borrowed money in reduction of the company's liabilities, but also on acquiescence[46] by the

---

[42] *Re National Permanent Benefit Building Society, ex p. Williamson* (1869) L.R. 5 Ch.App. 309; *Sinclair* v. *Brougham* [1914] A.C. 398. The lender can fall back on a proprietary remedy: see *Sinclair* v. *Brougham*, above, pp. 83 *et seq.*

[43] See above, pp. 538 *et seq.*, for a discussion of the statutory provisions.

[44] (1860) L.R. 4 Ch.App. 748. See the observations on this case by Kay J. in *Yorkshire Railway Waggon Co.* v. *Maclure* (1881) 19 Ch.D. 478, 487 (a decision reversed on appeal (1882) 21 Ch.D. 309). But see *Portsea Island Building Society* v. *Barclay* [1894] 3 Ch. 86, affd. [1895] 2 Ch. 298; cf. *Re Victoria Permanent Benefit Building, Investment & Freehold Land Society* (1870) L.R. 9 Eq. 605.

[45] At p. 761.

[46] At p. 759. Malins V.-C. at first instance had relied on acquiescence (see (1869) L.R. 4 Ch.App. 748, 752n.); the acquiescence of the shareholders was to be inferred from the authorisation of

shareholders in the borrowing.[47] But although such acquiescence or ratification on the part of the shareholders might have validated a borrowing which was beyond the powers of the directors, it could not have had the same effect on a borrowing which was beyond the powers of the company itself. Indeed, 13 years later subrogation was made available to a lender where there was no evidence of acquiescence by the shareholders of the borrowing company. In this case, *Blackburn Benefit Building Society* v. *Cunliffe, Brooks & Co.*,[48] Lord Selborne L.C. explained the relationship of the equity to the doctrine of *ultra vires* in the following terms[49]:

> "And I think that the consistency of the equity allowed in *Re Cork and Youghal Ry.* with the general rule of law that persons who have no borrowing powers cannot, by borrowing, contract debts to the lenders, may be shown in this way. The test is: Has the transaction really added to the liabilities of the company? If the amount of the company's liabilities remains in substance unchanged, but there is, merely for the convenience of repayment, a change of the creditor, there is no substantial borrowing in the result, so far as relates to the position of the company. Regarded in that light, it is consistent with the general principle of equity, that those who pay legitimate demands which they are bound in some way or other to meet, and have had the benefit of other people's money advanced to them for that purpose, shall not retain that benefit so as, in substance, to make those other people pay their debts."[50]

The formative decisions suggest that the basis of equity's intervention was "a principle recognised in the old cases, beginning with *Marlow* v. *Pitfeild*[51] . . . that . . . inasmuch his money had gone to pay debts, which would be recoverable at law, he could come into a Court of Equity and stand in the place of those

---

the issue of the bonds at a company meeting. The idea of acquiescence may have been suggested to the court by the citation to it of *Re Magdalena Steam Navigation Co.* (1860) Johns. 690. But in that case there was no *ultra vires* borrowing, rather an issue of securities by directors of a company without the authority of the company. Acquiescence may well be relevant in such a case, but cannot, we suggest, affect a borrowing which is *ultra vires* the company itself.

[47] See also Sir G. M. Giffard L.J. at pp. 762–763: see, too, his statement of the law in *Re National Permanent Benefit B.S.* (1869) L.R. 5 Ch.App. 309, 313.

[48] (1882) 22 Ch.D. 61; see also (1884) 9 App.Cas. 857. The more recent cases are *Re Airedale Co-operative Worsted Manufacturing Society Ltd.* [1933] Ch. 639; *Caledonian Community Credit Union* v. *Haldimand Feed Mill Ltd.* 45 D.L.R. 3d 676 (1974).

[49] (1882) 2 Ch.D. 61, 71. See, however, the criticism in Street, *The Doctrine of Ultra Vires*, pp. 379 et seq.

[50] The lender could not rely on the rule in *Clayton's Case* (1816) 1 Mer. 572, see above, p. 88, to discover how much of the borrowed money had been used in paying the borrowing company's debts. The lender may also obtain relief in equity where the company has used the borrowed money to pay debts accruing after the date of its receipt: see *Barones Wenlock and Ors.* v. *River Dee Co.* (1887) 19 Q.B.D. 155, applied in *Re Lough Neagh Ship Co.* [1895] 1 I.R. 533.

[51] (1719) 1 P.Wms. 558; and *cf.* above, p. 627, n. 85.

creditors whose debts had been so paid."[52] The plaintiff's right was said to be "an equity" or based on an "equitable principle"[53]; and in *Baroness Wenlock* v. *River Dee Co. Ltd.*,[54] the Court of Appeal described the plaintiff as being "subrogated to the rights of these creditors." But it was not until *Re Wrexham, Mold and Connah's Quay Railway Co.*[55] that the question of the nature of the right of an *ultra vires* lender became critical to the decision of a particular case. In that case A, who had made an *ultra vires* and unsecured loan to a company, B, sought to be subrogated to the rights of C, a secured creditor, who had been paid with his money. This was a bold claim; if admitted, it would have placed A in a better position than an *intra vires* unsecured creditor. It is not surprising, therefore, that the Court of Appeal rejected it. Rigby L.J. thought that "the great preponderance of authority shows that the doctrine of subrogation has very little, if anything at all, to do with the equity really enforced in the cases, and that there is, at any rate, no authority for any subrogation to the securities or priorities of the creditors paid off."[56] Rigby L.J. was not correct in asserting that precedent denied the relevance of subrogation[57]; but he was right in stating that the court had never preferred an *ultra vires* unsecured creditor over general creditors. Lindley M.R.'s[58] approach was much more pragmatic:

> "The subrogation theory has been had recourse to in order to account for the decisions ultimately arrived at; but that theory was not really wanted in order to justify them. It was, however, adequate for the purposes for which it was used, and as applied to the cases before the Courts, it led to just results. But, if logically followed out in other cases, it leads to consequences not only not foreseen by those who had recourse to it, but to results so startling that I cannot accept the theory as sound. There is no decision yet in which it has been applied so as to defeat any innocent person, nor so as to place the lender in a better position than that in which he would have been if his loan had not been prohibited."

The Court of Appeal did, however, allow A to succeed in equity to C's personal claim against the company, B, and to claim as a general creditor. This was a most proper result. What was regrettable was the court's assumption that *to subrogate* A to C must inevitably mean that A must succeed to C's charge over B's property. Subrogation is, in our view, a flexible remedy which may enable A to succeed in equity to C's personal claim against B, as *Marlow* v. *Pitfeild*[59]

---

[52] *Re National Permanent Benefit B.S., ex p. Williamson* (1869) 5 Ch.App. 309, 313, *per* Giffard L.J.
[53] *e.g. Blackburn and District Benefit B.S.* v. *Cunliffe, Brooks & Co.* (1885) 22 Ch.D. 61, 70–71, *per* Lord Selborne.
[54] (1887) 19 Q.B.D. 155, 166, *per curiam* (Fry L.J.).
[55] [1899] 1 Ch. 440.
[56] At p. 455.
[57] See above, pp. 625 *et seq.*
[58] At p. 447.
[59] (1719) 1 P.Wms. 558; see above, p. 636.

illustrates, or to C's lien or charge over B's property, as in *Thurstan's*[60] case. What is the appropriate remedy must depend on the facts of each case. It is never appropriate to allow an *ultra vires* unsecured lender to succeed to the rights of secured creditors.

---

[60] [1903] A.C. 6; see above, p. 633.

SECTION THREE

WHERE THE DEFENDANT HAS ACQUIRED A BENEFIT THROUGH HIS OWN WRONGFUL ACT

CHAPTER 32

INTRODUCTION

IN this Section we shall consider restitutionary claims against wrongdoers. The injured party seeks to recover the benefit gained by the wrongdoer from his wrong. There may be little coincidence between the loss which he suffered and the benefit which the wrongdoer gained. It is because the wrongdoer has made this gain, in circumstances where the injured party may have suffered little or no loss, that he will normally wish to pursue his restitutionary claim. His claim may be a claim at law, but more frequently it will be equitable. In some situations he will be content with an order that the defendant makes restitution of the value of the benefits received or accounts for the profits gained from his wrongful act. In others, he may plead that the wrongdoer, or a person claiming through him, is a constructive trustee of an identifiable asset[1] or that he must account, as a constructive trustee, for money which he has received but which is no longer identifiable in his hands.[2] He may be anxious to do so for a variety of reasons: the defendant is insolvent[3]; the "trust" property has increased in value[4]; the statute of limitations has tolled his claim unless the wrongdoer is held to be a trustee[5]; a constructive trustee may have to pay compound interest on the sums due; and a writ may be served on him even though he is out of the jurisdiction.[6]

Some wrongdoers are treated more sternly than others. Equity has characterised the conduct of those who repudiate their undertaking to hold property on trust for others as fraudulent.[7] Fiduciaries are stripped of their enrichment because there is a mere possibility they may have abused their position of trust and because the court concludes that it is necessary to punish them. So, equity has formulated Draconian rules to ensure that a fiduciary shall never profit at his principal's expense. The trustee is the fiduciary whose conduct is most scrupulously overseen; even the honest trustee, who acts in the best interests of the trust, may be held to be a trustee of gains which the trust itself could never have made. And trust law will often determine whether other fiduciaries have abused their fiduciary responsibilities.[8]

---

[1] *Cf.* above, Chap. 2.
[2] *Ibid.*
[3] See above, pp. 86 *et seq.*
[4] See below, p. 87.
[5] See Chap. 43.
[6] See below, p. 671.
[7] Chap. 34.
[8] See below, pp. 654 *et seq.*

A defendant may acquire confidential information because and only because he is a fiduciary. In contrast, a plaintiff may confide information to another in the course of a business or personal relationship. The confidant may not thereby become a fiduciary. But, even if he is not, he is not permitted to make use of information to the prejudice of the confider. The liability of the confidant who innocently exploits that information is less severe than that of the confidant who consciously exploits it.[9]

It is not surprising that criminals are never allowed to benefit from their crimes, and the courts will not hesitate to find that they are trustees of any identifiable benefit. But what is a *benefit* may be a matter for dispute; and a victim's (or his representatives') claim against a third party has failed on the ground that the benefit was not gained at the victim's (or his representatives') expense.[10]

Some but not all tortfeasors must disgorge the gain made from the tortious act. We conclude, however, that in principle there should normally be no objection to compelling, in the appropriate case, any tortfeasor to account for the gain from the tort, and, in some situations, to hold an identifiable gain on trust for the injured party.[11]

A defendant may acquire a benefit in breach of contract. The circumstances in which a plaintiff may obtain restitution of benefits so acquired have already been considered in an earlier Chapter of this book.[12]

---

[9] See below, pp. 690–692.

[10] Query whether a claim to recover sums paid to the criminal who sells his memoirs to a tabloid will fail for this reason: see below, pp. 711–712.

[11] Chap. 38.

[12] Chap. 18: see also above, p. 71, where we set out our reasons for treating the subject in this way.

CHAPTER 33

BENEFITS ACQUIRED IN BREACH OF FIDUCIARY RELATIONSHIPS

(A) Introduction

"There is a broad principle of equity developed by this court in order to ensure that trustees or agents shall not retain a profit made in the course of or by means of their office."[1] This principle has been established for some 250 years. It extends not only to trustees and agents but to all fiduciaries, and is applied in a wide variety of circumstances.

English judges have wisely never attempted to formulate a comprehensive definition of who is a fiduciary.[2] Certain relationships are well known to be fiduciary: trustee and beneficiary; a member of the Security Services and the Crown[3]; director and the company[4]; senior management employee and the company[5]; promoter and the company[6]; solicitor and client[7]; agent (including a

---

[1] *Phipps* v. *Boardman* [1964] 1 W.L.R. 993, 1010, *per* Wilberforce J. In this Chapter we have only attempted a general survey of the case law. The topic is sufficiently large to command for itself a complete textbook: See P. D. Finn, *Fiduciary Obligations*, which is a comprehensive, if now somewhat dated, survey.

[2] See *Ex p. Dale* (1879) 11 Ch.D. 772, 778, *per* Fry J.; *Re Coomber* [1911] 1 Ch. 723, 728, *per* Fletcher Moulton L.J. See, generally, Brunyate, *Limitation of Actions in Equity*, pp. 81–94, 102–103; [1962] C.L.J. 69, [1963] C.L.J. 119 [L. S. Sealy]; (1975) 25 U.T.L.J. 1 [Weinrib]; (1975) 53 Can.B.R. 771 [Beck]; P. D. Finn, *Fiduciary Obligations*, pp. 1–14; J. C. Shepherd, *Law of Fiduciaries*; A.J. Oakley, *Constructive Trusts*, Chap. 3; J. R. Maurice Gautreau, *Demystifying the Fiduciary Mystique* (1989) 68 Con.B.R. 1.

[3] *Att.-Gen.* v. *Guardian Newspapers Ltd. (No. 2)* [1990] 1 A.C. 109 (the *Spycatcher* case): see below, p. 662. *Cf.* Mr. Frank Snepp and the CIA: *Snepp* v. *United States* (1980) 444 U.S. 507.

[4] *e.g. Selangor United Rubber Estates Ltd.* v. *Cradock (No. 3)* [1968] 1 W.L.R. 1555. See, generally, Harold Marsh, Jr., "Are Directors Trustees?" (1966) 22 *The Business Lawyer* 35; L. S. Sealy, "The Director as Trustee" [1967] C.L.J. 83. But directors-elect are not fiduciaries: see *Lindgren* v. *L. & P. Estates Ltd.* [1968] Ch. 572.

[5] *Sybron Corp.* v. *Rochem Ltd.* [1984] Ch. 112, 127, *per* Stephenson L.J.; *Canadian Aero-Services Ltd.* v. *O'Malley* 1973) 40 D.L.R. (3d) 371, 381, *per* Laskin J. (S. Ct. of Canada).

[6] *Lydney and Wigpool Iron Ore Co.* v. *Bird* (1886) 33 Ch.D. 85, 94, *per curiam* (Lindley L.J.). *Cf. Daly* v. *Sydney Stock Exchange* (1986) 160 C.L.R. 371 (stockbroker and investor).

[7] *McMaster* v. *Byrne* [1952] 1 All E.R. 1362, P.C.; *Brown* v. *I.R.C.* [1965] A.C. 244. But contrast *Swain* v. *Law Society* [1983] 1 A.C. 598.

self-appointed agent[8]) and principal[9]; partner and co-partner[10]; mortgagee and mortgagor.[11] Conversely, the courts may be reluctant to find a fiduciary relationship between businessmen who enter into commercial dealings with each other.[12] But, exceptionally,[13] even in such a case, the nature of the transaction[14] between the parties, in particular the nature of the obligations incurred by one party to act for another,[15] may lead to the conclusion that one party is in a position of trust towards the other. The class of fiduciary relationships is never closed.[16] Yet, as Justice Frankfurter once said[17]:

> "To say that a man is a fiduciary only begins analysis; it gives direction to further inquiry. To whom is he a fiduciary? What obligations does he owe as a fiduciary? In what respect has he failed to discharge these obligations? And what are the consequences of his deviation from duty?"

To state that no man "who stands in a position of trust towards another [can], in matters affected by that position, advance his own interests (*e.g.* by making a profit) at the other's expense"[18] is, therefore, to initiate a complex inquiry.[19]

---

[8] *English* v. *Dedham Vale Properties Ltd.* [1978] 1 W.L.R. 93.

[9] In the sense that every agent owes a duty of loyalty to his principal: *Lowther* v. *Lowther* (1806) 13 Ves. 95, 103, *per* Lord Erskine. *Cf.* sub-agents (*Powell & Thomas* v. *Evans Jones & Co.* [1905] 1 K.B. 11) and bailees (*Re Hallett's Estate* (1880) 13 Ch.D. 696). But agents may not always be fiduciary agents: *Lord Napier and Ettrick* v. *R.F. Kershaw Ltd.* [1993] 1 All E.R. 385, H.L.; see Bowstead, *Agency*, pp. 156 *et seq.*; Meagher, Gummow and Lehane, *Equity*, §§ 538–545.

[10] *Bentley* v. *Craven* (1853) 18 Beav. 75. And parties to a joint venture: *Holiday Inns Inc.* v. *Yorkstone Properties (Harlington)* (1974) 232 E.G. 951; *Meinhard* v. *Salmon*, 164 N.E. 545 (1928). For the Australian authorities, see Lehane in Finn's *Essays in Equity*, pp. 96 *et seq.*

[11] *Farrars* v. *Farrars Ltd.* (1888) 40 Ch.D. 395.

[12] *Cf. Appleby* v. *Cowley, The Times*, April 14, 1982, (head of barristers' chambers owed no fiduciary obligation towards tenants); and, in particular, *United States Surgical Corp.* v. *Hospital Products International Pty. Ltd.* (1984) 58 A.L.J.R. 587 (High Ct. of Australia). See also *Pine Pass Oil* v. *Pacific Petroleum* (1968) 70 D.L.R. (2d) 196; *Jirna Ltd.* v. *Mister Do-Nut of Canada Ltd.* (1973) 40 D.L.R. (3d) 303.

[13] *Cf. Reid-Newfoundland Co.* v. *Anglo-American Telegraph Co. Ltd.* [1912] A.C. 555; *Liggett* v. *Kensington* [1993] 1 N.Z.L.R. 257, C.A.; *LAC Minerals* v. *International Corona Resources Ltd.* (1989) 61 D.L.R. (4th) 14 (S. Ct. of Canada); *Broomfield* v. *Kossow*, 212 N.E. 2d 556 (1965).

[14] A fiduciary relationship may arise "whenever the plaintiff *entrusts* to the defendant a job to be performed": *Re Reading's Petition of Right* [1949] 2 K.B. 232, 236, *per* Asquith L.J. (italics supplied). And *cf. Tito* v. *Waddell (No. 2)* [1977] Ch. 106, 229–230, *per* Megarry V.-C. and *Liggett* v. *Kensington* [1993] 1 N.Z.L.R. 257, 281, *per* Gault J. ("Generally it is appropriate to look for circumstances in which one person has undertaken to act in the interests of another or conversely one has communicated an expectation that another will act to protect or promote his or her interests.")

[15] *United States Surgical Corp.* v. *Hospital Products Pty. Ltd.* [1983] 2 N.S.W.L.R. 157, 207–209, C.A.; (1984) 58 A.L.J.R. 587, 597–598, *per* Gibbs C.J., 619–621, *per* Deane J., 628, *per* Dawson J. (On the facts, the New South Wales Court of Appeal found a fiduciary relationship. But the High Court of Australia concluded that the relationship was simply contractual); contrast *LAC Minerals Ltd.* v. *International Corona Resources Ltd.* (1989) 61 D.L.R. (4th) 14 (S. Ct. of Canada). See Finn, *op. cit.* p. 201; Lehane in Finn's *Essays in Equity*, pp. 95–108.

[16] *English* v. *Dedham Vale Properties Ltd.* [1978] 1 W.L.R. 93, 110, *per* Slade J.

[17] *S.E.C.* v. *Chenery Corp.*, 318 U.S. 80, 85–86 (1943). See also *Canadian Aero-Services Ltd.* v. *O'Malley* (1973) 40 D.L.R. (3d) 371, 391, *per* Laskin J.

[18] *Robinson* v. *Randfontein Estates Gold Mining Co. Ltd.*, 1921 A.D. 168, 179, *per* Innes C.J.

[19] For an analysis, see "Unjust Enrichment and the Fiduciary's Duty of Loyalty" (1968) 84 L.Q.R. 472 [Jones].

In this Chapter we shall discuss the more important cases where the courts have held that a fiduciary allowed his duty and interest to conflict[20] and where he has been required to make restitution.[21] Has the fiduciary made use of his *position* to obtain an advantage which he otherwise would not have obtained? Has he used, for his own profit, *property* which belongs in equity to his beneficiary? In answering these questions it is said to be irrelevant that the fiduciary has acted honestly and in the beneficiary's best interests, that the profit would not have been made without the fiduciary's own personal skill and judgment, that the beneficiary as well as the fiduciary benefited from what the fiduciary did, and that the beneficiary could never have obtained the benefit himself.[22] A fiduciary's duty of loyalty is "unbending and inveterate"[23]; equity's rule is "inflexible ... and must be applied inexorably by this court."[24] "The safety of mankind"[25] requires that a court should not be required to determine whether a fiduciary acted honestly or whether the beneficiary did, or did not, suffer any injury because of the fiduciary's dealings, for "no court is equal to the examination and ascertainment"[26] of these facts.[27] As Lord Chancellor King cynically remarked in *Keech* v. *Sandford*,[28] where a trustee had personally taken a lease after the lessor's refusal to grant a new term to the trust: "[F]or I very well see, if a trustee, on the refusal to renew, might have a lease to himself, few trust estates would be renewed to *cestui que use*."

Yet, judges have accepted that equity's rule may "be departed from in many cases, without any breach of morality, without any wrong being inflicted, and without any consciousness of wrongdoing."[29] If a fiduciary has been honest and his enrichment has not been gained at his beneficiary's expense, a court may conclude that there was no conflict between fiduciary duty and self-interest.[30] But there have been occasions when even an honest fiduciary, who has not been unjustly enriched at the beneficiary's expense, has been deprived of his gains in order to deter others from temptation.[31] Equity's inflexible rule

---

[20] *Cf. Boardman* v. *Phipps* [1967] 2 A.C. 46, 172, *per* Lord Upjohn: see below, pp. 663–665.

[21] It is beyond the scope of this book to consider his potential liability in contract or in tort. *Cf. Nocton* v. *Lord Ashburton* [1914] A.C. 392; *Hedley Byrne & Co.* v. *Heller & Partners* [1964] A.C. 465; *North & South Trust Co.* v. *Berkeley* [1971] 1 W.L.R. 470.

[22] *Boardman* v. *Phipps* [1967] 2 A.C. 46.

[23] *Meinhard* v. *Salmon*, 249 N.Y. 456, 464, 164 N.E. 545, 546, *per* Cardozo C.J. (1928).

[24] *Parker* v. *McKenna* (1874) L.R. 10 Ch. 96, 124–125, *per* James L.J.

[25] *Ibid.*

[26] *Ex p. James* (1803) 8 Ves. 337, 345, *per* Lord Eldon L.C.; but *cf.* below, pp. 649–650.

[27] This principle is modified and limited if a fiduciary is known to serve two principals: see *Boulting* v. *Association of Cinematographic, Television and Allied Technicians* [1963] 2 Q.B. 606; *North & South Trust Co.* v. *Berkeley* [1971] 1 W.L.R. 470; (Contrast the position of an estate agent who may act for both vendor and purchaser: see *Kelly* v. *Cooper* [1992] 3 W.L.R. 936, P.C.); Finn, *op. cit.* Chap. 22.

[28] (1728) Cas. *temp.* King 61, 62: see below, p. 655.

[29] *Bray* v. *Ford* [1896] A.C. 44, 51, *per* Lord Herschell. See also *Boardman* v. *Phipps* [1967] 2 A.C. 46, 123, *per* Lord Upjohn; *Holder* v. *Holder* [1968] Ch. 353, 392, *per* Harman L.J., 397–398, *per* Danckwerts L.J., 402, *per* Sachs L.J.; *Phelan* v. *Middle States Oil Corp.*, 220 F. 2d 593, 602–603, *per* Judge Learned Hand (1955).

[30] (1968) 84 L.Q.R. 472, 481 *et seq.* [Jones].

[31] *Boardman* v. *Phipps* [1967] 2 A.C. 46: see below, pp. 663–665.

is designed to strip a fiduciary of his unjust enrichment and to prevent the mere possibility that a fiduciary may have abused his position of trust.

The more intense the fiduciary relationship, the more vigilant is the court's surveillance of the conduct of the fiduciary. The relationship of trustee and beneficiary is so sensitive that the duties of a trustee have been widely defined to guard against the mere possibility of a conflict of interest[32]; and the analogy of trust law has been important in determining the duties of other fiduciaries, particularly directors.[33] But in relationships where the fiduciary element is less intense, and where the fiduciary has acted honestly and in his beneficiary's best interests, the courts may be more reluctant to find a potential conflict of interest.[34] The court must draw the boundaries of the particular fiduciary relationship, a task which may be difficult if the relationship is an ad hoc one,[35] and does not stem from any agreement between the parties concerned.[36]

Moreover, the equitable principles should not be perceived to be as if they were written in stone. As Laskin J. said in the Supreme Court of Canada[37]: "I do not regard [the older cases] as providing a rigid measure whose literal terms must be met in assessing succeeding cases. . . . In this, as in other branches of law, new fact situations may require formulation of existing principle to maintain its vigour in the new setting."

The English authorities suggest that a fiduciary will hold any benefit made from the abuse of his fiduciary position or from the use of his beneficiary's property as a constructive trustee. It is, arguably, a harsh conclusion to impose a constructive trust on gains made by an honest fiduciary who has acted in his principal's best interests.[38] But, as the law now stands, the only exception to

---

[32] *Keech* v. *Sandford* (1728) Cas. *temp.* King 61; but see *Holder* v. *Holder* [1968] Ch. 353: below, pp. 649–650.

[33] In particular, *Keech* v. *Sandford* (1728) Cas. *temp.* King 61, which was applied "in full force" in *Regal (Hastings) Ltd.* v. *Gulliver* [1942] 1 All E.R. 378: see below, pp. 656–658.

[34] *Cf. Consul Developments Pty. Ltd.* v. *D.P.C. Estates Pty. Ltd.* (1975) 49 A.L.J.R. 49. On the burden of proof, see *Pelrine* v. *Arron* [1969] 3 D.L.R. (3d) 713.

[35] As the facts of cases like *Boardman* v. *Phipps* [1967] 2 A.C. 46 (see below, pp. 663–665) and *Swain* v. *The Law Society* [1983] 1 A.C. 598 demonstrate.
In the latter case Oliver L.J. suggested ([1982] 1 W.L.R. 17, 37) that a court should make three inquiries:
   "what one has to do is to ascertain first of all whether there was a fiduciary relationship and, if there was, from what it arose and what, if there was any, the trust property was; and then to inquire whether that of which an account is claimed either arose, directly or indirectly, from the trust property itself or was acquired not only in the course of, but by reason of, the fiduciary relationship."
The House of Lords reversed the Court of Appeal's decision and held that the Law Society did not have to account for commissions received from insurance companies in respect of premiums paid by solicitors under the Law Society's indemnity scheme. The Law Society was not a fiduciary, but was performing a public duty. However, Lord Brightman approved Oliver L.J.'s statement of principle quoted in this footnote: [1983] A.C. 598, 619.

[36] *Cf. Aas* v. *Benham* [1891] 2 Ch. 244.

[37] *Canadian Aero-Services Ltd.* v. *O'Malley* (1973) 40 D.L.R. (3d) 371, 383.

[38] (1968) 84 L.Q.R. 472 [Jones] (for a different view, see Sir Peter Millett, *Bribes and Secret Commissions* in Vol. 1 of *Frontiers of Liability* (ed. Birks), pp. 9–10); *United States Surgical Corp.* v. *Hospital Products Pty. Ltd.* [1983] 2 N.S.W.L.R. 157, 238 (N.S.W.C.A.); (1984) 156 C.L.R. 41; *Chan* v. *Zacharia* (1984) 154 C.L.R. 178, 204–205, *per* Deane J. (cited below, p. 664, n. 91).

the general rule[39] is in favour of the dishonest fiduciary: a fiduciary who receives a sum as a bribe from a third party must account for, but is not a trustee of, that sum.[40] In some circumstances a fiduciary may be liable for the profits which others make. So, a trustee and a third party who consciously participate in a breach of trust will be jointly and severally liable to the beneficiaries.[41] However, in *Regal (Hastings) Ltd.* v. *Gulliver*,[42] the House of Lords held that an honest director was not liable for the profits made by third parties from his purchase of shares on their behalf, when the third parties had no notice of his unwitting breach of fiduciary duty. But if the director had acted dishonestly, it should be less objectionable to impose on him such a penal liability; for one of the objects of equity's inflexible rule is to deter fiduciaries from contemplating even the possibility of allowing self-interest to prevail over loyalty.[43]

(B) The Liability of a Fiduciary Who Abuses His Position of Trust

A fiduciary who uses his position of trust to acquire a benefit for himself holds that benefit on constructive trust for his beneficiary. This general principle[44] applies to all fiduciaries and to a wide variety of situations.

The conduct of trustees and executors is most scrupulously overseen; and there are many examples in the reports where trustees have been compelled to disgorge gains made from their fiduciary position. For this reason a trustee may not normally be remunerated for his services,[45] and a trustee of shares who uses his voting rights *qua* shareholder to secure his election to the board of the company holds his fees on constructive trust.[46] The duty of loyalty owed by other fiduciaries can be as comprehensive. At times, however, the wide principle that equity's duty of loyalty is inexorable may have been over-zealously applied, to punish an honest fiduciary who has acted in his benefi-ciary's best interests.[47] Equity's rules are not immutable. Their "precise scope ... must be moulded according to the nature of the [fiduciary] relation-ship."[48]In each case it should be critical to ascertain "the subject-matter over

---

See also The Hon. Mr. Justice J. B. Kearney, "Accounting for a Fiduciary's Gains in Commer-cial Contexts" in *Equity and Commercial Relationships* (ed. Finn), Chap. 7; and contrast R. P. Austin, "Fiduciary Accountability for Business Opportunities", in the same volume Chap. 6.

[39] See above, pp. 643–646.

[40] *Lister* v. *Stubbs* (1890) 45 Ch.D. 1; criticised below, pp. 668–669.

[41] Trustees are jointly and severally liable for breach of trust.

[42] [1942] 1 All E.R. 378: see below, pp. 656–658.

[43] *Cf. Re Philadelphia & Western Ry.*, 64 F.Supp. 738, 741, *per* Judge Kirkpatrick (1946).

[44] Snell, *op. cit.* pp. 284 *et seq.*

[45] See, *e.g. Re Macadam* [1946] Ch. 73.

[46] *Williams* v. *Barton* [1927] 2 Ch. 9. But the trust instrument may expressly or implicitly allow him to keep the fees: see, *e.g. Re Llewellin's Will Trusts* [1949] Ch. 225.

[47] *New Zealand Netherlands Society* v. *Kuys* [1973] 1 W.L.R. 1126, 1130, *per curiam*, Lord Wilberforce, P.C. See also *Knight* v. *Earl of Plymouth* (1747) 1 Dick. 120, 126–127, *per* Lord Hardwicke L.C.; *Albion Steel and Wire Co.* v. *Martin* (1875) 1 Ch.D. 580, 585–585, *per* Jessel M.R. For a fuller discussion, see (1968) 84 L.Q.R. 472 [Jones].

[48] *New Zealand Netherlands Society* v. *Kuys* [1973] 1 W.L.R. 1126, 1130, P.C. *Cf. Boulting* v. *Association of Cinematograph, Television and Allied Technicians* [1963] 2 Q.B. 606.

which the fiduciary obligations extend"; "the character of the venture or undertaking" may also depend on the agreement between, and the course of dealing pursued by, the parties.[49] So the scope of a director's or an agent's fiduciary duty may depend not only on the nature of the particular fiduciary relationship, but also on the terms of any agreement by which the fiduciary is engaged.[50]

We shall now consider the more important instances where a fiduciary has been held to have abused his position of trust. They are where he uses his position:

(1) to buy property belonging to the beneficiary;
(2) to buy the beneficiary's beneficial interest;
(3) to sell the beneficiary his own property;
(4) to compete with the beneficiary;
(5) to acquire confidential information;
(6) to speculate with his beneficiary's property;
(7) to enter into a transaction with a third party;
(8) to make a secret profit.

1. Purchase of a Beneficiary's Property by a Fiduciary: "the Self-dealing Rule"[51]

It is said to be a:

"rule of universal application, that no one, having [fiduciary] duties to discharge, shall be allowed to enter into engagements in which he has, or can have, a personal interest conflicting, or which may possibly conflict, with the interests of those whom he is bound to protect. So strictly is this principle adhered to, that no question is allowed to be raised as to the fairness or unfairness of a contract so entered into."[52]

The cases suggest, however, that purchases by trustees or executors are scrutinised more carefully than purchases by other fiduciaries.[53]

(a) A Trustee's Purchase of Trust Property

Lord Eldon's statement that trustees may never buy trust property, however fair the price, however scrupulous the mode of sale, and however honest be the trustee, has frequently been approved.[54] Consequently, even purchases by

---

[49] Birtchnell v. Equity Trustees, Executors and Agency Co. Ltd. (1929) 42 C.L.R. 384, 408, per Dixon J.; see also Boardman v. Phipps [1967] 2 A.C. 46, 129–130, per Lord Upjohn.

[50] Cf. Gluckstein v. Barnes [1900] A.C. 240; Boulting v. Association of Cinematograph, Television and Allied Technicians [1963] 2 Q.B. 606; United States Surgical Corp. v. Hospital Products International Pty. Ltd. (1984) 156 C.L.R. 141.

[51] Tito v. Waddell (No. 2) [1977] Ch. 106, 241, per Megarry V.-C.

[52] Aberdeen Ry. v. Blaikie (1854) 1 Macq. H.L. 461, 471–472, per Lord Cranworth L.C. See, generally, Finn, Fiduciary Obligations, §§ 394 et seq.

[53] See below, p. 652.

[54] Fox v. Mackreth (1789–91) 2 Bro.C.C. 400; Ex p. Lacey (1802) 6 Ves. 625; Ex p. James (1803) 8 Ves. 337; Williams v. Scott [1900] A.C. 499; Wright v. Morgan [1926] A.C. 788. The cases are

trustees at a public auction[55] or at a price fixed by an independent valuation,[56] have been set aside; for it is said that it is not possible to tell on the evidence available to the court "whether [the trustee] has made an advantage or not."[57]

But it is not true to say that a trustee may *never* buy trust property, for the purchase is not void but voidable by the beneficiaries within a reasonable time.[58] Lord Cairns L.C. accepted[59] that there is no rule of law that a trustee shall not buy property from his *cestui que trust*; but, "if challenged in proper time, Equity will examine into it, will ascertain the value that was paid by the trustee, and will throw upon the trustee the onus of proving that he gave full value and that all information was laid before the *cestui que trust* when it was sold." The trustee must disclose all that he knows about the property, its actual and potential value and every fact which may weigh with a vendor in determining whether to sell and the price at which to sell.[60] He must give the beneficiary "all that reasonable advice against himself, that he would have given . . . against a third person."[61] Even if a trustee acts honestly, he may find that a court, in later proceedings, will conclude that he suppressed a material fact.[62]

There are dicta which suggest that the trustee's duty to make full and proper disclosure is discharged if he makes full disclosure to his co-trustees instead of the beneficiaries.[63] In our view these dicta should not be followed. "If the connection between the trustee and beneficiary does not satisfactorily appear to have been dissolved, it is in the choice of the *cestui que trusts*, whether they will take back the property, or not"[64]; and that connection can only be dissolved with the beneficiaries' consent. Any other conclusion may lead to collusion between trustees, to the detriment of the beneficiaries. Similar considerations have led the courts to hold that directors must, in the absence of express provision in the company's articles, make disclosure to members of the company; disclosure to co-directors is not enough.[65]

Even if there has been full and proper disclosure, the beneficiaries must still consent to the sale. That is the general rule. But it appears that exceptionally the court may uphold the purchase if it thinks it just to do so even though a beneficiary, to whom full disclosure had been made, did not consent. In *Holder*

---

collected in Pettit, *Equity and the Law of Trusts*, pp. 379–381, and *Scott on Trusts*, Vol. II, § 170.1.

[55] *Whichcote* v. *Lawrence* (1798) 3 Ves. 740; *Ex p. Lacey* (1802) 6 Ves. 625.

[56] *Williams* v. *Scott* [1900] A.C. 499.

[57] *Ex p. Lacey* (1802) 6 Ves. 625, 627, *per* Lord Eldon.

[58] *Campbell* v. *Walker* (1800) 5 Ves. 678, 682, *per* Lord Eldon; *Morse* v. *Royal* (1806) 12 Ves. 355.

[59] *Thomson* v. *Eastwood* (1877) 2 App.Cas. 215, 236. See too *Tito* v. *Waddell (No. 2)* [1977] Ch. 106, 225, 240–244, *per* Megarry V.-C.

[60] *Randall* v. *Errington* (1805) 10 Ves. 423; *Life Association of Scotland* v. *Siddal* (1861) 3 De G. F. & J. 58, 74, *per* Turner L.J.

[61] *Gibson* v. *Jeyes* (1801) 6 Ves. 266, 278, *per* Lord Eldon; *Cane* v. *Allen* (1814) 2 Dow. 288, 289, cited in Finn, *Fiduciary Obligations*, § 439.

[62] *Cf. Boardman* v. *Phipps* [1967] 2 A.C. 46: see below, pp. 663–665.

[63] *Boardman* v. *Phipps* [1967] 2 A.C. 46, 93, *per* Viscount Dilhorne, 117, *per* Lord Guest.

[64] *Ex p. Lacey* (1802) 6 Ves. 625, 627, *per* Lord Eldon. *Cf. Boardman* v. *Phipps* [1967] 2 A.C. 46, 104, *per* Lord Cohen.

[65] *Cf. Guinness plc.* v. *Saunders* [1990] 2 A.C. 663 (an example of strict construction).

v. *Holder*[66] the defendant was an executor who had renounced his executorship but not before he was guilty of technical acts of intermeddling.[67] He was also the sitting tenant of a farm which he later bought at an auction, which had been arranged by the remaining executors, for a price which was said to be "probably higher than anyone not a sitting tenant would give."[68] The plaintiff, one of the residuary legatees, sought to set aside the sale. The Court of Appeal, reversing Cross J., found that he had agreed to the defendant buying the farm.[69] But the principal and independent ground of the decision was that equity's rule that a trustee or executor must not buy property was not "unbending and inveterate"[70] and that the transaction would be upheld if it was, as this was, fair and reasonable. Harman L.J. considered the facts "very special"; "for the beneficiaries never looked to [the defendant] to protect their interests," and the defendant had never acquired any special knowledge *qua* executor.[71] Danckwerts and Sachs L.JJ. went further. Danckwerts L.J. refused to accept Lord Eldon's justification for the penal rule, namely, that it is quite impossible to ascertain whether the trustee has acted honestly or not. Chancery judges are daily engaged "in ascertaining the knowledge and intentions" of parties to proceedings.

> "It is said that it makes no difference, even though the sale may be fair and honest and may be made at a public auction. . . . But the court can sanction such a purchase [under the Trustee Act 1925, s.57] and if the court can do that . . . there can be no more than a practice that the court should not allow a trustee to bid. . . . It is a matter for the discretion of the judge."[72]

Sachs L.J. agreed that Lord Eldon's rule appears on analysis to be one of practice as opposed to one going to the jurisdiction of the court. Today the tendency of the court is "to lean more and more against such rigidity of rules as can cause patent injustice."[73] It is debatable whether the observations of Danckwerts and Sachs L.JJ., although sensible and pragmatic, will be followed. They are not easy to reconcile with the old law which has stood for over 200 years.[74] Moreover, the facts of *Holder* v. *Holder* were indeed very special; the defendant had never purported to act as an executor,[75] the beneficiary was found to have acquiesced in the sale, and all the Lords Justices thought that counsel's admission that the defendant had not renounced his executorship in

---

[66] [1968] Ch. 353.
[67] Including the drawing of cheques, the indorsement of some insurance policies, and instructing solicitors to act for the estate.
[68] At p. 392, *per* Harman L.J.
[69] [1968] Ch. 353, 394–395, *per* Harman L.J., 399, *per* Danckwerts L.J., 404–406, *per* Sachs L.J.
[70] *Meinhard* v. *Salmon*, 249 N.Y. 456, 464, *per* Cardozo C.J. (1928).
[71] At pp. 391–392.
[72] At p. 398.
[73] At pp. 402–403.
[74] See cases cited above, n. 54.
[75] *Re Thompson's Settlement* [1986] Ch. 99, 115–116, *per* Vinelott J.

time had been misguided.[76] Although the court regarded acquiescence as a distinct issue, it must be an open question whether the court would have exercised its discretion in the defendant's favour if it had held that the plaintiff had not agreed to the purchase.[77]

A trustee cannot retire from his trust with the object of buying trust property,[78] but a trustee who has retired may buy trust property provided that he does not use information which he acquired *qua* trustee and which he has not disclosed to his beneficiaries.[79] The court is suspicious of any *sub rosa* purchase. A trustee's sale or property to a company which he controls[80] or to a third party to hold on trust for him is voidable[81]; and a sale to a trustee's wife, though not *ipso facto* voidable, should be treated with suspicion and should be set aside unless the trustee can convince the court that he has not in any way abused his fiduciary position.[82] A trustee may buy trust property if the trust instrument[83] or statute[84] authorises him to do so.[85]

The beneficiary's remedies

A beneficiary who succesfully impeaches the sale has a number of alternative remedies:

(1) If the trustee has resold the property, he can be made to account for any profit with interest.[86]

(2) If the property is unsold, the beneficiary, at least if he is absolutely entitled, may insist on the property being reconveyed to the trust. If the beneficiary is one of several beneficiaries, he may have no right to insist on reconveyance without the other beneficiaries' consent; for if the property could not subsequently be resold at a higher price "the

---

[76] [1968] Ch. 353, 392, *per* Harman L.J., 397, *per* Danckwerts L.J. 401, *per* Sachs L.J.

[77] *Cf. Re Tabone* [1968] V.R. 168. In *Holder* v. *Holder* [1968] Ch. 353, 375, Cross J. refused to allow the executor to bid on the resale when an adult beneficiary objected.

[78] *Spring* v. *Pride* (1864) 4 De G. J. & Sm. 395; *Wright* v. *Morgan* [1926] A.C. 788; *Re Mullholland's Will Trusts* [1949] 1 All E.R. 460.

[79] *Re Boles and British Land Co.'s Contract* [1902] 1 Ch. 244.

[80] *Silkstone & Haigh Moor Coal Co.* v. *Edey* [1900] 1 Ch. 167. *Cf. Farrars* v. *Farrars Ltd.* (1888) 40 Ch.D. 395; *Tito* v. *Waddell (No. 2)* [1977] Ch. 106, 241, *per* Megarry V.-C.

[81] *Michoud* v. *Girod* (1846) 4 How 503.

[82] *Cf. Tito* v. *Waddell (No. 2)* [1977] Ch. 106, 240, *per* Megarry V.-C.: ("one must look at the realities.")

[83] Such a clause may be strictly construed: *cf. Wright* v. *Morgan* [1926] A.C. 788, P.C. and *Guinness plc.* v. *Saunders* [1990] 2 A.C. 663; but contrast *Movitex Ltd.* v. *Bulfield* [1988] BCLC 104 (modification by articles of association not void under (then) s.205 of Companies Act 1948).

[84] *e.g.* Settled Land Act 1925, s.68.

[85] The Law Reform Committee recommended that trusts, with common trustees, should be able to do business with one another, "with the common trustees playing such part as is thought fit, provided that the market value of any property dealt with has been certified by a truly independent valuer as being the proper market price for that property" and the common trustees are not beneficiaries: 23rd Report, *The Powers and Duties of Trustees*, Cmnd. 8733 (1982) § 3.59.

[86] *Hall* v. *Hallett* (1784) 1 Cox 134; *Ex p. James* (1803) 8 Ves. 337, 351, *per* Lord Eldon.

beneficiaries would be worse off than if the claim had never been made."[87]

(3) If the property is unsold, a new sale may be ordered under the court's direction. If "it realises more than the reserve fixed by the court [which is normally what the trustee paid], the surplus belongs to the trust, whereas if it realises less, [the trustee] will be held to his bargain."[88] The court will give credit for any capital improvements made by the trustee.[89] In principle the beneficiary's enrichment should be deemed to be the cost of the improvements or the difference between the improved and unimproved value of the land, whichever is the lesser sum. He has neither requested nor freely accepted the improvements, but he is deemed to have received an incontrovertible benefit to this extent. *Holder* v. *Holder*[90] supports this conclusion, although earlier authorities would allow the cost of the improvements.[91] The trustee's right to obtain restitution does not appear to depend on whether he acted in good faith or not.[92] It is odd that a trustee who has acted in bad faith should be in a more favourable position than a bona fide improver of another's land.[93]

(b) *Purchase by Fiduciaries (other than Trustees) of Property of their Beneficiaries*

Such purchases will be upheld if the fiduciary pays a fair price, has not abused his position in any way, and has made full disclosure of his interest and of any information which he possesses about the property.[94] The onus is on the fiduciary to discharge this burden of proof.

To whom disclosure must be made depends on the particular fiduciary relationship; for example, a director must, subject to the articles of association, make disclosure to the members at a general meeting,[95] and an agent must disclose any relevant matter to his principal.[96] The fiduciary's beneficiary must also consent. A beneficiary of full age who has had independent advice may be deemed to have consented to the purchase; the fact that he did not have independent advice is, however, not conclusive evidence that he did not consent.[97]

---

[87] *Holder* v. *Holder* [1968] Ch. 353, 370–371, *per* Cross J.

[88] *Ibid.* at p. 371, *per* Cross J.

[89] *O'Sullivan* v. *Management Agency and Music Ltd.* [1985] Q.B. 428, 466, *per* Fox L.J. This was conceded in *Holder* v. *Holder* [1968] Ch. 353, 373, where, however, the executor acted throughout in good faith and thought he had disclaimed.

[90] *Holder* v. *Holder* [1968] Ch. 353, 373.

[91] *Ex p. Hughes* (1802) 6 Ves. 616, 624; *Luddy's Trustee* v. *Peard* (1886) 33 Ch.D. 500, 522, *per* Kay J. But *cf. Robinson* v. *Ridley* (1821) 6 Madd. 2.

[92] See, particularly, *Luddy's Trustee* v. *Peard* (1886) 33 Ch.D. 500 (the defendant was solicitor to a bankrupt).

[93] See above, Chap. 5.

[94] *Tito* v. *Waddell (No. 2)* [1977] Ch. 106, 225, 241, *per* Megarry V.-C.

[95] *Att.-Gen.* v. *Dudley* (1815) G.Coop. 146; *Edwards* v. *Meyrick* (1842) 2 Hare 60; *Smedley* v. *Varley* (1857) 23 Beav. 358; *Dunne* v. *English* (1874) L.R. 18 Eq. 524, 533, *per* Jessel M.R.; *McPherson* v. *Watt* (1877) L.R. 3 App.Cas. 254; *Movitex Ltd.* v. *Bulfield* [1988] BCLC 104.

[96] *Cf. Guinness plc.* v. *Saunders* [1990] 2 A.C. 663.

[97] *Jacobus Marler Estates* v. *Marler* (1913) (1916) 85 L.J.P.C. 167n.

2. PURCHASE FROM THE BENEFICIARIES OF THEIR BENEFICIAL INTERESTS: "THE FAIR DEALING RULE"[98]

A trustee or fiduciary may buy a beneficiary's beneficial interest if he is able to prove "distinctly and honestly . . . that he had removed himself from the character of trustee"[99] or fiduciary. He can discharge this onus by showing that he has concealed no facts, that the beneficiary has had independent advice, that he has given an adequate price, and that he has not in any way abused his fiduciary position.[1] If the trustee or fiduciary fails to fulfil these conditions, the beneficiary's remedies are similar to those exercisable by him when a purchase by a trustee of trust property is impeached.[2]

3. SALES TO BENEFICIARIES OF TRUSTEES' OR FIDUCIARIES' OWN PROPERTY

Because the law has always demanded the highest measure of good faith from trustees and other fiduciaries in their dealings with their beneficiaries, sales of their property to their beneficiaries may be set aside[3] if there is no full and proper disclosure of their interest in the property.[4] This rule is so stringent that it is not necessary for the beneficiary to show that the price was unfair or that the trustee or fiduciary acted dishonestly.[5] As Romilly M.R. once said, a fiduciary "will not be allowed to place himself in a situation which, under ordinary circumstances, would tempt a man to do that which is not the best for his principal."[6] Any other rule might lead the fiduciary to use his beneficiary as a "dumping ground" for his own unsuccessful or dubious investments, or otherwise to promote his own interests at his beneficiary's expense.[7]

For these reasons a beneficiary can always rescind the sale for non-disclosure of interest. Alternatively, he may want to reach the profits which the fiduciary has made from the sale; this will be a particularly attractive remedy if he can no

---

[98] *McMaster* v. *Byrne* [1952] 1 All E.R. 1362, P.C. Query whether it is a defence to show that disclosure would not have affected the beneficiary's decision: see *New Zealand Netherlands Society* v. *Kuys* [1973] 1 W.L.R. 1122, 1125, *per* Lord Wilberforce; *Walden Properties Ltd.* v. *Beaver Properties Pty. Ltd.* [1973] 2 N.S.W.L.R. 815, 847, *per* Hutley J.A.

[99] *Sanderson* v. *Walker* (1807) 13 Ves. 601, *per* Lord Eldon L.C. See, generally, *Chalmer* v. *Bradley* (1819) 1 J. & W. 51, 68, *per* Plumer M.R.

[1] These principles were laid down in *Coles* v. *Trecothick* (1804) 9 Ves. 234; *Randall* v. *Errington* (1805) 10 Ves. 423; *Morse* v. *Royal* (1806) 12 Ves. 355; *Wright* v. *Carter* [1903] 1 Ch. 27. See also *Tito* v. *Waddell (No. 2)* [1977] Ch. 106, 240–242, *per* Megarry V.-C.

[2] See above, p. 651.

[3] *Rothschild* v. *Brookman* (1831) 2 Dow & Cl. 188; *Bentley* v. *Craven* (1853) 18 Beav. 75; *King, Viall & Benson* v. *Howell* (1910) 27 T.L.R. 114; *Armstrong* v. *Jackson* [1917] 2 K.B. 822; *Hely-Hutchison* v. *Brayhead Ltd.* [1968] 1 Q.B. 549. See also *Cornet* v. *Cornet*, 269 Mo. 298 (1916); *McKenzie* v. *McDonald* [1927] V.L.R. 134.

[4] *Imperial Mercantile Credit Association* v. *Coleman* (1873) L.R. 6 H.L. 189; *Gray* v. *New Augarita Porcupine Mines* [1952] 3 D.L.R. 1; [1958] C.L.J. 93, 99 [Wedderburn]. *Cf.* above, p. 649.

[5] *Gillett* v. *Peppercorne* (1840) 3 Beav. 78, 83–84, *per* Lord Langdale M.R.

[6] *Bentley* v. *Craven* (1853) 18 Beav. 75, 76–77.

[7] *Cornet* v. *Cornet*, 269 Mo. 298 (1916).

longer rescind the transaction, for example, because *restitutio in integrum* is not possible.[8] Whether a beneficiary can require a fiduciary to disgorge his profits appears to turn on whether the fiduciary acquired the property before or after he became a fiduciary. A fiduciary who sells to a beneficiary property acquired after he became a fiduciary is "estopped from saying that he originally bought the property on his own behalf, or otherwise than for and on behalf of [the beneficiary]."[9] The profit, which is the difference between the sale and purchase prices, belongs to the beneficiary because he is buying, and paying for, "that which was already [his] own."[10]

Conversely, if the property had been acquired before the vendor became a fiduciary, the beneficiary cannot recover the profit made on the sale,[11] in the absence of fraud, misrepresentation, duress, or undue influence; to allow the beneficiary to recover that sum would enable him to make an entirely new bargain.[12] Today, given the desired fusion of legal and equitable remedies,[13] the courts may take a different view and conclude that a beneficiary should recover the profit. The beneficiary's claim is not "to be recouped part of the price as price," nor is it an "attempt in any way to vary the contract."[14] The trustee has acted in breach of his fiduciary duty, and should, for that simple reason, account for his profit.

4. TRANSACTIONS WITH A THIRD PARTY IN BREACH OF A FIDUCIARY DUTY

A fiduciary may abuse his position of trust by diverting a contract, purchase or other opportunity from his beneficiary to himself. If he does so, he is deemed to hold that contract, purchase, or opportunity on trust for the beneficiary. It is

---

[8] *Re Cape Breton* (1885) 29 Ch.D. 795; *Burland* v. *Earle* [1902] A.C. 83; *Tracey* v. *Mandalay Proprietary Ltd.* (1953) 88 C.L.R. 215.

[9] *Re Cape Breton* (1885) 29 Ch.D. 795, 804, *per* Cotton L.J. *Sed quaere* if the fiduciary sells unauthorised investments.

[10] *Ibid.*; see also *Tyrrel* v. *Bank of London* (1862) 10 H.L.C. 26.

[11] *Re Cape Breton* (1885) 29 Ch.D. 795, 805, *per* Cotton L.J.; *Robinson* v. *Randfontein Estates* [1921] A.C. 188. The company law cases, where the property was acquired by the vendor when he was not yet the plaintiff's fiduciary but was soon to become so, suggest the same conclusion: see *Albion Steel & Wire Co.* v. *Martin* (1875) 1 Ch.D. 580; *Re Cape Breton* (1885) 29 Ch.D. 795. And *cf. Lindgren* v. *L. & P. Estates Ltd.* [1968] Ch. 572.

[12] *Re Cape Breton* (1885) 29 Ch.D. 795; *Tracey* v. *Mandalay Pty. Ltd.* (1953) 88 C.L.R. 215, 241, *per curiam.*

[13] *United Scientific Holdings Ltd.* v. *Burnley B.C.* [1978] A.C. 904; *Lipkin Gorman (A Firm)* v. *Karpnale Ltd.* [1991] 2 A.C. 548, 580–581, *per* Lord Goff.

[14] *Cf. Re Cape Breton* (1885) 29 Ch.D. 795, 809, *per* Bowen L.J., dissenting; *Nocton* v. *Ashburton* [1914] A.C. 932. And see *Cavendish-Bentick* v. *Fenn* (1887) 12 App.Cas. 652, 669–671, *per* Lord McNaughten; *Re Leeds & Hanley Theatres of Varieties* [1902] 2 Ch. 809; [1963] C.L.J. 119, 135 [Sealy]. *Proprietary Mines Ltd.* v. *MacKay* [1939] 3 D.L.R. 215; *Jacobus Marler Estates* v. *Marler* (1913) (1916) 85 L.J.C.P. 167n. A sale may also be set aside on the ground that the fiduciary did not give independent advice: see *City of Toronto* v. *Bowes* (1858) 11 Moo. 463, 517–519, *per* Knight Bruce L.J.; but *cf. City of Edmonton* v. *Hawrelak* (1975) 54 D.L.R. (3d) 45.

irrelevant that the fiduciary acted in good faith, or that the beneficiary did not have any funds to acquire it, or that a third party had refused to deal with the beneficiary.[15]

These principles were established in the famous case of *Keech* v. *Sandford*,[16] which has profoundly influenced this branch of the law. In that case the lessor refused to renew a lease to the trust but allowed the trustee to renew it for his own personal benefit. Lord King L.C. held that, in these circumstances, the trustee must hold the lease for the benefit of the beneficiary, even though the landlord had previously refused to make a new lease to him *qua* trustee.[17] The basis of *Keech* v. *Sandford* was, therefore, a principle of public policy; the position of the trustee gave him access to the landlord, and gave him an advantage he could unscrupulously use for his own profit.[18]

The *ratio decidendi* of that case has been rigorously applied. For example, it is immaterial that the old lease has already expired,[19] or that the terms of the old lease were different from the new,[20] or that it was not customary to renew the lease.[21] Indeed, if a trustee buys the reversion of a lease renewable by custom or contract, he holds that reversion on trust for the beneficiaries even though he acted in good faith[22]; and the same rule may apply to his purchase of the reversion on any lease.[23]

Fiduciaries, other than trustees, who renew leases for their own benefit, hold the renewed lease on trust unless they can show that they did not in any way abuse their fiduciary position.[24] An extreme illustration is *Thompson's Trustee* v. *Heaton*,[25] where Pennycuick V.-C. held that the former partner of a now dissolved partnership, who had acquired the reversion of a lease, the lease having been an undistributed asset of the former partnership, must hold the reversion on trust for all the former partners. "The fiduciary relation [between partners] arises not from a trust of property but from the duty of good faith which each partner owes to the other"[26]; and a former partner owes that same

---

[15] *Canadian Aero-Services Ltd.* v. *O'Malley* (1973) 40 D.L.R. (3d) 371, 392, *per* Laskin J. See, generally, [1963] C.L.J. 119, 129 [Sealy].

[16] (1728) Cas. *temp.* King 61.

[17] *Keech* v. *Sandford* (1728) Cas. *temp.* King 61, 62; see also *Re Jarvis* [1958] 1 W.L.R. 815.

[18] *Blewett* v. *Millett* (1774) 7 Bro.P.C. 367, 373, *per curiam*.

[19] *Edwards* v. *Lewis* (1747) 3 Atk. 538.

[20] *Eyre* v. *Dolphin* (1813) 2 Ball. & B. 290, 298, *per* Lord Manners; *James* v. *Dean* (1805) 11 Ves. 383, (1808) 15 Ves. 236. *Cf. Giddings* v. *Giddings* (1826–1827) 3 Russ. 241.

[21] *Killick* v. *Flexney* (1792) 4 Bro.C.C. 161.

[22] *Phillips* v. *Phillips* (1885) 29 Ch.D. 673; *Bevan* v. *Webb* [1905] 1 Ch. 620; (1905) 21 L.Q.R. 258 [W. G. Hart].

[23] *Protheroe* v. *Protheroe* [1968] 1 W.L.R. 519, C.A., where the earlier cases were not, however, cited: see S. Cretney, "The Rationale of *Keech* v. *Sandford*" (1969) 33 Conv. 161.

[24] This principle embraces renewals by a partner (*Clegg* v. *Fishwick* (1849) 1 M. & G. 294; *Clegg* v. *Edmonson* (1857) 2 De G. M. & J. 787, 807; *Chan* v. *Zacharia* (1984) 154 C.L.R. 178); mortgagor or mortgagee (*Leigh* v. *Burnett* (1885) 29 Ch.D. 231); joint tenant or tenant in common (*Palmer* v. *Young* (1684) [1903] 2 Ch. 65n.); or a tenant for life (*Lloyd-Jones* v. *Clarke-Lloyd* [1919] 1 Ch. 424).

[25] [1974] 1 W.L.R. 605; criticised in (1976) 54 Can.B.R. 158 [Weinrib]; *Chan* v. *Zacharia* (1984) 154 C.L.R. 178.

[26] At p. 613.

duty to his former partners in respect of undistributed property of a dissolved partnership.

There is some authority that a person who is not a fiduciary but who is in a "special position" to "other persons interested" will be required to hold a renewed lease on trust for the "persons interested"[27] unless he can show that he did not in fact abuse his position. It is not clear who may occupy such a special position. In Re Biss,[28] Romer L.J. gave as instances of persons occupying a special position, a tenant for life under a settlement, a partner, and a mortgagee.[29] These are curious examples since such persons may be in a fiduciary position to the remaindermen, co-partners, and mortgagor respectively.[30] It is not easy, therefore, to predict who will be deemed to be in "a special position" to another; certainly they do not include persons "simply . . . engaged in ordinary commercial transactions."[31] Moreover, even if there is a separate class of "persons interested," their duty of loyalty extends only to renewal of leases and not to the purchase of freehold reversions.[32]

The principle enunciated in Keech v. Sandford has been most influential outside its immediate facts. It has been invoked to deprive a trustee of the advantage obtained from buying an incumbrance over trust property,[33] an agent of property which he had been commissioned to buy by his principal,[34] and a former managing director of the benefit of a profitable contract.[35] In company law, its analogy has been very persuasive, as the leading case of Regal (Hastings) Ltd. v. Gulliver[36] shows. The appellant company owned a cinema in Hastings, and wished to acquire two more cinemas, with a view to selling the property of the company as a going concern. For the purposes of acquiring the cinemas a subsidiary company was formed. The landlord was prepared to offer the subsidiary a lease of these properties but required the directors to guarantee the rent, unless the subsidiary's paid-up capital was £5,000. The appellant company, which was to hold all the shares of the subsidiary company, could only afford to subscribe in cash for 2,000 shares; and the directors did not want to give personal guarantees for the rest. Accordingly the plan was financed in another way. The company took up 2,000 shares, and the directors (on their own behalf and on behalf of certain third parties) and the company solicitor took up the other 3,000 shares. This arrangement was formalised by a resolu-

---

[27] Re Biss [1903] 2 Ch. 40, 61, per Romer L.J. (The defendant was entitled on an intestacy; he acquired the renewal after the lessor had refused the administratrix.)

[28] At pp. 61–63.

[29] Cf. Snell, Equity, op. cit. pp. 246–247.

[30] Chan v. Zacharia (1984) 154 C.L.R. 178.

[31] Keith Henry & Co. Proprietary Ltd. v. Stuart Walker & Co. Proprietary Ltd. (1958) 100 C.L.R. 342, 350–351, per curiam; Savage v. Dunningham [1974] Ch. 181 (flat-sharing arrangement).

[32] Thompson's Trustee v. Heaton [1974] 1 W.L.R. 605, 614, per Pennycuick V.-C.

[33] Ex p. Lacey (1802) 6 Ves. 625; Pooley v. Quilter (1858) 2 De G. & J. 327. See also Anon. (1707) 1 Salk. 155.

[34] Dunne v. English (1874) L.R. 18 Eq. 524; James v. Smith [1891] 1 Ch. 384; Regier v. Campbell-Stuart [1939] Ch. 766.

[35] Industrial Development Consultants Ltd. v. Cooley [1972] 1 W.L.R. 443.

[36] [1942] 1 All E.R. 378.

tion at a board meeting, at which the solicitor was present, and the shares were duly paid up and allotted. The directors and the solicitor acted throughout in good faith and in the best interests of the appellant company. Shortly afterwards the shares in the appellant company and its subsidiary were sold. From the sale of their shares in the subsidiary, the directors and solicitor made a profit of £2 16s. 1d. per share. In this action the appellant company, now controlled by the purchasers, sought to recover this profit from the former directors and the solicitor.

The House of Lords held that the directors, but not the solicitor, must disgorge[37] the profits which they had personally made to the company, for the opportunity and special knowledge to acquire the shares had come to them *qua* fiduciaries. As Lord Russell of Killowen said[38]:

> "The rule of equity which insists on those who by use of a fiduciary position make a profit, being liable to account for that profit, in no way depends on fraud, or absence of bona fides; or upon such questions or considerations as whether the profit would or should otherwise have gone to the plaintiff, or whether the profiteer was under a duty to obtain the source of the profit for the plaintiff, or whether he took a risk or acted as he did for the benefit of the plaintiff, or whether the plaintiff has in fact been damaged or benefited by his action. The liability arises from the mere fact of a profit having, in the stated circumstances, been made. The profiteer, however, honest and well intentioned, cannot escape the risk of being called upon to account. . . .
>
> I am of the opinion that the directors standing in a fiduciary relationship to Regal [the appellant company] in regard to the exercise of their powers as directors, and having obtained these shares by reason and only by reason of the fact that they were directors of Regal, and in the course of the execution of that office, are accountable for the profits which they have made out of them. The equitable rule laid down in *Keech* v. *Sandford* . . . applies to them in full force."

The solicitor, however, was not a fiduciary.[39] He had taken the shares at the director's request, and was not compelled to account for his profits. The chairman of the company who had bought his shares only as a nominee of third parties was also not liable to account to the appellant company. "Neither the shares nor the profit ever belonged to [him]."[40]

The company's claim appeared to lack all merit. The purchasers of the shares:

> "receive[d] in one hand part of the sum which ha[d] been paid by the other. For the shares in Amalgamated [the subsidiary] they paid

---

[37] There was no claim that the profits belonged in equity to the company: see [1967] C.L.J. 83, 98, n. 85 [Sealy]. *Cf. Cook* v. *Deeks* [1916] A.C. 554: see below, p. 658.

[38] At pp. 386, 389.

[39] It is odd that the solicitor was not deemed to be a fiduciary: contrast *Boardman* v. *Phipps* [1967] 2 A.C. 46; see below, pp. 663–665.

[40] At p. 390, *per* Lord Russell of Killowen.

£3 16s. 1d. per share, yet part of that sum may be returned to the group, though not necessarily to the individual shareholders by reason of the enhancement in the value of the shares in Regal—an enhancement brought about as a result of the receipt by the company of the profit made by some of its former directors on the sale of Amalgamated shares."[41]

Only Lord Porter, from whose speech this quotation is taken, chose to mention this point. He recognised that Regal, and hence its purchasers, had received an "unexpected windfall." But, he concluded,[42] "whether it be so or not, the principle that a person occupying a fiduciary relationship shall not make a profit by reason thereof is of such vital importance that the possible consequence in the present case is in fact as it is in law an immaterial consideration."[43]

A further example of the stringency of the principle that a fiduciary cannot buy property for himself when he ought to have bought it for the beneficiary is *Cook* v. *Deeks*,[44] which also concerned dealings by directors. Three directors of a company obtained a certain contract in their own names to the exclusion of the company. Subsequently, as a result of their control of three-quarters of the shareholding, they were able to ensure that a resolution was passed by the company confirming the deal and stating that the company had no interest in the particular contract. The Judicial Committee of the Privy Council found that the directors were "guilty of a distinct breach of duty in the course they took to secure the contract, and that they cannot retain the benefit of such contract for themselves, but must be regarded as holding it on behalf of the company."[45] Lord Buckmaster, who delivered the advice of the Board, went on to consider the effect of the resolution. He said that a distinction must be drawn between two classes of cases, namely, the "case of a director selling to his company property which was in equity as well as at law his own, and which he could dispose of as he thought fit," and the "case of a director dealing with property which, though his own at law, in equity belonged to his company."[46] In *Cook* v. *Deeks* the property belonged in equity to the company, so that "even supposing it be not *ultra vires* of a company to make a present to its directors, it appears quite certain that directors holding a majority of votes would not be permitted to make a present to themselves."[47] A fraud cannot be committed on the minority shareholders through the mechanism of a resolution passed by the

---

[41] At p. 394.
[42] *Ibid.*
[43] *Cf. Abbey Glen Corp.* v. *Stumborg* (1978) 85 D.L.R. (3d) 35 (S.Ct. of Alberta, App.Div.).
[44] [1916] 1 A.C. 554; see also *Aberdeen Town Council* v. *Aberdeen University* (1877) 2 App.Cas. 544; *Daniels* v. *Daniels* [1978] 1 W.L.R. 73.
[45] At p. 563.
[46] At p. 563. *Cf. North West Transportation Ltd.* v. *Beatty* (1887) 12 App.Cas. 589; *Burland* v. *Earle* [1902] A.C. 83, which illustrates the application of Lord Buckmaster's first class. See also [1958] C.L.J. 93, 94–106 [K. W. Wedderburn].
[47] At p. 564, citing *Menier* v. *Hooper's Telegraph Works* (1874) L.R. 9 Ch. 350.

majority of the shareholders ratifying the conduct of the directors.[48] Seemingly, in such cases, the fiduciary is entitled to his expenses, such as the cost of acquisition.[49]

We have seen that in English law it is not open to a director to plead that his company was neither legally nor financially in a position to acquire the property which he had acquired through the use of his fiduciary position.[50] Similarly, it is no defence that a third party refused to deal with the company.[51] But other common law jurisdictions have not always treated directors so severely. They have emphasised that directors are business men, and have consequently accepted that directors who act in good faith may retain benefits which their company could not, or would not, accept. The directors cannot be said to be unjustly enriched and it is undesirable to impose on them a penal liability. Representative of these cases is *Peso Silver Mines Ltd.* v. *Cropper*[52] where the Supreme Court of Canada refused to hold that a director who had acted honestly was a trustee of a mining claim which the board, of which he was a member, had previously refused to take up. As Bull J.A. said in the lower court[53]:

> "I do not consider it enlightened to extend the application of these principles [in *Keech* v. *Sandford*] beyond their present limits. That the principles, and the strict rules applicable to trustees upon which they are based, are salutary cannot be disputed, but care should be taken to interpret them in the light of modern practice and way of life."

It may be debatable whether *Peso Silver Mines* v. *Cropper* was correctly decided.[54] But it is undoubtedly desirable that such policy questions should be openly debated rather than buried in the mechanical application of a penal rule

---

[48] *Ngurli Ltd.* v. *McCann* (1954) 90 C.L.R. 425. *Cf. Regal (Hastings) Ltd.* v. *Gulliver* [1942] 1 All E.R. 378: see above, p. 656, n. 37. *Cf. Essays* (ed. Burrows), pp. 225–227 [Goode].

[49] See above, pp. 32–34 and see below, pp. 663–665; Goode, *op. cit.* n. 48.

[50] *Keech* v. *Sandford* (1728) Cas. *temp.* King 61: see above, p. 655; *Boardman* v. *Phipps* [1967] 2 A.C. 46: see below, pp. 662–664.

[51] *Industrial Development Consultants Ltd.* v. *Cooley* [1972] 1 W.L.R. 443; *Abbey Glen Property Co.* v. *Stumborg* (1978) 85 D.L.R. (3d) 35 (S.Ct. of Alberta, App.Div.); Lehane in Finn's *Essays in Equity*, pp. 104–105.

[52] (1966) 58 D.L.R. (2d) 1; see (1968) 84 L.Q.R. 472, 490–492. For a criticism of *Peso Silver Mines*, see (1971) 49 Can.B.Rev. 80 and (1975) 53 Can.B.R. 771 [Beck]. See also *Canadian Aero Services Ltd.* v. *O'Malley* (1974) 40 D.L.R. (3d) 371, 390, *per* Laskin J.; and *cf. Irving Trust Co.* v. *Deutsch*, 73 F.2d. 121, 124, *per* Judge Swan (1934).

[53] (1966) 56 D.L.R. (2d) 117, 154–155. *Cf. Regal (Hastings) Ltd.* v. *Gulliver* [1942] 1 All E.R. 378 at p. 381, where Viscount Sankey cited the unreported judgment of Lord Greene M.R., who took a similar view to that of Bull J.A.

[54] See, generally, (1967) 30 M.L.R. 450 [Prentice]; (1971) 49 Can.B.R. 80 [Beck]; (1979) 42 M.L.R. 711 [Sullivan]. *Queensland Mines Ltd.* v. *Hudson* (1978) 52 A.L.J.R. 399, P.C. is, however, a comparable case, where a director was allowed to retain mining licences which his company rejected because of liquidity difficulties. The Privy Council held that the director had acted outside the scope of his fiduciary duties. Moreover, the board of directors had consented.

of equity, which was formulated from cases concerned with attempts by trustees to renew for their own benefit leases which belonged to the trust.[55]

5. COMPETITION WITH THE BENEFICIARY

It is often stated that no fiduciary can carry on a business which competes with that carried on by his beneficiary. This principle has received statutory recognition in the Partnership Act 1890, s.30; but its application to other fiduciaries is not entirely free from uncertainty.

In *Re Thomson*,[56] the testator carried on the business of a yacht broker, which he directed his executors and trustees, one of whom was the defendant Allen, to continue after his death. The lease of the business premises expired after the testator's death; the business was then transferred to new premises, the lease of which was later granted, without the knowledge of Allen's fellow-trustees, to Allen, who claimed to carry on business as a yacht broker in his personal capacity and to exclude the other trustees from the premises. Before the hearing Allen surrendered the lease to the testator's next-of-kin, so that the only question before the court was whether the plaintiffs, his co-executors, could recover their costs; costs would be awarded if Allen could not carry on business in his personal capacity in competition with the testator. Clauson J. held on the facts that Allen was under a duty not to compete and must pay the plaintiffs' costs. He said that it was a rule of universal application that a fiduciary:

> "shall not be allowed to enter into any engagement in which he has or can have a personal interest conflicting, or which possibly may conflict, with the interests of those whom he is bound to protect. . . . Having regard to the special nature of a yacht agent's business, it appears to me clear that I am bound to answer that question by saying that, by starting such a business and entering into such engagements, Mr. Allen would have been entering into engagements which would conflict, or certainly possibly might conflict, with the interests of the beneficiaries under the will, because he would be obtaining for himself chances of earning a commission which, but for such competition, might be obtained for the beneficiaries under the will."[57]

In *Re Thomson*, a clash of interest was inevitable; for the testator's business was so highly specialised that, if the executor did compete, the testator's business must inevitably have suffered. In other cases this may not be so.[58] It is therefore doubtful whether there is an absolute rule against a trustee or an

---

[55] Cf. *Abbey Glen Property Corp.* v. *Stumborg* (1978) 85 D.L.R. (3d) 35 (S.Ct. of Alberta, App.Div.).

[56] [1930] 1 Ch. 203.

[57] At pp. 215–216; see also *Aberdeen Ry.* v. *Blakie Bros.* (1854) 1 Macq. 461, 471–472, *per* Lord Cranworth L.C.; *Bell* v. *Lever Bros.* [1932] A.C. 161, 195, *per* Lord Blanesburgh.

[58] Cf. *Re Irish* (1888) 40 Ch.D. 49, 51, *per* North J.; and contrast *Bell* v. *Lever Bros.* [1932] A.C. 161, 195, *per* Lord Blanesburgh and [1967] C.L.J. 83, 97 [Sealy].

executor carrying on a business in competition with his beneficiary.[59] But a trustee who is forbidden in the trust instrument to compete should not be able to escape that prohibition by resigning and then starting a new business.[60]

A company's articles of association should require its directors to devote themselves full time to the company's business. This is prudent because the older authorities suggest that a director, at least if he is a non-executive director, may work for a rival company.[61] But Lord Denning[62] has expressed the view that, if he does so, he may act "in a manner oppressive to other shareholders." Moreover, the Court of Appeal has held, in *Hivac Ltd.* v. *Park Royal Scientific Instruments Ltd.*,[63] that a servant may be enjoined from working, even in his spare time, for a competitor if this "would inflict great harm on his employer's business"[64]; he would then be in breach of his implied contractual obligation of good faith. If the older authorities are followed, a non-executive director may compete with his company but a subordinate employee may not.[65]

If the fiduciary breaks his duty by competing in this fashion, he must hold any profits so made on trust for his beneficiary; for the profits are the profits of the beneficiary's business which have been lost by the competition of the fiduciary.[66]

6. MISUSE OF, AND SPECULATION WITH, THE PROPERTY OF THE BENEFICIARIES

If a trustee or fiduciary uses the property of his beneficiary in any form of speculation, the beneficiary will be entitled to all the profits that the trustee or fiduciary makes through his use of the beneficiary's property.[67] So a trustee who uses trust money to buy shares in his own name will hold the property, and any profits earned thereon, as trustee for the beneficiary.[68] Indeed a fiduciary who makes any use of his beneficiary's property, such as exploiting a chattel for profit,[69] without his principal's informed consent, is liable to make restitution. The beneficiary may, at his election, recover the profit which the fiduciary

---

[59] *Cf. Moore* v. *M'Glynn* [1894] 1 I.R. 74, *per* Chatterton V.-C.

[60] *Cf.* above, p. 651.

[61] *London and Mashonaland Exploration Co.* v. *New Mashonaland Exploration Co.* [1891] 1 W.N. 165, approved in *Bell* v. *Lever Bros.* [1932] A.C. 161, 195, *per* Lord Blanesburgh.

[62] *Scottish Co-operative Wholesale Society Ltd.* v. *Meyer* [1959] A.C. 324, 366–367. For a critique, see (1992) 55 M.L.R. 506 [Christie], citing *Consul Developments* v. *D.P.C. Estates Ltd.* (1975) 132 C.L.R. 373, 394, *per* Gibbs J.

[63] [1946] Ch. 169.

[64] At p. 178, *per* Lord Greene M.R.

[65] See above, n. 61.

[66] *Somerville* v. *Mackay* (1810) 16 Ves. 382. See also *Dean* v. *MacDowell* (1877) 8 Ch.D. 345, 353, *per* Cotton L.J.; *Trimble* v. *Goldberg* [1906] A.C. 494; *Restatement of Restitution*, § 199. But *cf. Thomas Marshall (Exports) Ltd.* v. *Guinle* [1979] Ch. 227 (where there was a breach of an express agreement).

[67] See *Brown* v. *I.R.C.* [1965] A.C. 244; and *cf. Reid-Newfoundland Co.* v. *Anglo-American Telegraph Co. Ltd.* [1912] A.C. 555.

[68] *Cf. Re Oatway* [1903] 2 Ch. 356: see above, p. 87.

[69] *Shallcross* v. *Oldham* (1862) 2 J. & H. 609 (master using ship without the owner's consent).

makes from the use of that property or a sum which represents a reasonable hiring fee.[70] The fiduciary is only liable for that part of the profit which is attributable to the misuse of his principal's property, as distinct from that part which is the product of his own contribution[71]; but the burden appears to be on him to demonstrate what that proportion is.[72] It is not clear what is the basis upon which the court will make such an apportionment.[73] Only in exceptional circumstances will an allowance be made for the fiduciary's skilled contribution.[74] In contrast, a non-fiduciary agent is not accountable for profits made through the use of his principal's money, although he is under a duty to account for the money and any interest.[75]

7. USE OF CONFIDENTIAL INFORMATION

In this section we shall be concerned with those cases where a fiduciary acquires, in the course of the fiduciary relationship, confidential information which he exploits for his own profit.[76] A member of the British Security Services uses confidential information, acquired while in MI5, in his best selling book *Spycatcher*[77]; a milkman copies the list of his employer's customers[78]; a laboratory assistant leaks to a rival firm his employer's trade secret[79]; a consulting geologist uses information, acquired while prospecting, to obtain a mining lease on his own behalf[80]; a director speculates in his company's shares, using unpublished information about a potential take-over bid.[81] In all these cases the fiduciary has been unjustly enriched; it is irrelevant that the beneficiary has suffered no loss.[82]

On occasions it may be difficult to determine whether the information was received "in a fiduciary capacity, and [whether] its use would place [the fiduciary] in a position where his duty and his interest might possibly con-

---

[70] Cf. *Strand Electric and Engineering Co.* v. *Brisford Entertainments* [1952] 2 Q.B. 248: see below, p. 726.

[71] *Vyse* v. *Foster* (1872) L.R. 8 Ch.App. 309, 331, *per* James L.J., cited in Finn, *Fiduciary Obligations*, §§ 264–270.

[72] *Lupton* v. *White* (1808) 1 Ves. 432; *Cooke* v. *Addison* (1869) L.R. 7 Eq. 466.

[73] Cf. below, pp. 691–692.

[74] *Guinness plc* v. *Saunders* [1990] 2 A.C. 663: see above, pp. 32–33; see below, pp. 664–665. *O'Sullivan* v. *Management Agency and Music Ltd.* [1985] Ch. 428: see above, p. 33; see below, p. 665.

[75] *Yorks Ry. Co.* v. *Hudson* (1853) 16 Beav. 485; *Kirkham* v. *Peel* (1881) 44 L.T. 195.

[76] See Chap. 36 for a discussion of what is confidential information. In that Chapter we shall consider a party's liability in restitution where information is given to him in confidence and where there is no subsisting fiduciary relationship between the parties. On the difficulty of proving whether the information is confidential, see *Langsing Linde Ltd.* v. *Kerr* [1991] 1 W.L.R. 251, C.A. and cf. *English* v. *Dedham Vale Properties Ltd.* [1978] 1 W.L.R. 93, 105.

[77] *Att.-Gen.* v. *Guardian Newspapers Ltd.* (*No. 2*) [1990] 1 A.C. 109, discussed in Jones, "Breach of Confidence—after *Spycatcher*" [1989] C.L.P. 49.

[78] *Robb* v. *Green* [1895] 2 Q.B. 315.

[79] Cf. *United Indigo Chemical Co.* v. *Robinson* (1932) 49 R.P.C. 178.

[80] *Surveys and Mining Ltd.* v. *Morrison* [1969] Qd.R. 470.

[81] Cf. *Diamond* v. *Oreamuno*, 301 N.Y.S. 2d 78 (1969) (Ct. of Appeals of N.Y.); and generally, (1968) 84 L.Q.R. 272 [Jones].

[82] *English* v. *Dedham Vale Properties Ltd.* [1978] 1 W.L.R. 93, 112, *per* Slade J.

flict."[83] However, the courts appear to be so sensitive to the mere possibility that a fiduciary may have abused his position of trust that they have deprived an honest fiduciary of profits which have been gained at the expense of a third party. *Boardman* v. *Phipps*[84] was such a case. The testator died leaving an estate which induced a substantial but minority holding of shares in a private company. The defendants, who were the family solicitor and a beneficiary of a trust established under the will, advised the trustees that the trust's interests could only be adequately protected if the trust were represented on the board of the company; but this plan failed. The trustees then rejected their suggestion to acquire the majority shares, on the ground that they had neither the financial means nor the power in law to do so. The defendants, with at least the passive concurrence of the majority of the trustees, decided to buy the shares themselves. So they entered into negotiations with the directors, the majority shareholders, purporting in the very initial stages of the negotiations to represent the trust; it was at this stage that they obtained a list of the names of the company's shareholders. The protracted negotiations, during which the defendants incurred considerable personal expense, were eventually successful, and the defendants acquired the majority shares. Subsequently, the company declared a substantial capital dividend; even after the declaration, the shares were worth more than what the defendants had paid for them. The House of Lords held, by a majority, that the defendants must disgorge their profit to the trust. Lord Cohen, Lord Hodson and Lord Guest concluded that the defendants had acquired their knowledge and the opportunity to acquire the shares while purporting to represent the trust.[85] In particular, Boardman, as solicitor, was in a fiduciary relationship to the trustees so that there was a potential conflict of interest.[86] Consequently, it did not matter that they had acted honestly; that the trust did not want to buy, and could not have bought, the shares; that the trust benefited materially from the defendants' intervention; and that the defendants' profits had been made at the expense of third parties, the directors. Moreover, the confidential information which they had acquired belonged to the trust and they had exploited it for their own profit.[87] Viscount Dilhorne and Lord Upjohn dissented. In their view, the defendants' conflict of interest was theoretical rather than real; the defendants' fiduciary duty ended when they failed to secure to secure the representation of the trust on the board of the company, and their profits had been made through their

---

[83] *Boardman* v. *Phipps* [1967] 2 A.C. 46, 129, *per* Lord Upjohn. See also *New Zealand Netherlands Society* v. *Kuys* [1973] 1 W.L.R. 1122, 1125, *per* Lord Wilberforce; *Swain* v. *Law Society* [1982] 1 W.L.R. 17, 37, *per* Oliver L.J., [1983] A.C. 598, 619, *per* Lord Brightman. Contrast *Aas* v. *Benham* [1891] 2 Ch. 244.

[84] [1967] 2 A.C. 46.

[85] This was the principal ground on which the majority (Lord Cohen, Lord Hodson and Lord Guest) decided the case.

[86] In that he might have been asked for his advice on whether an approach should be made to the court to buy additional shares: at p. 103, *per* Lord Cohen, at p. 111, *per* Lord Hodson. For a cogent criticism, see Finn, *Fiduciary Obligations*, § 567.

[87] At p. 107, *per* Lord Hodson; at p. 115 *per* Lord Guest. Lord Cohen and Lord Upjohn denied that information was property "in the strict sense of that word": at pp. 102 and 127–128.

own initiative, skill and financial courage.[88] The House agreed that the defendants were, however, entitled to payment, on a liberal scale, for their work and skill in obtaining the shares and the profits therefrom.[89] In Lord Denning M.R.'s words, in the Court of Appeal, the beneficiary's claim that the defendants had been unjustly enriched should not "extend further than the justice of the case demands."[90]

Boardman v. *Phipps* is an important illustration of how rigorously English courts interpret the "scope and ambit" of a fiduciary's duty of loyalty. We have sympathy with the vigorous dissent that, on these facts, equity's rule was harshly and indiscriminately applied.[91] But, as the decision of the House of Lords in *Guinness plc* v. *Saunders*[92] demonstrates, there is little evidence that the courts are ready to treat more kindly the honest fiduciary. Indeed, only in "exceptional circumstances" should a court remunerate a trustee.[93] *Boardman* v. *Phipps* was such a circumstance because the facts of that case could "not provide any encouragement to trustees to put themselves in a position where their duties as trustees conflicted with their interests."[94] It was assumed that Mr. Ward, the Guinness director, had also acted in good faith and that his services had benefited the company and its shareholders. Nevertheless he had, in entering his service contract with the company, placed himself in a position where there was an inevitable conflict of interest. The House refused to exercise its equitable jurisdiction to grant him an allowance. But the facts of *Guinness plc* v. *Saunders* were, against the background of the Guinness trial and the pending application to extradite Mr. Ward from the United States, highly exceptional. It is to be hoped that the conflict of interest rule will not be so

---

[88] *Cf. Docker* v. *Somes* (1835) 2 Myl. & K. 655, 668, *per* Lord Brougham; *Willett* v. *Blandford* (1842) 1 Hare 253, 271–272, *per* Wigram V.-C. See also *Re Jarvis* [1958] 1 W.L.R. 815; *Re Berkeley Applegate (Investment) Consultants* [1989] Ch. 32.

[89] [1967] 2 A.C. 46, 102, *per* Lord Cohen, 112, *per* Lord Hodson; *Re Duke of Norfolk Settlement Trusts* [1982] Ch. 61.

[90] [1965] Ch. 992, 1020; but *cf.* Russell L.J. at p. 1032. There is earlier authority to support the conclusion that the honest fiduciary should be given an allowance: see *Brown* v. *Litton* (1711) 1 P.Wms. 140; *Crawshay* v. *Collins* (1808) 15 Ves. 18; *Wedderburn* v. *Wedderburn (No. 4)* (1856) 22 Beav. 84. But see now *Guinness plc* v. *Saunders* [1990] 2 A.C. 663, discussed in the text. In the U.S.A., the courts have restricted the allowances available to a conscious wrongdoer: see, in particular, *L. P. Larson Jr. & Co.* v. *William Wrigley Jr. & Co.*, 277 U.S. 97, 97–98, *per* Holmes J. (1927); but *cf. Re Lewis's Estate*, 72 A. 2d 80 (1950).

[91] In *Chan* v. *Zacharia* (1984) 154 C.L.R. 178, 204–205. Deane J. considered that it "may still be arguable" in the High Court of Australia that "the liability to account for a personal benefit or gain obtained or received by use or by reason of fiduciary position, opportunity or knowledge will not arise in circumstances where it would be unconscientious to assert it or in which, for example, there is no possible conflict between personal interest and fiduciary duty, and it is plainly in the interests of the person to whom the fiduciary duty is owed that the fiduciary obtain for himself rights or benefits which he is absolutely precluded from seeking or obtaining for the person to whom the fiduciary duty is owed." *Cf.* the approach of the U.S. Supreme Court in *Manufacturers Trust Co.* v. *Becker*, 338 U.S. 304 (1949), discussed in (1968) 84 L.Q.R. 472, 479 *et seq.* [Jones]; and *Pine Pass Oil* v. *Pacific Petroleum* (1968) 70 D.L.R. (2d) 196. And see Finn, *op. cit.* §§ 551–559. Contrast Birks, *Introduction*, p. 341.

[92] [1990] 2 A.C. 663.

[93] At p. 695, *per* Lord Templeman.

[94] At p. 701, *per* Lord Goff.

rigorously applied as to deny an allowance to honest fiduciaries who have acted in the best interests of, and enriched, their principals. Indeed, in an appropriate case, as the Court of Appeal envisaged in *O'Sullivan* v. *Management Agency and Music Ltd.*,[95] that allowance might even include a profit element.[96]

The beneficiary will normally be anxious to enjoin the fiduciary from making further use of the confidential information.[97] But, if the fiduciary has used the information, the beneficiary may seek an account of the profits made by the fiduciary. A fiduciary who has consciously made use of confidential information will have to account.[98] *Boardman* v. *Phipps* suggests that even an honest fiduciary will be compelled not only to account but to hold any profits made from the use of the confidential information on constructive trust for the beneficiary.[99] In our view, the honest fiduciary's liability should not, in such case, be so extensive but should be limited to a personal liability for the profits made.[1] However, the beneficiary should have an election of claiming a reasonable price for the use of the confidential information, if that is a more favourable remedy.[2]

A third party who receives confidential information from a fiduciary, in circumstances when he knows that that information was given to him in breach of the trust, should be jointly and severally liable with the fiduciary; he therefore holds any profits which he has made from the use of the information as a constructive trustee for the beneficiary. Whether a third-party purchaser is liable if he ought to have known that the information was given in breach of trust is an open question and may be dependent on whether "information" is deemed to be property.[3] The extent of the liability of the innocent volunteer is also uncertain.[4] A beneficiary cannot recover from a fiduciary who innocently imparted confidential information the profits which he has thereby enabled an innocent third party to make[5]; but if the fiduciary consciously passed confidential information to an innocent third party, it is arguable that the fiduciary should be made liable for those profits.

---

[95] [1985] Q.B. 428; *cf. Boardman* v. *Phipps* [1965] Ch. 992, 1030–1031, *per* Pearson L.J.
[96] See above, pp. 32–33 for a full discussion of these questions.
[97] *Cf. Liquid Veneer Co.* v. *Scott* (1912) 29 R.P.C. 639; *Amber Size & Chemical Co. Ltd.* v. *Menzel* [1913] 1 Ch. 239: below, pp. 686 *et seq.*
[98] *Cf. Peter Pan Manufacturing Corp.* v. *Corsets Silhouette Ltd.* [1964] 1 W.L.R. 96: see below, p. 691.
[99] See [1965] Ch. 992, 1006; and *cf.* [1964] 1 W.L.R. 993, 1018, *per* Wilberforce J. The House of Lords confirmed the decree of Wilberforce J.
[1] See above, p. 646.
[2] *Cf. Seager* v. *Copydex Ltd.* [1967] 1 W.L.R. 923; [1969] 1 W.L.R. 809: see below, pp. 690–693.
[3] See above p. 663 and below, pp. 695–696.
[4] *Cf.* below, pp. 670 *et seq.*
[5] *Regal (Hastings) Ltd.* v. *Gulliver* [1942] 1 All E.R. 378: see above, pp. 655–657.

8. Secret Commissions: Bribes

To accept a secret commission, which we shall call a bribe,[6] is inconsistent with the fiduciary duty owed by a fiduciary to his beneficiary. It is also inconsistent with the duty of a non-fiduciary agent to his principal.[7] The principal can rescind any transaction which his agent made, on his behalf, with the briber and which was induced by the bribe. He must, however, be able to restore the *status quo ante*. If the agent has subsequently accounted to, and handed over, the bribe to his principal, the principal is not required to give credit to the briber for the bribe; for he may elect whether or not to treat the bribe as part of the bargained for consideration.[8]

If the agent does not account for the bribe, he can be compelled to do so. The "court will presume . . . that they [the agents] were influenced by the bribe: and this presumption is irrebuttable."[9] It is irrelevant that the principal suffered no loss from the corrupt bargain; for the fiduciary will have been unjustly enriched.[10] Thus, in *Williams* v. *Barton*,[11] a trustee who received a secret commission was required to account for that commission to the trust estate, as was a director, in *The Metropolitan Bank* v. *Heiron*,[12] to his company.

These principles have been extended so as to catch secret payments to persons not normally regarded as fiduciaries or agents. In *Att.-Gen.* v. *Goddard*,[13] a policeman who was employed to watch and to report on houses of ill-fame and who had been accepting bribes with distressing frequency, was required to hand these sums to the Crown. Similarly, in *Reading* v. *Att.-Gen.*[14] the suppliant was an ex-sergeant of the R.A.M.C. who had received large sums of money for his assistance in smuggling illicit goods into Cairo. Wearing his full uniform, he used to ride through Cairo in a lorry carrying the goods; and his presence enabled it to pass the civil police without inspection. The money which he received for these services was seized by the military authorities, and

---

[6] For the purposes of the civil law a bribe means the payment of a secret commission: see *Industries and General Mortgage Co. Ltd.* v. *Lewis* [1949] 2 All E.R. 573, 575, *per* Slade J.; but see *Logicrose Ltd.* v. *Southend United Football Club Ltd.* [1988] 1 W.L.R. 1256, 1260, *per* Millett J.

[7] *De Bussche* v. *Alt* (1878) 8 Ch.D. 286; *Salomons* v. *Pender* (1865) 3 H. & C. 639; *Kimber* v. *Barber* (1872) 8 Ch.App. 56; *Thompson* v. *Meade* (1891) 7 T.L.R. 698; *Erskine, Oxenford & Co.* v. *Sachs* [1901] 2 K.B. 504; *Powell & Thomas* v. *Evans Jones & Co.* [1905] 1 K.B. 11; *Regier* v. *Campbell-Stuart* [1939] 1 Ch. 766. And *cf. Headway Construction Co.* v. *Downham* (1974) 223 E.G. 675.

[8] *Logicrose Ltd.* v. *Southend United Football Club Ltd.* [1988] 1 W.L.R. 1256.

[9] *Hovenden & Sons* v. *Millhoff* (1900) 83 L.T. 41, 43, *per* Romer L.J.

[10] See *Parker* v. *McKenna* (1874) 10 Ch.App. 96; *Re North Australian Territory Company* [1892] 1 Ch. 322, 327, *per* Kekewich J.; *Reading* v. *Att.-Gen.* [1948] 2 K.B. 268, affd. in the Court of Appeal [1949] 2 K.B. 232, affd. in the House of Lords [1951] A.C. 507. See also *Restatement of Agency* (2d) §§ 404, 404A; *Restatement of Restitution*, § 197.

[11] [1927] 2 Ch. 9: see also *Re Smith* [1896] 1 Ch. 71; *Chandler* v. *Bradley* [1897] 1 Ch. 315; *Shepherd* v. *Harris* [1905] 2 Ch. 310.

[12] (1880) L.R. 5 Ex.D. 319.

[13] (1929) 98 L.J.K.B. 743; see at p. 745, *per* Rowlatt J.

[14] [1948] 2 K.B. 268, affd. in the Court of Appeal [1949] 2 K.B. 232, affd. in the House of Lords [1951] A.C. 507. *Reading* v. *Att.-Gen.* was cited, with approval, in the colourful case of *Jersey City* v. *Hague*, 18 N.J. 584 (1955), on which see (1968) 84 L.Q.R. 472, 476, n. 25 [Jones].

in this action he petitioned for its return. Denning J. held that there was no fiduciary relationship between the suppliant and the Crown, but that its absence was immaterial. "The uniform of the Crown, and the position of the man as servant of the Crown, were the sole reasons why he was able to get this money, and that is sufficient to make him liable to hand it over to the Crown."[15]

In the Court of Appeal, counsel argued that the Crown could only succeed if there was a fiduciary relationship and that Denning J.'s proposition of law was without authority. Asquith L.J., who delivered the court's judgment, was not convinced by this argument. In any event, he thought that the term fiduciary relationship should here be used "in a very loose, or at all events a very comprehensive, sense,"[16] and, assuming it was necessary, "such a relationship subsisted in this case as to the user of the uniform and the opportunities and facilities attached to it; and that the suppliant obtained the sums claimed by acting in breach of the duties imposed by that relation."[17] Such reasoning had the desirable effect of preventing Reading from recovering his ill-gotten gains.[18] The speeches in the House of Lords in the same case confirm that the status of a fiduciary may, in such circumstances, be easily acquired.[19]

The beneficiary or principal may also sue the fiduciary and briber for damages for fraud, under which he can recover the amount of the actual loss sustained.[20] The Court of Appeal[21] has more than once expressed the view that the principal's remedies against the agent and briber are cumulative, so that he can recover from the agent the bribe[22] *and* from the agent and briber, jointly and severally, damages for loss suffered.[23] However, the Privy Council has more recently held[24] that this conclusion is inconsistent with the decision of the House of Lords in *United Australia Ltd.* v. *Barclays Bank Ltd.*,[25] and that the principal's remedies are alternative and not cumulative and consequently he must elect between them.[26]

---

[15] [1948] 2 K.B. 268. See Lord Denning's comment on this case in *Phipps* v. *Boardman* [1965] Ch. 992, 1019; and *cf. Tito* v. *Waddell (No. 2)* [1978] Ch. 106, 229–230, *per* Megarry V.-C.

[16] [1949] 2 K.B. 232, 236. He then held that the authorities showed that a fiduciary relation existed in such cases as *Shallcross* v. *Oldham* (1862) 2 J. & H. 609; *Att.-Gen.* v. *Goddard* (1929) 98 L.J.K.B. 743; *Powell & Thomas* v. *Evan Jones & Co.* [1905] 1 K.B. 11.

[17] [1949] 2 K.B. 232, 238; see also at p. 236, quoted above, p. 644, n. 14.

[18] See Meagher, Gummow and Lehane, *op. cit.* § 524.

[19] [1951] A.C. 507, 514, 516, *per* Lord Porter, 517, *per* Lord Norman, 517–518, *per* Lord Oaksey, 518, *per* Lord Radcliffe.

[20] *Mahesan* v. *Malaysia Housing Society* [1979] A.C. 374, 383, *per* Lord Diplock, P.C.

[21] *Salford Corp.* v. *Lever* [1891] 1 Q.B. 168; *Grant* v. *The Gold Exploration and Development Syndicate Ltd.* [1900] 1 Q.B. 233; *Hovenden & Sons* v. *Milhoff* (1900) 83 L.T. 41.

[22] And, certainly if a fiduciary, he must account for any profit which he makes in consequence: (1979) 95 L.Q.R. at 549 [Needham].

[23] In *Hovenden & Sons* v. *Milhoff* (1900) 83 L.T. 41, 43, Romer L.J. considered that the price is loaded against the principal by at least the amount of the bribe. *Sed quaere* whether this is "a hybrid form of legal wrong" and that damages in tort should simply be for the actual loss sustained: *Mahesan* v. *Malaysia Housing Society* [1979] A.C. 374, 381.

[24] *Mahesan* v. *Malaysia Housing Society* [1979] A.C. 374; see also Bowstead, *Agency*, p. 422.

[25] [1941] A.C. 1: see below, p. 732.

[26] *Cf.* (1979) 95 L.Q.R. 68 [Tettenborn], who argues in favour of double recovery; contrast (1979) 95 L.Q.R. 536 [Needham].

Neither of these actions will lie if there has been full and proper disclosure to the beneficiary or principal.[27] If he knew of, and either expressly or impliedly[28] assented to, the retention of the bribe, the fiduciary or agent may retain it, for it is no longer a bribe. But there must have been full and proper disclosure to all parties,[29] and if any fact is suppressed, the disclosure is not full and proper.

The recipient of a bribe, at least if it is paid in money,[29a] does not hold it on trust for his beneficiary or principal. In *Lister & Co.* v. *Stubbs*,[30] the principal, in an action to recover secret commissions from his agent, claimed to follow them into their product, namely certain investments, and sought an injunction restraining the agent from dealing with the investments or an order directing him to bring them into court. The Court of Appeal refused to grant these remedies. The secret commissions did not belong in equity to the principal. The agent was merely under a duty to account for them to his principal; the relationship of the parties was that of creditor and debtor.[31]

This decision emphatically marks off the secret commission cases from those where the fiduciary misapplies "trust property," for example, by using confidential information, by competing with the beneficiary or by speculating with the trust property. Because the secret commission does not "belong" to the beneficiary, it is said that he cannot take any profit made by the fiduciary through its use; he is only entitled to the amount of the bribe itself. Moreover, he has no preferential rights in bankruptcy, for he cannot trace the money[32] and the statute of limitations runs against him.[33] His only remedy is either to claim the money as had and received to his use[34] or to recover the money in a personal claim in equity.[35]

The Court of Appeal, in *Lister* v. *Stubbs*, assumed that the principal's title "depends on it being established *by a decree of a competent court* that the fraud of

---

[27] [1963] C.L.J. 119, 135 [L. S. Sealy].

[28] *Baring* v. *Stanton* (1876) 3 Ch.D. 502, following *Great Western Insurance Co. of New York* v. *Cunliffe* (1874) 9 Ch.App. 525; *Stubbs* v. *Slater* [1910] 1 Ch. 632.

[29] And see the cases cited above, p. 649.

[29a] See below, p. 669, n. 43.

[30] (1890) 45 Ch.D. 1.; followed in *Re Att.-Gen.'s Ref. No. 1 of 1985* [1986] 2 W.L.R. 733, 742, 743; *Iran Shipping Lines* v. *Denby* [1987] 1 Lloyd's Rep. 367; *Att.-Gen. for Hong Kong* v. *Reid* [1992] N.Z.L.R. 385, C.A.

[31] *Ibid.* at pp. 14–15, *per* Lindley L.J.; see also *Re Smith* [1896] 1 Ch. 71, 77, *per* Kekewich J. Contrast the authorities, discussed in the text at p. 669, n. 43, which were not cited to the court.

[32] *Lister & Co.* v. *Stubbs* (1890) 45 Ch.D. 1, 15, *per* Lindley L.J.; *Powell & Thomas* v. *Evan Jones & Co.* [1905] 1 K.B. 11.

[33] *Metropolitan Bank* v. *Heiron* (1880) L.R. 5 Ex.D. 319: see below, Chap. 43.

[34] It was argued in *Reading* v. *Att.-Gen.* that no promise could be implied in these circumstances. The argument was rejected and a promise was "implied" by some of the members of both the Court of Appeal and the House of Lords. Their reasoning may fairly be described as highly artificial: see [1949] 2 K.B. 232, 237, *per* Asquith L.J., [1951] A.C. 507, 515–516, *per* Lord Porter, 517, *per* Lord Normand, 517, *per* Lord Oaksey, 518, *per* Lord Radcliffe. *Cf.* [1948] 2 K.B. 268, 275, *per* Denning J., whose reasoning is much simpler and more satisfying.

[35] *Boston Deep Sea Fishing & Ice Co.* v. *Ansell* (1888) 39 Ch.D. 339, 367, *per* Bowen L.J. But *cf. Att.-Gen.* v. *Goddard* (1929) 98 L.J.K.B. 743, 746, where Rowlatt J. said that the action lay in equity only; and see Asquith L.J.'s comment on that passage in *Reading* v. *Att.-Gen.* [1949] 2 K.B. 232, 237; and *Mahesan* v. *Malaysia Housing Society* [1979] A.C. 374, 383, *per* Lord Diplock.

the trustee has given the *cestui que trust* a right to the money[36]; ownership should not be confused with obligation."[37] As an unbroken line of authority dating from *Keech* v. *Sandford* in 1728 demonstrates, an honest fiduciary, such as Mr. Boardman, who is deemed to have abused his position of trust, is a constructive trustee of his profits, even though he acted in the best interests of the trust and his beneficiary gained over £20,000 from his intervention.[38] In contrast, the corrupt agent or Sergeant Reading[39] is simply obliged to account for the value of his bribe. This is not a just conclusion. A fiduciary must transfer property received *qua* fiduciary to his principal. This obligation is specifically enforceable, for equity regards that as done which ought to be done. Only if the fiduciary has authority to deal with the proceeds of a sale as if they are his own should the relationship between him and his principal be that of debtor and creditor.[40] For example, as against the purchaser, a vendor is entitled to treat the bribe, promised or paid, as part of the purchase price, though he is not bound to do so. There is no reason why he should not have a similar right against his corrupt agent. Similarly, if it is the purchaser's agent who is bribed, the purchaser should be entitled to treat the bribe as a rebate of the purchase price or as excess consideration which he unknowingly provided.[41] Clearly, the agent has been unjustly enriched for he has breached his duty of loyalty to his principal in accepting the bribe, and, in our view, should hold the bribe money on trust for his principal.[41a]

In any event *Lister* v. *Stubbs* should have no application if the fiduciary obtains the bribe for the use of the beneficiaries' property.[42] And there are cases which hold that a company whose director has received a bribe of its shares from a dishonest promoter may claim from the director those shares or their highest value whilst in his hands; the shares are deemed to belong to the company.[43]

---

[36] *Metropolitan Bank Ltd.* v. *Heiron* (1880) 5 Ex.D. 319, 325, *per* Cotton L.J. (italics supplied). *Semble*, once there is a decree, the defendant becomes a trustee of the bribe for his principal.

[37] *Lister & Co.* v. *Stubbs* (1890) 45 Ch.D. 1, 15, *per* Lindley L.J.

[38] *Boardman* v. *Phipps* [1967] 2 A.C. 46: see above, pp. 662–664.

[39] *Reading* v. *Att.-Gen.* [1951] A.C. 507: see above, pp. 666–667.

[40] Sir Peter Millett, *Bribes and Secret Commissions*, Vol. I, *Frontiers of Liability* (ed. Birks), pp. 1–32. Sir Peter also emphasises that proprietary remedies have never been restricted to persons who seek to recover their own property; hence the constructive trust which arises in favour of the contracting purchaser of land. For a contrary view, see Goode, *Property and Unjust Enrichment* in *Essay on Restitution* (ed. Burrows) pp. 215 *et seq.*; and Birks, *Introduction*, pp. 388–389.

[41] *Logicrose* v. *Southend United Football Club* [1988] 1 W.L.R. 1257, 1263–4, *per* Millett J.

[41a] See above, p. 658.

[42] *Cf. Re Canadian Oil Works Corp.* (1875) L.R. 10 Ch. 593, 600 *per* James L.J. In *D.P.C. Estates Pty. Ltd.* v. *Grey and Consul Development Pty. Ltd.* [1974] 1 N.S.W.L.R. 443, 471, Hardie and Hutley JJ.A., in the New South Wales Supreme Court, described *Lister & Co.* v. *Stubbs* as anomalous and not to be extended to such a case. The High Court of Australia left the question open: (1975) 132 C.L.R. 373. But see *Daly* v. *The Stock Exchange* (1980) 160 C.L.R. 371, 379, *per* Gibbs J. For another view, see Birks, *Introduction*, pp. 388–389; *Essays* (ed. Burrows) pp. 241–242 [Goode].

[43] *Re Morvah Consols Tin Mining Co.* (1875) 2 Ch.D. 1, 6, *per* Mellish L.J., 7, *per* Brett J.; *Eden* v. *Ridsdales Railway Lamp and Lighting Co. Ltd.* (1889) 23 Q.B.D. 368. The courts did not appear to be constrained by the English company law rule that a company cannot own its own shares; but *cf. Hay's Case* (1875) L.R. 10 Ch.App. 593; *Archer's Case* [1892] 1 Ch. 322; *Re London*

The principles set out in this section apply to fiduciaries, non-fiduciary agents, civil servants, policemen and members of the armed forces. But, where the parties are not in such a relationship, a plaintiff cannot reach the secret profit made by a defendant simply because the defendant has been guilty of commercial sharp dealing. So, in the Ontario case of *Jirna Ltd.* v. *Mister Do-Nut of Canada Ltd.*[44] the plaintiffs, who had entered into a franchise agreement with the defendants whereby the plaintiffs agreed to buy supplies and materials from distributors nominated by the defendants, failed in their attempt to recover the secret rebate given by those distributors to the defendants.

(C) The Liability of a Stranger Who Receives Trust Property Transferred to Him in Breach of Trust

A stranger is deemed to *receive* trust property if he receives it for his own benefit in the sense that he sets up "a title of his own to the funds which he has received."[45] Subject to any appropriate defences, in particular bona fide purchase and change of position, the beneficiaries of the trust or the principal of the fiduciary can follow the trust property provided that they can identify it in the stranger's hands. We have discussed the scope of the proprietary claim in Chapter 2 of this book.[46] In this section we shall consider what is the personal liability of the stranger to account for the value of the property which he received; this inquiry is critical if the property can no longer be identified.

1. IN WHAT CIRCUMSTANCES WILL THE STRANGER BE HELD TO BE A CONSTRUCTIVE TRUSTEE?

The beneficiaries or the principal may be anxious to persuade the court that the stranger is a constructive trustee for more than one reason. First, the stranger will not be able to defend himself by pleading that the claim is

---

South Western Canal Ltd. [1911] 1 Ch. 346. *Cf. Logicrose Ltd.* v. *Southend United Football Club* [1988] 1 W.L.R. 1256, where Millett J. concluded that "there cannot in truth be any real difference between the secret payment to the agent of a sum additional to the purchase price and the payment to him of part of the purchase price of which his principal is unaware": see above, p. 669.

[44] 40 D.L.R. (3d) 303 (1973). But *cf.* the cases cited above, p. 644, n. 13 which point to a different

. Savin [1985] 2 N.Z.L.R. 41, 69, *per* Sir Clifford Richmond; see also *kson* [1990] Ch. 265, 291–293, *per* Millett J.

 stranger who knowingly receives trust property from the stranger who hering a fraudulent breach of trust. We shall not be concerned with the h seek to impose liability on the stranger (including a fiduciary's agent) rust in circumstances where trust property passed through his hands ceive that property for his own benefit.

statute-barred.[47] Secondly, a constructive trustee will be liable to pay interest, which may be at a higher rate than the rate of the court's special account.[48] Thirdly, trustees are jointly and severally liable for all the loss suffered by the trust. Fourthly, they cannot defend themselves by saying that any loss is too remote.[49] Fifthly, a court may be more ready to exercise its discretion to order an account of profits made from the exploitation of a fiduciary position; such an order was made against *The Sunday Times* which had published extracts from *Spycatcher* and had knowingly participated in Wright's breach of trust.[50] Sixthly, the trust property may have increased in value. Seventhly, Order 11, r.(1)(*t*) specifically permits the service of a writ outside the jurisdiction against the defendant as constructive trustee.

A stranger will be so liable if he received the property with the knowledge that it was transferred to him in breach of trust. Certainly, he will be liable as a constructive trustee if he had actual knowledge of the breach of trust, if he wilfully shut his eyes to that obvious fact or if he wilfully and recklessly failed to make such inquiries as an honest and reasonable man would have made and which would have led him to conclude that property had been transferred to him in breach of trust. He may also be deemed to be a constructive trustee "if the circumstances are such that an honest and reasonable man would have inferred that the moneys were probably trust moneys and were being mis-applied. . . . "[50a]; or ought to have known that the moneys were transferred in breach of trust.[51] However, it cannot be said with confidence that this is settled law. In *Carl-Zeiss Stiftung* v. *Herbert Smith & Co. (No. 2)*[52] Edmund Davies L.J. said the fiduciary must act with a "want of probity," having actual knowledge of the breach of trust or wilfully and recklessly shutting his eyes to that obvious fact, or wilfully and recklessly failing to make the inquiries which a reasonable man would have made and which would have led to the conclusion

---

[47] See Limitation Act 1980, s.20: discussed below, Chap. 43.

[48] For a recent illustration, see *Guardian Ocean Cargoes Ltd.* v. *Banco de Brasil SA* [1992] T.L.R. 129, *per* Hirst J., following *Wallersteiner* v. *Moir (No. 2)* [1975] Q.B. 373. See generally, Hayton and Marshall, *Cases and Commentary on the Law of Trusts*, pp. 779–780. If the stranger is simply under a personal liability to account, he may exceptionally not be liable to pay interest: see above, p. 584.

[49] *Caffrey* v. *Darby* (1801) 6 Ves. 488.

[50] *Att.-Gen.* v. *Guardian Newspapers Ltd. (No. 2)* [1990] 1 A.C. 109: see [1989] C.L.P. 49, 55–60 [Jones] and see below, p. 691.

[50a] *Eagle Trust plc* v. *Securities Ltd.* [1992] 4 All E.R. 488, 509, *per* Vinelott J.

[51] For the authorities, see, *inter alia*, Peter Gibson J.'s well-known classification in *Baden* v. *Société pour Favoriser le Developpement du Commerce et de l'Industrie en France SA* (1982) [1992] 4 All E.R. 161, 231, upon which see *Agip (Africa) Ltd.* v. *Jackson* [1992] 4 All E.R. 385, 403, *per* Millett J. and *Polly Peck International plc* v. *Nadir (No. 2)* [1992] 4 All E.R. 769, 777, *per* Scott L.J. See also *Manchester Trust* v. *Furness* [1895] 2 Q.B. 539, 545; *Thomson* v. *Clydesdale Bank Ltd.* [1893] A.C. 282; *John* v. *Dodwell & Co.* [1918] A.C. 563; *Nelson* v. *Larholt* [1948] 1 K.B. 339; *Belmont Finance* v. *Williams Furniture (No. 2)* [1980] 1 All E.R. 393, 405, 410; *International Sales Ltd.* v. *Marcus* [1982] 3 All E.R. 551, 557–558.

[52] [1969] 2 Ch. 276, 301.

that the property was transferred in breach of trust.[53] And in *Re Montague's Settlements*[54] Megarry V.-C. agreed that "the basic question is whether the conscience of the recipient is sufficiently affected to justify the imposition of a trust."[55] This conclusion is not unattractive. To hold that the stranger is a constructive trustee is to impose upon him a liability which is more onerous than to make him personally liable to make restitution.[56] And, as will be seen, to hold that he is not a constructive trustee may not absolve him of all liability; subject to defences, a stranger who receives trust property transferred in breach of trust should be obliged to make restitution of the value of the property received.[57] It is true that if the trust property can be identified in the stranger's hands, the beneficiaries can, again subject to defences, follow the property and claim it as theirs in equity whether or not the stranger knew of the breach of trust.[58] For Megarry V.-C. this asymmetry is in principle acceptable; tracing determines rights of property while the imposition of personal liability under a constructive trust goes beyond mere property rights.[59]

2. Is the Stranger under a Personal Liability to make Restitution?

A stranger, who is not a bona fide purchaser, should be liable to make restitution to the beneficiaries of a trust. It is well settled that the beneficiaries can trace their property, normally money, into his hands. In principle the stranger should be personally liable to make restitution and it should not matter whether he had no notice that the property was transferred to him in breach of trust. He has been unjustly enriched at the beneficiaries' expense; for their money has been paid to him in breach of trust.

At common law the recipient's liability is a strict one. So, a fiduciary who has paid money under a mistake of fact[60] may recover a like sum from the recipient; and the beneficiaries of the trust may compel him to exercise his legal right to sue at law.[61] A fiduciary's claim at law must, however, fail if money has been paid under a mistake of law.[62]

In equity, as has been seen, a recipient is, in two limited situations,

---

[53] See also Sachs L.J. at p. 299.
[54] [1987] Ch. 264, 284. *Cf. Lipkin Gorman (A Firm)* v. *Karpnale Ltd.* [1987] 1 W.L.E. 987; *Barclays Bank plc* v. *Quincare Ltd.* (1988) [1992] 4 All E.R. 363; *Cowan de Groot Properties Ltd.* v. *Eagle Trust plc.* [1992] 4 All E.R. 700, 759–760, *per* Knox J.; *Polly Peck International plc* v. *Nadir (No. 2)* [1992] 4 All E.R. 769, 777, *per* Scott L.J.
[55] In the view of the Vice-Chancellor he does not act with a want of probity if he had genuinely forgotten a critical fact which he once knew.
[56] See above, Chap. 29 and pp. 670–671.
[57] See above, pp. 670–671.
[58] For a critical comment, see (1987) 50 M.L.R. 217 [Harpum].
[59] *Re Montague's Settlements* [1987] Ch. 264, 272.
[60] See above, pp. 107–108, where we reject the argument that *ignorance* may ground a restitutionary claim.
[61] *Re Robinson* [1911] 1 Ch. 502, 507–508, *per* Warrington J.
[62] See above, pp. 154–155.

personally liable to make restitution even though a fiduciary has paid money under a mistake of law. First, a trustee may deduct from future payments to a beneficiary any over-payments paid to him under a mistake of law; possibly a beneficiary may be also able to recover in equity these moneys from his co-beneficiary, provided that he joins the trustee as a party to the suit.[63] Secondly, there is the *Diplock* personal claim, which enables next-of-kin and other beneficiaries to recover from recipients who had been paid moneys under a mistake of law. The scope of the equitable claim is uncertain and it is subject to irrational limitations; for example, the plaintiffs must first have exhausted their remedies against the fiduciaries who distributed the property in breach of trust.[64]

Given the desired fusion of legal and equitable remedies,[64a] the courts should now recognise that in equity, as at law, the recipient of trust money should be required to make restitution of the sums paid to him. He has been unjustly enriched at the beneficiaries' expense. In principle his liability should be a strict one. It should be irrelevant whether the sums were paid because of the trustee's mistake of fact (possibly even if the mistake was of law) or because the trustee knew that he was committing a breach of trust; and it should be no defence that the recipient had no notice of the breach of trust. However, if he knew of the breach of trust he will also be held to be a constructive trustee, whose liability to make restitution is far more onerous than that of an innocent volunteer, whose only duty should be to make restitution.[65] Moreover, the innocent volunteer is protected by such defences as change of position. In our view if he has acted honestly, having no knowledge of the breach of trust, he should be allowed to plead the defence of change of position even though he should, as a reasonable man, have realised that the money had been transferred to him in breach of trust.[66] It is true that there is no authority which directly supports such a broad equitable restitutionary claim; equally there is no authority which denies it. If it were recognised, then the two special cases cited above would be seen as equitable ghosts of the past.

Finally the beneficiaries should, in principle, be able to compel a third party, claiming through the immediate recipient to make restitution if they can prove that he received their money.[67]

---

[63] See above, pp. 154–155.
[64] See Chap. 29.
[64a] See above, p. 654.
[65] See above, p. 671. *Cf. Agip (Africa) Ltd.* v. *Jackson* [1990] Ch. 265, 291–293, *per* Millett J.; (1991) 107 L.Q.R. 71, 80–83, [Sir Peter Millet].
[66] See below, pp. 744–745.
[67] *Cf.* above, Chap. 2 (on the scope of the action for money had and received), and pp. 385–387.

Chapter 34

BENEFITS ACQUIRED IN BREACH OF AN UNDERTAKING TO HOLD PROPERTY FOR THE BENEFIT OF ANOTHER

A CONVEYS land to B. B undertakes to hold the land on trust for A or for a third party, T. Such an undertaking may be specifically enforceable if the proper formalities have been observed. But even if they have not, equity will not allow their absence to defeat the trust. The repudiation of an oral undertaking to hold land for the benefit of the transferor or a third party has consistently been characterised in equity as fraudulent conduct. In equity it has never been necessary to demonstrate that the transferee was dishonest; it is enough that he changed his mind.[1]

Equity would never allow a defendant to use a statute as a cloak for fraud. For this reason equity enforced, despite the express provisions of the Statute of Frauds 1677 and the Wills Act 1837, which required writing in due form, the undertaking of the heir at law, the devisee or the legatee who had promised to hold property for the benefit of another. "The Court of Equity ... may in notorious cases declare a legatee, that has obtained a legacy by fraud, to be a trustee for another; as if the drawer of a will should insert his own name instead of the name of the legatee." It would "declare a trust upon such a will" as it would in the case of "the legatee promising the trustee to stand as a trustee for another."[2] To repudiate the undertaking was a "species of fraud."[3] Equity's jurisdiction to enforce a trust, which was not evident on the face of the will, was then originally founded "on personal fraud."[4] In 1929 the House of Lords laid to rest any doubts as to the validity of the half secret trust, where the trust but not its terms was evident on the face of the will and where the legatee would probably not benefit from the breach of his undertaking. "The application of the principle of equity was logical, and was justified by the same considerations as in the cases of fraud and absolute gifts."[5] So, if fraud was the reason for equity's intervention, "that does not mean that fraud is [nowadays] an essential ingredient for the application of the doctrine."[6]

---

[1] See above, pp. 473–474. One of the earliest cases, decided soon after the Statute of Frauds, is *Thynn* v. *Thynn* (1684) 1 Vern. 296.

[2] *Marriot* v. *Marriot* (1726) Gilb.Rep. 203.

[3] *Chamberlain* v. *Agar* (1813) 2 Ves. & Beav. 259, 262.

[4] *McCormick* v. *Grogan* (1869) L.R. 4 H.L. 82, 97, *per* Lord Westbury.

[5] *Blackwell* v. *Blackwell* [1929] A.C. 318, 335, *per* Viscount Sumner.

[6] *Re Snowden* [1979] Ch. 528, 536, *per* Megarry V.-C.

The defendant to whom land is conveyed *inter vivos* and who repudiates his oral undertaking to hold land for the benefit of another is said to be a constructive trustee of the land; hence he cannot rely on section 53(1)(*b*) of the Law of Property Act 1925, which requires trusts of land to be evidenced in writing,[7] to defeat the trust.[8] But if the secret trust arises under a will or on an intestacy it is uncertain whether the trust is characterised as an express or a constructive trust; the characterisation is critical if the subject-matter of the trust is land. The few cases are not conclusive.[9] What should be clear is that the trustee should never be permitted to invoke the statute to enrich himself.[10] What is unclear is whether an appellate court will conclude that it is giving effect to the intention of the testator, and consequently characterise the trust as an express trust, or that, given the history of equity's intervention, it will hold that it is a constructive trust. The latter conclusion ensures that the trust will be upheld; furthermore, form is not allowed to prevail over substance.[11] No conclusion should turn on whether the trust is a fully or half secret trust; the rationalisation of the law in *Blackwell* v. *Blackwell*[12] would suggest a harmony rather than a disharmony of characterisation.

A similar body of law governs mutual wills; for example, where two parties make wills, leaving property of the first to die to the survivor for life, and after the survivor's death to named beneficiaries. The survivor is held to be a constructive trustee. The agreement to create the mutual will determines (a) what property is subject to the trusts, and (b) what are the beneficial interests of the trusts.[13]

---

[7] If they are not so evidenced, they are unenforceable by action.

[8] Law of Property Act 1925, s.53(2); *Bannister* v. *Bannister* [1948] 2 All E.R. 133, C.A.: see above, pp. 473–474.

[9] In *Ottaway* v. *Norman* [1972] Ch. 698, a case of a fully secret trust, the absence of writing was not raised; in contrast, in the briefly reported *Re Baillie* (1886) 2 T.L.R. 660, North J. held that a half secret trust was an express trust and had to be evidenced in writing. *Cf. Re Cleaver* [1981] 1 W.L.R. 939 (mutual wills).

[10] *Cf. Bannister* v. *Bannister* [1948] 2 All E.R. 133.

[11] *Cf. Vandervell* v. *I.R.C.* [1967] 2 A.C. 291, interpreting s.53(1)(*c*) of the Law of Property Act 1925.

[12] See above, n. 5.

[13] *Birmingham* v. *Renfrew* (1936) 57 C.L.R. 666; *Re Cleaver* [1981] 1 W.L.R. 939. For a full discussion, see Hayton and Marshall, *op. cit.* pp. 105–112.

CHAPTER 35

BENEFITS ACQUIRED BY REPREHENSIBLE MEANS

THERE can be no doubt that an English court will restrain a person from publishing information which he has obtained by means which are illegal and criminal. That was the fate of the Daily Mirror Group, which had knowingly acquired tapes which were the fruits of the illegal tapping of Mr. Francome's telephone.[1] In such cases a plaintiff may also be able to claim an account of profits, a *quantum meruit* or damages[2]; he may also demand that documents or chattels be handed over to him.[3]

However, a defendant may obtain confidential information by means which are not illegal but which could be justly characterised as reprehensible. An English court would, we suggest, have no hesitation in granting a plaintiff relief if the defendant's conduct could be characterised as tortious; for example, if he obtained information through implanting a trespassory electronic device[4] or through some act of deception.[5] But what if the defendant commits no tort but simply infringes the plaintiff's privacy? The point arose in *Bernstein* v. *Skyways & General Ltd.*[6] The defendant took, from a height of several hundred feet, aerial photographs of the plaintiff's house without his permission, and unsuccessfully attempted to sell them to him. The plaintiff's claim for damages for trespass and to enjoin the defendant from entering the air space above his house failed. Griffiths J. held that the defendant's aircraft had not interfered with the plaintiff's use or intended use of the land; an owner's rights extend only to such height as is necessary for the ordinary use and enjoyment of his land. "There is . . . no law against taking a photograph."[7] But the judge did contemplate that:

> "if the circumstances were such that a plaintiff was subjected to the harassment of constant surveillance of his house from the air, accompanied by the photographing of his every activity, I am far from saying that

---

[1] *Francome* v. *Mirror Group Newspapers Ltd.* [1984] 1 W.L.R. 892: see below, pp. 669–670.

[2] *Cf.* above, pp. 690–694.

[3] *Cf. Franklin* v. *Giddens* [1978] Qd. 72 (defendant stole bud-wood from the plaintiff's orchards; he was ordered to deliver up, for destruction, the productive bud-wood).

[4] *Cf.* The Younger Report of the Committee on Privacy, Cmnd. 5012 (1972), §§ 563, 629–630 (proposed civil wrong to obtain information in this way).

[5] *Cf. ITC Film Distributors* v. *Video Exchange Ltd.* [1982] Ch. 431, 437, *per* Warner J.

[6] [1978] Q.B. 479. Contrast *Exchange Telegraph Co. Ltd.* v. *Howard* (1906) 22 T.L.R. 25 (injunction to restrain the surreptitious obtaining of information collected by the plaintiff), discussed in Gurry, *op. cit.* at pp. 50–54.

[7] At p. 488.

the court would not regard such a monstrous invasion of his privacy as an actionable nuisance for which they would give relief."[8]

Bernstein provides a sharp contrast to the American case of *E.I. du Pont de Nemours & Co. Inc.* v. *Rolfe Christopher*,[9] where the United States Court of Appeals, Fifth Circuit, rejected the argument that, for an appropriation of trade secrets to be wrongful there must be a trespass, other illegal conduct, or breach of confidential relationship. In that case the defendant was engaged in aerial industrial espionage. The Court held, applying the *Restatement of Torts* paragraph 757,[10] that a defendant could be enjoined from making use of information obtained by "improper means." "Commercial privacy must be protected from espionage which could not have been reasonably anticipated or prevented."[11]

It would be most regrettable if an English court could not reach a similar conclusion. And yet it may be inferred from the *Bernstein* case that in English law a non-trespassory act, such as the act in that case and in *du Pont de Nemours*, is an innocent act which a defendant may, at least in some circumstances, exploit. It may well be, however, that a distinction can properly be drawn between conduct which invades another's privacy (*Bernstein*) and conduct designed to purloin confidential information (*du Pont de Nemours*).

---

[8] At p. 489. The Committee on Privacy and Related Matters, Cmnd. 1102, (1990) [the Calcutt Committee] recommended (para. 6.33) that:
". . . the following three forms of physical intrusion should be criminal offences in England and Wales:
  (a) entering private property, without the consent of the lawful occupant, with intent to obtain personal information with a view to its publication;
  (b) placing a surveillance device on private property, without the consent of the lawful occupant, with intent to obtain personal information with a view to its publication; and
  (c) taking a photograph, or recording the voice, of an individual who is on private property, without his consent, with a view to its publication with intent that the individual shall be identifiable."
The Calcutt Committee also considered (para. 6.38) that it would be:
"We would, nevertheless, consider it intolerable that a victim of any of the proposed offences in *paragraph* 6.33 should have no redress against the publisher of any material so obtained. We therefore *recommend* that there should be a statutory right of action for 'anyone having a sufficient interest' (the phrase used by Lord Denning, the Master of the Rolls, in *Chief Constable of Kent* v. *V.* [1983] Q.B. 34). Such a person should be able to apply for an injunction against publication or, if the material has already been published, for damages or an account of profits."
The Calcutt Committee concluded, however, that "an overwhelming case for introducing a statutory tort of infringement of privacy has not so far been made out." But that recommendation was made "on the assumption that the improved scheme for self-regulation recommended in chapter 15 will be made to work. Should this fail, the case for a statutory tort of infringement of privacy might have to be reconsidered": see chapter 12, particularly para. 12.5.
[9] 431 F.2d 1012 (1970). (The defendants had taken, at another's instigation, aerial photographs of the plaintiff's plant, which was in the course of construction. The plaintiff sought damages and injunctive relief.)
[10] There is no comparable section in the *Restatement of Torts* 2d.
[11] At pp. 1014–1016, *per curiam* (Goldberg C.J.). *Cf. Lopez* v. *United States*, 373 U.S. 427, 450, *per* Brennan J., dissenting (1950).

"Privacy" is a personal interest which English law will protect only in exceptional circumstances.[12] "Confidential information," which is only gained by the expenditure of time and money, is in contrast an economic interest which English law is anxious to protect. The court's ultimate conclusion whether conduct is or is not "reprehensible" may, therefore, depend, not only on what a person does and why he does it, but on the nature of the interest which he infringes.

[12] See above, p. 676.

CHAPTER 36

BENEFITS ACQUIRED IN BREACH OF ANOTHER'S CONFIDENCE

1. INTRODUCTION[1]

A PERSON (the confider) imparts information in confidence (a secret) to another (the confidant). The confidant may be an employee, agent, or fiduciary of the confider, or a mere stranger; and the nature of the relationship between the parties may determine the basis of the confidant's restitutionary claim and the remedy which a court may grant. The context of the litigation is predictable: the confider's fear that the confidant will exploit confidence or the realisation that confidence has already been exploited.[2]

What is a Secret?

There are secrets which one individual may impart to another in the course of a business or personal relationship. These are *private* secrets. In contrast, there are *public* or *State* secrets which are highly sensitive and which, if revealed, may endanger the security of a nation.

Private secrets

The majority of reported cases concern private secrets. Economically, the most valuable of these are trade secrets and literary ideas. The most precious are the intimate secrets of the confider's private life.

It is impossible to define a *trade secret*.[3] "Secret processes of manufacture provide obvious examples, but innumerable other pieces of information are capable of being trade secrets, though the secrecy of some information may only be short lived."[4] It is clear that it need not be so novel that it could be patented.[5] However, the secret must represent "in some considerable degree

---

[1] Francis Gurry, *Breach of Confidence* (Clarendon Press, 1984), is a leading work: see now Allison Coleman *Legal Protection of Trade Secrets* (1992). See also The Law Commission, *Breach of Confidence*, (Law Com. No. 110), Cmnd. 8388 (criticised in Gurry, *op. cit.* Appendix II. For the social and economic justification for protecting trade secrets, see Gurry, *op. cit.* 6–12; *Kewanee Oil Corp.* v. *Bicron Corp.* 416 U.S. 470 (1974), below, p. 702.

[2] On the distinction between legal professional privilege and the law relating to confidentiality, in the context of inadvertent but involuntary disclosure by lawyers of the information relating to their clients, see *Webster* v. *James Chapman & Co.* [1989] 3 All E.R. 939; discussed in (1991) 107 L.Q.R. 99 [Newbold].

[3] *Faccenda Chicken Ltd.* v. *Fowler* [1987] Ch. 117, 138, *per curiam*, C.A.

[4] *Ibid.*

[5] Conversely, it may be a trade secret even though it could have been patented.

[the confider's] independent efforts."[6] If the "whole result" is original,[7] it is immaterial that its "separate features or ingredients"[8] have been published or that it is described as "simple."[9] Moreover, the information "must be judged in light of the usage and practices of the particular industry or trade concerned."[10]

These are necessarily general guidelines. For example, it is not easy to distinguish the trade secret which an employee must never exploit from his "know-how," the skill, knowledge and experience acquired in the course of his career, which he may exploit.[11] In determining whether information is a trade secret the court may take into account a number of factors: the nature of the employment and the duties of the employee; the nature of the information itself; whether the employer impressed upon the employee the confidentiality of the information; and "whether the information is part of a package and the remainder of the package is not confidential" so that the alleged secret cannot be separated from the know-how. The courts have also distinguished the trade secret, which has a "sufficiently high degree of confidentiality," from "information which is given to or acquired by the employee while in his employment, and [which] in particular may cover information which is only 'confidential' in the sense that an unauthorised disclosure of such information to a third party while the employment subsisted would be a clear breach of the duty of good faith."[12]

Any description of the *literary idea* must be similarly generous. It must not be trivial tittle-tattle.[13] It has been said, more positively, that "the content of the idea [must be] clearly identifiable, original, of potential commercial attractiveness and capable of being realised in actuality." But "[n]either the originality nor the quality of an idea is in any way affected by the form in which it is expressed."[14]

Information about the confider's *private life*, which is not known to the world, is certainly a secret which the law should and does protect. The submission that it does not "protect information which relates to the sexual conduct or proclivities of an individual, save to the extent that such conduct takes place between married partners," has been firmly rejected.[15] Today there "is no common view that sexual conduct of any kind between consenting adults is grossly immoral." "Only in a case where there is still a generally accepted

---

[6] *Coco v. A. N. Clark (Engineers) Ltd.* [1969] R.P.C. 41, 47–48, *per* Megarry J.
[7] *Ansell Rubber Co. Pty. Ltd. v. Allied Rubber Industries Ltd.* [1967] V.L.R. 37, 49, *per* Gowans J.: see too *Under-Water Welders & Repairers Ltd. v. Street & Longthorne* [1968] R.P.C. 498, 506–507, *per* Buckley J.
[8] *Cranleigh Precision Engineering Ltd. v. Bryant* [1966] R.P.C. 81, 89–90, *per* Roskill J.; *cf. Coco v. A. N. Clark (Engineers) Ltd.* [1969] R.P.C. 41, 47, *per* Megarry J.
[9] *Coco v. A. N. Clark (Engineers) Ltd.* [1969] R.P.C. 41, 47, *per* Megarry J.
[10] *Thomas Marshall (Exports) Ltd. v. Guinle* [1979] 1 Ch. 237, 248, *per* Megarry V.-C.
[11] *Faccenda Chicken Ltd. v. Fowler* [1987] Ch. 117.
[12] *Ibid.* at p. 136. See also *Universal Thermosensors Ltd. v. Hibben* [1992] 1 W.L.R. 840.
[13] *Coco v. A. N. Clark (Engineers) Ltd.* [1969] R.P.C. 41, 48, *per* Megarry J.
[14] *Fraser v. Thames Television Ltd.* [1984] Q.B. 44, 65–66, *per* Hirst J. (use of a new idea, orally communicated, for a TV series).
[15] *Stephens v. Avery* [1988] Ch. 449, 452, *per* Sir Nicolas Browne-Wilkinson V.-C.

moral code can the court refuse to enforce rights in such a way as to offend that generally accepted code."[16]

Public or State secrets

As will be seen,[17] an English court jealously guards public secrets. Members of the security forces are under a duty of secrecy, rather than of confidence, which embraces information which was imparted to them by another or unearthed by their own endeavours.[18] Does this duty embrace all information which is imparted or unearthed? Such is the range of governmental information that there cannot be a single rule governing the publication of such a variety of matters. However, as a generalisation, it may be said that if publication of the information should obstruct the English form of government or impede the Government's powers and functions, that information will be protected; for example, if publication would endanger national security or the Government's relations with foreign countries.[19]

Does a secret cease to be a secret if it is published to the world?

"Ideas, however unpopular or unpalatable, once released and however released into the open air of free discussion and circulations, cannot for ever be effectively proscribed as if they were a virulent disease."[20] Or as Megarry J., less dramatically, said[21]: "something which is public property and public knowledge cannot *per se* provide any foundation for proceedings for breach of confidence." That is undoubtedly the general principle. However, information will be protected if there has only been a limited disclosure, for example, to a lecture audience or to members of a trade association. In each case it is a question of degree.[22] Moreover, a court may restrain a confidant from subsequently using information if he, or possibly even a third party, is responsible for its publication.[23]

The decision of the Court of Appeal in *Schering Chemicals Ltd.* v. *Falkman Ltd.*[24] is some authority for another and larger exception to the general principle that information in the public domain loses any hall mark of confidentiality. For in that case some, if not all, of the information imparted was in law "public property."

[16] *Ibid.* at pp. 453–454.
[17] See below, p. 700.
[18] *Att.-Gen.* v. *Guardian Newspapers Ltd. and others (No. 2)* [1990] 1 A.C. 109, 144, *per* Scott J.
[19] *Att.-Gen.* v. *Jonathan Cape Ltd.* [1976] 1 Q.B. 752, 770–771, *per* Lord Widgery C.J.
[20] *Att.-Gen.* v. *Guardian Newspapers Ltd.* [1987] 1 W.L.R. 1248, 1321, *per* Lord Oliver.
[21] *Coco* v. *A. N. Clark (Engineers) Ltd.* [1969] R.P.C. 41, 47, *per* Megarry J., citing *Saltman Engineering Co. Ltd.* v. *Campbell Engineering Co. Ltd.* (1948) 65 R.P.C. 203, 215, *per* Lord Green M.R.
[22] *Franchi* v. *Franchi* [1967] R.P.C. 149, 152–153, *per* Cross J. *Cf.* Restatement of Torts, § 757, discussed in *Ansell Rubber Co. Pty. Ltd.* v. *Allied Rubber Industries Pty. Ltd.* [1972] R.P.C. 811, 825–826: *cf.* below, p. 687.
[23] See below, pp. 689–690.
[24] [1982] Q.B. 1.

The plaintiffs had entered into a contract with Falkman, whereby Falkman agreed to train executives to defend the plaintiffs against criticism of their marketing, and application of, a pregnancy testing drug which had now been withdrawn from the market. The plaintiffs provided Falkman with detailed information about the drug, telling Falkman of "any doubts expressed in any quarter, internal or external, as to its use as a hormone pregnancy test." Falkman expressly agreed to preserve its confidentiality. Falkman recruited Elstein who was experienced in television journalism; and Elstein in turn acquired from Falkman's training courses most, if not all, of the same information. Within a month Elstein (who denied any knowledge of Falkman's promise of confidentiality) had approached a TV company with a proposal for a documentary "based largely on my memory of the courses." Elstein and the TV company asked the plaintiffs to cooperate in the production. The plaintiffs finally refused to do so, and sought an injunction to prevent the showing of the TV film.[25] The Court of Appeal, Lord Denning M.R. dissenting, granted an interlocutory injunction until the trial. Templeman L.J. concluded that when Elstein agreed to take part in Falkman's training programmes he impliedly promised[26] the plaintiffs not to use the information, whether confidential or not, for the very purpose which the plaintiffs sought to avoid, namely bad publicity in the future.[27] Republication of information critical of the plaintiffs would always be unwelcome. Shaw L.J. did not, however, base his judgment on the ground that Elstein had either expressly or impliedly promised the plaintiffs not to publicise information received from Falkman. Elstein was in a position of trust and had abused that trust. In his view it was cynical, if not specious, to argue that Elstein was not bound by any bond of confidence simply because the information was in the public domain.

> "Even in the commercial field, ethics and good faith are not to be regarded as merely opportunist or expedient. In any case, though facts may be widely known, they are not ever-present in the minds of the public. To extend the knowledge or to revive the recollection of matters which may be detrimental or prejudicial to the interests of some person or organisation is not to be condoned because the facts are already known to some and linger in the memory of others."[28]

---

[25] Falkman did not contest that the information supplied by the plaintiffs should be kept confidential. It was conceded that the television company was in the same position as Elstein.

[26] It was a triable issue whether he had made an express promise.

[27] At pp. 36–37.

[28] At p. 28. In *Allen-Qualley* v. *Shellmar Products Co.* 31 F. 2d 293 (1929), re-hearing denied, 87 F. 2d 104 (1936) (CCA 7th), the plaintiff disclosed in confidence to the defendant details of a machine to make candy wraps. Neither party knew that a patent had been issued to a third party, and that this patent had anticipated the plaintiff's apparent trade secret. The defendant, in consequence of what the plaintiff told him, searched the patent register, learnt of the patent and bought it from the third party. He was ordered to assign the patent to the plaintiff, on payment of the purchase price, and enjoined from making, using, or selling wraps made by the patented process. The defendant had abused his position of trust and confidence; it was not necessary to find a binding contract. In language which anticipated Shaw L.J.'s, in *Schering Chemicals Ltd.* v. *Falkman Ltd.*, the Circuit Court of Appeals for the Seventh Circuit said: "If men in the

The majority judgments in *Schering Chemical* case have been criticised. In *Att.-Gen.* v. *Guardian Newspapers* Lord Oliver qualified Shaw L.J.'s generous principle.[29] He agreed that, "even where the very information sought to be used has previously been made public, there may be circumstances in which the recipient, by contract or conduct, comes under a fiduciary obligation to refrain from unauthorised republication ... [But,] in so far as the majority judgments suggest that, apart from direct obligation or complicity in the breach of a direct obligation, information in the public domain can be the subject matter of a claim for breach of confidence ... I would, for my part, prefer the powerful dissenting judgment of Lord Denning M.R." [30] If this qualification of *Schering* is accepted, then a court will have to determine whether the confidant or a third party is under a fiduciary obligation not to republish information which is in the public domain. If there is an existing fiduciary relationship, that question is easily answered; the confider will be granted the equitable remedy which he seeks. But if it is only contract which binds the confider and the original confidant, then that contract will not normally create a "fiduciary obligation." Consequently, a court will not then enjoin the confidant or any third party from republishing the information imparted.[31]

2. THE BASIS AND SCOPE OF THE RESTITUTIONARY CLAIM

A confider may seek a remedy against his immediate confidant or against a third party who was given or bought the information which the confidant had imparted. The particular remedy which he seeks may determine the ground of his restitutionary claim.

In many situations the confidant will have, expressly or impliedly, contracted to preserve the confidentiality of the information imparted. An employee who has been told a trade secret may well be in such a position.[32] But

---

business world are to respect the rights of others, if we are to insist upon morality in commercial dealings, if honesty is to prevail in commercial intercourse between citizens, a court of equity must put the stamp of disapproval upon what defendant has done here,": at p. 296, *per* Judge Lindley.

[29] [1987] 1 W.L.R. 1248, 1319.

[30] *Ibid. Cf. Att.-Gen.* v. *Guardian Newspapers Ltd.* [1987] 1 W.L.R. 1248, 1263, *per* Browne-Wilkinson V.-C. See also *Att.-Gen.* v. *Guardian Newspapers (No. 2)* [1990] 1 A.C. 109, 177, *per* Donaldson M.R.: "if the confider is ... the source of the confidant's knowledge, the law may confer a right of confidentiality unless and until the information is acquired by the confidant from other sources."

[31] But *cf.* the broader dicta of Sir Nicholas Browne-Wilkinson V.-C. in the court below: is the duty of confidentiality enforceable by injunction notwithstanding that the information is in the public domain, in particular, has there been a breach of contract (enforceable by injunction) or a participation in a breach of trust?: [1987] 1 W.L.R. 1248, 1264.

[32] *United Sterling Corp. Ltd.* v. *Felton and Mannion* [1974] R.P.C. 162, 167, *per* Brightman J.; *Reid & Sigrist Ltd.* v. *Moss & Mechanism Ltd.* (1932) 49 R.P.C. 461, 481, *per* Luxmoore J.; *Faccenda Chicken Ltd.* v. *Fowler* [1987] Ch. 117, C.A. (see above, p. 679). *Cf. Lamb* v. *Evans* [1893] 1 Ch. 218; Partnership Act 1890, s.29. The existence of an obligation at common law may not exclude an obligation in equity: see *Ackroyds (London) Ltd.* v. *Islington Plastics Ltd.* [1962] R.P.C. 97; Gurry, *op. cit.* pp. 39–46. Conversely, it does not follow that an employee who improperly works for another must disclose to his employer confidential information obtained from that other: *cf.*

in others it will be difficult, if not impossible, to spell out a contract[33]; for example, the confidant may have received the information in the course of tentative negotiations which subsequently collapsed or a third person may have received the information from the confidant but not the confider.[34]

It has been said that confidential information is property; confiders own their ideas.[35] In the *Spycatcher* case, Sir Nicolas Browne-Wilkinson V.-C.'s analysis was similarly "in the traditional terms of equitable rights over property"; for the personal obligation of confidence could give rise "to a property right, *i.e.* an equitable interest in the property in relation to which the duty exists."[36] Certainly, the courts have, in some contexts, said that confidential information is "property"; a trade secret can form the subject-matter of a trust, it can be sold or assigned, and it passes to the owner's trustee in bankruptcy[37]; and it also has been characterised as "property" to protect the owner from predatory and surreptitious raids of strangers.[38] But to categorise information as property does not necessarily satisfactorily solve such complex questions as the scope of the liability of a confidant or a third person to make restitution or whether bona fide purchase is a good defence to the restitutionary claim of the confider.

Most judges have been more ready to find the basis of the restitutionary claim in a broad principle of equity. As Lord Denning said, in *Seager* v. *Copydex Ltd.*,[39] in a much quoted passage[40]:

> "The law on this subject . . . depends on the broad principle of equity that he who has received information in confidence shall not take unfair advantage of it. He must not make use of it to the prejudice of him who gave it without obtaining his consent."

This principle is sufficiently generous to impose a duty of good faith on a confidant who received information from the confider but who was not bound by any contractual obligation to keep that information secret. For example, the confidant may have been a person who had entered into abortive negotiations

---

North & South Trust Co. v. *Berkeley* [1971] 1 W.L.R. 470; *Kelly* v. *Cooper* [1992] 3 W.L.R. 936, P.C.

[33] *Schering Chemicals Ltd.* v. *Falkman Ltd.* [1982] Q.B. 1: see above, p. 681.

[34] *Seager* v. *Copydex Ltd.* [1967] 1 W.L.R. 923, C.A., see below, p. 692.

[35] *e.g. Dean* v. *Macdowell* (1878) 8 Ch.D. 345, 354, *per* Cotton L.J.; *Aas* v. *Benham* [1891] 2 Ch. 244, 258, *per* Bowen L.J.; *Boardman* v. *Phipps* [1967] 2 A.C. 46, 107, *per* Lord Hodson, 115, *per* Lord Guest.

[36] *Att.-Gen.* v. *Guardian Newspapers Ltd.* [1987] 1 W.L.R. 1248, 1264.

[37] See, *e.g. Green* v. *Folgham* (1823) 1 Sim. & Stu. 398; *Bryson* v. *Whitehead* (1823) 1 Sim. & Stu. 74; *Re Keene* [1922] 2 Ch. 475.

[38] *Exchange Telegraph Co. Ltd.* v. *Howard* (1906) 22 T.L.R. 375, *per* Buckley J. *Cf.* above, p. 663.

[39] [1967] 1 W.L.R. 923. See also the Court of Appeal's decision in *Saltman Engineering Co. Ltd.* v. *Campbell Engineering Co. Ltd.* (1948) 65 R.P.C. 20, 216, *per* Lord Greene M.R.

[40] At p. 931. See also *Boardman* v. *Phipps* [1967] 2 A.C. 46, 127, *per* Lord Upjohn; and *cf.* p. 103, *per* Lord Cohen; *Att.-Gen.* v. *Guardian Newspapers Ltd.* (*No. 2*) [1990] 1 A.C. 109; *Moorgate Tobacco Co.* v. *Philip Morris Ltd.* (1984) 56 A.L.R. 193 (H. Ct. of Aust.). *Fraser* v. *Evans* [1969] 1 Q.B. 349, 362, *per* Lord Denning M.R.

with the confider. Indeed a third party to whom the confidant had given the information may, in some circumstances, be similarly bound.[41]

Broad though the principle is it leaves unresolved a number of questions. Prominent among these is whether a confidant or a third party is deemed to owe a duty of confidence if he did not realise and could not, as a reasonable man, have realised that, in using the information, he was acting "to the prejudice of him who gave it." There is no reported decision which so holds. But dicta suggest that he will owe an equitable duty of confidence if he ought to have known that the information was being given to him in confidence.[42] Once that duty exists, it would appear that his liability is a strict one; he is then in breach of that duty if he unconsciously exploits the secret.[43] However, as will be seen, the defendant's honesty may be material in determining what is the appropriate remedy and whether he can successfully plead the defences of bona fide purchase and change of position.[44]

It is also questionable whether Lord Denning's principle is wide enough to include "certain situations, beloved of law teachers, where an obviously confidential document is wafted by an electric fan out of a window into a crowded street or when an obviously confidential document, such as a private diary, is dropped in a public place, and then picked up by a passer-by." In the *Spycatcher* case Lord Goff concluded, *obiter*, that the passer-by may not be free to use the information in the document or diary. He said[45]:

> "I start with the broad general principle (which I do not intend in any way to be definitive) that a duty of confidence arises when confidential information comes to the knowledge of a person (the confidant) in circumstances where he has notice, or is held to have agreed, that the information is confidential, with the effect that it would be just in all the circumstances that he should be precluded from disclosing the information to others. I have used the word 'notice' advisedly, in order to avoid the (here unnecessary) question of the extent to which actual knowledge is necessary; though I of course understand knowledge to include circumstances where the confidant has deliberately closed his eyes to the obvious."

These examples are distinguishable from the situation where a stranger by chance overhears a confidential conversation; he is then in no position to close his ears to what he hears. The confider is the victim of his own carelessness.

---

[41] As in *Seager* v. *Copydex*, see below, p. 692.
[42] *Coco* v. *A. N. Clark (Engineers) Ltd.* [1969] R.P.C. 41, 48, *per* Megarry J. See also *Yates Circuit Foil Co.* v. *Electrofoils Ltd.* [1976] F.S.R. 345, 380, *per* Whitford J.; *G. D. Searle & Co., Ltd.* v. *Celltech Ltd.* [1982] F.S.R. 92, 108, *per* Brightman L.J. *Cf. Stevenson, Jordan & Harrisons Ltd.* v. *MacDonald & Evans* (1951) 68 R.P.C. 190, 195, *per* Lloyd-Jacob J.; *Printers & Finishers Ltd.* v. *Holloway* [1965] R.P.C. 239, 252, *per* Cross J. The argument, that a confidant acts innocently if he could not have known that he was breaking confidence, was not apparently pressed in *Seager* v. *Copydex Ltd.* [1967] 1 W.L.R. 923; see (1970) 86 L.Q.R. 463, 475–477 [Jones]; Gurry, *op. cit.* pp. 115 *et seq.*
[43] See below, p. 692.
[44] See below, Chap. 40.
[45] *Att.-Gen.* v. *Guardian Newspapers Ltd. (No. 2)* [1990] 1 A.C. 109, 281.

There will be, of course, difficult borderline cases; for example, if the fluttering letter is not "obviously confidential" but its reader realises that it contains confidential information.[46]

3. REMEDIES

It is only the confider who may seek a remedy for breach of confidence; for that reason a third party cannot restrain the defendant from publishing confidential information which he had gathered as D's consultant.[47] If the confider can establish a breach of confidence, then he may seek an injunction, an order requiring the delivery up or destruction of materials and documents, an *Anton Piller* order, an accounting of profits or a *quantum meruit*, or damages for loss suffered. Moreover, he may go further and ask the court to hold that the confidant is a constructive trustee of identifiable assets or to impose a lien over those assets.

The confider may seek more than one remedy: for example, an injunction, an order for delivery up or destruction, an *Anton Piller* order *and* a monetary award. But he may on occasion have to elect his remedy; he cannot be awarded both an accounting of profits and damages for the confidant's breach of his duty of confidence.[48]

(a) *Injunction*

The well-known principles established by the House of Lords in the *American Cyanimid* case[49]; whether the plaintiff can show a good arguable case, whether the defendant would be adequately compensated by an award of damages if the injunction was improvidently granted, whether the plaintiff would be similarly protected if it were denied, and where the balance of convenience lies in granting an injunction, will determine whether a confider will be granted an

---

[46] It is also implicit in Lord Denning's principle that the confidant must "receive the information in confidence." Consequently, the "little man" who spontaneously writes to a company giving it his new idea for a washing powder may fail in his claim for restitution on the ground that he acted officiously. However, a court may be persuaded to conclude that, if the company which received the information used it knowing that its informant expected some payment if it were used, then it could be said to have impliedly agreed to pay for the information or to have freely accepted the services, knowing that the informant expected payment. *Cf. Johnson* v. *Heat and Air Systems Ltd.* (1941) 58 R.P.C. 229 (contract implied in fact.) Recovery has been allowed in some American jurisdictions in circumstances where it was open to the defendant to accept or reject the benefit. Having used the idea, he was said to have freely accepted the idea, knowing that payment was expected for its use. The plaintiff has also recovered on the ground that the defendant has "appropriated" the plaintiff's property right in the idea. Palmer, *op. cit.* Vol. II, § 10. 11 discusses the cases.

[47] *Fraser* v. *Evans* [1969] 1 Q.B. 349.

[48] *Neilson* v. *Betts* (1870) L.R. 5 H.L. 1, 22, *per* Lord Westbury; *Peter Pan Manufacturing Corp.* v. *Corsets Silhouette Ltd.* [1963] R.P.C. 45, 58, *per* Pennycuick J. *Cf. Lewis Trusts* v. *Bambers Stores Ltd.* [1983] F.S.R. 453, 459–460 (damages for conversion and for breach of copyright). *Semble* the election is not final until judgment: *cf. United Australia Ltd.* v. *Barclays Bank Ltd.* [1941] A.C. 1; see below, p. 732.

[49] *American Cyanimid Co.* v. *Ethicon Ltd.* [1975] A.C. 396.

interlocutory injunction.[50] However, if an interlocutory motion will have the effect of finally disposing of the matter, then a court "may require a plaintiff to do more than prove that there is a serious question to be tried."[51] In determining whether damages would adequately compensate the plaintiff, a court may take into account such factors as his position in the market, whether he was seeking the injunction in respect of misuse which had already occurred or against any further misuse,[52] and whether the secret is a mere idea or is already embodied in a marketed secret. The nature of the information is also critical; for example, personal secrets, if published, may cause the plaintiff uncompensatable damage.[53] The impact of an injunction on the defendant's business enterprise is another factor of particular significance; if it would put an end to his business, a court will be reluctant to grant interlocutory relief.[54]

It is said that a final injunction will not be awarded if damages are an adequate remedy. But courts do not normally hesitate to enjoin wrongdoers, and a dishonest confidant can certainly be so described. So if a confidant consciously exploits a trade secret an injunction will normally be granted unless the information has contributed only minimally to the success of his operations.[55] If the confidant acted honestly but unwittingly betrayed confidence, the confider may be denied an injunction, at least if the secret was only one of many ideas used by the confidant in developing a product which had been extensively marketed.[56] An injunction may also be denied if the parties have acted on the assumption that the "fruits of any confidential information were to sound in monetary compensation to the communicator." As Megarry J. once said[57]:

"If the duty is a duty not to use the information without consent, then it may be the proper subject of an injunction restraining its use, even if there is an offer to pay a reasonable sum for that use. If, on the other hand, the duty is merely a duty not to use the information without paying a reasonable sum for it, then no such injunction should be granted."

Similar principles should determine whether a literary idea is protected by an injunction. But he who reveals the secrets of his private life may suffer no financial harm from their publication; it may show "him in a favourable light

[50] *Lawrence David Ltd.* v. *Ashton* [1991] 1 All E.R. 385.
[51] See Gurry, *op. cit.* pp. 385 *et seq.* for the case law.
[52] *Universal Thermosensors Ltd.* v. *Hibben* [1992] 1 W.L.R. 840. The injunction will be denied if it is sought in respect of misuse which has already occurred.
[53] *Duchess of Argyll* v. *Duke of Argyll* [1967] Ch. 302.
[54] Gurry, *op. cit.* p. 406.
[55] See, generally, *Printers & Finishers Ltd.* v. *Holloway* [1965] R.P.C. 239; *Cranleigh Precision Engineering Ltd.* v. *Bryant* [1966] R.P.C. 81; *Duchess of Argyll* v. *Duke of Argyll* [1967] Ch. 302; *Distillers' Co. Ltd.* v. *Times Newspapers Ltd.* [1975] 1 Q.B. 613, 621, *per* Talbot J.
[56] *Seager* v. *Copydex Ltd.* [1967] 1 W.L.R. 923, [1969] 1 W.L.R. 809, see below, pp. 692–694.
[57] *Coco* v. *A. N. Clark (Engineers) Ltd.* [1969] R.P.C. 41, 50, *per* Megarry J., (a case where the confidant had acted honestly). *Cf.* (1975) 6 International Review of Industrial Property and Copyright Law 43 [Cornish].

but [may] gravely injure some relation or friend of his whom he wishes to protect."[58] Most people would regard the details of their and their intimates' sexual life as "high on their list of those matters which they regard as confidential,"[59] and would endorse Lord Keith's dictum that it is sufficient detriment if confidential information is disclosed to persons whom the confider "would prefer not to know of it."[60]

There has been much debate whether an injunction should be discharged if the confidential information ceases to be confidential.[61] It is clear that if the disclosure to the world is the act of the confider, then the confidant is discharged from his duty of confidence.[62] But what if it is a third party who discloses the information? At one time it was thought, on the authority of *Cranleigh Precision Engineering Ltd.* v. *Bryant*,[63] that the confidant may still be bound by the bond of confidence; but Lord Goff has recently doubted whether that decision supports so wide a proposition.[64] However, in the *Spycatcher* case the majority of the House of Lords were prepared perpetually to enjoin the confidant,[65] Mr. Wright, who had disclosed State secrets. The secrets were State secrets, and Mr. Wright had grossly betrayed Her Majesty's trust. Lord Goff alone concluded that once the "subject-matter is gone . . . the obligation is therefore also gone; all that is left is the remedy or remedies for breach of the obligation."[66]

The significance of private secrets once published, may not become immediately apparent to persons who learn of it. In contrast, the confidant is under no such disadvantage. If he is not perpetually enjoined, he may nonetheless be enjoined for a period of time which will prevent him using the secret as a "spring board" to get a "head start" over the world.[67] But the injunction should not extend beyond the period of time for which the advantage might reasonably be expected to continue; once the secret has been fully disclosed, there is no further reason to enjoin the erstwhile confidant.[68]

---

[58] *Coco* v. *A. N. Clark (Engineers) Ltd.* [1969] R.P.C. 41, 48, *per* Megarry J. *Cf.* the same judge's observations in *Thomas Marshall (Exports) Ltd.* v. *Guinle* [1979] 1 Ch. 237, 248.

[59] *Stephens* v. *Avery* [1988] Ch. 449, 454, *per* Browne-Wilkinson V.-C.

[60] *Att.-Gen.* v. *Guardian Newspapers Ltd. (No. 2)* [1990] 1 A.C. 109, 255–256.

[61] *Cf.* above, pp. 681–683, discussing the situation where the information disclosed was already in the public domain.

[62] *O. Mustad & Son* v. *Allcock and Dosen (1928)* [1963] R.P.C. 41.

[63] [1966] R.P.C. 81. *Cf. Speed Seal Products Ltd.* v. *Paddington* [1985] 1 W.L.R. 1327, C.A., where the confidant disclosed the secret.

[64] *Att.-Gen.* v. *Guardian Newspapers Ltd. (No. 2)* [1990] 1 A.C. 109, 285–287. See also Gurry, *op. cit.* pp. 245–252.

[65] *Att.-Gen.* v. *Guardian Newspapers Ltd. (No. 2)* [1990] 1 A.C. 109, 259.

[66] *Att.-Gen.* v. *Guardian Newspapers Ltd. (No. 2)* [1990] 1 A.C. 109, 287.

[67] *Terrapin Ltd.* v. *Builders' Supply Co. (Hayes) Ltd.* [1960] R.P.C. 128, 130, *per* Roxburgh J.; *Cranleigh Precision Engineering Ltd.* v. *Bryant* [1966] R.P.C. 81, 97, *per* Roskill J. But *cf. Potters-Ballotini* v. *Weston-Baker* [1979] R.P.C. 202, 206–207, *per* Lord Denning M.R.; *Harrison* v. *Project and Design Co. (Redcar) Ltd.* [1978] F.S.R. 81.

[68] Gurry, *op. cit.* pp. 245–252.

There are dicta which suggest that a confider must also show that he has suffered some detriment before an injunction is granted.[69] But the better view is that it is "sufficient detriment to the confider that information given in confidence is to be disclosed to persons whom he would prefer not to know of it, even though the disclosure would not be harmful to him in any positive way."[70]

Whether the injunction sought be interlocutory or final, the confider must be able to identify "with particularity the trade secret or similar confidential information to which he lays claim. The terms of any injunction must also be capable of being framed in sufficient detail to enable the defendant to know exactly what information he is not free to use."[71] It is because of the difficulty of drawing the line between information which is confidential and information which is not that employers take from employees covenants not to work for a competitor for a limited time after their employment has ceased.[72]

(b) Delivery Up or Destruction of Materials and Documents: and Anton Piller Orders

It is not uncommon for a court to order a confidant, often an employee, to deliver up the confider's documents to his solicitor or, if the documents are the confidant's but may provide evidence against him, to allow the confider's solicitor to take copies of them. A court may also require an undertaking that documents are preserved pending further order.

There are also cases in the reports where the court has ordered the destruction of documents (for example, copies of confidential documents) or of products or machinery embodying confidential information. This is a socially wasteful remedy which, for that reason, will not be readily granted.[73] The dishonest confidant may be treated less indulgently, but even he may escape this sanction if he can show that the secret did not contribute significantly to the manufactured article or product.[74]

The courts now recognise that *Anton Piller* orders, which are granted *ex parte* and which enable a confider to invade the sanctity of the confidant's home and to seize his documents and chattels, smack of Star Chamber justice and should

---

[69] *Att.-Gen.* v. *Guardian Newspapers Ltd. (No. 2)* [1990] 1 A.C. 109, 270, *per* Lord Griffiths. *Cf.* Lord Goff at p. 282 (who considered that it may not always be necessary).

[70] *Ibid.* at p. 256, *per* Lord Keith. It is true that the context of this observation was a state secret; and in such a case the harm to the national interest can hardly be said to be pecuniary. But, in our view, it is commendable as a general principle.

[71] *Lock International plc* v. *Beswick* [1989] 1 W.L.R. 1268, 1274, *per* Hoffmann J. See also *Lawrence David Ltd.* v. *Ashton* [1991] 1 All E.R., 385, 393, *per* Balcombe L.J.; *Littlewoods Organisation Ltd.* v. *Harris* [1977] 1 W.L.R. 1472, 1479, *per* Lord Denning M.R.

[72] For the consequences of the distinction between the protection of confidence and the protection of information protected by a negative covenant not to publish, see *Att.-Gen.* v. *Barker* [1990] 3 All E.R. 257, C.A.

[73] *Saltman Engineering Co. Ltd.* v. *Campbell Engineering Co. Ltd.* (1948) 65 R.P.C. 203, 219, *per curiam*.

[74] Gurry, *op. cit.* Chap. XXI discusses the cases, which include: *Prince Albert* v. *Strange* (1849) 2 De Gex & Sm. 652; *Reid and Sigrist Ltd.* v. *Moss and Mechanism Ltd.* (1932) 49 R.P.C. 461.

be granted only in exceptional circumstances, where there is a "paramount need" to do so.[75] In trade secret litigation employers have used them "to launch a pre-emptive strike to crush the unhatched competition in the egg by causing severe strains on the financial and management resources of the defendants or even a withdrawal of financial support."[76] Indeed even if it can be shown that the defendant acted dishonestly, an *Anton Piller* order may still be refused; for there must be "a *proportionality* between the perceived threat to the plaintiff's rights and the remedy granted."[76a]

(c) *Monetary Awards*

An account of profits or a quantum meruit claim

A confider may ask not only for an injunction but for an account of profits made from the use of the confidential information, or a sum which represents the reasonable value of the information which has been imparted.

"The purpose of ordering an account of profits . . . is to prevent an unjust enrichment."[77] It appears that the court has discretion whether or not to order an accounting of profits,[78] which is a difficult, laborious and expensive operation.[79] A confider will seek this remedy if he has suffered little or no damage.[80] But it is not entirely clear when an account will be considered appropriate. If a confidant has consciously broken confidence and if the information has materially contributed to the confidant's profits, an account may be ordered.[81] Conversely, the court has refused to order a confidant, who acted honestly but foolishly and did not realise that he was breaking the confider's confidence, to account for his profits.[82] It is undesirable to elevate this distinction into a hard and fast rule.[83] For example, a court may consider the plaintiff's economic interests deserve the protection which an accounting of profits affords, even though the defendant did not consciously break confidence.[84]

---

[75] *Columbia Pictures Industries Inc.* v. *Robinson* [1987] Ch. 38, 69–76, *per* Scott J.; *Lock International plc* v. *Beswick* [1989] 1 W.L.R. 1268; *Universal Thermosensors Ltd.* v. *Hibben* [1992] 1 W.L.R. 840.

[76] *Lock International plc* v. *Beswick* [1989] 1 W.L.R. 1268, 1281, *per* Hoffman J.

[76a] *Ibid.*

[77] *My Kinda Town Ltd.* v. *Soll* [1982] F.S.R. 147, 156, *per* Slade J. (where the claim was for passing off); revs'd [1983] R.P.C. 407, C.A. (no passing off).

[78] *Seager* v. *Copydex Ltd.* [1967] 1 W.L.R. 923, 932, *per* Lord Denning M.R.

[79] *Cf. Siddell* v. *Vickers* (1892) 9 R.P.C. 152, 162–163, *per* Lindley L.J.; *cf.* above p. 28. For a discussion of the American cases describing the various methods of taking an account, see 72 North Western U.L.R. 1004, 1020–1022 (1978).

[80] This possibility was not considered by the court in *Woodward* v. *Hutchins* [1977] Q.B. 752, which was, however, only an application for an interlocutory injunction.

[81] *Peter Pan Manufacturing Corp.* v. *Corsets Silhouette Ltd.* [1964] 1 W.L.R. 96, followed in *A.B. Consolidated Ltd.* v. *Europe Strength Food Co. Pty. Ltd.* [1978] 2 N.Z.L.R. 515.

[82] *Seager* v. *Copydex Ltd.* [1967] 1 W.L.R. 923, 932, where the mistake may have been one of mixed fact and law; *cf.* pp. 931 and 932.

[83] See above, pp. 32–34.

[84] Contrast Copyright Designs and Patents Act 1988, ss.97 and 233; Patents Act 1977, s.62(1); and *A. E. Spalding & Bros. Ltd.* v. *A. W. Gamage Ltd.* (1915) 32 R.P.C. 273, 283, *per* Lord Parker of Waddington.

It has been said that the court will "ordinarily direct the account in a form wide enough to include all profits made by the defendant from his tortious acts or breaches of confidence."[85] If the defendant's profits are attributable solely to his use of the plaintiff's confidential information, then he must disgorge all those profits. So, in *Peter Pan Manufacturing Corporation* v. *Corsets Silhouette Ltd.*,[86] the defendant was required to account for a sum which was the difference between his receipts from the sale of brassieres, made from the plaintiff's designs, and the cost of manufacturing the goods. The accounting becomes much more difficult if it is evident that some of the defendant's profits are attributable to his own efforts and ideas as well as to his use of the plaintiff's confidential information.[87] But difficulty and expense should not of themselves be allowed to defeat the plaintiff's claim for an accounting.[88] It is proper that the burden should be on the confidant to show what proportion of the profits is attributable to factors other than the use of the confidential information.[89] But, in many cases, "this is obviously a matter which cannot be determined by mathematical calculation or with absolute accuracy. At best, the result can only be an approximation."[90] The confider should sue as soon as he knows of the breach of confidence; he should not be allowed to stand by and permit the confidant to make his profits for him.[91]

We have discussed earlier in this book what deductions a wrongdoer, such as a dishonest confidant,[92] can claim. What are *net* profits may not be easy to determine. For example, in the *Spycatcher* case,[93] it is debatable whether the net profits were all the net profits made by *The Sunday Times* from the issue which contained the extract from *Spycatcher*, or only the percentage of profits attributable to the increased circulation of that issue in consequence of the publication of the extract from Mr. Wright's book.[94]

---

[85] *My Kinda Town* v. *Soll* [1982] F.S.R. 147, 154, *per* Slade J., who discusses the authorities in the context of a passing-off claim (reversed on the ground that there was no passing off, in [1983] R.P.C. 407).

[86] [1963] R.P.C. 45, followed in *House of Spring Gardens Ltd.* v. *Point Blank Ltd.* [1983] R.P.C. 489 (High Court of Ireland).

[87] The difficulties are described in *Siddell* v. *Vickers* (1892) 9 R.P.C. 152, 162–163, *per* Lindley L.J. *Cf.* Oliver L.J.'s observations on the form of the account ordered by Slade J. in *My Kinda Town Ltd.* v. *Soll* [1983] R.P.C. 407, 432, C.A.; *reversing* [1983] R.P.C. 15, [1982] F.S.R. 147.

[88] *Cf. Chaplin* v. *Hicks* [1911] 2 K.B. 786. (A court must award damages even if assessment is difficult.)

[89] *Cf. Peter Pan Manufacturing Corp.* v. *Corsets Silhouette Ltd.* [1964] 1 W.L.R. 96, 108–109, *per* Pennycuick J.; *cf.* above, pp. 32–34 and 86.

[90] *Watson, Laidlow & Co. Ltd.* v. *Pott, Cassels and Williamson* (1914) 31 R.P.C. 104, 114, *per* Lord Atkinson; *cf. Sheldon* v. *M.G.M. Pictures Corp.* 309 U.S. 390, 408, *per* Hughes C.J. (1940); *Duplate Corp.* v. *Triplex Safety Glass Co.*, 298 U.S. 448, at 456–458 (1935); *cf.* the cases on restitutionary claims arising from tortious acts, below, Chap. 38.

[91] *Cf. Beard* v. *Turner* (1866) 13 L.T.(N.S.) 746, 750, *per* Wood V.-C. (a trade mark case); *Electrolux Ltd.* v. *Electrix Ltd.* (1953) 70 R.P.C. 158.

[92] See below, pp. 32–34.

[93] *Att.-Gen.* v. *Guardian Newspapers Ltd. (No. 2)* [1990] 1 A.C. 109.

[94] For a discussion, see [1989] C.L.P. 49, 55–60 [Jones].

Instead of an account, a confider may elect to recover the reasonable value of the information imparted.[95] Whether a confider so elects, as distinct from seeking an account of profits, will depend on whether a *quantum meruit* award is a more attractive remedy; for example, if the defendant has earned little or no profits, or on the particular facts an accounting is peculiarly complicated and protracted. However, it appears from *Seager* v. *Copydex Ltd.*,[96] that the court has a discretion,[97] if the confidant has acted honestly, to limit the confider's claim to the market value of the information imparted. In that case the plaintiff told the defendant's employees about his idea[98] for a new type of carpet grip. The defendant subsequently developed a similar grip but unwittingly made use of the plaintiff's ideas. The Court of Appeal refused to order an account of profits, but held that the defendant could not make use of the information without paying for it. Although the Court accepted that the basis of the plaintiffs' claim was the defendant's breach of his equitable duty of confidence, it also accepted the analogy of the law of conversion of goods and concluded that damages should be awarded calculated by the market value of the information imparted, and that, once the damages were assessed and paid, the "confidential information belongs to [the confidant]."[99] In our view it would have been happier if the Court had rejected the analogy of the law of conversion and had instead made a *quantum meruit* award.[1] If the basis of the confider's right is not property but the confidant's equitable duty of good faith, it is not evident that the confidant must make restitution if he uses confidential information innocently, having no reason to believe that, in doing so, he is betraying another's confidence; and we have suggested that he should not be so liable.[2] Moreover, it may not be just in every case to conclude that information *belongs* to the confidant once damages are assessed and paid. For there may be circumstances where it is proper both to grant an injunction as to the future and a *quantum meruit* claim for the value of the benefits conferred during the time when the confidant was not enjoined.[3] Whether an injunction should or should not be granted is a question which is independent of whether there should be a *quantum meruit* award, although its resolution may indirectly determine the amount of that award.

---

[95] For an unusual illustration, see *Materese* v. *Moore-McCormack Lines Ltd.* 158 F. 2d 631 (1946), discussed in (1970) 86 L.Q.R. 488–489 [Jones].

[96] [1967] 1 W.L.R. 923; [1969] 1 W.L.R. 809.

[97] See above, pp. 32–34.

[98] Some of the information given by plaintiff was in the public domain.

[99] [1969] 1 W.L.R. 809, 813, *per* Lord Denning M.R. See also *Universal Thermosensors Ltd.* v. *Hibben* [1992] 1 W.L.R. 840. The Vice-Chancellor awarded compensatory damages based on the "user principle."

[1] Cf. *Craven-Ellis* v. *Canons Ltd.* [1936] 2 K.B. 403, 412, *per* Greer L.J.; see above, p. 478.

[2] See above, p. 685.

[3] If the defendant had at first acted reasonably in thinking he could utilise the information, he may still be enjoined from using the information in the future. The *quantum meruit* claim may then fail; the defendant should be under no liability unless and until he knew that he was breaking confidence and, thereafter, he will be enjoined from using the information. See the authorities cited below.

Damages

Damages are awarded for the loss which the confider has suffered. How that loss is to be measured may depend, however, on the basis of the restitutionary claim. If the confidant is in breach of contract he will, as a general principle, recover his expectation loss. The burden is on him to prove that loss. And in *Universal Thermosensors Ltd.* v. *Hibben*,[4] Sir Donald Nicholls V.-C. rejected the submission that there

> "arises an irrebuttable presumption that any business resulting from the orders derives from the wrongful use of the confidential information and that the defendants are liable in damages accordingly.... Whether particular business obtained by a defendant was obtained as a result of misuse by him of a plaintiff's confidential information is essentially a question of fact in each case."[5]

But what if there is no contractual relationship between the plaintiff and the defendant? In the *Spycatcher* case[6] the House of Lords endorsed Lord Denning's principle in *Seager* v. *Copydex Ltd.*[7] that the obligation to respect confidence was an independent equitable principle; nonetheless in *Seager* the award of damages was based on the analogy of the law of conversion.

It is another question whether a court can only award expectation damages in addition to or in substitution for equitable relief or whether it now has an inherent jurisdiction in equity to do so. It can award damages in addition to or in lieu of any equitable remedy.[8] Today an English court may well award damages[9] even though it is inappropriate to grant equitable relief.[10] Indeed the Court of Appeal of New Zealand has recently said that for breach of confidence "a full range of remedies should be available, as appropriate, no matter whether they originated in common law, equity or statute."[11]

---

[4] [1992] 1 W.L.R. 840.
[5] At pp. 850–851. But the Vice-Chancellor thought, not surprisingly, that any court would view with scepticism the contention that a defendant who had chosen to use a list, stolen from the plaintiff, had already carried some of the information in his own head and that looking at that list for any particular name or names was quite superfluous and unnecessary. Moreover, any doubts and obscurities arising from the evidence are likely to be resolved against the defendant.
[6] *Att.-Gen.* v. *Guardian Newspapers Ltd.* [1990] 1 A.C. 109.
[7] [1967] 1 W.L.R. 923: see above, p. 684.
[8] *Saltman Engineering Co. Ltd.* v. *Campbell Engineering Co. Ltd.* (1948) 65 R.P.C. 203, C.A.; *Cranleigh Precision Engineering Co. Ltd.* v. *Bryant* [1966] R.P.C. 81. Gurry, *op. cit.* Chap. XXIII discusses the case law.
[9] *United Scientific Holdings Ltd.* v. *Burnley Borough Council* [1978] A.C. 904.
[10] *Nichrotherm Electrical Co. Ltd.* v. *Percy* [1956] R.P.C. 272, 279–281, *per* Harman J. The point was left open by Lord Evershed M.R. in the Court of Appeal: see [1957] R.P.C. 207, 213–214. See also *Seager* v. *Copydex Ltd. (No. 2)* [1969] 1 W.L.R. 809; see above, p. 692. But see *English* v. *Dedham Vale Properties Ltd.* [1978] 1 W.L.R. 93, 111, (where Slade J. doubted that a court has power to award damages in lieu of an account).
[11] *Acquaculture Corp.* v. *New Zealand Green Mussel Co. Ltd.,* [1990] 3 N.Z.L.R. 299, 301, *per* Cooke P., cited in (1991) 107 L.Q.R. 209, 210 [Beatson]: see also *LAC Minerals Ltd.* v. *International Resources Ltd.* (1989) 61 D.L.R. (4th) 14 (below, p. 694).

There may be concurrent liability for breach of contract and liability in tort. So, where a confidant is in breach of his contractual bond of confidence, the court may nonetheless act on the assumption that the information was the property of the confider which the confidant had converted.[12] "The general rule ... in relation to 'economic' torts is that the measure of damages is to be, so far as possible, that sum of money which will put the injured party in the same position as he would have been if he had not sustained the wrong."[13] The position of the particular confider must, however, always be considered. For example, a plaintiff manufacturer will be entitled to his lost profits if he can demonstrate that his confidant used the information to become his competitor and had thereby deprived him of those profits. But if, as in *Seager* v. *Copydex Ltd.*,[14] the confidant was content to licence another to use the information, then the measure of damages will be "the price that he could have commanded for that information."[15]

(d) *Proprietary Claims*

The confidant may be declared to be a constructive trustee of specific assets, or a lien may be imposed over those assets.[16] In determining whether to grant a proprietary remedy, the court should consider whether it is the appropriate remedy.

In particular, it should be a significant consideration that the confidant had consciously broken confidence. In *LAC Minerals Ltd.* v. *International Corona Resources Services Ltd.*[17] the Supreme Court of Canada granted a confider a proprietary remedy. La Forest J, giving the leading judgment, held that it was appropriate to impose a constructive trust over land which the confidant had bought because it had been told in confidence that the land was potentially gold bearing.[18] The circumstances were exceptional: the land was unique, damages were difficult to assess and the interests of the confider were more fully protected by a proprietary remedy. Moreover, to impose a trust over the land would deter other confidants who might be tempted to break confidence. La Forest J. concluded that the trust should be imposed simply because there was a breach of confidence; it was not necessary to find that the confidant was the confider's fiduciary. The historic division between law and equity should not impede the grant of the appropriate remedy. No English court has gone so

---

[12] *Dowson & Mason Ltd.* v. *Potter* [1986] 1 W.L.R. 1419, 1426, *per* Slade L.J.

[13] *General Tire and Rubber Co.* v. *Firestone Tyre and Rubber Co. Ltd.* [1975] 1 W.L.R. 819, 824, *per* Lord Wilberforce.

[14] [1969] 1 W.L.R. 809; see above, p. 692.

[15] *Dowson & Mason Ltd.* v. *Potter* [1986] 1 W.L.R. 1419, 1420 *per* Sir Edward Eveleigh, explaining *Seager* v. *Copydex Ltd.*

[16] See Chap. 2 above, where these arguments are fully developed.

[17] (1989) 61 D.L.R. (4th) 14; noted in [1990] L.M.C.L.Q. 4 [Davies] 460 [Birks].

[18] Lamer and Wilson JJ. concurred. McIntyre and Sopinka JJ. dissented (there was no pre-existing right of property or fiduciary relationship).

far. But there are dicta[19] which may persuade an English court to endorse the reasoning of the majority of the Supreme Court of Canada.

A court should be more reluctant to grant a proprietary remedy if the confidant has not consciously broken confidence. In any event, if he is insolvent, a court should hesitate to grant a lien over his unencumbered assets to secure a sum which represents the profits earned from his exploitation of the information, as distinct from a sum which represents the market value of the information imparted.[20]

4. DEFENCES

Bona fide purchase is not generally a defence to a personal restitutionary claim and, in particular, to one based on breach of confidence.[21] *Change of position* is a general defence to any restitutionary claim. *Disclosure in the public interest* is a defence which is particularly important in this context and its scope has, in recent years, been the subject of much litigation. A confider's claim may also fail if he has been guilty of some impropriety or of laches.

(a) *Change of Position*

English law has now accepted that change of position is a general defence to all restitutionary claims. It is a defence which is independent of the defence of estoppel and bona fide purchase.[22] A defendant who did not know and ought not to have known that he was betraying another's confidence acts honestly. He may then plead change of position. In our view, a defendant who is honest but ought to have known of the breach of confidence should also be allowed to invoke the defence.[23]

(b) *Bona Fide Purchase*

It is not at all clear from the decided cases whether bona fide purchase is a defence to a restitutionary claim based on another's breach of confidence.[24] If the basis of that claim is that the confider retains an equitable proprietary interest in the information imparted, then it should be a good defence.[25]

---

[19] *Lipkin Gorman (A Firm)* v. *Karpnale Ltd.* [1991] 2 A.C. 548, 580–581, *per* Lord Goff; *Agip (Africa) Ltd.* v. *Jackson* [1990] Ch. 265, 289, *per* Millett J.

[20] See above, pp. 93 *et seq.*

[21] But it is a defence if the plaintiff's personal claim is based on his legal title to money: see above, pp. 41–43.

[22] *Lipkin Gorman (A Firm)* v. *Karpnale Ltd.* [1991] 2 A.C. 548, H.L.: see above, p. 82 and see below, Chap. 40.

[23] See below, pp. 744–745. In *Seager* v. *Copydex Ltd.* [1969] 1 W.L.R. 809 the plaintiff may not have been granted an injunction or an account of profits because the honest defendant had spent money in marketing the carpet grip: see below, p. 692.

[24] *Hubbard* v. *Vosper* [1972] 2 Q.B. 84 and *Church of Scientology* v. *Kaufman* [1973] R.P.C. 627, discussed by Gurry, *op. cit.* pp. 353–357. See also (1985) 5 I.P.R. 353, 385.

[25] *Morrison* v. *Moat* (1851) 9 Hare 241, 263, *per* Turner V.-C.; *Printers and Finishers Ltd.* v. *Holloway* [1965] R.P.C. 239, 253, *per* Cross J. (*semble*): Cf. *Stewart* v. *Hook*, 45 S.E. 369, 370, *per* Candler J. (1903); *Homer* v. *Crown Cork & Seal Co. of Baltimore City*, 141 A. 425, 431, *per* Parke J. (1928); *Lamont Carliss & Co.* v. *Bonnie Blend Chocolate Corp.*, 238 N.Y.S. 78 (1929),

However, if the law on the subject depends, as it appears to depend, on the broad principle of equity that he who has received information in confidence shall not take unfair advantage of it,[26] then bona fide purchase should not be a defence. It is only a defence to a personal claim which is based on the plaintiff's title to money.[27] But is bona fide purchase a change of position which defeats such a claim? A court may reach a number of different conclusions, depending on whether it wishes to protect a bona fide purchaser in these circumstances. For example, it may enjoin the bona fide purchaser from using the secret, but impose a term that the plaintiff reimburses him the purchase price; if it denies an injunction, it may require the purchaser to pay the plaintiff the difference between the reasonable value of the information imparted and the purchase price. A more radical conclusion is that bona fide purchase is never a change of position which renders it inequitable to grant restitution, for the purchaser has his personal claim against the confidant who sold the information to him.[28] In our tentative view, this conclusion would endanger the certainty and sanctity of commercial transactions, and should be rejected.

(c) *Disclosure in the Public Interest*[29]

The confidant's duty to act in good faith is not absolute but qualified; and the courts have recognised that the confidant may, in some circumstances, be under a duty to disclose confidential information. Any duty of confidence is "overridden by the duty to obey the law."[30] Consequently, a doctor must disclose information acquired in confidence in his professional capacity in judicial proceedings under the Road Traffic Act 1972,[31] and banks must answer questions about their customers' accounts under the Bankers' Books Evidence Act 1879.[32] In such circumstances a confidant is under a statutory duty to make disclosure. Indeed he may exceptionally owe a common law duty of care to another to do so. For example, a psychiatrist may be under a duty to disclose confidential information given by his patient if he considers, from what he has learnt in confidence, that another's life or safety is endangered.[33]

---

243 N.Y.S. 764 (1930). See, generally, *Restatement of Torts*, § 758(b): and *cf. International Tools Ltd.* v. *Kollar* (1968) 67 D.L.R. (2d) 386.

[26] *Seager* v. *Copydex Ltd.* [1967] 1 W.L.R. 923, 931, see above, pp. 684, 692.

[27] See Chaps. 2 and 41.

[28] See the New South Wales decision of *Wheatley* v. *Bell* (1982) [1984] F.S.R. 16, following a dictum of Lord Denning M.R. in *Fraser* v. *Evans* [1969] 1 Q.B. 349, 361, where a bona fide purchaser was enjoined.

[29] It is beyond the scope of this work to consider whether a person can be compelled in judicial proceedings to disclose confidential information or the source of that information: see generally *British Steel Corp.* v. *Granada Television Ltd.* [1982] A.C. 1096; Contempt of Court Act 1981, s.10.

[30] *Parry-Jones* v. *The Law Society* [1969] 1 Ch. 1, 9, *per* Diplock J., *Hunter* v. *Mann* [1974] Q.B. 767. See also *Tournier* v. *National Provincial & Union Bank of England* [1924] 1 K.B. 461.

[31] s.168(2), interpreted in *Hunter* v. *Mann* [1974] Q.B. 767.

[32] s.7.

[33] *Cf. Tarasoff* v. *Regents of University of California*, 529, p. 2d 553, 561 (1974) ("The protective privilege ends where the public peril begins.")

More frequently he may be permitted at common law to disclose confidential information, if it is in public interest so to do. At one time it was thought that disclosure was permissible in the public interest only if it were necessary to reveal or prevent crime.[34] In Page Wood V.C.'s oft-quoted phrase: there is "no confidence as to the disclosure of iniquity."[35] Today it is accepted that it is not "an essential ingredient of this defence that the plaintiffs should have been guilty of iniquitous conduct"[36]; and that "iniquity" is "merely an instance of just cause and excuse for breaking confidence."[37] "There are some things which may be required to be disclosed in the public interest in which event no confidence can be prayed in aid to keep them secret."[38]

The modern case law begins with the Court of Appeal's decision in *Initial Services Ltd.* v. *Putterill.*[39] In that case, the defendant, who was the plaintiff's former sales manager, supplied information to a newspaper, alleging that there was a ring among certain laundry undertakings to keep up prices, and that the plaintiff's company had used, in a circular to its customers, the introduction of selective employment tax as an excuse for making extra profits. The Court of Appeal refused to strike out the defence that the plaintiff's circular misled the public and that it was in the public interest to disclose information which the defendant had received in confidence. There is an obligation on "every member of the society to discover every design which may be formed, contrary to the laws of the society, to destroy the public welfare."[40] Whether disclosure is in the public interest should be determined at the date when disclosure is sought; it is possible, therefore, that subsequent events will make it "unreasonable" to continue to enforce a stipulation of confidence.[41]

There is now a body of case law which gives substance to this broadly phrased defence and which provides illustrations of situations where it has been held that there is "just cause and excuse for breaking confidence." It is permissible to disclose confidential information which is essentially nothing more than medical quackery endangering the health of the public, and for which the confider demands large fees[42]; or that some impending chemical or

---

[34] *Weld-Blundell* v. *Stephens* [1919] 1 Q.B. 520, 527, *per* Bankes L.J.
[35] *Gartside* v. *Outram* (1856) 26 L.J. Ch. 113, 114 and 116 (employer defrauding his customers).
[36] *Lion Laboratories Ltd.* v. *Evans* [1985] Q.B. 526, 550, *per* Griffiths L.J. See below, pp. 698–701 for a further discussion.
[37] *Fraser* v. *Evans* [1969] 1 Q.B. 349, 362, *per* Lord Denning M.R. For this reason some observations in some earlier cases may no longer be good law: see below, p. 698.
[38] *Ibid.*
[39] [1968] 1 Q.B. 396.
[40] *Annesley* v. *Earl of Anglesea* (1743) 17 State Trials 1139, 1223–1246, cited in [1968] 1 Q.B. 396, 405, *per* Lord Denning M.R. *Semble* it may be enough that the confidant has "reasonable grounds" for his belief that it is in the public interest to make the disclosure: see *Malone* v. *Commissioner of Police of the Metropolis (No. 2)* [1979] Ch. 344.
[41] *Dunford & Elliott Ltd.* v. *Johnson* [1977] 1 Lloyd's Rep. 505, 509, *per* Lord Denning M.R., invoking the analogy of the doctrine of restraint of trade. *Cf. Att.-Gen.* v. *Jonathan Cape Ltd.* [1976] 1 Q.B. 752, see below, p. 700.
[42] *Cf. Hubbard* v. *Vosper* [1972] 2 Q.B. 84; *Beloff* v. *Pressdram Ltd.* [1973] 1 All E.R. 241; *Church of Scientology of California* v. *Kaufman* [1973] R.P.C. 635.

other disaster is about to burst on an unexpecting world.[43] In *Lion Laboratories Ltd.* v. *Evans*[44] the Court of Appeal refused to grant an interlocutory injunction to enjoin former employees from publishing alleged confidential information which cast doubt on the reliability of a device, extensively used by the police, which measured the level of a person's intoxication. The confider's interest in the preservation of his confidence must be balanced against "the countervailing interest of the public in being kept informed of matters which are of real public concern." Stephenson L.J. concluded that four further considerations should be borne in mind[45]:

> "First, there is a wide difference between what is interesting to the public and what it is in the public interest to make known: *per* Lord Wilberforce in *British Steel Corporation* v. *Granada Television Ltd.* [1981] A.C. 1096 at 1168. The public are interested in many private matters which are no real concern of theirs and which the public have no pressing need to know. Secondly, the media have a private interest of their own in publishing what appeals to the public and may increase their circulation or the numbers of their viewers or listeners; and (I quote from the judgment of Sir John Donaldson M.R. in *Francome* v. *Mirror Group Newspapers Ltd.* [1984] 1 W.L.R. 892, 898 ' . . . they are peculiarly vulnerable to the error of confusing the public interest with their own interest.' Thirdly, there are cases in which the public interest is best served by an informer giving the confidential information, not to the press, but to the police or some other responsible body, as was suggested by Lord Denning M.R. in the *Initial Services Ltd.* v. *Putterill* and by Sir John Donaldson M.R. in the *Francome* case. Fourthly, it was said by Page Wood V.-C. in *Gartside* v. *Outram* (1856) 26 L.J. Ch. 113 at 114, 'there is no confidence as to the disclosure of iniquity'; and though [counsel] concedes on the plaintiffs' behalf that, as Salmon L.J. said in *Initial Services* v. *Putterill* (1967) [1968] 1 Q.B. 396 at 410, 'what was iniquity in 1856 may be too narrow, or too wide, in 1967,' and in 1984 extends to serious misdeeds or grave misconduct, he submits that misconduct of that kind is necessary to destroy the duty of confidence or excuse the breach of it, and nothing of that sort is alleged against the plaintiffs in the evidence now before the court. . . . [But] I agree with the judge in rejecting the 'no iniquity, no public interest rule' and in respectfully adopting what Lord Denning M.R. said in *Fraser* v. *Evans* [1969] 1 Q.B. 349, 362 ' . . . [Iniquity] is merely an instance of a just cause and excuse for breaking confidence."

But the court must be satisfied that there is "a legitimate ground for supposing it in the public interest"[46] to disclose the information. There was a

---

[43] *Malone* v. *Commissioner of Police of the Metropolis (No. 2)* [1979] Ch. 344, 362, *per* Megarry V.-C.
[44] [1985] Q.B. 526.
[45] At p. 537, 538.
[46] *Woodward* v. *Hutchins* [1977] W.L.R. 760, 764, *per* Lord Denning M.R., cited in *Lion Laboratories Ltd.* v. *Evans* [1985] Q.B. 526, 538, *per* Stephenson L.J. See also at p. 550 *per*

legitimate ground in *Lion Laboratories*: if the information was not published, members of the public might be wrongly convicted and imprisoned. The Court dismissed the argument that, as in libel, no injunction should be granted if justification is pleaded. The action for breach of confidence is significantly different in character from that of defamation.[47] In defamation, a plaintiff is saying that untrue and defamatory statements have been made about him; in breach of confidence, he is saying that "statements which are about to be published are statements about events which have happened and have been disclosed in breach of confidence."[48]

In *Lion Laboratories* v. *Evans* the Court of Appeal accepted that the circumstances must be exceptional before the defence could succeed. Certainly, a defendant may never publish documents which a plaintiff disclosed to third parties, on discovery, in pending litigation between them[49]; and it appears that the public interest can never justify revealing a trade secret, such as a valuable chemical formula, even though it might be beneficial to the public to do so.[50] Indeed, in *Schering Chemicals Ltd.* v. *Falkman*,[51] the majority of the Court of Appeal rejected Lord Denning M.R.'s view that it was in the public interest to allow the defendant to make use of information given in confidence about a pregnancy drug now withdrawn from the market, even though that information was technically in the public domain[52]; it would undoubtedly have been a different matter if the drug had still been on the market.[53] More recently, in

---

Griffiths L.J. The Court accepted that this would also be a defence to an action for breach of copyright.

[47] In *Woodward* v. *Hutchins* and *Fraser* v. *Evans* [1969] 1 Q.B. 362, Lord Denning M.R. had said that a plaintiff cannot avoid the salutary rule of law in libel, that no injunction should be granted, where the defendant intends to justify by framing the case in breach of confidence." But in *Khashoggi* v. *Smith* [1980] C.A. Transcripts 58, *Francombe* v. *Mirror Newspapers Ltd.* [1984] 1 W.L.R. 892 and *Lion Laboratories Ltd.* v. *Evans* [1985] Q.B. 526, the Court of Appeal emphasised that the issues in the two claims were very different: see text above.

[48] *Khashoggi* v. *Smith* (1980) 124 S.J. 149, C.A., *per* Sir David Cairns, cited in *Lion Laboratories Ltd.* v. *Evans* [1985] Q.B. 526, 551, *per* O'Connor L.J.

[49] *Distillers' Co.* v. *Times Newspapers Ltd.* [1975] 1 Q.B. 613, 622, *per* Talbot J. *Cf. Marcel* v. *Commissioner of Police of the Metropolis* [1992] 2 W.L.R. 50; *Re Barlow Clowes Gilt Managers* [1991] 4 All E.R. 385.

[50] *Church of Scientology of California* v. *Kaufman* [1973] R.P.C. 635, 649, *per* Goff J.; *cf.* above, n. 43 and contrast below, p. 702. In the U.S.A. the courts have rejected the argument that Federal patent law pre-empts the state law of trade secrets: see *Painton* v. *Bournes Inc.*, 442 F. 2d 216 (CCA2 1971) and *Kewanee Oil Corp.* v. *Bicron Corp.*, 416 U.S. 470 (1974), where the economic arguments for the protection of trade secrets are developed: see below, p. 702. See too Art. 10(2) of the European Convention for the Protection of Human Rights and Fundamental Freedoms (Rome, November 4, 1950; TS 71 (1953); Cmd. 8969).

[51] [1982] Q.B. 1.

[52] See above, p. 681.

[53] There is authority that an employee should not reveal information that his employer has been negligent: see *Weld-Blundell* v. *Stephens* [1919] 1 Q.B. 520, 535, *per* Warrington L.J., [1920] A.C. 956, 965, *per* Viscount Finlay; *Distillers' Co.* v. *Times Newspapers Ltd.* [1975] 1 Q.B. 613, 622, *per* Talbot J. It is true that "negligence" may not amount to an "iniquity." But today it may be in the public interest to disclose that a confider is negligent, for example, if the public's health would be endangered by the marketing of unsafe drugs: see text above.

Francome v. *Mirror Group Newspapers Ltd.*,[54] the Court of Appeal emphatically dismissed the argument that confidential information illegally obtained by wire tapping could be published by the Daily Mirror before trial, since it demonstrated that the plaintiff had been guilty of an "iniquity" in that he had breached the rules of racing and was possibly guilty of criminal offences. The excuse of public interest could not justify a breach of the criminal law.

It is doubtful whether it can ever be said that it is in the public interest to disclose the secrets, acquired in confidence, of another's sexual life.[55] However, the Court of Appeal has held that those who seek publicity cannot "complain if a servant or employee of theirs afterwards discloses the truth about them."[56] Yet the fact that persons present themselves to the world "in a favourable light" should not absolve their confidants from the bond of confidence.[57]

There is a real danger that the recognition of a "shadowy defence" of public interest may encourage confidants to equate their private interests with those of the public.[58] There is indeed "a wide difference between what is interesting to the public and what it is in the public interest to make known."[59] English courts have been particularly sensitive to this distinction when the secret is a public or State secret. In *British Steel Corporation* v. *Granada Television Ltd.*[60] the House of Lords accepted as proper Granada's concession that British Steel, if it had acted in time, could have obtained an injunction preventing Granada from publishing documents, leaked by a mole, relating to British Steel's, a public corporation's, management and Governmental involvement in its affairs. Indeed, in the *Spycatcher* case, Lord Griffiths did not envisage any circumstances when it could be said to be in the public interest to publish State secrets acquired in confidence; not even trivia should be published for "what may appear to the writer to be trivial may in fact be the one missing piece in the jigsaw sought by some hostile intelligence agency."[61] Similarly, Lord Goff, while admitting the possibility of a successful public interest defence, found it very difficult to envisage the circumstances in which the facts would justify such a defence.[62] The House of Lords did not suggest, as did Lord Widgery C.J. in *Att.-Gen.* v. *Jonathan Cape*,[63] that it was for the Crown to demonstrate that it was in the public interest that a secret should remain a secret. But in England, where there is no First Amendment which jealously protects free

---

[54] [1984] 1 W.L.R. 892.

[55] See *Stephens* v. *Avery* [1988] Ch. 449: see above, p. 680.

[56] *Woodward* v. *Hutchins* [1977] 1 W.L.R. 760, 764, *per* Lord Denning M.R. See also *Lennon* v. *News Group Newspapers Ltd.* [1978] F.S.R. 573; *Khashoggi* v. *Smith* (1980) 124 S.J. 149, C.A.

[57] *Cf. Stephens* v. *Avery* [1988] Ch. 449.

[58] *Lion Laboratories* v. *Evans* [1985] Q.B. 526, 551, *per* Griffiths L.J.

[59] *Ibid.* at p. 537, *per* Stephenson L.J.: see above, p. 698.

[60] [1981] A.C. 1096, 1168, *per* Lord Wilberforce, 1202, *per* Lord Fraser. Contrast Lord Salmon, dissenting, at pp. 1185–1186.

[61] *Att.-Gen.* v. *Guardian Newspapers Ltd. (No. 2)* [1990] 1 A.C. 109, 269.

[62] *Ibid.* at p. 283.

[63] [1976] 1 Q.B. 752. But contrast *Distillers Co. (Biochemicals Ltd.)* v. *Times Newspapers Ltd.* [1975] 1 Q.B. 613, 623, *per* Talbot J.

speech, that burden should be on the confidant who pleads the defence. In *Jonathan Cape* the court found that Cabinet discussions which had taken place some 10 to 11 years ago were no longer protected.[64] In *Commonwealth of Australia* v. *John Fairfax & Sons Ltd.*[65] the High Court of Australia went so far as to say that publication of stale State secrets was positively a good thing, encouraging healthy political debate which is at the heart of the democratic process. Private individuals, but not governments, may be protected from embarrassing disclosures. But the line between national security and governmental embarrassment is a thin one and can be drawn differently by different judges and different jurisdictions.

It has been suggested that whether disclosure is permissible in the public interest may depend on the motives of the confidant, for example, whether he is acting "out of malice or spite" or is attempting to sell the information for reward.[66] But that consideration has not deterred the Court of Appeal; it has, on more than one occasion, refused to enjoin an avaricious confidant from selling his secret to a newspaper.[67] It has also been said, in this context, that the recipient must have a proper interest to receive the information. In *Francome* v. *Mirror Group Newspapers Ltd.*, Sir John Donaldson M.R. concluded that it "is impossible to see what public interest would be served by publishing the contents of the tapes which would not equally be served by giving them to the police or to the Jockey Club. Any wider publication could only serve the interests of the Daily Mirror."[68] But in that case the Postmaster-General had statutory authority to authorise disclosure of that information.[69] In other circumstances, where such limited disclosure is not possible, it is difficult to see why the spite or cupidity of a confidant or the prurient interest of the recipient should be critical, if it is in the public interest that the information should be disclosed.[70]

Many of the cases which illustrate the scope of the defence of public interest concern applications to prevent publication of information before trial. One of the reasons which the Court of Appeal gave for denying the injunction in *Woodward* v. *Hutchins*[71] and *Lion Laboratories Ltd.* v. *Evans*[72] was that damages were an adequate remedy. It should not, we think, be inferred that the defence

---

[64] At pp. 763 *et seq.*

[65] (1981) 55 A.L.J.R. 45.

[66] *Initial Services* v. *Putterill* [1968] 1 Q.B. 396, 406, *per* Lord Denning M.R. *Cf. Church of Scientology of California* v. *Kaufman* [1973] R.P.C. 635, 660, *per* Goff J.; *Malone* v. *Commissioner of Police of the Metropolis (No. 2)* [1979] Ch. 344, 375–377, *per* Megarry V.-C. But see the authorities cited above, nn. 47 and 48.

[67] See cases cited above, nn. 47 and 48.

[68] [1984] 1 W.L.R. 892, 898, cited with approval in *Lion Laboratories Ltd.* v. *Evans* [1984] Q.B. 526, 537, *per* Stephenson L.J.

[69] *Cf. W.* v. *Egdell* [1990] Ch. 359 (duty of confidence to patient overridden, duty to disclose to public authorities); *Re a Company's Application* [1989] Ch. 477, (disclosure to Inland Revenue).

[70] *Cf. Woodward* v. *Hutchins* [1977] 1 W.L.R. 760. See also *British Steel Corp.* v. *Granada Television Ltd.* [1981] A.C. 1096, 1202, *per* Lord Fraser.

[71] [1977] 1 W.L.R. 760; see above, p. 699.

[72] [1985] Q.B. 526; see above, p. 698.

of public interest would not have been a sufficient defence to an action for damages or other monetary relief. It would be very odd if public interest was only a limited defence.[73] In principle it should be an absolute defence, otherwise confidants who should disclose secrets might be deterred from doing so by the prospect of an order to account for profits or an award of damages. In the Court of Appeal of New Zealand Sir Robin Cooke P. was "unwilling to accept that in this class of case, when the publication . . . is both true and in the public interest, a newspaper should have to pay damages or account for any profits."[74]

Some conclusions

It has been said that the possibility of an action for breach of confidence is a "not insubstantial check on freedom of speech" and on the exploitation of ideas in the commercial and industrial sphere.[75] We doubt whether it is a *substantial* check on freedom of speech when the confidant has voluntarily assumed the obligation of confidence and has consciously exploited information knowing that it was confidential. Indeed, in the specific context of trade secrets, the economic evidence accepted by the Supreme Court of the United States in *Kewanee Oil Co.* v. *Bicron Corporation*[76] is a clear refutation of that argument and is a convincing demonstration that the common law which protects trade secrets is essential if industrial invention is to be encouraged and is to flourish.

We are of the view that this is a branch of the common law which should be allowed to develop in a gradualist manner, on a case by case basis. However, there is one area where legislative intervention would be welcome, indeed, in the view of some commentators, is necessary. The courts have been wise not to encourage confidants to invoke, as a higher law, the doctrine that confidence may be broken if it is in the public interest to do so. This defence should rarely if ever succeed where the information imparted is a State secret. Whether it should ever be a defence that it is in the public interest to publish a State secret is a question of great sensitivity, so sensitive that it should be answered by Parliament and not by the courts.

---

[73] *Cf.* Justice Douglas' dissent in *Kewanee Corp.* v. *Bicron Corp.* 416 U.S. 470, 498–499, (1974); and (1984) 4 O.J.L.S. 361, 363–364 [Cripps].

[74] *Att.-Gen. (U.K.)* v. *Wellington Newspapers Ltd.* [1988] 1 N.Z.L.R. 129, 177.

[75] Law Commission, Report, No. 110.

[76] 416 U.S. 470 (1974). For an analysis, see Francis Gurry's excellent Ph.D. thesis, deposited in the University Library at Cambridge.

CHAPTER 37

BENEFITS ACCRUING TO A CRIMINAL FROM HIS CRIME[1]

1. THE COMMON LAW RULE OF FORFEITURE[1a]

"IT appears to me," said Fry L.J. in *Cleaver* v. *Mutual Reserve Fund Life Association*,[2] "that no system of jurisprudence can with reason include amongst the rights which it enforces rights directly resulting to the person asserting them from the crime of that person."[3] No criminal can retain a benefit which accrues to him from crime.[4] But this imprecise principle has not been easy to apply. It is clear that a killer who is found not guilty of murder by reason of insanity does not forfeit his rights, since this verdict constitutes an acquittal.[5] In contrast, there has been much debate whether the forfeiture principle should have any application if the criminal has no *mens rea* but is nevertheless found guilty of a criminal offence. This problem may arise if the accused is found guilty of involuntary manslaughter. Some judges have rejected any such

---

[1] Burrows is of the opinion that this topic should not form part of the law of restitution. First, the courts are seeking to prevent rather than to reverse an unjust enrichment; but it may be fortuitous whether those claiming through the criminal have or have not yet been enriched. Secondly, he argues that the wrong is against the state and not against a particular individual; but there is no suggestion in the case law that a restitutionary claim should in principle be denied for this reason: see *The Law of Restitution*, p. 380.

[1a] The Theft Act 1968, s.28, gives a criminal court power to order property to be restored to its rightful owner. Its technical and complex provisions are beyond the scope of a work on restitution. For a discussion and criticism, see *Profits of Crime and their Recovery, Report of a Committee chaired by Sir Derek Hodgson* (London, 1984), Chap. 7. See Police (Property) Act 1897; and (on powers of forfeiture), Powers of Criminal Courts Act 1973, ss.30, 43 as amended by the Criminal Justice Act 1988, s.104, and (on confiscation orders) Criminal Justice Act 1988, ss.71, 76 and 78, Drug Trafficking Offences Act 1986, ss.1 *et seq*.

[2] [1892] 1 Q.B. 147, 156, quoted, with approval, in *Beresford* v. *Royal Insurance Co.* [1938] A.C. 586, 596, *per* Lord Atkin. For discussions of the application of the *Cleaver* principle, see (1973) 89 L.Q.R. 235 [Youdan] and (1974) 37 M.L.R. 481 [Earnshaw and Pace].

[3] It is the criminal who normally benefits from his crime. But it may be that an innocent third party is the beneficiary. Unless he is a bona fide purchaser, his innocence does not protect him if it can be shown that he would not have gained the property but for the crime and that he has no independent claim: *cf. Bridgman* v. *Green* (1757) Wilm. 58; *Huguenin* v. *Baseley* (1807) 14 Ves. 273.

[4] *St. John Shipping Corp.* v. *Joseph Rank Ltd.* [1957] 1 Q.B. 267, 292, *per* Devlin J. See also *Haseldine* v. *Hosken* [1933] 1 K.B. 822; *Askey* v. *Golden Wine Co.* [1948] 2 All E.R. 35; *Restatement of Restitution*, §§ 3 and 140. See also *Beresford's Case* [1937] 2 K.B. 197, 220; *Cointat* v. *Myham & Sons* [1913] 2 K.B. 220; *Marles* v. *Philip Trant & Sons Ltd.* [1954] 1 Q.B. 29, 39–30, *per* Denning L.J.; and contrast *Howard* v. *Shirlstar Container Transport Ltd.* [1990] 3 All E.R. 366, C.A.

[5] Criminal Procedure (Insanity) Act 1964, s.1.

distinction. To accept it would be to encourage "what ... would be very noxious—a sentimental speculation as to the motives and degree of moral guilt of a person who has been justly convicted."[5a] So, in *Re Giles*,[6] Pennycuick V.-C. refused "to analyse the ground upon which the courts have established this rule of public policy. It is sufficient to say that the rule has been established and that the deserving of punishment and moral culpability are not necessary ingredients of the type of crime to which this rule applies, that is, culpable homicide, murder or manslaughter." Consequently, he held that a person convicted of manslaughter could not benefit under his victim's will even though he was found guilty through diminished responsibility. But dicta in other decisions have rejected the conclusion that a conviction of manslaughter necessarily entails "the consequence that the person convicted will be barred from all succession to any benefit under the will or intestacy of the person whom he or she has killed and from succession to any interest of the deceased jointly."[7] "Manslaughter is a crime which varies infinitely in its seriousness."[8] For that reason, in *Re K (deceased)*, Vinelott J. and the Court of Appeal could not accept counsel's submission that the forfeiture rule should never apply to any case of involuntary manslaughter. The forfeiture rule will then apply if the person guilty of manslaughter was "guilty of deliberate, intentional and unlawful violence or threats of violence,"[9] even though that person did not intend to kill or to do grievous bodily harm.[10]

Conviction of murder may be conclusive of guilt in any civil proceedings.[11] However, an acquittal in criminal proceedings, which may not be admissible in evidence in civil litigation,[12] should not lead a civil court to conclude that a person must necessarily benefit under the will or an intestacy of a deceased person. An acquittal in criminal proceedings establishes that there was not proof beyond a reasonable doubt but it does not establish that there was not proof on the preponderance of the evidence that a person committed the crime. So, in *Re Sigsworth*,[13] Sigsworth had committed suicide before his trial for murder; and in *Gray* v. *Barr*[14] the defendant had been acquitted both of murder and manslaughter. Nevertheless Sigworth's representatives were not

---

[5a] *In the Estate of Hall* [1914] P. 1, 7, *per* Hamilton L.J.

[6] [1972] Ch. 544. See also *Re Holgate* (1971), unreported but discussed in (1974) 37 M.L.R. 481 [Earnshaw and Pace].

[7] *Re K (deceased)* [1985] Ch. 85, 98, *per* Vinelott J., applying *Gray* v. *Barr (Prudential Assurance Co. Ltd., third party)* [1970] 2 Q.B. 626, 640, *per* Geoffrey Lane J.; [1971] 2 Q.B. 554, 581, *per* Salmon L.J.

[8] *Gray* v. *Barr* [1971] 2 Q.B. 554, 581, *per* Salmon L.J.

[9] *Gray* v. *Barr* [1970] 2 Q.B. 626, 640, *per* Geoffrey Lane J.

[10] *Re K (deceased)* [1985] Ch. 85, [1985] 3 W.L.R. 234, C.A. But the Court of Appeal granted relief against the forfeiture: see below, p. 706.

[11] See Civil Evidence Act 1968, ss.11 and 13; and *cf. McIlkenny* v. *Chief Constable of Midlands* [1980] Q.B. 283.

[12] *Cf. Hollington* v. *Hewthorn* [1943] K.B. 587 (which concerned, however, a conviction). The Civil Evidence Act 1968 does not deal with this question, so the common law is unchanged.

[13] [1935] 1 Ch. 89: see below, p. 707.

[14] [1971] 2 Q.B. 554: see above, n. 7.

allowed to claim on his victim's intestacy and Barr was denied an indemnity from his insurers under a "hearth and home" policy.

The basis of the common law forfeiture rule is then that it is against public policy to allow a criminal to benefit from his crime. But Parliament has recently, in the Forfeiture Act 1982, questioned its wisdom, at least in its most Draconian formulation, and has rejected the argument that its relaxation would be "harmful and dangerous."[15]

2. THE FORFEITURE ACT 1982

This statute, which began as a private member's bill, was prompted by the plight of the morally blameless widow who killed her husband and in consequence forfeited social welfare benefits.[16] The court now has power under section 2(1) to make an order modifying the forfeiture rule where it has precluded a person, who has unlawfully killed another, from acquiring an interest in property.[17] But "nothing in this Act . . . shall affect the application of the forfeiture rule in the case of a person who stands convicted of murder."[18] Moreover:

> "The court shall not make an order under this section modifying the effect of the forfeiture rule in any case unless it is satisfied that, having regard to the conduct of the offender and of the deceased and to such other circumstances as appear to the court to be material, the justice of the case requires the effect of the rule to be so modified in that case."[19]

In *Re K (deceased)*,[20] Vinelott J. took into account, in determining whether to exercise his discretion, the facts that the wife, who had unlawfully killed her husband, was then greatly distressed, that she was a loyal wife who had been consistently and grievously assaulted by her deceased husband, and that there were no other persons for whom the deceased was under a moral duty to

---

[15] *Cf. Re Giles* [1972] Ch. 544, 552–553, *per* Pennycuick V.-C.

[16] *R.* v. *Chief National Insurance Commissioner, ex p. O'Connor* [1981] Q.B. 758.

[17] Persons who unlawfully aid, abet, counsel and procure are within the Act: s.1(2). S.2(4) defines what is an "interest in property," referred to in subsection (1). It is:–
> "(a) any beneficial interest in property which (apart from the forfeiture rule) the offender would have acquired—
>   (i) under the deceased's will (including as respects Scotland, any writing having testamentary effect) or the law relating to intestacy or by way of ius relicti, ius relictae or legitim;
>   (ii) on the nomination of the deceased in accordance with the provisions of any enactment;
>   (iii) as a donatio mortis causa made by the deceased; or
>   (iv) under a special destination (whether relating to heritable or moveable property); or
>   (b) any beneficial interest in property which (apart from the forfeiture rule) the offender would have acquired in consequence of the death of the deceased, being property which, before the death, was held on trust for any person."

[18] s.5. *Cf. Re H, decd.* [1990] Fam. Law 175 (where the killing was not deliberate).

[19] s.2(2); and see below, p. 630 for s.2(5).

[20] [1985] Ch. 85.

provide, and that the deceased's family wished her to benefit under the will. The Court of Appeal[20a] concluded that he was right to do so, and that the 1982 Act did not limit his discretion to make an award of an amount no greater than the sum she would obtain on divorce or under the Inheritance (Provision for Family and Dependants) Act 1975.

These sections of the Act came into force on October 13, 1982.[21]An order under section 2 may, however, be made even though the unlawful killing occurred before that date.[22] But by section 2(7) no order can be made which will have the effect of depriving a person (other than the offender or a person claiming through him) of an interest in property acquired, before the coming into force of section 2, in consequence of the forfeiture rule. In *Re K, (deceased)*[23] the Court of Appeal, affirming Vinelott J., held that: "the word 'acquired' in section 2(7) is used to denote property which has been actually transferred to a person entitled thereto by virtue of the operation of the [forfeiture] rule or who has thereby acquired an indefeasible right to have it transferred to him or to her." It did not therefore extend to property which, when section 2(7) came into force, was held by the deceased's personal representatives, who had not completed the administration of the estate.[24]

The court shall not have power to make an order modifying the forfeiture rule "unless proceedings for the purpose are brought before the expiry of the period of three months beginning with [the conviction of the person convicted]."[25] Although the sub-section is not free from ambiguity, it appears to be intended to govern the case where it is the convicted person who initiates the proceedings seeking relief from forfeiture; the limitation period only runs from his, and not an accomplice's, conviction.

The Act also makes provision for applications to be made under other statutes, such as the Inheritance (Provision for Family and Dependants) Act 1975 and the Matrimonial Causes Act 1973.[26] Regulations may also be made under the Act to enable a Commissioner to determine whether the forfeiture rule applies to social security benefits.[27]

[20a] [1986] Ch. 180, C.A.

[21] s.7(2).

[22] s.7(4).

[23] [1985] Ch. 85, 99; [1986] Ch. 180, C.A.; contrast *Re Royse, decd.* [1985] Ch. 22.

[24] Vinelott J. expressed no opinion whether a present or future interest in property settled by will, which had vested in personal representatives or trustees on completion of administration, was "accquired" within the meaning of s.2(7).

[25] s.2(3).

[26] s.3 The question may arise whether reasonable provision has been made by the deceased in his will for his spouse found guilty of involuntary manslaughter. This must be determined before the forfeiture rule is applied. If there has been, then the court must consider whether it should exercise its discretion under s.2(1): *Re Royse, decd.* [1985] Ch. 22; *Re K (deceased)* [1985] Ch. 85, 101.

[27] s.4.

3. SPECIFIC PROBLEMS ARISING FROM SUCCESSION TO PROPERTY ON DEATH[28]

The application of the common law principle of *Cleaver's* case[29] has been of particular importance in administration of estates,[30] and it will continue to be so if a person has been convicted of murder.[31] So, in *In the Estate of Cunigunda (otherwise Cora) Crippen (deceased)*,[32] Sir Samuel Evans P. refused a grant of administration of the murdered wife's estate to Miss Le Neve, the murderer's sole executrix, who claimed the grant on the ground that she was entitled to the wife's estate as the murderer's legatee. This principle of public policy, which precludes a murderer from claiming under his victim's will, also precludes him from taking any benefit on his victim's intestacy. In *Re Sigsworth*,[33] the murderer killed his mother, who in her will left everything to him. He would also have taken on his mother's intestacy. The murderer then committed suicide. Clauson J. held that his estate could not take under the mother's will or on her intestacy under the Administration of Estates Act 1925, for the general words of that statute must be read and construed subject to the principle that a criminal cannot reap the fruits of his crime.

The conclusion in *Re Sigsworth* is unimpeachable because the murderer died without issue. But if he had left issue, it is not clear from the decision whether those issue would have taken with the murderer's brother as the next-of-kin of the intestate. It is true that persons claiming through a murderer should have no rights to any benefits from his crime, but they should not be deprived of any independent right of succession. Professor Scott's resolution[34] of this problem is persuasive. His solution is to allow the next-of-kin of the murderer to take provided that they would have taken as next-of-kin of the murdered person if the murderer had pre-deceased his victim. In our view this is a just result, which is consistent with the decision in *Cleaver* v. *Mutual Reserved Fund Life Association*.[35] In that case, the assured had taken out an insurance on his life for the benefit of his wife, who later murdered him. The assured's executors claimed under the policy and the insurance company pleaded that the executors were attempting to benefit from the wife's crime. The Court of Appeal rejected this argument. Between the executors and the insurance company, the question of public policy did not arise. The objects of the trust could no longer be performed, since the wife by her crime had rendered the trust in her favour

---

[28] See, generally, (1973) 89 L.Q.R. 235 [Youdan].
[29] [1892] 1 Q.B. 147, 156 (see above, n. 2 and text).
[30] See, *e.g. Re Dellow's Will Trusts* [1964] 1 W.L.R. 451.
[31] See above, p. 705.
[32] [1911] P. 108.
[33] [1935] 1 Ch. 89, 92, citing Fry L.J. in *Cleaver's Case*, see above; and *Re Pitts* [1931]. 1 Ch. 546, 550, *per* Farwell J., refusing to follow *Re Houghton* [1915] 2 Ch. 173, *per* Joyce J. See also *Davitt* v. *Titcumb* [1990] Ch. 110; see below, n. 48.
[34] *Scott on Trusts*, § 187; *Restatement of Restitution*, § 187. But see *In the Estate of Robertson* (1963) 107 S.J. 318.
[35] [1892] 1 Q.B. 147.

incapable of performance. But the rights of the executors were distinct from and independent of those of the wife.[36] They were entitled to succeed to the policy moneys, which, however, they held on trust for the deceased's estate and the beneficiaries therein, excluding the wife's estate.[37]

Two other cases illustrate the importance of distinguishing "dependent" from "independent" rights of succession. In both the court had to determine the consequence of striking out the criminal beneficiary from the trust, in order to identify the persons on whose behalf the trustee should hold the property to which the criminal was no longer entitled. In *Re Peacock*,[38] a testator was murdered by his wife, who then committed suicide. He left in his will a class gift to "my wife, my son and step-son," subject to certain conditions. The question which the court was required to decide was whether the wife should be struck out of the class, or whether her share was vested but passed as on her intestacy because she was disabled from taking. Upjohn J., although he favoured the latter conclusion,[39] felt bound by authority to accept that the wife's share failed, so that the remaining members of the class succeeded to her share.[40] In our view, Upjohn J.'s hesitation was unjustified. To have reached any other conclusion would have enabled those claiming through the wife, on her intestacy, to have taken her share, and to have benefited from her crime. Those persons entitled to her intestacy should have succeeded only if they had an independent right of succession as surviving members of the class.[41] Vaisey J., in the earlier case of *Re Callaway*,[42] was also much attracted by the argument that the share of the criminal had vested but that public policy did not allow him to enjoy it. But his solution would have been to allow the Crown to take as *bona vacantia*.[43] In that case, the testatrix bequeathed her whole estate to her daughter, who murdered her and committed suicide. The daughter's brother claimed a declaration that he was entitled on his mother's intestacy, to the exclusion of the Crown. Vaisey J. granted it only because authority compelled him to do so, even though he said that, as a result, the brother was benefiting from his sister's crime. But the brother's claim was not through his sister but as next-of-kin of his mother. To have allowed the Crown to take would not only have been contrary to the current of

---

[36] At p. 159, *per* Fry L.J.
[37] A similar conclusion would seemingly have been reached if the wife had been a third party, for whose benefit a contract had been entered into: *cf.* Lord Esher M.R. at p. 153, Fry L.J. at pp. 157–158.
[38] [1957] Ch. 310.
[39] At p. 315.
[40] In these circumstances, therefore, there is no lapse: see *Re Woods* [1931] 2 Ch. 138.
[41] *Fell* v. *Biddolph* (1875) L.R. 10 C.P. 701, 709–710, *per* Jessel M.R.; *Re Coleman and Jarrom* (1876) 4 Ch.D. 165, 173, decisions which Upjohn J. followed. *Cf. Re Sigsworth* [1935] Ch. 89.
[42] [1956] Ch. 559; see (1956) 72 L.Q.R. 475.
[43] At pp. 563–564. The germ of this idea appears in *Re Sigsworth* [1935] Ch. 89, where Clauson J. adjourned the case to allow the Crown to be joined as defendant, to argue that the share should pass as *bona vacantia*.

authority, but would have indirectly reversed the policy of the Forfeiture Act 1870, which abolished forfeiture in cases of felony.

The distinction, which the Court of Appeal drew in *Cleaver's* case between rights dependent on and rights independent of the criminal act, is crucial. It would meet the case posited by Vaisey J. in *Re Callaway*,[44] where T, who is murdered by R, is a life tenant of property held on trust for sale for T for life, remainder to R. In such a case R, or his successor, should not thereby be able to accelerate his remainder, but at the same time should not be deprived of it since it was acquired independently of the felonious act.[45] A possible solution is to require the trustees to hold the property on the trusts of T's will, excluding R, for the period of T's life expectancy at the moment before his death, and thereafter for R.[46] A more difficult case will arise if one joint tenant murders another. In *Re K (deceased)*[47] Vinelott J. accepted the concession of counsel that the forfeiture rule operated to sever the joint tenancy in the proceeds of sale and the rent and profits until sale; the surviving joint tenant held the beneficial interest in the property on trust, half for himself and half for the person entitled to the share of his victim.[48] Commonwealth authorities have reached a similar conclusion.[49] In contrast, the *Restatement of Trusts 2d*[50] would allow the survivor only one-half of the income from the property for life on the ground that he might, in the natural course of events, have died before the joint tenant whom he murdered. In all these cases the legal title in the property passes to the wrongdoer, but a constructive trust is imposed in order to prevent his unjust enrichment.[51]

Today, many of the persons who feature in these cases would not be convicted of murder and would consequently seek to ask the court to make an

---

[44] [1956] Ch. 559, 563.

[45] *Aliter* if the remainder was contingent, since then the murderer might have pre-deceased his victim without ever having fulfilled the contingency: see *Scott on Trusts*, § 493.

[46] See, generally, *Scott on Trusts*, pp. 3204–3207; *Restatement of Restitution*, § 188. (1973) 89 L.Q.R. at 250–251 [Youdan].

[47] [1985] Ch. 85, 100.

[48] In *Davitt* v. *Titcumb* [1990] Ch. 110 Scott J. held that the defendant, a tenant in common who had murdered his wife, could not be deprived of that vested interest. But he could not claim any part of the proceeds of an insurance policy on his wife's life. The policy money had been paid to the mortgagee who used it to discharge a very large part of the mortgage debt. The house was subsequently sold. The personal representatives of the deceased wife were held to be entitled to the equity of redemption to the exclusion of the defendant. It was their money which had been used to pay off the mortgage debt, and they were entitled to contribution from the defendant. The judge was not required to decide whether the appropriate contribution was one half of the policy moneys, or his share of the proceeds of the sale of the house. In principle, they should bear the burden of their joint debt in proportion to their beneficial interests. See above, Chaps. 12 and 13.

[49] *Schobelt* v. *Barber* (1966) 60 D.L.R. (2d) 519; *Re Pechar, decd.* [1969] N.Z.L.R. 574; *Rasmanis* v. *Jurewitsch* [1968] 2 N.S.W.R. 166. In all these cases the court concluded that the survivor held an undivided share on trust for the deceased's next of kin other than the offender.

[50] § 493.2.

[51] *Cleaver* v. *Mutual Reserve Fund Life Association* [1892] 1 Q.B. 147, 158, *per* Fry L.J. A bona fide purchaser from the wrongdoer would, therefore, be protected: for a discussion, see (1973) 89 L.Q.R. at 255–256 [Youdan].

order under section 2 of the Forfeiture Act 1982, modifying the common law
forfeiture rule. In particular, section 2(5) provides that:

> "An order under this section may modify the effect of the forfeiture rule in
> respect of any interest in property to which the determination referred to
> in subsection (1) above relates and may do so in either or both of the
> following ways, that is—
> (a) where there is more than one such interest, by excluding the applica-
>   tion of the rule in respect of any (but not all) of those interests; and
> (b) in the case of any such interest in property, by excluding application
>   of the rule in respect of part of the property."

This is a most obscure subsection. In *Re K, (deceased)*[52] Vinelott J. concluded
that it is:

> "intended to enlarge the power conferred by subsection (1)[53] by making it
> clear that the court is not bound either to relieve against the operation of
> the forfeiture rule altogether or not to relieve against the operation of the
> rule at all. The draftsman assumed that subsection (1) alone conferred
> power to relieve an applicant from the operation of the rule in respect of
> the entirety of all interests affected by the rule. Subsection 5 then in effect
> enlarges the court's powers."[54]

4. PROFITS FROM THE CRIME

In the cases discussed in the previous section the criminal, and persons
claiming through him, were seeking to benefit on the victim's intestacy or
under the victim's will, or to enlarge a beneficial interest under a trust. In
contrast, there is no reported civil decision in this country where the criminal
has been deprived of profits gained from exploiting the crime after the victim's
death. There are statutory provisions, such as the Criminal Justice Act 1988,[55]
which enable the Crown, but not the victim or his representatives, to seek
confiscation orders, and the Crown and the Court have power to compensate
the victim from the proceeds of the confiscation.[56]

Take the case of the notorious murderer who sells his story to a tabloid
newspaper. Do the victim's personal representatives have any common law
claim to recover the blood money? The murderer has certainly been enriched;
he would not have gained the profit but for the murder of his victim; and the
ground of the claim is murder, the most heinous of wrongful acts. It may be

---

[52] [1985] Ch. 85, 100.
[53] See above, p. 705.
[54] The Court of Appeal did not comment on the judge's interpretation of this subsection. It held,
construing s.2(7) of the Act, that the interests of the residuary beneficiaries had not been
"acquired" before the 1980 Act came into force. The Court had discretion, therefore, to grant
relief against forfeiture.
[55] See above, n. 1a; see below, p. 712.
[56] Powers of Criminal Courts Act 1973, as amended, s.30 (Court) and s.43A (Crown). There is also
the Criminal Injuries Compensation Board: see Criminal Justice Act 1988, ss.108 *et seq.*

that his lurid tale contains details of a deprived life which led him to a life of crime, or other personal details not directly related to the murder. But a court should treat him with the utmost severity and deny him any allowances, rejecting any argument that part of the gain which he made was the product of such extraneous details. At the very least the burden should be imposed on him to demonstrate whether his story would ever have been published at all but for the notoriety accompanying his crime; and, if so, the percentage of profits attributable to material unrelated, directly or undirectly, to the crime.[57]

The objection to recognition of a restitutionary claim is that the gain made by the criminal is made from his contract with his publisher and not from his crime.[58] His enrichment is indirect, not direct. But that may not be a fatal objection to a restitutionary claim.[59] In the United States there is attractive and analogous authority which holds that a defendant who induces a third party to breach his contract with the plaintiff must disgorge the profits which are the product of that tortious act[60]; it was his wrongful act which enabled him to enter into a profitable contract with the third party. Similarly, the murderer would not have been in a position to make his contract but for his crime. Other objections are, we consider, equally unpersuasive.[61] The criminal may not be enriched, for he may have used his gains to pay his legal costs or to support his family. But no criminal can invoke the defence of change of position.

Other persons, such as the criminal's publishers and ghost writers, may also benefit from the criminal act. That others have benefited does not exculpate the criminal. But it raises the question whether persons claiming through him should also disgorge their gains. The facts of the Canadian case of *Rosenfeld* v. *Olsen*,[62] are quite a remarkable illustration of third persons benefiting from information which the criminal would not have obtained but for the crime. The plaintiffs had obtained, under the Family Compensation Act, an unsatisfied judgment against Olsen who had murdered their children. In this action they claimed funds which were held on trust for the benefit of Olsen's wife and children. The trust had been established and funded by the Royal Canadian Mounted police. The RCMP had made these payments in return for Olsen telling them where he had buried the murdered children. The Court of Appeal of British Columbia held that their claim against the trustees must fail. The trust fund was not a benefit gained at the plaintiff's expense since they had not

---

[57] *Cf.* below, p. 727 suggesting a similar principle if the wrongdoer is a tortfeasor if he is an infringer of another's intellectual property; and see above, p. 691.

[58] "Criminal Anti-Profit Laws: Some Thoughts in Favour of Their Constitutionality" (1988) 76 Cal. L.R. 1353 [Okuda], cited and endorsed in "Confiscating the Literary Proceeds of Crime" [1992] Crim. L.R. 96 [Freiberg].

[59] See above, pp. 57–58.

[60] See below, pp. 724–725.

[61] For a contrary view, see the articles cited in n. 58, above.

[62] (1986) 25 D.L.R. (4th) 472.

suffered a "corresponding deprivation." But if a claim is based on the defendant's wrongdoing, it is not necessary to prove that there is a coincidence between loss suffered and benefit gained. The defendants had been enriched. the gain had been made a the expense of the plaintiffs' children, and through their children, at the plaintiffs' expense. It is true that the defendants were innocent of the crime; but they were claiming through the criminal and were benefiting from his wrongful act. Their position should be no different from that of Ethel Le Neve.[63] In concluding, on comparable facts, that a restitutionary claim should succeed, an English court may be guided by the analogy of section 71(4) of the Criminal Justice Act 1988 which states, in the context of the Crown's application for a confiscation order, that "a person benefits from an offence,[64] if he obtains property as a result of or in connection with its commission. . . . "

For these reasons there is much to be said for the view that publishers and ghost writers of a criminal's memoirs who have contracted with the criminal must account for their profits. If the court is ready to grant such an allowance,[65] the burden is on them to demonstrate what proportion of that gain is attributable to their skills and labour. Their position is quite different from writers who use an horrendous murder as the basis of a novel or play and who have never contracted with the criminal. In England no defendant can plead the First Amendment.[65a] Nonetheless the principles which it embodies may persuade an English court, if it is minded to recognise a restitutionary claim, also to recognise a defence that it is in the public interest that the book, play, film, etc., should be published; the analogy of the law of breach of confidence may guide the court; it is a defence which should be accepted only in the clearest of circumstances.[66]

It may be said that these problems are best solved by legislation. But it is most unlikely that legislation will be enacted in this country. Furthermore, the

---

[63] See above, p. 707.

[64] See Freiberg, above, n. 58. In this article he discusses the litigation involving Pat Pottle and Michael Randle who wrote the book, *The Blake Escape: How We Freed George Blake and Why*. They were paid £30,000 by the publishers. Having been indicted for offences relating to the escape, the Crown obtained a charging order over their homes, under the Criminal Justice Act 1988, ss.76 and 78. Their application to discharge it, on the ground that the £30,000 was not a benefit within the meaning of the statute, was unsuccessful. Section 71(4) of the 1988 Act provides that "a person benefits from an offence if he obtains property as a result of or *in connection with its commission* and his benefit is the value of the property so obtained" (emphasis supplied). It was held that the £30,000 was property connected with the alleged offences. However, Randle and Pottle were later acquitted and with their acquittal the charging order was discharged.

[65] Even an honest fiduciary is granted an allowance only in *exceptional* circumstances: see above, pp. 32–35.

[65a] In the U.S.A. over half of the states have imposed, by statute, an involuntary trust over any profits generated by a criminal's novels, plays, films, etc. The proceeds are held on trust for victims who can establish claims for damages against the criminal. Some statutes have, however, been held to be unconstitutional: see, *e.g. Simon and Schuster inc.* v. *Members of the New York State Crime Victims Board*, 112 S.Ct. 501 (1991).

[66] See below, pp. 700 *et seq.*

example of other jurisdictions demonstrates the pitfalls for its draftsman.[67] So, it may be a good thing that the burden will fall on the courts to build on existing common law principles so as to ensure that no criminal should benefit, directly or indirectly, from his crime.[68]

---

[67] On which see, Freiberg: above, n. 58.

[68] We do not see any tension between the acceptance of the restitutionary claim and the Forfeiture Act 1980: see above, p. 705. The court's discretion to modify the forfeiture rule arises where it precludes a morally blameless person from *acquiring* an interest in property. But the analogy of the statute may persuade the court (*cf.* above, p. 712, n. 64) to conclude that it should only grant the restitutionary claim in circumstances where it would not have allowed, at common law, a criminal to benefit from his crime.

CHAPTER 38

TORT AND RESTITUTIONARY CLAIMS

"A PERSON upon whom a tort has been committed and who brings an action for the benefits received by the tortfeasor is sometimes said to 'waive the tort.' "[1] "Waiver of tort" is a misnomer.[2] A party only waives a tort in the sense that he elects to sue in restitution to recover the defendant's unjust benefit rather than to sue in tort to recover damages[3]; he has a choice of alternative remedies. But the tort is not extinguished. Indeed it is said that it is a *sine qua non* of both remedies that he should establish that a tort has been committed.[4]

The earliest cases, which anticipated the early cases of "waiver of tort," concerned usurpers of offices[5] who had appropriated fees to which the plaintiff was entitled.[6] Though there had been cases before *Howard* v. *Wood*[7] in 1679, it was that decision which finally settled, though not without some doubt and misgiving,[8] that an action for money had and received would lie for the profits of the office wrongfully usurped, as an alternative to trover or case. The authority of such cases persuaded Holt C.J., in *Lamine* v. *Dorrell*,[9] to allow a plaintiff, whose goods had been converted, to waive the tort and recover in quasi-contract the price for which they were sold. In that case the torts waived

---

[1] *Restatement of Restitution,* § 525, cited by Viscount Simon in *United Australia Ltd.* v. *Barclays Bank Ltd.* [1941] A.C. 1, 18. Apparently this was the first time that the *Restatement* was referred to by an English judge; see Lord Denning (who was counsel for the appellants in that case) in (1949) 1 J.S.P.T.L. 258, 265–266.

[2] Occasional judicial doubts have been voiced as to its propriety; see, *e.g. Lamine* v. *Dorrell* (1701) 2 Ld.Raym. 1216, 1217, *per* Holt C.J.; *Burnett* v. *Lynch* (1826) 5 B. & C. 589, 608–609, *per* Littledale J.; *Neate* v. *Harding* (1851) 6 Ex. 349, 352, *per* Martin B.; *cf.* Woodward, op. cit. p. 438 and below, p. 715.

[3] *United Australia Ltd.* v. *Barclays Bank Ltd.* [1941] A.C. 1, 13, *per* Viscount Simon, 28, *per* Lord Atkin, 48, *per* Lord Porter.

[4] *Oughton* v. *Seppings* (1830) 1 B. & Ad. 241; *Turner* v. *Cameron's Coalbrook Steam Coal Co.* (1850) 5 Ex. 932; *Commercial Banking Co. of Sydney* v. *Mann* [1961] A.C. 1; *Chesworth* v. *Farrer* [1967] 1 Q.B. 407, 417, *per* Edmund Davies J. See also *Tooley* v. *Windham* (1591) Cro.Eliz. 206. *Cf. Heilbut* v. *Nevill* (1870) L.R. 5 C.P. 478; Winfield, *Province,* pp. 175–176.

[5] But see Jackson, op. cit. pp. 9–11, citing the use of the writ of account against receivers (of money) who had committed fraudulent conversion.

[6] Jackson, op. cit. pp. 61–64; for a discussion of these cases, see above, Chap. 28.

[7] (1679) 2 Lev. 245. For the basis of the plaintiff's restitutionary claim in these cases, see above, Chap. 28.

[8] See above, p. 577.

[9] (1701) 2 Ld.Raym. 1216.

were detinue and trover. Thereafter,[10] the courts permitted waiver of other torts, including trespass to goods[11] and to land,[12] and deceit.[13]

A plaintiff could, by waiving the tort, gain procedural[14] as well as substantive advantages; for example, it was a useful method of circumventing short limitation periods and the old common law rule that tortious actions died with the person.[15] Today there are other reasons why a plaintiff may want to sue in restitution rather in tort, one of the most important of which is that it may enable him to obtain restitution of a benefit gained by the tortfeasor from the tortious act in circumstances where he has suffered little or no loss.[16]

Some jurists have questioned whether a plaintiff should be allowed this election. Corbin condemned it as a "trick or legerdemain,"[17] and Prosser was unhappy that a plaintiff could, by waiving a technical trespass, strip the defendant of profits which he could never have himself gained.[18] Such criticisms are based on the hitherto accepted principle that the restitutionary claim is parasitic, in the sense that its existence is dependent on it being demonstrated that a tort has been committed. Even if it is admitted that the restitutionary claim is parasitic, it should not follow, for example, that the restitutionary claim should be statute-barred simply because the tortious claim is statute-barred, or that a tortfeasor should not be compelled to disgorge the profits gained from his tortious act.[19]

Indeed it has been argued[20] in recent years that the courts should recognise the existence of an independent restitutionary claim which is simply based on the wrongful acquisition of a benefit[21] and that the so-called waiver of tort cases

---

[10] For a discussion of the early authorities, see Jackson, op. cit. pp. 72–76.

[11] *Oughton* v. *Seppings* (1830) 1 B. & Ad. 241; *cf. Lindon* v. *Hooper* (1776) 1 Cowp. 414; see above, n. 4.

[12] *Powell* v. *Rees* (1837) 7 Ad. & El. 426.

[13] *Hill* v. *Perrott* (1810) 3 Taunt. 274; *Abbots* v. *Barry* (1820) 2 Brod. & B. 369; *cf. Clarke* v. *Dickson* (1858) E.B. & E. 148.

[14] Both the plaintiff and the defendant enjoyed procedural advantages; the plaintiff did not have to disclose his claim with the same particularity, and the defendant could plead the general issue. Indeed, in *Lindon* v. *Hooper* (1776) 1 Cowp. 414, 418 (see above, p. 273), Lord Mansfield held that money had and received could not lie to recover money paid for the release of cattle damage feasant, though the distress was unlawful, because the defendant would be "surprised" at the trial. See Jackson, *op. cit.* pp. 71–72, 80–81; Winfield, *Province*, p. 144; and (1984) 100 L.Q.R. 653, 656 *et seq.* [Hedley], who argues that waiver was a defendant's plea, "barring liability when the plaintiff could have sued in tort," which plea did not survive (should not have survived?) the abolition of the forms of action.

[15] Now abolished by the Law Reform (Miscellaneous Provisions) Act 1934. But see *Chesworth* v. *Farrer* [1967] 1 Q.B. 407 see below, p. 728.

[16] See below, pp. 726–727.

[17] *Waiver of Tort in Suit in Assumpsit*, 19 Yale L.J. 221, 235 (1910): see below, p. 728.

[18] *Torts* (5th ed., 1984), pp. 672 *et seq.*

[19] See below, pp. 726 *et seq.*

[20] Beatson, *The Use and Abuse of Unjust Enrichment*, op. cit. pp. 212 *et seq.*

[21] *Cf. Brocklebank* v. *R.* [1925] 1 K.B. 52, above, p. 246, where it is difficult to identify an "accepted" tort.

are simply examples of this broader category.[22] This analysis is jurisprudentially most attractive. But it is doubtful whether English law is sufficiently mature to adopt this general principle, although, in analysing this body of law, we shall look for guidance to other situations where English law has compelled other recognised wrongdoers,[22a] such as a fiduciary or a confidant, to make restitution.

1. What Torts Can Form the Basis of a Restitutionary Claim?

(a) *The Historical Legacy*

In *Hambly* v. *Trott*,[23] Lord Mansfield stated the general principle in the following words:

> "If it is a sort of injury by which the offender acquires no gain to himself at the expense of the sufferer, as beating or imprisoning a man, etc., there, the person injured has only a reparation for the *delictum* in damages to be assessed by a jury. But, where besides the crime, property is acquired which benefits the testator, there an action for the value of the property shall survive against the executor."

Later authority is said to have imposed two artificial limits on this general principle. First, it has been said that waiver is only possible if the defendant tortfeasor has received a specific sum of money.[24] Historically, this conclusion was justifiable[25] because the appropriate form of action was for money had and received, but the consequences of this reasoning were startling even to those who enunciated it. Thus it would prevent a tortfeasor who converted the plaintiff's goods and exchanged them for other goods from being sued in quasi-contract. To avoid these procedural difficulties a "receipt of money" was tacitly assumed on the most unlikely facts. The value of the labour of an apprentice, whom the defendant had seduced into his service, was recovered in *Lightly* v. *Clouston*[26] and *Foster* v. *Stewart*,[27] in an action for money had and received; and in *Powell* v. *Rees*,[28] Denman C.J. refused counsel leave to

---

[22] Beatson, *The Use and Abuse of Unjust Enrichment*, pp. 212 *et seq.*

[22a] For Burrows, the hall-mark of a wrong is that the injured party can be compensated for the loss he has suffered in consequence of what the plaintiff has done: *The Law of Restitution*, p. 378.

[23] (1776) 1 Cowp. 371, 376.

[24] See, *inter alia*, *Thompson* v. *Spender* (1767) Buller N.P. 129; *Nightingal* v. *Devisme* (1770) 5 Burr. 2589; Jackson, p. 77.

[25] See Lord Mansfield in *Nightingal* v. *Devisme* (1770) 5 Burr. 2589, 2592: the action for money had and received to the use of the plaintiff "will not lie in the present case where no money was received."

[26] (1808) 1 Taunt. 112, 114, *per* Sir James Mansfield C.J.

[27] (1814) 3 M. & S. 191. These decisions were criticised by Bowen L.J. in *Phillips* v. *Homfray* (1883) 24 Ch.D. 439, 462. But *cf. Restatement of Restitution*, §§ 134–135.

[28] (1837) 7 A. & E. 426; see, generally, *Norris* v. *Napper* (1704) 2 Ld.Raym. 1007; *Andrew* v. *Robinson* (1812) 3 Camp. 199; *Hill* v. *Perrott* (1810) 3 Taunt. 274; *Abbots* v. *Barry* (1820) 2 Brod. & B. 367; *Neate* v. *Harding* (1851) 6 Ex. 349; *Russell* v. *Bell* (1842) 10 M. & W. 340, 352, *per* Abinger C.B.

There are two 19th century cases. *Ferguson* v. *Carrington* (1829) 9 B. & C. 59 and *Strutt* v. *Smith*

question a jury's finding that coal, which had been converted, had been sold at the market price.[29] Today such procedural limitations should not artificially limit the restitutionary claim. The courts should no longer have need to resort to transparent fictions to award restitution of benefits obtained through the defendant's tortious act.[30]

Secondly, at one time it was said that a restitutionary claim does not lie if the tortfeasor has merely gained a negative benefit from his wrongful act and, in particular, if he has benefited from the use and occupation of land during a period of adverse possession.[31] *Phillips* v. *Homfray*[32] is the authority cited to support these propositions. In *Phillips* v. *Homfray* the defendants, in a cross-suit, sought injunctive and other relief against the plaintiffs, who owned a colliery business in partnership. The plaintiffs, who had unsuccessfully sought specific performance of a contract of sale, had removed coal from the defendants' land and, in doing so, had used their passages. The Vice-Chancellor refused the injunction but directed, as against the surviving partners, three inquiries[32a] as to:

(1) the quantities and market value of the coal removed by the plaintiffs from under the defendants' land;

(2) the quantities of coal conveyed through the use of passages under the defendants' land; and

(3) the amount which ought to be paid for carriage of the coal (a "way-leave") and royalty in respect of the use of these passages.

But one of the partners had died since the filing of the suit. The Vice-Chancellor directed only the first inquiry against his estate. On appeal Lord Hatherley L.C. affirmed the Vice-Chancellor's decrees; the tortious claims, the basis of the second and third inquiries, had died with the tortfeasor. On the subsequent death of another partner, the suit was revived against his executrix, who moved that the second and third inquiries be stayed.[33] The Court of

---

(1834) 1 C.M. & R. 312, which support the proposition that a person could not sue in *indebitatus assumpsit* for goods sold and delivered until the period of credit given by the contract had expired even though the contract had been induced by fraud. As Parke B. said, "if they treat the transaction as a contract at all they must take the contract altogether, and be bound by the specified terms" (p. 315). But such a contract must be immediately voidable. If the plaintiff can sue for trover, he should be able to waive the tort and obtain restitution forthwith of the defendant's unjust benefit. See also *Clarke* v. *Dickson* (1858) 1 E.B. & E. 148; Street, *Damages*, pp. 258–259.

[29] For a full citation of American authorities, see Reporters' Notes to the *Restatement of Restitution*, p. 189; Palmer, *op. cit.* Vol. I, Chap. 2.

[30] But see below, pp. 718–719.

[31] There were two other reasons why, at one time, courts refused to recognise a quasi-contractual claim. Courts were reluctant to determine title to land in *assumpsit* actions: see (1889) 2 Harv.L.R. 1 [Ames]; Matthew Bacon, *Abridgement* (7th ed.), Vol. 1, p. 339. Again, it was said that, as a disseisor purported to take possession as of right, the trespass could not therefore be waived and an imaginary contract substituted for it: see below, p. 719. But the historical antecedents of *assumpsit* should not today bar a restitutionary claim; and the implied contract theory is now seen to be, what it always was, a fallacy: see above, p. 5.

[32] (1871) 6 Ch.App. 770; (1883) 24 Ch.D. 439; (1890) 44 Ch.D. 694; [1892] 1 Ch. 465.

[32a] There was a fourth inquiry which is not relevant to this discussion.

[33] Before the litigation was finally resolved all the partners, the original plaintiffs, had died.

Appeal refused to order the second and third inquiries. In the view of the majority of the Court of Appeal the success of the claim was not dependent upon the particular form of action, whether it was based on the deceased's tortious act or upon any "implied contract or duty." For the deceased partner's estate could not be said to have "swollen" from the use of the way-leaves. As Bowen L.J. said[34]:

> "If such alternative form of action could be conceived it must be either an action for the use, by the Plaintiff's permission, of the Plaintiff's roads and passages . . . Or it must be in the shape of an action for money had and received, based upon the supposition that funds are in the hands of the executors which properly belong in law or in equity to the Plaintiffs. We do not believe that the principle of waiving a tort and suing in contract can be carried further than this—that a plaintiff is entitled, if he chooses it, to abstain from treating as a wrong the acts of the defendant in cases where, independently of the question of wrong, the plaintiff could make a case for relief."

The Lord Justice thought that the difficulties of extending the principle of the "waiver of tort" cases were "insuperable."[35]

> "The circumstances under which [the trespasser] used the road appear to us to negative the idea that he meant to pay for it. Nor have the assets of the deceased Defendant been necessarily swollen by what he has done. He saved his estate expense, but he did not bring into it any additional property or value belonging to another person."[36]

In contrast, Baggallay L.J., in his dissenting judgment, concluded, relying on *Hambly* v. *Trott*,[37] that an account should lie; for a "gain or acquisition to the wrongdoer by the work and labour of another does not necessarily, if it does at all, imply a diminution of the property of such other person." He continued[38]:

> "I cannot appreciate the reasons upon which it is insisted that, although executors are bound to account for any accretions to the property of their testator derived directly from his wrongful act, they are not liable for the amount of value of any other benefit which may be derived by his estate from or by reason of such wrongful act . . . A gain or acquisition to the wrongdoer by the work and labour of another does not necessarily, if it does at all, imply a diminution of the property of such other person. Whether the amount of the wayleave which a person could reasonably be called upon to pay for the use for the carriage of his minerals over the roads of another would be a fair measure of the gain or acquisition to the

---

[34] (1883) 24 Ch.D. 439, 461, delivering the judgment of himself and Cotton L.J.
[35] *Ibid.* at p. 462.
[36] *Ibid.* at pp. 462–463. Moreover, an account in equity (which the defendant had originally sought) would only lie if the defendant "has something in his hands representing the plaintiff's property or the proceeds or value of it. But if there were any such it could be recovered at law as well as in equity": at p. 463.
[37] (1776) 1 Cowp. 371; see above, p. 716.
[38] (1883) 24 Ch.D. 439, 471–472.

property of the person who has so used them without paying any way-leave, is a question which it is not necessary to decide. I entertain no doubts as to there being ample means of ascertaining the amount of gain or acquisition to the property of a person so using the roads of another."

The issue before the Court of Appeal was, therefore, whether any form of action survived the trespasser's death. Baggallay L.J. thought an account did lie and that it did not matter that the benefit did not involve a diminution of the owner's assets, a conclusion which a modern lawyer should endorse.

Bowen L.J.'s rejection of the defendants' request for the second and third inquiries was for reasons which may have been then valid, but which can no longer be supported. At common law an action for money had and received would lie only if the plaintiff had received the defendants' money, and he had not; but today no court will allow a restitutionary claim to founder because of the limitations of the old forms of action or deny that the saving of expense is a benefit. Now that the *actio personalis* rule has been abolished, there remains the objection that no contract can be implied between the parties because the deceased was a trespasser who, by setting up an adverse title, negatived the implication of a contract; such a contract had to be based on the plaintiff's permission. Today the so-called implied contract is seen to be what it always was, a fiction,[39] its assumption that the claimant, by suing in quasi-contract, had ratified the trespasser's acts is fallacious.[40] In *United Australia Ltd.* v. *Barclays Bank Ltd.*[41] the House of Lords exorcised that particular ghost. Once exorcised, the dicta in *Phillips* v. *Homfray* do not stand in the way of the acceptance of the principle that a tortfeasor should be personally liable to make restitution for any benefit gained at the plaintiff's expense, whether that benefit be positive or negative. This makes good legal as well as economic sense.[42]

Moreover, there is some authority which supports this view, and allows a plaintiff to recover for the use and hire of equipment which the defendant refused to return to him. In the old case of *Rumsey* v. *The North Eastern Railway*[43] the tortfeasor was required to pay a sum which represented the reasonable hiring charge of a chattel. The plaintiff had taken a first-class excursion ticket on the railway, which was issued on the express condition that

---

[39] See above, pp. 5 *et seq.*
[40] *Ibid.* for discussion of the "implied contract" heresy.
[41] [1941] A.C. 1, 18, *per* Viscount Simon, 28–29, *per* Lord Atkin; discussed below, p. 732. But see *Morris* v. *Tarrant* [1971] 2 Q.B. 143, 158, *per* Lane J.
[42] Some jurisdictions in the U.S.A. have adopted and extended Baggallay L.J.'s reasoning: see *Raven Red Ash Coal Co.* v. *Ball*, 39 S.E. 2d 231 (1946); *Edwards* v. *Lee's Administrators*, 96 S.W. 2d 1028 (1936). *Cf.* the cases where the defendant trespassed on the plaintiff's land for the purpose of acquiring geological information about mineral deposits: *Shell Petroleum Co.* v. *Skully*, 71 F. 2d 772 (1934); *Angelloz* v. *Humble Oil & Ref. Co.*, 199 So. 656 (1940); *Phillips Petroleum Co.* v. *Cowden*, 241 F. 2d 586 (1957).
Civilian jurisdictions are ready to allow restitution: see *Le Roux* v. *Van Biljon* [1956] (2) S.A. 17 (T.); Req. December 11, 1928 (D.Hebd. 1929, 18), (cited [1934] 5 C.L.J. 204, 214 [Gutteridge and David]): (1962) 36 Tul.L.Rev. 605, 644 [Nicholas].
[43] (1863) 14 C.B. (N.S.) 641. See also *Hambly* v. *Trott* (1776) 1 Cowp. 371, 375, *per* Lord Mansfield.

he could carry no luggage. He did in fact take luggage and was caught in the act. The defendants, who had seized his luggage, claimed a lien over it and refused to give it up, save on payment of its charges. The plaintiff then brought an action for damages for the unlawful detention of his luggage. The Court of Common Pleas dismissed the claim. Erle C.J. held[44] that the facts raised an implied promise by the plaintiff to pay a reasonable sum for the carriage of the luggage. But Williams J. treated the facts as analogous to waiver of tort; the plaintiff intended to defraud the company and "the fraud of the plaintiff was equivalent to a request to carry the portmanteau for hire."[45]

More recently, in *Strand Electric and Engineering Co. Ltd.* v. *Brisford Entertainments Ltd.*,[46] the plaintiffs were allowed to recover the full market rate for hiring equipment which the defendant had refused to return.[47] Denning L.J. described the plaintiffs' claim as one "for restitution rather than an action of tort," and he rejected the argument that the plaintiffs could not recover because they would not have used the equipment during the period of detention.[48] The defendant's liability should not be limited to the loss suffered by the plaintiff.

(b) *A Question of Principle: should all Tortfeasors Disgorge the Benefits Gained from their Torts?*

A plaintiff may obtain restitution of the benefits gained from the following tortious acts: conversion and detinue (wrongful interference with goods)[49]; trespass to land and to goods[50]; deceit[51]; (probably) passing off and injurious falsehood[52]; and (possibly) inducing a breach of contract.[53] No innocent party has sought to recover the benefit gained by a defendant who committed the

---

[44] At p. 650; see also Willes J. at p. 653.

[45] At p. 652. An unusual and analogous case is *Ablah* v. *Eyman*, 365 P. 2d 181 (1961), where the Supreme Court of Kansas allowed the plaintiff to waive the tort of replevin. The defendant had wrongfully replevied the defendant's working papers. "The value must be determined by its value to the user."

[46] [1952] 2 Q.B. 246.

[47] A comparable measure of damages is now recoverable in tort: Torts (Interference with Goods) Act 1977, s.3; *Hillesden Securities Ltd.* v. *Ryjack Ltd.* [1983] 1 W.L.R. 959.

[48] At p. 255. The two other members of the Court of Appeal treated the claim as a claim in detinue. For Somervell L.J. the nearest analogy was a claim for mesne profits (at p. 252). The judgment of Romer L.J. is even more narrowly couched (at p. 257). He left open the question what would have been the position if the property was non-profit earning or if the plaintiff had never applied it to non-remunerative purposes. (But contrast *The Medina* [1900] A.C. 113, 117, *per* Earl of Halsbury.) In *Stoke-on-Trent Council* v. *W. & J. Wass Ltd.* [1988] 3 All E.R. 394 (see below, pp. 722–723), Nourse L.J. preferred their analysis.

[49] *Lamine* v. *Dorrell* (1701) 2 Ld.Raym. 1216; *United Australia Ltd.* v. *Barclays Bank Ltd.* [1941] A.C. 1; see above, pp. 713–714.

[50] *Oughton* v. *Seppings* (1830) 1 B. & Ad. 241; *Powell* v. *Rees* (1837) 7 Ad. & El. 426; see above, p. 715.

[51] *Hill* v. *Perrott* (1810) 3 Taunt. 274; *Abbots* v. *Barry* (1820) 2 Brod. & B. 369. *Cf. Clarke* v. *Dixon* (1858) E.B. & E. 148; see above, p. 715.

[52] We know of no authority, but it is a proprietary tort. *Cf.* an action for patent infringement where it is presumed that the sales made by the infringer were taken from the patent owner: *Watson, Laidlaw & Co. Ltd.* v. *Pott, Cassels and Williamson* (1914) 31 R.P.C. 104, 120, *per* Lord Shaw; *Meters Ltd.* v. *Metropolitan Gas Meter Ltd.* (1911) 28 R.P.C. 157, C.A.

[53] There is no English case. But see *Federal Sugar Refining Co.* v. *The United States Equalisation Board*, 268 F. 575 (1920) (S.D.N.Y.), discussed below, p. 724.

torts of defamation or nuisance,[54] although these are torts which may enrich a tortfeasor. In contrast, assault, battery and negligence do not, although exceptionally they may do so.[55]

Some writers have sought to rationalise this body of common law in economic terms. Professor Palmer has suggested that it is necessary to determine whether the plaintiff's interest "is of a type for which it is normal to acquire a right of user by purchase,"[56] in other words, whether it has any market value. Professor Birks's explanation is somewhat similar: is the tort an "anti-enrichment" tort?; "was the prevention of the enrichment which the defendant had acquired a main purpose behind the wrong which he has committed?" At the same time he accepts that no wrongdoer should be allowed to retain a gain if he deliberately set out to enrich himself by committing the wrongful act—a significant exception to his principle of "anti-enrichment."[57]

Few common law courts have rationalised the law in these terms; and no English court has sought to weave any sophisticated golden thread to unite the cases on "waiver of tort." In *Hambly* v. *Trott*,[58] Lord Mansfield was content to contrast the position of the tortfeasor who "acquires no gain" with that of the tortfeasor who acquires property which benefits him. In our view, English courts should adopt a similar principle: namely, if it can be demonstrated that a tortfeasor has gained a benefit and that benefit would not have been gained but for the tort, he should be required to make restitution. If adopted, it may be possible for the injured party to recover the benefit gained by a defendant from tortious acts which have not hitherto formed the basis of a restitutionary claim; for example, nuisance or defamation.

In *Kirk* v. *Todd*[59] the plaintiff failed to recover damages from the estate of the tortfeasor who had polluted his stream. Sir George Jessel M.R. thought "this is a very hard case"; but any claim must die with the tortfeasor.[60] That bar no longer exists. The plaintiff's interest infringed by the defendant's tortious act is a proprietary interest. The benefit thereby gained is the expense which the tortfeasor saved or even the profits gained from the tortious act.[61] In an appropriate case a restitutionary claim should then lie.[62]

---

[54] See below, pp. 721–722.

[55] *e.g.* money may be paid to a dangerously belligerent thief; or a thug may have been paid £15,000 for assaulting the plaintiff and see below, p. 725.

[56] Palmer, *op. cit.* Vol. I, § 2.10. For the position in French and German law, see Zweigert and Kötz, *op. cit.* Vol. II, pp. 232 *et seq.*

[57] *Introduction*, pp. 328–329. The quotation is at p. 329. Burrows, *The Law of Restitution*, pp. 394–396, follows Jackman in [1989] C.L.J. 302: restitution is justified if it protects "facilitative institutions"; and facilitative institutions are "power conferring facilities for the creation of private arrangements between individuals, such as contracts, trusts and private property." If this is to conclude, for example, that a person's reputation and privacy are less deserving of the law's protection, then we do not find it a convincing test for determining whether restitution should be allowed or denied.

[58] (1776) 1 Cowp. 371; see above, p. 716.

[59] (1882) 21 Ch.D. 484.

[60] At p. 488.

[61] If he is a conscious wrongdoer: see above, pp. 32–33 and below, p. 727.

[62] But see below, p. 725 for a possible limitation of this principle.

A defamatory statement injures reputation, not property. There has been no attempt in England to recover the benefit gained from the publication of a defamatory statement,[63] and in the few reported cases in the United States the plaintiff has been unsuccessful.[64] It is said that a plaintiff has no economic interest in his reputation. But the law does protect his reputation and the only question is whether it is desirable that the courts should recognise a restitutionary claim to further this purpose. It is true that it is most unlikely that a person would ever license another to defame him; but it does not follow that a defamer should be allowed to retain a gain earned from bringing another into hatred, ridicule and contempt.[65] As the Court of Appeal has recently recognised,[66] an award of damages for loss of reputation may be a crude and arbitrary remedy. In contrast, to compel a defamer to disgorge the gain from the tort is to grant a nicely fashioned remedy which does not punish him. As yet English law appears to deny the possibility of such a restitutionary claim, while permitting an award of exemplary damages if it is found that the defamer's conduct has been calculated to make a profit which may exceed the compensation payable by him to the plaintiff.[67] It is a distinct question whether the defendant's gain is the product of the publication of the libel.[68]

Hitherto the courts have been reluctant to contemplate the possibility of novel restitutionary claims for benefits gain from tortious acts. Instead counsel have sought to persuade the court that the benefit gained by the tortfeasor is the measure of the loss suffered by the plaintiff from the tortious act.[69] On occasion a court has accepted that argument, but more frequently has rejected it on the grounds that it may give a plaintiff a right to substantial damages where no loss had been suffered.[70] This was the fate of the Stoke-on-Trent City Council, which unsuccessfully sought damages from W. & J. Wass Ltd., who

---

[63] *Cf. Broadway Approvals v. Odhams Press Ltd.* [1965] 1 W.L.R. 805; *McCarey v. Associated Newspapers Ltd.* [1965] 2 Q.B. 86.

[64] *Hart v. E. P. Dutton*, 93 N.Y.S. 871 (2d) (1949), aff'd 98 N.Y.S. 2d 773 (1949). The plaintiff's claim, which was based on an alleged libel in the defendant's book, failed for reasons which we do not find persuasive: damages would be an adequate remedy; the tortious action was already statute-barred; and the restitutionary claim would impose unacceptable hazards on publishers. However, damages may be less than adequate; it is accepted that a plaintiff may take advantage of the longer "contractual" limitation period (see below, p. 728) even though his tort claim is barred; and it is not easy to see why a restitutionary claim is an unacceptable hazard when in England and in the U.S.A. he may be compelled to pay exemplary damages: *Broome v. Cassell Ltd.* [1972] A.C. 1027.

[65] This will not deprive either party of his right to a jury trial. He may elect his remedy, on which see below, p. 732.

[66] *Sutcliffe v. Pressdram Ltd.* [1991] 1 Q.B. 153, C.A.

[67] *Cassell Ltd. v. Broome* [1972] A.C. 1027.

[68] See below, p. 723. A comparable problem would arise if an English court were to accept that it is tortious conduct to exploit for profit another's personality without his permission. In the U.S.A. a restitutionary claim has been recognised: see *Zacchini v. Scripps-Howard Broadcasting Co.*, 433 U.S. 562 (1977).

[69] *Cf.* the "wayleave" and patent authorities, cited in *Stoke-on-Trent City Council v. W. & J. Wass Ltd.* [1988] 3 All E.R. 394, 398–399, 402–403.

[70] *Stoke-on-Trent City Council v. W. & J. Wass Ltd.* [1988] 3 All E.R. 394, 401–402, *per* Nourse L.J.

had knowingly and repeatedly infringed its exclusive proprietary right to hold a retail market.[71] The Court of Appeal was not persuaded that substantial damages, measured by the fee which the Council would have demanded if it had been asked for its licence to hold such a market, should be awarded, when it was evident that the Council had suffered only nominal damage. In Nourse L.J.'s opinion, to accept this principle would "revolutionise the tort of nuisance by making it unnecessary to prove loss. Moreover, if the principle were to be applied in nuisance, why not in other torts where the defendant's wrong can work to his own profit, for example in defamation?[72] But the Lord Justice did admit the possibility that "the English law of tort, more especially the so-called 'proprietary torts,' will in due course make a more deliberate move towards recovery based not on loss suffered by the plaintiff but on the unjust enrichment of the defendant."[73]

The claim for damages in cases like *Stoke-on Trent City Council* conceals a claim to strip a defendant of his unjust enrichment.[74] In our view there is much to be said for the recognition of a restitutionary claim. A plaintiff should be allowed to recover the benefit gained by the defendant from his tortious act if he can show that the benefit was the product of the tort. It should be irrelevant that he suffered no, or little, loss. The decision of the Court of Appeal in the *Stoke-on-Trent City Council* case is a harsh one. A tortfeasor who had consistently flouted in a most calculated and cynical fashion the plaintiff's exclusive right was allowed to retain the benefit gained from the tort. Indeed the benefit gained, which he should have been required to disgorge, should have been the profits which W. & J. Wass Ltd. made from the tort, rather than the licence fee which the plaintiff would have demanded from an honest licensee.[75]

(c) *When is the Benefit from a Tortious Act Gained at the Plaintiff's Expense?*

The problem of determining whether a benefit from a tortious act has been gained at the plaintiff's expense may arise in a number of contexts.[76] The question—would the defendant have gained the benefit but for the tort?—does not always admit an easy answer. A defendant may admit liability but claim that it was his intellectual and financial contributions which generated the benefit gained by him; for example, the plaintiff may have been defamed in only one paragraph of a best-selling novel, 500 pages long. But the court have, in other contexts, overcome these difficulties and have apportioned profits if it was necessary to do so. In the *Spycatcher*[77] case the House of Lords held that the *Sunday Times* must account for its profits when it published an extract from the book of that name, knowing that it contained confidential information

---

[71] At pp. 395–396.
[72] At p. 401.
[73] At p. 402.
[74] *Cf.* above, pp. 415 *et seq.*
[75] See above, pp. 31–35, for a full discussion.
[76] See above, pp. 720 *et seq.*
[77] *A.-G.* v. *Guardian Newspapers Ltd.* (*No. 2*) [1990] 1 A.C. 109. See above, pp. 32–33.

acquired by the author, the Crown's fiduciary, while working for MI5. The House was not deterred by the fact that the taking of the account would be an arduous task. And the courts have also not been deterred in making an apportionment when confronted with defendants who, having infringed another's trade mark or copyright, pleaded that their profits were the result of their contribution rather than the fruits of the infringement.[78] The burden should be on the infringer[79] to prove the manner and degree of his contribution.

Similarly, it may be a finely balanced question whether the benefit gained was the product of the tort or the defendant's independent dealings with a third party.[80] This question arose in the United States in *Federal Sugar Refining Co.* v. *United States Sugar Equalisation Board*.[81] The plaintiff had contracted to sell a quantity of sugar to the Norwegian government for 6.60 cents per pound. It was alleged that the defendant induced the Norwegian government to repudiate its contract with the plaintiff and to buy the same quantity of sugar from them for 11 cents a pound. The defendant was able to do this because it had exclusive power to issue a licence for the export of sugar from the United States. From this sale the defendant made a net profit of $219,744. In his complaint the plaintiff sought to recover that profit. The complaint was held good on a demurrer. Judge Mayer rejected the argument that nothing had been

> "taken away from plaintiff and added to the treasury of defendant. The point is whether defendant unjustly enriched itself by doing a wrong to plaintiff in such manner and in such circumstances that in equity and good conscience defendant should not be permitted to retain that by which it has been enriched. . . ."[81a]

It was irrelevant that the plaintiff had made a losing contract, for the prevailing market price at the date when the plaintiff was bound to deliver the sugar appeared to be 8.12 cents per pound. "The action is not for damages for breach of contract, but for the profit which the defendant is alleged to have made as the result of its alleged wrongful acts.[82] The court did not expressly ask whether the defendant's gain was made at the expense of the Norwegian government or at the expense of the plaintiff. But the court must have concluded that it was made at the plaintiff's expense; if the defendant had not

---

[78] *e.g. Watson, Laidlaw & Co. Ltd.* v. *Pott, Cassels and Williamson* (1914) 31 R.P.C. 104, 114, *per* Lord Atkinson: see above, p. 691.

[79] *Cf. Lupton* v. *White* (1808) 15 Ves. 432; *Peter Pan Manufacturing Corp.* v. *Corsets Silhouette Ltd.* [1964] 1 W.L.R. 96: see above, p. 691.

[80] *The Restatement of Restitution* § 133 left open this question.

[81] 268 F. 575, 582, (1920) (S.D.N.Y.). See also *Caskie* v. *Philadelphia Rapid Transit Co.*, 184 A. 17 (1936) (S.Ct. of Pa.); *Second National Bank of Toledo* v. *M. Samuel & Sons Inc.*, 12 F. 2d 963 (1926); *Scymanski* v. *Dufault*, 491 P. 2d 1050 (1971) (where a constructive trust was imposed); *National Merchandising Corp.* v. *Leyden*, 348 N.E. 2d 771, 775–776 (1976).

[81a] At p. 582.

[82] At p. 583.

induced the Norwegian government to break its contract with the plaintiff, it would never have had the opportunity of contracting with the Norwegian government and making the profit it did. The restitutionary claim succeeded even though the benefit was indirectly gained at the plaintiff's expense.[83]

In the *Federal Sugar* case, and in the other cases hitherto discussed in this Chapter, the tortfeasor injured one identifiable individual. Tortious acts or omissions may, however, cause damage to a number, even a very large number, of people. The Ford Motor Company manufactured its *Pinto* but did not make a necessary modification to it even though it would have cost only $15.30 to have done so.[84] It was later held, in litigation brought by a Pinto owner who was injured in a crash, that Ford was grossly negligent in failing to have made the modification. Again, a factory belches smoke and fumes over an area which covers thousands of neighbouring households; its owner had previously rejected a proposal to install an anti-pollution device on the ground of expense. The owner is later held liable in nuisance.

In these examples there are formidable difficulties in measuring the benefit gained at the expense of each injured party. What is the benefit gained by Ford at the expense of the *first* injured owner to recover against the company? Is it $15.30 multiplied by the number of defective Pintos which were manufactured? Or is it $15.30? Is it relevant that the owner may have brought the car more cheaply because Ford did not make the modification; or, conversely, that if Ford had installed the device and charged a higher price, its sales would have dropped? And what do later Pinto owners who are injured recover?[85]

The factory which creates a nuisance poses a comparable problem. What is the factory owner's benefit gained at each householder's expense? Is it the sum which the factory owner would have had to pay each owner for the privilege of polluting his property? Or is it a proportion of the owner's profits, or the sum which he has saved from not installing the anti-pollution device? Does the owner of a nearby mansion recover more than the owner of a nearby terraced house?[86]

The difficulties confronting a court in measuring and valuing the benefit gained by Ford and the factory owner in these two examples persuade us that, where there is the probability of multiple plaintiffs who suffer injury or loss from the same tortious act, a restitutionary claim should be denied. If it is not known how many people are likely to be injured or to sue the tortfeasor any valuation of the benefit gained at the expense of *this* plaintiff may be conjectural. Furthermore, any judicial inquiry, with the complex economic evidence which may be introduced, will be inefficient.[87]

---

[83] See above, pp. 57–58.
[84] This hypothetical is based on *Grimshaw* v. *Ford Motor Co.*, 119 Cal.App. 3d 757 (1981); the plaintiff was awarded compensatory and punitive damages.
[85] *Cf.* Laycock, *Modern American Remedies* (Boston, 1985), pp. 137–138; Palmer, *op. cit.* Vol. I, § 2.10; 80 Col.L.R. 504, 554–555 (1980) [Friedmann].
[86] *Cf.* Palmer, *op. cit.* Vol. I, pp. 137–138; see also 80 Col.L.R. 504, 555 (1980) [Friedmann].
[87] See generally Posner, *Economic Analysis of Law.*

2. The Advantages of Bringing a Restitutionary Claim

(a) *Quantum Meruit Claims: Accounting of Profits*

There are a number of reasons why a plaintiff may wish to claim the benefit which a tortfeasor has gained from the tortious act, though they are fewer than they were.[88] He will be most anxious to do so if the tortfeasor's gain is greater than his loss. One objection to allowing such a claim is said to be that the law should not protect so generously the plaintiff's interest which has been infringed,[89] particularly if he suffered little or no loss. We reject the conclusion that damages are an adequate remedy,[90] and conclude that in principle a restitutionary claim should normally be recognised.

A plaintiff may claim on a *quantum meruit* the amount which a tortfeasor saves.[91] So, in *Strand Electric and Engineering Co.* v. *Brisford Entertainments*,[92] the plaintiff was allowed to recover from the defendant a reasonable hiring fee in respect of the chattel which he had converted. He did not claim that he was entitled to recover the profits which the defendant had gained from the wrongful act. If the defendant had consciously exploited the plaintiff's chattel an accounting might well have been a more appropriate remedy.

In *Re Simms*,[93] all the members of the Court of Appeal concluded that the claim that the tortfeasor should account for his profits must fail on the ground that the plaintiff's election to treat the defendant as a tortfeasor prevented the plaintiff from treating him as his agent, and therefore from establishing the promise necessary for the success of an action for money had and received.[94] In *United Australia Ltd.* v. *Barclays Bank Ltd.*,[95] the House of Lords repudiated this view of the basis of the quasi-contractual action. In principle, there is no reason why a restitutionary claim should not lie in an appropriate case. Moreover, in *Phillips* v. *Homfray*,[96] the Court of Appeal ordered the executors of a trespasser to account for the profits from the act of trespass, namely the market value of the coal, after all just allowances and expenses, taken from the injured parties' land.

---

[88] See above, p. 715.

[89] See above, pp. 715, 721.

[90] It is true that a court may now assess damages more generously than it did in the past, *e.g.* in awarding mesne profits: *cf.* above, p. 719.

[91] See above, p. 3.

[92] [1952] 2 Q.B. 246; but see above, pp. 719–720 and n. 48.

[93] [1934] Ch. 1.

[94] In *Re Simms* the defendant had used his own money and skills in the performance of the contracts, and, it appears, it could not be determined with accuracy to what extent he took advantage of the bankrupt's work. But *Re Simms* is no authority for denying an accounting if it is demonstrable that the profits earned are clearly attributable to the use of the plaintiff's property. Moreover, in comparable cases, the burden was on the wrongdoer to prove what percentage of the profits was the product of his own independent efforts or the use of his own property: see above, pp. 35, 691. However, in *Re Simms*, Romer L.J. concluded (at p. 33), in our view wrongly, that the tortfeasor should not be liable to make restitution.

[95] [1941] A.C. 1; see below, p. 732.

[96] [1892] 1 Ch. 465: see above, p. 716.

In analogous situations, a defendant has been compelled to disgorge profits gained from the improper exploitation of a trade secret and a trade mark.[97] The sparse common law suggests that it is only the wrongdoer who knowingly breaks confidence who must account.[98] The Patent Act 1977[99] and the Copyright, Designs and Patents Act 1988[1] draw a somewhat similar distinction. This body of law also suggests that the burden is on the wrongdoer to demonstrate that the profits, or a proportion of them, are the product of his own independent efforts or the use of his own property.[2] "This is obviously a matter which cannot be determined by mathematical calculation or with absolute accuracy. At best, the result can only be an approximation."[3] Even if the wrongdoer fails to discharge that burden, the court may exceptionally grant him reasonable remuneration.[4] Moreover, an account is a discretionary remedy, and it should always be open to a court to deny it even though the tortfeasor was a conscious wrongdoer.

Conversely, if the tortfeasor has innocently caused harm to another, for example, if he has used that other's chattel or land profitably, then it should normally be more appropriate to require him to pay the fee which that other would have demanded for a licence to do what he did.[5] But exceptionally a court may require even an innocent tortfeasor to account. So, an innocent converter who buys a chattel from a thief will be accountable for the profits made from any subsequent resale; similarly a fiduciary is, though for different reasons, liable to account if he innocently exploits his fiduciary office. The plaintiff's economic interest in the title to his own chattel justifies the account; and a fiduciary must be compelled to disgorge his gain in order to dissuade other fiduciaries from the temptation of profiting from their position of trust.[6]

(b) *Avoiding Statutory or Common Law Bars to a Restitutionary Claim*

A tortfeasor may defend himself by invoking a statutory or common law bar which appears to defeat the injured party's restitutionary claim. For example, he may point to a statutory provision or a common law rule which grants him immunity from any tortious claim. But a restitutionary claim should not necessarily fail simply because the claim in tort would fail. The *raison d'être* of the statutory or common law bar is critical. It may be to safeguard the

---

[97] *Peter Pan Manufacturing Co.* v. *Corsets Silhouette Ltd.* [1964] 1 W.L.R. 96: see below, p. 691; *Edelsten* v. *Edelsten* (1863) 1 De G.J. & Sm. 185, 189–190, *per* Lord Westbury.
[98] See above, pp. 690–692.
[99] ss.61 and 62 (patents).
[1] ss.96 and 97 (copyright).
[2] See above, p. 691.
[3] *Watson, Laidlaw & Co.* v. *Pott, Cassels and Williamson* [1914] 31 R.P.C. 104, 114, *per* Lord Atkinson.
[4] *Guinness plc* v. *Saunders* [1990] 2 A.C. 663. But contrast *O'Sullivan* v. *Management Agency & Music Ltd.* [1985] Q.B. 428; see above, pp. 32–35.
[5] *Cf.* above, pp. 31–32.
[6] See above, Chap. 33.

defendant only from a claim for damages which may seriously impede his social, political or economic activities.[7] It would then be an illegitimate extension of the policy of the statutory provision to reject the restitutionary claim and allow the defendant to retain his benefit. On the other hand, that claim should fail if it would frustrate or circumvent the policy of the statute or common law rule which denies the tortious claim. In every case the court should expressly address these questions, as did the House of Lords in the *Universe Sentinel*[8] case. In that case the House rejected the restitutionary claim, concluding that the sections of the Trade Union and Labour Relations Act 1974 "afford an indication . . . of where public policy requires that line to be drawn." That conclusion is debatable[9]; but the analysis of the questions to be answered cannot be faulted.[10]

We turn now to discuss particular statutory or common law bars to a restitutionary claim, the most important of which is the Limitation Act 1980.[11]

The Limitation Act

A plaintiff's claim in tort may be barred by lapse of time when a restitutionary claim may not. An illustration of such a case is *Chesworth* v. *Farrer*.[12] In this action a bailor made a claim against the administrator of the bailee's estate, alleging that certain antiques had not been accounted to her or had been lost. Her cause of action in tort was statute-barred since proceedings had not been brought against the deceased bailee, "not later than six months after his personal representative took out representation."[13] Nevertheless Edmund Davies J. held that the plaintiff could waive the tort and claim the proceeds of the wrongful sale. The action for money had and received was "an action analogous to one brought in contract, regarding which the *actio personalis* rule

---

[7] *Cf.* above, pp. 252–253.

[8] [1983] 1 A.C. 366. See too *Dimskal Shipping Co. S.A.* v. *International Transport Workers' Federation, The Evia Luck* [1991] 4 All E.R. 871, 874–875, *per* Lord Templeman, 884–885, *per* Lord Goff: see above, pp. 252–253 and below, p. 731.

[9] See above, pp. 252–253. *Cf.* Birks, *op. cit.* pp. 349–351.

[10] A legislature may confer immunity from a suit in tort for other reasons. For example, immunity may be based on a close family relationship, such as a husband and wife: contrast *Chandler* v. *Chandler* [1951] Queensland W.N. 20 (restitutionary claim denied) with *Barnet* v. *Barnet* 12 P.D. 565 (1958) (discussed in (1980) 80 Col.L.R. 504, 540, n. 198 [Friedmann], where the Israeli Supreme Court allowed recovery). For the cases concerning claims against the U.S.A., see Palmer, *op. cit.* Vol. I, para. 2.3.

[11] At one time tortious claims were not provable in bankruptcy or in the winding-up of an insolvent company. But if the claimant waived the tort, he could prove to the extent of the benefits received by the tortfeasor. However, today unliquidated claims are provable; for, in determining whether any liability in tort is a bankruptcy debt or a debt in the winding up of a company, "the bankrupt shall be deemed to become subject to that liability by reason of an obligation incurred at the time when the cause of action accrued": Insolvency Act 1986 s.382(1), (2) and Insolvency Rules 1986, Rule 13.12. If the benefit gained by the tortfeasor is greater than the loss suffered by the claimant, he will naturally prove for that larger sum.

[12] [1967] 1 Q.B. 407.

[13] Law Reform (Miscellaneous Provisions) Act 1934, s.1(3), now repealed: see Proceedings against Estates Act 1970, s.1.

does not apply."[14] Jurisdictions in the United States have reached a similar conclusion.[15]

Some judges and jurists have, however, been critical of the use of waiver as a means of circumventing the limitation period appropriate to the tortious action. In *Beaman* v. *A.R.T.S. Ltd.*,[16] Denning J. rejected the argument that section 3 of the Limitation Act 1939,[17] which provided that no action may be brought in conversion after six years from the date of the original conversion, could "be evaded by a mere change in the form of remedy. An owner cannot escape the effect of the statute by assuming to waive the tort of conversion and to sue for money had and received." Corbin had expressed similar views many years earlier.[18] In 1910 he wrote:

> "The cause of action is a tort, and the tort exists as the cause of action and must be proved as the cause of action from first to last. No trick or legerdemain on the part of the plaintiff can change the tort into a contract. Neither can the law do this ... The fact that it has been used to dodge the rule that a personal action dies with the person, or to expand the right of set off which the common law technically and inconveniently limited, is no ground for using it to nullify a legislative act [*i.e.* the statute of limitation] based on sound public policy."

It is not always easy to determine why a shorter limitation period is required for tortious action than for contractual or restitutionary actions. But there is no reason to conclude that, in principle, the actions in tort and in restitution should necessarily terminate at the same time. Whether they do so may depend on the nature of the particular tort. Take the case of the defendant who converts the plaintiff's goods. "For the sake of the integrity of ordinary commercial transactions and the protection of the purchasers of goods it is desirable that at some time (within a relatively short period) the title to a chattel be unencumbered from the consequences of a previous theft. There is no such compelling reason for haste in decreeing restitution for unjust enrichment— which is a continuous wrong, not a single and completed act."[19] Such reasoning, which is supported by cases such as *Chesworth* v. *Farrer*,[20] would lead to the conclusion that in restitution the limitation period should not begin to run until the tortfeasor had received the proceeds of the tort.[21] If this principle is accepted, there must be one *caveat* to it, namely, that if the right to sue in tort is

---

[14] [1967] 1 Q.B. 407, 416. But see below, pp. 729–730.
[15] *Dentist Supply Co.* v. *Cornelius*, 119 N.Y.S. 2d 570, aff'd. 116 N.E. 2d 238 (1953) (S.Ct. of N.Y.); (1956) 2 N.Y. Law Forum 40 [Teller]. But *cf. Hart* v. *E. P. Dutton & Co.*, 93 N.Y.S. 2d 871 (1949); see above, p. 722, n. 64.
[16] [1948] 2 All E.R. 89, 92–93. *Cf. Waterhouse* v. *Keen* (1825) 4 B. & C. 200, discussed in (1984) 100 L.Q.R. 653, 663 [Hedley].
[17] See now Limitation Act 1980, s.3.
[18] *Waiver of Tort and Suit in Assumpsit*, (1910) 19 Yale L.J. 221, 235–236 [Corbin].
[19] K. York, *Extension of Restitutional Remedies in the Tort Field* (1952) 4 U.C.L.A.L.R. 499, 554. *Contra*, Birks, *Introduction*, p. 349.
[20] [1967] 1 Q.B. 407.
[21] *Cf. Loughman* v. *Town of Pelham*, 126 F. 2d 714 (1942).

barred before the proceeds of sale are received, the restitutionary right should also be barred. For example, A converts B's chattel on August 1, 1980 and sells it on September 1, 1987, receiving the proceeds of sale on January 1, 1988. When A sells the chattel, B's title is already barred. However, if A had sold the chattel on September 1, 1985, but did not receive the proceeds of sale until September 1, 1986, the limitation period governing his restitutionary claim will run from that latter date.[22]

These problems should, of course, have been anticipated in the Limitation Act 1980. Unfortunately, successive Limitation Acts have not recognised the independent existence of many restitutionary claims, which judges have therefore found necessary to squeeze into those sections of the statute which deal with contractual claims.[23]

Torts committed abroad

An act done in a foreign country is actionable as a tort in England only if it would be so actionable if committed in England and is actionable by the *lex loci delicti commissi*.[24] The courts have not yet been asked to determine what is the relevant conflictual rule which governs a restitutionary claim to recover the tortfeasor's enrichment. Dicey and Morris's text on *Conflict of Laws*, although stating the general rule that the proper law of the obligation is the law of the country where the enrichment occurs, is "doubtful" whether it applies if the ground of the restitutionary claim is a tortious act; the restitutionary claim should succeed only if the tortious claim for damages would have succeeded.[25]

If a tort is committed abroad, the only connection with England may be that the defendant is within the jurisdiction of the English court. If the tort is committed abroad and if the tortfeasor has enriched himself abroad, the relevance of English law in determining the success of the restitutionary claim is not immediately apparent. If the restitutionary claim is not parasitic and not dependent upon the tort,[26] then the law where the enrichment occurs should be the appropriate law.[26a] This is not to deny that it may not always be a simple task to determine where that place is. For example, in consequence of D's tortious threat in Sweden, P pays $4000 into D's bank account in Paris. The bank is a branch of an Italian bank. D is domiciled and resident in France. In

---

[22] *Cf.* Woodward, *op. cit.* § 294 and Keener, *op. cit.* pp. 177–178. This admittedly produces curious results. In the example quoted, there would be a period from August 1, 1986 (when the six-year period had elapsed) to September 1, 1986 when B would be without a remedy.

[23] See below, Chap. 43.

[24] *Phillips* v. *Eyre* (1870) L.R. 6 Q.B. 1; *Boys* v. *Chaplin* [1971] A.C. 356.

[25] Rule 203(1): see the comment on the Rule at p. 1351.

[26] See above, pp. 715–716.

[26a] Contrast Burrows, *The Law of Restitution*, p. 492, who suggests that the choice of law rule should be the "*the law of the country where the plaintiff's loss and the defendant's gain occur . . .* Where the loss (or wrong) and gain occur in different countries other factors must then be taken into account, such as domicile, residence or place of business of the parties. If this too fails to give a clear answer the *lex fori* should perhaps be applied *faute de mieux*." In our view the courts should not be tempted by such a counsel of perfection which must inevitably breed great uncertainty as to what is the applicable law.

our view, the country where the money is deposited is prima facie the law where the enrichment occurs.

In *Dimskal Shipping Co. S.A.* v. *International Transport Workers' Federation, The Evia Luck*[27] there was a threat to black a ship in a Swedish port. In order to prevent the threat being implemented, the owners contracted to make, and did make, payments into the respondents' bank account in England. The proper law of the agreement was English, and by English law the threat of blacking constituted illegitimate economic pressure. In contrast, the threat was lawful by Swedish law. The House of Lords, Lord Templeman dissenting, upheld the owners' claim to avoid the contract and to recover the moneys paid thereunder. As the defendants conceded, the only relevant law was the proper law of the contract, English law; and by that law the contract was voidable for economic duress. The House, therefore, rejected the submission that the act must be illegitimate both by English law and by Swedish law, the law of the place where the threat was made.

Even if it were to be held that, as a general rule, a restitutionary claim based on a tortious act can succeed only if it is actionable in England and in the *lex loci delicti commissi*, the *Evia Luck* case is authority for the rule that an English court will only look to the proper law of any contract entered into in consequence of illegitimate pressure to determine whether it is voidable and whether any payment made under it can be recovered. But what if in *The Evia Luck* the appellants had paid the money without formally contracting to do so? There must be a *scintilla temporis* when they must have agreed to do so[28]; and the court will then have to determine what is the proper law of that implied agreement, which seemingly will determine whether a restitutionary claim will succeed.

The owners did not base their restitutionary claim on the ground that the respondents' act was tortious, and Lord Goff accepted that illegitimate pressure, which amounted to duress, was not necessarily actionable as a tort.[29] But their Lordships did not suggest that their conclusion would have been different if the threat would also have been characterised as tortious.[30-31]

Assignment of claims

It is possible that the apparent prohibition on assignment of bare claims to damages in tort, will not defeat a restitutionary claim to recover the benefit gained from a tortious act.

---

[27] [1991] 4 All E.R. 871.
[28] See Beatson, *op. cit.* p. 107; see above, pp. 240–241.
[29] At p. 881; and see above, pp. 252–253.
[30-31] Lord Goff rejected the argument that the conflictual rule governing tortious claims (see above, p. 730) should determine whether the restitutionary claim should succeed. Not only conduct which constitutes duress may not be tortious, but, in a claim grounded in tort, in contrast to a claim on a contract governed by English law, the "only fact which brings in English law at all is the fact that the defendant is amenable to the jurisdiction of the English court": at p. 881. The question did not, therefore, arise whether a restitutionary claim based on a tortious act must be actionable by English law and the *lex loci delicti commissi*.

3. Election

In *Lamine* v. *Dorrell*,[32] Holt C.J. said:

> "If an action of trover should be brought by the plaintiff for these debentures after judgment in this *indebitatus assumpsit*, he may plead this recovery in bar of the action of trover, in the same manner as it would have been a good plea in bar for the defendant to have pleaded to the action of trover, that he sold the debentures and paid to the plaintiff in satisfaction. But it may be a doubt if this recovery can be pleaded before execution."

This view of the law did not go unchallenged. A dictum of Bovill C.J. in *Smith* v. *Baker*[33] suggested that the mere commencement of an action was a sufficient election. But in *United Australia Ltd.* v. *Barclays Bank Ltd.*,[34] Holt C.J.'s view of the law was vindicated. A cheque which was payable to the appellants was indorsed by Emons, the appellants' secretary, in favour of M. F. G. Trust Ltd. and was later collected, received and paid by the respondents. The appellants brought an action for money lent or had and received against M. F. G. Trust Ltd. for the amount of the cheque, alleging that Emons had indorsed the cheque without authority. The action was, however, discontinued by the appellants before final judgment. They then commenced this second action against the respondents for damages for conversion of the cheque. At first instance and in the Court of Appeal, the respondents contended successfully that the appellants had waived irrevocably their right to sue in tort. But the House of Lords rejected this plea. The House expressly disapproved of Bovill C.J.'s dictum, which Lord Wright[35] was later to stigmatise as having "no merit except a delusive appearance of precision and a certain crispness of language."

Viscount Simon said[36]:

> "There is nothing conclusive about the form in which the writ is issued, or about the claims made in the statement of claim. A plaintiff may at any time before judgment be permitted to amend. . . . At some stage of the proceedings the plaintiff must elect which remedy he will have. There is, however, no reason of principle or convenience why that stage should be deemed to be reached until the plaintiff applies for judgment. . . .
>
> To avoid misunderstanding, I must add that I do not think that the respondents in the present case would escape liability, even if judgment had been entered in the appellant company's earlier action against

[32] (1701) 2 Ld.Ray. 1216, 1217. *Cf. Ernest Scragg & Sons Ltd.* v. *Perseverance Banking & Trust Co. Ltd.* [1973] 2 Lloyd's Rep. 101, 103, *per* Lord Denning M.R.
[33] (1873) L.R. 8 C.P. 350, 355; *cf. Ferguson* v. *Carrington* (1829) 9 B. & C. 59; *Rice* v. *Read* [1900] 1 Q.B. 54; (1900) 16 L.Q.R. 160 [Griffiths], 269 [Galbraith].
[34] [1941] A.C. 1. This decision exhaustively reviews previous authority, save *Bradley & Cohn Ltd.* v. *Ramsay* (1912) 106 L.T. 771. *Cf.* the South Australian case of *Militz* v. *Bowering-Wood* [1954] S.A.S.R. 175; (1955) 18 M.L.R. 1 [Fridman].
[35] (1941) 57 L.Q.R. 184, 189.
[36] [1941] A.C. 1, 19, 21; see also Lord Porter at p. 50. *Cf.* Keener, *op. cit.* pp. 212–213.

M. F. G. What would be necessary to constitute a bar, as Bayley J. pointed out in *Morris* v. *Robinson*,[37] would be that, as the result of such judgment or otherwise, the appellant should have received satisfaction."

Election is not, therefore, final[38] until judgment is satisfied.[39]

4. PROPRIETARY CLAIMS

We have already discussed the principles which should determine whether a court should impose a trust or a lien over the defendant's assets.[40] As a general principle, such a remedy should be granted, not only to protect the plaintiff's pre-existing equitable title, but if it is just, in the context of the plaintiff's claim against the particular defendant, to allow him the additional benefits which flow from the grant of that remedy. If the courts continue to insist on a fiduciary relationship, a restitutionary proprietary claim against a tortfeasor may be defeated *in limine*.[41] However, that condition is easily satisfied.[42] The plaintiff must nonetheless be able to identify his property. If he waives a proprietary tort, such as conversion, he may be able to do so. But the tortfeasor's enrichment may not be the proceeds of the sale of a chattel; it may simply be the saving of an expense which he would otherwise have incurred. If equity's traditional rules are applied,[43] the plaintiff's proprietary claim will fail, even though the defendant is a conscious tortfeasor and intended to enrich himself. In such circumstances the court may, however, grant him a lien over his unencumbered assets to secure the plaintiff's claim that the defendant should make restitution of the benefit gained.[44] The court may possibly be

---

[37] (1824) 3 B. & C. 196, 205.

[38] In *John* v. *Dodwell & Co.* [1918] A.C. 563, Lord Haldane had expressed doubts (at pp. 570–571) whether a plaintiff who had waived a tort against an agent could subsequently sue a third party in tort; for the waiver could be interpreted as amounting to a ratification of the actions of the agent. In a comparable situation, where the plaintiff had obtained an unsatisfied judgment against a third party in quasi-contract, the Court of Appeal held, in *Veschures Creameries Ltd.* v. *Hull and Netherlands Steamship Co.* [1921] 2 K.B. 608, that the plaintiff could not later sue an agent in tort. But the assertion that the waiver is tantamount to ratification so as to bar a subsequent action is to resurrect once more the heresy of implied contract (on which see above, pp. 5 *et seq.* In our view the *Veschures Creameries* case must be regarded as wrongly decided; it is puzzling that both Lord Atkin and Lord Porter should have approved it in the *United Australia* case: see [1941] A.C. 1, 31–32, 51–52. *Cf. Ernest Scragg & Sons Ltd.* v. *Perseverance Banking Trust Co. Ltd.* [1973] 2 Lloyd's Rep. 101, 103, *per* Lord Denning M.R.

[39] Consistently, the receipt of the proceeds of a settlement between the parties may constitute a final election: see *Lythgoe* v. *Vernon* (1860) 5 H. & N. 180. *Cf. Smith* v. *Baker* (1873) L.R. 8 C.P. 350.

[40] See above, Chap. 2.

[41] *Cf.* above, pp. 83 *et seq.*

[42] See above, pp. 93–94.

[43] See above, pp. 86 *et seq.*

[44] Such a conclusion cannot be reached if a court continues to insist on a "proprietary base" to support the injured person's claim. *Cf.* above, pp. 95 *et seq.*

more ready to impose a lien over assets if the defendant is solvent. If he is insolvent it is arguable that any proprietary claim should be limited to the amount of the loss the plaintiff has suffered. To allow him to capture the benefit gained, if greater than the loss suffered, would ignore the legitimate interests of the general creditors.[45]

---

[45] *Cf.* above, pp. 95–102.

PART III

DEFENCES

CHAPTER 39

INTRODUCTION

THE defences which may defeat a claim to restitution[1] are: change of position; estoppel; bona fide purchase; the running of time and laches; and *res judicata*.[2] The House of Lords has recently recognised change of position as a general defence to restitutionary claims[3] and it is predictable that, as it develops pragmatically, it will come to play a most significant role in the law of restitution, far more significant than estoppel has played in the past. We shall discuss the inter-relationship between this defence, estoppel and bona fide purchase.[4]

We have already commented in the opening Chapter of this book[5] on the role of the defences of illegality[6] and contracting out.[7] Illegality may bar a restitutionary claim; and a person can contract out of his right of restitution in the same way as he can agree not to enforce most other rights conferred upon him by statute or common law. Moreover, it has also been seen that a person may make a payment with the intention of closing a transaction, in which case his restitutionary claim will fail.[8]

Unless the parties enter into an agreement to the contrary, the *death* of a party should not in itself terminate a restitutionary claim.[9] Minority, however, should not necessarily constitute a bar to such a claim. A loan of money to a minor to buy necessaries may be recovered to the extent that the money has been applied in the purchase of necessaries.[10] It is true that a restitutionary claim cannot be used to enforce indirectly a bargain which the law has avoided,[11] but this is a limit which is independent of, and distinct from, a defence of incapacity. *Cowern* v. *Nield*[12] does, however, suggest that *incapacity* will defeat a claim for money had and received[13] even where there has been a

---

[1] And see the limiting principles, above, pp. 44 *et seq.*
[2] *Cf. Restatement of Restitution,* § 139.
[3] *Lipkin Gorman (A Firm)* v. *Karpnale Ltd.* [1991] 2 A.C. 548; see below, p. 740.
[4] See below, pp. 746–747 and 762.
[5] See above, p. 3.
[6] See above, pp. 62–63.
[7] See above, pp. 44–50.
[8] See above, pp. 50–51.
[9] *Cf. Restatement of Restitution,* § 149(2).
[10] *Marlow* v. *Pitfeild* (1719) 1 P.Wms. 558: see above, p. 627; see also the cases concerning *ultra vires* loans, above, pp. 634 *et seq.*
[11] See above, pp. 62 *et seq.*
[12] [1912] 2 K.B. 419.
[13] But not an action *ex delicto.*

total failure of consideration. In that case[14] the plaintiff failed to recover from a minor trader the price of goods which the minor had failed to deliver, as required under the terms of a contract void under the Infants Relief Act 1874; for the action was held to be *ex contractu*, and a minor "is not, except in certain cases, liable on contracts made by him."[15] In our opinion, for reasons already stated,[16] this case was wrongly decided and should be overruled. The theory of implied contract has not survived the House of Lords decision in *United Australia Ltd.* v. *Barclays Bank Ltd.*,[17] and to have allowed recovery on the ground of the total failure of consideration would not have indirectly enforced the void contract.

---

[14] See above, p. 531.
[15] At p. 424, *per* Bray J.
[16] See above, pp. 531–532.
[17] [1941] A.C. 1; see above, pp. 732–733.

CHAPTER 40

CHANGE OF POSITION AND ESTOPPEL

(A) Change of Position

IN *Moses* v. *Macferlan*[1] Lord Mansfield stated that the action for money had and received will only lie when it is inequitable for the defendant to retain the money which the plaintiff claims. So, the defendant "may defend himself by every thing which shows that the plaintiff, *ex aequo et bono*, is not entitled to the whole of his demand, or to any part of it."[2] In the past, analytically-minded judges, hostile to the Mansfield "heresy," were reluctant to admit so generous a defence, finding "little help in such generalities."[3] Indeed, the Court of Appeal appeared to have rejected it in *Durrant* v. *Ecclesiastical Commissioners for England and Wales*,[4] which the same court later followed in *Baylis* v. *Bishop of London*.[5]

However, it is not true to say that English law has never accepted the concept of change of position. It has been influential in some areas, both at law and in equity. An analogous principle underlies the rule that rescission of a transaction will not be granted unless *restitutio in integrum* is possible[6]; an equitable proprietary claim is, in some situations, defeated by an innocent recipient's change of position[7]; and there has also been statutory recognition of the defendant's change of position.[8] Again, there are two groups of cases where change of position has played a decisive part in the development of the law, although it does not entirely explain the decisions: a restitutionary claim will be defeated if an agent, having innocently received money from the plaintiff, accounts to his principal before notice of the plaintiff's restitutionary claim[9]; and if a plaintiff has paid the defendant money on a forged bill of exchange but the defendant has changed his position before receiving notice of his claim.[10]

---

[1] (1760) 2 Burr. 1005.
[2] *Ibid.* p. 1010: see also *Freeman* v. *Jeffries* (1869) L.R. 4 Ex. 189, 197, *per* Kelly C.B.
[3] *Re Diplock, sub nom. Ministry of Health* v. *Simpson* [1951] A.C. 251, 276, *per* Lord Simonds.
[4] (1880) 6 Q.B.D. 234.
[5] [1913] 1 Ch. 127, C.A.
[6] See above, pp. 60–62.
[7] See above, pp. 90–91.
[8] Law Reform (Frustrated Contracts) Act 1943, ss.1, 2, discussed in *B.P.* v. *Hunt* [1979] 1 W.L.R. 783, 800, 804, *per* Robert Goff J.; see above, p. 451; Perpetuities and Accumulations Act 1964, s.2(2).
[9] See below, pp. 750 *et seq.*
[10] See below, pp. 755 *et seq.*

The reluctance of the courts to recognise change of position as a general defence to restitutionary claims was understandable in the light of the history of the development of the law of restitution in this country.[11] But recent years have seen the recognition of the importance of restitutionary claims founded upon a principle of unjust enrichment. It was predictable that the House of Lords would follow the example of other common law jurisdictions which had recognised the defence.[12] In *Lipkin Gorman (A Firm)* v. *Karpnale Ltd.* the House expressly recognised the defence and accepted it as a general defence to all restitutionary claims.[13]

Their Lordships agreed that "it would be unwise to attempt to define its scope in abstract terms, but better to allow the law on the subject to develop on a case by case basis."[14] It was Lord Goff who analysed in depth the nature and scope of the defence. After noting the hitherto limited acceptance of the defence[15] and the limitations of estoppel,[16] he said[17]:

> "I am most anxious that, in recognising this defence to actions of resti-
> tution, nothing should be said at this stage to inhibit the development of
> the defence on a case by case basis, in the usual way. It is, of course, plain
> that the defence is not open to one who has changed his position in bad
> faith, as where the defendant has paid away the money with knowledge of
> the facts entitling the plaintiff to restitution; and it is commonly accepted
> that the defence should not be open to a wrongdoer. These are matters
> which can, in due course, be considered in depth in cases where they arise
> for consideration. They do not arise in the present case. Here there is no
> doubt that the respondents have acted in good faith throughout, and the
> action is not founded upon any wrongdoing of the respondents. It is not
> however appropriate in the present case to attempt to identify all those
> actions in restitution to which change of position may be a defence. A
> prominent example will, no doubt, be found in those cases where the
> plaintiff is seeking repayment of money paid under a mistake of fact; but I
> can see no reason why the defence should not also be available in principle
> in a case such as the present, where the plaintiff's money has been paid by
> a thief to an innocent donee, and the plaintiff then seeks repayment from
> the donee in an action for money had and received. At present I do not

---

[11] See above, pp. 90–92.
[12] See below, pp. 740, n. 14 and 741.
[13] [1991] 2 A.C. 548, 558–559, *per* Lord Bridge; 562–563, *per* Lord Templeman; 567–568, *per* Lord Griffiths and Lord Ackner; 577–583, *per* Lord Goff.
[14] At p. 558, *per* Lord Bridge. *Cf.* the dicta of the High Court of Australia in *David Securities Pty Ltd.* v. *Commonwealth Bank of Australia* (1992) 66 A.L.J.R. 768, 780, where it is pointed out that in Canada and some of the states of the U.S.A., it is necessary to point to *specific* expenditure; in other states of the U.S.A. a defendant can rely on the defence even though he cannot "precisely identify the expenditure caused by the mistaken payments." And see below, p. 741.
[15] See the authorities cited above, p. 739.
[16] See below, p. 746.
[17] At pp. 579–580; applied in *Home Office* v. *Ayres* [1992] I.C.R. 175.

wish to state the principle any less broadly than this: that the defence is available to a person whose position has so changed that it would be inequitable in all the circumstances to require him to make restitution, or alternatively to make restitution in full. I wish to stress however that the mere fact that the defendant has spent the money, in whole or in part, does not of itself render it inequitable that he should be called upon to repay, because the expenditure might in any event have been incurred by him in the ordinary course of things. I fear that the mistaken assumption that mere expenditure of money may be regarded as amounting to a change of position for present purposes has led in the past to opposition by some to recognition of a defence which in fact is likely to be available only on comparatively rare occasions. In this connection I have particularly in mind the speech of Lord Simonds in *Ministry of Health* v. *Simpson* [1951] A.C. 251, 276."

Lord Goff has not then committed himself to the proposition that the defence should, as it is in some jurisdictions, be restricted to situations where the defendant has "altered his position *in reliance on* the validity of the payment."[18] His cautious formulation of the defence is in the spirit of Article 142(1) of the *Restatement of Restitution*, which reads as follows: "(1) The right of a person to restitution from another because of a benefit received is terminated or diminished if, after receipt of the benefit, circumstances have so changed that it would be inequitable to require the other to make full restitution."

It is clear from this, and Lord Goff's, formulation, that the defence is a general defence.[18a] It will be most frequently invoked by recipients of mistaken

---

[18] *Cf.* New Zealand Judicature Act 1908, s.94B, as amended (italics supplied); see also Western Australia Trustee Act 1962, s.65(8) and Property Law Act 1969, s.125. See also the similar language of the Supreme Court of Canada in *Rural Municipality of Storthoaks* v. *Mobil Oil Canada Ltd.* (1975) 55 D.L.R. (3d) 1, 13, *per curiam* (Martland J.): has the defendant "materially changed its circumstances *as a result of the receipt of* the money"? (italics supplied).
As the High Court of Australia recently said, in the context of a claim to recover money paid under a mistake of law, "a defence of change of position is necessary to ensure that enrichment of the recipient of the payment is prevented only in circumstances where it would be unjust . . . the defence of change of position is relevant to the enrichment of the defendant precisely because its central element is that the defendant has acted to his or her detriment on the *faith of the receipt*": *David Securities Pty Ltd.* v. *Commonwealth Bank of Australia* (1992) 66 A.L.J.R. 768, 780.

[18a] *Westdeutsche Landesbank Girozentrale* v. *The Council of the London Borough of Islington* (February 12, 1993, unrep.: see above p. 541) is one of the first cases where a court was required to consider the scope and application of the defence of change of position. The plaintiff had entered into "swap" contracts with the defendant, and to safeguard its position had made a back-to-back contract with another bank. Hobhouse J. held, *obiter*, that this contract was "wholly independent" of the plaintiff's transaction with the defendant. The plaintiff could not therefore rely on its existence to support its defence to the defendant's counterclaim that it would be inequitable to require it to make restitution since it had changed its position.
The judge also rejected the defendant's submission that "to order restitution would be inconsistent with the statutory policy that the finances of local authorities should be regulated on an annual basis" and that, consequently, it would be unjust for the tax payers of the current year to pay for a benefit received by the Council many years before and indirectly enjoyed by residents of that year or the following year. In the judge's view the relevant statutory provisions required

payments. But it may be invoked in other contexts, for example, by a confidant who acts honestly but unwittingly betrays a confidence.[19]

An unusual example of its application is exemplified by the facts of *Lipkin Gorman* itself. In that case Cass, a partner of a firm of solicitors, was authorised to draw cheques on its clients' account. He did so, without the firm's authority, and used the cash to gamble at the defendant casino. The House of Lords held that the plaintiff firm could, subject to defences, recover its money.[19a] The defendant casino was not a bona fide purchaser; the gaming contracts were rendered void by section 18 of the Gaming Act 1845. However, the defendant casino, being an innocent donee, could rely on the defence of change of position. The firm of solicitors was therefore entitled to recover their money to the extent of the casino's winnings from the gambler, and in determining what were those winnings attention should be "focused upon the overall position" of the casino[20]:

> "When in such circumstances the plaintiff seeks to recover from the casino the amount of several bets placed with it by a gambler with his money, it would be inequitable to require the casino to repay in full without bringing into account winnings paid by it to the gambler on any one or more of the bets so placed with it."[21]

Other jurisdictions which have recognised the defence suggest some of the fundamental questions which English courts may have to answer in future years. These include:

(1) Paragraph 818(2) of the BGB states that: "if the return of that which was received is no longer possible due to its condition, or if the recipient is on other grounds not able to return it, he has to replace its value." However, paragraph 818(3) then goes on to provide that: "the obligation to disgorge or replace the value is excluded to the extent that the recipient is no longer enriched." It is said that "the underlying legislative idea is that the enrichment claim, being based simply on equity, should not cause any loss to the defendant."[22] Consequently, any economic misfortunes suffered by the recipient of the benefit as a result of his dealings with what he has received are borne by the plaintiff:

> "Thus the recipient's duty is terminated or diminished if what he has received is destroyed, embezzled, or confiscated ... ; if he lends the

---

any deficit on the defendant's income and expenditure account to be carried forward. So, in any subsequent year, residents will be obliged either to pay an increased rate or suffer a diminution in the defendant's expenditure during that year. Moreover, the defendant had established a suspense account to satisfy any successful restitutionary claim. The judge also rejected the submission that, as the swap loan was erroneously treated as if were interest received upon a capital loan, there had been an under-payment of housing subsidy to the defendant.

[19] See above, p. 695.

[19a] The claim for money had and received was based on the plaintiff firm's common law title: see above, pp. 82–83.

[20] At pp. 581–583, *per* Lord Goff.

[21] At pp. 582–583. But see Birks, "The English recognition of unjust enrichment" [1991] Lloyd's Maritime and Commercial Law Quarterly 473.

[22] Zweigert and Kötz, *op. cit.* Vol. II, p. 275.

money he receives to a trickster or invests it in an industrial enterprise which is dismantled after the war . . . ; if he makes a gift of the goods he received or sells them at a loss . . . ; if he spends money on what he received in the belief that he was entitled to keep it . . . ; if he increases his standard of living . . . ; surrenders claims . . . , or assumes obligations from which he cannot free himself without loss . . . In brief, the plaintiff must bear the risk of all the events which negative or neutralise the economic benefit accruing to the defendant."[23]

So, "German law focuses on the estate of the enrichment-debtor as a whole, and defines enrichment as the 'surviving net gain' ('Saldo'), after comparing the difference between the current value of the debtor's estate with the value that it would have had but for the enriching fact."[23a]

In the United States the courts have, by and large, reached a similar conclusion and have found a change of circumstances in those situations, outlined above, where German law concluded that the enrichment had disappeared.[24]

---

[23] *Ibid.* The judicial citations to be found in the text have been omitted. "The courts have, however, restricted the ambit of §818(3) in the case of synallagmatic agreements that are void or are subsequently avoided. This they have done by developing the so-called '*Saldotheorie*'. . . . The '*Saldotheorie*', however, provides that S may subtract the value of his or her own performance from the amount owed to B in terms of the latter's enrichment claim": D. P. Visser, "Responsibility to Return Lost Enrichment," 1992, Acta Juridica 175, 187. For a different view, see P. Birks, *Restitution — The Future*, Chap. 6, pp. 141–143, who would deny the defence if money paid under mistake of fact is immediately stolen by a third party; in his view the loss is not then causally related to the enrichment received. Professor Birks distinguishes between change of position as a defence to a claim that the defendant has been *enriched* (he includes under this head: where the defendant has given exchange-value to the plaintiff; bona fide purchase; where defendant has spent the money [value expended]; ministerial receipt; and supervening loss) from a claim that in consequence of the change of position his enrichment is not *unjust* (detrimental reliance-related change of position, based on the analogy of estoppel). We reject the strict causation test as too stringent; of course, if there has been a detrimental change of position a defendant may successfully plead change of position although the defence may not be, depending upon the extent of the reliance, a complete defence: contrast *Avon C.C.* v. *Howlett* [1983] 1 W.L.R. 605: discussed below, p. 746.

[23a] "Responsibility to Return Lost Enrichment," 1992, Acta Juridica 175, 187 [D.P. Visser], who also discusses the Roman and Roman-Dutch law. See also Reinhard Zimmermann, *The Law of Obligations: Roman Foundations of the Civilian Tradition*, pp. 895–901.

[24] Palmer, *op. cit.* Vol. III, p. 524.
American courts have not accepted the *Restatement of Restitution's* caveat in art. 141(2), namely that "change of circumstances may be a defense or a partial defense if the conduct of the recipient was not tortious and he was no more at fault for his receipt, retention or dealing with the subject matter than was the claimant." They have wisely avoided weighing the relative faults of the parties to the litigation.
For the position in Austria and France, whose courts may take the payer's fault into account, see Zweigert and Kötz, *op. cit.* pp. 281–282.
Cf. Bishop and Beatson, "Mistaken Payments in the Law of Restitution" (1986) 36 Univ. of Toronto L.J. 149, who argue that the courts should be concerned with isolating the potential loss to the recipient if restitution is granted rather than inquiring what is the benefit gained by the recipient at the plaintiff's expense. "On this approach," they conclude that the "courts would take into account the fault of the parties and would be likely to adopt a method of apportioning payments." They offer an economic analysis, and conclude that the defence does

In contrast, German jurists as distinguished as Rabel and Flume,[25] have criticised these decisions and have argued that a person should take responsibility for his own "economic conduct,"[26] a philosophy, embodied in the Roman law principle, still followed in Austria, France and Italy, that the recipient of money transferred without justification remains absolutely liable to repay it.[27]

A central question is this: should an English court consider whether a recipient acted foolishly or recklessly but in the honest belief that an asset was his to dispose of as he thought fit? We are inclined to the view that it would be unwise to attempt such an inquiry, and that a court should only determine whether there has been such a change of position that it would be inequitable to require the defendant to make restitution. What is foolish and reckless may often be determined with the doubtful benefit of judicial hindsight, and may require the courts to make economic judgments which they are not equipped to make. Moreover, it may well lead the courts to weigh in the balance the relative fault of both parties (for example, the plaintiff's gross negligence in making a mistaken payment against the defendant's decision to invest it imprudently), with the inevitable temptation of reaching ad hoc moral judgments.[28]

(2) The defence is said not to be open to one who has changed his position in bad faith. Case law will crystallise what is meant by *bad faith*. For example, "apart from the case where a claim has already been instituted, the BGB imposes the stricter liability for bad faith only where the defendant was fully aware that there was no legal justification for his receipt (§ 819, par. 1), and the courts do not regard mere knowledge of the facts which destroy the justification for the transfer as sufficient (see RG WarnRspr. 1918 No. 24; RG UW 1931, 529)." In contrast, the "Austrian and Swiss codes remove the privilege if the recipient 'should have reckoned on restitution' (Art. 64 OR) or 'should in the circumstances have suspected . . . that the transfer was in error' (1437 ABGB)."[29]

---

not take into account all changes of position which a person may suffer. See also Beatson, *The Use and Abuse of Unjust Enrichment*, Chap. 6.

[25] Cited in Zweigert and Kötz, *op. cit.* Vol. II, pp. 285–286.

[26] *Cf.* Dawson, "Restitution without Enrichment" (1981) 61 Boston Univ. L.R. 563, who argues that only gifts, and not economic exchanges, should amount to change of position. But, as Professor Visser says (see above, n. 23): in German law, loss of enrichment is "an exceptional defence in circumstances where care has been taken to ensure that it is equitable to place the risk for the loss of enrichment on the creditor." He then adds: "This is strongly reminiscent . . . of Lord Goff's vision of the new defence of change of position as one which will find only limited application." But Lord Goff's remarks are more cautious than Professor Visser would seemingly allow: see the passage cited in the text, above, p. 740.

[27] Zweigert and Kötz, *op. cit.* Vol. II, p. 276.

[28] Contrast "Restitution without enrichment," 61 Boston Univ. L.R. 571–573 (1981) [Dawson], who considers that the court should take into account the defendants' fault with Visser, above n. 23a, who thinks it should not. And for a more cautious view see Burrows, *The Law of Restitution*, p. 430: only where the defendant "was clearly more at fault" should his conduct be relevant.

[29] Zweigert and Kötz, *op. cit.* Vol. II, pp. 275–276.

In English law it has been held that beneficiaries of a trust were deemed to have acquiesced in a breach of trust when they knew all the facts but did not appreciate their legal significance.[30] It does not follow that the beneficiaries acted in bad faith in such circumstances. It is our tentative conclusion that the honest, if foolish, defendant who, knowing all the facts, ought to have surmised that he should make restitution of the value of the benefit conferred should be allowed, in an appropriate case, to invoke the defence of change of position. He has not acted with a want of probity.[31]

(3) Since change of position is a *defence* to a restitutionary claim, in principle the burden should be on the defendant to demonstrate that he has changed his position. But, as Slade L.J. pointed out in *Avon County Council* v. *Howlett*[32] it may be difficult for him to prove that he has altered his mode of life or undertaken certain onerous commitments in consequence of the receipt of a payment. In the United States there have been instances in which the evidence was not clear that a defendant has altered his standard of living but where the courts have reached the sympathetic conclusion that because of a "sudden addition to his resources, the defendant may have and probably did spend more for living expenses than he otherwise would have spent."[33] In a similar situation, an English court is likely to make a comparable finding of fact.

(4) If a claimant can identify his asset in the defendant's hands, then it will not normally be inequitable to require the defendant to give it back. But exceptionally, it may. For example, he may have received money under mistake and in consequence altered his standard of living but left untouched the money he received from the payer.[34]

(5) Jurists have suggested that the status of a particular defendant should be taken into account in determining whether the defence of change of position is or is not open to him. It has, for example, been argued that a defendant who is rich and powerful, such as a multi-national corporation, should never be allowed the defence.[35] We are not attracted by such an absolute principle, although we readily concede that it may be difficult for such a person to satisfy a court that the defence should succeed.[36]

Some persons are certainly privileged. But it is a distinct question whether a restitutionary claim should fail because they are privileged rather than because they have changed their position. We have already seen, for example, that the plea of *minority* defeated a restitutionary claim even though the minor's conduct was characterised as reprehensible.

---

[30] *Re Pauling's Settlement Trusts* [1962] 1 W.L.R. 86; *cf.* above, pp. 671–672.
[31] *Cf.* above, p. 673.
[32] [1983] 1 W.L.R. 605, 621–622.
[33] Palmer, *op. cit.* Vol. III, pp. 525–526, citing *Moritz* v. *Horsman*, 9 N.W. 2d 868 (1943).
[34] *Cf. Avon County Council* v. *Howlett* [1983] 1 W.L.R. 605, 621–622, *per* Slade L.J.; see below, pp. 746–747.
[35] Bishop and Beatson, *op. cit.* (1986) 36 Univ. of Toronto L.J. 149, cited above, n. 24.
[36] *Cf. ibid.*

(B) Common Law Estoppel

1. INTRODUCTION: THE FUTURE OF COMMON LAW ESTOPPEL AND THE LAW OF RESTITUTION

Before the recognition of the defence of change of position a plaintiff was on occasions compelled to rely on the defence of estoppel. But as a defence to restitutionary claims it suffers from many limitations. It is, as a general rule,[37] said to depend upon the existence of a representation of fact[38] by one party to another, in reliance upon which the representee has so changed his position that it is inequitable for the representor to go back on his representation. But it is often with difficulty that a court has found that a plaintiff made a representation, for example, that the defendant was entitled to money paid to him and, then only as a general rule, in the limited context of claims based on the plaintiff's mistake of fact.

Moreover, in *Avon County Council* v. *Howlett*,[39] where the plaintiffs had paid money under a mistake of fact, the Court of Appeal held that estoppel cannot operate *pro tanto* "with the effect that if, for example, the defendant has innocently changed his position by disposing of part of the money, a defence of estoppel would provide him with a defence to the whole of his claim. Considerations such as these provide a strong indication that, in many cases, estoppel is not an appropriate concept to deal with the problem"[40] which arises when a defendant seeks to invoke a defence of change of position.

It is predictable that, in the future, a defendant who has changed his position will rarely, if ever, seek to plead that the plaintiff is estopped. Change of position is a much more flexible defence. Moreover, it is a general defence to all restitutionary claims, whereas estoppel is, in practice, limited to claims based on mistake. And, unlike estoppel, it is not dependent upon the requirement of a representation (or exceptionally a breach of duty) which led the defendant to change his position.

The defences are not then complementary. However, there is a tension between them. Let us assume that A pays £3,000 to B under a mistake of fact. B changes his position by spending £1,000; but £2,000 remains in his bank account. He has changed his position *pro tanto* and should make restitution of £2,000. But if he is allowed a defence of estoppel, then A's restitutionary claim

---

[37] Exceptionally a plaintiff may be estopped if he has been guilty of a breach of duty which he owed to the defendant: see below, pp. 747–748.

[38] The courts have been ingenious in finding a representation of fact, although the mere payment of money under mistake is not in itself such a representation. In some situations it may then be impossible to spell out a representation. Such were the facts of *Re Diplock* [1951] A.C. 251, where the next-of-kin had made no representation to the charities who were not allowed a general defence of change of position. Similarly, in *Lipkin Gorman (A Firm)* v. *Karpnale Ltd.* [1991] 2 A.C. 548, it could not be said that the firm of solicitors had made any representation to the casino, but in this case the innocent donee was now protected by the defence of change of position: see above, p. 742.

[39] [1983] 1 W.L.R. 605.

[40] *Lipkin Gorman (A Firm)* v. *Karpnale Ltd.* [1991] 2 A.C. 548, 579, *per* Lord Goff.

is defeated *in limine*. This cannot be a just conclusion. It may well be that a court will avoid the dilemma by finding that the payer has not made a representation sufficient to support an estoppel. More radically, the House of Lords may conclude that *Avon County Council* v. *Howlett*[41] cannot stand with *Lipkin Gorman (A Firm)* v. *Karpnale Ltd.*[42] and should be overruled.

These questions are for the future. But they present the authors of this book with a dilemma. To what extent, if at all, should the discussion of the law of estoppel be jettisoned? We have concluded that, given that *Lipkin Gorman* was decided only in June 1991, the appropriate course to follow in this edition is to include a short statement of the relevant general principles governing estoppel. We have retained the full discussion of the two special groups of cases, on agency and bills of exchange, for they have developed their own special rules and cannot be entirely explained on the ground of change of position.

2. ESTOPPEL AS A DEFENCE AT COMMON LAW

The following conclusions may be drawn from the cases on estoppel:

(1) The plaintiff will be estopped from asserting his claim to restitution if the following conditions are satisfied:

(a) The plaintiff must generally have made a representation of fact which led the defendant to believe that he was entitled to treat the money as his own.[42a] Sometimes a representation may be implicit in the payment itself in the light of the surrounding circumstances,[43] for example, where it is made in response to a claim by the recipient, or follows upon an account showing the money as due to the recipient. In contrast, a paying bank does not impliedly represent, by honouring a cheque, that it is genuine or that its customer's signature is genuine, even if the cheque is presented for special collection.[44] A mistaken payment is not in itself a representation which gives rise to an estoppel. There must, therefore, normally be some further indication of the defendant's supposed title other than the mere fact of payment.[45]

Even if there is no representation of fact, the plaintiff may be estopped if he has been guilty of a breach of a duty which he owed to

---

[41] [1983] 1 W.L.R. 605.

[42] [1991] 2 A.C. 548.

[42a] See above, n. 38

[43] See Scrutton L.J.'s view of the facts in *Holt* v. *Markham* [1923] 1 K.B. 504, and Asquith J.'s apparent acceptance of the second representation in *Weld-Blundell* v. *Synott* [1940] 2 K.B. 107; and *cf. Sidney Bolsom Investment Trust Ltd.* v. *E. Karmios & Co. Ltd.* [1956] 1 Q.B. 529, 540–541, *per* Denning L.J.

[44] *National Westminster Bank Ltd.* v. *Barclays Bank Ltd.* [1975] Q.B. 654.

[45] *R. E. Jones Ltd.* v. *Waring & Gillow Ltd.* [1926] A.C. 670. In *Transvaal & Delagoa Bay Investment Co.* v. *Atkinson* [1944] 1 All E.R. 579, Atkinson J. suggested (at p. 585) that the plaintiff must have "expressly or impliedly represented to the defendant that the money paid was truly due and owing to the defendant."

the defendant.[46] Whether such a duty exists is a question of law. There is "no basis for any suggestion that a bank owes a duty of care to a payee in deciding to honour a customer's cheque, at any rate when this appears to be regular on its face."[47]

(b) The defendant must have, bona fide without notice of the plaintiff's claim, consequently changed his position. Examples of changes in position include: being in receipt of payments over a period of time and spending them in such a manner as to have altered his mode of living[48]; paying the money over to a third party to whom the defendant believed he had a duty to pay it and from whom there was no practical means of recovering it[49]; investing the money in a company which has since gone into liquidation.[50]

The burden of proof imposed on the defendant to demonstrate such a change of position could, if stringently imposed, be difficult to discharge.[51] In *Avon County Council* v. *Howlett*,[52] Slade L.J. recognised that a bona fide defendant who receives a benefit (often, in these circumstances, a mistaken payment), which prima facie he must disgorge, may find it "very difficult ... subsequently to recall and identify retrospectively" in what way its receipt has led him to alter his mode of living and to incur burdensome extra commitments and expenditure. "He may even have done so, while leaving some of the particular moneys paid to him by the plaintiff untouched. If the pecuniary amount of his prejudice has to be precisely quantified by the defendant in such circumstances, he may be faced with obvious difficulties of proof."

---

[46] *Skyring* v. *Greenwood & Cox* (1825) 4 B. & C. 281, 291, *per* Bayley J.; *Coventry Shepherd & Co.* v. *Great Eastern Rly.* (1883) 11 Q.B.D. 776; *Mercantile Bank of India Ltd.* v. *Central Bank of India Ltd.* [1938] A.C. 287. It is not easy to reconcile the *obiter dictum* of Asquith J. in *Weld-Blundell* v. *Synott* [1940] 2 K.B. 107, 114–115, that breach of duty is *essential* to raise such an estoppel, with the judgments in *The Deutsche Bank (London Agency)* v. *Beriro & Co.* (1985) 1 Com.Cas. 123, 255 and *Holt* v. *Markham* [1923] 1 K.B. 504.
Similar observations were made by Lord Sumner, in *R. E. Jones Ltd.* v. *Waring & Gillow Ltd.* [1926] A.C. 670, 693 (see above, p. 135 for a full statement of the facts). The third edition of this book analysed in detail this aspect of the decision (at pp. 701–703), and concluded that the only discernible *ratio decidendi* of the part of the case concerned with estoppel is that on the facts there was no sufficient representation by the appellants leading the respondents to change their position. We expressed the view that the reasoning of the dissentients, Viscount Cave and Lord Atkinson, to support their conclusion that there was a representation, is more persuasive. *Cf.* *Lipkin Gorman (A Firm)* v. *Karpnale Ltd.* [1991] 2 A.C. 548, 579, *per* Lord Goff.
[47] *National Westminster Bank Ltd.* v. *Barclays Bank Ltd.* [1975] Q.B. 654, 662, *per* Kerr J.
[48] *Skyring* v. *Greenwood & Cox* (1825) 4 B. & C. 281; *Lloyds Bank* v. *Brooks* (1950) 6 *Legal Decisions Affecting Bankers* 161; *Avon County Council* v. *Howlett* [1983] 1 W.L.R. 605. But *cf.* *United Overseas Bank* v. *Jiwani* [1976] 1 W.L.R. 964.
[49] *The Deutsche Bank (London Agency)* v. *Beriro & Co.* (1895) 1 Com.Cas. 123, 255.
[50] *Holt* v. *Markham* [1923] 1 K.B. 504.
[51] In *Avon County Council* v. *Howlett* [1983] 1 W.L.R. 605, 609, Cumming-Bruce L.J. concluded that, if the defence were raised, the burden would then be on the payer to show that it was inequitable for the recipient to retain the money. This is a radical conclusion which is contrary to the principle that a defendant must establish his own defence.
[52] [1983] 1 W.L.R. 605, 621–622; *cf.* above, p. 745.

(c) The payment must not have been primarily caused by the fault of the defendant.[53] For example, the defendant may have knowledge of unusual and exceptional circumstances surrounding a particular transaction, such as the presentation of a cheque, which could not have been known to the plaintiff.[54] He may also obtain possession of money by a wrongful act, or mislead the plaintiff by some mis-representation that the money is due.

(2) The effect of such an estoppel will generally be to defeat the claim altogether. Indeed, in *Avon County Council* v. *Howlett*[55] the Court of Appeal held, on the particular facts, that estoppel may not operate *pro tanto*. In that case the plaintiffs paid instalments amounting to £1,007 to the defendant under mistake. The defendant claimed that the plaintiffs were estopped from recovering any of the moneys. They had made a representation of fact which led him to believe that he was entitled to the money, and in good faith he had changed his position relying on that representation. It was specifically pleaded in his defence that he had only spent about £546 of the £1,007. The trial judge, Sheldon J., found, however, as a fact that by the date of the hearing the defendant had spent all the money overpaid; yet his counsel declined an invitation to amend the pleadings to put the defence on a broader basis.[56] So, the judge was compelled to hold that it would not be inequitable to require the defendant to disgorge the balance of £460. The Court of Appeal reversed that decision. In Slade L.J.'s view[57]:

> "the authorities suggest that, in cases where estoppel by representation is available as a defence to a claim for money had and received, the courts . . . do not treat the operation of the estoppel as being restricted to the precise amount of the detriment which the representee proves he has suffered in reliance on the representation."[58]

Eveleigh and Slade L.JJ. concluded that the question whether estoppel could operate *pro tanto* had already been decided in *Greenwood* v. *Martins Bank Ltd.*,[59] where a bank's customer was:

> "estopped from asserting that a cheque with which he has been debited is a forgery, because of his failure to inform the bank in due time, so that it could have recourse to the forger, the debit will stand for the whole amount and not merely that which could have been recovered from the forger."[60]

---

[53] *Larner* v. *London County Council* [1949] 2 K.B. 683, 689, *per* Denning L.J.
[54] *National Westminster Bank Ltd.* v. *Barclays Bank Ltd.* [1975] Q.B. 654, 676–677, *per* Kerr J.
[55] [1983] 1 W.L.R. 605.
[56] [1983] 1 W.L.R. 605, 616.
[57] At p. 622.
[58] [1932] 1 K.B. 371, [1933] A.C. 51, H.L.
[59] At p. 622, *per* Slade L.J.
[60] *Ibid.*

Estoppel is a rule of evidence which precluded a representor averring facts contrary to his own representation. Slade L.J. also regarded *Skyring* v. *Greenwood*[61] and *Holt* v. *Markham*[62] as further authority for the proposition that estoppel cannot operate *pro tanto*; the fact that in these cases there was no exact inquiry into the alteration of each defendant's financial position suggested that such an inquiry was irrelevant and inappropriate.[63]

It is doubtful whether these three decisions support Eveleigh and Slade L.JJ.'s statement of principle. In *Greenwood* v. *Martins Bank Ltd.* the bank had not received any benefit but had suffered loss, which it could not recoup from the forger and which it recouped by debiting its customer's accounts; in contrast, in *Avon County Council* v. *Howlett*, the plaintiff sought to recover money from a recipient who had been enriched by the receipt of the payment. In *Skyring* v. *Greenwood* and *Holt* v. *Markham* there is no judicial statement that estoppel by representation could not operate *pro tanto*; and it is reading a great deal into their uncertain facts to say that the courts, in these cases, regarded it as immaterial whether all the money had been spent or not. In our view it is regrettable that estoppel should be regarded as a rule of evidence which defeats a plaintiff's claim *in limine*.[64]

(C) Two Special Groups of Cases

(a) *The Cases on Agency: Recovery from Agents and Persons in an Analogous Position: Payment to the Principal.*[64a]

An agent[65] who has received money on his principal's behalf may, if the money

---

[61] (1825) 4 B. & C. 281.

[62] [1923] 1 K.B. 504, [1933] A.C. 51, H.L.

[63] At p. 624, *per* Slade L.J.

[64] Both Eveleigh L.J. and Slade L.J. conceded that in some circumstances the conclusion that there could not be a *pro tanto* estoppel could result in injustice; for example where the sums sought to be recovered were so large as to bear no relation to any detriment which the defendant could have suffered. In such circumstances it may be unconscionable for the defendant to retain the money (at p. 612, *per* Eveleigh L.J.; *cf.* at pp. 609–610, *per* Cumming-Bruce L.JJ.). Slade L.J. left open the question whether the court had jurisdiction to exact an undertaking from the defendant to repay his "profit": at pp. 624–625, citing *R. E. Jones Ltd.* v. *Waring and Gillow Ltd.* [1926] A.C. 670, 885, *per* Viscount Cave L.C. Arguably, such important reservations destroy the credibility of the principle that an estoppel cannot operate *pro tanto*.

[64a] In Burrows' view the defence of payment over is distinct from that of change of position: *The Law of Restitution*, pp. 484–486. We agree that this is a body of law governed by its own principles, and we have always treated it as a "special" case. But it does have many of the manifestations of the defence of change of position, and for that reason we discuss it in this Chapter.

[65] Including a banker, receiver, solicitor, churchwarden, parish officer, excise officer, sheriff or collecting bank: see *Whitbread* v. *Brooksbank* (1774) 1 Cowp. 66; *Greenway* v. *Hurd* (1792) 4 T.R. 553; *Townson* v. *Wilson* (1808) 1 Camp. 396, *semble*; *Horsfall* v. *Handley* (1818) 8 Taunt. 136; *Chappell* v. *Poles* (1837) 2 M. & W. 867, *semble*; *Davys* v. *Richardson* (1888) 21 Q.B.D. 202; *D. Owen & Co.* v. *Cronk* [1895] 1 Q.B. 265; *Kleinwort, Sons & Co.* v. *Dunlop Rubber Co.* (1907) 97 L.T. 263; *Kerrison* v. *Glyn Mills, Currie & Co.* (1911) 81 L.J.K.B. 465; *Marshall Shipping Co.* v. *Board of Trade* [1923] 2 K.B. 343; *National Westminster Bank Ltd.* v. *Barclays Bank Ltd.* [1975] Q.B. 654, commenting on *Bank of Montreal* v. *The King* (1907) 38 S.C.R. 258. See also

was not due, be liable to refund it.[66] But if the agent, before learning of the claim, has paid it over to his principal[67] or done something equivalent thereto or otherwise altered his position in relation to his principal on the faith of the payment, he will have a good defence to the claim and the claimant will have to sue the principal.[68] In *Australia & New Zealand Banking Group Ltd.* v. *Westpac Banking Corporation*[69] the High Court of Australia expressly rejected the argument that the defence of payment over can succeed only if it can be shown that the agent had sustained some identifiable and unjust detriment if he were required to refund the mistaken payment.[70] The defence is not available if the agent received the money as principal, or the consequence of some wrongdoing to which he was a party or of which he had knowledge[71]; in such cases he will remain liable to the claimant even though he has accounted to his principal.

The basis of the agent's defence may have originally been change of position. But special rules have now been developed,[72] and the cases can no longer be so simply explained.[73]

The defence has been made available to agents in many different situations.[74] A striking case is *Gowers* v. *Lloyds and National Provincial Foreign*

Peto v. *Blades* (1814) 5 Taunt. 657, 659, *per* Gibbs C.J.; but *cf.* the criticisms in *Baylis* v. *Bishop of London* [1913] 1 Ch. 127, 134, 136. 140, C.A.

[66] *Kleinwort, Sons & Co.* v. *Dunlop Rubber Co.* (1907) 97 L.T. 263, 264, *per* Lord Atkinson. See also *Pollard* v. *The Bank of England* (1871) L.R. 6 Q.B. 623, 630, *per* Blackburn J.; *Continental Caoutchouc & Gutta Percha Co.* v. *Kleinwort, Sons & Co.* (1904) 90 L.T. 474, 476, *per* Collins M.R.

[67] If the agent uses the mistaken payment to pay a debt owed by his principal to him and is authorised so to do, he can still rely on the defence. *Continental Caoutchouc & Gutta Percha Co.* v. *Kleinwort Sons & Co.* (1904) 9 Com.Cas. 240, 242, *per* Collins M.R.

[68] *Buller* v. *Harrison* (1777) 2 Cowp. 565. The earliest cases in which the exception was applied were *Pond* v. *Underwood* (1705) 2 Ld.Raym. 1210; *Cary* v. *Webster* (1721) 1 Str. 480. In *Jacob* v. *Allen* (1703) 1 Salk. 27, however, a different rule had prevailed, and that case was approved in *Att.-Gen.* v. *Perry* (1733) 2 Com. 481. In *Sadler* v. *Evans* (1766) 4 Burr. 1984, Lord Mansfield preferred *Pond* v. *Underwood* to *Jacob* v. *Allen*, and the exception was finally established in *Buller* v. *Harrison*, where Lord Mansfield relied (at p. 568) on the unreported case of *Muilman* v. *Anon*. See also *Stevenson* v. *Mortimer* (1778) 2 Cowp. 805, 806, *per* Lord Mansfield.

[69] (1988) 62 A.L.J.R. 292.

[70] At p. 299.

[71] This rider to the exception was established in *Snowdon* v. *Davis* (1808) 1 Taunt. 359; for other cases see below, pp. 754–755.

[72] See below, pp. 753 *et seq.*

[73] (1930–1931) 45 Harv.L.Rev. 1333, 1345–1349 [Cohen]; *Restatement of Restitution*, § 143. In the agency cases the problem is, generally, not whether it would be inequitable to proceed against the defendant at all, it is to choose which of two alterantive defendants shall be liable.

[74] *Pond* v. *Underwood* (1705) 2 Ld.Ray. 1210 (action against an administrator's agent who collected testator's debts before discovery of the will); *Cary* v. *Webster* (1721) 1 Str. 480 (action against servant who had misapplied money); *Sadler* v. *Evans* (1766) 4 Burr. 1984 (action to recover quitrent said to be due); *Greenway* v. *Hurd* (1792) 4 T.R. 553 (action to recover overpayments of excise duty); *Horsfall* v. *Handley* (1818) 8 Taunt. 136 (action against church-warden to recover dues); *East India Co.* v. *Tritton* (1824) 3 B. & C. 280 (action to recover money paid away by agent without authority); *Ex p. Bird* (1851) 4 De G. & Sm. 273 (petition to prove in bankruptcy in respect of money paid in discounting forged bills); *Holland* v. *Russell* (1861) 1 B. & S. 424, affd. Ex.Ch. (1863) 4 B. & S. 14 (action by underwriter to recover insurance money paid under policy voidable for non-disclosure); *Shand* v. *Grant* (1863) 15 C.B.(N.S.) 324 (action to recover simple overpayment); *Davys* v. *Richardson* (1888) 21 Q.B.D. 202 (recovery of money taken out of court in good faith but without an order); *D. Owen & Co.* v. *Cronk* [1895] 1 Q.B.

Bank Ltd.[75] The plaintiffs were Crown Agents for the Colonies, entrusted with the task of paying pensions to colonial officers. They carried out this duty by forwarding receipt forms to each pensioner at the time when a payment became due, and the pensioner would present the form together with a certificate, signed by a competent person, which certified that the pensioner was still alive. The payment would then be made. A pensioner named Gibson used to present his receipt forms and certificates through his bank, the defendants, who then received the pension payments on his behalf. After his death, forged receipt forms and certificates were sent to the bank, and the money thereby collected by the bank was paid over by them to the supposed principal. Neither the bank nor the Crown Agents were aware of the fraud, but on discovering it the agents sought to recover the money from the bank as paid under a mistake of fact. The Court of Appeal held that they could not recover, for the bank had paid the money away to their "principal." The defence applied to protect them even though the ultimate recipient of the money was not the principal they believed they were acting for but some fraudulent person posing as that principal.

To invoke the defence, however, it is not enough that the agent has simply credited his principal with the money received on his behalf[76]; the money must have been paid over to the principal or something equivalent must have occurred. Thus, in *Holland* v. *Russell,*[77] the defendant paid to his principal part of certain money he had received from the plaintiff; for another part, he had allowed the principal credit in a settled account,[78] and a third part he had expended, with his principal's authority, on his principal's behalf. Each of these dealings was held to be equivalent to payment over to the principal, and the agent was not liable to the plaintiff in respect of any part of the money. Any

---

265 (action to recover money paid under duress of goods); *Gowers* v. *Lloyds and National Provincial Foreign Bank Ltd.* [1938] 1 All E.R. 766 and *Transvaal & Delagoa Bay Investment Co.* v. *Atkinson* [1944] 1 All E.R. 579 (actions to recover money paid as a consequence of fraud). See also *National Westminster Bank Ltd.* v. *Barclays Bank Ltd.* [1975] Q.B. 654, 673, *per* Kerr J., commenting on *Bank of Montreal* v. *The King* (1907) 38 S.C.R. 258. And *cf. Whitbread* v. *Brooksbank* (1744) 1 Cowp. 66; *Edden* v. *Read* (1813) 3 Camp. 338; *Goodall* v. *Lowndes* (1844) 6 Q.B. 464; *Fitzpatrick* v. *M'Glone* [1897] 2 I.R. 542, 551, *per* Palles C.B.

[75] [1938] 1 All E.R. 766.

[76] *Buller* v. *Harrison* (1777) 2 Cowp. 565; *Cox* v. *Prentice* (1815) 3 M. & S. 344; *Kleinwort, Sons & Co.* v. *Dunlop Rubber Co.* (1907) 97 L.T. 263; *Bavins, Junr. & Sims* v. *London & South Western Bank Ltd.* [1900] 1 Q.B. 270; *Scottish Metropolitan Assurance Co. Ltd.* v. *P. Samuel & Co. Ltd.* [1923] 1 K.B. 348. See also *Kerrison* v. *Glyn Mills, Currie & Co.* (1911) 81 L.J.K.B. 465, and *Restatement of Agency,* 2d, § 339, comment f.

In *Australia and New Zealand Banking Group Ltd.* v. *Westpac Banking Corp.* (1988) 62 A.L.J.R. 292, 295, the High Court of Australia emphasised that a court should look to the substance, not to the form, of the transaction.

[77] (1861) 1 B. & S. 424, affd. Ex.Ch. (1863) 4 B. & S. 14. See also *Taylor* v. *Metropolitan Ry.* [1906] 2 K.B. 55.

[78] Similarly if new credit is given: *Buller* v. *Harrison* (1777) 2 Cowp. 565, 568, *per* Lord Mansfield. See also *Kleinwort, Sons & Co.* v. *Dunlop Rubber Co.* (1907) 97 L.T. 263, 265–266, *per* Lord Atkinson; *Scottish Metropolitan Assurance Co. Ltd.* v. *P. Samuel & Co. Ltd.* [1923] 1 K.B. 348, 355–356, *per* Bailhache J., who distinguished the giving of time from the giving of new credit; *Barclays Bank Ltd.* v. *W. J. Simms & Sons Ltd.* [1980] Q.B. 677, 690, *per* Robert Goff J.

true alteration of position by an agent in relation to his principal should, therefore, be sufficient to establish the defence.

The burden is on the agent to show that there has been a payment over.[79] If he has done so, the High Court of Australia in *Australia and New Zealand Banking Group* v. *Westpac Banking Corp.*[80] concluded it was far from self-evident that the agent should take effective steps to recover the money from his principal once he was aware of the mistake.[81]

There are certain cases where it is settled that the defence has no application. These are as follows:

Where the agent has been dealing as principal

Where the agent has been dealing as a principal in the transaction with the plaintiff, the fact that he may have accounted for the money he received from the plaintiff or passed it on to another will not provide him with a defence.[82] Such a defence is only available to one who not only was dealing as an agent in the transaction, but who was also acting on behalf of a disclosed principal.[83] Thus, a bishop who received money from a sequestrator, and applied it in providing for the spiritual needs of a benefice and in payments to the trustee in bankruptcy of its incumbent, was held to be a principal in the transaction and unable to take advantage of the doctrine.[84] And where money has been received by a trustee and paid over by him to the beneficiary, it has been held that the proper person to be sued by the payer for recovery of the money is the trustee, who is the principal.[85]

It is evident that these are well-established principles. But Professor Palmer's conclusion that "the imposition of liability on an innocent agent does violence to the principles of unjust enrichment" is persuasive.[86] It is conjectural whether the acceptance of the general defence of change of position will persuade the courts that the defence should be open to an agent of an undisclosed principal.

---

[79] However, in *Australia and New Zealand Banking Group* v. *Westpac Banking Corp.* (1988) 62 A.L.J.R. 292, 296, the High Court of Australia left open the question whether the nature and scope of the business of a modern commercial bank (*e.g.* the fact that banks carried on a business for profit and immediately gave a customer credit on presentation of a cheque) suggested that the burden should be on the paying bank to demonstrate that the agent [the payee's bank] had not paid the money over to his principal.

[80] (1988) 62 A.L.J.R. 292, 299.

[81] See also *Continental Caoutchouc & Gutta Percha Co.* v. *Kleinwort Sons & Co.* (1904) 9 Com.Cas. 240, C.A.

[82] *Gurney* v. *Womersley* (1854) 4 E. & B. 133; *Royal Exchange Assurance* v. *Moore* (1863) 8 L.T. 242; *Newall* v. *Tomlinson* (1871) L.R. 6 C.P. 405; *King* v. *Stewart* (1892) 66 L.T. 339; *Continental Caoutchouc & Gutta Percha Co.* v. *Kleinwort, Sons & Co.* (1904) 90 L.T. 474; *The Dominion Bank* v. *The Union Bank of Canada* (1908) 40 Can.S.C.R. 366; *Baylis* v. *Bishop of London* [1913] 1 Ch. 127. See also *Wakefield* v. *Newbon* (1844) 6 Q.B. 276; *Smith* v. *Sleap* (1844) 12 M. & W. 585. For the American law, which is similar, see *Restatement of Agency*, 2d, § 341.

[83] *Newall* v. *Tomlinson* (1871) L.R. 6 C.P. 405.

[84] *Baylis* v. *Bishop of London* [1913] 1 Ch. 127.

[85] *King* v. *Stewart* (1892) 66 L.T. 339.

[86] *Op. cit.* Vol. III, pp. 519–523.

Where the money is retained by the agent, or paid over by him after notice of the plaintiff's claim

Where the agent retains the money, he has in no way changed his position[87] unless the payment has been retained under an account settled with his principal; similarly, where the agent has paid the money over to his principal but has received it back again so that his position is as it was before he paid it over, he is liable to be sued.[88] Nor can the defence be successfully pleaded if he has paid the money over to his principal after receiving notice of the plaintiff's claim.[89]

Where the agent has received the money in consequence of some wrongdoing to which he was a party or of which he had knowledge

Where the money comes into the agent's hands as a consequence of some wrongdoing to which he was a party or of which he had knowledge, he cannot take advantage of the defence.

This exception, which was established in *Snowdon* v. *Davis*,[90] a case concerned with duress of goods,[91] has been applied in many other cases of wrongdoing. Thus the agent was not protected where the money was paid to him to obtain fulfilment of a duty which he was bound to perform for nothing[92]; where he received the money under an illegal contract[93]; where the money came into his hands as executor *de son tort*[94]; or was received by him in fraud of creditors. The agent is deprived of the defence not only where he indulged in wrongdoing for his own purposes,[95] but also where he acted simply on his principal's behalf.[96] If, however, he has been merely a conduit-pipe for the payment of the money to the principal, he can plead the defence even though the money has been obtained as a result of wrongdoing, provided that the agent neither participated in the wrongdoing nor knew about it. So where the manager of a company's business compelled the plaintiffs by duress of goods to pay what they claimed to be an extortionate sum for work which the company had done for them, and that sum was paid to the receiver of the company who paid it into the company's account without any notice of

---

[87] *Buller* v. *Harrison* (1777) 2 Cowp. 565.
[88] *British American Continental Bank* v. *British Bank for Foreign Trade* [1926] 1 K.B. 328.
[89] *Continental Caoutchouc & Gutta Percha Co.* v. *Kleinwort, Sons & Co.* (1904) 90 L.T. 474, 477, *per* Romer L.J.; see also *Nizam of Hyderabad, etc.* v. *Jung* [1957] Ch. 185, 239, *per* Evershed M.R., 248, *per* Romer L.J., revd. [1958] A.C. 379.
[90] (1808) 1 Taunt. 359.
[91] Another case of duress of goods is *Oates* v. *Hudson* (1851) 6 Ex. 346. See also *Smith* v. *Sleap* (1844) 12 M. & W. 585; *Wakefield* v. *Newbon* (1844) 6 Q.B. 276; *Close* v. *Phipps* (1844) 7 M. & G. 586.
[92] *Steele* v. *Williams* (1853) 8 Ex. 625; see above, p. 246.
[93] *Miller* v. *Aris* (1800) 3 Esp. 231; *Townson* v. *Wilson* (1808) 1 Camp. 396; *Chappell* v. *Poles* (1837) 2 M. & W. 867.
[94] *Sharland* v. *Mildon* (1846) 15 L.J.Ch. 434; *cf. Padget* v. *Priest and Porter* (1787) 2 T.R. 97.
[95] *Smith* v. *Sleap* (1844) 12 M. & W. 585; *Wakefield* v. *Newbon* (1844) 6 Q.B. 276.
[96] *Oates* v. *Hudson* (1851) 6 Ex. 346.

the duress, it was held that the receiver could successfully plead the payment over in an action against him by the plaintiffs for money had and received.[97]

In *Snowden* v. *Davis*, Mansfield C.J. said that the reason why the defence did not avail an agent in a case of wrongdoing was that in such circumstances the money has not been paid to the use of the person to whom the agent has paid it over. "The plaintiff pays it under the terror of process, to redeem his goods, not with an intent that it should be delivered over to any one in particular."[98] This explanation is, however, also true of the case where the agent is a mere conduit-pipe, and yet there the agent is entitled to take advantage of the defence. It, therefore, seems preferable today to say that the defence is one which is available only where it is inequitable that the agent should be compelled to refund the money, and that can hardly be the case where he has participated in or had knowledge of the wrongdoing in consequence of which the money has come into his hands.

(b) *Bills of Exchange*

Special principles have developed concerning the presentation of bills of exchange, "which are not mere forgeries *in toto* but contain at least one genuine signature and which have been negotiated to at least one innocent holder."[99] These principles apply only to "negotiable instruments proper"; they have no application to forged cheques which are not negotiable instruments but mere sham pieces of paper[1] nor to a simple unindorsed cheque, payment of which is countermanded by the drawer.[2] Prominent among the cases on bills of exchange is *Price* v. *Neal*.[3] In that case, the plaintiff sued the defendant to recover two sums of £40 each, paid to the defendant upon two bills of exchange of which the plaintiff was drawee. The defendant, as indorsee for valuable consideration of the first bill, presented it for payment on the day it became due, and the plaintiff paid the money and took it up. The plaintiff also accepted the second bill and indorsed it to the defendant for valuable consideration; subsequently, he also paid the money due upon that bill, and took it up. In fact, both bills had been forged by a third party. The plaintiff sought to recover the £80 he had so paid to the defendant, who had acted throughout in good faith without notice of the forgeries.

Lord Mansfield held that in neither case could the plaintiff recover his money. He said[4]:

---

[97] *D. Owen & Co.* v. *Cronk* [1895] 1 Q.B. 265; see also *Ex p. Bird* (1851) 4 De G. & Sm. 273.
[98] (1808) 1 Taunt. 359, 363.
[99] *National Westminster Bank Ltd.* v. *Barclays Bank Ltd.* [1975] Q.B. 654, 666, *per* Kerr J.
[1] *Imperial Bank of Canada* v. *Bank of Hamilton* [1903] A.C. 49; *Imperial Bank of India* v. *Abeyesinghe* (1927) 29 Ceylon L.R. 257; *National Westminster Bank Ltd.* v. *Barclays Bank Ltd.* [1975] Q.B. 654; see above, p. 749.
[2] *Barclays Bank Ltd.* v. *W. J. Simms & Sons Ltd.* [1980] 1 Q.B. 677, 702–703, *per* Robert Goff J., applying Bills of Exchange Act 1882, s.50(2)(c).
[3] (1762) 3 Burr. 1354; see also *Jenys* v. *Fawler* (1733) 2 Str. 946.
[4] At p. 1357. See also *Ancher* v. *Bank of England* (1781) 2 Doug. 637, discussed in Holden, *History of Negotiable Instruments*, pp. 120–122.

" . . . It can never be thought unconscientious in the defendant to retain this money, when he has once received it upon a bill of exchange indorsed to him for a fair and valuable consideration, which he had bona fide paid, without the least privity or suspicion of any forgery.

Here was no fraud: no wrong. It was incumbent upon the plaintiff to be satisfied 'that the bill drawn upon him was the drawer's hand,' before he accepted or paid it: but it was not incumbent upon the defendant, to inquire into it. . . . The plaintiff lies by, for a considerable time after he has paid these bills; . . . He made no objection to them at the time of paying them. Whatever neglect there was, was on his side. . . . The defendant had actual encouragement from the plaintiff himself, for negotiating the second bill, from the plaintiff's having without any scruple or hesitation paid the first. . . . If there was no neglect in the plaintiff, yet there is no reason to throw off the loss from one innocent man upon another innocent man . . . "

Lord Mansfield, as is evident from this quotation, relied on a multiplicity of reasons.[5] In later cases,[6] however, the emphasis has been transferred to the change in the defendant's position because of delay by the plaintiff in discovering and giving notice of the forgery. Thus, in *Cocks* v. *Masterman*,[7] a bill, which purported to have been accepted by Sewell and Cross, was presented to the plaintiffs as their bankers on the day it became due and they duly paid the amount of the bill to the defendants, the bankers of the holders. The next day the plaintiffs discovered that the acceptance was forged, and they at once gave notice of that fact to the defendants. The plaintiffs sought to recover from the defendants the money so paid to them as paid under a mistake of fact, but the Court of King's Bench held they were not entitled to succeed. Bayley J., who delivered the judgment of the court, said[8]:

" . . . We are all of the opinion that the holder of a bill is entitled to know, on the day when it becomes due, whether it is an honoured or dishonoured bill, and that, if he receive the money and is suffered to retain it during the whole of that day, the parties who paid it cannot recover it back. The holder, indeed, is not bound by law (if the bill be dishonoured by the acceptor) to take any steps against the other parties to the bill till the day after it is dishonoured. But he is entitled so to do, if he thinks fit, and the parties who pay the bill ought not by their negligence to deprive the holder of any right or privilege."

---

[5] *National Westminster Bank Ltd.* v. *Barclays Bank Ltd.* [1975] Q.B. 654, 667–668, *per* Kerr J. *Cf.* *Simms* v. *Anglo-American Telegraph Co.* (1883) 11 Q.B.D. 327.

[6] *Smith* v. *Mercer* (1815) 6 Taunt. 76; *Cocks* v. *Masterman* (1829) 9 B. & C. 902; *Mather* v. *Lord Maidstone* (1856) 18 C.B. 273; *Morison* v. *London County and Westminster Bank Ltd.* [1914] 3 K.B. 356; *London & River Plate Bank* v. *Bank of Liverpool* [1896] 1 Q.B. 7; *Bank of Montreal* v. *R.* (1907) 38 Can.S.C.R. 258. See also *Pooley* v. *Brown* (1862) 31 L.J.C.P. 134.

[7] (1829) 9 B. & C. 902.

[8] At pp. 908–909. See also *Wilkinson* v. *Johnson* (1824) 3 B. & C. 428.

The concluding words of this passage suggest that the judges thought negligence in the plaintiffs to be an essential prerequisite of this defence.[9] But it is clear from Lord Mansfield's judgment in *Price* v. *Neal*[10] that what he regarded as essential was not presence of fault in the plaintiff, but absence of fault in the defendant; and in *London & River Plate Bank* v. *Bank of Liverpool*,[11] Mathew J. held that the defence is independent of the plaintiff's negligence. In that case Mathew J. expressed the view that the foundation of the defence is estoppel. He said of *Price* v. *Neal*[12] that, "if the plaintiff in that case so conducted himself as to lead the holder of the bill to believe that he considered the signature genuine, he could not afterwards withdraw from that position."[13] There is force in this view, which gives effect to the expressions in the context of the particular cases, that a drawee ought to know his drawer's signature,[14] a banker his customer's,[15] an acceptor his own.[16] In these cases the holder may be in a less favourable position to ascertain the signature's authenticity. On the other hand, it is difficult to maintain that the drawee of a bill ordinarily represents by payment the genuineness of the signatures of indorsees on the bill.[17] However, in *London & River Plate Bank* v. *Bank of Liverpool*,[18] where the plaintiffs paid the defendants on a bill, the indorsements on which, so it appeared some months later, had been forged, Mathew J. held that the plaintiffs were precluded from recovering the payment. If the basis of the *Price* v. *Neal* line of cases is the doctrine of estoppel, some doubt must be cast upon this decision.[19]

In a defence based on estoppel, the defendant must be able to show that his position has been changed for the worse. But it has been said[20] that, if notice of forgery is not given until the day after payment, it will be presumed that the position of the holder has altered; and in *London & River Plate Bank* v. *Bank of Liverpool*, Mathew J. was of opinion[21] that, even if notice is given on the day of payment, the defendant may rely on the defence if he can show that his position has actually been altered. This presumption of change of position after the day of payment has led some American writers to suggest that the ultimate basis of

---

[9] See also *Smith* v. *Mercer* (1815) 6 Taunt. 76, 80, *per* Dallas J.

[10] (1762) 3 Burr. 1354.

[11] [1896] 1 Q.B. 7.

[12] (1762) 3 Burr. 1354.

[13] *London & River Plate Bank* v. *Bank of Liverpool* [1896] 1 Q.B. 7, 10–11.

[14] *Price* v. *Neal* (1762) 3 Burr. 1354; *cf.* Bills of Exchange Act 1882, s.54.

[15] *Smith* v. *Mercer* (1815) 6 Taunt. 76.

[16] *Mather* v. *Lord Maidstone* (1856) 18 C.B. 273.

[17] *Cf. Jones* v. *Ryde* (1814) 5 Taunt. 488; *Bruce* v. *Bruce* (1814) 5 Taunt. 495; *Gompertz* v. *Bartlett* (1853) 2 E. & B. 849; *Gurney* v. *Womersley* (1854) 4 E. & B. 133.

[18] [1896] 1 Q.B. 7.

[19] In the United States, where the case law is much more voluminous and the rules have been greatly elaborated, the defence has not been extended to cases of forged indorsement: see *Restatement of Restitution*, § 35. And see Lord Wright's comment in his *Legal Essays and Addresses*, pp. 41–42; and *Robinson* v. *Yarrow* (1817) 7 Taunt. 455.

[20] *Cocks* v. *Masterman* (1829) 9 B. & C. 902, 908–909, *per* Bayley J.: see above, p. 756.

[21] [1896] 1 Q.B. 7, 11–12.

the doctrine is not estoppel or change of position, but "the policy of maintaining confidence in the security of negotiable paper, by making the time and place of acceptance or payment the time and place for the final settlement, as between drawee and holder, of the question of the genuineness of the drawer's signature."[22] But in English law there are indications that it is necessary to show an actual change of position before the defence can be invoked. Thus, in *Imperial Bank of Canada* v. *Bank of Hamilton*,[23] the Privy Council obviously regarded the rule as laid down by Mathew J. as very stringent, and expressed some doubts whether it should be so rigorously applied.[24] In that case, it was held that, in the case of a simple forged cheque, the rule had in any event no application. Lord Lindley said[25]:

> "The cheque for the larger amount was a simple forgery; and Bauer, the drawer and forger, was not entitled to any notice of its dishonour by non-payment. There were no indorsers to whom notice of dishonour had to be given. The law as to the necessity of giving notice of dishonour has, therefore, no application. The rule laid down in *Cocks* v. *Masterman*, and recently reasserted in even wider language by Mathew J. in *London & River Plate Bank* v. *Bank of Liverpool*, has reference to negotiable instruments, on the dishonour of which notice has to be given to some one, namely, to some drawers or indorser, who would be discharged from liability unless such notice were given in proper time. Their lordships are not aware of any authority for applying so stringent a rule to any other cases. Assuming it to be as stringent as is alleged in such cases as those above described, their lordships are not prepared to extend it to other cases where notice of the mistake is given in reasonable time, and no loss has been occasioned by the delay in giving it."

Similarly, in *Leeds & County Bank Ltd.* v. *Walker*,[26] Denman J. held that the rule in *Cocks* v. *Masterman* had no application in the case of money paid upon an altered Bank of England note, because nobody other than the Bank of England could possibly be held liable on such a note; in the event, therefore, of the Bank repudiating liability on the recovery of an alteration, there was no question of steps being taken or rights lost against any other party.

There is, therefore, something to be said for the view that the defendant must, before he can rely on the defence, show that his position has actually

---

[22] Woodward, *op. cit.* p. 137; *First National Bank of Portland* v. *Noble*, (1946) 179 Or. 26; *Restatement of Restitution* § 30; *Uniform Commercial Code*, § 3–406, § 3–407, § 3–148; (1891) 4 Harv.L.Rev. 297, 299–300 [Ames]; Keener, pp. 154–158. See also Lord Wright, *Legal Essays and Addresses*, pp. 41–42. Contrast Farnsworth, (1960) 60 Col.L.R. 284, 302 who justifies the rule as the best way of spreading loss.

[23] [1903] A.C. 49. See also *National Westminster Bank Ltd.* v. *Barclays Bank International Ltd.* [1975] Q.B. 654; *Barclays Bank* v. *W. J. Simms & Son Ltd.* [1980] 1 Q.B. 677.

[24] At pp. 56–58, *per* Lord Lindley. See also the reservations of Viscount Cave L.C. in *R. E. Jones Ltd.* v. *Waring & Gillow Ltd.* [1926] A.C. 670, 684.

[25] At p. 58.

[26] (1883) 11 Q.B.D. 84. See also *Wilkinson* v. *Johnson* (1824) 3 B. & C. 428; *Phillips* v. *Im Thurn* (1866) L.R. 1 C.P. 463.

been changed for the worse. The old view that, where notice of the forgery has not been given on the day of payment, the defendant's position is presumed to have been altered, may yet be discarded. And if Mathew J.'s application of the defence to cases of forged indorsement were also to be rejected, the decisions would be consistent not only with the cases on estoppel[27] but with the defence of change of position.

---

[27] *London & River Plate Bank* v. *Bank of Liverpool* [1896] 1 Q.B. 7: see above, p. 757.

CHAPTER 41

BONA FIDE PURCHASE

A restitutionary proprietary claim[1] will normally be defeated if the defendant is a bona fide purchaser, since it would not then be just to impose a constructive trust or a lien over assets in his hands.

Whether a bona fide purchase will defeat a personal claim in restitution is a question which arises less frequently.[2] In many of the situations discussed earlier in this book, it will transparently have no relevance; for example, there is little scope for any such defence when a benefit has been conferred under an ineffective transaction.[3] But, exceptionally, a plea of bona fide purchase may defeat even a personal claim in restitution. As Lord Mansfield said in *Clarke* v. *Shee*,[4] "where money or notes are paid bona fide, and upon a valuable consideration they shall never be brought back by the true owner." And, in *Nelson* v. *Larholt*,[5] Denning J. was prepared to accept that an action for money had and received or an equitable personal claim against a defendant who had in good faith received assets of the estate from a fraudulent executor would be defeated if the defendant could prove that he was a bona fide purchaser.

For these reasons it is necessary to consider briefly the principles of the equitable doctrine of bona fide purchase.

Equitable claims are only enforceable against a purchaser in whom the legal title[6] is vested if that person's conscience is affected by notice of the equitable interest. A defendant, before he can rely on bona fide purchase, must, therefore, prove that he is a purchaser for value and that he had no notice of any equitable interest. The giving of value, which includes not only money and money's worth[7] but also marriage consideration,[8] need not be simultaneous

---

[1] See above, Chap. 2.

[2] In New South Wales it has been held that bona fide purchase may not be a defence to an action based on the defendant's breach of confidence: see *Wheatley* v. *Bell* (1982) [1984] F.S.R. 16, citing *Frazer* v. *Evans* [1969] 1 Q.B. 349, 361, *per* Lord Denning M.R. It is doubtful if an English court would endorse this principle: see *Stevenson Jordan & Harrison Ltd.* v. *Macdonald & Evans* (1951) 68 R.P.C. 190: see above, pp. 695–696.

[3] See above, Chap. 2.

[4] (1774) 1 Cowp. 197, 200; *Lipkin Gorman (A Firm)* v. *Karpnale Ltd.* [1991] 2 A.C. 548.

[5] [1948] 1 K.B. 339; see above, p. 575, n. 22 and other cases there cited. And *cf.* the scope of the action for money had and received: see above, Chap. 2.

[6] In certain limited cases a purchaser of "any interest in the land" for value takes free from equitable interests previously created, unless such equitable interest has been registered under the Land Charges Act before the completion of his purchase: see Land Charges Act 1972, ss.4(5), 17.

[7] In certain cases, value must be money or money's worth: see Land Charges Act 1972, s.4(6).

[8] *Pullan* v. *Koe* [1913] 1 Ch. 9.

with the transfer of the property; it may precede or succeed the transfer provided that at the date when value is given or the date of the transfer, whichever is the later, the purchaser was not fixed with notice.[9] After he has notice of any equitable interest, a purchaser cannot improve his position by giving value for the transfer.[10]

At common law, notice was equated with honesty.[11] This criterion has been accepted by the Bills of Exchange Act 1882, which states that "a thing is deemed to be done in good faith within the meaning of this Act, where it is in fact done honestly, whether it is done negligently or not."[12] So, constructive notice will not prevent the holder of a bill being a holder in due course, provided that he does not act in bad faith.[13] In equity, however, notice has been more generously defined. A defendant may be deemed to have constructive or imputed notice of equitable interests affecting land. A person is deemed to have constructive notice if he deprives himself of actual knowledge by failing to carry out[14] or by abstaining from carrying out[15] the usual and proper inquiries which would have been conducted by a reasonable and prudent purchaser. He has imputed notice of equitable interests of which his agent has actual or constructive notice, provided that the agent acquired such notice in the course of the particular transaction or purchase.[16] It is a distinct question whether a person who receives trust money is personally liable in equity if he has "notice" that the money was transferred in breach of trust.[17]

This distinction between notice at law and in equity is based on sound principle. As Lindley L.J. said[18]:

"The equitable doctrines of constructive notice are common enough when dealing with land and estates, with which the court is familiar; but there have been repeated protests against the introduction into commercial transactions of anything like an extension of these doctrines, and the

---

[9] *Ratcliffe* v. *Barnard* (1871) L.R. 6 Ch. App. 652.
[10] The doctrine of *tabula in naufragio* may assist a purchaser without notice of an equitable interest who subsequently acquires the legal title, even though at the date of the acquisition of the legal title he had notice of the equitable interest. The implications of this doctrine for factoring companies are discussed in (1976) 92 L.Q.R. 528, 556 [Goode], (1977) 93 L.Q.R. 324 [Donaldson], and (1977) 93 L.Q.R. 487 [Goode].
[11] *Nelson* v. *Larholt* [1948] 1 K.B. 339, 343–344, *per* Denning J.
[12] s.90.
[13] It is often not open to a banker to say that he is a "holder in due course." But the Bills of Exchange Act 1882, as amended, contains special provisions for their protection in certain situations: see Bills of Exchange Act 1882, ss.80, 82; Cheques Act 1957, s.4; *Midland Bank Ltd.* v. *Reckitt* [1933] A.C. 1.
[14] Law of Property Act 1925, s.199; Land Charges Act 1974, s.4. see also *Jones* v. *Smith* (1841) 1 Hare 43, 45, *per* Wigram V.-C.
[15] *West* v. *Reid* (1843) 2 Hare 249, 257–258, *per* Wigram V.-C.; *Oliver* v. *Hinton* [1899] 2 Ch. 264; Law of Property Act 1925, s.199. Land Charges Act 1974, s.4.
[16] Law of Property Act 1925, s.199; Land Charges Act 1974, s.4. see also *Fuller* v. *Bennett* (1843) 2 Hare 394.
[17] See above, pp. 671–672.
[18] *Manchester Trust* v. *Furness* [1895] 2 Q.B. 539, 545; see also *London Joint Stock Bank* v. *Simmons* [1892] A.C. 201, 221, *per* Lord Herschell; *Shields* v. *The Governor & Co. of the Bank of Ireland* [1901] 1 I.R. 222.

protest is founded on good sense. In dealing with estates in land title is everything, and it can be leisurely investigated; in commercial transactions possession is everything, and there is no time to investigate title; and if we were to extend the doctrine of constructive notice to commercial transactions we should be doing infinite mischief and paralysing the trade of the country."[19-20]

In equity, if the purchaser can satisfy the court that he gave value and that he had no notice, not only he, but all persons claiming through him, may rely on bona fide purchase, even though the persons claiming through him had notice of the equitable interest.[21] But if a purchaser with notice sells to a bona fide purchaser, he cannot successfully plead the defence if he later buys the property back from him.[22]

English law has now recognised a defence of change of position.[23] It has been said that the defence of bona fide purchase is "simply the paradigm change of position defence, and that the true rule is that equity will not permit a defendant to set up title to property in which the plaintiff has a beneficial interest unless he has given value or otherwise changed his position to his detriment without notice, actual or constructive, of the plaintiff's interest."[24] But the defences are distinct defences.[25] Neither common law nor equity normally inquires into the adequacy of the consideration which a purchaser provides.[26] But such an inquiry would be central to any defence based solely on a defence of change of position, for it is a defence which operates to discharge, wholly or in part,[27] a defendant's duty to make restitution.

[19-20] But see Mr. Justice L.J. Priestley, "The Romalpa Clause and the Quistclose Trust" in *Equity and Commercial Relationships* (ed. Finn), Chap. 8 and *cf.* Mr. Justice Kearney, "Accounting for Fiduciary's Gains in Commercial Contexts" in the same volume, Chap. 7, and above, pp. 671–672.

[21] *Wilkes* v. *Spooner* [1911] 2 K.B. 473.

[22] *Barrows' Case* (1880) 14 Ch.D. 432, 445, *per* Jessel M.R.; *cf. Restatement of Restitution,* § 176.

[23] *Lipkin Gorman (A Firm)* v. *Karpnale Ltd.* [1991] 2 A.C. 548; see above, Chap. 40.

[24] Sir Peter Millett, *Tracing the Proceeds of Fraud,* (1991) 107 L.Q.R. 71, 82.

[25] *Lipkin Gorman (A Firm)* v. *Karpnale Ltd.* [1991] 2 A.C. 548, 580–581, *per* Lord Goff.

[26] *Basset* v. *Nosworthy* (1673) Rep. temp. Finch 102; *Midland Bank* v. *Green* [1981] A.C. 513.

[27] Contrast the operation of the defence of estoppel: see above, pp. 746 *et seq.*

CHAPTER 42

RES JUDICATA AND ELECTION

1. Res Judicata

Interest reipublicae ut sit finis litium. This maxim is as important in the law of restitution as in any other branch of English private law. In *Moses* v. *Macferlan*[1] Lord Mansfield recognised that "it is most clear 'that the merits of a judgment can never be overhaled by an original suit, either at law or in equity.' Till the judgment is set aside, or reversed, it is conclusive, as to the subject-matter of it, to all intents and purposes." The original cause of action between the actual parties[2] merges in the final judgment and they are estopped between themselves from litigating that point again.

Once the judgment has become final, it cannot be challenged on the ground that it was wrong. However, in *Moses* v. *Macferlan*[3] itself it was decided that the unsuccessful party might still bring an action for money had and received against the successful party to recover the amount of the judgment, for, as Lord Mansfield said, "the ground of this action is not, 'that the judgment is wrong'—but 'that . . . the defendant ought not in justice to keep the money.' "[4] But the facts of that case were exceptional. Moses had indorsed to Macferlan four several promissory notes, made to Moses by Jacob, to enable Macferlan to recover the money in his name against Jacob. Macferlan agreed that Moses should not be prejudiced by his indorsements. Notwithstanding this agreement, Macferlan "summoned . . . Moses to the Court of Conscience" upon the indorsements. The Court of Conscience rejected the defence based on the agreement, "thinking they had no power to judge of it," and gave judgment against Moses, whose agent paid the money into court. Subsequently, in the Court of King's Bench, Moses sought to recover the money from Macferlan in *indebitatus assumpsit*. The court held that he must succeed, since the defendant was obliged by the ties of natural justice and equity to refund the money.

---

[1] (1760) 2 Burr. 1005, 1009.
[2] A judicial decision *inter partes* will estop not only the actual parties but also all who are jointly, though not severally, liable with either party: see, generally, Spencer Bower, *Res Judicata*, pp. 201–203, 382–390; *Restatement of Restitution*, § 147.
[3] (1760) 2 Burr. 1005.
[4] At p. 1009. *Cf. Marriot* v. *Hampton* (1797) 7 T.R. 269, where money paid under threat of legal process was held irrecoverable. Such a case is an example of voluntary payment rather than *res judicata*: see *Ward & Co.* v. *Wallis* [1900] 1 Q.B. 675, 678, *per* Kennedy J.; see above, pp. 50–51.

Lord Mansfield's decision, although just, was a blatant attack upon, and a *de facto* reversal of, the judgment of a competent court,[5] and his observations have not been accepted as authority for any exception to the principle of *res judicata*. In *Phillips* v. *Hunter*,[6] Eyre C.J. refused to "subscribe to the authority of that case."[7] He said[8]: "I believe that judgment did not satisfy Westminster Hall at the time; I could never subscribe to it; it seems to me to unsettle foundations."[9]

2. ELECTION

A plaintiff may have a choice of remedies, each of which will, if he succeeds in his suit, compensate him for the loss of a certain benefit; for example, he may be able to claim for damages in tort or claim restitution of the defendant's benefit as money had and received to his use.[10] If the plaintiff chooses one remedy rather than another, his election will only be final if he has proceeded to judgment and the judgment has been satisfied.[11]

---

[5] See C. H. S. Fifoot, *Lord Mansfield*, pp. 143, 155; and J. Oldham, *The Mansfield Manuscripts*, Vol. I, p. 258.

[6] (1795) 2 H.Bl. 402.

[7] *Ibid.* at p. 414.

[8] *Ibid.* at p. 416.

[9] See also *Munt* v. *Stokes* (1792) 4 T.R. 561; *Brisbane* v. *Dacres* (1813) 5 Taunt. 143, 160, *per* Heath J.; *Cobden* v. *Kendrick* (1791) 4 T.R. 431.

[10] See above, Chap. 38.

[11] *United Australia Ltd.* v. *Barclays Bank Ltd.* [1941] A.C. 1: see above, p. 732. *Cf. Mahesan S/O Thambiah* v. *Malaysia Government Officers' Co-operative Housing Society Ltd.* [1979] A.C. 374: see above, p. 667.

CHAPTER 43

STATUTES OF LIMITATION AND LACHES[1]

THE primary criterion for the application of statutes of limitation was originally procedural. All claims in *assumpsit* were deemed to fall within section 3 of the Limitation Act 1623, and had to be brought "within six yeares next after the cause of such accions or suit." In certain cases, for example, where the equitable remedy was similar to the legal remedy or where the equitable remedy was in aid of legal rights, the Court of Chancery was content to apply the analogy of this statute and its successors[2] to bar claims in equity which were not expressly barred at law.[3] A principal's suit for an account against a non-fiduciary agent was accordingly barred after six years,[4] as was an action by one *cestui que trust* against his fellow *cestui que trust* who had been overpaid because of the mistake of the trustees.[5] Purely equitable claims were and are,[6] however, barred only by laches, an equitable doctrine which defeats stale demands where a party has slept upon his rights.[7] Equity adopts no fixed time-bar, but considers the circumstances of each case in determining whether there is delay amounting to laches. "Two circumstances, always important in such cases, are the length of the delay and the nature of the acts done during the interval, which might affect either party and cause a balance of justice or injustice in taking the one course or the other."[8]

The old law of limitations, and to some extent the equitable doctrine of laches,[9] have been profoundly affected by the Limitation Acts 1939 and 1965, now consolidated in the Limitation Act 1980. These statutes, however, do not solve a significant number of the limitation problems to which restitutionary claims give rise. Indeed, there is not even a general section, akin to section 3 of the Act of 1623, which previously governed all *assumpsit* claims.[10] In the past, the courts were compelled to interpret the Limitation Act 1939 in a somewhat cavalier fashion in an effort to achieve consistency. The tendency has been,

---

[1] See, generally, H. M. McLean, "Limitation of Actions in Restitution" [1989] C.L.J. 472.
[2] *e.g.* Real Property Limitation Acts 1833 and 1874; Civil Procedure Act 1833.
[3] *Hovenden* v. *Annesley* (1806) 2 Sch. & Lef. 607.
[4] *Lockey* v. *Lockey* (1719) Pr.Ch. 518; *Knox* v. *Gye* (1871) L.R. 5 H.L. 656.
[5] *Re Robinson* [1911] 1 Ch. 502; and *cf. Baker* v. *Courage & Co.* [1910] 1 K.B. 56.
[6] Subject to very limited exceptions; see, *e.g.* below, pp. 766, 768.
[7] *Smith* v. *Clay* (1767) Amb. 645; Brunyate, *op. cit.* pp. 1–23.
[8] *Lindsay Petroleum Co.* v. *Hurd* (1874) L.R. 5 P.C. 221, 239–240, *per* Sir Barnes Peacock, approved in *Erlanger* v. *New Sombrero Phosphate Co.* (1878) 3 App.Cas. 1218, 1279, *per* Lord Blackburn.
[9] The doctrine of laches is preserved by the Limitation Act 1980, s.36(2).
[10] See above, pp. 3–4, for the scope of *assumpsit* claims.

wherever possible, to apply a six-year period of limitation. Thus actions for money had and received were squeezed into section 2(1)(*a*) of the 1939 Act (now section 5 of the Limitation Act 1980), which stated that "actions founded on simple contract" are barred after six years. In *Re Diplock*,[11] Lord Greene M.R. was prepared to assume that these words "must be taken to cover actions for money had and received, formerly actions on the case. . . . The assumption must, we think, be made, though the words used cannot be regarded as felicitous." And in *Kleinwort Benson Ltd.* v. *The Borough Council of Sandwell*[12] Hobhouse J. held that the words "action founded on simple contract" within section 5 of the Limitation Act 1980 "are sufficiently broad to cover an action for money had and received." In reaching this conclusion the ambiguity of the statutory provision enabled him to look to *Hansard* for guidance as to its meaning.[12a] In the debate on the Limitation Act 1939, the precursor of the 1980 Act, the Solicitor-General stated that the statute was intended to implement the recommendations of the Fifth Interim Report of the Law Revision Committee and, in particular, the recommendation "that the period for all actions founded in tort or simple contract (including quasi-contract) . . . should be six years . . ."

Seemingly, therefore, the remaining quasi-contractual claims will be barred after six years[12b] unless the Limitation Act 1980 provides, as it does in some cases,[13] an alternative limitation period. Claims to recover trust property are also barred after six years.[14] If, however, the claim is to personal estate of a deceased person, the limitation period is 12 years.[15] Generally,[16] purely equitable claims are still only barred by laches; but, in practice, equity will follow the analogy of the statutory period of limitation.[17]

The plaintiff's cause of action will normally accrue when he pays money to the defendant, or to the defendant's use, or when he supplied goods or services, as the case may be,[18] or when the defendant is paid money for which he must account to the plaintiff. If a plaintiff seeks rescission when time begins to run may depend on the grounds for rescission. In *Lakshmijit* v. *Sherani*,[19] the Privy Council held that time runs from the date when the

---

[11] [1948] Ch. 465, 514; below, p. 775.
[12] February 12, 1993, unrep.: see above, p. 541.
[12a] *Pepper* v. *Hart* [1992] 3 W.L.R. 1032, H.L.
[12b] See *Amantilla Ltd.* v. *Telefusion plc.* (1987) 9 Con.L.R. 139 (H.H. Judge Davies Q.C.), interpreting s.29(5)(c) of the Limitation Act 1980 (acknowledgment of debts), where a *quantum meruit* claim was said to be an action for a liquidated sum and fell within the section; the sum was of a sufficiently contractual description to be ascertained by the court. For an historical explanation, see (1988) 8 Oxford. Jo. L.S. 312, 316 [Ibbetson].
[13] Particularly in cases of mistake or fraud or breach of trust: see below, pp. 767–769 and 776 *et seq.*
[14] s.21(3). The subsection has no application to an action by the Att.-Gen. to enforce a charitable trust: *Att.-Gen.* v. *Cocke* [1988] Ch. 414.
[15] s.22(a), discussed below, p. 775.
[16] But see below, pp. 766, 768.
[17] See, *e.g. Molloy* v. *Mutual Reserve Life Insurance Co.* (1906) 94 L.T. 756, 762, *per* Romer L.J.
[18] *Baker* v. *Courage & Co. Ltd.* [1910] 1 K.B. 56; *Maskell* v. *Horner* [1915] 3 K.B. 106; *Brueton* v. *Woodward* [1941] 1 K.B. 680.
[19] [1974] A.C. 605.

plaintiff communicated to the defendant his intention to rescind. The facts of that case were, however, unusual. The plaintiff had contracted to sell land to the defendant by instalments. The defendant defaulted. Under the terms of the contract, the plaintiff was permitted to elect either to sue for the purchase money or to rescind and retake possession, retaining the instalments already paid. He did nothing; and the defendant remained in possession of the land for over 12 years. The plaintiff then sought to rescind the contract, and sued for possession; the defendant pleaded that he had acquired the title by adverse possession. The Privy Council rejected this defence and gave judgment for the plaintiff. The analogy of *Car and Universal Finance Co. Ltd.* v. *Caldwell*[20] persuaded the court that time did not run against the plaintiff until he had unequivocally communicated to the defendant that he was rescinding the agreement. Communication was necessary because rescission "alters the rights and obligations of both parties to the sale agreement, since it puts an end to the purchaser's right to possession of the land and prevents any further instalment of the purchase price becoming due."[21] Until such communication was made the defendant remained entitled to possession. In our view, however, there is much force in the dissent of Viscount Dilhorne. He distinguished *Caldwell's* case on the ground that it concerned a contract voidable for fraud, where the defrauded party was not able to communicate his intention to rescind, and concluded that time should run against the plaintiff as soon as his right to rescind arose. On the facts, this was when there was the requisite default[22] under the agreement. English courts are traditionally reluctant to allow the claim of a squatter that he has acquired a good title by adverse possession. The Privy Council's decision in *Lakshmijit* v. *Sherani* is such a case; it is possible that future cases will limit the principle which it formulates to claims against adverse possessors.

The Limitation Act 1980[23] makes special provision when persons suffer from legal disabilities. In most cases,[24] the six-year limitation period runs from the date the person ceases to be under a disability or dies, whichever event occurs first.

Further generalisation is impossible. The state of the law of limitation compels us to provide a catalogue of heads of restitution claims and their appropriate limitation periods.

1. Where the Defendant has Acquired a Benefit from or by the Act of the Plaintiff

(a) *Recovery of Benefits Conferred Under a Mistake*

At common law, in cases of mistaken payments time ran from the date when

---

[20] [1965] 1 Q.B. 525: see above, pp. 204–205.
[21] [1974] A.C. 605, 616, *per curiam* (Lord Cross).
[22] *Ibid.* at pp. 616–618.
[23] See ss.28, 38(2), (3), (4).
[24] For special cases, see Preston & Newsom *op. cit.* Chap. VII; Franks, *op. cit.* pp. 209–215.

the payment was made and not from the date when the mistake was, or ought reasonably have been, discovered.[25] Equity adopted the same rule if the equitable claim was strictly analogous to a common law claim.[26] But if the plaintiff was seeking purely equitable relief, such as rescission or rectification, time did not run until he had, or ought reasonably to have, discovered the mistake.[27]

This conflict has been largely resolved by section 32(1)(c) of the Limitation Act 1980, which reads as follows:

> "Subject to subsection (3) below[28] where, in the case of any action for which a period of limitation is prescribed by this Act. . . .
>
>   (c) the action is for relief from the consequences of a mistake, the period of limitation shall not begin to run until the plaintiff has discovered . . . the mistake . . . or could with reasonable diligence have discovered it."

Section 32(1)(c), therefore, applies only if the Act prescribes a period of limitation. For quasi-contractual claims this will generally be the six-year period prescribed by section 5.[29] But not all equitable claims to recover benefits conferred by mistake fall within that section.[30] Only claims for equitable relief analogous to common law claims are within section 5 and section 32(1)(c).[31] Purely equitable claims for relief from mistake are, therefore, only barred by laches[32]; unless they are to the personal estate of a deceased person, when they fall within section 22(a), which is of much wider ambit than section 5 and governs "*any*[33] claim to the personal estate of a deceased person." The distinction, however, is academic[34]; for whether the claim falls within section 32(1)(c) or is barred by laches, time will not run until the plaintiff has discovered the mistake or *could, with reasonable diligence, have discovered it*. It has been said that "it is impossible to devise a meaning or construction to be put on those [italicised] words which can generally be applied in all contexts."[35]

---

[25] *Baker* v. *Courage & Co. Ltd.* [1910] 1 K.B. 56.

[26] *Re Robinson* [1911] 1 Ch. 502; *Re Mason* [1928] Ch. 385, 392–393, *per* Romer J., affd. [1929] 1 Ch. 1.

[27] *Brooksbank* v. *Smith* (1836) 2 Y. & C.Ex. 58; *Denys* v. *Shuckburgh* (1840) 4 Y. C.Ex. 42.

[28] This subsection protects the bona fide purchaser and any person claiming through him: see below, p. 770.

[29] See above, pp. 765–766.

[30] See *Re Diplock* [1948] Ch. 465, 514–516, where the Court of Appeal assumed that s.32(1)(c) applied to the facts. The House of Lords left open the question; the subsection "presents many problems": [1951] A.C. 251, 277, *per* Viscount Simonds: see below, p. 769, nn. 41, 42.

[31] s.36(1).

[32] *Smith* v. *Clay* (1767) Amb. 645, 648, *per* Lord Camden; *Erlanger* v. *New Sombrero Phosphate Co.* (1878) 3 App.Cas. 1218; *Caird* v. *Moss* (1886) 33 Ch.D. 22, 29, *per* Kay J.; *Case* v. *Case* (1889) 61 L.T. 789, 791, *per* Kay J.; Brunyate, pp. 1–23, 185 *et seq.*; Franks, pp. 236–237. For the effect of lapse of time on the right to rescind contracts induced by misrepresentation, see below, pp. 768–769.

[33] Italics supplied.

[34] But *cf. Peco Arts Inc.* v. *Hazlitt Gallery Ltd.* [1983] 1 W.L.R. 1315, 1327, *per* Webster J.

[35] *Peco Arts Inc.* v. *Hazlitt Gallery Ltd.* [1983] 1 W.L.R. 1315, 1323, *per* Webster J.

In *Peco Arts Inc.* v. *Hazlitt Gallery Ltd.*,[36] where that observation was made, the claim was for the return of money paid under a shared mistake of fact. The buyer sought the return of the purchase price for a drawing which was thought to be by Ingres but was in fact a reproduction, Webster J. concluded that "the words which we have put in italics,"[36a] mean the doing of that which an ordinarily prudent buyer and possessor of a valuable work of art would do having regard in to the circumstances, including the circumstances of the purchase." In determining whether the buyer had acted with reasonable diligence, the acts or omissions of the buyer's agents cannot be attributed to him.[37]

In *Phillip-Higgins* v. *Harper*,[38] Pearson J. held that section 26(*c*) of the Limitation Act 1939, (now s.32(1)(*c*) of the 1980 Act),

> "applies only where the mistake is an essential ingredient of the cause of action, so that the statement of claim sets out, or should set out, the mistake and its consequences and prays for relief from those consequences."

Section 26(*c*) did not apply to the facts of *Phillip-Higgins* v. *Harper*, where the defendant had underpaid the plaintiff, who had not realised what payments were due to her. The plaintiff's action was not for "relief from the consequences of a mistake," but to recover moneys due to her under a contract. "The cause of action is the same as if she sued for each unpaid balance on its due date."[39] This reasoning, if logical, does produce some odd results, as Pearson J. appreciated. It means that "a person who has by mistake paid too much can take advantage of the section whereas a person who has by mistake received too little and made no protest cannot take advantage of the section."[40] Yet, in *Re Diplock*,[41] the Court of Appeal assumed that, if section 2 of the Limitation Act 1939 had been applicable, the next-of-kin, who had not been paid because of the executors' mistake, could have invoked s.26(*c*).[42] To reach that desirable result, it will be necessary to read generously the words, "the action is for relief from the consequences of a mistake," so as to conclude that it is sufficient to show circumstances from which law or equity will grant relief from mistake.[43]

---

[36] *Ibid.* Contrast *Leaf* v. *International Galleries* [1950] 2 K.B. 86, distinguished by Webster J., at pp. 1323–1324: see above, p. 206.

[36a] See above, p. 768.

[37] *Ibid.* at p. 1326.

[38] [1954] 1 Q.B. 411, 419; affd., without reasons reported, in [1954] 2 All E.R. 51n.

[39] *Ibid.* at pp. 418–419.

[40] *Ibid.* at p. 419.

[41] [1948] Ch. 465, 514–516: see above, p. 775. But, in the House of Lords, Viscount Simonds left open the question whether s.26(*c*) (now s.32(1)(*c*) of the Limitation Act 1980 was applicable: see above, p. 768).

[42] For s.2 (now Limitation Act 1980, s.5) see above, p. 766. The Court held, however, that the relevant section was s.20 of the Limitation Act 1939 (now Limitation Act 1980, s.22(*a*)), on which see below, p. 775.

[43] Franks, *op. cit.* p. 207.

In *Peco Arts Inc.* v. *Hazlitt Gallery Ltd.* the representation was not part of the contract and the buyer was held to have acted with reasonable diligence on discovering the mistake. But what if the attribution had formed a term of the contract and there had been a shared mistake as to the attribution? In *Peco Arts*[44] Webster J. suggested that

> "it may well be the case that ... in those circumstances section 32(1)(c) does not apply either because it is not a mistake within the meaning of that subsection or because, where goods are sold with a condition or warranty as to attribution which is broken because the seller is under a mistake, the price paid is not to be regarded as money paid in consequence of a mistake."

The judge concluded that any other result would be "contrary to the interests of normal trading." This may be so.[45] Yet in these circumstances a buyer is surely seeking relief from the consequences of a mistake and would not have bought the painting but for the mistaken attribution. Moreover, Webster J.'s suggested construction, if accepted, produces the odd result that a buyer who buys a painting with an attribution which is a term of the contract may be, for the purpose of limitation, in a worse position than the buyer whose seller made no contractual representation.[46]

An innocent purchaser for valuable consideration of property, or any person claiming through him, is protected "if he did not at the time of the purchase know or have reason to believe that the mistake had been made."[47]

In *Freeman* v. *Jeffries*[48] it was suggested that a formal demand is necessary before an action to recover money paid under a mistake will lie and, therefore, before the limitation period will run. We have already given our reasons for doubting this suggestion.[49] In our view, no demand should be necessary and it is striking that, in the limitation cases, the dicta in *Freeman* v. *Jeffries*, when invoked, have been distinguished.[50]

(b) *Recovery of Benefits Conferred under Compulsion*

Duress and undue influence

Actions to recover money paid under duress fall within section 5 and are therefore barred after six years from the date of the payment to the defendant. But a claim to set aside a transaction because of undue influence, being purely

---

[44] [1983] 1 W.L.R. 1315, 1323.

[45] *Cf. Leaf* v. *International Galleries* [1950] 2 K.B. 86, 96, *per* Evershed M.R.: see above, p. 206.

[46] This *may* be so; for it was conceded in *Peco Arts* that the money could be recovered, having been paid under "common mistake."

[47] Limitation Act 1980, s.32(3).

[48] (1869) L.R. 4 Ex. 189: see above, pp. 125–126.

[49] *Ibid.*

[50] *Baker* v. *Courage & Co. Ltd.* [1910] K.B. 56, 65, *per* Hamilton J., followed in *Anglo-Scottish Beet Sugar Corporation* v. *Spalding U.D.C.* [1937] 2 K.B. 607, 628–630, *per* Atkinson J. See also *Re Mason* [1928] Ch. 385, 392, *per* Romer J.; *Re Blake* [1932] 1 Ch. 54, 60, *per* Maugham J.

equitable, is only defeated by the claimant's laches.[51] Any claim to the personal estate of a deceased person is barred after 12 years.[52]

Contribution

Claims for contribution may be made:

    (1) at law or in equity, where the parties are liable *in solidum* for the same *debt*;

    (2) under the Civil Liability (Contribution) Act 1978, where the parties are liable to compensate another for *damages*;

    (3) under the Maritime Conventions Act 1911;

    (4) for general average.

Different periods of limitation will apply depending on the nature of the contribution claim.

(1) At law or in equity: liability of the obligors for the same debt

Any claim for contribution which arises from a contract[53] between two parties will be barred after six years, since it is an action "founded on simple contract" within section 5 of the Limitation Act 1980. Not all contribution claims, however, depend on contract. Indeed the genesis of the right of contribution in equity was, as we have seen, unjust enrichment,[54] and contribution claims between co-obligors, such as co-sureties, were sustained even though there was no contract between them.[55] In these circumstances, section 5 would appear to be inapplicable,[56] unless it could be said that, as soon as the claim lies, a debt arises between the parties.[57] This reasoning is artificial, and it may be more attractive to hold that the equitable doctrine of laches should apply.[58] It is an open question whether equity will then follow the analogy of section 5 of the Limitation Act 1980, when the limitation period is six years, or of section 10 of the same statute, which states that no action to recover contribution under the Civil Liability (Contribution) Act 1978 shall be brought more than two years from the accrual of the right to contribution. Time will, in any event, not begin to run until the liability to contribute arises. For example, the fact that a co-surety's obligation *vis-à-vis* the principal debtor is statute-barred does not mean that his duty to contribute is also barred; that duty arises from the time when the claimant surety discharges more than his share of the common debt.[59]

---

[51] *Allcard* v. *Skinner* (1887) 36 Ch.D. 145; see also *Wright* v. *Vanderplank* (1856) 8 De G.M. & G. 133; *Turner* v. *Collins* (1871) L.R. 7 Ch. 329; Brunyate, *op. cit.* pp. 254–257.

[52] Limitation Act 1980, s.22a.

[53] Such as partnership: see *Knox* v. *Gye* (1872) L.R. 5 H.L. 656, and *cf. Gordon* v. *Gonda* [1955] 1 W.L.R. 885.

[54] See above, pp. 304–307.

[55] See above, pp. 307–308.

[56] *Cf.* Limitation Act 1980, s.36(2).

[57] *Robinson* v. *Harkin* [1896] 2 Ch. 415, 426, *per* Stirling J.

[58] *Cf. Gardner* v. *Brooke* [1897] 2 I.R. 6, 14, *per* O'Brien J.

[59] *Wolmerhausen* v. *Gullick* [1893] 2 Ch. 514: see also *Carter* v. *White* (1883) 25 Ch.D. 666; *cf. Restatement of Restitution*, § 83, ill.3. Similarly, it should be immaterial that the surety

(2) *Under the Civil Liability (Contribution) Act 1978*

A claim to contribution must generally be brought within two years from the date on which the statutory right of action for contribution accrues: Limitation Act 1980, s.10(1). The statute further provides that the date on which this right accrues ("the relevant date") shall be ascertained as follows[60]:

> "(3) If the person in question is held liable in respect of that damage—
> (*a*) by a judgment given in any civil proceedings; or
> (*b*) by an award made on any arbitration;
> the relevant date shall be the date on which the judgment is given, or the date of the award (as the case may be).
>
> For the purposes of this subsection no account shall be taken of any judgment or award given or made on appeal in so far as it varies the amount of damages awarded against the person in question.
>
> (4) If, in any case not within subsection (3) above, the person in question makes or agrees to make any payment to one or more persons in compensation for that damage (whether he admits any liability in respect of the damage or not), the relevant date shall be the earliest date on which the amount to be paid by him is agreed between him (or his representative) and the person (or each of the persons, as the case may be) to whom the payment is to be made."

(3) *General average contribution*

If there is a general average clause of the contract, then any action is time-barred after six years from the accrual of the cause of action.[61] If there is no such clause, it is an open question whether the contributing parties are time-barred only in the event of laches,[62] or are treated as falling within section 5 of the Limitation Act 1980 and are accordingly time-barred after the expiration of six years from the date on which the cause of action accrued. It has been held[63] that the cause of action accrues on the occurrence of the sacrifice in respect of which contribution is claimed, whether the claim is based upon liability at common law or under a general average clause. The effect of the average adjustment is not to postpone the accrual of the cause of action until the adjustment is completed: it is merely to quantify the amount of the parties' respective contributions.[64] But if a consignee executes a Lloyd's standard form

---

claiming contribution becomes a surety after his co-surety's liability was so barred. See above, pp. 309–312.

[60] Limitation Act 1980, s.10(3), (4).

[61] Limitation Act 1980, s.5.

[62] *Cf.* salvage claims see below, p. 773.

[63] *Chandris* v. *Argo Insurance Co.* [1963] 2 Lloyd's Rep. 65 at pp. 76 *et seq.*, in which Megaw J. relied on the terms of s.66 of the Marine Insurance Act 1906; *Castle Insurance Co. Ltd.* v. *Hong Kong Islands Shipping Co. Ltd.* [1984] A.C. 226, P.C. See also *Det Forenede Dampskibsselskab* v. *Insurance Co. of North America* (1929) A.M.C. 58; *Liman* v. *India Supply Mission* [1975] 1 Lloyd's Rep. 220 (U.S.D.C.).

[64] *Noreuro Traders Ltd.* v. *E. Hardy & Co.* (1923) 16 Ll.L.R. 319.

average bond, in consideration of the release of cargo, he undertakes a fresh obligation to contribute to general average.[65]

(4) *Under the Maritime Conventions Act 1911*

No action for contribution shall lie in respect of any damages for loss of life or personal injuries "unless proceedings therein are commenced within one year of the date of payment."[66]

The running of time may be postponed, whatever the nature of the contribution claim, if there is mistake or fraud or deliberate concealment,[67] or if the plaintiff is under a disability.[68]

Compulsory discharge

A claim for reimbursement from a person whose liability the claimant has compulsorily discharged must presumably be brought within six years of the payment which was made to the defendant's use.

(c) *Recovery of Benefits Conferred in an Emergency without Request*

Any claim at law for recompense, or any equitable claim analogous to such a legal claim, must be brought within six years of the date when the benefit was conferred.[69]

Salvage claims are not, however, governed by the Limitation Act 1980. Section 8 of the Maritime Conventions Act 1911, provides that:

"No action shall be maintainable to enforce any claim or lien against a vessel or her owners in respect of any damage or loss to another vessel, her cargo or freight, or any property on board her, or damages for loss of life or personal injuries suffered by any person on board her, caused by the fault of the former vessel, whether such vessel be wholly or partly in fault, or in respect of salvage services, unless proceedings therein are commenced within two years from the date when the damage or loss or injury was caused or the salvage services were rendered. .... "

On the face of the section, it is doubtful whether all actions in respect of salvage services are time-barred after expiry of the two-year period, or only such actions as are brought against a vessel or her owners. If the latter construction were correct, salvage claims against, for example, cargo only, would not be caught by the section. It has, however, been held[70] by a majority of the High Court of Australia that the former construction is applicable to an Australian

---

[65] *Castle Insurance Co. Ltd.* v. *Hong Kong Islands Shipping Co. Ltd.* [1984] A.C. 226, P.C.
[66] s.8.
[67] See above, pp. 766, 768; see below, pp. 776 *et seq.*; Limitation Act 1980, s.32.
[68] Limitation Act 1980, s.28.
[69] Limitation Act 1980, s.5. *Aliter* if the claim is a claim to a personal estate of a deceased person: see s.22(*a*).
[70] *Burns, Philp & Co. Ltd.* v. *Nelson & Robertson Pty. Ltd.* (1957–58) 98 C.L.R. 495, [1958] 1 Lloyd's Rep. 342.

statutory provision[71] in identical language. If, and in so far as, salvage claims are not caught by the section, they will only be time-barred in the event of laches.[72]

By a proviso of section 8 of the Act of 1911, the court has power, in certain specified circumstances, to extend the period within which the proceedings may be brought.[73]

(d) *Recovery of Benefits Conferred under Ineffective Sources of Obligation*

Contracts

Quasi-contractual actions to recover benefits conferred under ineffective transactions prima facie fall within section 5 and are, therefore, barred after six years from the date when the benefit is conferred.[74]

A claim for purely equitable relief, such as rectification, is barred by the plaintiff's laches.

In *Kleinwort Benson Ltd.* v. *The Borough of Sandwell*[74a] Hobhouse J. considered the scope of section 35 of the 1980 Act which provides:

> "(1) For the purpose of this Act, any new claim made in the course of any action shall be deemed to be a separate action and to have been commenced . . . on the same date as the original action.
>
> (2) In this section a new claim means any claim by way of set-off or counterclaim. . . ."

The judge held, following a dictum of Lord Denning M.R. in *Henriksens Rederi A/S* v. *Rolimpex*,[74b] that "set-off" is used in subsection (2) to denote a "legal set-off and not an equitable set-off. That is a legal set-off as permitted by the statutes of set-off." Nonetheless it may be possible to raise equitable set-off as a separate equitable defence. For "nothing in this Act shall affect any equitable jurisdiction to refuse relief on the ground of acquiescence or otherwise."[74c]

Trusts

If the trust fails, the settlor, or if he is dead his personal representatives, must pursue their claim within six years of the date when the trust fails,[75] unless the suit is a claim to the personal estate of a deceased person, when the limitation

---

[71] Australian Navigation Act 1912–1953, s.396(1).
[72] *The Royal Arch* (1857) Swab. 269, 285, *per* Dr. Lushington; *The Kong Magnus* [1891] P. 223.
[73] An extension of time was refused in *The Vadne* [1960] 1 Lloyd's Rep. 260.
[74] *Cf. B.P. Exploration Co. (Libya) Ltd.* v. *Hunt (No. 2)* [1983] 2 A.C. 352 (cause of action under s.1(3) of the Law Reform (Frustrated) Contracts Act 1943 accrues at the date of frustration); *Guardian Ocean Cargoes Ltd.* v. *Banco do Brasil (No. 2), The Times*, March 19, 1992 (cause of action, based on total failure of consideration, accrues at the date of the failure of consideration); and see above, pp. 765–766. Exceptionally, the claim may fall within Limitation Act 1980, s.22(*a*); see below, p. 775.
[74a] See below, pp. 541, 766.
[74b] [1974] Q.B. 233, 245, 246.
[74c] Limitation Act 1980, s.36(2).
[75] s.21(3), being an action by a beneficiary to recover trust property.

period is 12 years.[76] In certain cases, however, no limitation period will apply to bar the claim.[77]

2. WHERE THE DEFENDANT HAS ACQUIRED FROM A THIRD PARTY BENEFITS FOR WHICH HE MUST ACCOUNT TO THE PLAINTIFF

Under section 23 of the Limitation Act 1980, "an action for an account shall not be brought after the expiration of any time limit under this Act which is applicable to the claim which is the basis of the duty to account." The accounting party is only liable to account for moneys received during the limitation period, although it may be necessary to go behind that period to ascertain his liability for that period.

(a) *Attornment*

If the plaintiff claims property which the defendant holds for him because of an attornment, the limitation period is probably six years from the date of the attornment.[78]

(b) *Subrogation*

If a claimant is subrogated[79] to another's right of action against a third party he can be in no better position than that other; so that if that other's right of action is barred, the claimant will also be barred. If a claimant is subrogated to a fund, such as securities in a creditor's hands, his claim, if personal, will probably be barred after six years from the date when he pays the creditor[80]; but, if proprietary, his claim will presumably only be barred by laches.

(c) *Claims of Beneficiaries and Others under a Trust or in the Administration of an Estate*

If a beneficiary under an *inter vivos* trust claims from a third party trust money paid to that third party, he must pursue his claim within six years from the date of the payment of the money.[81] There are, however, special provisions relating to claims to the personal estate of deceased persons. These claims are governed by section 22(*a*) and must be brought within 12 years "from the date on which the right to receive the share or interest accrued."[82] It was this section which both the Court of Appeal and the House of Lords held applicable in *Re Diplock*,[83] where the next-of-kin claimed from charities money which the

---

[76] s.22(*a*).
[77] *e.g.* if there is a mistake (see above, pp. 767–770), fraud or deliberate concealment (see below, pp. 776–778) or breach of a fiduciary relationship (see below, pp. 778–779).
[78] s.5, *semble*: see above, pp. 765–766.
[79] See above, Chap. 31.
[80] On the basis that the claim will be for money had and received and will be held to fall within s.5 of the Limitation Act 1980.
[81] Limitation Act 1980, s.21(3): see below, pp. 778, 780.
[82] This phrase can give rise to difficult questions of interpretation: see Franks, *op. cit.* pp. 50–51.
[83] [1948] Ch. 465, 512–513, C.A., [1951] A.C. 251, 276, *per* Lord Simonds.

executors had paid to them under a mistake. This construction led to the bizarre conclusion that the period began to run from the same "date as that from which the statute runs in the case of a claim against a personal representative, and without regard to the time when the moneys belonging to the claimant were in fact wrongly paid to the recipient."[84] It is even more strange that a creditor whose debtor dies has a period of 12 years in which to bring his suit, whereas if his debtor had remained alive, the limitation period would have been merely six years.[85] The running of time may be postponed if there is mistake[86] or fraud or deliberate concealment.[87]

3. WHERE THE DEFENDANT HAS ACQUIRED A BENEFIT THROUGH HIS OWN WRONGFUL ACT

The normal period of limitation which governs a plaintiff's claim in all these cases[88] is six years,[89] unless the claim is one to the personal estate of a deceased person, when it is 12 years.[90] If, however, there is fraud or fraudulent concealment, the running of the limitation period is postponed, while in certain cases of breach of fiduciary relationship no statutory limitation period whatsoever applies.[90a]

(a) *Fraud or Deliberate Concealment*

Section 32 of the Limitation Act 1980 provides:

"(1) Subject to subsection (3) below,[91] where in the case of any action for which a period of limitation is prescribed by this Act, either—
(a) the action is based upon the fraud of the defendant; or
(b) any fact relevant to the plaintiff's right of action has been deliberately concealed from him by the defendant . . .
the period of limitation shall not begin to run until the plaintiff has discovered the fraud, concealment . . . or could with reasonable diligence have discovered it.

---

[84] *Ibid.* at p. 513; see also [1951] A.C. 251, 276–277, *per* Lord Simonds.
[85] The relationship of s.22(*a*) to s.21(3) (see above, nn. 41, 42) could be clearer: *e.g.* it is arguable that, if a personal representative is a trustee, then the limitation period is six years, as provided by s.21(3); see below, p. 778. This argument, however, ignores the excluding words of s.21(3) that the section does not apply where a "period of limitation is prescribed by any other provision of this Act": *cf.* Preston and Newsom, *op. cit.* pp. 187–188, with Franks, *op. cit.* p. 49.
[86] See above, pp. 767–770.
[87] See below, pp. 776–778. If the recipient is a constructive trustee, no limitation period may apply: see below, pp. 779–780 for proprietary claims.
[88] Including cases of waiver of tort; acquisition of benefits through crime; breaches of fiduciary duty.
[89] Limitation Act 1980, ss.5, 21(3) (but see above, n. 85); *Chesworth* v. *Farrar* [1967] 1 Q.B. 407: see above, p. 728.
[90] Limitation Act 1980, s.22(*a*).
[90a] See below, p. 778.
[91] This subsection protects the bona fide purchaser: see below, p. 778, 780.

References in this subsection to the defendant include references to the defendant's agent and to any person through whom the defendant claims and his agent.

(2) For the purposes of subsection (1) above, deliberate commission of a breach of duty in circumstances in which it is unlikely to be discovered for some time amounts to deliberate concealment of the facts involved in that breach of duty."

For section 32(1) and (2) to apply, the plaintiff has, therefore, to prove fraud or a deliberate concealment of relevant facts, and this must be a necessary or relevant allegation[92] in his claim.[93] Fraud does not necessarily involve any moral turpitude. The concept embraces a "wide range of conduct which before the statute was regarded in equity as so dishonest as to prevent the Statute of Limitations (or its analogous application in equity) from coming into operation."[94] Unconscionable conduct or the abuse of a special relationship between the parties may lead the court to a finding of fraud.[95] If a party is conscious that what he is doing may well be wrongful, his conduct may be characterised as fraudulent.[96]

A defendant need not behave fraudulently before he can be said to have "deliberately concealed" any fact[97]; so, surreptitious extraction of minerals will amount to deliberate concealment if it is dishonest, furtive or otherwise unfair having regard to the relationship between the parties.[98] It appears that the defendant must have had actual knowledge of the facts and have deliberately concealed them[99]; indeed, a deliberate withholding of information may be a concealment in circumstances where the plaintiff has relied on the defendant's expertise.[1]

---

[92] *Beaman* v. *A.R.T.S. Ltd.* [1949] 1 K.B. 550; *G. L. Baker Ltd.* v. *Medway Building and Supplies Ltd.* [1958] 1 W.L.R. 1216.

[93] See, generally, *Tito* v. *Waddell (No. 2)* [1977] Ch. 106, 241 *et seq.*, *per* Megarry V.-C.

[94] *Beaman* v. *A.R.T.S. Ltd.* [1949] 1 K.B. 550, 559, *per* Lord Greene M.R.

[95] *Applegate* v. *Moss* [1971] 1 Q.B. 406, 413, *per* Lord Denning M.R., following *Kitchen* v. *R.A.F. Association* [1958] 1 W.L.R. 563; *King* v. *Victor Parsons & Co.* [1973] 1 W.L.R. 29, 34; *Bartlett* v. *Barclays Bank Trust Co. Ltd.* [1980] Ch. 515, 537, *per* Brightman J.

[96] *Beaman* v. *A.R.T.S. Ltd.* [1949] 1 K.B. 550, 572, *per* Singleton L.J.

[97] *Beaman* v. *A.R.T.S. Ltd.* [1949] 1 K.B. 550; *G. L. Baker Ltd.* v. *Medway Building and Supplies Ltd.* [1958] 1 W.L.R. 1216.

[98] s.26 of the Limitation Act 1939 spoke of the right of action "concealed by fraud." But the courts had interpreted that language to mean "an unconscionable failure to reveal": *Tito* v. *Waddell (No. 2)* [1977] Ch. 106, 244–245, *per* Megarry V.-C. See also *King* v. *Victor Parsons & Co.* [1973] 1 W.L.R. 29. 33–34, *per* Lord Denning M.R. The decisions interpreting s.26 of the 1939 Act are therefore still relevant although most of its problems of construction have now disappeared with the enactment of section 32(1)(*b*) and (2). The older cases include *Trotter* v. *Maclean* (1879) 13 Ch.D. 574; *Bulli Coal Mining Co.* v. *Osborne* [1899] A.C. 351. *Cf. Rains* v. *Buxton* (1880) 14 Ch.D. 537; *Dawes* v. *Bagnall* (1875) 23 W.R. 690; *Morton-Norwich Products Inc.* v. *Intercen Ltd. (No. 2)* [1981] F.S.R. 337.

[99] *Cf. King* v. *Victor Parsons & Co.* [1973] 1 W.L.R. 29, 36, *per* Megaw L.J.

[1] *Cf. Clark* v. *Woor* [1965] 2 All E.R. 353.

Time runs from the date when the fraud or deliberate concealment is discovered or could with reasonable diligence[2] have been discovered.[3]

The Limitation Act 1980 protects an innocent purchaser for valuable consideration, or any person claiming through him, from any action to recover the property or its value, or to enforce any charge against, or set aside any transaction affecting, any property,[4] "if he was not a party to the fraud or (as the case may be) to the concealment of the fact and did not at the time of the purchase know or have reason to believe that the fraud or concealment had taken place."[5]

(b) *Breach of Fiduciary Duty*

An action by a beneficiary "to recover trust property or in respect of any breach of trust, not being an action for which a period of limitation is prescribed by any other provision of this Act," must be brought within six years of the accrual of the right of action,[6] which is generally when the breach of trust has been committed.[7] But a claim to "an account simpliciter based on a fiduciary relationship and nothing more is not barred by any period of limitation."[8] A purchase by trustees of a beneficiary's beneficial interest is not a purchase of trust property and any action to set aside such a purchase is governed by the equitable doctrine of laches.[9] A right of action shall not be deemed to have accrued to any beneficiary entitled to a future interest in the trust property until the interest falls into possession.[10]

However, section 21(1) of the Limitation Act 1980 provides that:

"(1) No period of limitation prescribed by this Act shall apply to an action by a beneficiary under a trust, being an action:
(a) in respect of any fraud or fraudulent breach of trust[11] to which the trustee was a party or privy; or
(b) to recover from the trustee trust property or the proceeds thereof in the possession of the trustee,[12] or previously received by the trustee and converted to his use."[13]

---

[2] For the meaning of these words, in the context of a claim to recover money on the ground of common mistake, see *Peco Arts Inc.* v. *Hazlitt Gallery* [1983] 1 W.L.R. 1315; see above, pp. 769–770.

[3] Limitation Act 1980, s.32(1).

[4] *Ibid.* s.32(3)(a), (b).

[5] *Ibid.* s.32(4). This language removes some of the constructional difficulties arising from the Limitation Act 1939, s.26, on which see *Eddis* v. *Chichester Constable* [1969] 2 Ch. 345, 358, 364.

[6] Limitation Act 1980, s.21(3).

[7] *Re Swain* [1891] 3 Ch. 233; *Thorne* v. *Heard* [1894] 1 Ch. 599, affd. [1895] A.C. 495.

[8] *Att.-Gen.* v. *Cocke* [1988] Ch. 414, 421, *per* Harman J. In this case the will was proved in 1951.

[9] *Tito* v. *Waddell (No. 2)* [1977] Ch. 106, 246–250, *per* Megarry V.-C.

[10] s.21(3). Cf. *Re Pauling's Settlement Trusts* [1964] Ch. 303; *Tito* v. *Waddell (No. 2)* [1977] Ch. 106, 246–250, *per* Megarry V.-C.

[11] *Thorne* v. *Heard* [1895] A.C. 495. Cf. *Blair* v. *Bromley* (1847) 2 Ph. 354; *Moore* v. *Knight* [1891] 1 Ch. 547.

[12] *Re National Bank of Wales* [1899] 2 Ch. 629; *Re Clark* (1920) 150 L.T.Jo. 94; *Re Eyre-Williams* [1923] 2 Ch. 533; *Re Howlett* [1949] Ch. 767.

[13] *Moore* v. *Knight* [1891] 1 Ch. 547; *Re Gurney* [1893] 1 Ch. 590.

The scope of section 21(1)(*a*) is far from clear.[14] In *G. L. Baker Ltd.* v. *Medway Building and Supplies Ltd.*,[15] Danckwerts J., speaking of the similarly worded provision in the Limitation Act 1939, pointed out that it gave rise to "considerable difficulties of interpretation."

> "Is it a provision which only deals with proceedings against a trustee who was guilty of fraud, or does it also apply to a person who was not the original trustee but one who has acquired the trust property or payment which was fraudulently made out of the trust property?"[16]

Whereas the Trustee Act 1888[17] clearly dealt with both cases, "it is not at all clear whether the Act of 1939 has the same purpose but it may be so."[18]

Section 21(1)(*b*) of the 1980 Act specifically provides that no period of limitation shall apply to an action by a beneficiary under a trust, being an action "to recover from the trustee trust property or the proceeds of trust property in the possession of the trustee, or previously received by the trustee and converted to his use."[19] In the past, this rule could cause hardship if a trustee distributed in good faith the trust estate to all the known beneficiaries (of whom he was one), and who, he reasonably believed, constituted the whole class, and six years after that distribution an action was brought against him by a beneficiary who had just discovered his entitlement. In such a case, however, a trustee who has acted honestly and reasonably, is nowadays liable only for the excess over what would have been his "proper share" of the trust funds.[20]

For limitation purposes, the expressions "trust" and "trustee" include not only an express trustee but an implied, resulting and constructive trustee, a trustee *de son tort*, a personal representative, and any other fiduciary, such as a director, partner or fiduciary agent.[21]

4. PROPRIETARY CLAIMS

At common law a proprietary claim is nowadays generally pursued by means of an action of wrongful interference with goods[22] or an action of money had and received. Such actions fall within section 5 of the Limitation Act 1980.

---

[14] *e.g.* it is not clear whether a beneficiary's claim will be defeated by laches. *Semble* it will: see Limitation Act 1980, s.36(2); *Sleeman* v. *Wilson* (1871) L.R. 13 Eq. 36. Again, s.21(1) speaks of an action "by a beneficiary under a trust." *Quaere*, therefore, whether an action by a newly appointed trustee, who seeks to recover trust property from the other trustees, is within s.21(1)(*a*); *cf. Re Bowden* (1890) 45 Ch.D. 444: and see below, n. 19.

[15] [1958] 1 W.L.R. 1216.

[16] *Ibid.* 1221.

[17] Trustee Act 1888, s.8.

[18] [1958] 1 W.L.R. 1216, 1222.

[19] *Cf.* G. Elias, *Explaining Constructive Trusts*, pp. 117 *et seq.*, arguing that the law of limitations and laches, essentially the distinction between claims at law (governed by statute) and some claims in equity (laches), offers no coherent basis for determining whether the liability of a defendant should or should not be open-ended.

[20] s.21(2), which adopts the proposal of the Law Reform Committee, 21st Report, Cmnd. 6293, (1977), §§ 3.82–3.84.

[21] Limitation Act 1980, s.38; *cf.* Trustee Act 1925, s.68(17).

[22] Torts (Interference with Goods) Act 1977, ss.1 and 3.

Accordingly, a claimant has six years from the date when his right of action accrued to him to pursue his claim.

In the nineteenth century, it was accepted that a claimant's equitable right to follow property could be defeated only by his laches.[23] But if a beneficiary is claiming under an *inter vivos* trust, his proprietary claim seems to fall within section 21(3),[24] as an "action . . . to recover trust property," and is, therefore, barred after six years. A proprietary claim to personalty, arising from the administration of an estate, appears to fall within section 22(a),[25] being an "action in respect of any claim to the personal estate of a deceased person or to any share or interest in such estate," and is, therefore, barred after 12 years.[26] Sections 21(3) and 22(a) are, therefore, appropriate to govern pure proprietary claims based on equitable title.[27] But an equitable restitutionary proprietary claim, which is created in order to prevent unjust enrichment, arises when it is imposed by the court.[28] Under the old law comparable claims were only defeated by laches.[29] In our view that should still be the general principle today.

As in personal claims, the running of the limitation period may be postponed if there is mistake, fraud or deliberate concealment.[30]

---

[23] *March* v. *Russell* (1837) 3 Myl. & Cr. 31; *Bate* v. *Hooper* (1855) 5 De G.M. & G. 338; *Harris* v. *Harris (No. 2)* (1861) 29 Beav. 110.

[24] See above, p. 778.

[25] See above, p. 775.

[26] Franks, *op. cit.* p. 258. Proprietary claims to land are also barred after 12 years: see s.15(1).

[27] Some of the cases discussed in Chap. 33 (benefits acquired in breach of fiduciary relationships) would still be so described.

[28] See above, Chap. 2.

[29] *Beckford* v. *Wade* (1810) 17 Ves. 87, 96, *per* Grant M.R.; J. W. Brunyate, *Limitation of Actions in Equity*, pp. 51–53, 102–111.

[30] See above, pp. 767–770, 776–778.

BIBLIOGRAPHY
OF PRINCIPAL WORKS CITED

Abbot, C.: *Law Relating to Merchant Ships and Seamen* (14th ed., 1901, by B. Aspinall and H.S. Moore).

American Law Institute: *See Restatement*.

Ames, J.B.: *Lectures on Legal History* (1911).

Anson, Sir W.R.: *Principles of the English Law of Contract and of Agency* (26th ed., 1984, by A.G. Guest).

Arnould, Sir J.: *Law of Marine Insurance and Average* (*British Shipping Laws*, Vols. 9 and 10) (16th ed., 1981, by Sir M.J. Mustill and J.C.B. Gilman).

Ashburner, W.: *Principles of Equity* (2nd ed., 1933, by D. Browne).

Atiyah, P.S.: *Introduction to the Law of Contract* (4th ed., 1989).

—— *Sale of Goods* (8th ed., 1990).

—— *The Rise and Fall of Freedom of Contract* (1979).

Bacon, Mathew: *New Abridgement of the Law* (7th ed., 1832).

Beatson, J.: *The Use and Abuse of Unjust Enrichment* (1991).

Benjamin's *Sale of Goods* (3rd ed., 1987, by A.G. Guest and others).

Birks, P.: *An Introduction to the Law of Restitution* (1985).

—— *Restitution—The Future* (1992).

Blackstone, W.: *Commentaries on the Laws of England* (3rd ed., 1768–1769).

Bower, G. Spencer: *Doctrine of Res Judicata* (2nd ed., 1969, by Sir A.K. Turner).

Bower, G. Spencer, and Turner, Sir A.K.: *Law Relating to Estoppel by Representation* (3rd ed., 1977).

Bowstead, W.: *Digest of the Law of Agency* (*Common Law Library*, No. 7) (15th ed., 1985, by F.M.B. Reynolds).

Bracton, H. de: *De Legibus et Consuetudinibus Angliae* (ed. by G.E. Woodbine and translated by S.E. Thorne, 1969–1977).

Brice, G.: *Maritime Law of Salvage* (London, 1983).

Bromley, P.M.: *Family Law* (7th ed., 1987).

Brunyate, J.W.: *Limitation of Actions in Equity* (1932).

Buckland, W.W.: *Text Book of Roman Law from Augustus to Justinian* (3rd ed., 1963, by P.G. Stein).

Buckland, W.W., and McNair, A.D.: *Roman Law and Common Law: A Comparison in Outline* (2nd ed., 1952; reprinted with corrections, 1965).

Buckley on the Companies Acts (14th ed., 1981, by G. Brian Parker and Martin Buckley).

Bullen, E.: *Law of Distress for Rent* (2nd ed., 1899).

Bullen, E., and Leake, S.M.: *Precedents of Pleadings* (2nd ed., 1863; 3rd ed., 1868).

Burrows, A. (ed): *Essays on the Law of Restitution* (1991).

Burrows, A.: *The Law of Restitution* (1993).

Byles, Sir J.B.: *Law of Bills of Exchange* (26th ed., 1988, by F.R. Ryder and A. Bueno).

Cardozo, B.N.: *The Nature of the Judicial Process* (1921).

Cartwright, J. *Unequal Bargaining* (1991).

Carver, T.G.: *Carriage by Sea* (*British Shipping Laws*, Vols. 1 and 2) (13th ed., 1982, by R.P. Colinvaux).

Chalmers, Sir M.D.: *Marine Insurance Act, 1906* (9th ed., 1983, by E.R.H. Ivamy).

781

Chalmers, Sir M.D.: *Sale of Goods Act 1979* (18th ed., 1981, by M. Mark).
Cheshire, G.C., and Burn, E.H.: *Modern Law of Real Property* (14th ed., 1988, by E.H. Burn).
Cheshire, G.C., Fifoot, C.H.S., and Furmston, M.P.: *Law of Contract* (12th ed., 1991).
Chitty, J.: *Law of Contracts* (26th ed., 1989, by A.G. Guest and others).
Chorley, Lord, and Giles, O.C.: *Shipping Law* (8th ed., 1987, by N.J. Gaskell, C. Debattista and R.J. Swatton).
Coleman, A.: *The Legal Protection of Trade Secrets* (1992).
Cook, W.W.: *Logical and Legal Bases of the Conflict of Laws* (1943).
Corbin, A.L.: *Cases on the Law of Contract* (1947).
—— *Contracts* (8 vols. 1950–1964).
—— *Contracts* (1 vol. ed., 1952).
Cordery's *Law Relating to Solicitors* (8th ed., 1988, by F.T. Horne).
Corpus Juris Secundum (1936–).
Cretney, S.M., and Masson, J.M.: *Principles of Family Law* (5th ed., 1990).
Cross, R.: *Evidence* (7th ed., 1990, by C. Tapper).

Dart, J.H.: *Law Relating to Vendors and Purchasers* (8th ed., 1929, by E.P. Hewitt and M.R.C. Overton).
Dawson, J.P.: *Unjust Enrichment: A Comparative Analysis* (1951).
Dawson, J.P., and Palmer, G.E.: *Cases on Restitution* (1969).
Dicey, A.V., and Morris, J.H.C.: *Conflict of Laws* (11th ed., 1987, by L. Collins and others).

Elias, G.O.A.: *Explaining Constructive Trusts* (1990).

Falconbridge, J.D.: *Essays on the Conflict of Laws* (2nd ed., 1954).
Farnsworth, E. Allen: *Contracts* (2nd ed., 1990).
Fifoot, C.H.S.: *History and Sources of the Common Law: Tort and Contract* (1949).
—— *Lord Mansfield* (1936).
Finn, P.D.: *Fiduciary Obligations* (1977).
Finn, P.D. (ed): *Essays in Equity* (1985).
—— *Equity and Commercial Relationships* (1987).
—— *Essays on Restitution* (1990).

Gilmore, G.: *The Death of Contract* (1974).
Glanvil, R. de: *De Legibus et Consuetudinibus Regni Angliae* (ed., 1965, by G.D.G. Hall).
Gloag, W.M.: *The Law of Contract* (2nd ed., 1929).
Goode, R.M.: *Consumer Law* (1989).
Gray, C.M.: *Copyhold, Equity and the Common Law* (1963).
Gray, K.: *Elements of Land Law* (1987).
Gurry, F.: *Breach of Confidence* (1984).

Halsbury (Earl of): *Laws of England* (3rd ed., 1952–; 4th ed., 1973–).
Hanbury, H.G., and Maudsley, R.H.: *Modern Equity* (13th ed., 1989, by J.E. Martin).
Hart, H.L.A., and Honoré, A.M.: *Causation in the Law* (2nd ed., 1985).
Hayton and Marshall: *Cases and Commentary on the Law of Trusts* (9th ed., 1991, by D.J. Hayton).
Holden, J.M.: *History of Negotiable Instruments in English Law* (1955).
Holdsworth, Sir W.S.: *History of English Law* (1903–1965).
Hudson's *Building and Engineering Contracts* (10th ed., 1970, by I.N. Duncan Wallace).

Jackson, R.M.: *History of Quasi-Contract in English Law* (1936).
Jones, G.: *Restitution in Public and Private Law* (1991).
Jones, G., and Goodhart, W.: *Specific Performance* (1986).

Kahn-Freund, O.: *Law of Carriage by Inland Transport* (4th ed., 1965).
Keener, W.A.: *Quasi-Contracts* (1893).
Kennedy, W.R.: *Law of Civil Salvage* (5th ed., 1985, by D.W. Steel and F.D. Rose).
Kerly, Sir D.M.: *Law of Trade Marks and Trade Names* (12th ed., 1986, by T.A. Blanco White and Robin Jacob).
Kerr, W.W.: *Law of Fraud and Mistake* (7th ed., 1952, by J.G. Munroe and D.L. McDonnell).
Klippert, G.B.: *Unjust Enrichment* (1983).

Langdell, C.C.: *A Brief Survey of Equity Jurisprudence* (2nd ed., 1908).
Laycock, D.: *Modern American Remedies* (1985, with supplements).
Lewin, T.: *Practical Treatise on the Law of Trusts* (16th ed., 1964, by W.J. Mowbray).
Lindley, Lord, and Banks, R.C. I'Anson: *Law of Partnership* (16th ed., 1990).
Lowndes, R., and Rudolph, G.R.: *Law of General Average (British Shipping Laws*, Vol. 7) (10th ed., 1975, by Sir John Donaldson and others and 11th ed., 1990 by D.J. Wilson and J.H.S. Cooke).

Macgillivray, E.J., and Parkington, M.W.: *Insurance Law* (8th ed., 1988).
Maddaugh, P.D., and McCamus J.: *The Law of Restitution* (1990).
McGregor, H.: *Law of Damages* (15th ed., 1988).
Maitland, F.W.: *Equity* (2nd ed., 1936, revised by J. Brunyate).
—— *Forms of Action at Common Law* (1909).
Mann, F.A.: *Legal Aspect of Money* (5th ed., 1992).
Marsden, R.G.: *Law Relating to Collisions at Sea (British Shipping Laws*, Vol. 4) (11th ed., 1961, by K.C. McGuffie).
Marshall, O.R.: *Assignment of Choses in Action* (1950).
May, H.W., and Edwards, W.D.: *Law of Fraudulent and Voluntary Conveyances* (3rd ed., 1908).
Meagher, R.P., Gummow, W.M.C., and Lehane, J.R.: *Equity: Doctrines and Remedies* (2nd ed., 1984).
Megarry, Sir Robert, and Wade, Sir William: *Law of Real Property* (5th ed., 1984).
Meston, Lord: *Law Relating to Moneylenders* (5th ed., 1968).
Milsom, S.F.C.: *Historical Foundations of the Common Law* (2nd ed., 1981).
Morrison, C.B.M.: *Rescission of Contracts* (1916).
Munkman, J.H.: *Law of Quasi-Contracts* (1950).
Mustill, Sir M.J., and Boyd, S.C.: *Commercial Arbitration in England* (2nd ed., 1989).

Oakley, A.J.: *Constructive Trusts* (2nd ed., 1987).

Palmer's *Company Law* (25th ed., 1992, by G. Morse and others).
Palmer, G.E.: *Law of Restitution*, 4 vols. (1978, with annual supplements).
—— *Mistake and Unjust Enrichment* (1962).
Peiris, G.L.: *Some Aspects of the Law of Unjust Enrichment in South Africa and Ceylon* (1972).
Pettit, P.H.: *Equity and the Law of Trusts* (6th ed., 1989).
Plucknett, T.F.T.: *Concise History of the Common Law* (5th ed., 1956).
Pollock, Sir F.: *Principles of Contract* (13th ed., 1950, by P.H. Winfield).
Pollock, Sir F., and Maitland, F.W.: *History of English Law before Edward I* (2nd ed.).
Pollock, Sir F., and Mulla, D.F.: *Indian Contract and Specific Relief Acts* (10th ed., 1986, by J.L. Kapur).
Posner, R.: *Economic Analysis of Law* (4th ed., 1992).
Powell, R.: *Law of Agency* (2nd ed., 1961).

Restatement of the Law of Agency, 2d (1958).
Restatement of the Law of Contracts, 2d (1981).

Restatement of the Law of Restitution (1937).
Restatement of the Law of Trusts, 2d (1959).
Rolle, H.: *Abridgement* (1668 ed.).
Rowlatt on *The Law of Principal and Surety*: (4th ed., 1982, by David G.M. Marks and Gabriel S. Moss).
Ruoff, Sir T.B.F., and Roper, R.B.: *Registered Conveyancing* (5th ed., 1986).
Russell, F., and Walton, A.: *Law of Arbitration* (20th ed., 1982, by A. Walton).

Salmond, Sir J., and Heuston, R.F.V.: *Law of Torts* (20th ed., 1992).
Schulz, F.: *Classical Roman Law* (1951).
Scott, A.W.: *Law of Trusts* (4th ed., 1987).
Scrutton, Sir T.E.: *Charter Parties and Bills of Lading* (19th ed., 1984, by Sir Alan Mocatta and others).
Shepherd, J.C.: *The Law of Fiduciaries* (1981).
Sheppard, W.: *Touchstone of Common Assurances* (8th ed., 1826, by E.G. Atherly).
Sheridan, L.A.: *Fraud in Equity* (1957).
Simpson, A.W.B.: *History of the Common Law of Contract* (1975).
Smith, J.W.: *Leading Cases* (13th ed., 1929, by Sir T.W. Chitty and others).
Snell, E.H.T.: *Principles of Equity* (29th ed., 1990, by P.V. Baker and P.J. Langan).
Stoljar, S.J.: *The Law of Quasi-Contract* (2nd ed., 1989).
Story, J.: *Commentaries on Equity Jurisprudence* (2nd ed., 1893).
Street, H.: *Principles of the Law of Damages* (1962).
—— *The Law of Torts* (8th ed., 1988, by M. Brasier).
Street, J.H.A.: *Ultra Vires* (1930).
Sugden: *Vendors and Purchasers* (14th ed., 1962).

Treitel, G.H.: *The Law of Contracts* (8th ed., 1991).

Underhill, Sir A.: *Law Relating to Trusts and Trustees* (14th ed., 1989, by D.J. Hayton).

Viner, C.: *Abridgement of Law and Equity* (2nd ed., 1791).

Wade, J.W.: *Cases and Materials on Restitution* (2nd ed., 1966).
Waldock, C.H.M.: *Law of Mortgages* (2nd ed., 1950).
Walker, D.M.: *Principles of Scottish Private Law* (4th ed., 1988).
Waters, D.W.M.: *The Constructive Trust* (1964).
Williams, G.L.: *Criminal Law: The General Part* (2nd ed., 1961).
—— *Joint Obligations* (1949).
—— *Joint Torts and Contributory Negligence* (1950).
—— *Law Reform (Frustrated Contracts) Act, 1943* (1944).
—— *Liability for Animals* (1939).
Williams and Muir Hunter: *Law and Practice in Bankruptcy* (19th ed., 1979, by Muir Hunter and David Graham).
Williams, T.C.: *The Law Relating to Vendors and Purchasers* (4th ed., 1936, by the author and J.M. Lightwood).
Williston, S.: *Law of Contracts* (Revised ed., 1936–1938).
Winfield, Sir P.H.: *Province of the Law of Tort* (1931).
—— *Quasi-Contracts* (1952).
Winfield, Sir P.H., and Jolowicz, J.A.: *Tort* (13th ed., 1989, by W.V.H. Rogers).
Woodward, F.C.: *The Law of Quasi-Contracts* (1913).
Wright, Lord: *Legal Essays and Addresses* (1939).

Zweigert K., and Kötz H.: *An Introduction to Comparative Law*, 2 vols, transl. by T. Weir (2nd ed., 1987).

INDEX

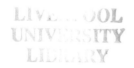
LIVERPOOL
UNIVERSITY
LIBRARY

LIVERPOOL
UNIVERSITY
LIBRARY